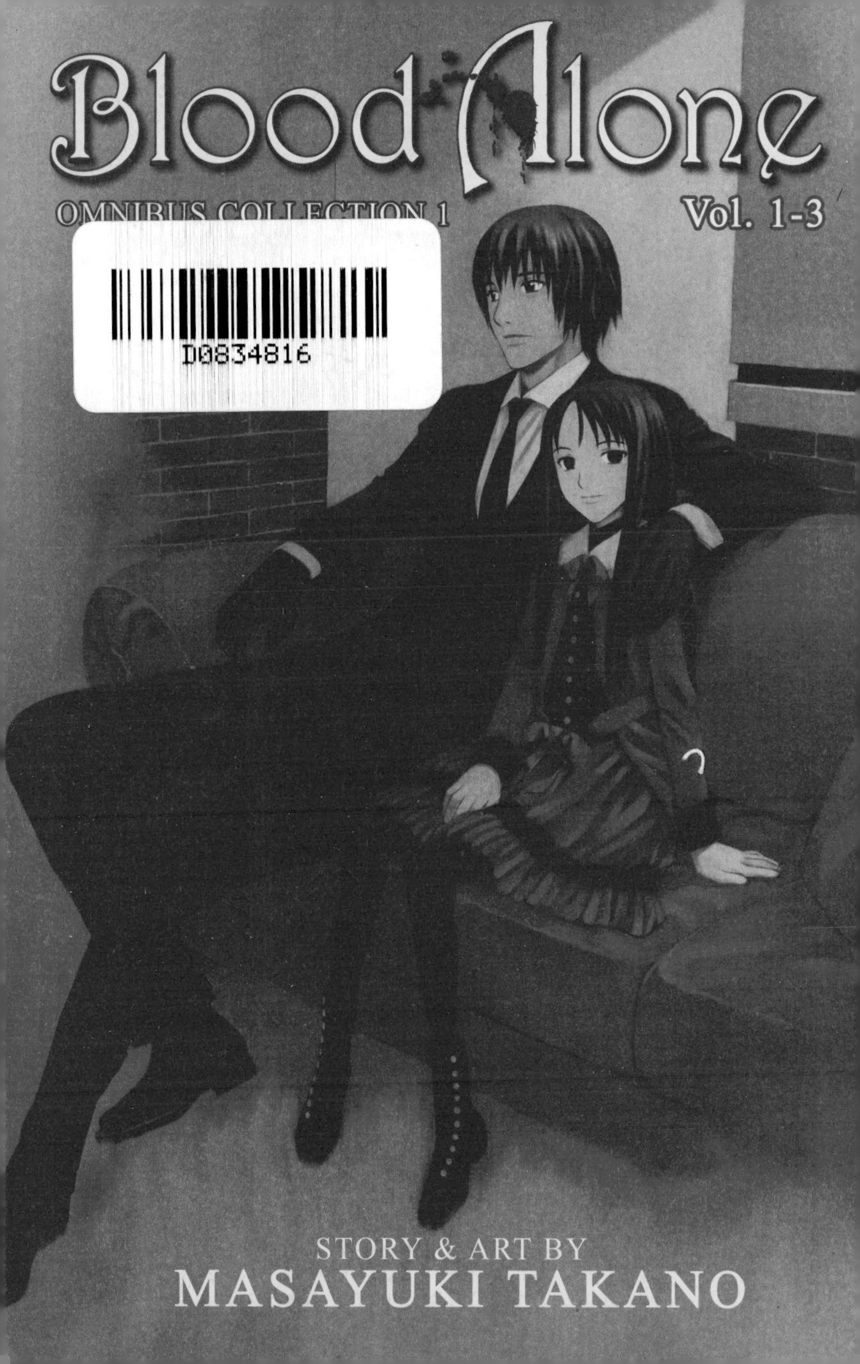
Blood Alone
OMNIBUS COLLECTION 1
Vol. 1-3
STORY & ART BY
MASAYUKI TAKANO

Blood Alone

OMNIBUS COLLECTION 1   Vol. 1-3

STORY & ART BY
MASAYUKI TAKANO

STAFF CREDITS

translation	Nan Rymer
adaptation	Shannon Fay
retouch & lettering	Roland Amago
cover design	Nicky Lim
layout	Bambi Eloriaga-Amago
copy editor	Shanti Whitesides
editor	Adam Arnold
publisher	Jason DeAngelis
	Seven Seas Entertainment

BLOOD ALONE OMNIBUS COLLECTION 1
Content originally published as Blood Alone Vol. 1-3.
Copyright © Masayuki Takano 2005-2006
First published in 2005-2006 by Media Works Inc., Tokyo, Japan.
English translation rights arranged with ASCII MEDIA WORKS.

Visit us online at www.gomanga.com.

ISBN: 978-1-934876-98-5

Printed in Canada

First Printing: May 2011

10 9 8 7 6 5 4 3 2 1

Contents

GLOSSARY

Absorbire	Vampire cannibalism, absorption
Aruhiek	An elder vampire
Aruta	Special powers possessed by an Elder
Adevaraht Kurai	The Eyes That See the Truth
Farumek	Glamour, a hypnotic trance used to bend a person to a vampire's will
Insegrod Spaldha	The Crimson Blade
Orphan	A vampire with no clan
Renfield	Vampire servant or thrall
Straruda	The element in a vampire's blood that gives them their powers
Sinacolda	A Renfield's master, a vampire who has shared its blood with a Renfield
Vanatoare	A vampire hunter or slayer

Blood Alone

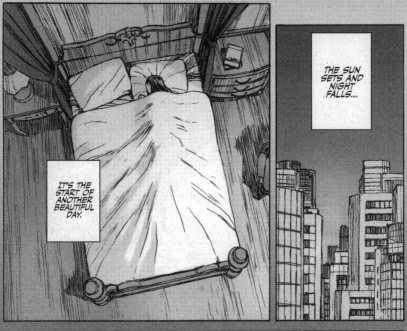

THE SUN SETS AND NIGHT FALLS...

IT'S THE START OF ANOTHER BEAUTIFUL DAY.

AND NEXT TO ME, HIS SLEEPING FACE BESIDE MINE--

PAT

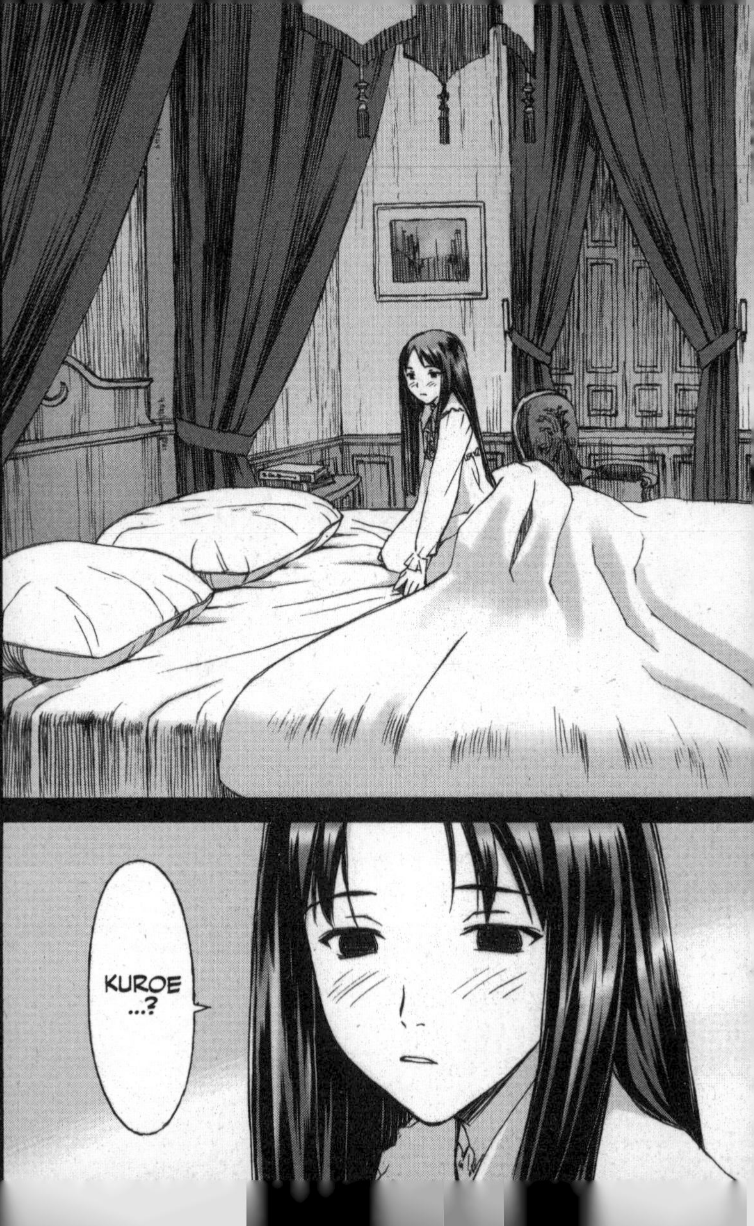
KUROE ...?

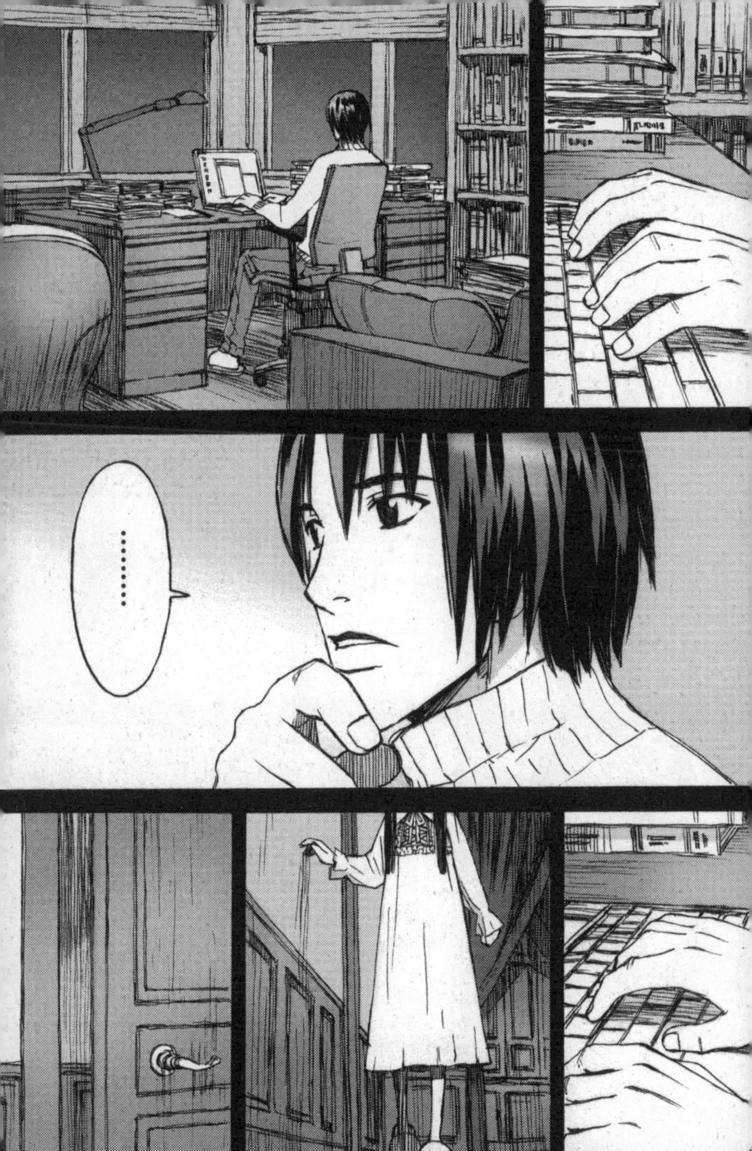
……

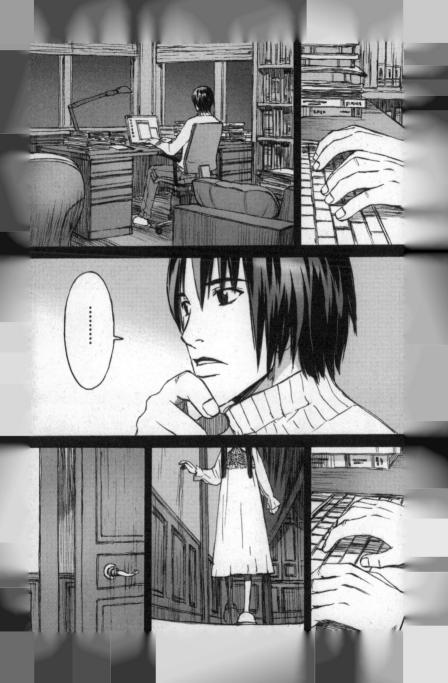

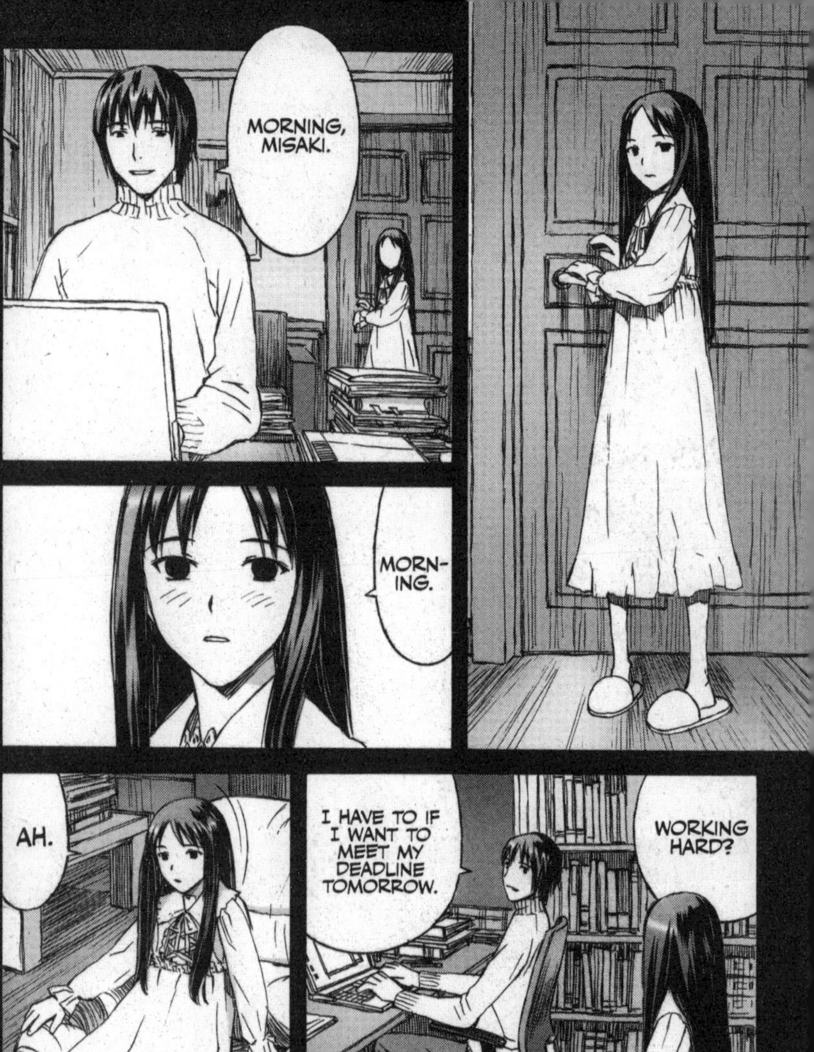
MORNING, MISAKI.
MORN-ING.
WORKING HARD?
I HAVE TO IF I WANT TO MEET MY DEADLINE TOMORROW.
ESPECIAL-LY SINCE I'M A BIT BEHIND...
AH.

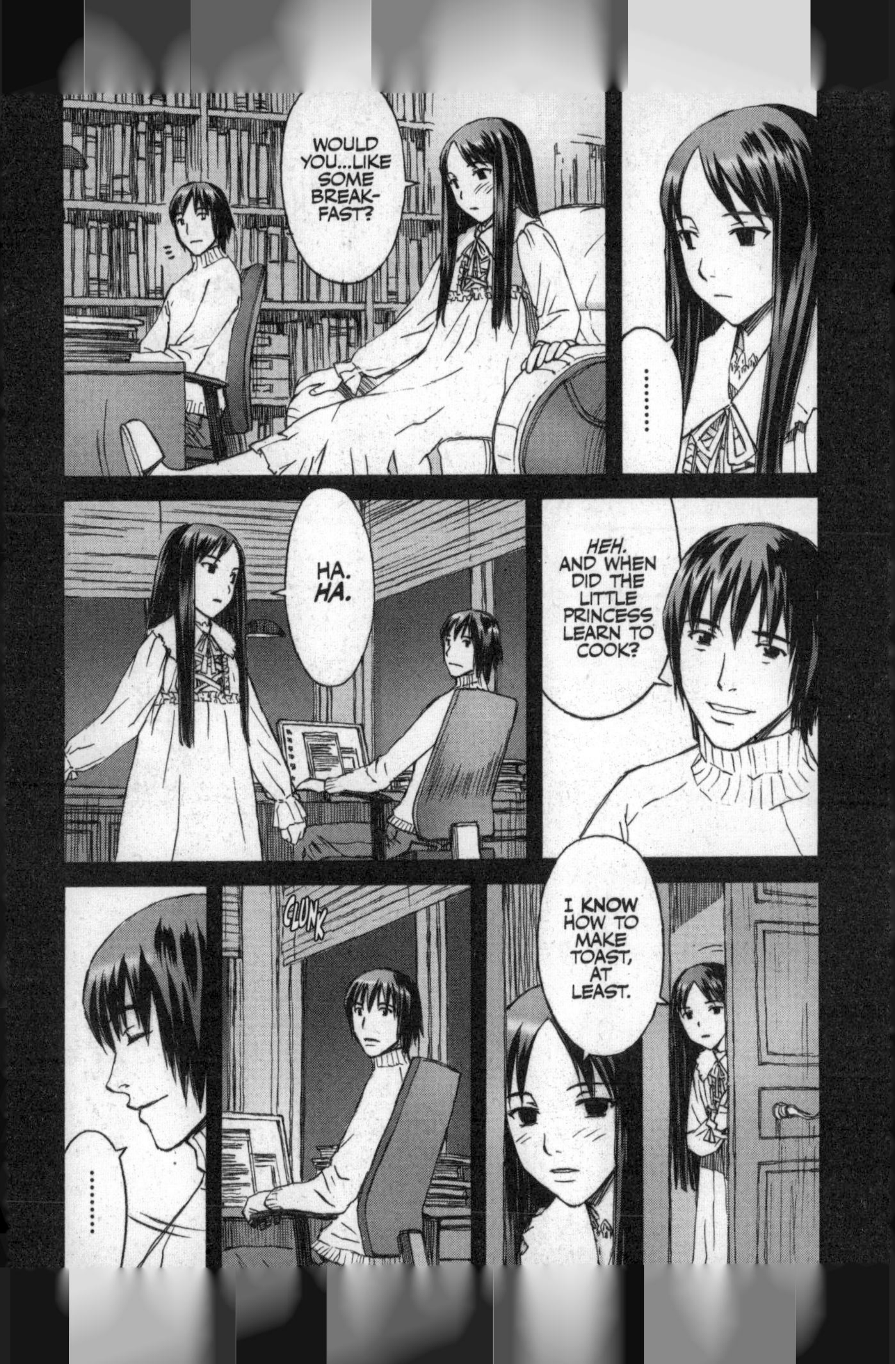
......
WOULD YOU...LIKE SOME BREAK-FAST?
HEH. AND WHEN DID THE LITTLE PRINCESS LEARN TO COOK?
HA. *HA.*
I KNOW HOW TO MAKE TOAST, AT LEAST.
CLUNK
......

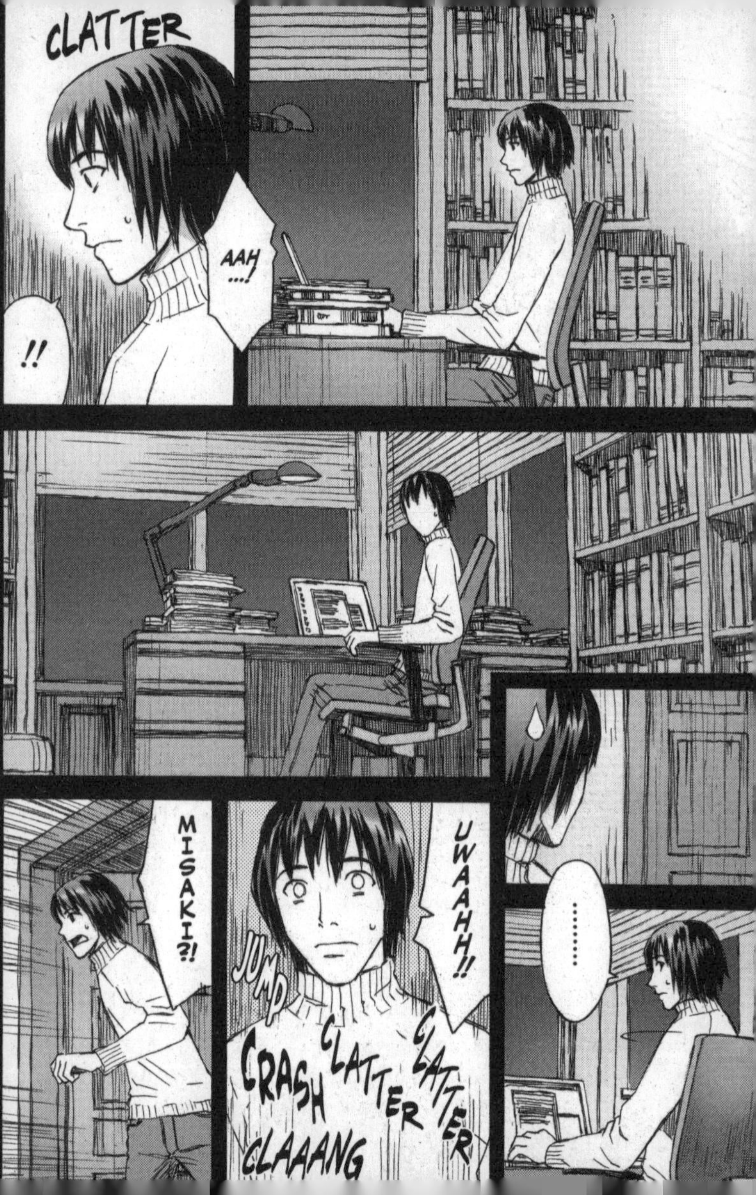
CLATTER
AAH ....!
!!
....
UWAAHH!!
JUMP
CLATTER
CLATTER
CRASH
CLAAANG
MISAKI?!

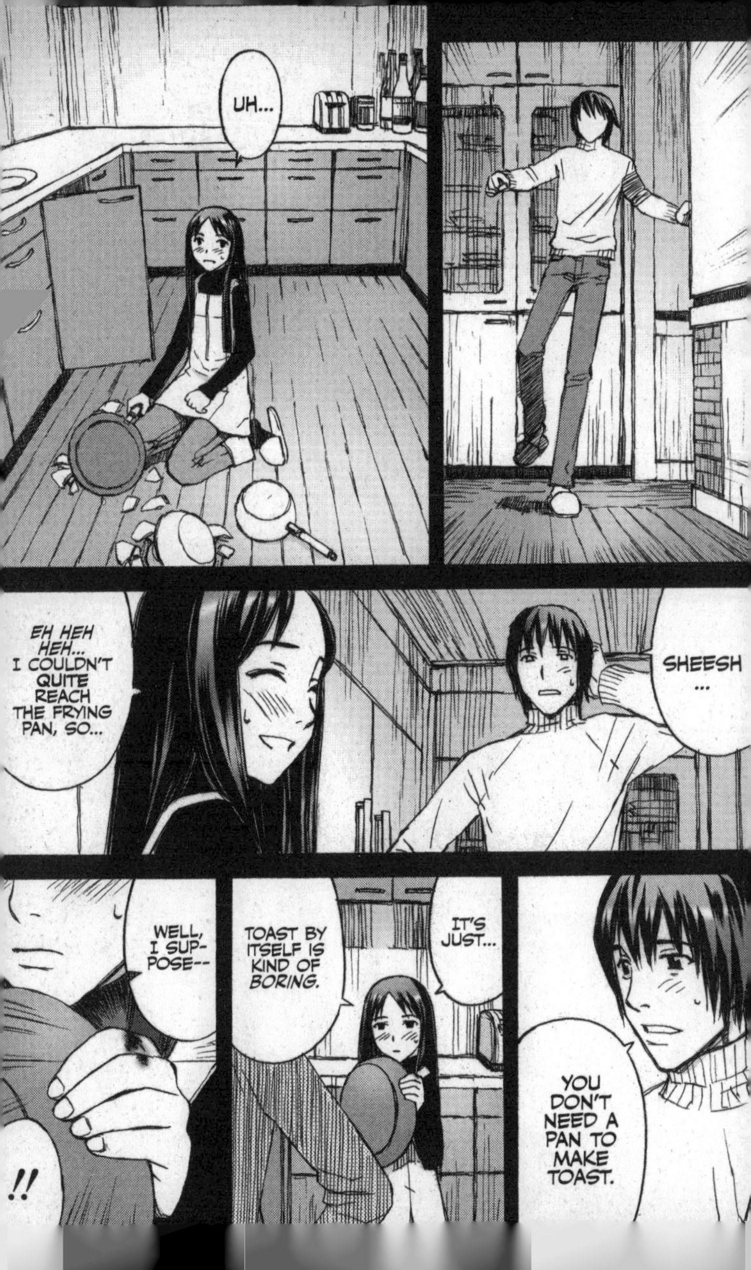
UH...
SHEESH ...
EH HEH HEH... I COULDN'T QUITE REACH THE FRYING PAN, SO...
YOU DON'T NEED A PAN TO MAKE TOAST.
IT'S JUST...
TOAST BY ITSELF IS KIND OF *BORING.*
WELL, I SUP-POSE--
!!

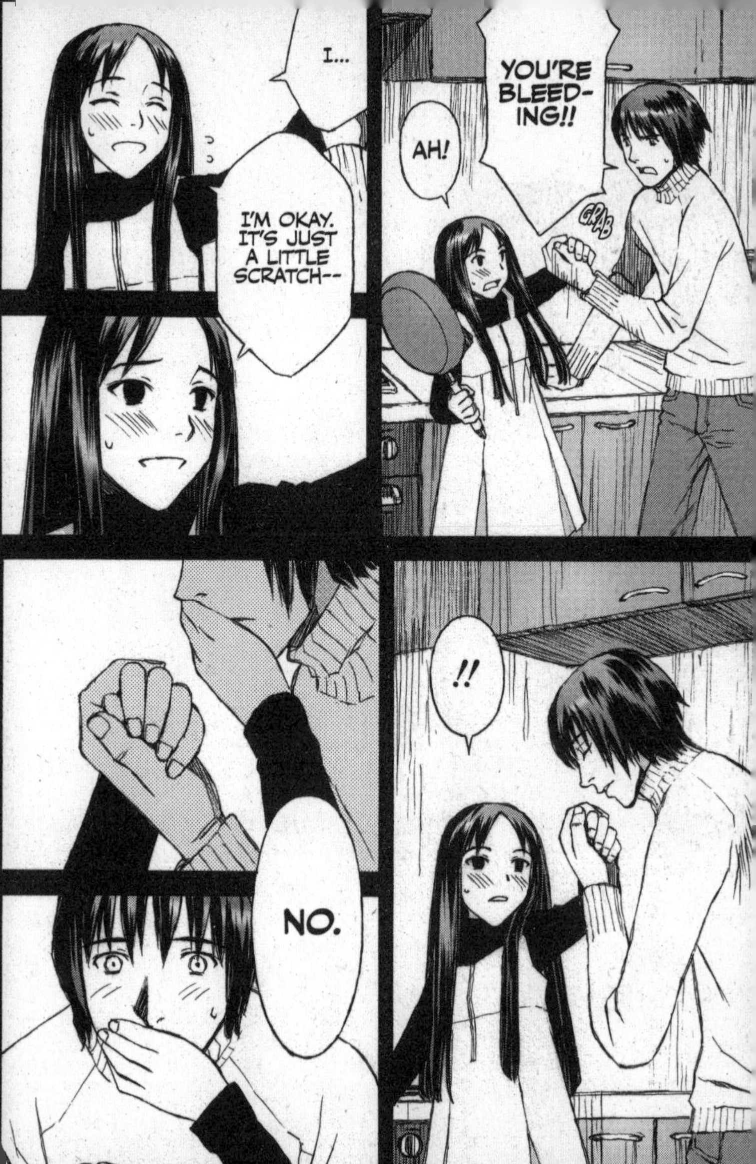
YOU'RE BLEED-ING!!
AH!
GRAB
I...
I'M OKAY. IT'S JUST A LITTLE SCRATCH--
!!
NO.

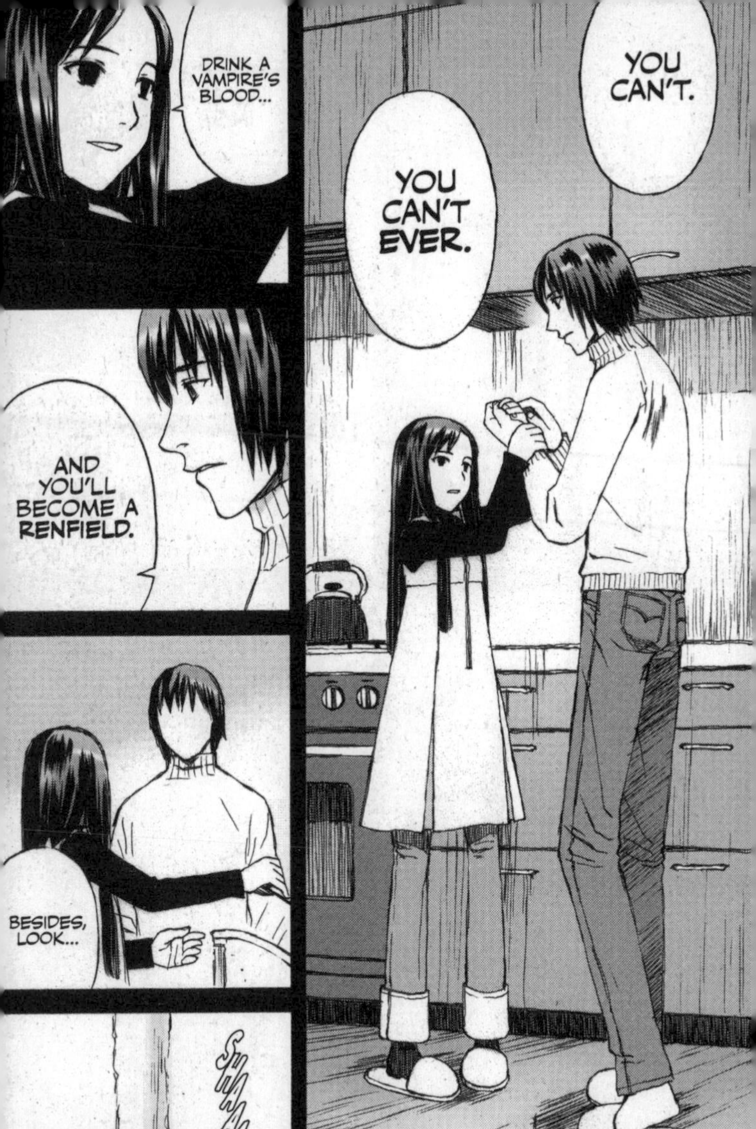
YOU CAN'T.
YOU CAN'T EVER.
DRINK A VAMPIRE'S BLOOD...
AND YOU'LL BECOME A RENFIELD.
BESIDES, LOOK...
SHAAA

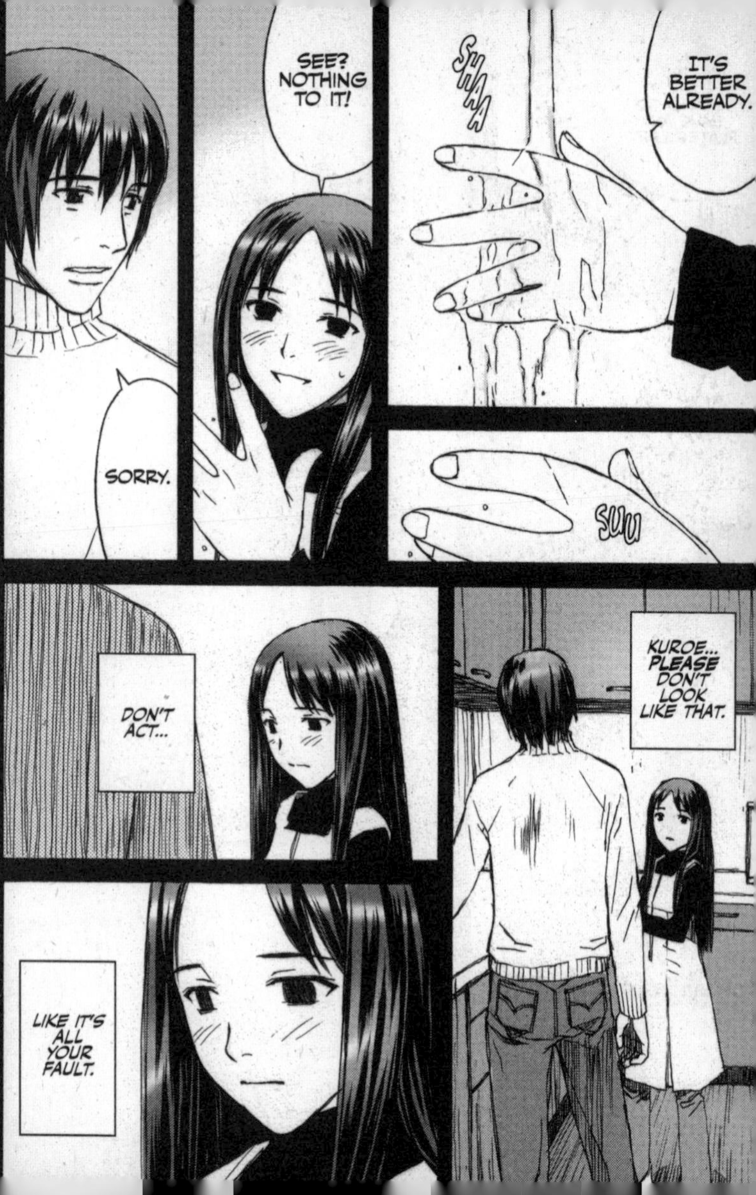
IT'S BETTER ALREADY.
SHAA
SUU
SEE? NOTHING TO IT!
SORRY.
KUROE... PLEASE DON'T LOOK LIKE THAT.
DON'T ACT...
LIKE IT'S ALL YOUR FAULT.

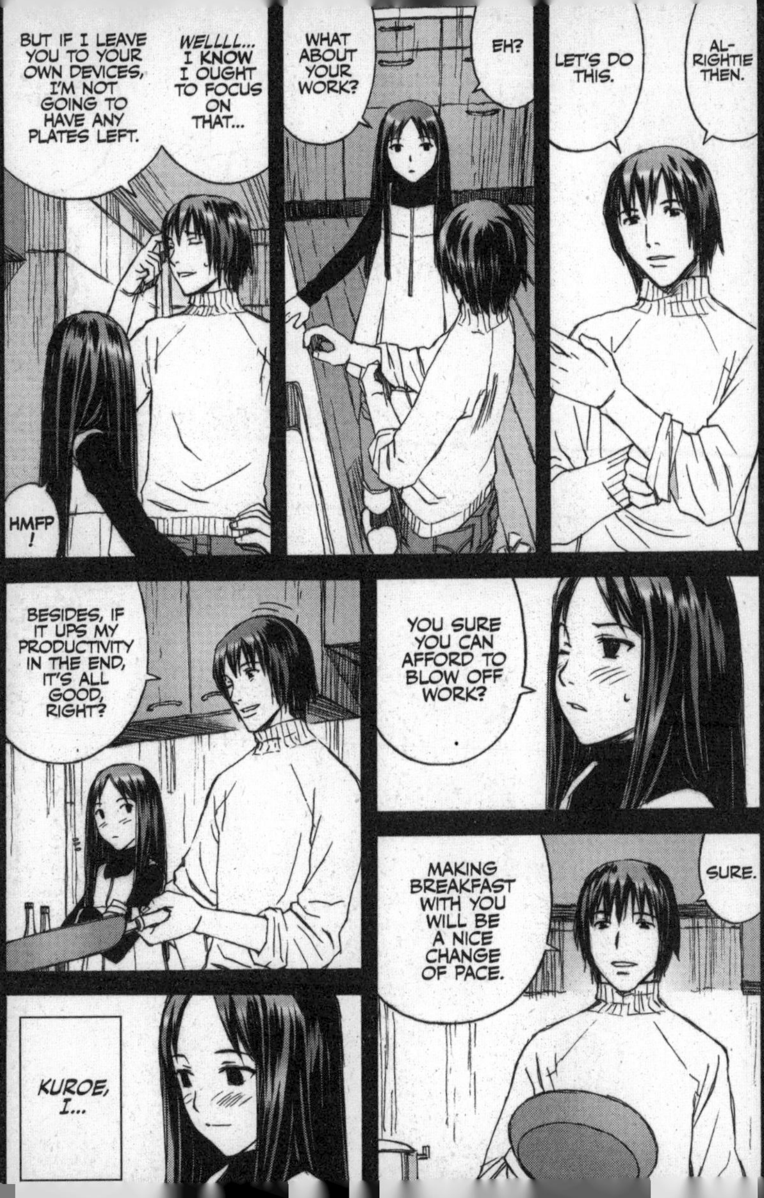
WELLLL... I KNOW I OUGHT TO FOCUS ON THAT...
BUT IF I LEAVE YOU TO YOUR OWN DEVICES, I'M NOT GOING TO HAVE ANY PLATES LEFT.
HMFP!
WHAT ABOUT YOUR WORK?
EH?
LET'S DO THIS.
AL-RIGHTIE THEN.
BESIDES, IF IT UPS MY PRODUCTIVITY IN THE END, IT'S ALL GOOD, RIGHT?
YOU SURE YOU CAN AFFORD TO BLOW OFF WORK?
MAKING BREAKFAST WITH YOU WILL BE A NICE CHANGE OF PACE.
SURE.
KUROE, I...

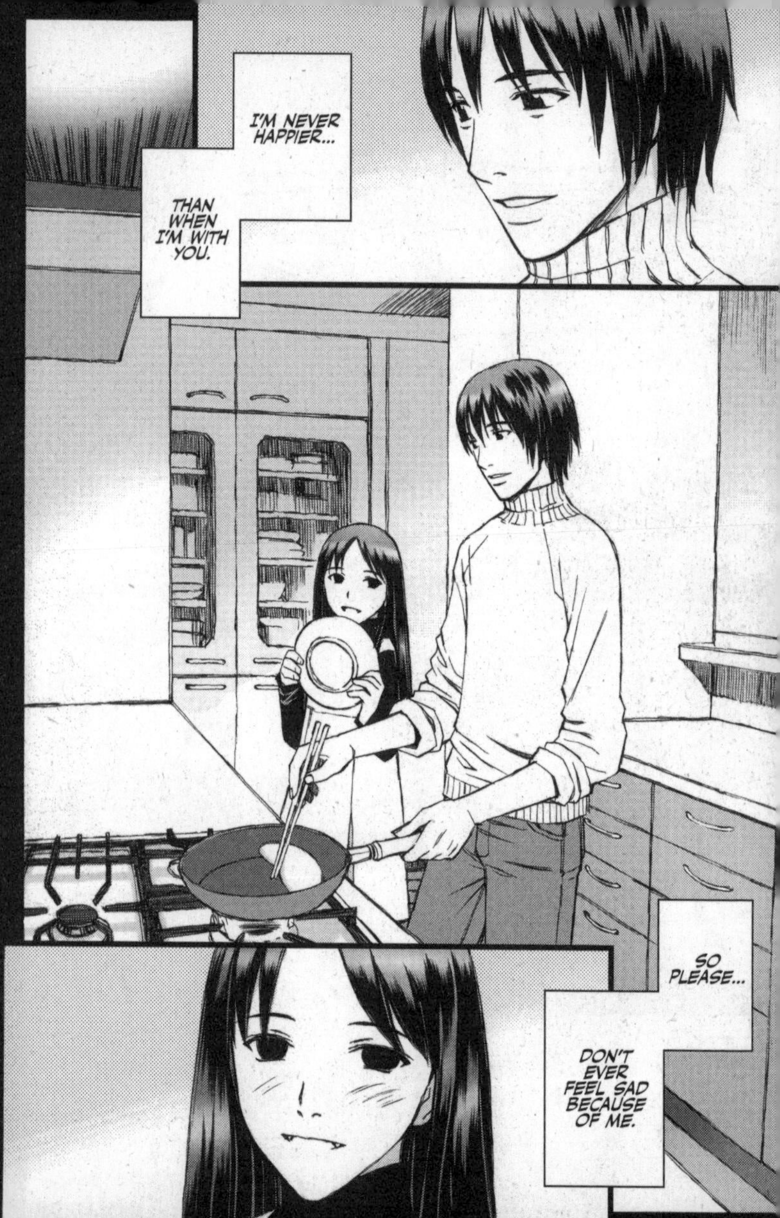
I'M NEVER HAPPIER...
THAN WHEN I'M WITH YOU.
SO PLEASE...
DON'T EVER FEEL SAD BECAUSE OF ME.

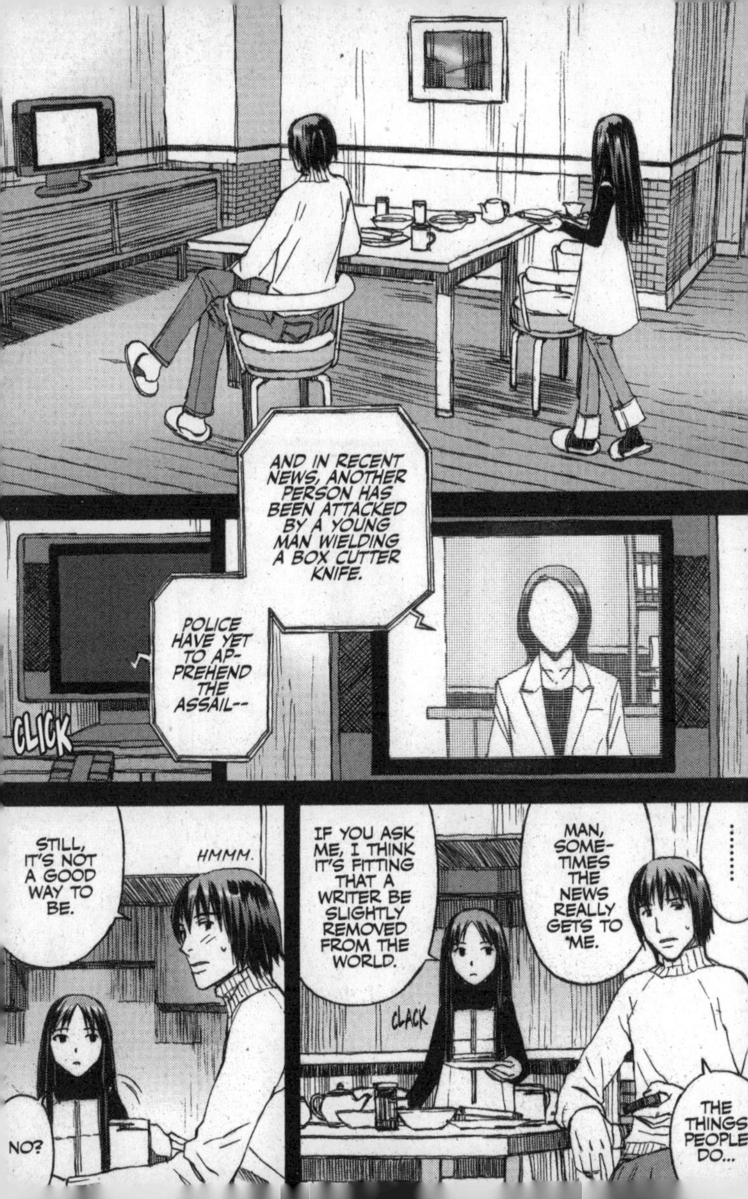
AND IN RECENT NEWS, ANOTHER PERSON HAS BEEN ATTACKED BY A YOUNG MAN WIELDING A BOX CUTTER KNIFE.
POLICE HAVE YET TO AP-PREHEND THE ASSAIL--
CLICK
......
MAN, SOME-TIMES THE NEWS REALLY GETS TO 'ME.
THE THINGS PEOPLE DO...
IF YOU ASK ME, I THINK IT'S FITTING THAT A WRITER BE SLIGHTLY REMOVED FROM THE WORLD.
CLACK
HMMM.
STILL, IT'S NOT A GOOD WAY TO BE.
NO?

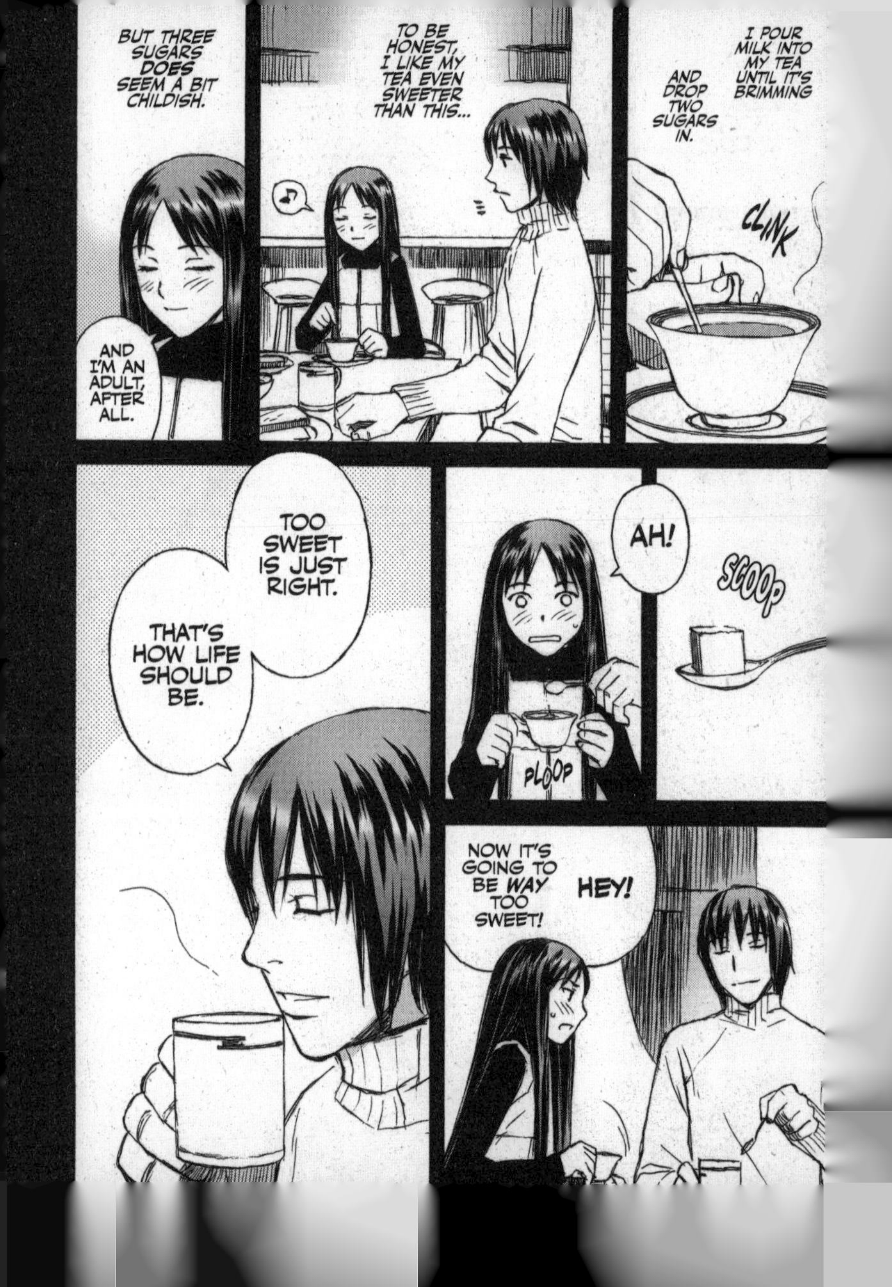

I POUR MILK INTO MY TEA UNTIL IT'S BRIMMING
AND DROP TWO SUGARS IN.
CLINK
TO BE HONEST, I LIKE MY TEA EVEN SWEETER THAN THIS...
BUT THREE SUGARS DOES SEEM A BIT CHILDISH.
AND I'M AN ADULT, AFTER ALL.
SCOOP
AH!
PLOOP
HEY!
NOW IT'S GOING TO BE WAY TOO SWEET!
TOO SWEET IS JUST RIGHT.
THAT'S HOW LIFE SHOULD BE.

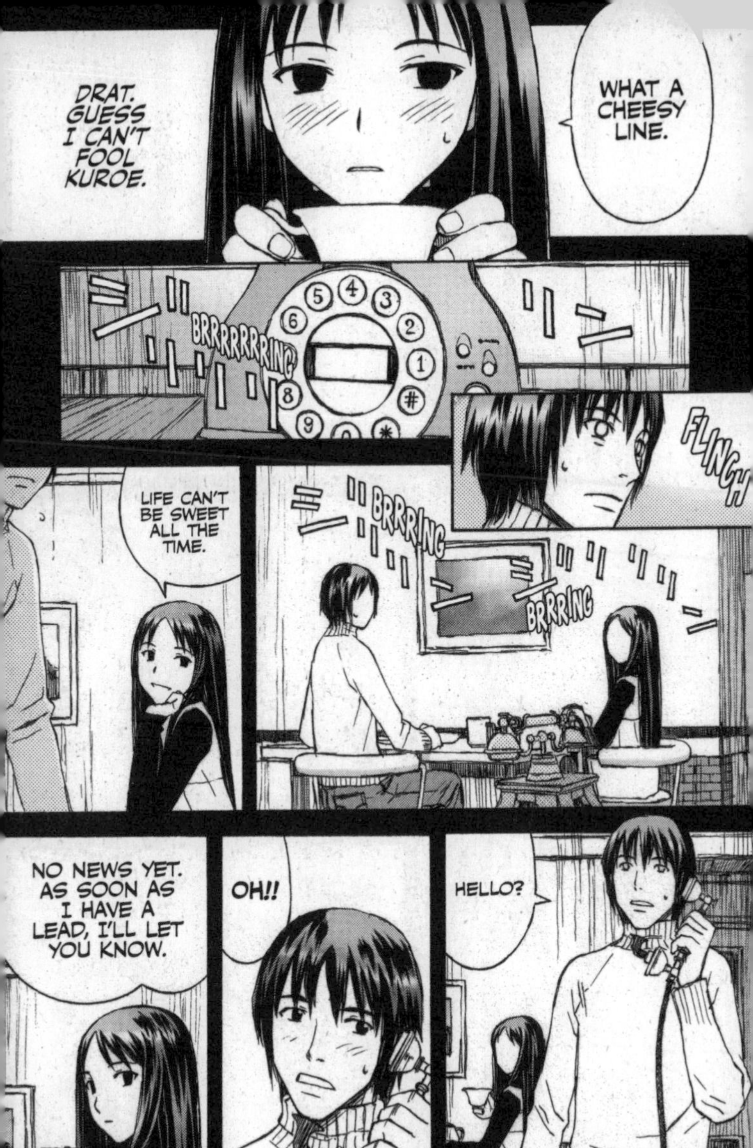
WHAT A CHEESY LINE.
DRAT. GUESS I CAN'T FOOL KUROE.
BRRRRRRRING
FLINCH
BRRRING
BRRRING
LIFE CAN'T BE SWEET ALL THE TIME.
HELLO?
OH!!
NO NEWS YET. AS SOON AS I HAVE A LEAD, I'LL LET YOU KNOW.

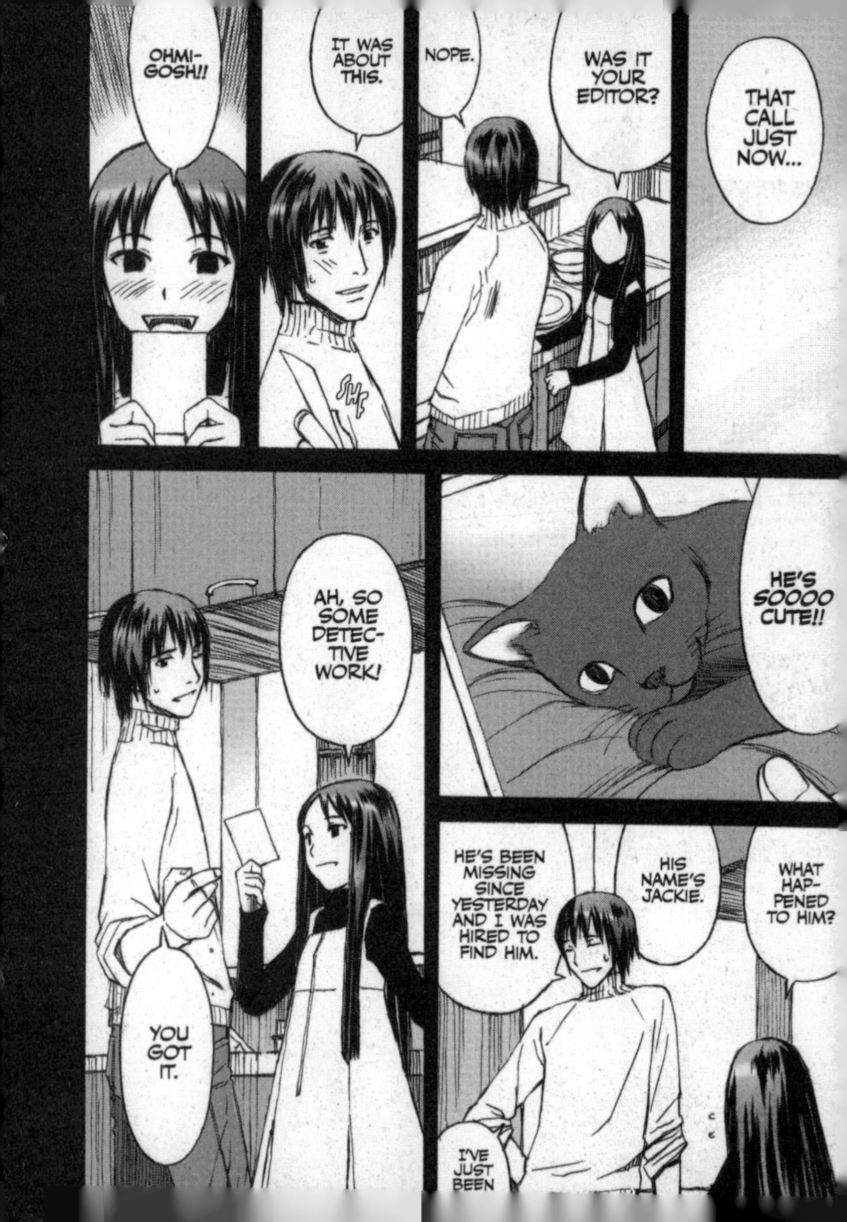
THAT CALL JUST NOW...
WAS IT YOUR EDITOR?
NOPE.
IT WAS ABOUT THIS.
OHMI-GOSH!!
HE'S SOOOO CUTE!!
WHAT HAP-PENED TO HIM?
HIS NAME'S JACKIE.
HE'S BEEN MISSING SINCE YESTERDAY AND I WAS HIRED TO FIND HIM.
I'VE JUST BEEN
AH, SO SOME DETEC-TIVE WORK!
YOU GOT IT.

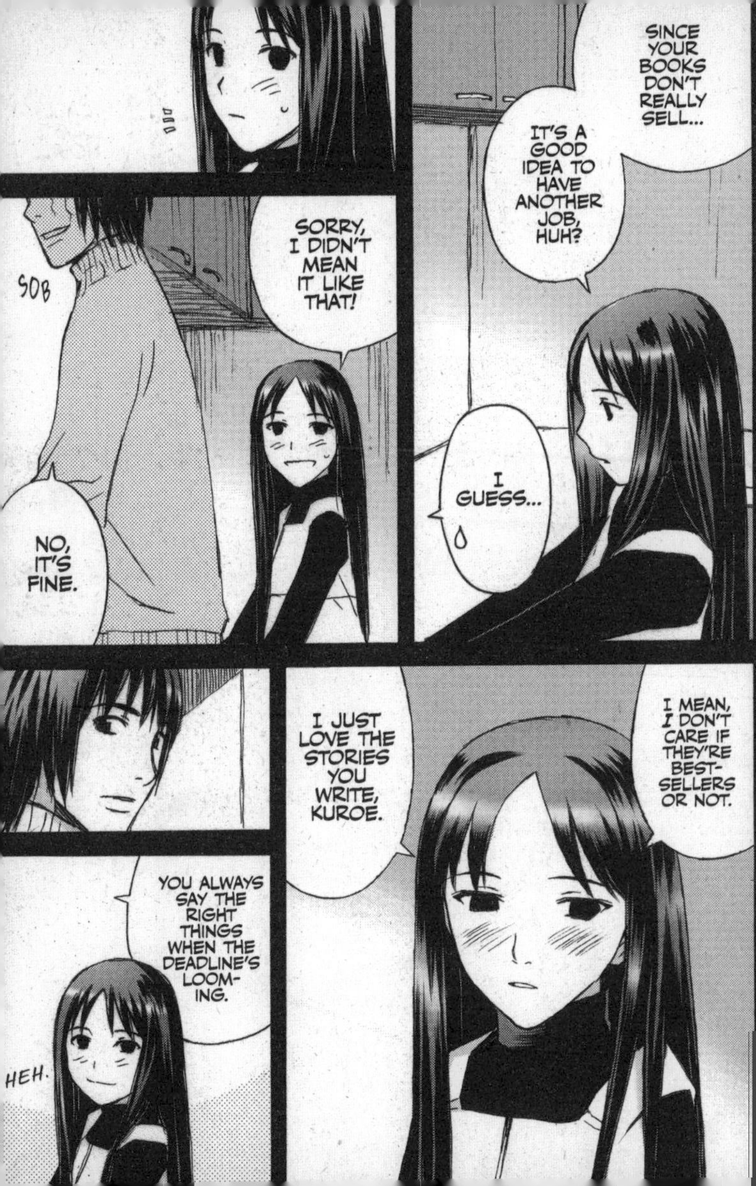
SINCE YOUR BOOKS DON'T REALLY SELL...
IT'S A GOOD IDEA TO HAVE ANOTHER JOB, HUH?
I GUESS...
SORRY, I DIDN'T MEAN IT LIKE THAT!
SOB
NO, IT'S FINE.
I MEAN, I DON'T CARE IF THEY'RE BEST-SELLERS OR NOT.
I JUST LOVE THE STORIES YOU WRITE, KUROE.
YOU ALWAYS SAY THE RIGHT THINGS WHEN THE DEADLINE'S LOOMING.
HEH.

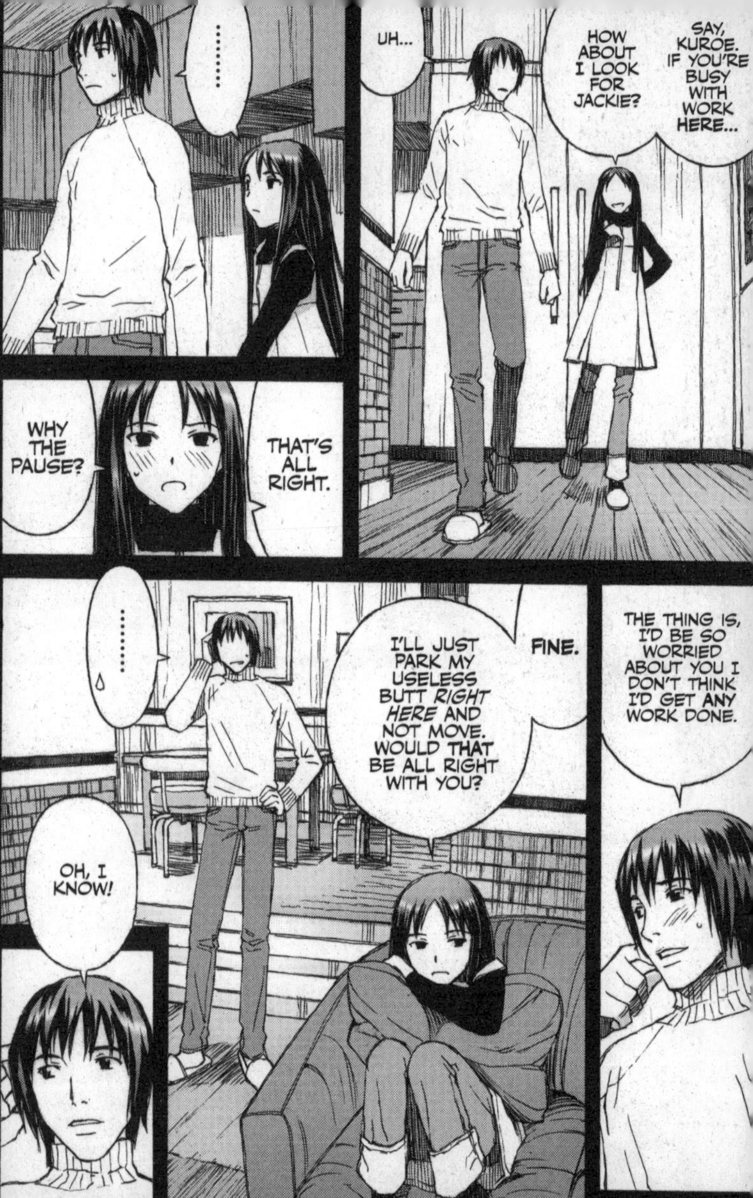
SAY, KUROE. IF YOU'RE BUSY WITH WORK HERE...
HOW ABOUT I LOOK FOR JACKIE?
UH...
......
THAT'S ALL RIGHT.
WHY THE PAUSE?
THE THING IS, I'D BE SO WORRIED ABOUT YOU I DON'T THINK I'D GET ANY WORK DONE.
FINE.
I'LL JUST PARK MY USELESS BUTT *RIGHT HERE* AND NOT MOVE. WOULD THAT BE ALL RIGHT WITH YOU?
......
OH, I KNOW!

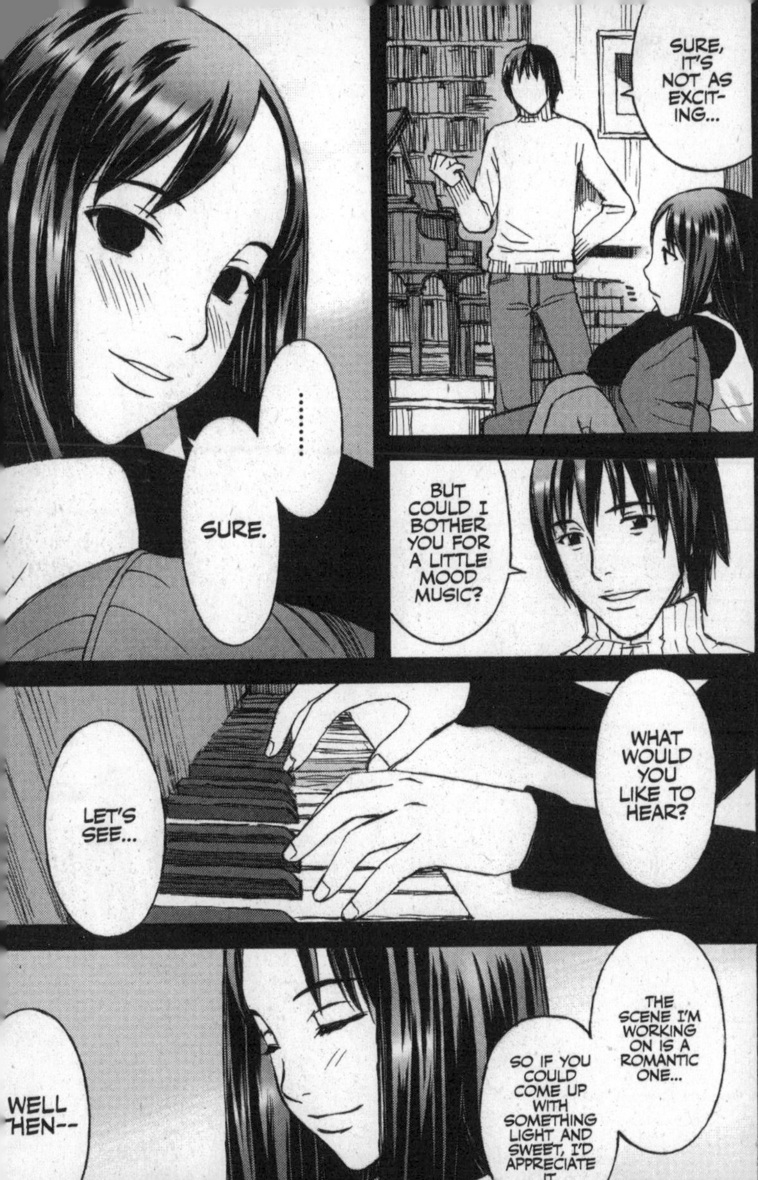

SURE, IT'S NOT AS EXCIT-ING...
BUT COULD I BOTHER YOU FOR A LITTLE MOOD MUSIC?
......
SURE.
WHAT WOULD YOU LIKE TO HEAR?
LET'S SEE...
THE SCENE I'M WORKING ON IS A ROMANTIC ONE...
SO IF YOU COULD COME UP WITH SOMETHING LIGHT AND SWEET, I'D APPRECIATE IT.
WELL THEN--

Episode 1
ORDINARY LIFE
An Ordinary Everyday

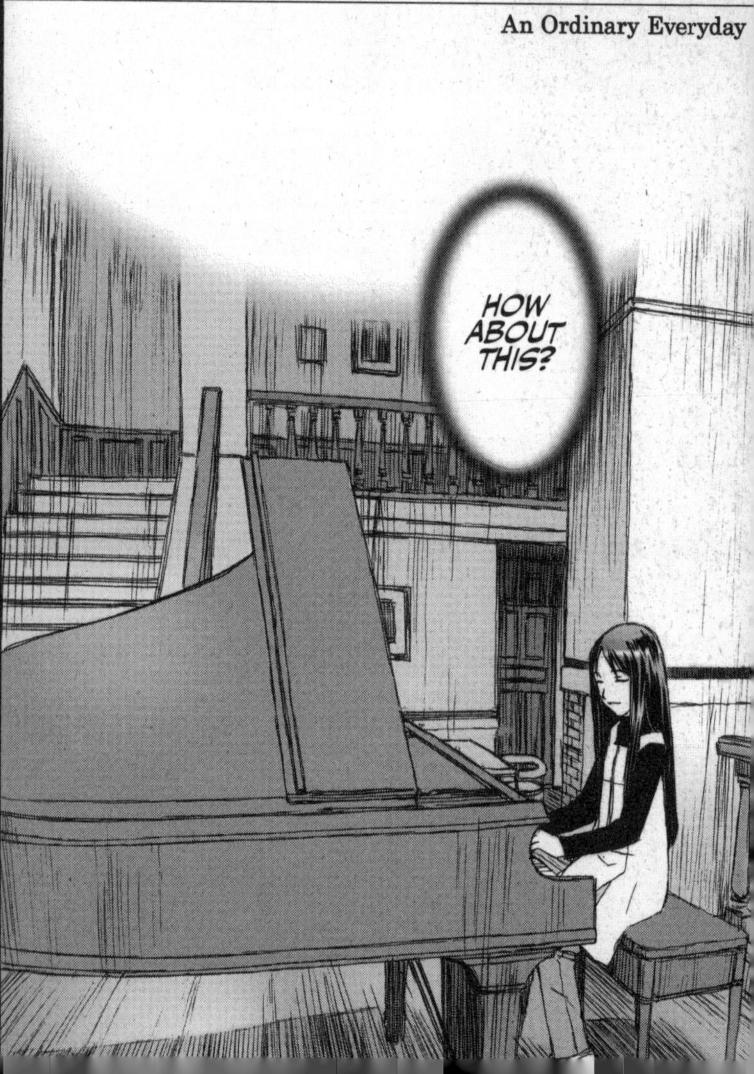
HOW ABOUT THIS?

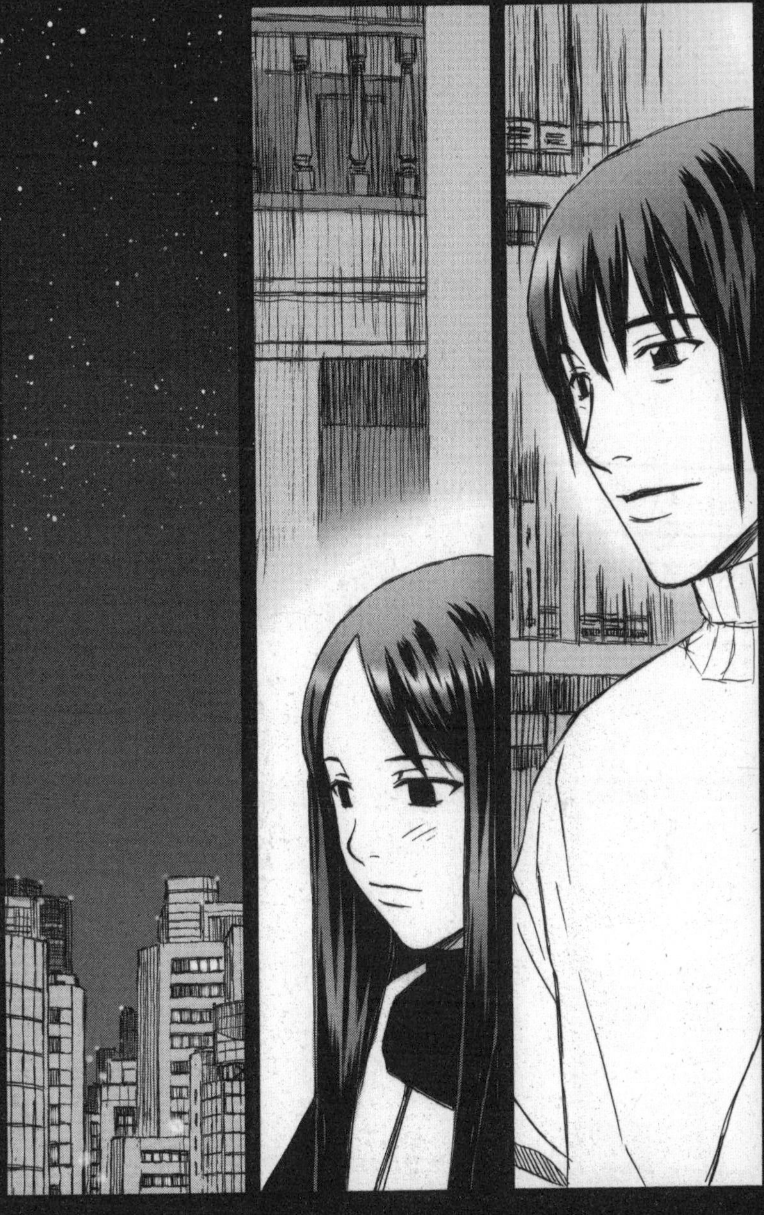

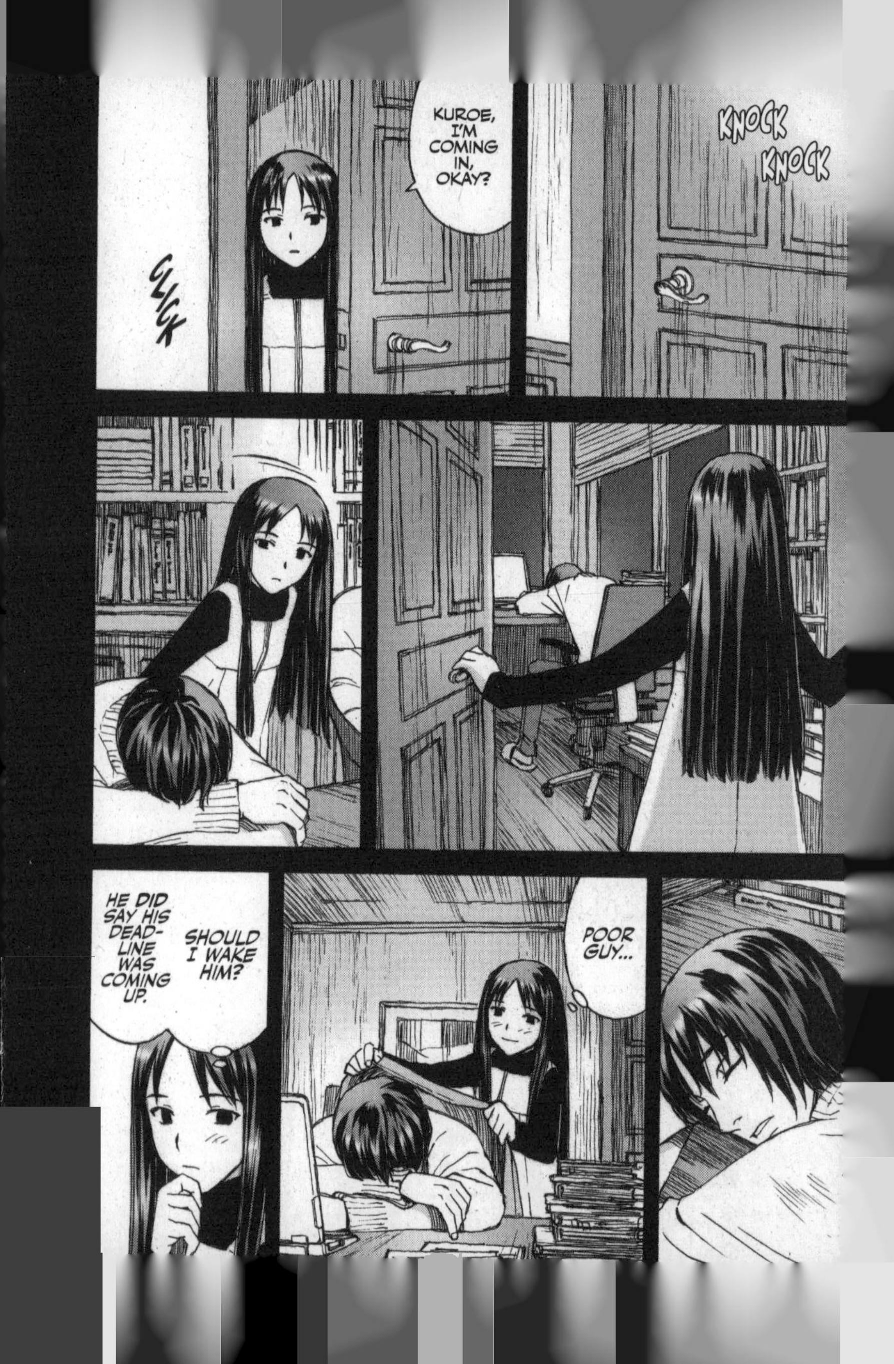
KNOCK KNOCK
KUROE, I'M COMING IN, OKAY?
CLICK
POOR GUY...
SHOULD I WAKE HIM?
HE DID SAY HIS DEAD-LINE WAS COMING UP.

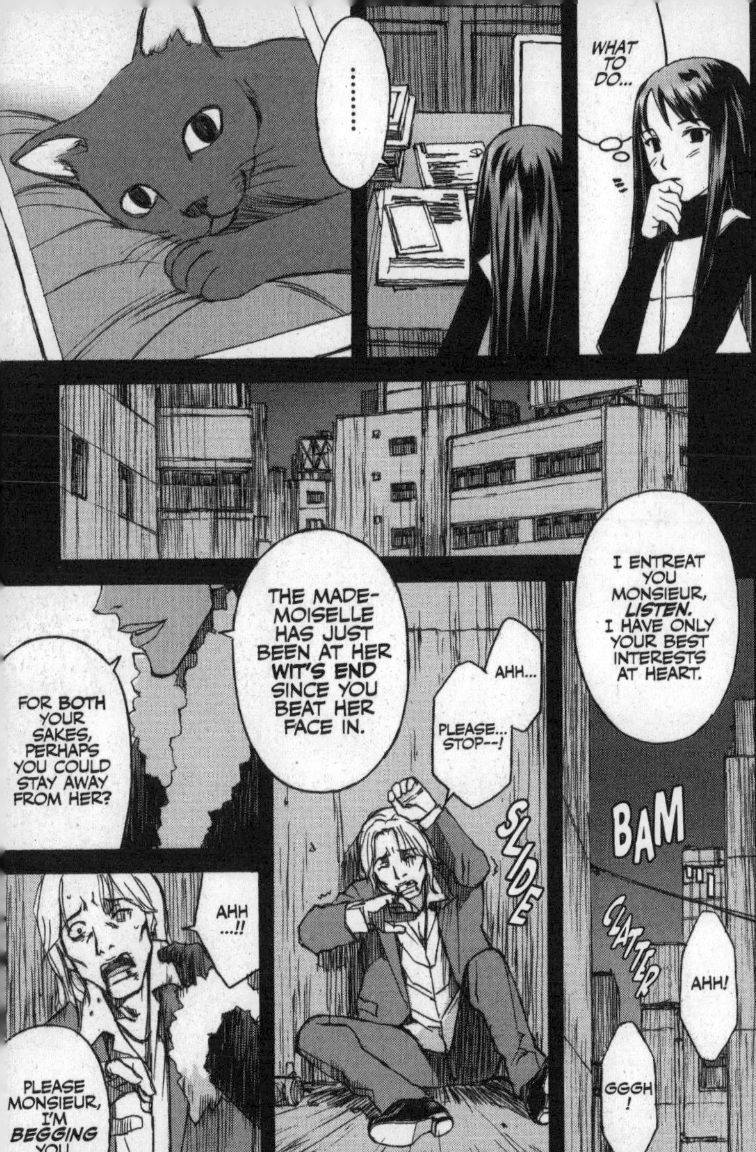
WHAT TO DO...
....
I ENTREAT YOU MONSIEUR, ***LISTEN.*** I HAVE ONLY YOUR BEST INTERESTS AT HEART.
BAM
CLATTER
AHH!
GGGH!
THE MADE-MOISELLE HAS JUST BEEN AT HER **WIT'S END** SINCE YOU BEAT HER FACE IN.
AHH...
PLEASE... STOP--!
SLIDE
FOR BOTH YOUR SAKES, PERHAPS YOU COULD STAY AWAY FROM HER?
AHH ...!!
PLEASE MONSIEUR, I'M ***BEGGING*** YOU.

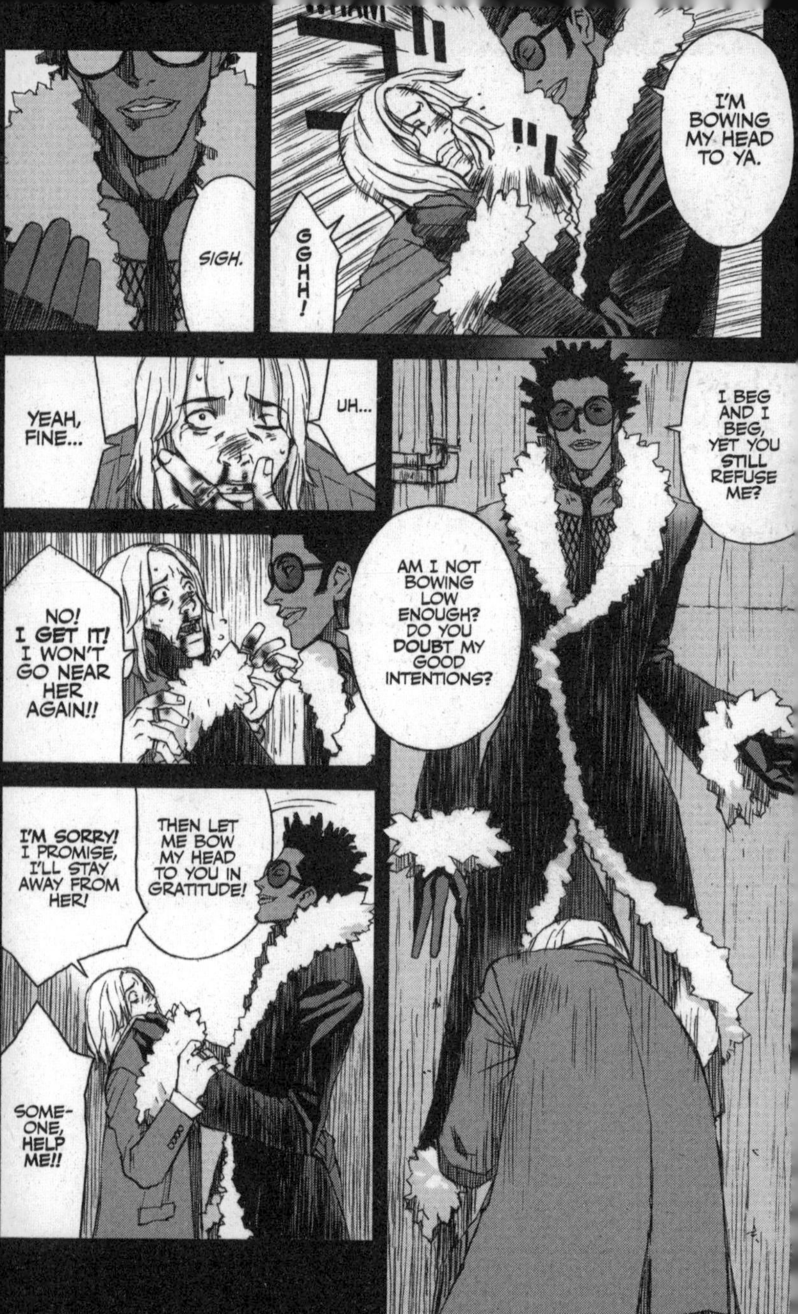
I'M BOWING MY HEAD TO YA.
GGHH!
SIGH.
I BEG AND I BEG, YET YOU STILL REFUSE ME?
AM I NOT BOWING LOW ENOUGH? DO YOU DOUBT MY GOOD INTENTIONS?
UH...
YEAH, FINE...
NO! I GET IT! I WON'T GO NEAR HER AGAIN!!
THEN LET ME BOW MY HEAD TO YOU IN GRATITUDE!
I'M SORRY! I PROMISE, I'LL STAY AWAY FROM HER!
SOME-ONE, HELP ME!!

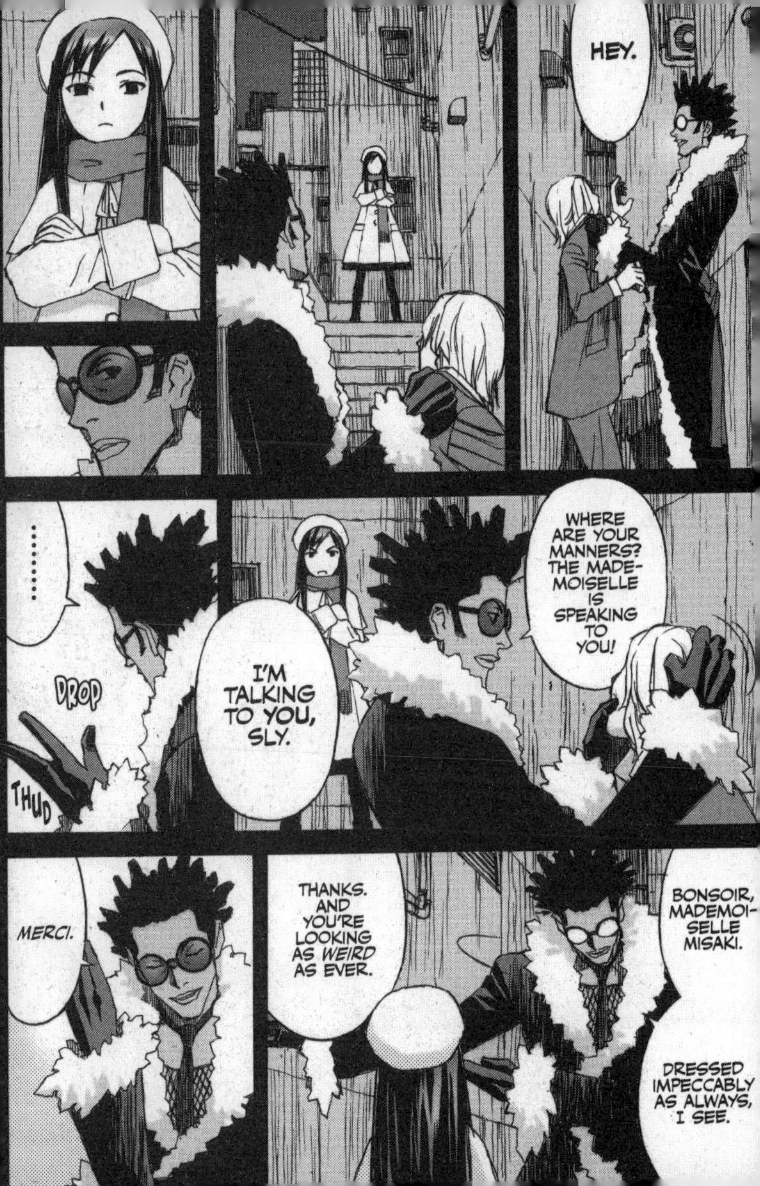
HEY.
WHERE ARE YOUR MANNERS? THE MADE-MOISELLE IS SPEAKING TO YOU!
I'M TALKING TO YOU, SLY.
......
DROP
THUD
BONSOIR, MADEMOI-SELLE MISAKI.
DRESSED IMPECCABLY AS ALWAYS, I SEE.
THANKS. AND YOU'RE LOOKING AS *WEIRD* AS EVER.
MERCI.

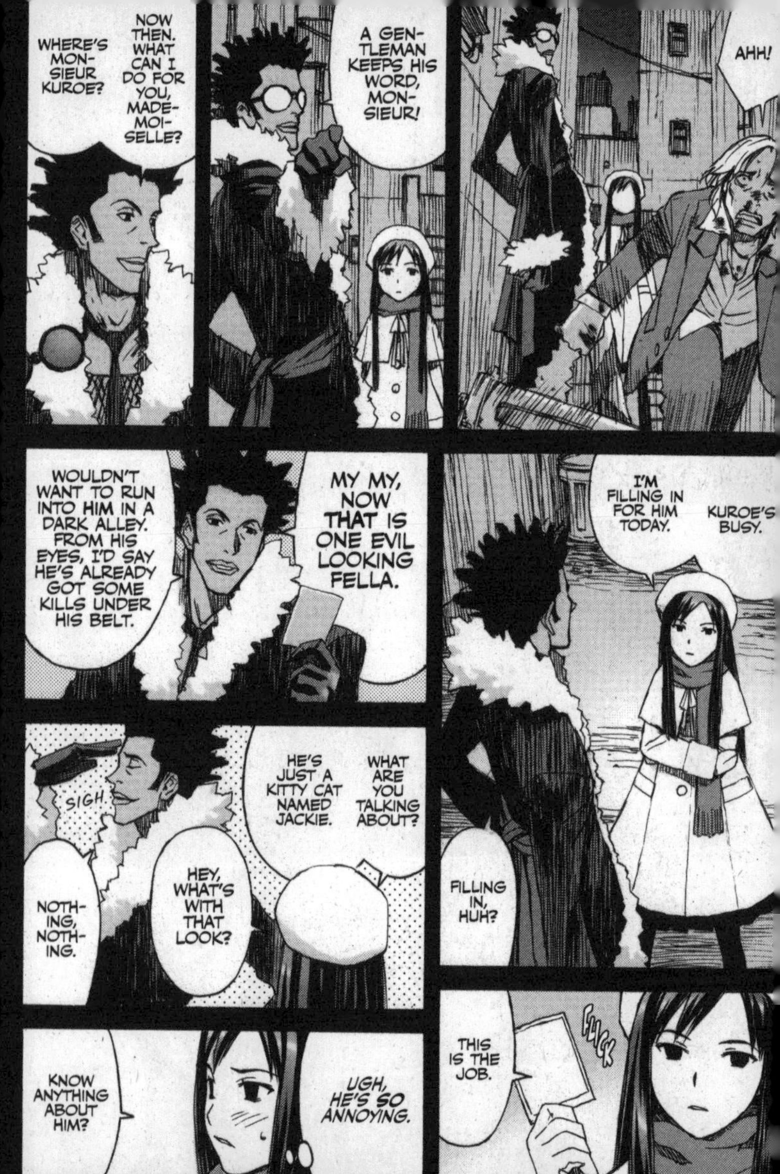
AHH!
A GENTLEMAN KEEPS HIS WORD, MONSIEUR!
NOW THEN. WHAT CAN I DO FOR YOU, MADEMOISELLE?
WHERE'S MONSIEUR KUROE?
KUROE'S BUSY.
I'M FILLING IN FOR HIM TODAY.
FILLING IN, HUH?
MY MY, NOW THAT IS ONE EVIL LOOKING FELLA.
WOULDN'T WANT TO RUN INTO HIM IN A DARK ALLEY. FROM HIS EYES, I'D SAY HE'S ALREADY GOT SOME KILLS UNDER HIS BELT.
WHAT ARE YOU TALKING ABOUT?
HE'S JUST A KITTY CAT NAMED JACKIE.
SIGH
HEY, WHAT'S WITH THAT LOOK?
NOTHING, NOTHING.
FLICK
THIS IS THE JOB.
UGH, HE'S SO ANNOYING.
KNOW ANYTHING ABOUT HIM?

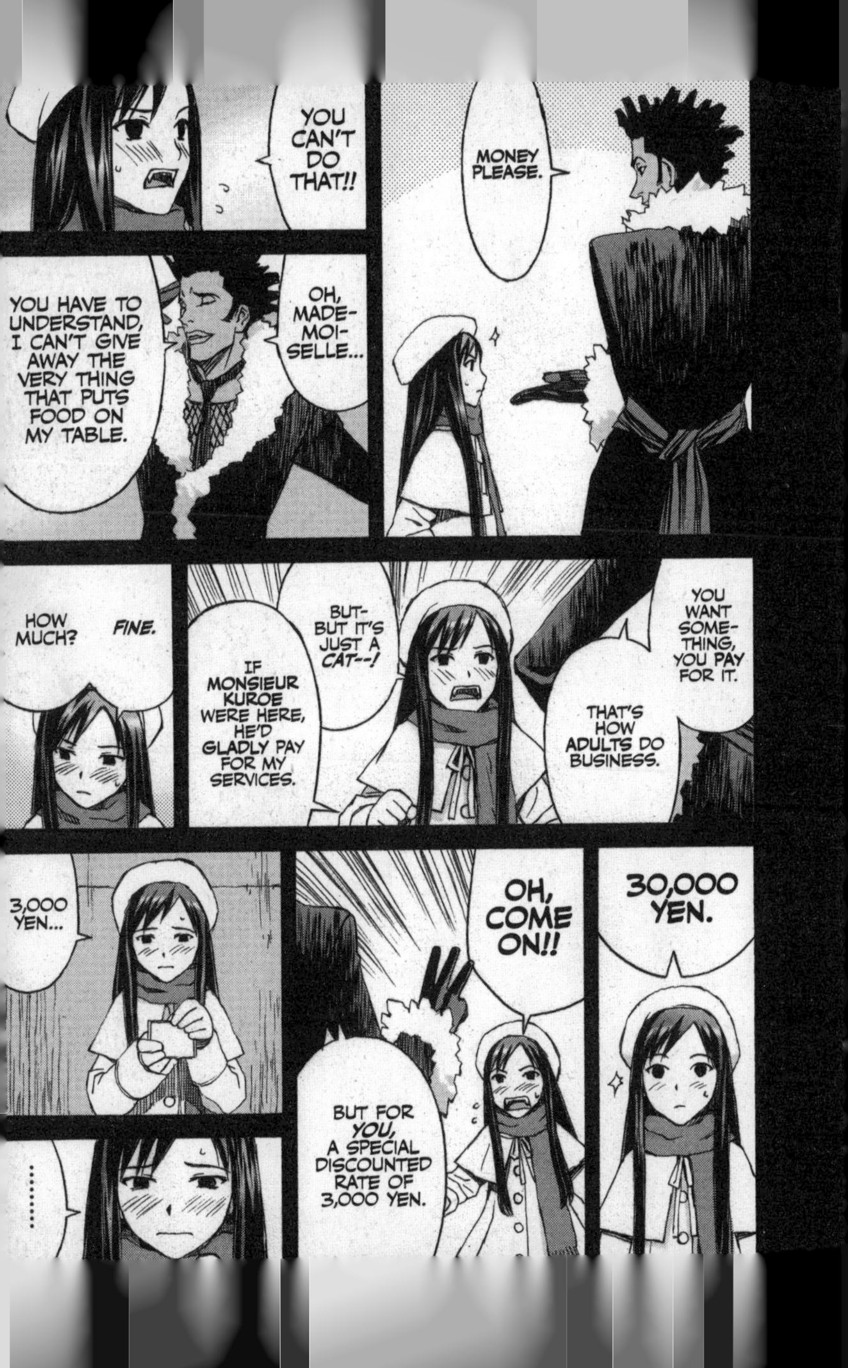
MONEY PLEASE.
YOU CAN'T DO THAT!!
OH, MADE-MOI-SELLE...
YOU HAVE TO UNDERSTAND, I CAN'T GIVE AWAY THE VERY THING THAT PUTS FOOD ON MY TABLE.
YOU WANT SOME-THING, YOU PAY FOR IT.
THAT'S HOW ADULTS DO BUSINESS.
BUT- BUT IT'S JUST A *CAT--!*
IF MONSIEUR KUROE WERE HERE, HE'D GLADLY PAY FOR MY SERVICES.
FINE.
HOW MUCH?
30,000 YEN.
OH, COME ON!!
BUT FOR *YOU*, A SPECIAL DISCOUNTED RATE OF 3,000 YEN.
3,000 YEN...
......

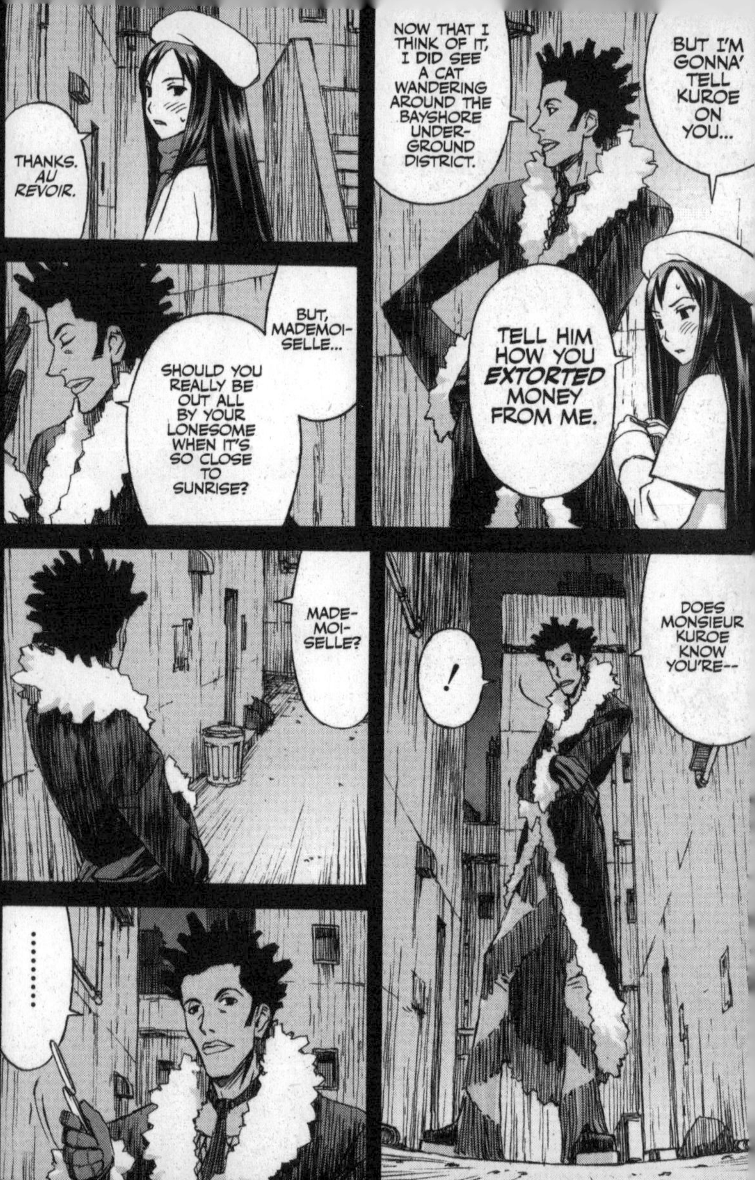
BUT I'M GONNA' TELL KUROE ON YOU...
NOW THAT I THINK OF IT, I DID SEE A CAT WANDERING AROUND THE BAYSHORE UNDER-GROUND DISTRICT.
TELL HIM HOW YOU *EXTORTED* MONEY FROM ME.
THANKS. AU REVOIR.
BUT, MADEMOI-SELLE...
SHOULD YOU REALLY BE OUT ALL BY YOUR LONESOME WHEN IT'S SO CLOSE TO SUNRISE?
DOES MONSIEUR KUROE KNOW YOU'RE--
!
MADE-MOI-SELLE?
....

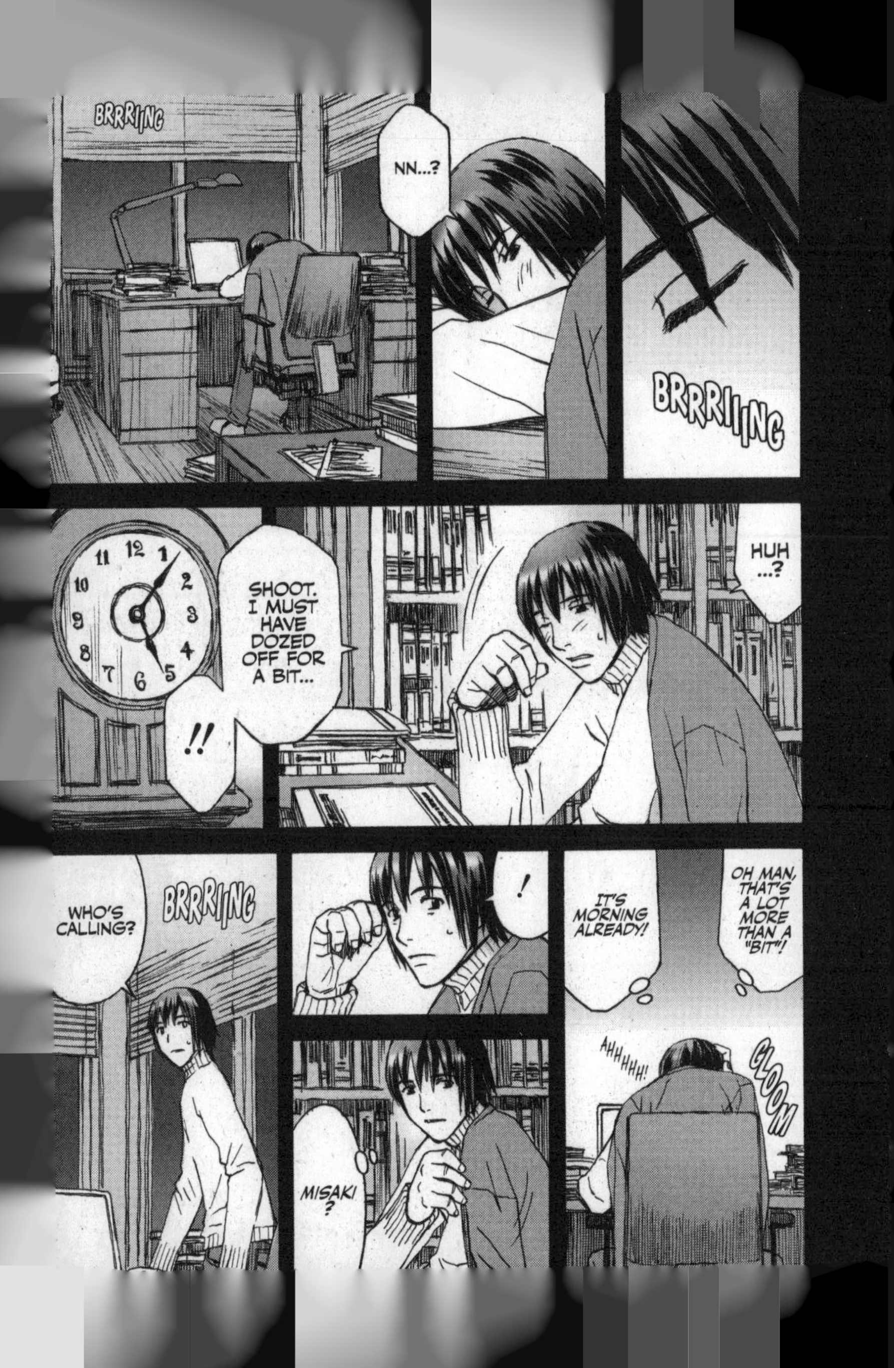
BRRRIIING
NN...?
BRRRIING
HUH ...?
SHOOT. I MUST HAVE DOZED OFF FOR A BIT...
!!
OH MAN, THAT'S A LOT MORE THAN A "BIT"!
IT'S MORNING ALREADY!
GLOOM
AHHHHH!
!
MISAKI ?
BRRRIING
WHO'S CALLING?

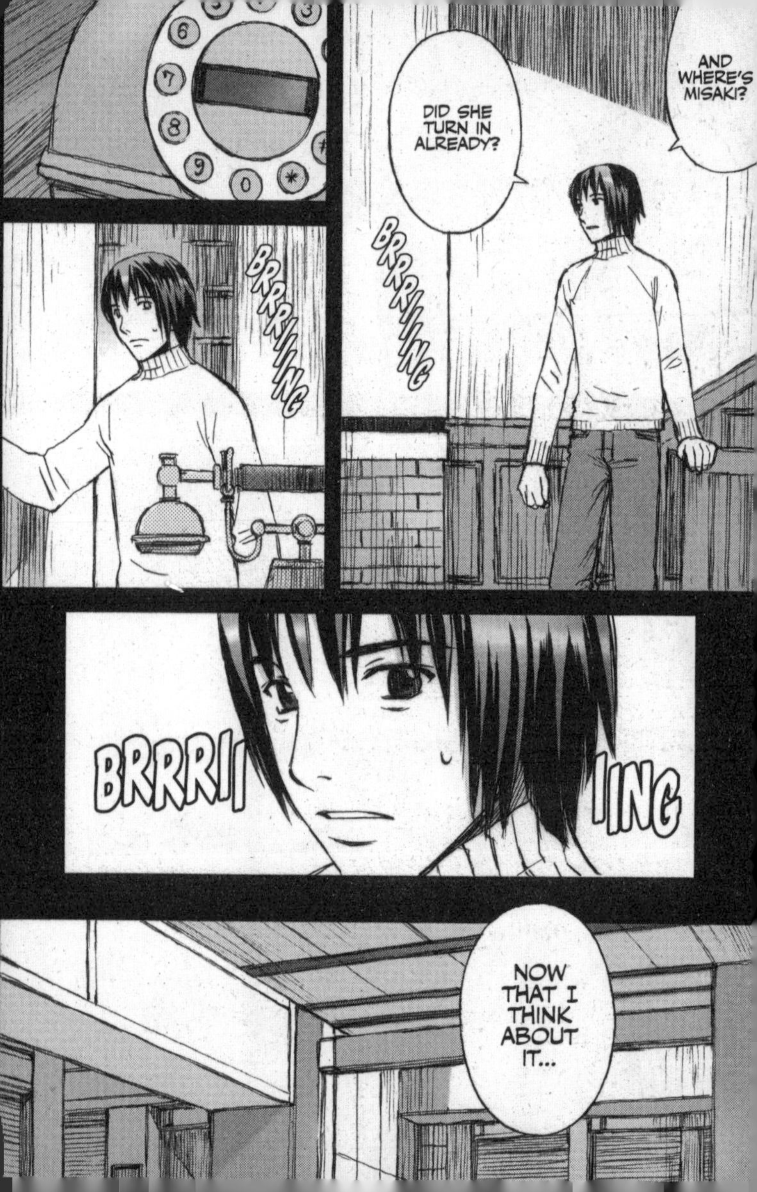
AND WHERE'S MISAKI?
DID SHE TURN IN ALREADY?
BRRRIIING
BRRRIIING
BRRRII
IING
NOW THAT I THINK ABOUT IT...

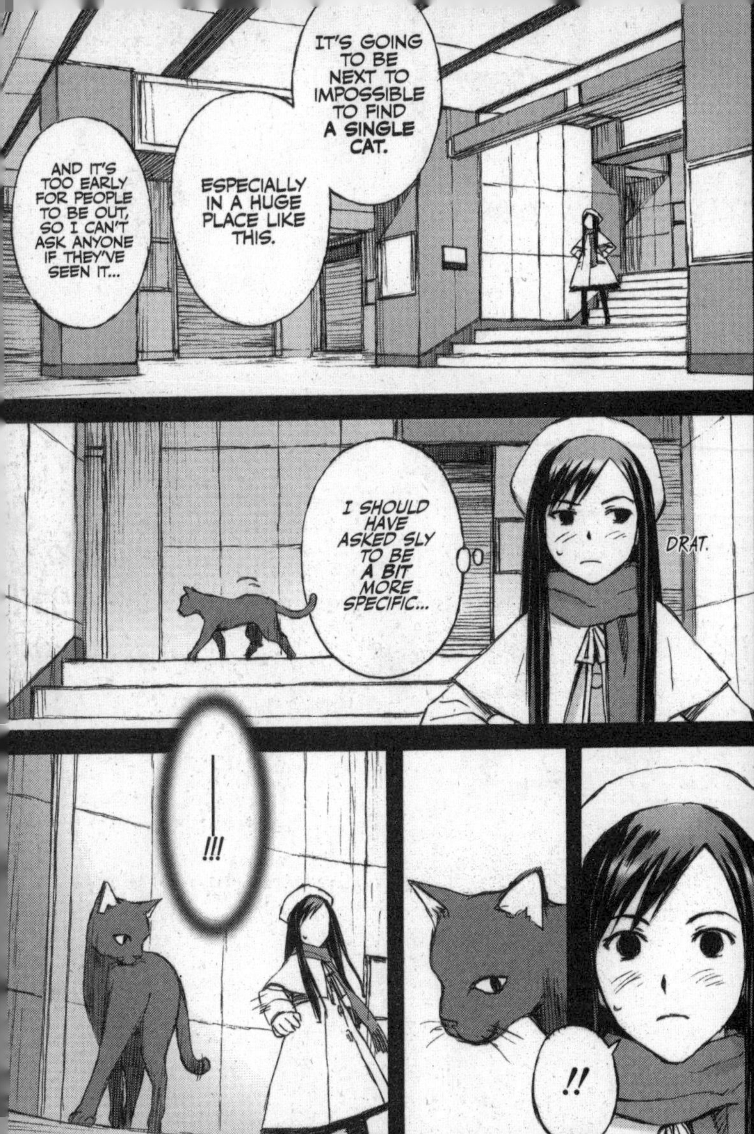
IT'S GOING TO BE NEXT TO IMPOSSIBLE TO FIND A SINGLE CAT.
ESPECIALLY IN A HUGE PLACE LIKE THIS.
AND IT'S TOO EARLY FOR PEOPLE TO BE OUT, SO I CAN'T ASK ANYONE IF THEY'VE SEEN IT...
I SHOULD HAVE ASKED SLY TO BE A BIT MORE SPECIFIC...
DRAT.
!!
—!!!

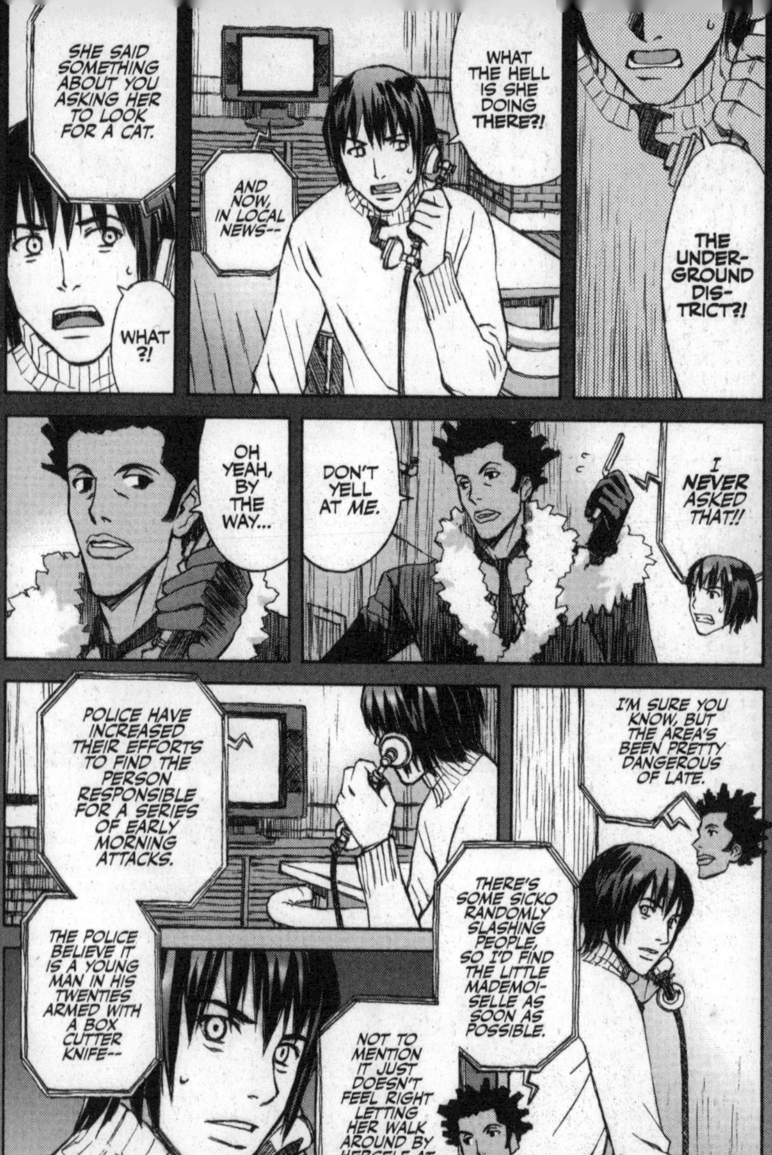
THE UNDER-GROUND DIS-TRICT?!
WHAT THE HELL IS SHE DOING THERE?!
AND NOW, IN LOCAL NEWS--
SHE SAID SOMETHING ABOUT YOU ASKING HER TO LOOK FOR A CAT.
WHAT?!
I NEVER ASKED THAT!!
DON'T YELL AT ME.
OH YEAH, BY THE WAY...
I'M SURE YOU KNOW, BUT THE AREA'S BEEN PRETTY DANGEROUS OF LATE.
THERE'S SOME SICKO RANDOMLY SLASHING PEOPLE, SO I'D FIND THE LITTLE MADEMOI-SELLE AS SOON AS POSSIBLE.
POLICE HAVE INCREASED THEIR EFFORTS TO FIND THE PERSON RESPONSIBLE FOR A SERIES OF EARLY MORNING ATTACKS.
THE POLICE BELIEVE IT IS A YOUNG MAN IN HIS TWENTIES ARMED WITH A BOX CUTTER KNIFE--
NOT TO MENTION IT JUST DOESN'T FEEL RIGHT LETTING HER WALK AROUND BY HERSELF AT THIS TIME OF DAY.

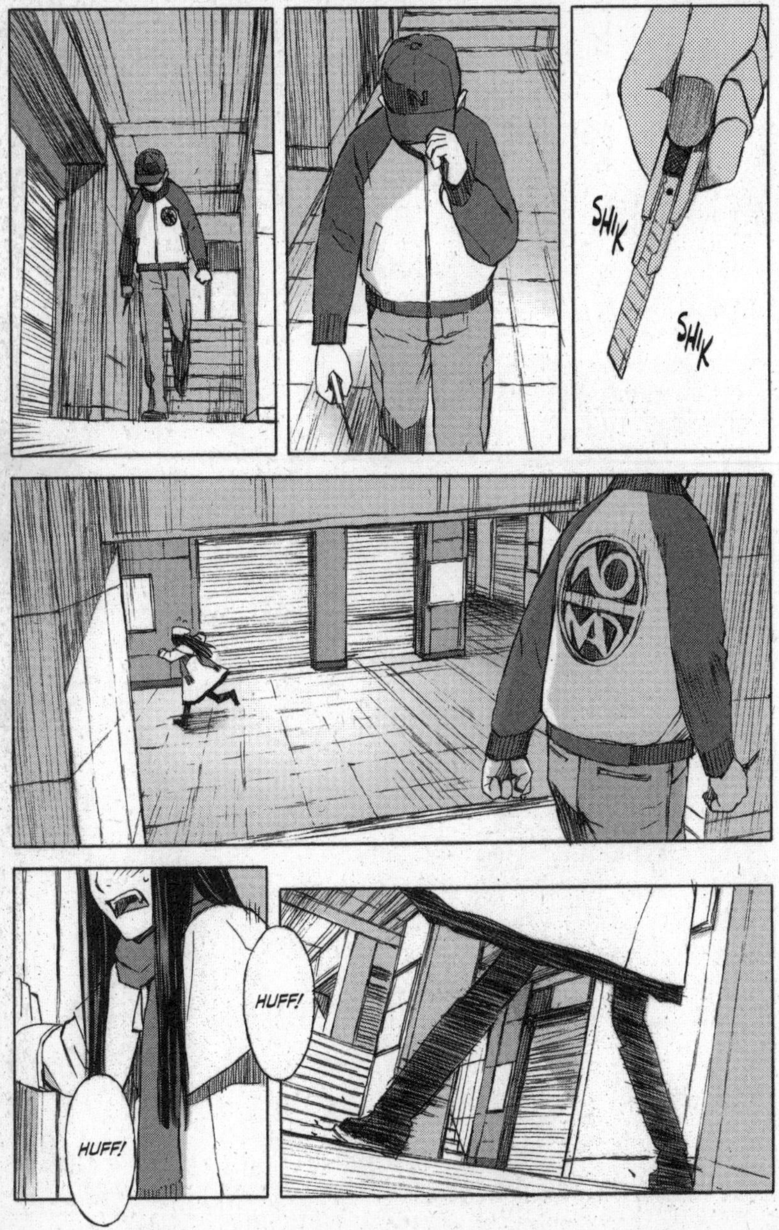
SHIK
SHIK
HUFF!
HUFF!

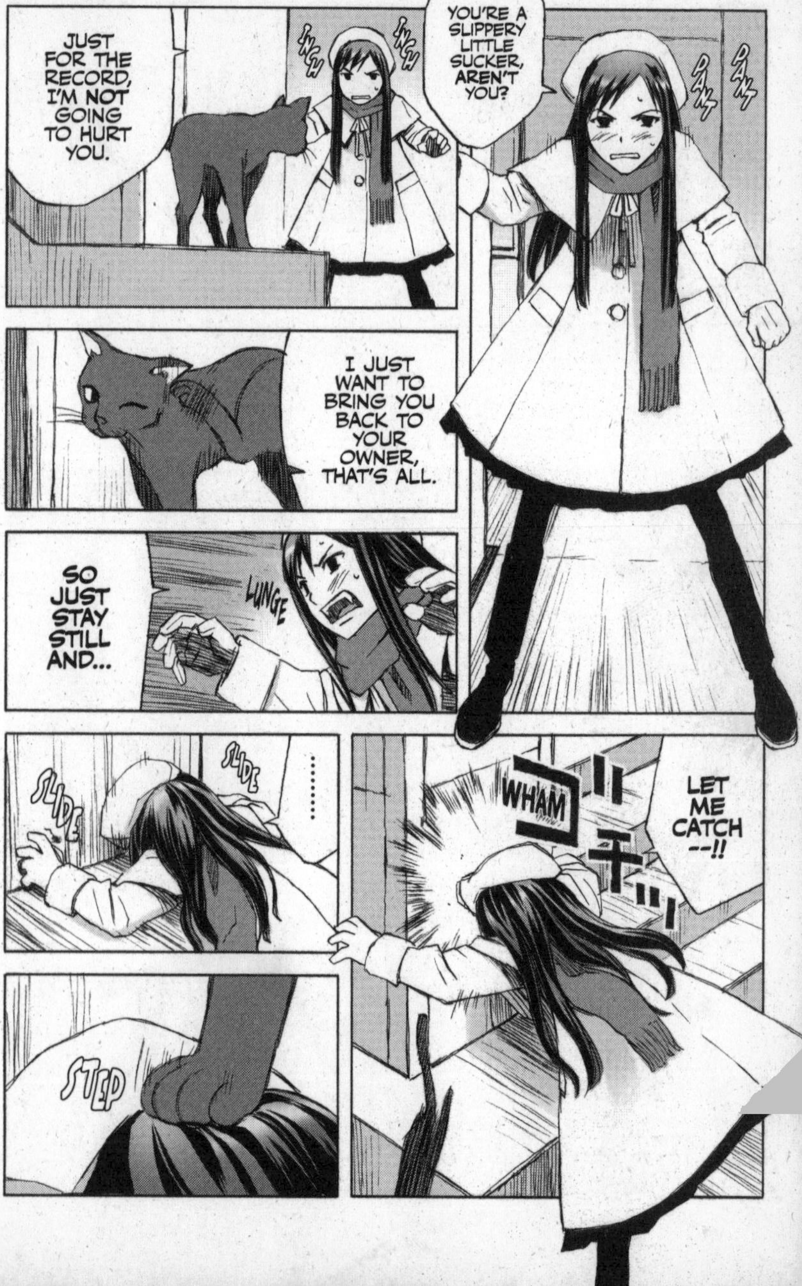

YOU'RE A SLIPPERY LITTLE SUCKER, AREN'T YOU?
PANT PANT
INCH INCH
JUST FOR THE RECORD, I'M NOT GOING TO HURT YOU.
I JUST WANT TO BRING YOU BACK TO YOUR OWNER, THAT'S ALL.
SO JUST STAY STILL AND...
LUNGE
LET ME CATCH --!!
WHAM
SLIDE
SLIDE
......
STEP

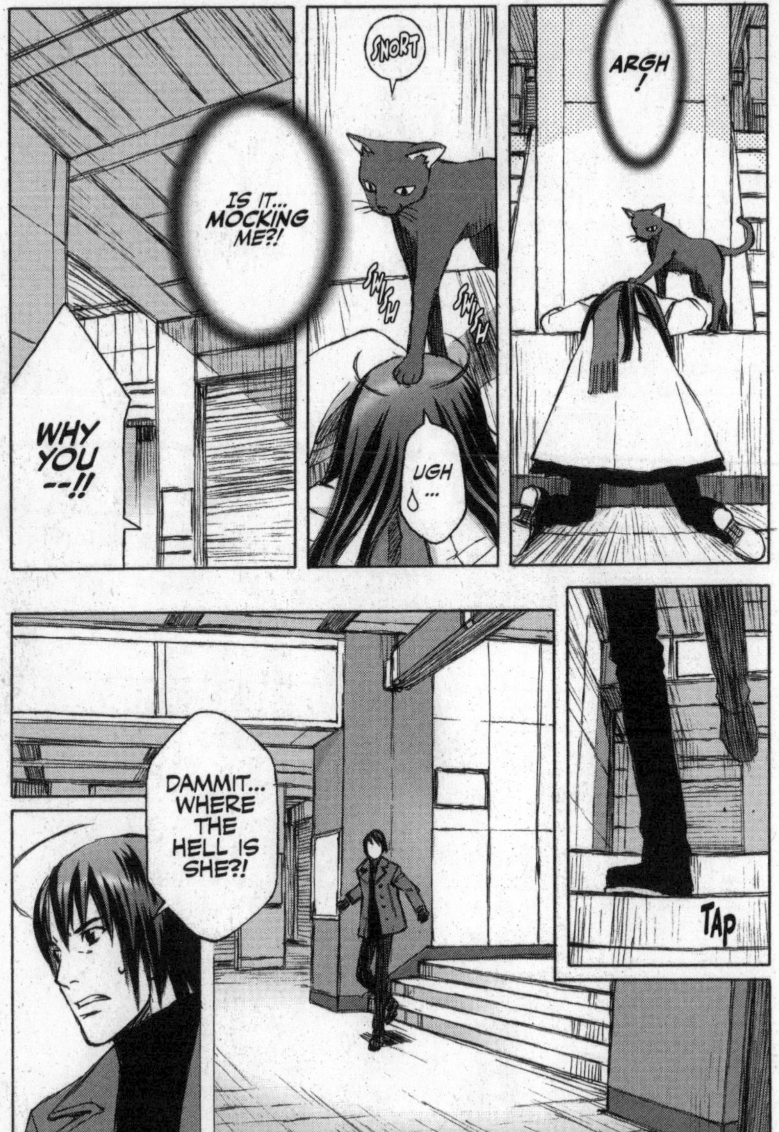
ARGH!
SNORT
IS IT... MOCKING ME?!
SWISH
SWISH
UGH...
WHY YOU--!!
TAP
DAMMIT... WHERE THE HELL IS SHE?!

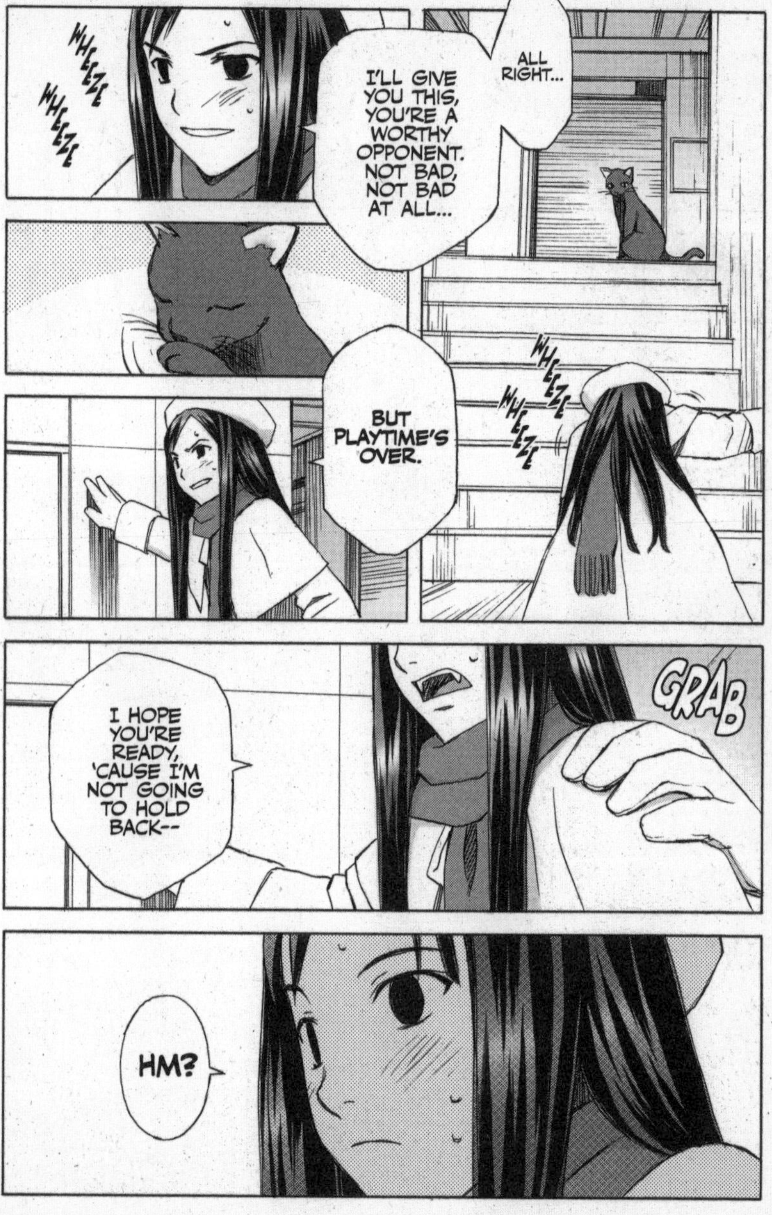
ALL RIGHT...
WHEEZE WHEEZE
I'LL GIVE YOU THIS, YOU'RE A WORTHY OPPONENT. NOT BAD, NOT BAD AT ALL...
WHEEZE WHEEZE
BUT PLAYTIME'S OVER.
GRAB
I HOPE YOU'RE READY, 'CAUSE I'M NOT GOING TO HOLD BACK--
HM?

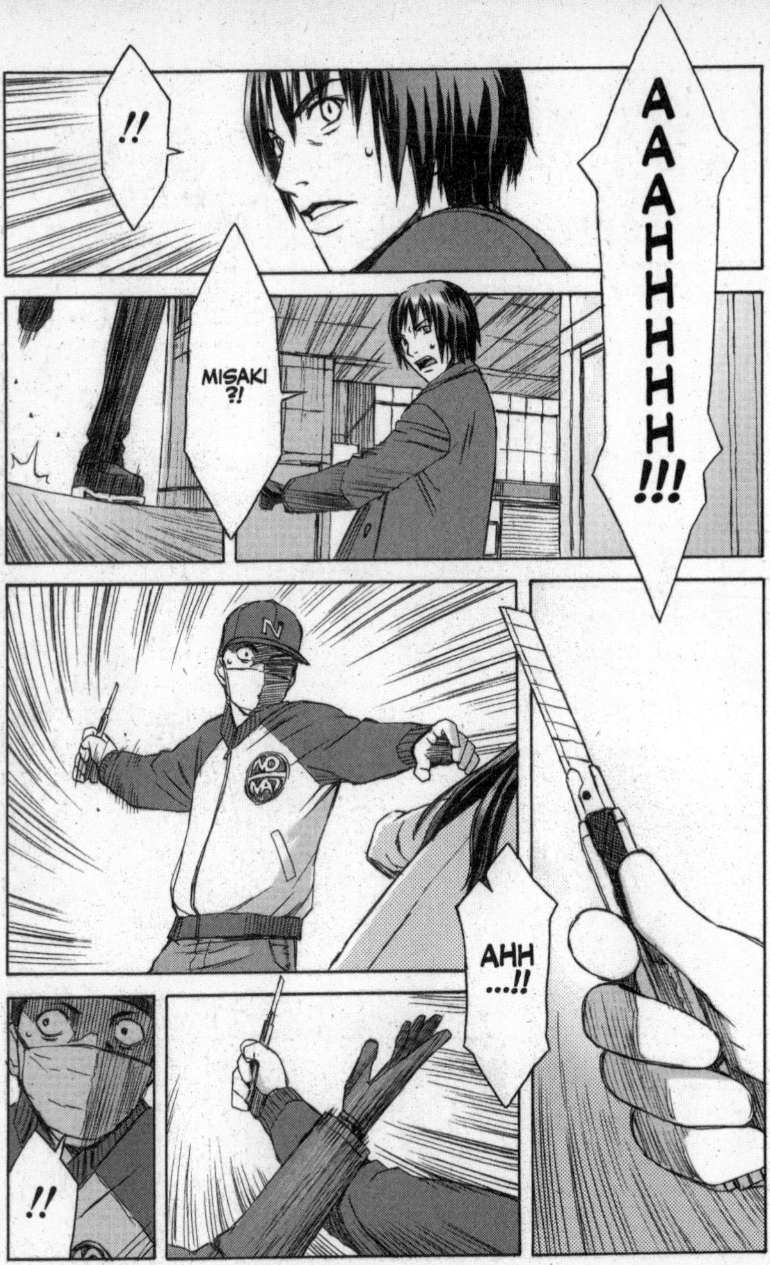

AAAHHHHHH!!!
!!
MISAKI?!
AHH...!!
!!

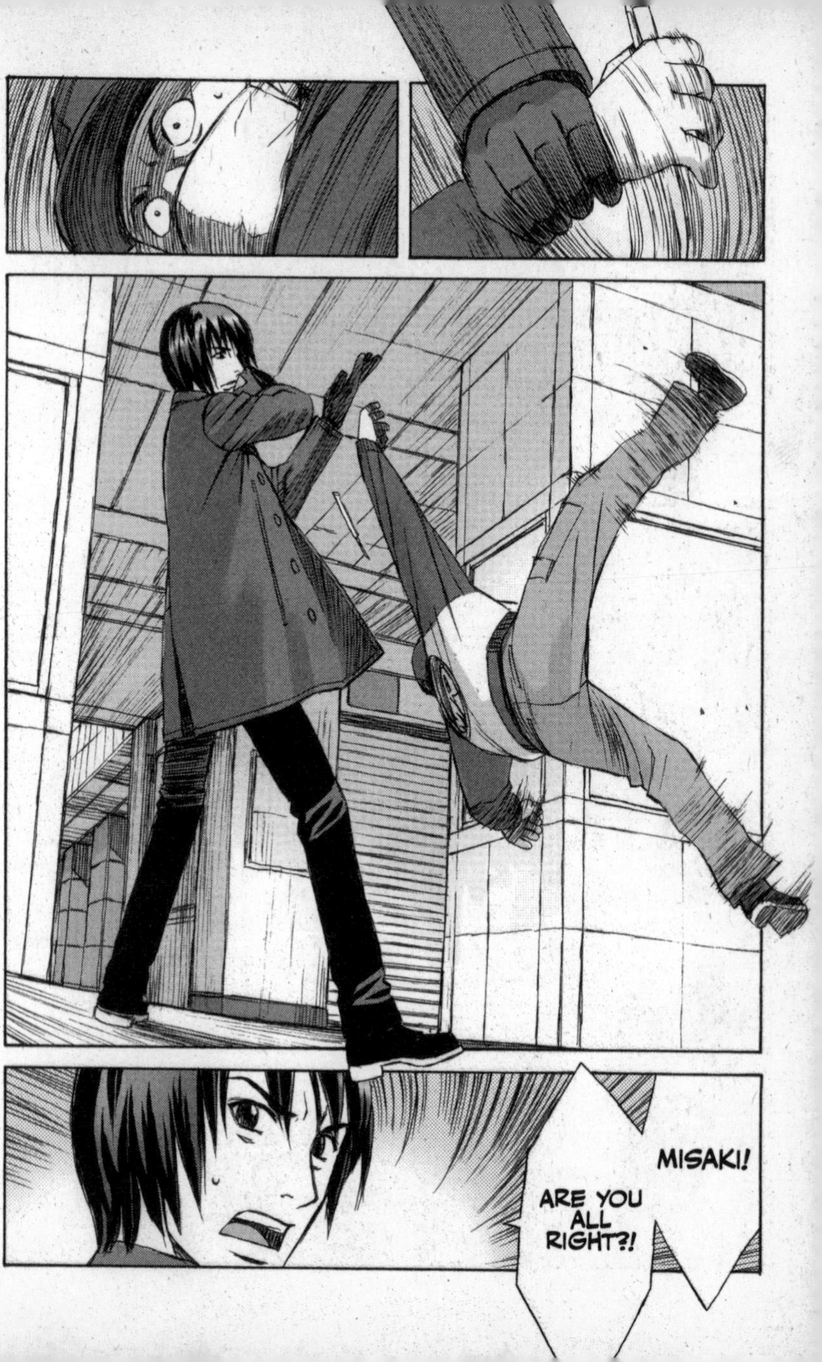
MISAKI!
ARE YOU ALL RIGHT?!

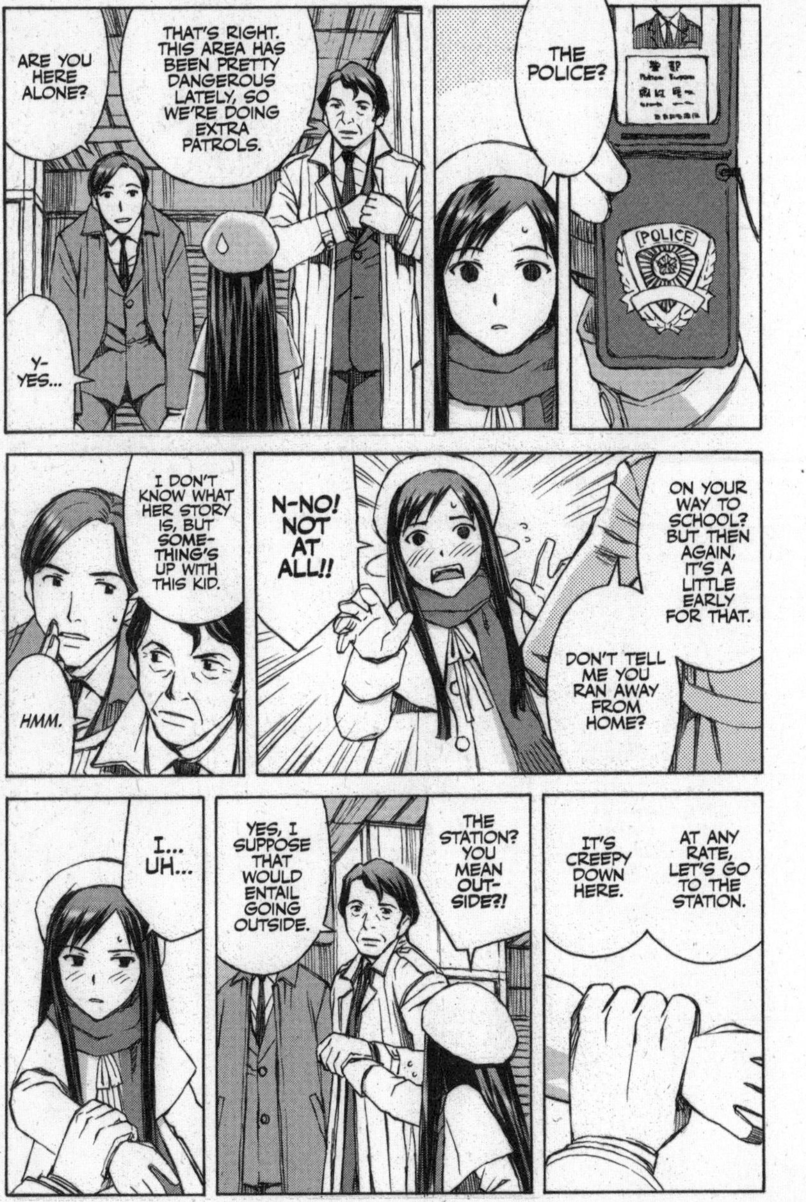
THE POLICE?
THAT'S RIGHT. THIS AREA HAS BEEN PRETTY DANGEROUS LATELY, SO WE'RE DOING EXTRA PATROLS.
ARE YOU HERE ALONE?
Y-YES...
POLICE
ON YOUR WAY TO SCHOOL? BUT THEN AGAIN, IT'S A LITTLE EARLY FOR THAT.
DON'T TELL ME YOU RAN AWAY FROM HOME?
N-NO! NOT AT ALL!!
I DON'T KNOW WHAT HER STORY IS, BUT SOME-THING'S UP WITH THIS KID.
HMM.
AT ANY RATE, LET'S GO TO THE STATION.
IT'S CREEPY DOWN HERE.
THE STATION? YOU MEAN OUT-SIDE?!
YES, I SUPPOSE THAT WOULD ENTAIL GOING OUTSIDE.
I... UH...

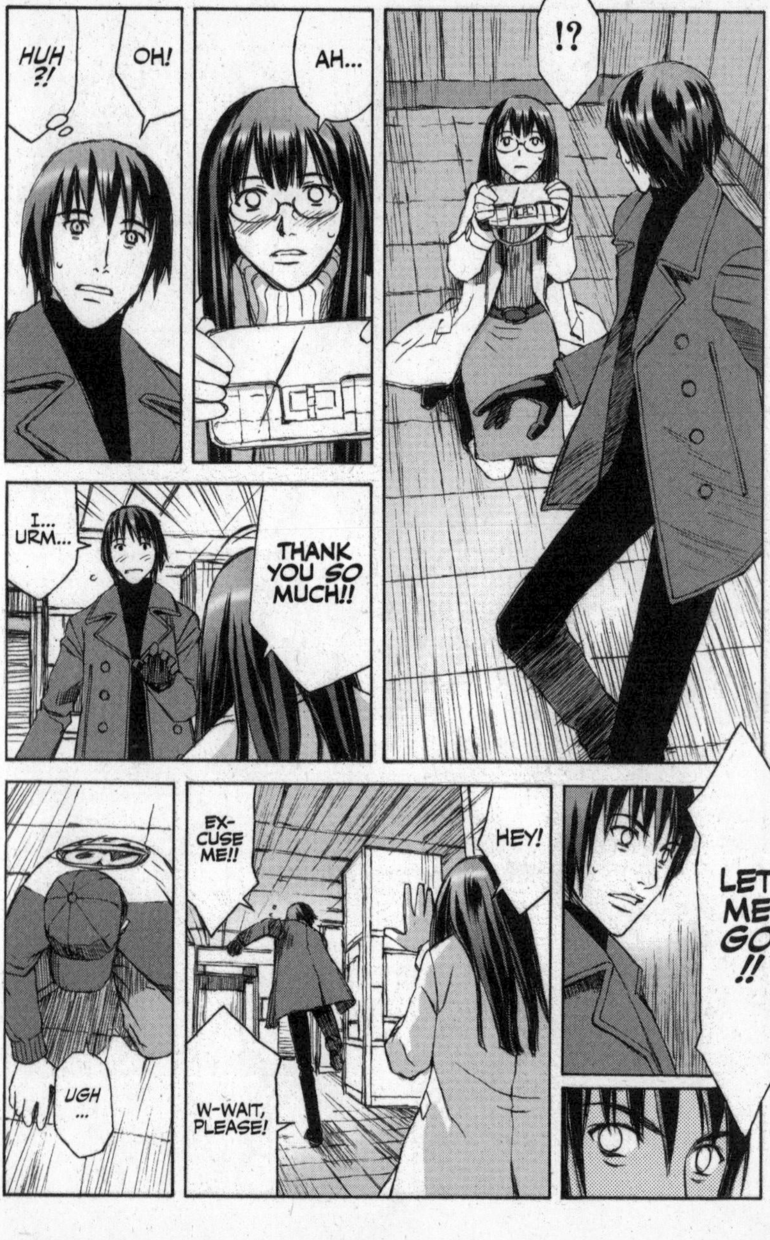
!?
AH...
OH!
HUH ?!
THANK YOU SO MUCH!!
I... URM...
LET ME GO !!
HEY!
EX-CUSE ME!!
W-WAIT, PLEASE!
UGH ...

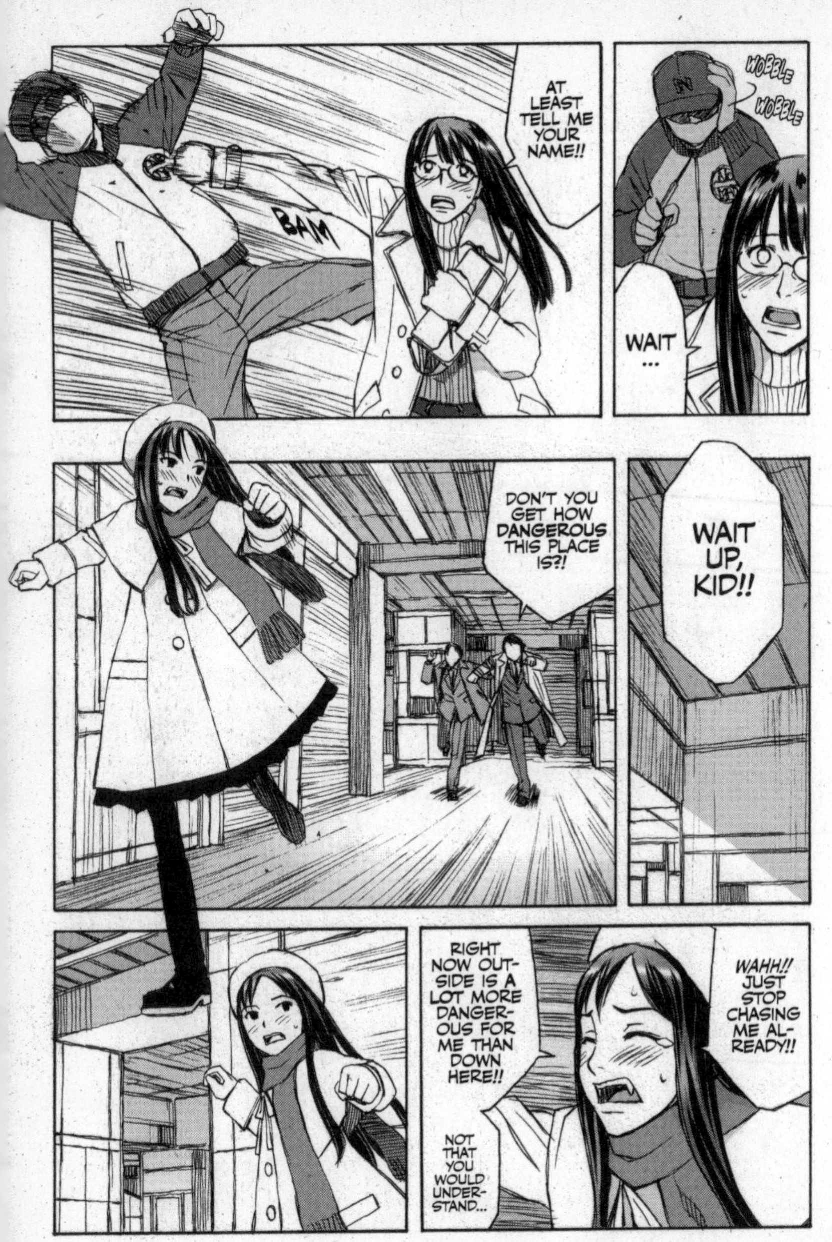
WOBBLE
WOBBLE
WAIT ...
AT LEAST TELL ME YOUR NAME!!
BAM
WAIT UP, KID!!
DON'T YOU GET HOW DANGEROUS THIS PLACE IS?!
WAHH!! JUST STOP CHASING ME AL-READY!!
RIGHT NOW OUT-SIDE IS A LOT MORE DANGER-OUS FOR ME THAN DOWN HERE!!
NOT THAT YOU WOULD UNDER-STAND...

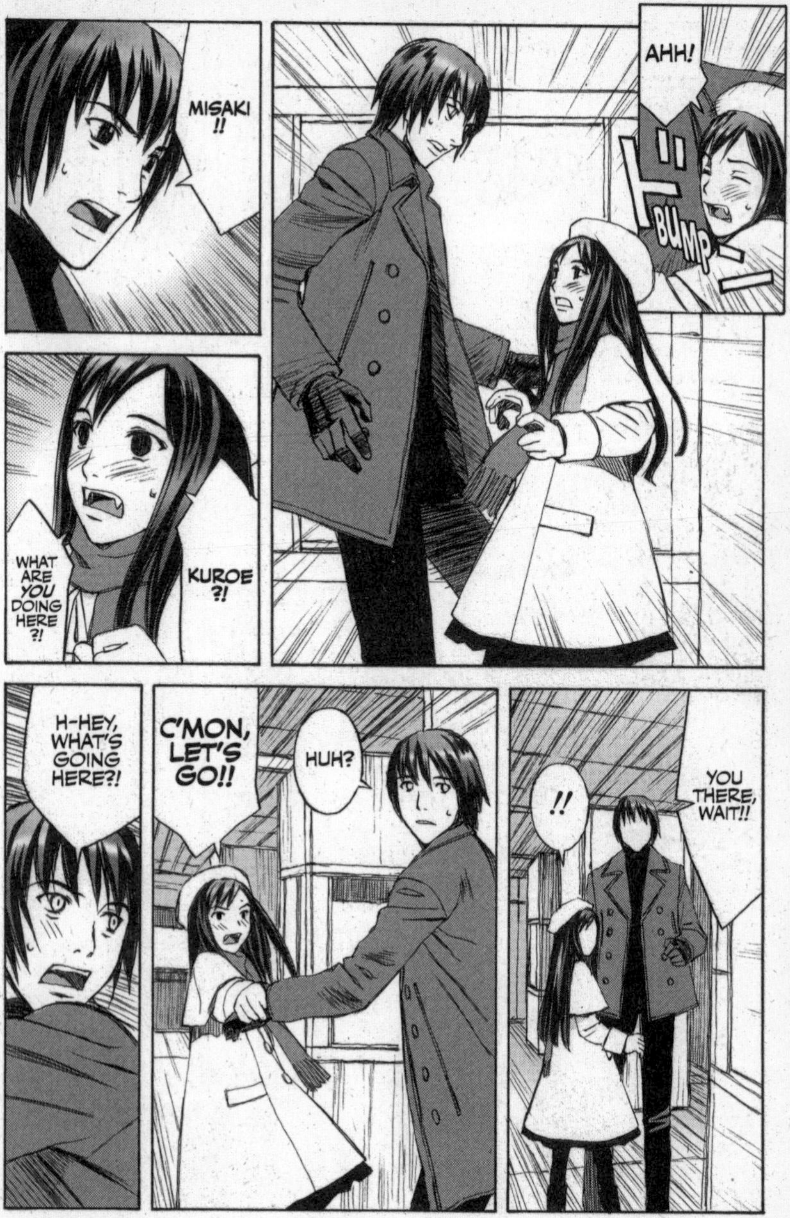
AHH!
BUMP
MISAKI!!
KUROE?!
WHAT ARE YOU DOING HERE?!
YOU THERE, WAIT!!
!!
HUH?
C'MON, LET'S GO!!
H-HEY, WHAT'S GOING HERE?!

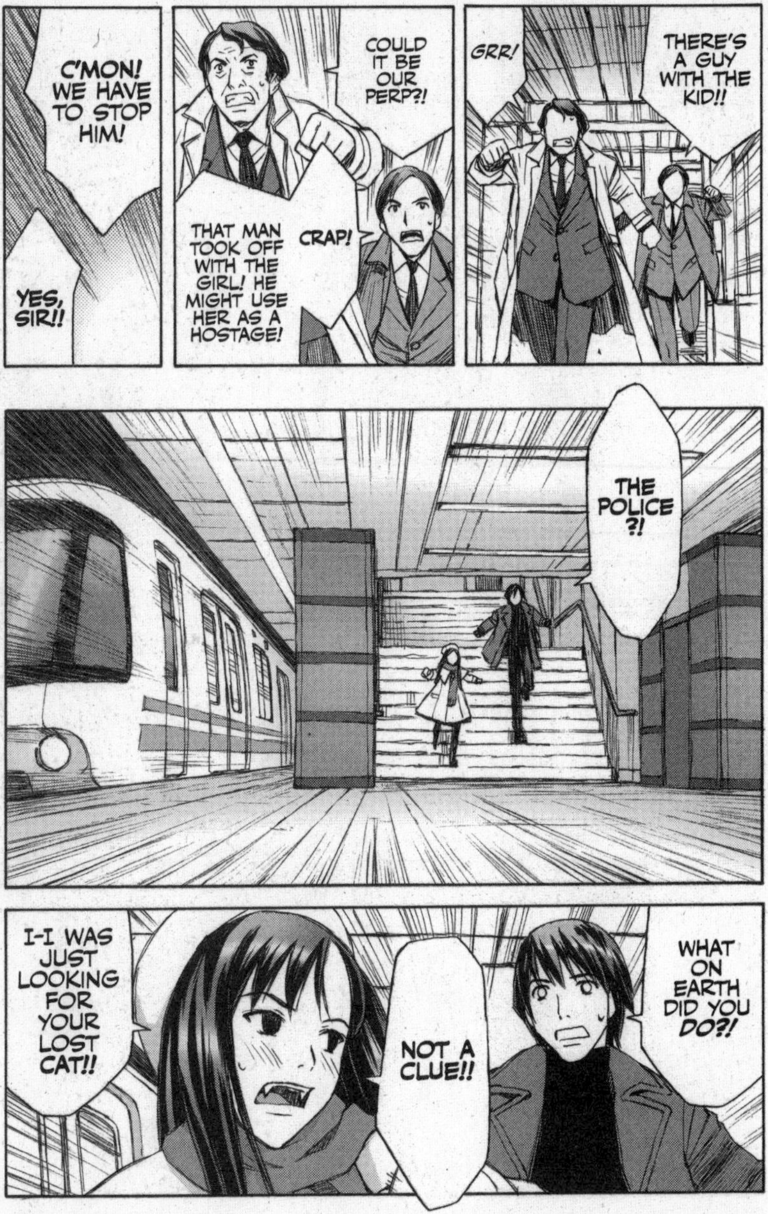
THERE'S A GUY WITH THE KID!!
GRR!
COULD IT BE OUR PERP?!
CRAP!
THAT MAN TOOK OFF WITH THE GIRL! HE MIGHT USE HER AS A HOSTAGE!
C'MON! WE HAVE TO STOP HIM!
YES, SIR!!
THE POLICE ?!
WHAT ON EARTH DID YOU *DO*?!
NOT A CLUE!!
I-I WAS JUST LOOKING FOR YOUR LOST CAT!!

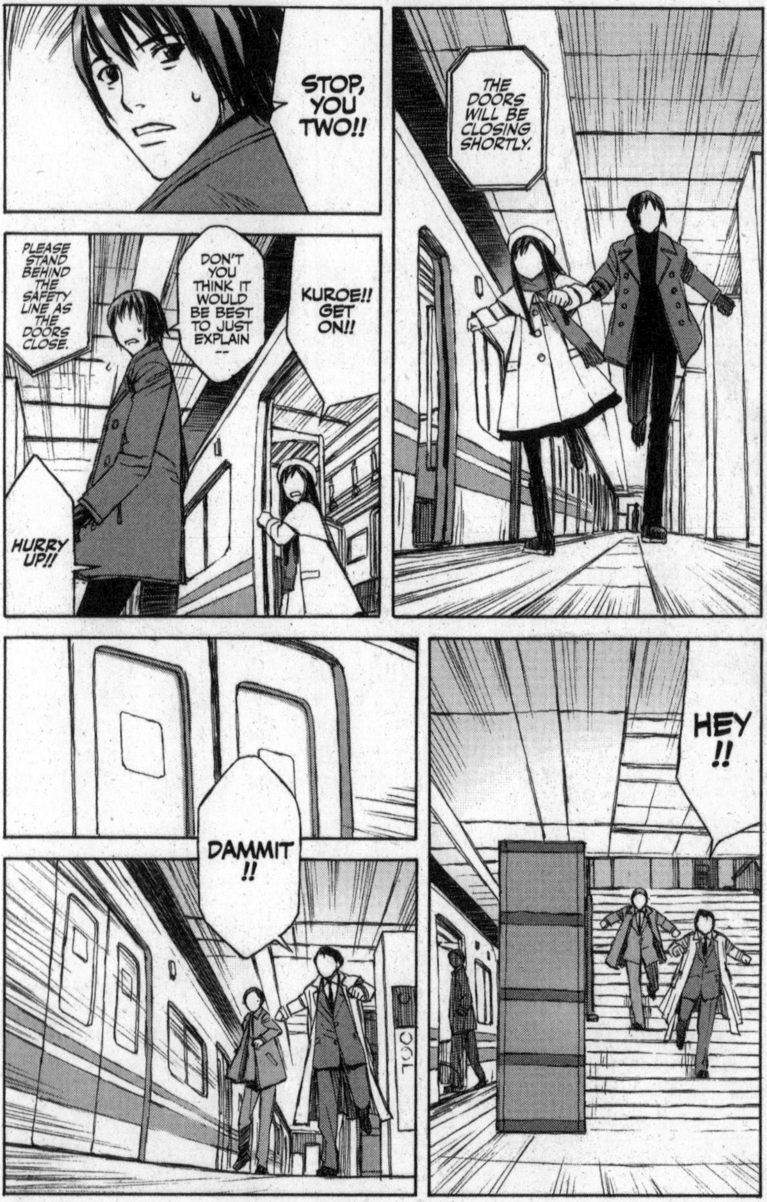
THE DOORS WILL BE CLOSING SHORTLY.
STOP, YOU TWO!!
KUROE!! GET ON!!
DON'T YOU THINK IT WOULD BE BEST TO JUST EXPLAIN --
PLEASE STAND BEHIND THE SAFETY LINE AS THE DOORS CLOSE.
HURRY UP!!
HEY!!
DAMMIT!!

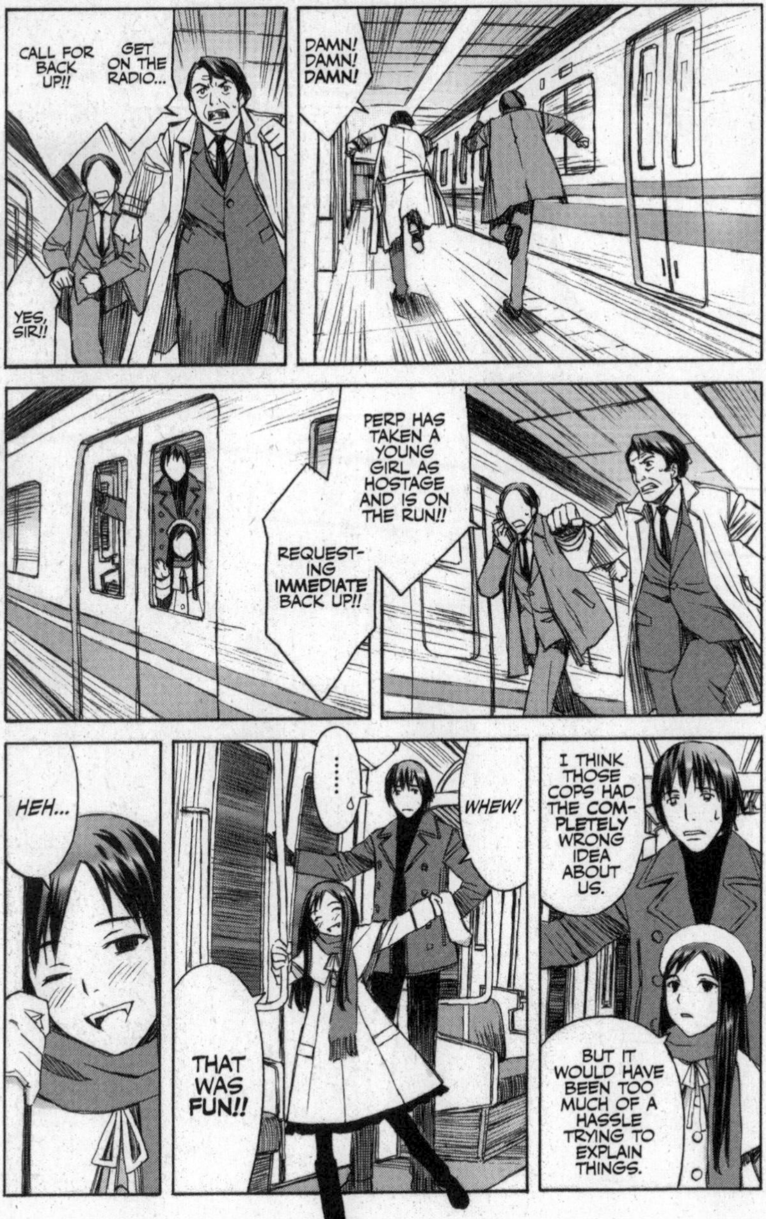
DAMN! DAMN! DAMN!
GET ON THE RADIO...
CALL FOR BACK UP!!
YES, SIR!!
PERP HAS TAKEN A YOUNG GIRL AS HOSTAGE AND IS ON THE RUN!!
REQUESTING IMMEDIATE BACK UP!!
I THINK THOSE COPS HAD THE COMPLETELY WRONG IDEA ABOUT US.
BUT IT WOULD HAVE BEEN TOO MUCH OF A HASSLE TRYING TO EXPLAIN THINGS.
WHEW!
......
THAT WAS FUN!!
HEH...

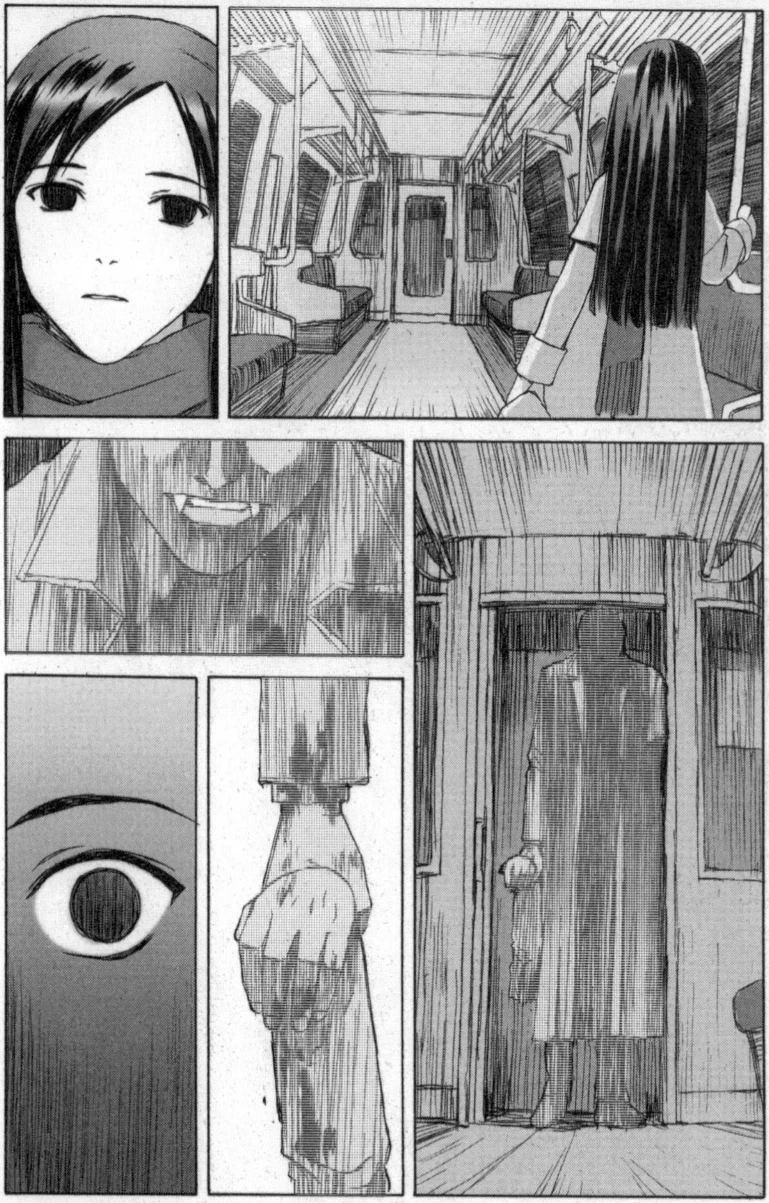

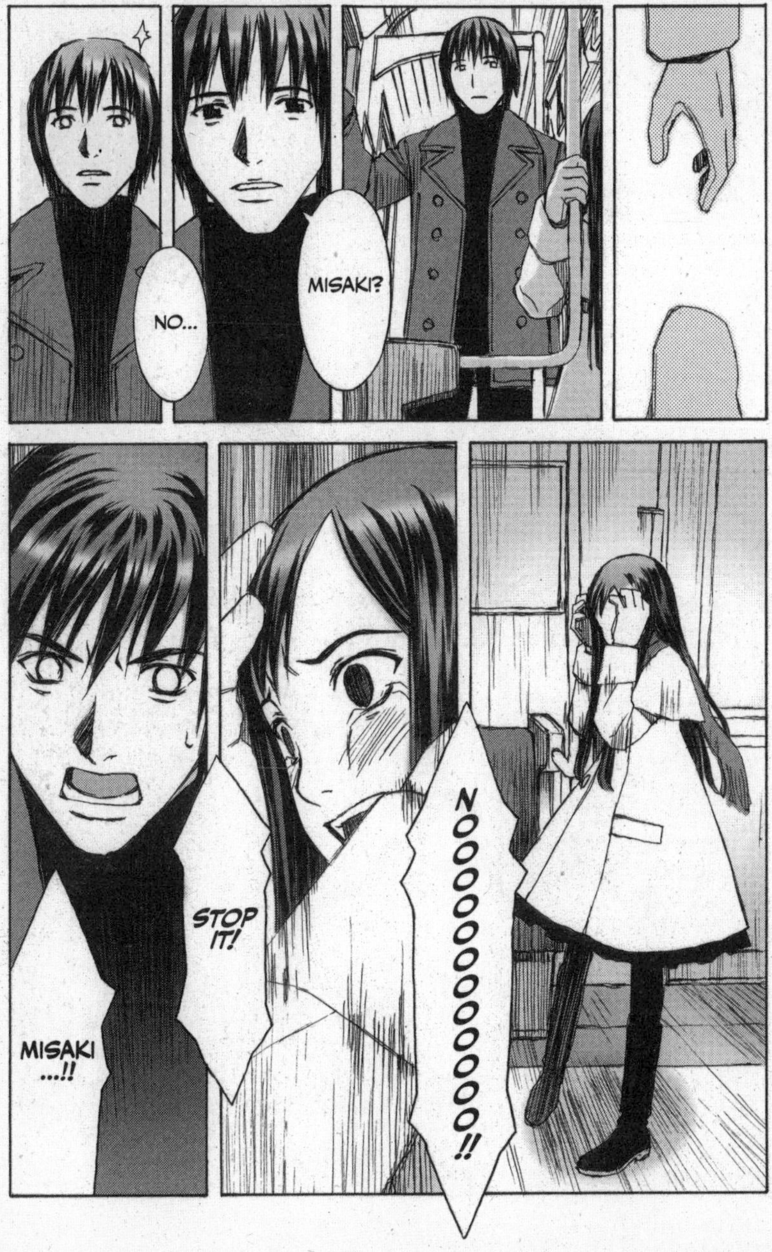
MISAKI?
NO...
NOOOOOOOOOOOOOO!!
STOP IT!
MISAKI ...!!

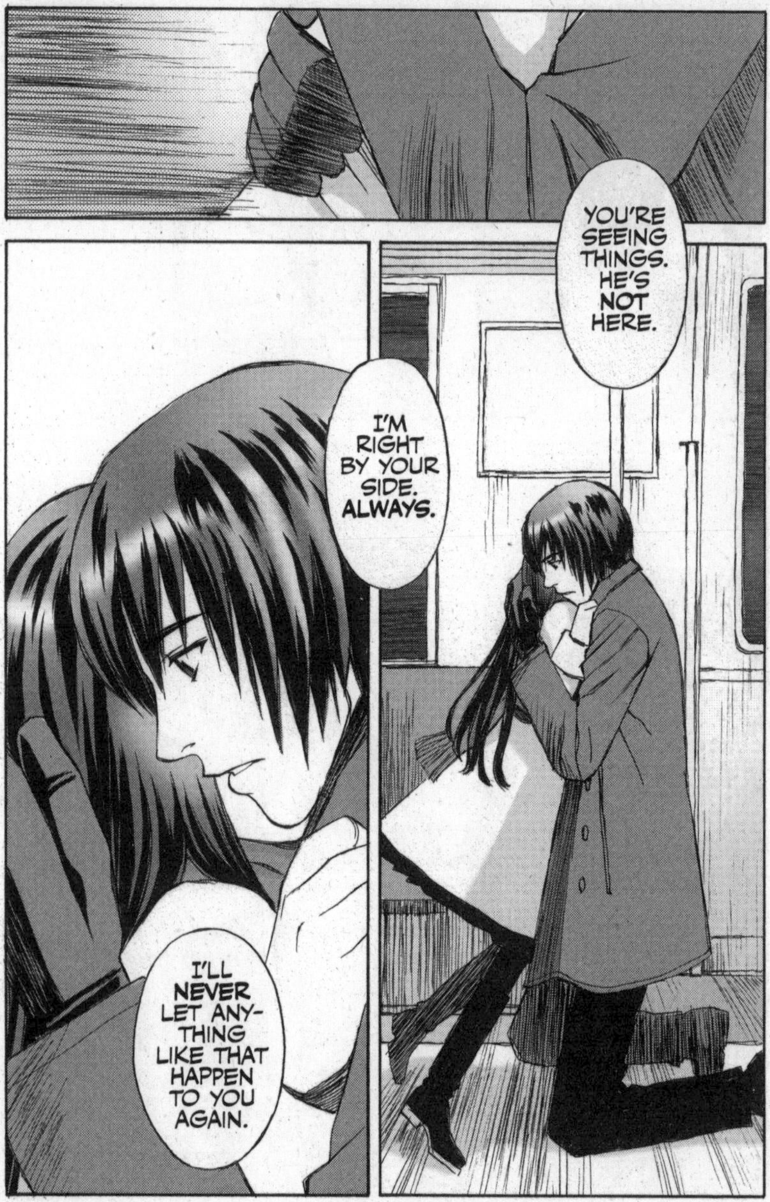
YOU'RE SEEING THINGS. HE'S NOT HERE.
I'M RIGHT BY YOUR SIDE. ALWAYS.
I'LL NEVER LET ANYTHING LIKE THAT HAPPEN TO YOU AGAIN.

...I'M OKAY.

Y-YEAH...

MISAKI?

GRIP

SOB

THANK YOU...

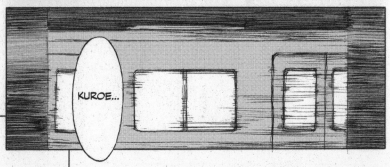

KUROE...

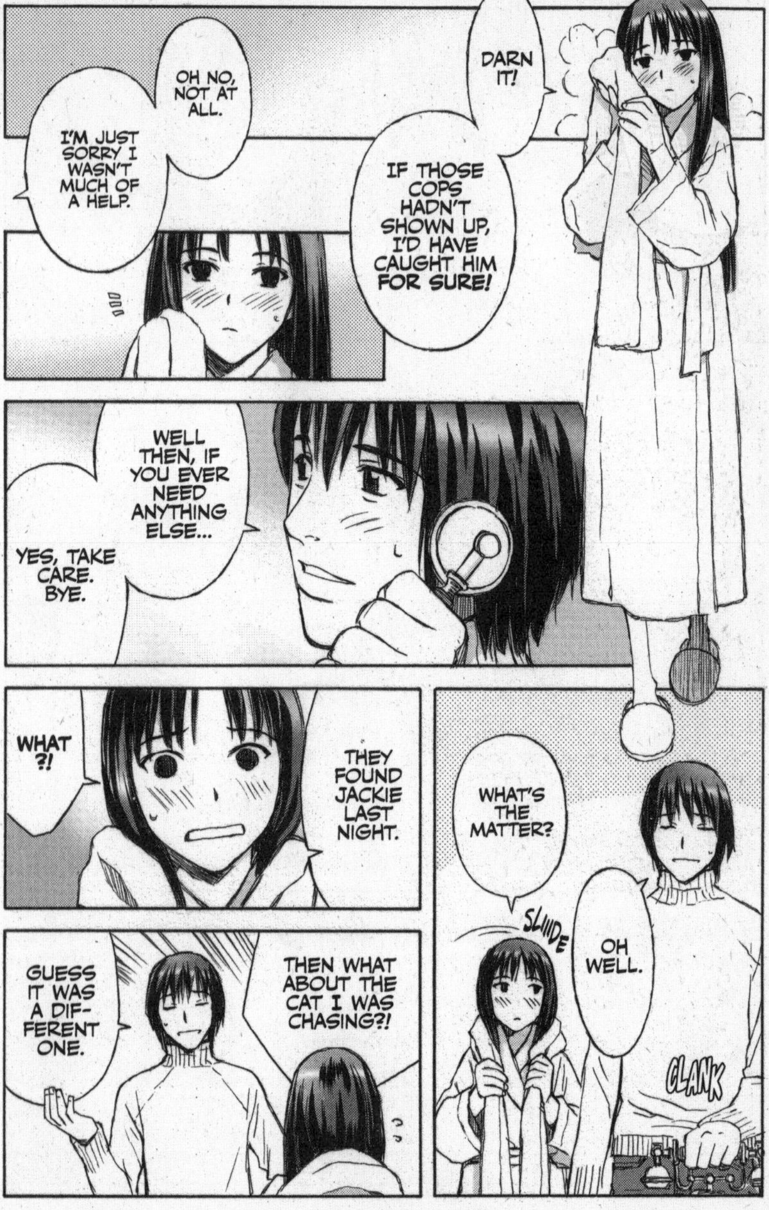
OH NO, NOT AT ALL.
I'M JUST SORRY I WASN'T MUCH OF A HELP.
WELL THEN, IF YOU EVER NEED ANYTHING ELSE...
YES, TAKE CARE. BYE.
DARN IT!
IF THOSE COPS HADN'T SHOWN UP, I'D HAVE CAUGHT HIM FOR SURE!
WHAT'S THE MATTER?
SLIIDE
OH WELL.
CLANK
THEY FOUND JACKIE LAST NIGHT.
WHAT ?!
THEN WHAT ABOUT THE CAT I WAS CHASING?!
GUESS IT WAS A DIF-FERENT ONE.

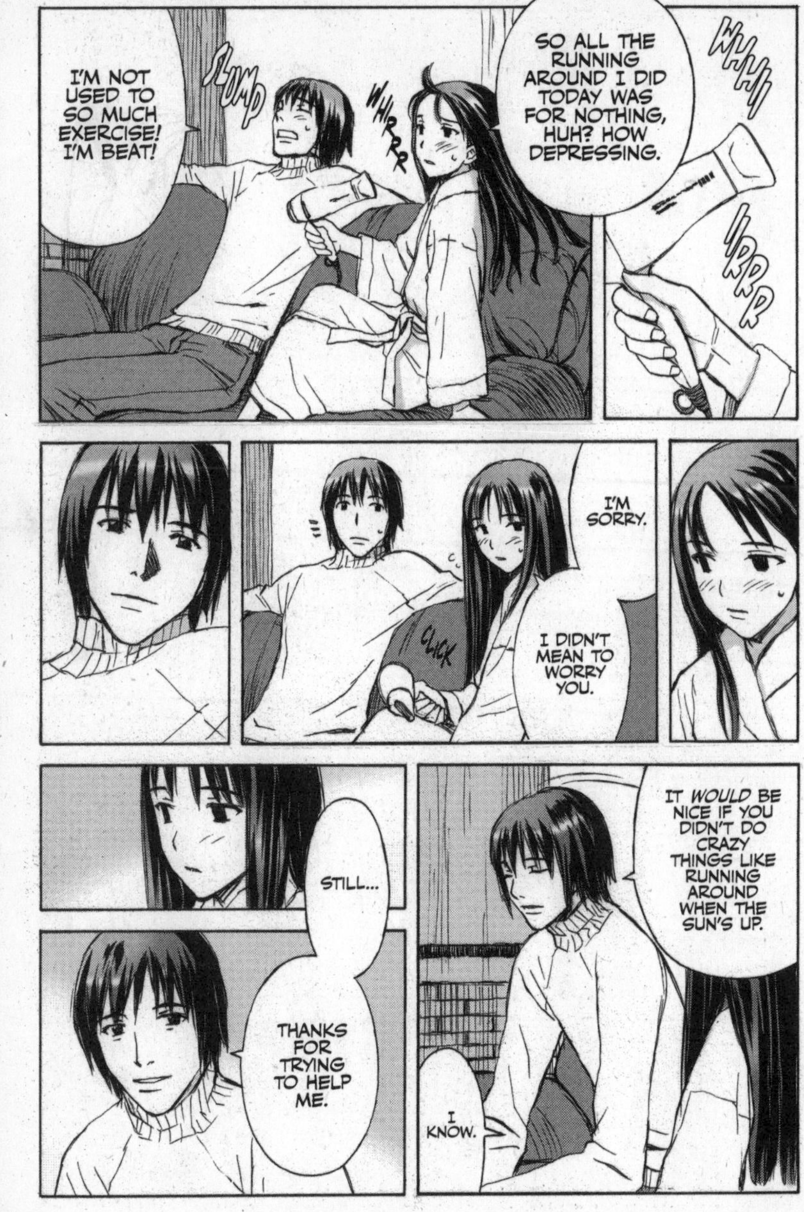
WHHHI
IRRRR
SO ALL THE RUNNING AROUND I DID TODAY WAS FOR NOTHING, HUH? HOW DEPRESSING.
WHIRRR
SLUMP
I'M NOT USED TO SO MUCH EXERCISE! I'M BEAT!
I'M SORRY.
I DIDN'T MEAN TO WORRY YOU.
CLICK
IT *WOULD* BE NICE IF YOU DIDN'T DO CRAZY THINGS LIKE RUNNING AROUND WHEN THE SUN'S UP.
I KNOW.
STILL...
THANKS FOR TRYING TO HELP ME.

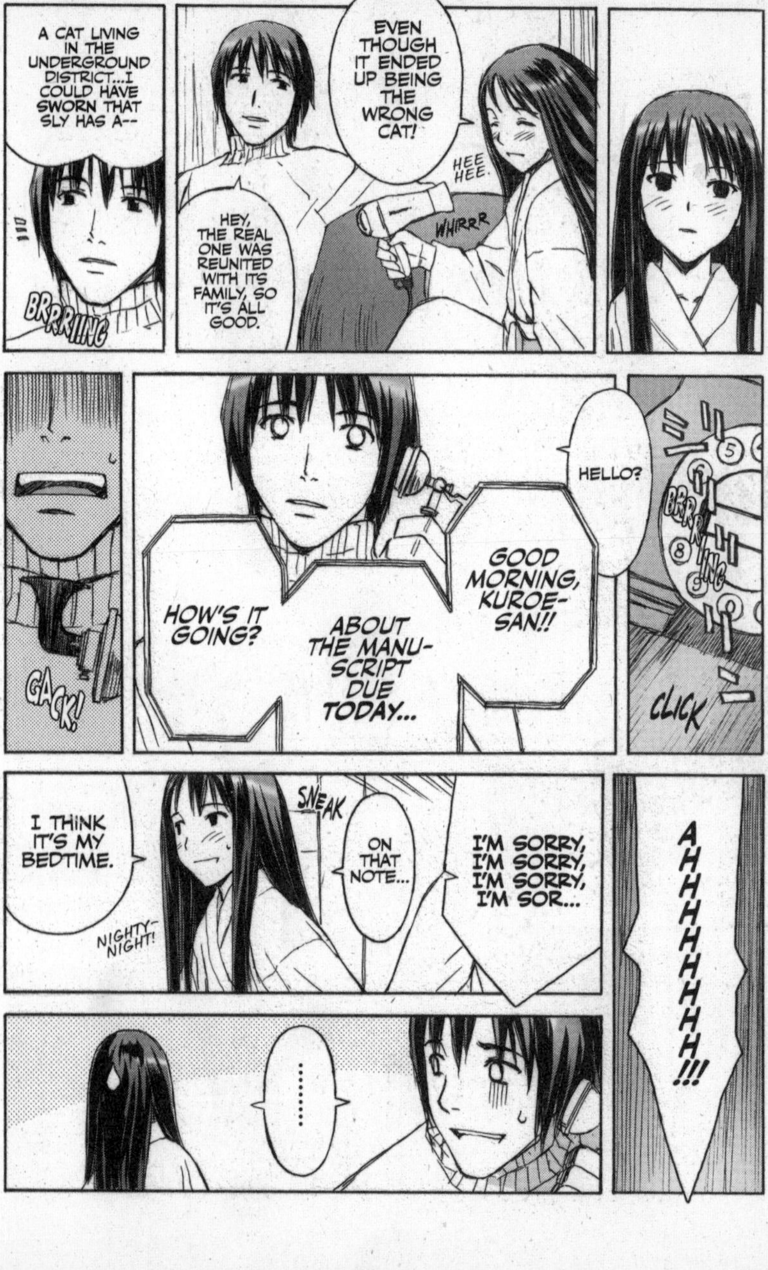
EVEN THOUGH IT ENDED UP BEING THE WRONG CAT!
HEE HEE.
WHIRRR
HEY, THE REAL ONE WAS REUNITED WITH ITS FAMILY, SO IT'S ALL GOOD.
A CAT LIVING IN THE UNDERGROUND DISTRICT...I COULD HAVE SWORN THAT SLY HAS A--
BRRRIING
BRRRRIIING
CLICK
HELLO?
GOOD MORNING, KUROE-SAN!!
HOW'S IT GOING?
ABOUT THE MANU-SCRIPT DUE TODAY...
GACK!
AHHHHHHHH!!!
I'M SORRY, I'M SORRY, I'M SORRY, I'M SOR...
SNEAK
ON THAT NOTE...
I THINK IT'S MY BEDTIME.
NIGHTY-NIGHT!
....

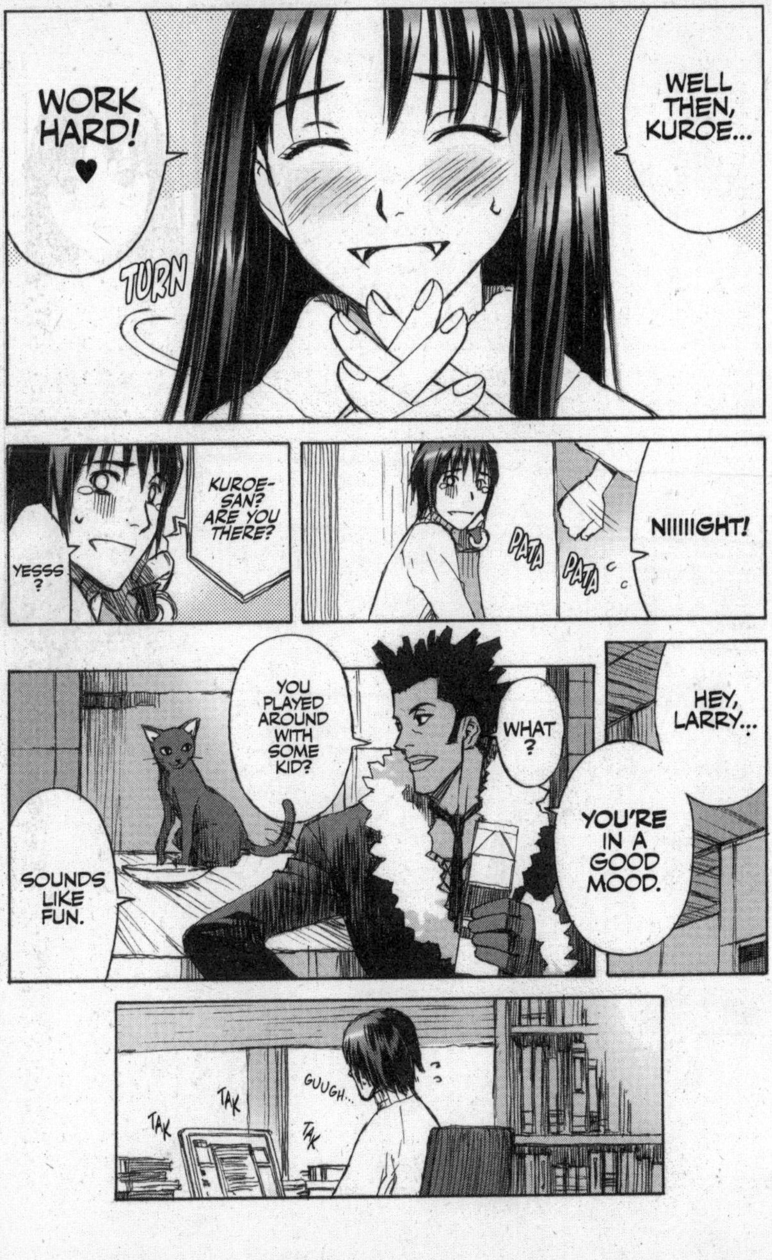
WELL THEN, KUROE...
WORK HARD! ♥
TURN
NIIIIGHT!
PATA
PATA
KUROE-SAN? ARE YOU THERE?
YESSS?
HEY, LARRY...
YOU'RE IN A GOOD MOOD.
WHAT?
YOU PLAYED AROUND WITH SOME KID?
SOUNDS LIKE FUN.
GUUGH...
TAK
TAK
TAK

Episode 2
LIVING THROUGH THE TWILIGHT
Living in the Twilight

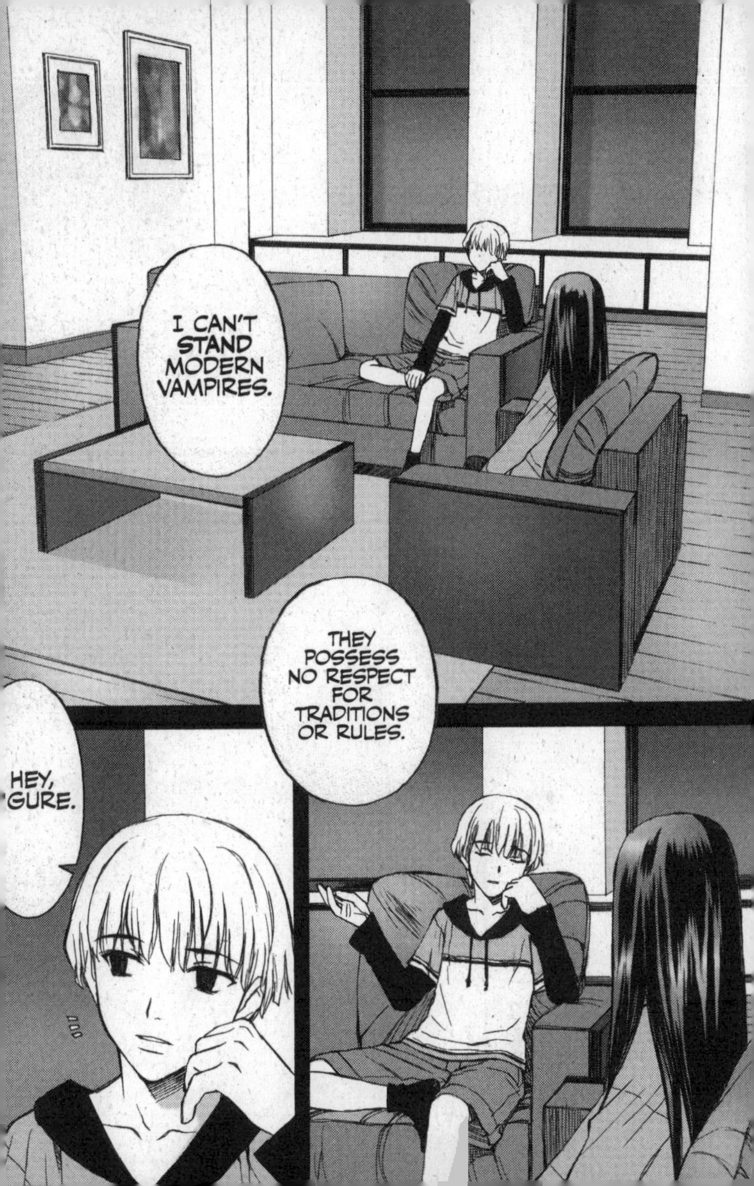
I CAN'T STAND MODERN VAMPIRES.
THEY POSSESS NO RESPECT FOR TRADITIONS OR RULES.
HEY, GURE.

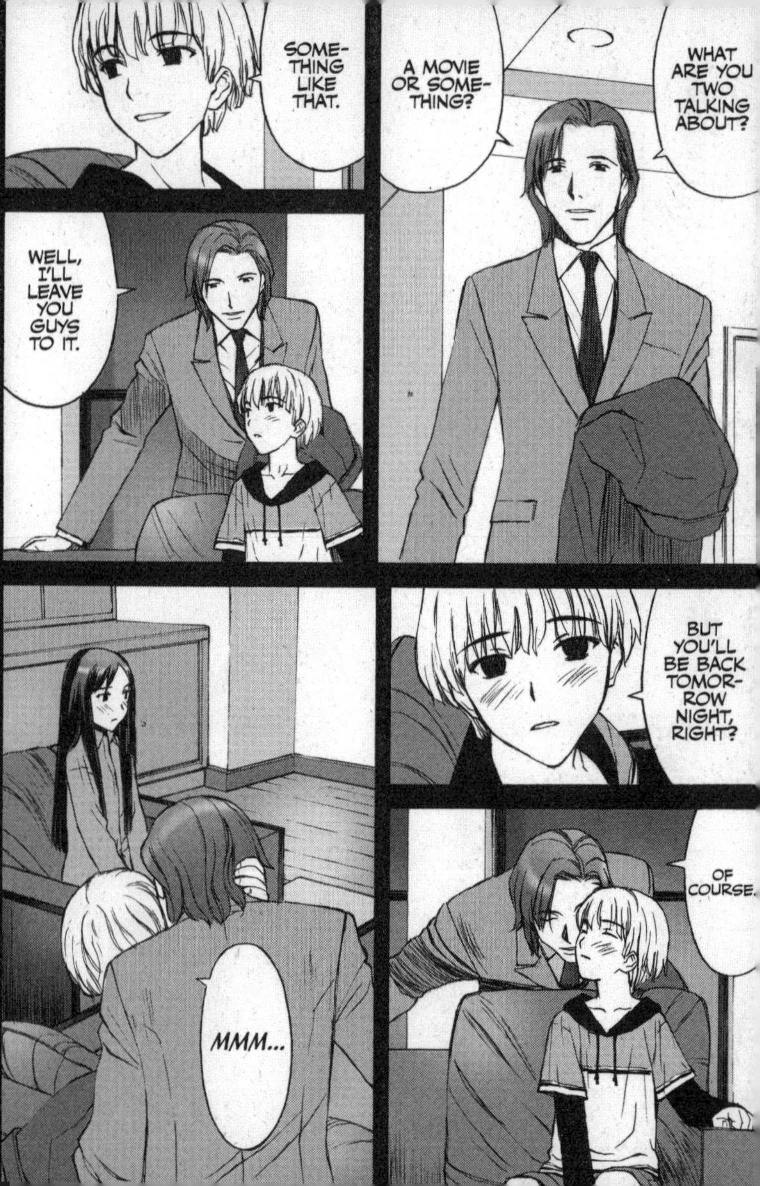
WHAT ARE YOU TWO TALKING ABOUT?
A MOVIE OR SOME-THING?
SOME-THING LIKE THAT.
WELL, I'LL LEAVE YOU GUYS TO IT.
BUT YOU'LL BE BACK TOMOR-ROW NIGHT, RIGHT?
OF COURSE.
MMM...

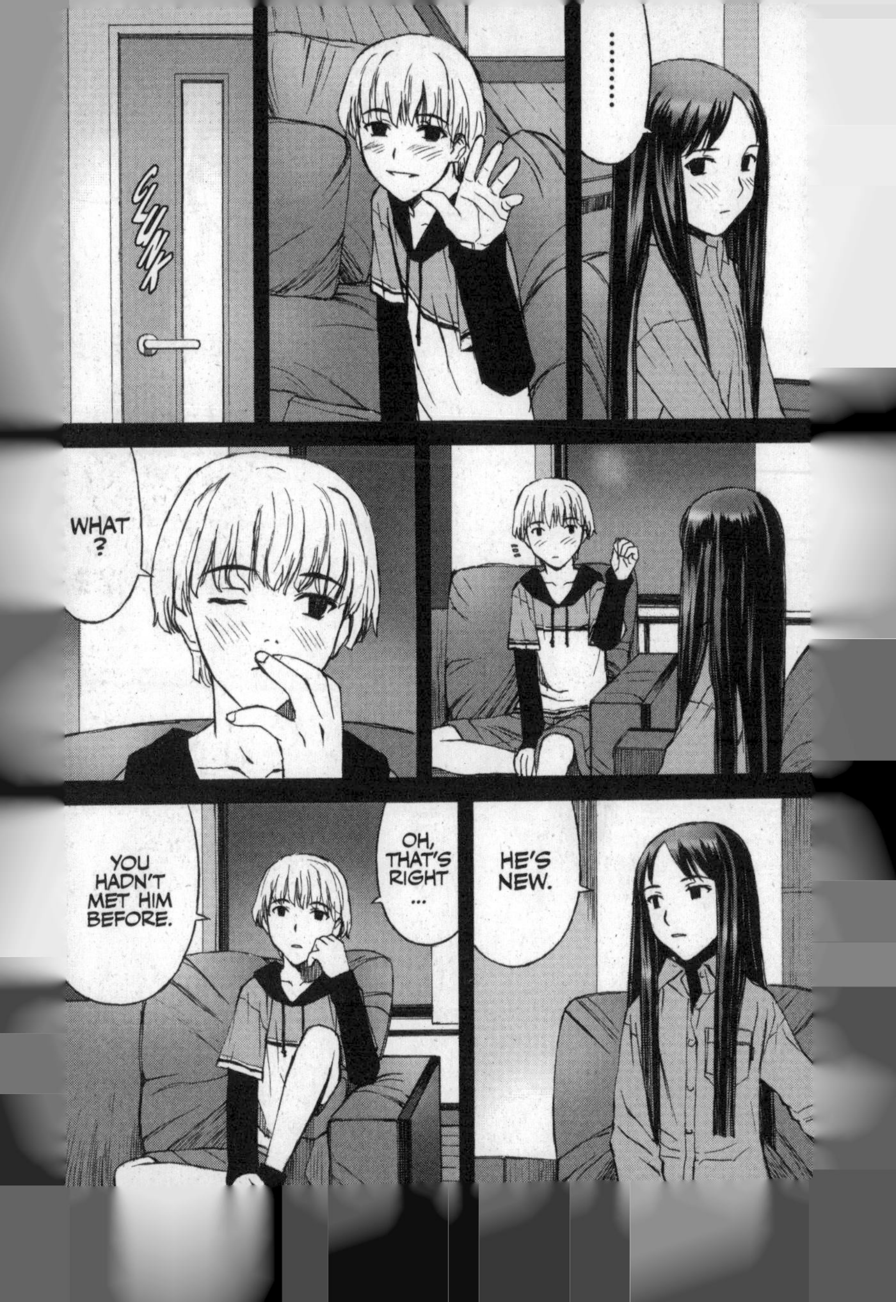
……
CLUNK
WHAT?
HE'S NEW.
OH, THAT'S RIGHT ...
YOU HADN'T MET HIM BEFORE.

HE'S ONE OF MY RENFIELDS.
A REN-FIELD, HUH?
WHAT DO YOU THINK? HE'S PRETTY CUTE, ISN'T HE?
IF YOU SAY SO.
TO ME, HE DOESN'T SEEM ALL THAT.
WELL...
COMPARED TO YOURS, I SUPPOSE HE'S PRETTY AVERAGE.

MINE?
OH, COME NOW!
YOU KNOW WHAT I'M TALKING ABOUT. THAT KUROE FELLOW.
YOU'VE GOT GOOD TASTE.
IF THE OPPORTUNITY EVER AROSE, I'D *LOVE* TO GET TO KNOW HIM BETTER.
DON'T TALK LIKE THAT.
I WAS JUST KIDDING.
EVEN *I'M* NOT GREEDY ENOUGH TO STEAL AWAY ANOTHER VAMPIRE'S PROPERTY.
I-IT'S NOT LIKE THAT!!
LIKE WHAT?
I MEAN ...

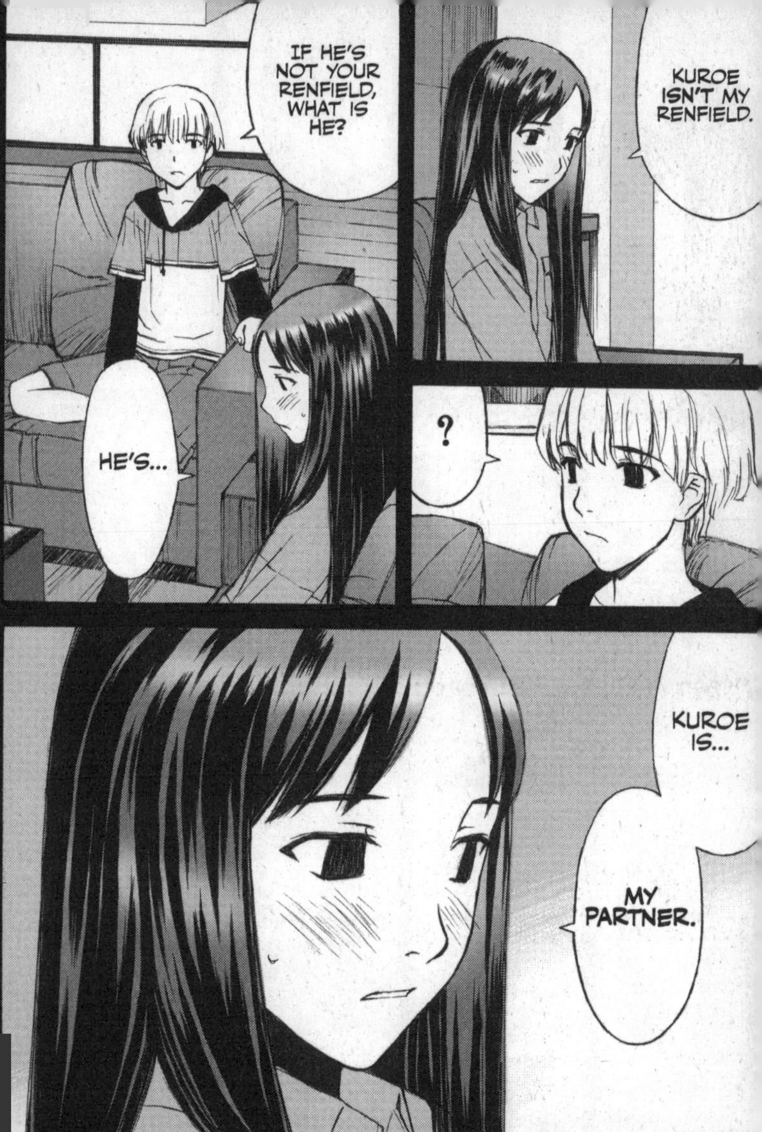
KUROE ISN'T MY RENFIELD.
?
IF HE'S NOT YOUR RENFIELD, WHAT IS HE?
HE'S...
KUROE IS...
MY PARTNER.

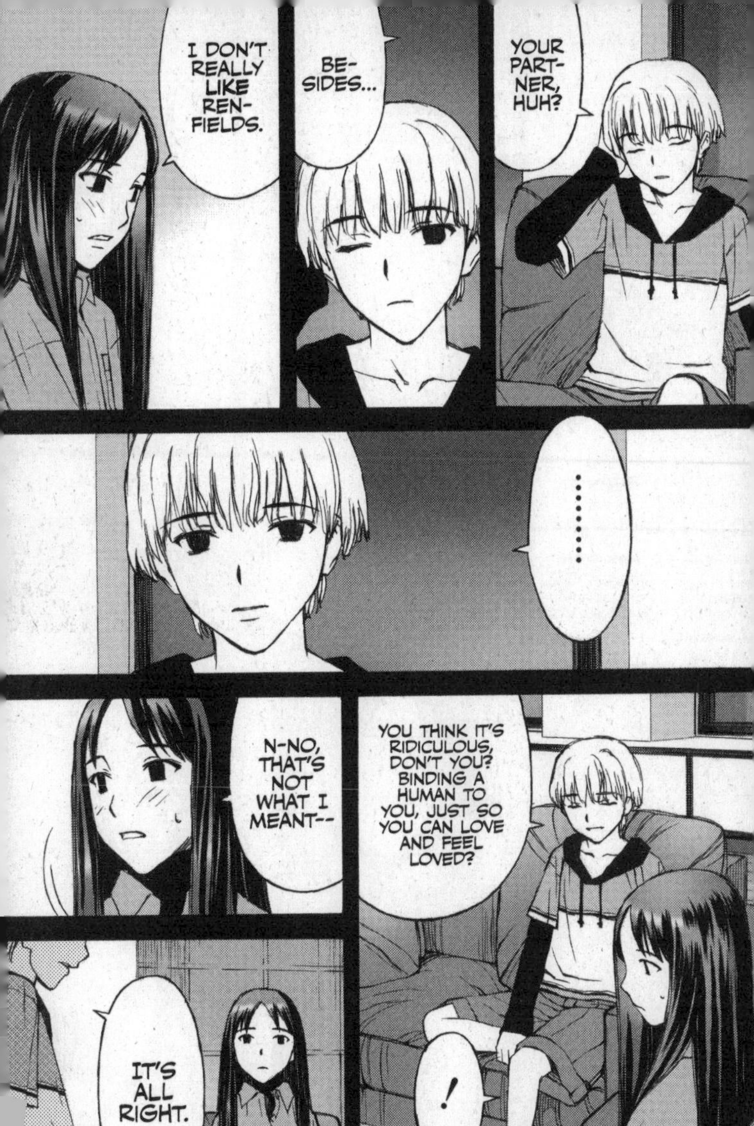
YOUR PARTNER, HUH?
BESIDES...
I DON'T REALLY LIKE RENFIELDS.
....
YOU THINK IT'S RIDICULOUS, DON'T YOU? BINDING A HUMAN TO YOU, JUST SO YOU CAN LOVE AND FEEL LOVED?
!
N-NO, THAT'S NOT WHAT I MEANT--
IT'S ALL RIGHT.

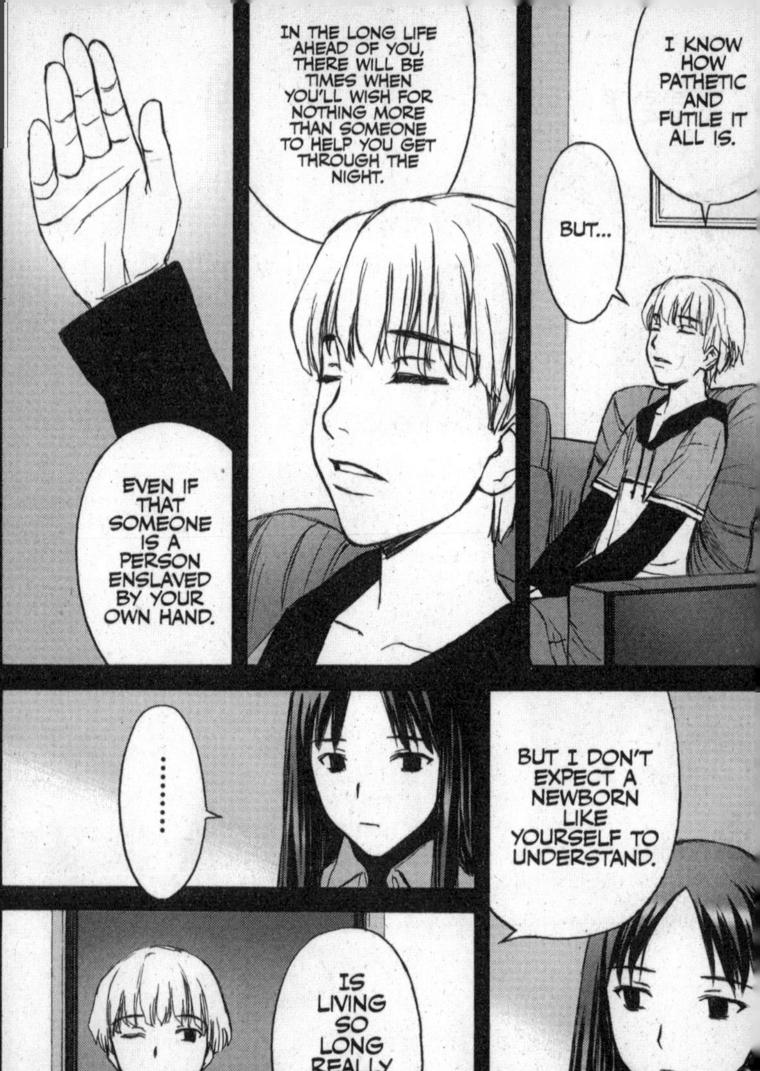
I KNOW HOW PATHETIC AND FUTILE IT ALL IS.
BUT...
IN THE LONG LIFE AHEAD OF YOU, THERE WILL BE TIMES WHEN YOU'LL WISH FOR NOTHING MORE THAN SOMEONE TO HELP YOU GET THROUGH THE NIGHT.
EVEN IF THAT SOMEONE IS A PERSON ENSLAVED BY YOUR OWN HAND.
BUT I DON'T EXPECT A NEWBORN LIKE YOURSELF TO UNDERSTAND.
....
IS LIVING SO LONG REALLY THAT BAD?

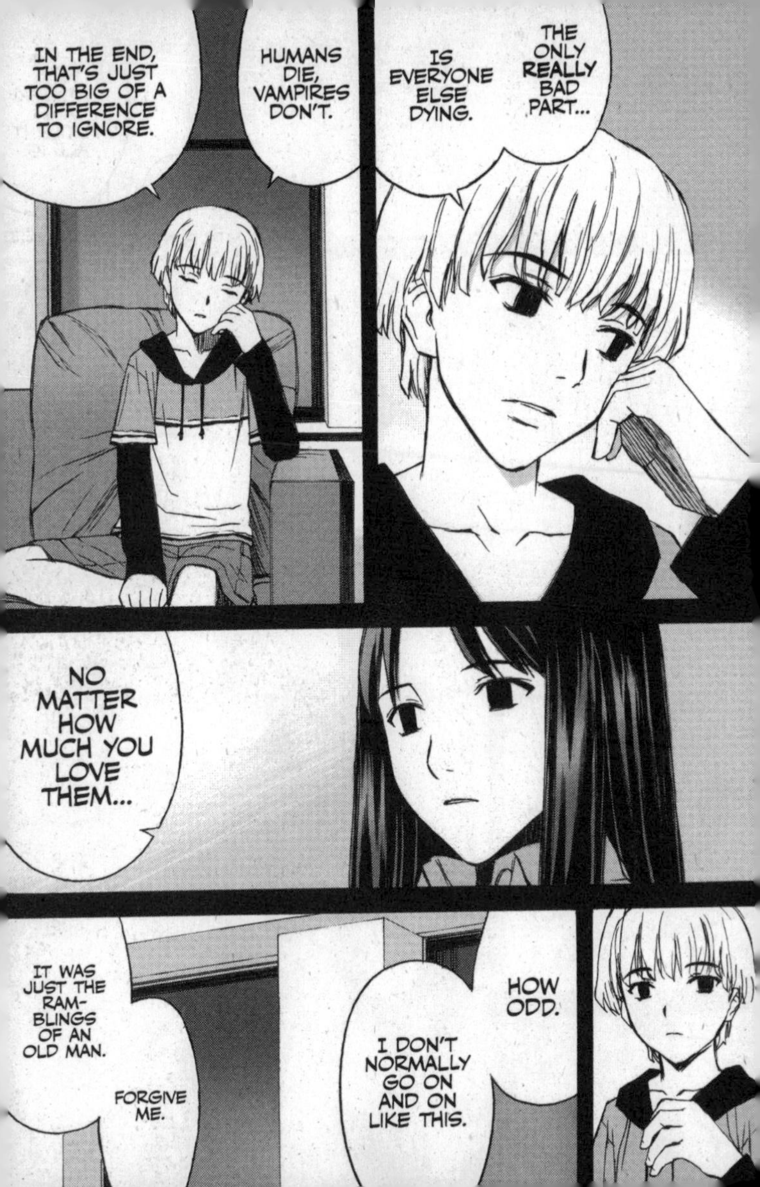
THE ONLY REALLY BAD PART...
IS EVERYONE ELSE DYING.
HUMANS DIE, VAMPIRES DON'T.
IN THE END, THAT'S JUST TOO BIG OF A DIFFERENCE TO IGNORE.
NO MATTER HOW MUCH YOU LOVE THEM...
HOW ODD.
I DON'T NORMALLY GO ON AND ON LIKE THIS.
IT WAS JUST THE RAM-BLINGS OF AN OLD MAN.
FORGIVE ME.

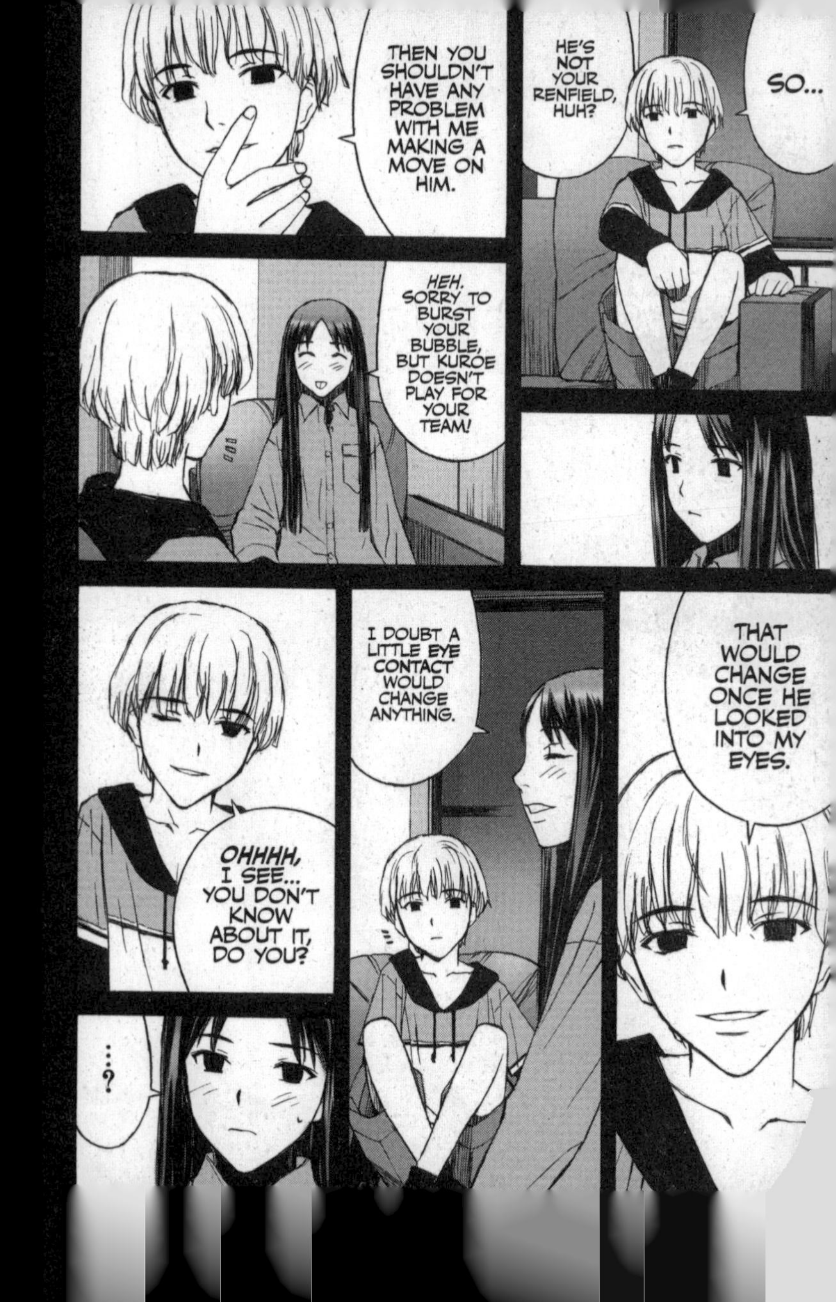
SO...
HE'S NOT YOUR RENFIELD, HUH?
THEN YOU SHOULDN'T HAVE ANY PROBLEM WITH ME MAKING A MOVE ON HIM.
HEH. SORRY TO BURST YOUR BUBBLE, BUT KUROE DOESN'T PLAY FOR YOUR TEAM!
THAT WOULD CHANGE ONCE HE LOOKED INTO MY EYES.
I DOUBT A LITTLE EYE CONTACT WOULD CHANGE ANYTHING.
OHHHH, I SEE... YOU DON'T KNOW ABOUT IT, DO YOU?
...?

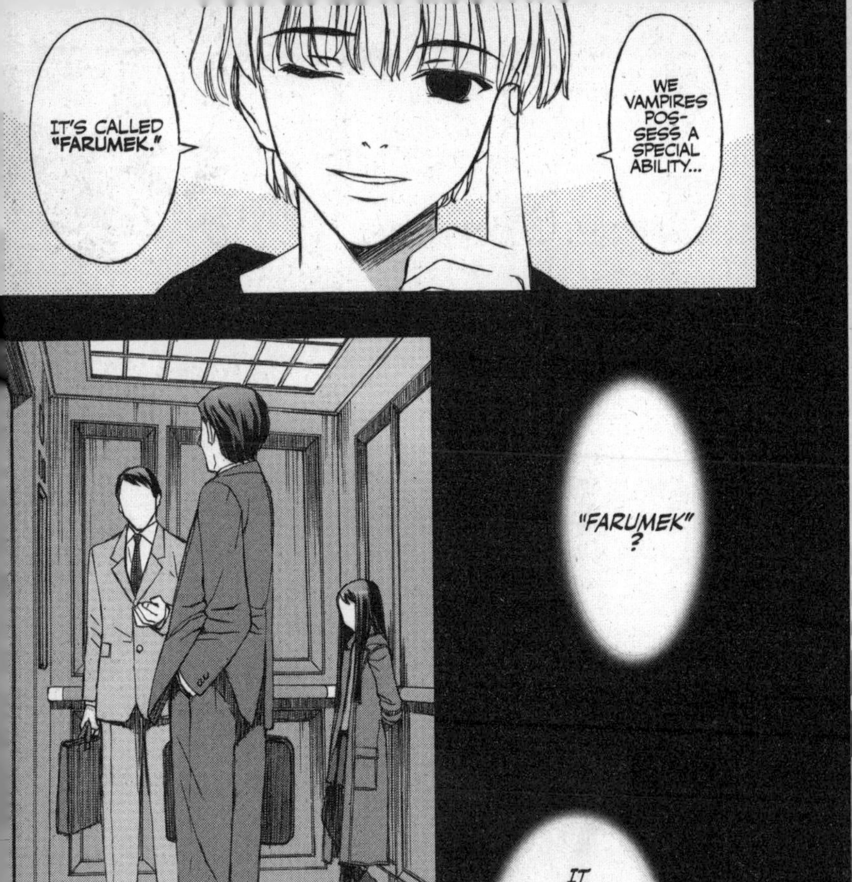
WE VAMPIRES POS-SESS A SPECIAL ABILITY...
IT'S CALLED "FARUMEK."
"FARUMEK"?
IT ALLOWS US TO CONTROL ANOTHER SIMPLY THROUGH OUR GAZE.
I CAN TEACH YOU, IF YOU WANT. IT'S NOT THAT HARD.

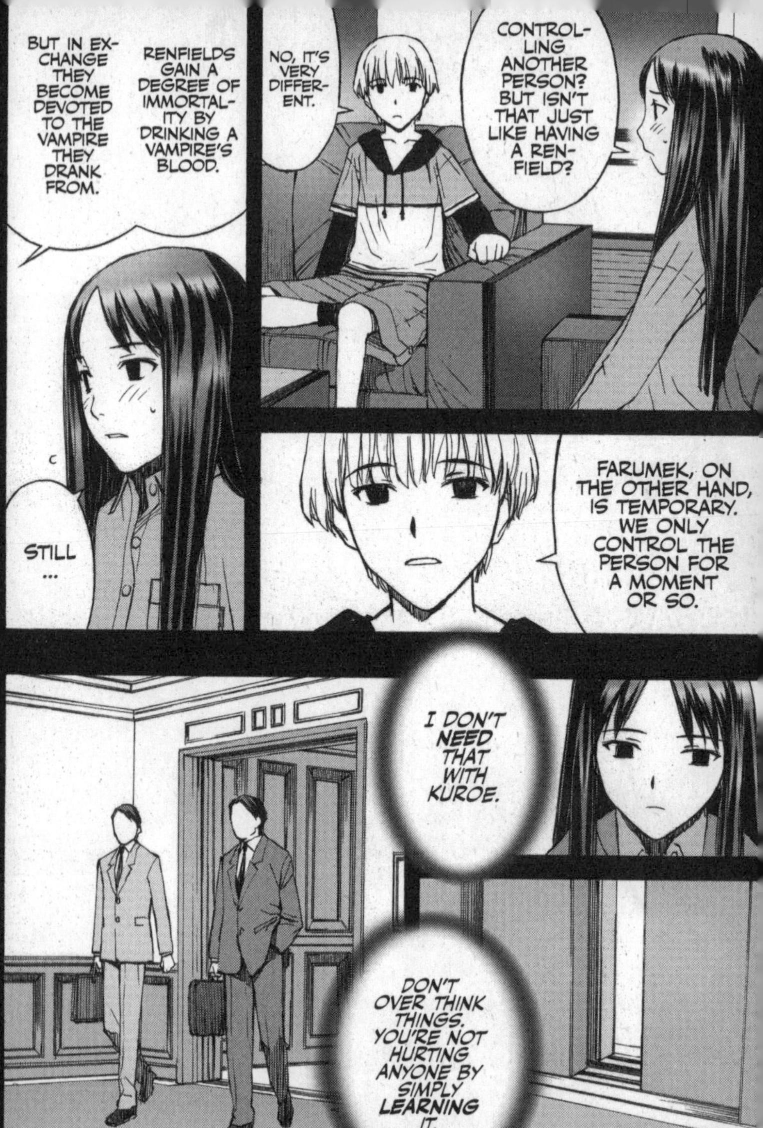
CONTROL-LING ANOTHER PERSON? BUT ISN'T THAT JUST LIKE HAVING A REN-FIELD?
NO, IT'S VERY DIFFER-ENT.
FARUMEK, ON THE OTHER HAND, IS TEMPORARY. WE ONLY CONTROL THE PERSON FOR A MOMENT OR SO.
RENFIELDS GAIN A DEGREE OF IMMORTAL-ITY BY DRINKING A VAMPIRE'S BLOOD.
BUT IN EX-CHANGE THEY BECOME DEVOTED TO THE VAMPIRE THEY DRANK FROM.
STILL ...
I DON'T NEED THAT WITH KUROE.
DON'T OVER THINK THINGS. YOU'RE NOT HURTING ANYONE BY SIMPLY LEARNING IT.

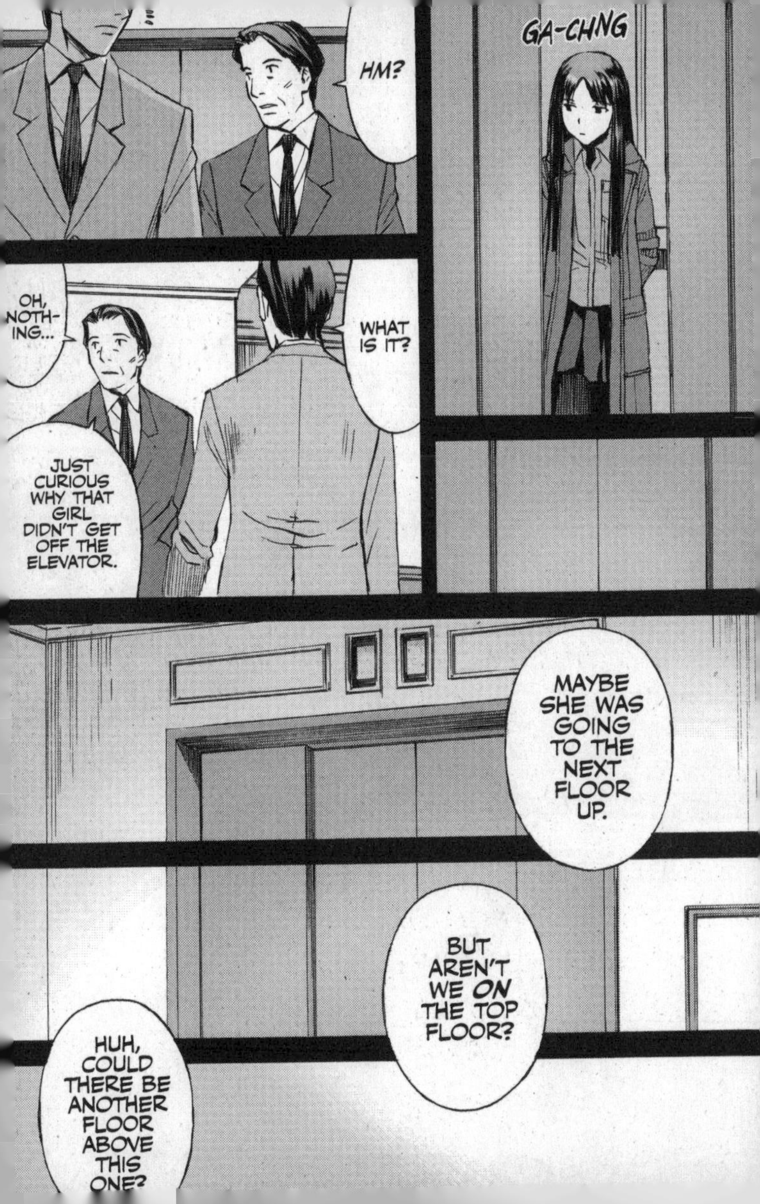
GA-CHNG
HM?
WHAT IS IT?
OH, NOTHING...
JUST CURIOUS WHY THAT GIRL DIDN'T GET OFF THE ELEVATOR.
MAYBE SHE WAS GOING TO THE NEXT FLOOR UP.
BUT AREN'T WE ON THE TOP FLOOR?
HUH, COULD THERE BE ANOTHER FLOOR ABOVE THIS ONE?

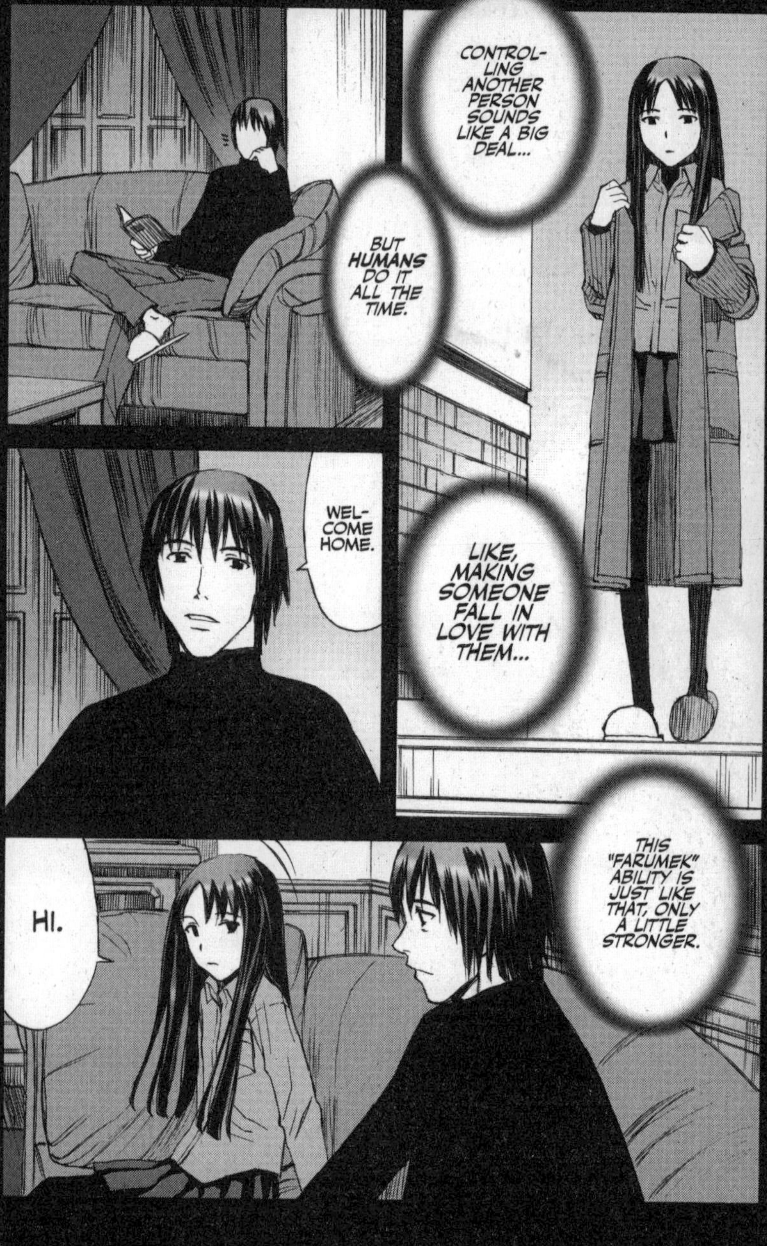
CONTROL-LING ANOTHER PERSON SOUNDS LIKE A BIG DEAL...
BUT HUMANS DO IT ALL THE TIME.
LIKE, MAKING SOMEONE FALL IN LOVE WITH THEM...
WEL-COME HOME.
THIS "FARUMEK" ABILITY IS JUST LIKE THAT, ONLY A LITTLE STRONGER.
HI.

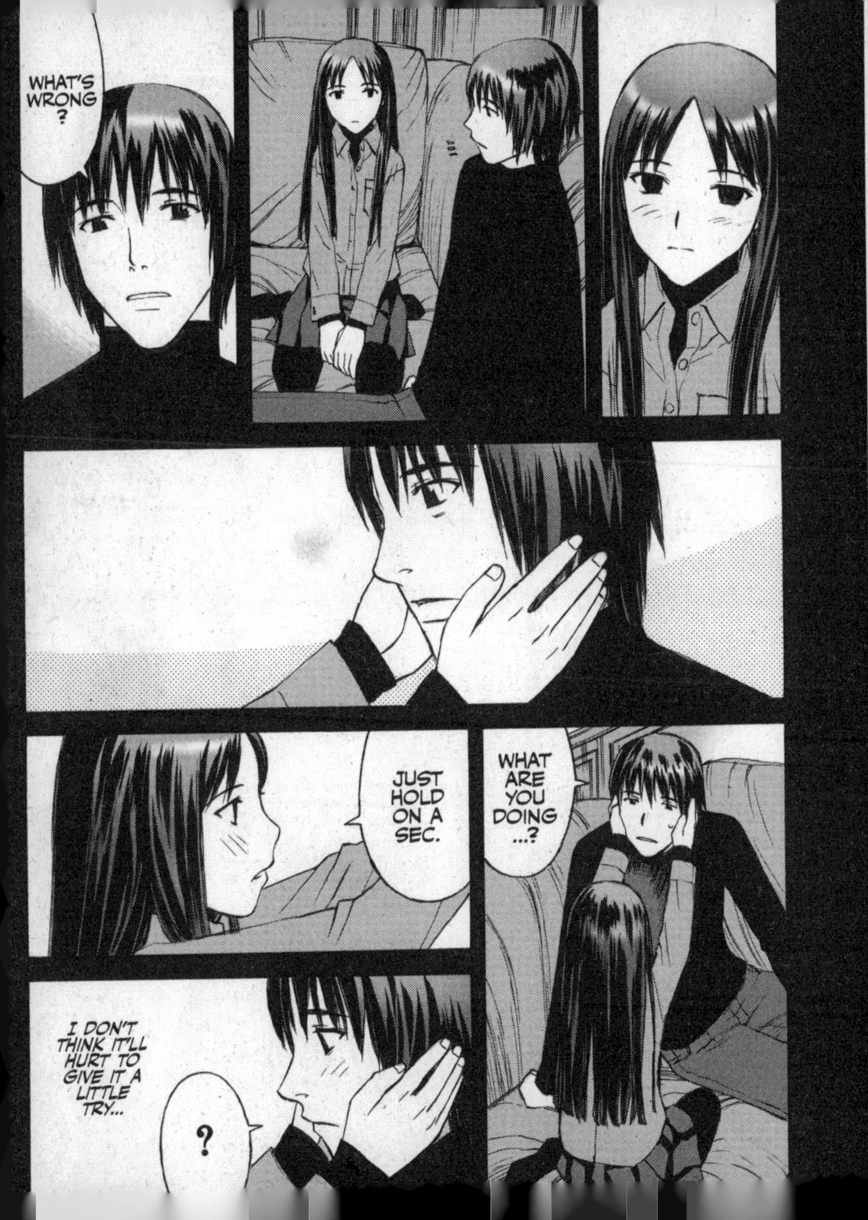
WHAT'S WRONG ?
WHAT ARE YOU DOING ...?
JUST HOLD ON A SEC.
I DON'T THINK IT'LL HURT TO GIVE IT A LITTLE TRY...
?

IT'S EASY.
!
JUST STARE INTO THEIR EYES AS IF YOU'RE GIVING AN ORDER...
AND THEY'LL DO ANYTHING AND EVERYTHING YOU SAY.
DID IT WORK?
WHAT I NEED...
IS A WAY TO TEST IT.

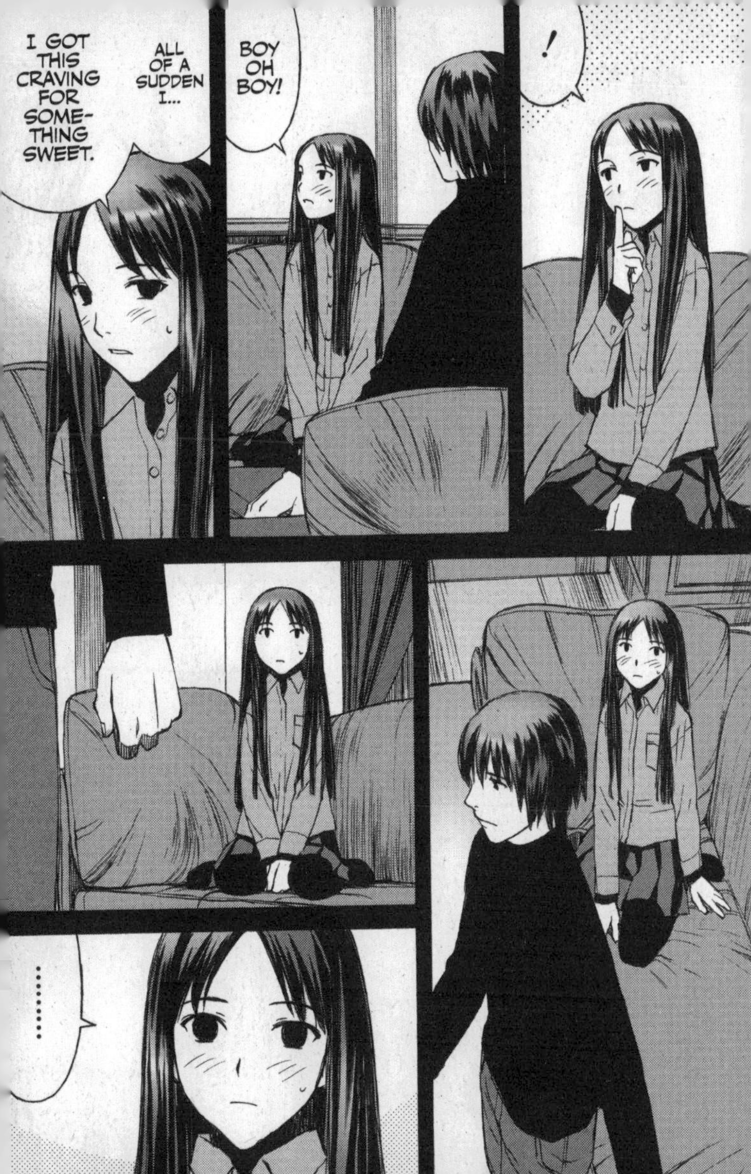
!
BOY OH BOY!
ALL OF A SUDDEN I...
I GOT THIS CRAVING FOR SOME-THING SWEET.
......

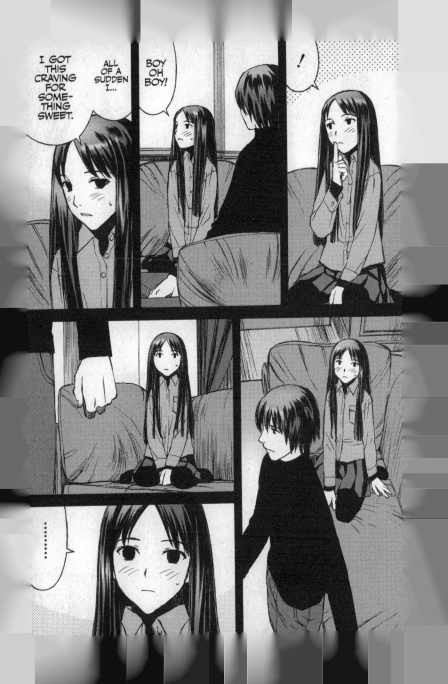

HERE YOU GO.

CLINK

IT... IT'S WORKING?!

!!

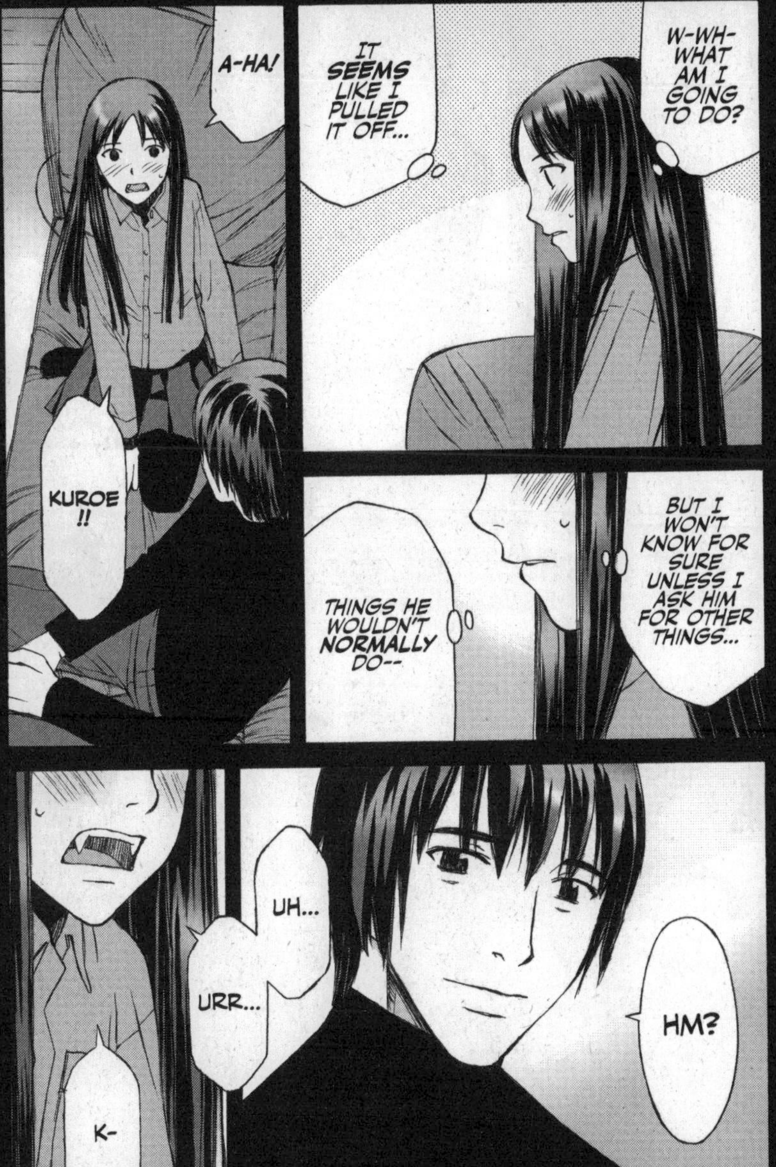
W-WH-WHAT AM I GOING TO DO?
IT SEEMS LIKE I PULLED IT OFF...
BUT I WON'T KNOW FOR SURE UNLESS I ASK HIM FOR OTHER THINGS...
THINGS HE WOULDN'T NORMALLY DO--
A-HA!
KUROE !!
HM?
UH...
URR...
K-

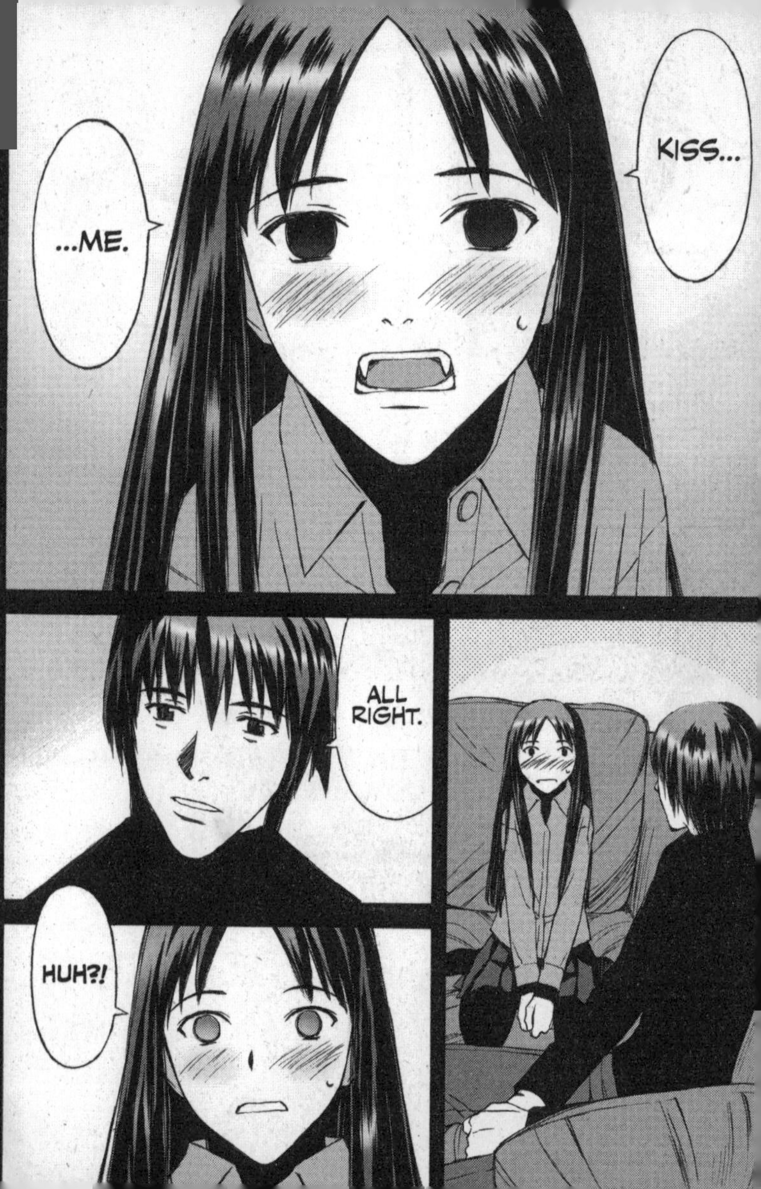
KISS...
...ME.
ALL RIGHT.
HUH?!

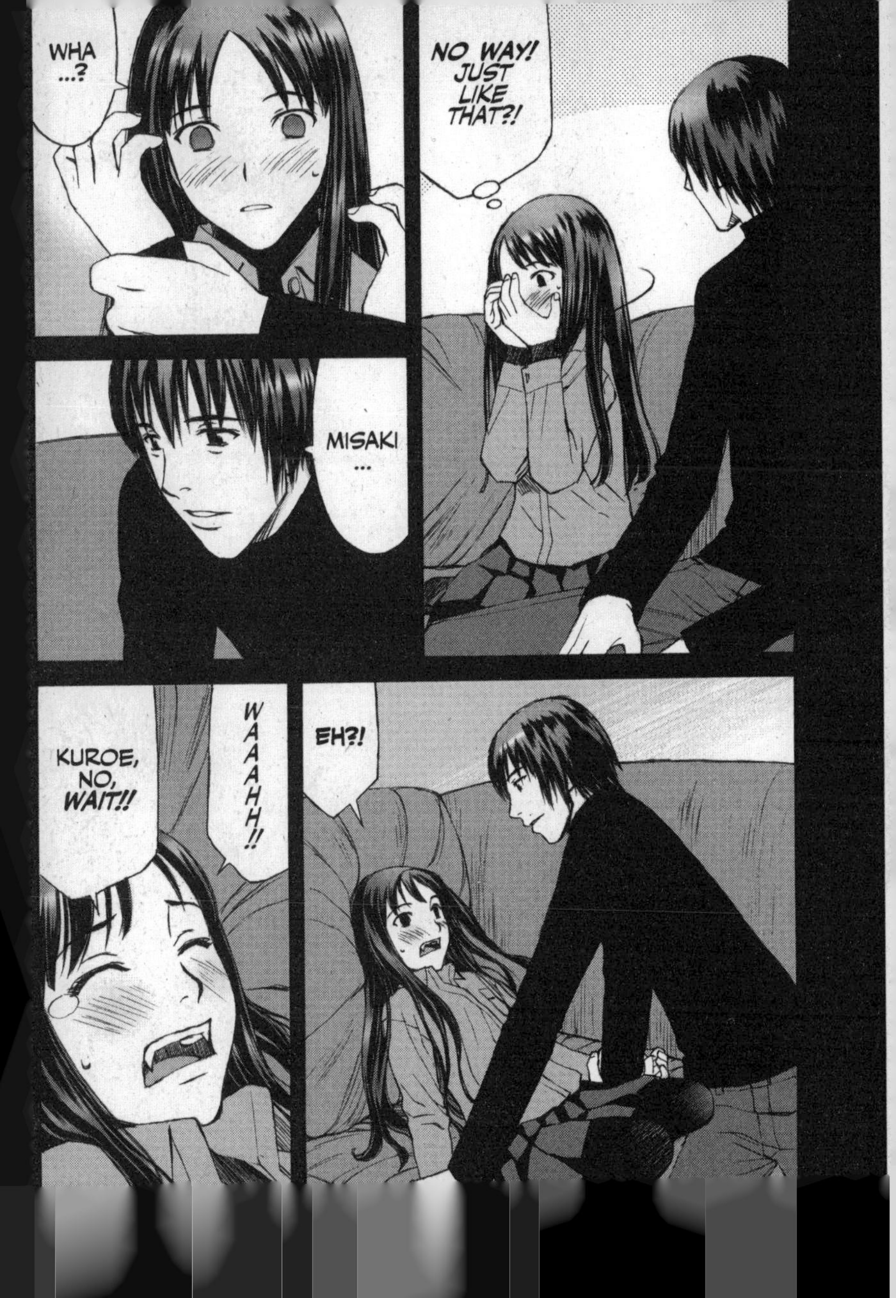
NO WAY! JUST LIKE THAT?!
WHA ...?
MISAKI ...
EH?!
WAAAAHH!!
KUROE, NO, WAIT!!

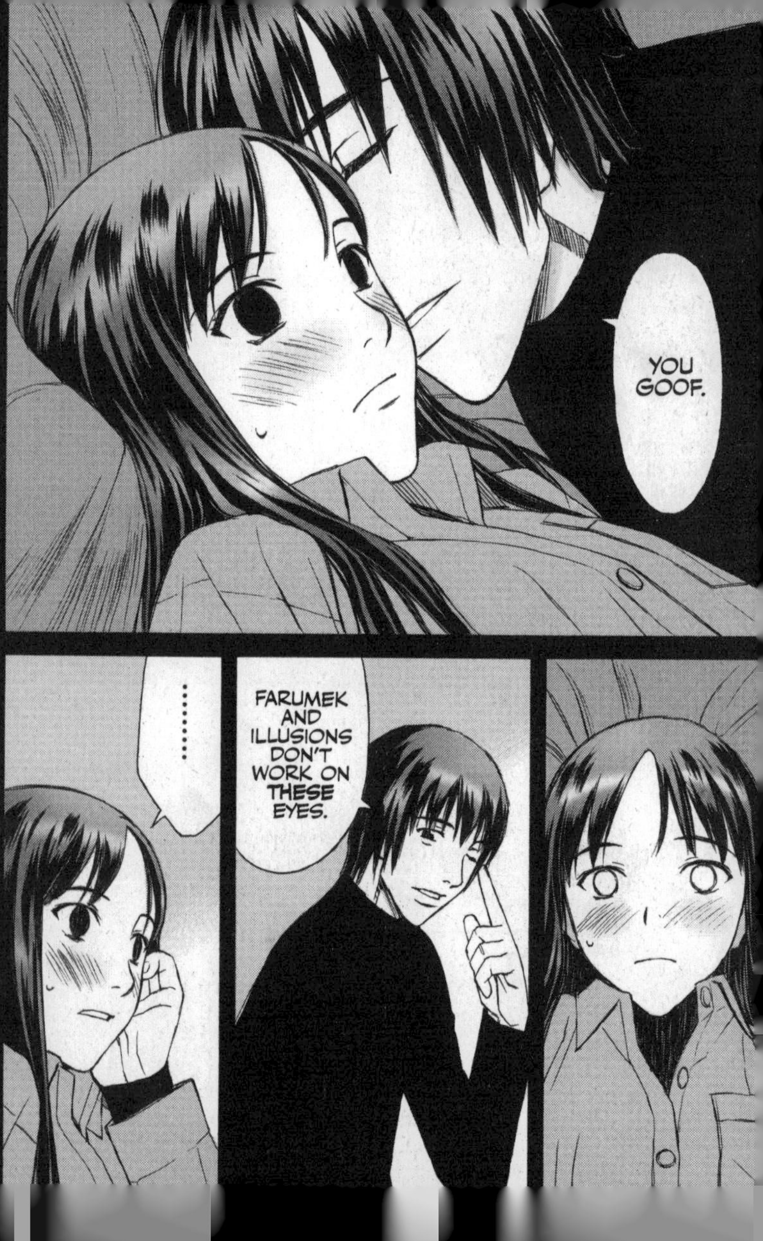
YOU GOOF.
FARUMEK AND ILLUSIONS DON'T WORK ON THESE EYES.
......

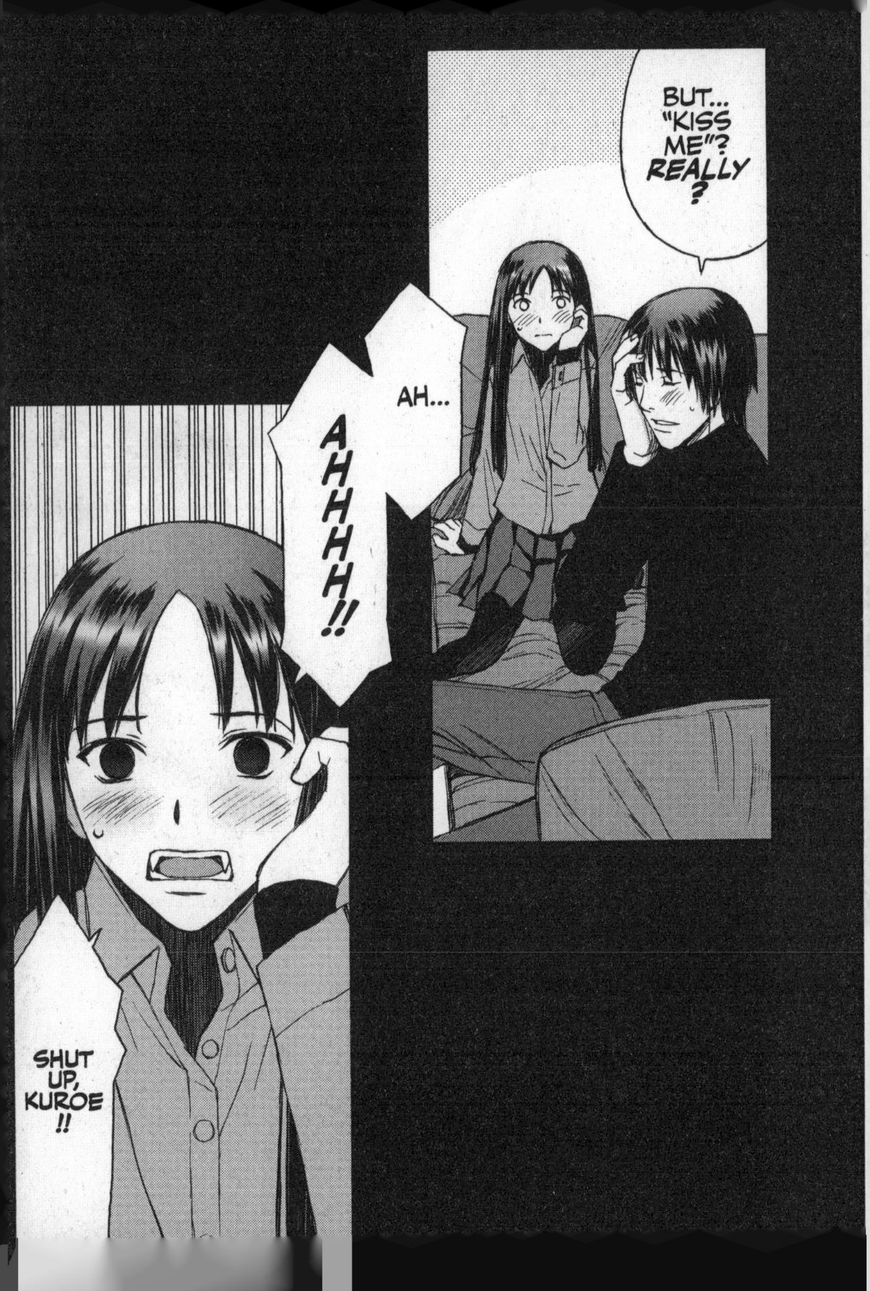
BUT... "KISS ME"? REALLY?
AH...
AHHHHH!!
SHUT UP, KUROE!!

Episode 3
SOUL SLAVE part 1
Slave of the Soul

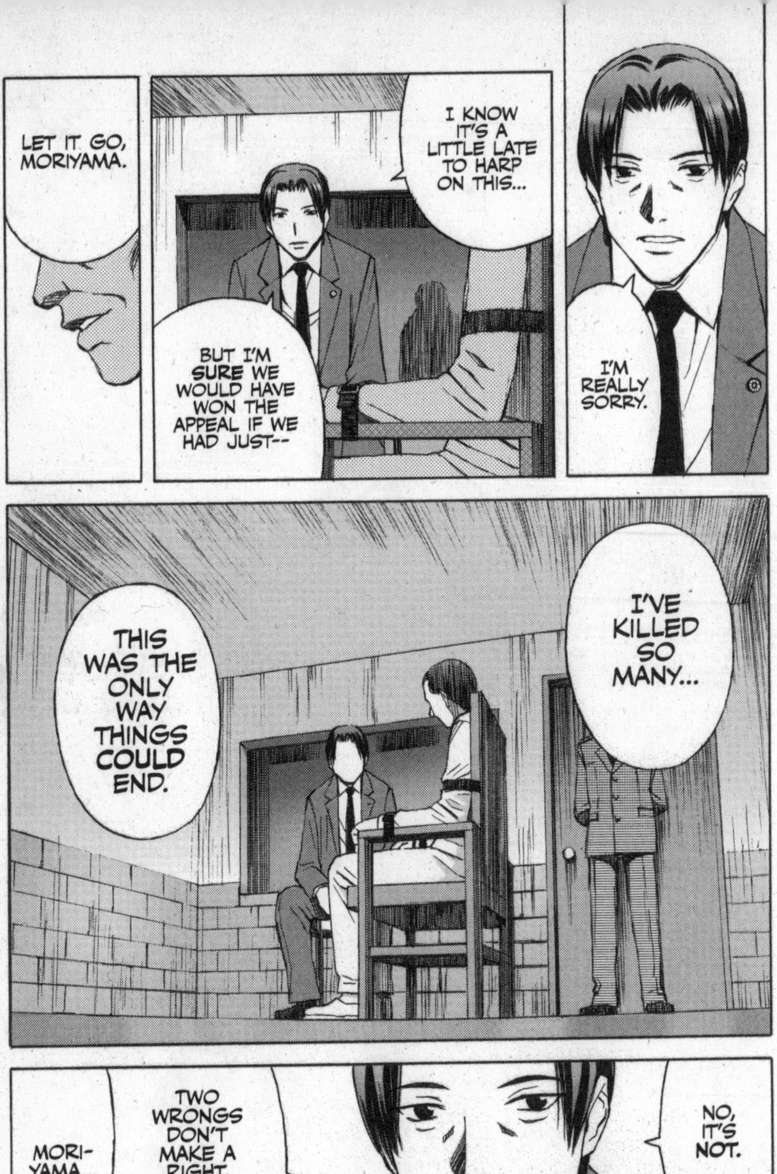
I'M REALLY SORRY.
I KNOW IT'S A LITTLE LATE TO HARP ON THIS...
BUT I'M SURE WE WOULD HAVE WON THE APPEAL IF WE HAD JUST--
LET IT GO, MORIYAMA.
I'VE KILLED SO MANY...
THIS WAS THE ONLY WAY THINGS COULD END.
NO, IT'S NOT.
TWO WRONGS DON'T MAKE A RIGHT, AND BY KILLING YOU--
MORI-YAMA...

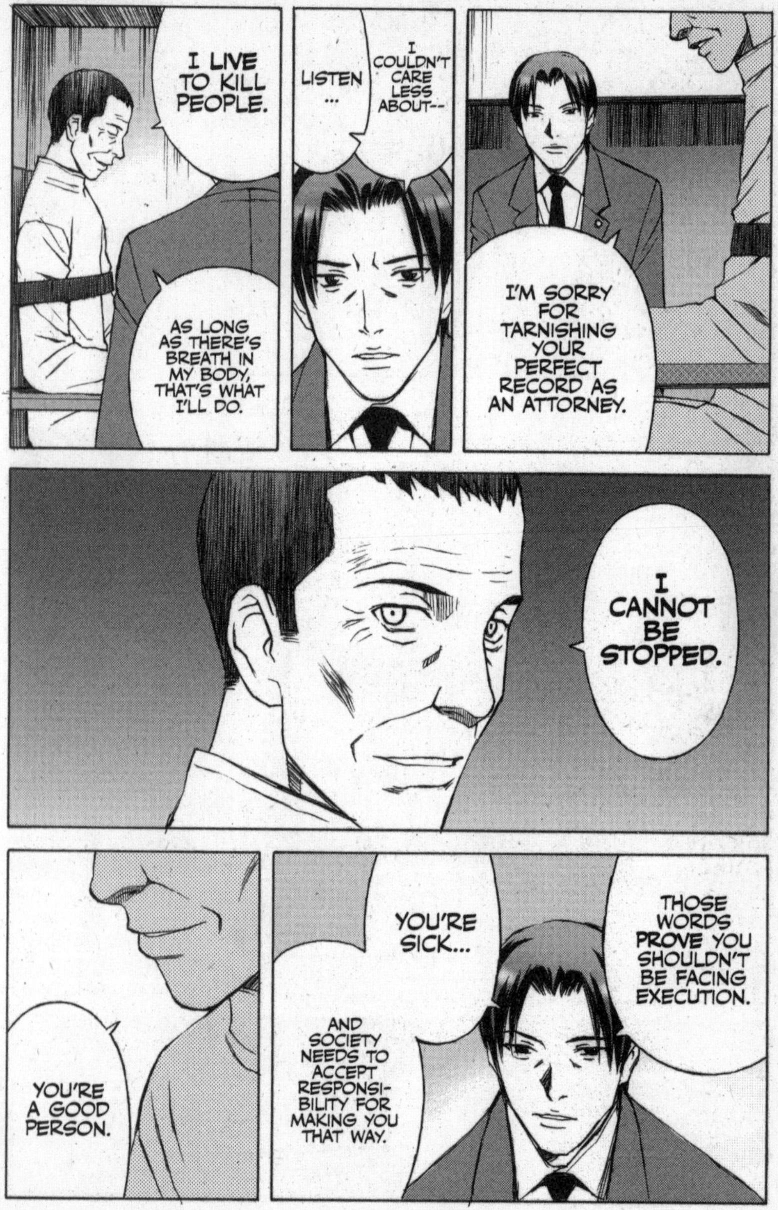
I'M SORRY FOR TARNISHING YOUR PERFECT RECORD AS AN ATTORNEY.
I COULDN'T CARE LESS ABOUT--
LISTEN ...
I LIVE TO KILL PEOPLE.
AS LONG AS THERE'S BREATH IN MY BODY, THAT'S WHAT I'LL DO.
I CANNOT BE STOPPED.
THOSE WORDS PROVE YOU SHOULDN'T BE FACING EXECUTION.
YOU'RE SICK...
AND SOCIETY NEEDS TO ACCEPT RESPONSI-BILITY FOR MAKING YOU THAT WAY.
YOU'RE A GOOD PERSON.

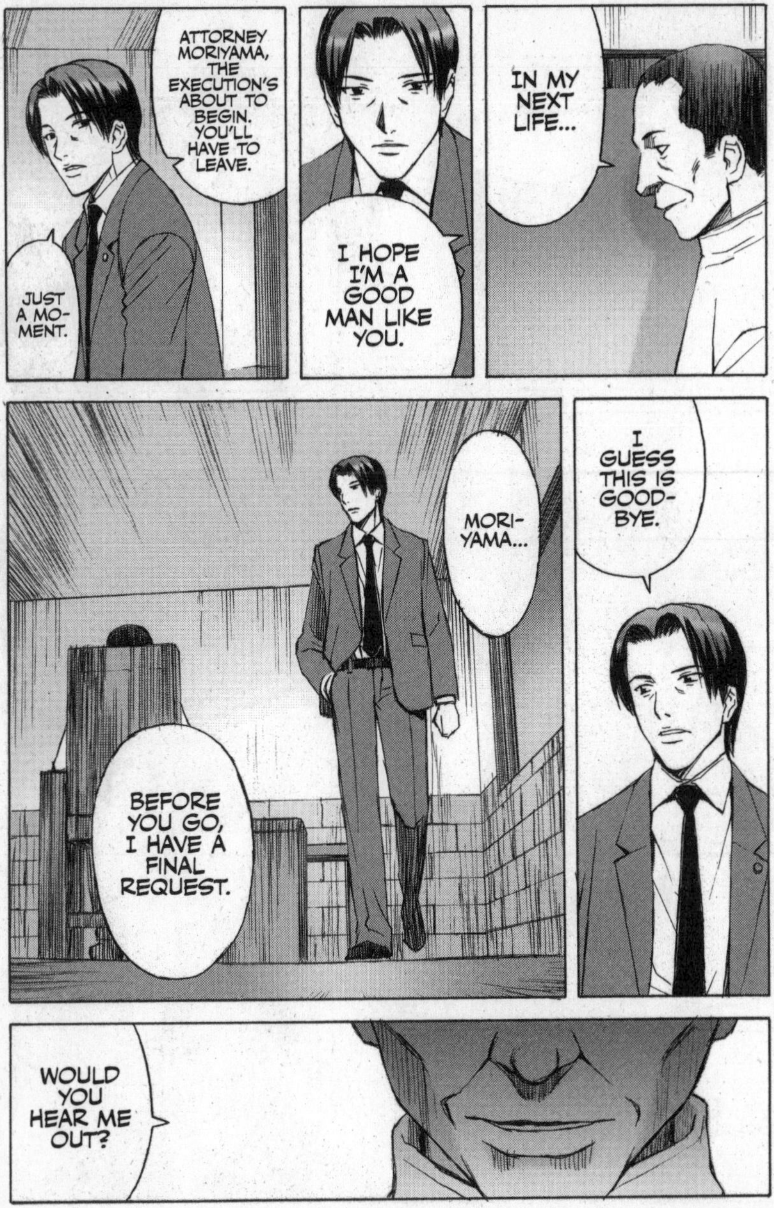
IN MY NEXT LIFE...
I HOPE I'M A GOOD MAN LIKE YOU.
ATTORNEY MORIYAMA, THE EXECUTION'S ABOUT TO BEGIN. YOU'LL HAVE TO LEAVE.
JUST A MO-MENT.
I GUESS THIS IS GOOD-BYE.
MORI-YAMA...
BEFORE YOU GO, I HAVE A FINAL REQUEST.
WOULD YOU HEAR ME OUT?

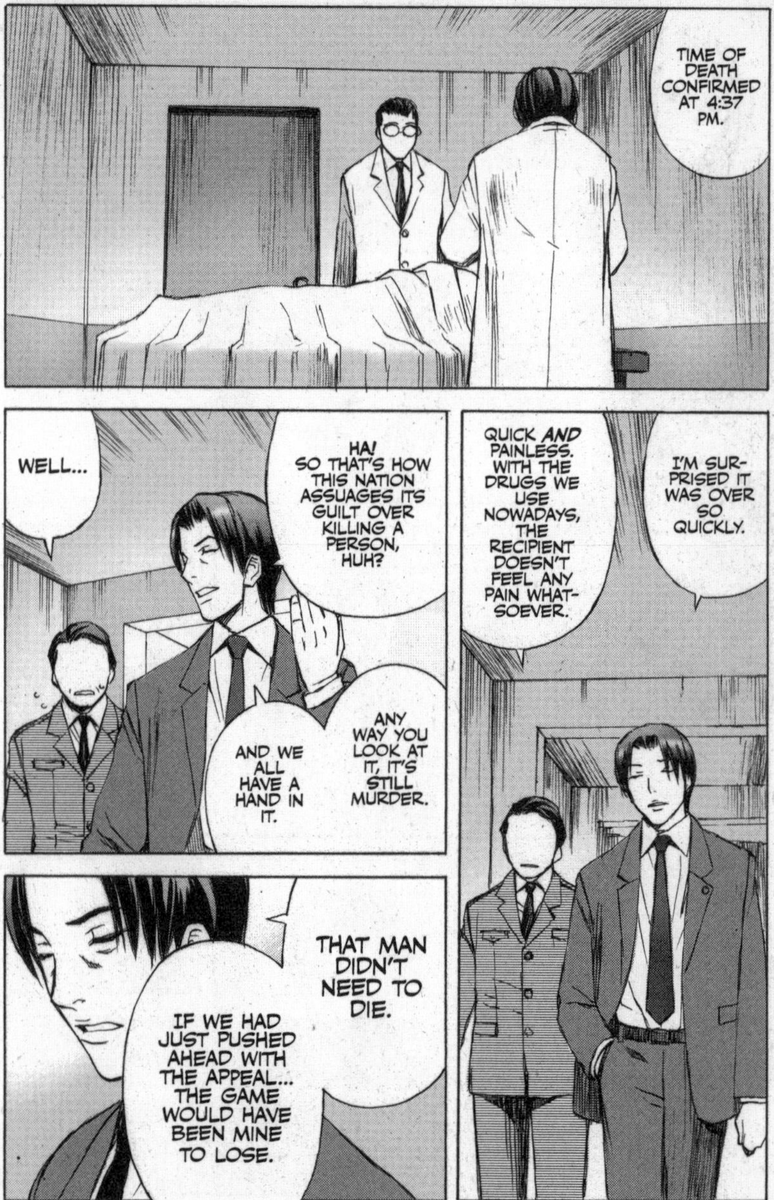

TIME OF DEATH CONFIRMED AT 4:37 PM.
I'M SURPRISED IT WAS OVER SO QUICKLY.
QUICK *AND* PAINLESS. WITH THE DRUGS WE USE NOWADAYS, THE RECIPIENT DOESN'T FEEL ANY PAIN WHATSOEVER.
HA! SO THAT'S HOW THIS NATION ASSUAGES ITS GUILT OVER KILLING A PERSON, HUH?
WELL...
ANY WAY YOU LOOK AT IT, IT'S STILL MURDER.
AND WE ALL HAVE A HAND IN IT.
THAT MAN DIDN'T NEED TO DIE.
IF WE HAD JUST PUSHED AHEAD WITH THE APPEAL... THE GAME WOULD HAVE BEEN MINE TO LOSE.

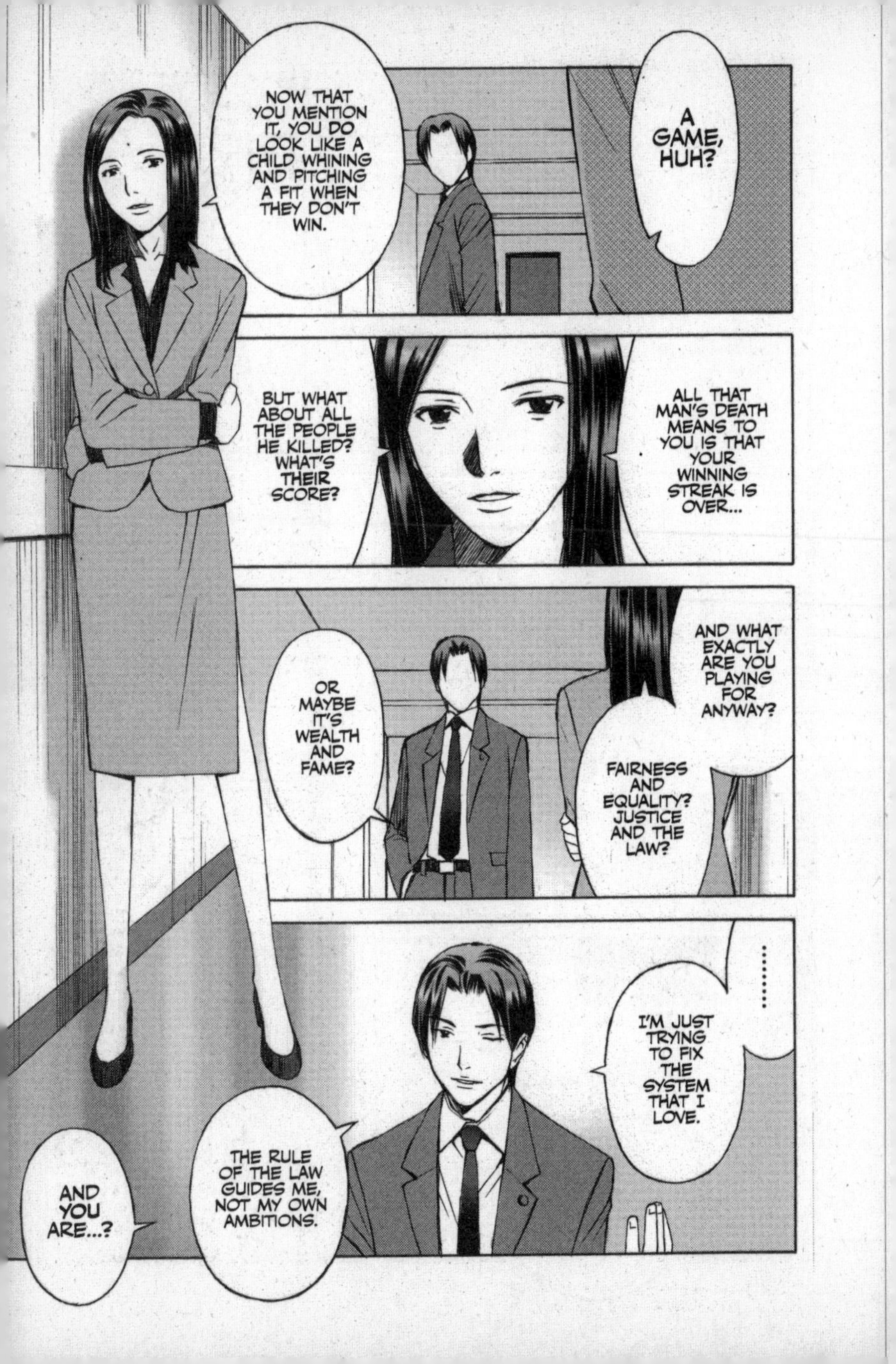
A GAME, HUH?
NOW THAT YOU MENTION IT, YOU DO LOOK LIKE A CHILD WHINING AND PITCHING A FIT WHEN THEY DON'T WIN.
ALL THAT MAN'S DEATH MEANS TO YOU IS THAT YOUR WINNING STREAK IS OVER...
BUT WHAT ABOUT ALL THE PEOPLE HE KILLED? WHAT'S THEIR SCORE?
AND WHAT EXACTLY ARE YOU PLAYING FOR ANYWAY?
FAIRNESS AND EQUALITY? JUSTICE AND THE LAW?
OR MAYBE IT'S WEALTH AND FAME?
......
I'M JUST TRYING TO FIX THE SYSTEM THAT I LOVE.
THE RULE OF THE LAW GUIDES ME, NOT MY OWN AMBITIONS.
AND YOU ARE...?

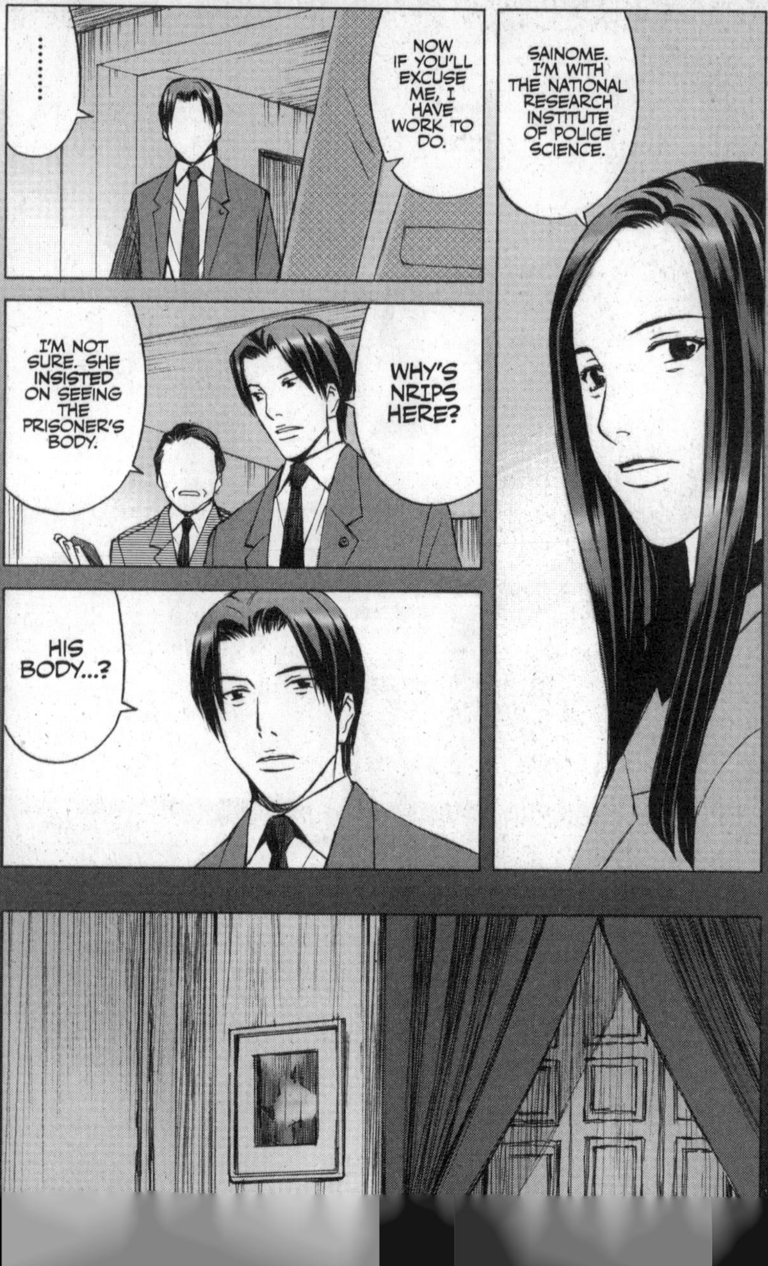
SAINOME. I'M WITH THE NATIONAL RESEARCH INSTITUTE OF POLICE SCIENCE.
NOW IF YOU'LL EXCUSE ME, I HAVE WORK TO DO.
......
WHY'S NRIPS HERE?
I'M NOT SURE. SHE INSISTED ON SEEING THE PRISONER'S BODY.
HIS BODY...?

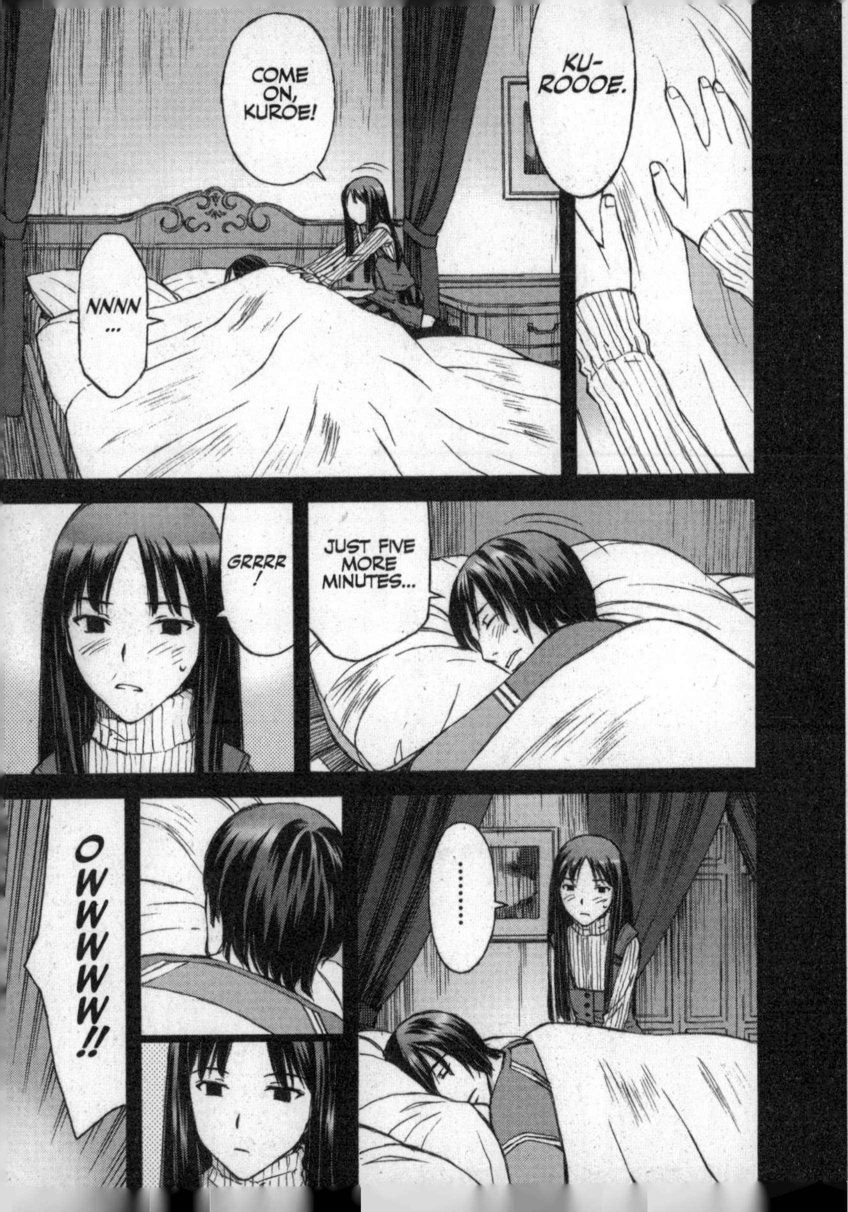
KU-ROOOE.
COME ON, KUROE!
NNNN...
JUST FIVE MORE MINUTES...
GRRRR!
....
OWWWWW!!

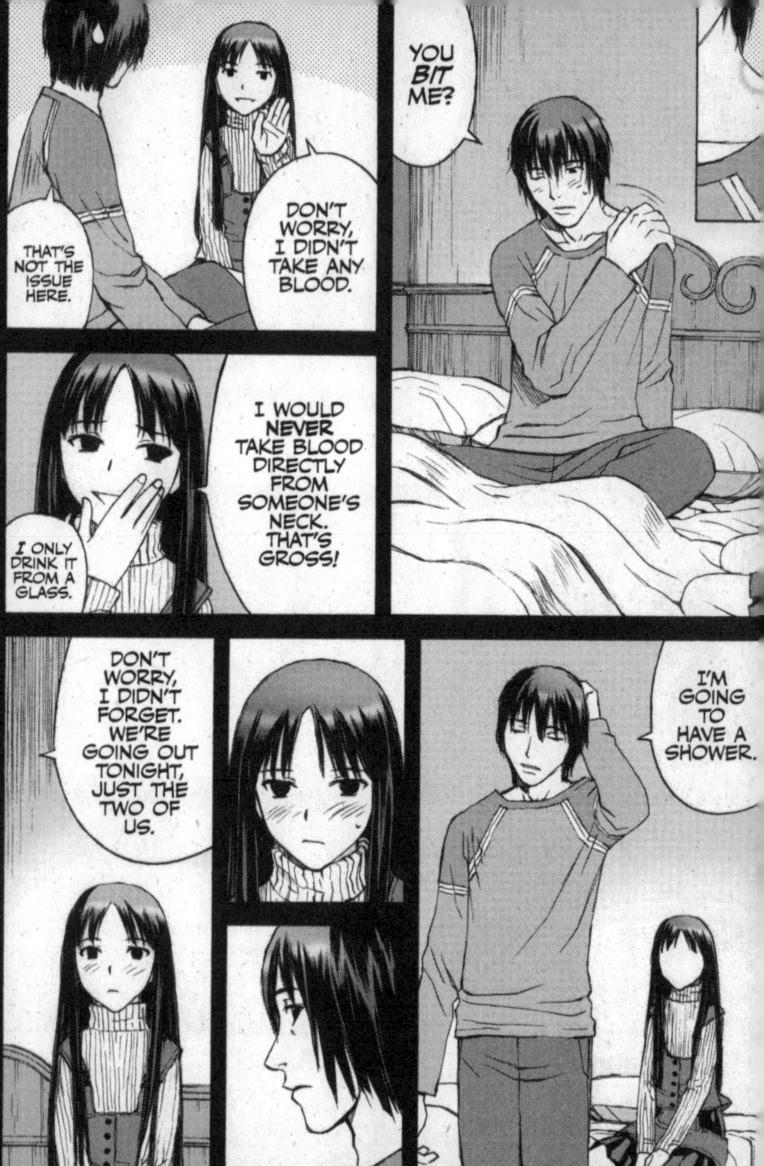
YOU *BIT* ME?
DON'T WORRY, I DIDN'T TAKE ANY BLOOD.
THAT'S NOT THE ISSUE HERE.
I WOULD **NEVER** TAKE BLOOD DIRECTLY FROM SOMEONE'S NECK. THAT'S GROSS!
I ONLY DRINK IT FROM A GLASS.
I'M GOING TO HAVE A SHOWER.
DON'T WORRY, I DIDN'T FORGET. WE'RE GOING OUT TONIGHT, JUST THE TWO OF US.

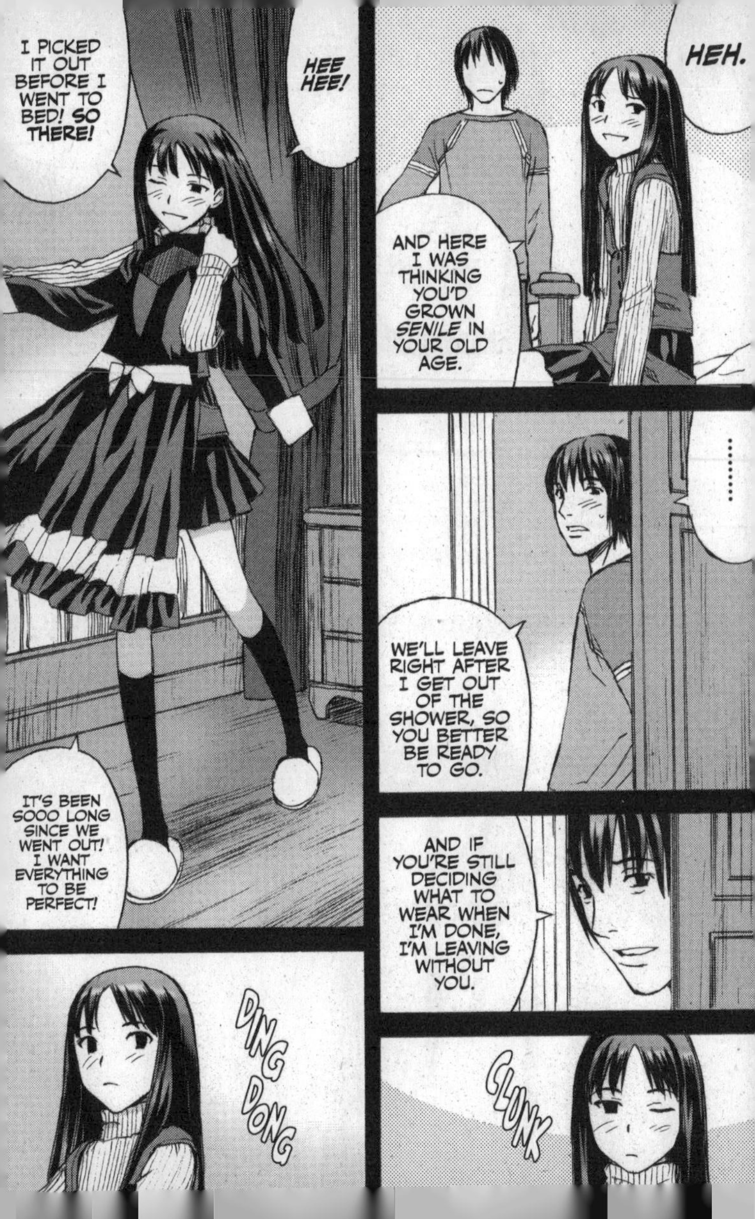
HEH.
AND HERE I WAS THINKING YOU'D GROWN SENILE IN YOUR OLD AGE.
HEE HEE!
I PICKED IT OUT BEFORE I WENT TO BED! SO THERE!
IT'S BEEN SOOO LONG SINCE WE WENT OUT! I WANT EVERYTHING TO BE PERFECT!
......
WE'LL LEAVE RIGHT AFTER I GET OUT OF THE SHOWER, SO YOU BETTER BE READY TO GO.
AND IF YOU'RE STILL DECIDING WHAT TO WEAR WHEN I'M DONE, I'M LEAVING WITHOUT YOU.
CLUNK
DING DONG

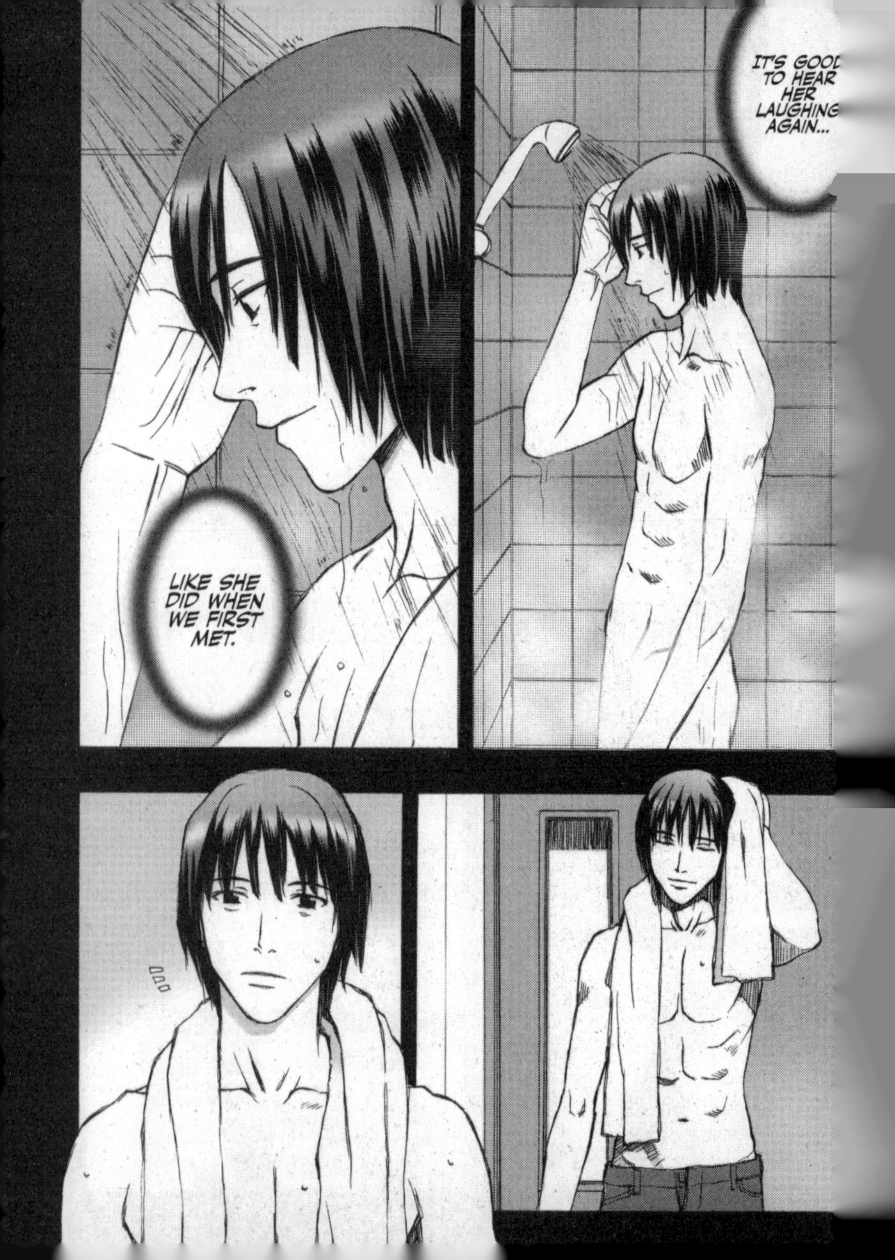
IT'S GOOD TO HEAR HER LAUGHING AGAIN...
LIKE SHE DID WHEN WE FIRST MET.

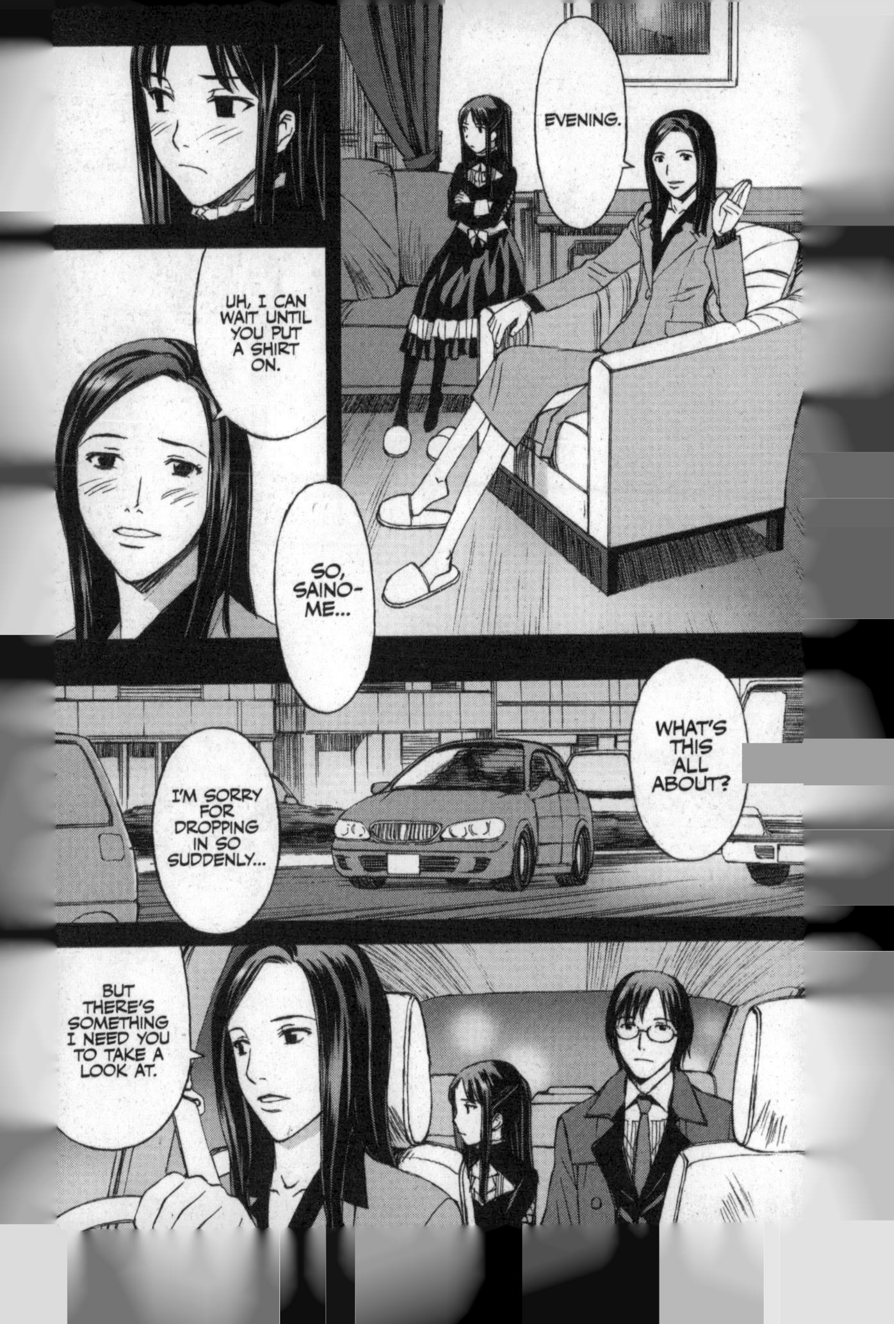
EVENING.
UH, I CAN WAIT UNTIL YOU PUT A SHIRT ON.
SO, SAINO-ME...
WHAT'S THIS ALL ABOUT?
I'M SORRY FOR DROPPING IN SO SUDDENLY...
BUT THERE'S SOMETHING I NEED YOU TO TAKE A LOOK AT.

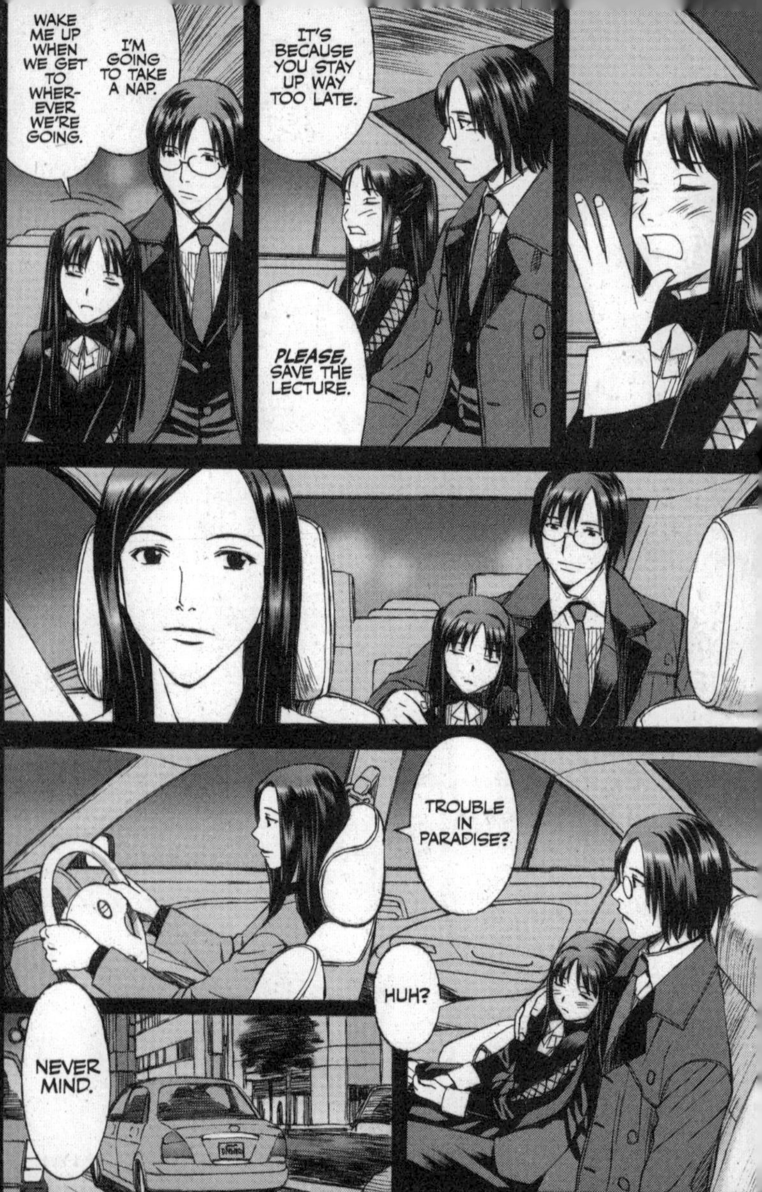
IT'S BECAUSE YOU STAY UP WAY TOO LATE.
PLEASE, SAVE THE LECTURE.
I'M GOING TO TAKE A NAP.
WAKE ME UP WHEN WE GET TO WHER-EVER WE'RE GOING.
TROUBLE IN PARADISE?
HUH?
NEVER MIND.

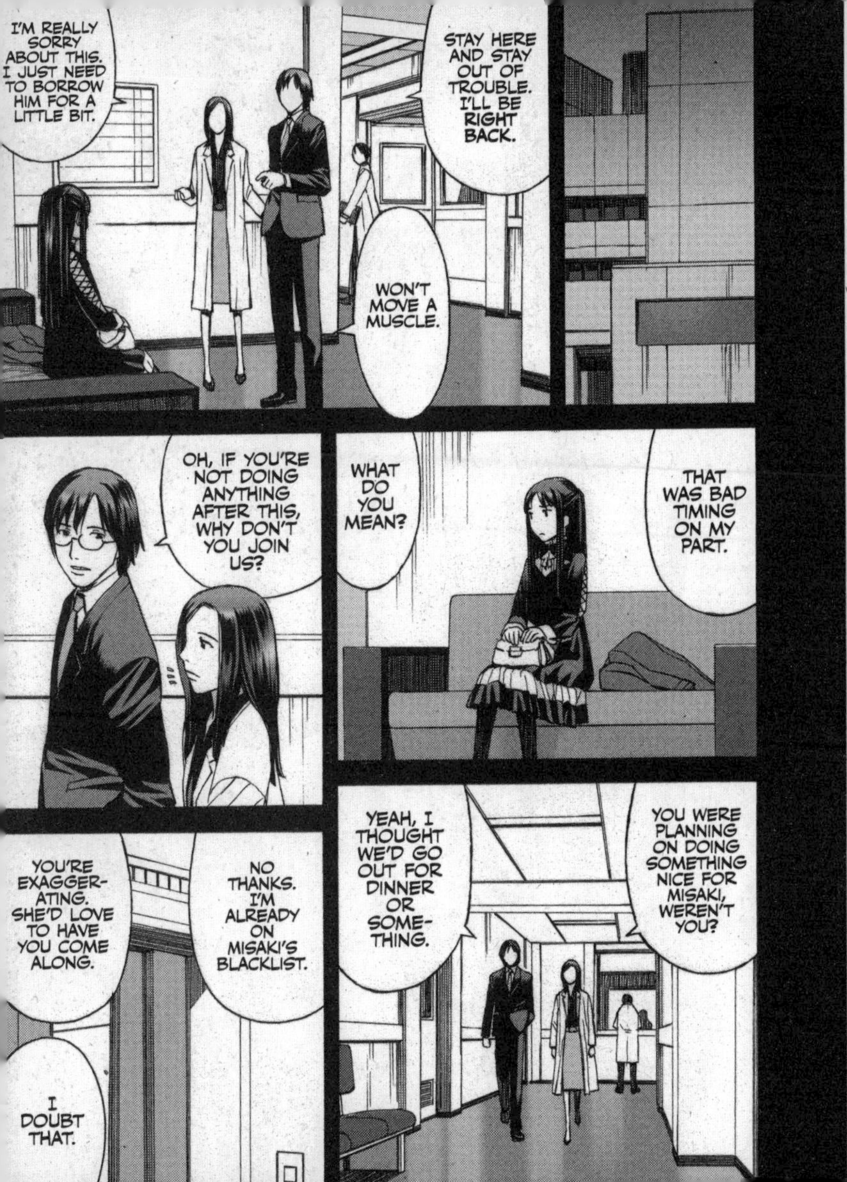
STAY HERE AND STAY OUT OF TROUBLE. I'LL BE RIGHT BACK.
WON'T MOVE A MUSCLE.
I'M REALLY SORRY ABOUT THIS. I JUST NEED TO BORROW HIM FOR A LITTLE BIT.
THAT WAS BAD TIMING ON MY PART.
WHAT DO YOU MEAN?
OH, IF YOU'RE NOT DOING ANYTHING AFTER THIS, WHY DON'T YOU JOIN US?
YOU WERE PLANNING ON DOING SOMETHING NICE FOR MISAKI, WEREN'T YOU?
YEAH, I THOUGHT WE'D GO OUT FOR DINNER OR SOME-THING.
NO THANKS. I'M ALREADY ON MISAKI'S BLACKLIST.
YOU'RE EXAGGER-ATING. SHE'D LOVE TO HAVE YOU COME ALONG.
I DOUBT THAT.

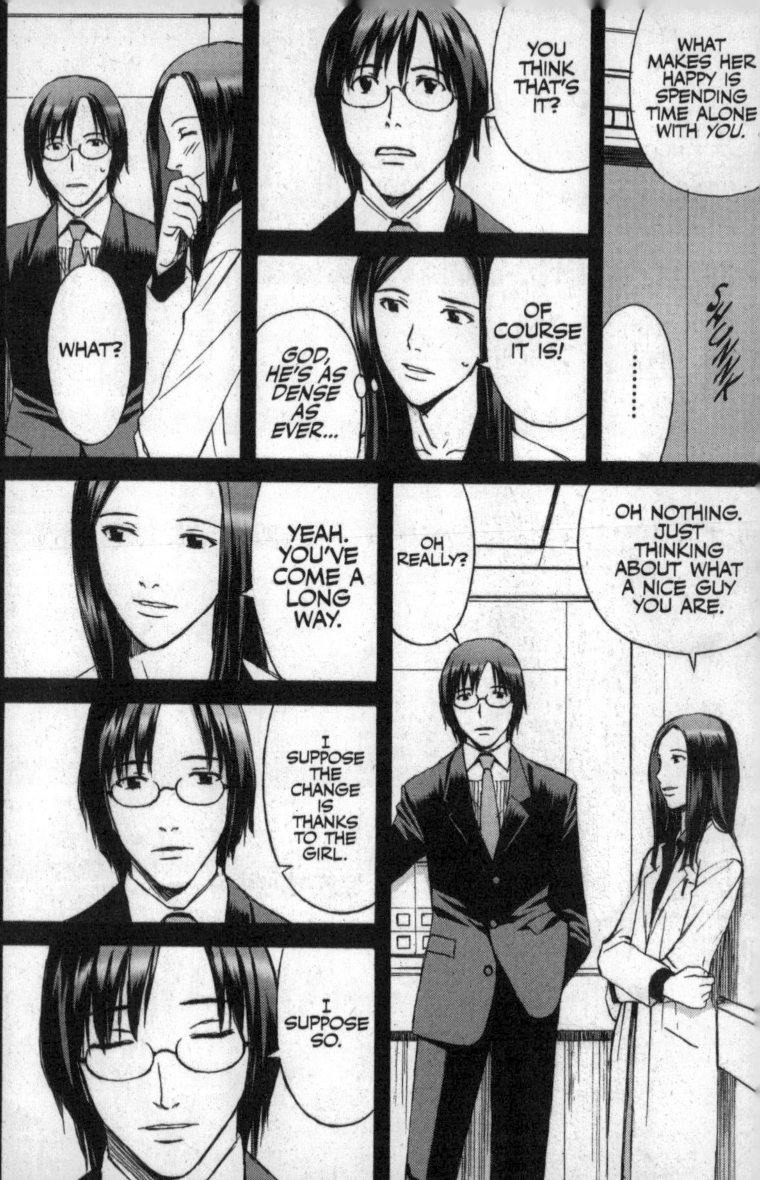
WHAT MAKES HER HAPPY IS SPENDING TIME ALONE WITH YOU.
......
SHUNK
YOU THINK THAT'S IT?
OF COURSE IT IS!
GOD, HE'S AS DENSE AS EVER...
WHAT?
OH NOTHING. JUST THINKING ABOUT WHAT A NICE GUY YOU ARE.
OH REALLY?
YEAH. YOU'VE COME A LONG WAY.
I SUPPOSE THE CHANGE IS THANKS TO THE GIRL.
I SUPPOSE SO.

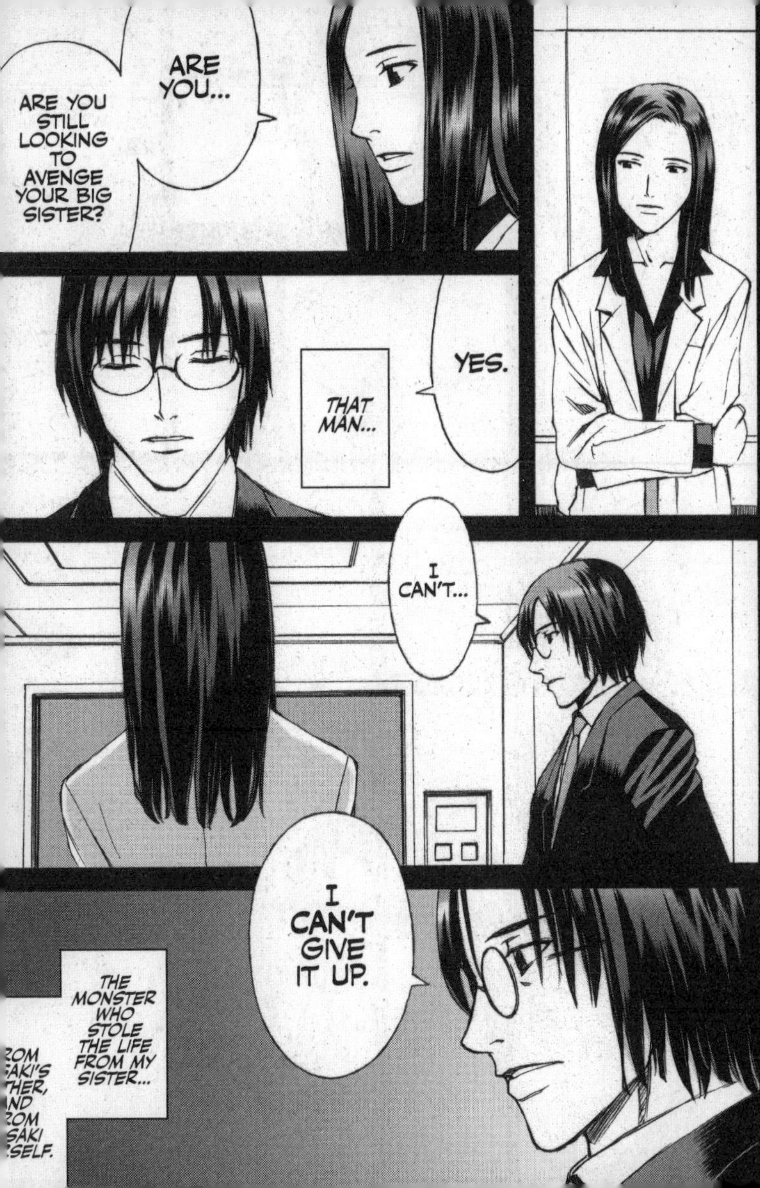
ARE YOU...
ARE YOU STILL LOOKING TO AVENGE YOUR BIG SISTER?
YES.
THAT MAN...
I CAN'T...
I CAN'T GIVE IT UP.
THE MONSTER WHO STOLE THE LIFE FROM MY SISTER...
ROM SAKI'S THER, ND ROM SAKI SELF.

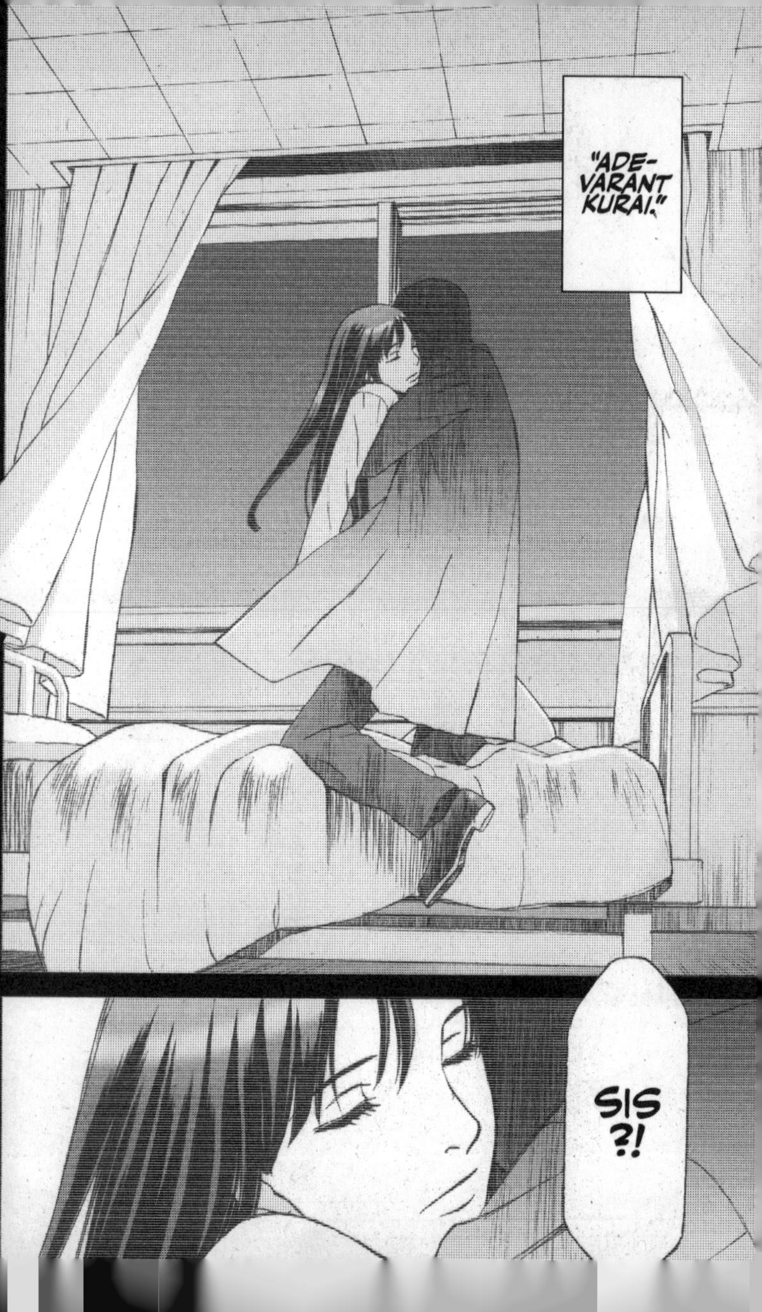
"ADE-
VARANT
KURAI."
SIS
?!

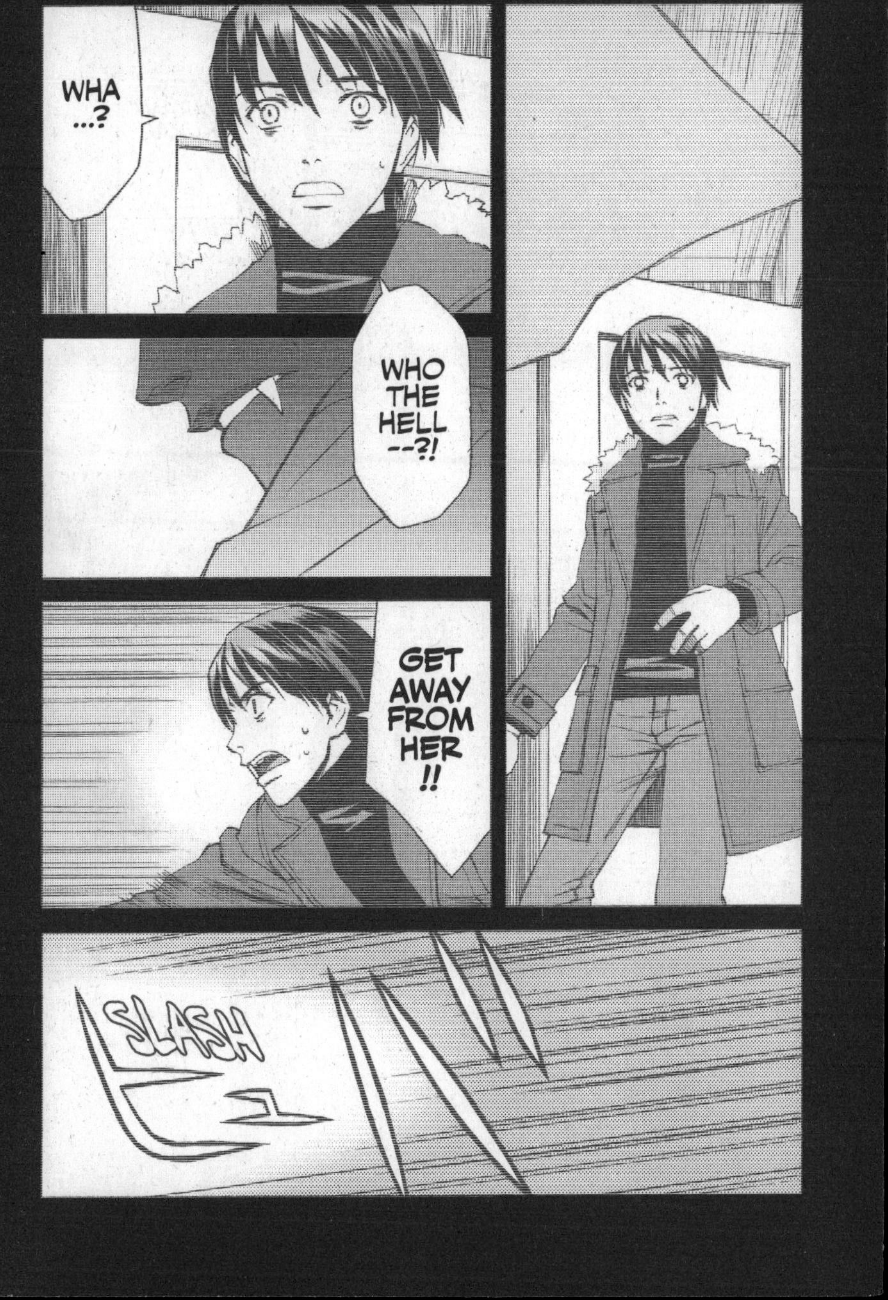
WHA ...?
WHO THE HELL --?!
GET AWAY FROM HER !!
SLASH

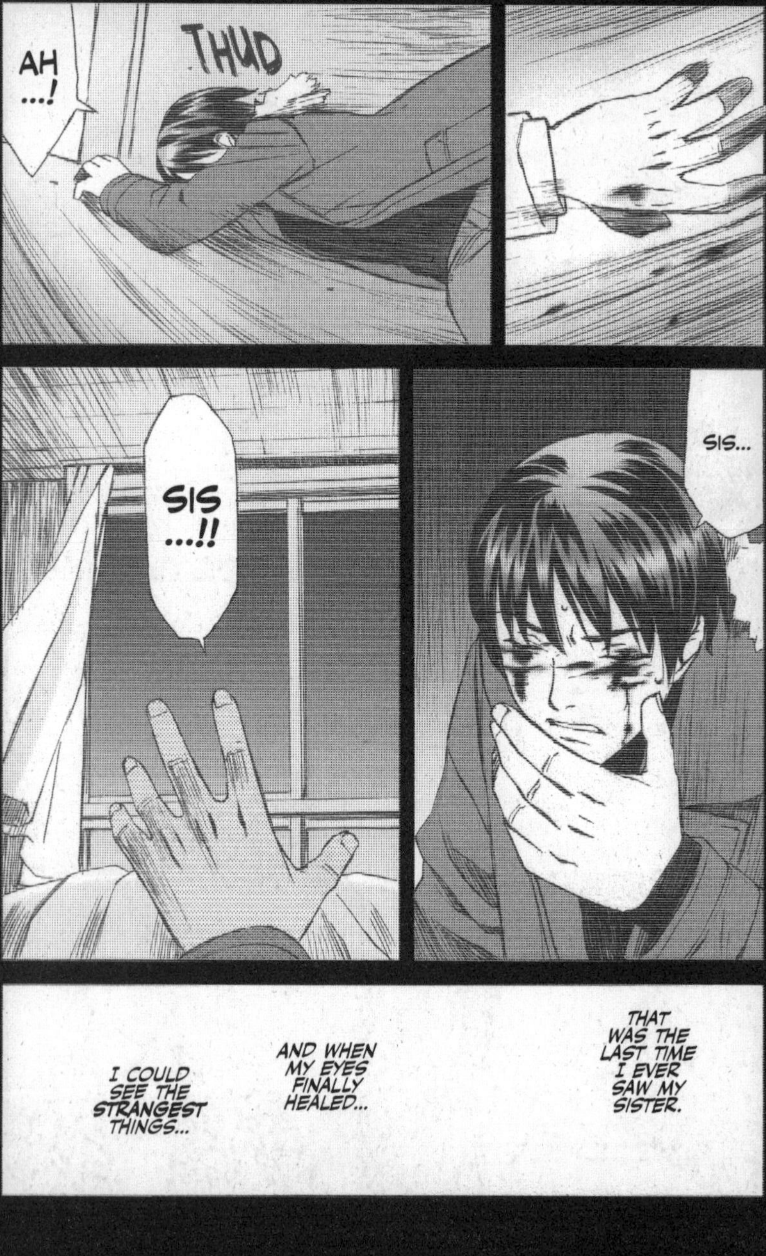
THUD
AH ...!
SIS...
SIS ...!!
THAT WAS THE LAST TIME I EVER SAW MY SISTER.
AND WHEN MY EYES FINALLY HEALED...
I COULD SEE THE STRANGEST THINGS...

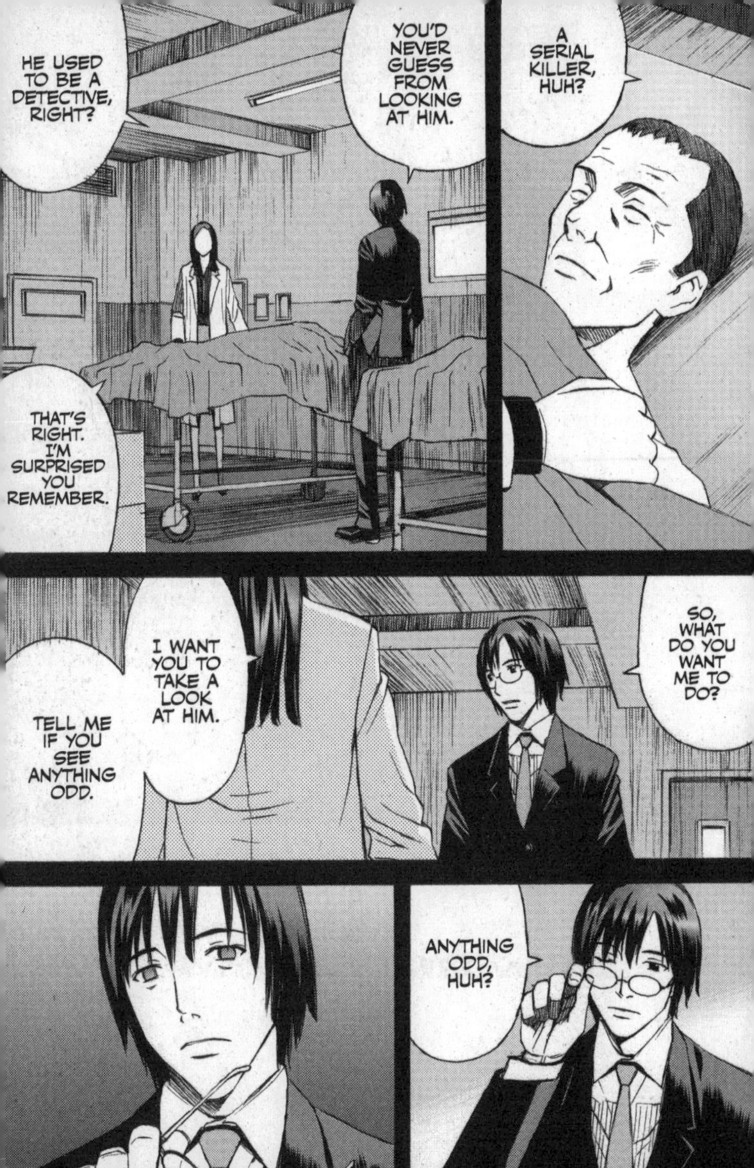
A SERIAL KILLER, HUH?
YOU'D NEVER GUESS FROM LOOKING AT HIM.
HE USED TO BE A DETECTIVE, RIGHT?
THAT'S RIGHT. I'M SURPRISED YOU REMEMBER.
SO, WHAT DO YOU WANT ME TO DO?
I WANT YOU TO TAKE A LOOK AT HIM.
TELL ME IF YOU SEE ANYTHING ODD.
ANYTHING ODD, HUH?

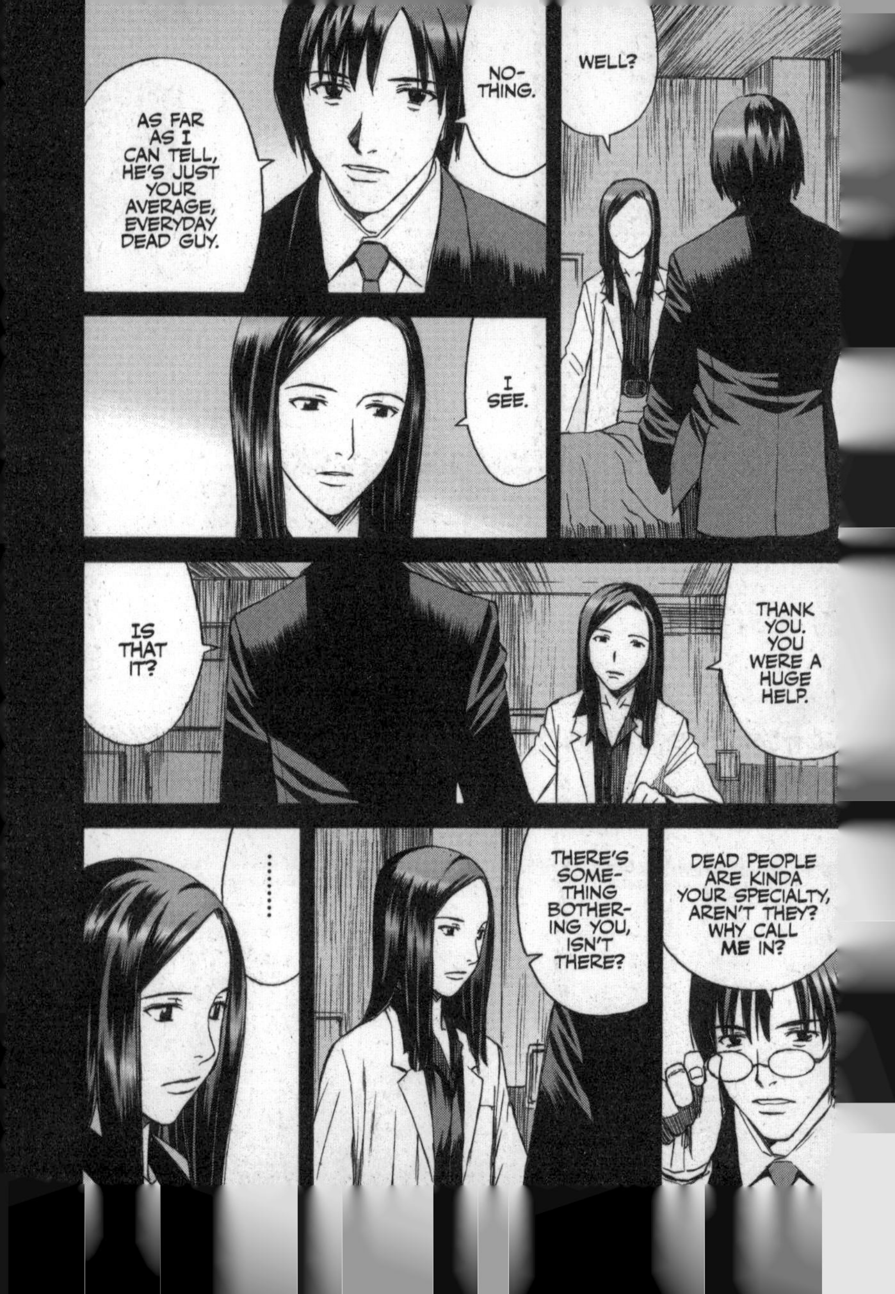
WELL?
NO-THING.
AS FAR AS I CAN TELL, HE'S JUST YOUR AVERAGE, EVERYDAY DEAD GUY.
I SEE.
THANK YOU. YOU WERE A HUGE HELP.
IS THAT IT?
DEAD PEOPLE ARE KINDA YOUR SPECIALTY, AREN'T THEY? WHY CALL ME IN?
THERE'S SOME-THING BOTHER-ING YOU, ISN'T THERE?
......

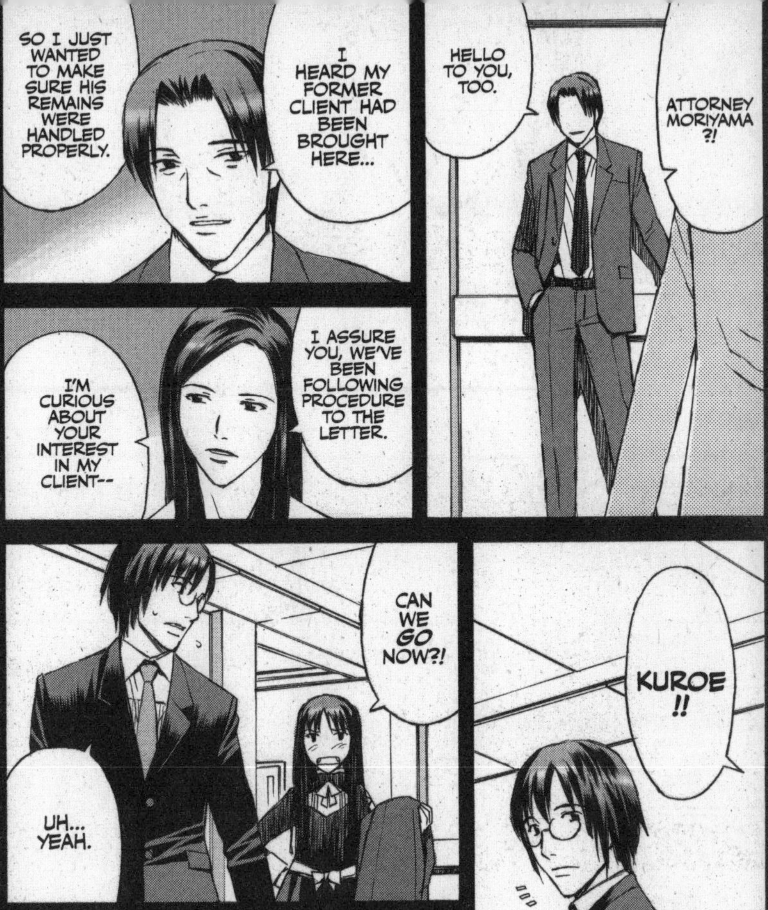
ATTORNEY MORIYAMA?!
HELLO TO YOU, TOO.
I HEARD MY FORMER CLIENT HAD BEEN BROUGHT HERE...
SO I JUST WANTED TO MAKE SURE HIS REMAINS WERE HANDLED PROPERLY.
I ASSURE YOU, WE'VE BEEN FOLLOWING PROCEDURE TO THE LETTER.
I'M CURIOUS ABOUT YOUR INTEREST IN MY CLIENT--
KUROE!!
CAN WE GO NOW?!
UH... YEAH.
THANKS, KUROE.
I'LL TALK TO YOU LATER.
HAVE A NICE NIGHT.

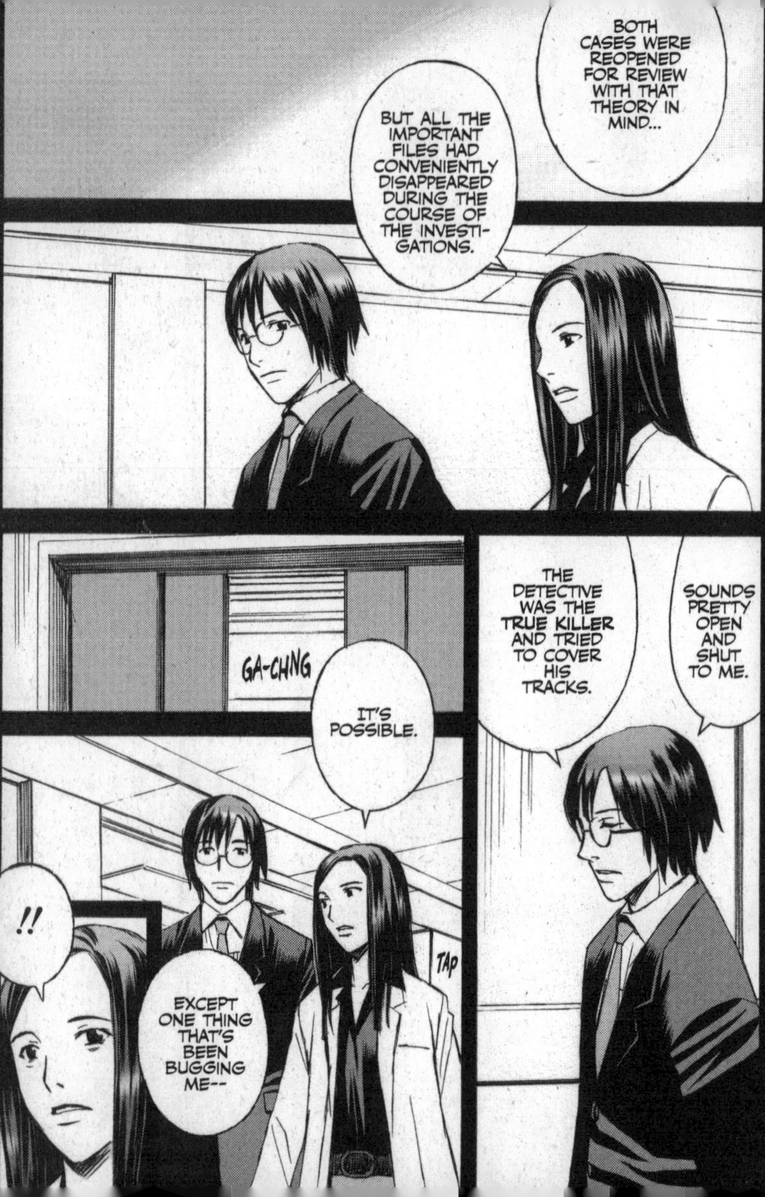
BOTH CASES WERE REOPENED FOR REVIEW WITH THAT THEORY IN MIND...
BUT ALL THE IMPORTANT FILES HAD CONVENIENTLY DISAPPEARED DURING THE COURSE OF THE INVESTI-GATIONS.
SOUNDS PRETTY OPEN AND SHUT TO ME.
THE DETECTIVE WAS THE **TRUE KILLER** AND TRIED TO COVER HIS TRACKS.
GA-CHNG
IT'S POSSIBLE.
TAP
EXCEPT ONE THING THAT'S BEEN BUGGING ME--
!!

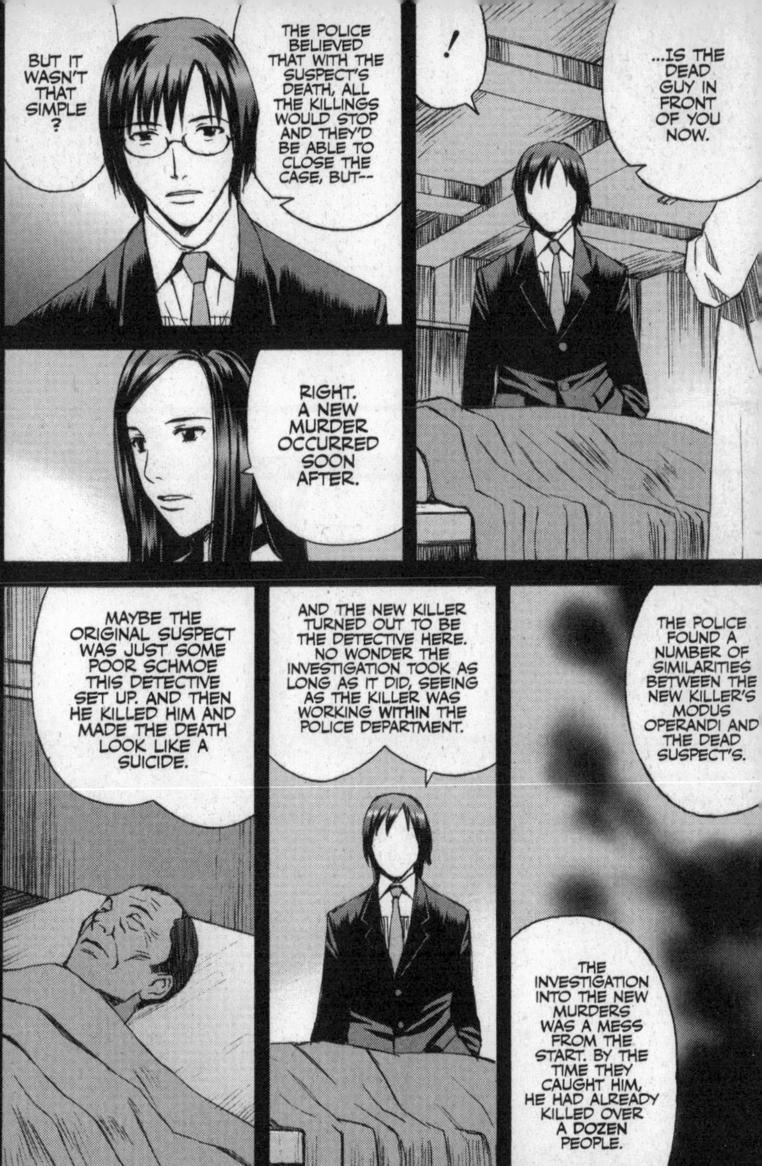

...IS THE DEAD GUY IN FRONT OF YOU NOW.
!
THE POLICE BELIEVED THAT WITH THE SUSPECT'S DEATH, ALL THE KILLINGS WOULD STOP AND THEY'D BE ABLE TO CLOSE THE CASE, BUT--
BUT IT WASN'T THAT SIMPLE?
RIGHT. A NEW MURDER OCCURRED SOON AFTER.
THE POLICE FOUND A NUMBER OF SIMILARITIES BETWEEN THE NEW KILLER'S MODUS OPERANDI AND THE DEAD SUSPECT'S.
THE INVESTIGATION INTO THE NEW MURDERS WAS A MESS FROM THE START. BY THE TIME THEY CAUGHT HIM, HE HAD ALREADY KILLED OVER A DOZEN PEOPLE.
AND THE NEW KILLER TURNED OUT TO BE THE DETECTIVE HERE. NO WONDER THE INVESTIGATION TOOK AS LONG AS IT DID, SEEING AS THE KILLER WAS WORKING WITHIN THE POLICE DEPARTMENT.
MAYBE THE ORIGINAL SUSPECT WAS JUST SOME POOR SCHMOE THIS DETECTIVE SET UP. AND THEN HE KILLED HIM AND MADE THE DEATH LOOK LIKE A SUICIDE.

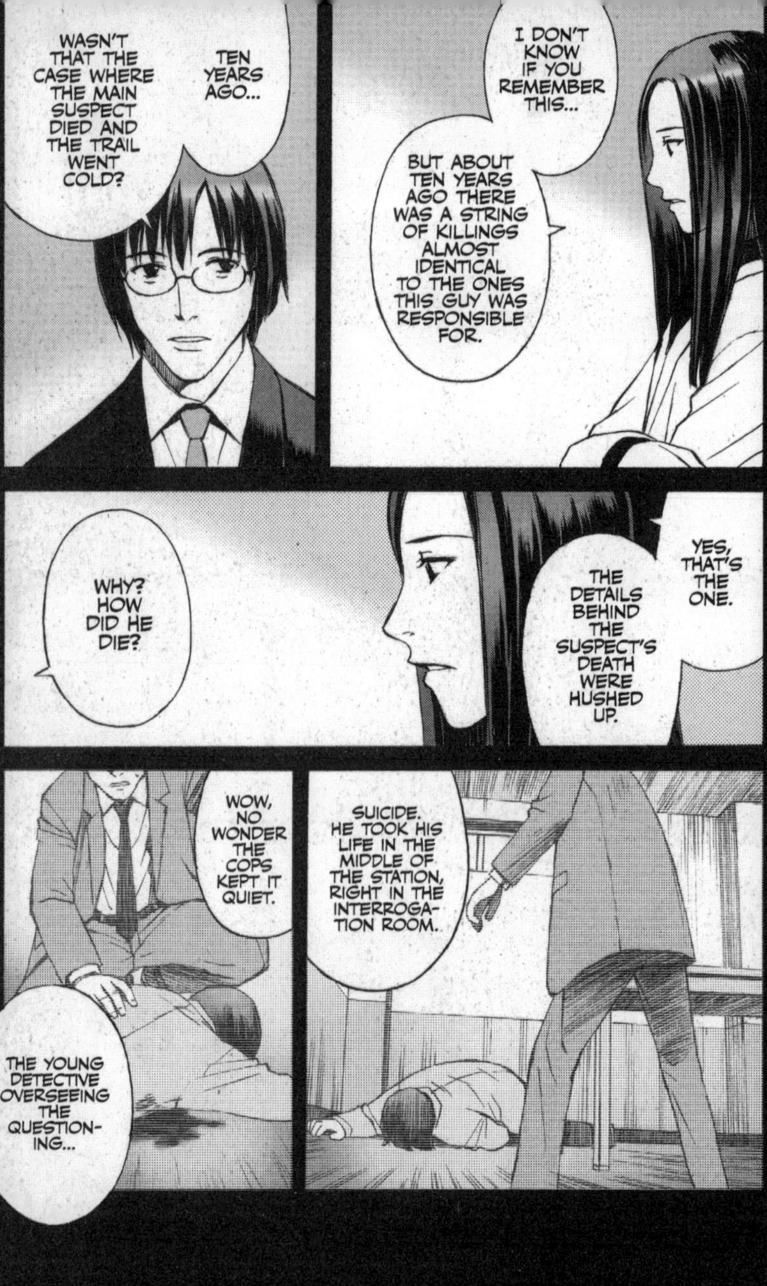
I DON'T KNOW IF YOU REMEMBER THIS...
BUT ABOUT TEN YEARS AGO THERE WAS A STRING OF KILLINGS ALMOST IDENTICAL TO THE ONES THIS GUY WAS RESPONSIBLE FOR.
TEN YEARS AGO...
WASN'T THAT THE CASE WHERE THE MAIN SUSPECT DIED AND THE TRAIL WENT COLD?
YES, THAT'S THE ONE.
THE DETAILS BEHIND THE SUSPECT'S DEATH WERE HUSHED UP.
WHY? HOW DID HE DIE?
SUICIDE. HE TOOK HIS LIFE IN THE MIDDLE OF THE STATION, RIGHT IN THE INTERROGATION ROOM.
WOW, NO WONDER THE COPS KEPT IT QUIET.
THE YOUNG DETECTIVE OVERSEEING THE QUESTIONING...

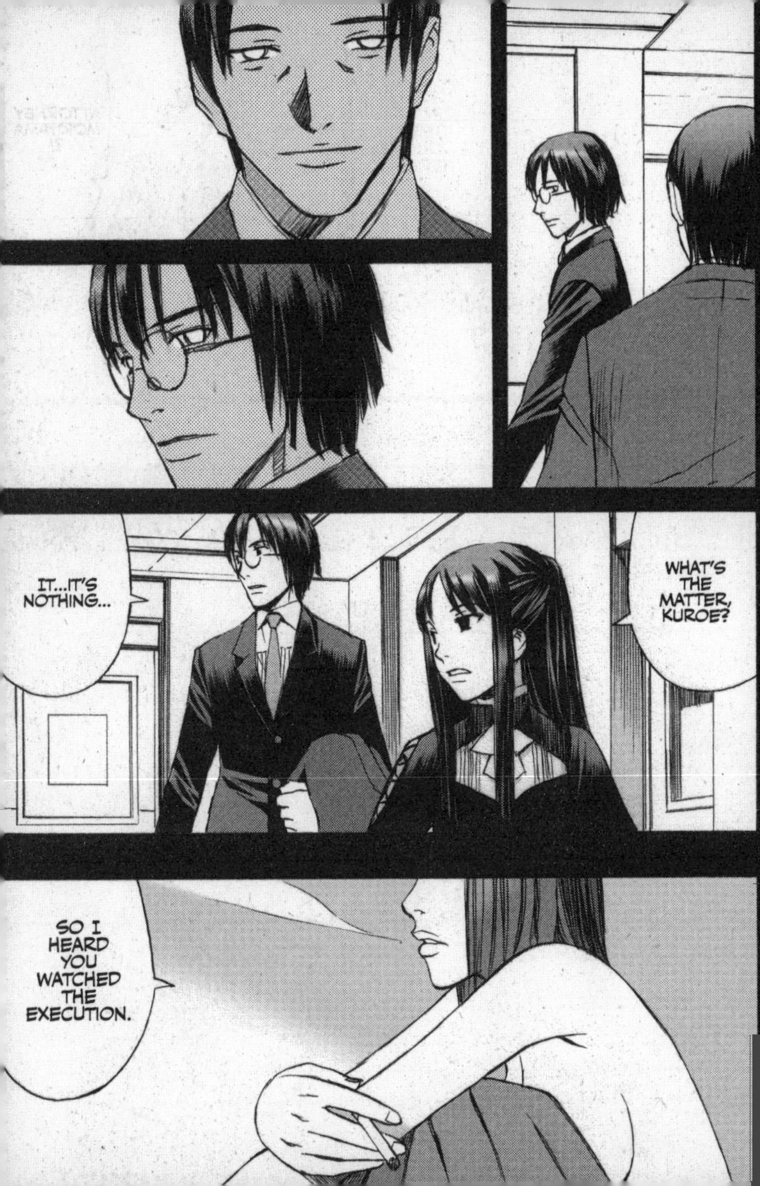
WHAT'S THE MATTER, KUROE?
IT...IT'S NOTHING...
SO I HEARD YOU WATCHED THE EXECUTION.

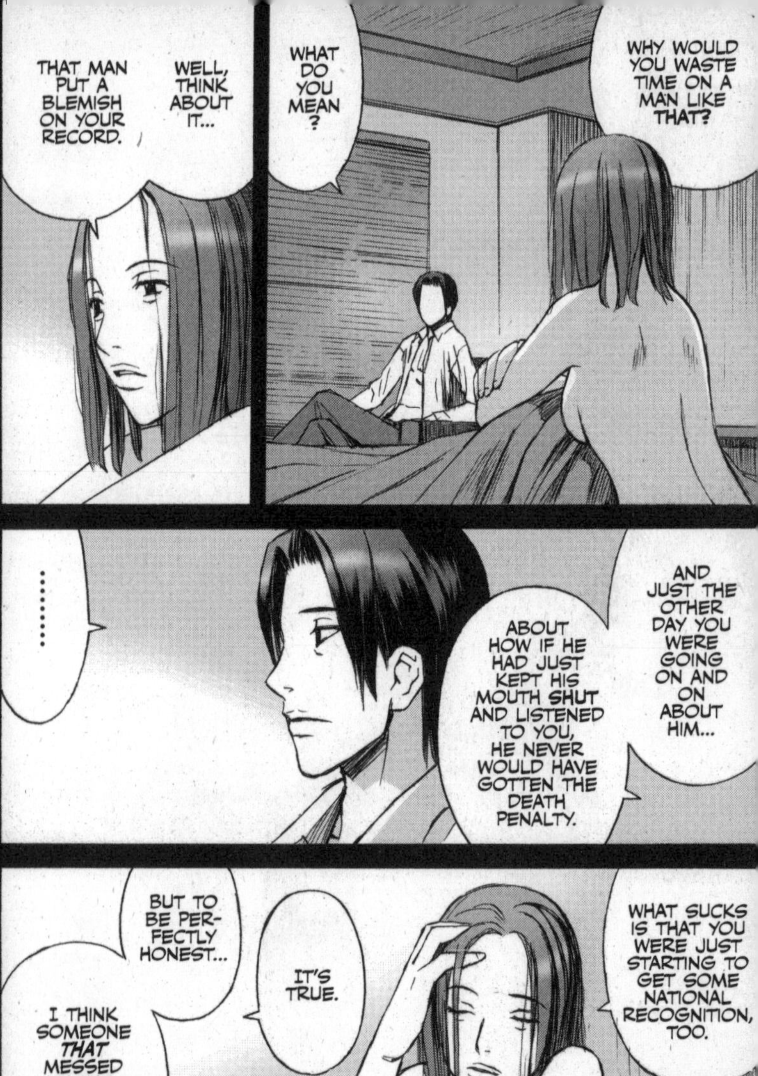
WHY WOULD YOU WASTE TIME ON A MAN LIKE **THAT?**
WHAT DO YOU MEAN?
WELL, THINK ABOUT IT...
THAT MAN PUT A BLEMISH ON YOUR RECORD.
AND JUST THE OTHER DAY YOU WERE GOING ON AND ON ABOUT HIM...
ABOUT HOW IF HE HAD JUST KEPT HIS MOUTH **SHUT** AND LISTENED TO YOU, HE NEVER WOULD HAVE GOTTEN THE DEATH PENALTY.
....
WHAT SUCKS IS THAT YOU WERE JUST STARTING TO GET SOME NATIONAL RECOGNITION, TOO.
IT'S TRUE.
BUT TO BE PER-FECTLY HONEST...
I THINK SOMEONE ***THAT*** MESSED IN THE HEAD **SHOULD** DIE.

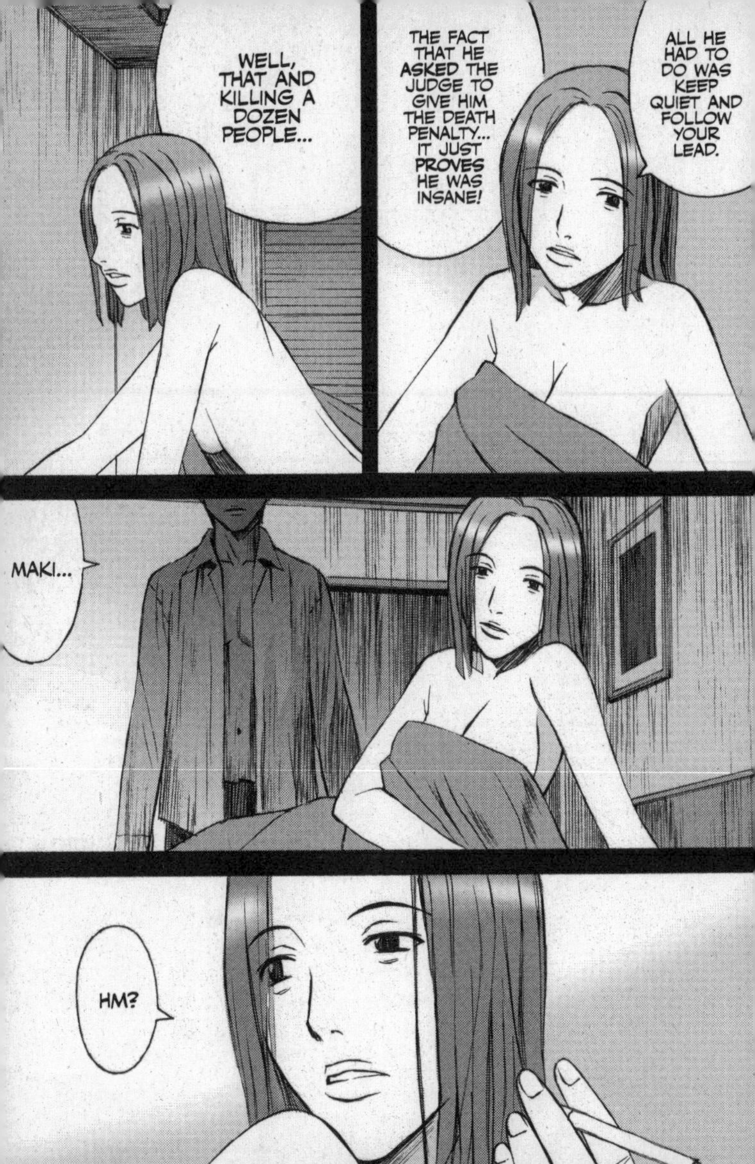
ALL HE HAD TO DO WAS KEEP QUIET AND FOLLOW YOUR LEAD.
THE FACT THAT HE ASKED THE JUDGE TO GIVE HIM THE DEATH PENALTY... IT JUST **PROVES** HE WAS INSANE!
WELL, THAT AND KILLING A DOZEN PEOPLE...
MAKI...
HM?

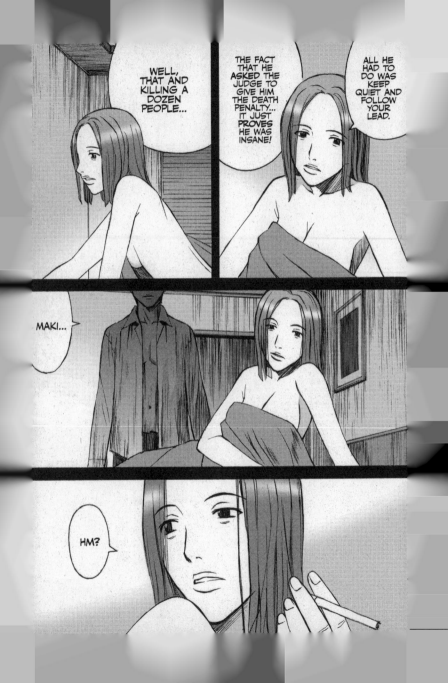

Episode 4
SOUL SLAVE part 2

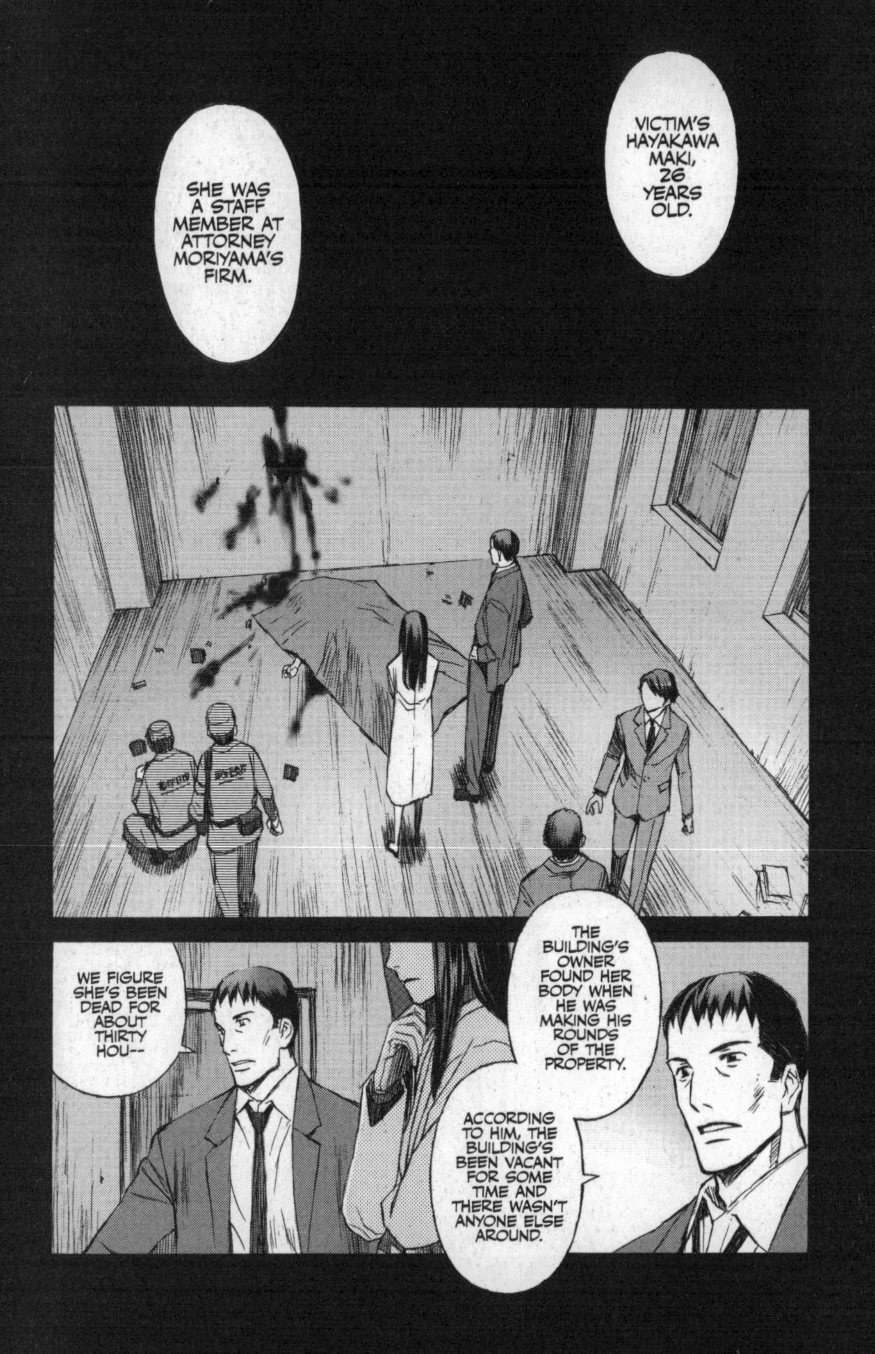
VICTIM'S HAYAKAWA MAKI, 26 YEARS OLD.
SHE WAS A STAFF MEMBER AT ATTORNEY MORIYAMA'S FIRM.
THE BUILDING'S OWNER FOUND HER BODY WHEN HE WAS MAKING HIS ROUNDS OF THE PROPERTY.
ACCORDING TO HIM, THE BUILDING'S BEEN VACANT FOR SOME TIME AND THERE WASN'T ANYONE ELSE AROUND.
WE FIGURE SHE'S BEEN DEAD FOR ABOUT THIRTY HOU--

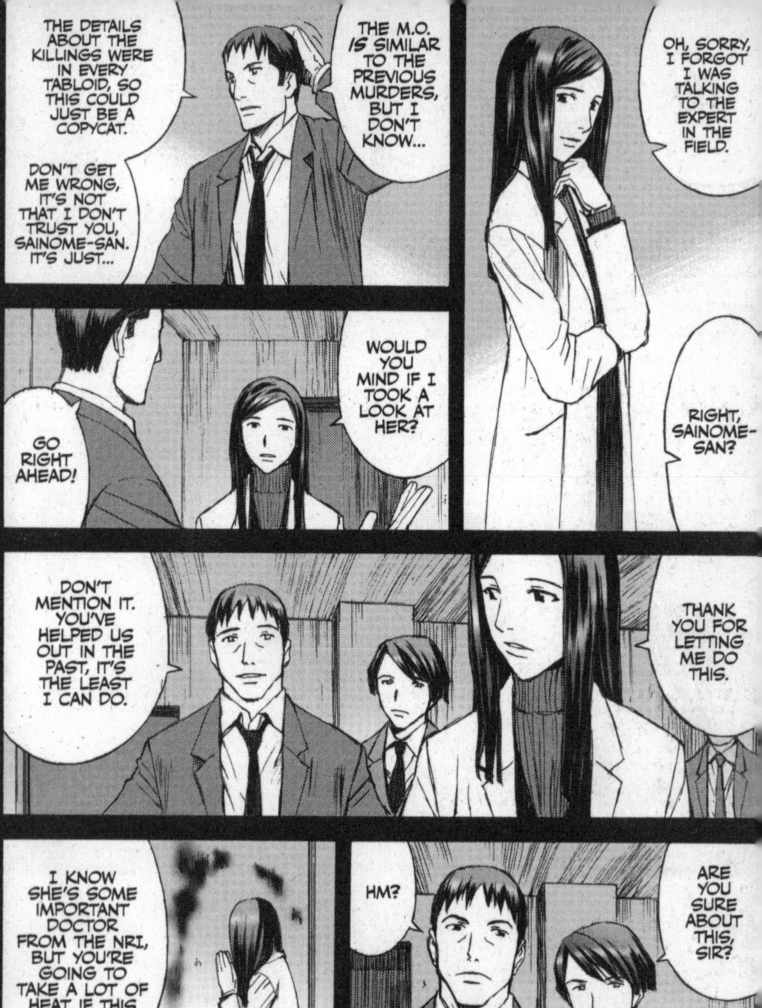
OH, SORRY, I FORGOT I WAS TALKING TO THE EXPERT IN THE FIELD.
RIGHT, SAINOME-SAN?
THE M.O. *IS* SIMILAR TO THE PREVIOUS MURDERS, BUT I DON'T KNOW...
THE DETAILS ABOUT THE KILLINGS WERE IN EVERY TABLOID, SO THIS COULD JUST BE A COPYCAT.
DON'T GET ME WRONG, IT'S NOT THAT I DON'T TRUST YOU, SAINOME-SAN. IT'S JUST...
WOULD YOU MIND IF I TOOK A LOOK AT HER?
GO RIGHT AHEAD!
THANK YOU FOR LETTING ME DO THIS.
DON'T MENTION IT. YOU'VE HELPED US OUT IN THE PAST, IT'S THE LEAST I CAN DO.
ARE YOU SURE ABOUT THIS, SIR?
HM?
I KNOW SHE'S SOME IMPORTANT DOCTOR FROM THE NRI, BUT YOU'RE GOING TO TAKE A LOT OF HEAT IF THIS GETS OUT.

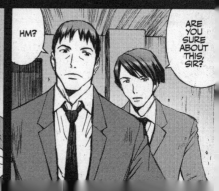

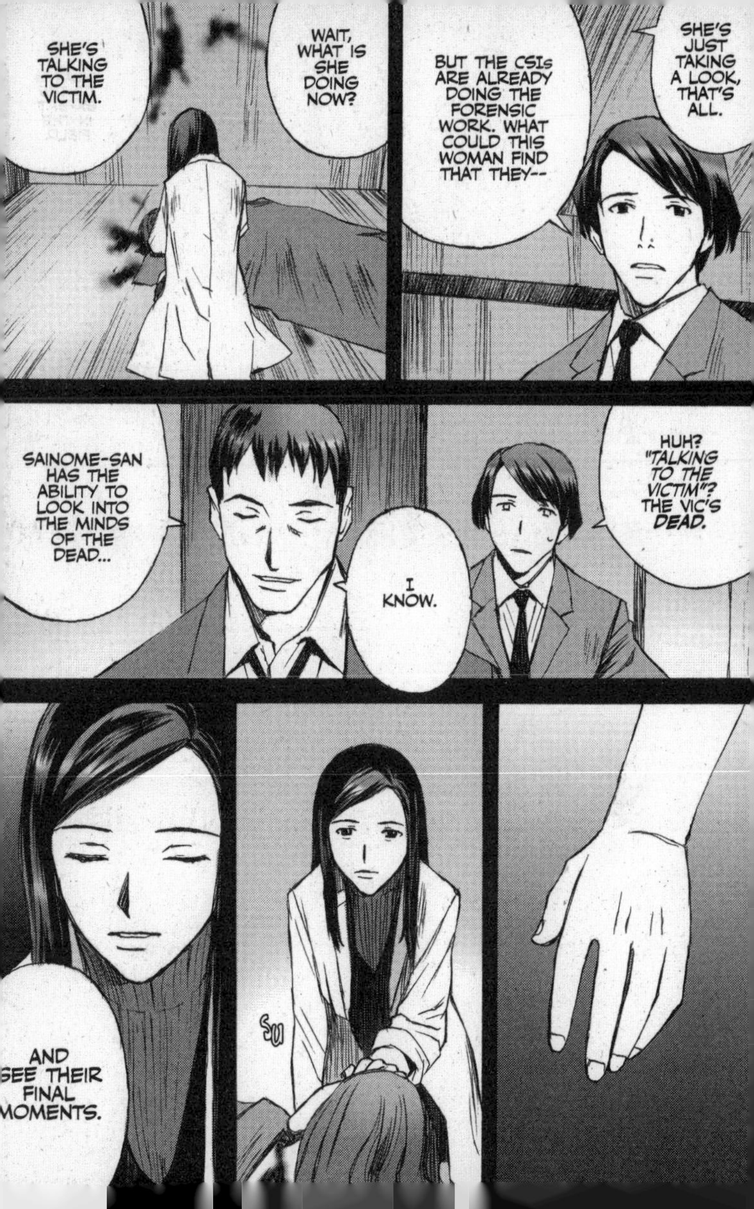
SHE'S JUST TAKING A LOOK, THAT'S ALL.
BUT THE CSIs ARE ALREADY DOING THE FORENSIC WORK. WHAT COULD THIS WOMAN FIND THAT THEY--
WAIT, WHAT IS SHE DOING NOW?
SHE'S TALKING TO THE VICTIM.
HUH? "TALKING TO THE VICTIM"? THE VIC'S DEAD.
I KNOW.
SAINOME-SAN HAS THE ABILITY TO LOOK INTO THE MINDS OF THE DEAD...
SU
AND SEE THEIR FINAL MOMENTS.

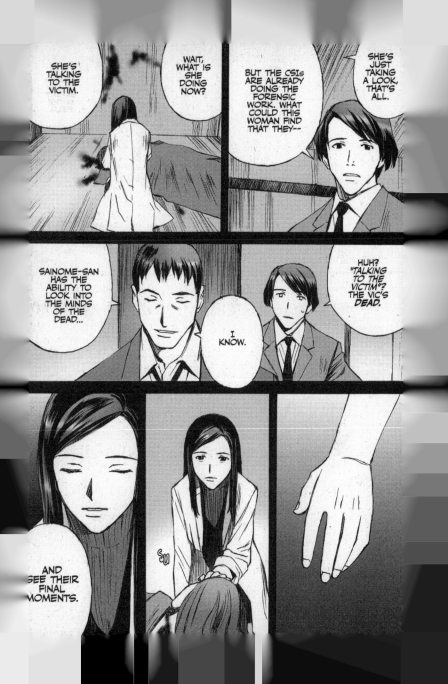

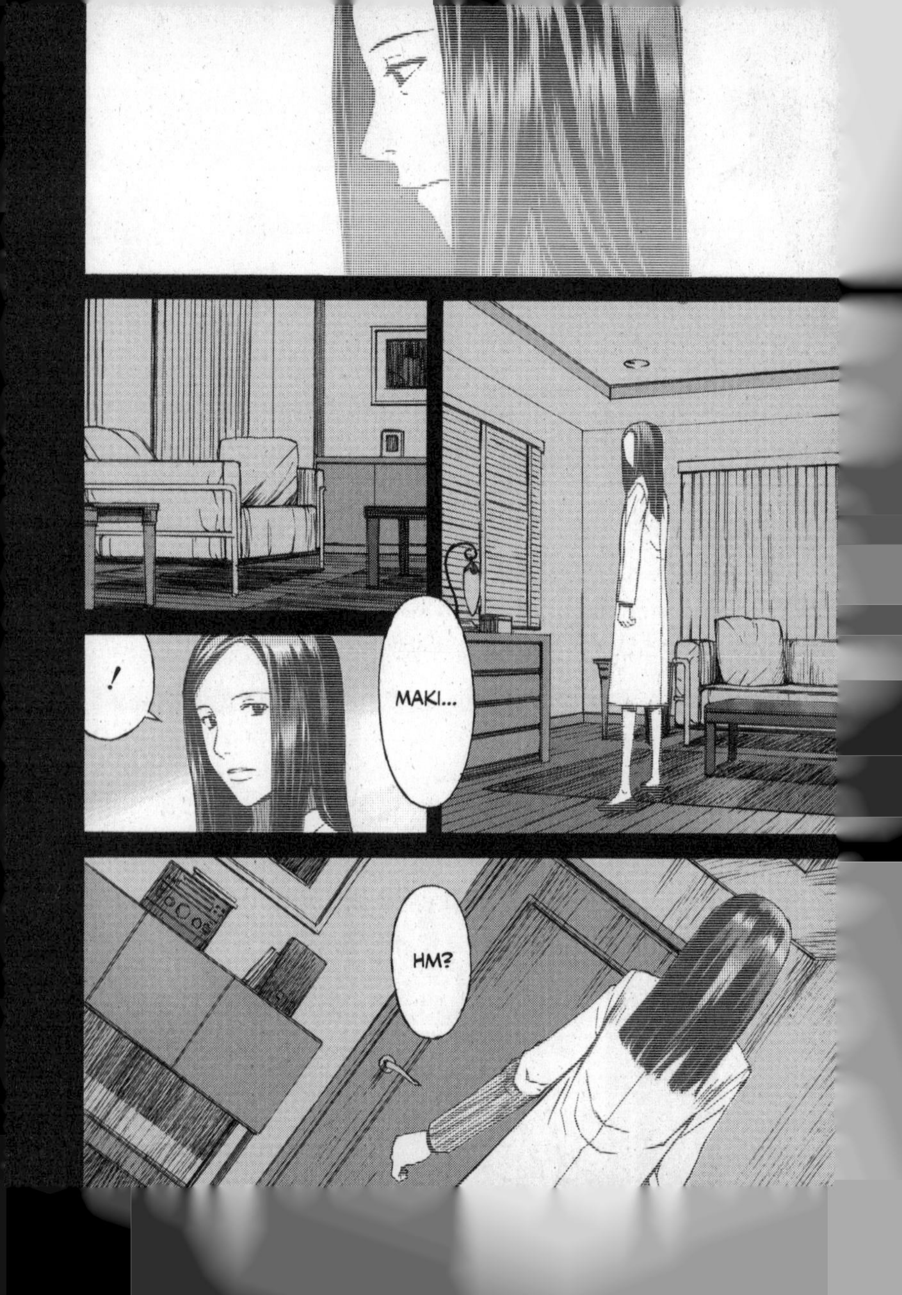
MAKI...
!
HM?

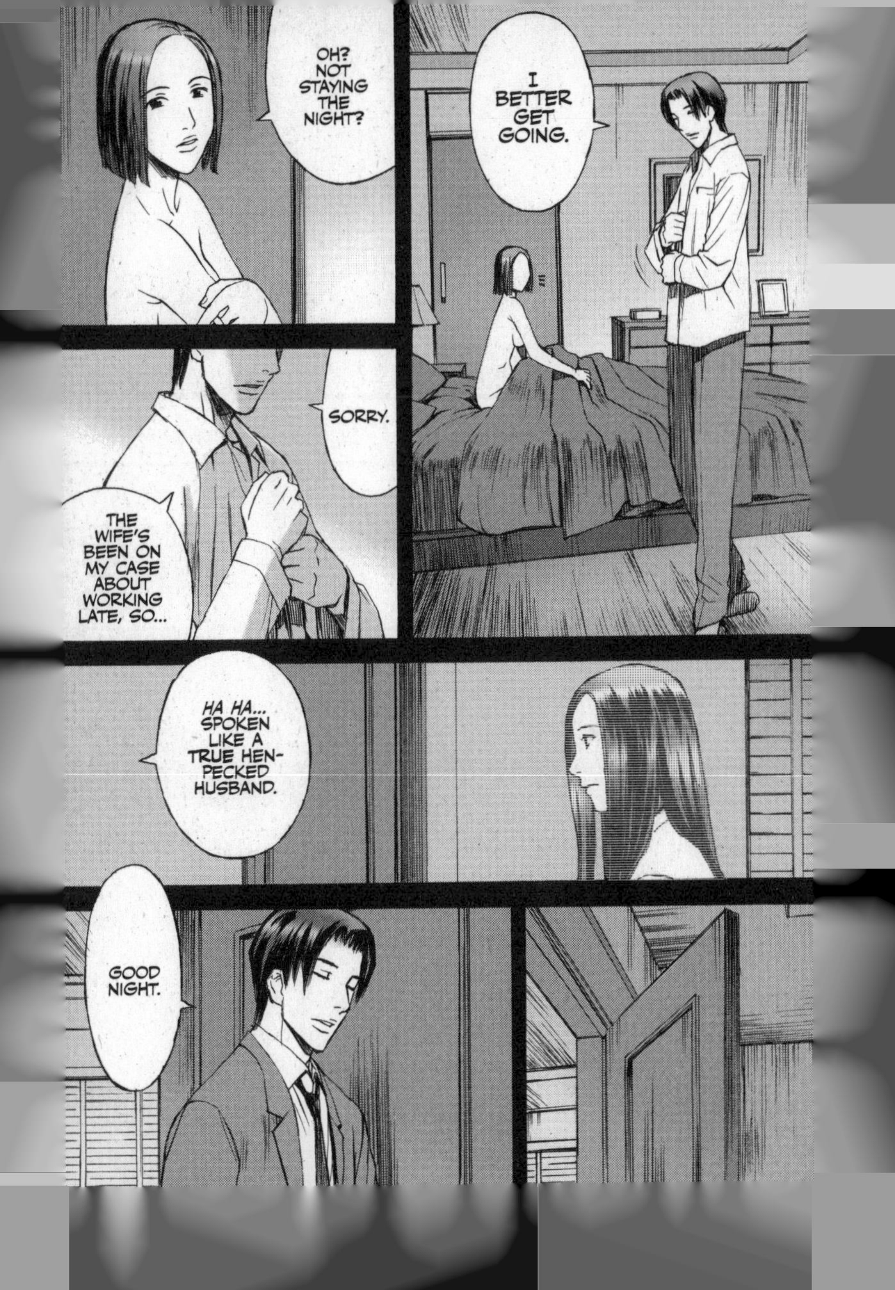
I BETTER GET GOING.
OH? NOT STAYING THE NIGHT?
SORRY.
THE WIFE'S BEEN ON MY CASE ABOUT WORKING LATE, SO...
HA HA... SPOKEN LIKE A TRUE HEN-PECKED HUSBAND.
GOOD NIGHT.

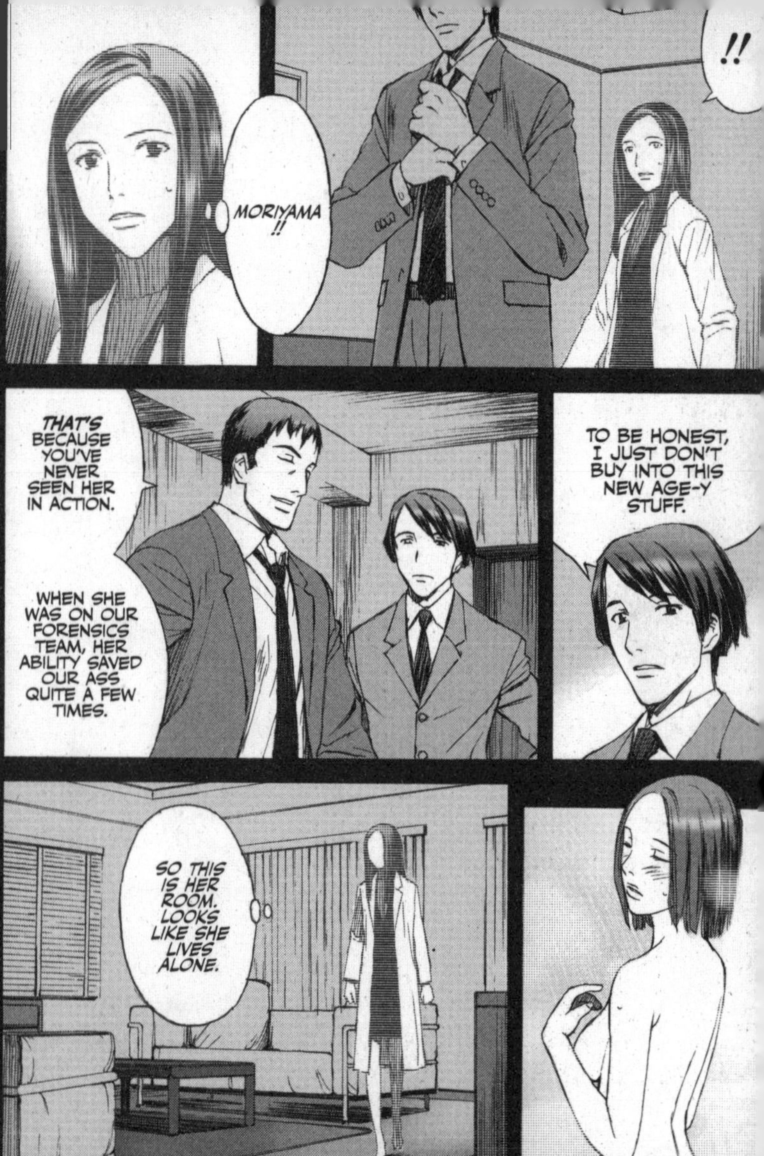
!!
MORIYAMA !!
TO BE HONEST, I JUST DON'T BUY INTO THIS NEW AGE-Y STUFF.
THAT'S BECAUSE YOU'VE NEVER SEEN HER IN ACTION.
WHEN SHE WAS ON OUR FORENSICS TEAM, HER ABILITY SAVED OUR ASS QUITE A FEW TIMES.
SO THIS IS HER ROOM. LOOKS LIKE SHE LIVES ALONE.

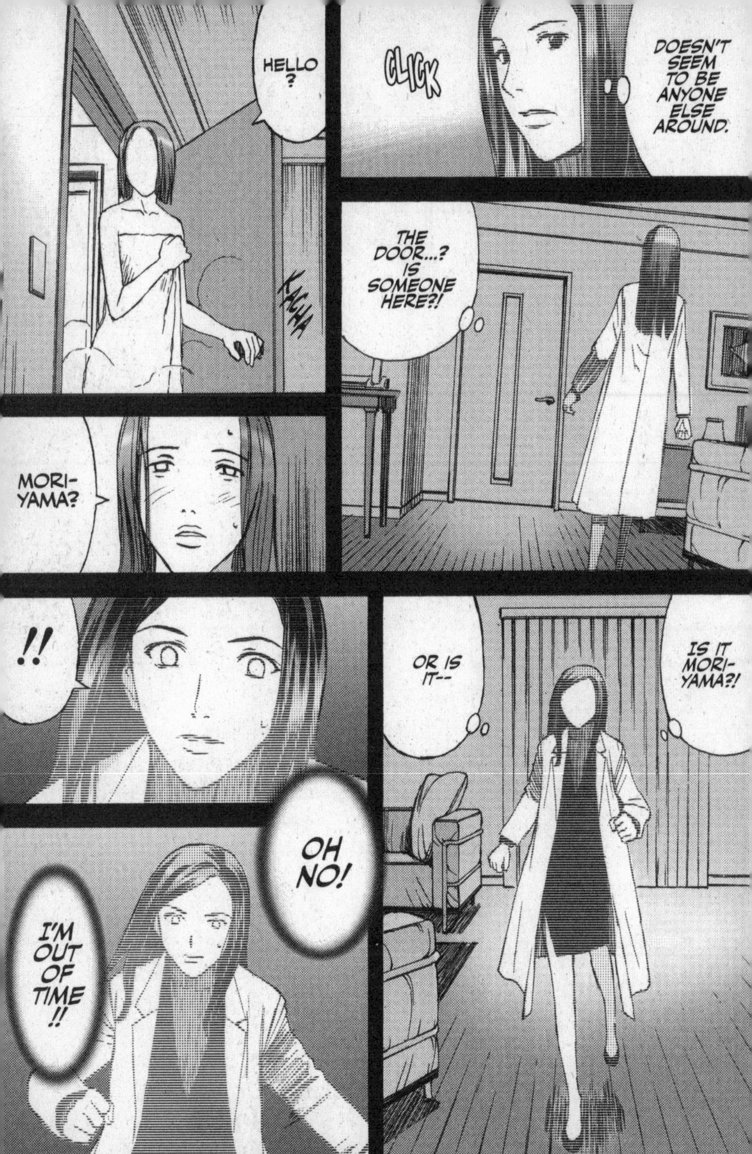
DOESN'T SEEM TO BE ANYONE ELSE AROUND.
CLICK
THE DOOR...? IS SOMEONE HERE?!
HELLO?
KACHA
MORI-YAMA?
IS IT MORI-YAMA?!
OR IS IT--
!!
OH NO!
I'M OUT OF TIME!!

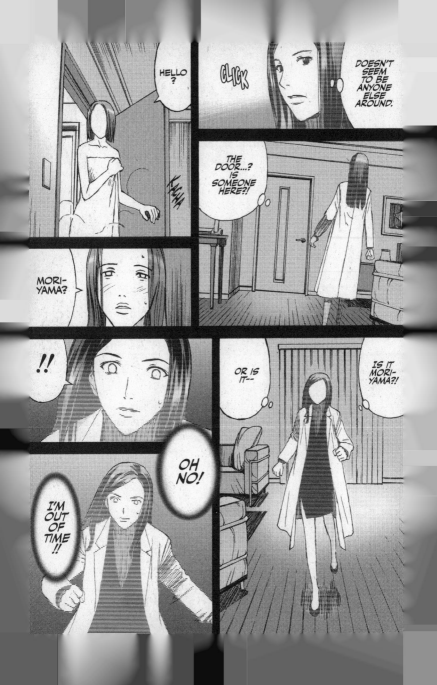

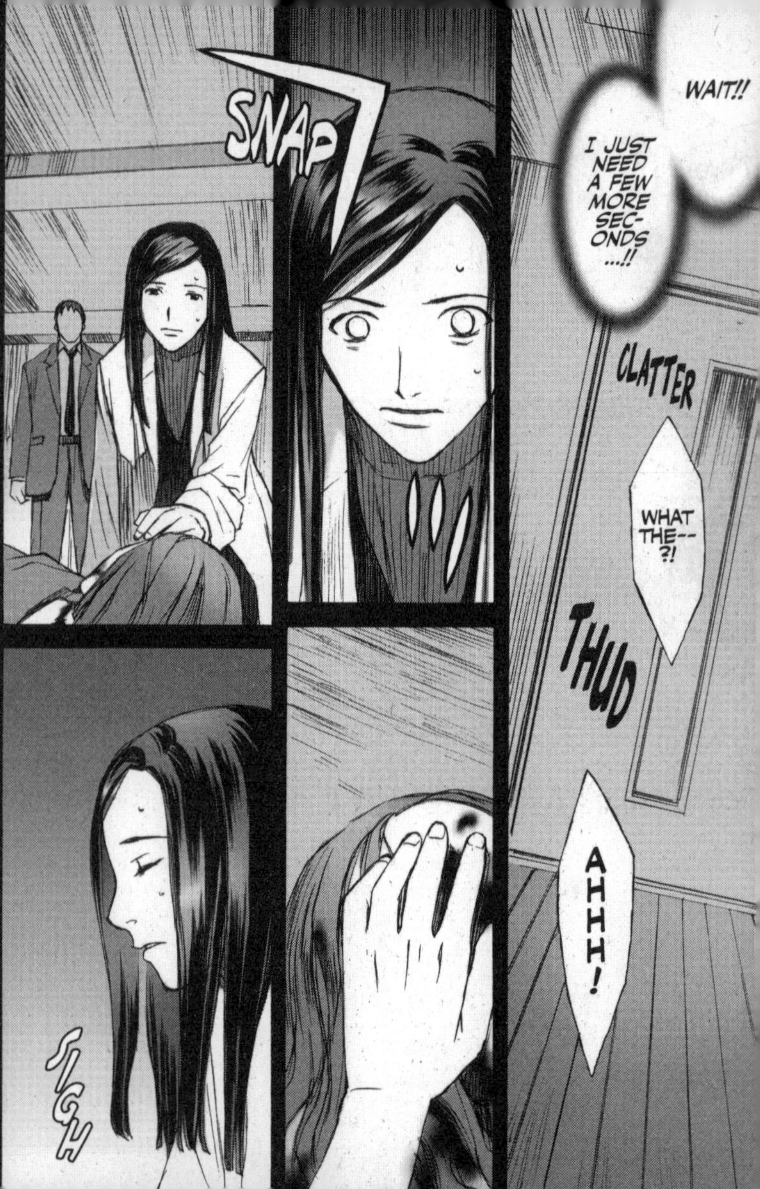
WAIT!!
I JUST NEED A FEW MORE SECONDS...!!
CLATTER
WHAT THE--?!
THUD
AHHH!
SNAP
SIGH

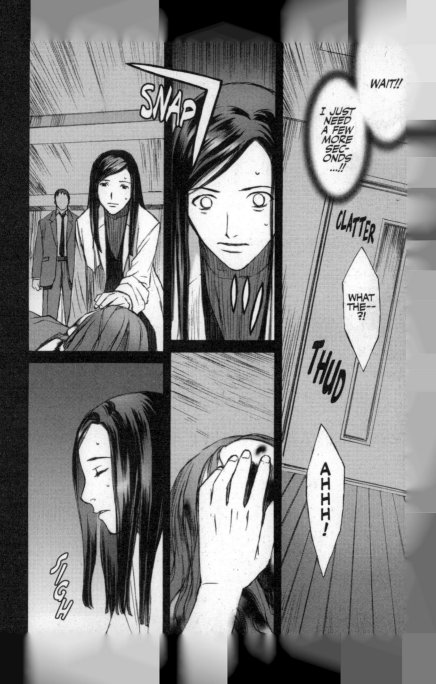

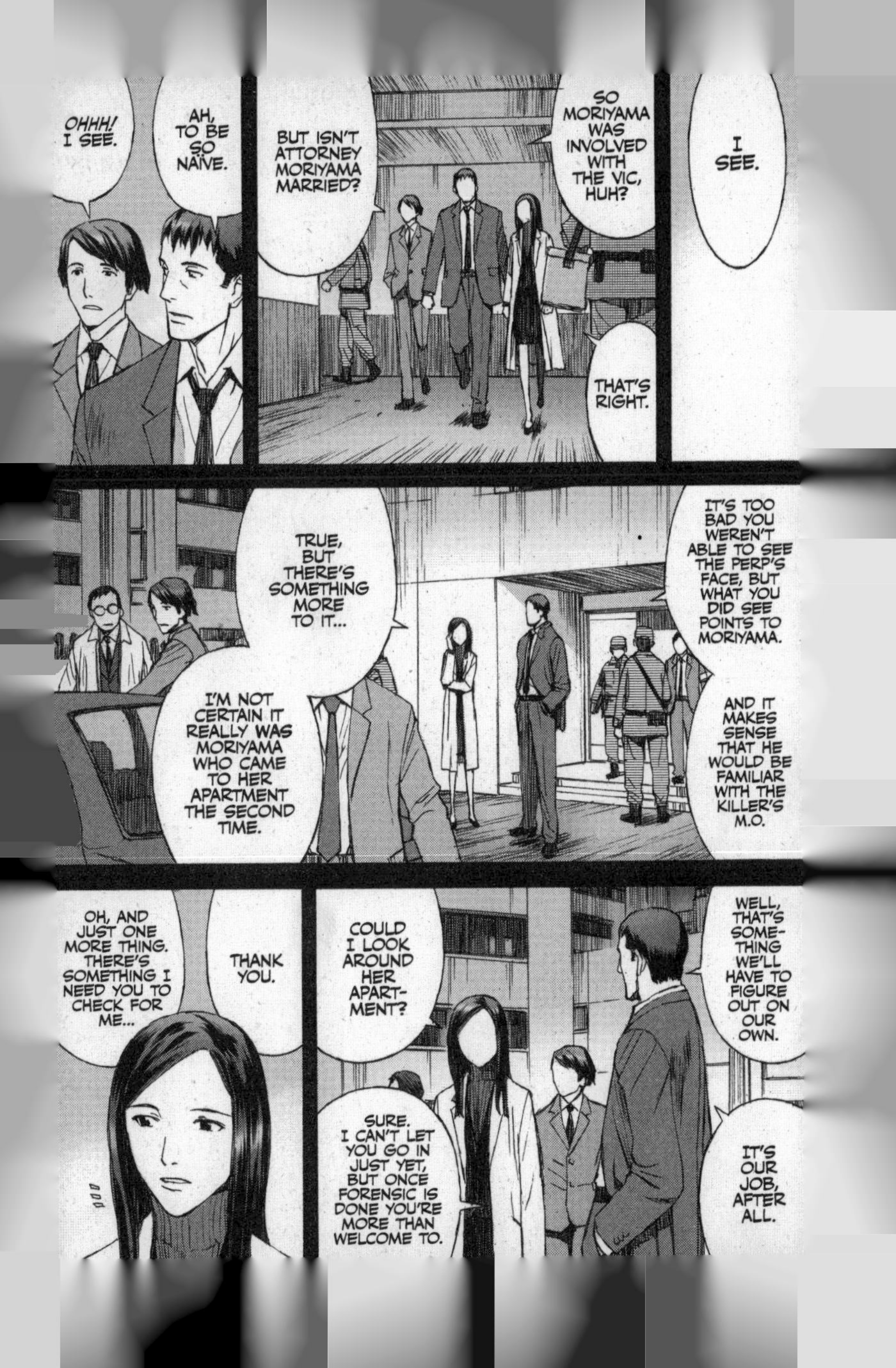
I SEE.
THAT'S RIGHT.
SO MORIYAMA WAS INVOLVED WITH THE VIC, HUH?
BUT ISN'T ATTORNEY MORIYAMA MARRIED?
AH, TO BE SO NAÏVE.
OHHH! I SEE.
IT'S TOO BAD YOU WEREN'T ABLE TO SEE THE PERP'S FACE, BUT WHAT YOU DID SEE POINTS TO MORIYAMA.
AND IT MAKES SENSE THAT HE WOULD BE FAMILIAR WITH THE KILLER'S M.O.
TRUE, BUT THERE'S SOMETHING MORE TO IT...
I'M NOT CERTAIN IT REALLY WAS MORIYAMA WHO CAME TO HER APARTMENT THE SECOND TIME.
WELL, THAT'S SOME-THING WE'LL HAVE TO FIGURE OUT ON OUR OWN.
IT'S OUR JOB, AFTER ALL.
COULD I LOOK AROUND HER APART-MENT?
SURE. I CAN'T LET YOU GO IN JUST YET, BUT ONCE FORENSIC IS DONE YOU'RE MORE THAN WELCOME TO.
THANK YOU.
OH, AND JUST ONE MORE THING. THERE'S SOMETHING I NEED YOU TO CHECK FOR ME...

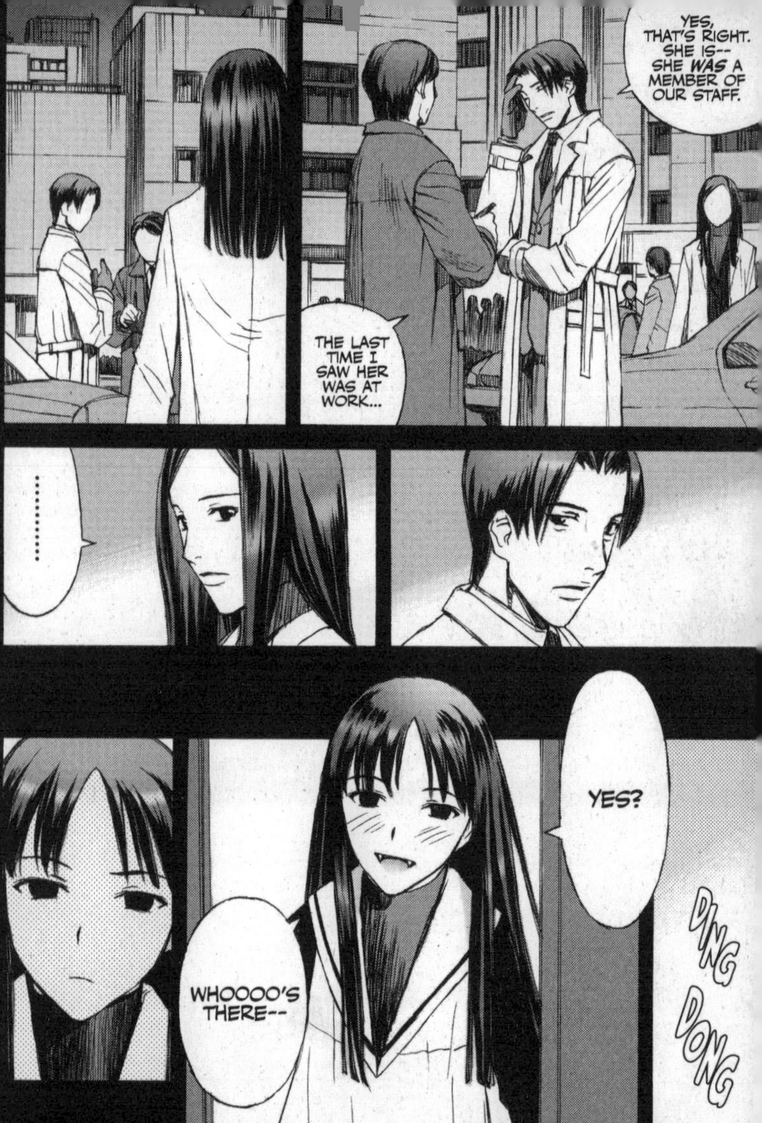
YES, THAT'S RIGHT. SHE IS-- SHE *WAS* A MEMBER OF OUR STAFF.
THE LAST TIME I SAW HER WAS AT WORK...
......
DING DONG
YES?
WHOOOO'S THERE--

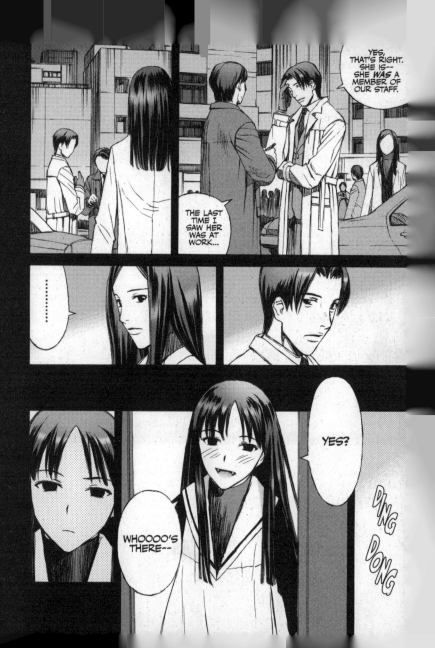

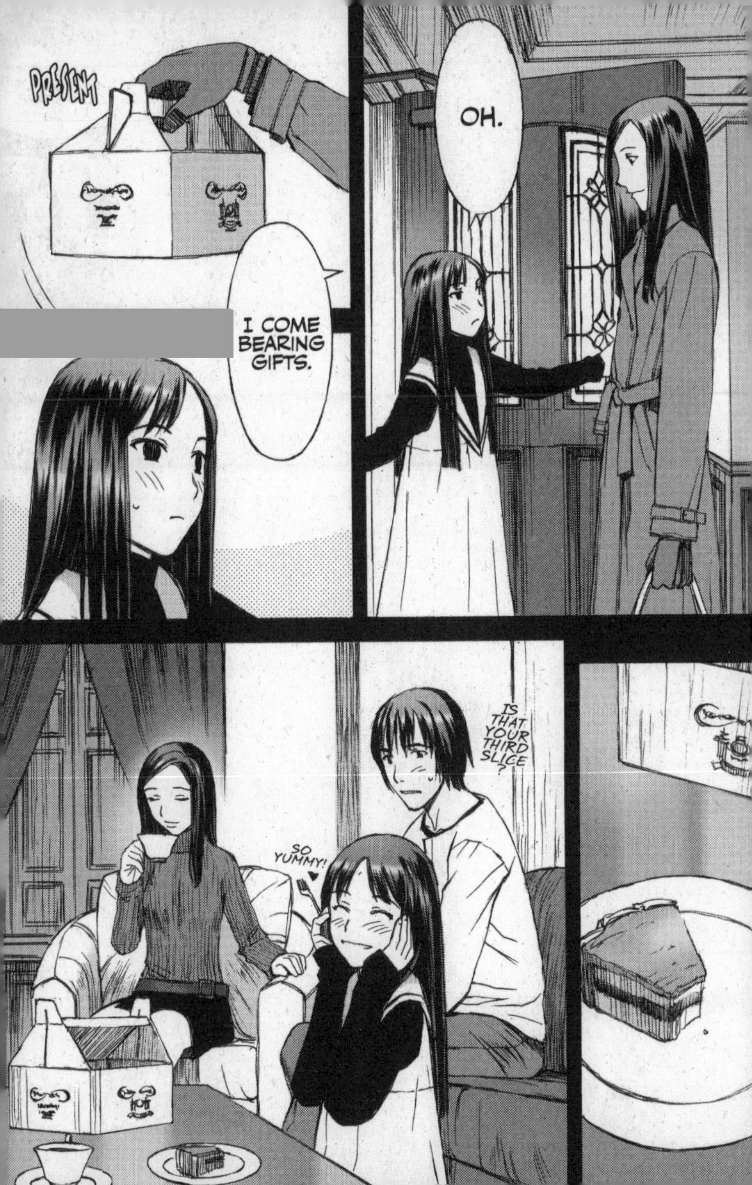
OH.
PRESENT
I COME BEARING GIFTS.
IS THAT YOUR THIRD SLICE?
SO YUMMY!

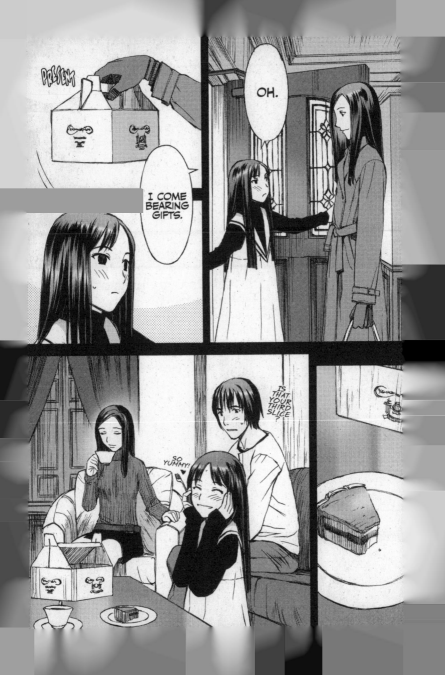

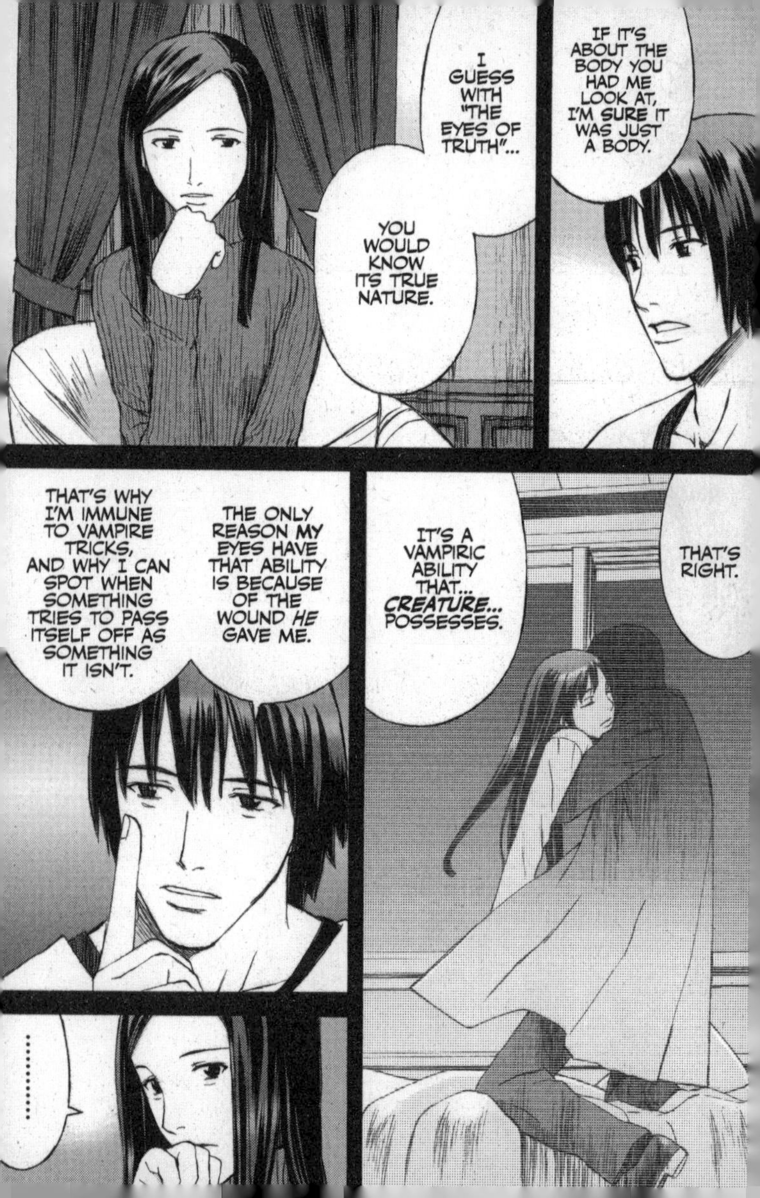
IF IT'S ABOUT THE BODY YOU HAD ME LOOK AT, I'M **SURE** IT WAS JUST A BODY.
I GUESS WITH "THE EYES OF TRUTH"...
YOU WOULD KNOW ITS TRUE NATURE.
THAT'S RIGHT.
IT'S A VAMPIRIC ABILITY THAT... ***CREATURE...*** POSSESSES.
THE ONLY REASON **MY** EYES HAVE THAT ABILITY IS BECAUSE OF THE WOUND *HE* GAVE ME.
THAT'S WHY I'M IMMUNE TO VAMPIRE TRICKS, AND WHY I CAN SPOT WHEN SOMETHING TRIES TO PASS ITSELF OFF AS SOMETHING IT ISN'T.
....

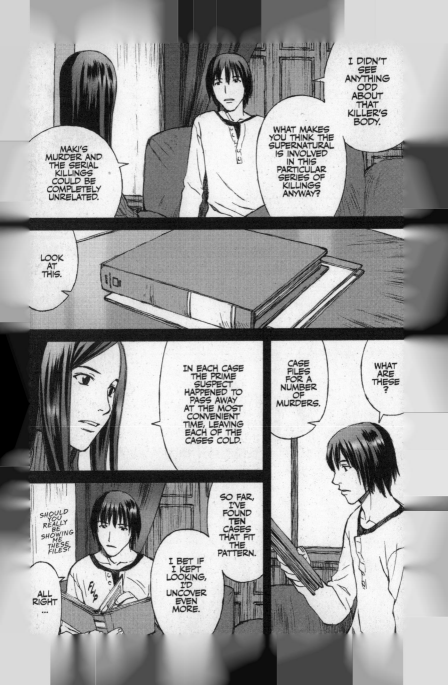

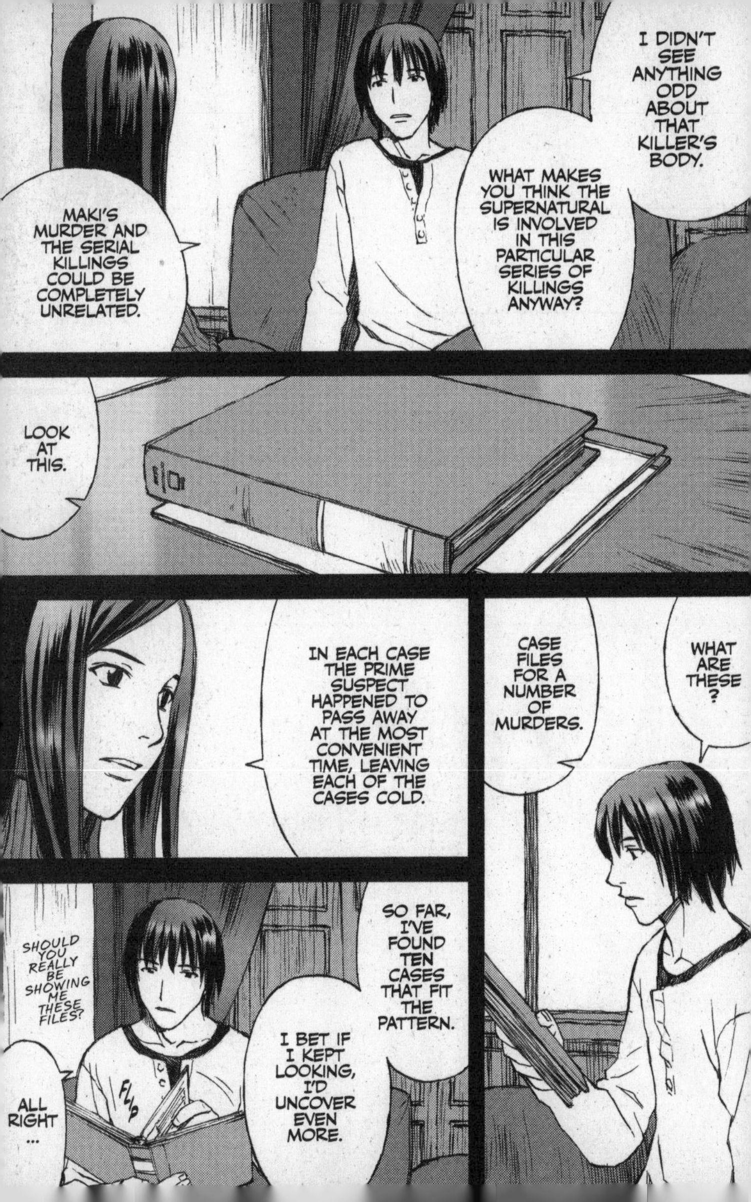
I DIDN'T SEE ANYTHING ODD ABOUT THAT KILLER'S BODY.
WHAT MAKES YOU THINK THE SUPERNATURAL IS INVOLVED IN THIS PARTICULAR SERIES OF KILLINGS ANYWAY?
MAKI'S MURDER AND THE SERIAL KILLINGS COULD BE COMPLETELY UNRELATED.
LOOK AT THIS.
WHAT ARE THESE?
CASE FILES FOR A NUMBER OF MURDERS.
IN EACH CASE THE PRIME SUSPECT HAPPENED TO PASS AWAY AT THE MOST CONVENIENT TIME, LEAVING EACH OF THE CASES COLD.
SO FAR, I'VE FOUND TEN CASES THAT FIT THE PATTERN.
I BET IF I KEPT LOOKING, I'D UNCOVER EVEN MORE.
SHOULD YOU REALLY BE SHOWING ME THESE FILES?
FLIP
ALL RIGHT ...

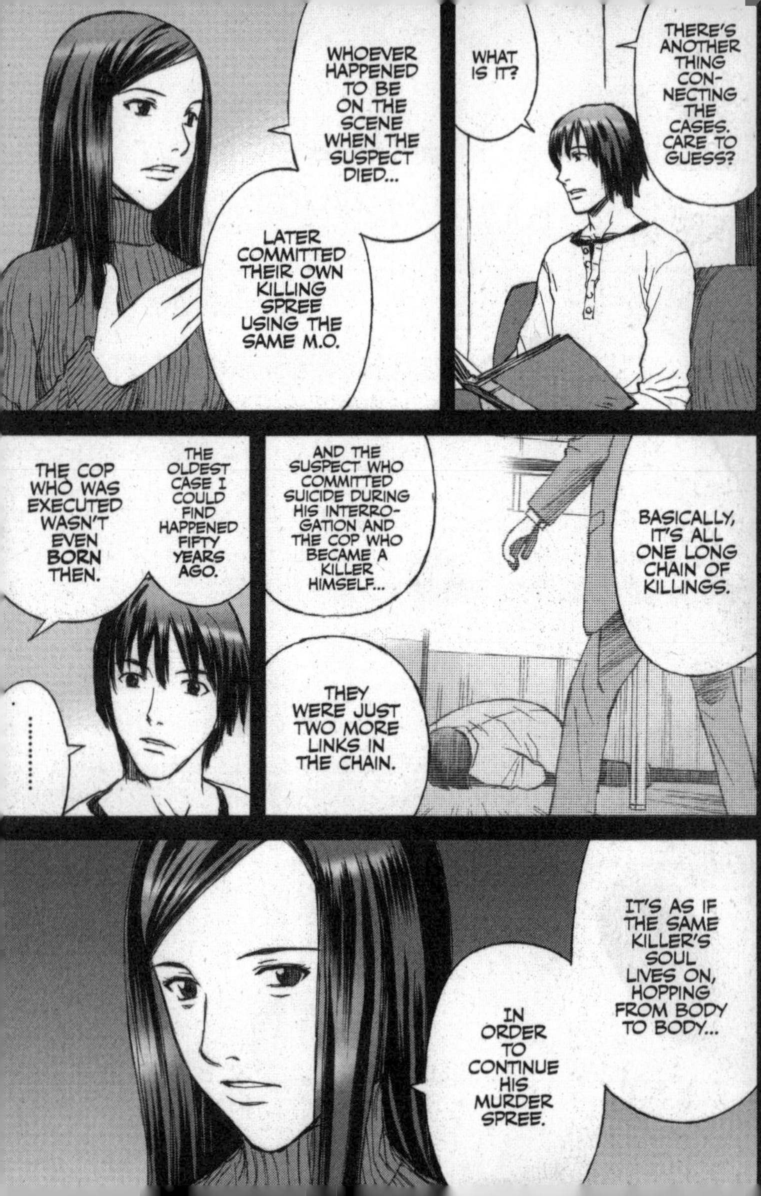
THERE'S ANOTHER THING CONNECTING THE CASES. CARE TO GUESS?
WHAT IS IT?
WHOEVER HAPPENED TO BE ON THE SCENE WHEN THE SUSPECT DIED...
LATER COMMITTED THEIR OWN KILLING SPREE USING THE SAME M.O.
BASICALLY, IT'S ALL ONE LONG CHAIN OF KILLINGS.
AND THE SUSPECT WHO COMMITTED SUICIDE DURING HIS INTERROGATION AND THE COP WHO BECAME A KILLER HIMSELF...
THEY WERE JUST TWO MORE LINKS IN THE CHAIN.
THE OLDEST CASE I COULD FIND HAPPENED FIFTY YEARS AGO.
THE COP WHO WAS EXECUTED WASN'T EVEN BORN THEN.
....
IT'S AS IF THE SAME KILLER'S SOUL LIVES ON, HOPPING FROM BODY TO BODY...
IN ORDER TO CONTINUE HIS MURDER SPREE.

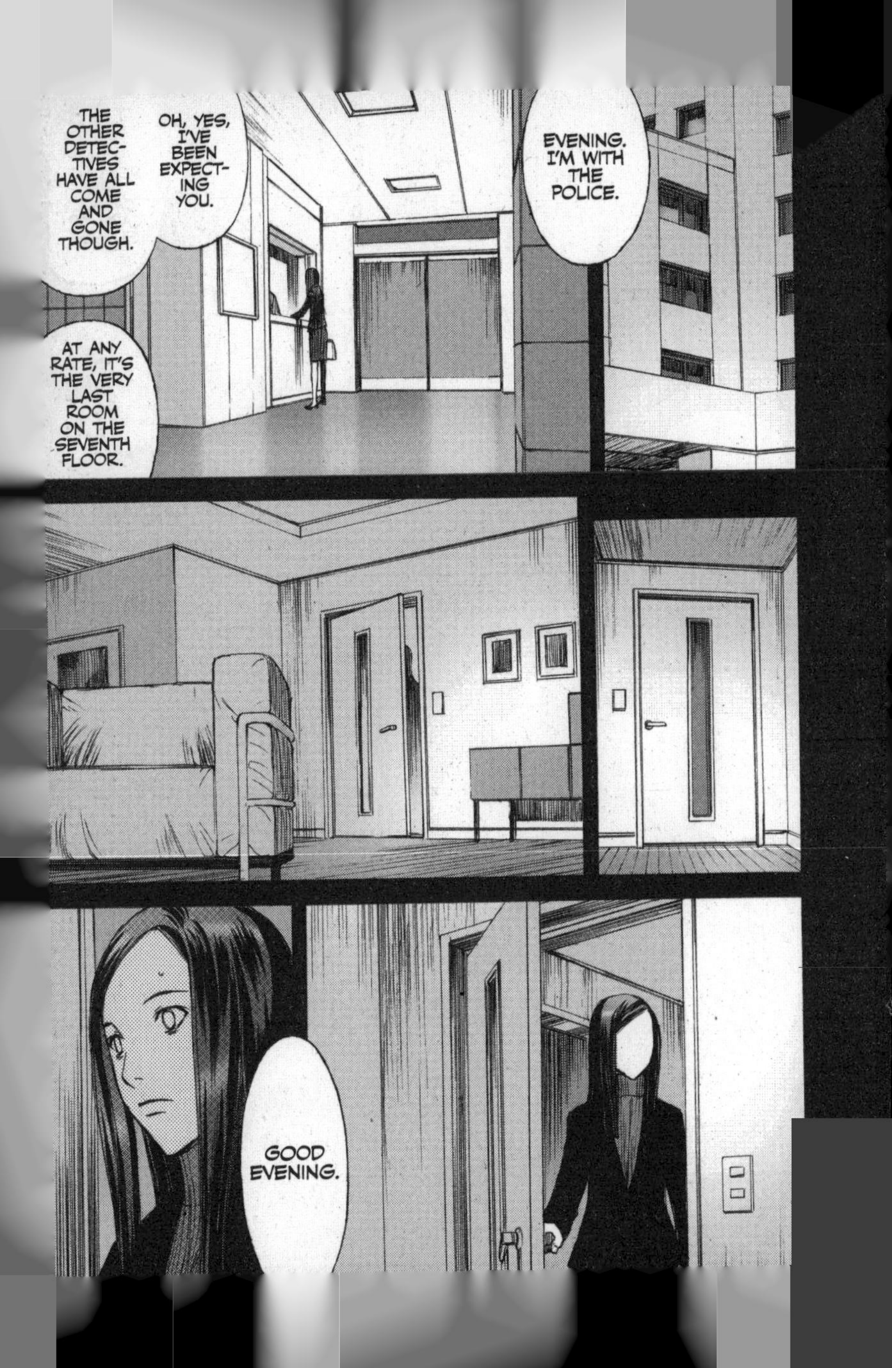
EVENING. I'M WITH THE POLICE.
OH, YES, I'VE BEEN EXPECTING YOU.
THE OTHER DETECTIVES HAVE ALL COME AND GONE THOUGH.
AT ANY RATE, IT'S THE VERY LAST ROOM ON THE SEVENTH FLOOR.
GOOD EVENING.

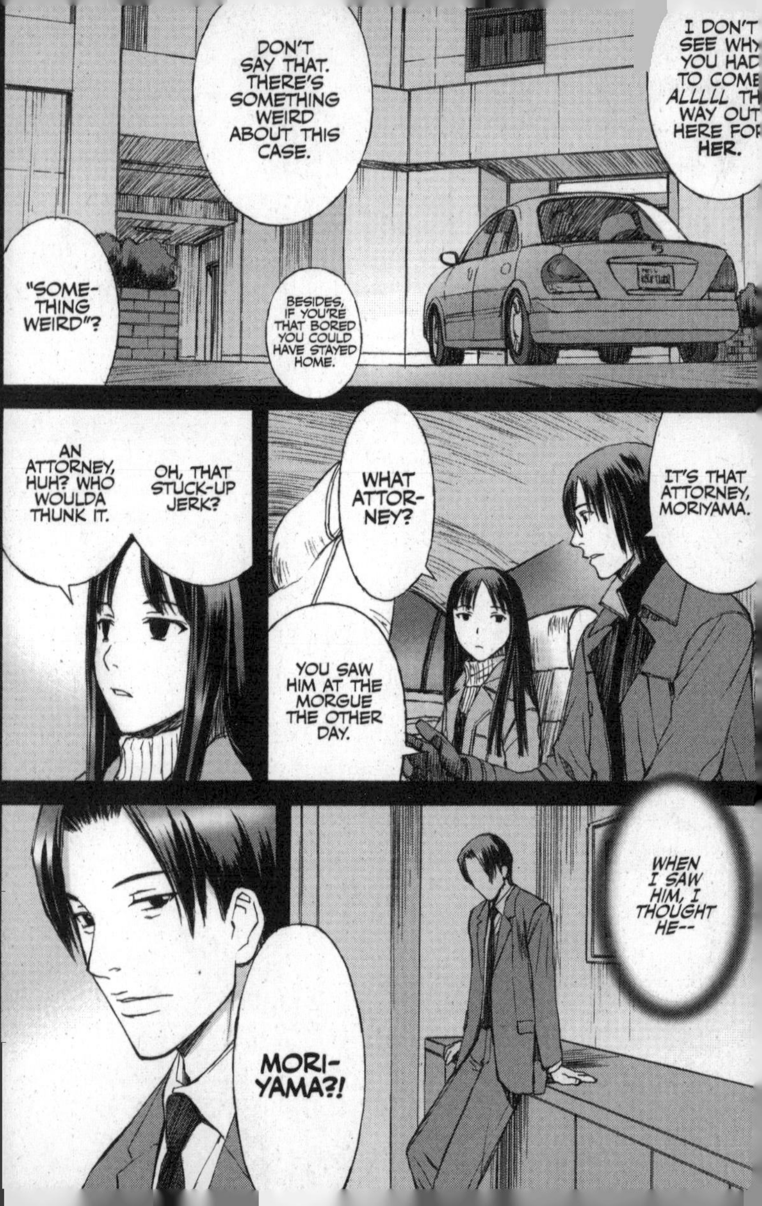
I DON'T SEE WHY YOU HAD TO COME ALLLLL TH WAY OUT HERE FOR HER.
DON'T SAY THAT. THERE'S SOMETHING WEIRD ABOUT THIS CASE.
BESIDES, IF YOU'RE THAT BORED YOU COULD HAVE STAYED HOME.
"SOME-THING WEIRD"?
IT'S THAT ATTORNEY, MORIYAMA.
WHAT ATTOR-NEY?
YOU SAW HIM AT THE MORGUE THE OTHER DAY.
OH, THAT STUCK-UP JERK?
AN ATTORNEY, HUH? WHO WOULDA THUNK IT.
WHEN I SAW HIM, I THOUGHT HE--
MORI-YAMA?!

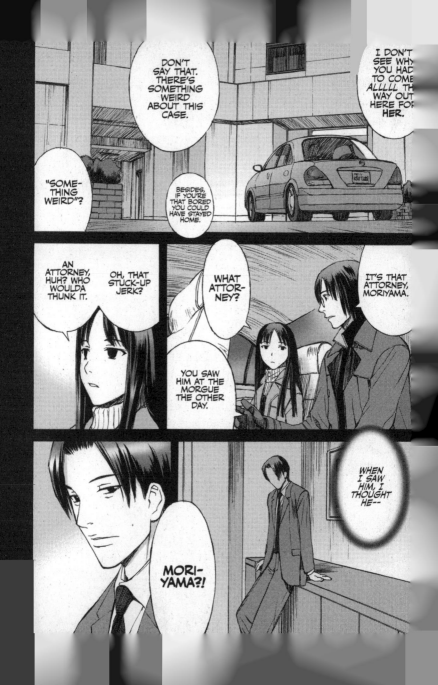

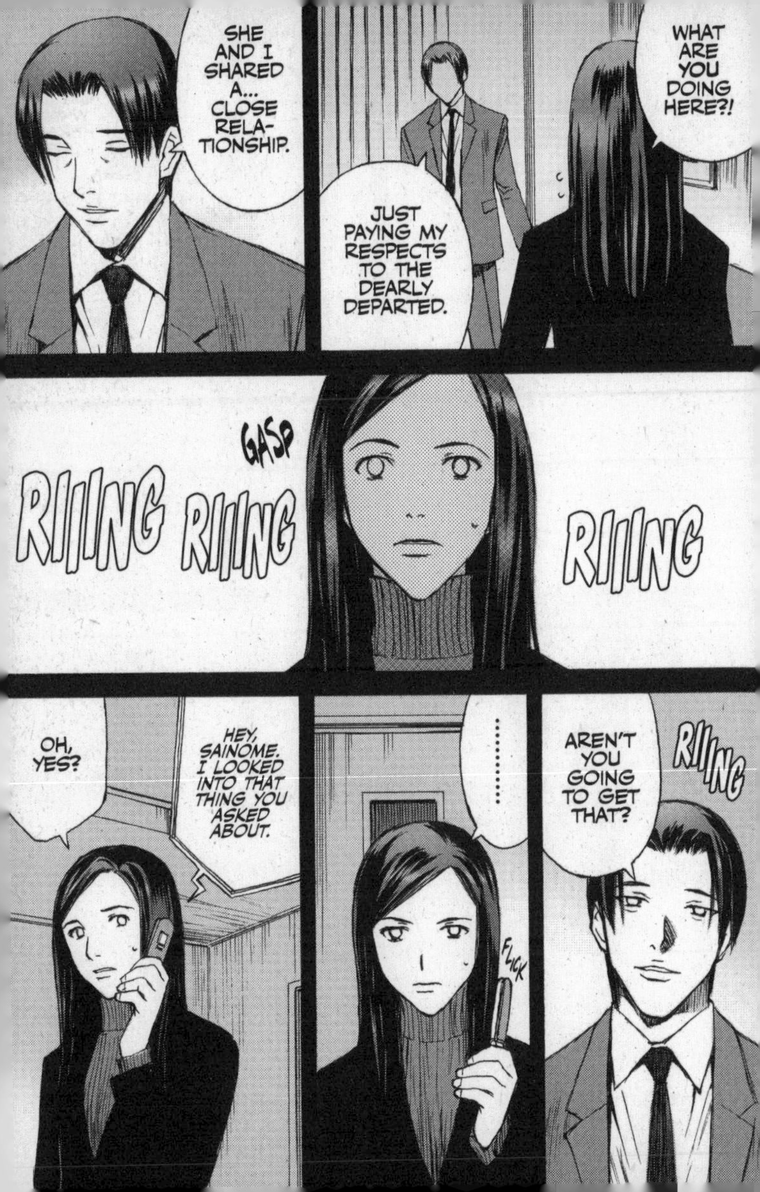
WHAT ARE YOU DOING HERE?!
JUST PAYING MY RESPECTS TO THE DEARLY DEPARTED.
SHE AND I SHARED A... CLOSE RELATIONSHIP.
RIIING
GASP
RIIING
RIIING
RIIING
AREN'T YOU GOING TO GET THAT?
......
FLICK
HEY, SAINOME. I LOOKED INTO THAT THING YOU ASKED ABOUT.
OH, YES?

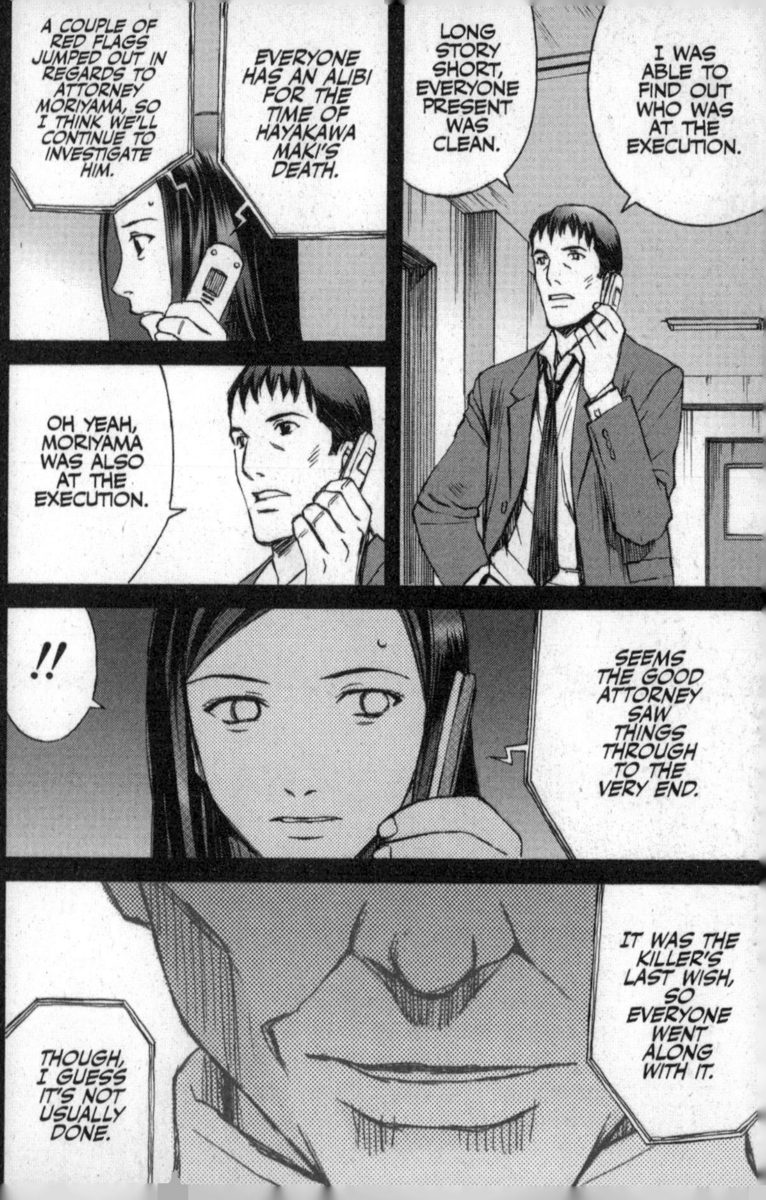
I WAS ABLE TO FIND OUT WHO WAS AT THE EXECUTION.
LONG STORY SHORT, EVERYONE PRESENT WAS CLEAN.
EVERYONE HAS AN ALIBI FOR THE TIME OF HAYAKAWA MAKI'S DEATH.
A COUPLE OF RED FLAGS JUMPED OUT IN REGARDS TO ATTORNEY MORIYAMA, SO I THINK WE'LL CONTINUE TO INVESTIGATE HIM.
OH YEAH, MORIYAMA WAS ALSO AT THE EXECUTION.
SEEMS THE GOOD ATTORNEY SAW THINGS THROUGH TO THE VERY END.
!!
IT WAS THE KILLER'S LAST WISH, SO EVERYONE WENT ALONG WITH IT.
THOUGH, I GUESS IT'S NOT USUALLY DONE.

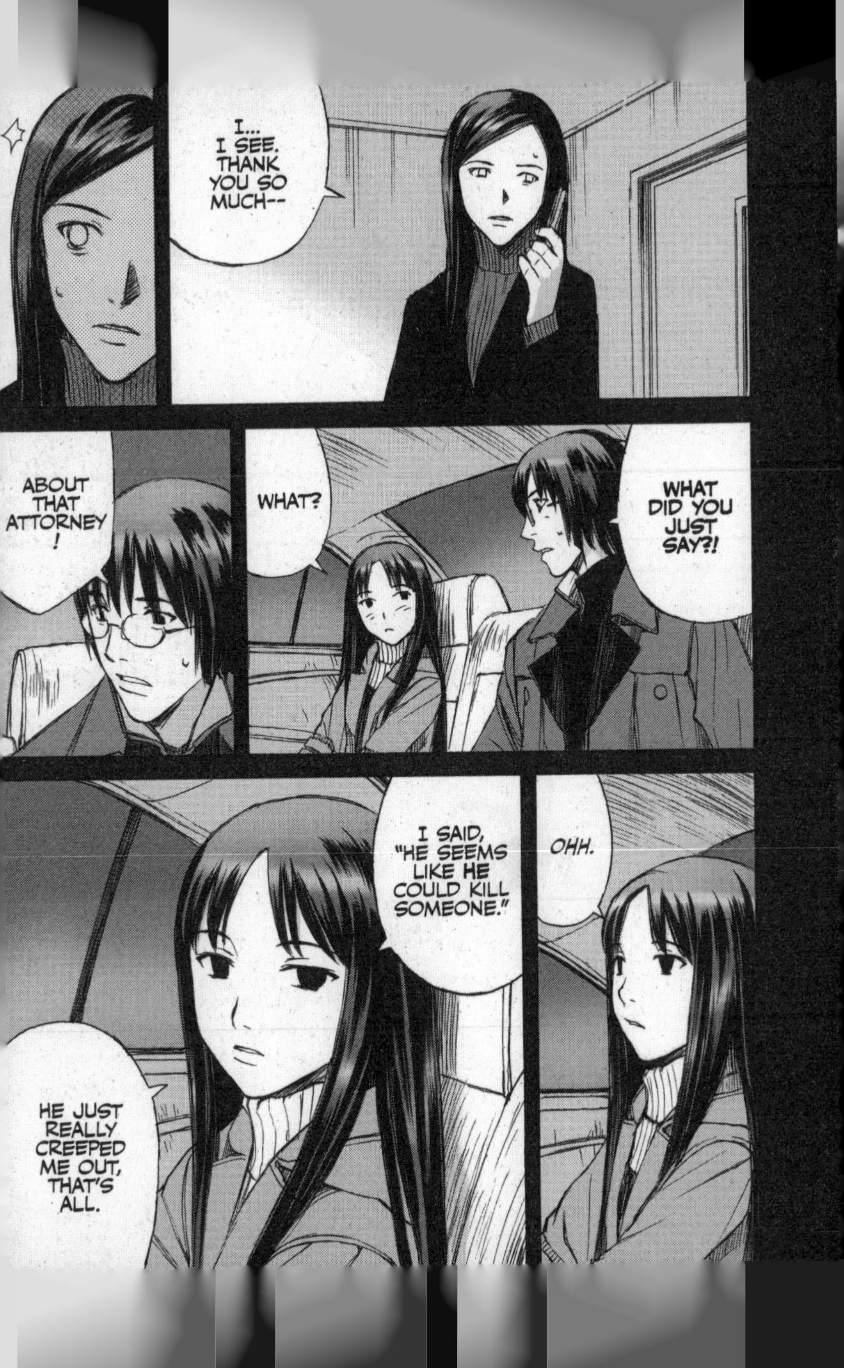
I... I SEE. THANK YOU SO MUCH--
WHAT DID YOU JUST SAY?!
WHAT?
ABOUT THAT ATTORNEY!
OHH.
I SAID, "HE SEEMS LIKE HE COULD KILL SOMEONE."
HE JUST REALLY CREEPED ME OUT, THAT'S ALL.

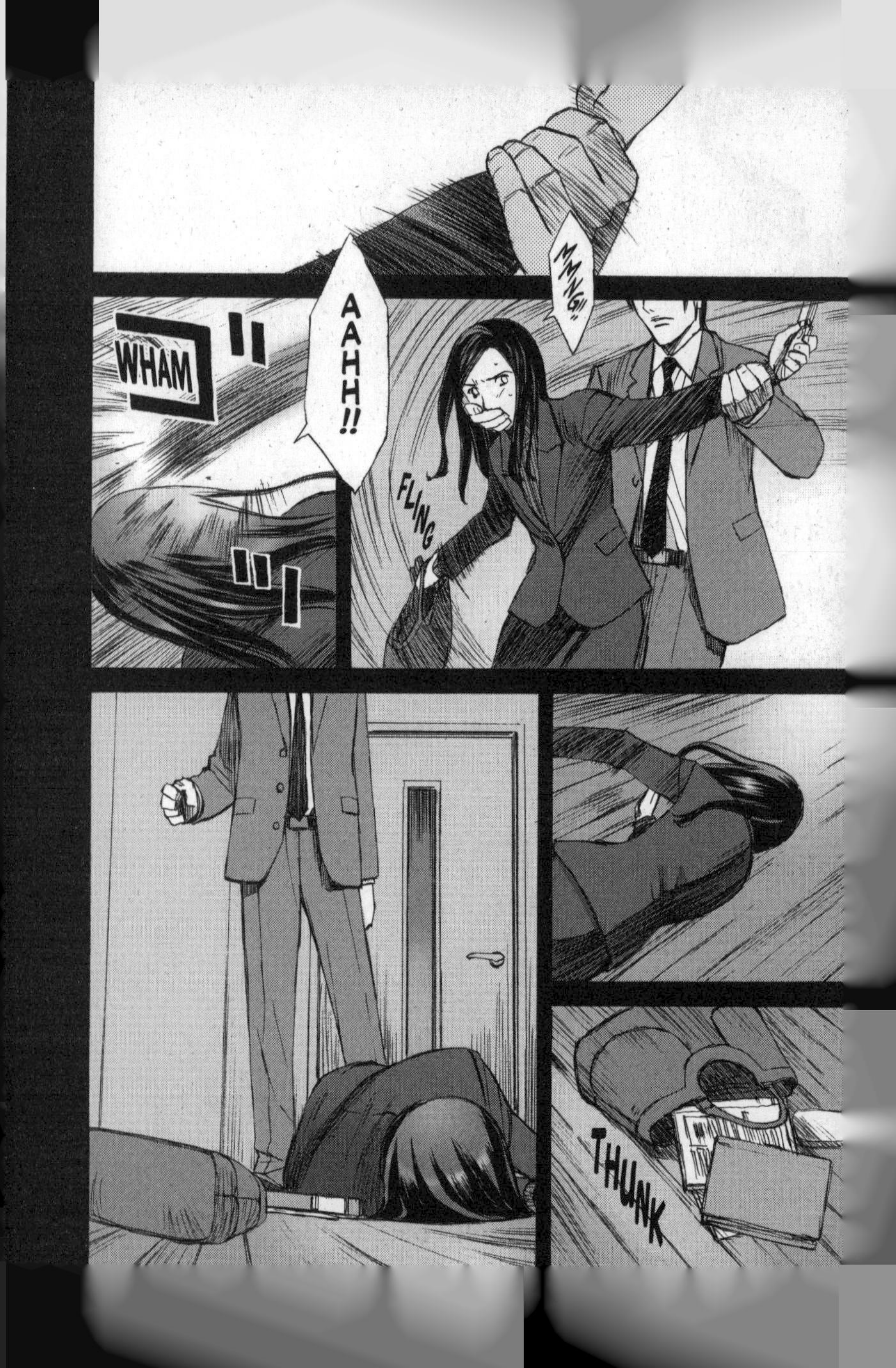
MMNG!!
AAHH!!
FLING
WHAM
THUNK

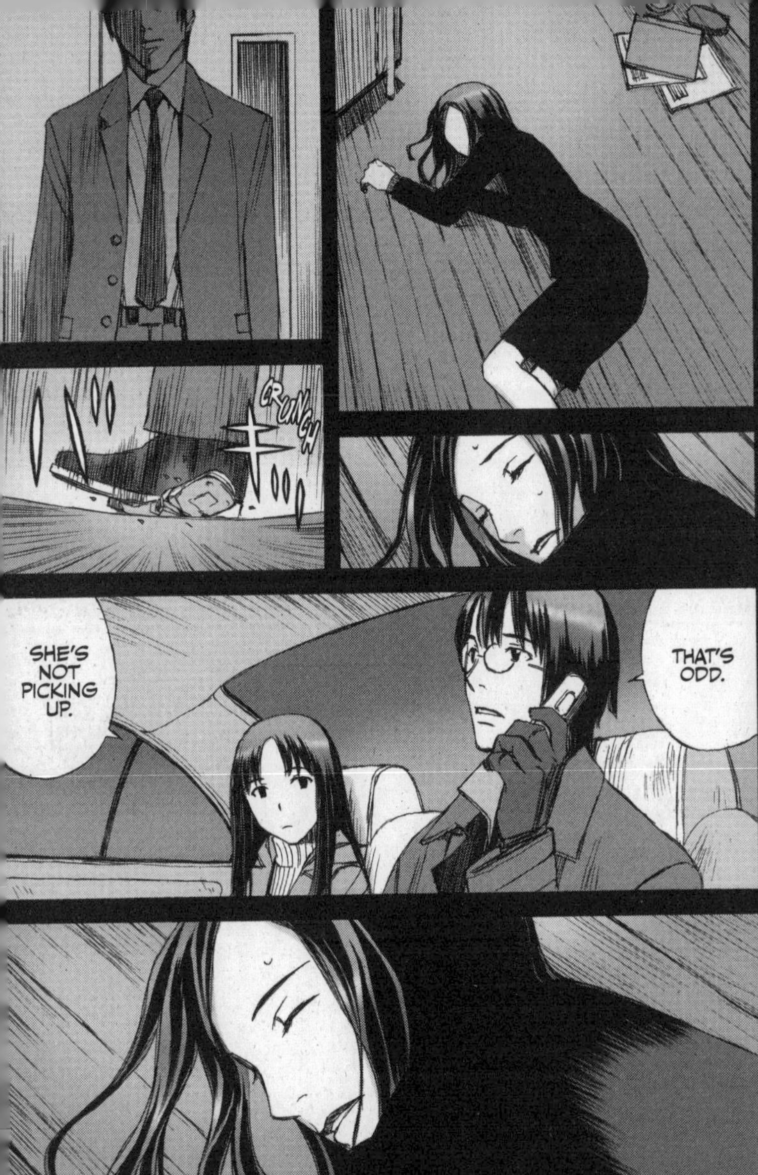
CRUNCH
THAT'S ODD.
SHE'S NOT PICKING UP.

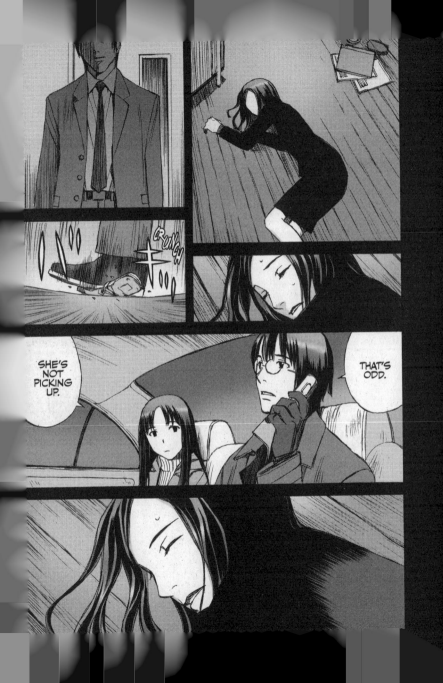

Episode 5
SOUL SLAVE part 3

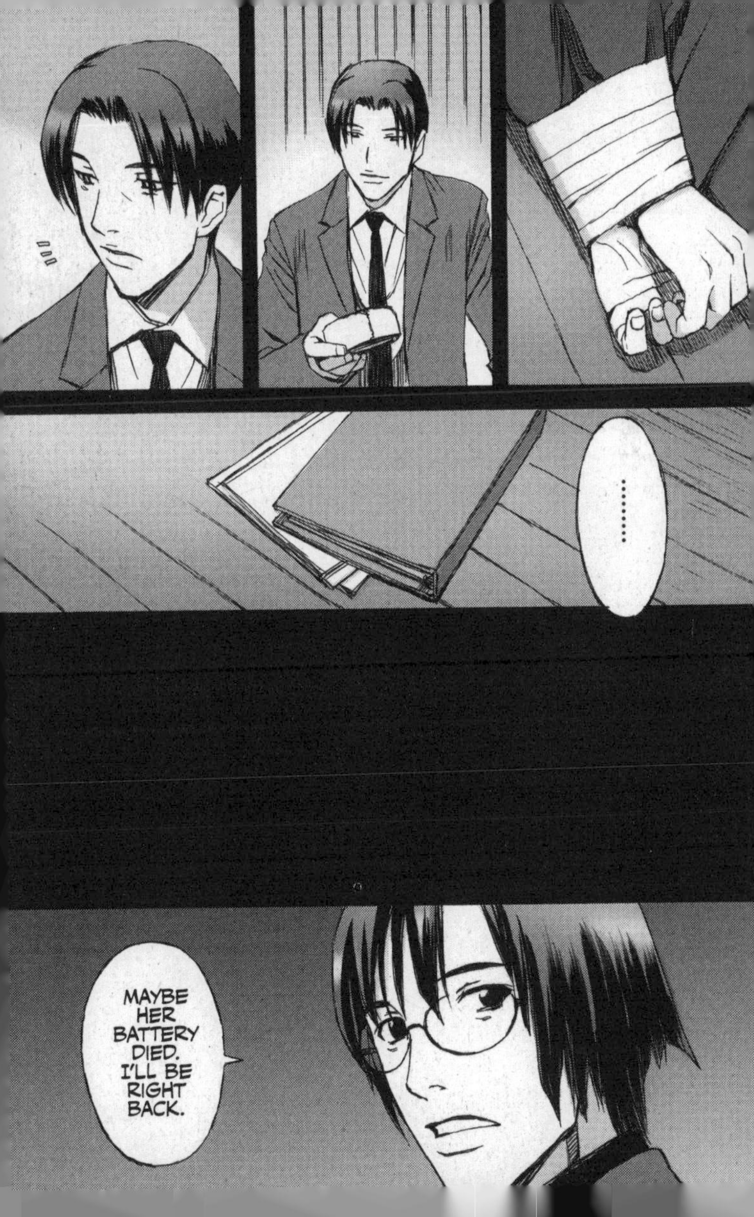
……
MAYBE HER BATTERY DIED. I'LL BE RIGHT BACK.

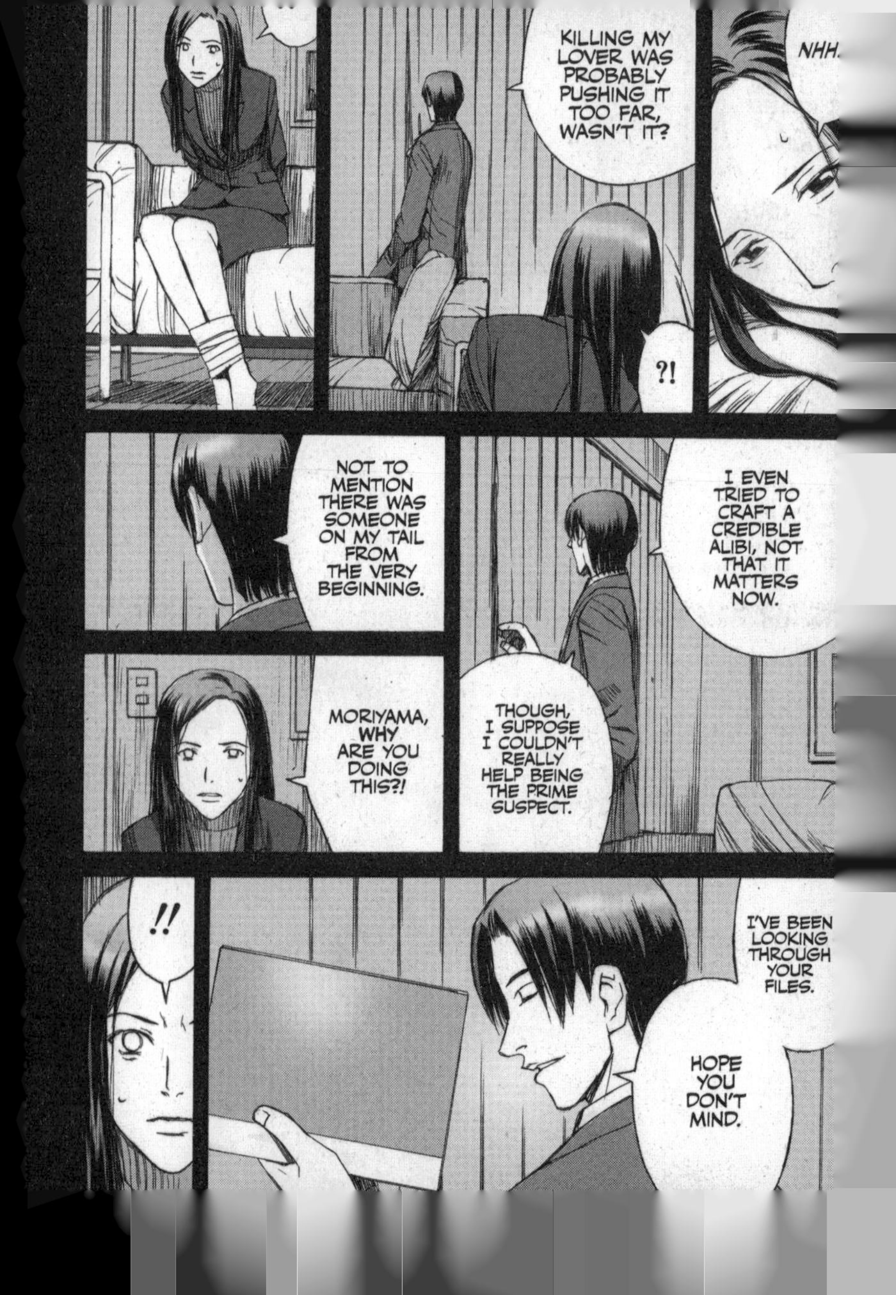
NHH.
KILLING MY LOVER WAS PROBABLY PUSHING IT TOO FAR, WASN'T IT?
?!
I EVEN TRIED TO CRAFT A CREDIBLE ALIBI, NOT THAT IT MATTERS NOW.
THOUGH, I SUPPOSE I COULDN'T REALLY HELP BEING THE PRIME SUSPECT.
NOT TO MENTION THERE WAS SOMEONE ON MY TAIL FROM THE VERY BEGINNING.
MORIYAMA, WHY ARE YOU DOING THIS?!
I'VE BEEN LOOKING THROUGH YOUR FILES.
HOPE YOU DON'T MIND.
!!

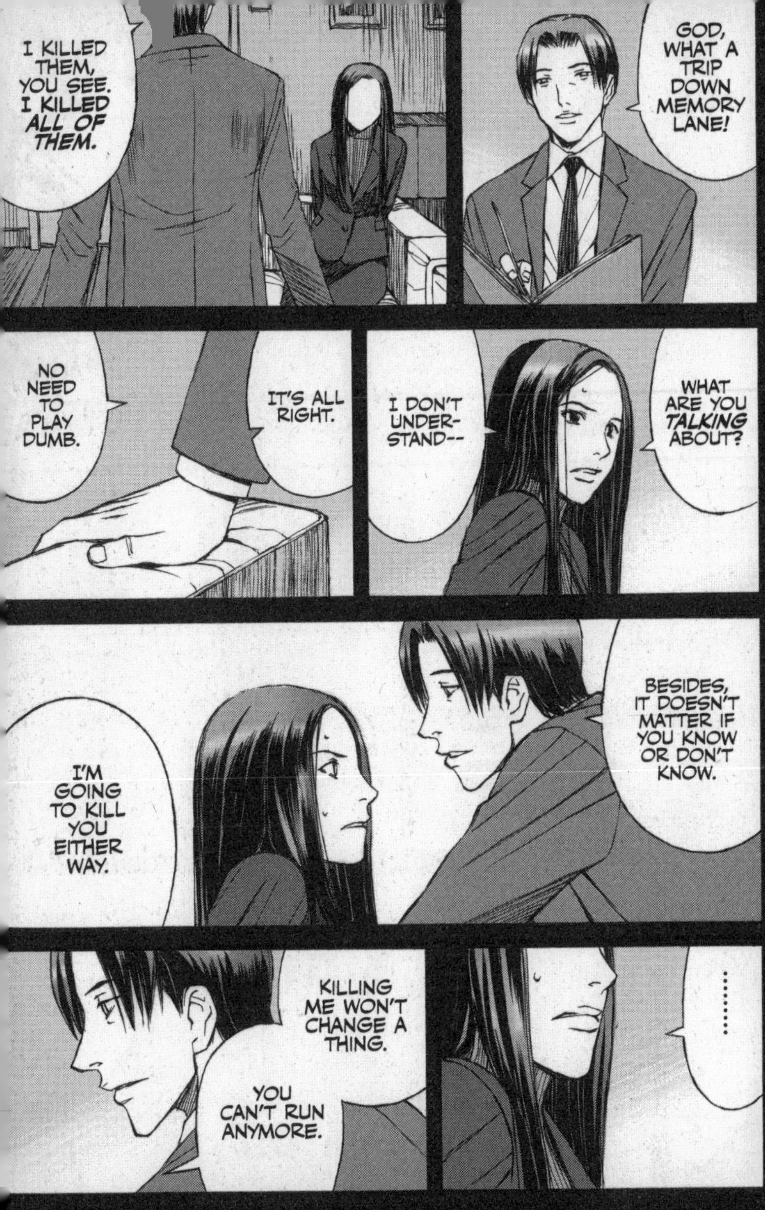
GOD, WHAT A TRIP DOWN MEMORY LANE!
I KILLED THEM, YOU SEE. I KILLED *ALL OF THEM.*
WHAT ARE YOU *TALKING* ABOUT?
I DON'T UNDER-STAND--
IT'S ALL RIGHT.
NO NEED TO PLAY DUMB.
BESIDES, IT DOESN'T MATTER IF YOU KNOW OR DON'T KNOW.
I'M GOING TO KILL YOU EITHER WAY.
......
KILLING ME WON'T CHANGE A THING.
YOU CAN'T RUN ANYMORE.

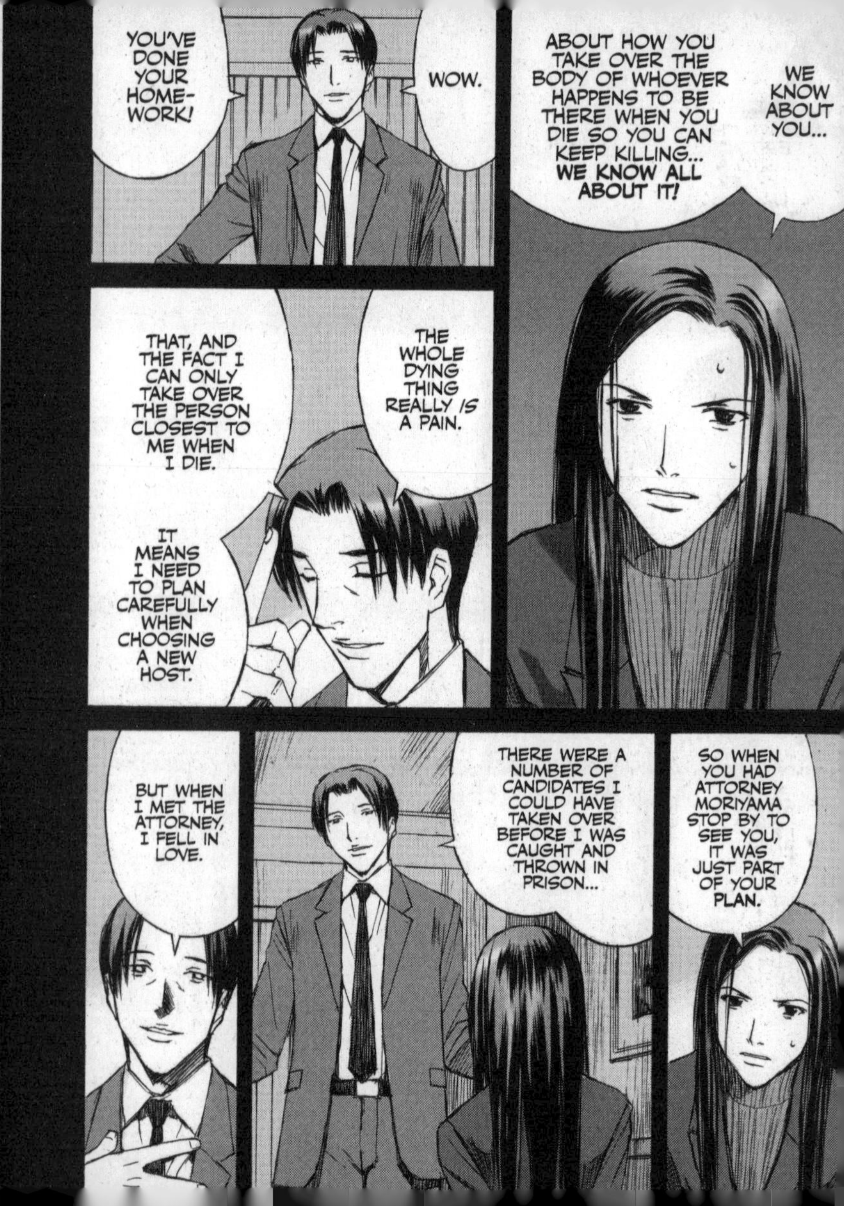
WE KNOW ABOUT YOU...
ABOUT HOW YOU TAKE OVER THE BODY OF WHOEVER HAPPENS TO BE THERE WHEN YOU DIE SO YOU CAN KEEP KILLING... **WE KNOW ALL ABOUT IT!**
WOW.
YOU'VE DONE YOUR HOME-WORK!
THE WHOLE DYING THING REALLY *IS* A PAIN.
THAT, AND THE FACT I CAN ONLY TAKE OVER THE PERSON CLOSEST TO ME WHEN I DIE.
IT MEANS I NEED TO PLAN CAREFULLY WHEN CHOOSING A NEW HOST.
SO WHEN YOU HAD ATTORNEY MORIYAMA STOP BY TO SEE YOU, IT WAS JUST PART OF YOUR PLAN.
THERE WERE A NUMBER OF CANDIDATES I COULD HAVE TAKEN OVER BEFORE I WAS CAUGHT AND THROWN IN PRISON...
BUT WHEN I MET THE ATTORNEY, I FELL IN LOVE.

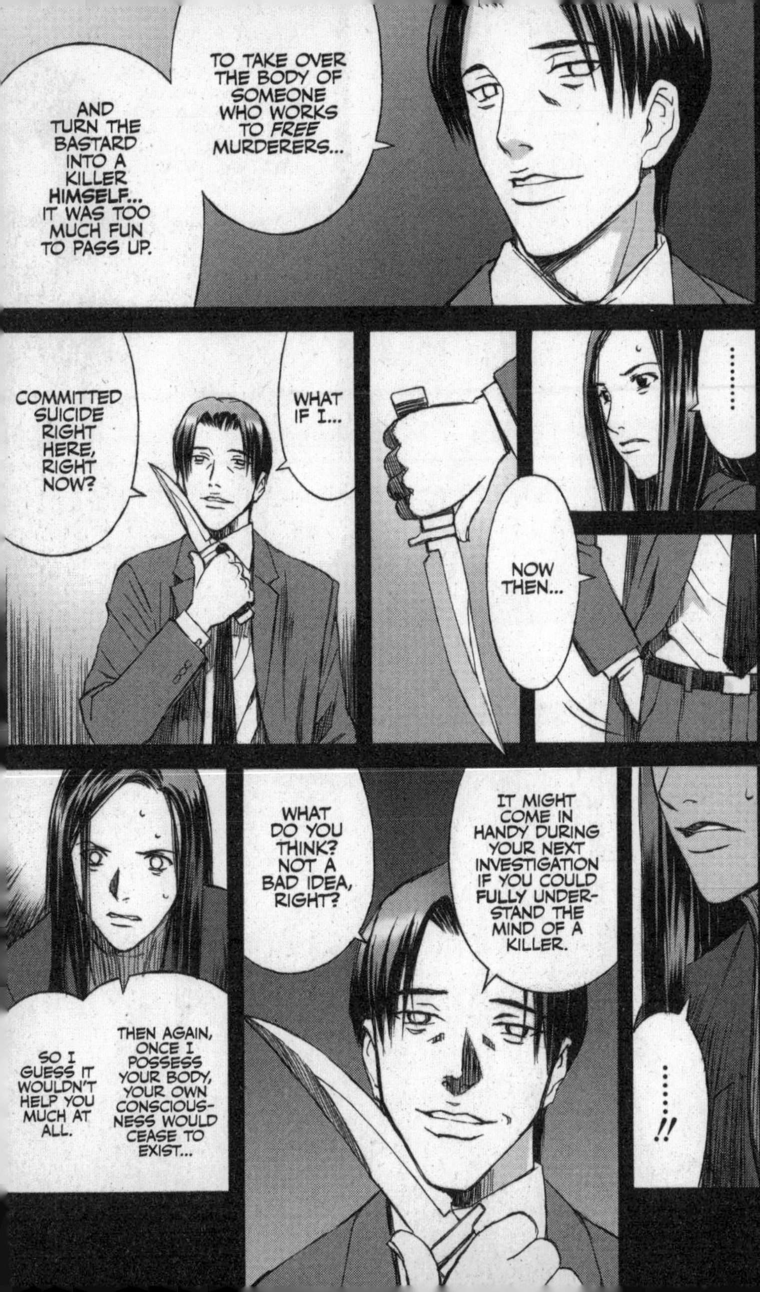
TO TAKE OVER THE BODY OF SOMEONE WHO WORKS TO *FREE* MURDERERS...
AND TURN THE BASTARD INTO A KILLER **HIMSELF**... IT WAS TOO MUCH FUN TO PASS UP.
......
NOW THEN...
WHAT IF I...
COMMITTED SUICIDE RIGHT HERE, RIGHT NOW?
......!!
IT MIGHT COME IN HANDY DURING YOUR NEXT INVESTIGATION IF YOU COULD FULLY UNDER-STAND THE MIND OF A KILLER.
WHAT DO YOU THINK? NOT A BAD IDEA, RIGHT?
THEN AGAIN, ONCE I POSSESS YOUR BODY, YOUR OWN CONSCIOUS-NESS WOULD CEASE TO EXIST...
SO I GUESS IT WOULDN'T HELP YOU MUCH AT ALL.

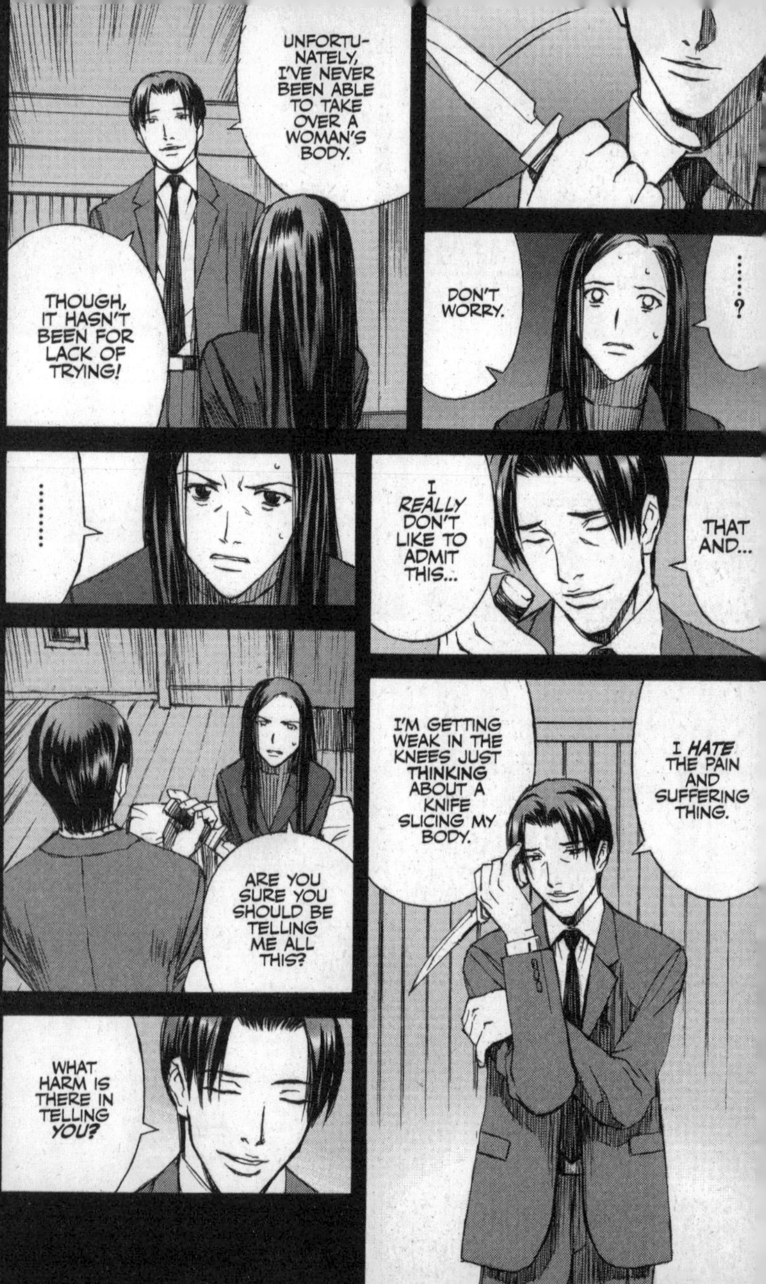
......?
DON'T WORRY.
UNFORTUNATELY, I'VE NEVER BEEN ABLE TO TAKE OVER A WOMAN'S BODY.
THOUGH, IT HASN'T BEEN FOR LACK OF TRYING!
THAT AND...
I *REALLY* DON'T LIKE TO ADMIT THIS...
....
I *HATE* THE PAIN AND SUFFERING THING.
I'M GETTING WEAK IN THE KNEES JUST THINKING ABOUT A KNIFE SLICING MY BODY.
ARE YOU SURE YOU SHOULD BE TELLING ME ALL THIS?
WHAT HARM IS THERE IN TELLING *YOU*?

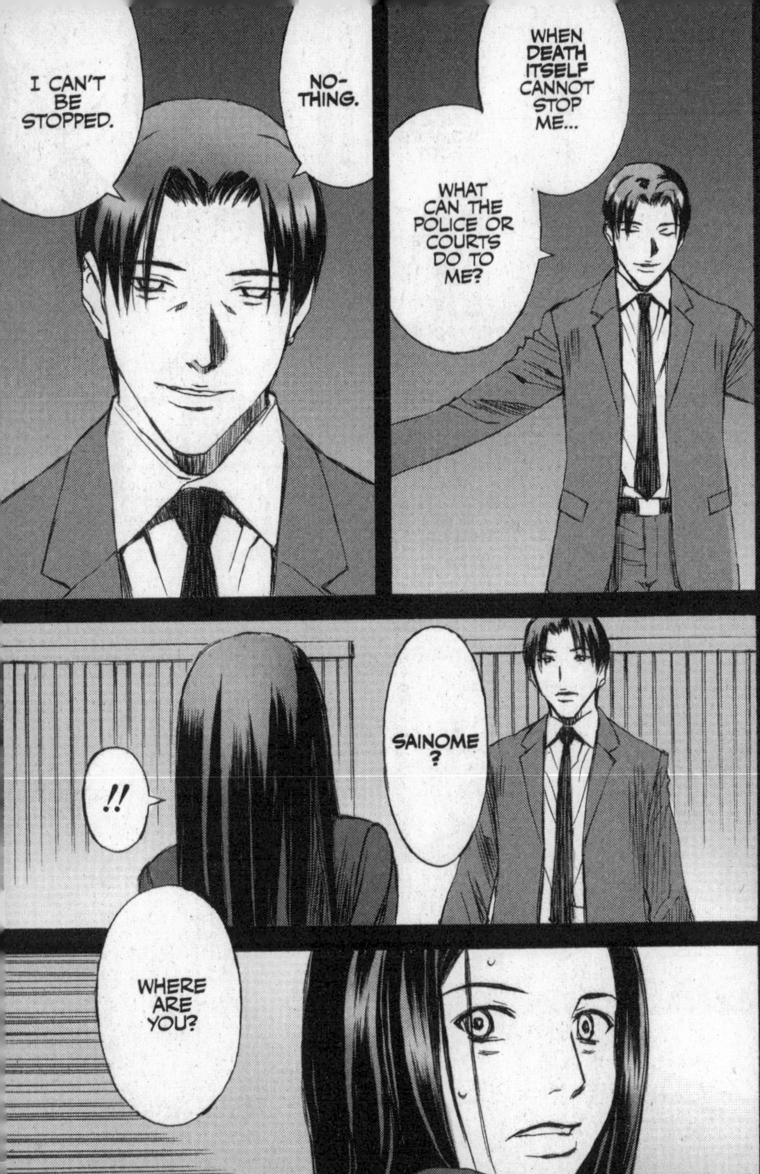
WHEN DEATH ITSELF CANNOT STOP ME...
WHAT CAN THE POLICE OR COURTS DO TO ME?
NO-THING.
I CAN'T BE STOPPED.
SAINOME?
!!
WHERE ARE YOU?

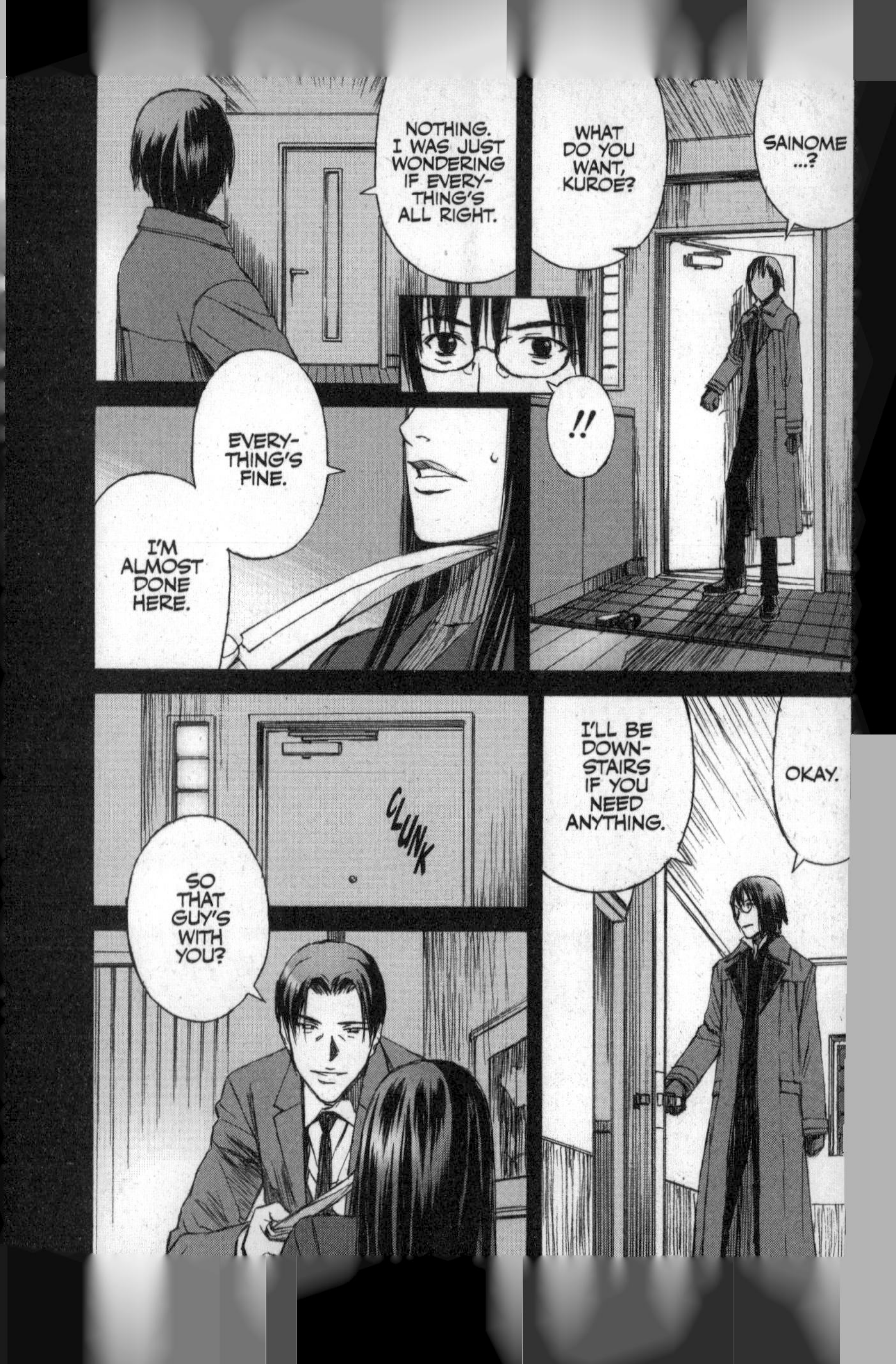
SAINOME ...?
WHAT DO YOU WANT, KUROE?
NOTHING. I WAS JUST WONDERING IF EVERY-THING'S ALL RIGHT.
!!
EVERY-THING'S FINE.
I'M ALMOST DONE HERE.
OKAY.
I'LL BE DOWN-STAIRS IF YOU NEED ANYTHING.
CLUNK
SO THAT GUY'S WITH YOU?

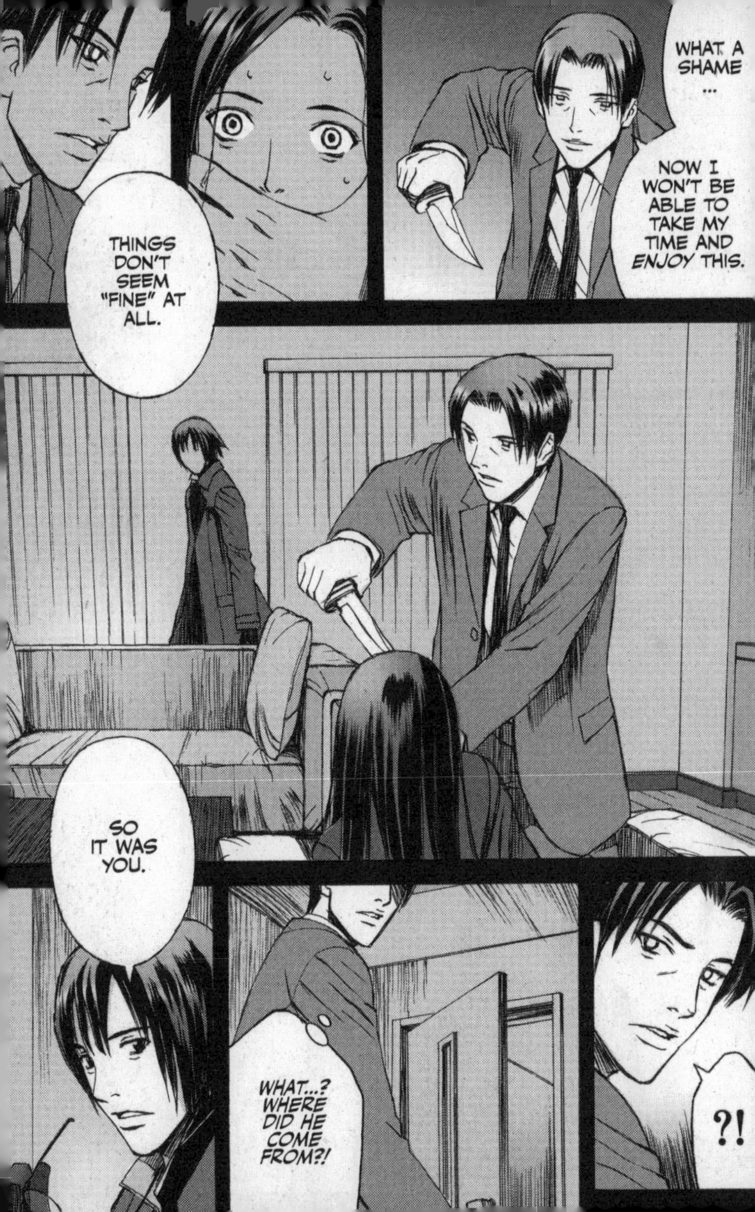
WHAT A SHAME ...
NOW I WON'T BE ABLE TO TAKE MY TIME AND *ENJOY* THIS.
THINGS DON'T SEEM "FINE" AT ALL.
?!
WHAT...? WHERE DID HE COME FROM?!
SO IT WAS YOU.

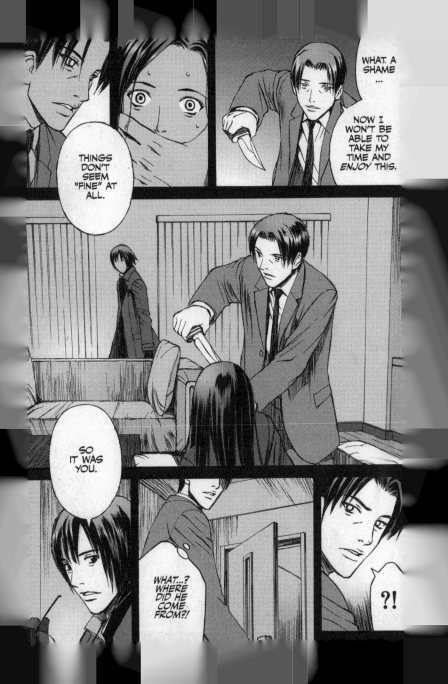

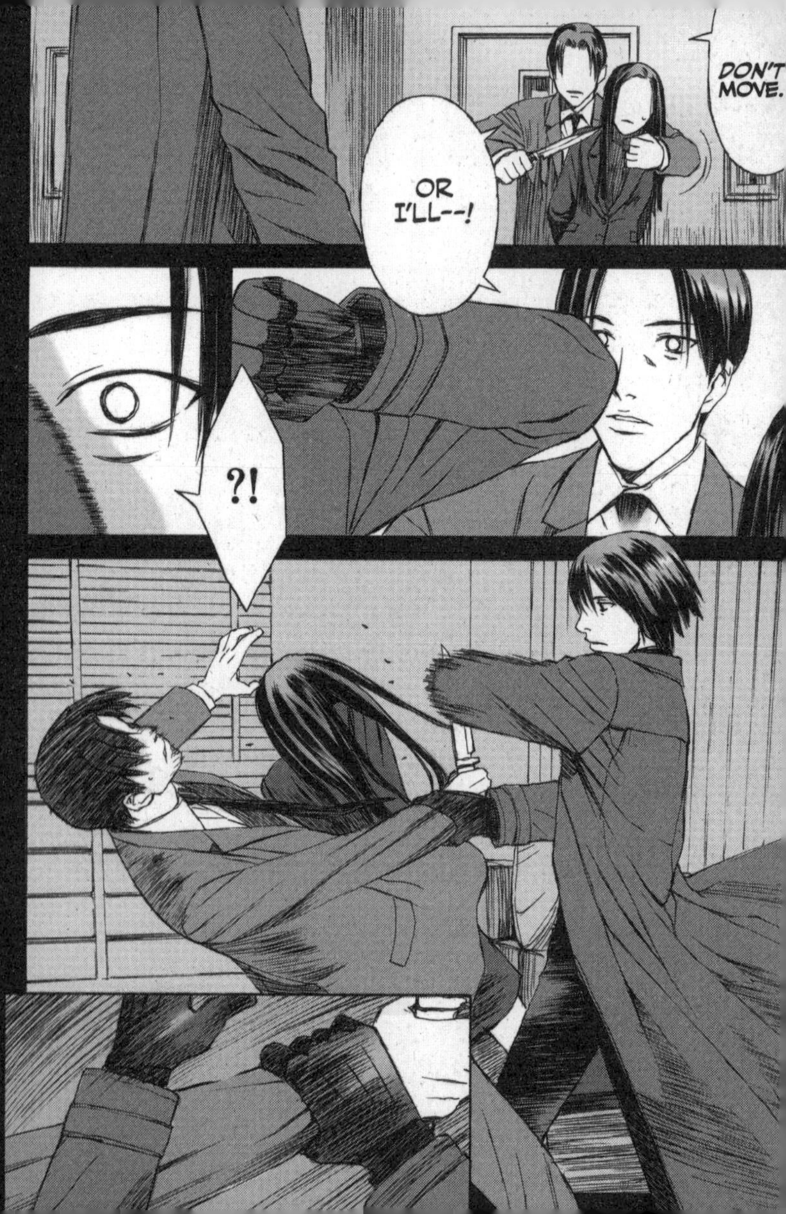
DON'T MOVE.
OR I'LL--!
?!

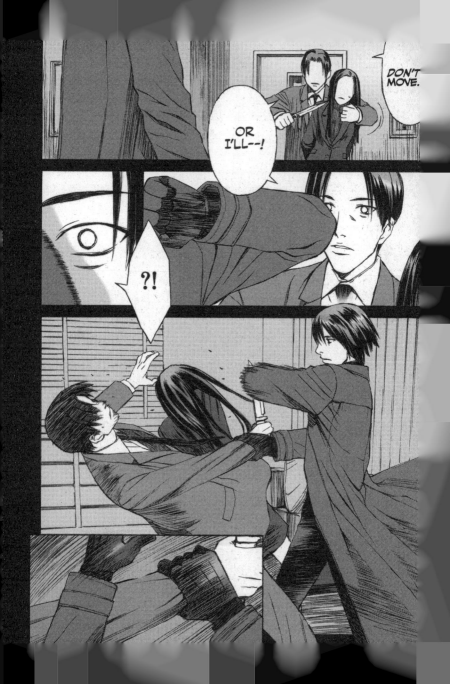

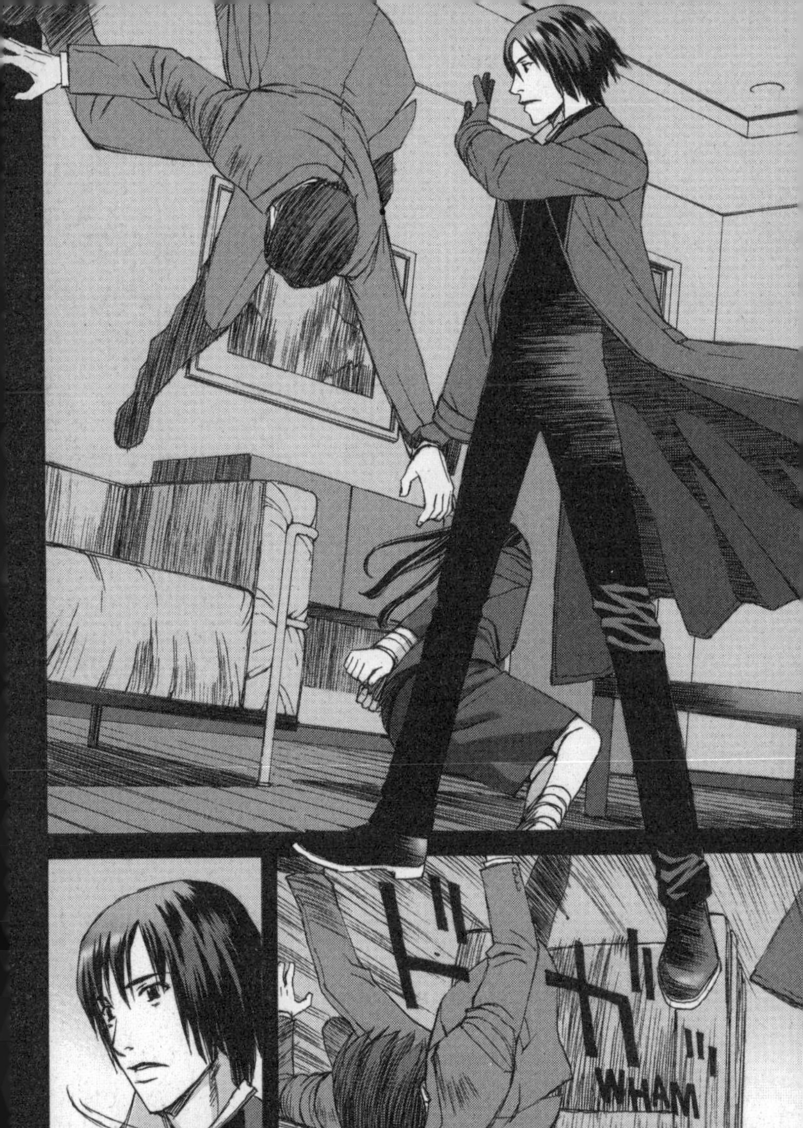
WHAM

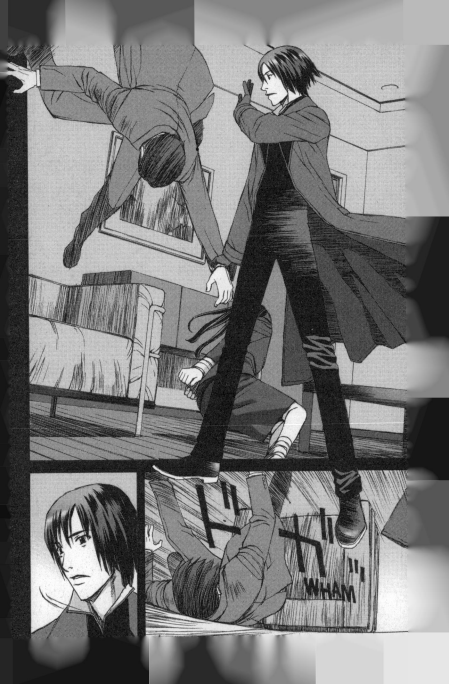

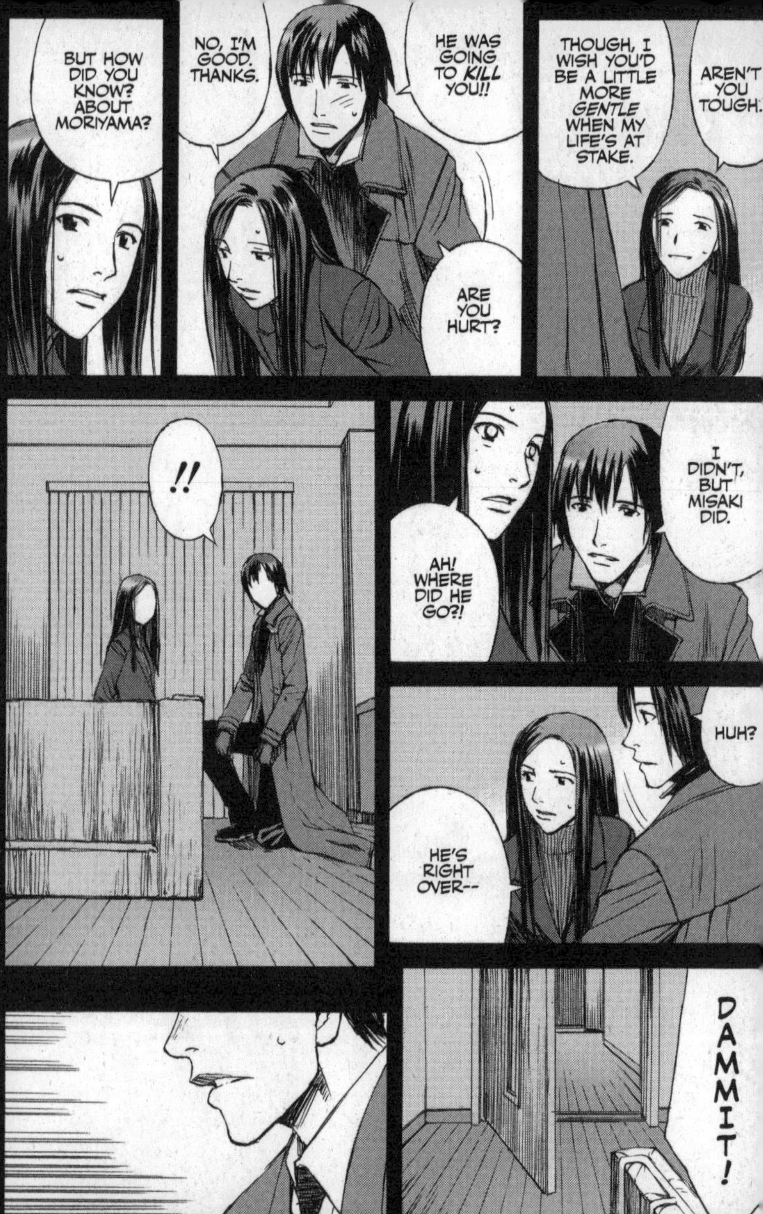
AREN'T YOU TOUGH.
THOUGH, I WISH YOU'D BE A LITTLE MORE GENTLE WHEN MY LIFE'S AT STAKE.
HE WAS GOING TO KILL YOU!!
ARE YOU HURT?
NO, I'M GOOD. THANKS.
BUT HOW DID YOU KNOW? ABOUT MORIYAMA?
I DIDN'T, BUT MISAKI DID.
AH! WHERE DID HE GO?!
HUH?
HE'S RIGHT OVER--
!!
DAMMIT!

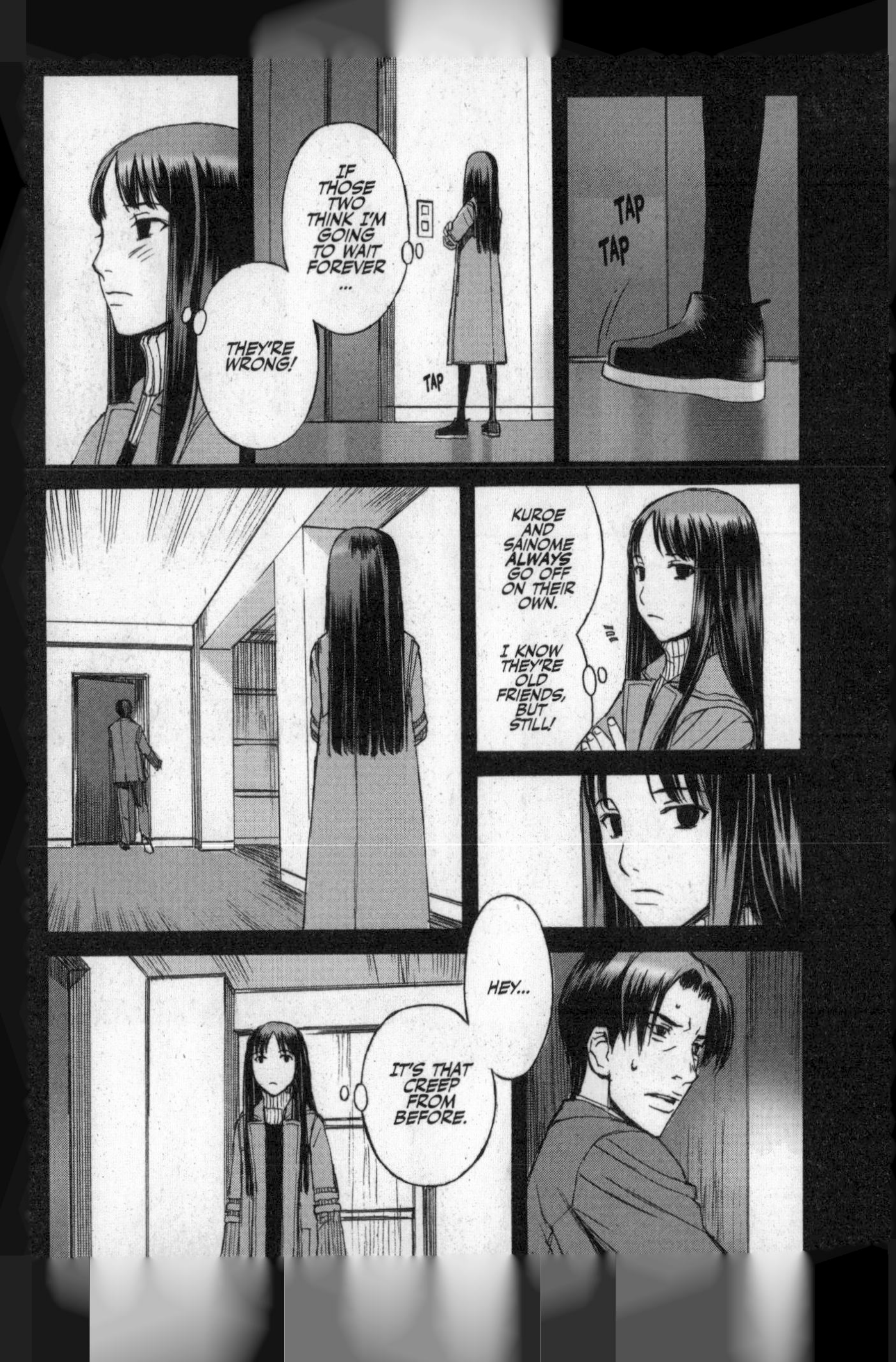
TAP
TAP
IF THOSE TWO THINK I'M GOING TO WAIT FOREVER ...
TAP
THEY'RE WRONG!
KUROE AND SAINOME ALWAYS GO OFF ON THEIR OWN.
I KNOW THEY'RE OLD FRIENDS, BUT STILL!
HEY...
IT'S THAT CREEP FROM BEFORE.

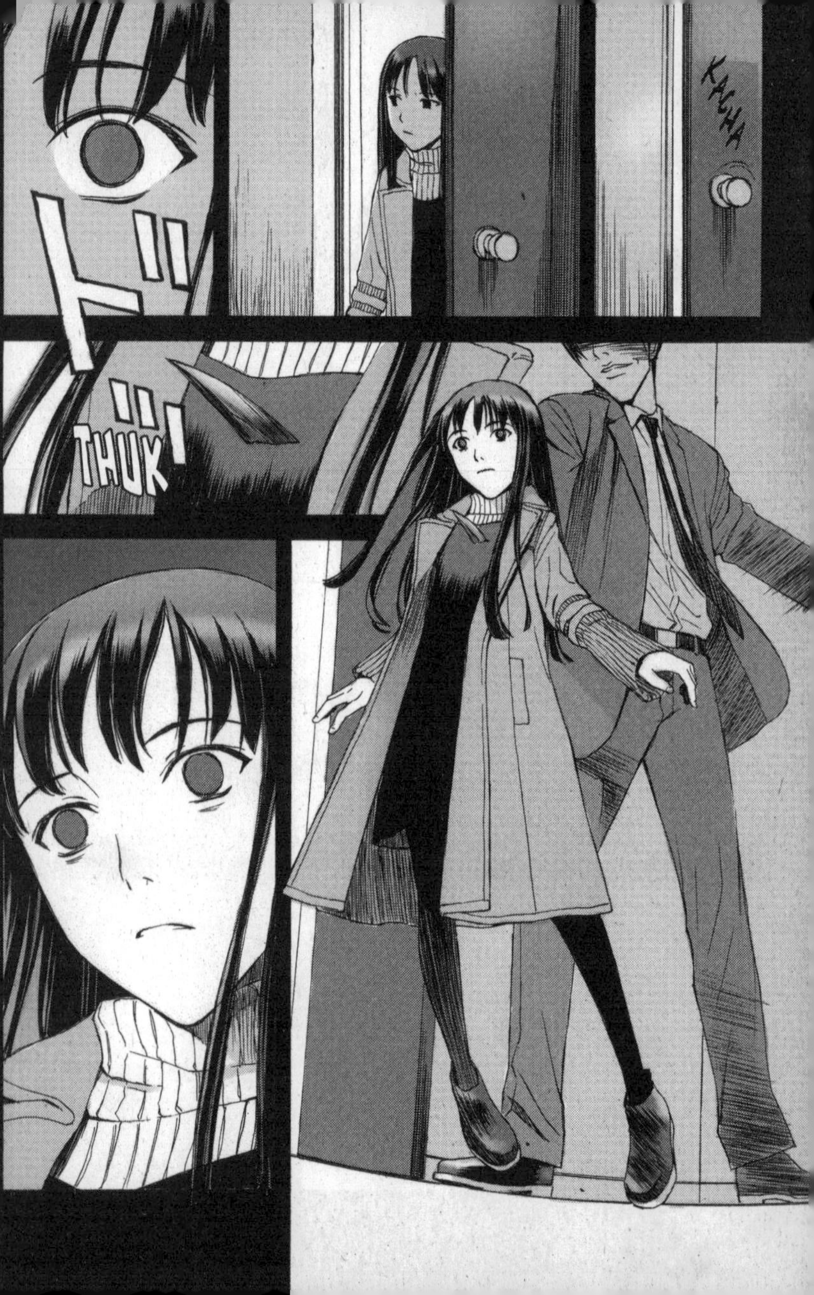
KACHA
THUK

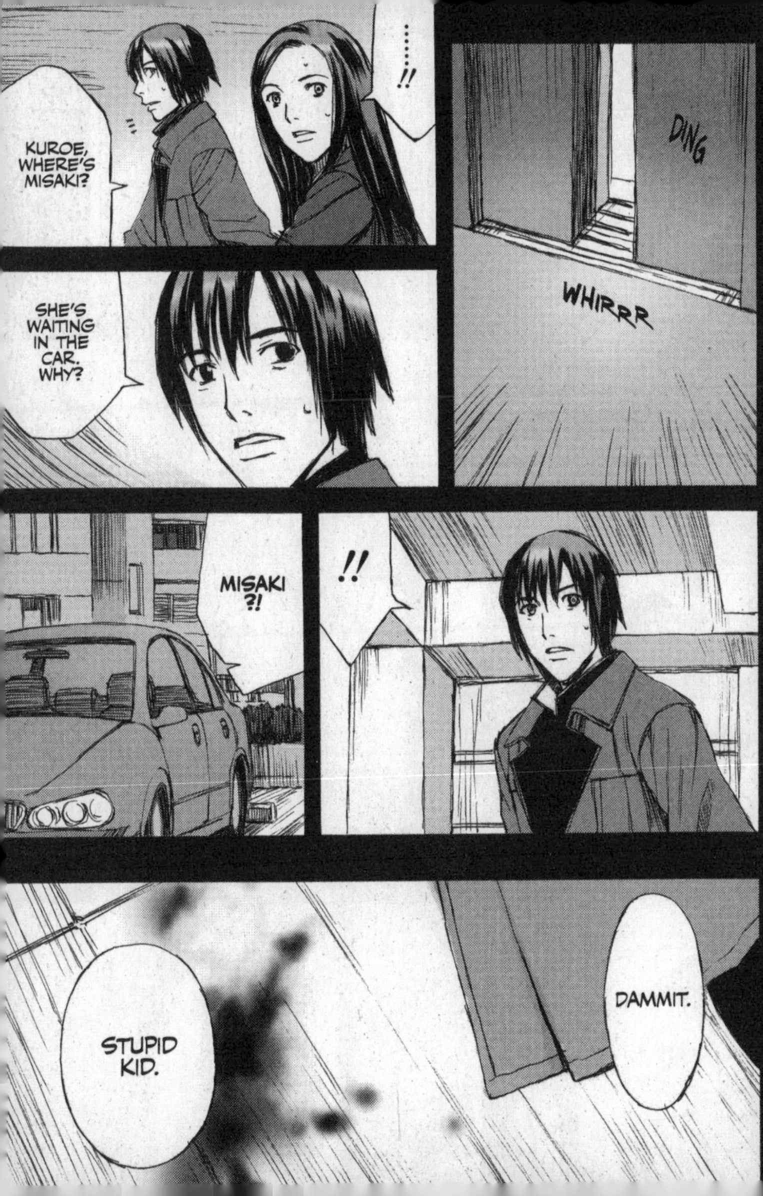
DING
WHIRRR
……!!
KUROE, WHERE'S MISAKI?
SHE'S WAITING IN THE CAR. WHY?
!!
MISAKI ?!
DAMMIT.
STUPID KID.

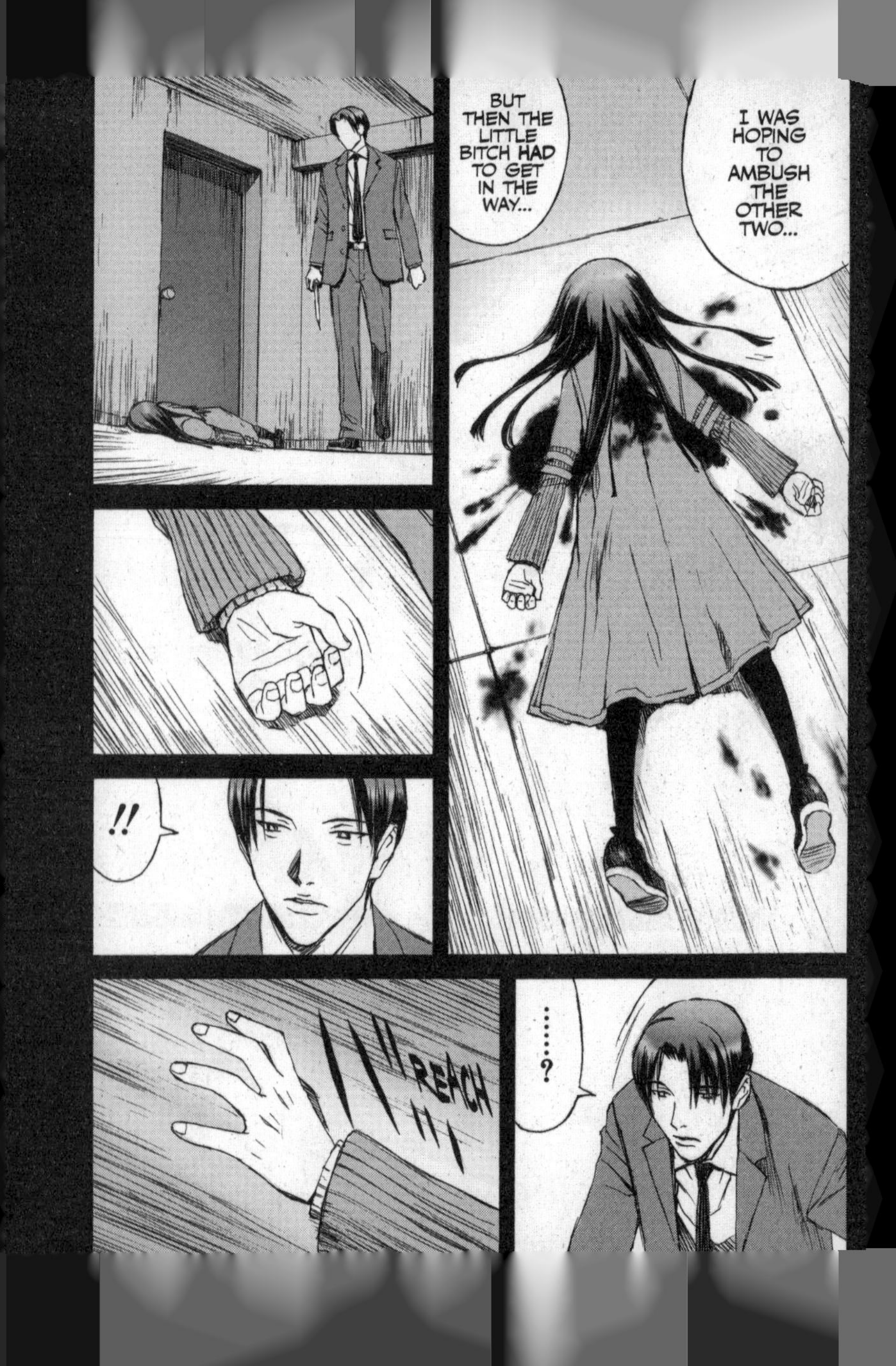
I WAS HOPING TO AMBUSH THE OTHER TWO...
BUT THEN THE LITTLE BITCH HAD TO GET IN THE WAY...
!!
......?
REACH

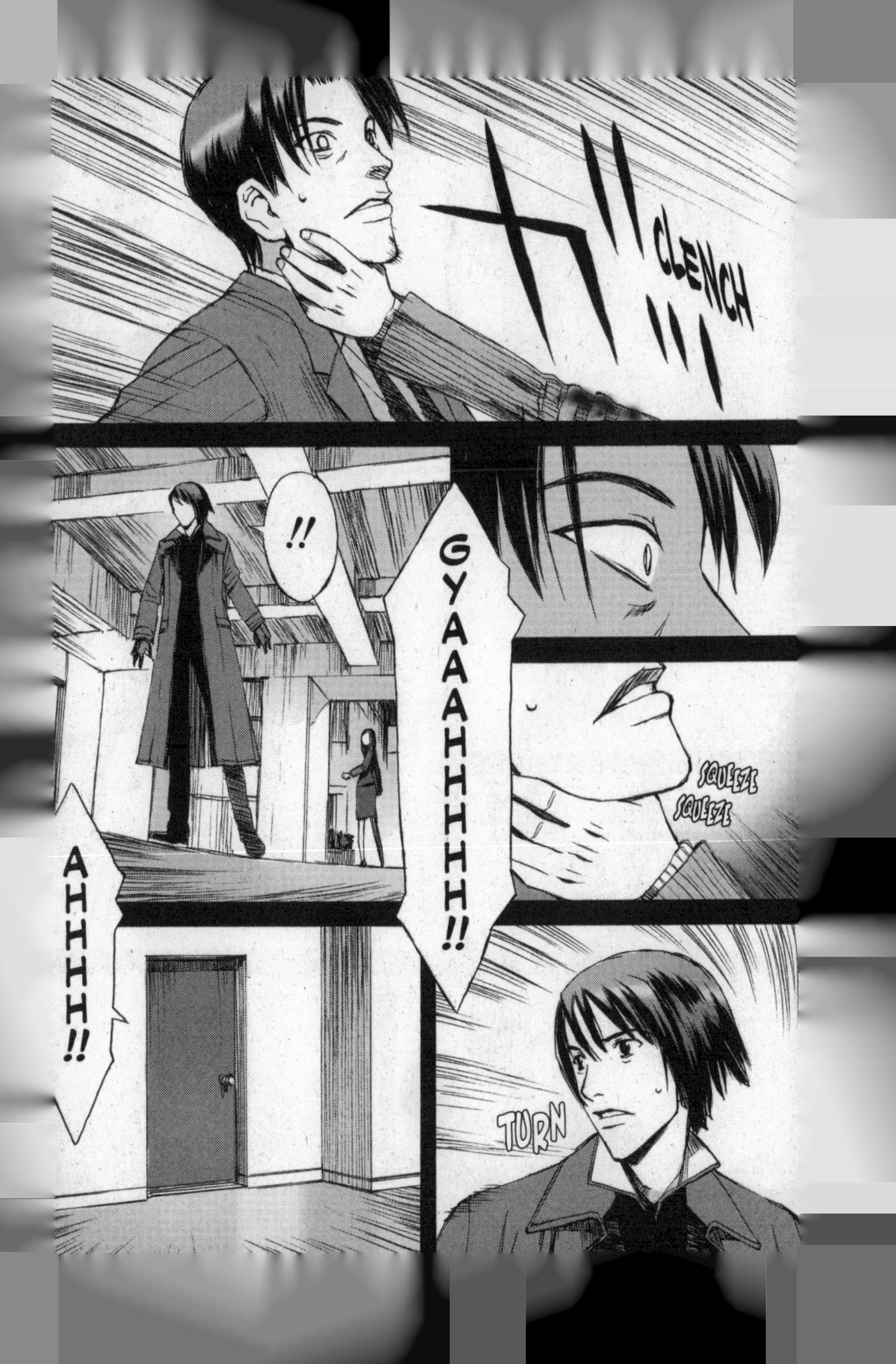
CLENCH
GYAAAHHHHHH!!
SQUEEZE
SQUEEZE
!!
AHHHHH!!
TURN

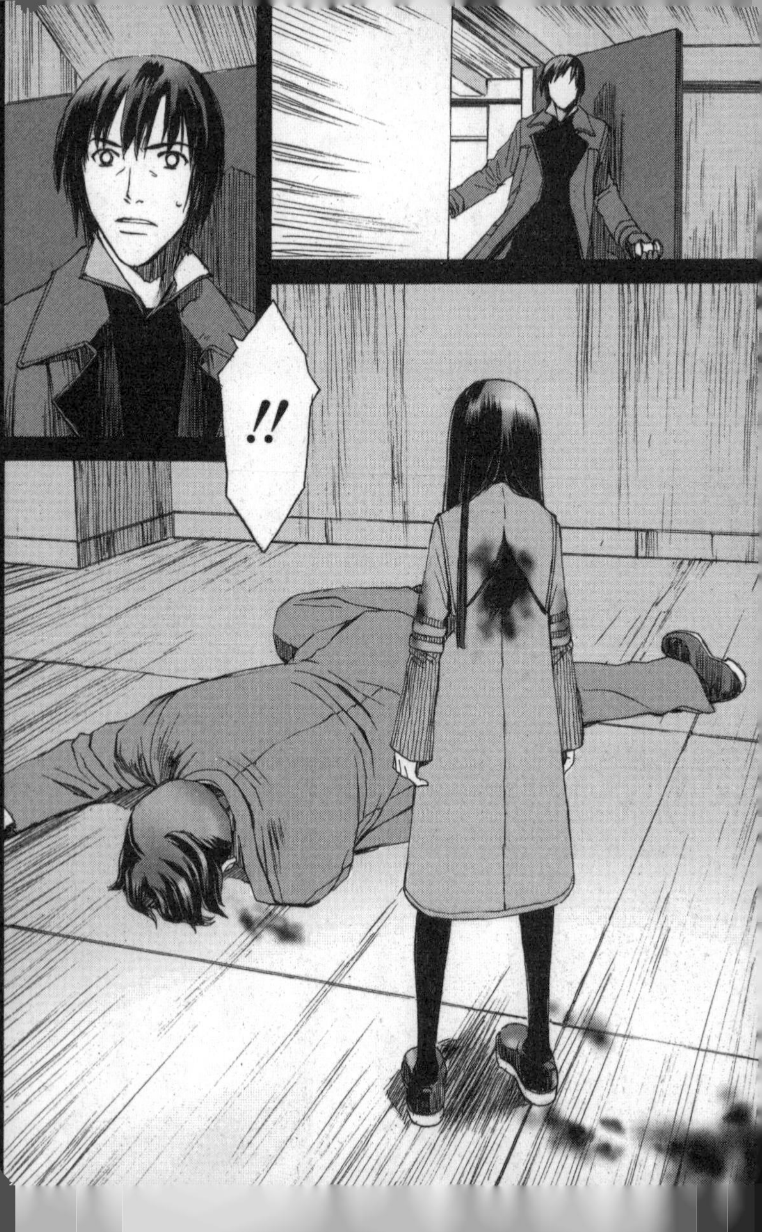
!!

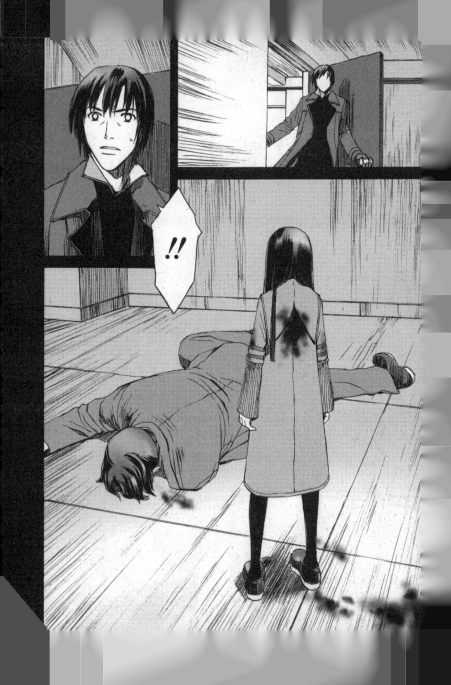

MISAKI
...

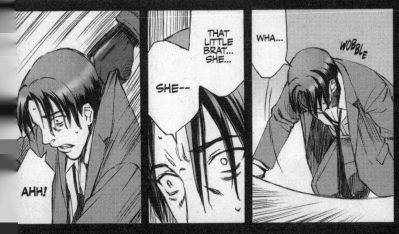

AHH!

SHE--

THAT LITTLE BRAT... SHE...

WHA...

WOBBLE

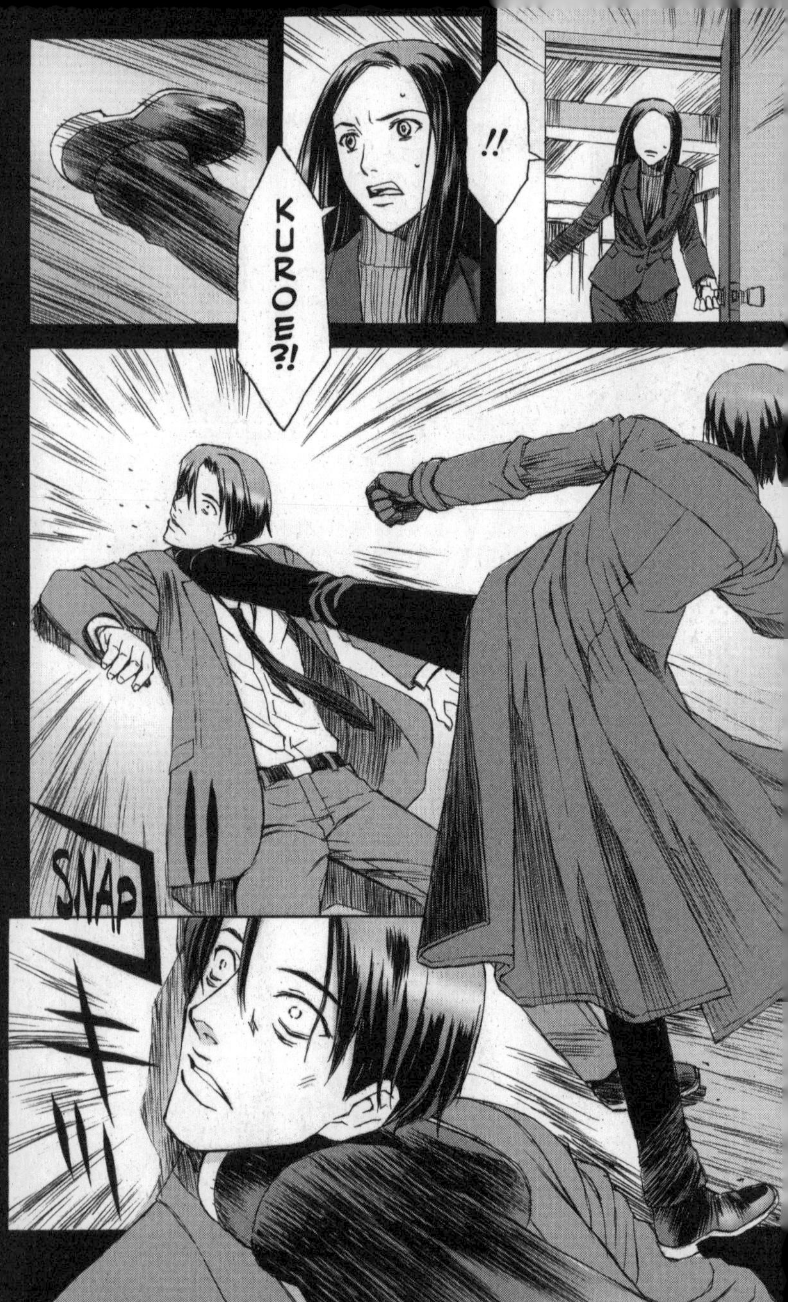
!!
KUROE?!
SNAP

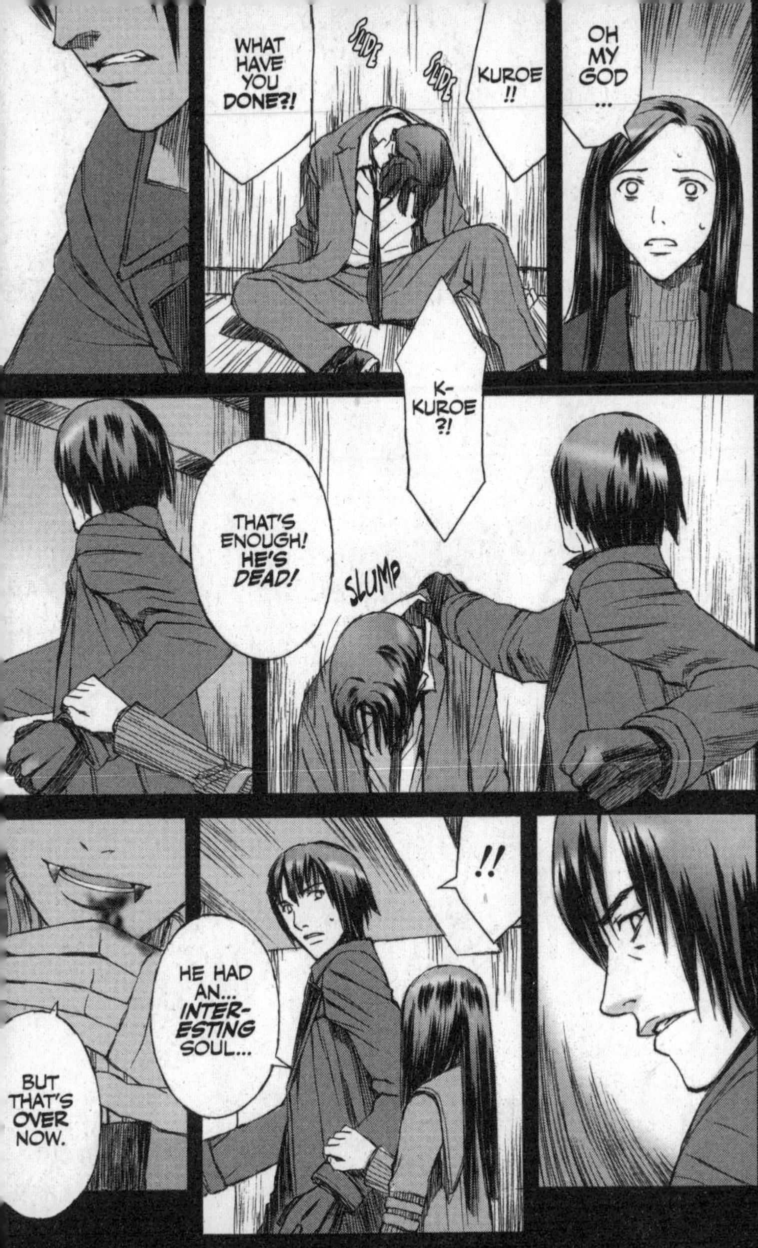
OH MY GOD ...
KUROE !!
SLIDE
SLIDE
WHAT HAVE YOU DONE?!
K-KUROE ?!
SLUMP
THAT'S ENOUGH! HE'S DEAD!
!!
HE HAD AN... INTER-ESTING SOUL...
BUT THAT'S OVER NOW.

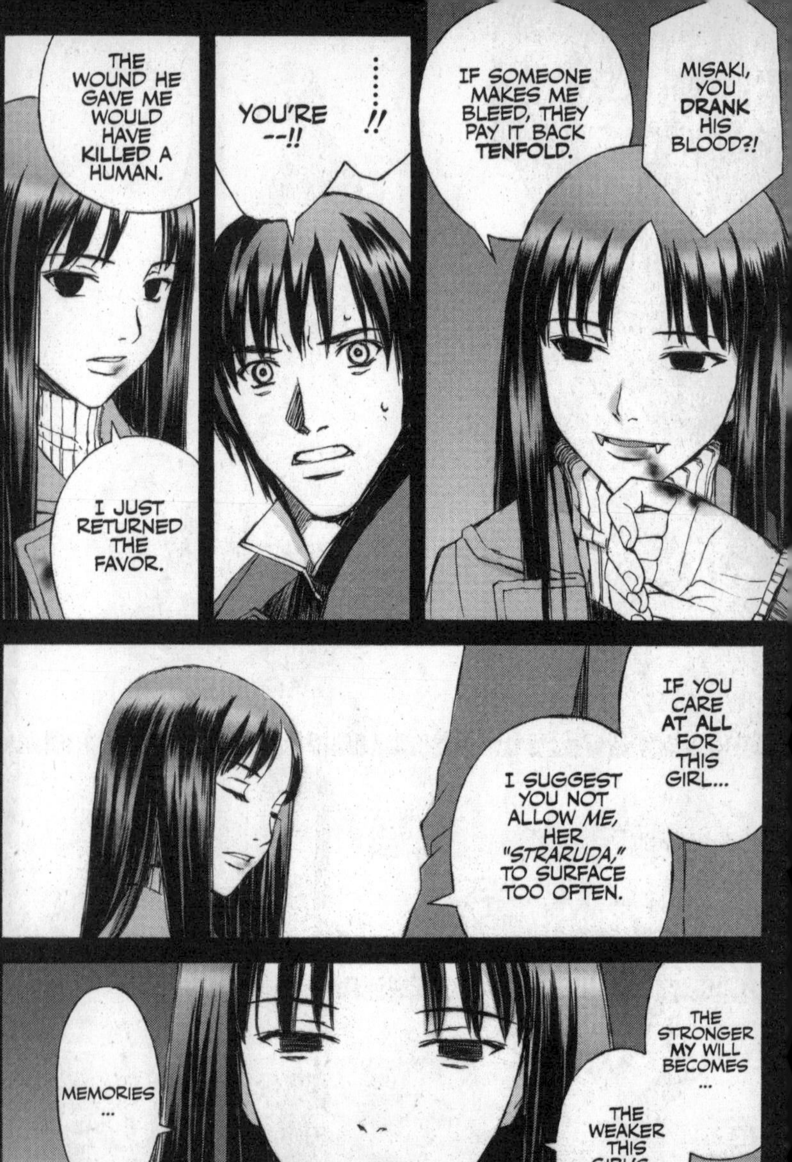
MISAKI, YOU DRANK HIS BLOOD?!
IF SOMEONE MAKES ME BLEED, THEY PAY IT BACK TENFOLD.
......!!
YOU'RE --!!
THE WOUND HE GAVE ME WOULD HAVE KILLED A HUMAN.
I JUST RETURNED THE FAVOR.
IF YOU CARE AT ALL FOR THIS GIRL...
I SUGGEST YOU NOT ALLOW ME, HER "STRARUDA," TO SURFACE TOO OFTEN.
THE STRONGER MY WILL BECOMES ...
THE WEAKER THIS GIRL'S...
MEMORIES ...

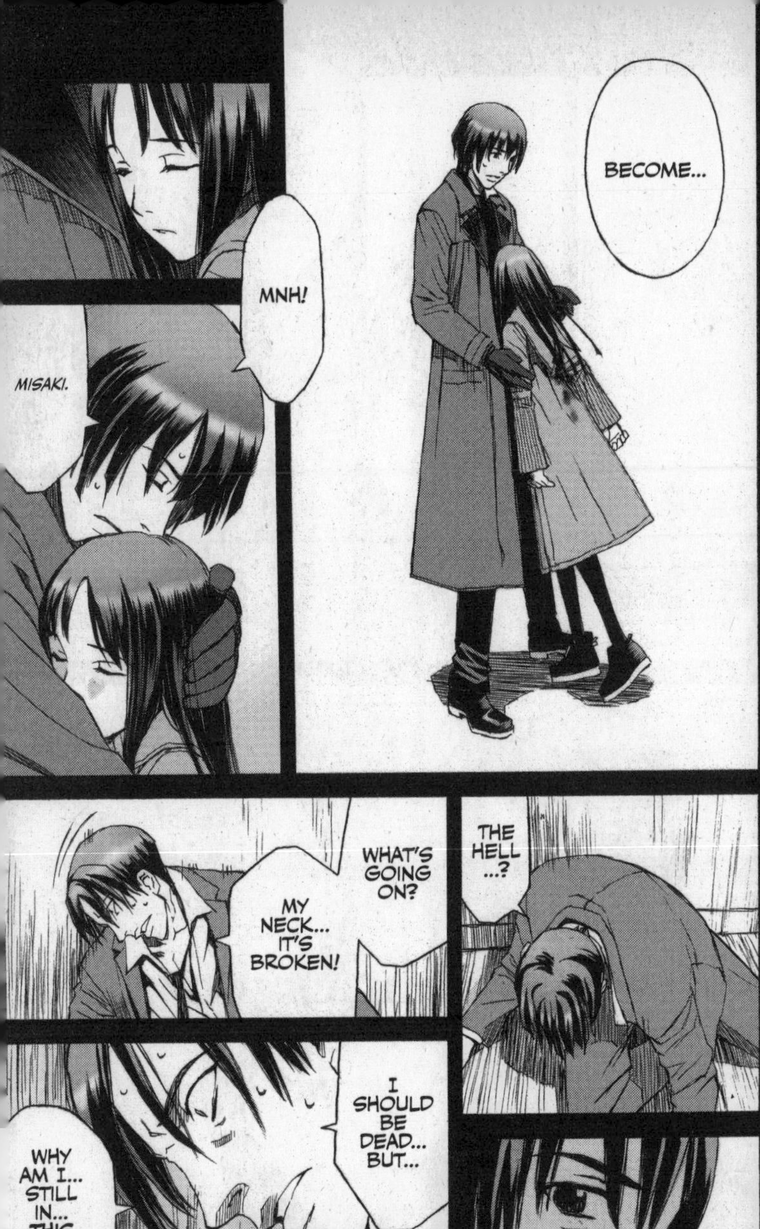
BECOME...
MNH!
MISAKI.
THE HELL ...?
WHAT'S GOING ON?
MY NECK... IT'S BROKEN!
I SHOULD BE DEAD... BUT...
WHY AM I... STILL IN... THIS BODY?!

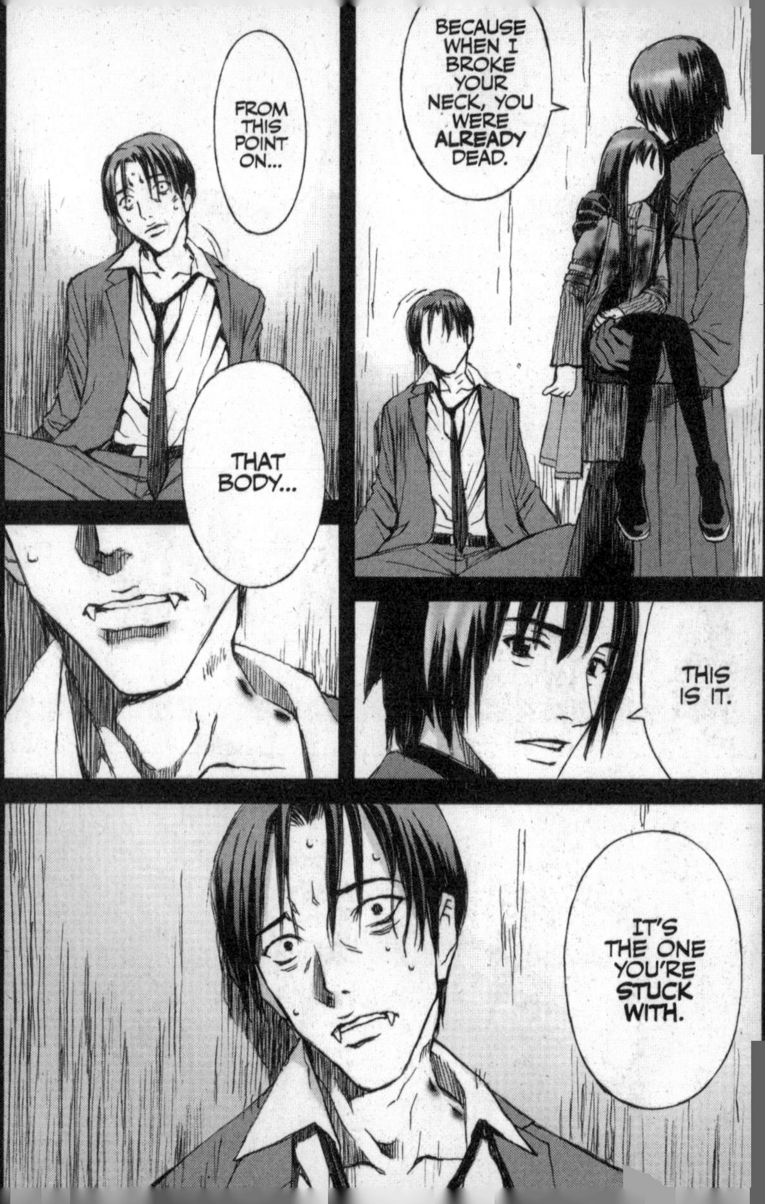
BECAUSE WHEN I BROKE YOUR NECK, YOU WERE ALREADY DEAD.
FROM THIS POINT ON...
THAT BODY...
THIS IS IT.
IT'S THE ONE YOU'RE STUCK WITH.

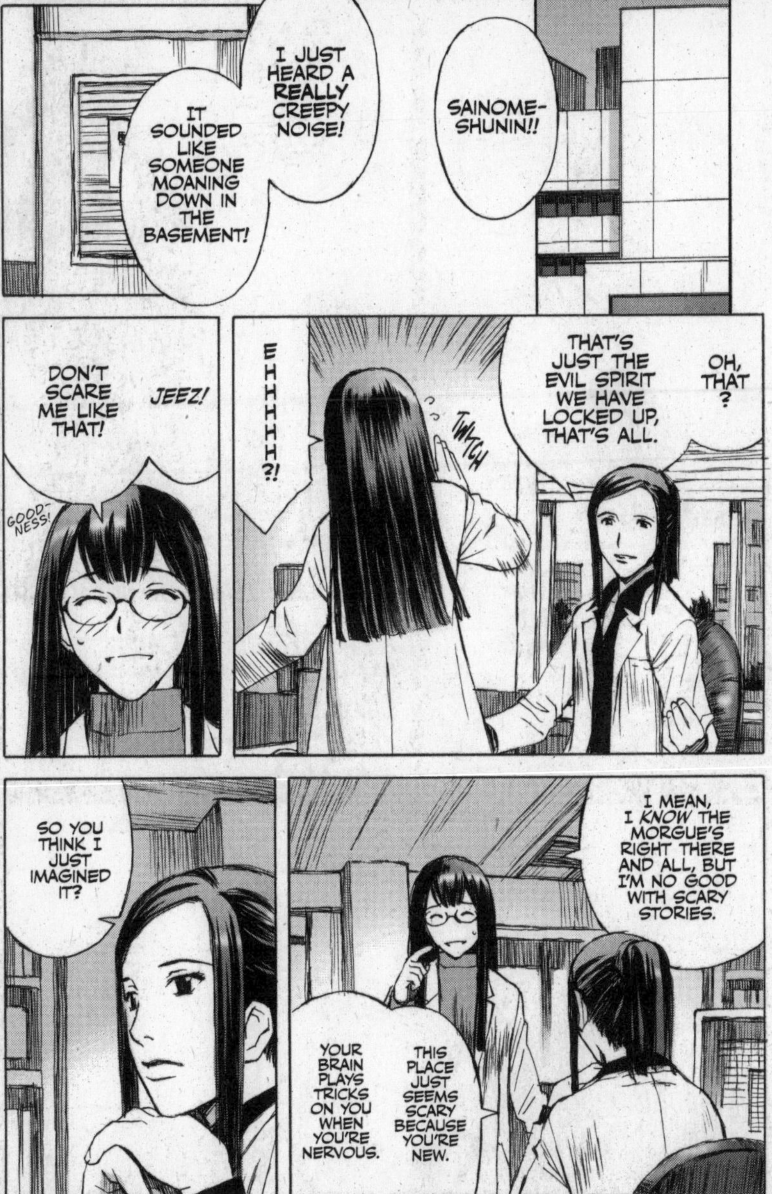
SAINOME-SHUNIN!!
I JUST HEARD A REALLY CREEPY NOISE!
IT SOUNDED LIKE SOMEONE MOANING DOWN IN THE BASEMENT!
OH, THAT?
THAT'S JUST THE EVIL SPIRIT WE HAVE LOCKED UP, THAT'S ALL.
TWITCH
EHHHHHH?!
JEEZ!
DON'T SCARE ME LIKE THAT!
GOOD-NESS!
I MEAN, I *KNOW* THE MORGUE'S RIGHT THERE AND ALL, BUT I'M NO GOOD WITH SCARY STORIES.
THIS PLACE JUST SEEMS SCARY BECAUSE YOU'RE NEW.
YOUR BRAIN PLAYS TRICKS ON YOU WHEN YOU'RE NERVOUS.
SO YOU THINK I JUST IMAGINED IT?

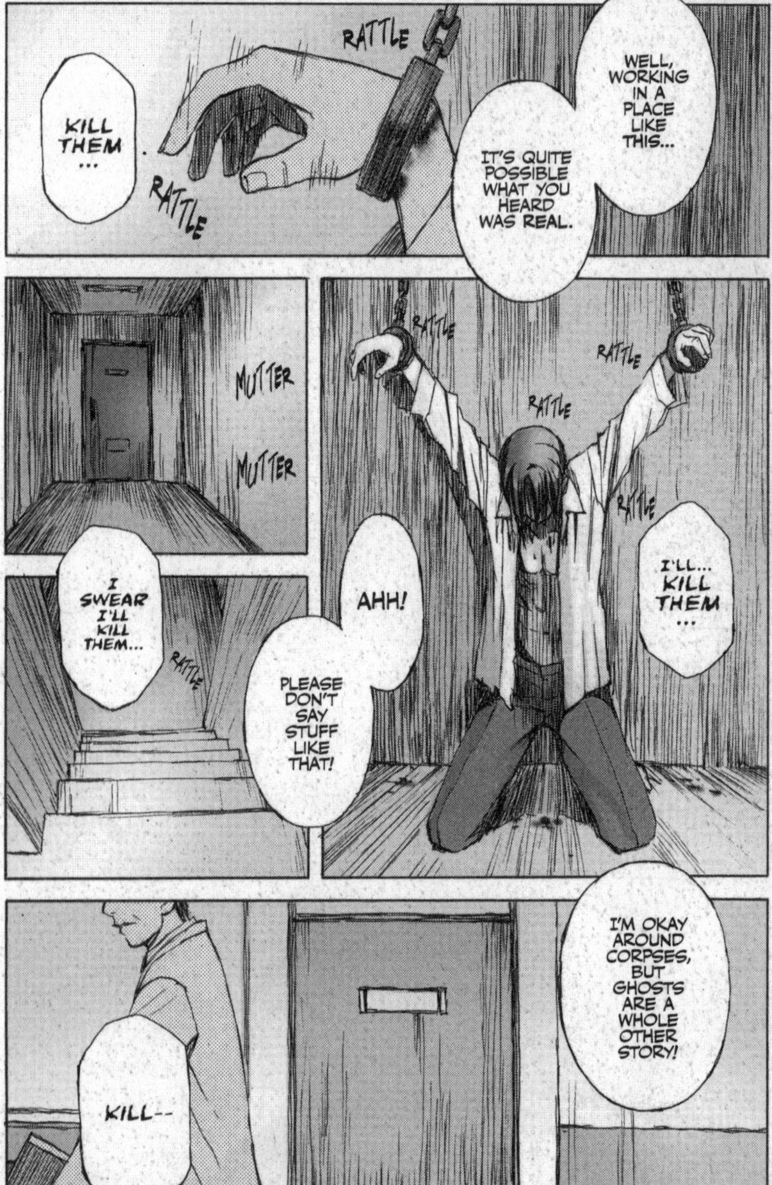
WELL, WORKING IN A PLACE LIKE THIS...
IT'S QUITE POSSIBLE WHAT YOU HEARD WAS REAL.
RATTLE
KILL THEM...
RATTLE
RATTLE
RATTLE
RATTLE
RATTLE
I'LL... KILL THEM...
AHH!
PLEASE DON'T SAY STUFF LIKE THAT!
MUTTER
MUTTER
I SWEAR I'LL KILL THEM...
RATTLE
I'M OKAY AROUND CORPSES, BUT GHOSTS ARE A WHOLE OTHER STORY!
KILL--

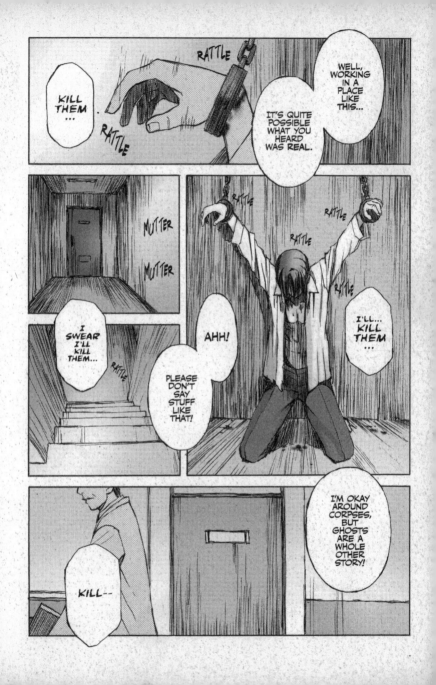

Episode 6
CLASP YOUR HAND
Until You Wake

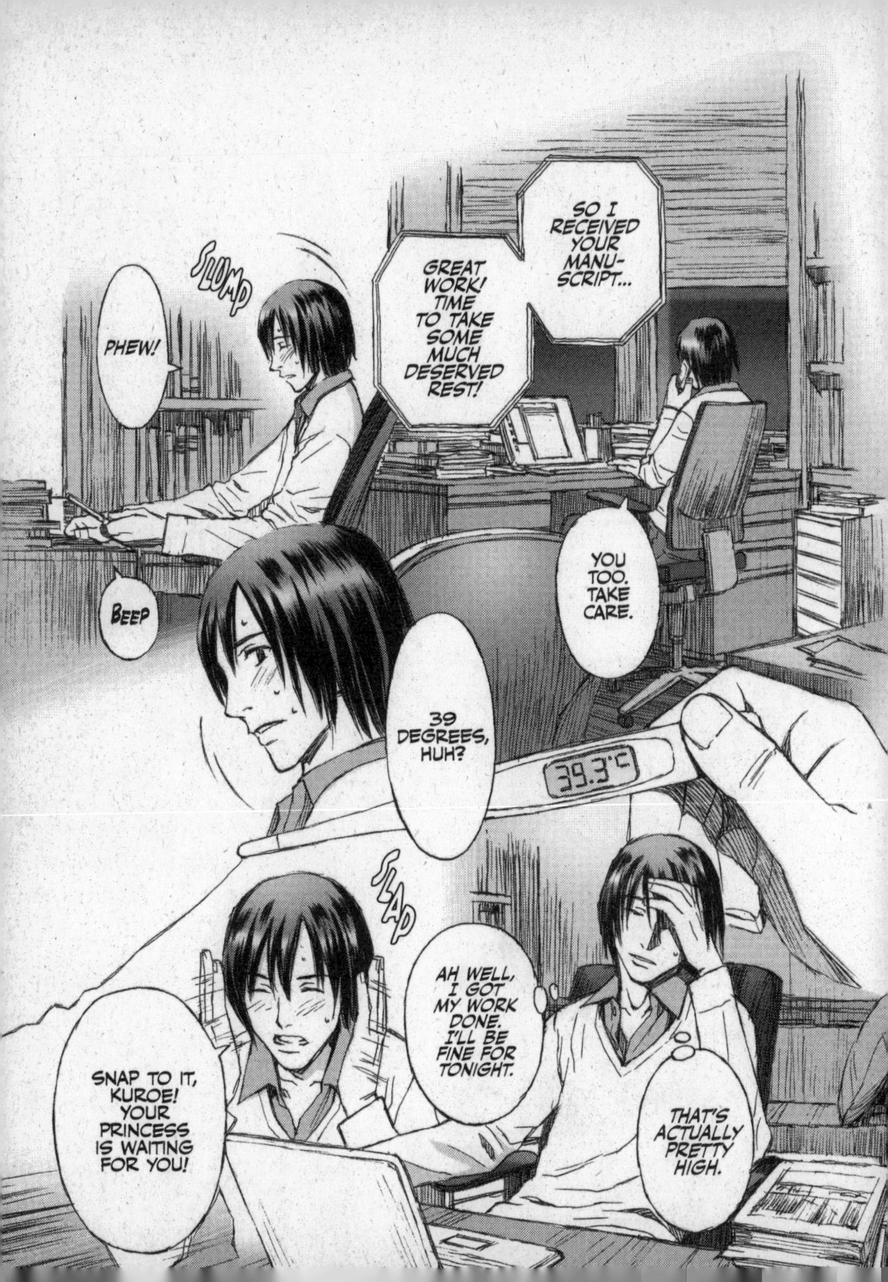
SO I RECEIVED YOUR MANU-SCRIPT...
GREAT WORK! TIME TO TAKE SOME MUCH DESERVED REST!
YOU TOO. TAKE CARE.
SLUMP
PHEW!
BEEP
39 DEGREES, HUH?
39.3°C
THAT'S ACTUALLY PRETTY HIGH.
AH WELL, I GOT MY WORK DONE. I'LL BE FINE FOR TONIGHT.
SLAP
SNAP TO IT, KUROE! YOUR PRINCESS IS WAITING FOR YOU!

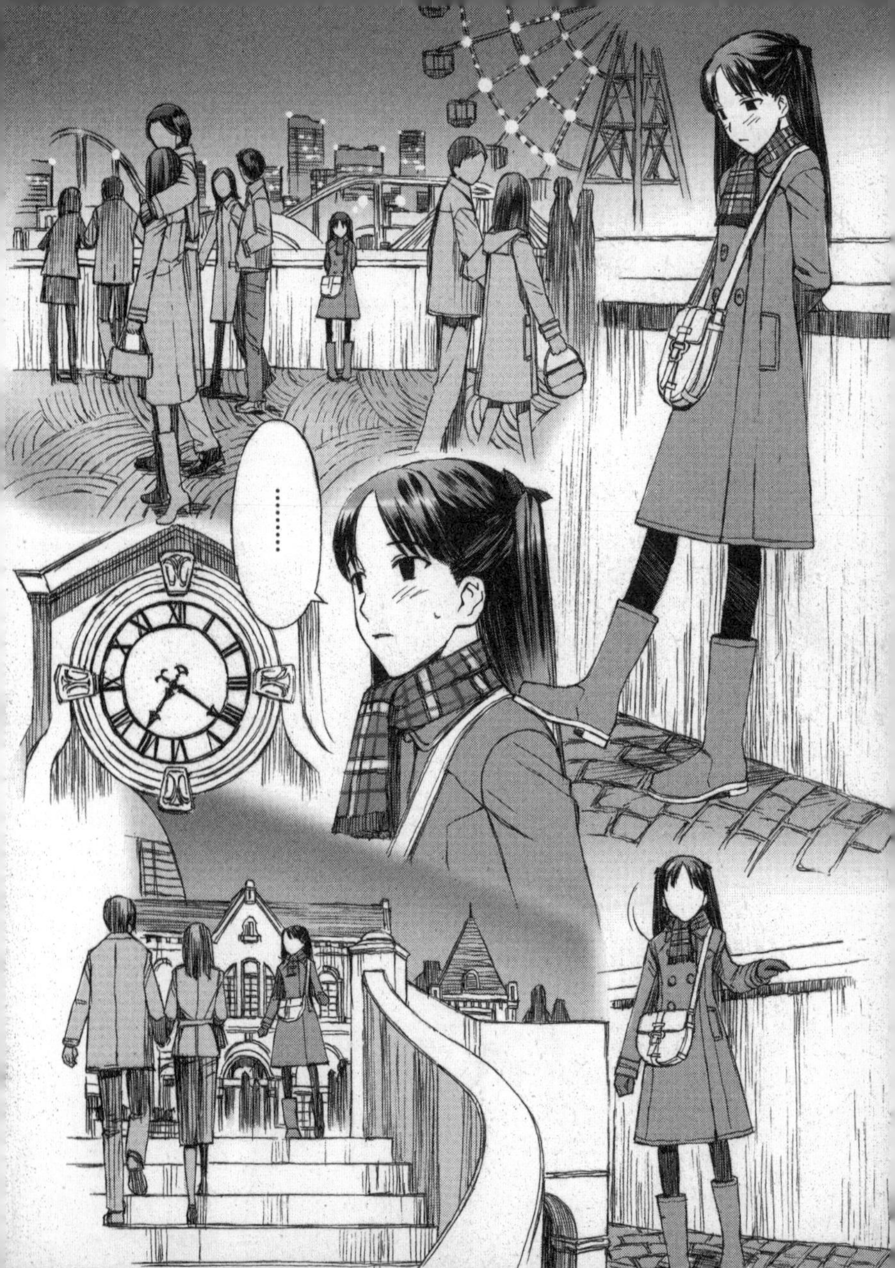
……

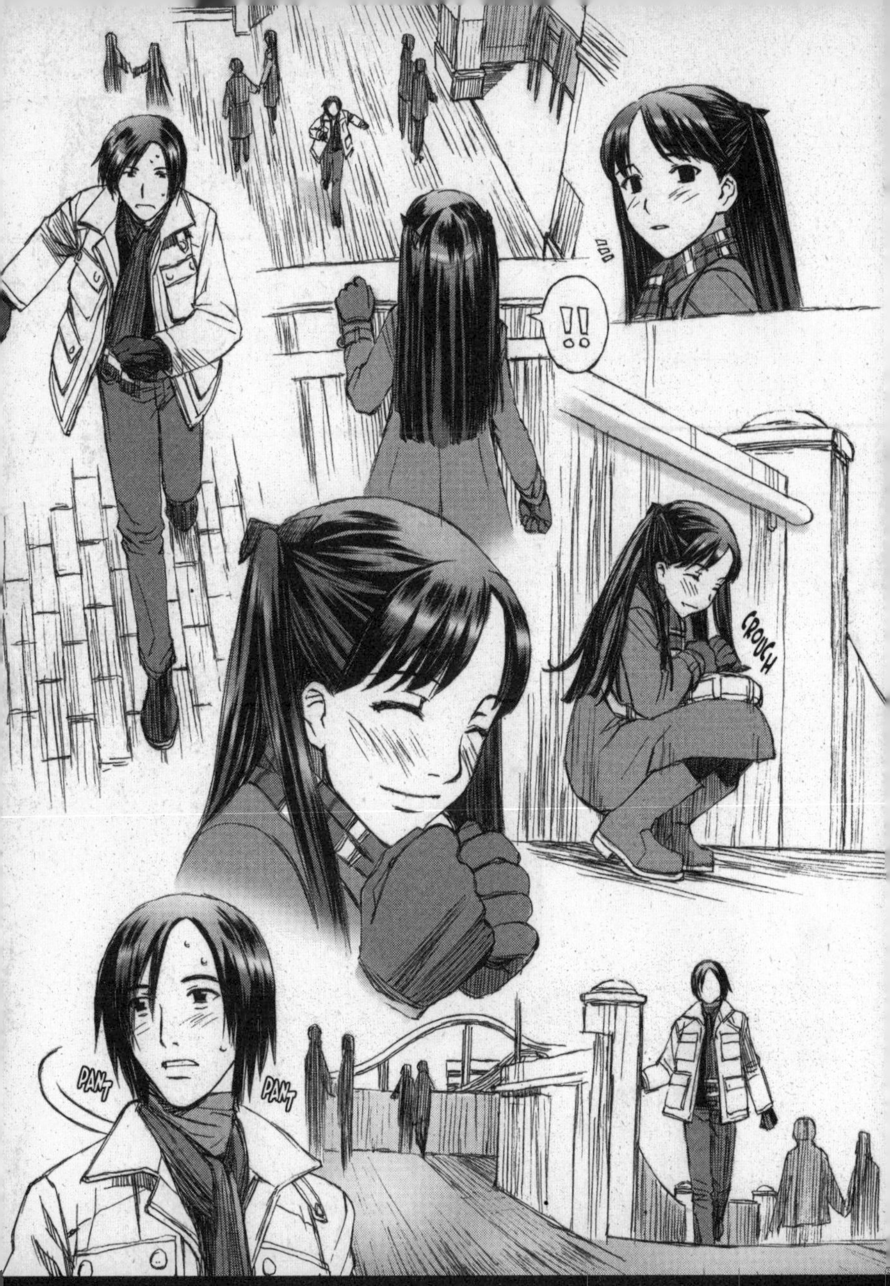
!!
CROUCH
PANT
PANT

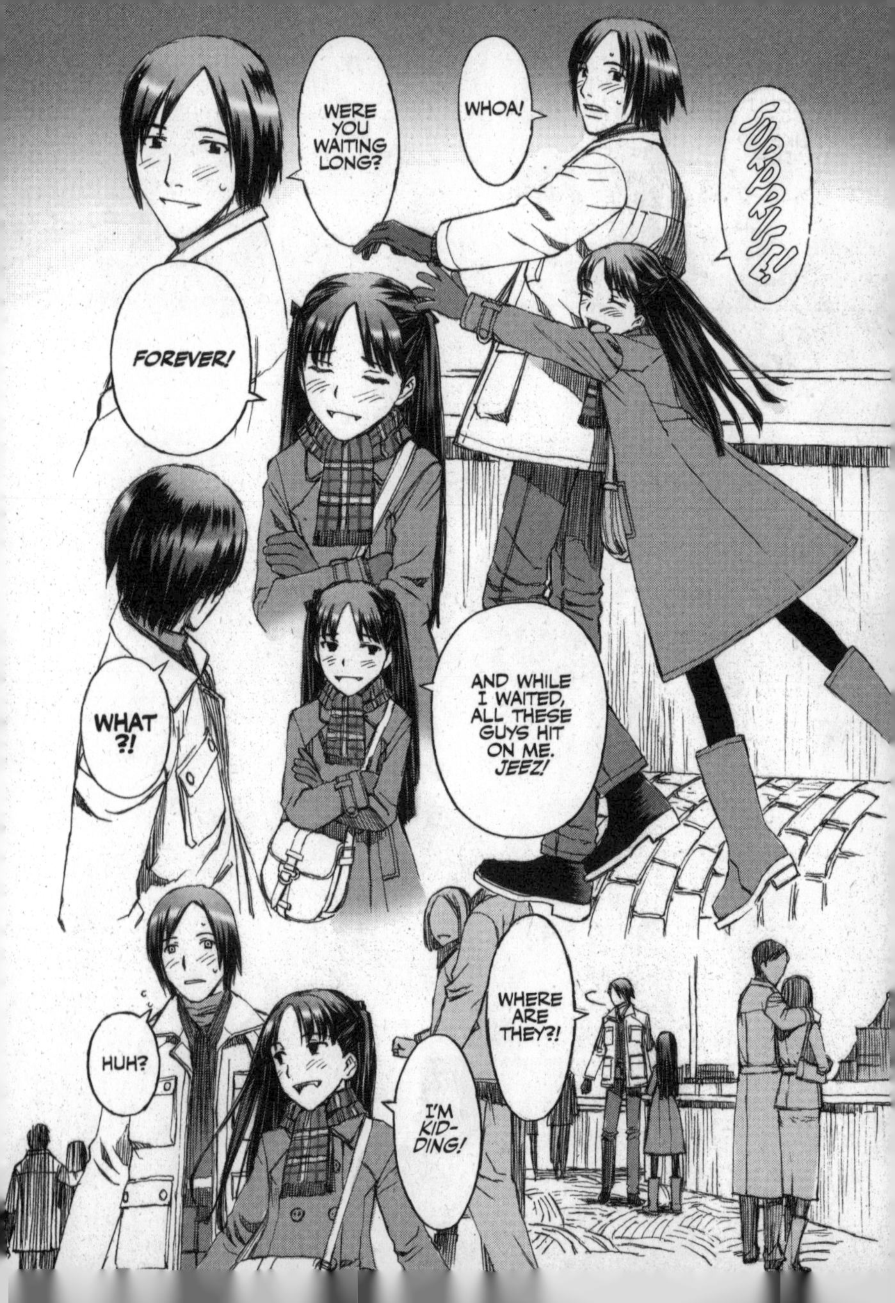
SURPRISE!
WHOA!
WERE YOU WAITING LONG?
FOREVER!
AND WHILE I WAITED, ALL THESE GUYS HIT ON ME. JEEZ!
WHAT?!
WHERE ARE THEY?!
I'M KID-DING!
HUH?

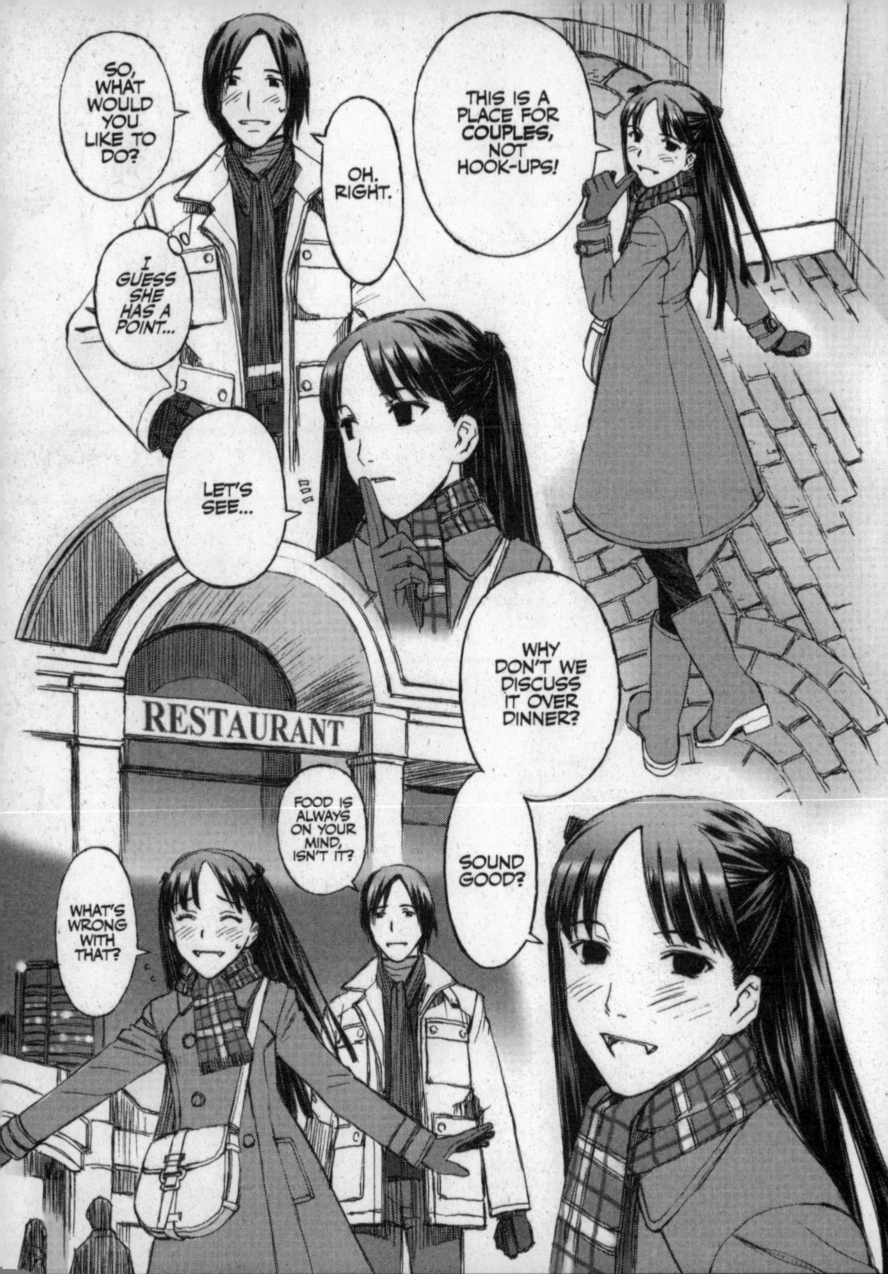
THIS IS A PLACE FOR COUPLES, NOT HOOK-UPS!
OH. RIGHT.
I GUESS SHE HAS A POINT...
SO, WHAT WOULD YOU LIKE TO DO?
LET'S SEE...
WHY DON'T WE DISCUSS IT OVER DINNER?
RESTAURANT
SOUND GOOD?
FOOD IS ALWAYS ON YOUR MIND, ISN'T IT?
WHAT'S WRONG WITH THAT?

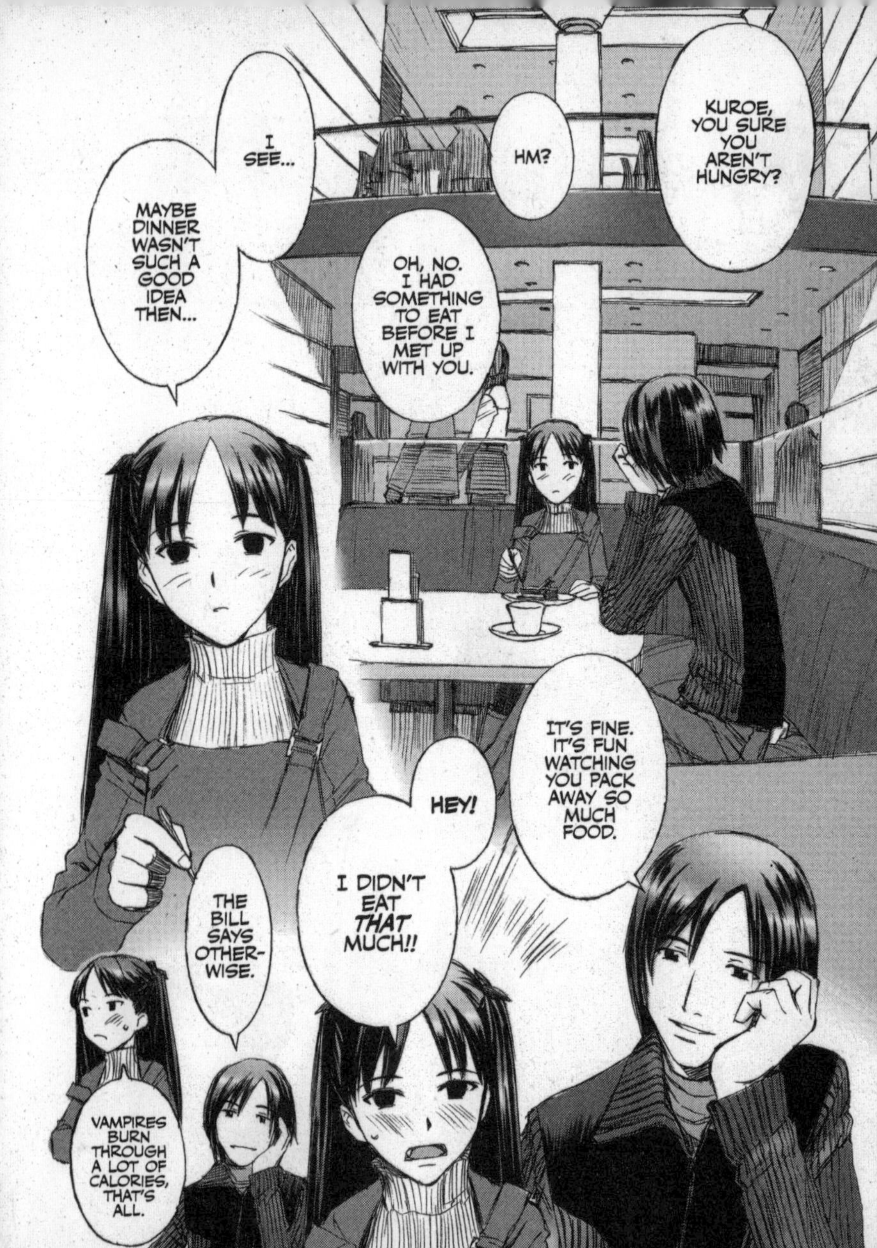
KUROE, YOU SURE YOU AREN'T HUNGRY?
HM?
OH, NO. I HAD SOMETHING TO EAT BEFORE I MET UP WITH YOU.
I SEE...
MAYBE DINNER WASN'T SUCH A GOOD IDEA THEN...
IT'S FINE. IT'S FUN WATCHING YOU PACK AWAY SO MUCH FOOD.
HEY!
I DIDN'T EAT *THAT* MUCH!!
THE BILL SAYS OTHER-WISE.
VAMPIRES BURN THROUGH A LOT OF CALORIES, THAT'S ALL.

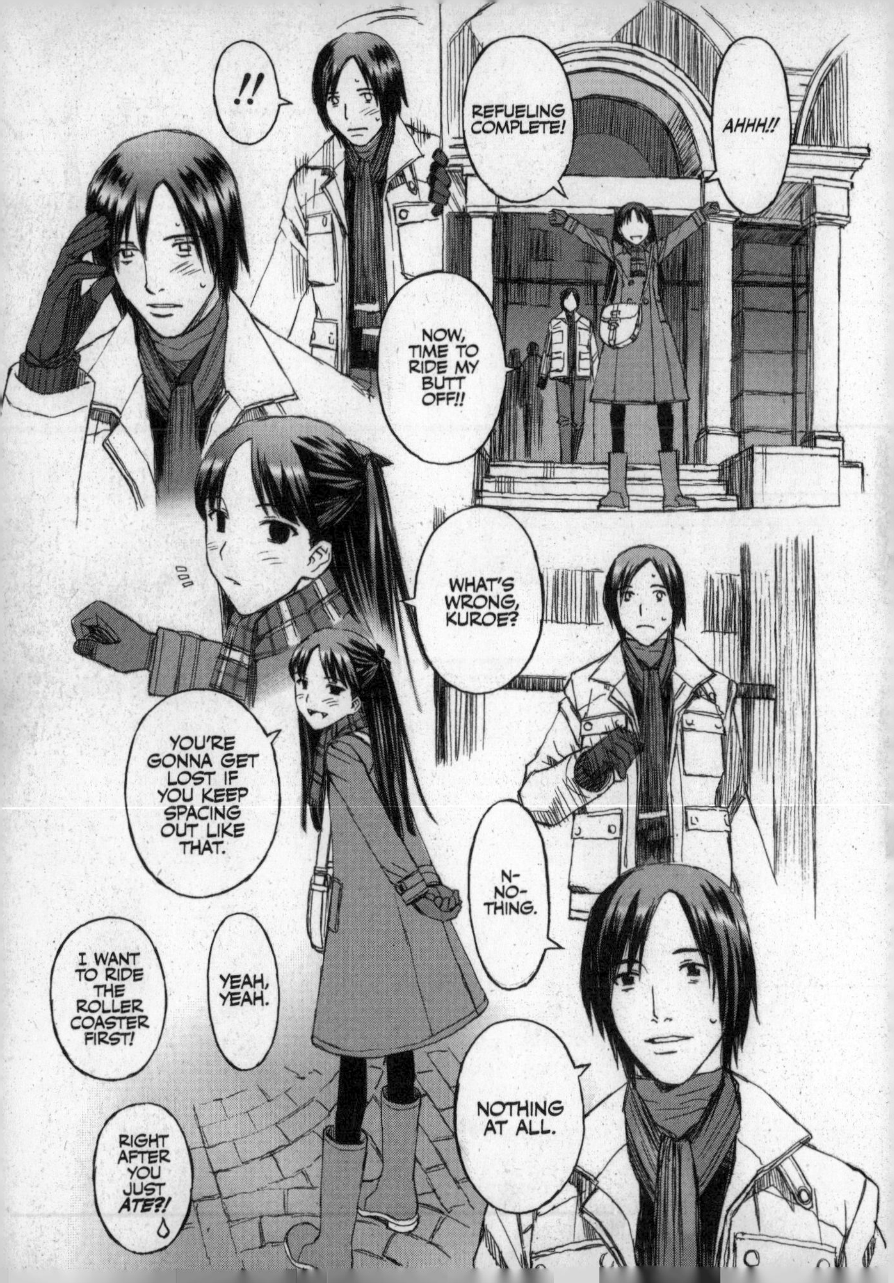
AHHH!!
REFUELING COMPLETE!
NOW, TIME TO RIDE MY BUTT OFF!!
!!
WHAT'S WRONG, KUROE?
N-NO-THING.
NOTHING AT ALL.
YOU'RE GONNA GET LOST IF YOU KEEP SPACING OUT LIKE THAT.
YEAH, YEAH.
I WANT TO RIDE THE ROLLER COASTER FIRST!
RIGHT AFTER YOU JUST ATE?!

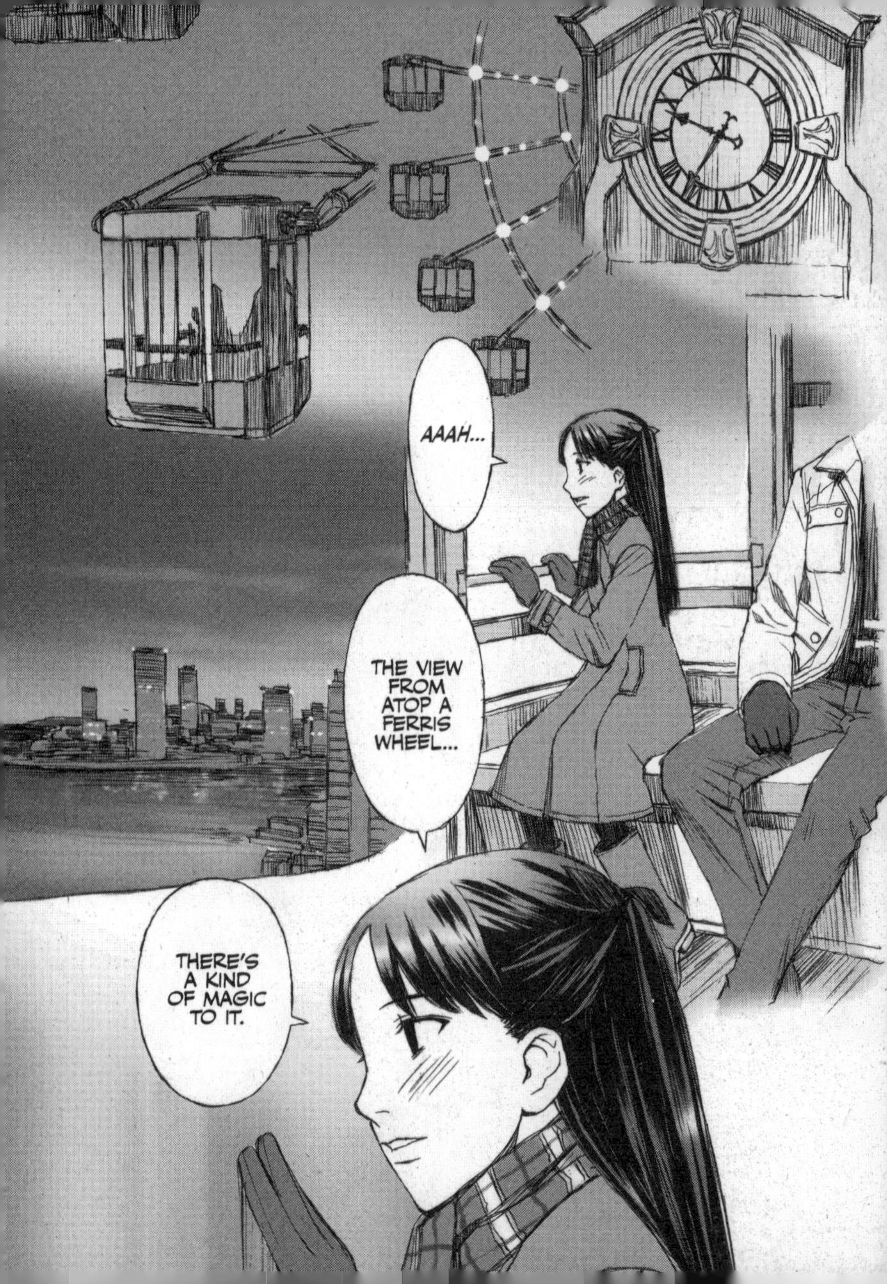
AAAH...
THE VIEW FROM ATOP A FERRIS WHEEL...
THERE'S A KIND OF MAGIC TO IT.

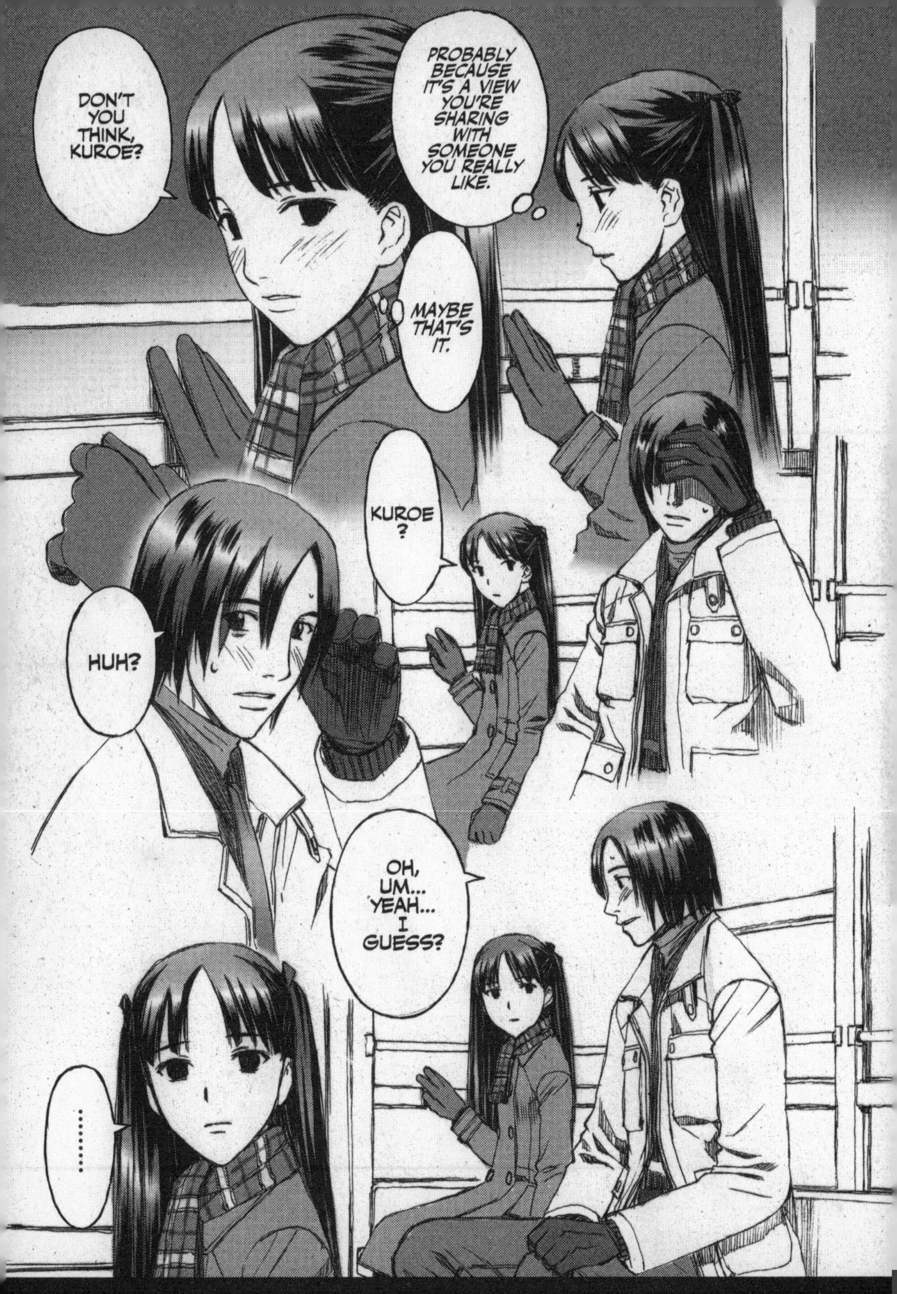
PROBABLY BECAUSE IT'S A VIEW YOU'RE SHARING WITH SOMEONE YOU REALLY LIKE.
DON'T YOU THINK, KUROE?
MAYBE THAT'S IT.
KUROE?
HUH?
OH, UM... YEAH... I GUESS?
....

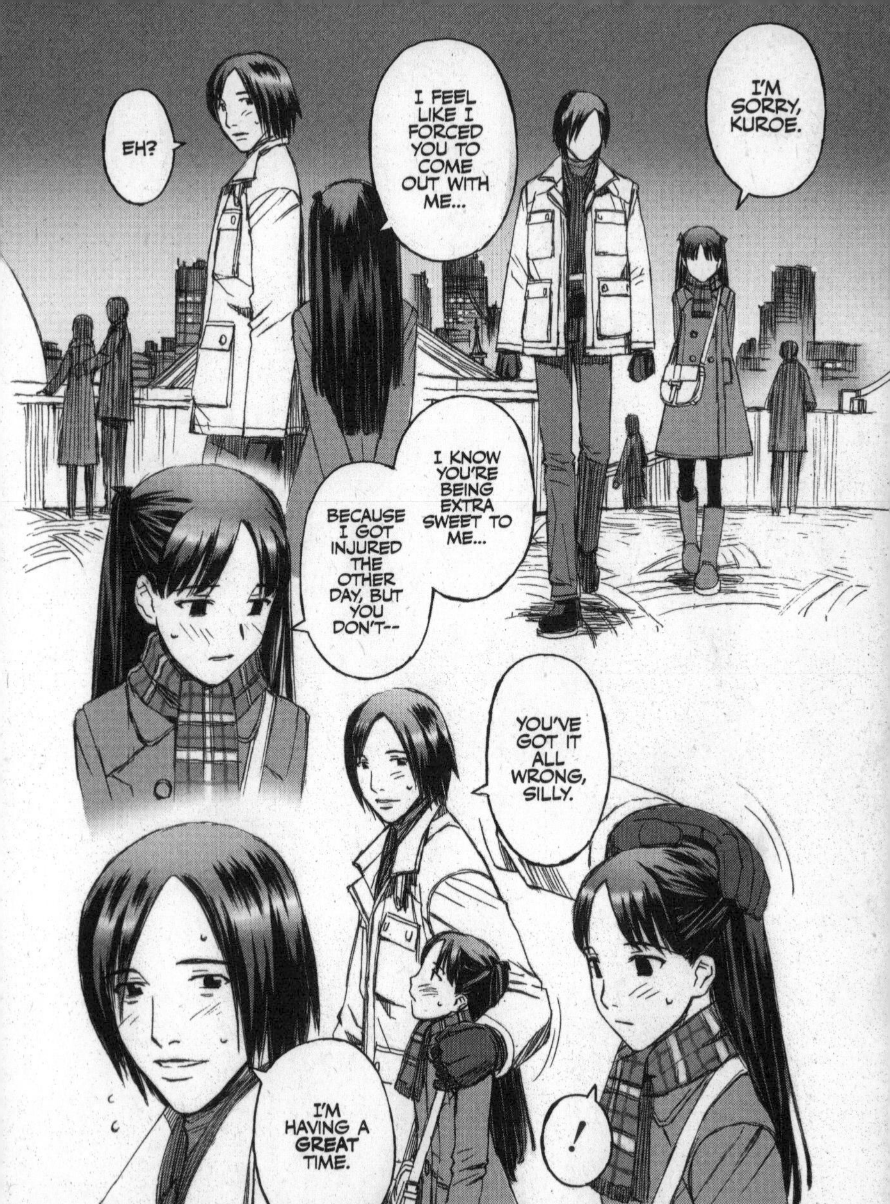
I'M SORRY, KUROE.
I FEEL LIKE I FORCED YOU TO COME OUT WITH ME...
EH?
I KNOW YOU'RE BEING EXTRA SWEET TO ME...
BECAUSE I GOT INJURED THE OTHER DAY, BUT YOU DON'T--
YOU'VE GOT IT ALL WRONG, SILLY.
I'M HAVING A GREAT TIME.
!

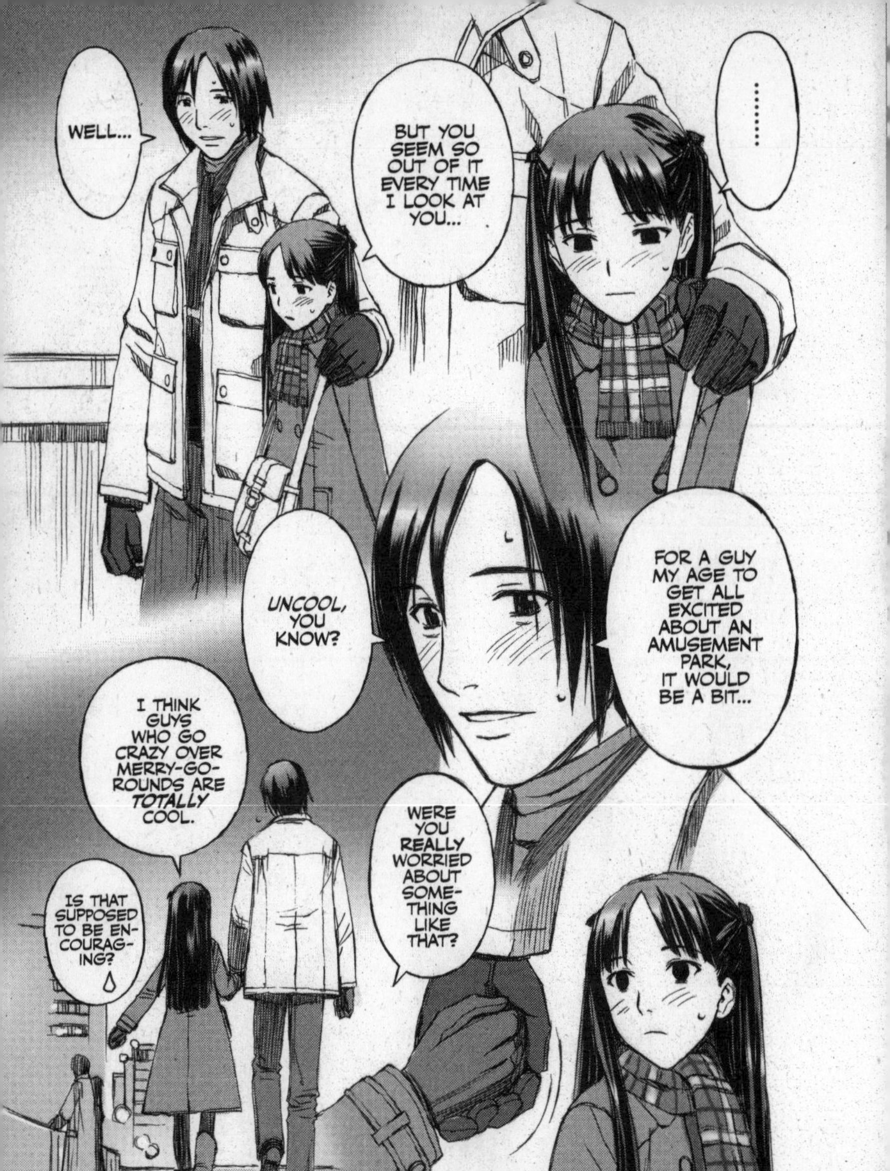
......
BUT YOU SEEM SO OUT OF IT EVERY TIME I LOOK AT YOU...
WELL...
FOR A GUY MY AGE TO GET ALL EXCITED ABOUT AN AMUSEMENT PARK, IT WOULD BE A BIT...
UNCOOL, YOU KNOW?
WERE YOU REALLY WORRIED ABOUT SOME-THING LIKE THAT?
I THINK GUYS WHO GO CRAZY OVER MERRY-GO-ROUNDS ARE *TOTALLY* COOL.
IS THAT SUPPOSED TO BE EN-COURAG-ING?

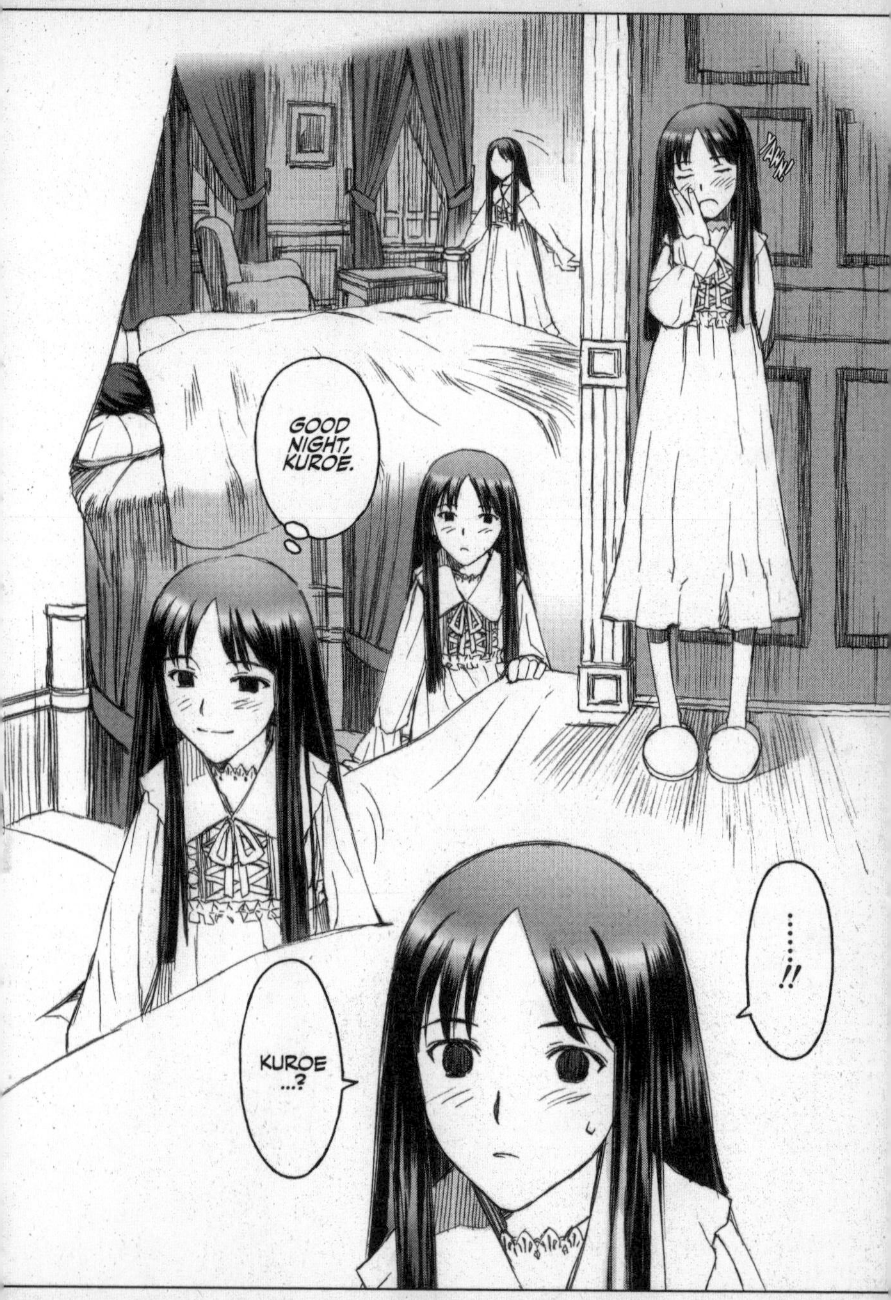
YAWN!
GOOD NIGHT, KUROE.
......!!
KUROE ...?

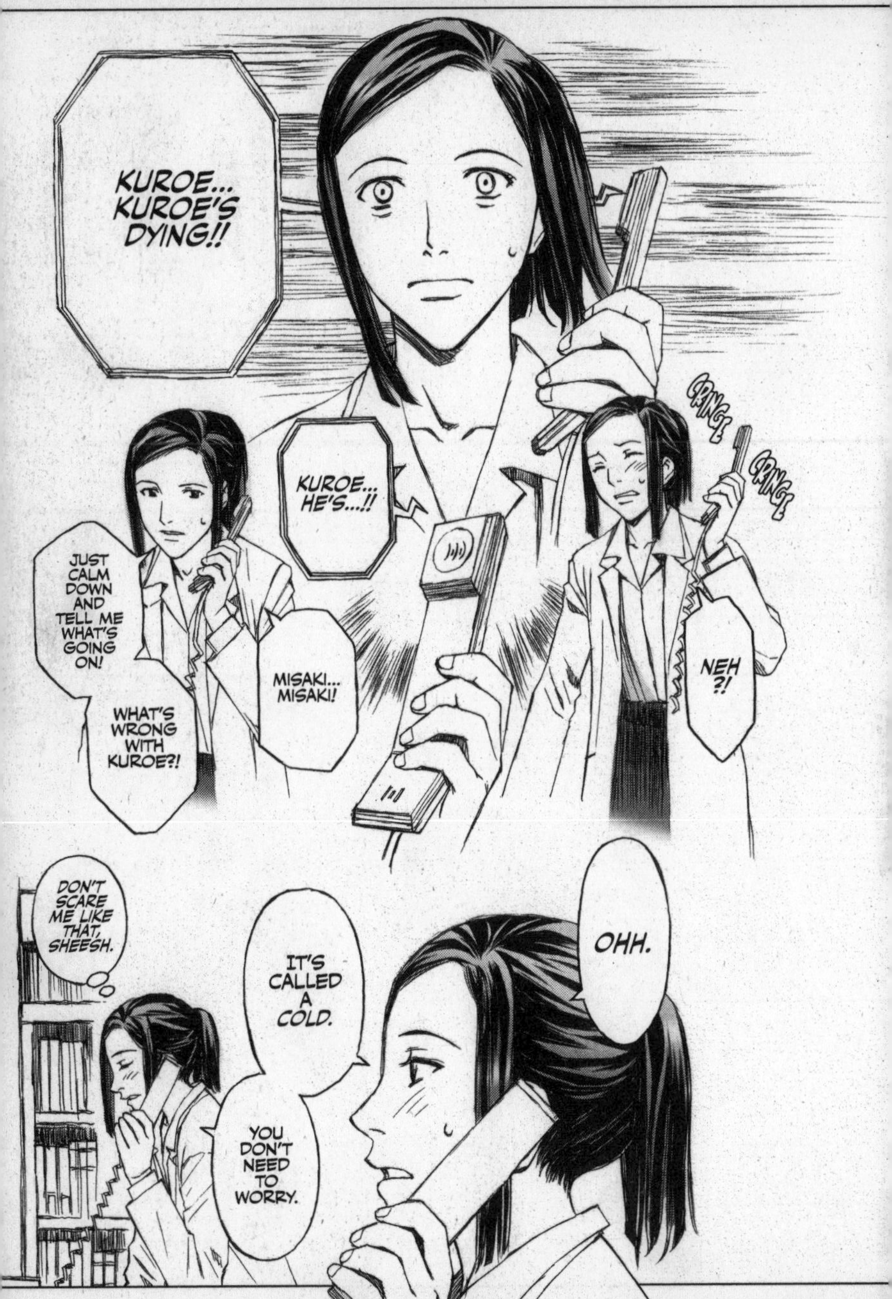
KUROE... KUROE'S DYING!!
CRINGE
CRINGE
NEH?!
KUROE... HE'S...!!
MISAKI... MISAKI!
JUST CALM DOWN AND TELL ME WHAT'S GOING ON!
WHAT'S WRONG WITH KUROE?!
OHH.
IT'S CALLED A COLD.
YOU DON'T NEED TO WORRY.
DON'T SCARE ME LIKE THAT, SHEESH.

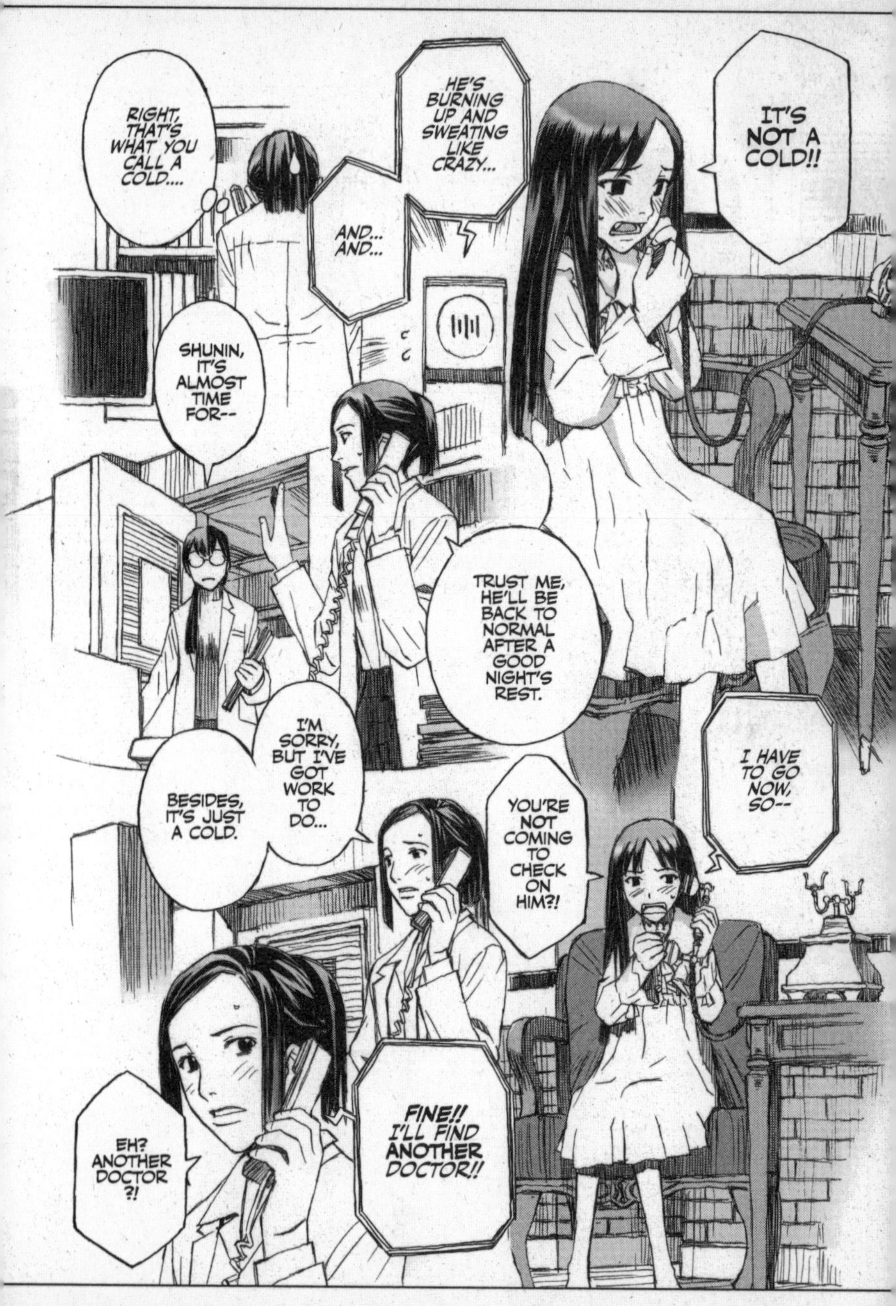
IT'S NOT A COLD!!
HE'S BURNING UP AND SWEATING LIKE CRAZY...
AND... AND...
RIGHT, THAT'S WHAT YOU CALL A COLD....
SHUNIN, IT'S ALMOST TIME FOR--
TRUST ME, HE'LL BE BACK TO NORMAL AFTER A GOOD NIGHT'S REST.
I HAVE TO GO NOW, SO--
YOU'RE NOT COMING TO CHECK ON HIM?!
I'M SORRY, BUT I'VE GOT WORK TO DO...
BESIDES, IT'S JUST A COLD.
FINE!! I'LL FIND ANOTHER DOCTOR!!
EH? ANOTHER DOCTOR?!

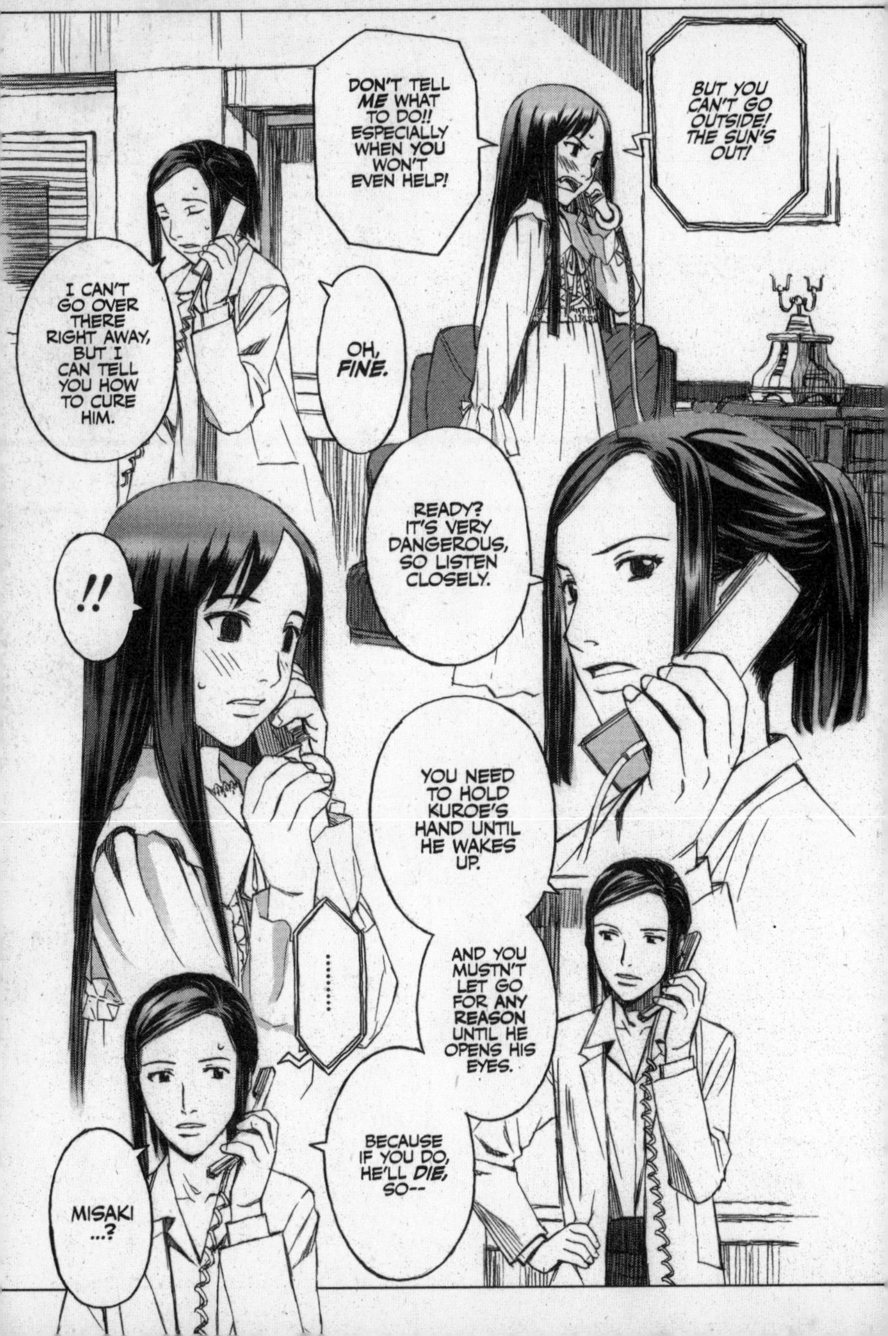
BUT YOU CAN'T GO OUTSIDE! THE SUN'S OUT!
DON'T TELL *ME* WHAT TO DO!! ESPECIALLY WHEN YOU WON'T EVEN HELP!
OH, *FINE.*
I CAN'T GO OVER THERE RIGHT AWAY, BUT I CAN TELL YOU HOW TO CURE HIM.
READY? IT'S VERY DANGEROUS, SO LISTEN CLOSELY.
YOU NEED TO HOLD KUROE'S HAND UNTIL HE WAKES UP.
!!
AND YOU MUSTN'T LET GO FOR ANY REASON UNTIL HE OPENS HIS EYES.
....
BECAUSE IF YOU DO, HE'LL *DIE,* SO--
MISAKI ...?

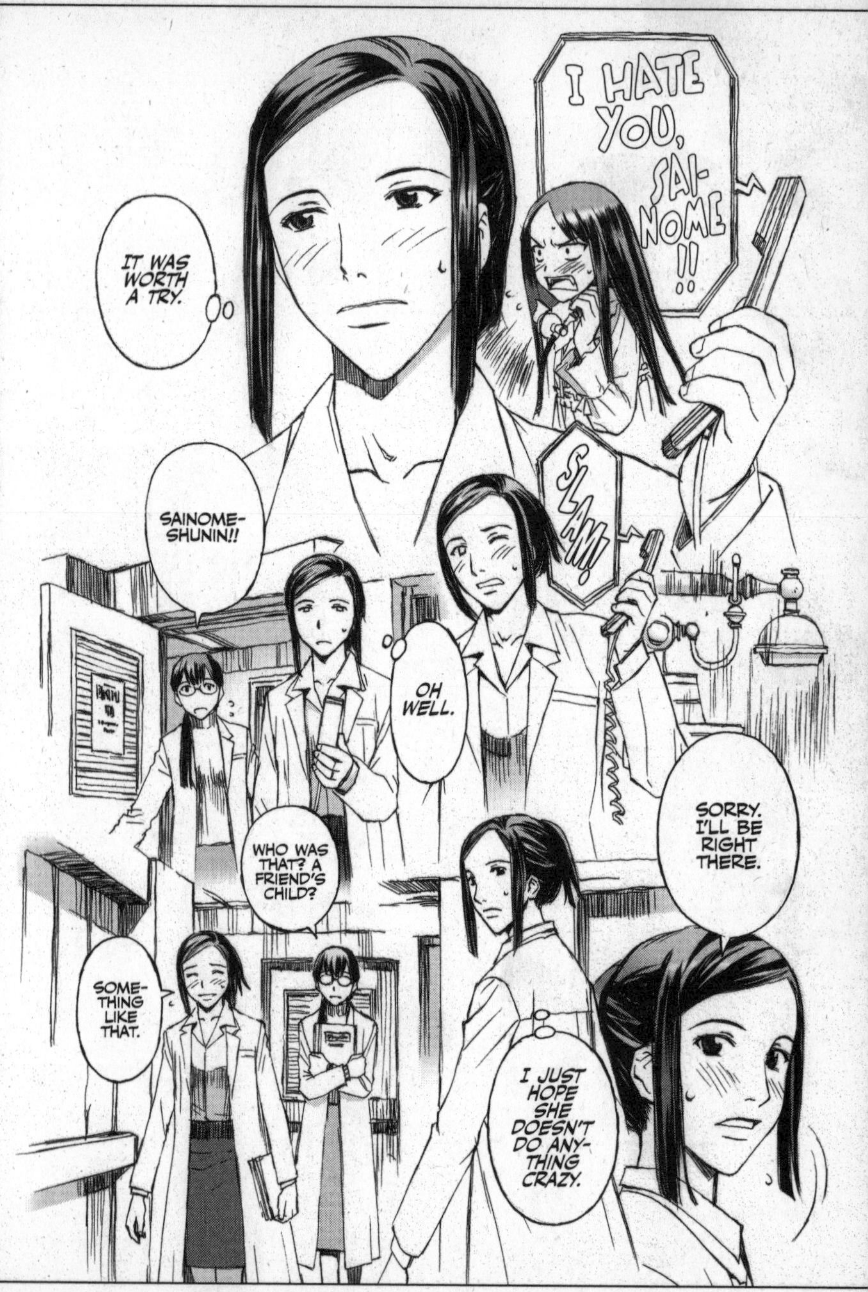
I HATE YOU, SAI-NOME!!
IT WAS WORTH A TRY.
SLAM!
OH WELL.
SAINOME-SHUNIN!!
SORRY. I'LL BE RIGHT THERE.
WHO WAS THAT? A FRIEND'S CHILD?
SOME-THING LIKE THAT.
I JUST HOPE SHE DOESN'T DO ANY-THING CRAZY.

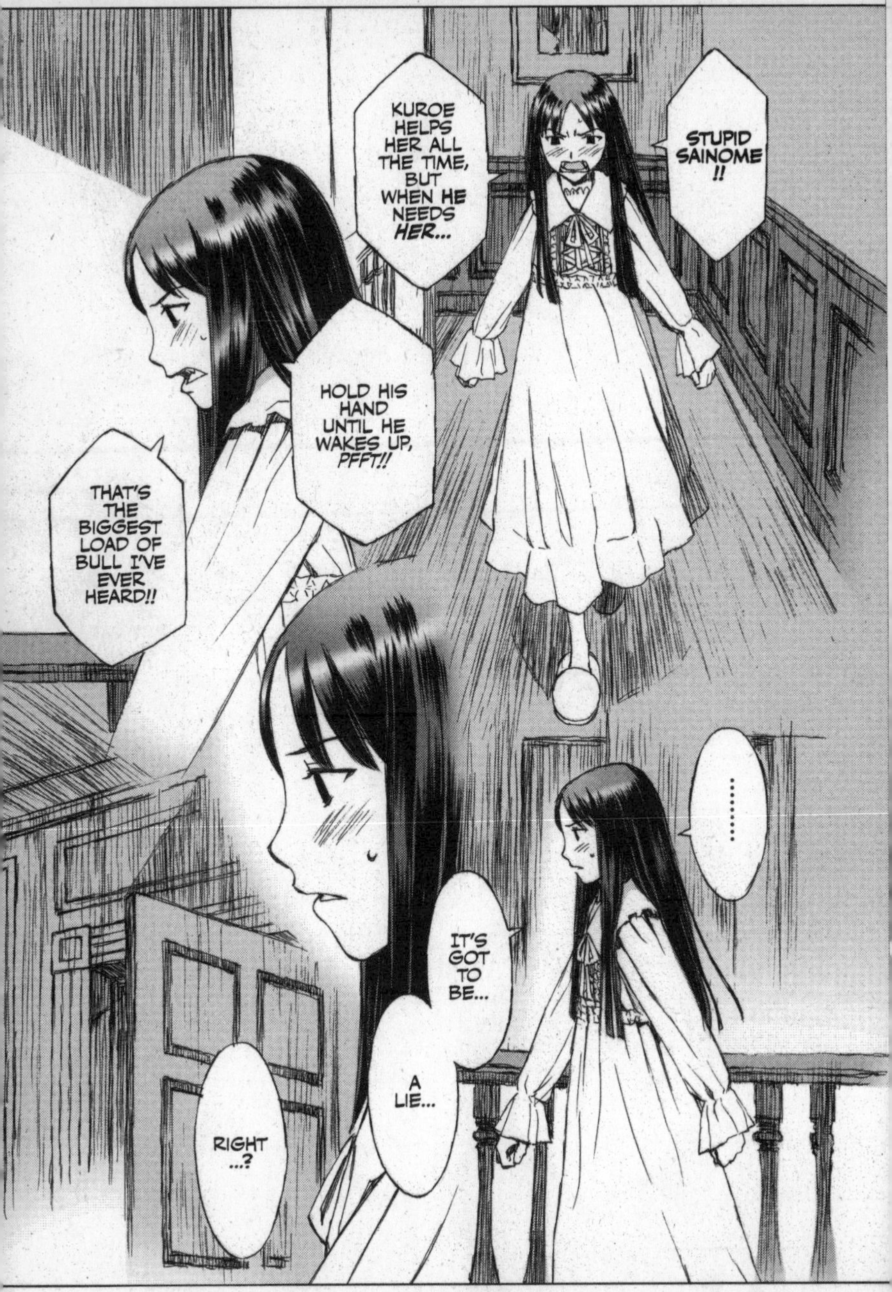
STUPID SAINOME!!
KUROE HELPS HER ALL THE TIME, BUT WHEN HE NEEDS *HER*...
HOLD HIS HAND UNTIL HE WAKES UP, *PFFT!!*
THAT'S THE BIGGEST LOAD OF BULL I'VE EVER HEARD!!
......
IT'S GOT TO BE...
A LIE...
RIGHT...?

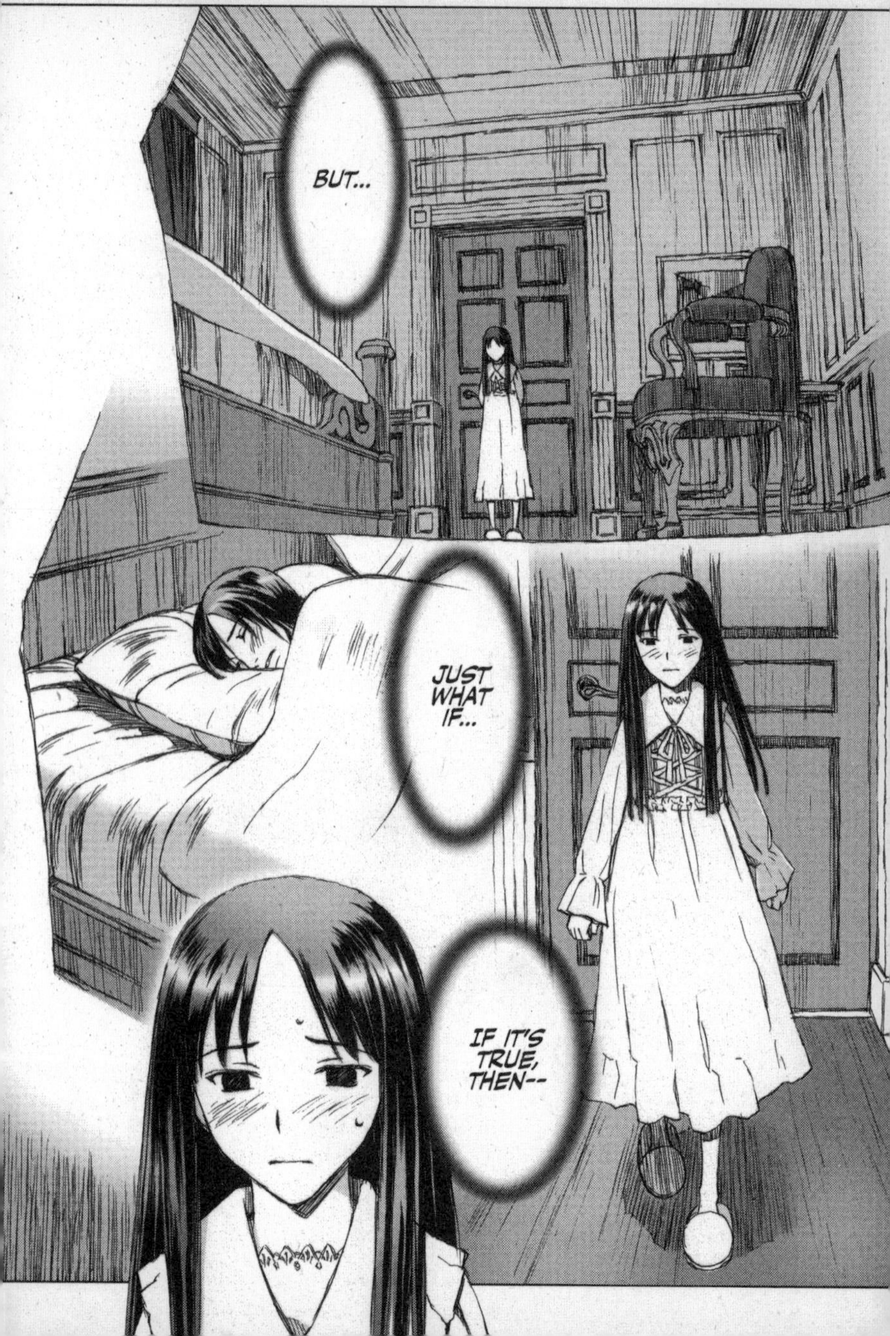
BUT...
JUST WHAT IF...
IF IT'S TRUE, THEN--

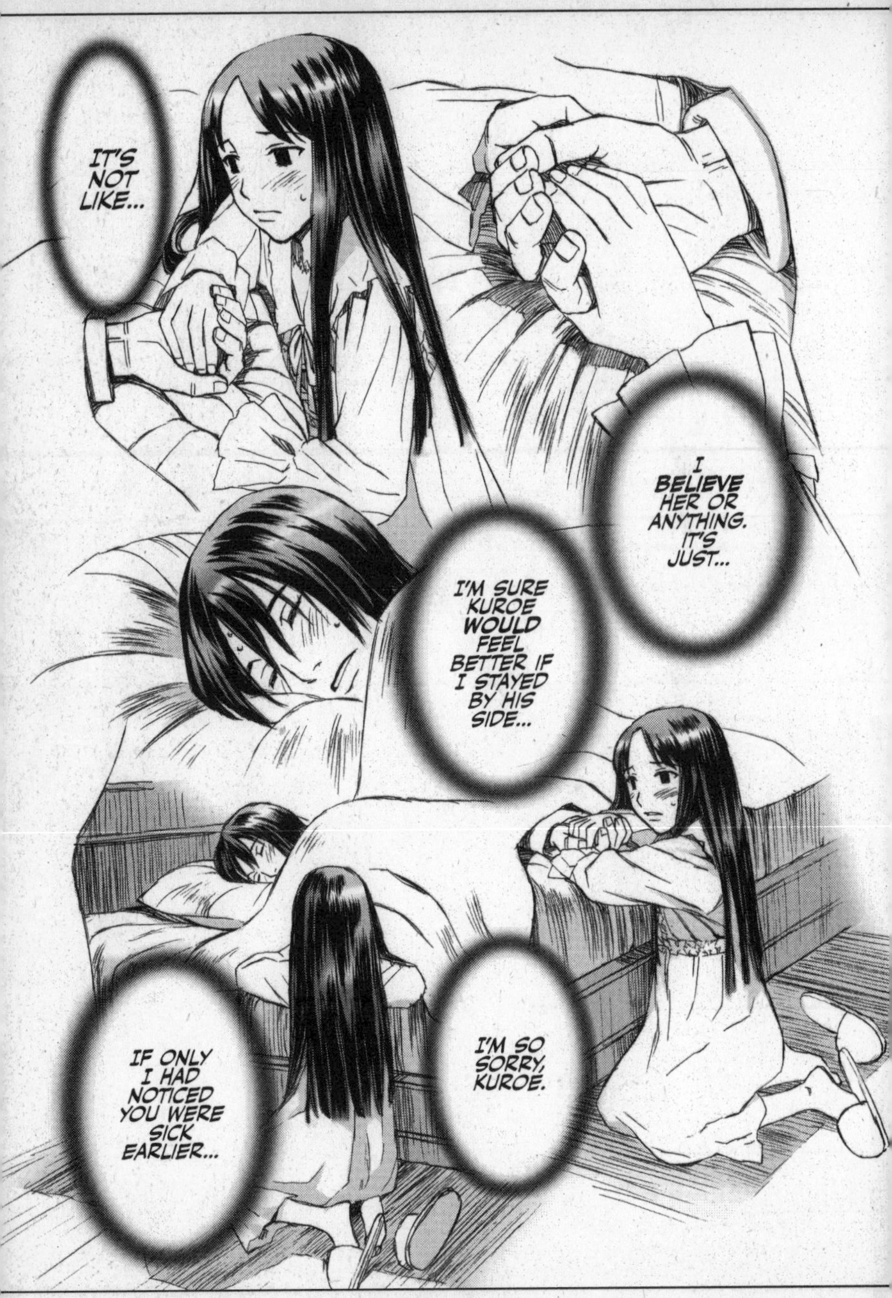
IT'S NOT LIKE...
I BELIEVE HER OR ANYTHING. IT'S JUST...
I'M SURE KUROE WOULD FEEL BETTER IF I STAYED BY HIS SIDE...
I'M SO SORRY, KUROE.
IF ONLY I HAD NOTICED YOU WERE SICK EARLIER...

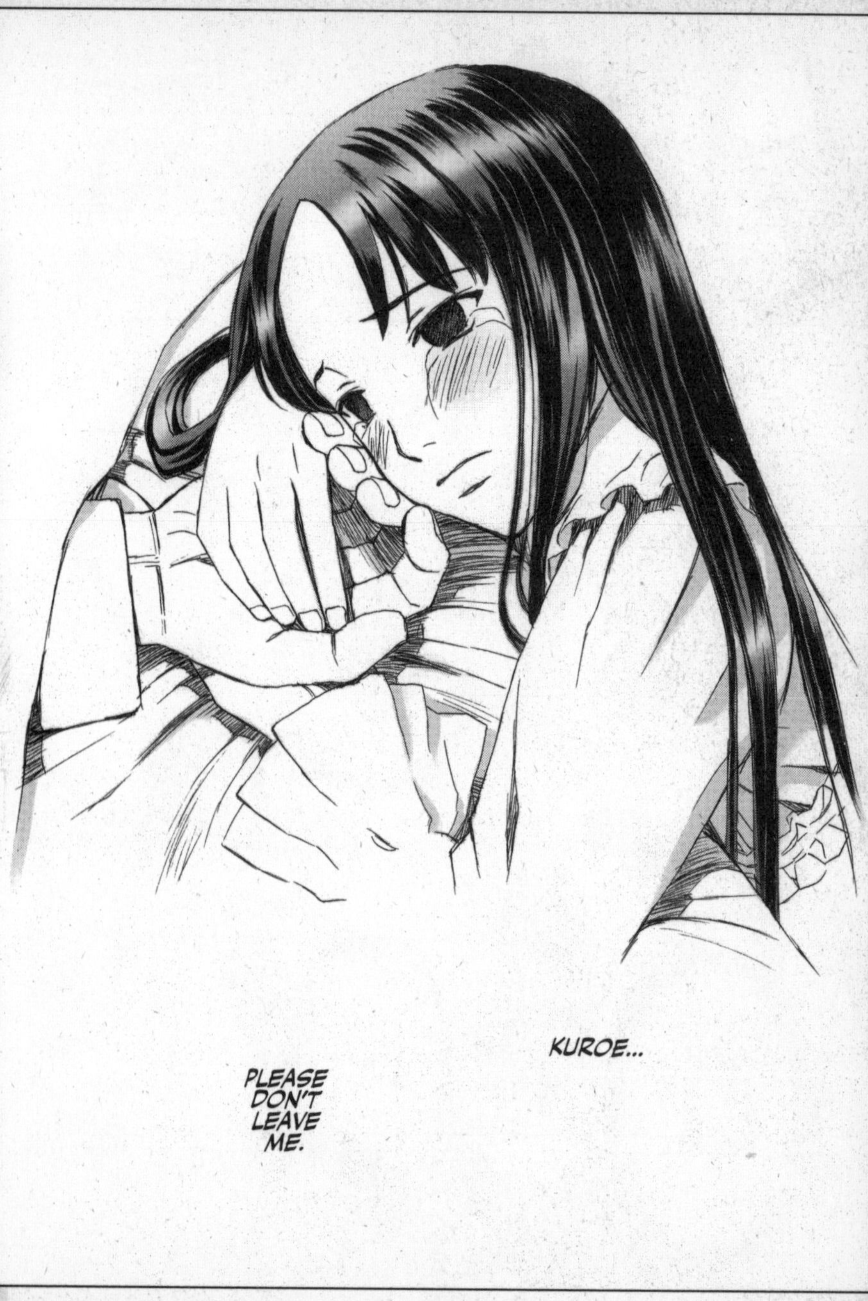
KUROE...
PLEASE DON'T LEAVE ME.

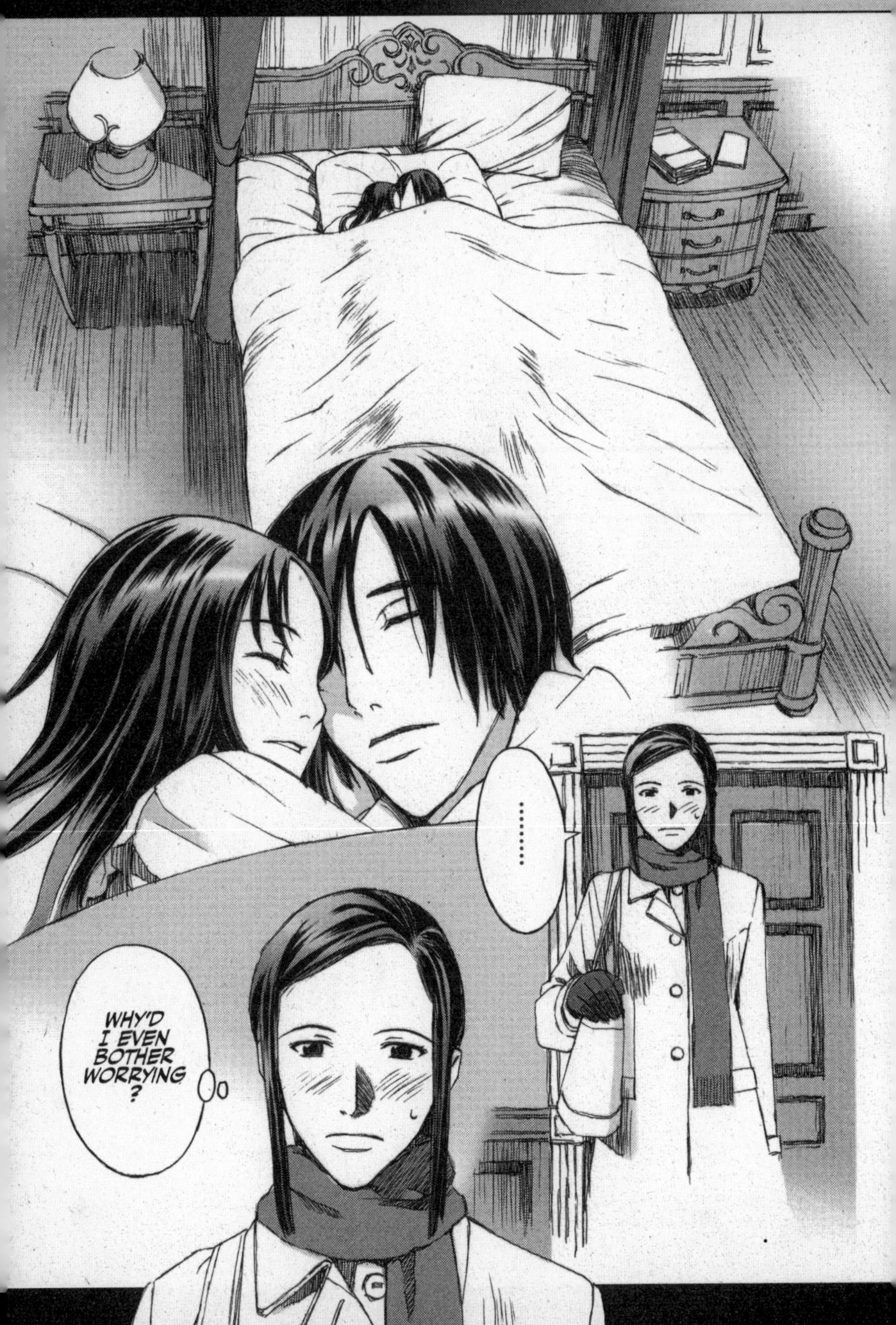
......
WHY'D I EVEN BOTHER WORRYING?

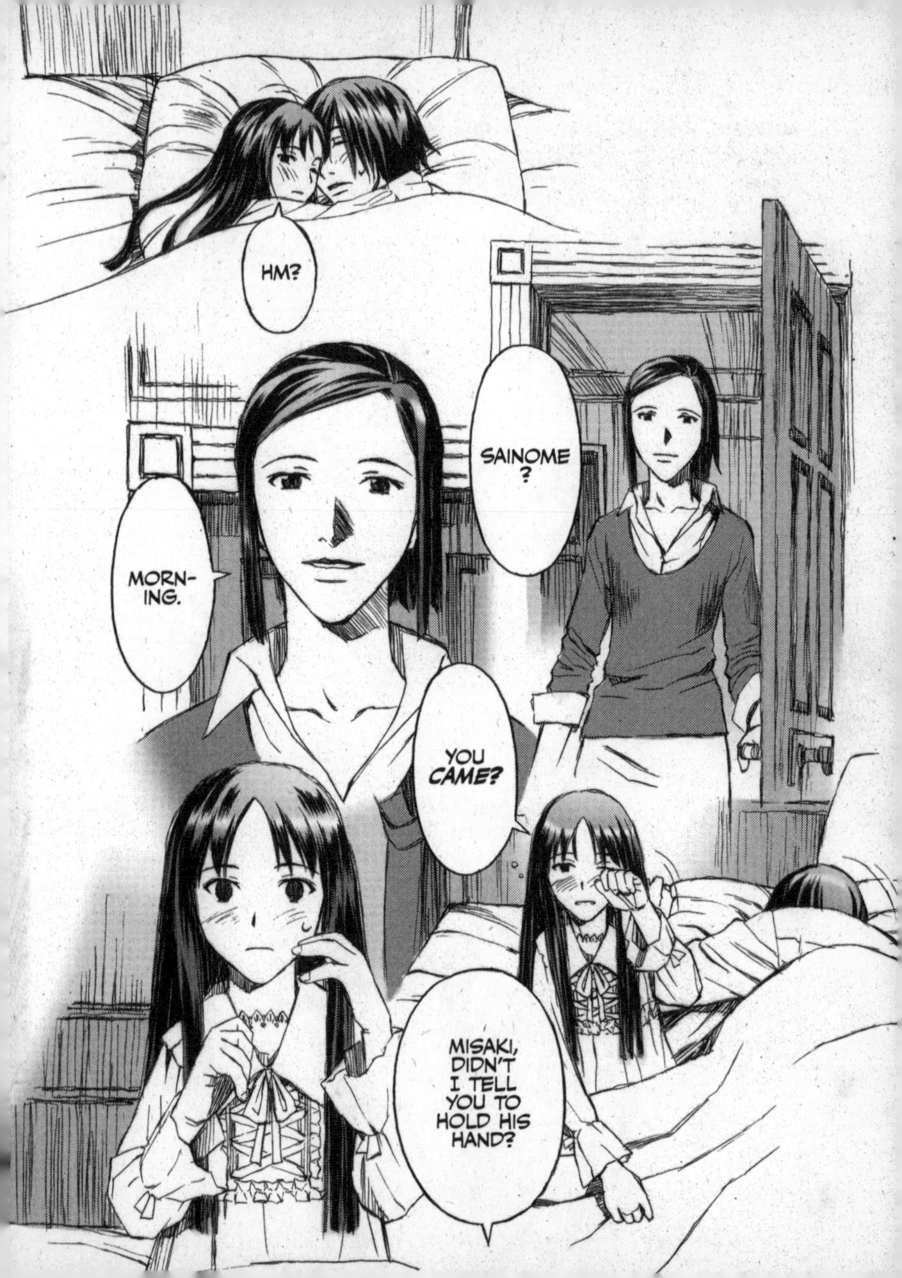
HM?
SAINOME?
MORNING.
YOU CAME?
MISAKI, DIDN'T I TELL YOU TO HOLD HIS HAND?

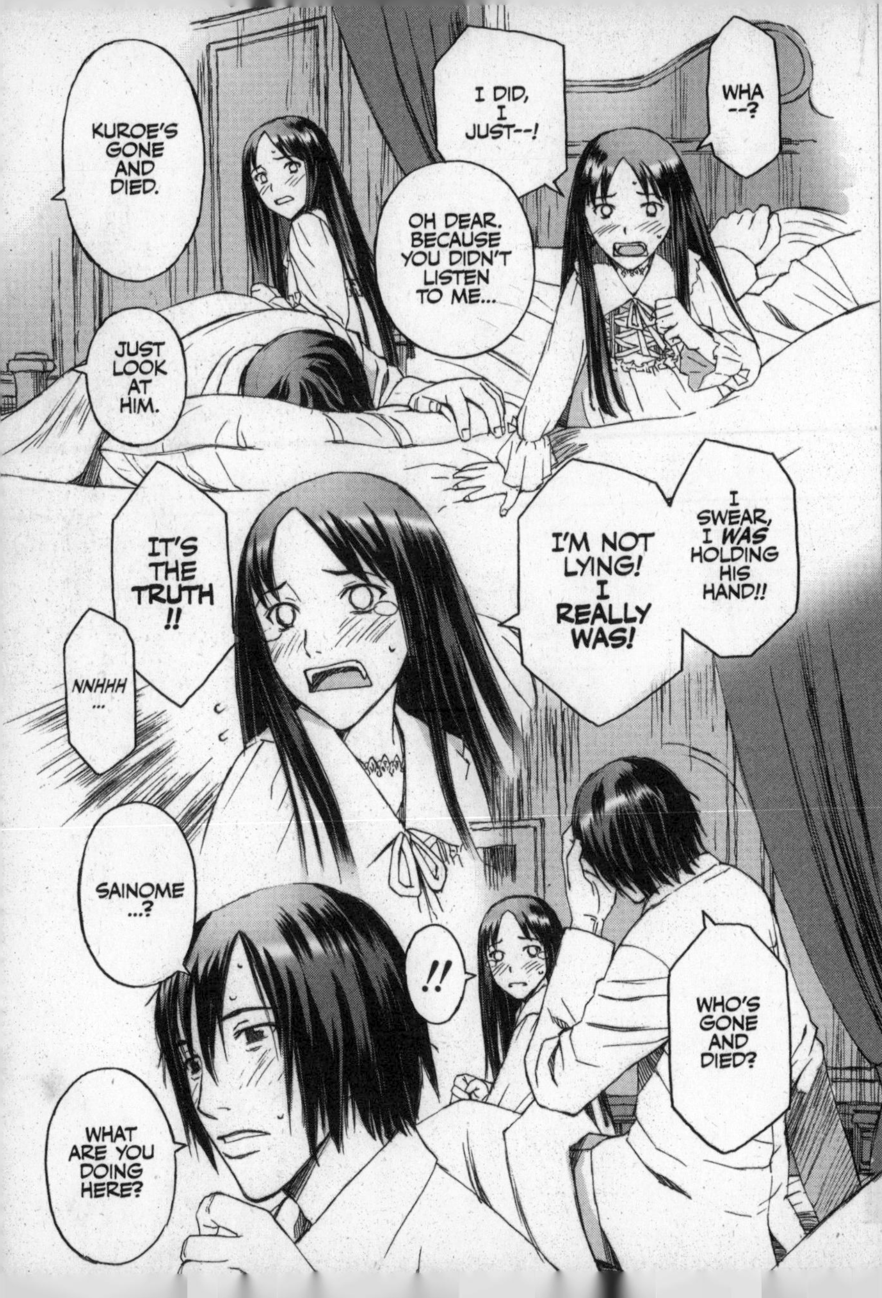
WHA --?
I DID, I JUST--!
KUROE'S GONE AND DIED.
OH DEAR. BECAUSE YOU DIDN'T LISTEN TO ME...
JUST LOOK AT HIM.
I SWEAR, I *WAS* HOLDING HIS HAND!!
I'M NOT LYING! I REALLY WAS!
IT'S THE **TRUTH** !!
NNHHH ...
WHO'S GONE AND DIED?
!!
SAINOME ...?
WHAT ARE YOU DOING HERE?

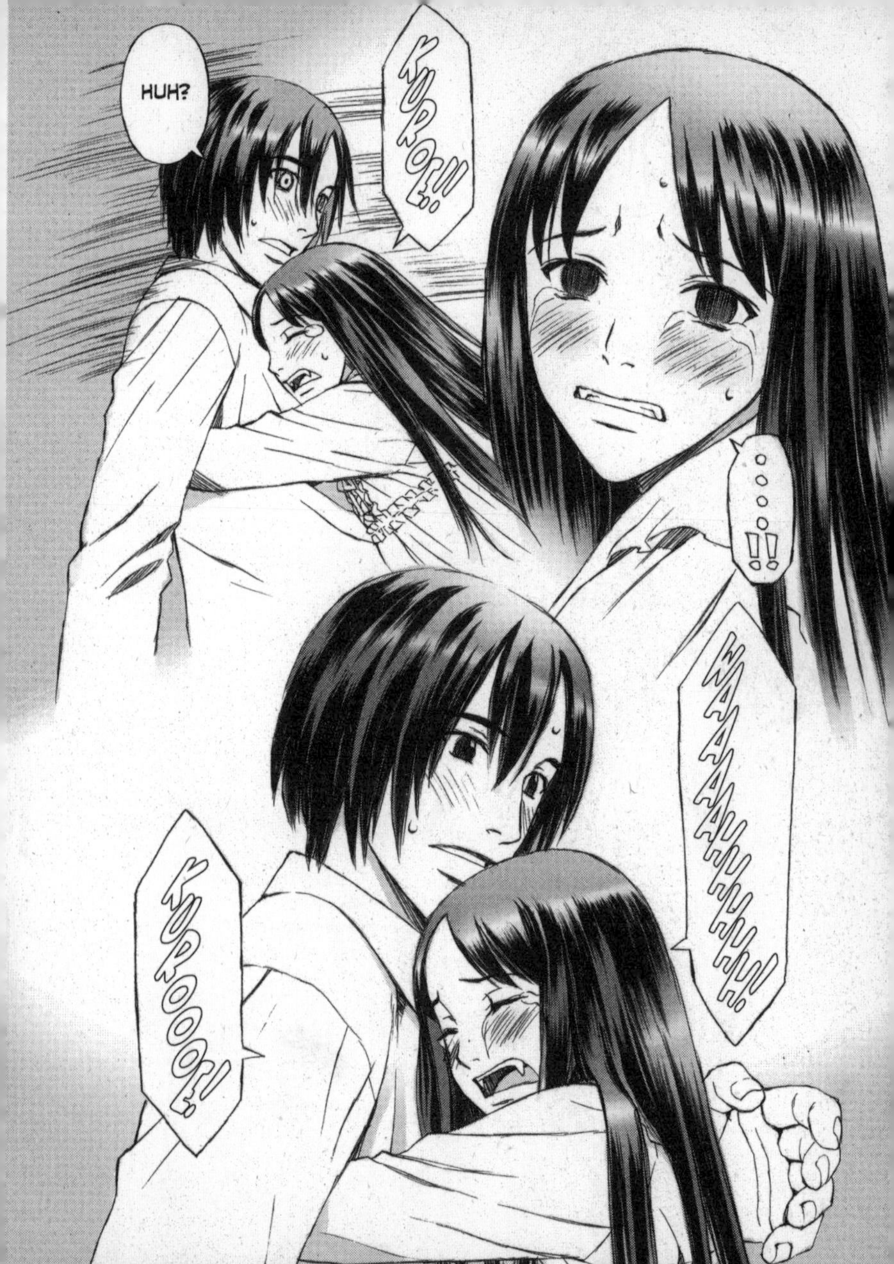
KUROE!!
HUH?
......!!
WAAAAHHHHH!
KUROOO!

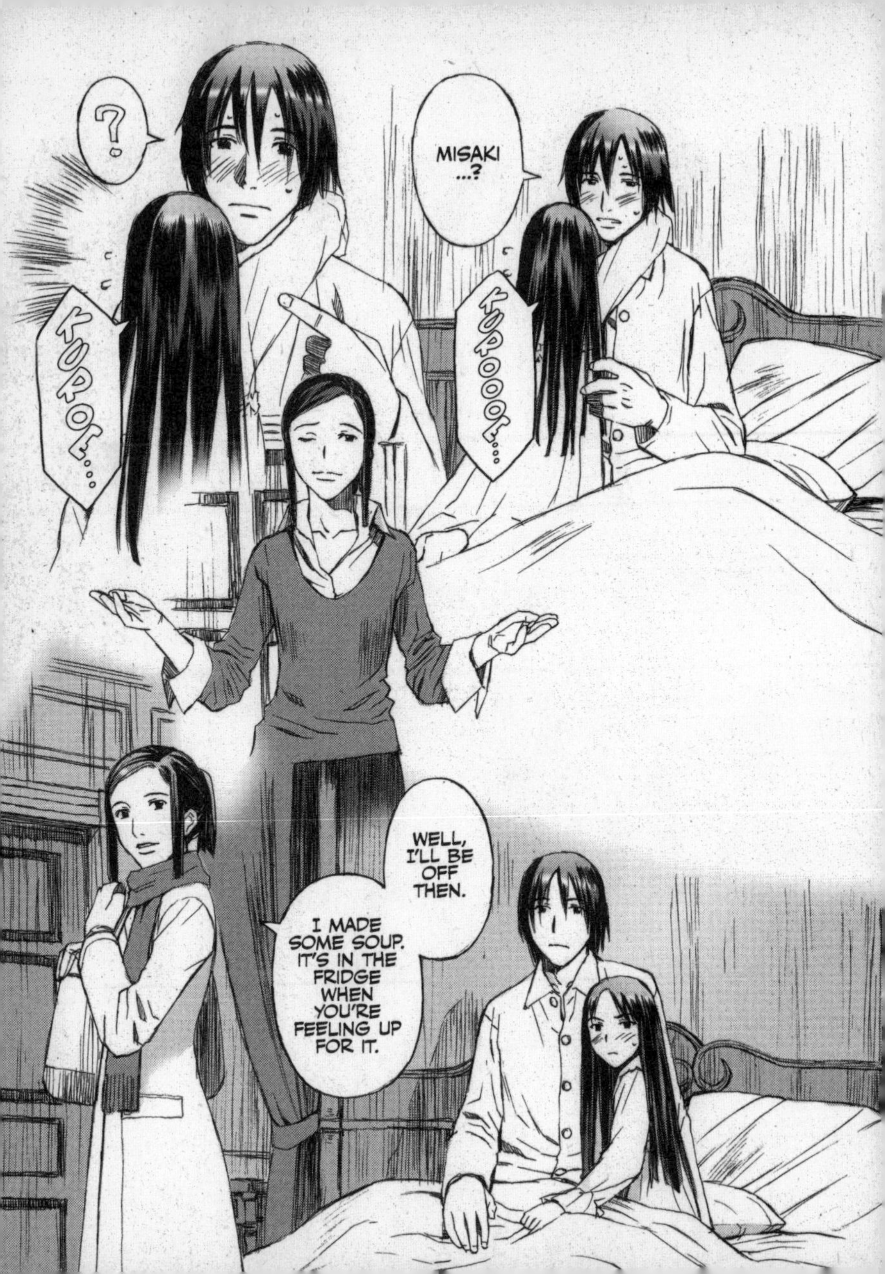
MISAKI ...?
KUROOOI...
?
KUROI...
WELL, I'LL BE OFF THEN.
I MADE SOME SOUP. IT'S IN THE FRIDGE WHEN YOU'RE FEELING UP FOR IT.

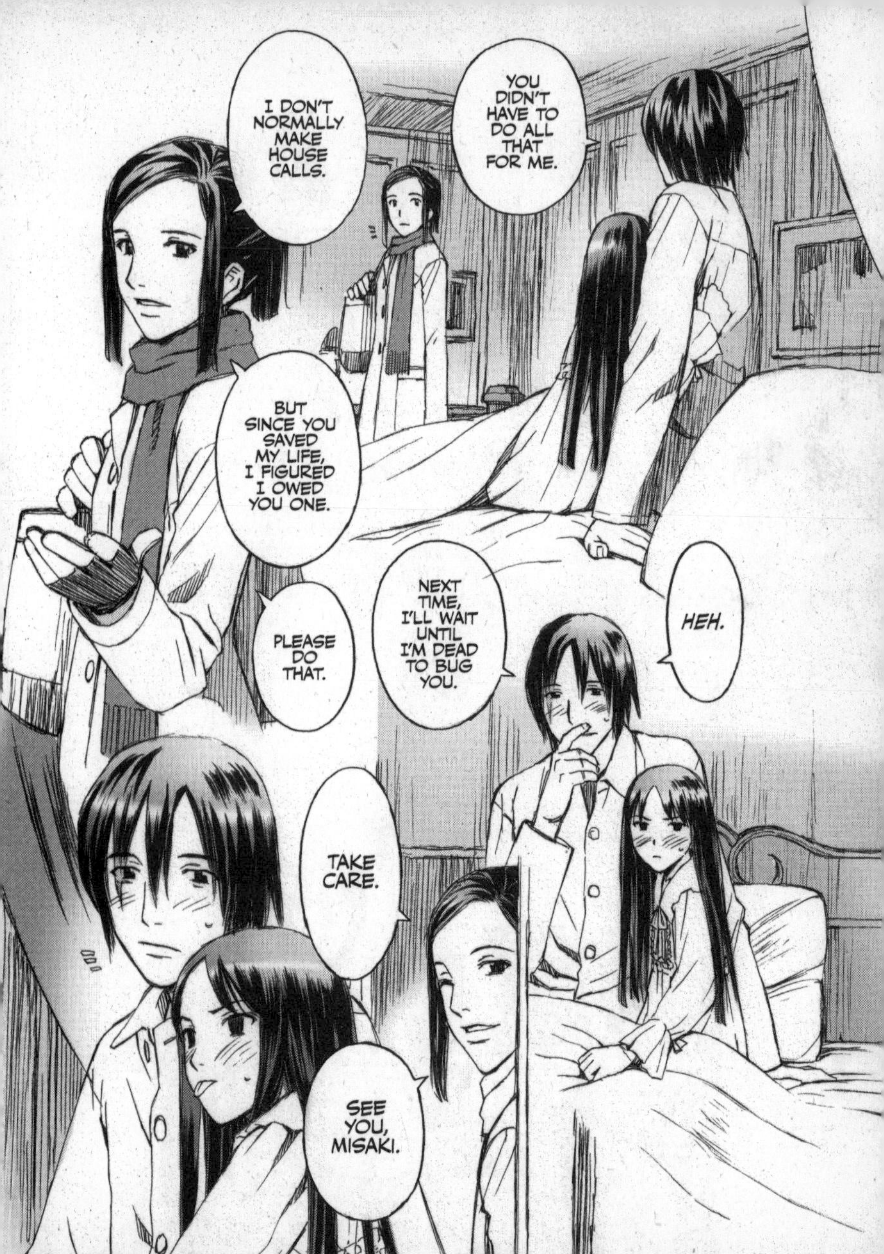
YOU DIDN'T HAVE TO DO ALL THAT FOR ME.
I DON'T NORMALLY MAKE HOUSE CALLS.
BUT SINCE YOU SAVED MY LIFE, I FIGURED I OWED YOU ONE.
HEH.
NEXT TIME, I'LL WAIT UNTIL I'M DEAD TO BUG YOU.
PLEASE DO THAT.
TAKE CARE.
SEE YOU, MISAKI.

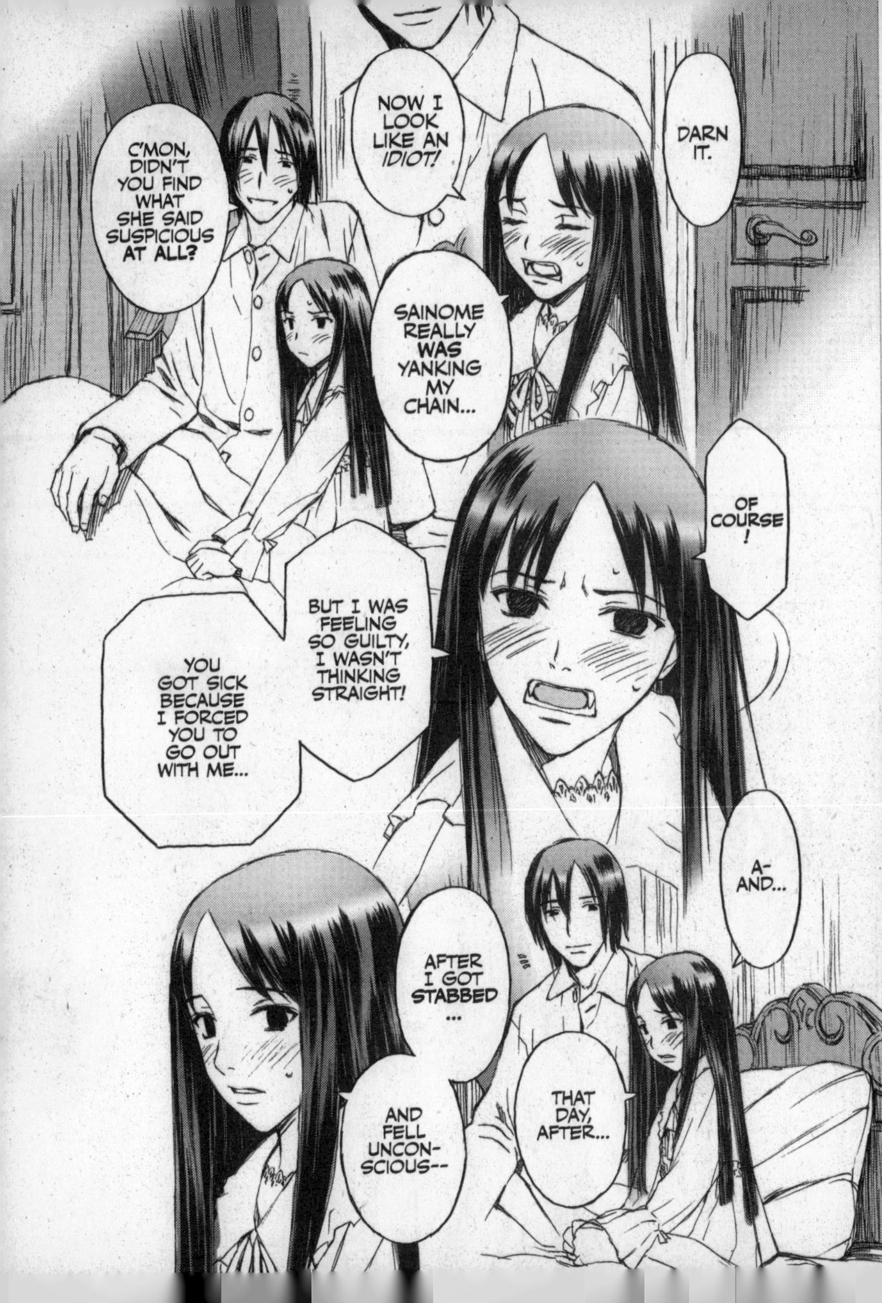
DARN IT.
NOW I LOOK LIKE AN *IDIOT!*
C'MON, DIDN'T YOU FIND WHAT SHE SAID SUSPICIOUS AT ALL?
SAINOME REALLY WAS YANKING MY CHAIN...
OF COURSE!
BUT I WAS FEELING SO GUILTY, I WASN'T THINKING STRAIGHT!
YOU GOT SICK BECAUSE I FORCED YOU TO GO OUT WITH ME...
A-AND...
THAT DAY, AFTER...
AFTER I GOT STABBED...
AND FELL UNCON-SCIOUS--

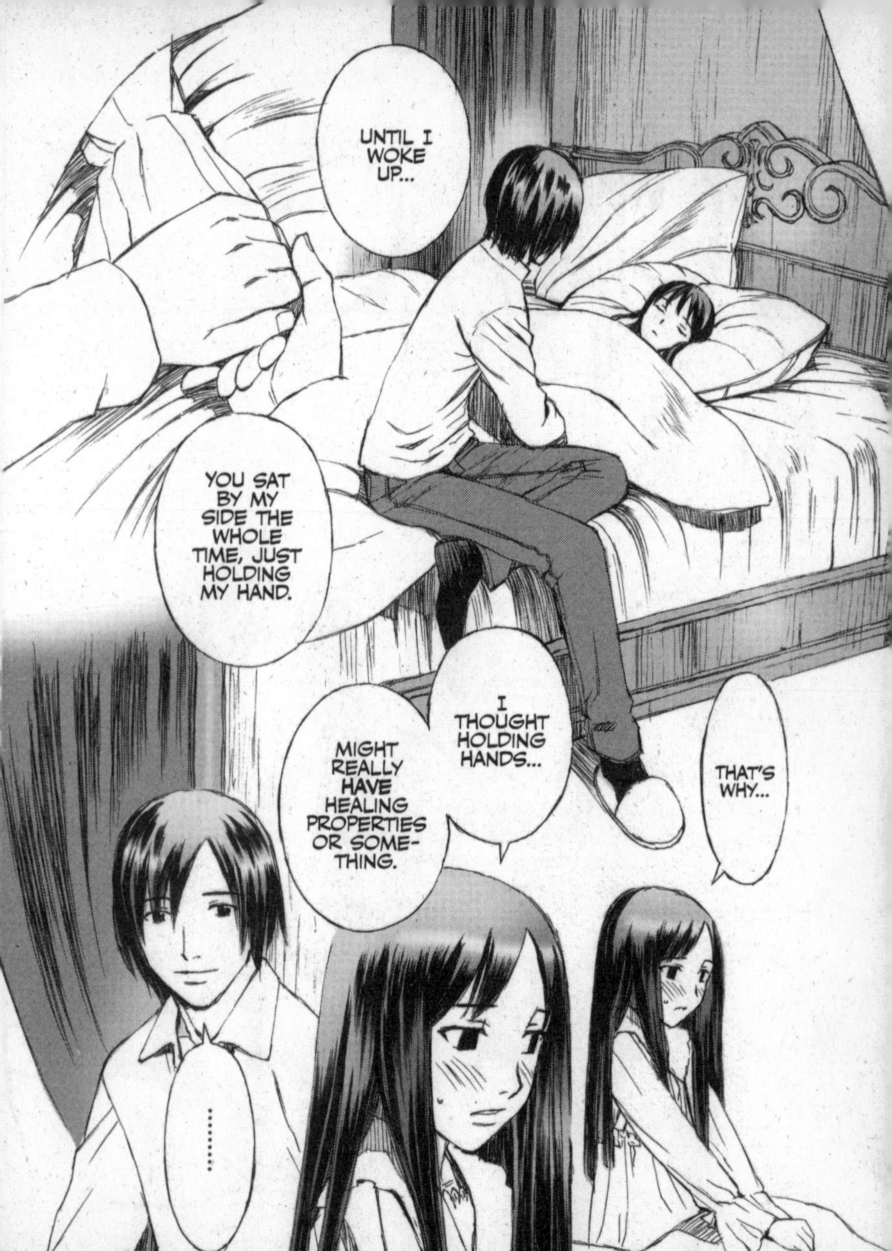
UNTIL I WOKE UP...
YOU SAT BY MY SIDE THE WHOLE TIME, JUST HOLDING MY HAND.
THAT'S WHY...
I THOUGHT HOLDING HANDS...
MIGHT REALLY HAVE HEALING PROPERTIES OR SOME-THING.
....

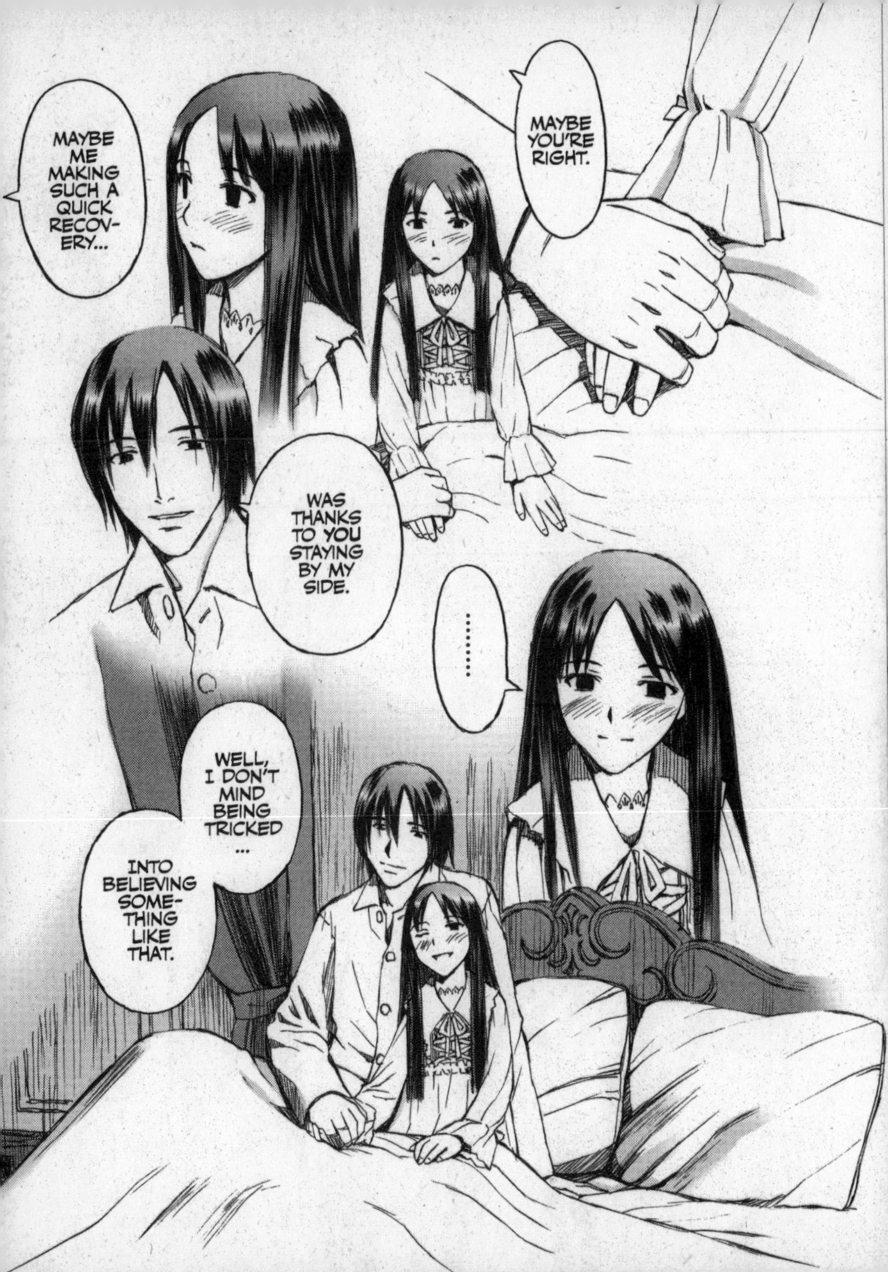
MAYBE YOU'RE RIGHT.
MAYBE ME MAKING SUCH A QUICK RECOVERY...
WAS THANKS TO YOU STAYING BY MY SIDE.
......
WELL, I DON'T MIND BEING TRICKED ...
INTO BELIEVING SOMETHING LIKE THAT.

Appendix

IN MY BED I SCREAM

Kuroe's Early Morning Return

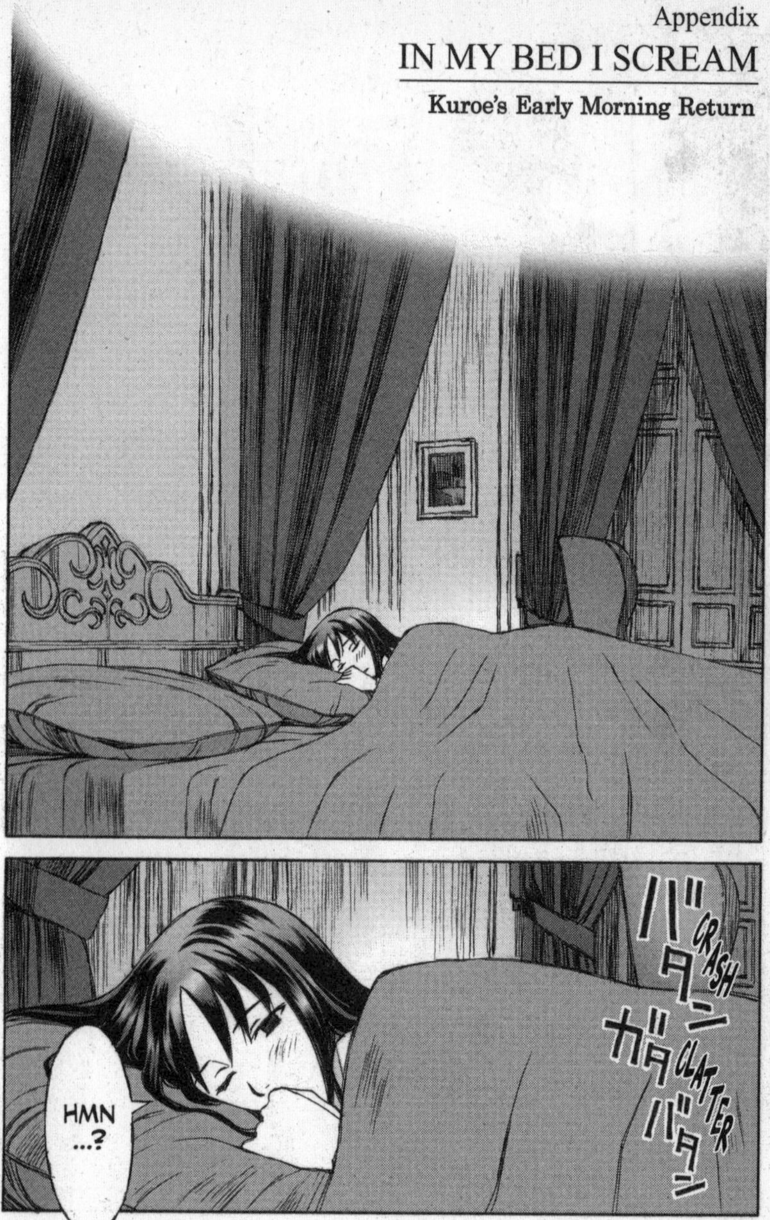
バ"タン
CRASH
ガタバタン
CLATTER
HMN ...?

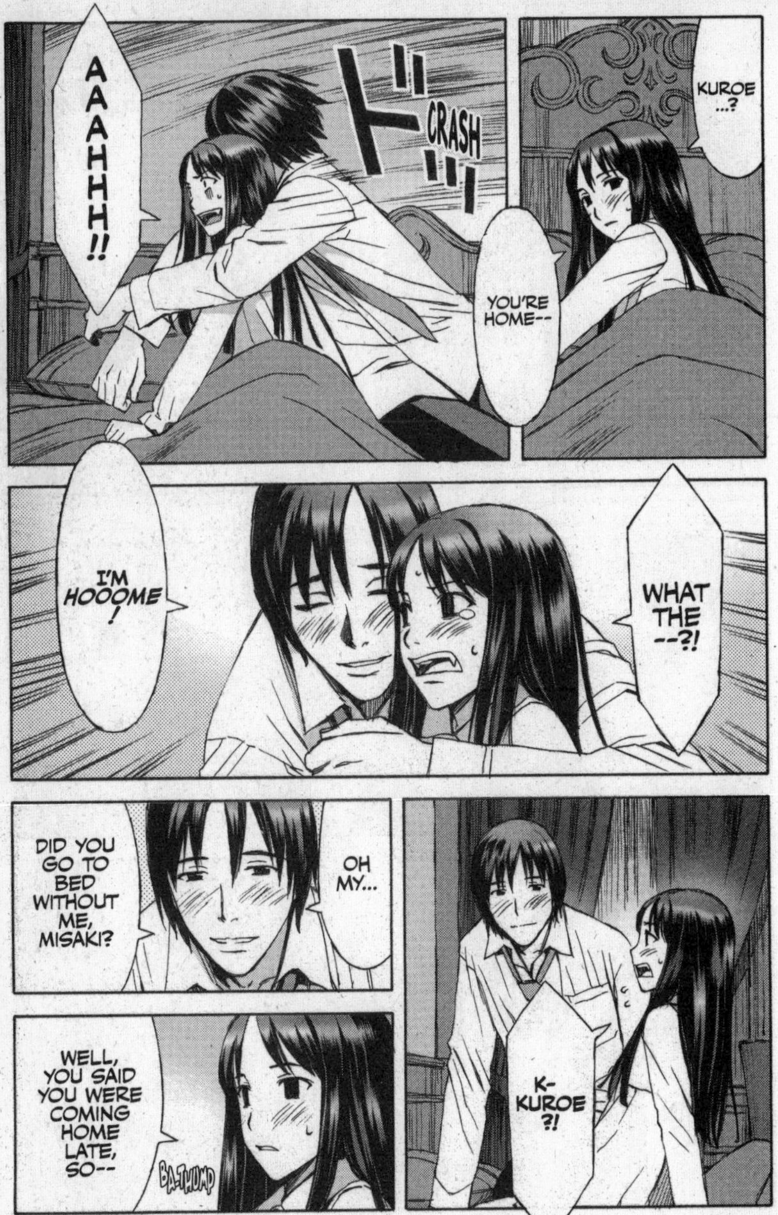
KUROE ...?
YOU'RE HOME--
CRASH
AAAHHH!!
WHAT THE --?!
I'M *HOOOME*!
K-KUROE?!
OH MY...
DID YOU GO TO BED WITHOUT ME, MISAKI?
WELL, YOU SAID YOU WERE COMING HOME LATE, SO--
BA-THUMP

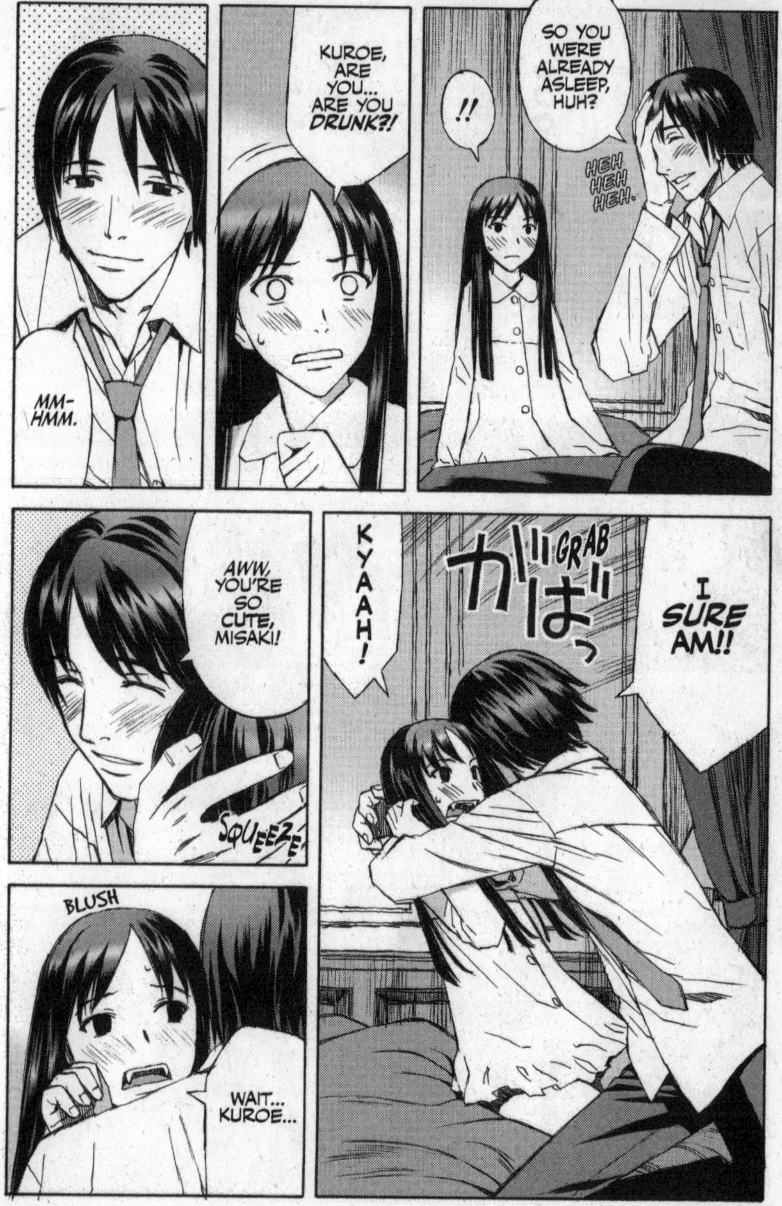
SO YOU WERE ALREADY ASLEEP, HUH?
HEH HEH HEH.
!!
KUROE, ARE YOU... ARE YOU DRUNK?!
MM-HMM.
I SURE AM!!
がばっ
GRAB
KYAAAH!
AWW, YOU'RE SO CUTE, MISAKI!
SQUEEZE
BLUSH
WAIT... KUROE...

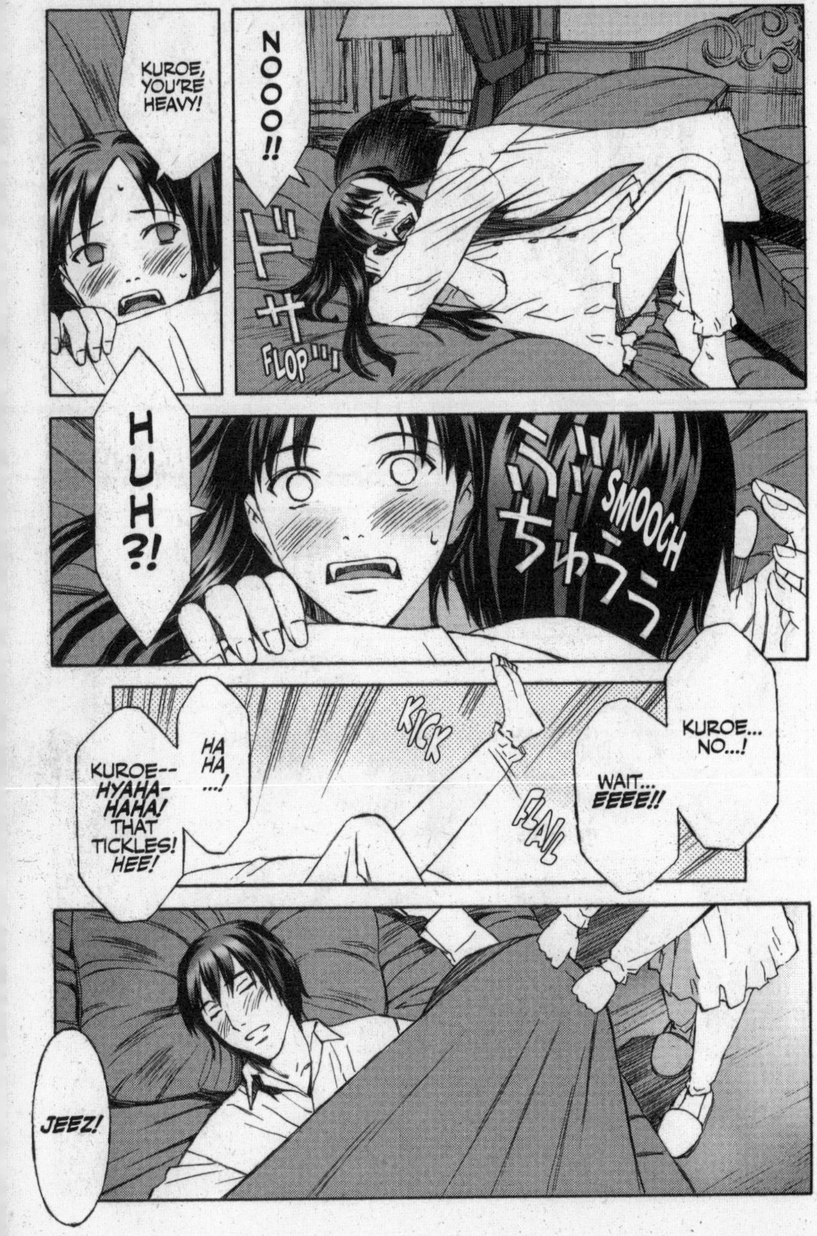
NOOOO!!
ドサ
FLOP
KUROE, YOU'RE HEAVY!
SMOOCH
HUH?!
KUROE... NO...!
WAIT... EEEE!!
KICK
FLAIL
HA HA...!
KUROE-- HYAHA-HAHA! THAT TICKLES! HEE!
JEEZ!

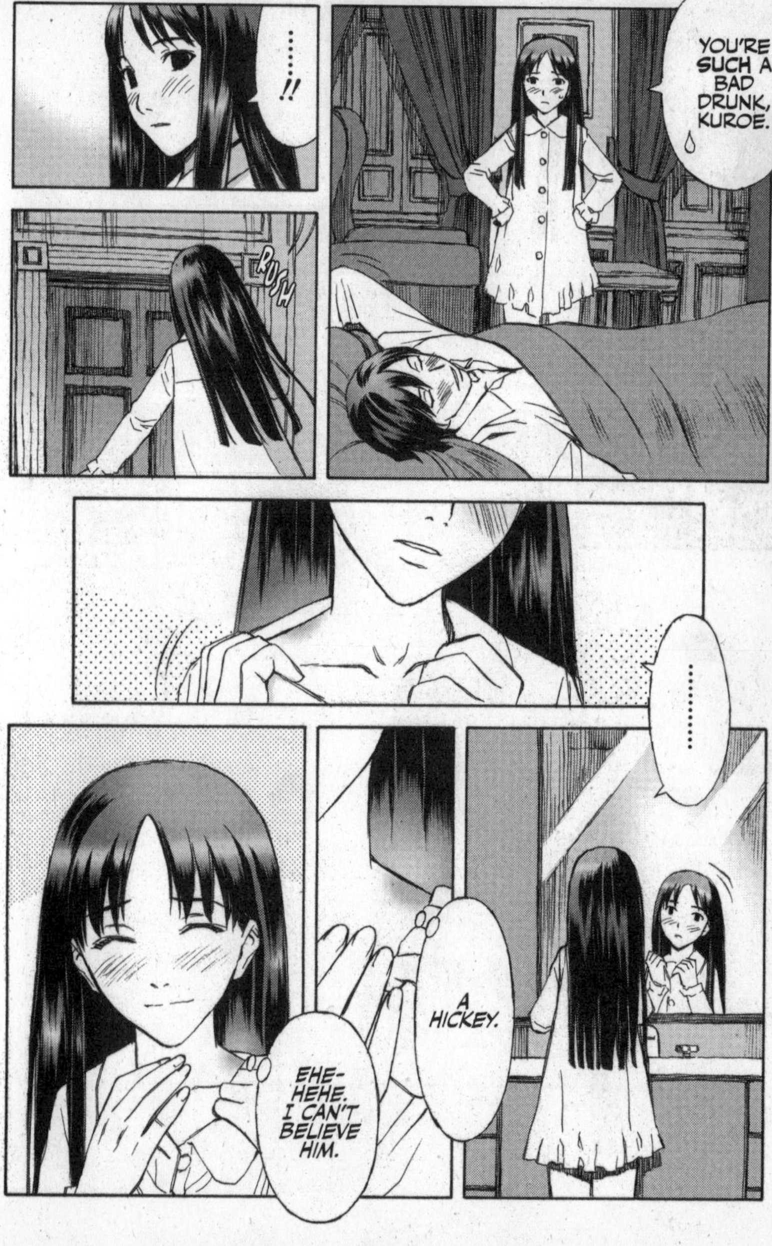
YOU'RE SUCH A BAD DRUNK, KUROE.
......!!
RUSH
......
A HICKEY.
EHEHEHE. I CAN'T BELIEVE HIM.

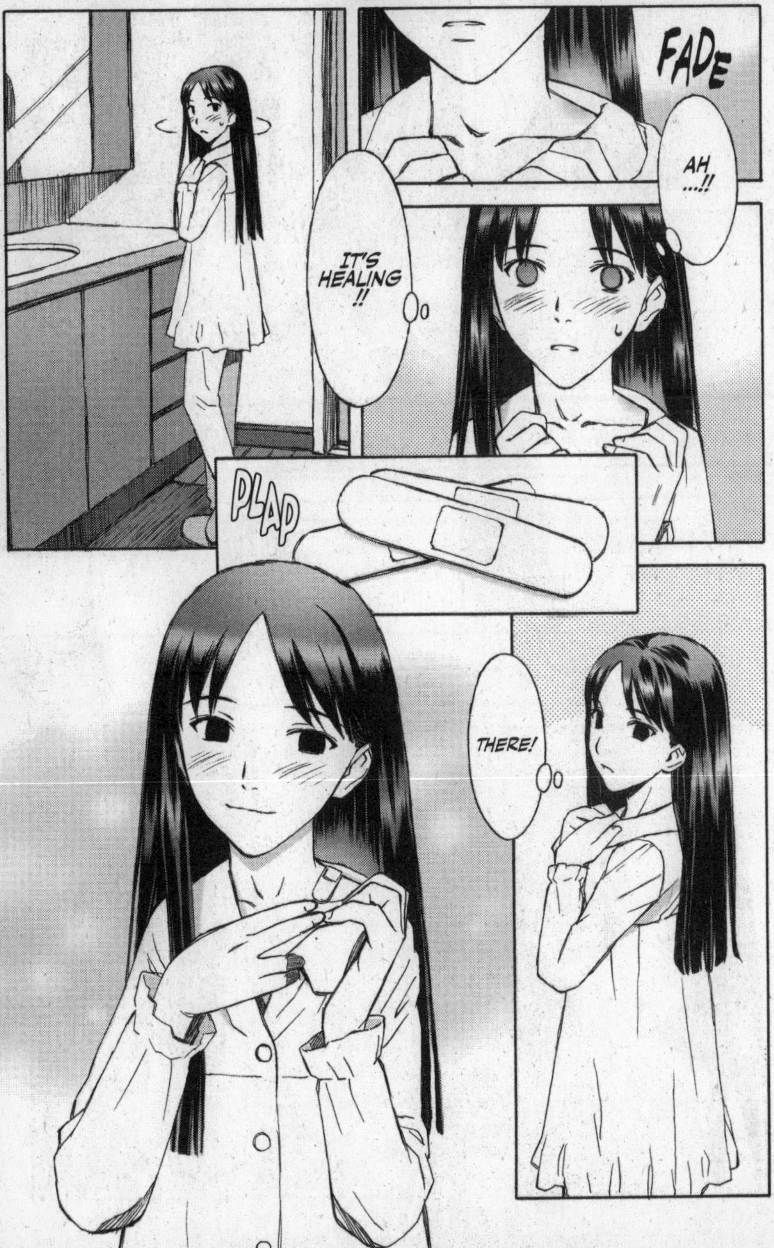
FADE
AH ...!!
IT'S HEALING !!
PLAP
THERE!

Blood Alone

Episode 7

YOU'RE ALL I NEED

Just to Be By Your Side

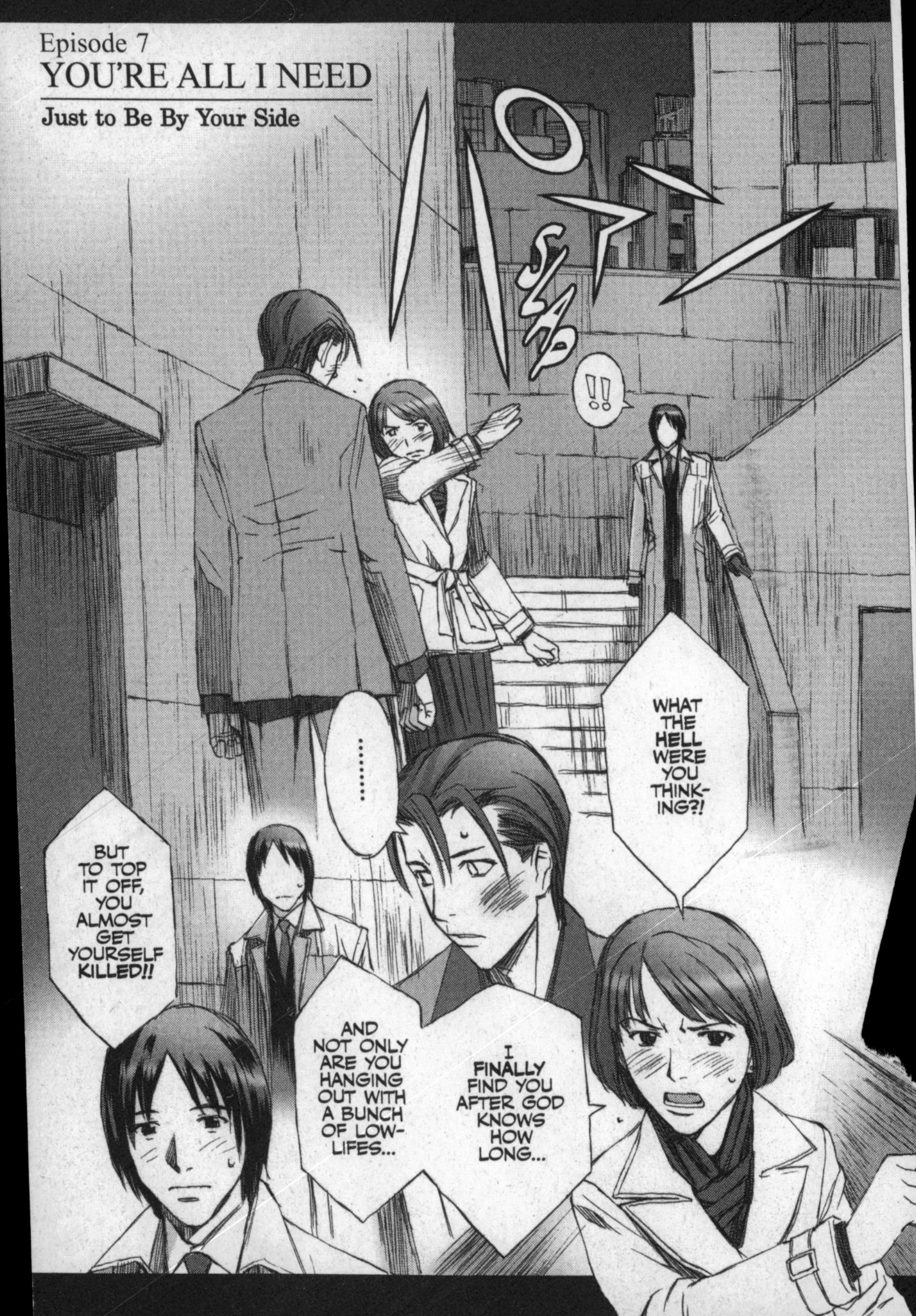
SLAP
!!
WHAT THE HELL WERE YOU THINK-ING?!
......
I FINALLY FIND YOU AFTER GOD KNOWS HOW LONG...
AND NOT ONLY ARE YOU HANGING OUT WITH A BUNCH OF LOW-LIFES...
BUT TO TOP IT OFF, YOU ALMOST GET YOURSELF KILLED!!

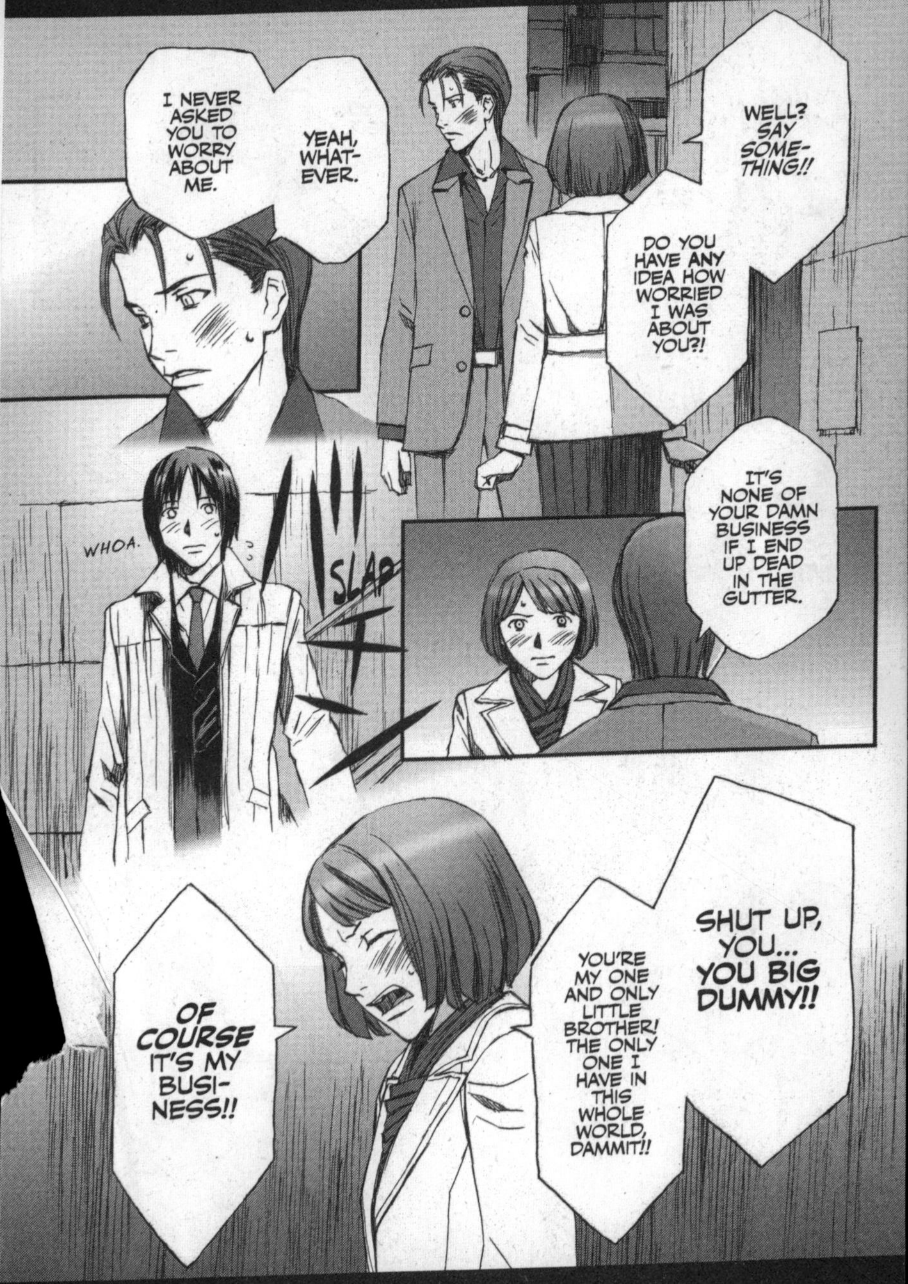
WELL? SAY SOME-THING!!
DO YOU HAVE ANY IDEA HOW WORRIED I WAS ABOUT YOU?!
YEAH, WHAT-EVER.
I NEVER ASKED YOU TO WORRY ABOUT ME.
IT'S NONE OF YOUR DAMN BUSINESS IF I END UP DEAD IN THE GUTTER.
SLAP
WHOA.
SHUT UP, YOU... YOU BIG DUMMY!!
YOU'RE MY ONE AND ONLY LITTLE BROTHER! THE ONLY ONE I HAVE IN THIS WHOLE WORLD, DAMMIT!!
OF COURSE IT'S MY BUSI-NESS!!

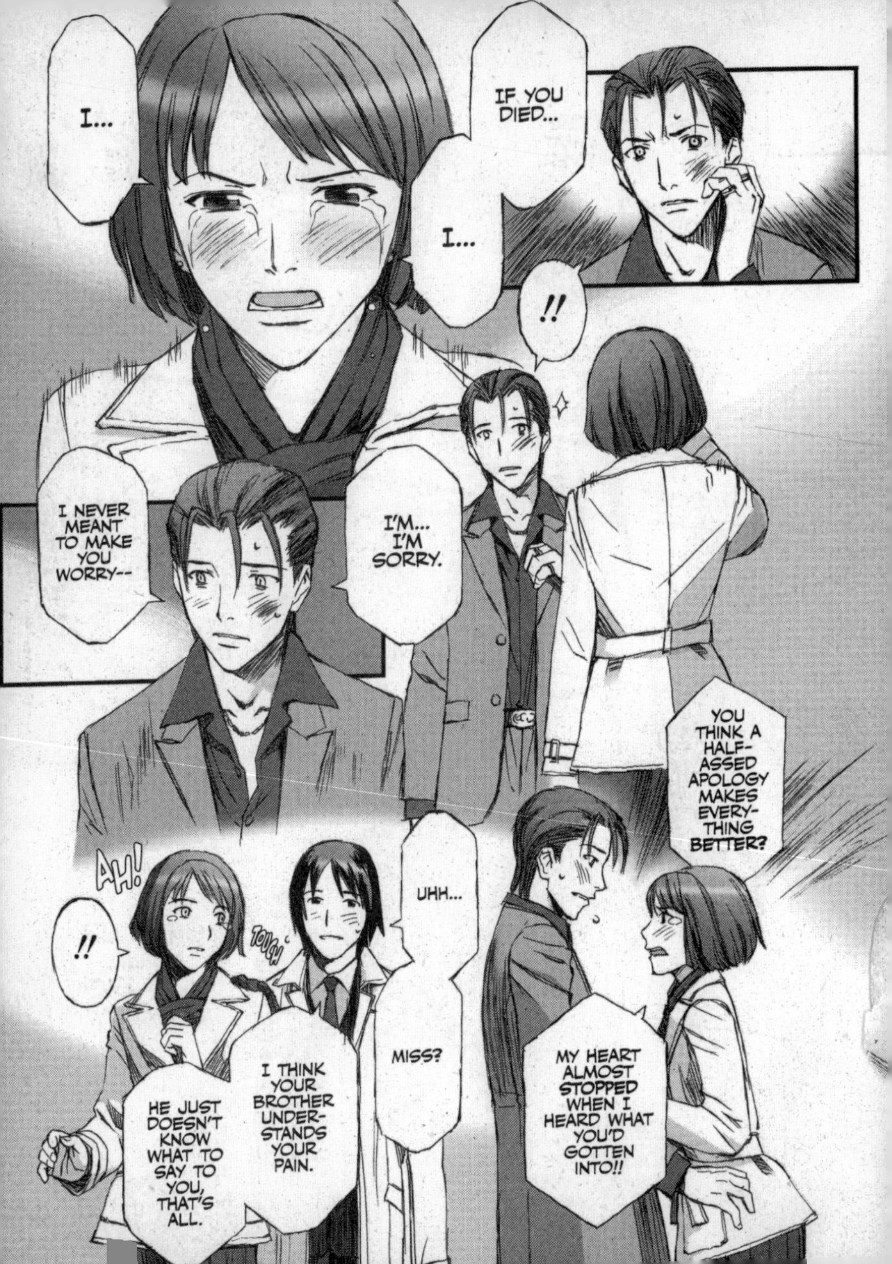
IF YOU DIED...
I...
I...
!!
I'M... I'M SORRY.
I NEVER MEANT TO MAKE YOU WORRY--
YOU THINK A HALF-ASSED APOLOGY MAKES EVERYTHING BETTER?
MY HEART ALMOST STOPPED WHEN I HEARD WHAT YOU'D GOTTEN INTO!!
UHH...
AH!
!!
TOUCH
MISS?
I THINK YOUR BROTHER UNDERSTANDS YOUR PAIN.
HE JUST DOESN'T KNOW WHAT TO SAY TO YOU, THAT'S ALL.

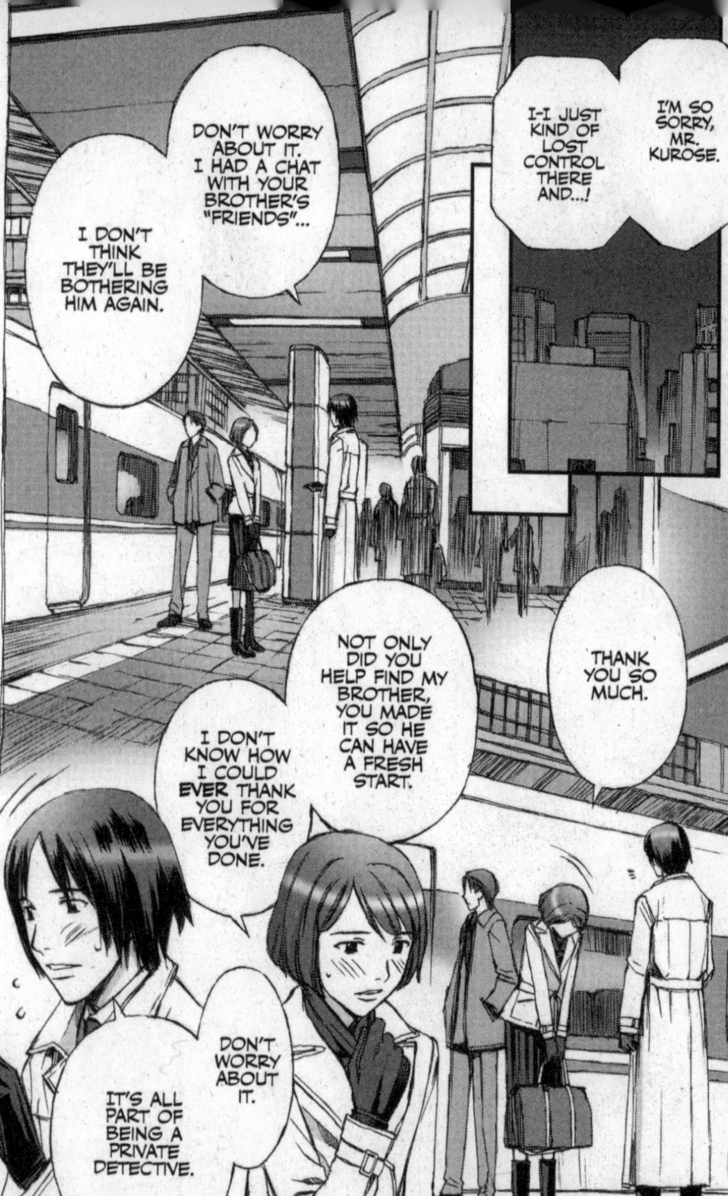
I'M SO SORRY, MR. KUROSE.
I-I JUST KIND OF LOST CONTROL THERE AND...!
DON'T WORRY ABOUT IT. I HAD A CHAT WITH YOUR BROTHER'S "FRIENDS"...
I DON'T THINK THEY'LL BE BOTHERING HIM AGAIN.
THANK YOU SO MUCH.
NOT ONLY DID YOU HELP FIND MY BROTHER, YOU MADE IT SO HE CAN HAVE A FRESH START.
I DON'T KNOW HOW I COULD **EVER** THANK YOU FOR EVERYTHING YOU'VE DONE.
DON'T WORRY ABOUT IT.
IT'S ALL PART OF BEING A PRIVATE DETECTIVE.

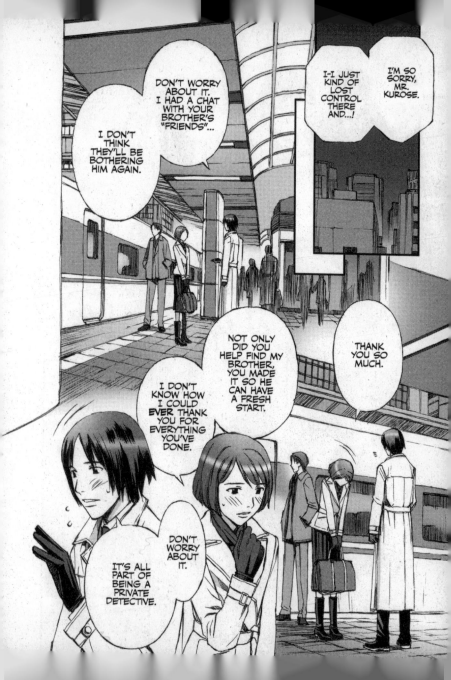

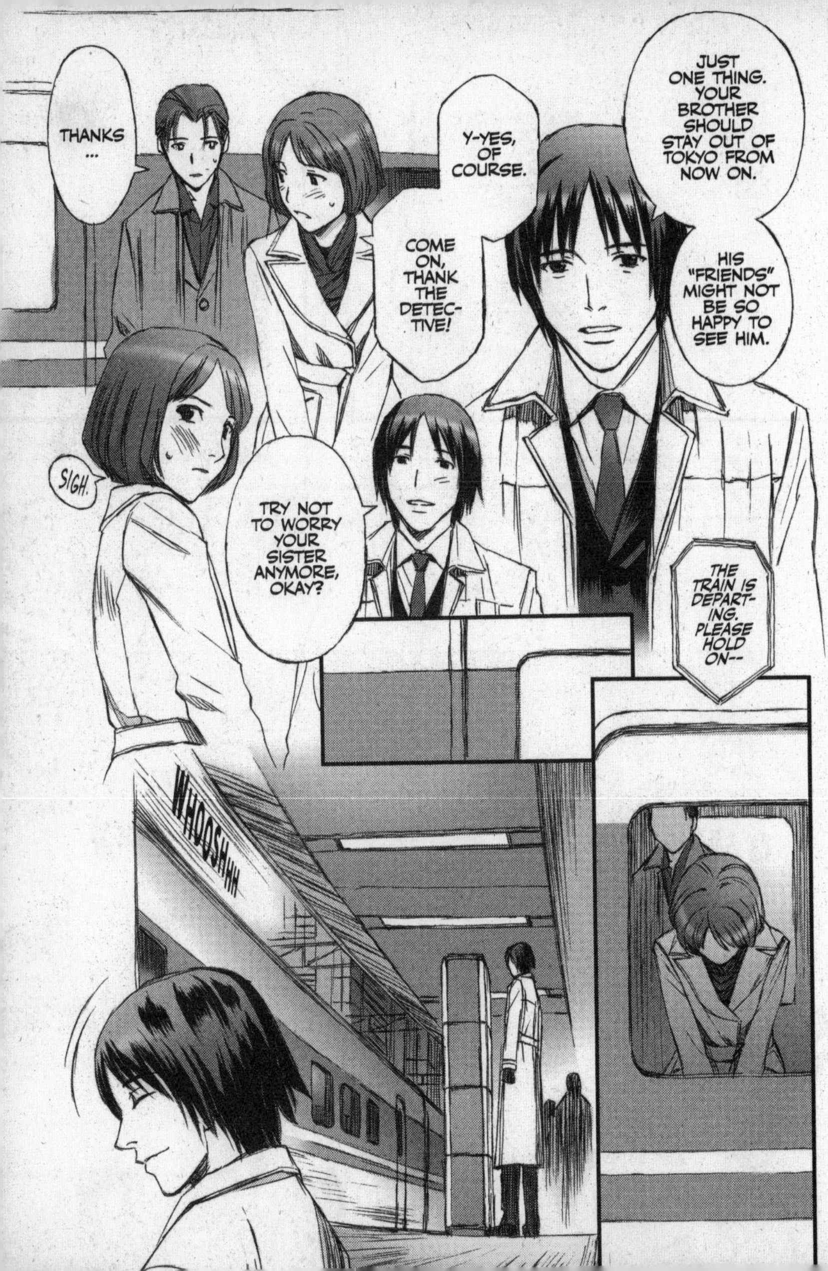
JUST ONE THING. YOUR BROTHER SHOULD STAY OUT OF TOKYO FROM NOW ON.
HIS "FRIENDS" MIGHT NOT BE SO HAPPY TO SEE HIM.
Y-YES, OF COURSE.
COME ON, THANK THE DETEC-TIVE!
THANKS ...
TRY NOT TO WORRY YOUR SISTER ANYMORE, OKAY?
SIGH.
THE TRAIN IS DEPART-ING. PLEASE HOLD ON--
WHOOSHHHH

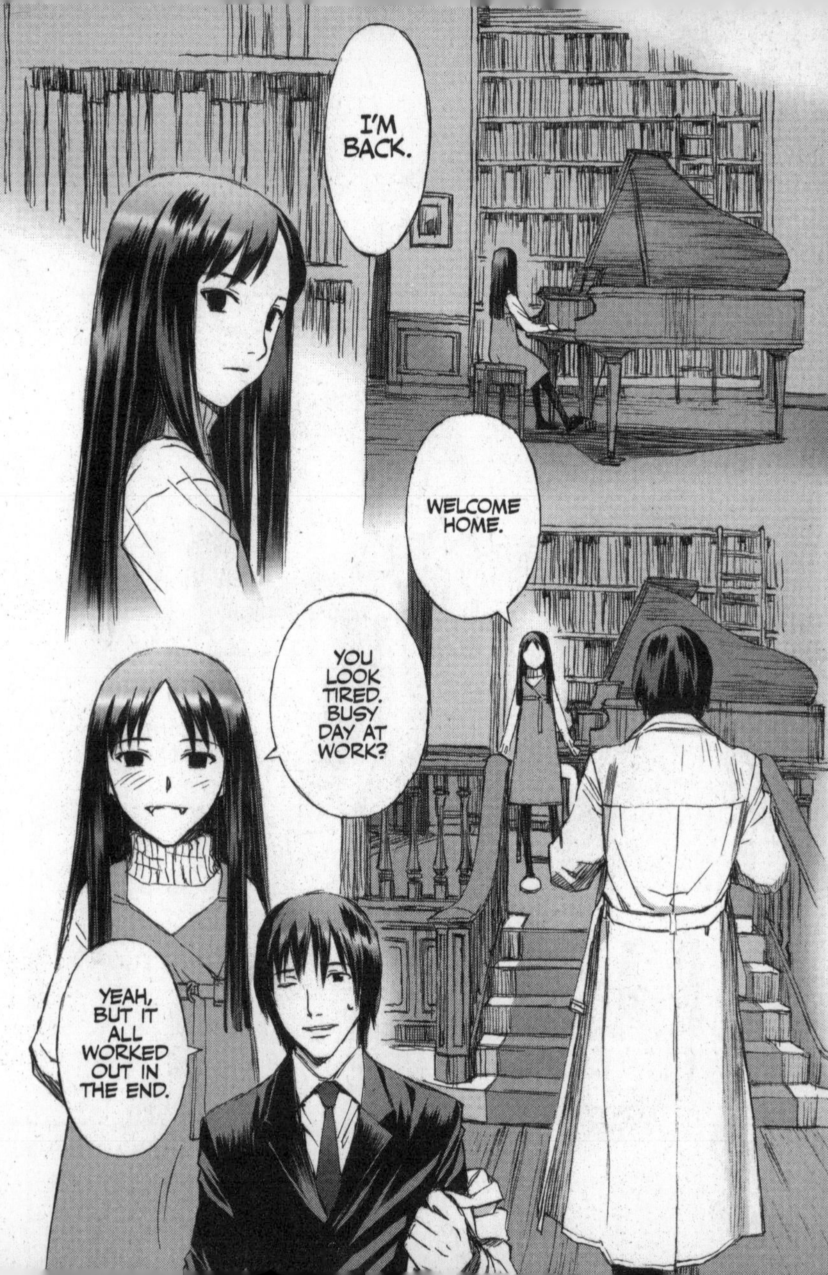
I'M BACK.
WELCOME HOME.
YOU LOOK TIRED. BUSY DAY AT WORK?
YEAH, BUT IT ALL WORKED OUT IN THE END.

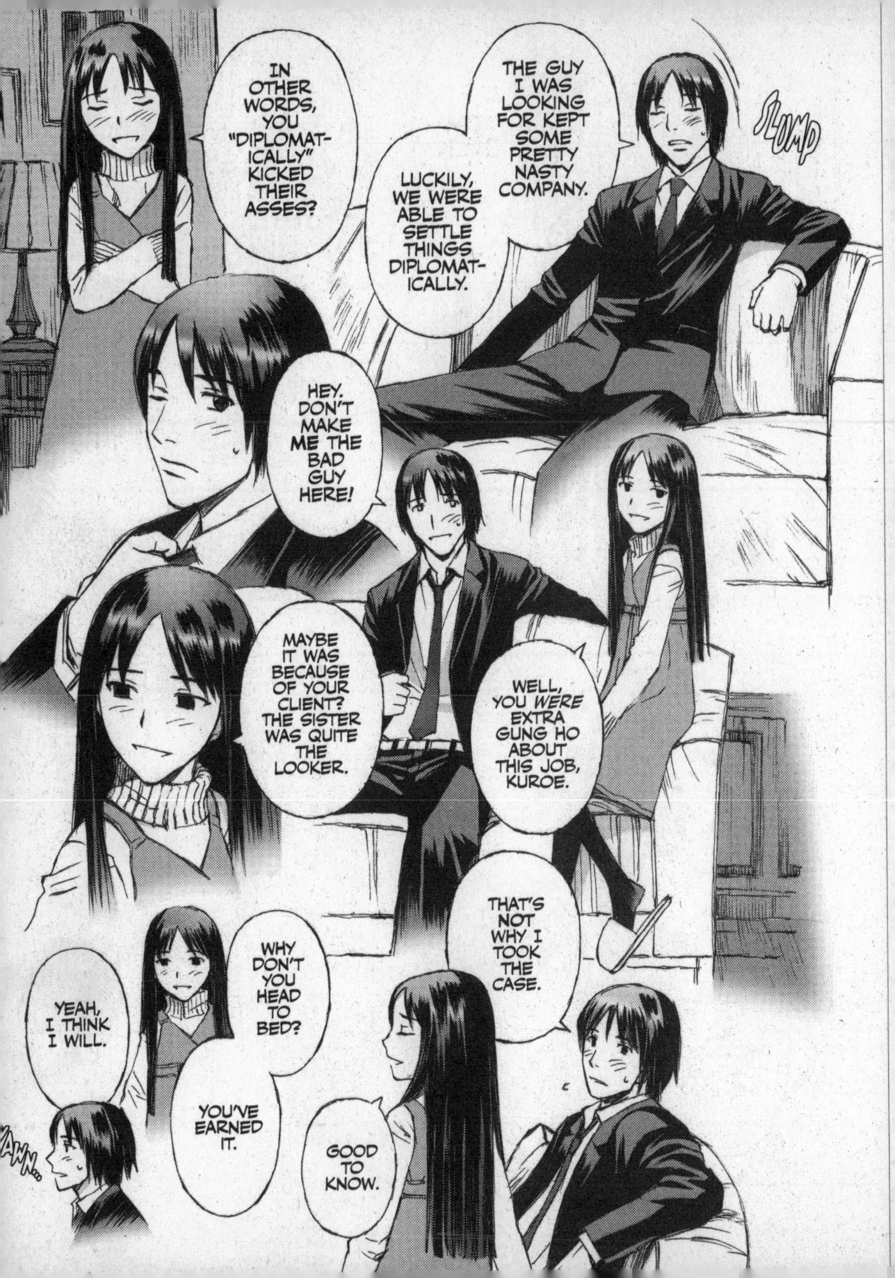

THE GUY I WAS LOOKING FOR KEPT SOME PRETTY NASTY COMPANY.
SLUMP
LUCKILY, WE WERE ABLE TO SETTLE THINGS DIPLOMATICALLY.
IN OTHER WORDS, YOU "DIPLOMATICALLY" KICKED THEIR ASSES?
HEY. DON'T MAKE ME THE BAD GUY HERE!
WELL, YOU *WERE* EXTRA GUNG HO ABOUT THIS JOB, KUROE.
MAYBE IT WAS BECAUSE OF YOUR CLIENT? THE SISTER WAS QUITE THE LOOKER.
THAT'S NOT WHY I TOOK THE CASE.
GOOD TO KNOW.
WHY DON'T YOU HEAD TO BED?
YOU'VE EARNED IT.
YEAH, I THINK I WILL.
YAWN...

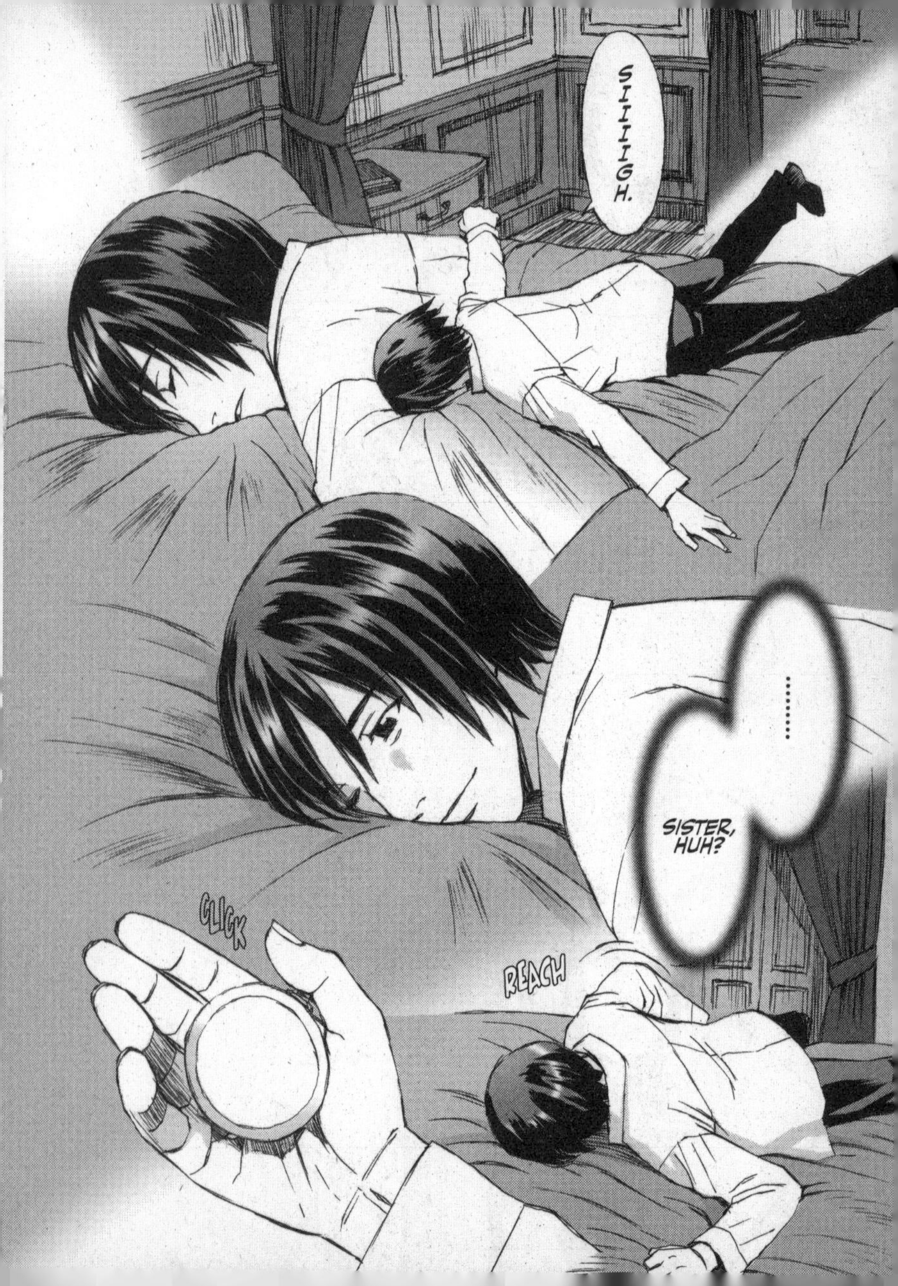
SIIIIGH.
......
SISTER, HUH?
REACH
CLICK

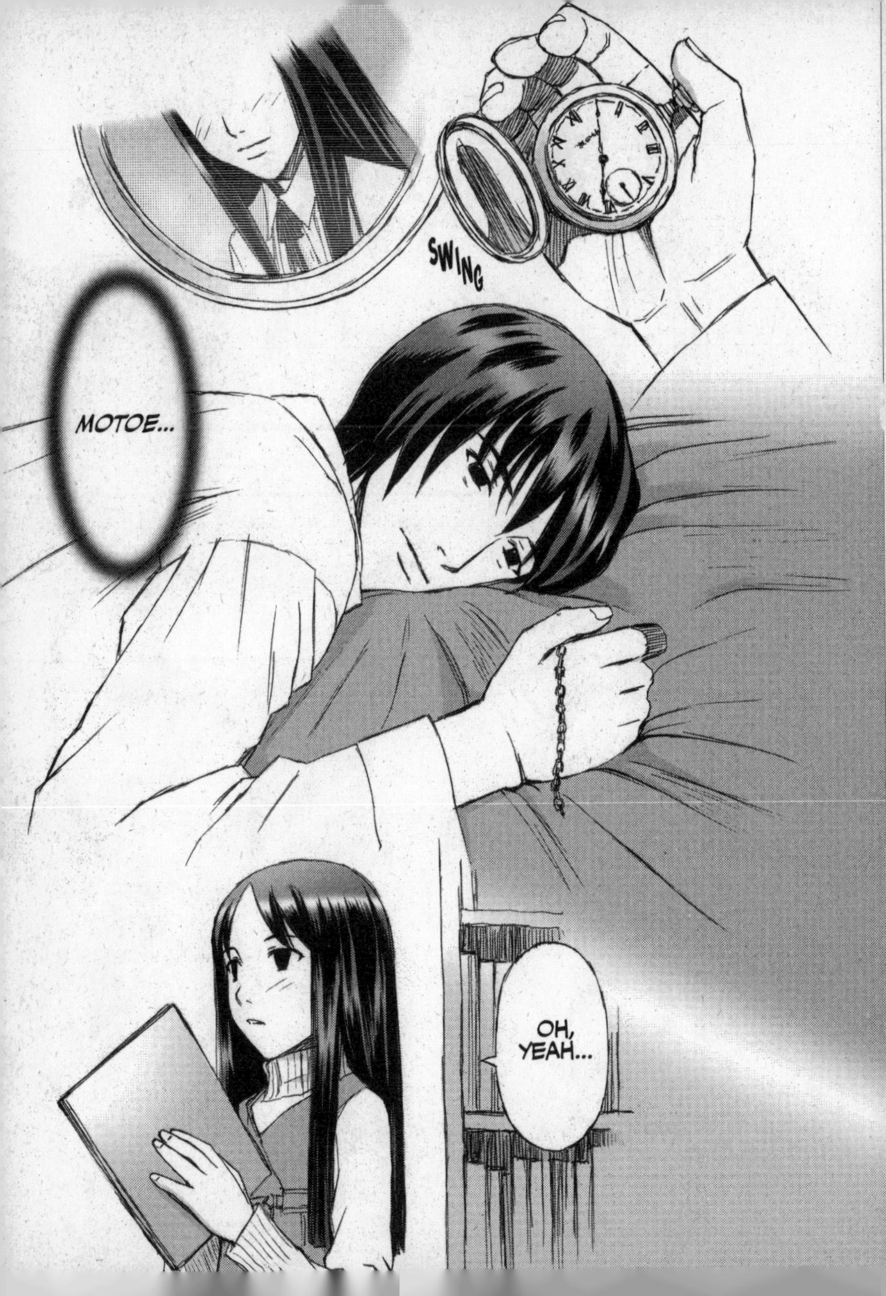
SWING
MOTOE...
OH, YEAH...

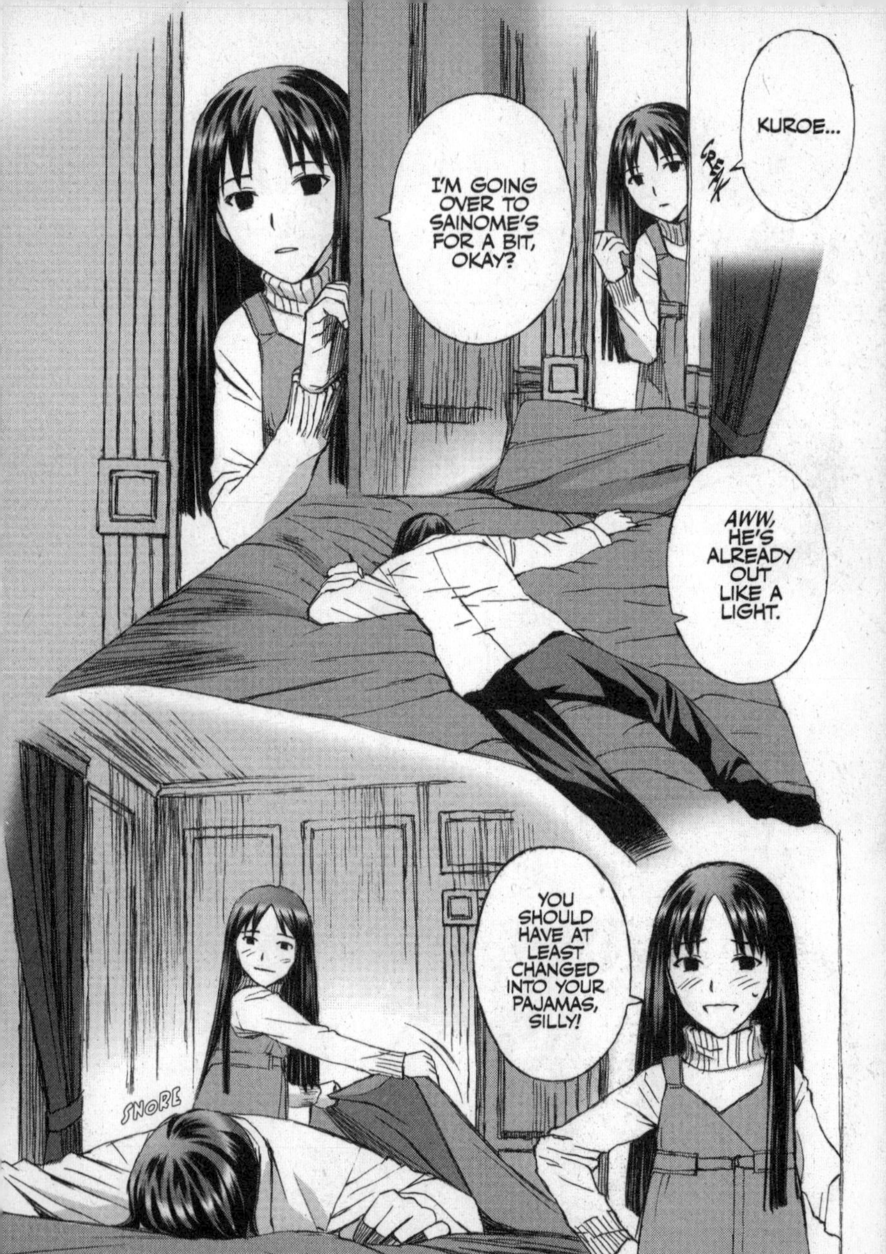
KUROE...
CREAK
I'M GOING OVER TO SAINOME'S FOR A BIT, OKAY?
AWW, HE'S ALREADY OUT LIKE A LIGHT.
YOU SHOULD HAVE AT LEAST CHANGED INTO YOUR PAJAMAS, SILLY!
SNORE

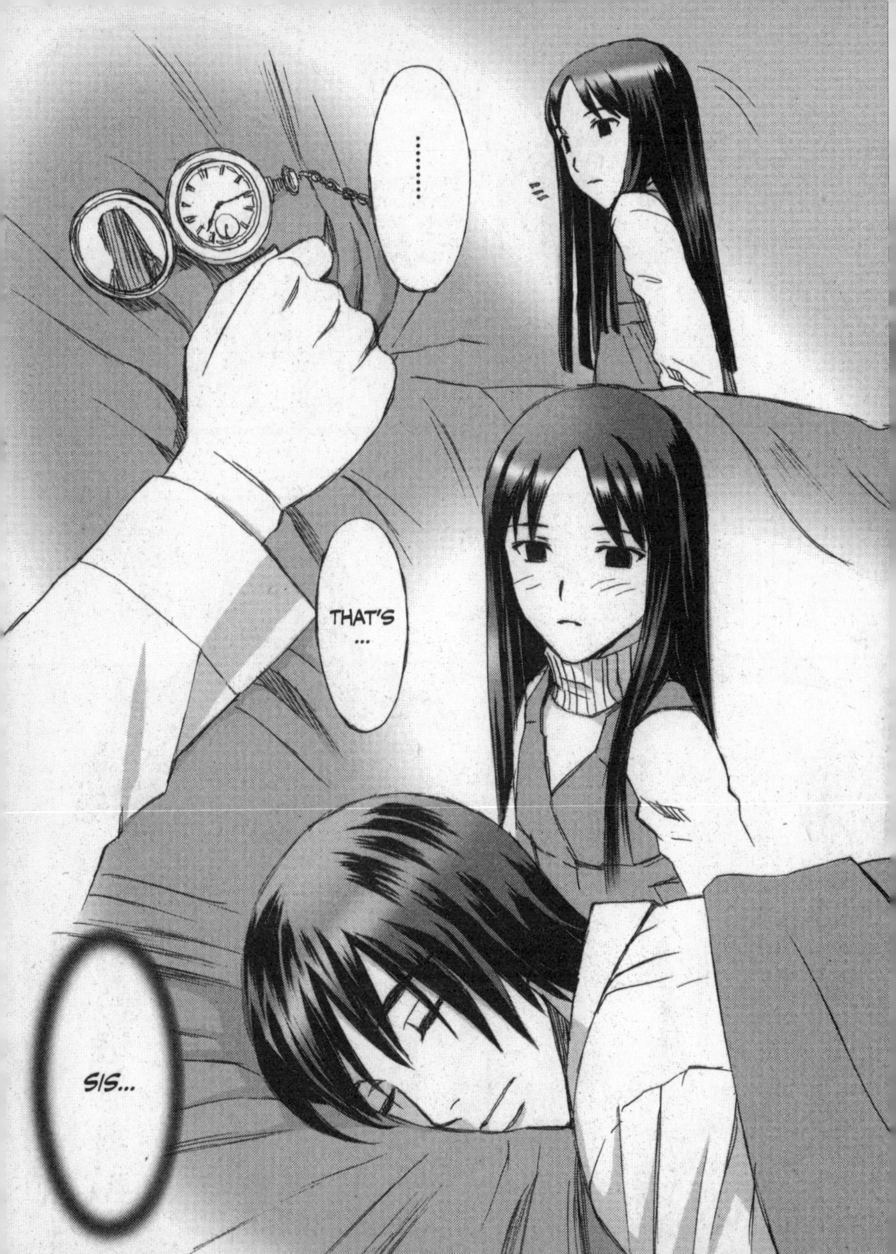
......
THAT'S ...
SIS...

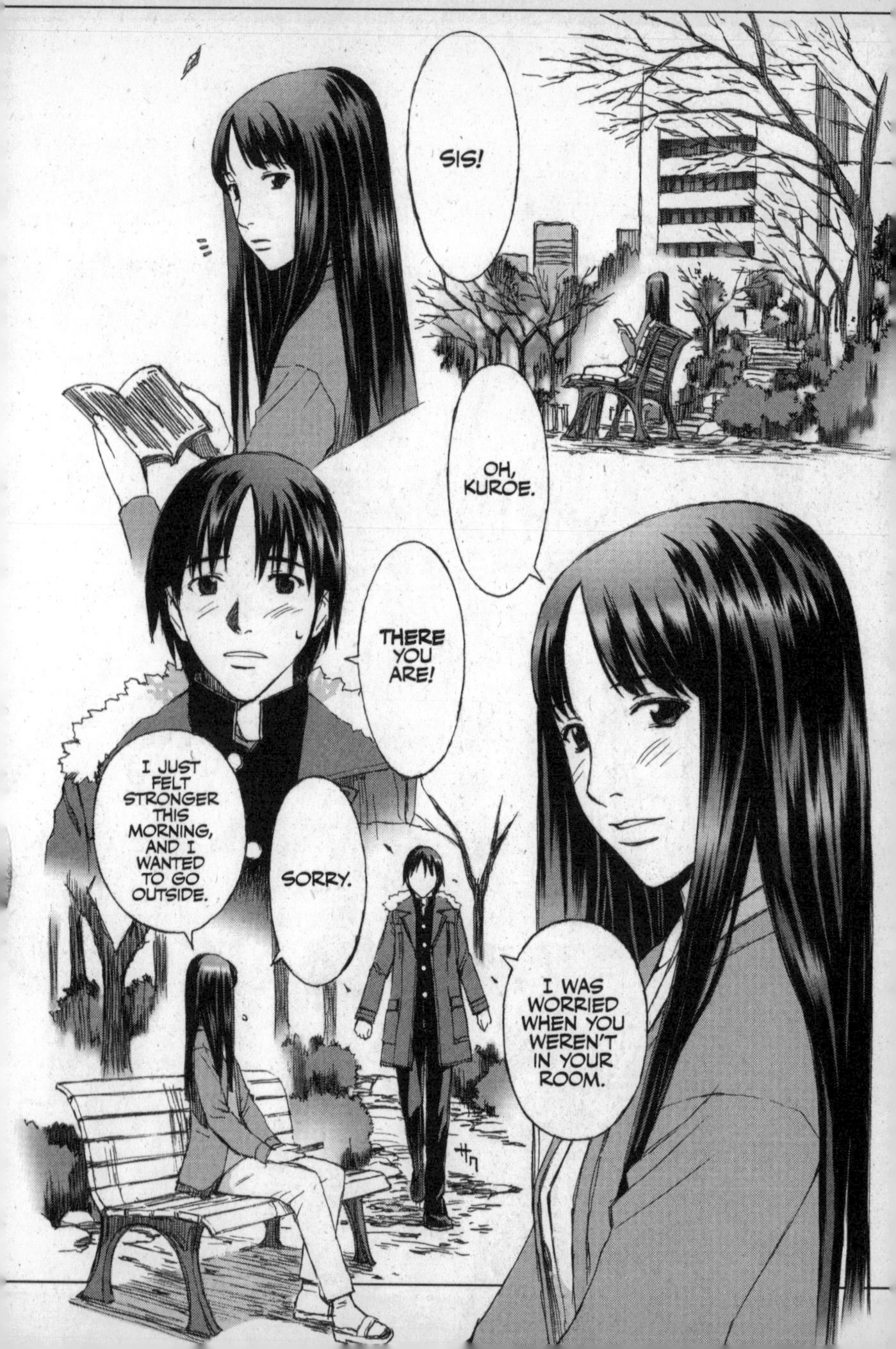
SIS!
OH, KUROE.
THERE YOU ARE!
I WAS WORRIED WHEN YOU WEREN'T IN YOUR ROOM.
SORRY.
I JUST FELT STRONGER THIS MORNING, AND I WANTED TO GO OUTSIDE.

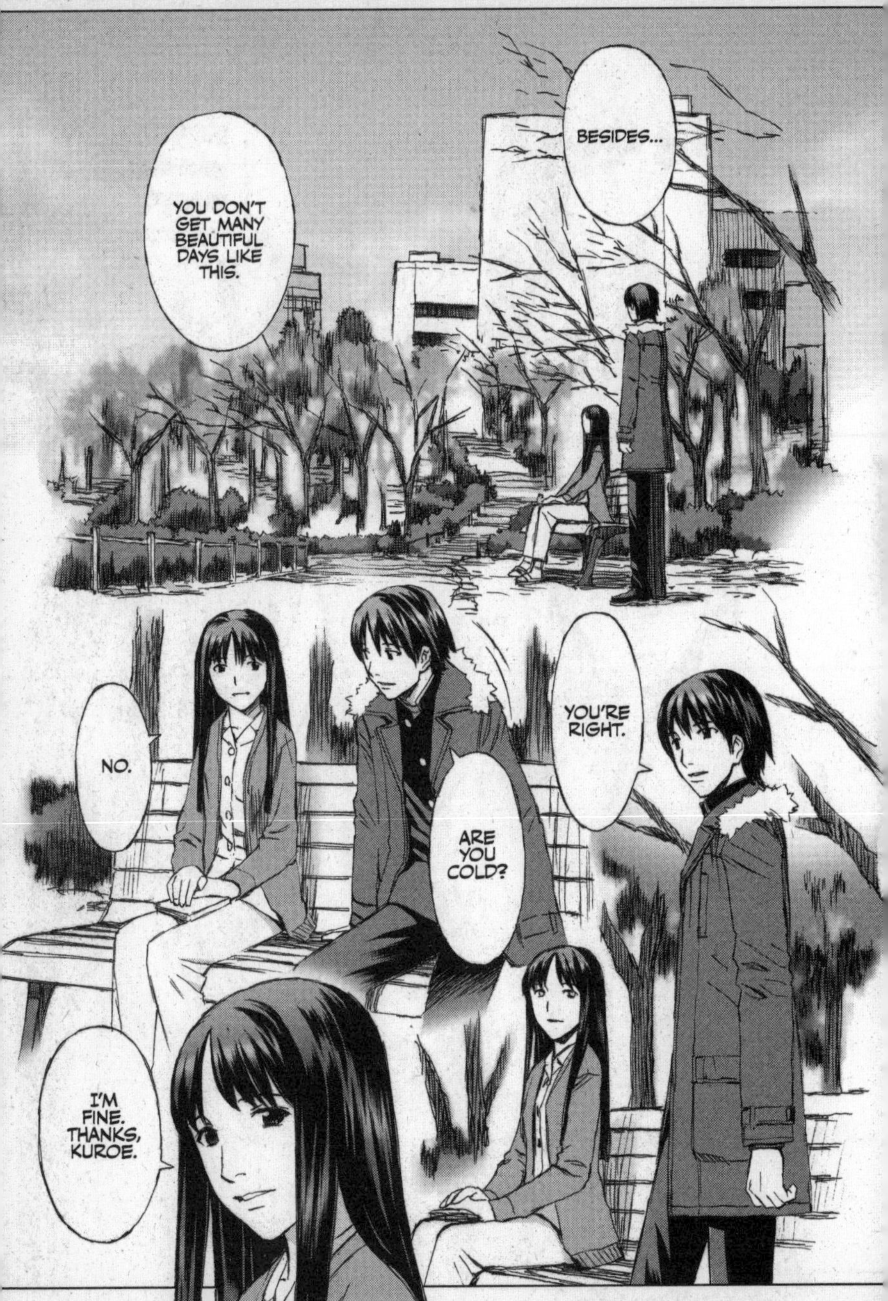
BESIDES...
YOU DON'T GET MANY BEAUTIFUL DAYS LIKE THIS.
YOU'RE RIGHT.
ARE YOU COLD?
NO.
I'M FINE. THANKS, KUROE.

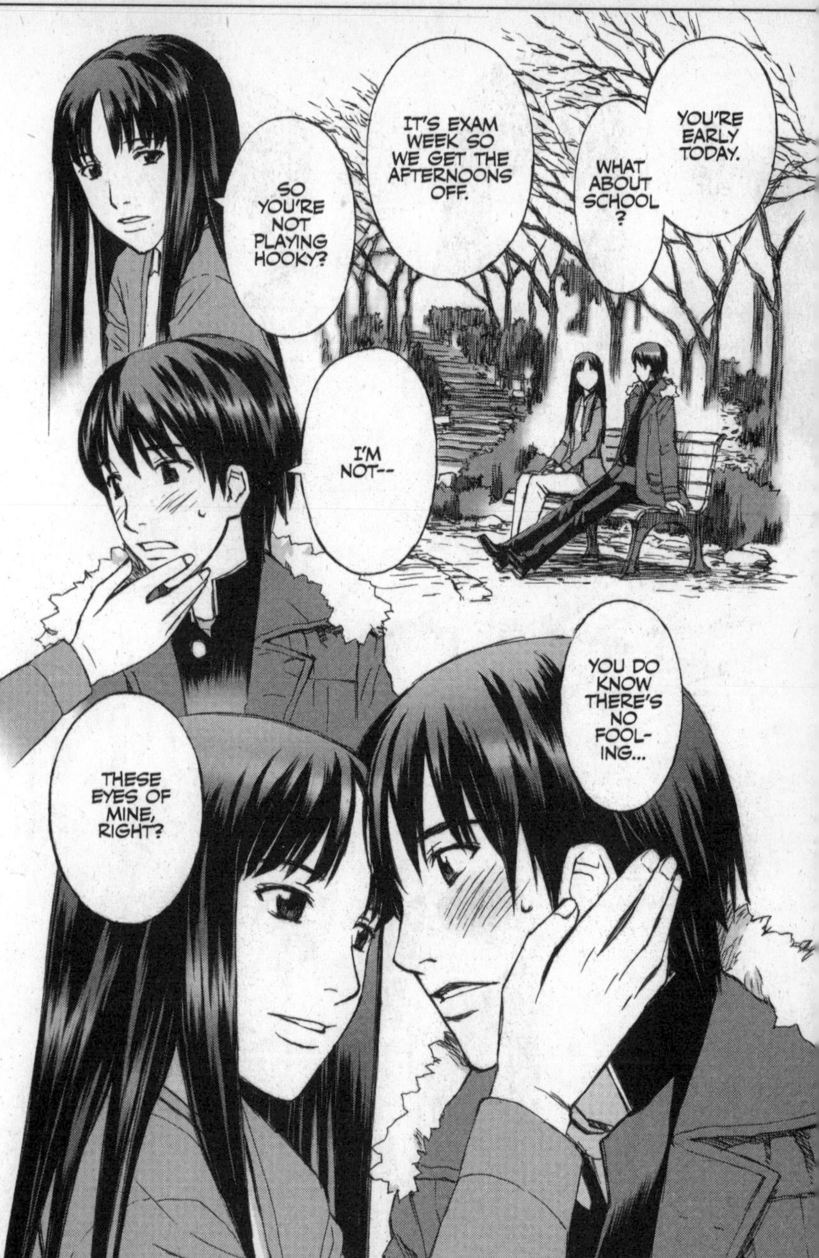
YOU'RE EARLY TODAY.
WHAT ABOUT SCHOOL?
IT'S EXAM WEEK SO WE GET THE AFTERNOONS OFF.
SO YOU'RE NOT PLAYING HOOKY?
I'M NOT--
YOU DO KNOW THERE'S NO FOOLING...
THESE EYES OF MINE, RIGHT?

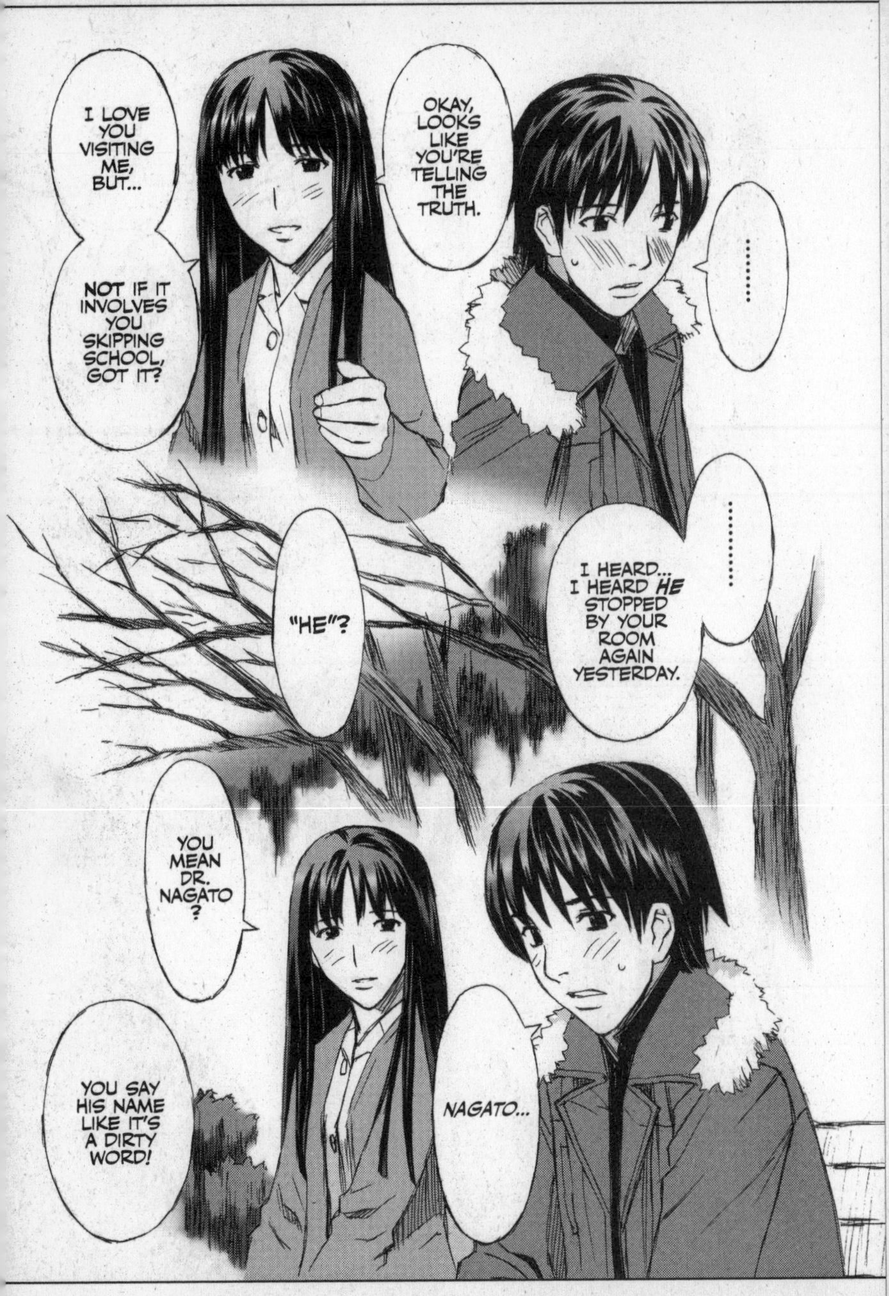
OKAY, LOOKS LIKE YOU'RE TELLING THE TRUTH.
......
I LOVE YOU VISITING ME, BUT...
NOT IF IT INVOLVES YOU SKIPPING SCHOOL, GOT IT?
......
I HEARD... I HEARD HE STOPPED BY YOUR ROOM AGAIN YESTERDAY.
"HE"?
YOU MEAN DR. NAGATO?
NAGATO...
YOU SAY HIS NAME LIKE IT'S A DIRTY WORD!

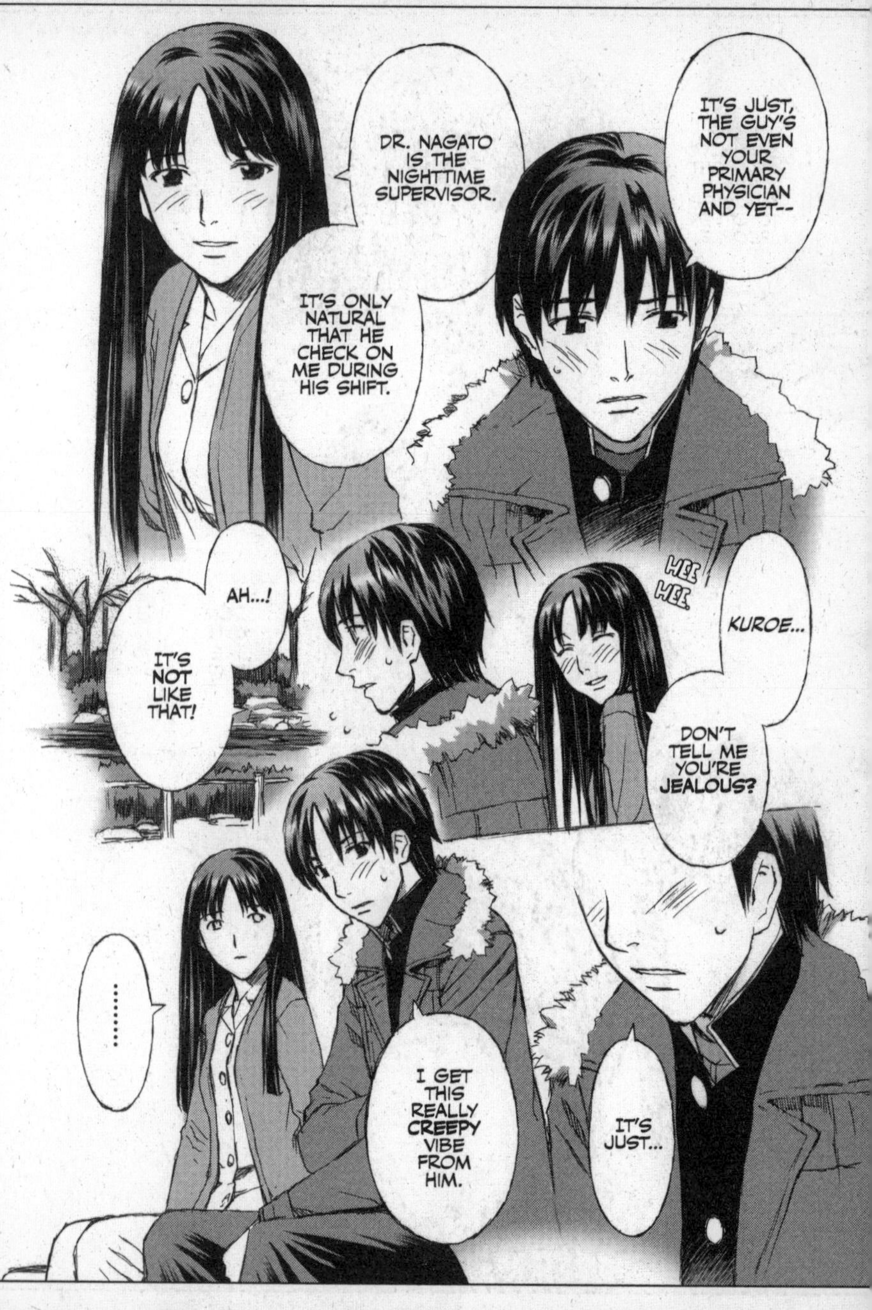
IT'S JUST, THE GUY'S NOT EVEN YOUR PRIMARY PHYSICIAN AND YET--
DR. NAGATO IS THE NIGHTTIME SUPERVISOR.
IT'S ONLY NATURAL THAT HE CHECK ON ME DURING HIS SHIFT.
HEE HEE.
KUROE...
DON'T TELL ME YOU'RE JEALOUS?
AH...!
IT'S NOT LIKE THAT!
IT'S JUST...
I GET THIS REALLY CREEPY VIBE FROM HIM.
....

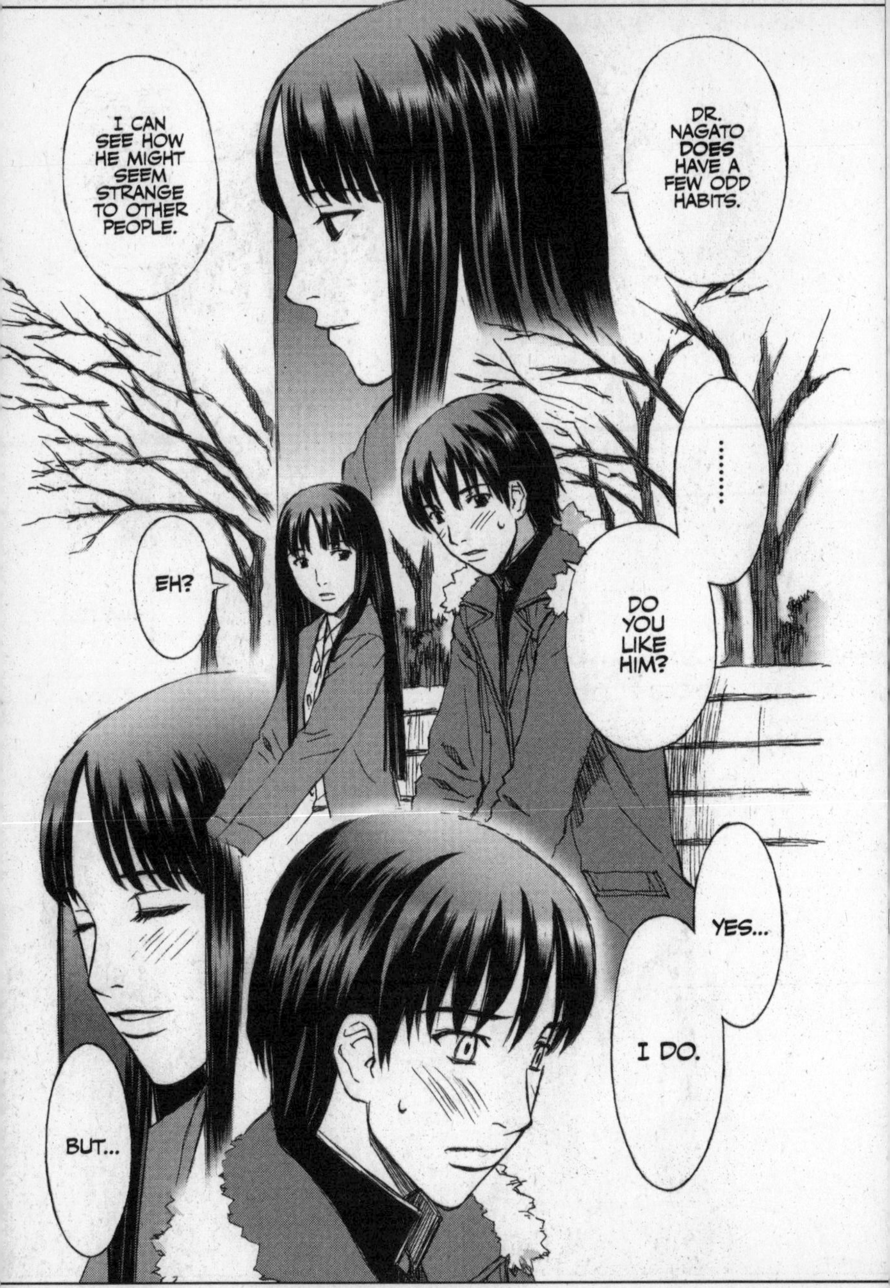
DR. NAGATO DOES HAVE A FEW ODD HABITS.
I CAN SEE HOW HE MIGHT SEEM STRANGE TO OTHER PEOPLE.
......
DO YOU LIKE HIM?
EH?
YES...
I DO.
BUT...

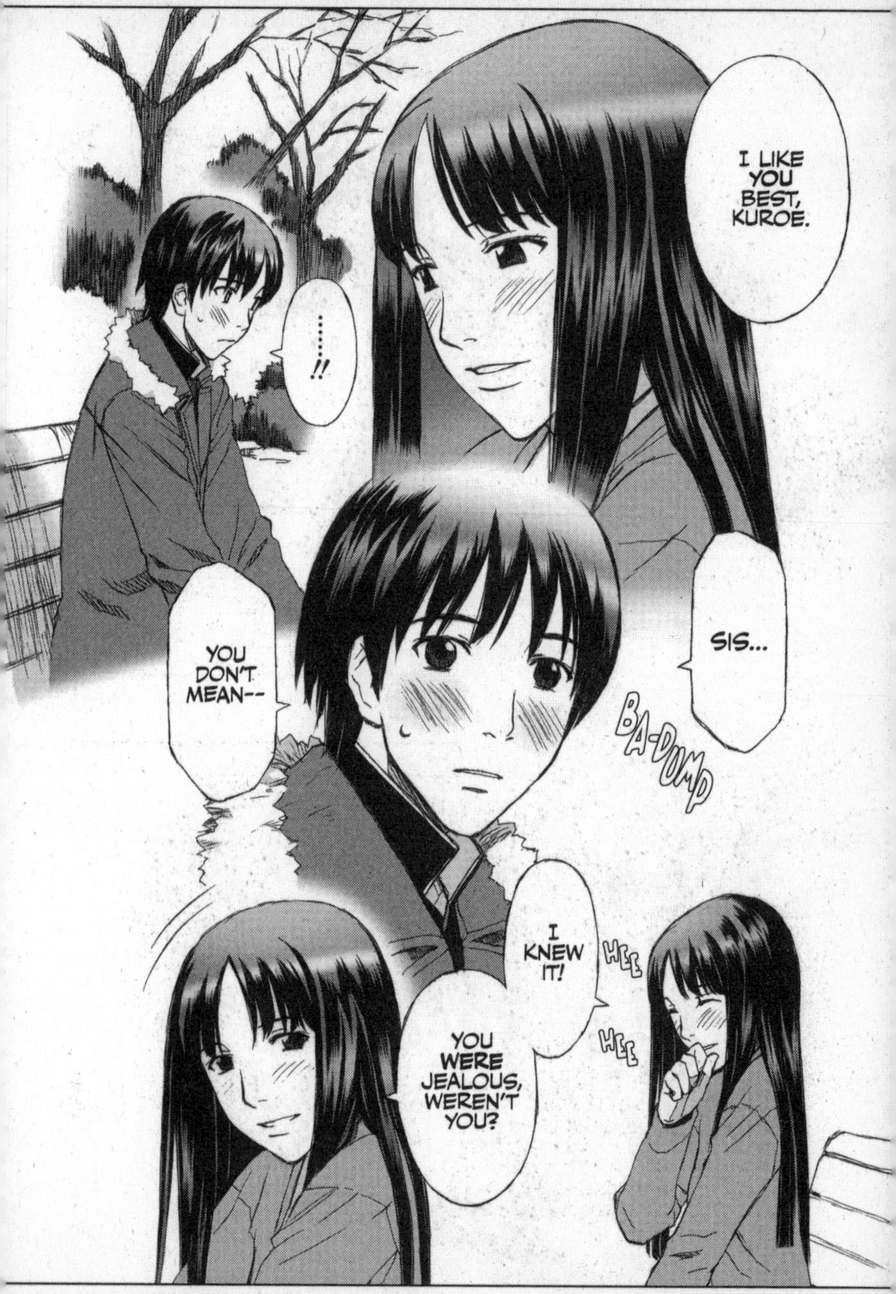
I LIKE YOU BEST, KUROE.
......!!
SIS...
BA-DUMP
YOU DON'T MEAN--
HEE
HEE
I KNEW IT!
YOU WERE JEALOUS, WEREN'T YOU?

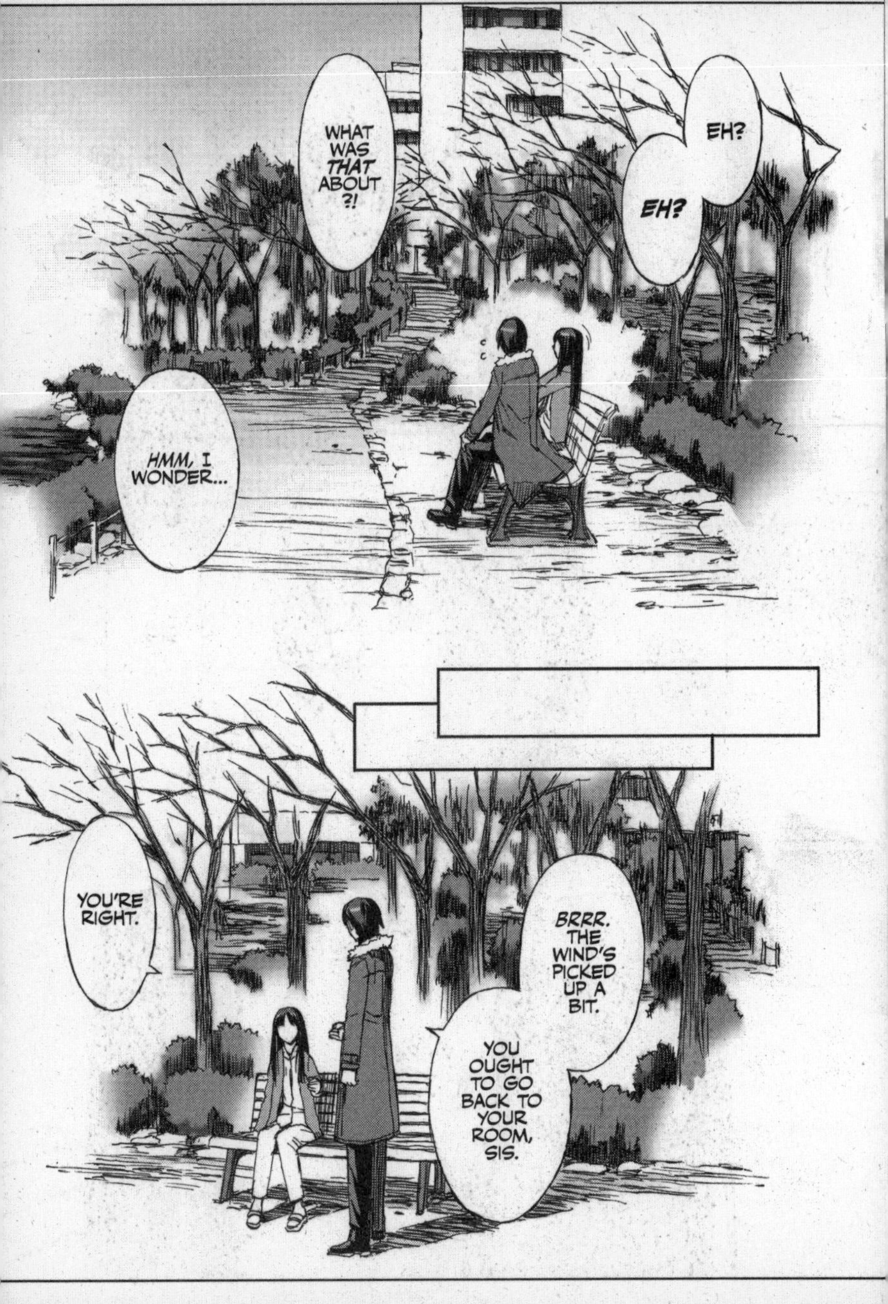
EH?
EH?
WHAT WAS *THAT* ABOUT ?!
HMM, I WONDER...
BRRR. THE WIND'S PICKED UP A BIT.
YOU OUGHT TO GO BACK TO YOUR ROOM, SIS.
YOU'RE RIGHT.

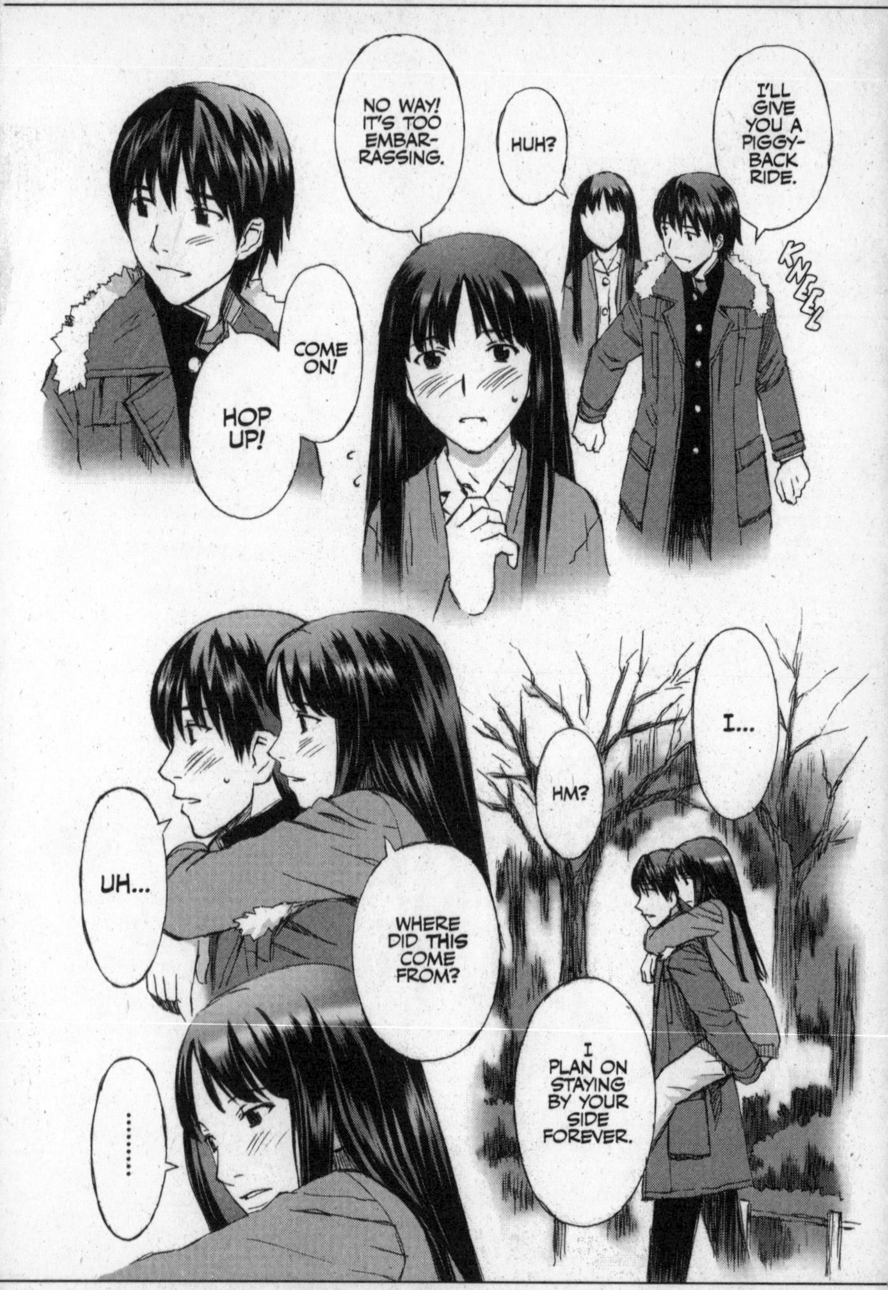
I'LL GIVE YOU A PIGGY-BACK RIDE.
KNEEL
HUH?
NO WAY! IT'S TOO EMBARRASSING.
COME ON!
HOP UP!
I...
HM?
I PLAN ON STAYING BY YOUR SIDE FOREVER.
WHERE DID THIS COME FROM?
UH...
......

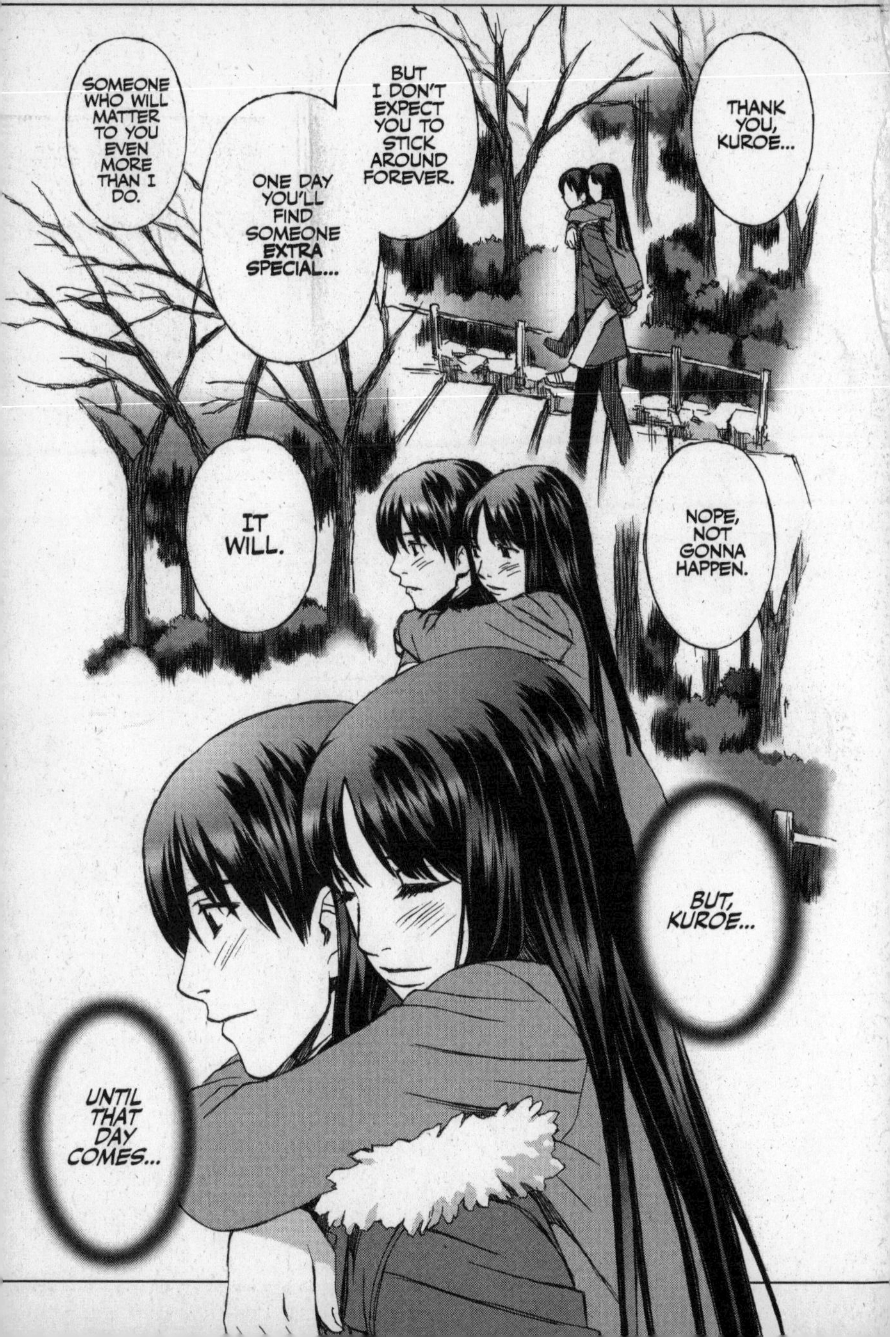
THANK YOU, KUROE...
BUT I DON'T EXPECT YOU TO STICK AROUND FOREVER.
ONE DAY YOU'LL FIND SOMEONE EXTRA SPECIAL...
SOMEONE WHO WILL MATTER TO YOU EVEN MORE THAN I DO.
NOPE, NOT GONNA HAPPEN.
IT WILL.
BUT, KUROE...
UNTIL THAT DAY COMES...

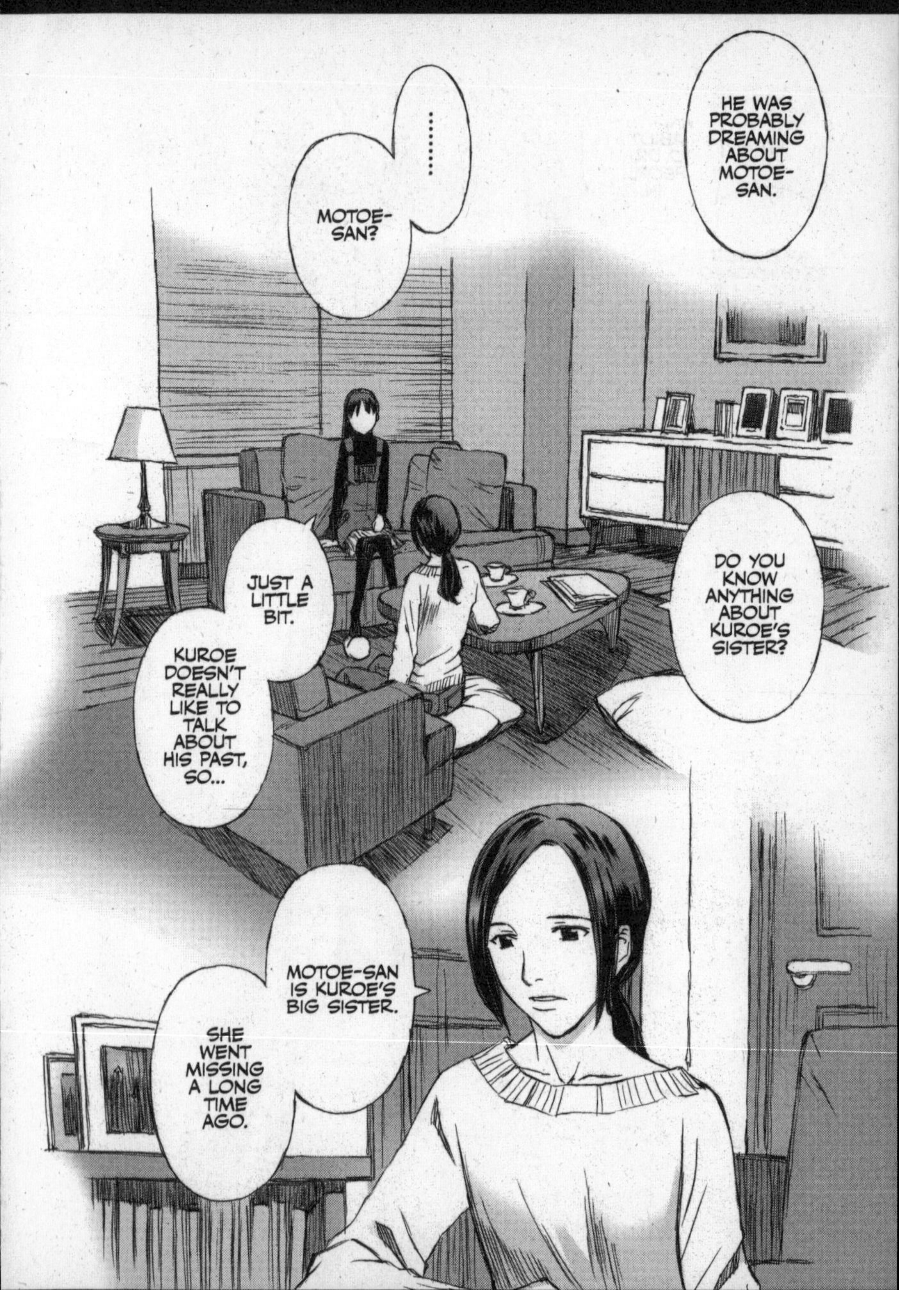
HE WAS PROBABLY DREAMING ABOUT MOTOE-SAN.
......
MOTOE-SAN?
DO YOU KNOW ANYTHING ABOUT KUROE'S SISTER?
JUST A LITTLE BIT.
KUROE DOESN'T REALLY LIKE TO TALK ABOUT HIS PAST, SO...
MOTOE-SAN IS KUROE'S BIG SISTER.
SHE WENT MISSING A LONG TIME AGO.

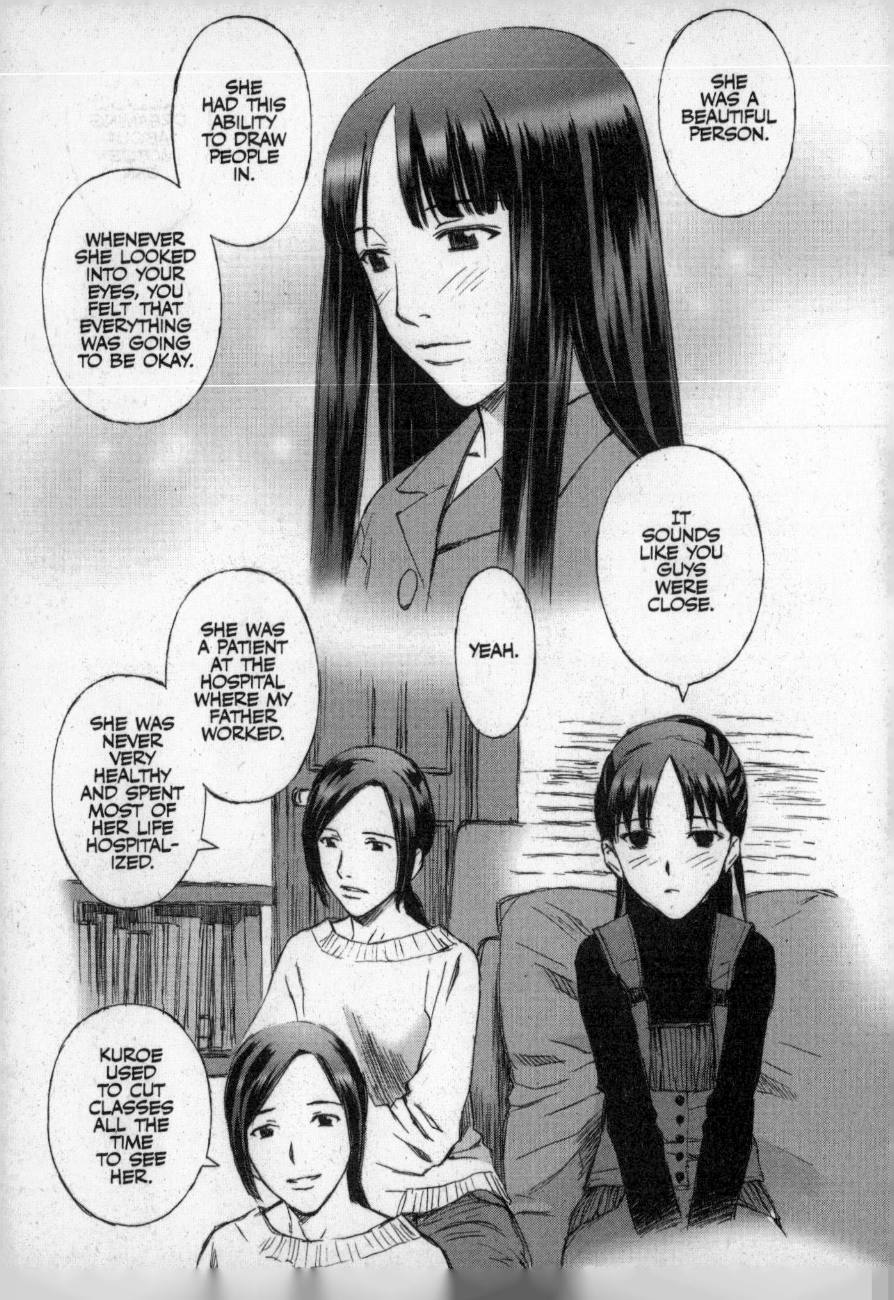
SHE WAS A BEAUTIFUL PERSON.
SHE HAD THIS ABILITY TO DRAW PEOPLE IN.
WHENEVER SHE LOOKED INTO YOUR EYES, YOU FELT THAT EVERYTHING WAS GOING TO BE OKAY.
IT SOUNDS LIKE YOU GUYS WERE CLOSE.
YEAH.
SHE WAS A PATIENT AT THE HOSPITAL WHERE MY FATHER WORKED.
SHE WAS NEVER VERY HEALTHY AND SPENT MOST OF HER LIFE HOSPITAL-IZED.
KUROE USED TO CUT CLASSES ALL THE TIME TO SEE HER.

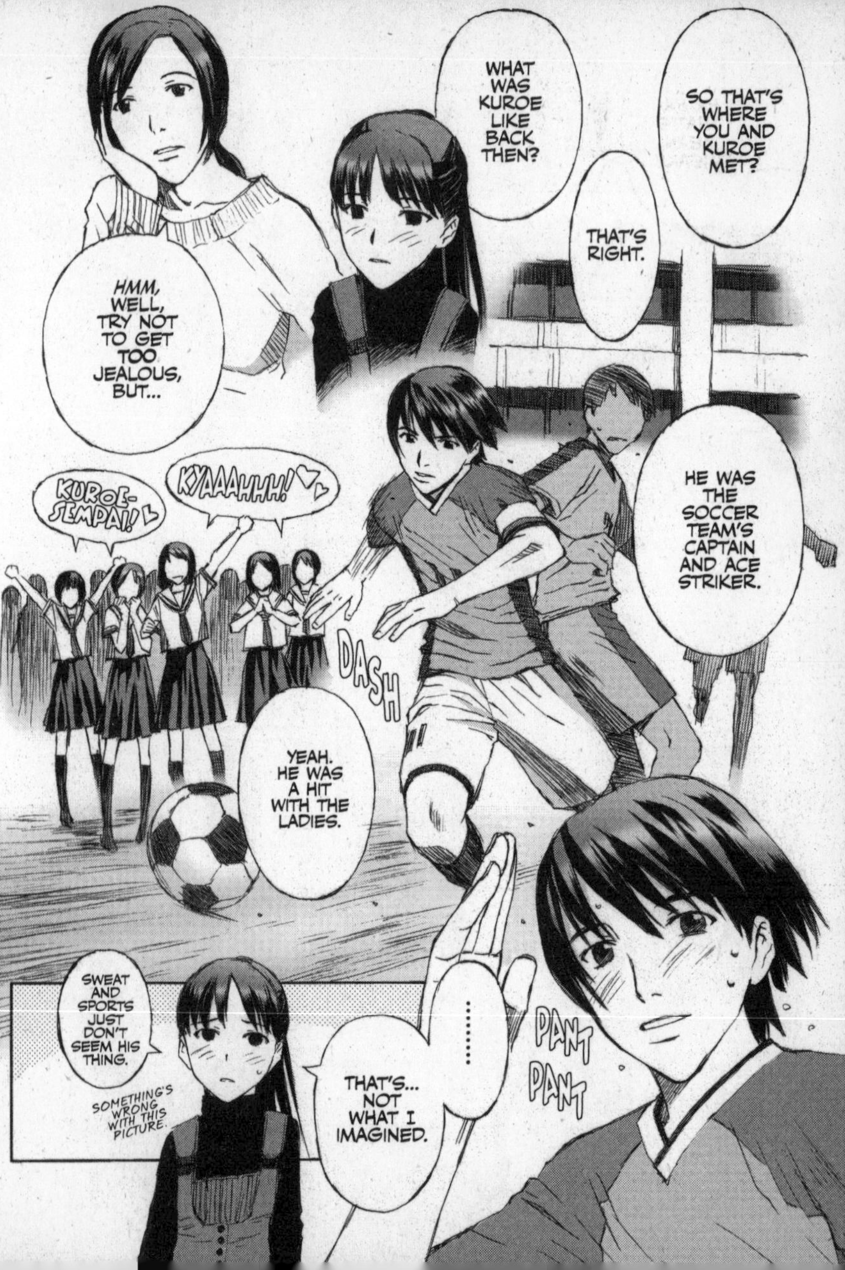
SO THAT'S WHERE YOU AND KUROE MET?
THAT'S RIGHT.
WHAT WAS KUROE LIKE BACK THEN?
HMM, WELL, TRY NOT TO GET TOO JEALOUS, BUT...
HE WAS THE SOCCER TEAM'S CAPTAIN AND ACE STRIKER.
KYAAAHHH!
KUROE-SEMPAI!
DASH
YEAH. HE WAS A HIT WITH THE LADIES.
PANT PANT
......
THAT'S... NOT WHAT I IMAGINED.
SWEAT AND SPORTS JUST DON'T SEEM HIS THING.
SOMETHING'S WRONG WITH THIS PICTURE.

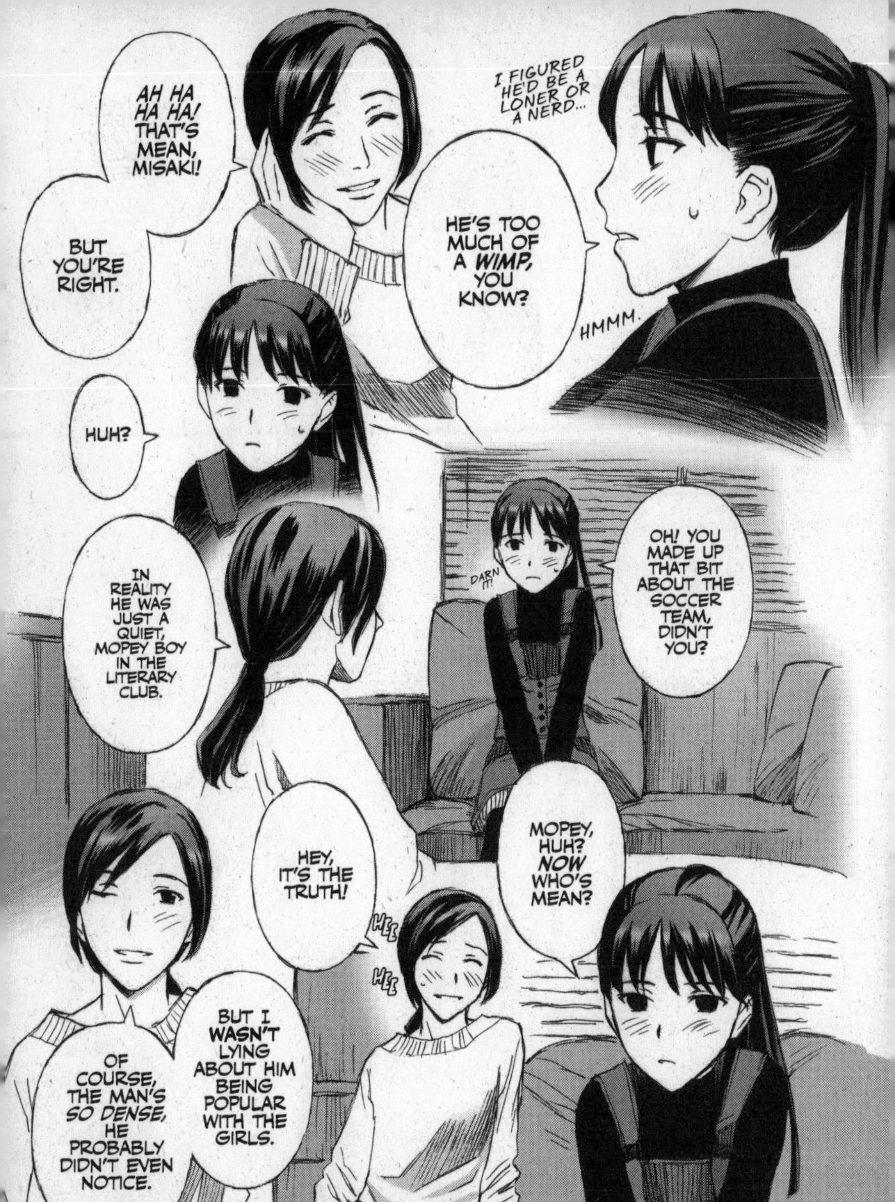
I FIGURED HE'D BE A LONER OR A NERD...
HE'S TOO MUCH OF A *WIMP*, YOU KNOW?
HMMM.
AH HA HA HA! THAT'S MEAN, MISAKI!
BUT YOU'RE RIGHT.
HUH?
OH! YOU MADE UP THAT BIT ABOUT THE SOCCER TEAM, DIDN'T YOU?
DARN IT!
IN REALITY HE WAS JUST A QUIET, MOPEY BOY IN THE LITERARY CLUB.
MOPEY, HUH? *NOW* WHO'S MEAN?
HEE
HEE
HEY, IT'S THE TRUTH!
BUT I WASN'T LYING ABOUT HIM BEING POPULAR WITH THE GIRLS.
OF COURSE, THE MAN'S *SO DENSE*, HE PROBABLY DIDN'T EVEN NOTICE.

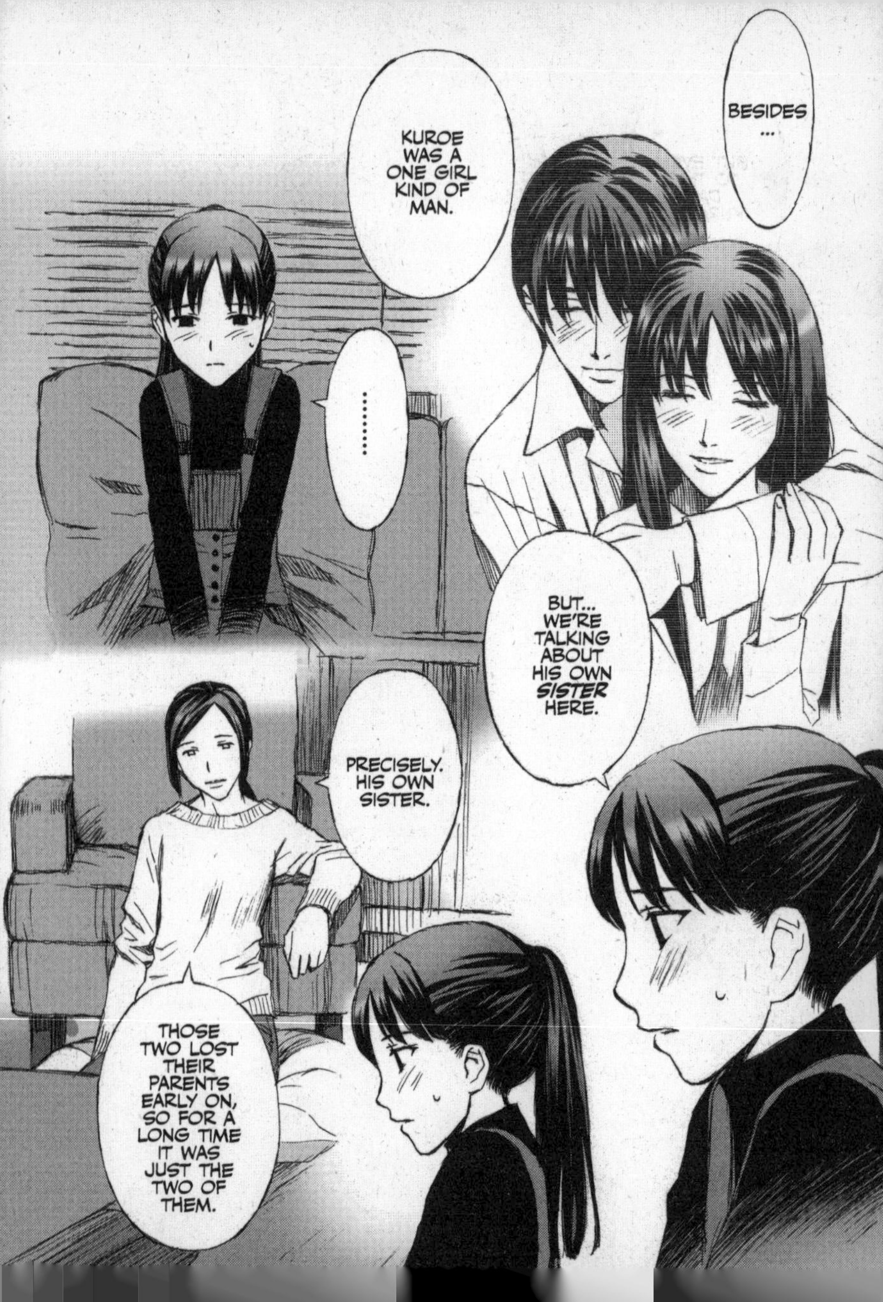
BESIDES...
KUROE WAS A ONE GIRL KIND OF MAN.
....
BUT... WE'RE TALKING ABOUT HIS OWN *SISTER* HERE.
PRECISELY. HIS OWN SISTER.
THOSE TWO LOST THEIR PARENTS EARLY ON, SO FOR A LONG TIME IT WAS JUST THE TWO OF THEM.

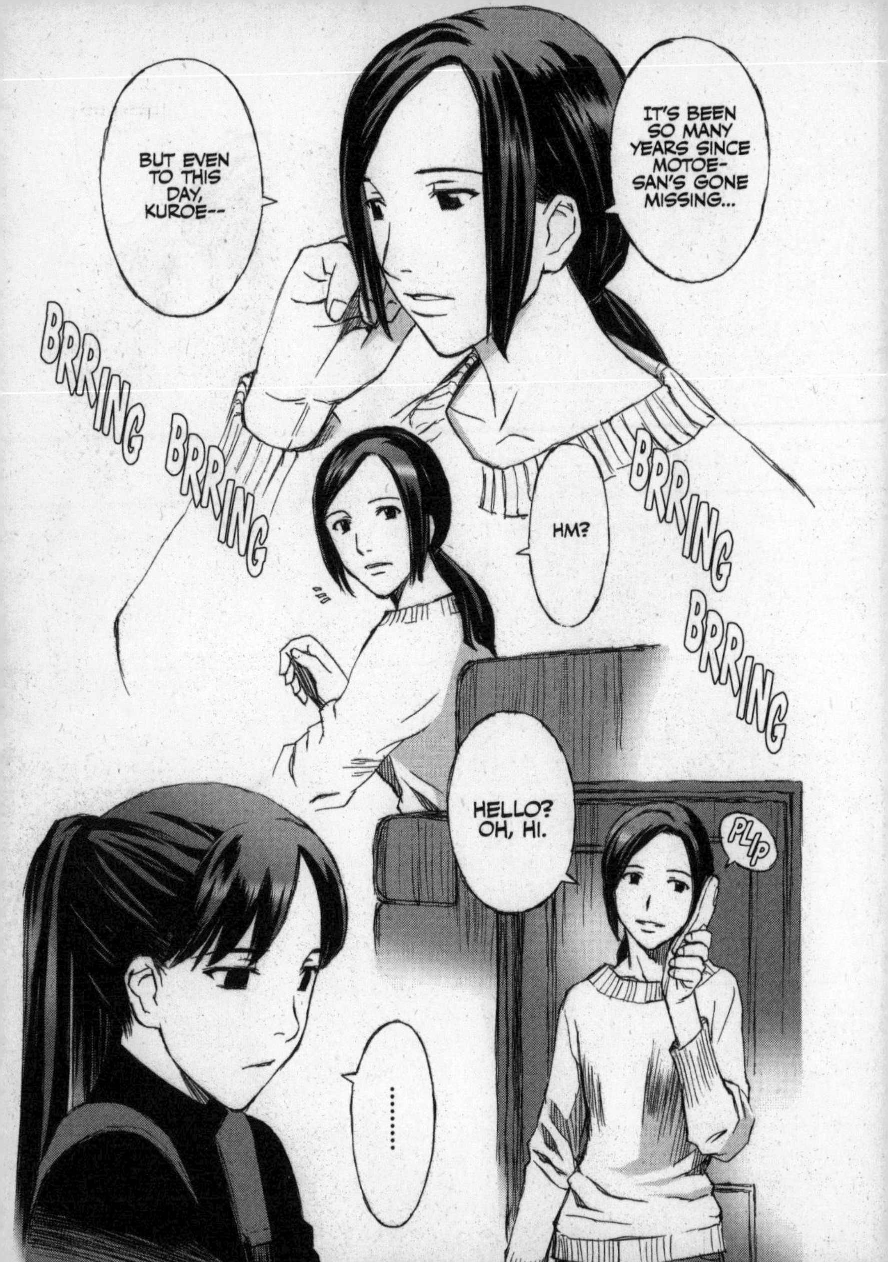
IT'S BEEN SO MANY YEARS SINCE MOTOE-SAN'S GONE MISSING...
BUT EVEN TO THIS DAY, KUROE--
BRRING BRRING
BRRING BRRING
BRRING BRRING
HM?
HELLO? OH, HI.
PLIP
......

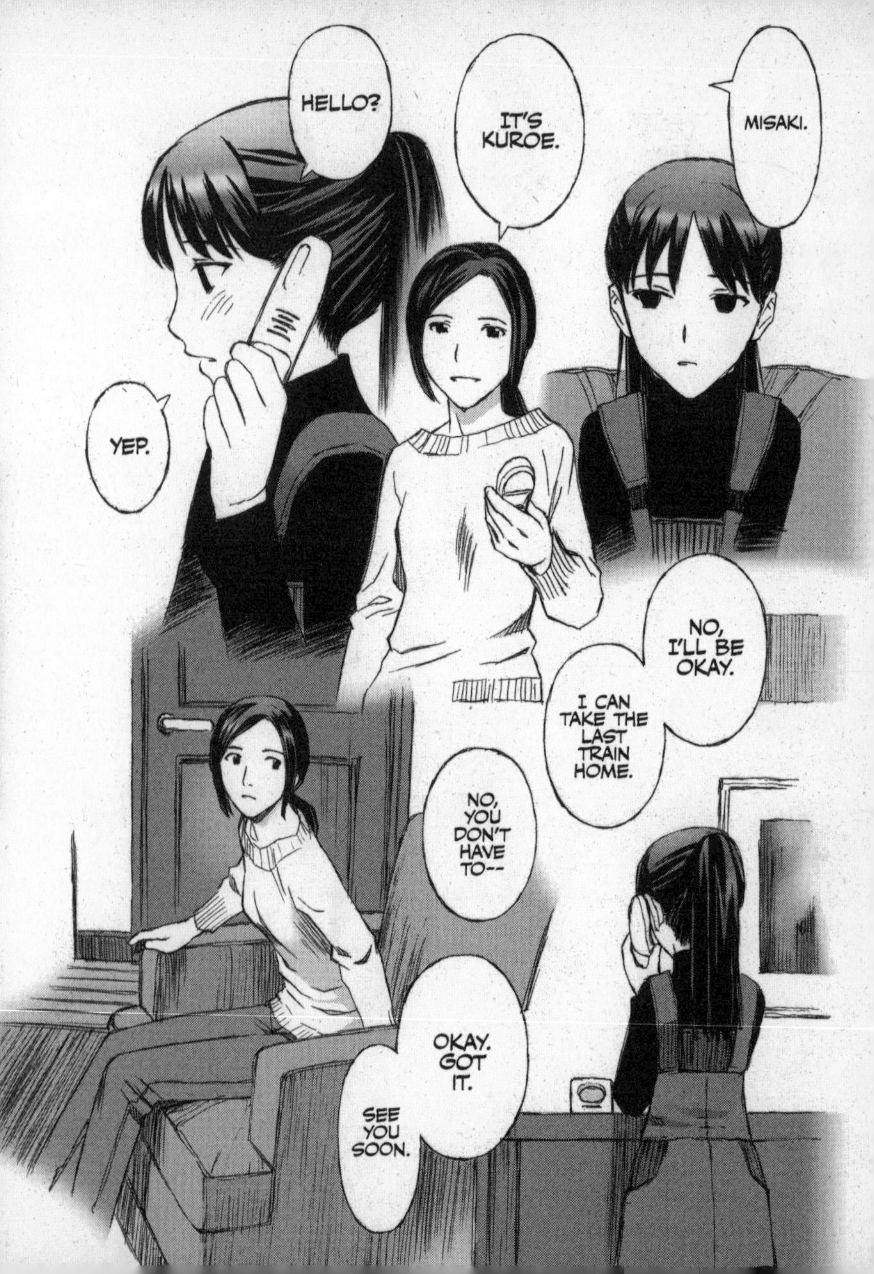
MISAKI.
IT'S KUROE.
HELLO?
YEP.
NO, I'LL BE OKAY.
I CAN TAKE THE LAST TRAIN HOME.
NO, YOU DON'T HAVE TO--
OKAY. GOT IT.
SEE YOU SOON.

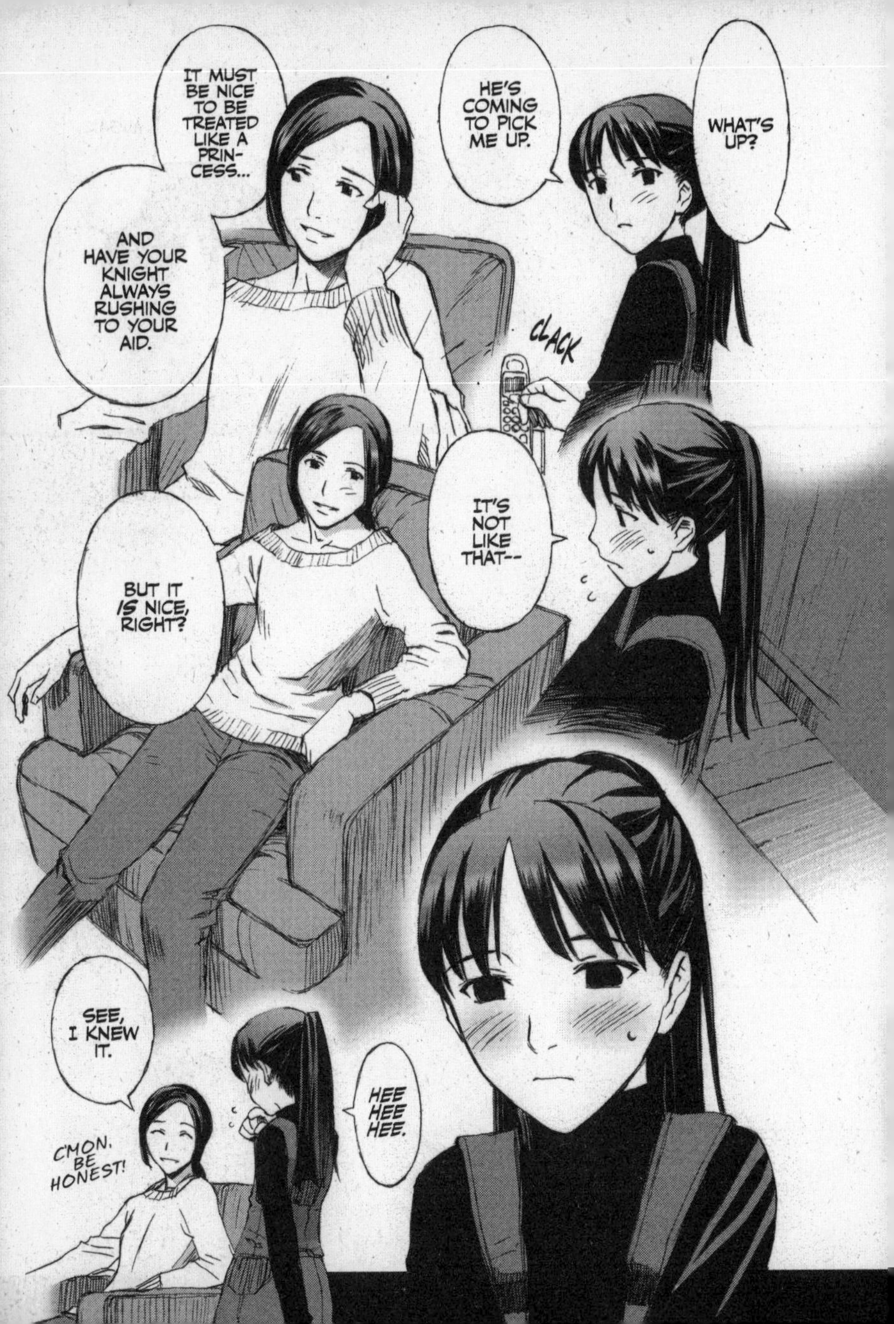
WHAT'S UP?
HE'S COMING TO PICK ME UP.
CLACK
IT MUST BE NICE TO BE TREATED LIKE A PRIN-CESS...
AND HAVE YOUR KNIGHT ALWAYS RUSHING TO YOUR AID.
IT'S NOT LIKE THAT--
BUT IT *IS* NICE, RIGHT?
SEE, I KNEW IT.
HEE HEE HEE.
C'MON, BE HONEST!

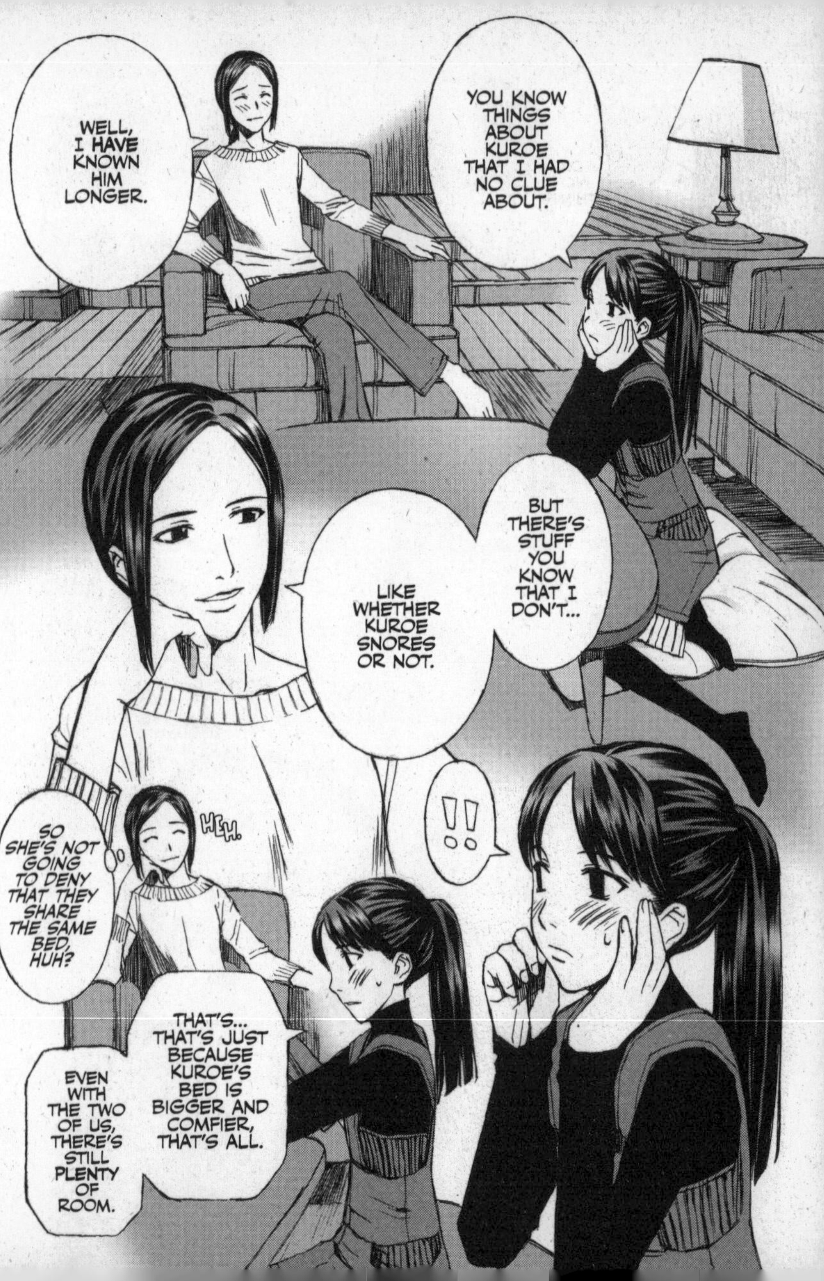
YOU KNOW THINGS ABOUT KUROE THAT I HAD NO CLUE ABOUT.
WELL, I HAVE KNOWN HIM LONGER.
BUT THERE'S STUFF YOU KNOW THAT I DON'T...
LIKE WHETHER KUROE SNORES OR NOT.
!!
HEH.
SO SHE'S NOT GOING TO DENY THAT THEY SHARE THE SAME BED, HUH?
THAT'S... THAT'S JUST BECAUSE KUROE'S BED IS BIGGER AND COMFIER, THAT'S ALL.
EVEN WITH THE TWO OF US, THERE'S STILL PLENTY OF ROOM.

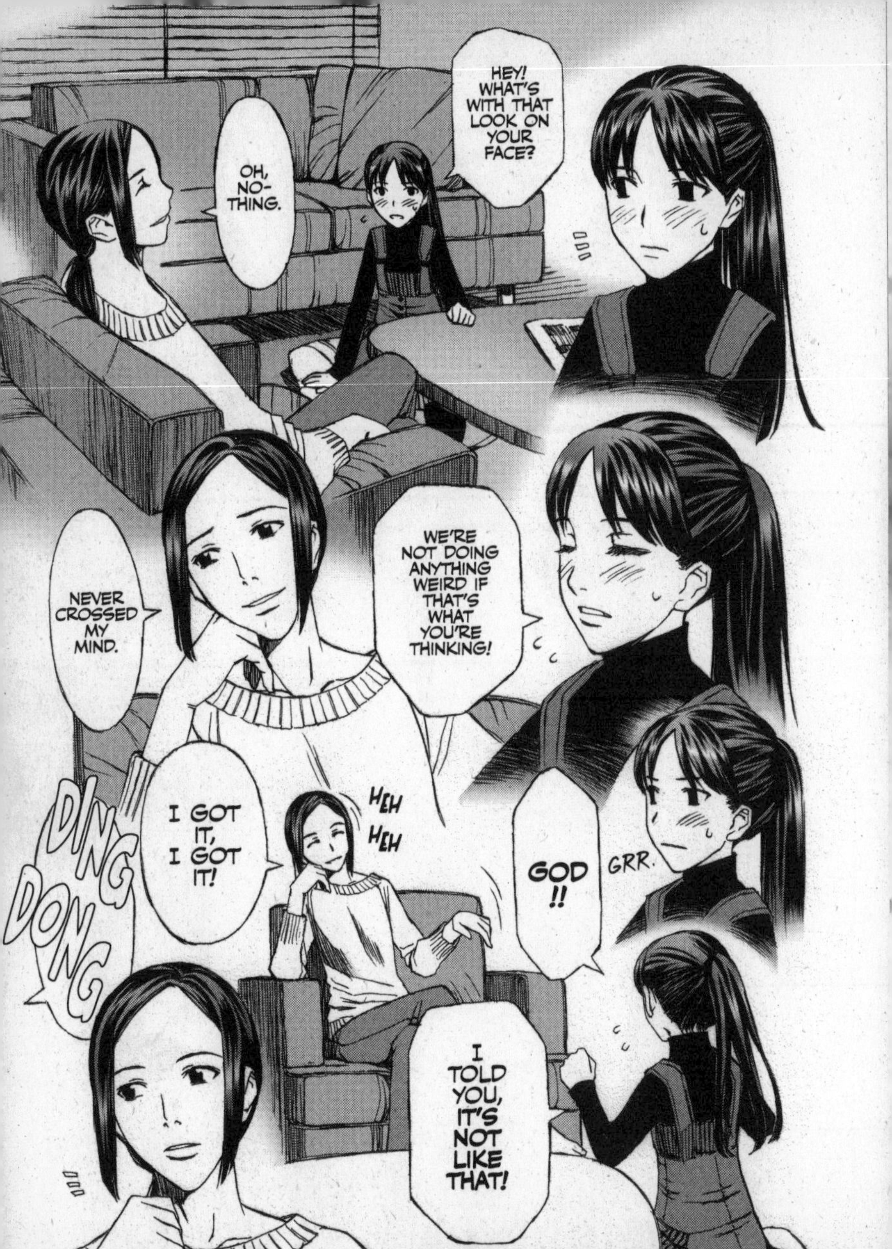
HEY! WHAT'S WITH THAT LOOK ON YOUR FACE?
OH, NO-THING.
WE'RE NOT DOING ANYTHING WEIRD IF THAT'S WHAT YOU'RE THINKING!
NEVER CROSSED MY MIND.
GRR.
GOD!!
I TOLD YOU, IT'S NOT LIKE THAT!
HEH HEH
I GOT IT, I GOT IT!
DING DONG

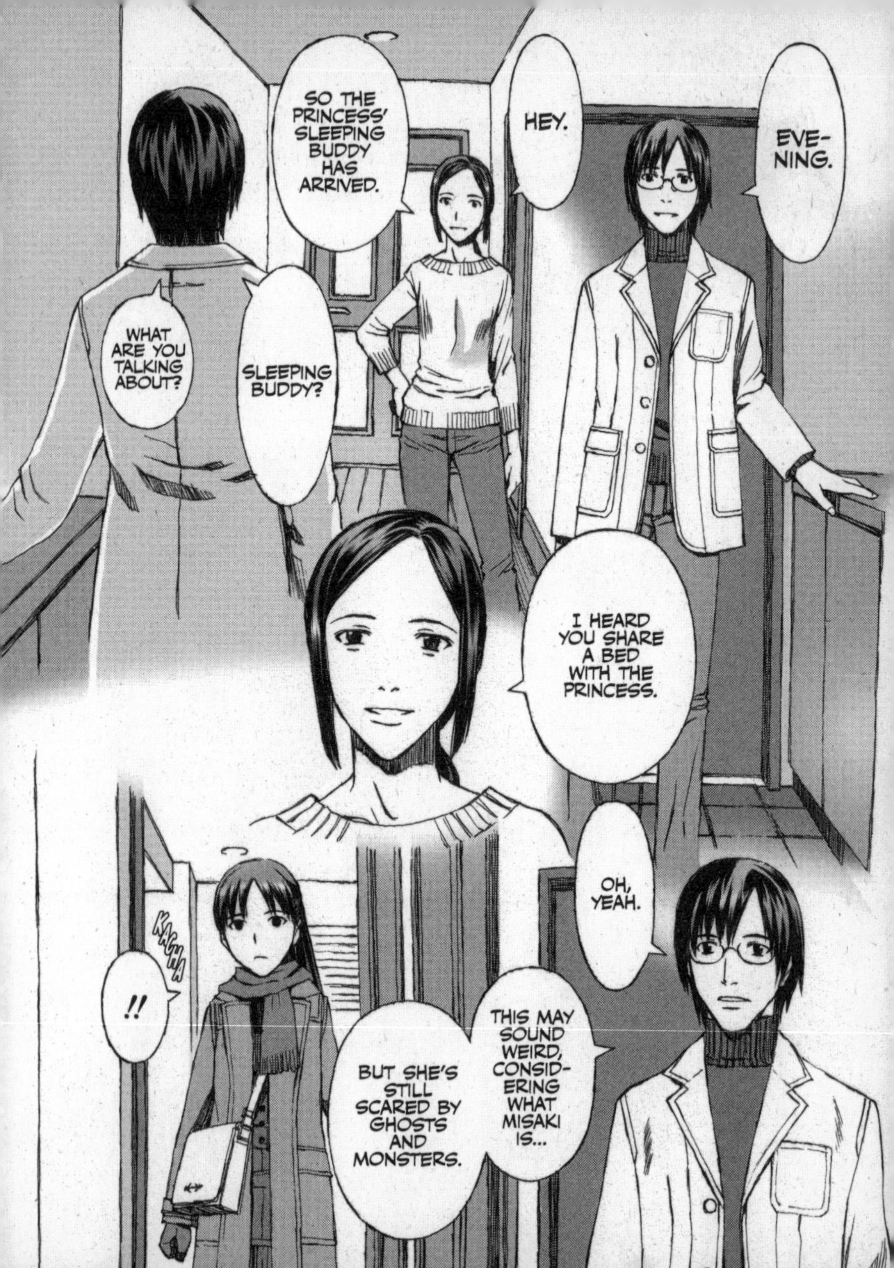
EVE-NING.
HEY.
SO THE PRINCESS' SLEEPING BUDDY HAS ARRIVED.
SLEEPING BUDDY?
WHAT ARE YOU TALKING ABOUT?
I HEARD YOU SHARE A BED WITH THE PRINCESS.
OH, YEAH.
THIS MAY SOUND WEIRD, CONSID-ERING WHAT MISAKI IS...
BUT SHE'S STILL SCARED BY GHOSTS AND MONSTERS.
KACHA
!!

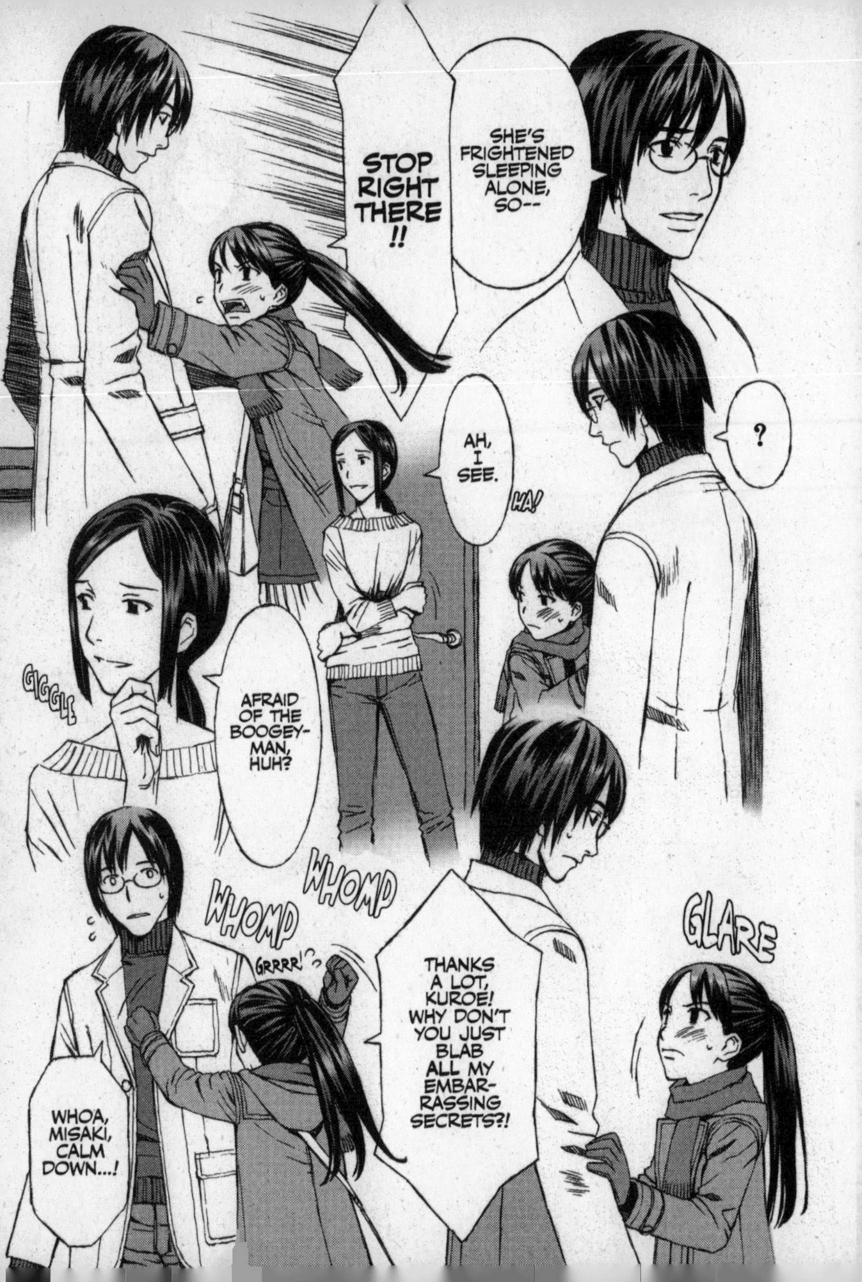
SHE'S FRIGHTENED SLEEPING ALONE, SO--
STOP RIGHT THERE!!
?
AH, I SEE.
HA!
AFRAID OF THE BOOGEY-MAN, HUH?
GIGGLE
GLARE
THANKS A LOT, KUROE! WHY DON'T YOU JUST BLAB ALL MY EMBAR-RASSING SECRETS?!
WHOMP
WHOMP
GRRRR!
WHOA, MISAKI, CALM DOWN...!

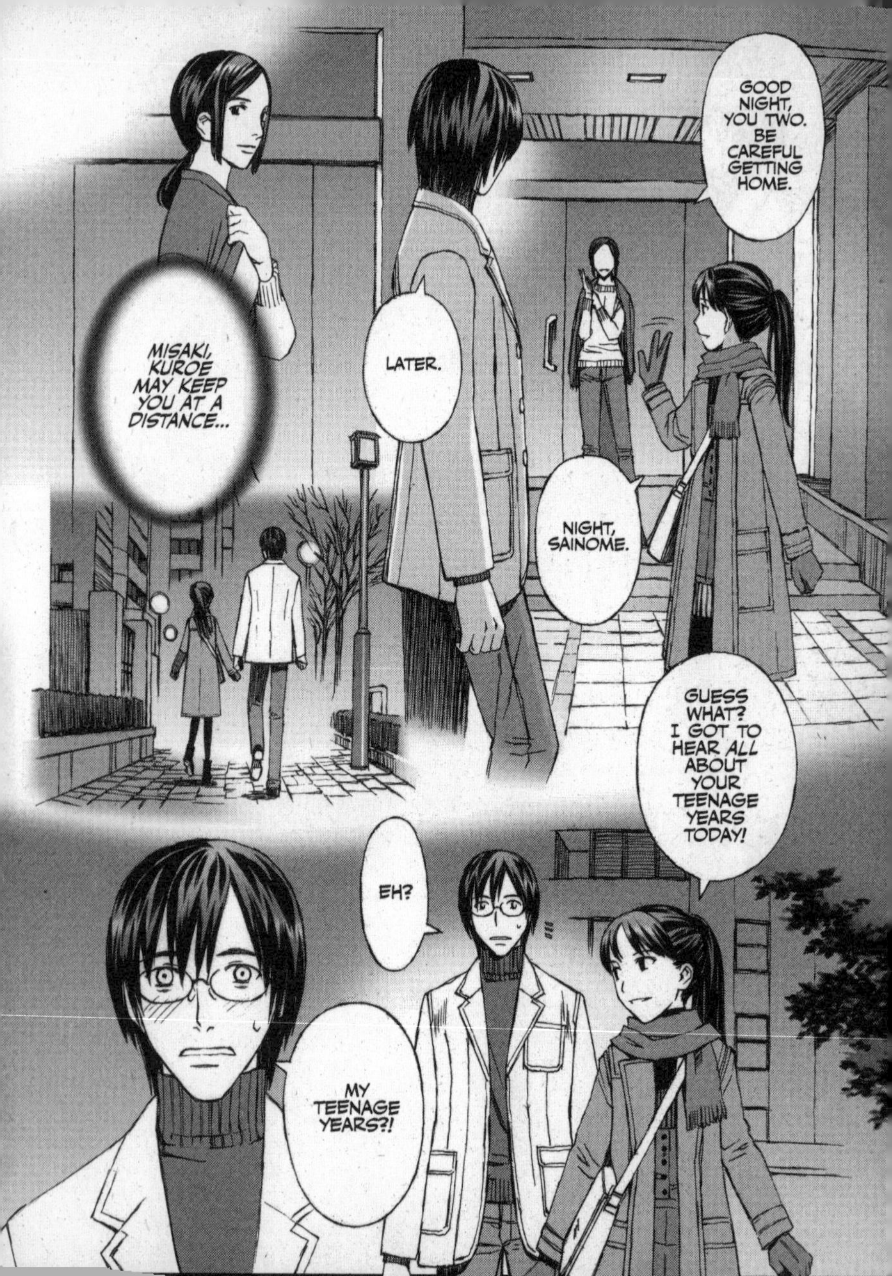
GOOD NIGHT, YOU TWO. BE CAREFUL GETTING HOME.
LATER.
NIGHT, SAINOME.
MISAKI, KUROE MAY KEEP YOU AT A DISTANCE...
GUESS WHAT? I GOT TO HEAR *ALL* ABOUT YOUR TEENAGE YEARS TODAY!
EH?
MY TEENAGE YEARS?!

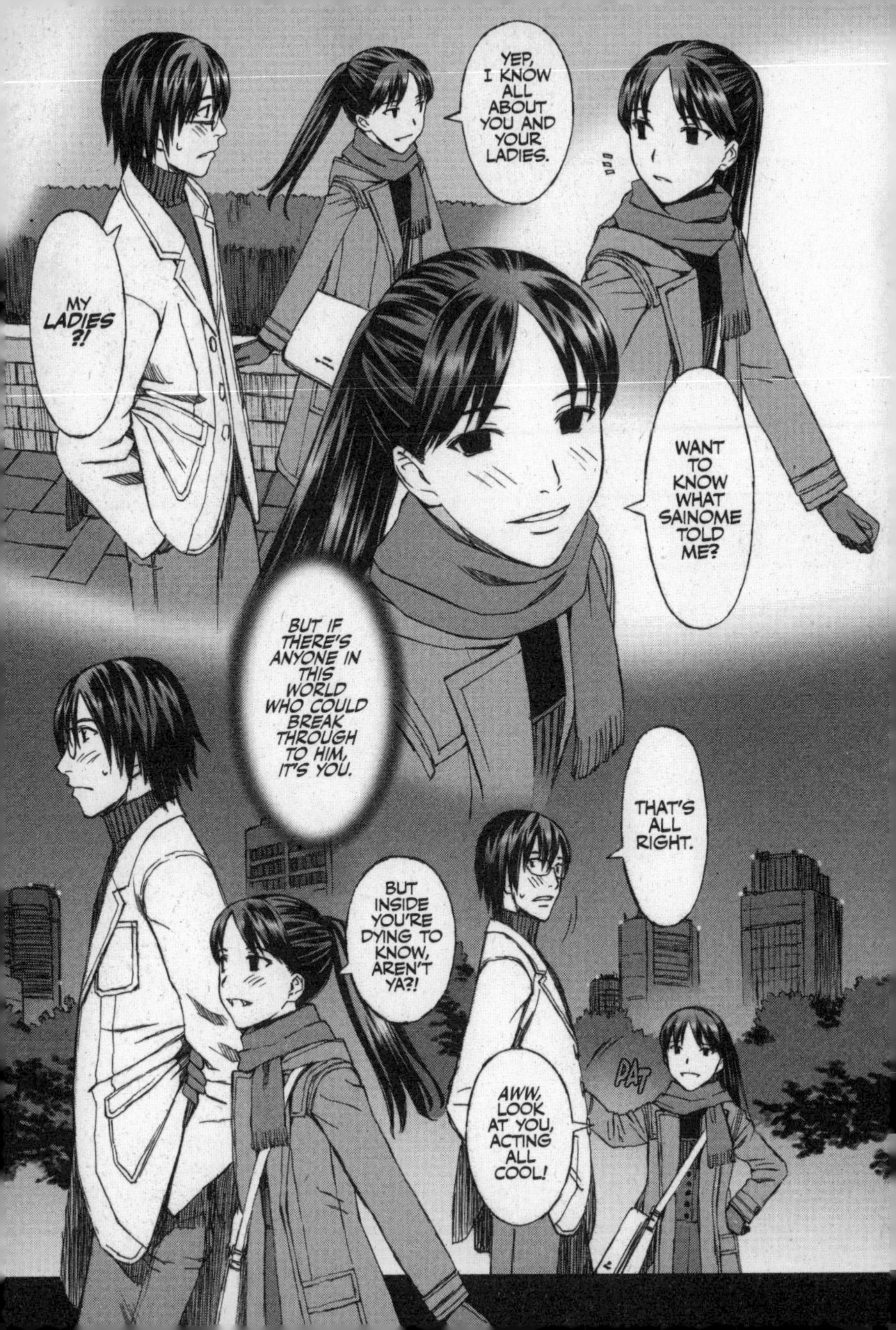
YEP, I KNOW ALL ABOUT YOU AND YOUR LADIES.
MY LADIES?!
WANT TO KNOW WHAT SAINOME TOLD ME?
BUT IF THERE'S ANYONE IN THIS WORLD WHO COULD BREAK THROUGH TO HIM, IT'S YOU.
THAT'S ALL RIGHT.
PAT
AWW, LOOK AT YOU, ACTING ALL COOL!
BUT INSIDE YOU'RE DYING TO KNOW, AREN'T YA?!

Episode 8
YOUR SMILE
The Smile I Don't Know

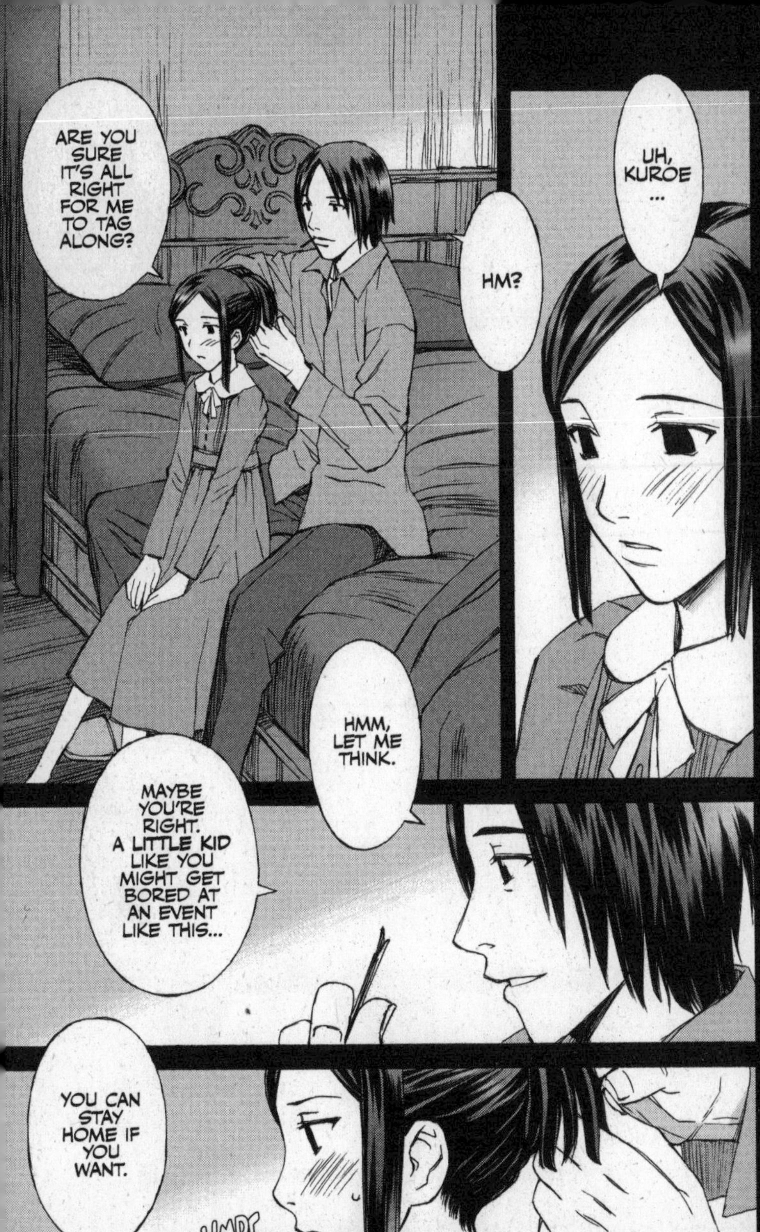
UH, KUROE ...
HM?
ARE YOU SURE IT'S ALL RIGHT FOR ME TO TAG ALONG?
HMM, LET ME THINK.
MAYBE YOU'RE RIGHT. A LITTLE KID LIKE YOU MIGHT GET BORED AT AN EVENT LIKE THIS...
YOU CAN STAY HOME IF YOU WANT.
HMPF

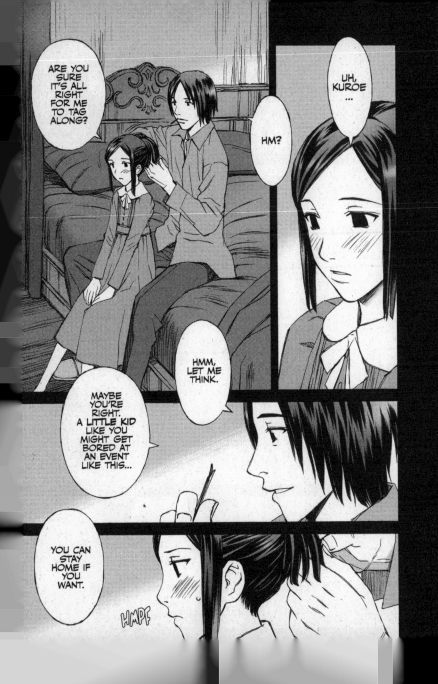

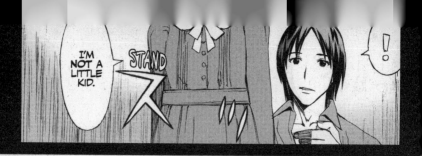

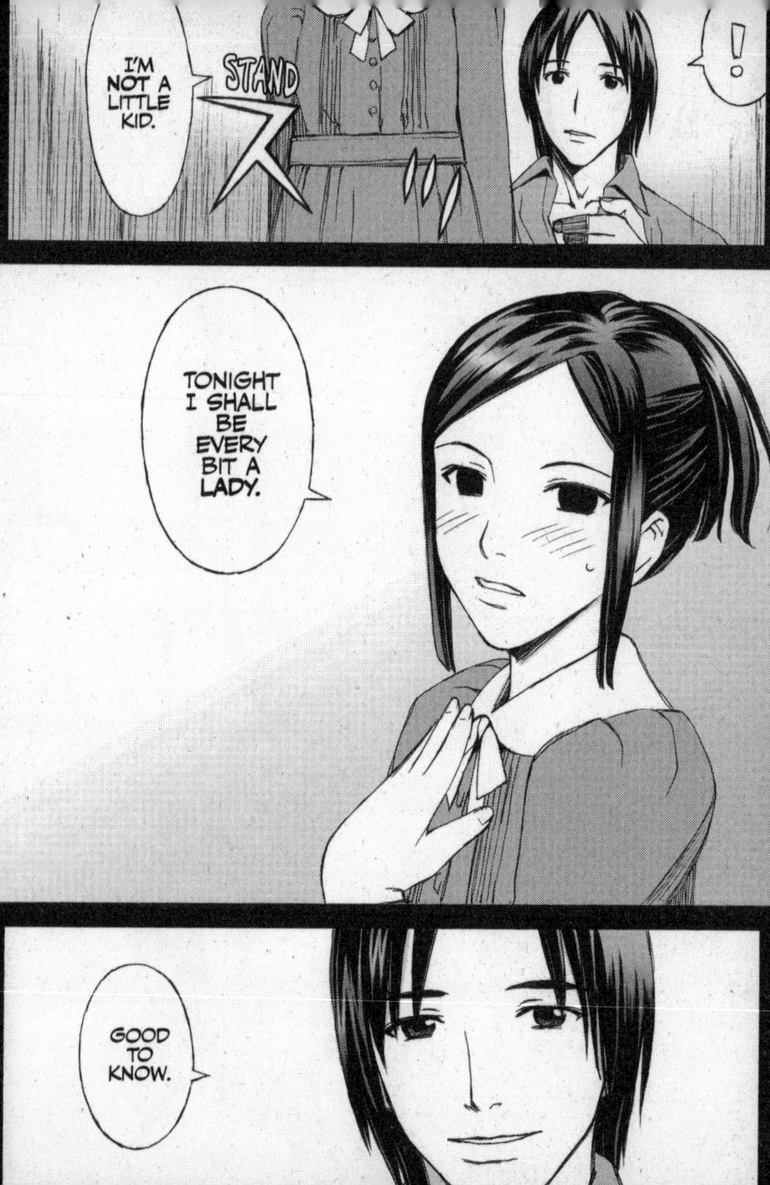
!
STAND
I'M NOT A LITTLE KID.
TONIGHT I SHALL BE EVERY BIT A LADY.
GOOD TO KNOW.

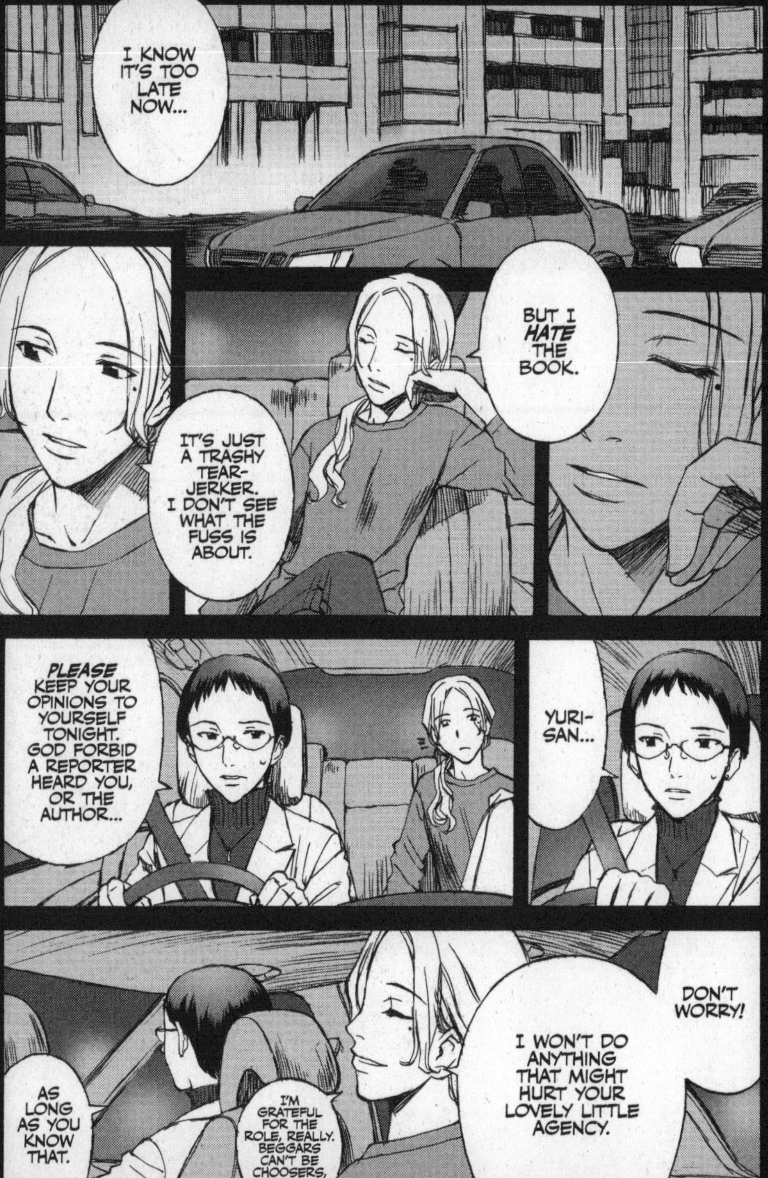
I KNOW IT'S TOO LATE NOW...
BUT I *HATE* THE BOOK.
IT'S JUST A TRASHY TEAR-JERKER. I DON'T SEE WHAT THE FUSS IS ABOUT.
YURI-SAN...
PLEASE KEEP YOUR OPINIONS TO YOURSELF TONIGHT. GOD FORBID A REPORTER HEARD YOU, OR THE AUTHOR...
DON'T WORRY!
I WON'T DO ANYTHING THAT MIGHT HURT YOUR LOVELY LITTLE AGENCY.
I'M GRATEFUL FOR THE ROLE, REALLY. BEGGARS CAN'T BE CHOOSERS, AFTER ALL.
AS LONG AS YOU KNOW THAT.

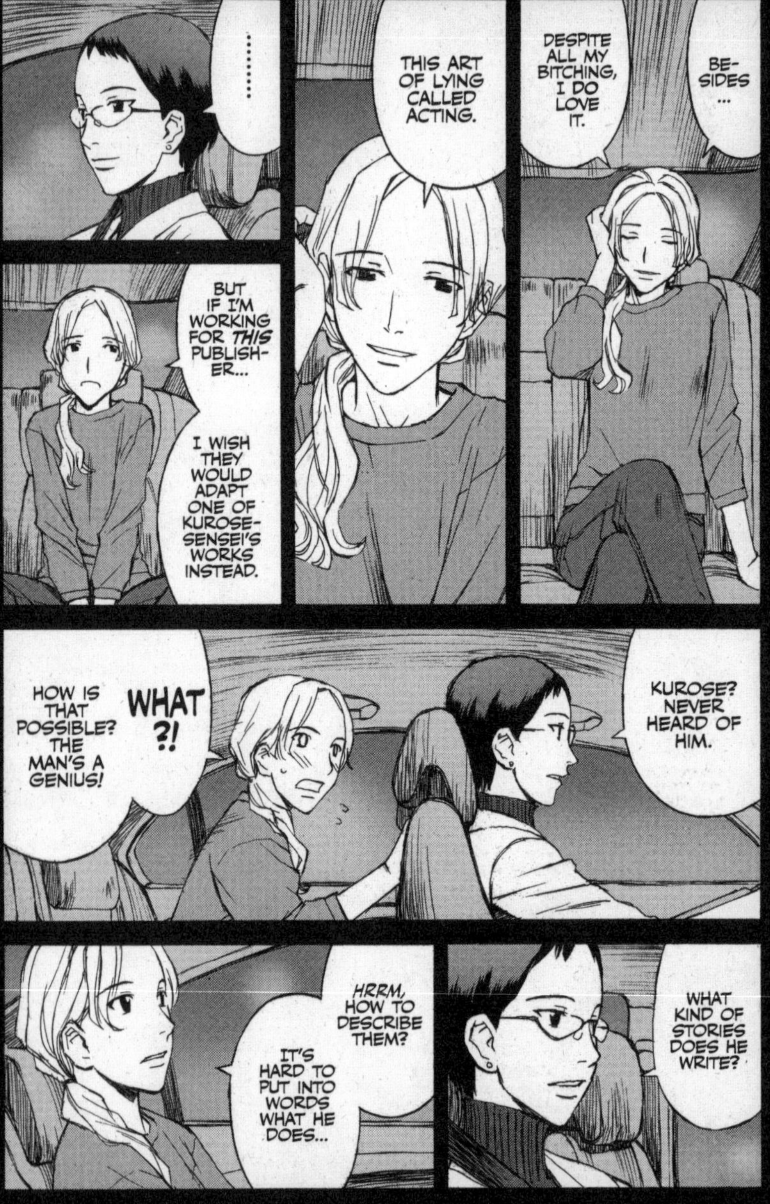
BE-SIDES...
DESPITE ALL MY BITCHING, I DO LOVE IT.
THIS ART OF LYING CALLED ACTING.
......
BUT IF I'M WORKING FOR *THIS* PUBLISHER...
I WISH THEY WOULD ADAPT ONE OF KUROSE-SENSEI'S WORKS INSTEAD.
KUROSE? NEVER HEARD OF HIM.
WHAT?!
HOW IS THAT POSSIBLE? THE MAN'S A GENIUS!
WHAT KIND OF STORIES DOES HE WRITE?
HRRM, HOW TO DESCRIBE THEM?
IT'S HARD TO PUT INTO WORDS WHAT HE DOES...

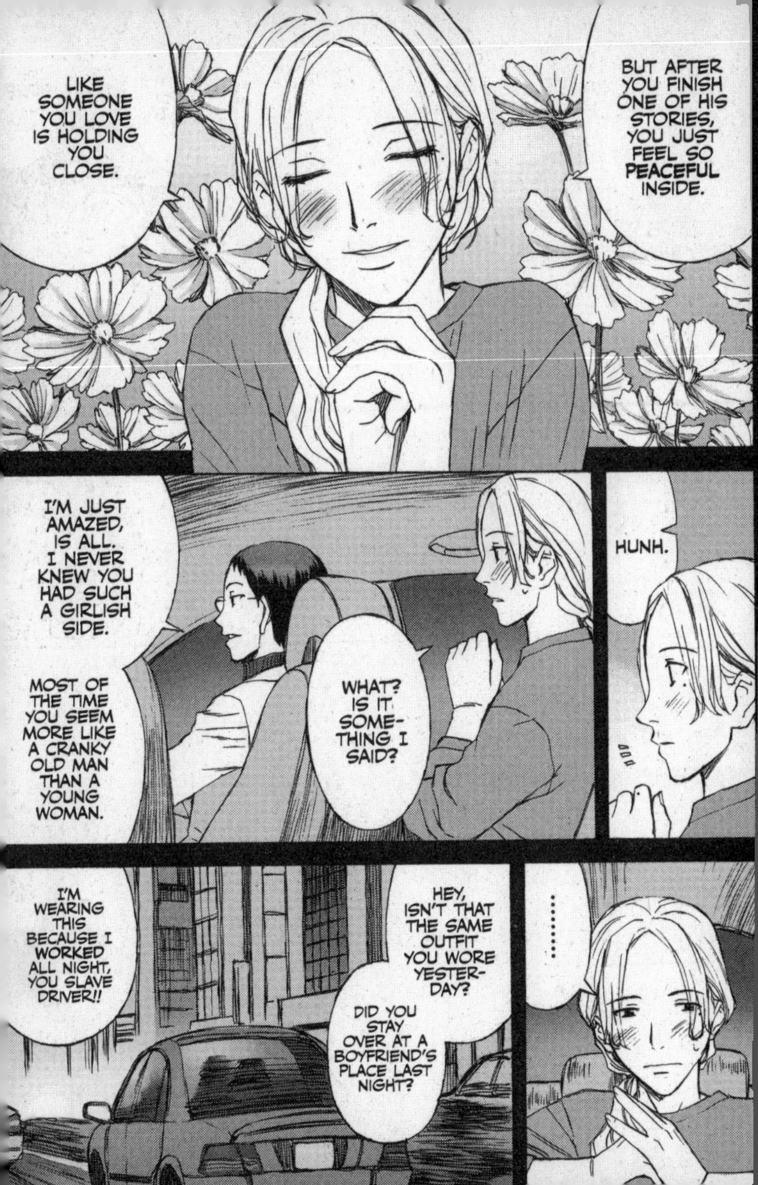
BUT AFTER YOU FINISH ONE OF HIS STORIES, YOU JUST FEEL SO PEACEFUL INSIDE.
LIKE SOMEONE YOU LOVE IS HOLDING YOU CLOSE.
HUNH.
WHAT? IS IT SOME-THING I SAID?
I'M JUST AMAZED, IS ALL. I NEVER KNEW YOU HAD SUCH A GIRLISH SIDE.
MOST OF THE TIME YOU SEEM MORE LIKE A CRANKY OLD MAN THAN A YOUNG WOMAN.
....
HEY, ISN'T THAT THE SAME OUTFIT YOU WORE YESTER-DAY?
DID YOU STAY OVER AT A BOYFRIEND'S PLACE LAST NIGHT?
I'M WEARING THIS BECAUSE I WORKED ALL NIGHT, YOU SLAVE DRIVER!!

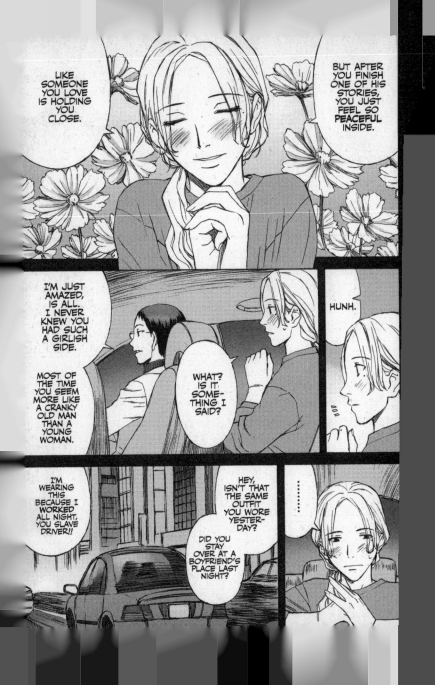

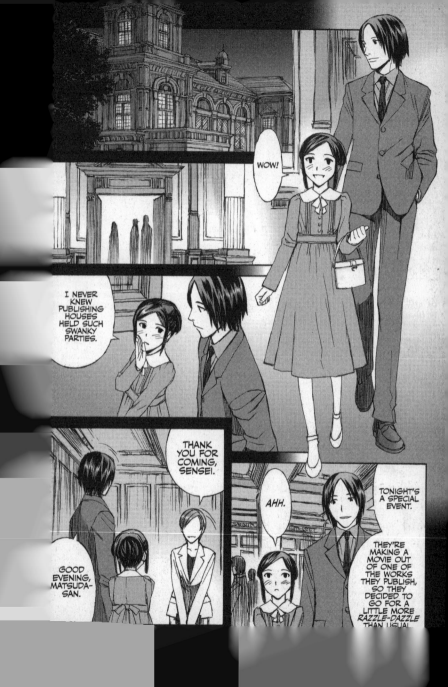

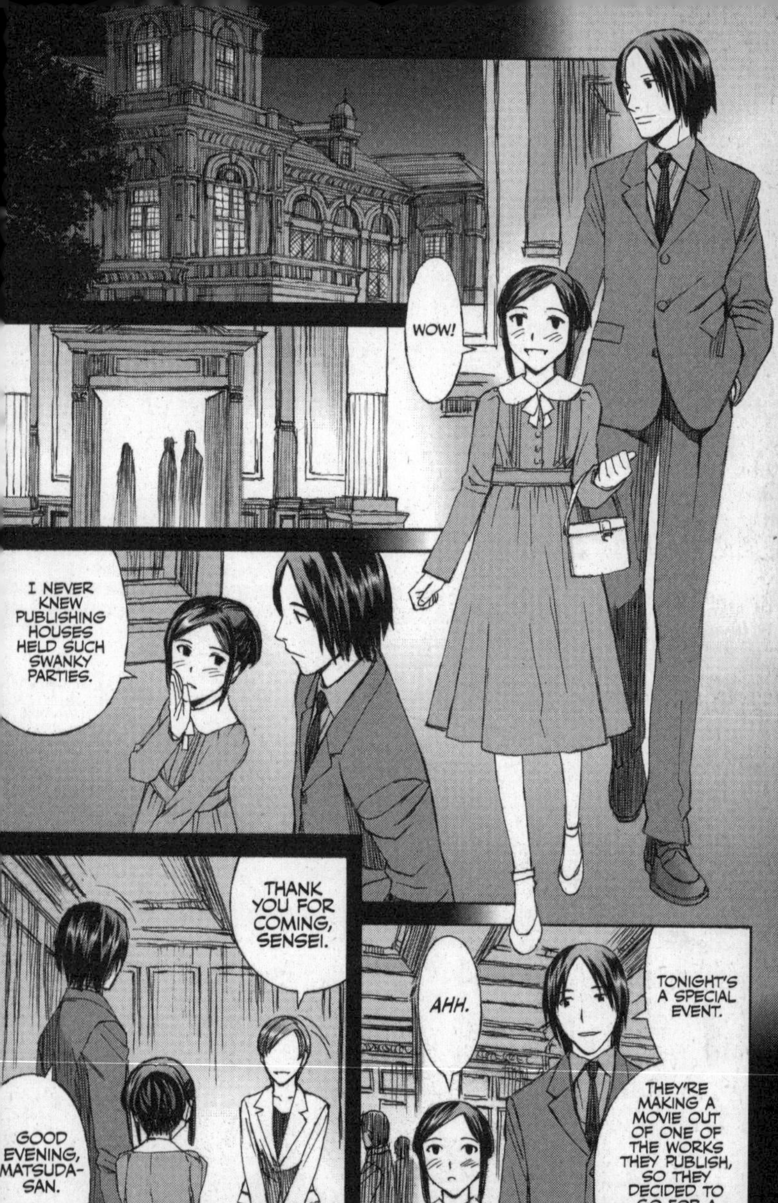
WOW!
I NEVER KNEW PUBLISHING HOUSES HELD SUCH SWANKY PARTIES.
TONIGHT'S A SPECIAL EVENT.
AHH.
THEY'RE MAKING A MOVIE OUT OF ONE OF THE WORKS THEY PUBLISH, SO THEY DECIDED TO GO FOR A LITTLE MORE *RAZZLE-DAZZLE* THAN USUAL.
THANK YOU FOR COMING, SENSEI.
GOOD EVENING, MATSUDA-SAN.

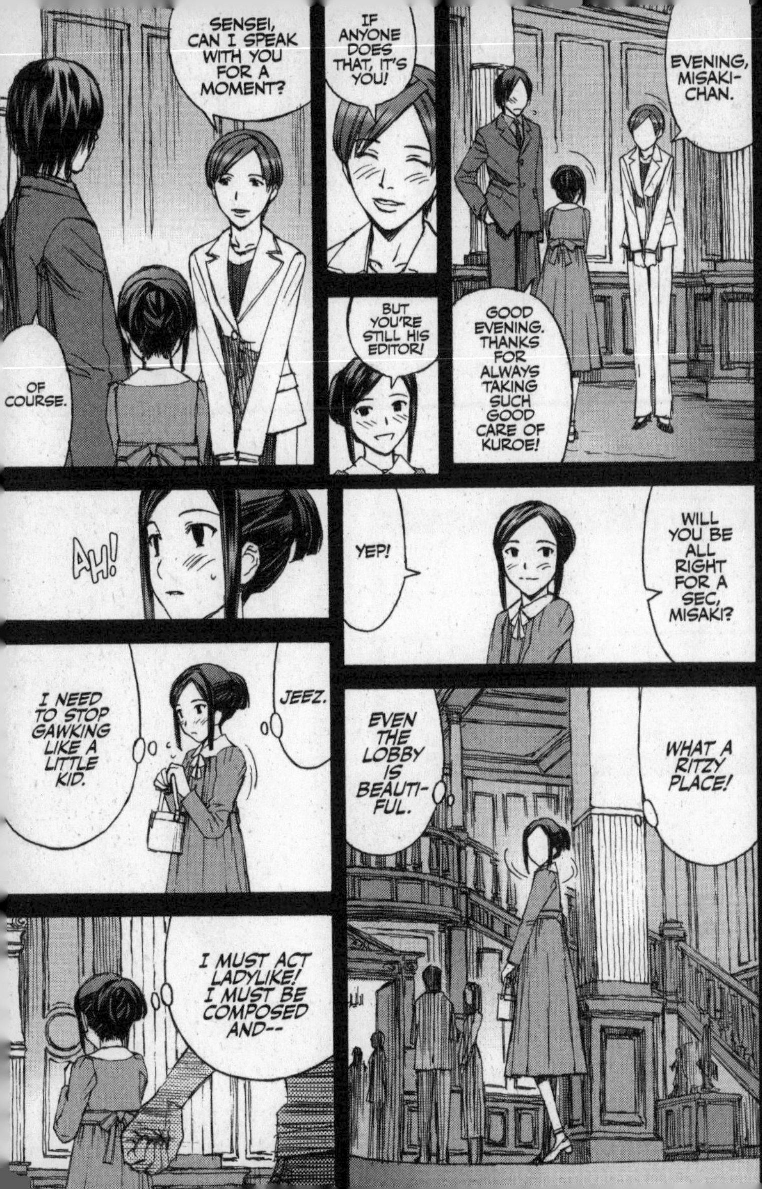
EVENING, MISAKI-CHAN.
GOOD EVENING. THANKS FOR ALWAYS TAKING SUCH GOOD CARE OF KUROE!
IF ANYONE DOES THAT, IT'S YOU!
BUT YOU'RE STILL HIS EDITOR!
SENSEI, CAN I SPEAK WITH YOU FOR A MOMENT?
OF COURSE.
WILL YOU BE ALL RIGHT FOR A SEC, MISAKI?
YEP!
AH!
WHAT A RITZY PLACE!
EVEN THE LOBBY IS BEAUTIFUL.
JEEZ.
I NEED TO STOP GAWKING LIKE A LITTLE KID.
I MUST ACT LADYLIKE! I MUST BE COMPOSED AND--

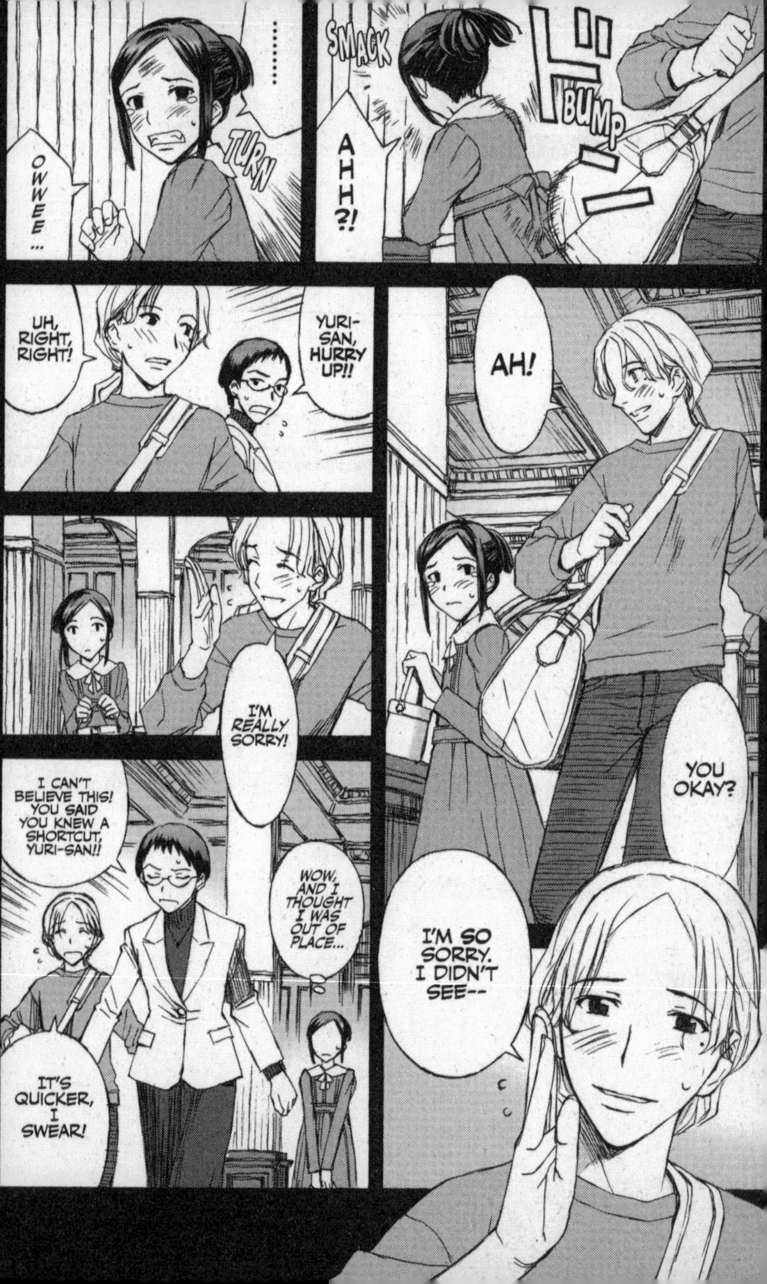

SMACK
BUMP
AHH?!
......
TURN
OWWEE...
AH!
YOU OKAY?
I'M SO SORRY. I DIDN'T SEE--
YURI-SAN, HURRY UP!!
UH, RIGHT, RIGHT!
I'M REALLY SORRY!
I CAN'T BELIEVE THIS! YOU SAID YOU KNEW A SHORTCUT, YURI-SAN!!
IT'S QUICKER, I SWEAR!
WOW, AND I THOUGHT I WAS OUT OF PLACE...

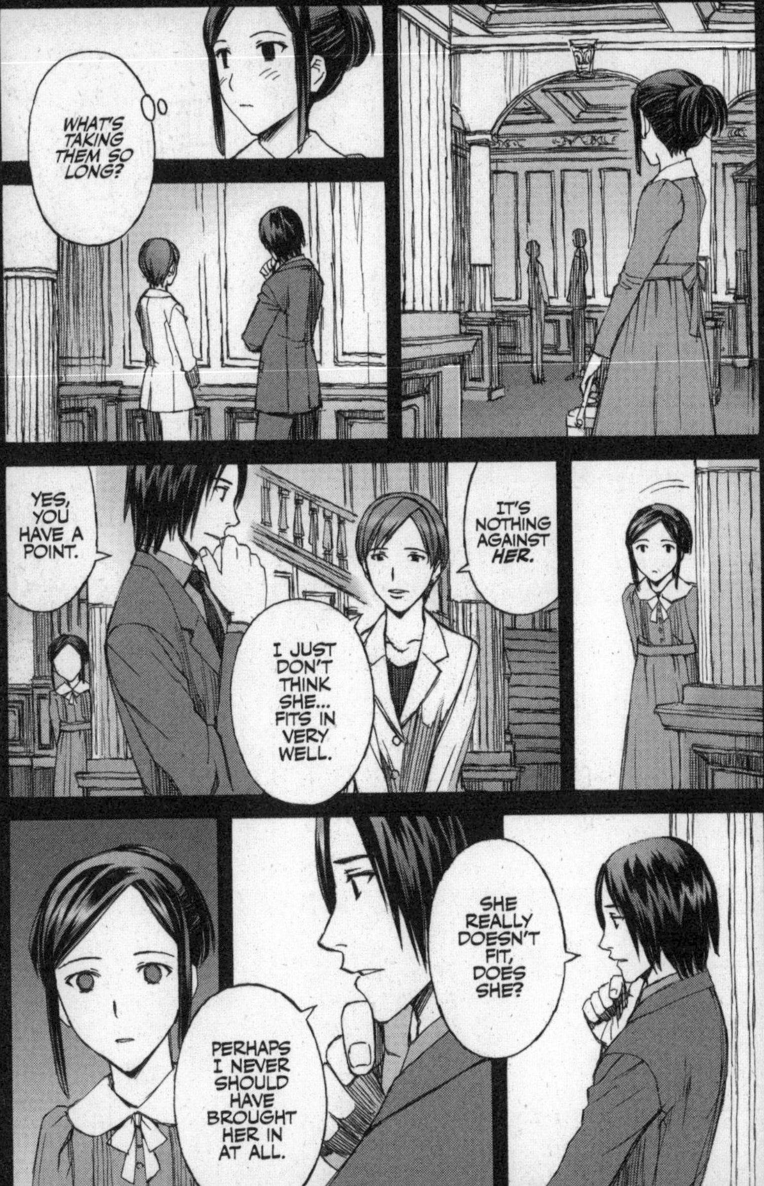
WHAT'S TAKING THEM SO LONG?
IT'S NOTHING AGAINST *HER.*
I JUST DON'T THINK SHE... FITS IN VERY WELL.
YES, YOU HAVE A POINT.
SHE REALLY DOESN'T FIT, DOES SHE?
PERHAPS I NEVER SHOULD HAVE BROUGHT HER IN AT ALL.

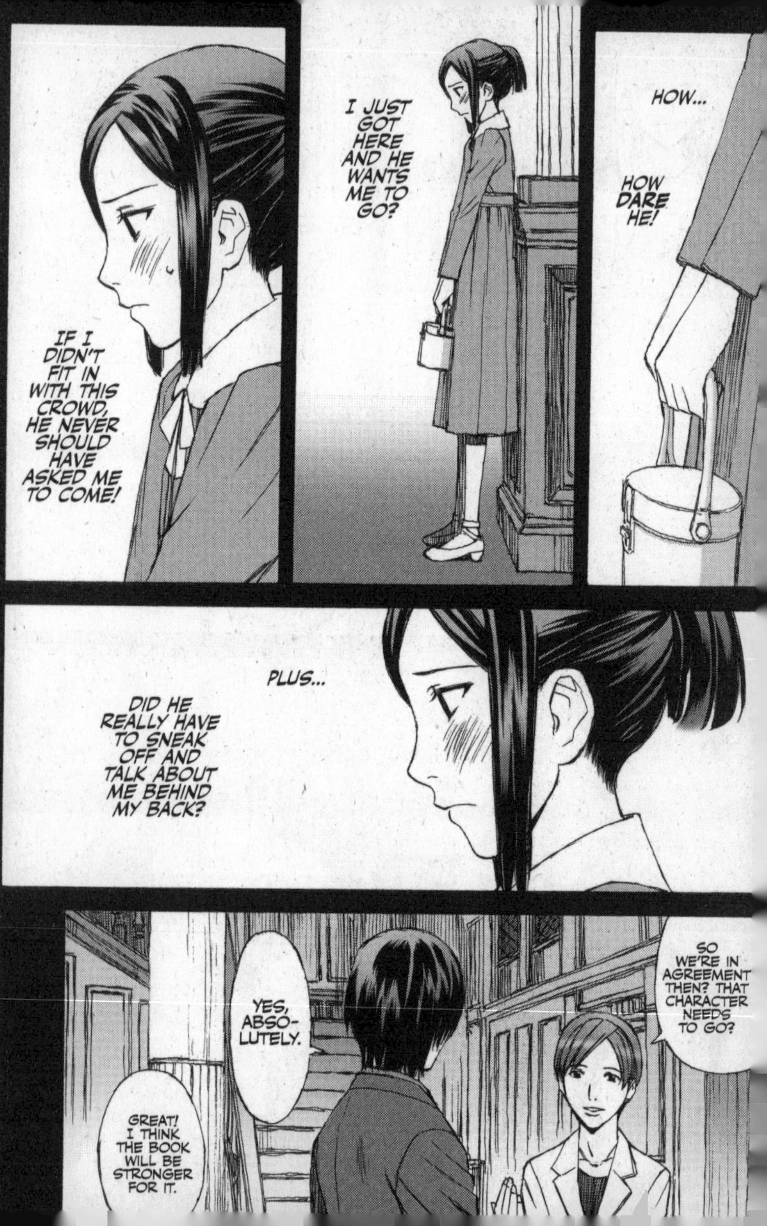
HOW...
HOW DARE HE!
I JUST GOT HERE AND HE WANTS ME TO GO?
IF I DIDN'T FIT IN WITH THIS CROWD, HE NEVER SHOULD HAVE ASKED ME TO COME!
PLUS...
DID HE REALLY HAVE TO SNEAK OFF AND TALK ABOUT ME BEHIND MY BACK?
SO WE'RE IN AGREEMENT THEN? THAT CHARACTER NEEDS TO GO?
YES, ABSOLUTELY.
GREAT! I THINK THE BOOK WILL BE STRONGER FOR IT.

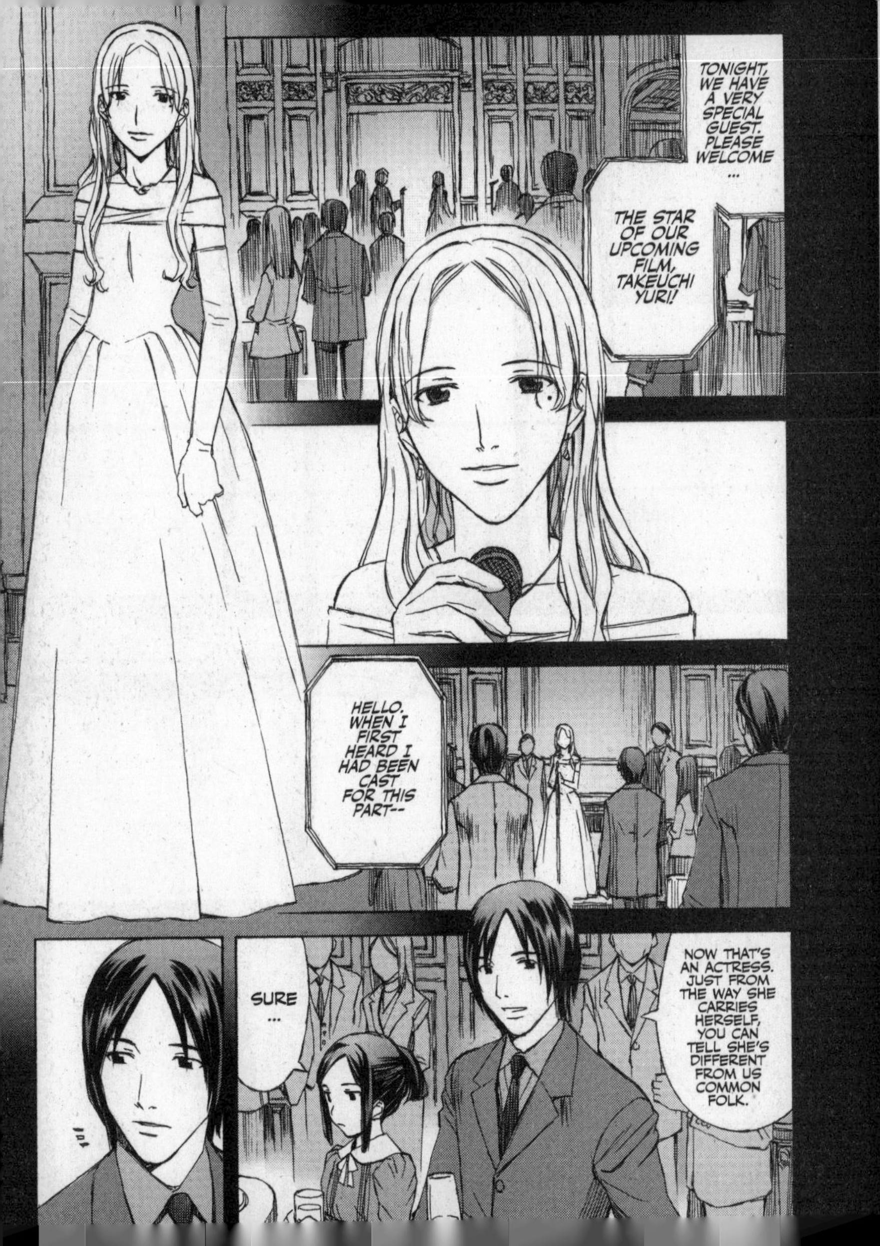
TONIGHT, WE HAVE A VERY SPECIAL GUEST. PLEASE WELCOME ...
THE STAR OF OUR UPCOMING FILM, TAKEUCHI YURI!
HELLO. WHEN I FIRST HEARD I HAD BEEN CAST FOR THIS PART--
NOW THAT'S AN ACTRESS. JUST FROM THE WAY SHE CARRIES HERSELF, YOU CAN TELL SHE'S DIFFERENT FROM US COMMON FOLK.
SURE ...

? SOMEONE LIKE HER FITS RIGHT IN AT A PLACE LIKE THIS.

OH, SENSEI--!!

WHAT'S WRONG? YOU'VE BEEN POUTING ALL NIGHT.

WHOOOOOO

AH, SURE--

THERE'S SOMEONE I ABSOLUTELY HAVE TO INTRODUCE YOU TO!

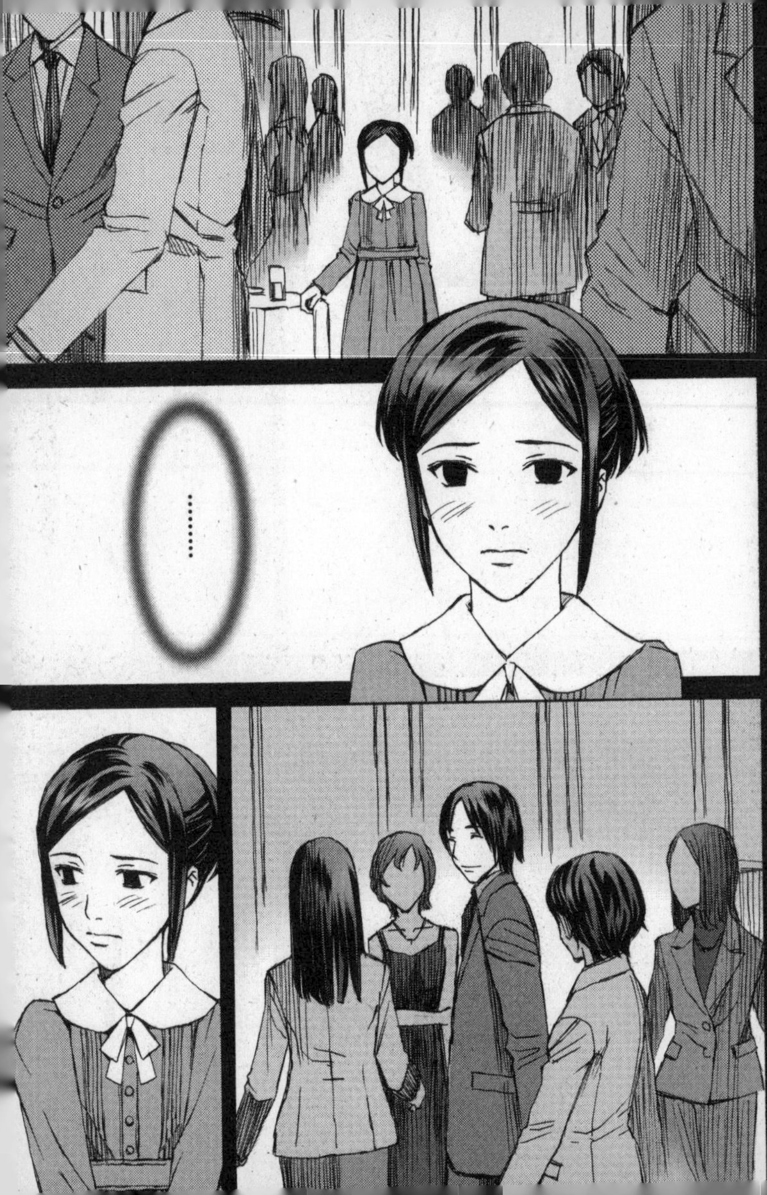
……

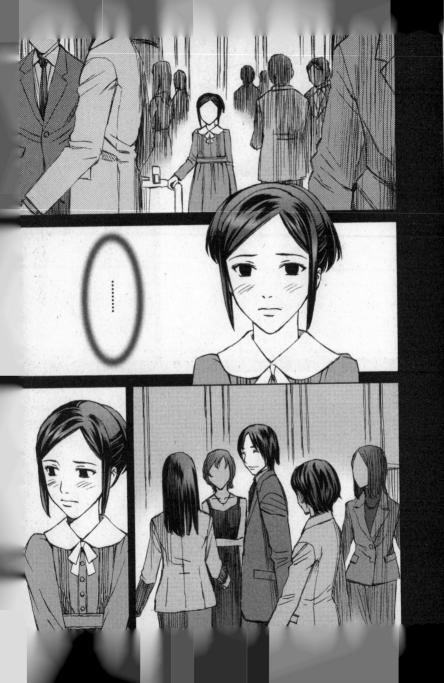

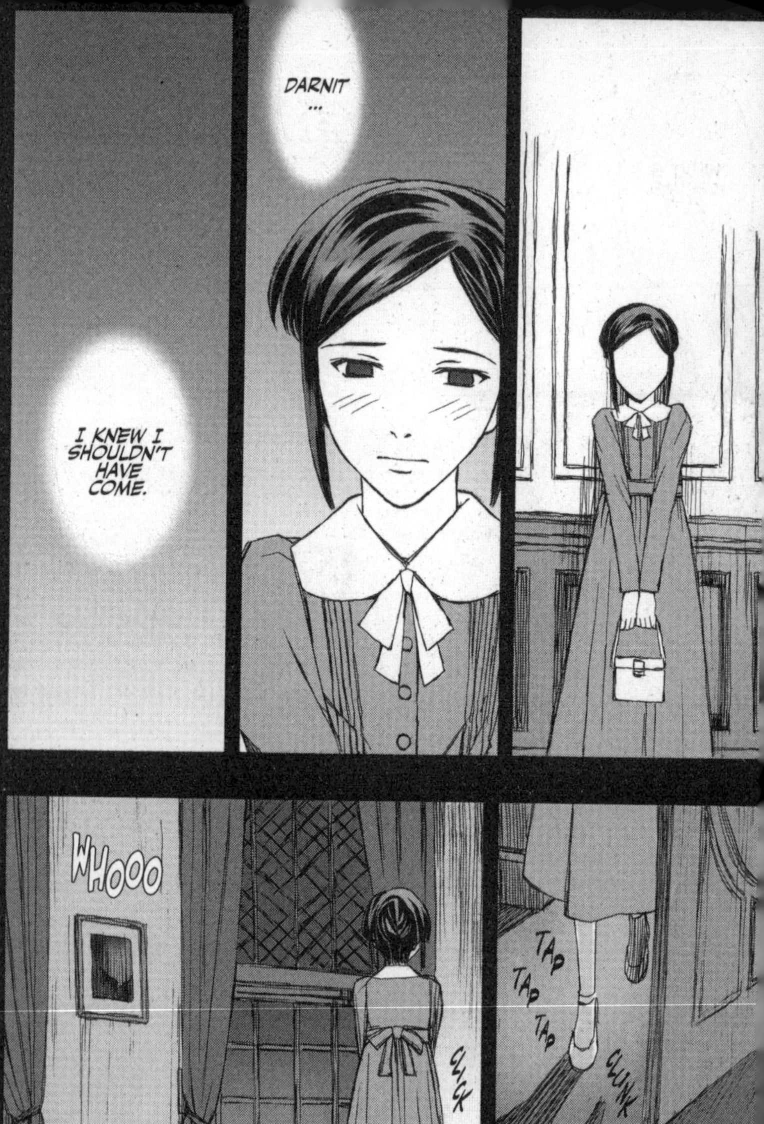
DARNIT ...
I KNEW I SHOULDN'T HAVE COME.
TAP
TAP TAP TAP
CLUNK
WHOOO
CLICK

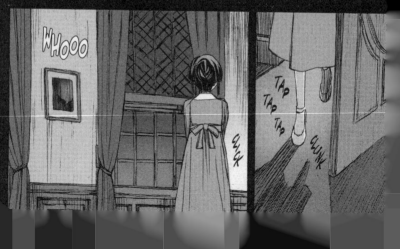

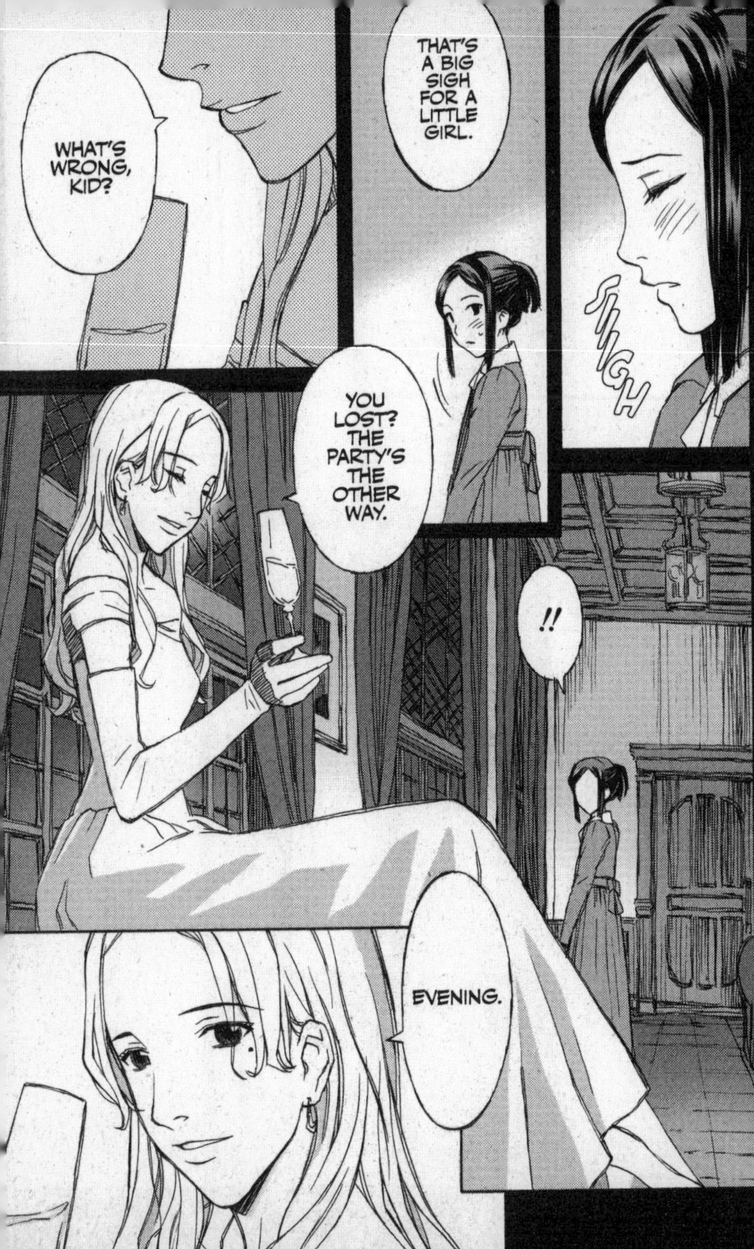
SIGH
THAT'S A BIG SIGH FOR A LITTLE GIRL.
WHAT'S WRONG, KID?
!!
YOU LOST? THE PARTY'S THE OTHER WAY.
EVENING.

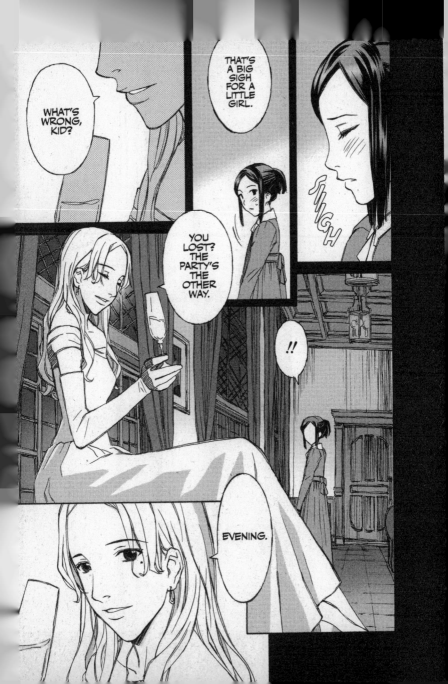

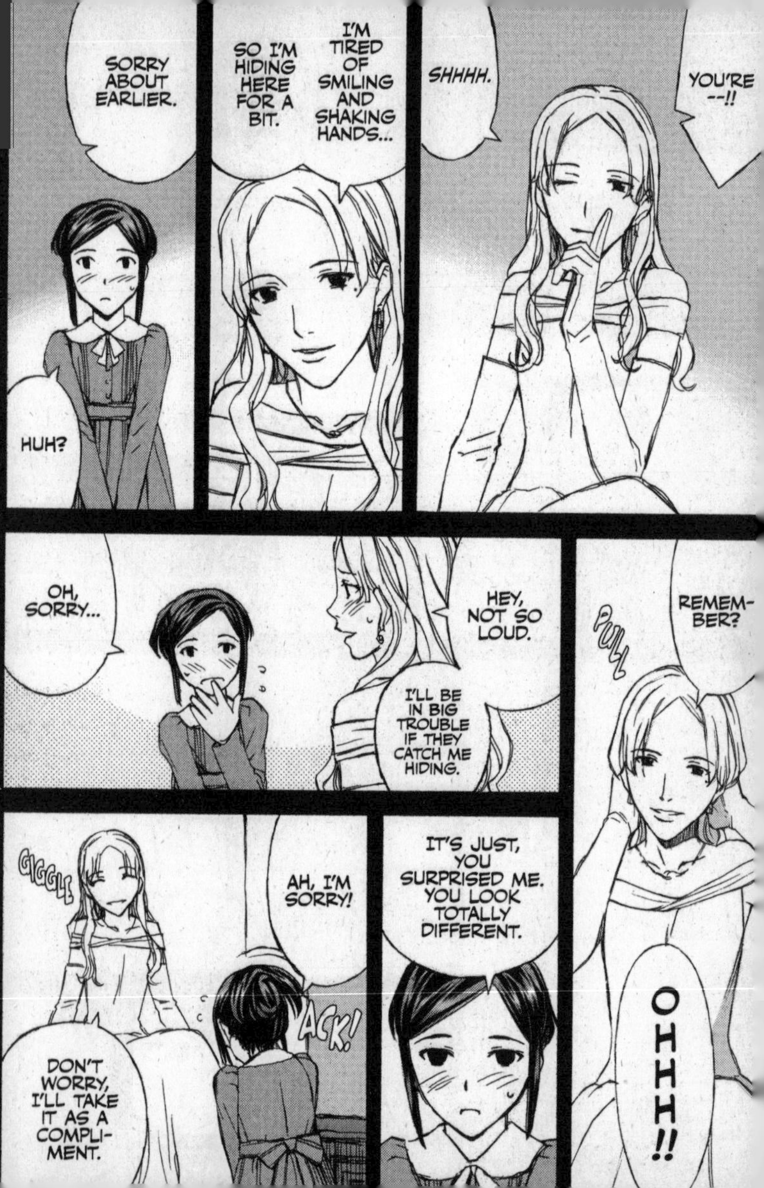
YOU'RE --!!
SHHHH.
I'M TIRED OF SMILING AND SHAKING HANDS...
SO I'M HIDING HERE FOR A BIT.
SORRY ABOUT EARLIER.
HUH?
REMEMBER?
PULL
OHHHH!!
HEY, NOT SO LOUD.
I'LL BE IN BIG TROUBLE IF THEY CATCH ME HIDING.
OH, SORRY...
IT'S JUST, YOU SURPRISED ME. YOU LOOK TOTALLY DIFFERENT.
AH, I'M SORRY!
ACK!
GIGGLE
DON'T WORRY, I'LL TAKE IT AS A COMPLIMENT.

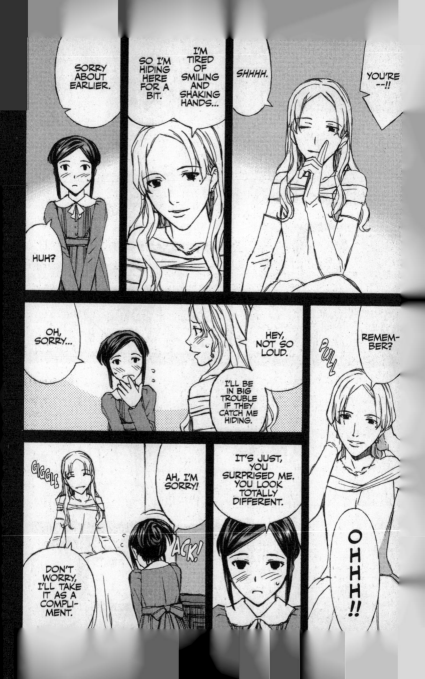

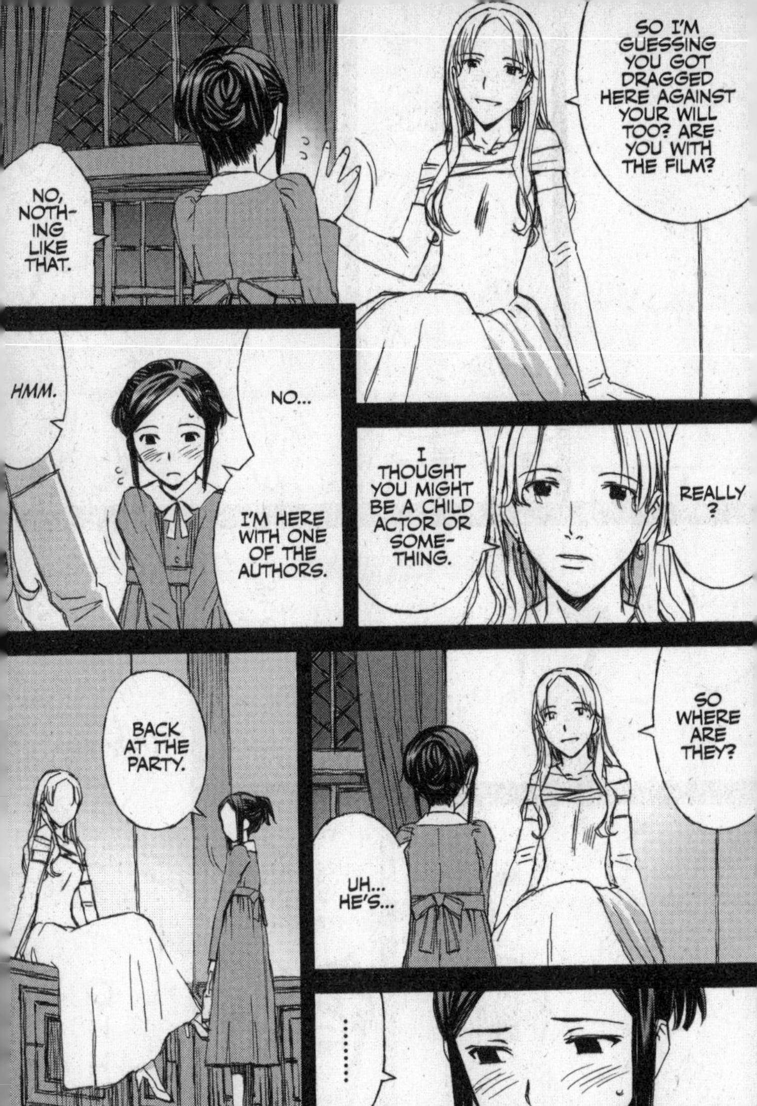
SO I'M GUESSING YOU GOT DRAGGED HERE AGAINST YOUR WILL TOO? ARE YOU WITH THE FILM?
NO, NOTHING LIKE THAT.
REALLY?
I THOUGHT YOU MIGHT BE A CHILD ACTOR OR SOMETHING.
NO...
I'M HERE WITH ONE OF THE AUTHORS.
HMM.
SO WHERE ARE THEY?
UH... HE'S...
......
BACK AT THE PARTY.

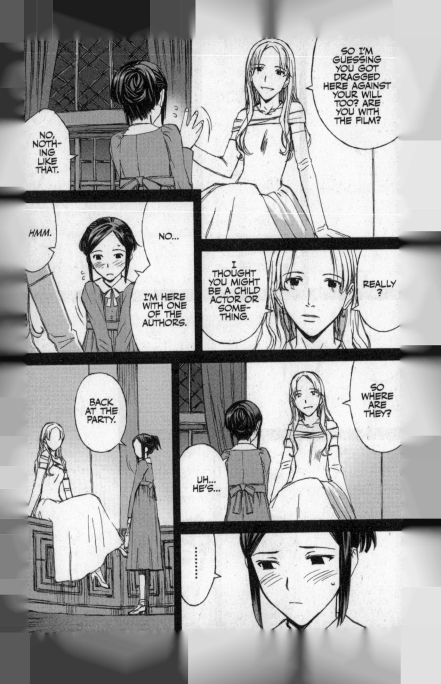

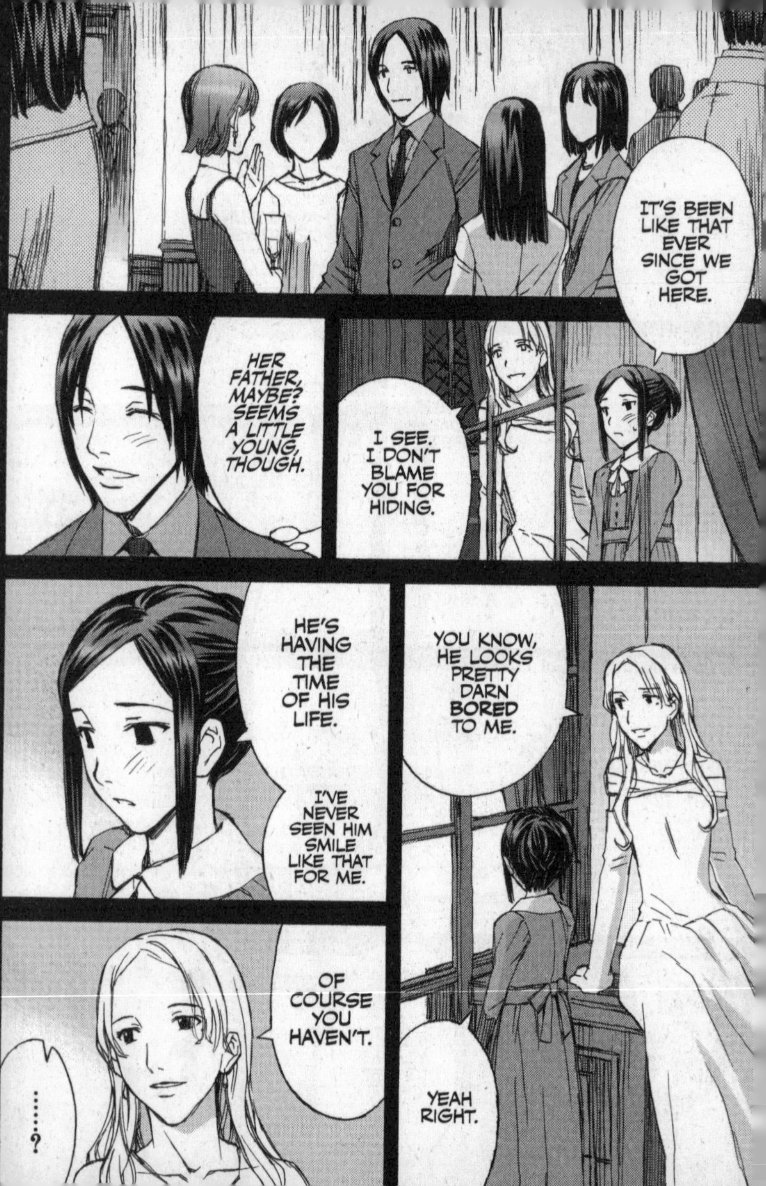
IT'S BEEN LIKE THAT EVER SINCE WE GOT HERE.
I SEE. I DON'T BLAME YOU FOR HIDING.
HER FATHER, MAYBE? SEEMS A LITTLE YOUNG, THOUGH.
YOU KNOW, HE LOOKS PRETTY DARN BORED TO ME.
YEAH RIGHT.
HE'S HAVING THE TIME OF HIS LIFE.
I'VE NEVER SEEN HIM SMILE LIKE THAT FOR ME.
OF COURSE YOU HAVEN'T.
......?

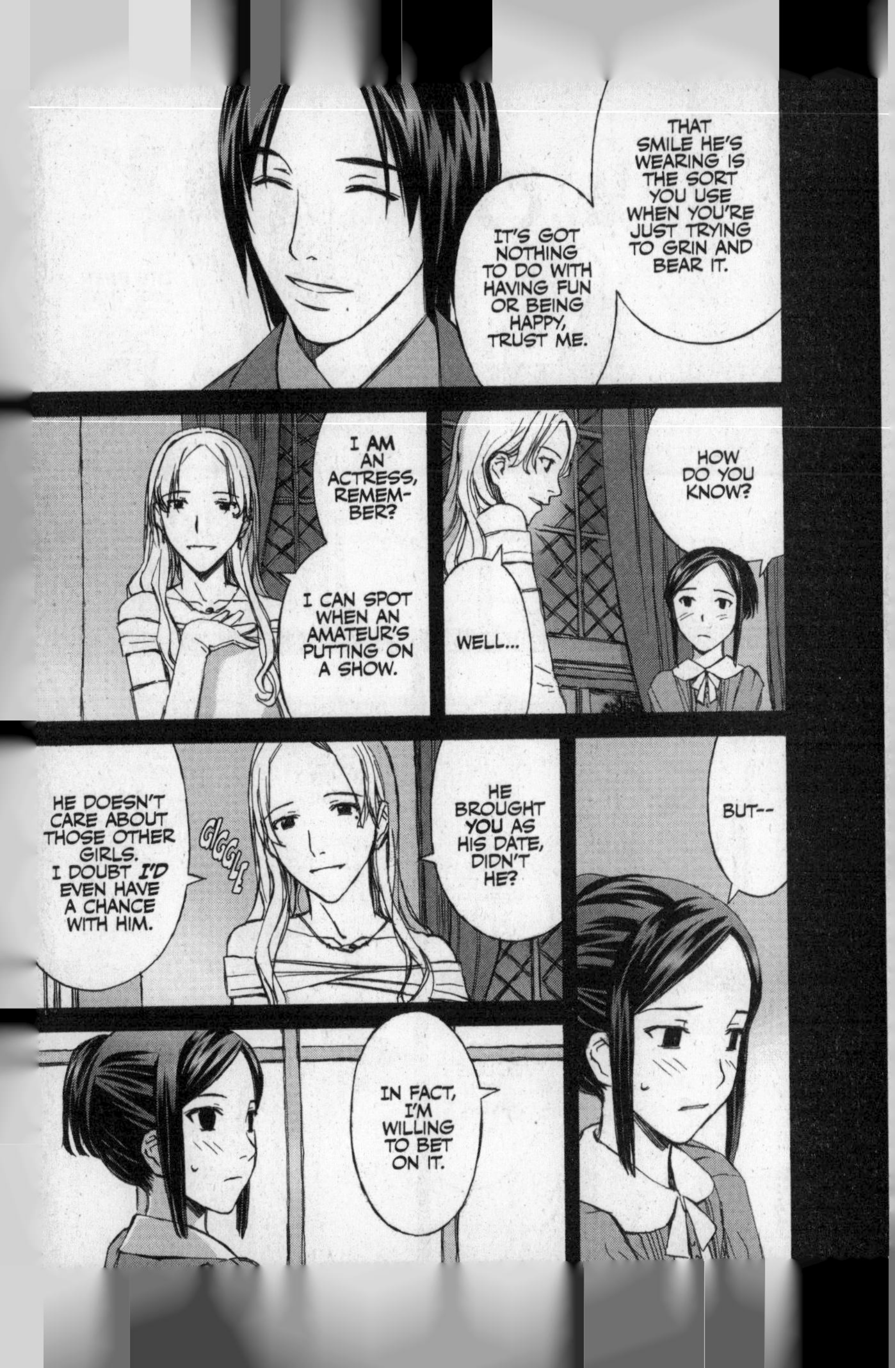
THAT SMILE HE'S WEARING IS THE SORT YOU USE WHEN YOU'RE JUST TRYING TO GRIN AND BEAR IT.
IT'S GOT NOTHING TO DO WITH HAVING FUN OR BEING HAPPY, TRUST ME.
HOW DO YOU KNOW?
WELL...
I AM AN ACTRESS, REMEMBER?
I CAN SPOT WHEN AN AMATEUR'S PUTTING ON A SHOW.
BUT--
HE BROUGHT YOU AS HIS DATE, DIDN'T HE?
GIGGLE
HE DOESN'T CARE ABOUT THOSE OTHER GIRLS. I DOUBT *I'D* EVEN HAVE A CHANCE WITH HIM.
IN FACT, I'M WILLING TO BET ON IT.

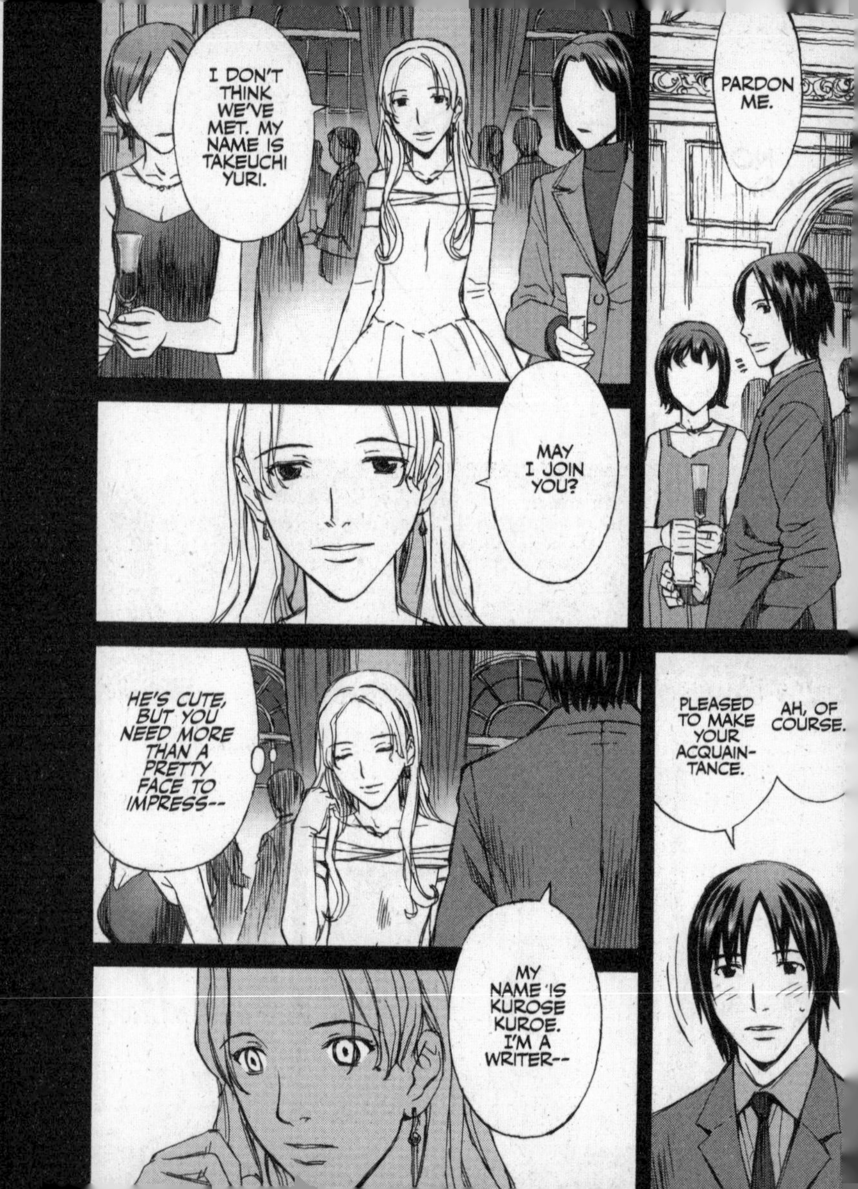
PARDON ME.
I DON'T THINK WE'VE MET. MY NAME IS TAKEUCHI YURI.
MAY I JOIN YOU?
AH, OF COURSE.
PLEASED TO MAKE YOUR ACQUAINTANCE.
HE'S CUTE, BUT YOU NEED MORE THAN A PRETTY FACE TO IMPRESS--
MY NAME IS KUROSE KUROE. I'M A WRITER--

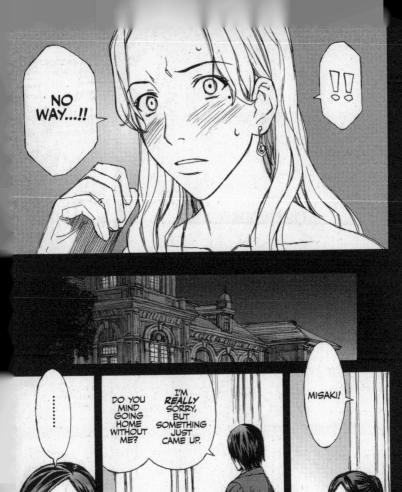

!!
NO WAY...!!
MISAKI!
I'M *REALLY* SORRY, BUT SOMETHING JUST CAME UP.
DO YOU MIND GOING HOME WITHOUT ME?
......

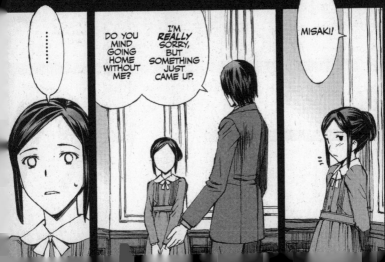

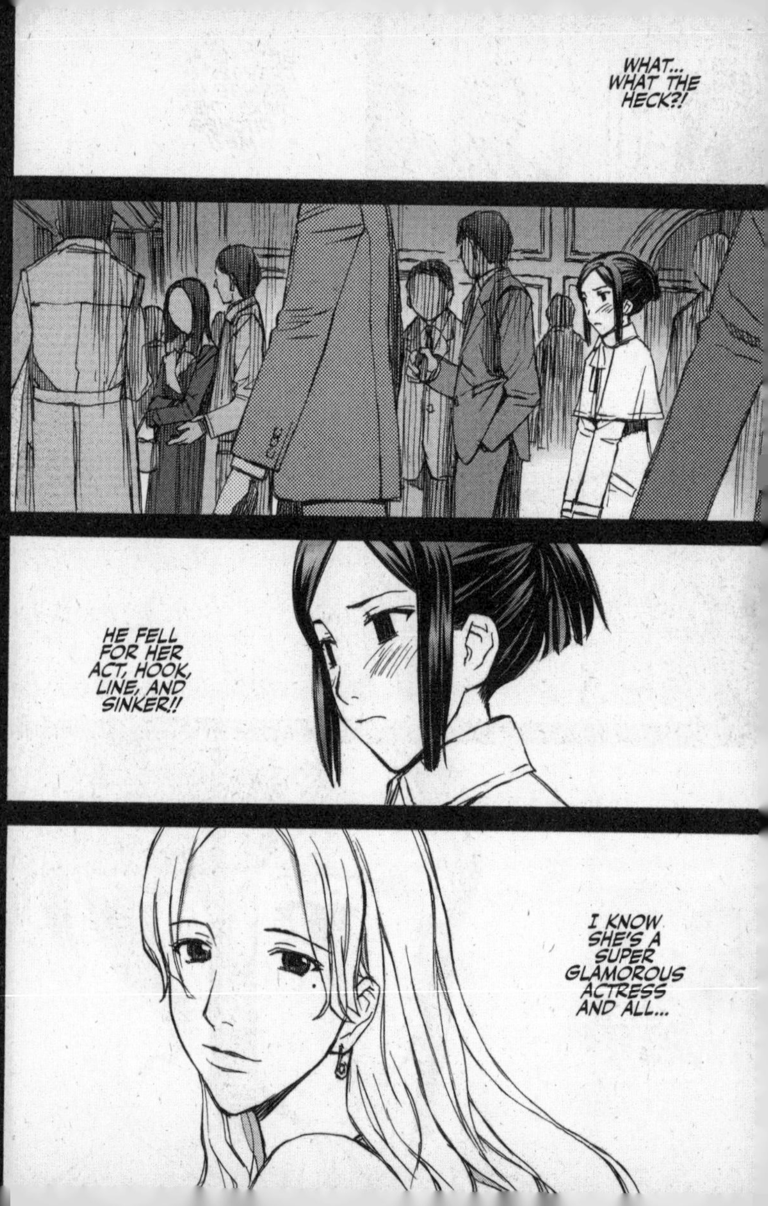
WHAT... WHAT THE HECK?!
HE FELL FOR HER ACT, HOOK, LINE, AND SINKER!!
I KNOW SHE'S A SUPER GLAMOROUS ACTRESS AND ALL...

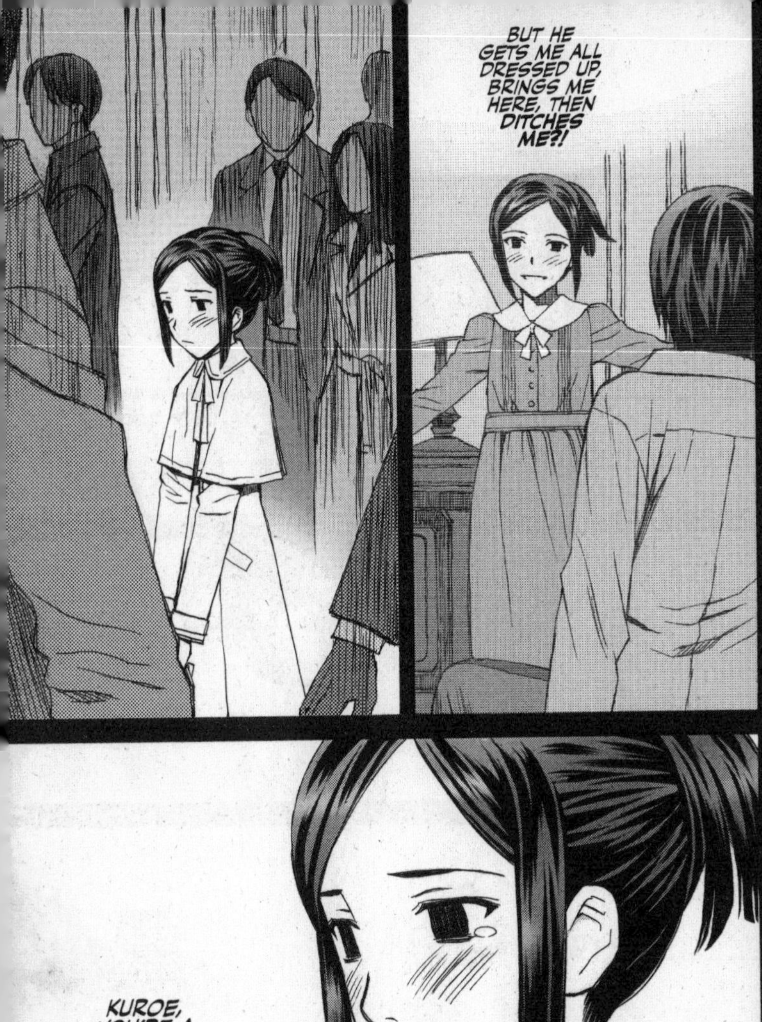
BUT HE GETS ME ALL DRESSED UP, BRINGS ME HERE, THEN DITCHES ME?!
KUROE, YOU'RE A JERK.

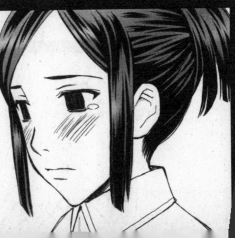

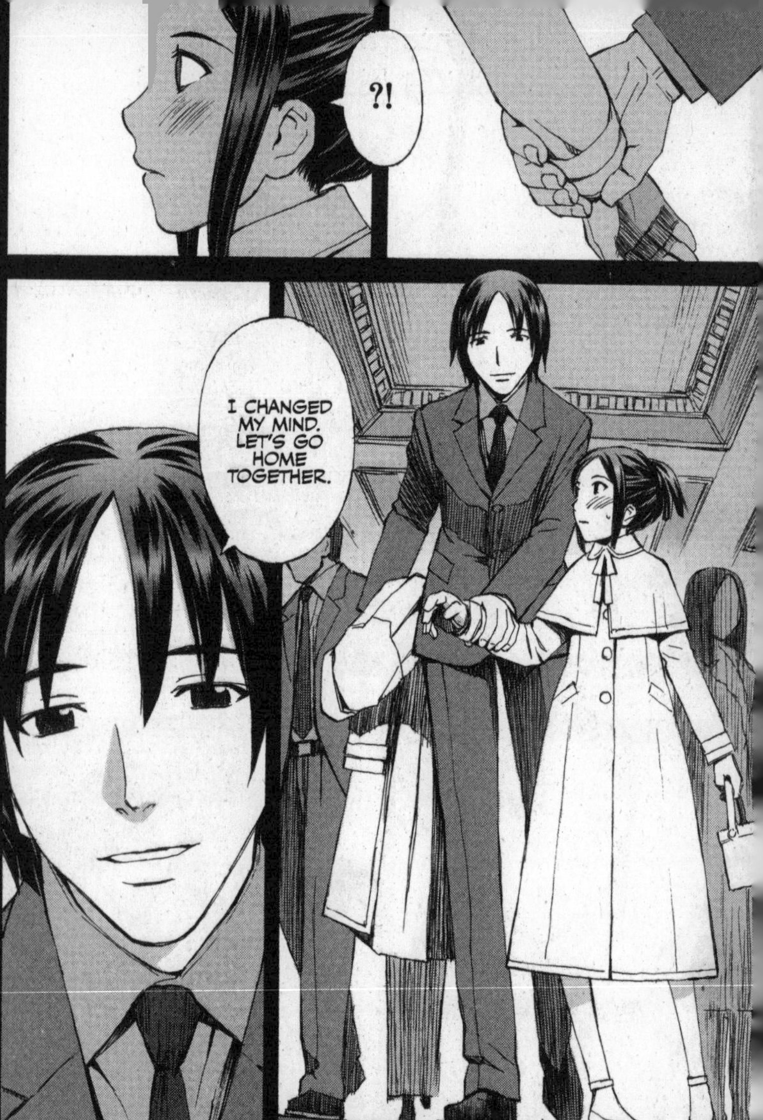
?!
I CHANGED MY MIND. LET'S GO HOME TOGETHER.

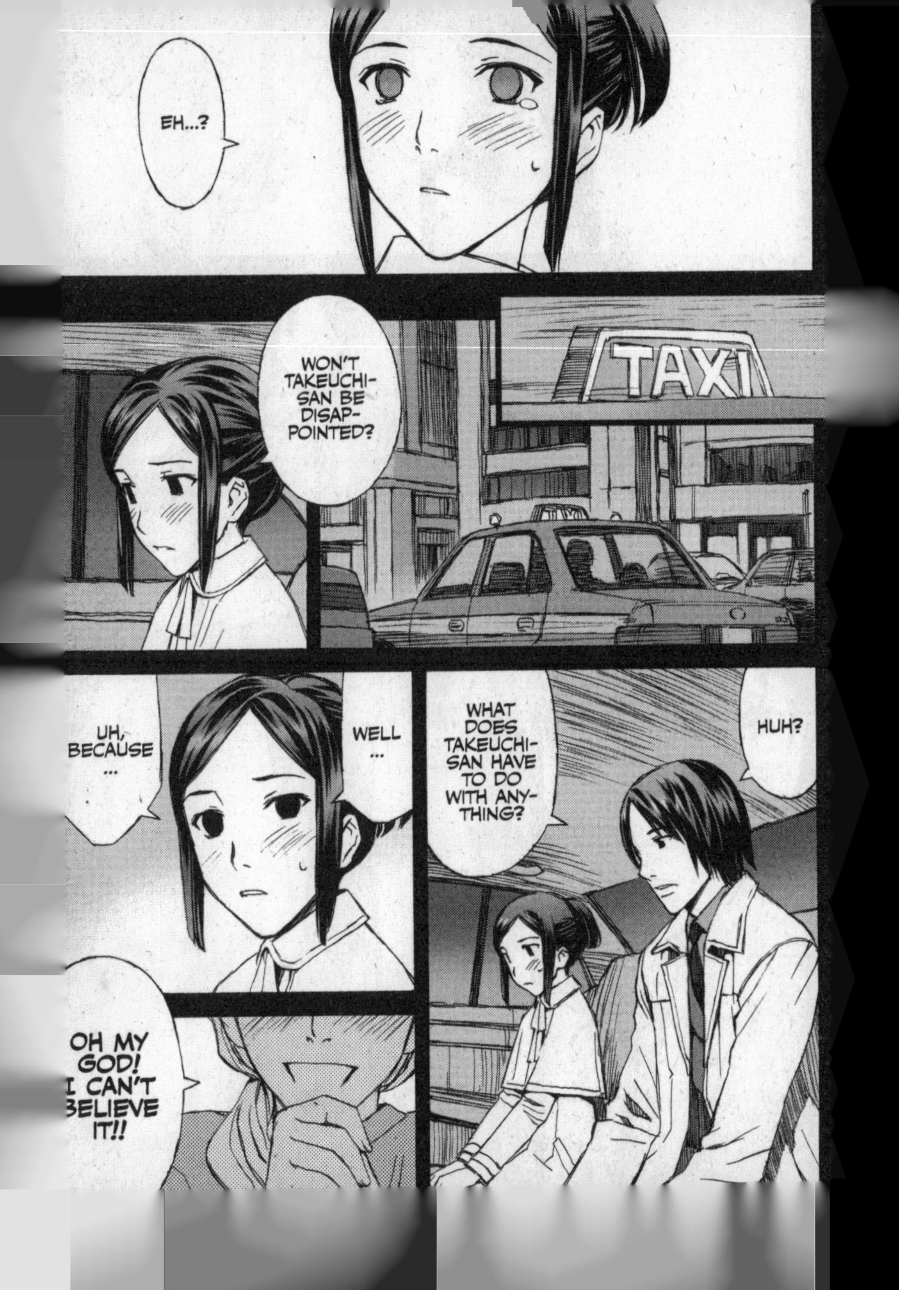
EH...?
TAXI
WON'T TAKEUCHI-SAN BE DISAP-POINTED?
HUH?
WHAT DOES TAKEUCHI-SAN HAVE TO DO WITH ANY-THING?
WELL ...
UH, BECAUSE ...
OH MY GOD! I CAN'T BELIEVE IT!!

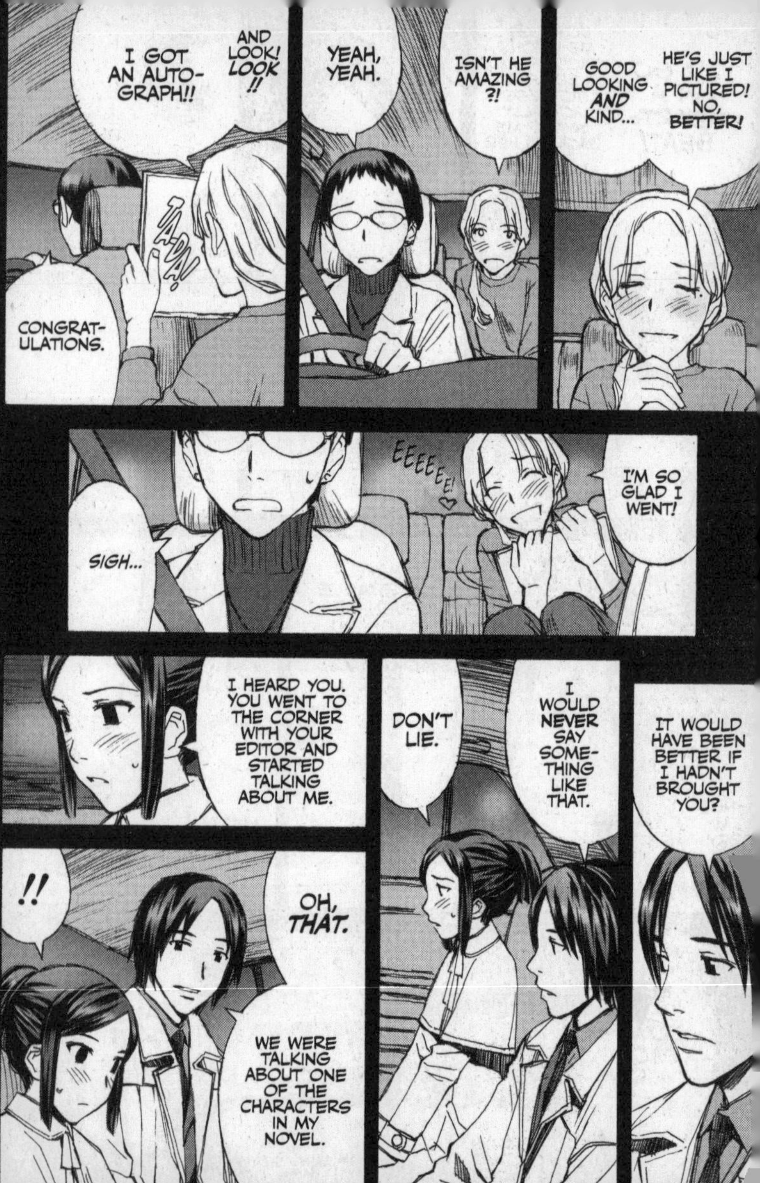
HE'S JUST LIKE I PICTURED! NO, BETTER!
GOOD LOOKING AND KIND...
ISN'T HE AMAZING ?!
YEAH, YEAH.
AND LOOK! LOOK!!
I GOT AN AUTO-GRAPH!!
TADA!
CONGRAT-ULATIONS.
I'M SO GLAD I WENT!
EEEEEE!
SIGH...
IT WOULD HAVE BEEN BETTER IF I HADN'T BROUGHT YOU?
I WOULD NEVER SAY SOME-THING LIKE THAT.
DON'T LIE.
I HEARD YOU. YOU WENT TO THE CORNER WITH YOUR EDITOR AND STARTED TALKING ABOUT ME.
OH, THAT.
!!
WE WERE TALKING ABOUT ONE OF THE CHARACTERS IN MY NOVEL.

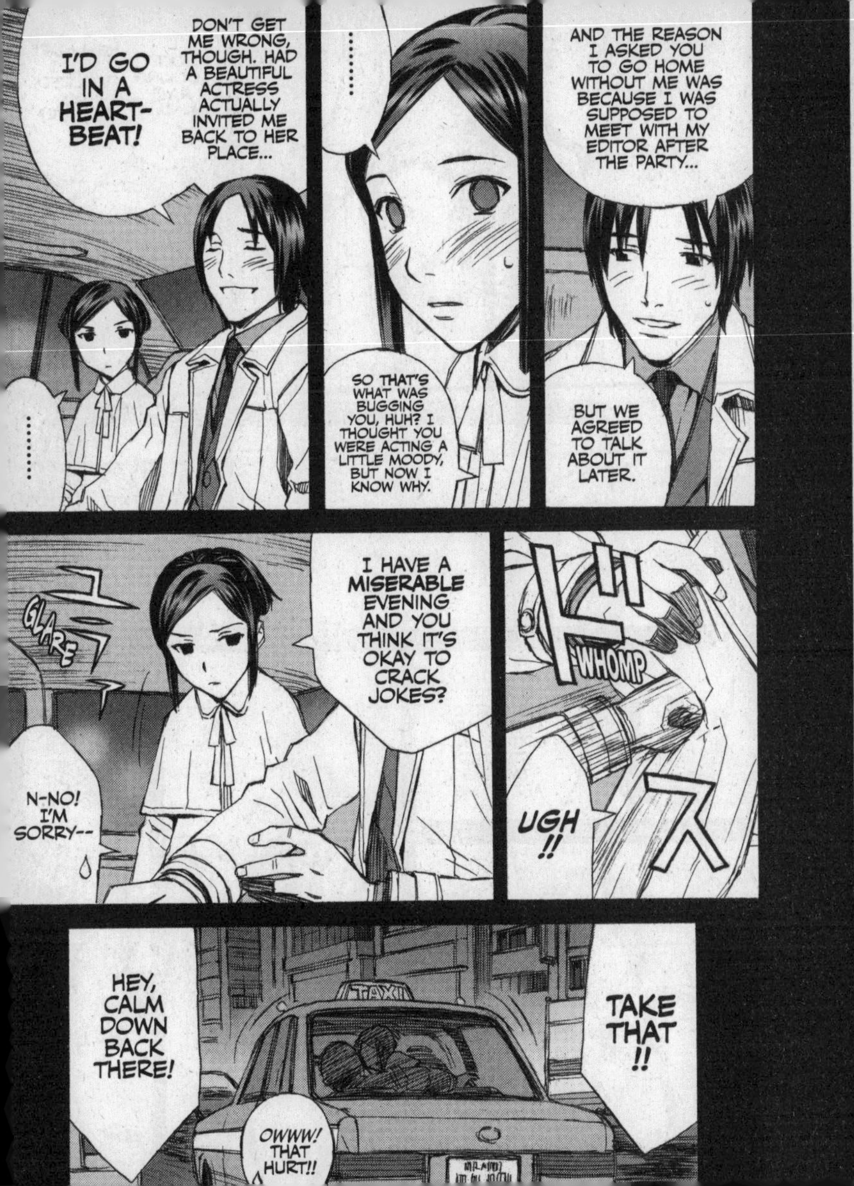
AND THE REASON I ASKED YOU TO GO HOME WITHOUT ME WAS BECAUSE I WAS SUPPOSED TO MEET WITH MY EDITOR AFTER THE PARTY...
BUT WE AGREED TO TALK ABOUT IT LATER.
......
SO THAT'S WHAT WAS BUGGING YOU, HUH? I THOUGHT YOU WERE ACTING A LITTLE MOODY, BUT NOW I KNOW WHY.
DON'T GET ME WRONG, THOUGH. HAD A BEAUTIFUL ACTRESS ACTUALLY INVITED ME BACK TO HER PLACE...
I'D GO IN A HEART-BEAT!
......
ドッ
WHOMP
ス
UGH!!
I HAVE A MISERABLE EVENING AND YOU THINK IT'S OKAY TO CRACK JOKES?
GLARE
N-NO! I'M SORRY--
TAKE THAT!!
TAXI
OWWW! THAT HURT!!
HEY, CALM DOWN BACK THERE!

Episode 9
ANOTHER FACE
Her Secret

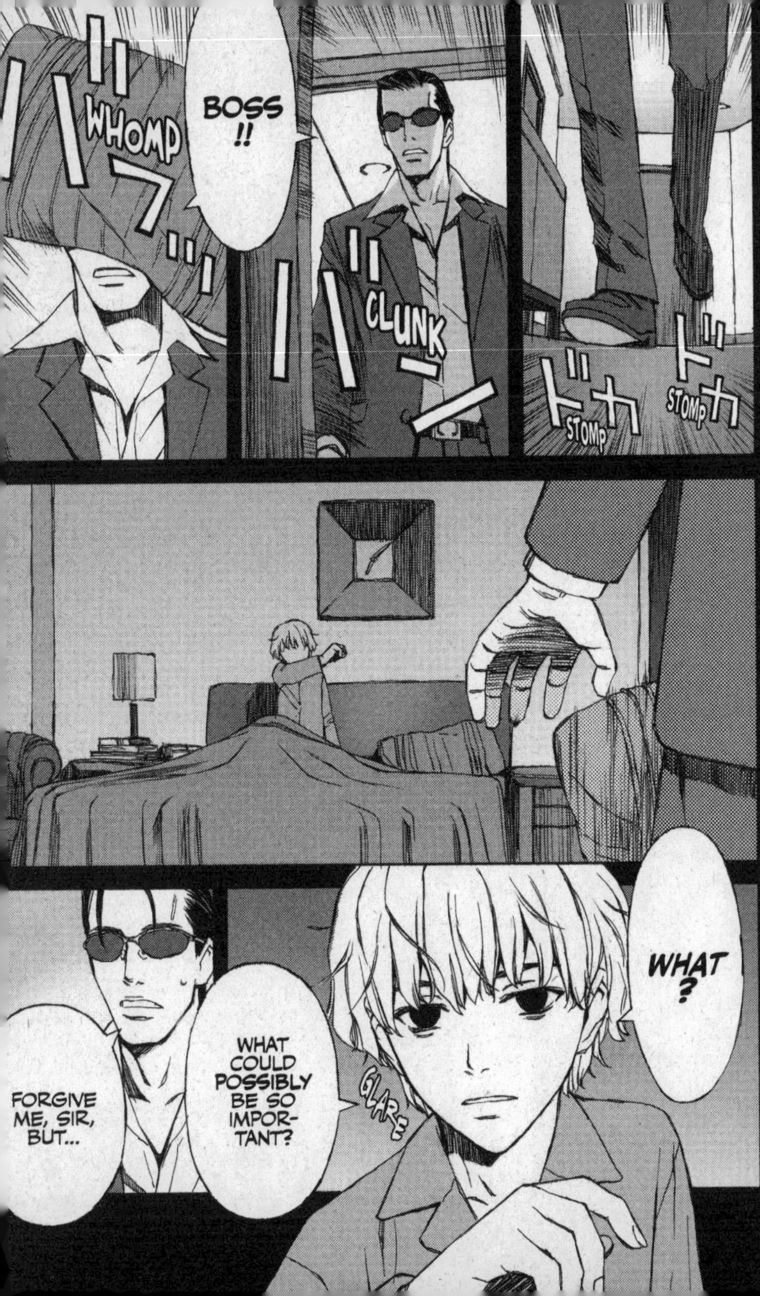
ドカ
STOMP
ドカ
STOMP
CLUNK
BOSS!!
WHOMP
WHAT?
GLARE
WHAT COULD POSSIBLY BE SO IMPORTANT?
FORGIVE ME, SIR, BUT...

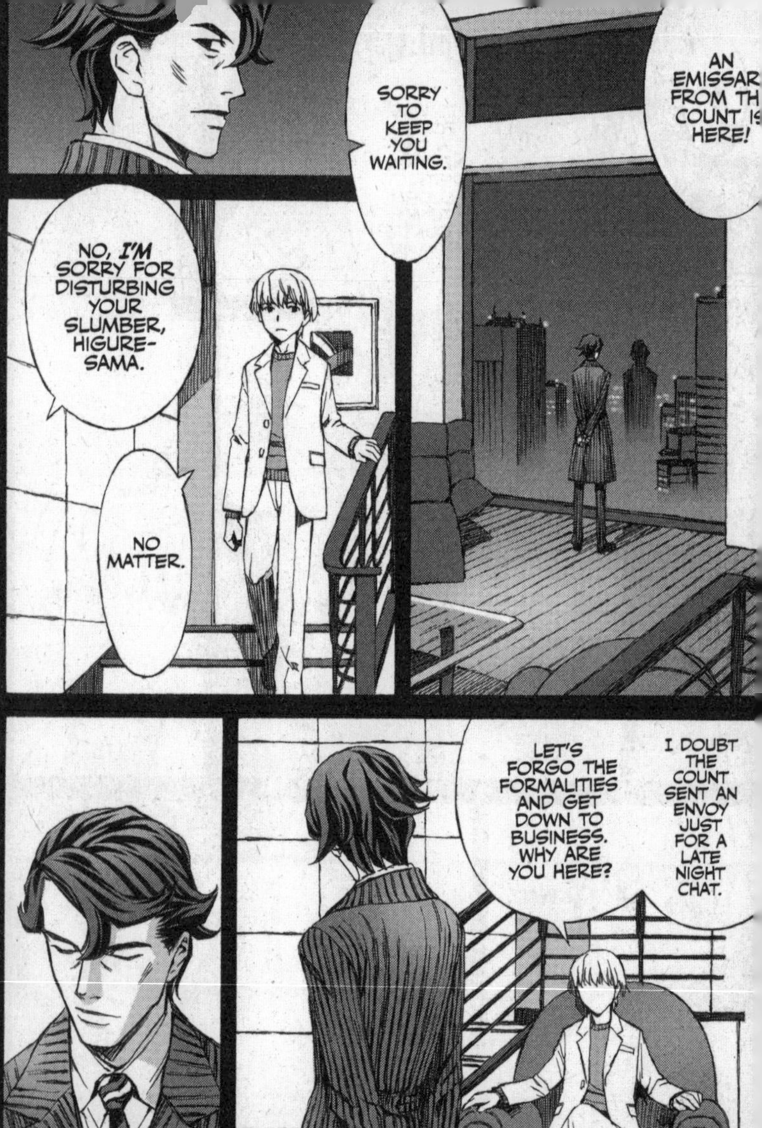
AN EMISSAR FROM TH COUNT IS HERE!
SORRY TO KEEP YOU WAITING.
NO, *I'M* SORRY FOR DISTURBING YOUR SLUMBER, HIGURE-SAMA.
NO MATTER.
I DOUBT THE COUNT SENT AN ENVOY JUST FOR A LATE NIGHT CHAT.
LET'S FORGO THE FORMALITIES AND GET DOWN TO BUSINESS. WHY ARE YOU HERE?

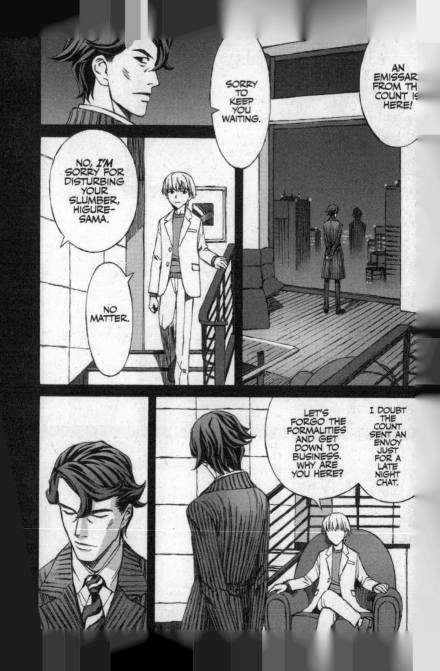

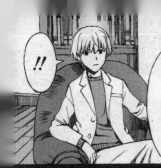

A DRAINED CORPSE WAS DISCOVERED A FEW HOURS AGO.
IT WAS FOUND IN THE NEUTRAL DISTRICT, CLOSE TO MY COUNT'S DOMAIN.
!!
......
HOW AWFUL. NONE OF MY BLOODLINE WOULD COMMIT SUCH A DISGUSTING CRIME.
OF COURSE NOT, SIR.
MOST LIKELY THIS IS THE WORK OF AN ORPHAN.
BUT SINCE IT DID TAKE PLACE IN THE NEUTRAL DISTRICT, WE THOUGHT IT ONLY PROPER IT BE BROUGHT TO YOUR ATTENTION, HIGURE-SAMA.
......
WITH YOUR ASSENT, OUR PEOPLE PLAN TO LAUNCH A FULL INVESTIGA-TION--
WAIT.
I *MAY* HAVE A LEAD.

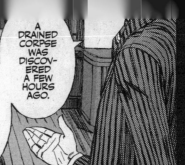

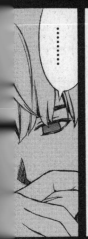

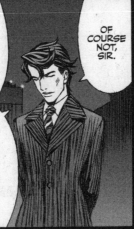

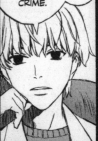

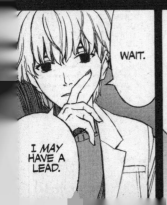

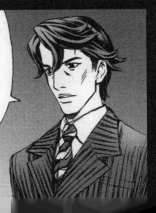

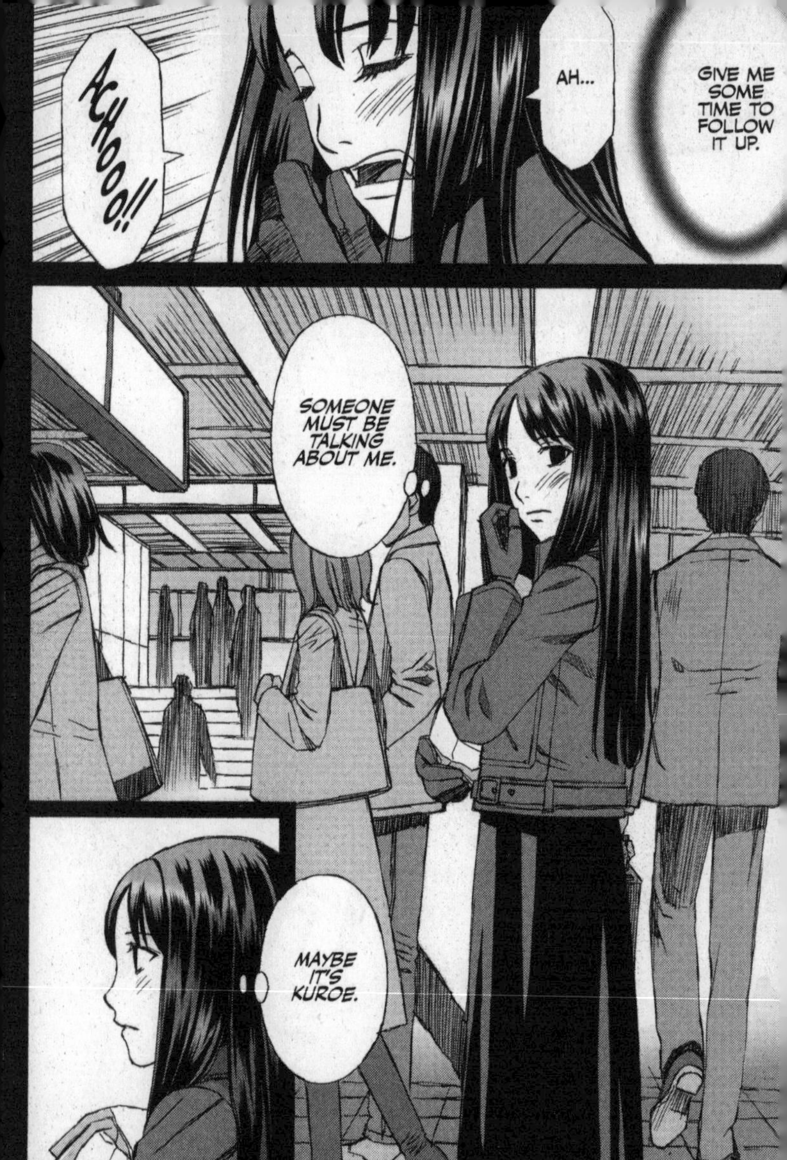
GIVE ME SOME TIME TO FOLLOW IT UP.
AH...
ACHOO!!
SOMEONE MUST BE TALKING ABOUT ME.
MAYBE IT'S KUROE.

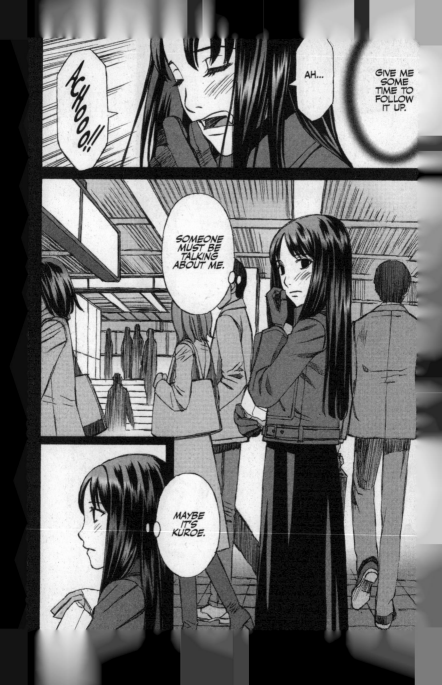

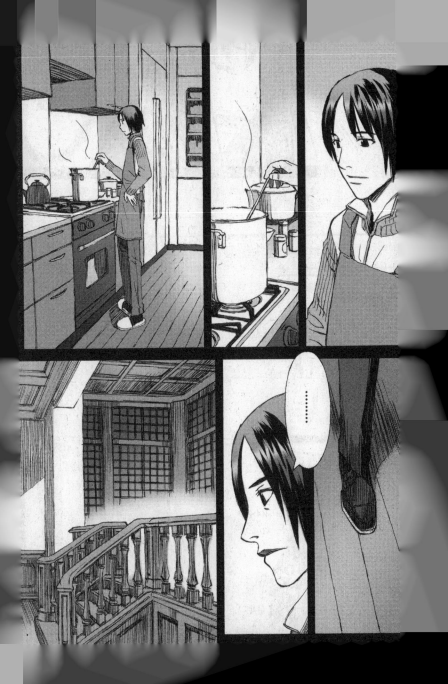

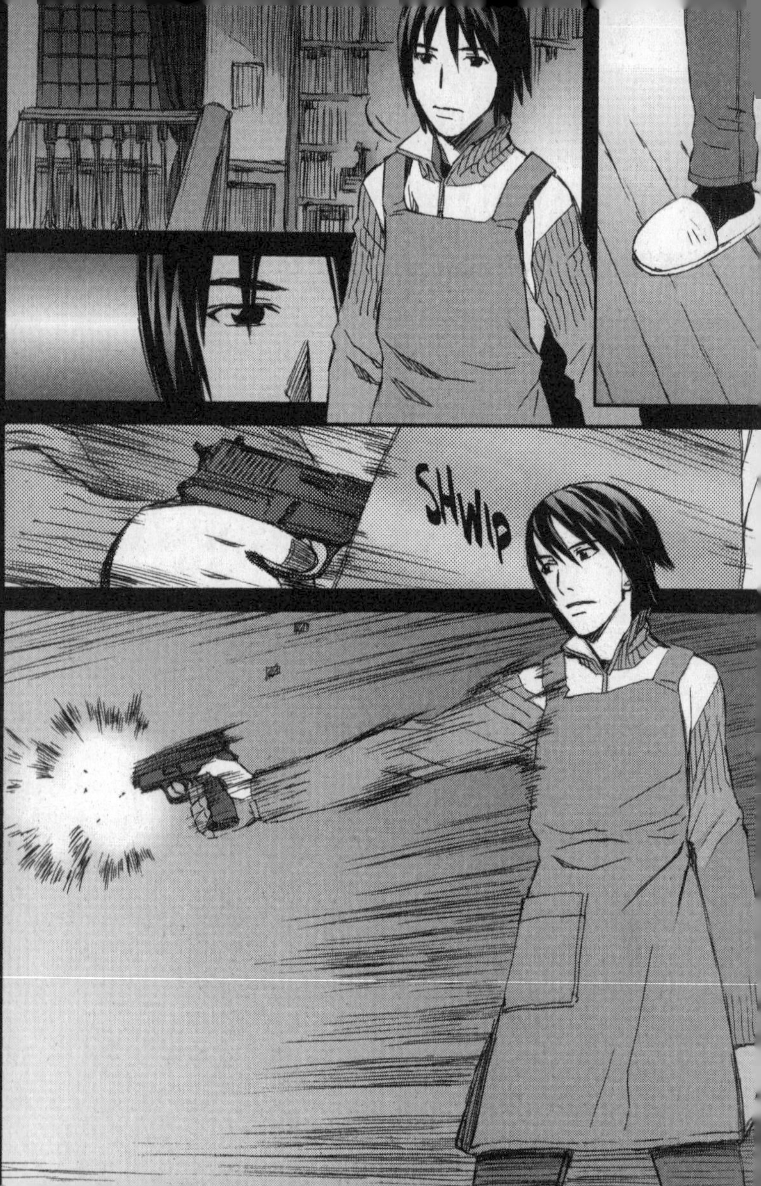
SHWIP

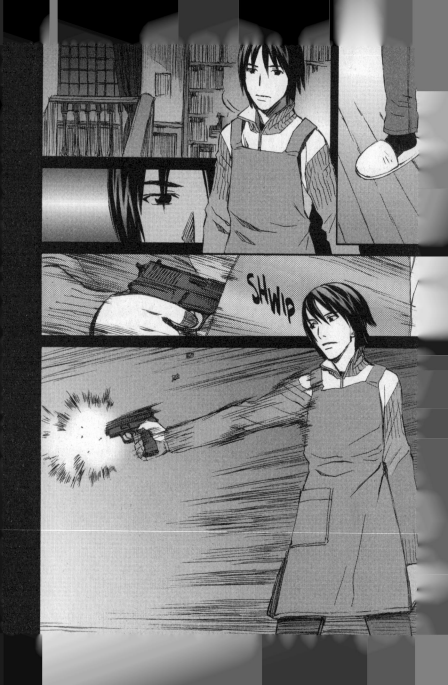

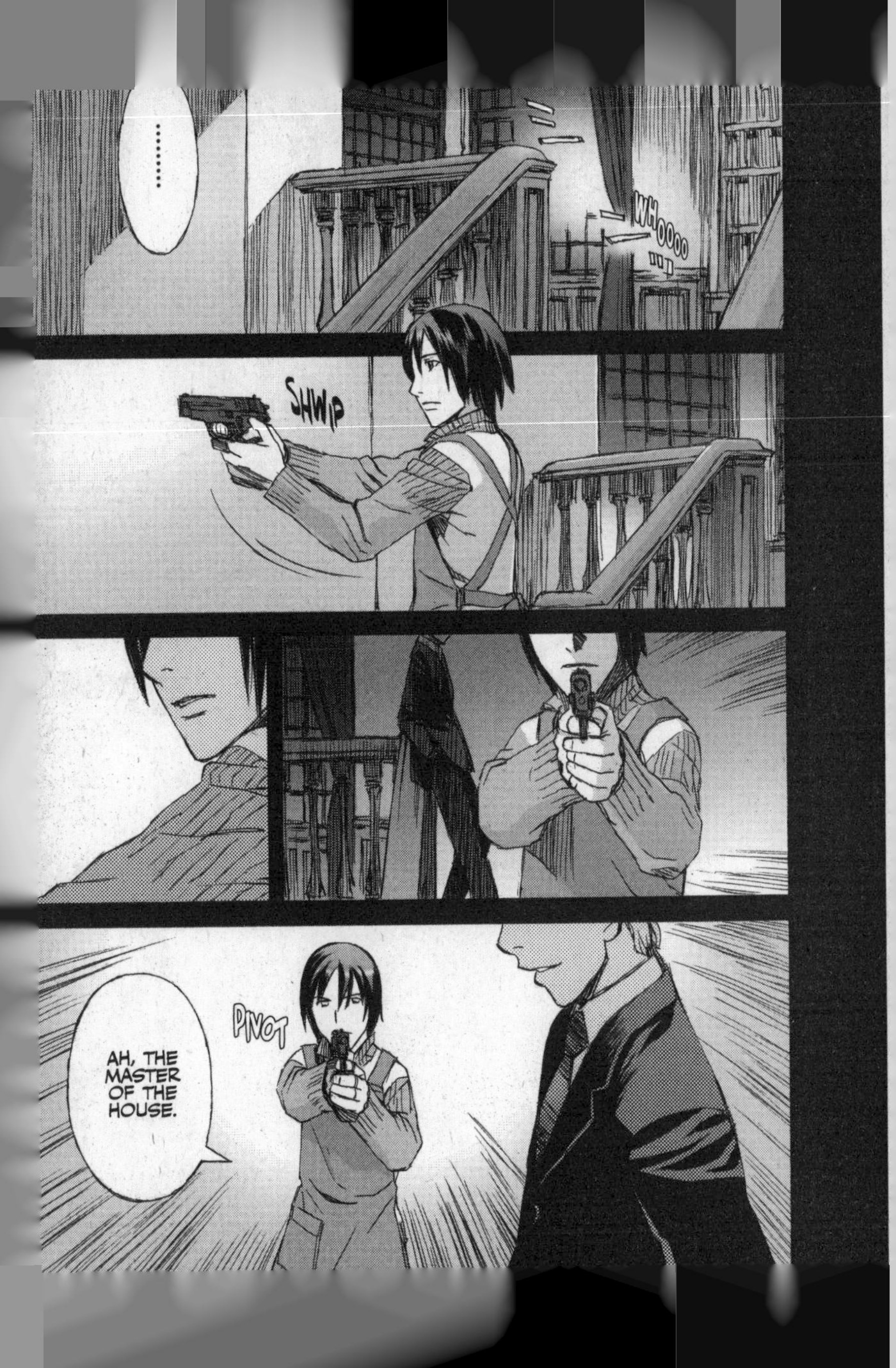
WHOOOO
......
SHWIP
PIVOT
AH, THE MASTER OF THE HOUSE.

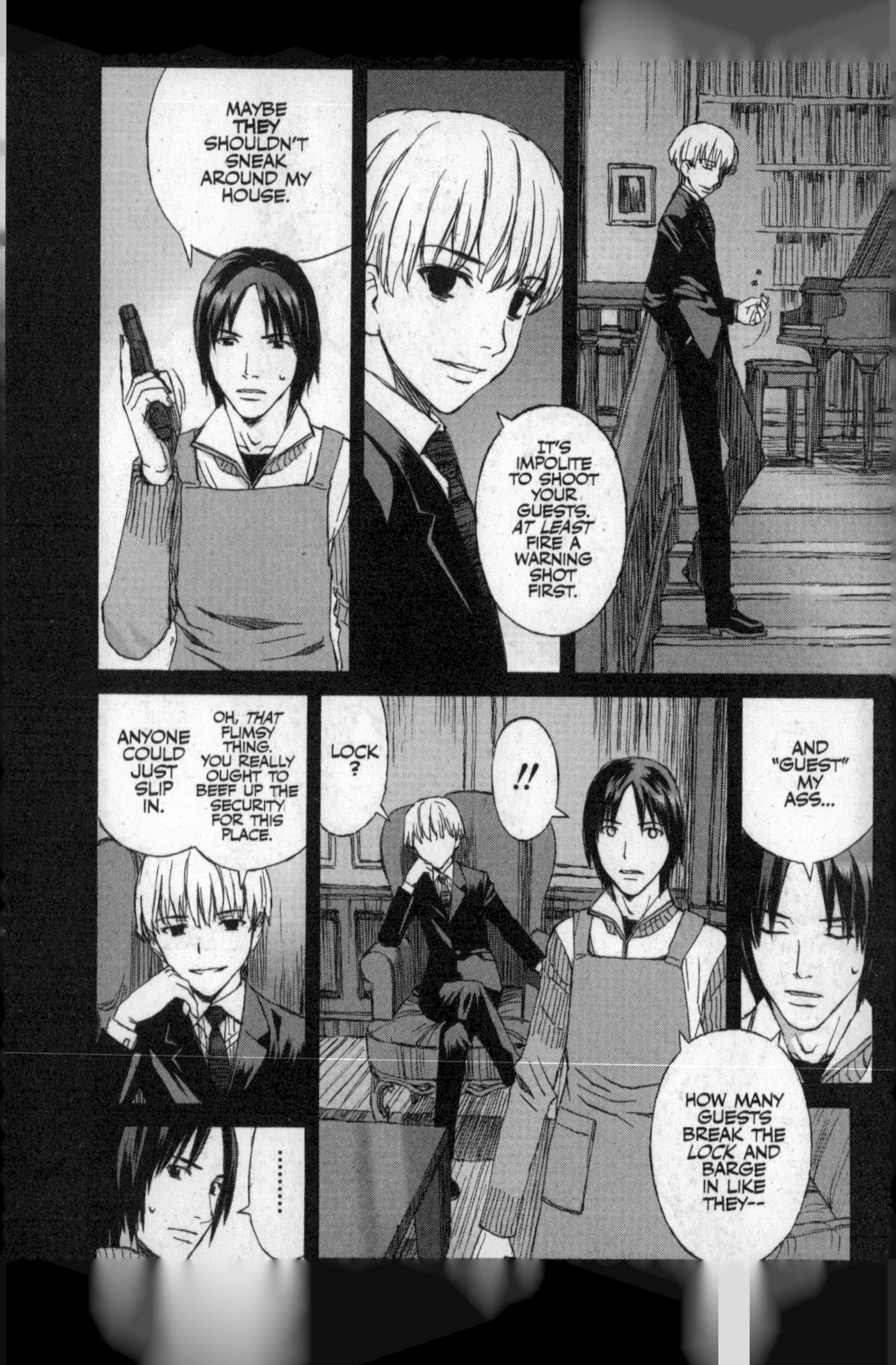
IT'S IMPOLITE TO SHOOT YOUR GUESTS. *AT LEAST* FIRE A WARNING SHOT FIRST.
MAYBE THEY SHOULDN'T SNEAK AROUND MY HOUSE.
AND "GUEST" MY ASS...
HOW MANY GUESTS BREAK THE *LOCK* AND BARGE IN LIKE THEY--
!!
LOCK ?
OH, *THAT* FLIMSY THING. YOU REALLY OUGHT TO BEEF UP THE SECURITY FOR THIS PLACE.
ANYONE COULD JUST SLIP IN.
......

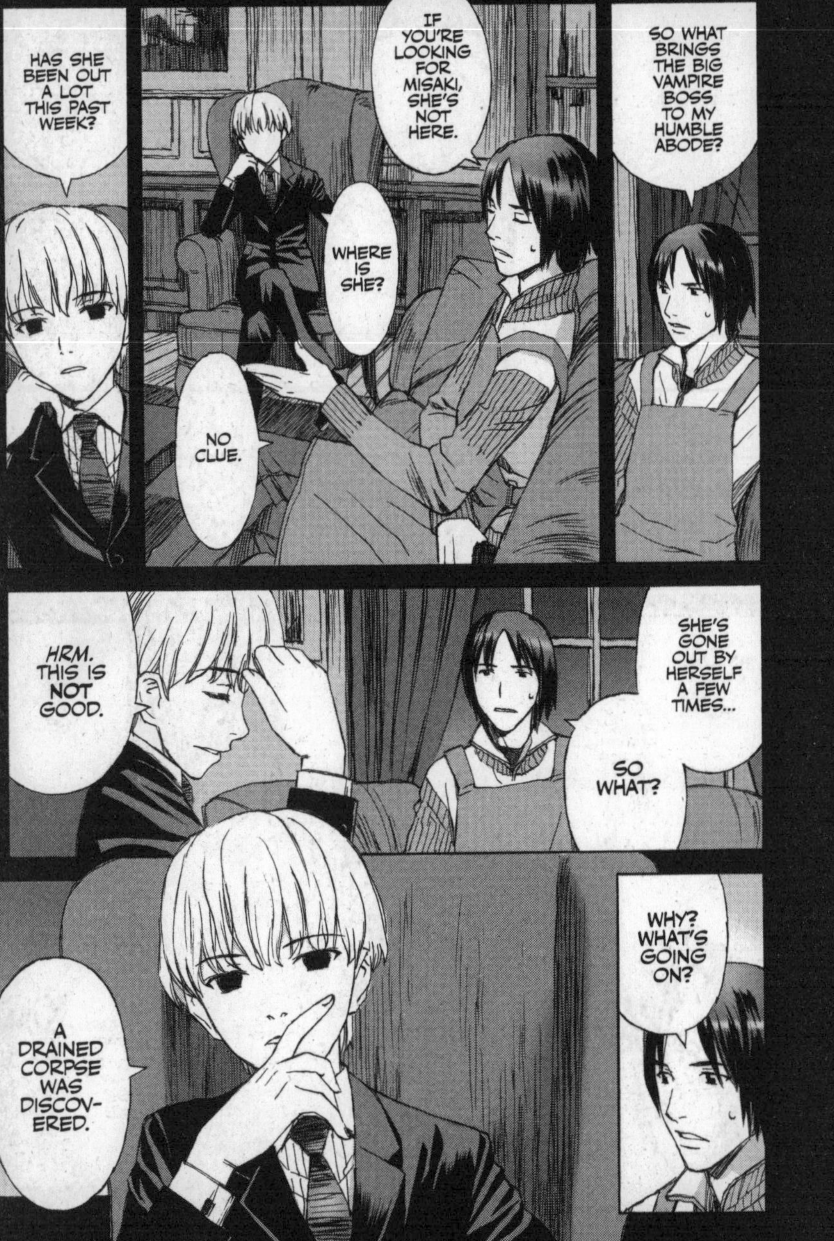
SO WHAT BRINGS THE BIG VAMPIRE BOSS TO MY HUMBLE ABODE?
IF YOU'RE LOOKING FOR MISAKI, SHE'S NOT HERE.
WHERE IS SHE?
NO CLUE.
HAS SHE BEEN OUT A LOT THIS PAST WEEK?
SHE'S GONE OUT BY HERSELF A FEW TIMES...
SO WHAT?
HRM. THIS IS **NOT** GOOD.
WHY? WHAT'S GOING ON?
A DRAINED CORPSE WAS DISCOV-ERED.

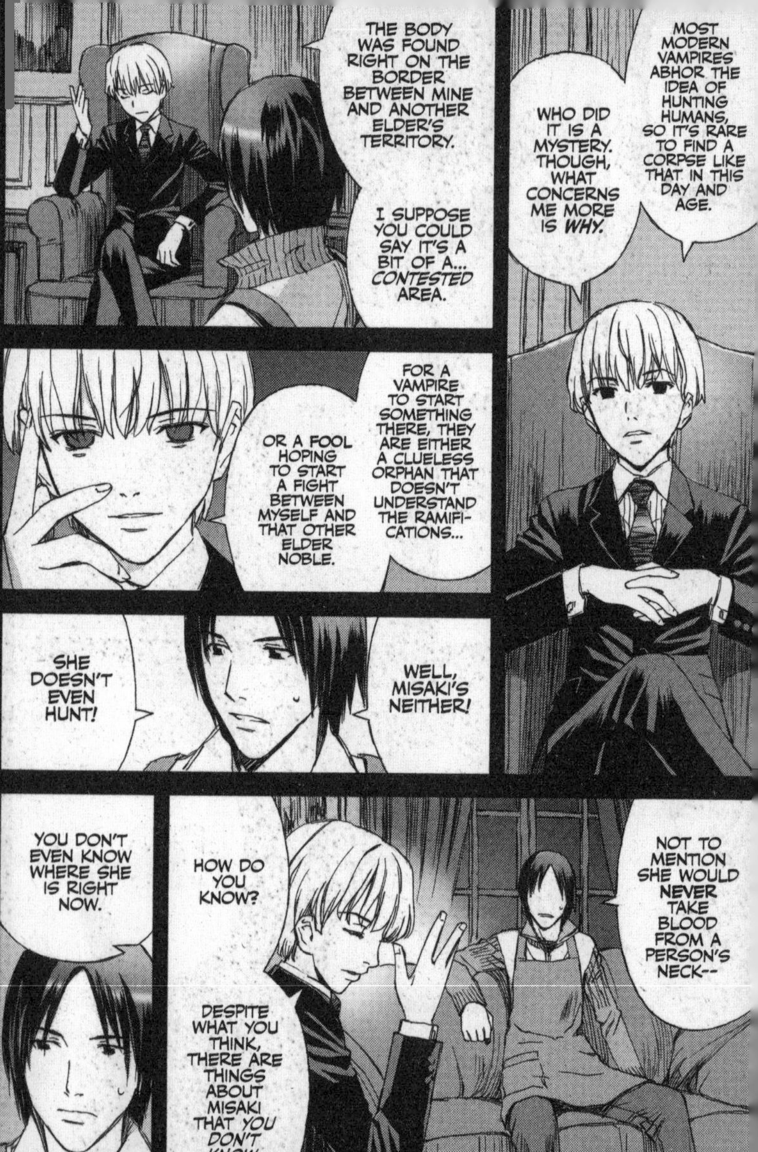
MOST MODERN VAMPIRES ABHOR THE IDEA OF HUNTING HUMANS, SO IT'S RARE TO FIND A CORPSE LIKE THAT IN THIS DAY AND AGE.
WHO DID IT IS A MYSTERY. THOUGH, WHAT CONCERNS ME MORE IS *WHY*.
THE BODY WAS FOUND RIGHT ON THE BORDER BETWEEN MINE AND ANOTHER ELDER'S TERRITORY.
I SUPPOSE YOU COULD SAY IT'S A BIT OF A... *CONTESTED* AREA.
FOR A VAMPIRE TO START SOMETHING THERE, THEY ARE EITHER A CLUELESS ORPHAN THAT DOESN'T UNDERSTAND THE RAMIFI-CATIONS...
OR A FOOL HOPING TO START A FIGHT BETWEEN MYSELF AND THAT OTHER ELDER NOBLE.
WELL, MISAKI'S NEITHER!
SHE DOESN'T EVEN HUNT!
NOT TO MENTION SHE WOULD NEVER TAKE BLOOD FROM A PERSON'S NECK--
HOW DO YOU KNOW?
DESPITE WHAT YOU THINK, THERE ARE THINGS ABOUT MISAKI THAT *YOU DON'T KNOW*.
YOU DON'T EVEN KNOW WHERE SHE IS RIGHT NOW.

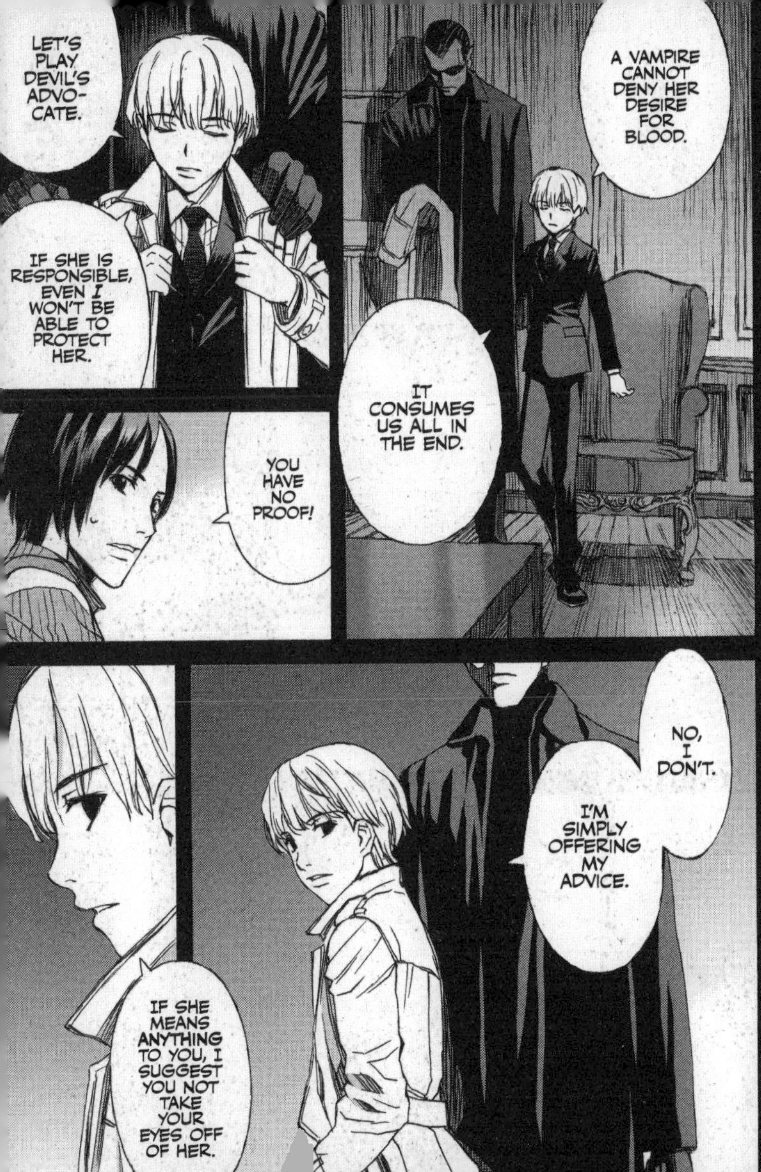
A VAMPIRE CANNOT DENY HER DESIRE FOR BLOOD.
IT CONSUMES US ALL IN THE END.
LET'S PLAY DEVIL'S ADVOCATE.
IF SHE IS RESPONSIBLE, EVEN *I* WON'T BE ABLE TO PROTECT HER.
YOU HAVE NO PROOF!
NO, I DON'T.
I'M SIMPLY OFFERING MY ADVICE.
IF SHE MEANS ANYTHING TO YOU, I SUGGEST YOU NOT TAKE YOUR EYES OFF OF HER.

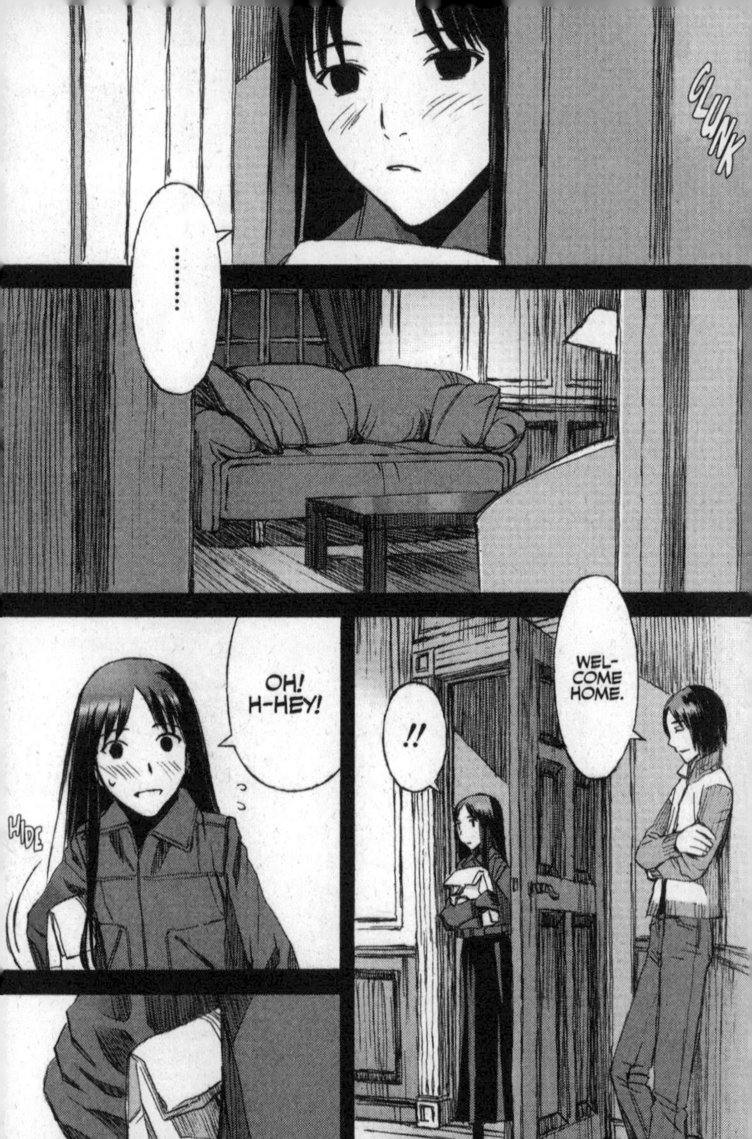
CLUNK
......
WEL-COME HOME.
!!
OH! H-HEY!
HIDE

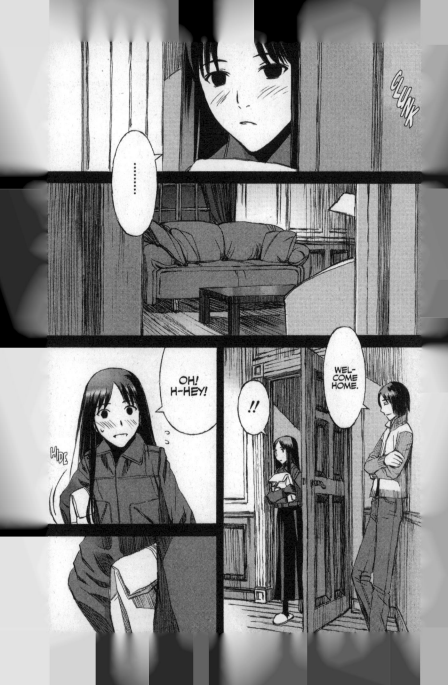

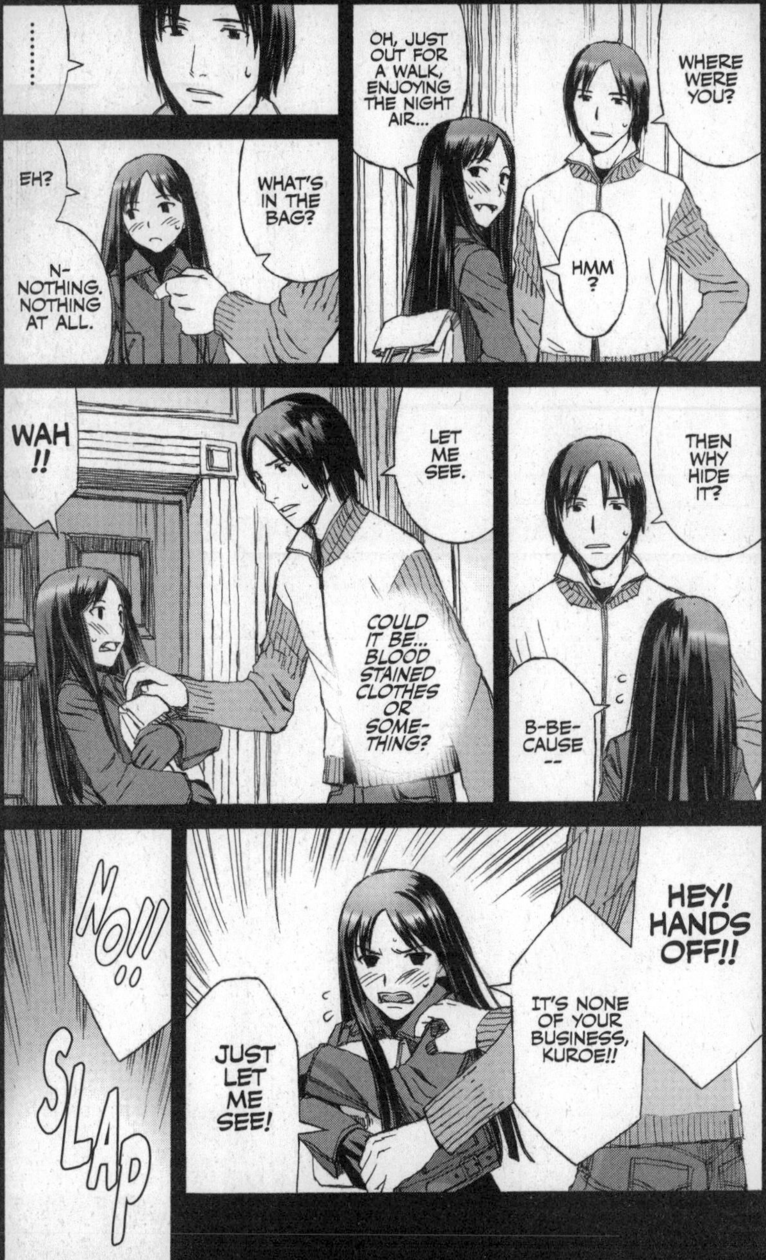
WHERE WERE YOU?
OH, JUST OUT FOR A WALK, ENJOYING THE NIGHT AIR...
HMM?
......
WHAT'S IN THE BAG?
EH?
N-NOTHING. NOTHING AT ALL.
THEN WHY HIDE IT?
B-BE-CAUSE --
LET ME SEE.
WAH!!
COULD IT BE... BLOOD STAINED CLOTHES OR SOME-THING?
HEY! HANDS OFF!!
IT'S NONE OF YOUR BUSINESS, KUROE!!
JUST LET ME SEE!
NO!!
SLAP

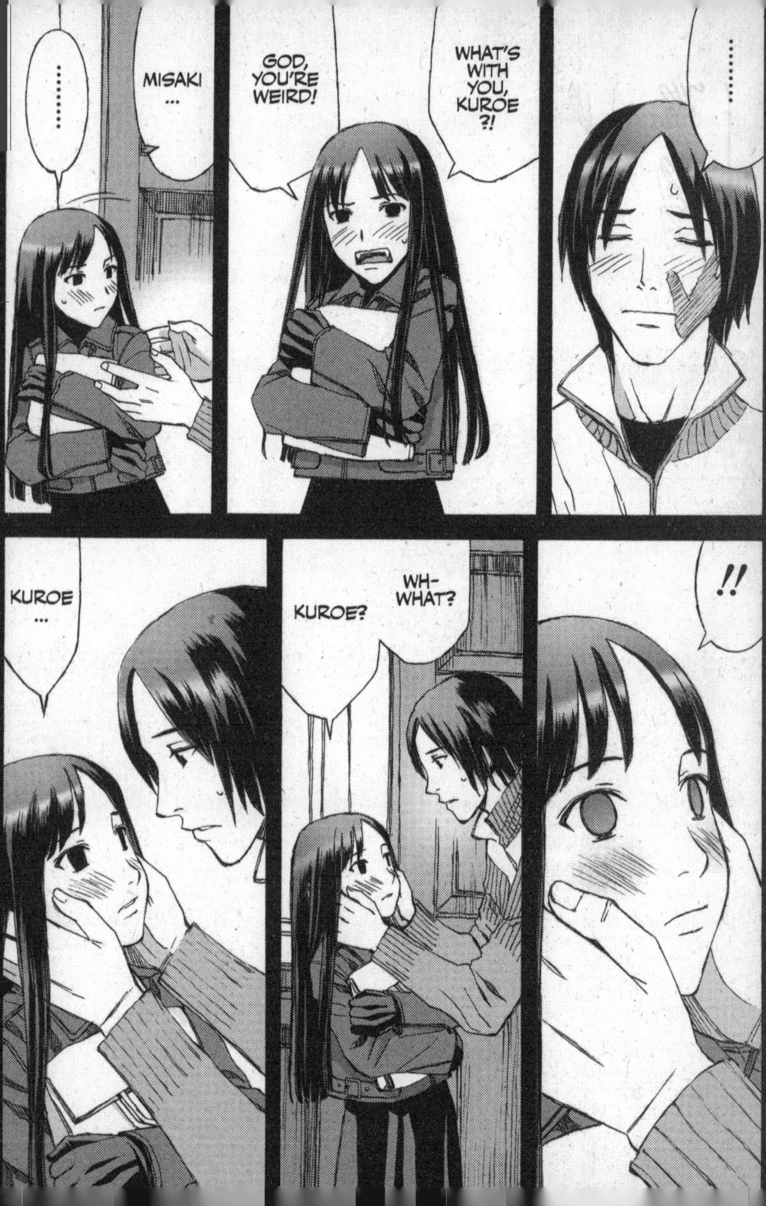
......
WHAT'S WITH YOU, KUROE ?!
GOD, YOU'RE WEIRD!
MISAKI ...
......
!!
WH- WHAT?
KUROE?
KUROE ...

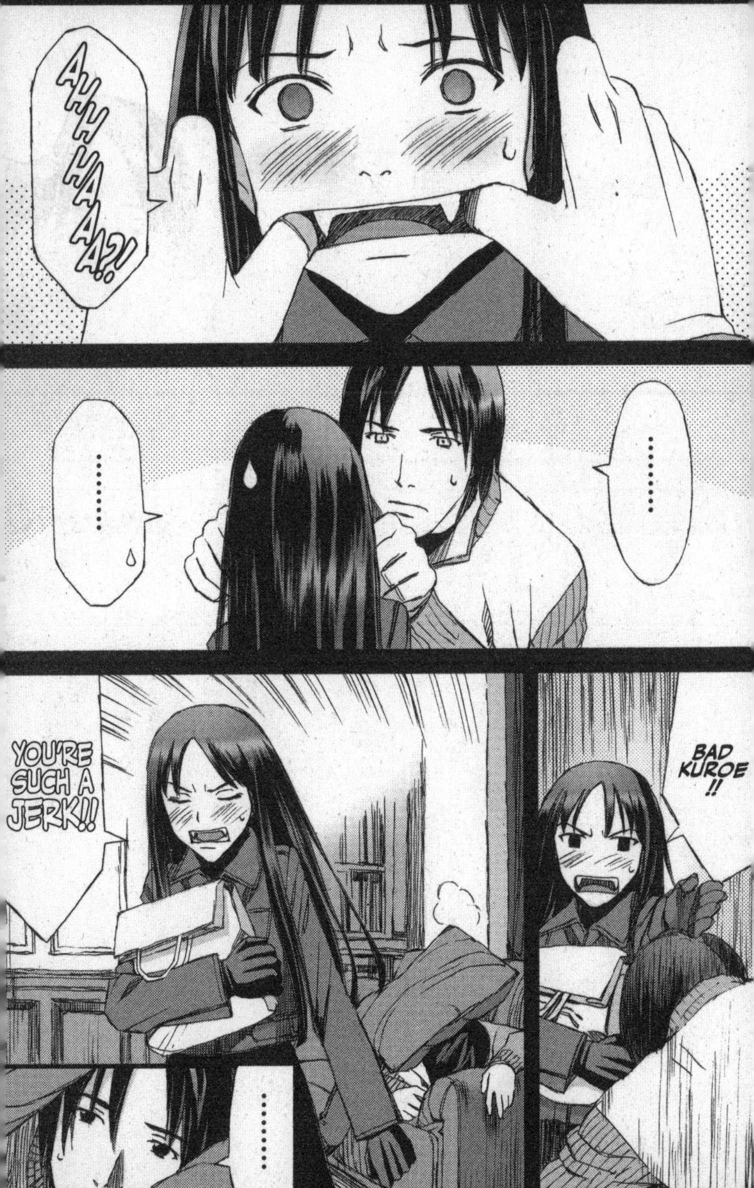
AHHHAAA?!
......
......
BAD KUROE!!
YOU'RE SUCH A JERK!!
......

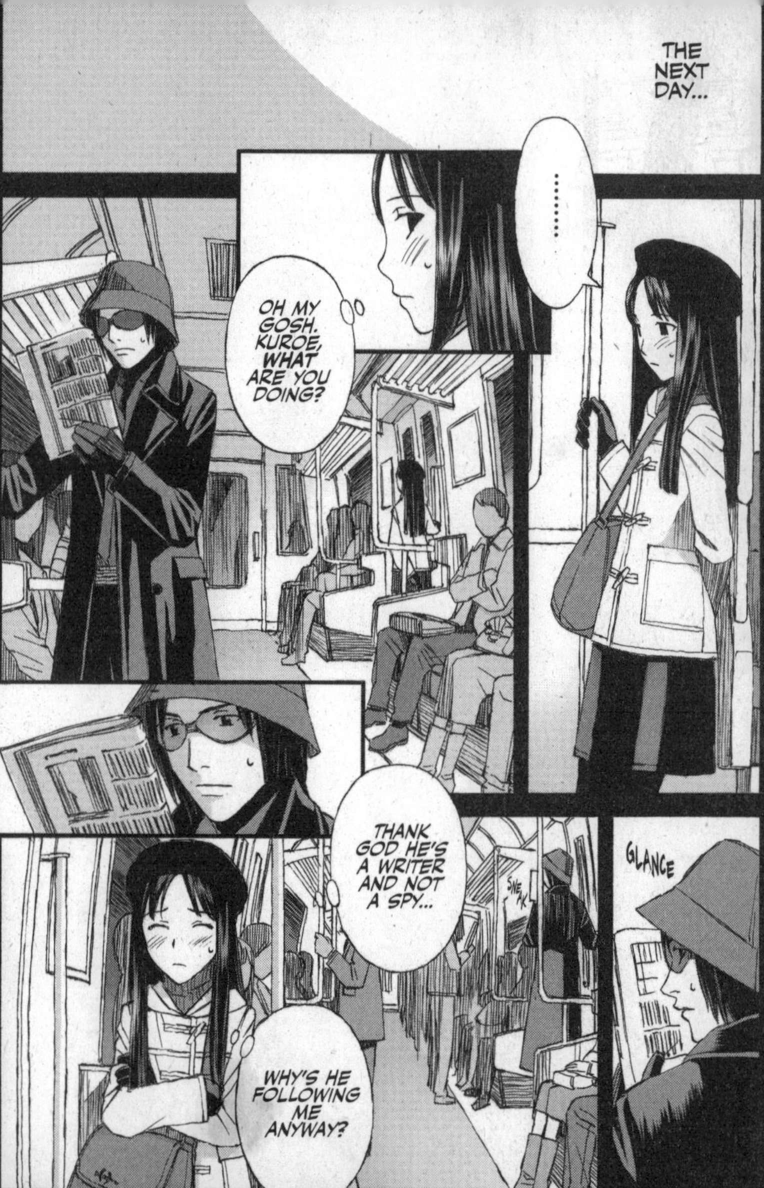
THE NEXT DAY...
......
OH MY GOSH. KUROE, WHAT ARE YOU DOING?
THANK GOD HE'S A WRITER AND NOT A SPY...
GLANCE
SNEAK
WHY'S HE FOLLOWING ME ANYWAY?

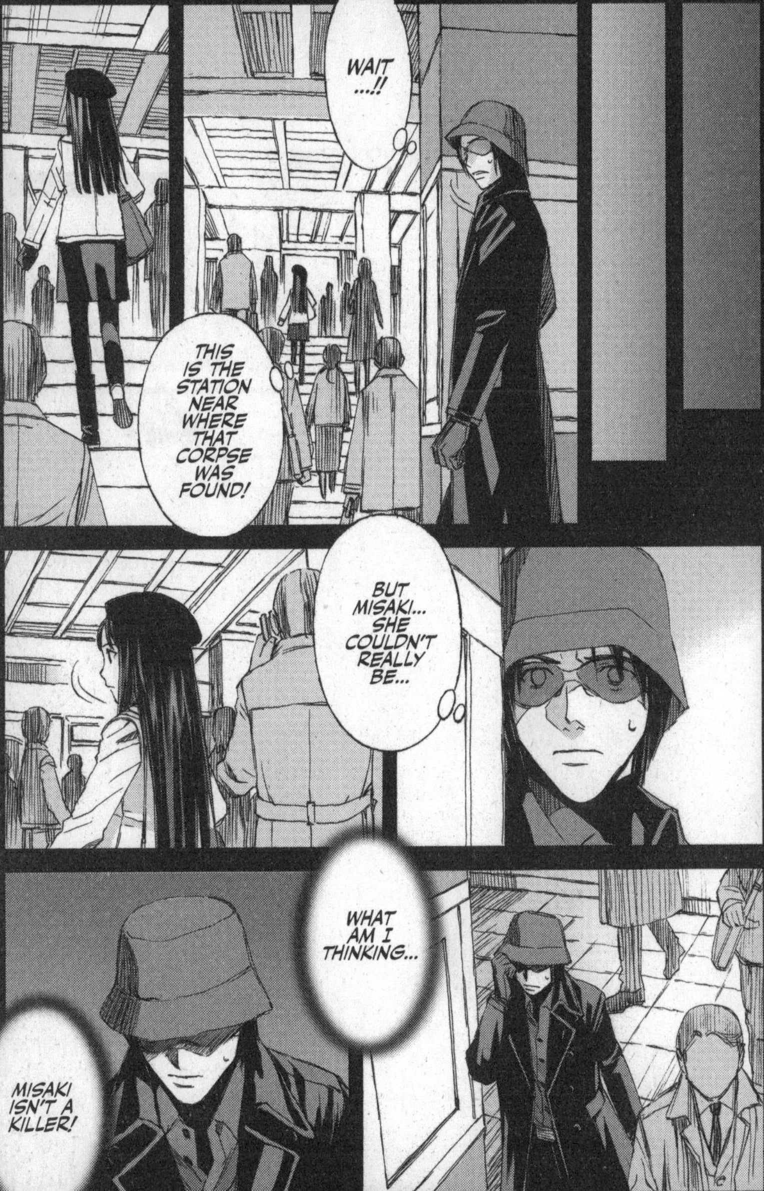
WAIT ...!!
THIS IS THE STATION NEAR WHERE THAT CORPSE WAS FOUND!
BUT MISAKI... SHE COULDN'T REALLY BE...
WHAT AM I THINKING...
MISAKI ISN'T A KILLER!

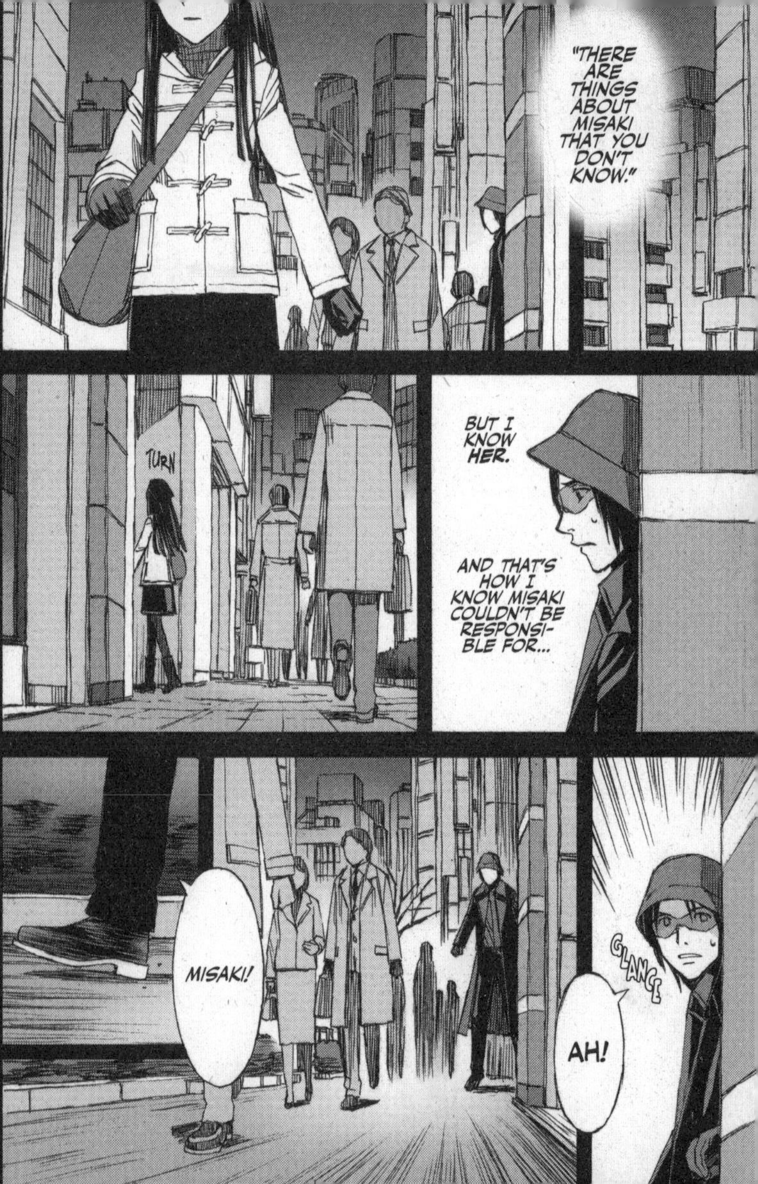
"THERE ARE THINGS ABOUT MISAKI THAT YOU DON'T KNOW."
BUT I KNOW HER.
AND THAT'S HOW I KNOW MISAKI COULDN'T BE RESPONSIBLE FOR...
TURN
GLANCE
AH!
MISAKI!

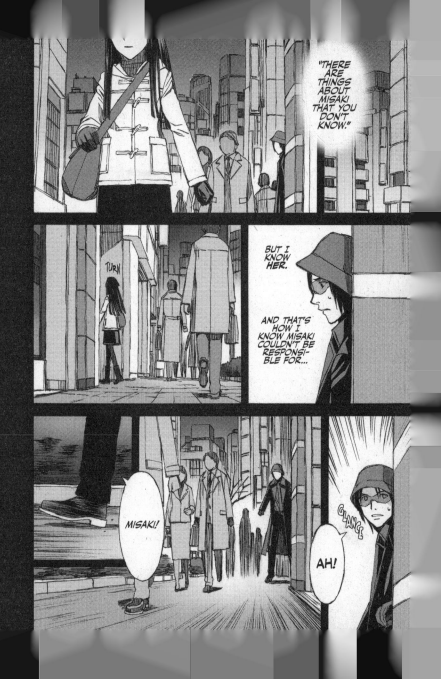

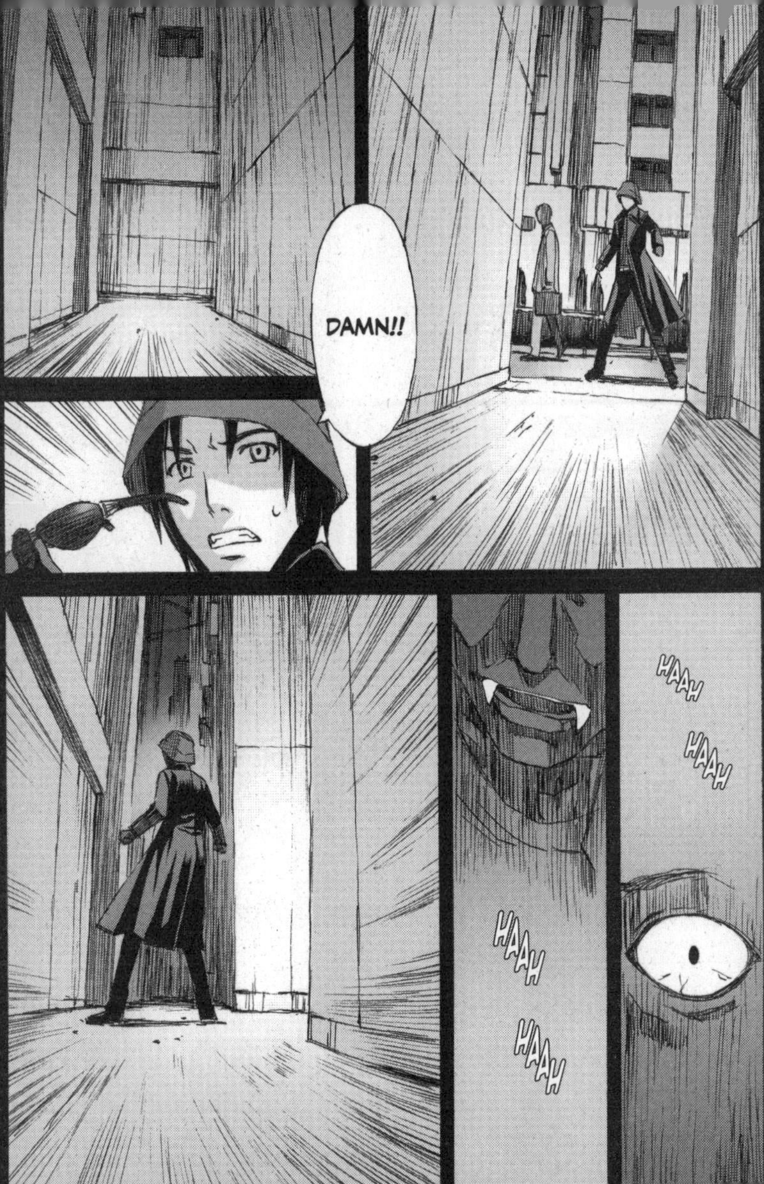
DAMN!!
HAAH
HAAH
HAAH
HAAH

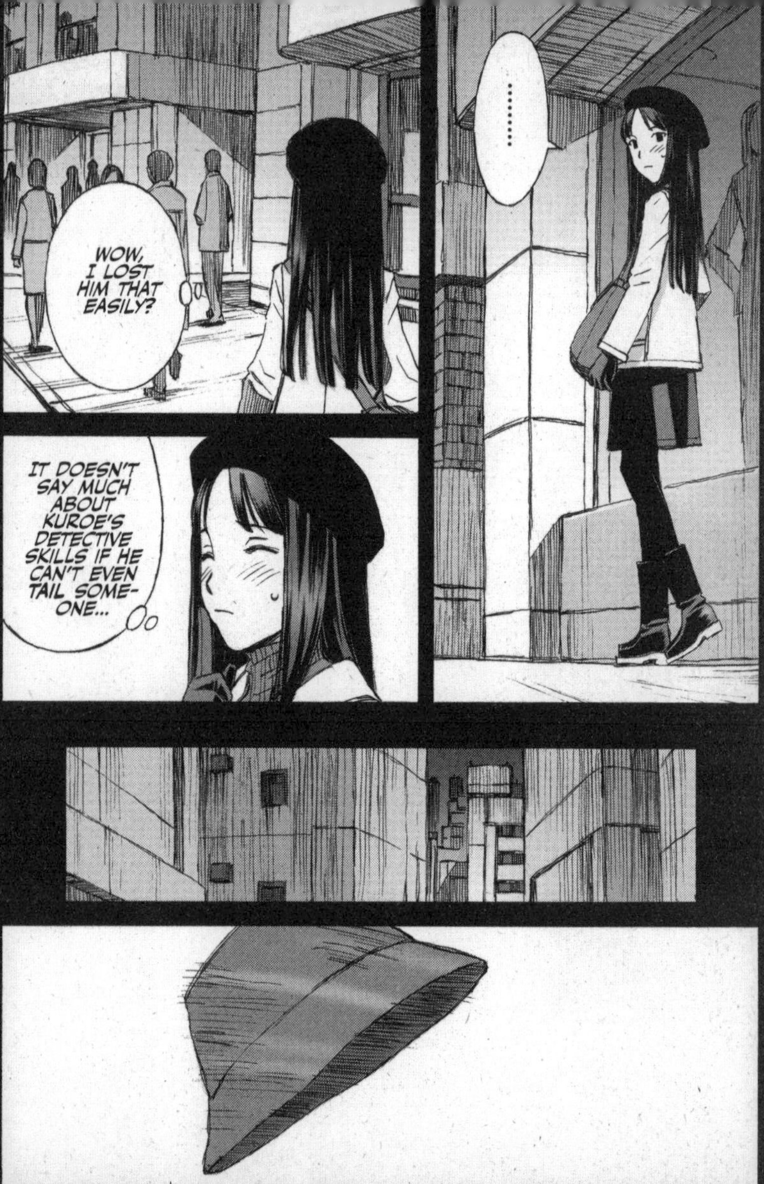
......
WOW, I LOST HIM THAT EASILY?
IT DOESN'T SAY MUCH ABOUT KUROE'S DETECTIVE SKILLS IF HE CAN'T EVEN TAIL SOME-ONE...

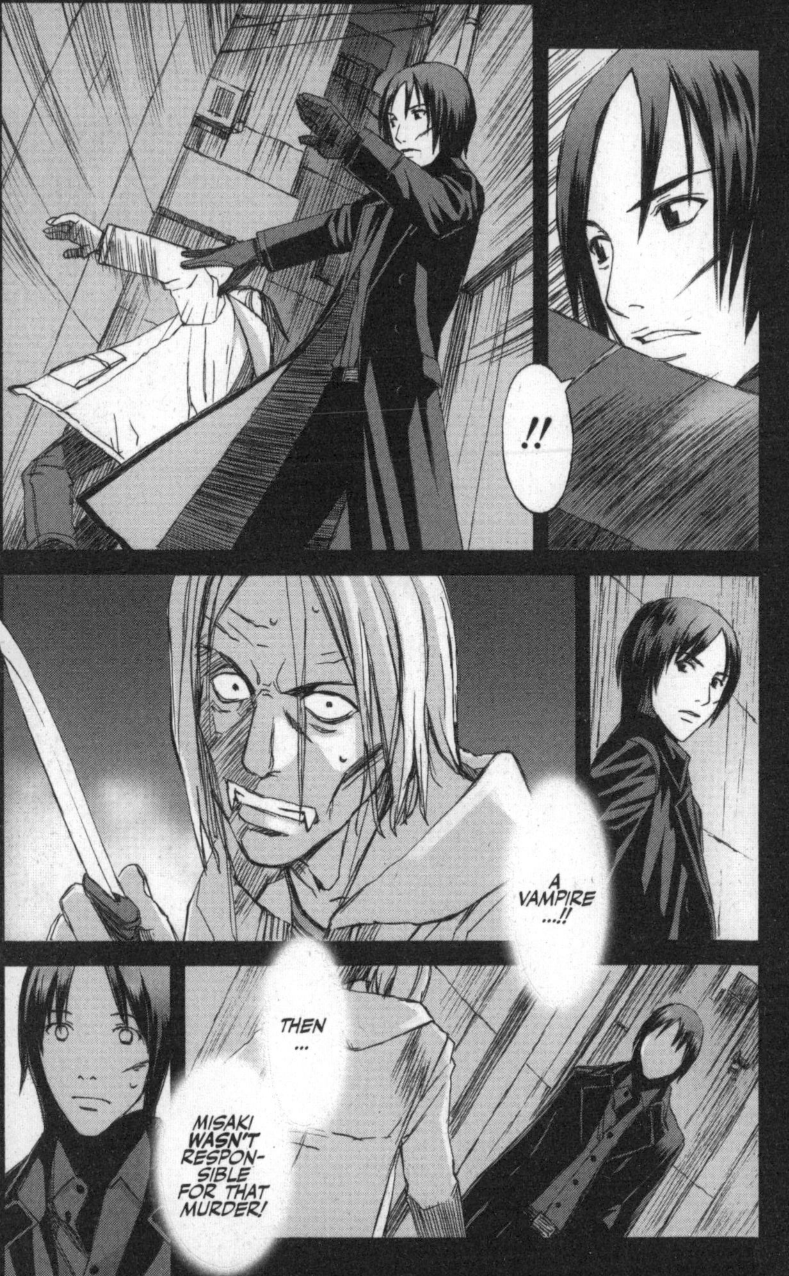
!!
A VAMPIRE ...!!
THEN ...
MISAKI WASN'T RESPONSIBLE FOR THAT MURDER!

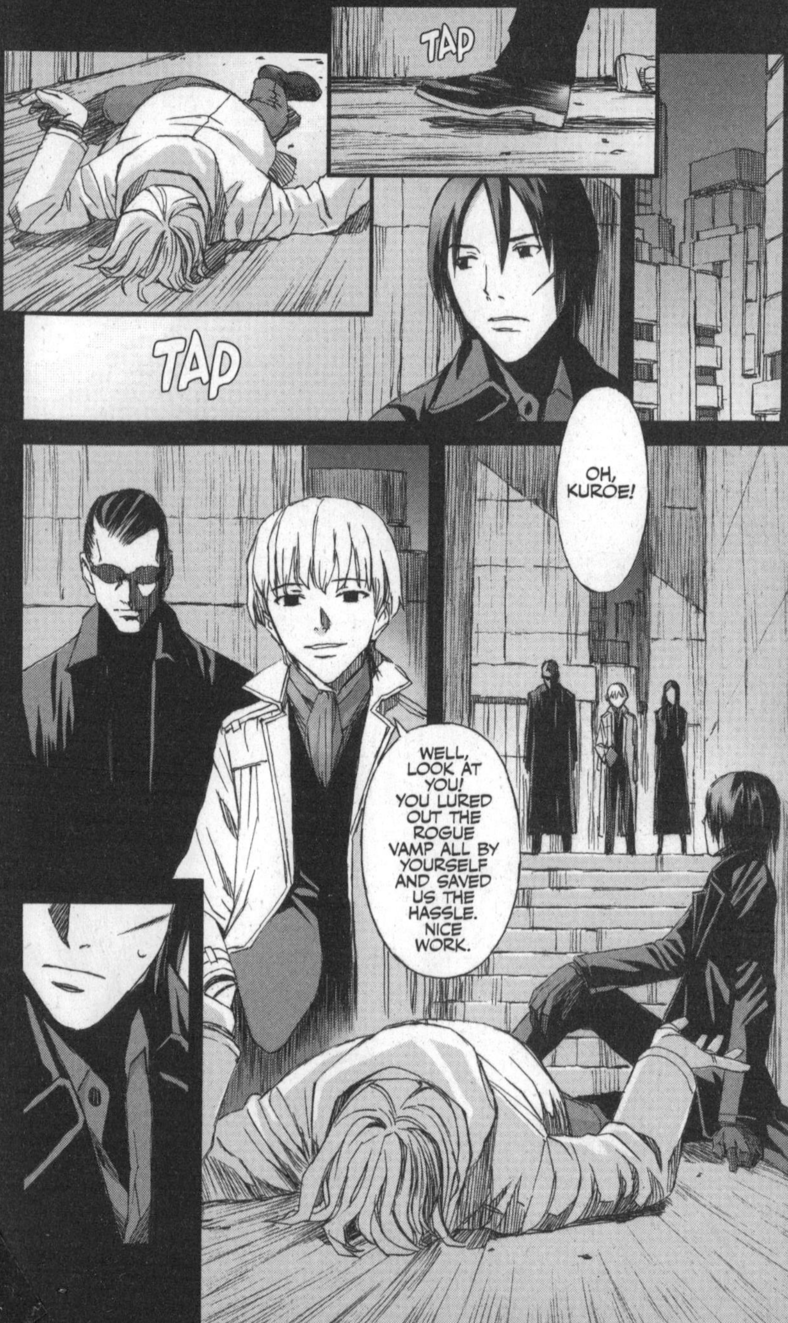
TAP
TAP
OH, KUROE!
WELL, LOOK AT YOU! YOU LURED OUT THE ROGUE VAMP ALL BY YOURSELF AND SAVED US THE HASSLE. NICE WORK.

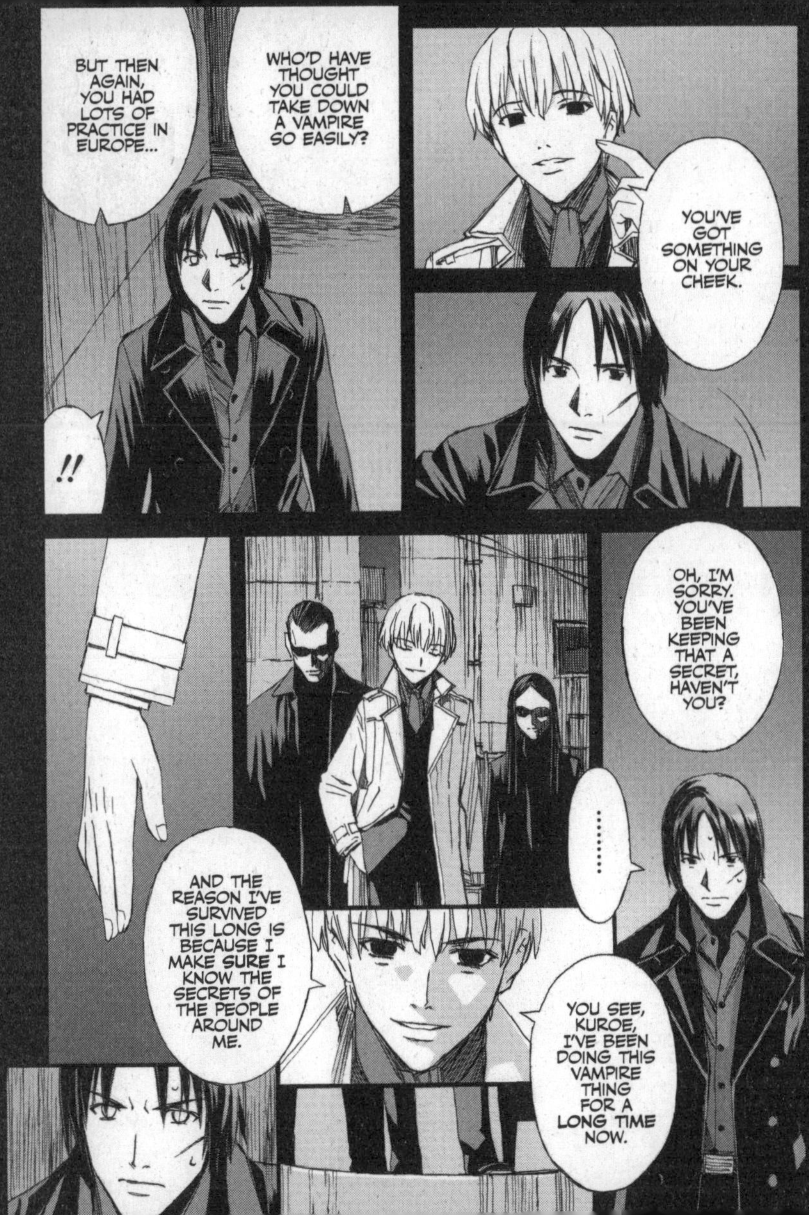
YOU'VE GOT SOMETHING ON YOUR CHEEK.
WHO'D HAVE THOUGHT YOU COULD TAKE DOWN A VAMPIRE SO EASILY?
BUT THEN AGAIN, YOU HAD LOTS OF PRACTICE IN EUROPE...
!!
OH, I'M SORRY. YOU'VE BEEN KEEPING THAT A SECRET, HAVEN'T YOU?
......
YOU SEE, KUROE, I'VE BEEN DOING THIS VAMPIRE THING FOR A LONG TIME NOW.
AND THE REASON I'VE SURVIVED THIS LONG IS BECAUSE I MAKE SURE I KNOW THE SECRETS OF THE PEOPLE AROUND ME.

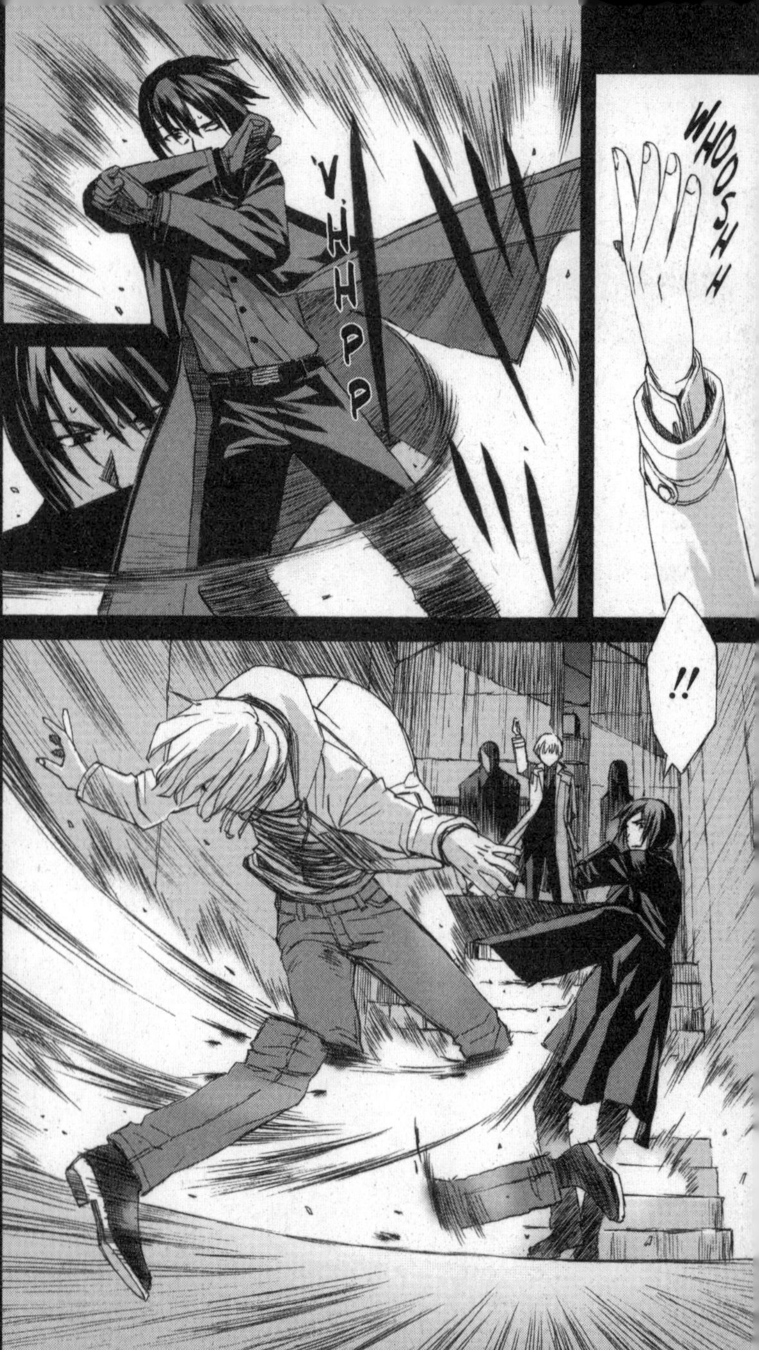
WHOOSHH
VHHPP
!!

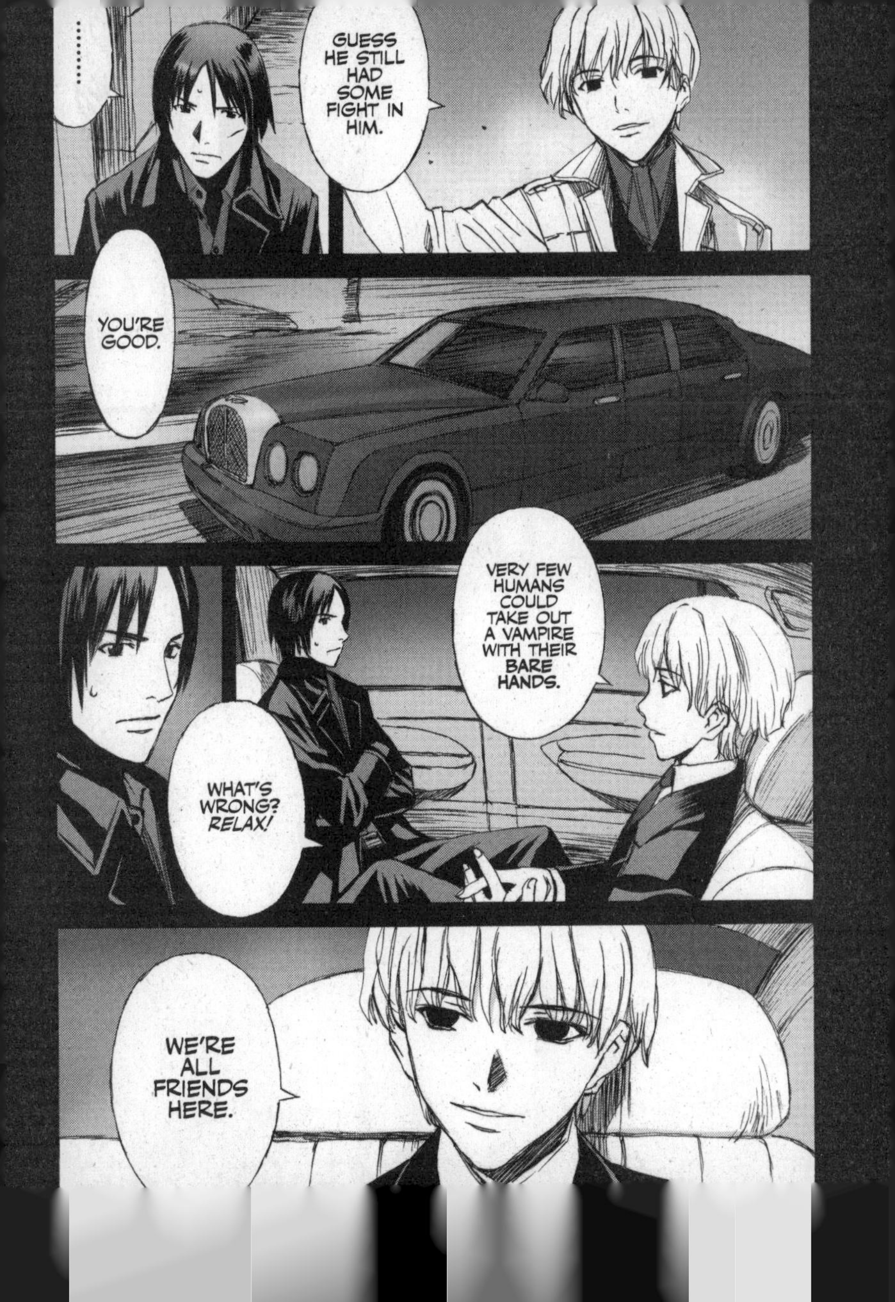

GUESS HE STILL HAD SOME FIGHT IN HIM.
......
YOU'RE GOOD.
VERY FEW HUMANS COULD TAKE OUT A VAMPIRE WITH THEIR BARE HANDS.
WHAT'S WRONG? *RELAX!*
WE'RE ALL FRIENDS HERE.

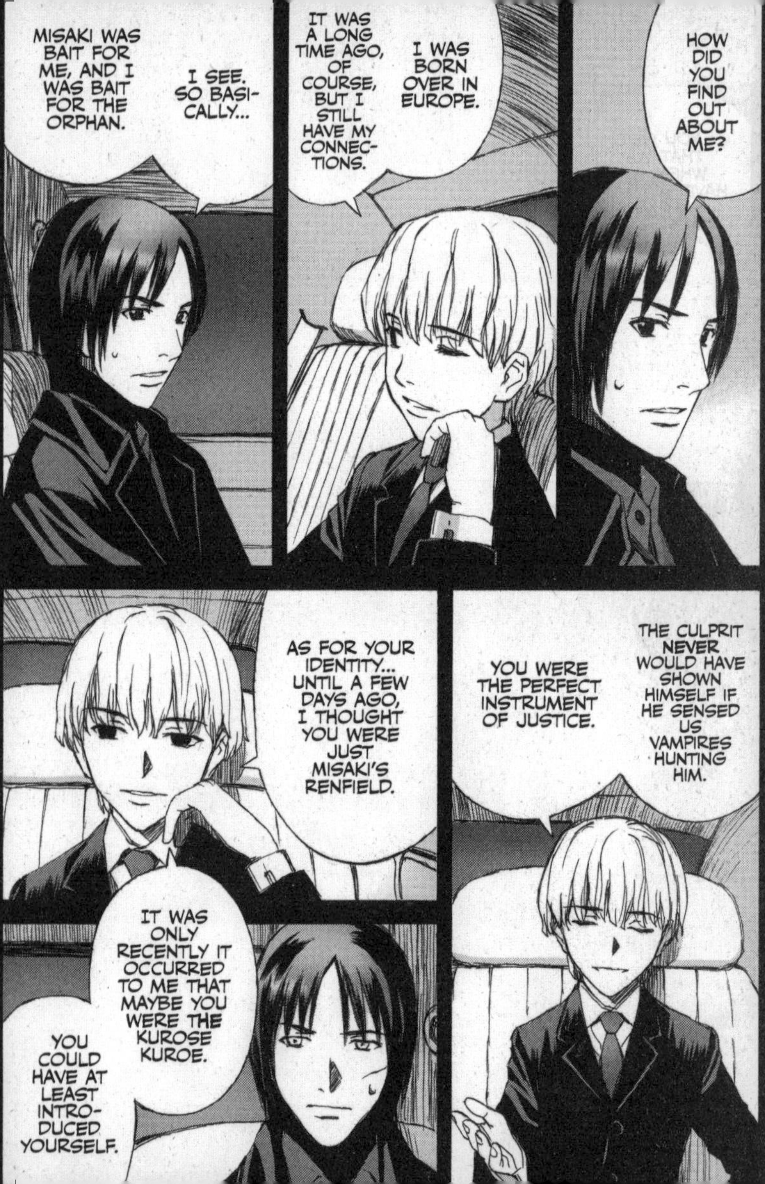
HOW DID YOU FIND OUT ABOUT ME?
I WAS BORN OVER IN EUROPE.
IT WAS A LONG TIME AGO, OF COURSE, BUT I STILL HAVE MY CONNECTIONS.
I SEE. SO BASICALLY...
MISAKI WAS BAIT FOR ME, AND I WAS BAIT FOR THE ORPHAN.
THE CULPRIT NEVER WOULD HAVE SHOWN HIMSELF IF HE SENSED US VAMPIRES HUNTING HIM.
YOU WERE THE PERFECT INSTRUMENT OF JUSTICE.
AS FOR YOUR IDENTITY... UNTIL A FEW DAYS AGO, I THOUGHT YOU WERE JUST MISAKI'S RENFIELD.
IT WAS ONLY RECENTLY IT OCCURRED TO ME THAT MAYBE YOU WERE THE KUROSE KUROE.
YOU COULD HAVE AT LEAST INTRODUCED YOURSELF.

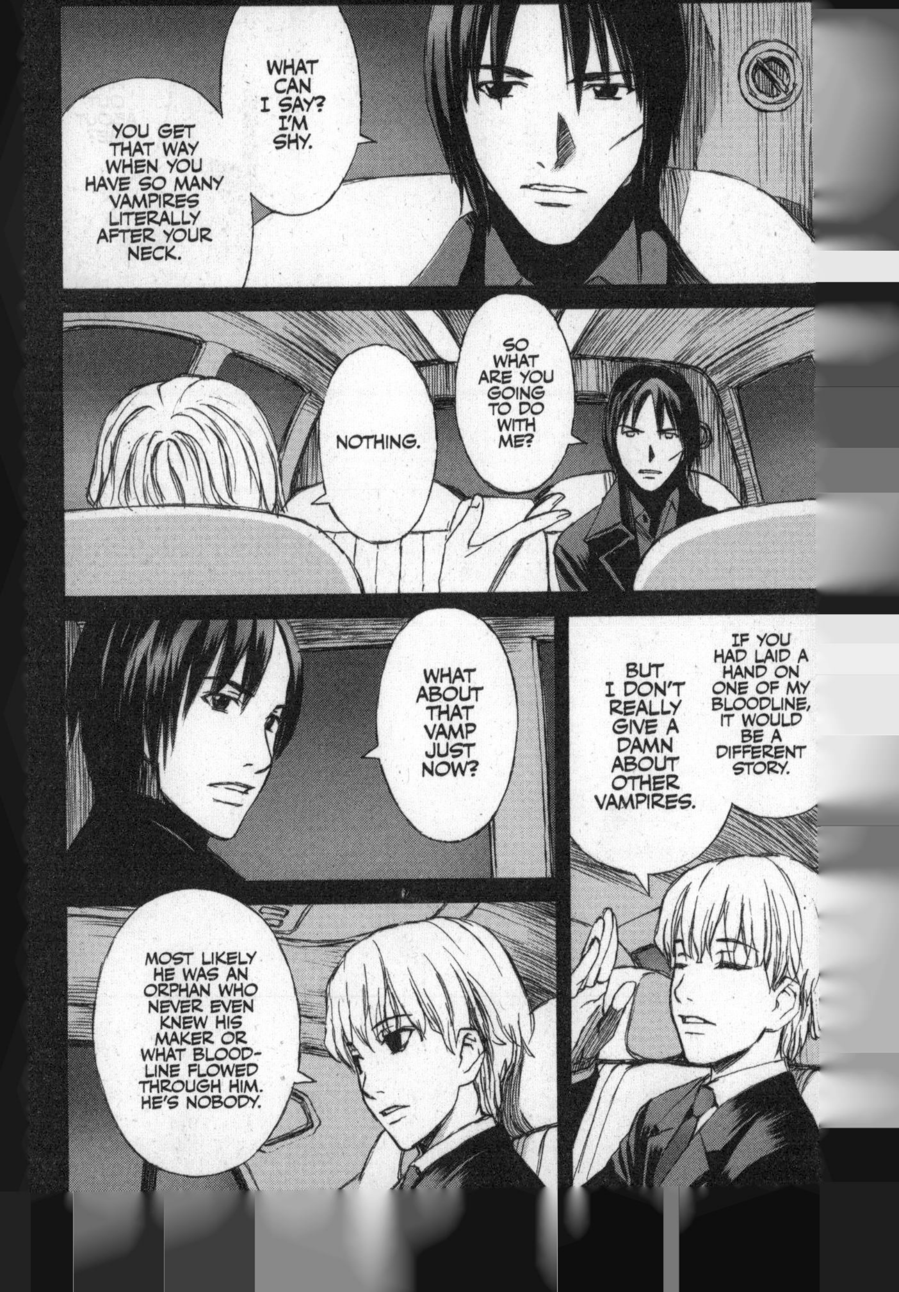
WHAT CAN I SAY? I'M SHY.
YOU GET THAT WAY WHEN YOU HAVE SO MANY VAMPIRES LITERALLY AFTER YOUR NECK.
SO WHAT ARE YOU GOING TO DO WITH ME?
NOTHING.
IF YOU HAD LAID A HAND ON ONE OF MY BLOODLINE, IT WOULD BE A DIFFERENT STORY.
BUT I DON'T REALLY GIVE A DAMN ABOUT OTHER VAMPIRES.
WHAT ABOUT THAT VAMP JUST NOW?
MOST LIKELY HE WAS AN ORPHAN WHO NEVER EVEN KNEW HIS MAKER OR WHAT BLOOD-LINE FLOWED THROUGH HIM. HE'S NOBODY.

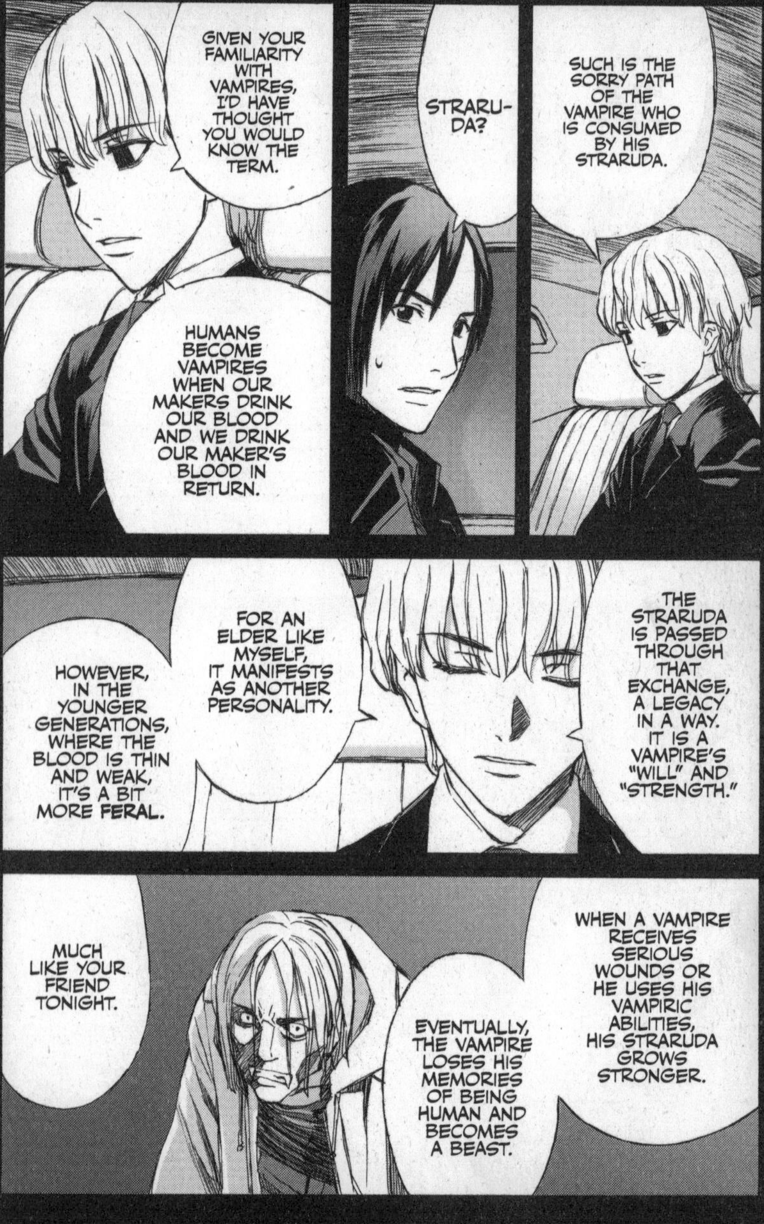
SUCH IS THE SORRY PATH OF THE VAMPIRE WHO IS CONSUMED BY HIS STRARUDA.
STRARU-DA?
GIVEN YOUR FAMILIARITY WITH VAMPIRES, I'D HAVE THOUGHT YOU WOULD KNOW THE TERM.
HUMANS BECOME VAMPIRES WHEN OUR MAKERS DRINK OUR BLOOD AND WE DRINK OUR MAKER'S BLOOD IN RETURN.
THE STRARUDA IS PASSED THROUGH THAT EXCHANGE, A LEGACY IN A WAY. IT IS A VAMPIRE'S "WILL" AND "STRENGTH."
FOR AN ELDER LIKE MYSELF, IT MANIFESTS AS ANOTHER PERSONALITY.
HOWEVER, IN THE YOUNGER GENERATIONS, WHERE THE BLOOD IS THIN AND WEAK, IT'S A BIT MORE FERAL.
WHEN A VAMPIRE RECEIVES SERIOUS WOUNDS OR HE USES HIS VAMPIRIC ABILITIES, HIS STRARUDA GROWS STRONGER.
EVENTUALLY, THE VAMPIRE LOSES HIS MEMORIES OF BEING HUMAN AND BECOMES A BEAST.
MUCH LIKE YOUR FRIEND TONIGHT.

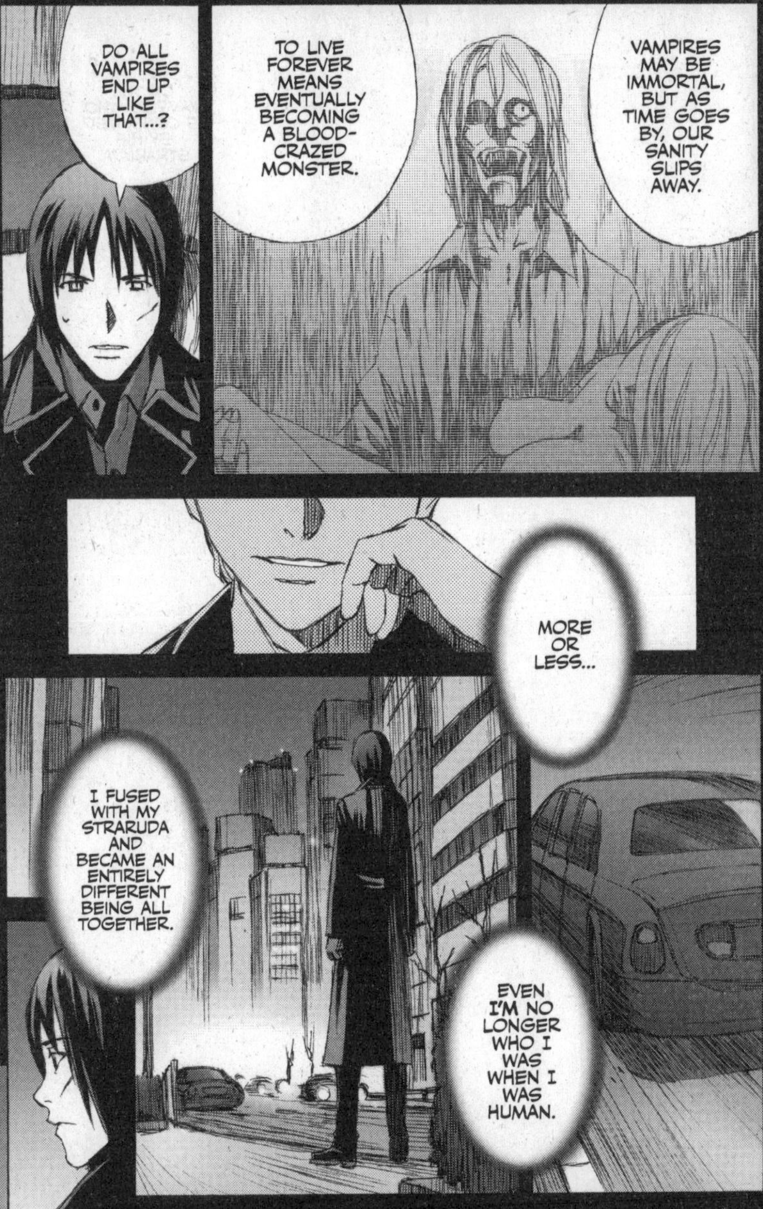
VAMPIRES MAY BE IMMORTAL, BUT AS TIME GOES BY, OUR SANITY SLIPS AWAY.
TO LIVE FOREVER MEANS EVENTUALLY BECOMING A BLOOD-CRAZED MONSTER.
DO ALL VAMPIRES END UP LIKE THAT...?
MORE OR LESS...
I FUSED WITH MY STRARUDA AND BECAME AN ENTIRELY DIFFERENT BEING ALL TOGETHER.
EVEN I'M NO LONGER WHO I WAS WHEN I WAS HUMAN.

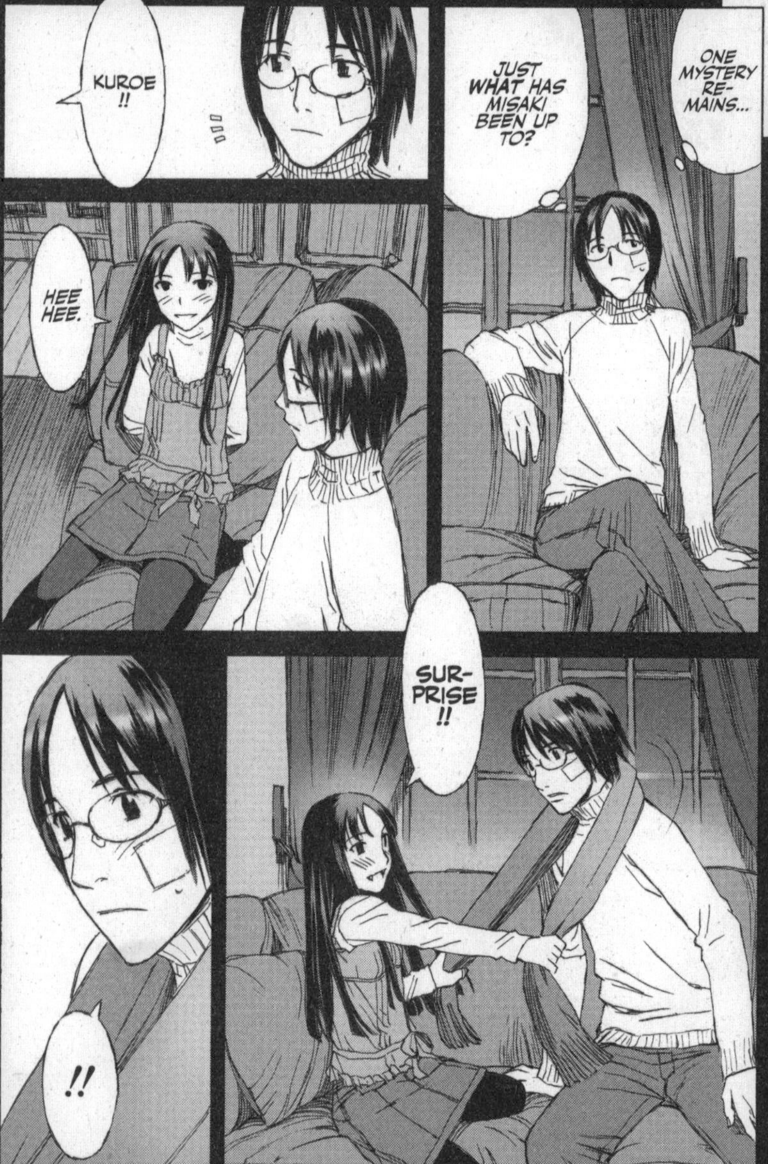

ONE MYSTERY RE-MAINS...
JUST WHAT HAS MISAKI BEEN UP TO?
KUROE !!
HEE HEE.
SUR-PRISE !!
!!

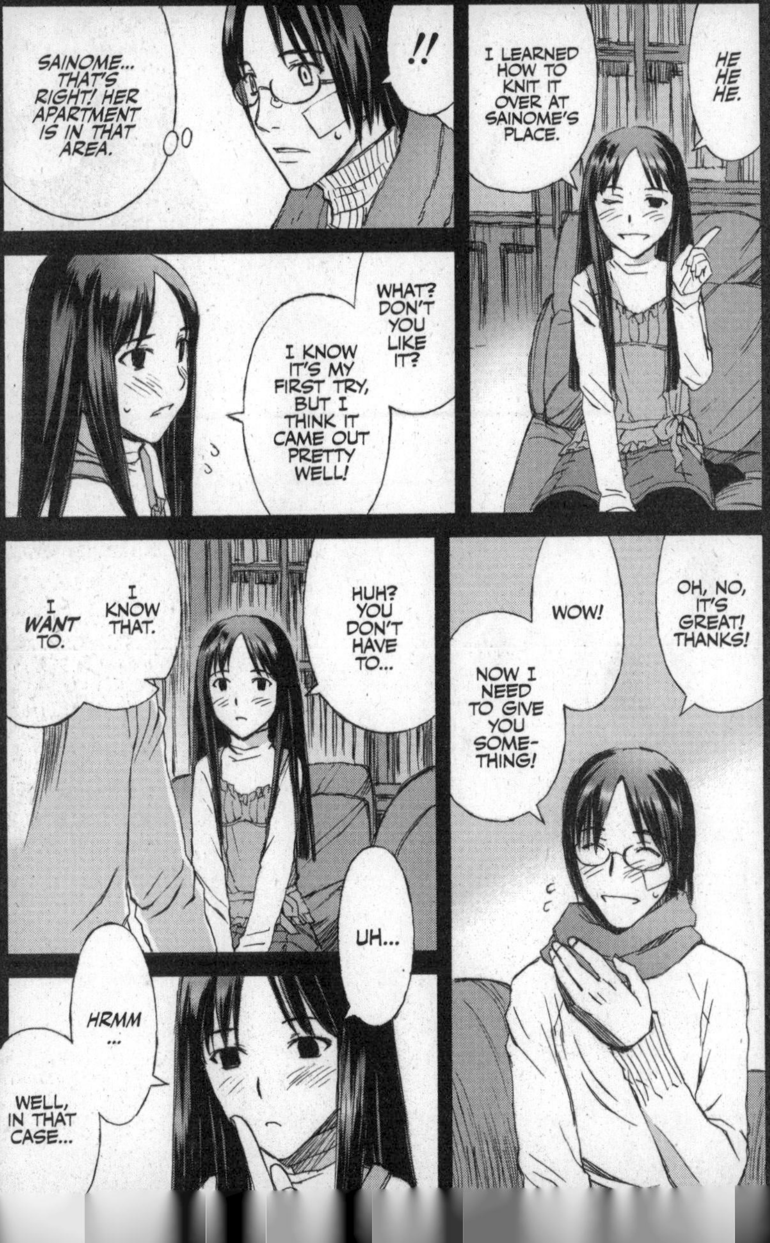
HE HE HE.
I LEARNED HOW TO KNIT IT OVER AT SAINOME'S PLACE.
!!
SAINOME... THAT'S RIGHT! HER APARTMENT IS IN THAT AREA.
WHAT? DON'T YOU LIKE IT?
I KNOW IT'S MY FIRST TRY, BUT I THINK IT CAME OUT PRETTY WELL!
OH, NO, IT'S GREAT! THANKS!
WOW!
NOW I NEED TO GIVE YOU SOME-THING!
HUH? YOU DON'T HAVE TO...
I KNOW THAT.
I *WANT* TO.
UH...
HRMM...
WELL, IN THAT CASE...

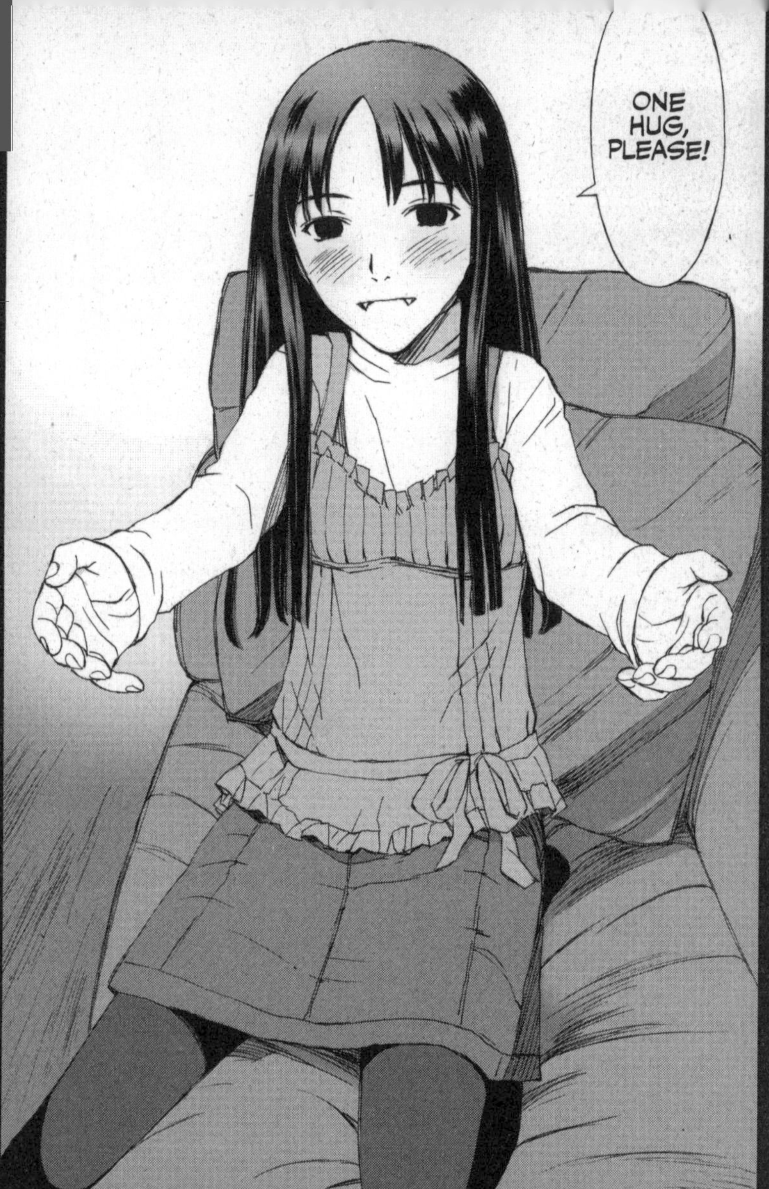
ONE HUG, PLEASE!

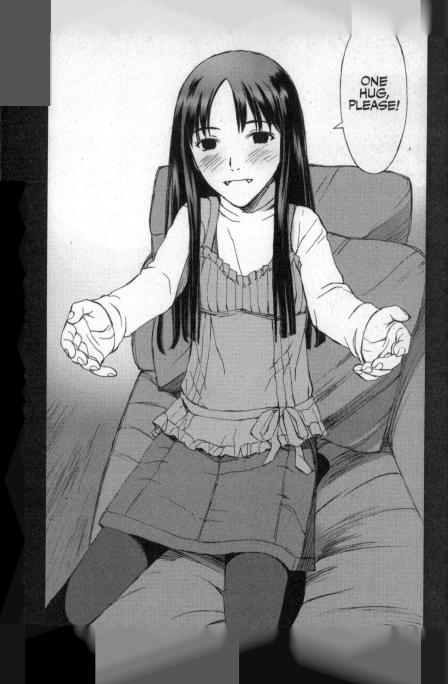

Episode 10
SWEET MUSIC
Music That Moves the Soul

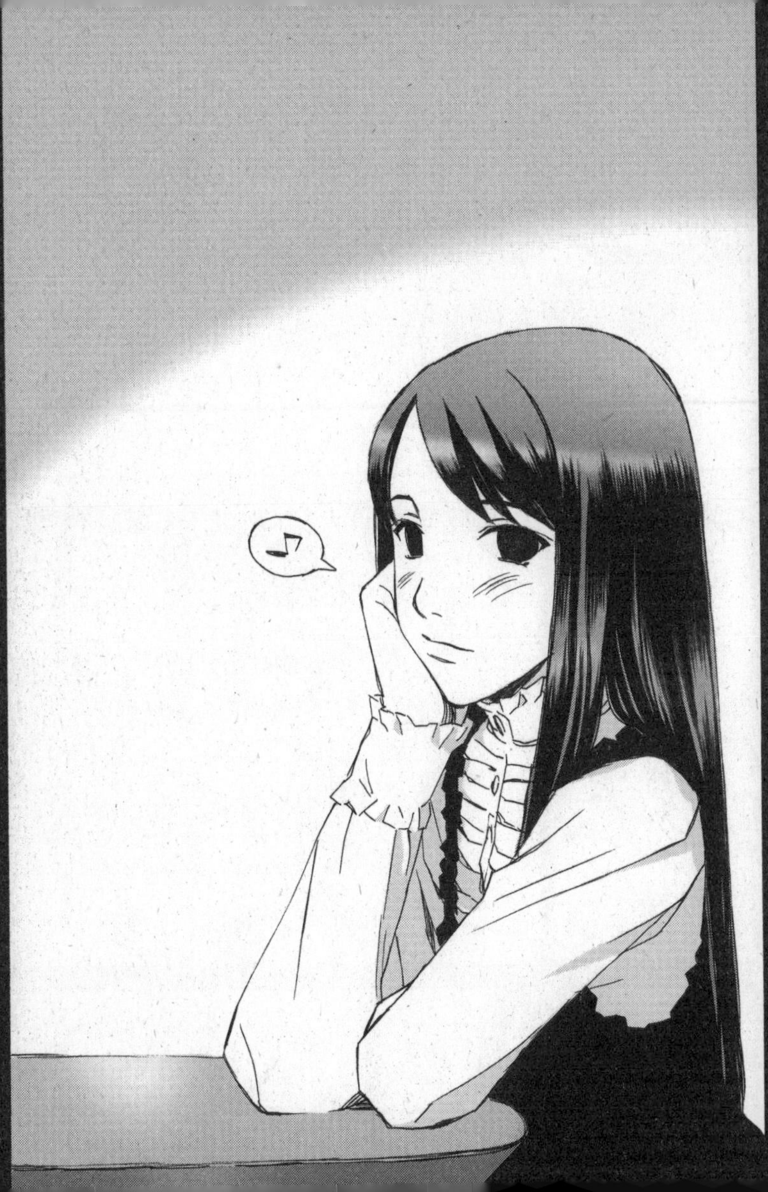

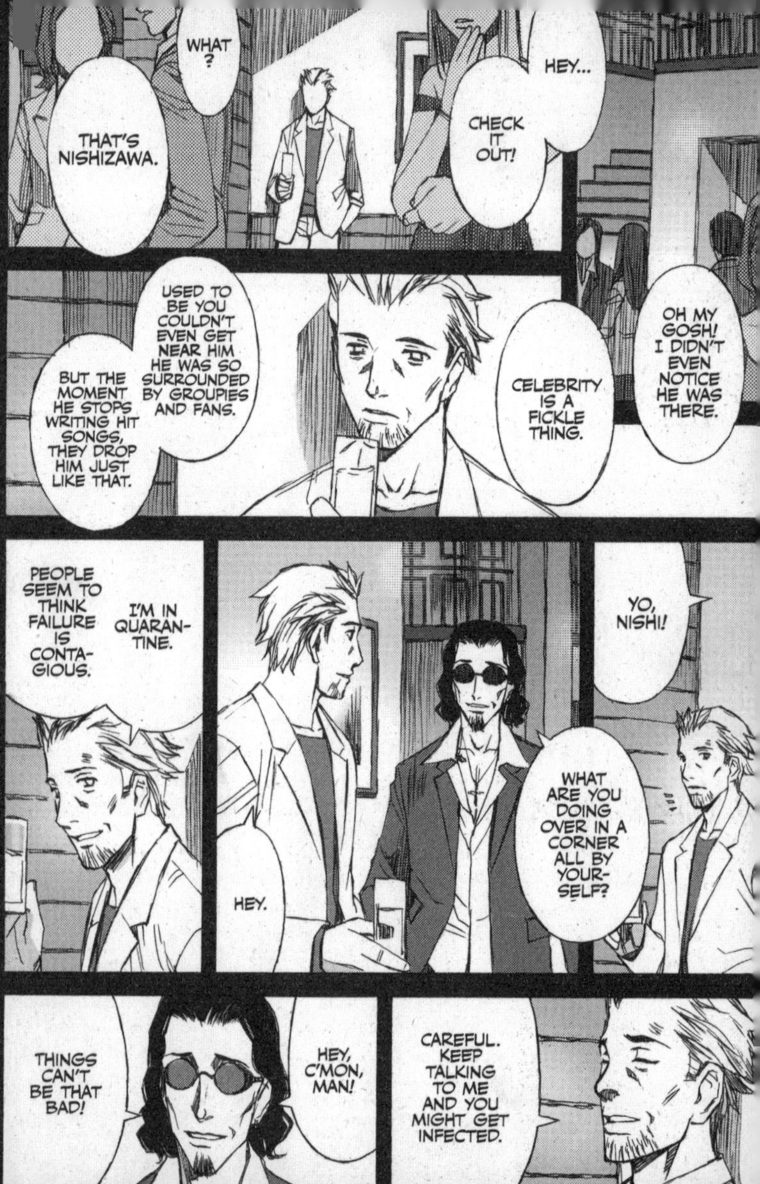
HEY...
CHECK IT OUT!
WHAT?
THAT'S NISHIZAWA.
OH MY GOSH! I DIDN'T EVEN NOTICE HE WAS THERE.
CELEBRITY IS A FICKLE THING.
USED TO BE YOU COULDN'T EVEN GET NEAR HIM HE WAS SO SURROUNDED BY GROUPIES AND FANS.
BUT THE MOMENT HE STOPS WRITING HIT SONGS, THEY DROP HIM JUST LIKE THAT.
YO, NISHI!
WHAT ARE YOU DOING OVER IN A CORNER ALL BY YOURSELF?
HEY.
I'M IN QUARANTINE.
PEOPLE SEEM TO THINK FAILURE IS CONTAGIOUS.
CAREFUL. KEEP TALKING TO ME AND YOU MIGHT GET INFECTED.
HEY, C'MON, MAN!
THINGS CAN'T BE THAT BAD!

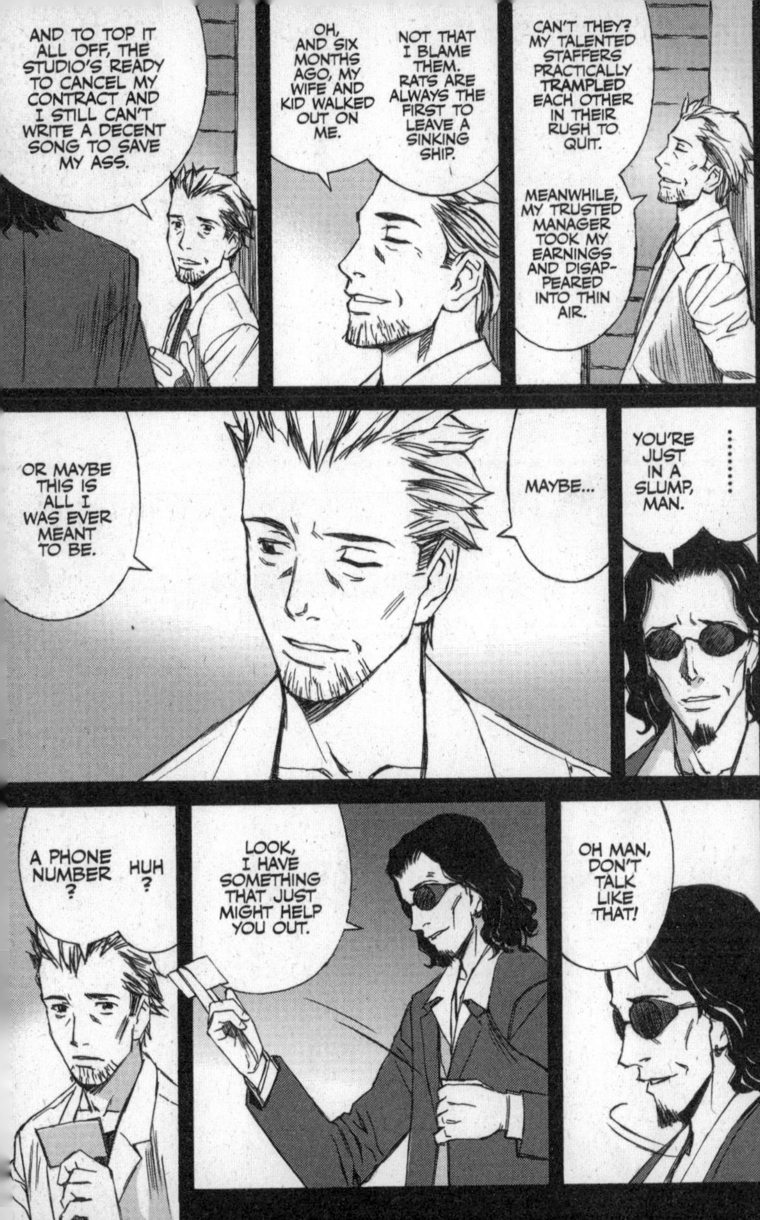

CAN'T THEY? MY TALENTED STAFFERS PRACTICALLY TRAMPLED EACH OTHER IN THEIR RUSH TO QUIT.
MEANWHILE, MY TRUSTED MANAGER TOOK MY EARNINGS AND DISAP-PEARED INTO THIN AIR.
NOT THAT I BLAME THEM. RATS ARE ALWAYS THE FIRST TO LEAVE A SINKING SHIP.
OH, AND SIX MONTHS AGO, MY WIFE AND KID WALKED OUT ON ME.
AND TO TOP IT ALL OFF, THE STUDIO'S READY TO CANCEL MY CONTRACT AND I STILL CAN'T WRITE A DECENT SONG TO SAVE MY ASS.
......
YOU'RE JUST IN A SLUMP, MAN.
MAYBE...
OR MAYBE THIS IS ALL I WAS EVER MEANT TO BE.
OH MAN, DON'T TALK LIKE THAT!
LOOK, I HAVE SOMETHING THAT JUST MIGHT HELP YOU OUT.
HUH?
A PHONE NUMBER?

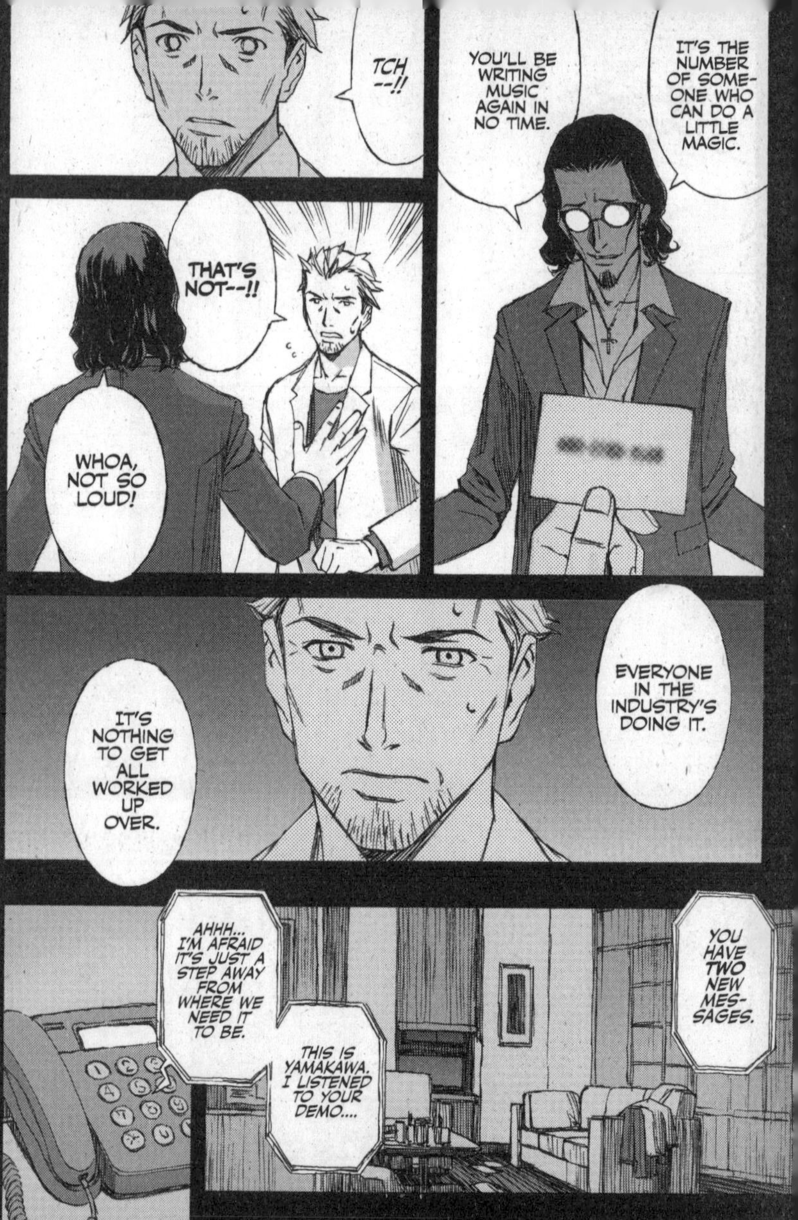
IT'S THE NUMBER OF SOMEONE WHO CAN DO A LITTLE MAGIC.
YOU'LL BE WRITING MUSIC AGAIN IN NO TIME.
TCH--!!
THAT'S NOT--!!
WHOA, NOT SO LOUD!
EVERYONE IN THE INDUSTRY'S DOING IT.
IT'S NOTHING TO GET ALL WORKED UP OVER.
YOU HAVE TWO NEW MESSAGES.
THIS IS YAMAKAWA. I LISTENED TO YOUR DEMO....
AHHH... I'M AFRAID IT'S JUST A STEP AWAY FROM WHERE WE NEED IT TO BE.

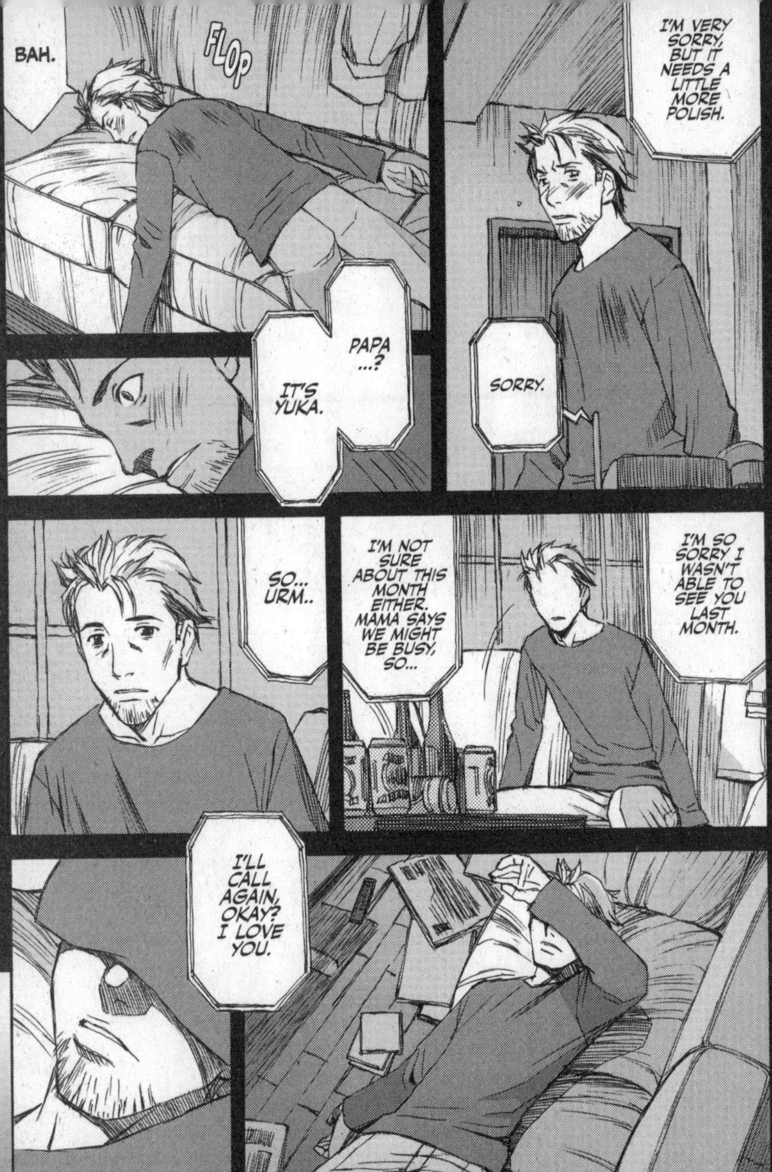
I'M VERY SORRY, BUT IT NEEDS A LITTLE MORE POLISH.
SORRY.
BAH.
FLOP
PAPA ...?
IT'S YUKA.
I'M SO SORRY I WASN'T ABLE TO SEE YOU LAST MONTH.
I'M NOT SURE ABOUT THIS MONTH EITHER. MAMA SAYS WE MIGHT BE BUSY, SO...
SO... URM..
I'LL CALL AGAIN, OKAY? I LOVE YOU.

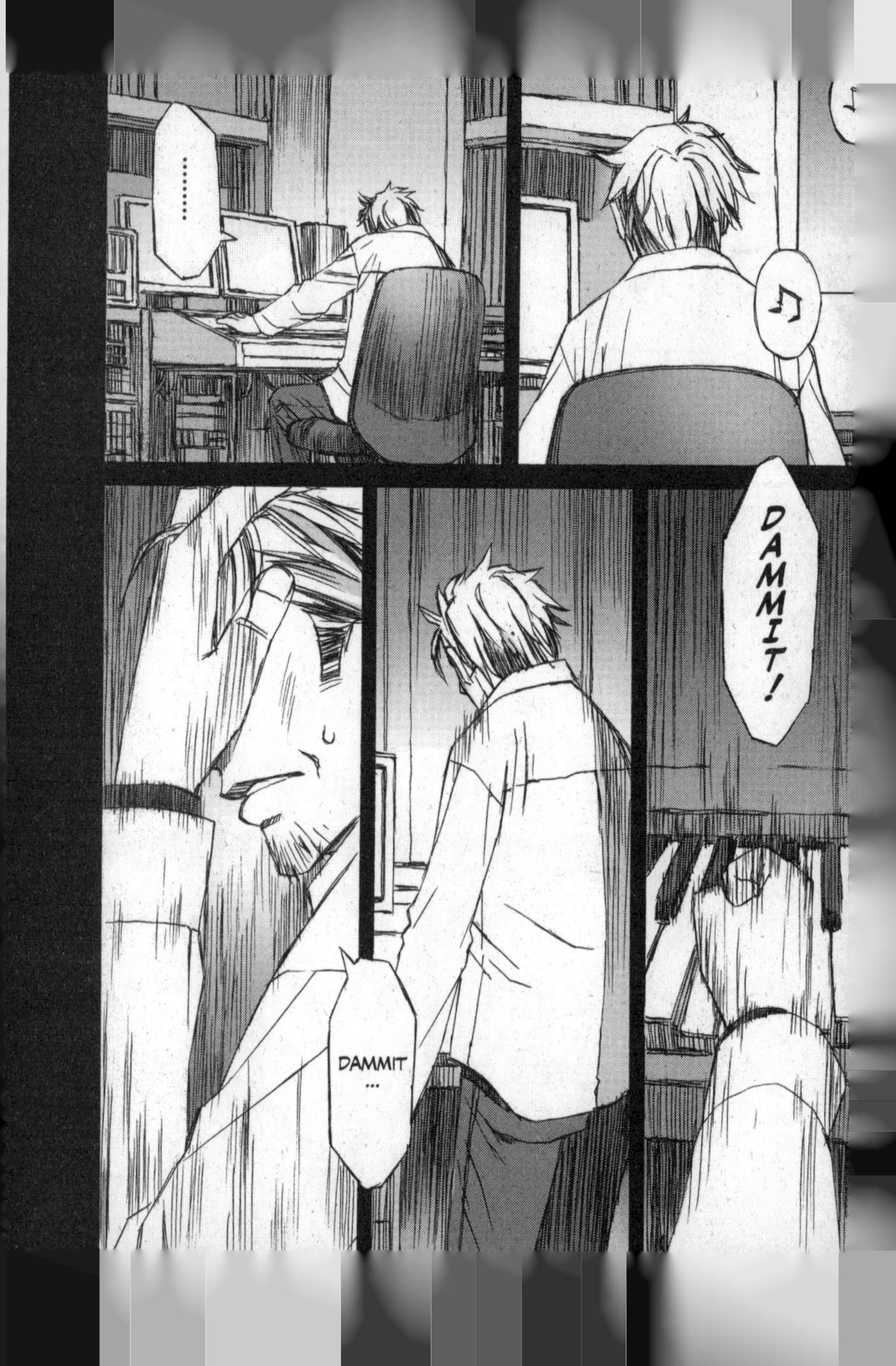

♫
....
DAMMIT!
DAMMIT ...

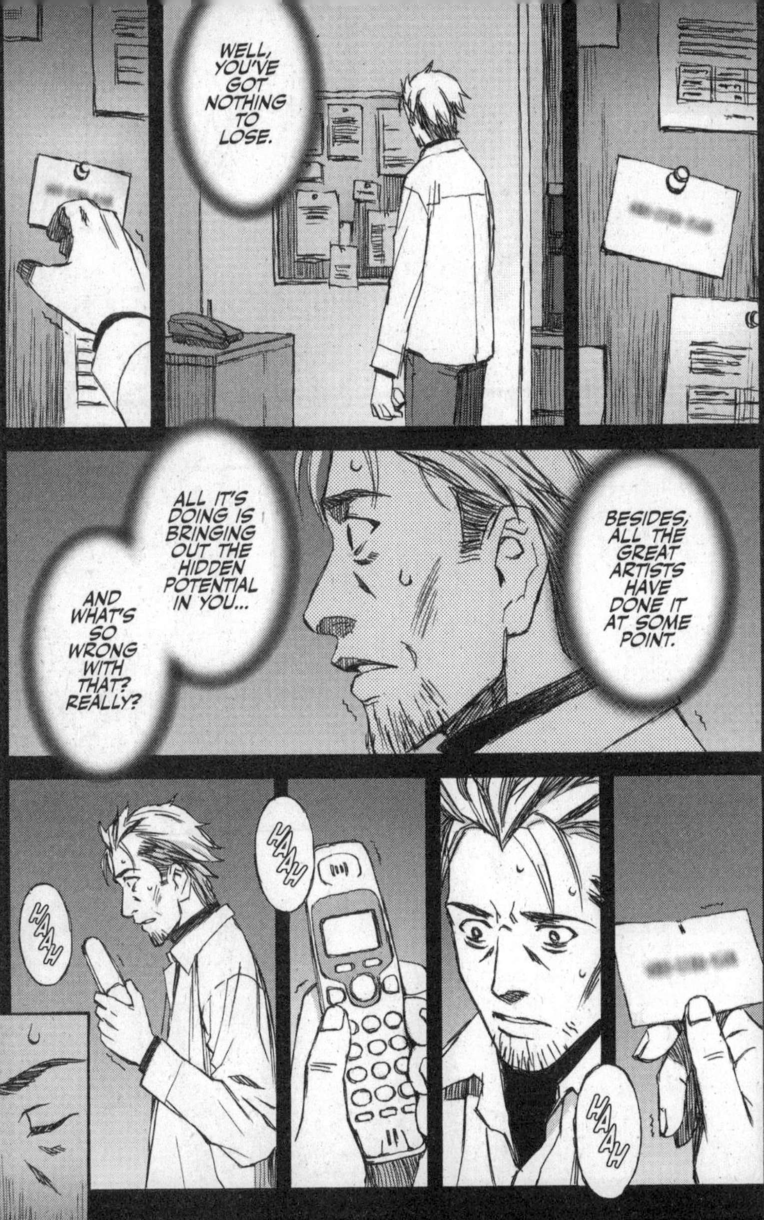
WELL, YOU'VE GOT NOTHING TO LOSE.
BESIDES, ALL THE GREAT ARTISTS HAVE DONE IT AT SOME POINT.
ALL IT'S DOING IS BRINGING OUT THE HIDDEN POTENTIAL IN YOU...
AND WHAT'S SO WRONG WITH THAT? REALLY?
HAAH
HAAH
HAAH

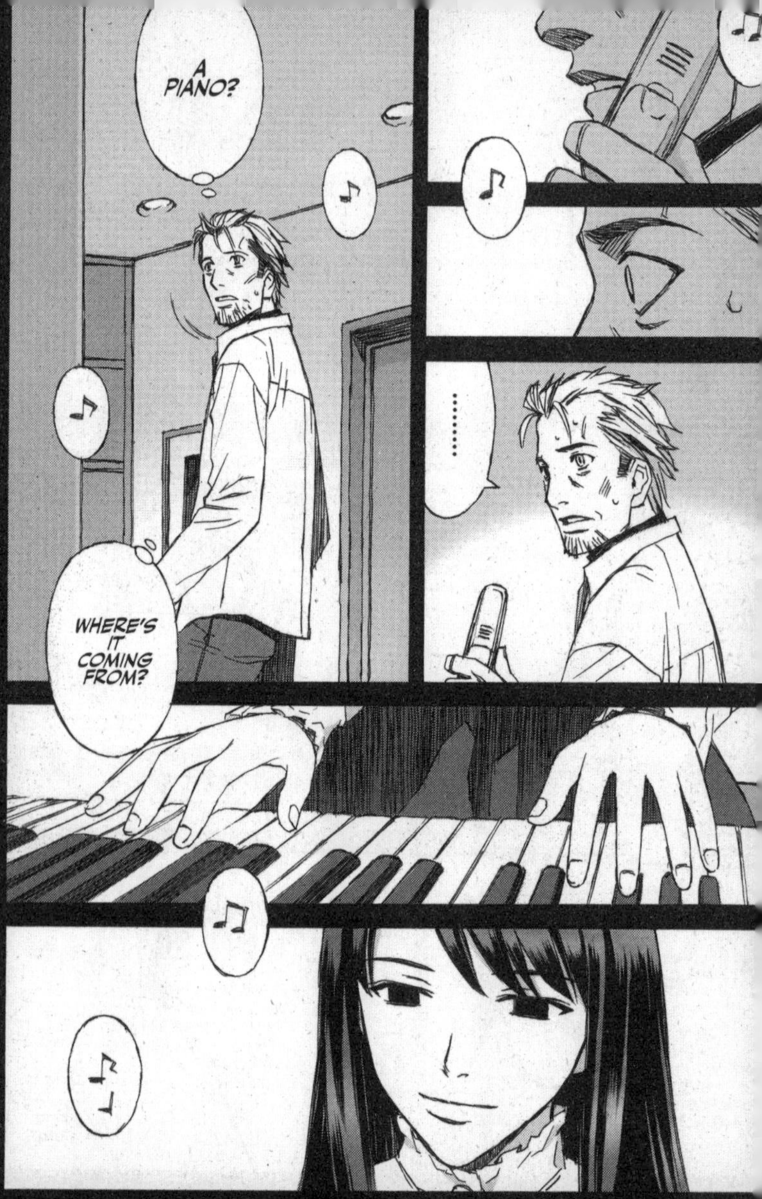

....
A PIANO?
WHERE'S IT COMING FROM?

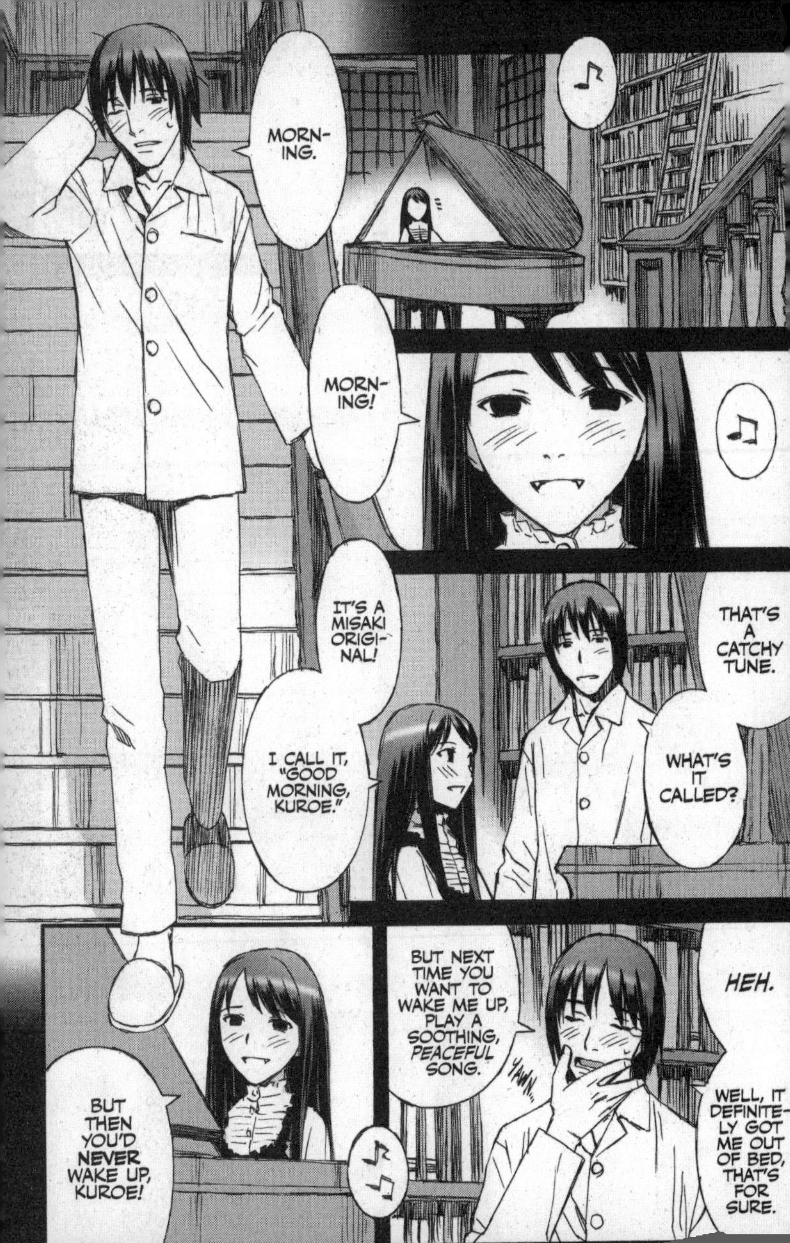
♪
MORNING.
MORNING!
♪
THAT'S A CATCHY TUNE.
WHAT'S IT CALLED?
IT'S A MISAKI ORIGINAL!
I CALL IT, "GOOD MORNING, KUROE."
HEH.
WELL, IT DEFINITELY GOT ME OUT OF BED, THAT'S FOR SURE.
YAWN
BUT NEXT TIME YOU WANT TO WAKE ME UP, PLAY A SOOTHING, *PEACEFUL* SONG.
♪ ♪
BUT THEN YOU'D **NEVER** WAKE UP, KUROE!

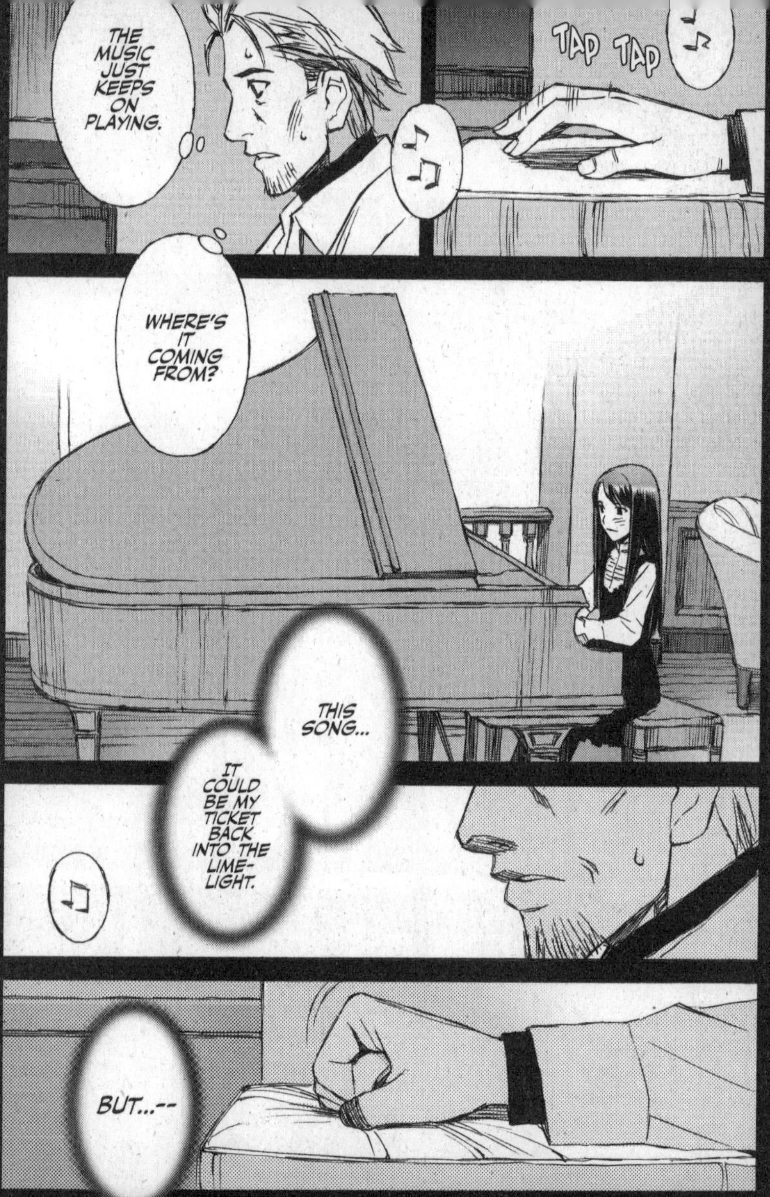
TAP TAP
THE MUSIC JUST KEEPS ON PLAYING.
WHERE'S IT COMING FROM?
THIS SONG...
IT COULD BE MY TICKET BACK INTO THE LIME-LIGHT.
BUT...--

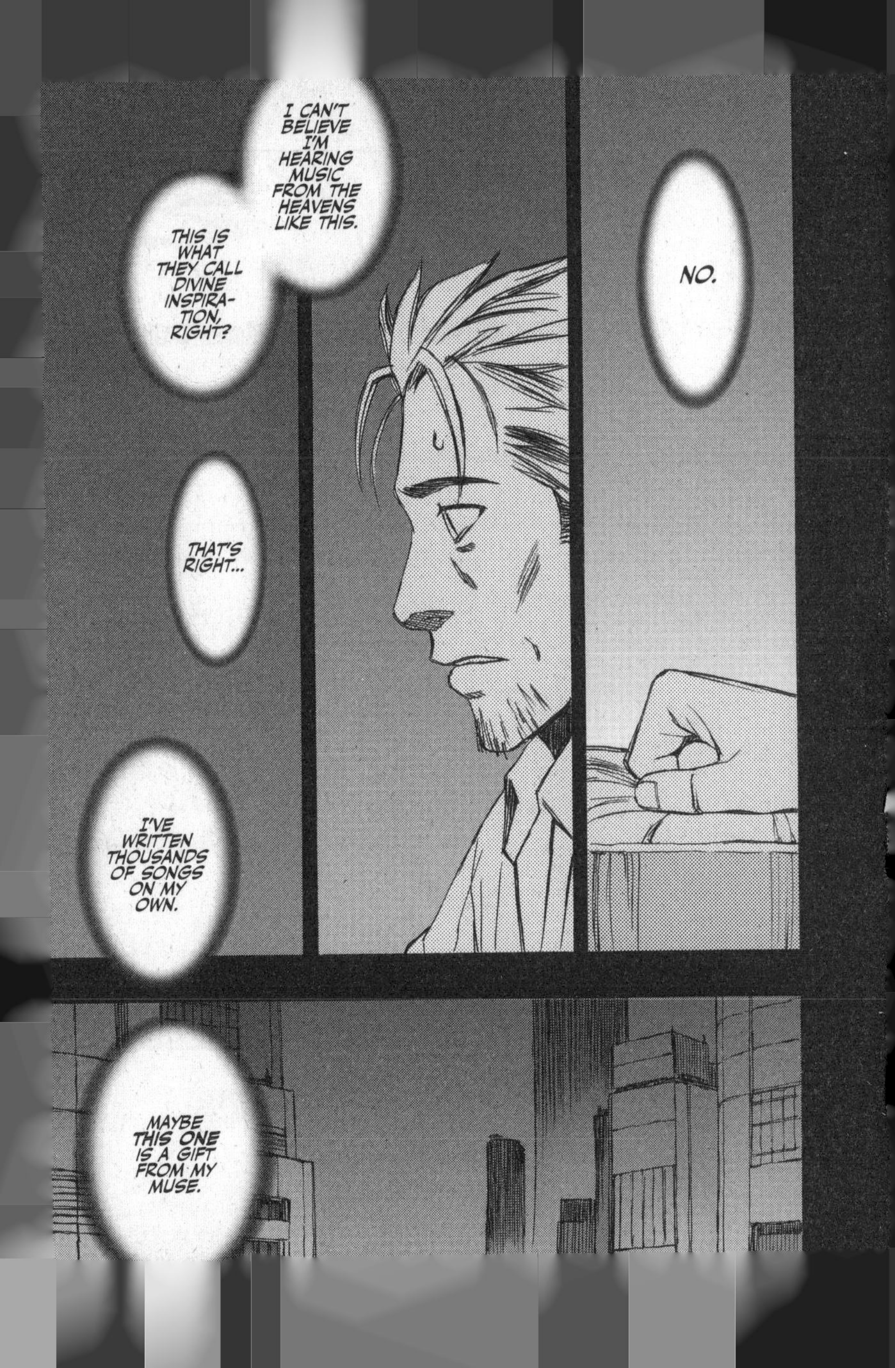
NO.
I CAN'T BELIEVE I'M HEARING MUSIC FROM THE HEAVENS LIKE THIS.
THIS IS WHAT THEY CALL DIVINE INSPIRA-TION, RIGHT?
THAT'S RIGHT...
I'VE WRITTEN THOUSANDS OF SONGS ON MY OWN.
MAYBE THIS ONE IS A GIFT FROM MY MUSE.

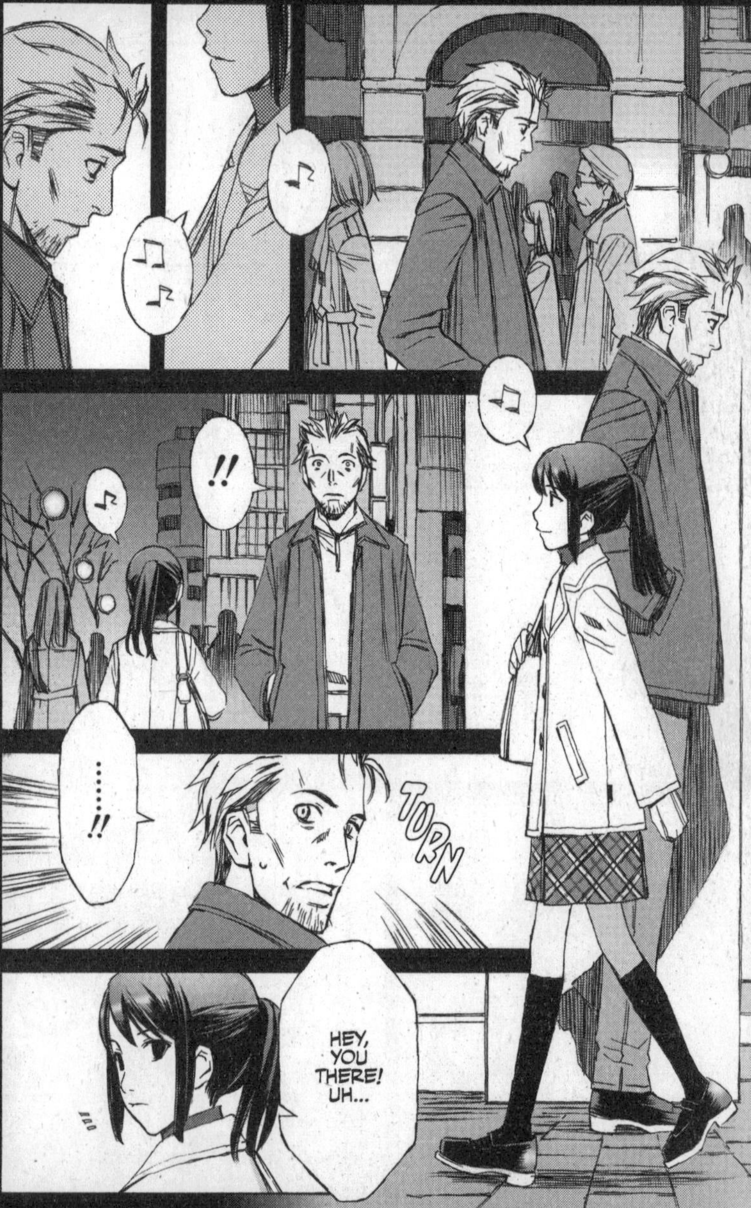
♪
♪ ♪
♪
♪
!!
......!!
TURN
HEY, YOU THERE! UH...

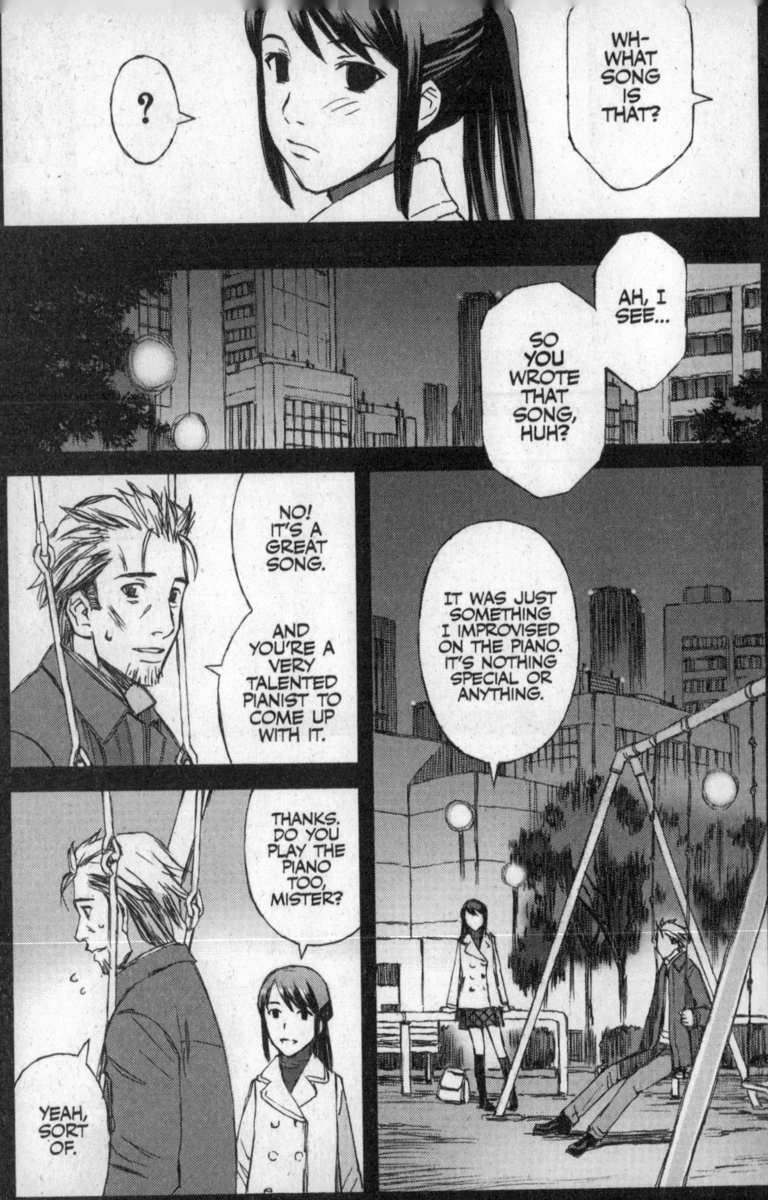
WH-WHAT SONG IS THAT?
?
AH, I SEE...
SO YOU WROTE THAT SONG, HUH?
IT WAS JUST SOMETHING I IMPROVISED ON THE PIANO. IT'S NOTHING SPECIAL OR ANYTHING.
NO! IT'S A GREAT SONG.
AND YOU'RE A VERY TALENTED PIANIST TO COME UP WITH IT.
THANKS. DO YOU PLAY THE PIANO TOO, MISTER?
YEAH, SORT OF.

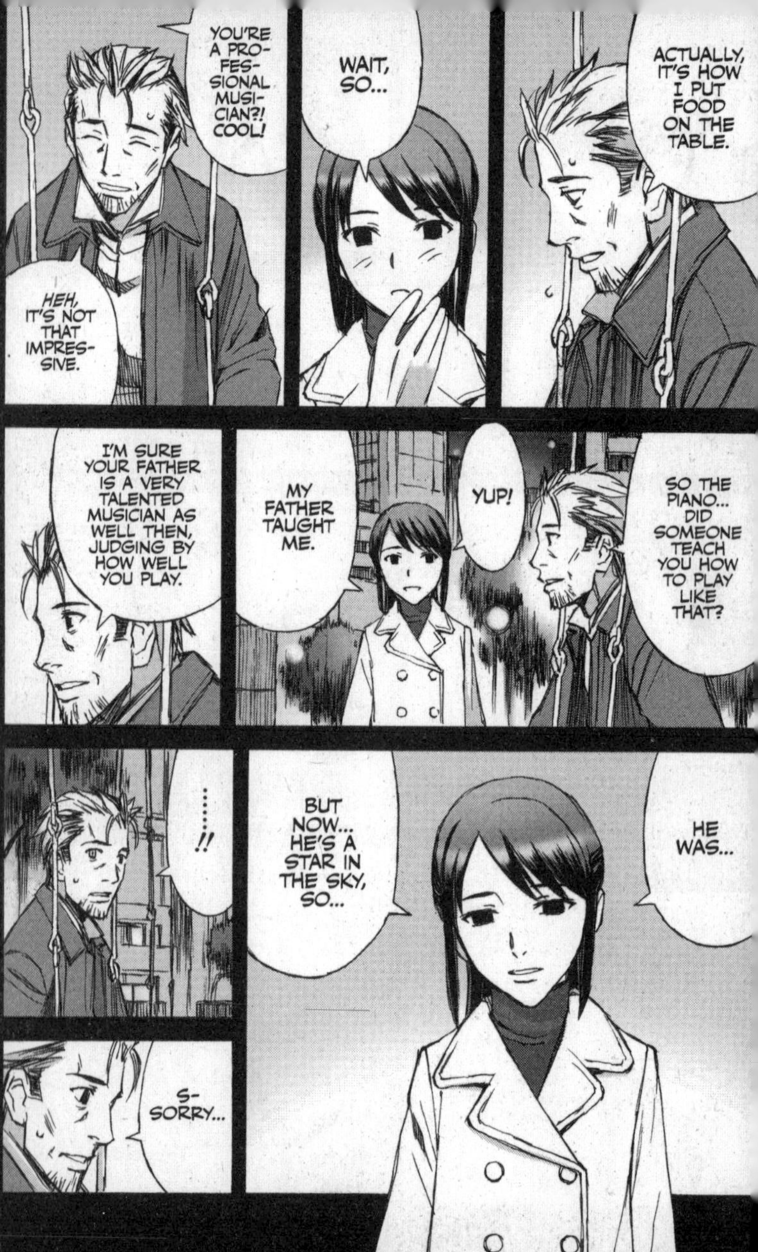
ACTUALLY, IT'S HOW I PUT FOOD ON THE TABLE.
WAIT, SO...
YOU'RE A PRO-FES-SIONAL MUSI-CIAN?! COOL!
HEH, IT'S NOT THAT IMPRES-SIVE.
SO THE PIANO... DID SOMEONE TEACH YOU HOW TO PLAY LIKE THAT?
YUP!
MY FATHER TAUGHT ME.
I'M SURE YOUR FATHER IS A VERY TALENTED MUSICIAN AS WELL THEN, JUDGING BY HOW WELL YOU PLAY.
HE WAS...
BUT NOW... HE'S A STAR IN THE SKY, SO...
......!!
S-SORRY...

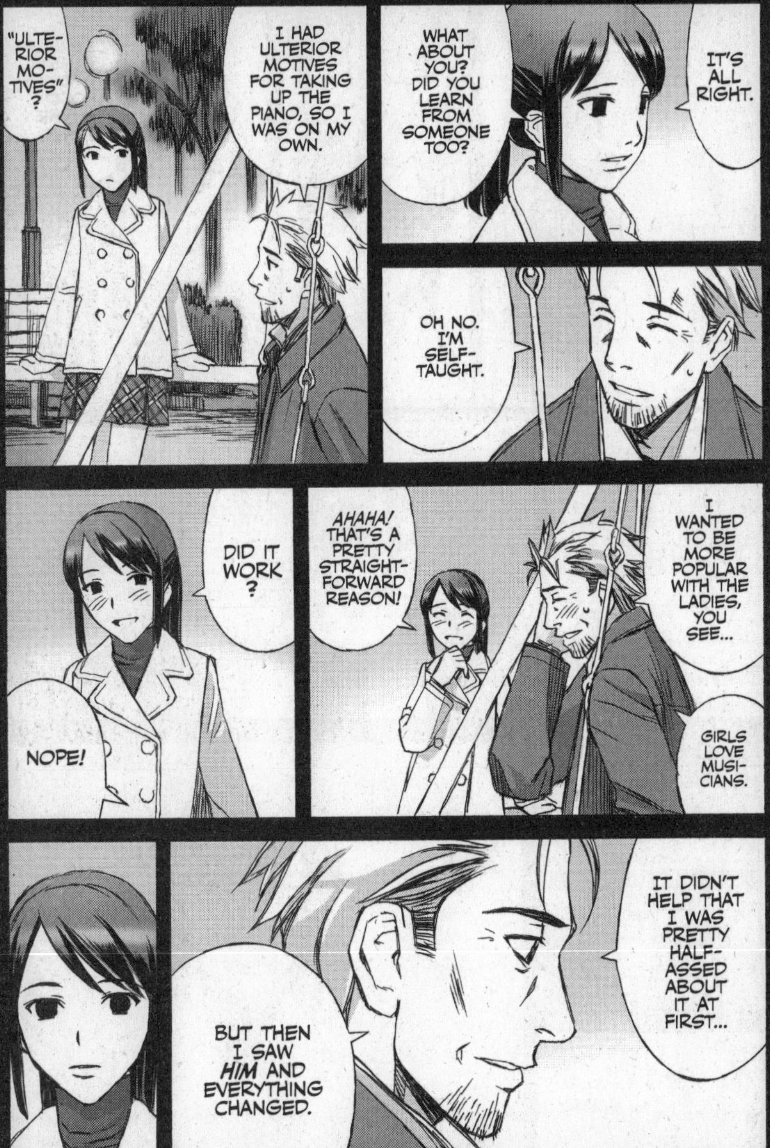
IT'S ALL RIGHT.
WHAT ABOUT YOU? DID YOU LEARN FROM SOMEONE TOO?
OH NO. I'M SELF-TAUGHT.
I HAD ULTERIOR MOTIVES FOR TAKING UP THE PIANO, SO I WAS ON MY OWN.
"ULTERIOR MOTIVES"?
I WANTED TO BE MORE POPULAR WITH THE LADIES, YOU SEE...
AHAHA! THAT'S A PRETTY STRAIGHTFORWARD REASON!
GIRLS LOVE MUSICIANS.
DID IT WORK?
NOPE!
IT DIDN'T HELP THAT I WAS PRETTY HALF-ASSED ABOUT IT AT FIRST...
BUT THEN I SAW *HIM* AND EVERYTHING CHANGED.

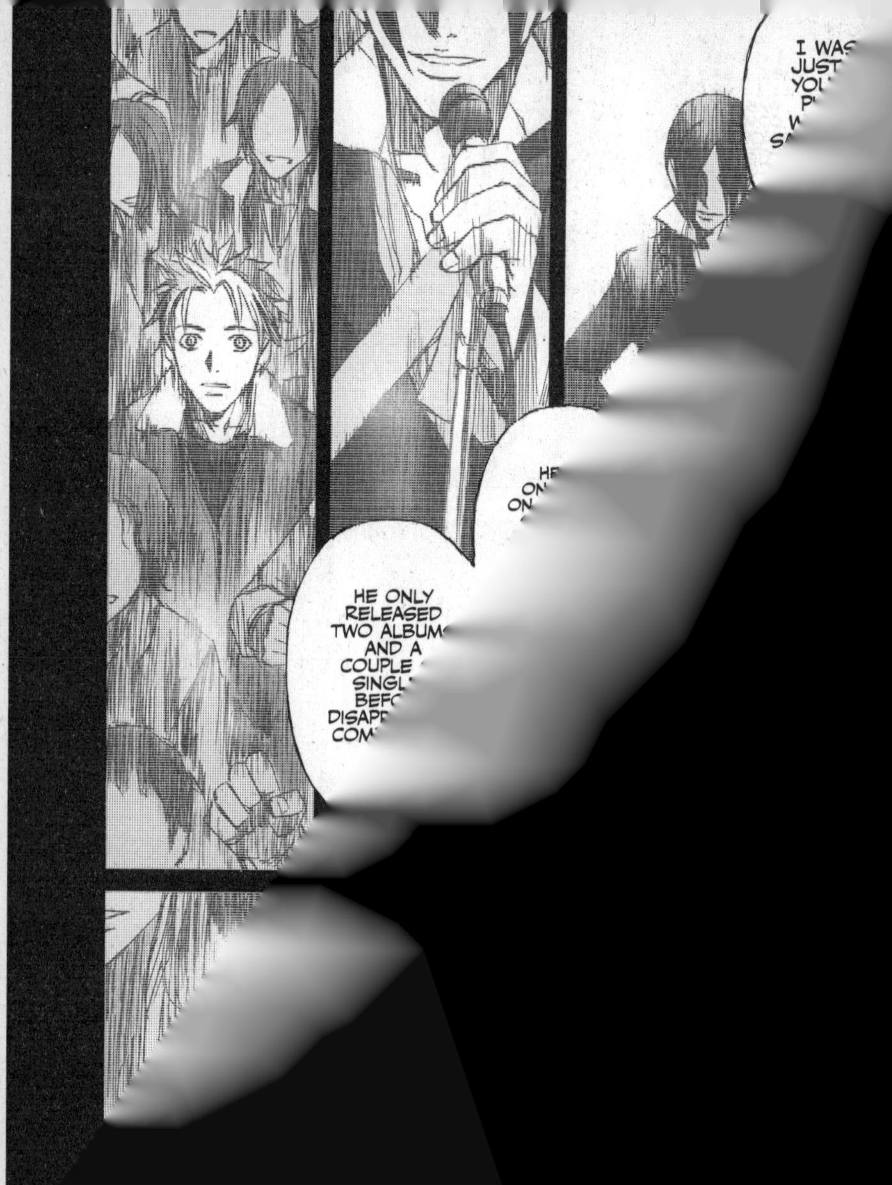
I WAS JUST
HE ONLY RELEASED TWO ALBUM AND A COUPLE

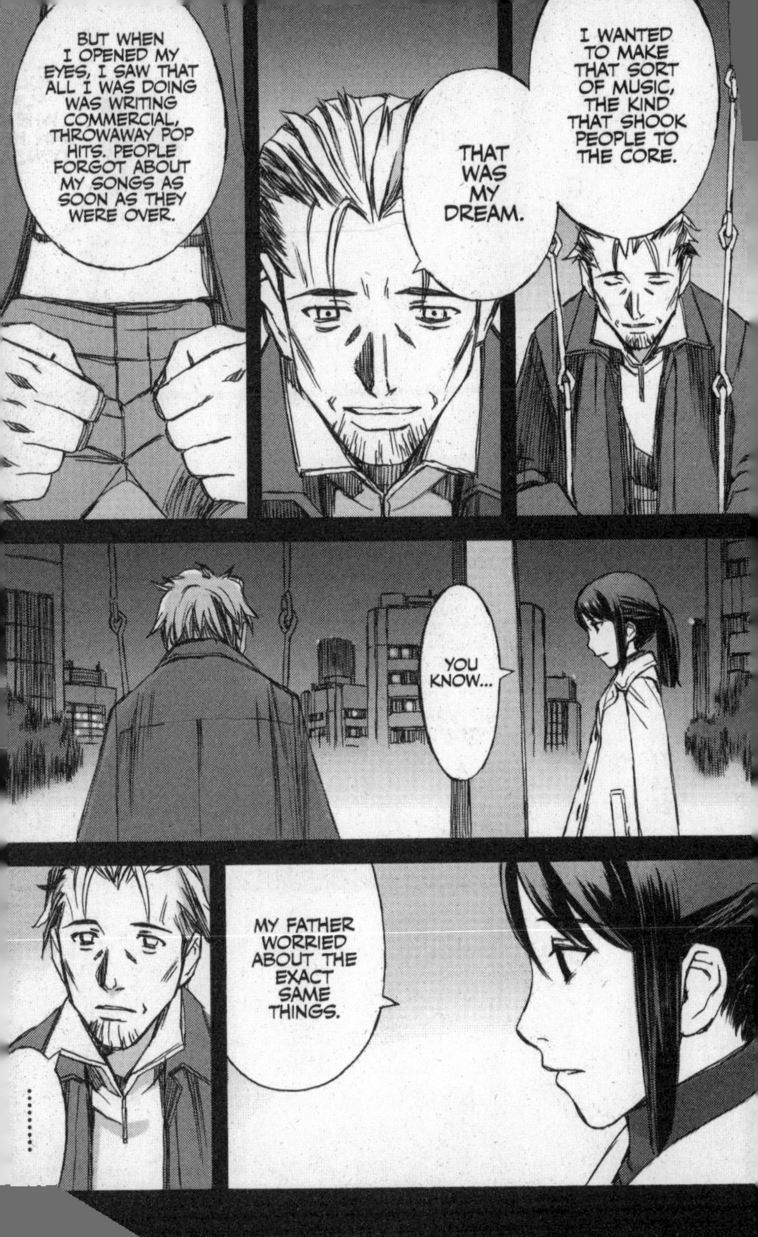
I WANTED TO MAKE THAT SORT OF MUSIC, THE KIND THAT SHOOK PEOPLE TO THE CORE.
THAT WAS MY DREAM.
BUT WHEN I OPENED MY EYES, I SAW THAT ALL I WAS DOING WAS WRITING COMMERCIAL, THROWAWAY POP HITS. PEOPLE FORGOT ABOUT MY SONGS AS SOON AS THEY WERE OVER.
YOU KNOW...
MY FATHER WORRIED ABOUT THE EXACT SAME THINGS.

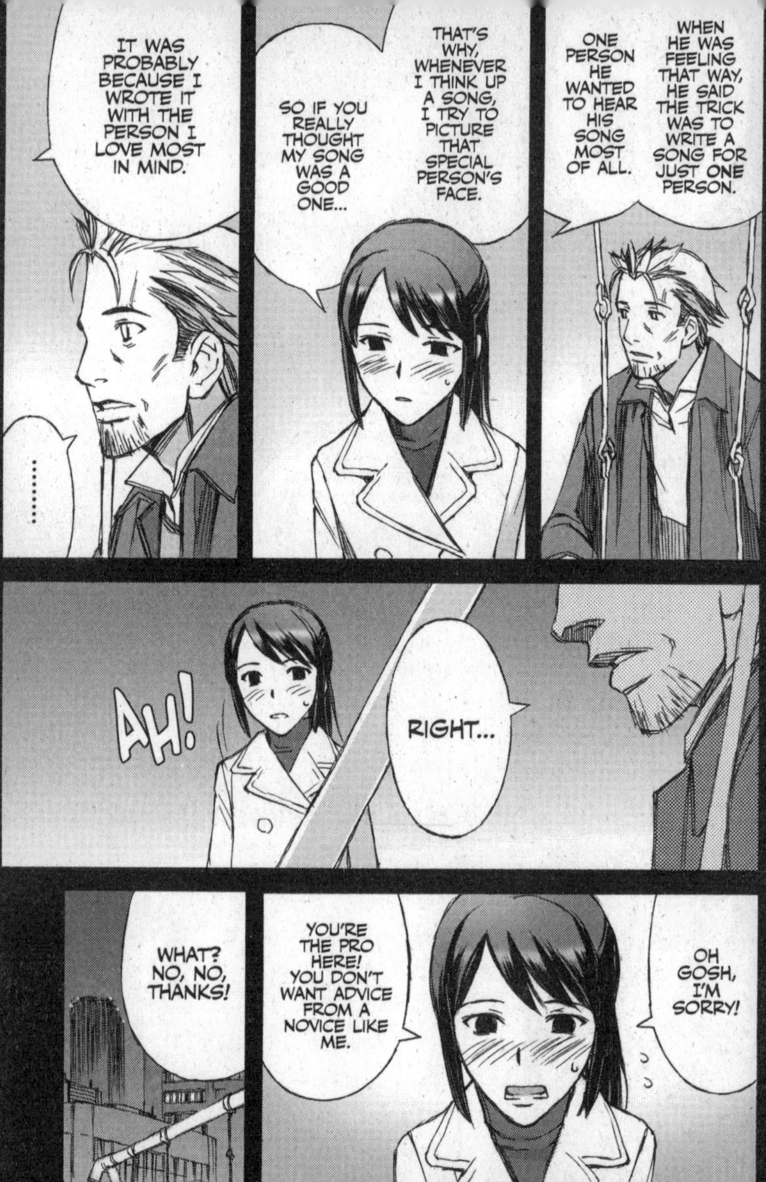
WHEN HE WAS FEELING THAT WAY, HE SAID THE TRICK WAS TO WRITE A SONG FOR JUST ONE PERSON.
ONE PERSON HE WANTED TO HEAR HIS SONG MOST OF ALL.
THAT'S WHY, WHENEVER I THINK UP A SONG, I TRY TO PICTURE THAT SPECIAL PERSON'S FACE.
SO IF YOU REALLY THOUGHT MY SONG WAS A GOOD ONE...
IT WAS PROBABLY BECAUSE I WROTE IT WITH THE PERSON I LOVE MOST IN MIND.
....
RIGHT...
AH!
OH GOSH, I'M SORRY!
YOU'RE THE PRO HERE! YOU DON'T WANT ADVICE FROM A NOVICE LIKE ME.
WHAT? NO, NO, THANKS!

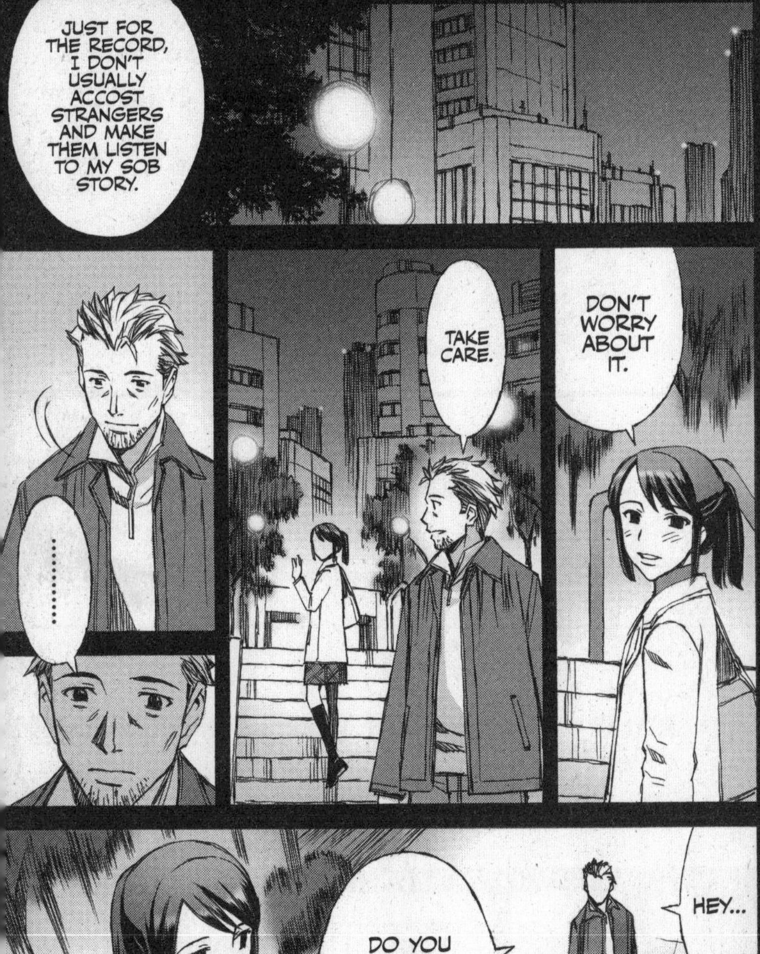
JUST FOR THE RECORD, I DON'T USUALLY ACCOST STRANGERS AND MAKE THEM LISTEN TO MY SOB STORY.
DON'T WORRY ABOUT IT.
TAKE CARE.
......
HEY...
DO YOU MIND TELLING ME YOUR FATHER'S NAME?

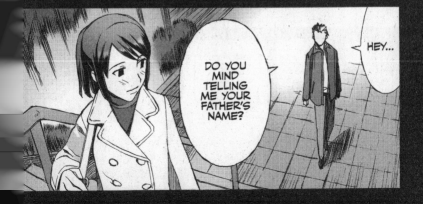

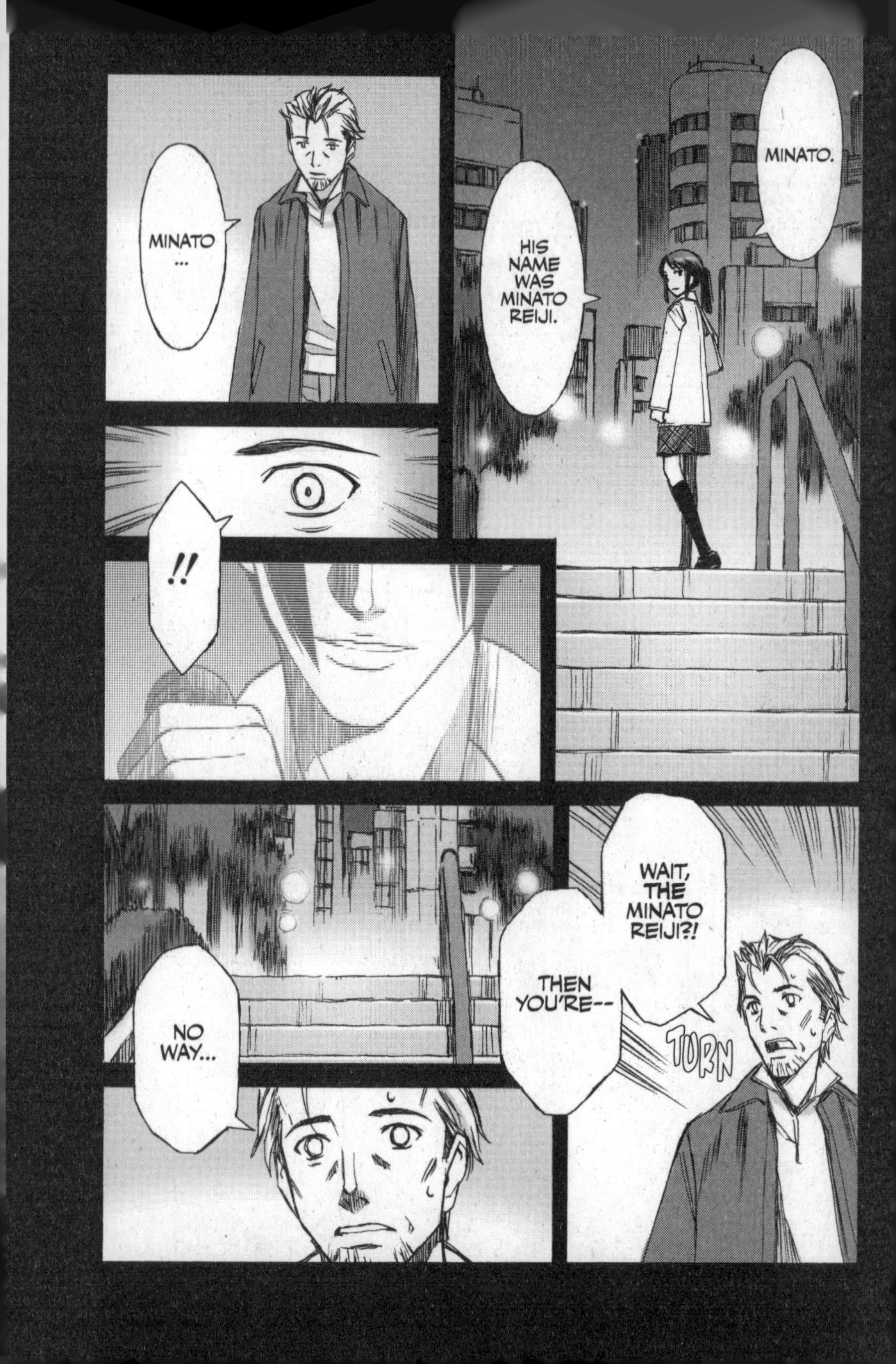
MINATO.
HIS NAME WAS MINATO REIJI.
MINATO ...
!!
WAIT, THE MINATO REIJI?!
THEN YOU'RE--
TURN
NO WAY...

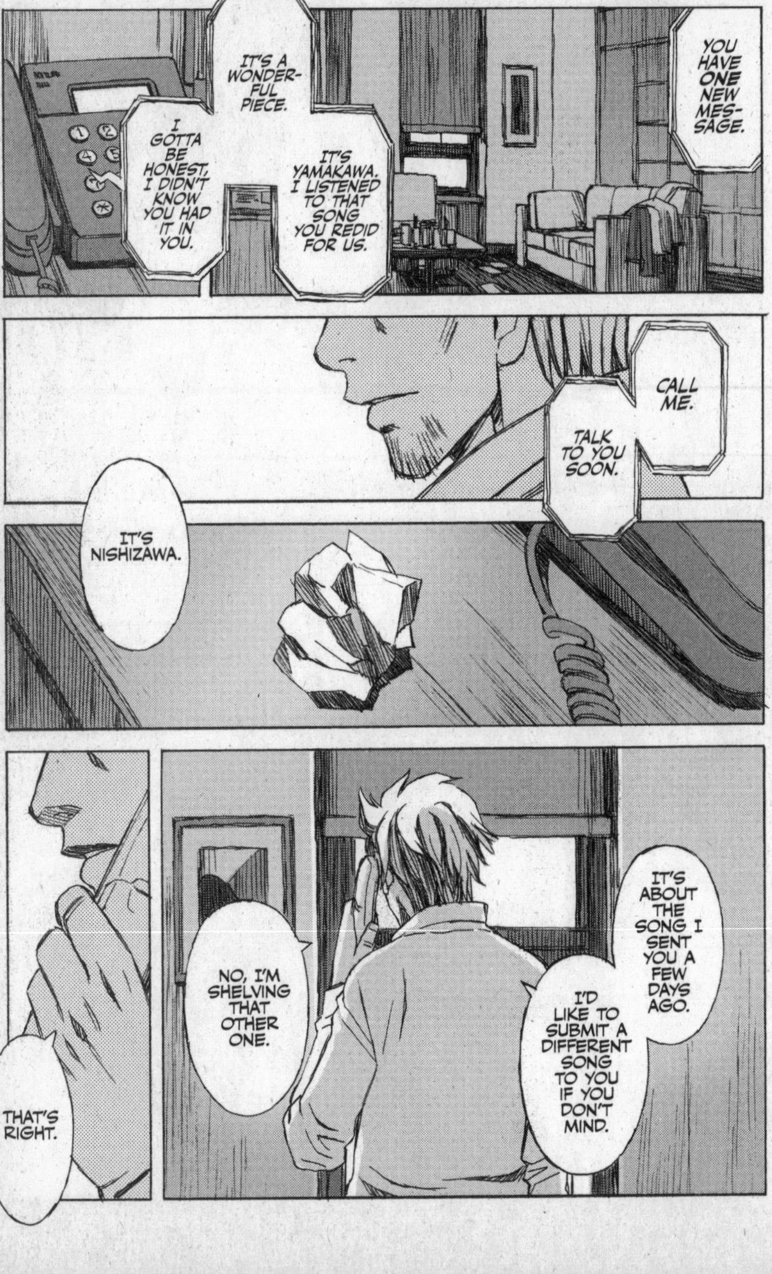
YOU HAVE ONE NEW MESSAGE.
IT'S YAMAKAWA. I LISTENED TO THAT SONG YOU REDID FOR US.
IT'S A WONDERFUL PIECE.
I GOTTA BE HONEST, I DIDN'T KNOW YOU HAD IT IN YOU.
CALL ME.
TALK TO YOU SOON.
IT'S NISHIZAWA.
IT'S ABOUT THE SONG I SENT YOU A FEW DAYS AGO.
I'D LIKE TO SUBMIT A DIFFERENT SONG TO YOU IF YOU DON'T MIND.
NO, I'M SHELVING THAT OTHER ONE.
THAT'S RIGHT.

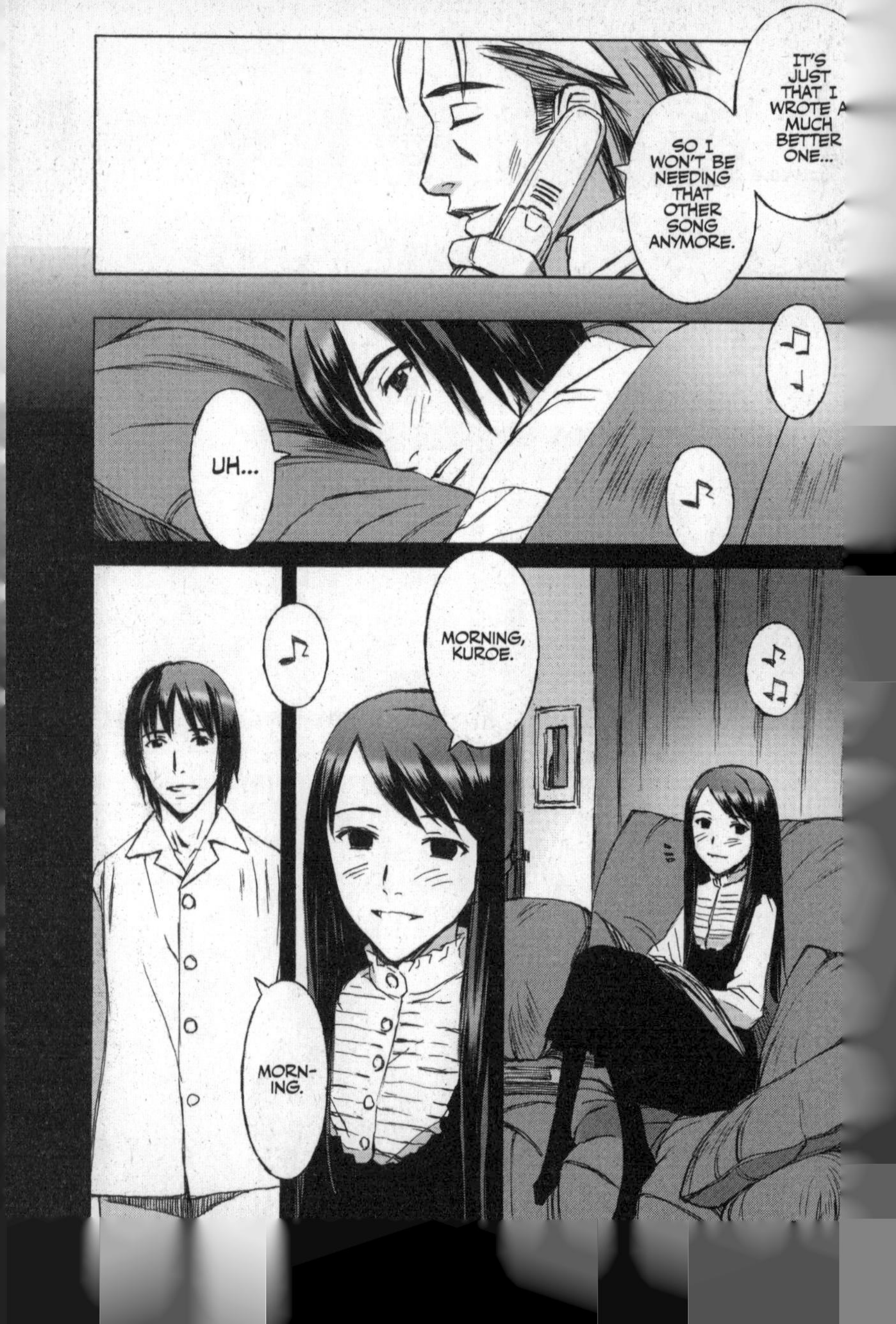
IT'S JUST THAT I WROTE A MUCH BETTER ONE...
SO I WON'T BE NEEDING THAT OTHER SONG ANYMORE.
UH...
MORNING, KUROE.
MORN-ING.

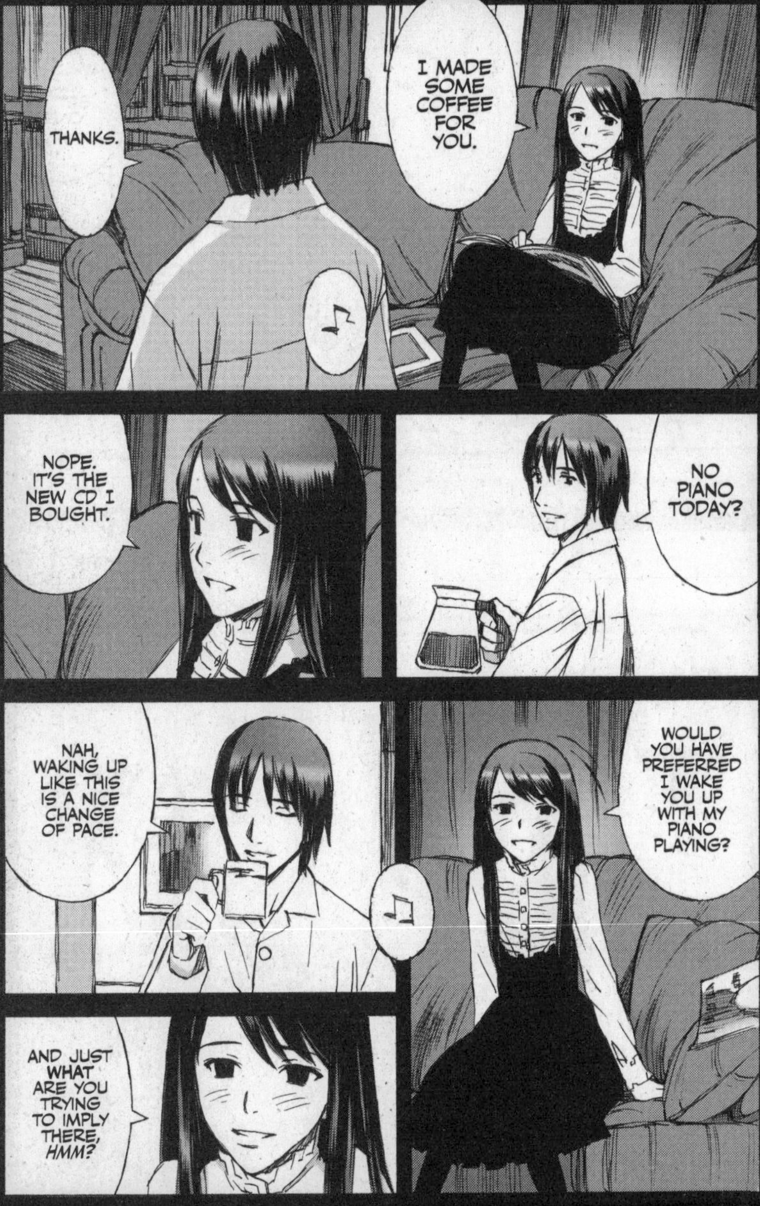
I MADE SOME COFFEE FOR YOU.
THANKS.
NO PIANO TODAY?
NOPE. IT'S THE NEW CD I BOUGHT.
WOULD YOU HAVE PREFERRED I WAKE YOU UP WITH MY PIANO PLAYING?
NAH, WAKING UP LIKE THIS IS A NICE CHANGE OF PACE.
AND JUST WHAT ARE YOU TRYING TO IMPLY THERE, *HMM?*

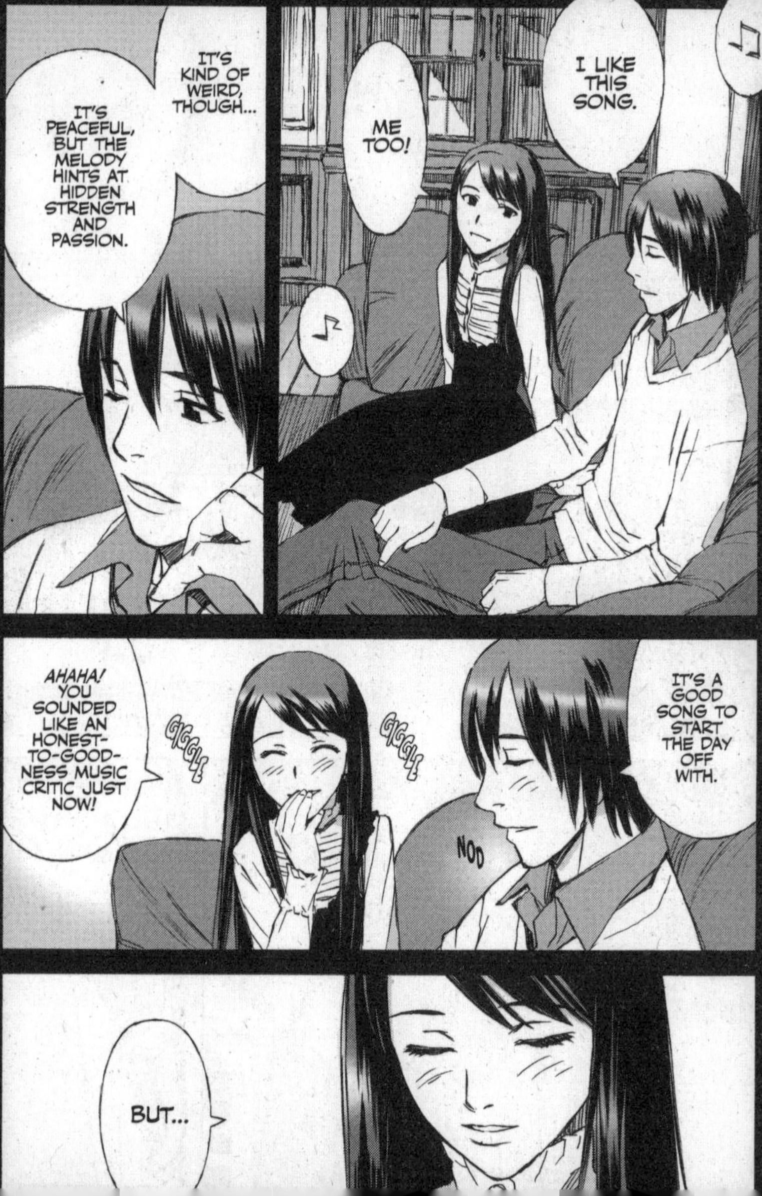
I LIKE THIS SONG.
ME TOO!
IT'S KIND OF WEIRD, THOUGH...
IT'S PEACEFUL, BUT THE MELODY HINTS AT HIDDEN STRENGTH AND PASSION.
IT'S A GOOD SONG TO START THE DAY OFF WITH.
NOD
GIGGLE
GIGGLE
AHAHA! YOU SOUNDED LIKE AN HONEST-TO-GOODNESS MUSIC CRITIC JUST NOW!
BUT...

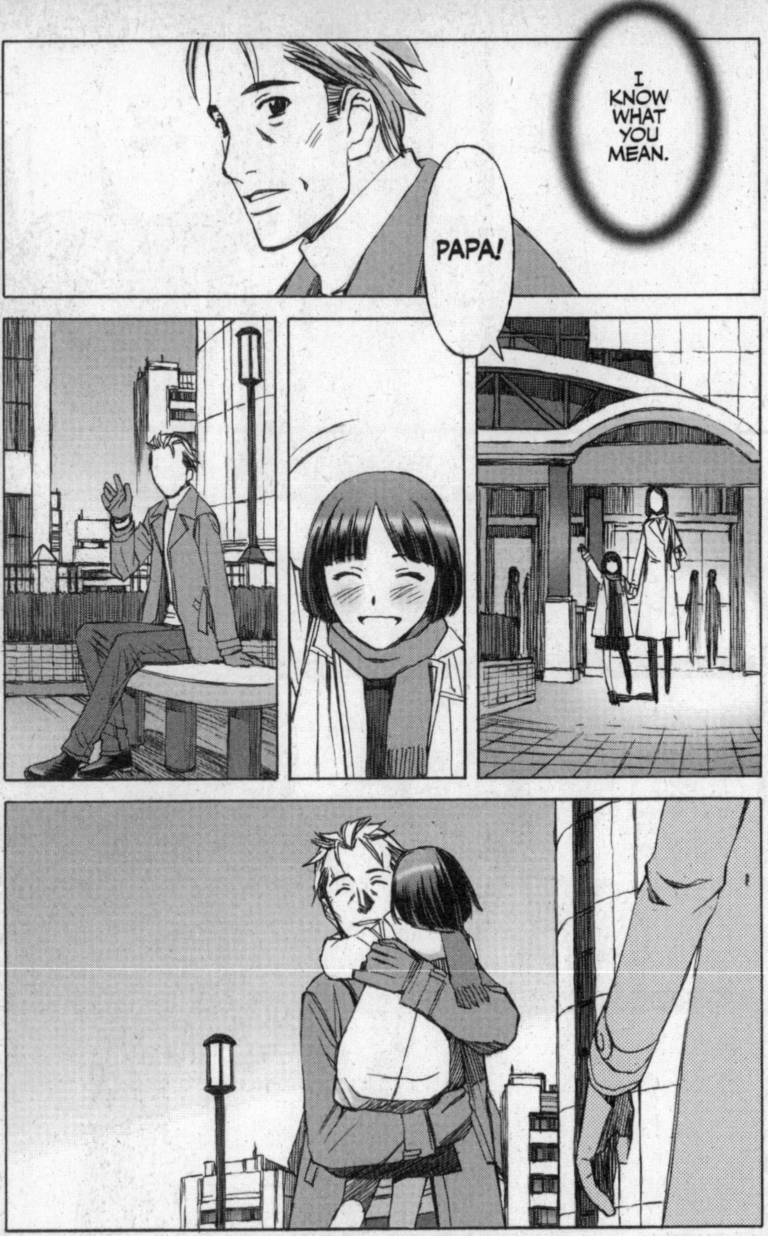
I KNOW WHAT YOU MEAN.
PAPA!

Episode 11
VALENTINE NIGHT
The Case of the Missing Chocolate

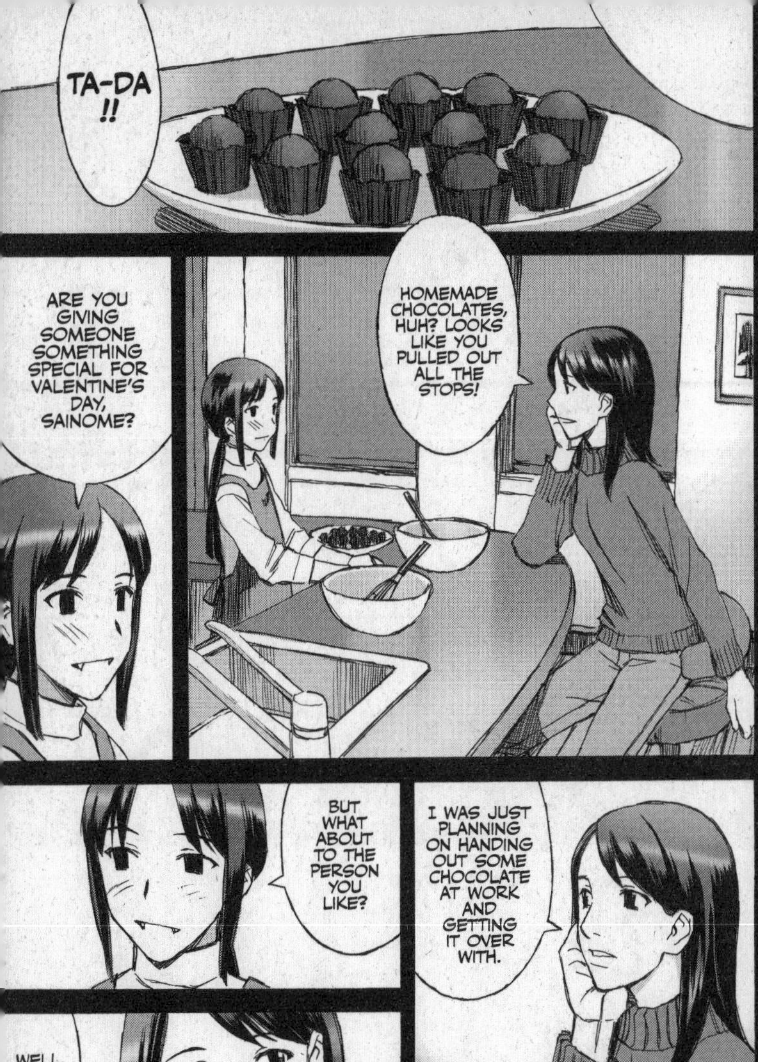
TA-DA !!
HOMEMADE CHOCOLATES, HUH? LOOKS LIKE YOU PULLED OUT ALL THE STOPS!
ARE YOU GIVING SOMEONE SOMETHING SPECIAL FOR VALENTINE'S DAY, SAINOME?
I WAS JUST PLANNING ON HANDING OUT SOME CHOCOLATE AT WORK AND GETTING IT OVER WITH.
BUT WHAT ABOUT TO THE PERSON YOU LIKE?
WELL, IN THAT CASE...

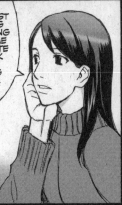

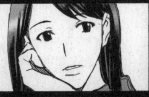

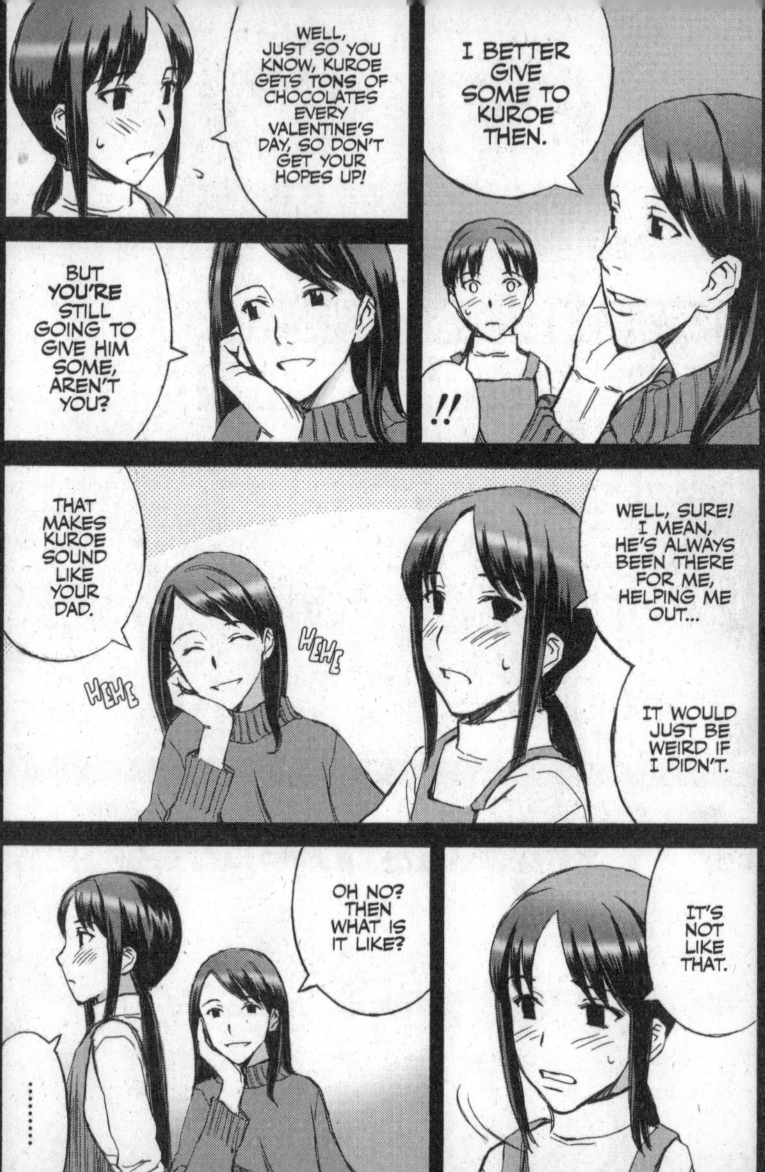
I BETTER GIVE SOME TO KUROE THEN.
!!
WELL, JUST SO YOU KNOW, KUROE GETS TONS OF CHOCOLATES EVERY VALENTINE'S DAY, SO DON'T GET YOUR HOPES UP!
BUT YOU'RE STILL GOING TO GIVE HIM SOME, AREN'T YOU?
WELL, SURE! I MEAN, HE'S ALWAYS BEEN THERE FOR ME, HELPING ME OUT...
IT WOULD JUST BE WEIRD IF I DIDN'T.
HEHE
THAT MAKES KUROE SOUND LIKE YOUR DAD.
HEHE
IT'S NOT LIKE THAT.
OH NO? THEN WHAT IS IT LIKE?
....

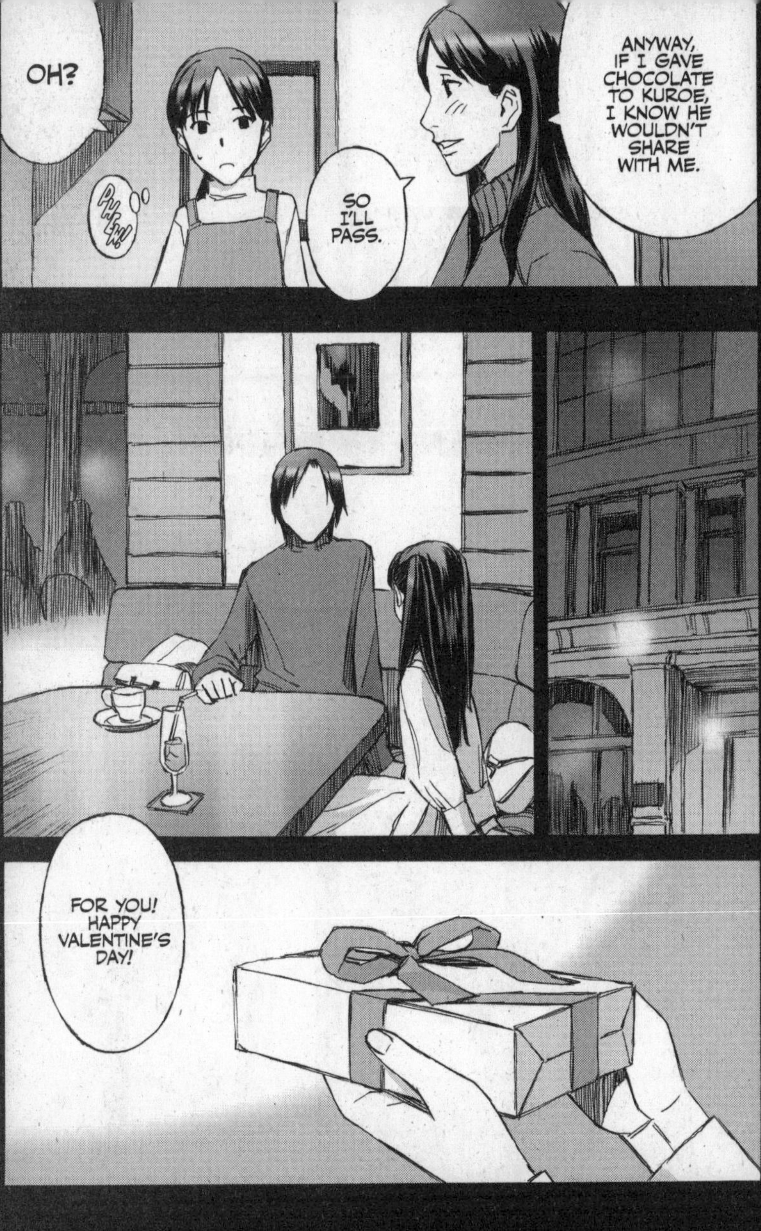
ANYWAY, IF I GAVE CHOCOLATE TO KUROE, I KNOW HE WOULDN'T SHARE WITH ME.
SO I'LL PASS.
OH?
PHEW!
FOR YOU! HAPPY VALENTINE'S DAY!

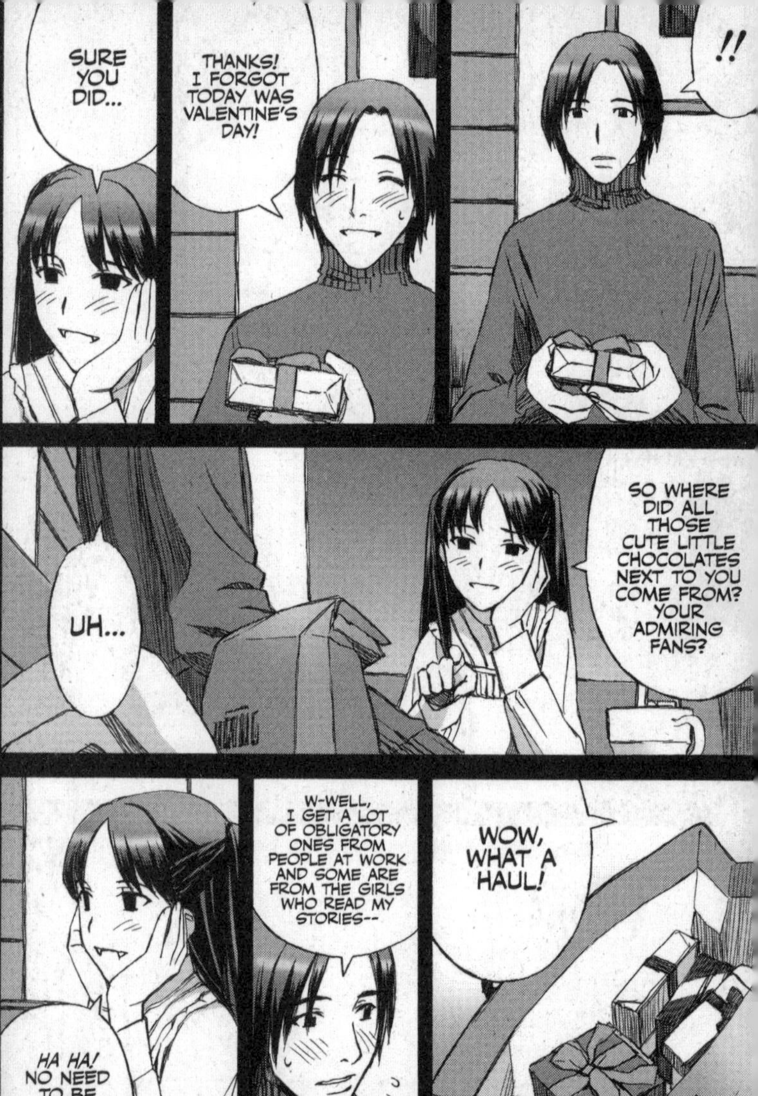
!!
THANKS! I FORGOT TODAY WAS VALENTINE'S DAY!
SURE YOU DID...
SO WHERE DID ALL THOSE CUTE LITTLE CHOCOLATES NEXT TO YOU COME FROM? YOUR ADMIRING FANS?
UH...
WOW, WHAT A HAUL!
W-WELL, I GET A LOT OF OBLIGATORY ONES FROM PEOPLE AT WORK AND SOME ARE FROM THE GIRLS WHO READ MY STORIES--
HA HA! NO NEED TO BE EMBAR-RASSED!

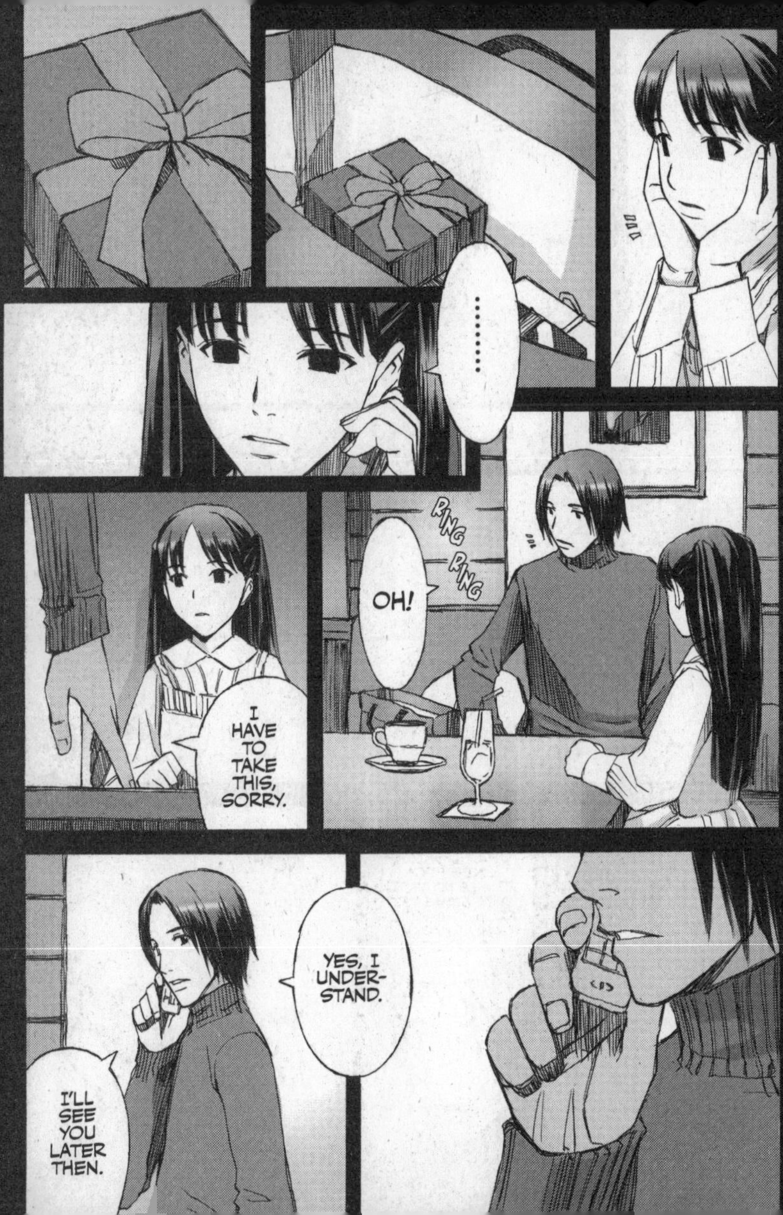
....
RING RING
OH!
I HAVE TO TAKE THIS, SORRY.
YES, I UNDERSTAND.
I'LL SEE YOU LATER THEN.

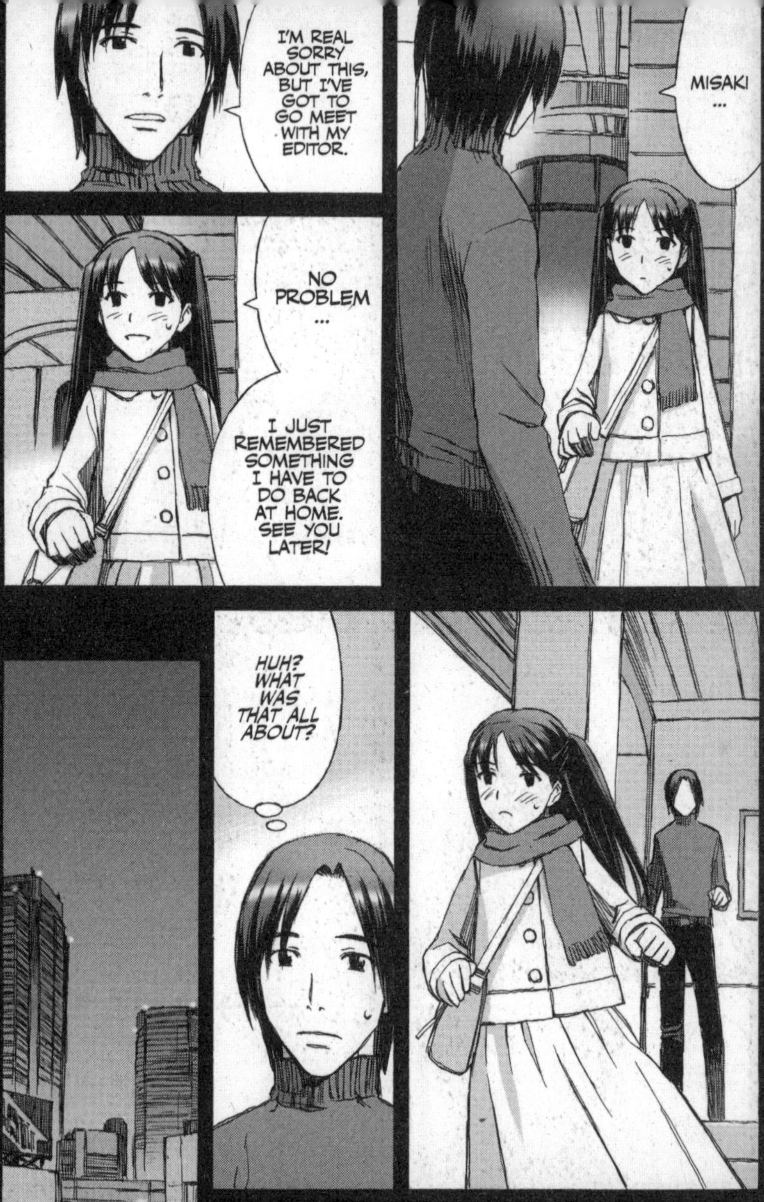
MISAKI ...
I'M REAL SORRY ABOUT THIS, BUT I'VE GOT TO GO MEET WITH MY EDITOR.
NO PROBLEM ...
I JUST REMEMBERED SOMETHING I HAVE TO DO BACK AT HOME. SEE YOU LATER!
HUH? WHAT WAS THAT ALL ABOUT?

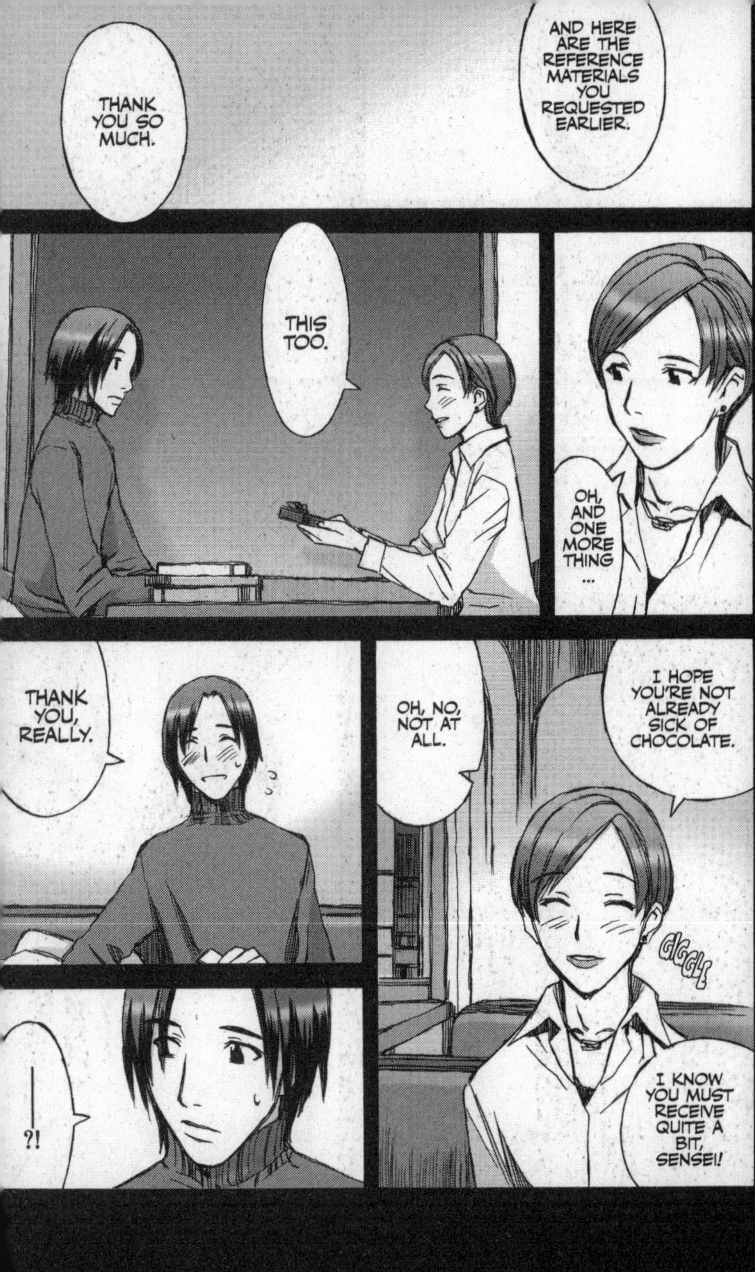
AND HERE ARE THE REFERENCE MATERIALS YOU REQUESTED EARLIER.
THANK YOU SO MUCH.
OH, AND ONE MORE THING ...
THIS TOO.
I HOPE YOU'RE NOT ALREADY SICK OF CHOCOLATE.
OH, NO, NOT AT ALL.
GIGGLE
I KNOW YOU MUST RECEIVE QUITE A BIT, SENSEI!
THANK YOU, REALLY.
—?!

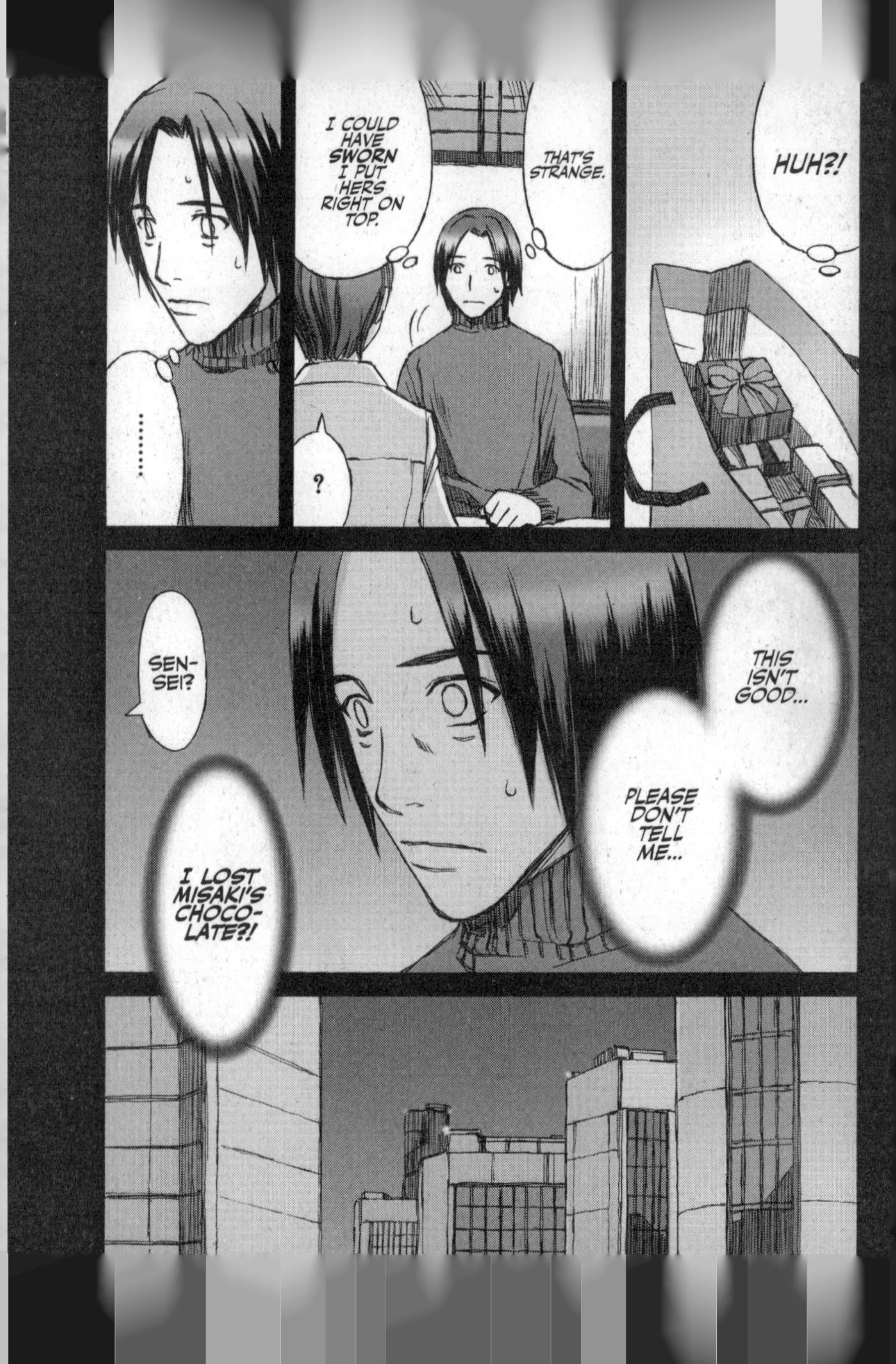
HUH?!
THAT'S STRANGE.
I COULD HAVE SWORN I PUT HERS RIGHT ON TOP.
?
......
THIS ISN'T GOOD...
PLEASE DON'T TELL ME...
I LOST MISAKI'S CHOCOLATE?!
SEN-SEI?

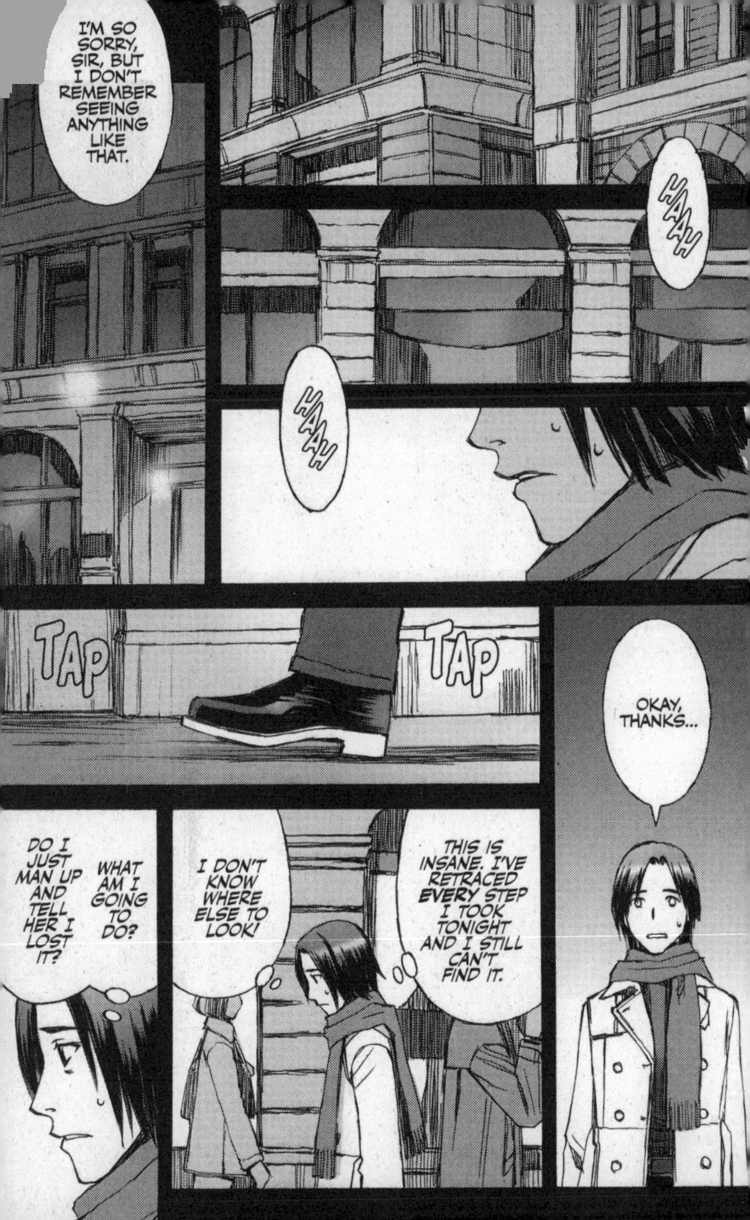
HAAH
HAAH
I'M SO SORRY, SIR, BUT I DON'T REMEMBER SEEING ANYTHING LIKE THAT.
OKAY, THANKS...
TAP
TAP
THIS IS INSANE. I'VE RETRACED **EVERY** STEP I TOOK TONIGHT AND I STILL CAN'T FIND IT.
I DON'T KNOW WHERE ELSE TO LOOK!
WHAT AM I GOING TO DO?
DO I JUST MAN UP AND TELL HER I LOST IT?

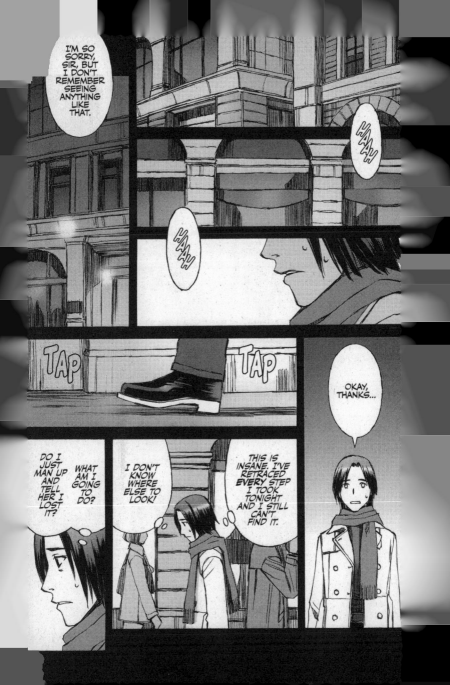

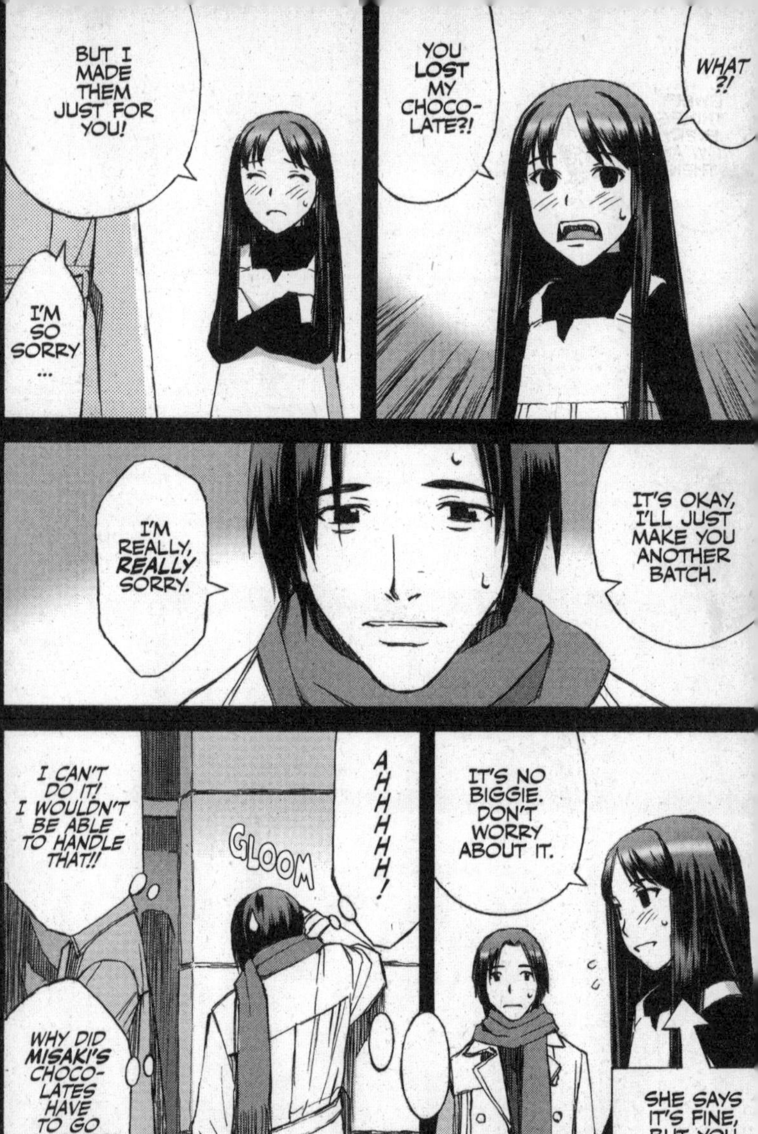
WHAT?!
YOU LOST MY CHOCOLATE?!
BUT I MADE THEM JUST FOR YOU!
I'M SO SORRY...
IT'S OKAY, I'LL JUST MAKE YOU ANOTHER BATCH.
I'M REALLY, REALLY SORRY.
IT'S NO BIGGIE. DON'T WORRY ABOUT IT.
SHE SAYS IT'S FINE, BUT YOU CAN TELL IT'S NOT.
AHHHHH!
GLOOM
I CAN'T DO IT! I WOULDN'T BE ABLE TO HANDLE THAT!!
WHY DID MISAKI'S CHOCOLATES HAVE TO GO MISSING?!

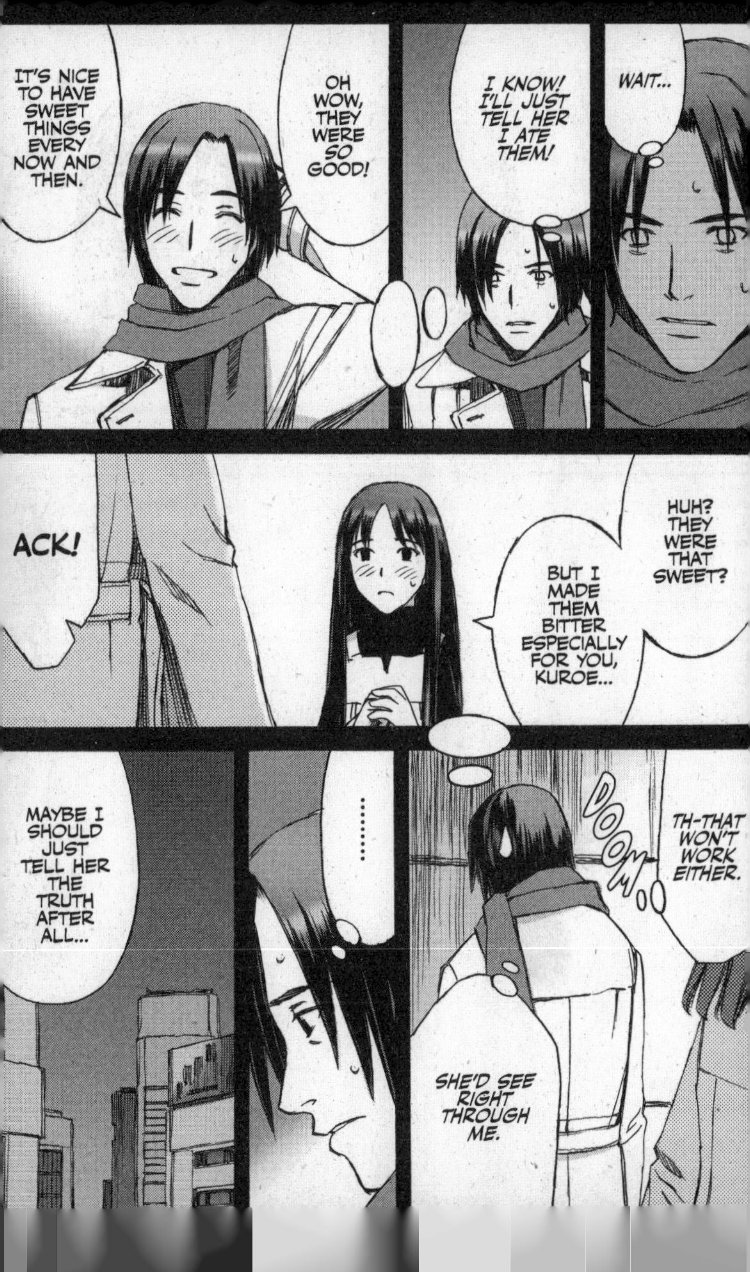
WAIT...
I KNOW! I'LL JUST TELL HER I ATE THEM!
OH WOW, THEY WERE SO GOOD!
IT'S NICE TO HAVE SWEET THINGS EVERY NOW AND THEN.
HUH? THEY WERE THAT SWEET?
BUT I MADE THEM BITTER ESPECIALLY FOR YOU, KUROE...
ACK!
TH-THAT WON'T WORK EITHER.
DOOM...
SHE'D SEE RIGHT THROUGH ME.
....
MAYBE I SHOULD JUST TELL HER THE TRUTH AFTER ALL...

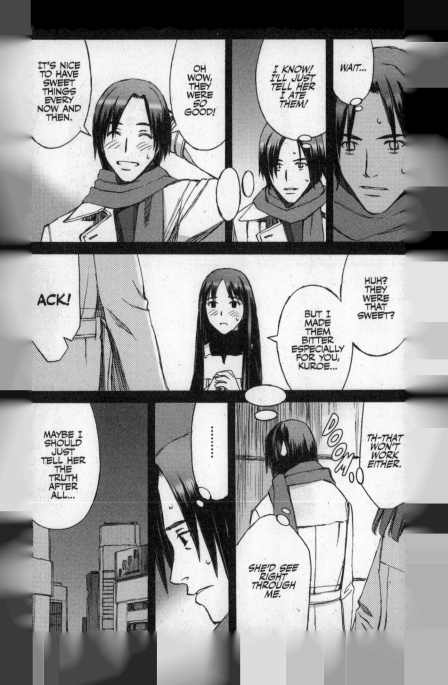

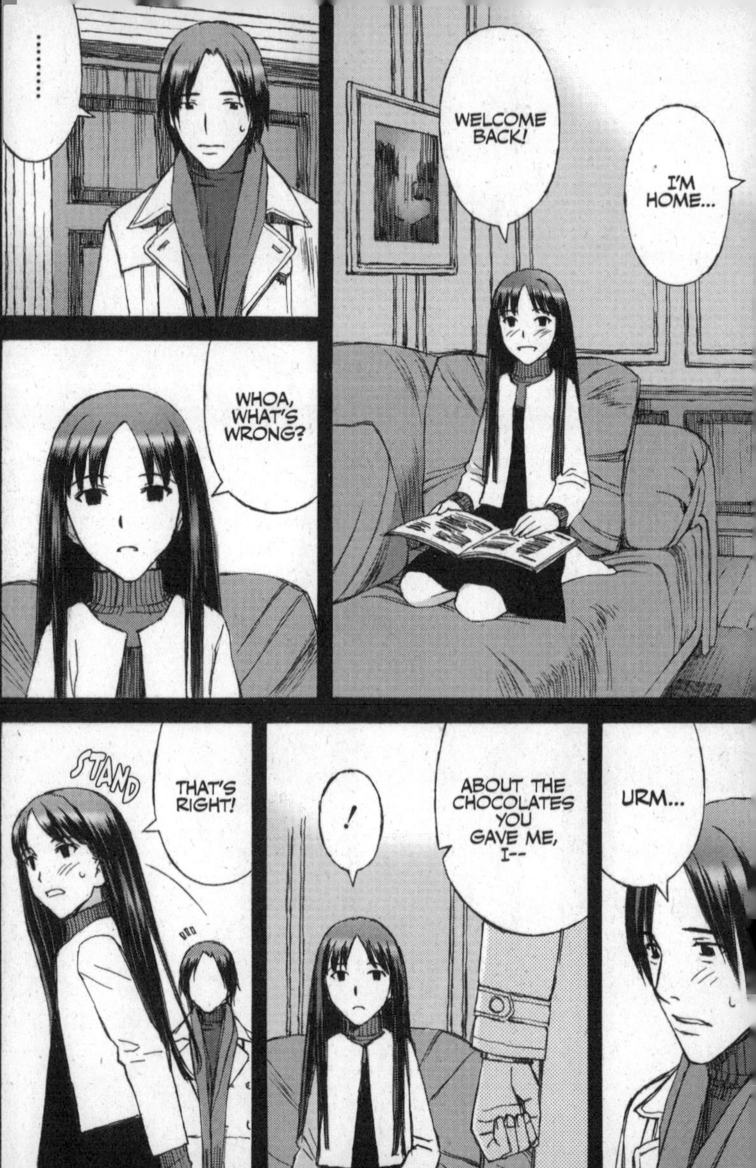
I'M HOME...
WELCOME BACK!
....
WHOA, WHAT'S WRONG?
URM...
ABOUT THE CHOCOLATES YOU GAVE ME, I--
!
THAT'S RIGHT!
STAND

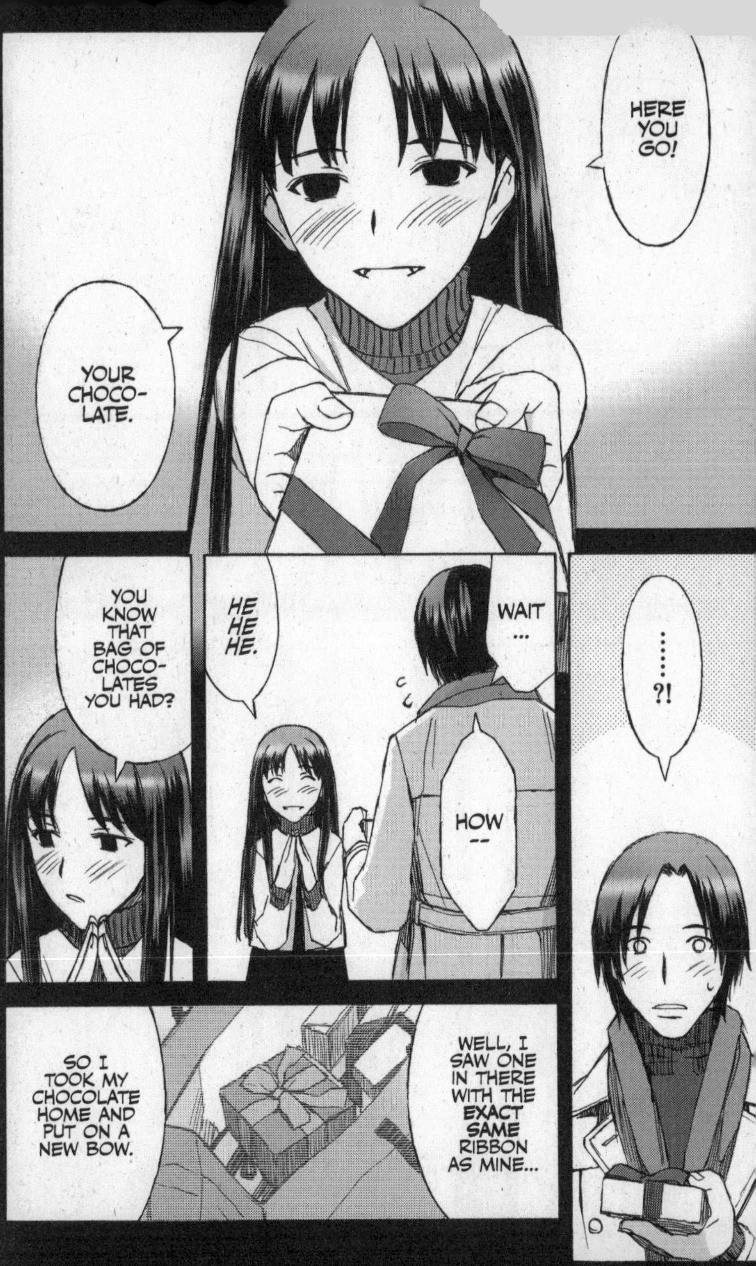
HERE YOU GO!
YOUR CHOCOLATE.
......?!
WAIT...
HE HE HE.
HOW --
YOU KNOW THAT BAG OF CHOCOLATES YOU HAD?
WELL, I SAW ONE IN THERE WITH THE **EXACT SAME** RIBBON AS MINE...
SO I TOOK MY CHOCOLATE HOME AND PUT ON A NEW BOW.

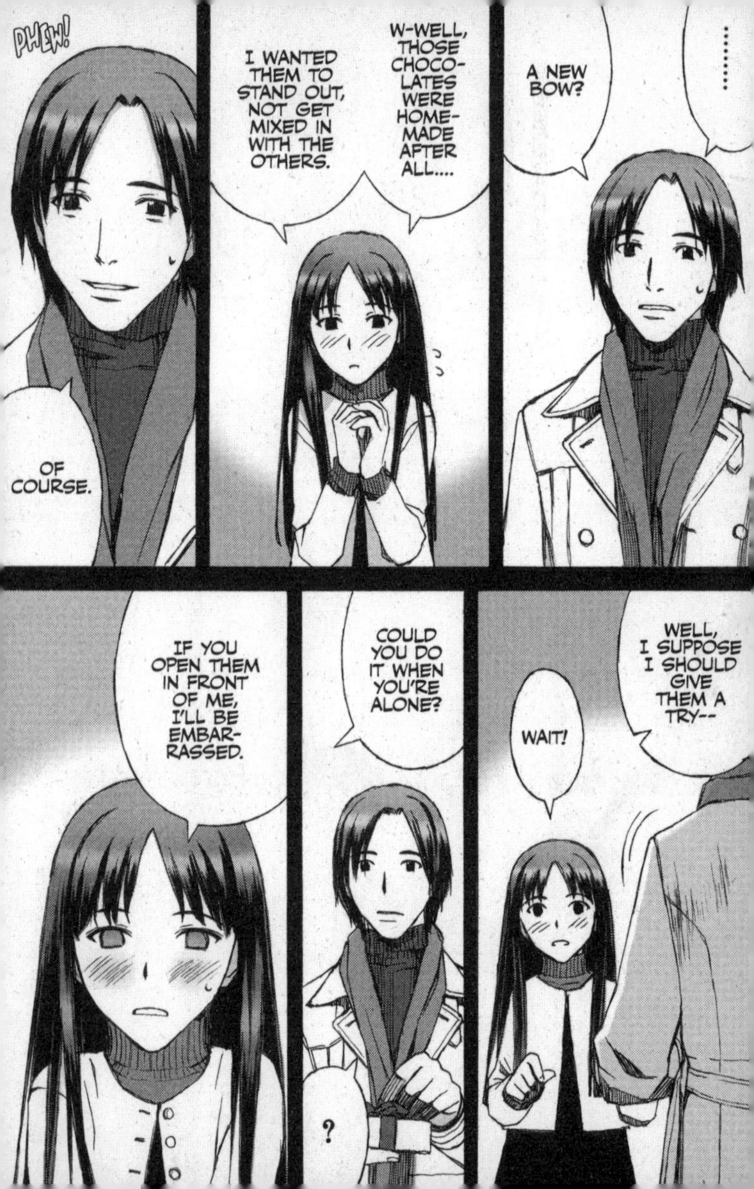
....
A NEW BOW?
W-WELL, THOSE CHOCOLATES WERE HOMEMADE AFTER ALL....
I WANTED THEM TO STAND OUT, NOT GET MIXED IN WITH THE OTHERS.
PHEW!
OF COURSE.
WELL, I SUPPOSE I SHOULD GIVE THEM A TRY--
WAIT!
COULD YOU DO IT WHEN YOU'RE ALONE?
?
IF YOU OPEN THEM IN FRONT OF ME, I'LL BE EMBARRASSED.

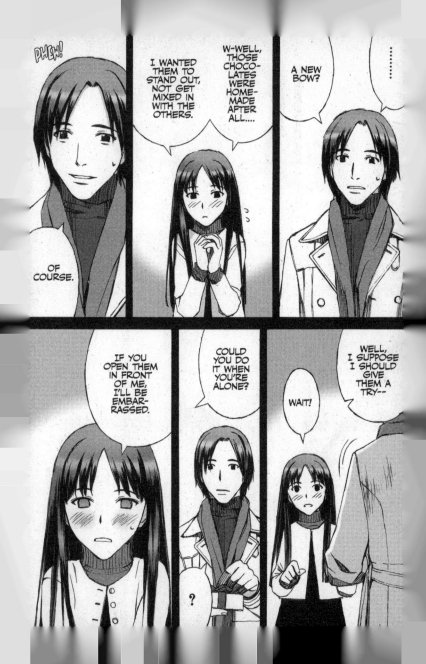

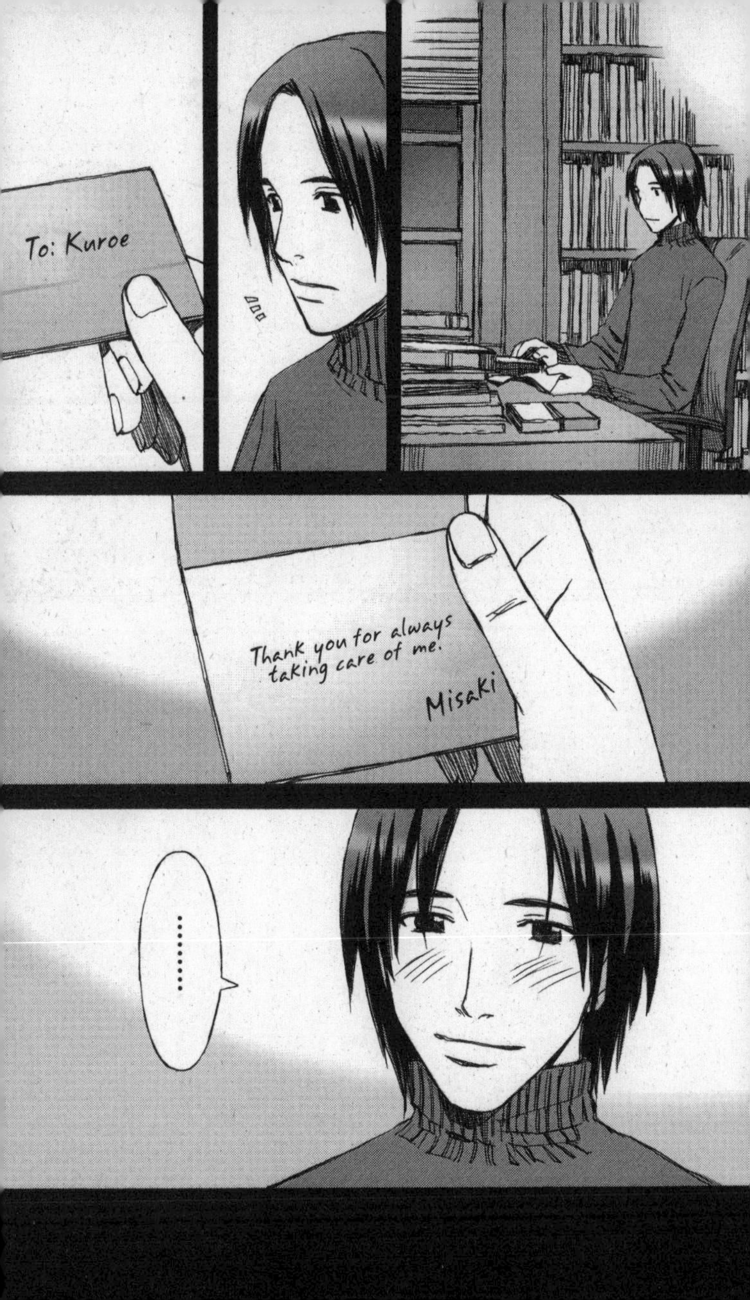
To: Kuroe
Thank you for always taking care of me.
Misaki
....

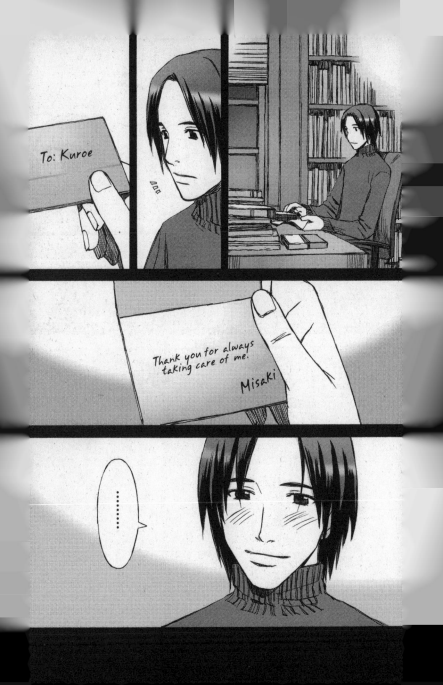

Episode 12
WHY CRY? part 1
The Crimson Blade

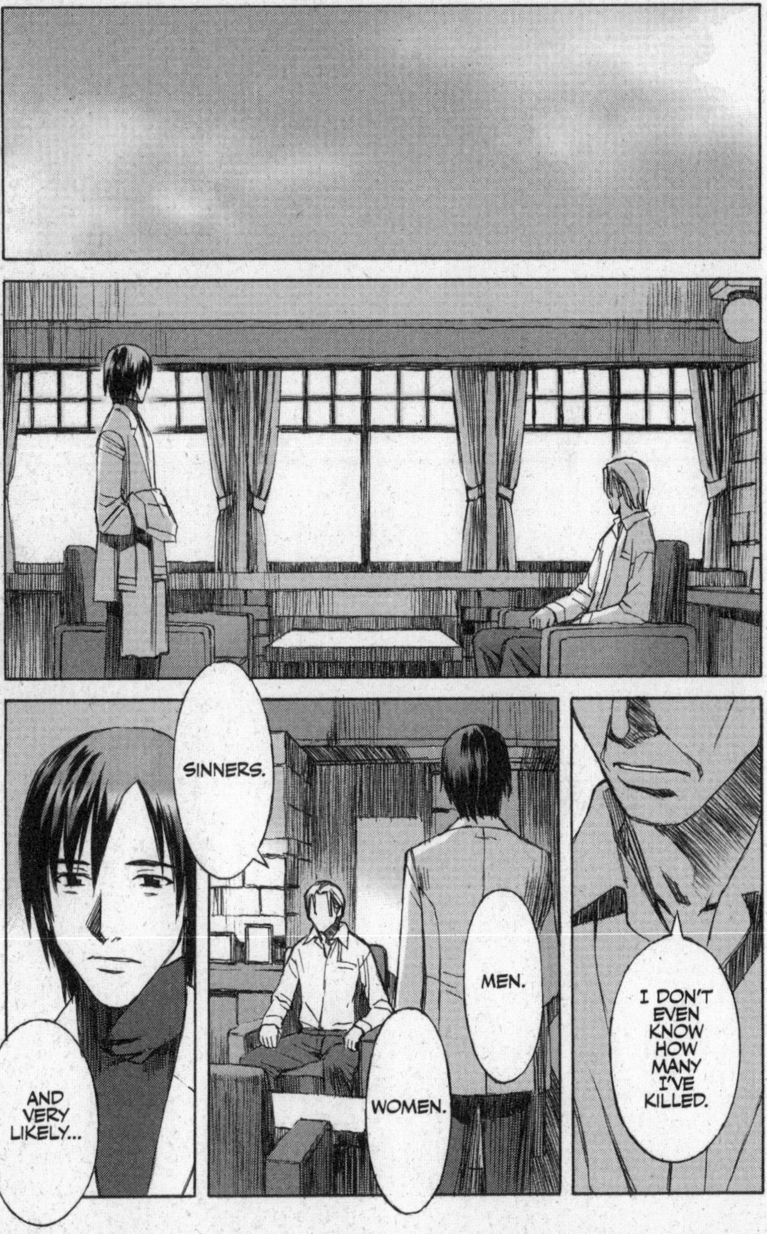
I DON'T EVEN KNOW HOW MANY I'VE KILLED.
SINNERS.
MEN.
WOMEN.
AND VERY LIKELY...

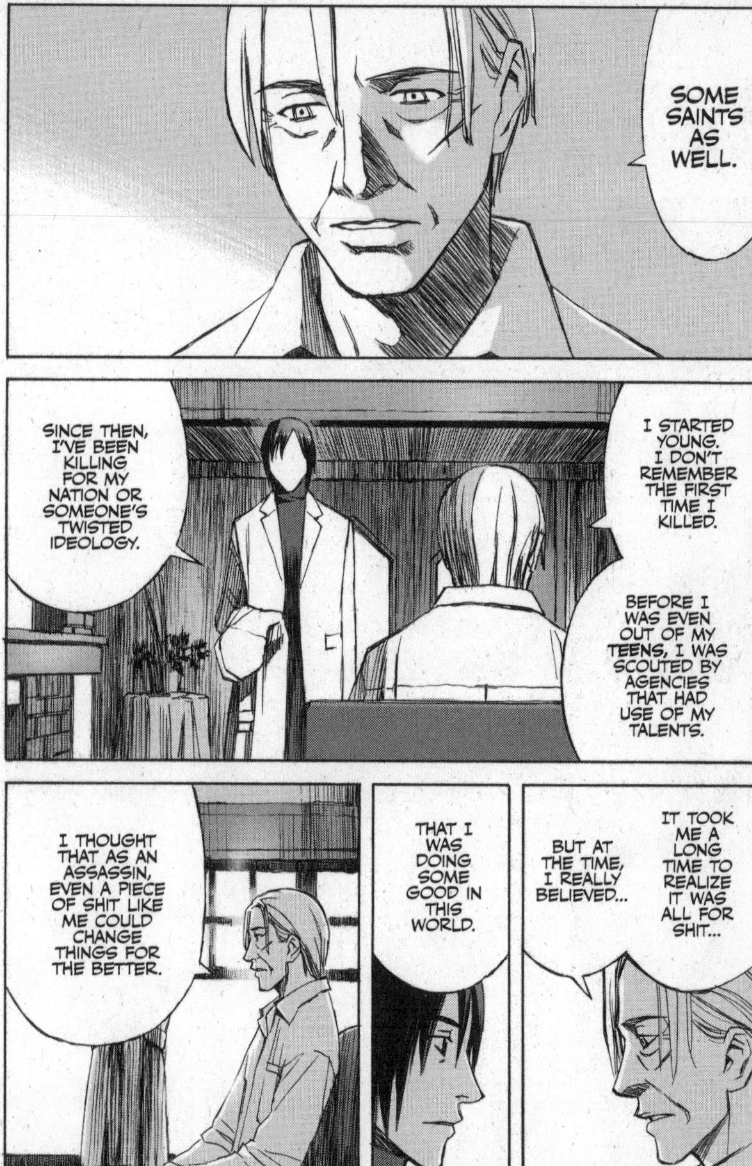
SOME SAINTS AS WELL.
I STARTED YOUNG. I DON'T REMEMBER THE FIRST TIME I KILLED.
BEFORE I WAS EVEN OUT OF MY TEENS, I WAS SCOUTED BY AGENCIES THAT HAD USE OF MY TALENTS.
SINCE THEN, I'VE BEEN KILLING FOR MY NATION OR SOMEONE'S TWISTED IDEOLOGY.
IT TOOK ME A LONG TIME TO REALIZE IT WAS ALL FOR SHIT...
BUT AT THE TIME, I REALLY BELIEVED...
THAT I WAS DOING SOME GOOD IN THIS WORLD.
I THOUGHT THAT AS AN ASSASSIN, EVEN A PIECE OF SHIT LIKE ME COULD CHANGE THINGS FOR THE BETTER.

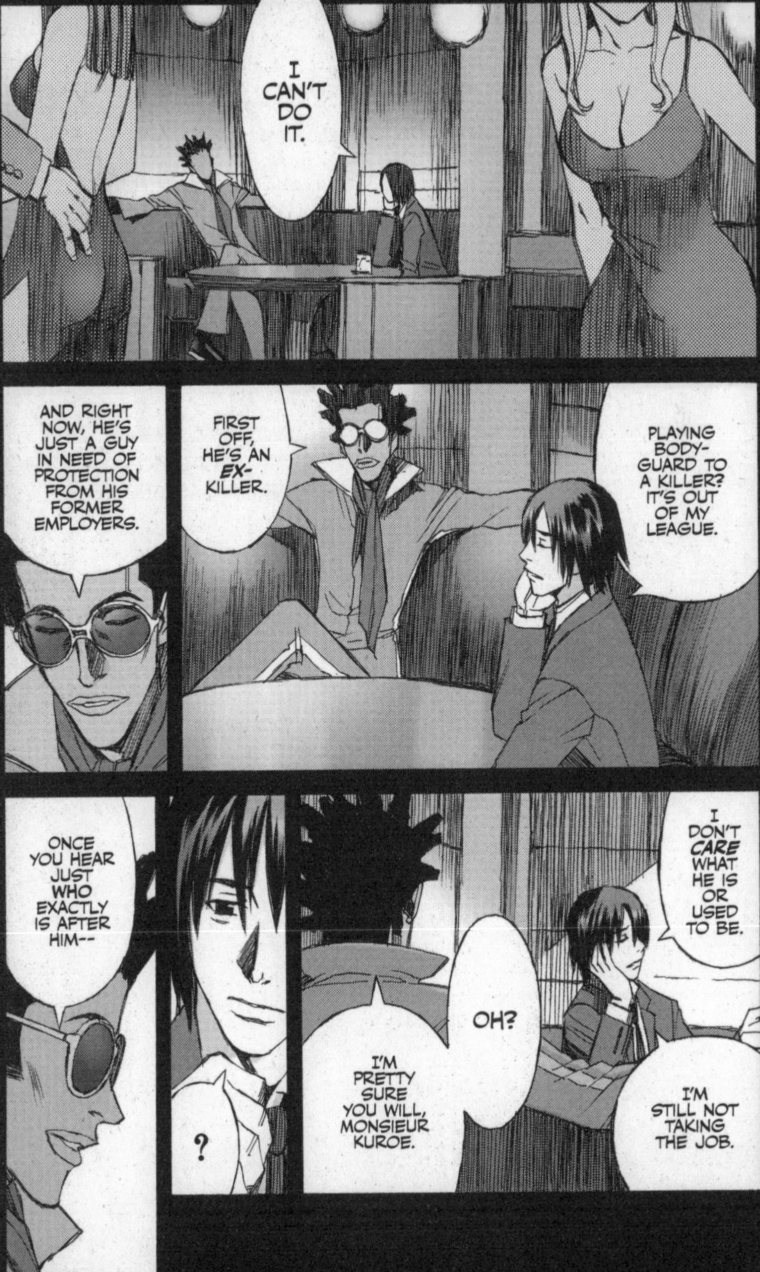
I CAN'T DO IT.
PLAYING BODY-GUARD TO A KILLER? IT'S OUT OF MY LEAGUE.
FIRST OFF, HE'S AN *EX*-KILLER.
AND RIGHT NOW, HE'S JUST A GUY IN NEED OF PROTECTION FROM HIS FORMER EMPLOYERS.
I DON'T *CARE* WHAT HE IS OR USED TO BE.
OH?
I'M STILL NOT TAKING THE JOB.
I'M PRETTY SURE YOU WILL, MONSIEUR KUROE.
?
ONCE YOU HEAR JUST WHO EXACTLY IS AFTER HIM--

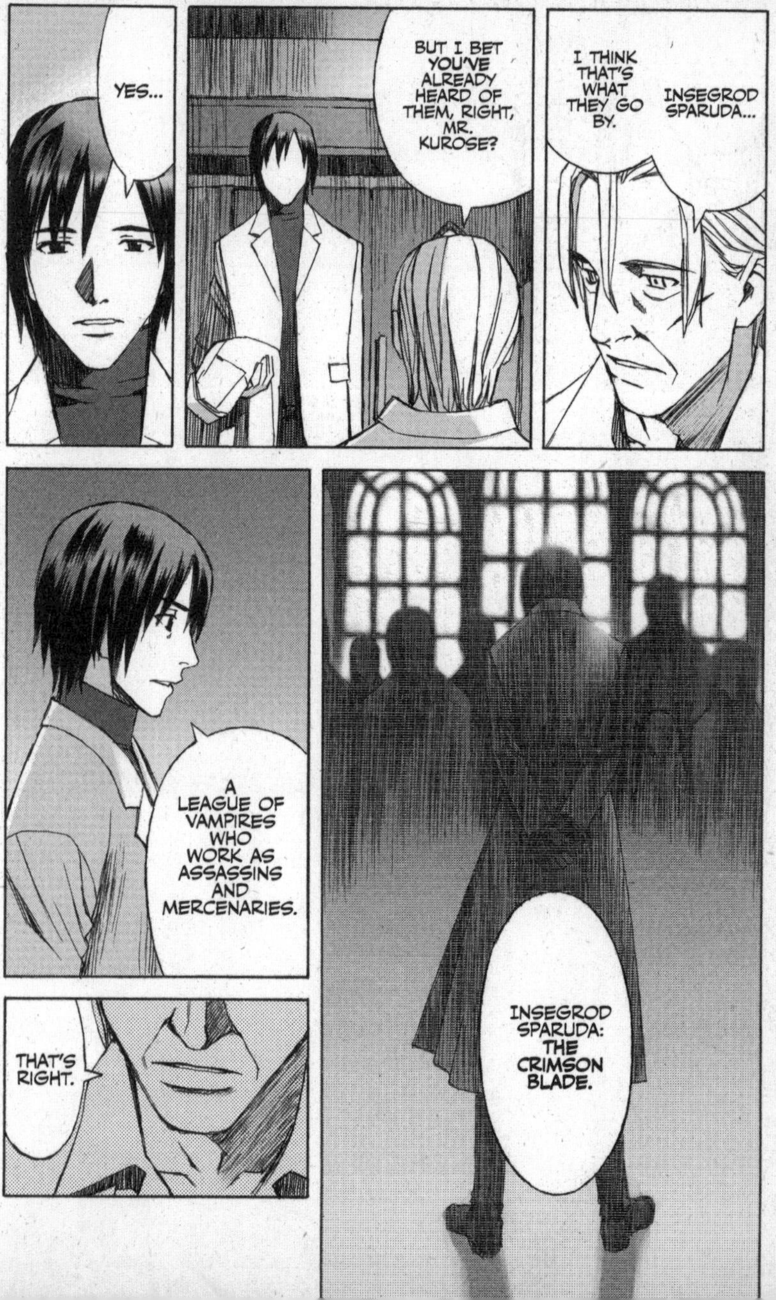
INSEGROD SPARUDA...
I THINK THAT'S WHAT THEY GO BY.
BUT I BET YOU'VE ALREADY HEARD OF THEM, RIGHT, MR. KUROSE?
YES...
INSEGROD SPARUDA: THE CRIMSON BLADE.
A LEAGUE OF VAMPIRES WHO WORK AS ASSASSINS AND MERCENARIES.
THAT'S RIGHT.

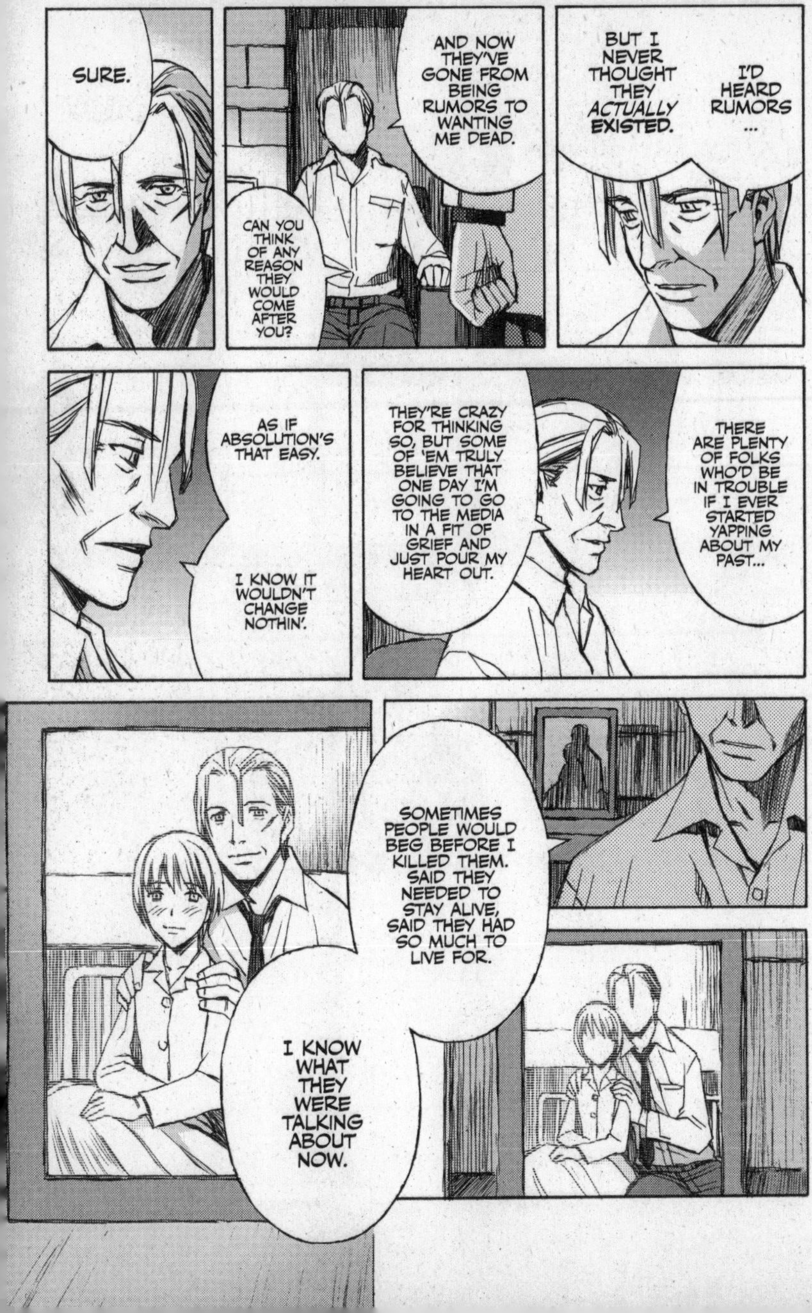
I'D HEARD RUMORS ...
BUT I NEVER THOUGHT THEY *ACTUALLY* EXISTED.
AND NOW THEY'VE GONE FROM BEING RUMORS TO WANTING ME DEAD.
CAN YOU THINK OF ANY REASON THEY WOULD COME AFTER YOU?
SURE.
THERE ARE PLENTY OF FOLKS WHO'D BE IN TROUBLE IF I EVER STARTED YAPPING ABOUT MY PAST...
THEY'RE CRAZY FOR THINKING SO, BUT SOME OF 'EM TRULY BELIEVE THAT ONE DAY I'M GOING TO GO TO THE MEDIA IN A FIT OF GRIEF AND JUST POUR MY HEART OUT.
AS IF ABSOLUTION'S THAT EASY.
I KNOW IT WOULDN'T CHANGE NOTHIN'.
SOMETIMES PEOPLE WOULD BEG BEFORE I KILLED THEM. SAID THEY NEEDED TO STAY ALIVE, SAID THEY HAD SO MUCH TO LIVE FOR.
I KNOW WHAT THEY WERE TALKING ABOUT NOW.

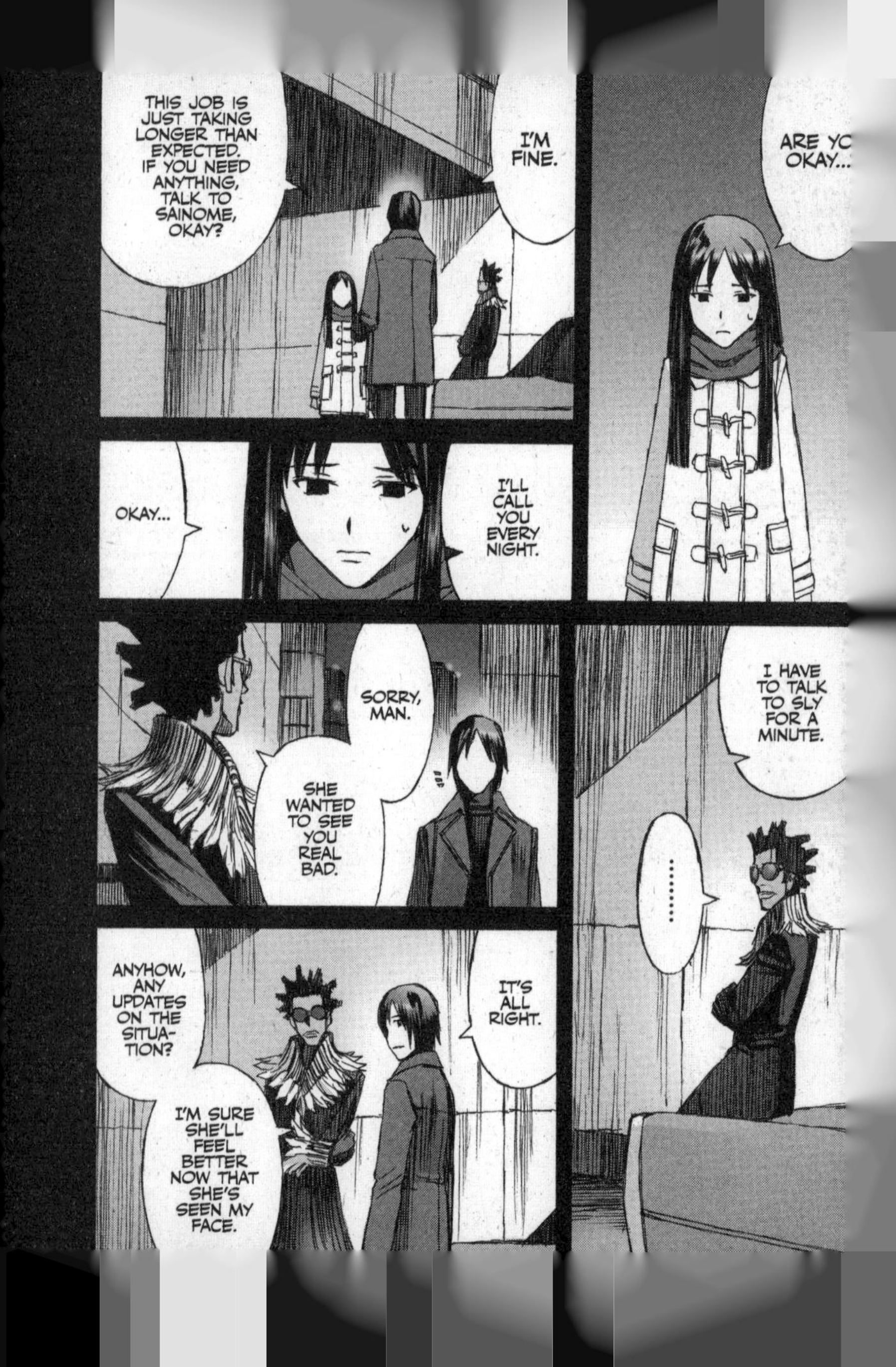
ARE YO
OKAY...
I'M FINE.
THIS JOB IS JUST TAKING LONGER THAN EXPECTED. IF YOU NEED ANYTHING, TALK TO SAINOME, OKAY?
I'LL CALL YOU EVERY NIGHT.
OKAY...
I HAVE TO TALK TO SLY FOR A MINUTE.
......
SORRY, MAN.
SHE WANTED TO SEE YOU REAL BAD.
IT'S ALL RIGHT.
ANYHOW, ANY UPDATES ON THE SITUA-TION?
I'M SURE SHE'LL FEEL BETTER NOW THAT SHE'S SEEN MY FACE.

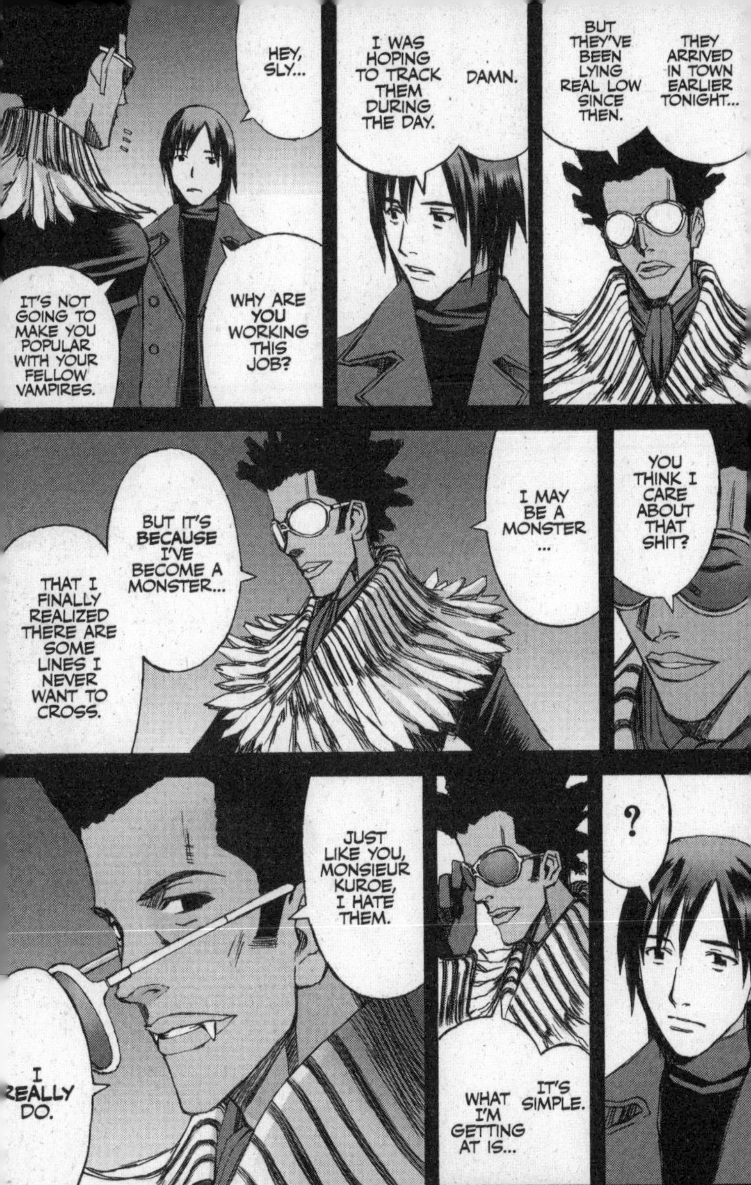
THEY ARRIVED IN TOWN EARLIER TONIGHT...
BUT THEY'VE BEEN LYING REAL LOW SINCE THEN.
DAMN.
I WAS HOPING TO TRACK THEM DURING THE DAY.
HEY, SLY...
WHY ARE YOU WORKING THIS JOB?
IT'S NOT GOING TO MAKE YOU POPULAR WITH YOUR FELLOW VAMPIRES.
YOU THINK I CARE ABOUT THAT SHIT?
I MAY BE A MONSTER ...
BUT IT'S BECAUSE I'VE BECOME A MONSTER...
THAT I FINALLY REALIZED THERE ARE SOME LINES I NEVER WANT TO CROSS.
?
IT'S SIMPLE.
WHAT I'M GETTING AT IS...
JUST LIKE YOU, MONSIEUR KUROE, I HATE THEM.
I REALLY DO.

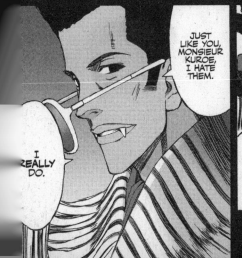

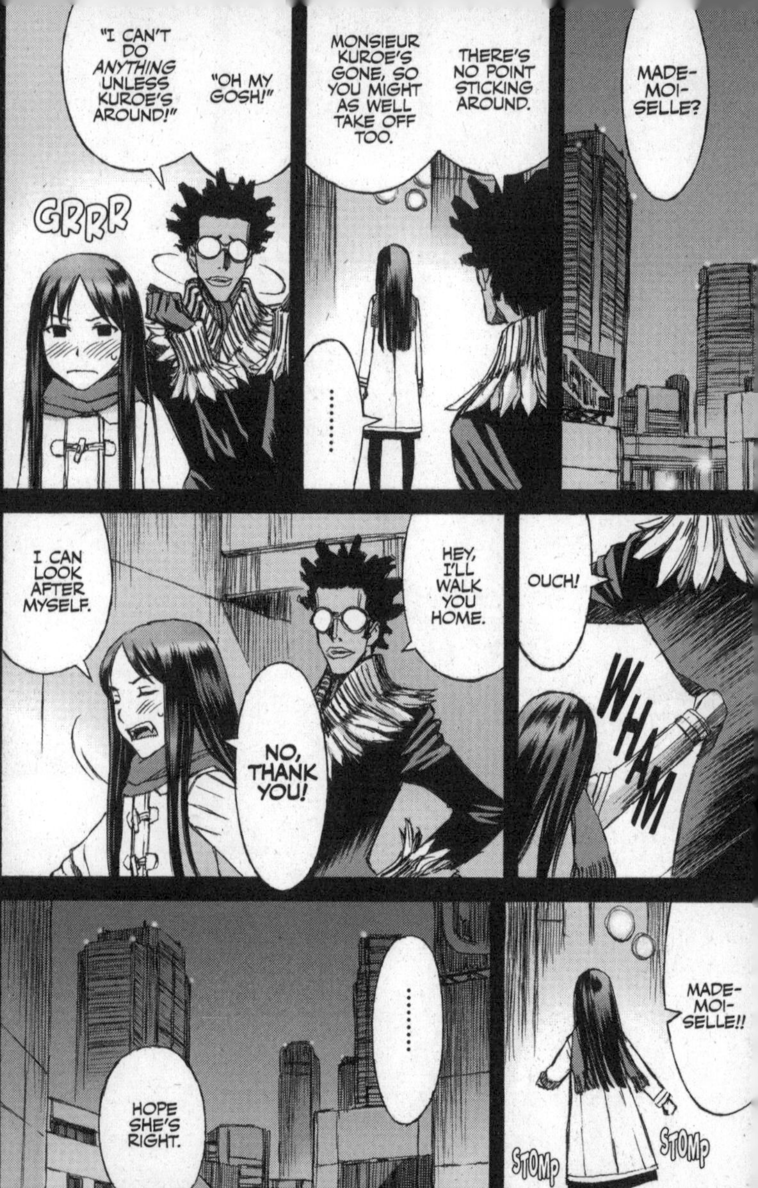
MADE-MOI-SELLE?
MONSIEUR KUROE'S GONE, SO YOU MIGHT AS WELL TAKE OFF TOO.
THERE'S NO POINT STICKING AROUND.
....
"I CAN'T DO *ANYTHING* UNLESS KUROE'S AROUND!"
"OH MY GOSH!"
GRRR
OUCH!
WHAM
HEY, I'LL WALK YOU HOME.
NO, THANK YOU!
I CAN LOOK AFTER MYSELF.
MADE-MOI-SELLE!!
STOMP
STOMP
....
HOPE SHE'S RIGHT.

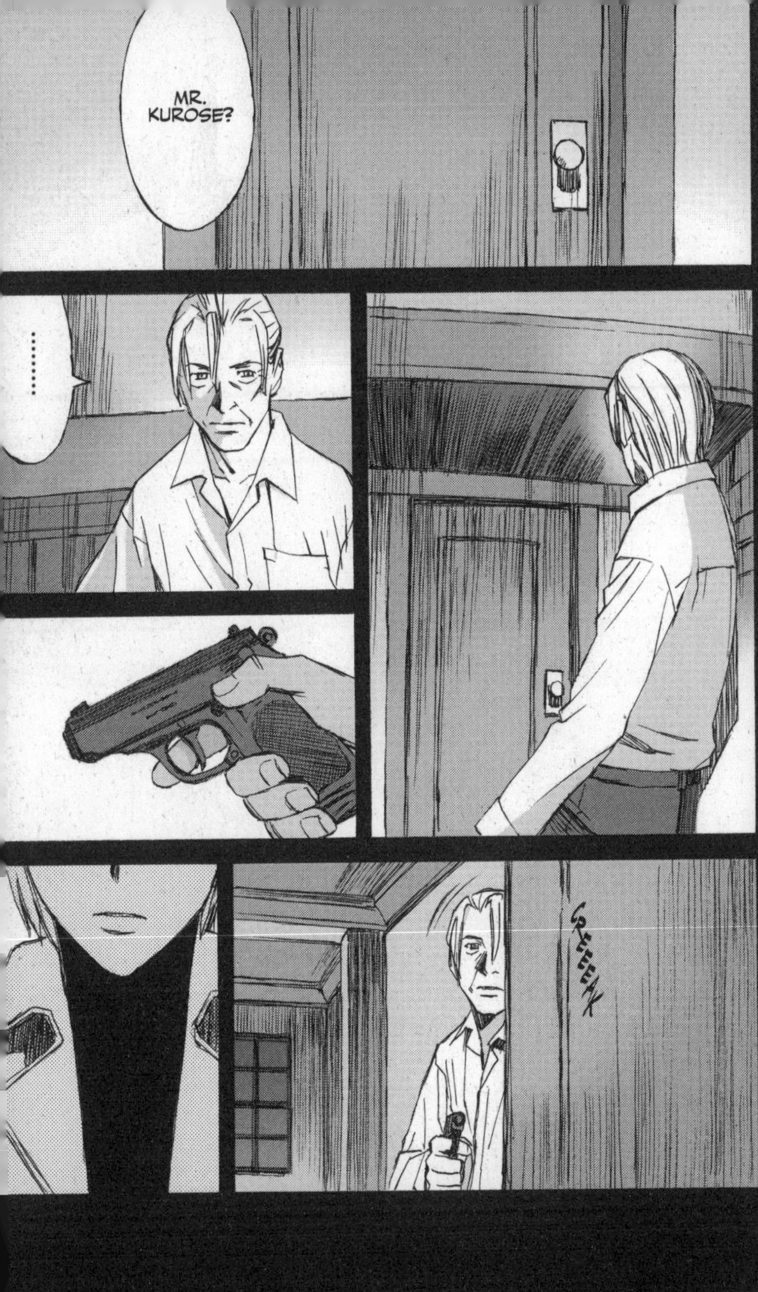
MR. KUROSE?
......
CREEEAK

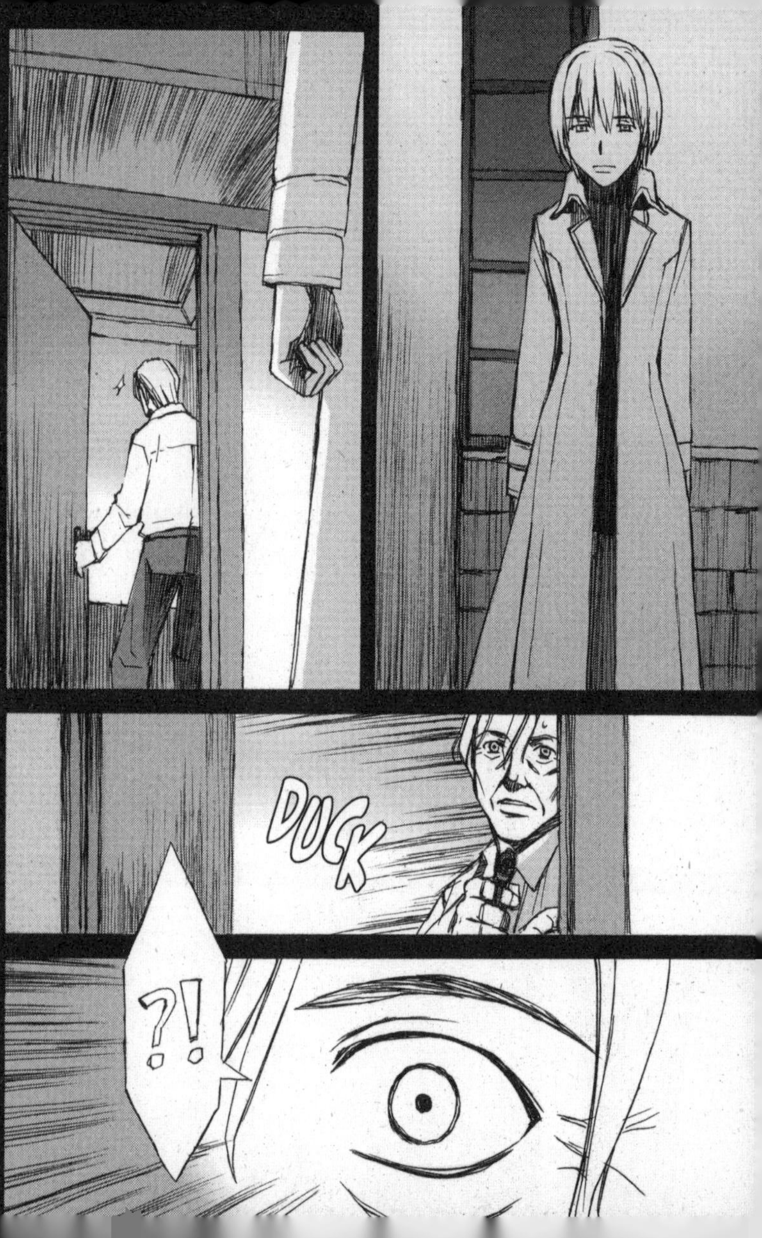
DUCK
?!

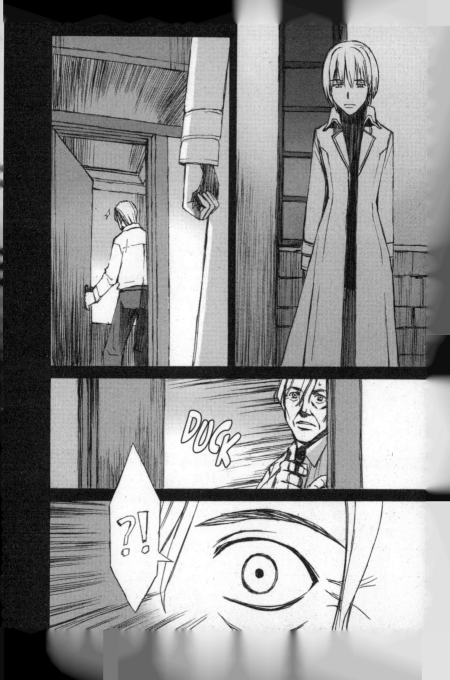

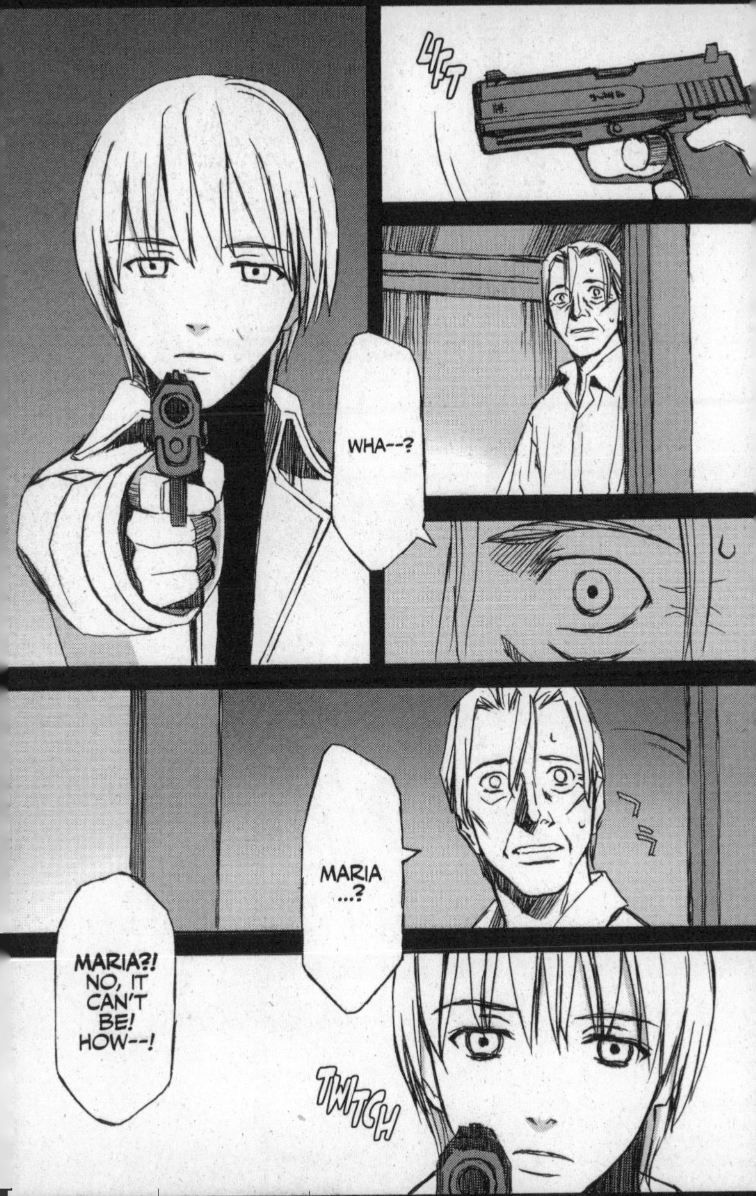
LIFT
WHA--?
MARIA ...?
MARIA?! NO, IT CAN'T BE! HOW--!
TWITCH

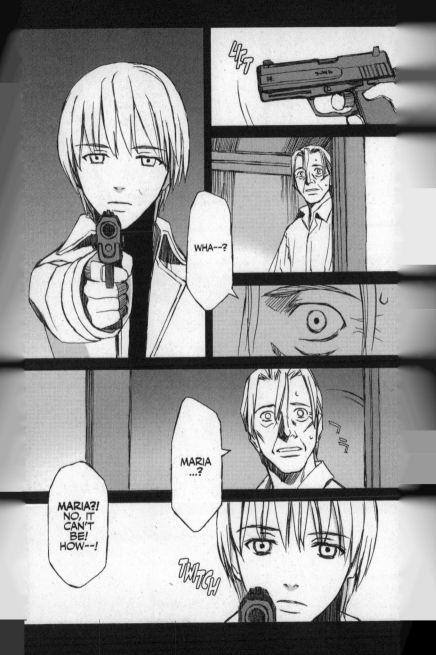

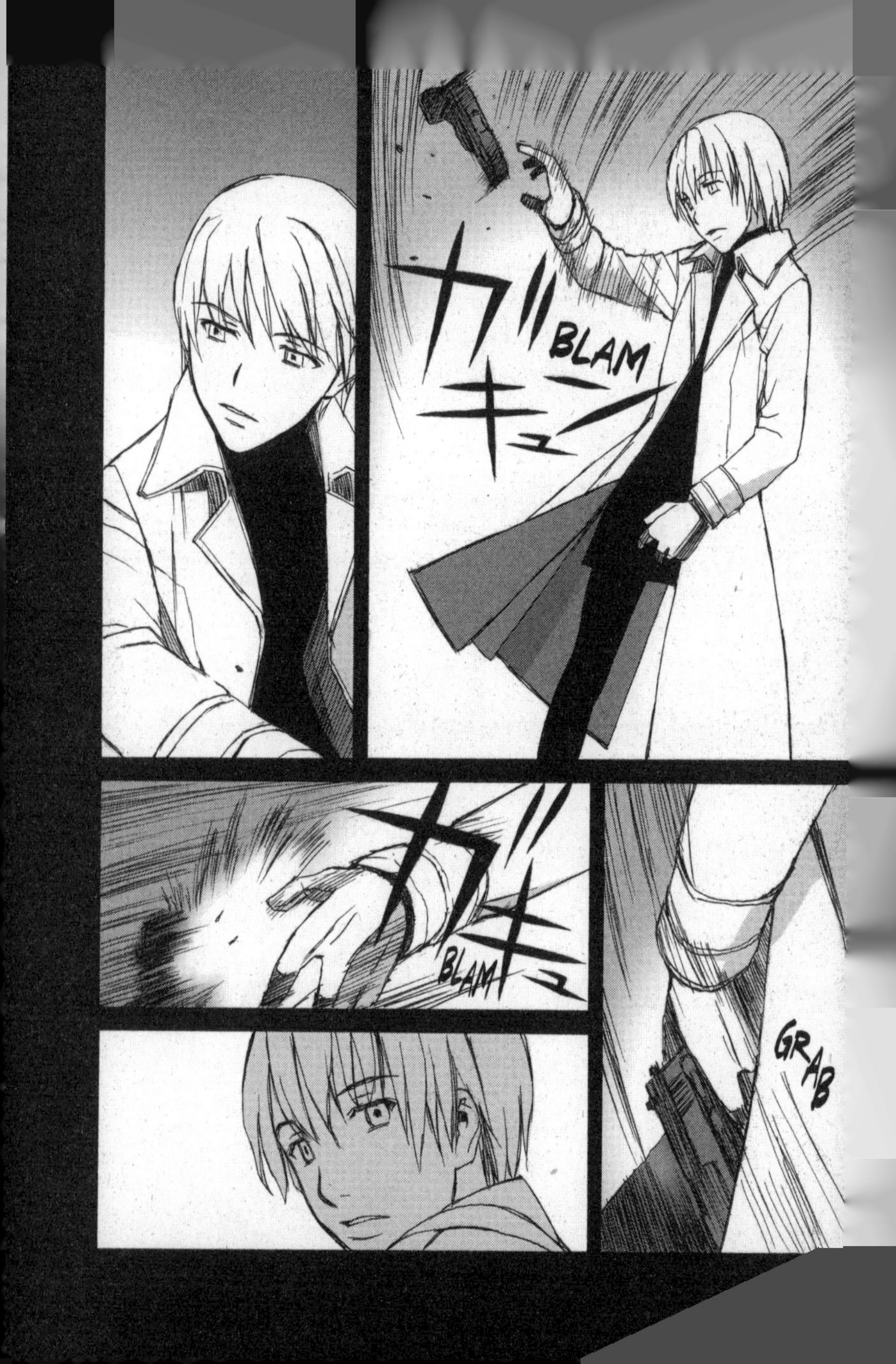
BLAM
GRAB
BLAM

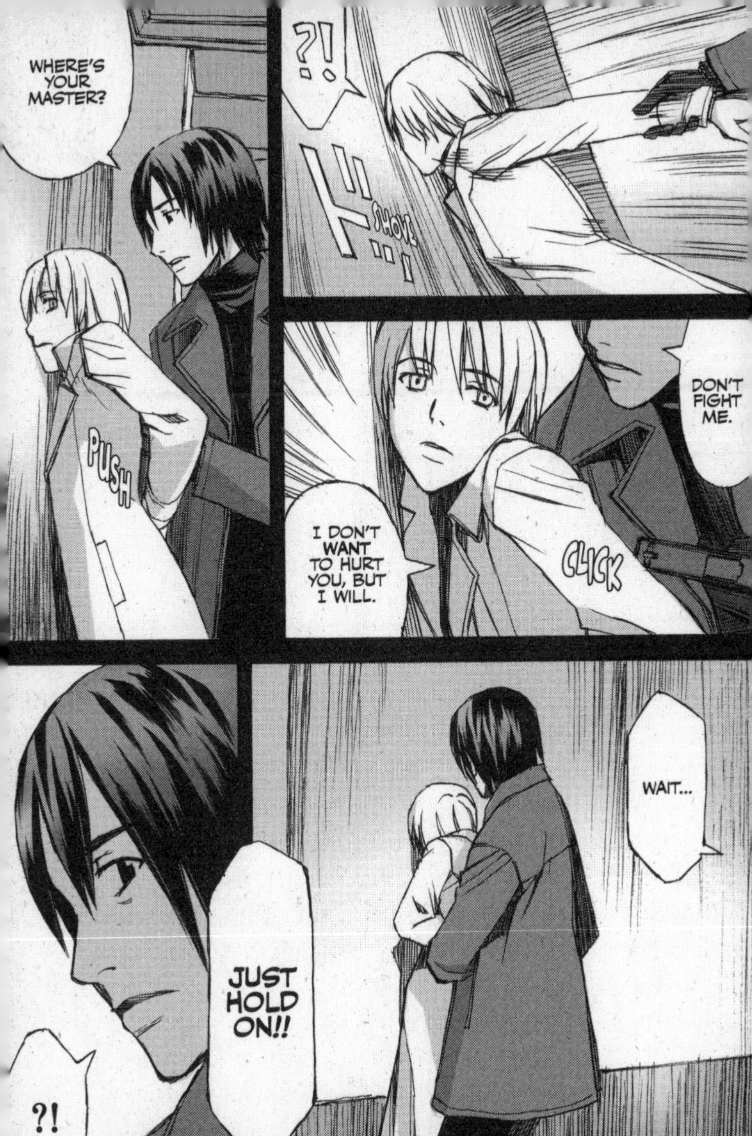
?!
SHOVE
DON'T FIGHT ME.
I DON'T WANT TO HURT YOU, BUT I WILL.
CLICK
WHERE'S YOUR MASTER?
PUSH
WAIT...
JUST HOLD ON!!
?!

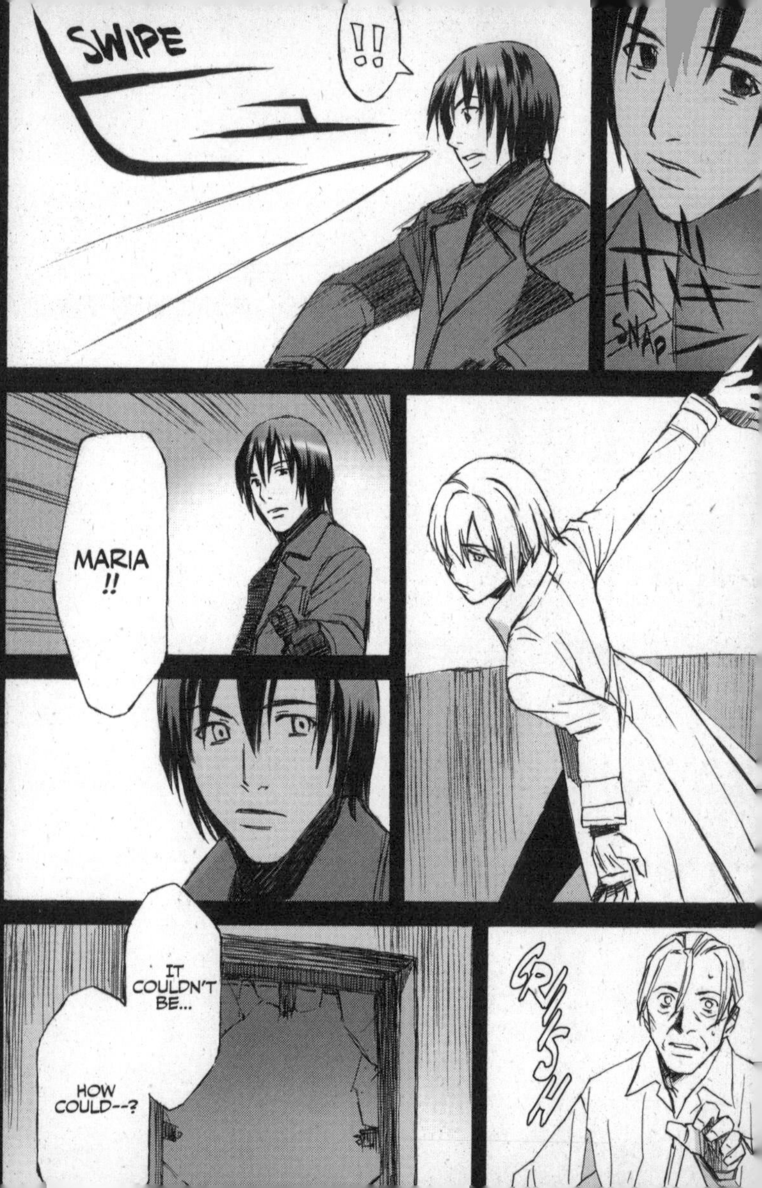
SNAP
SWIPE
!!
MARIA !!
CRUSH
IT COULDN'T BE...
HOW COULD--?

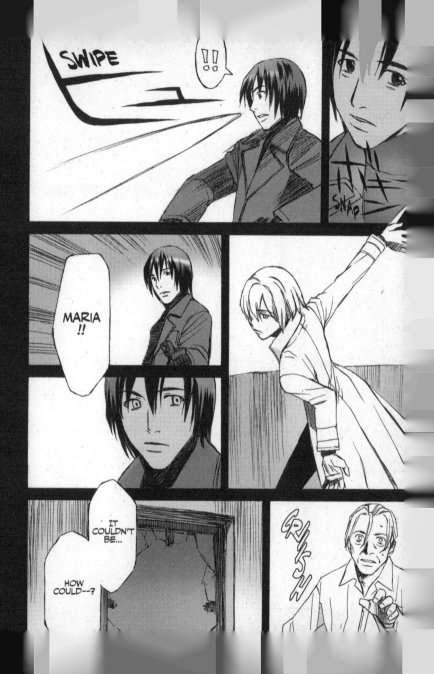

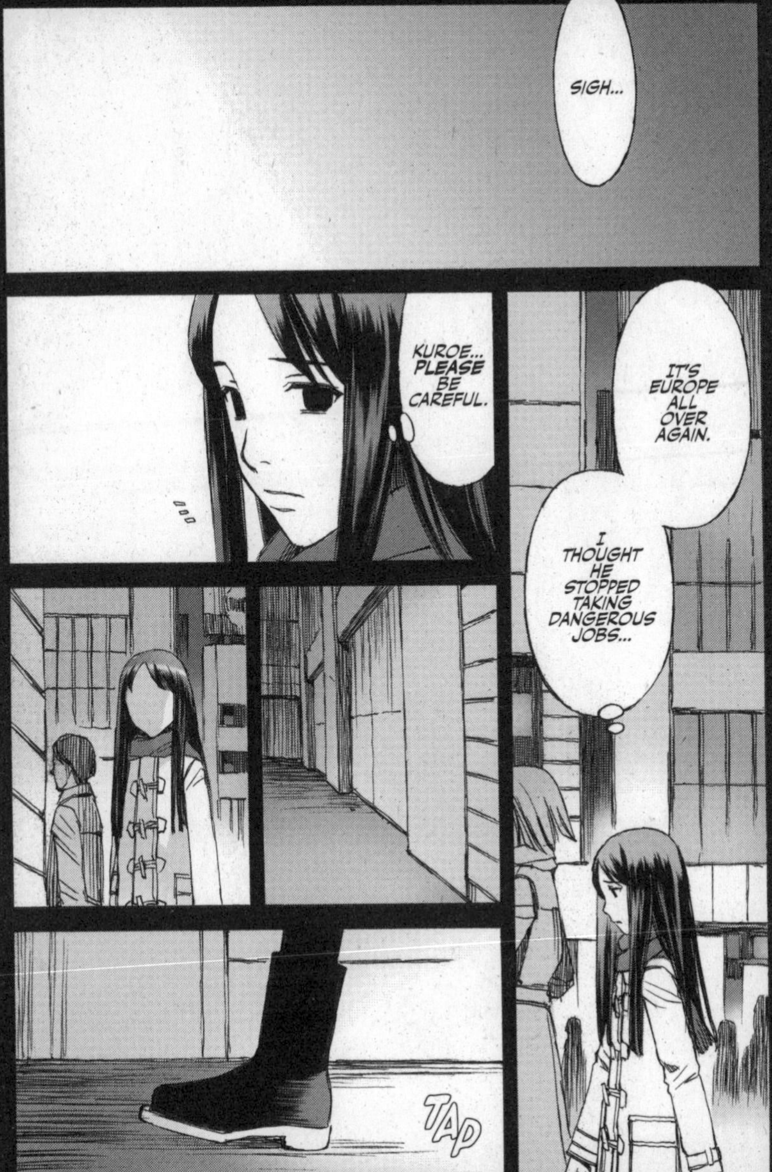
SIGH...
IT'S EUROPE ALL OVER AGAIN.
I THOUGHT HE STOPPED TAKING DANGEROUS JOBS...
KUROE... PLEASE BE CAREFUL.
TAP

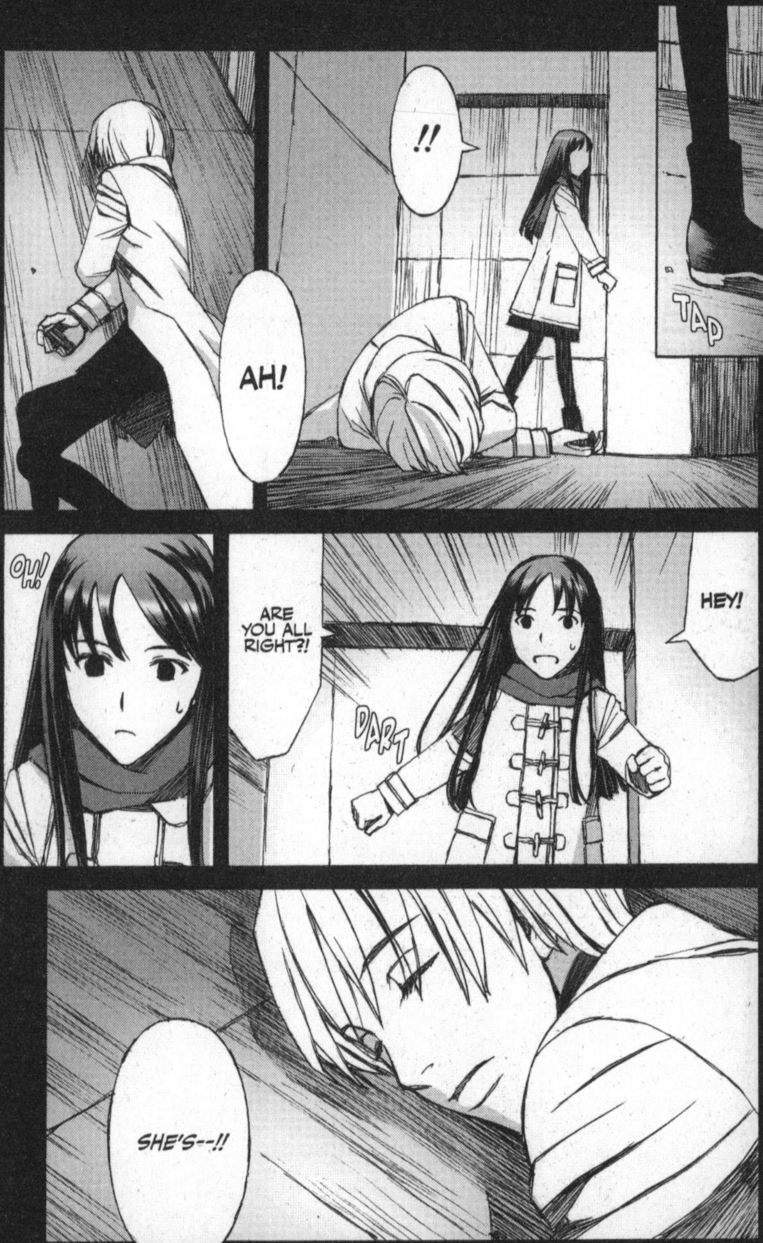
TAP
!!
AH!
HEY!
ARE YOU ALL RIGHT?!
DART
OH!
SHE'S--!!

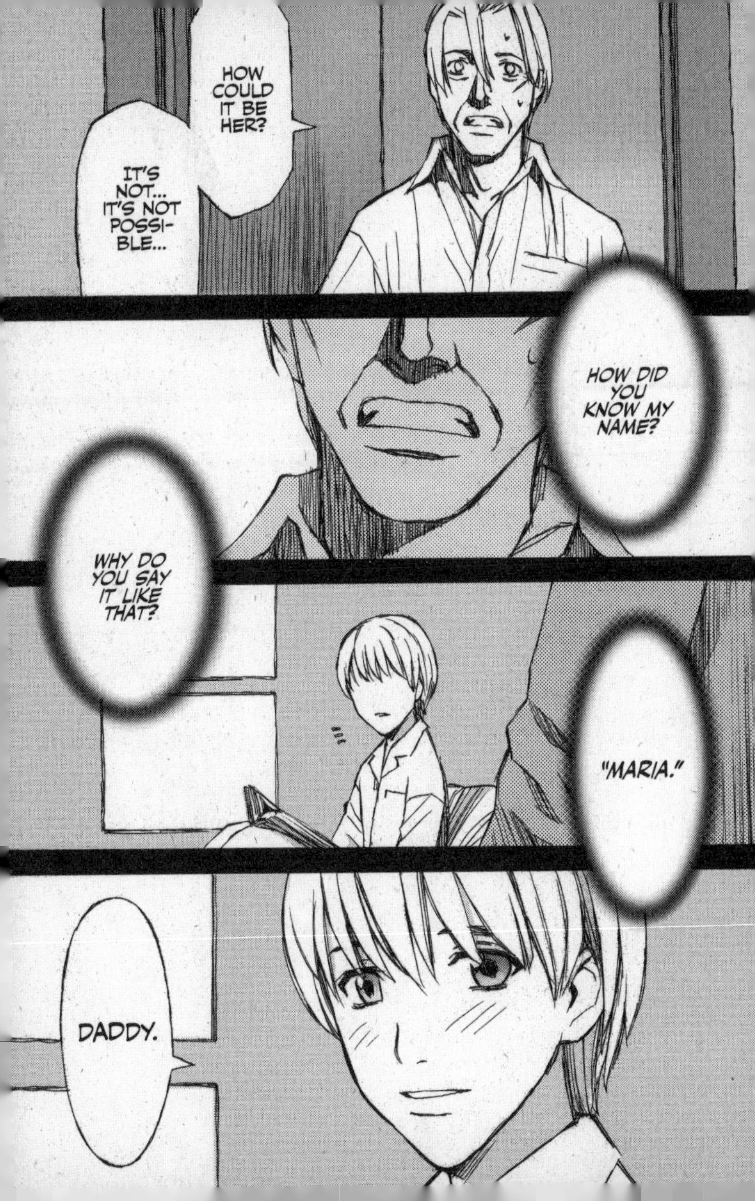
HOW COULD IT BE HER?
IT'S NOT... IT'S NOT POSSIBLE...
HOW DID YOU KNOW MY NAME?
WHY DO YOU SAY IT LIKE THAT?
"MARIA."
DADDY.

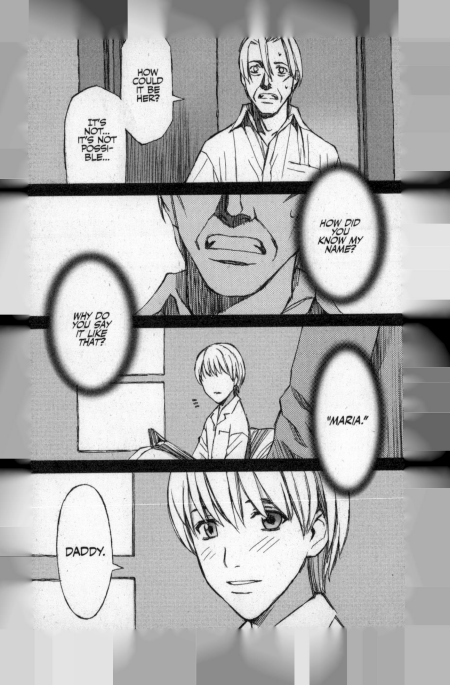

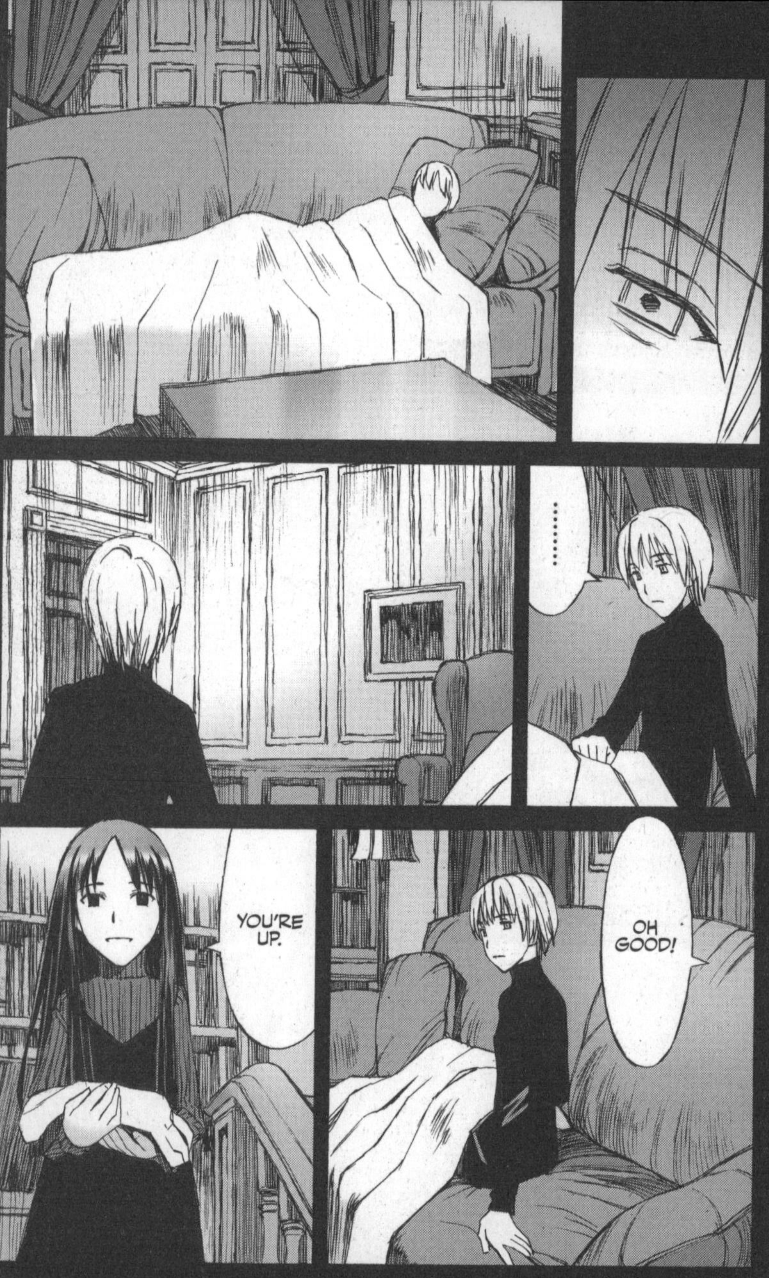
……
OH GOOD!
YOU'RE UP.

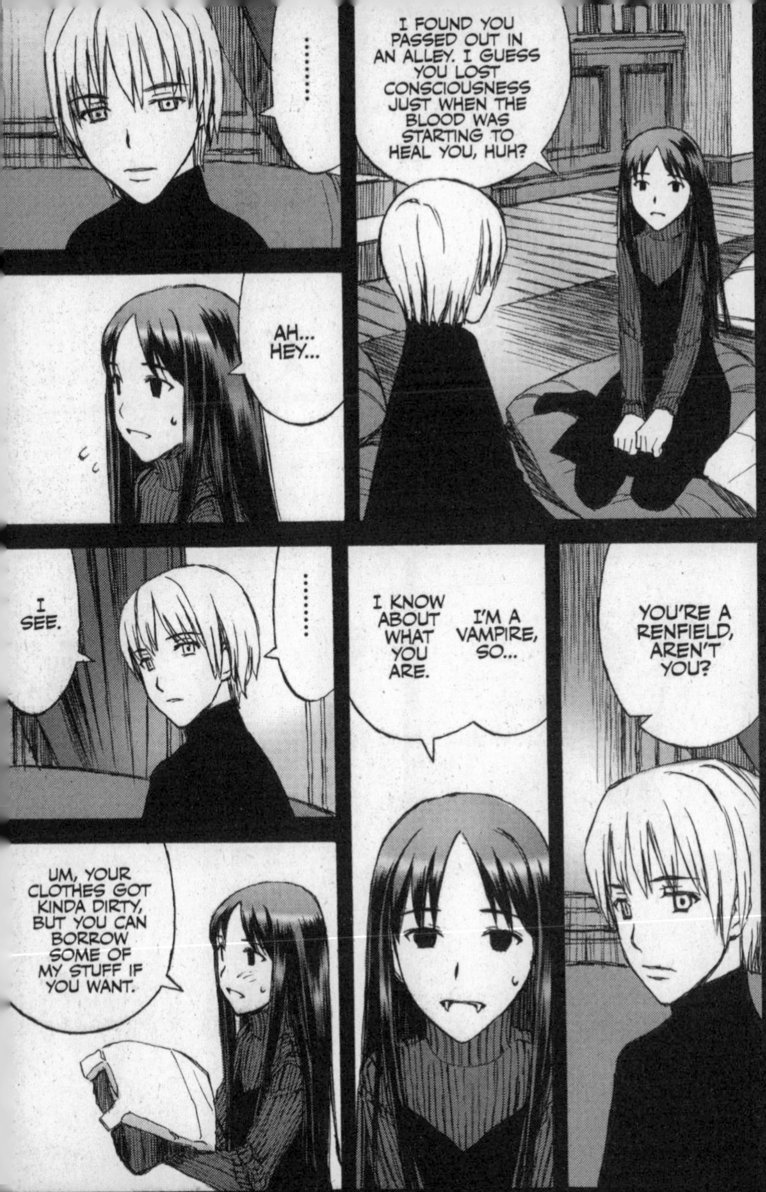
I FOUND YOU PASSED OUT IN AN ALLEY. I GUESS YOU LOST CONSCIOUSNESS JUST WHEN THE BLOOD WAS STARTING TO HEAL YOU, HUH?
......
AH... HEY...
YOU'RE A RENFIELD, AREN'T YOU?
I'M A VAMPIRE, SO...
I KNOW ABOUT WHAT YOU ARE.
......
I SEE.
UM, YOUR CLOTHES GOT KINDA DIRTY, BUT YOU CAN BORROW SOME OF MY STUFF IF YOU WANT.

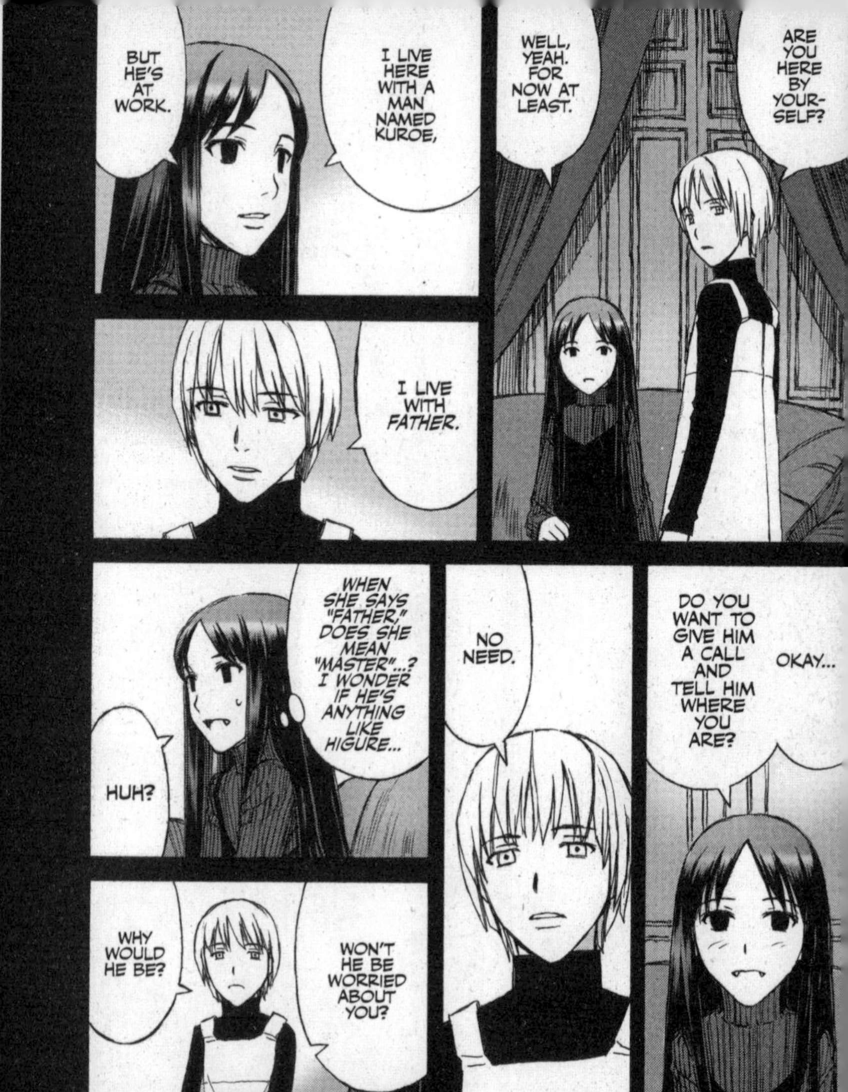
ARE YOU HERE BY YOURSELF?
WELL, YEAH. FOR NOW AT LEAST.
I LIVE HERE WITH A MAN NAMED KUROE,
BUT HE'S AT WORK.
I LIVE WITH *FATHER.*
DO YOU WANT TO GIVE HIM A CALL AND TELL HIM WHERE YOU ARE?
OKAY...
NO NEED.
WHEN SHE SAYS "FATHER," DOES SHE MEAN "MASTER"...? I WONDER IF HE'S ANYTHING LIKE HIGURE...
HUH?
WON'T HE BE WORRIED ABOUT YOU?
WHY WOULD HE BE?

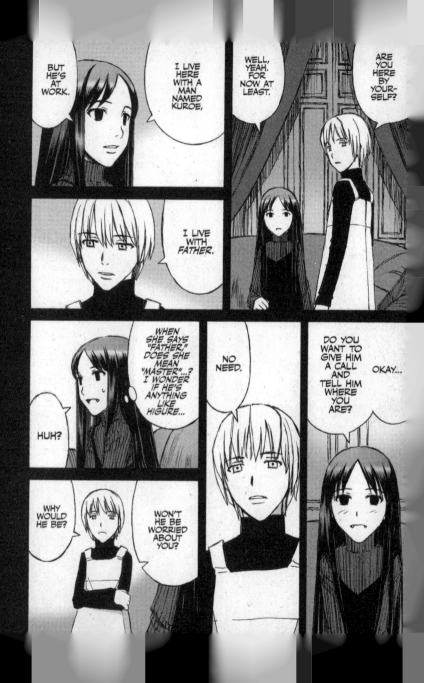

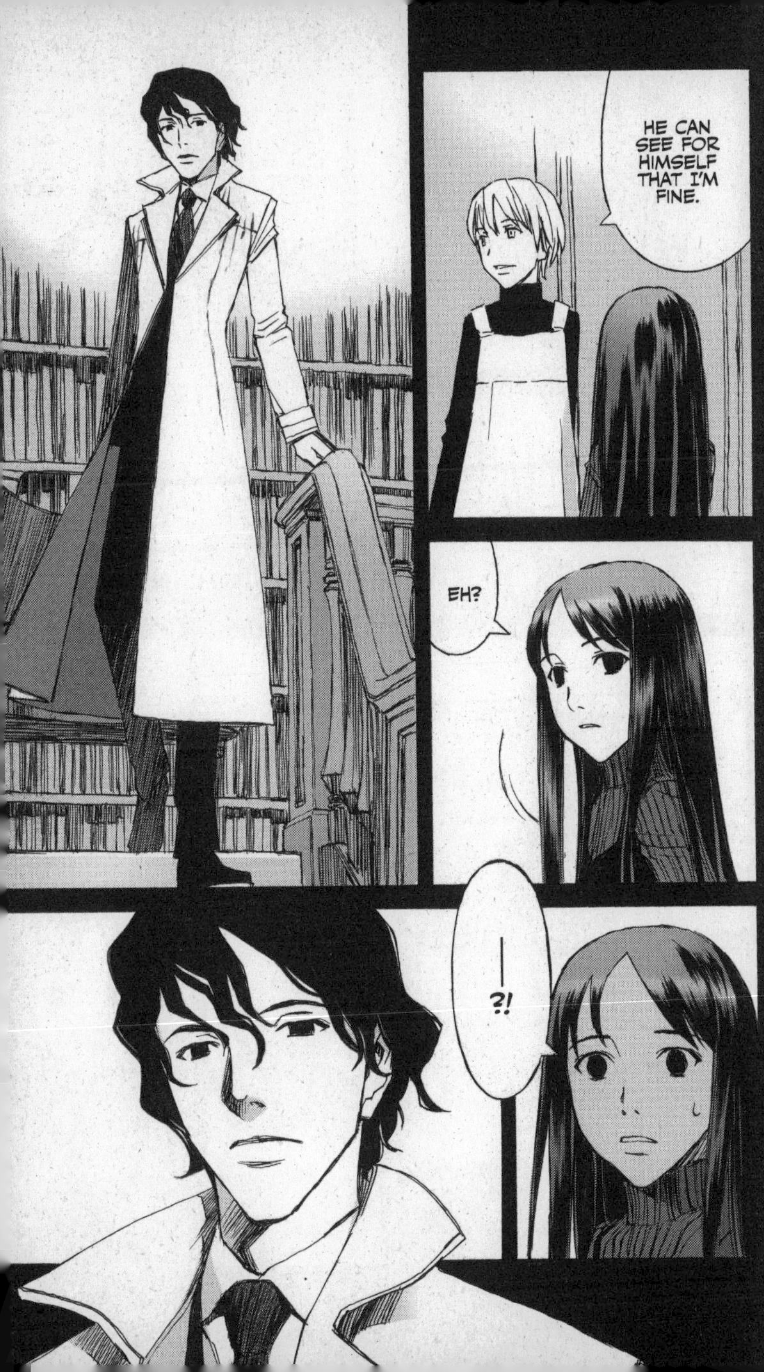
HE CAN SEE FOR HIMSELF THAT I'M FINE.
EH?
—?!

Episode 13

WHY CRY? part 2

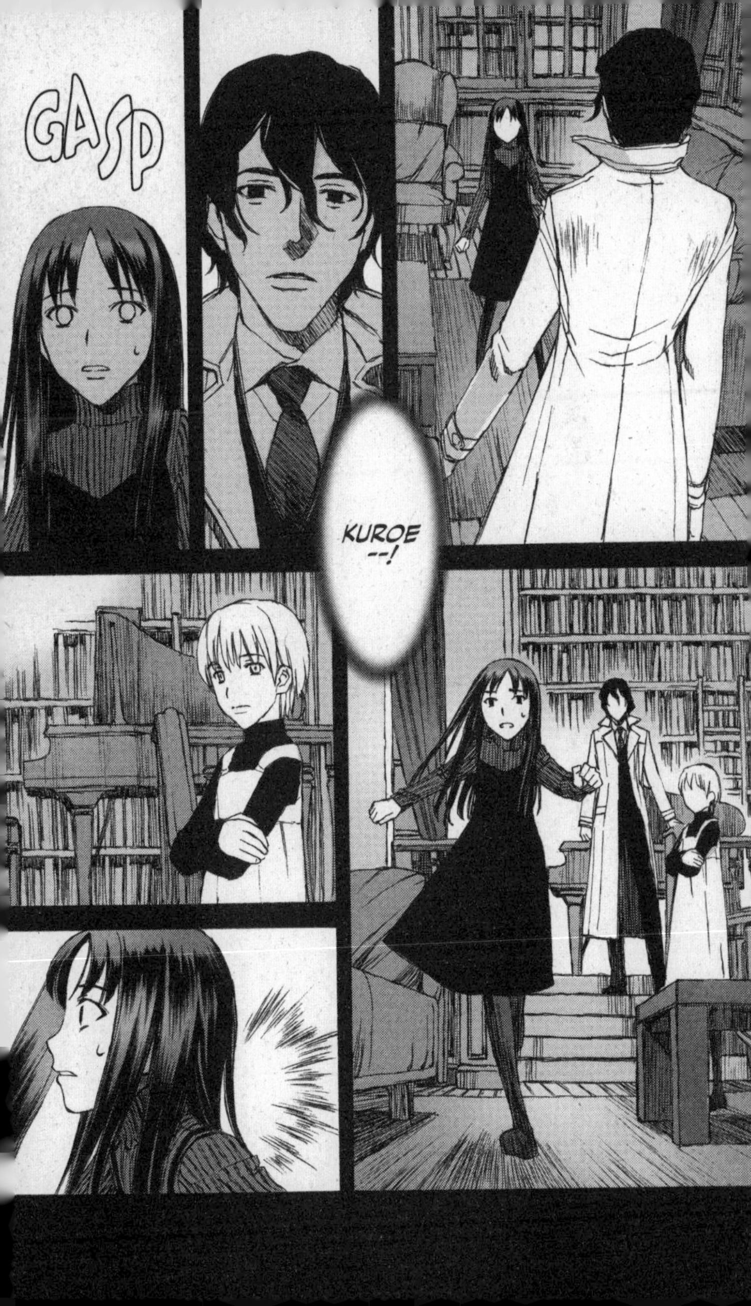
GASP
KUROE --!

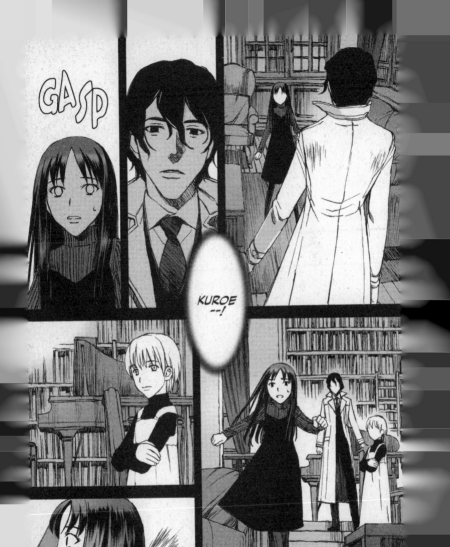

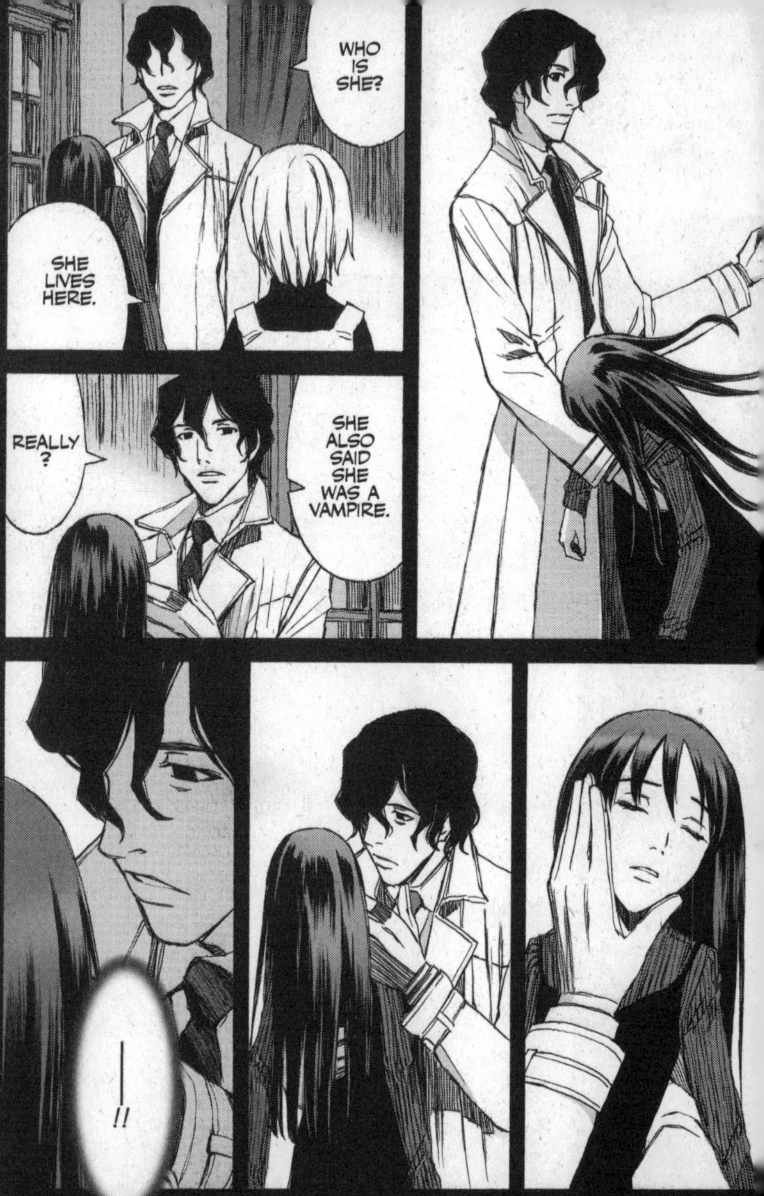
WHO IS SHE?
SHE LIVES HERE.
SHE ALSO SAID SHE WAS A VAMPIRE.
REALLY?
—!!

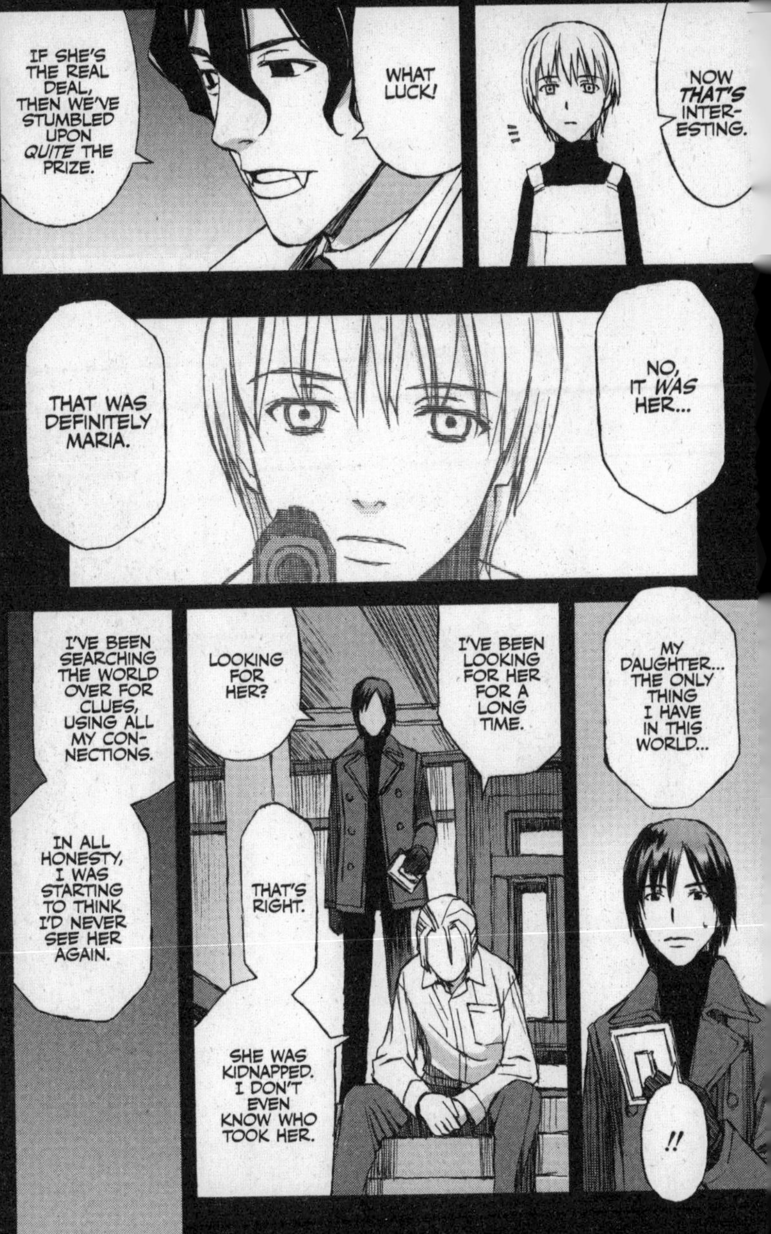

NOW *THAT'S* INTERESTING.
WHAT LUCK!
IF SHE'S THE REAL DEAL, THEN WE'VE STUMBLED UPON *QUITE* THE PRIZE.
NO, IT *WAS* HER...
THAT WAS DEFINITELY MARIA.
MY DAUGHTER... THE ONLY THING I HAVE IN THIS WORLD...
!!
I'VE BEEN LOOKING FOR HER FOR A LONG TIME.
LOOKING FOR HER?
THAT'S RIGHT.
SHE WAS KIDNAPPED. I DON'T EVEN KNOW WHO TOOK HER.
I'VE BEEN SEARCHING THE WORLD OVER FOR CLUES, USING ALL MY CONNECTIONS.
IN ALL HONESTY, I WAS STARTING TO THINK I'D NEVER SEE HER AGAIN.

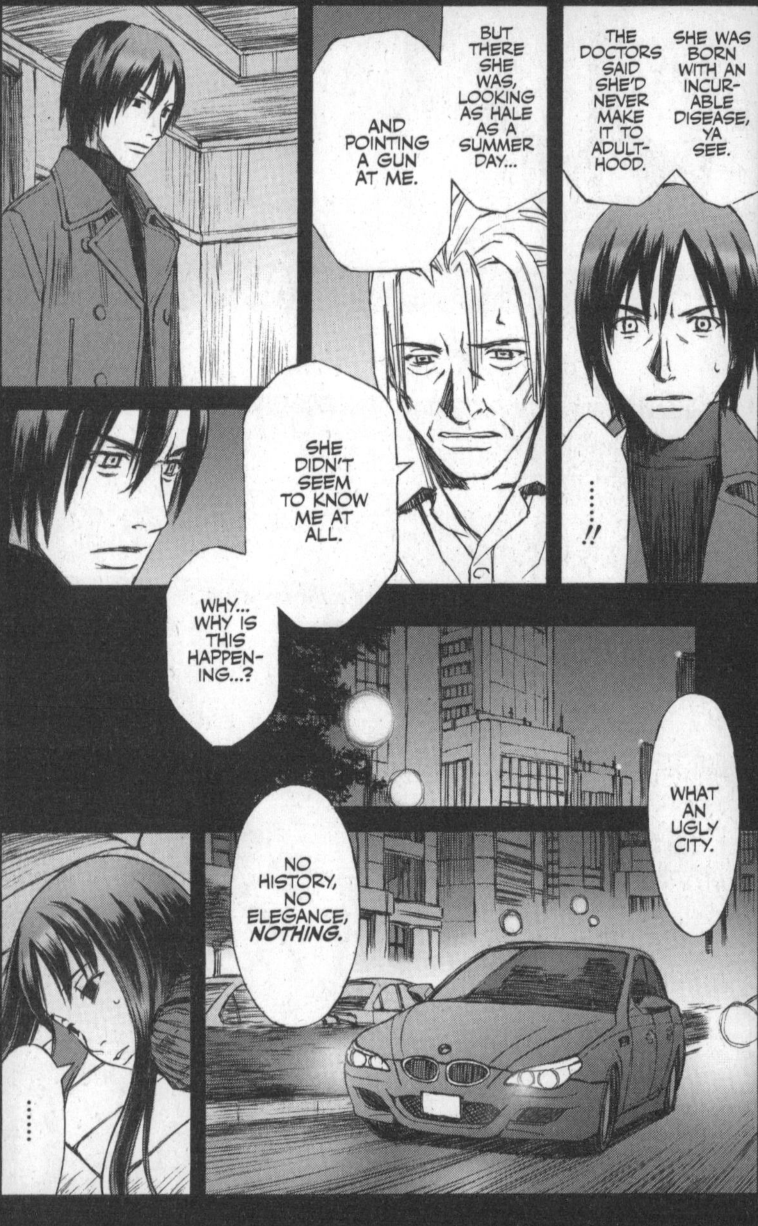
SHE WAS BORN WITH AN INCURABLE DISEASE, YA SEE.
THE DOCTORS SAID SHE'D NEVER MAKE IT TO ADULTHOOD.
......!!
BUT THERE SHE WAS, LOOKING AS HALE AS A SUMMER DAY...
AND POINTING A GUN AT ME.
SHE DIDN'T SEEM TO KNOW ME AT ALL.
WHY... WHY IS THIS HAPPENING...?
WHAT AN UGLY CITY.
NO HISTORY, NO ELEGANCE, *NOTHING.*
......

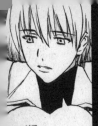

LET'S FINISH THIS SO WE CAN GET OUT OF HERE.
!!
......
THAT MAN...
HE ACTED LIKE HE KNEW ME.
HOW COULD HE?
HE MUST HAVE THOUGHT YOU WERE SOMEONE ELSE.
THAT'S RIGHT, I GOT CAPTURED BY THIS VAMPIRE...
YOU'RE RIGHT. I'M SO SORRY I DIDN'T COMPLETE MY MISSION.
BUT NEXT TIME...
I WILL KILL HIM.

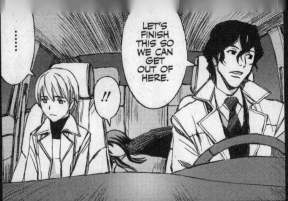

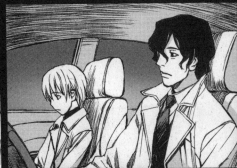

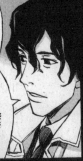

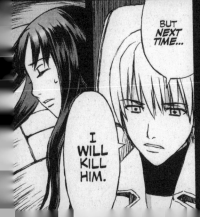

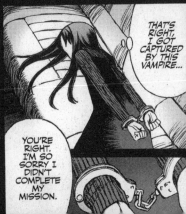

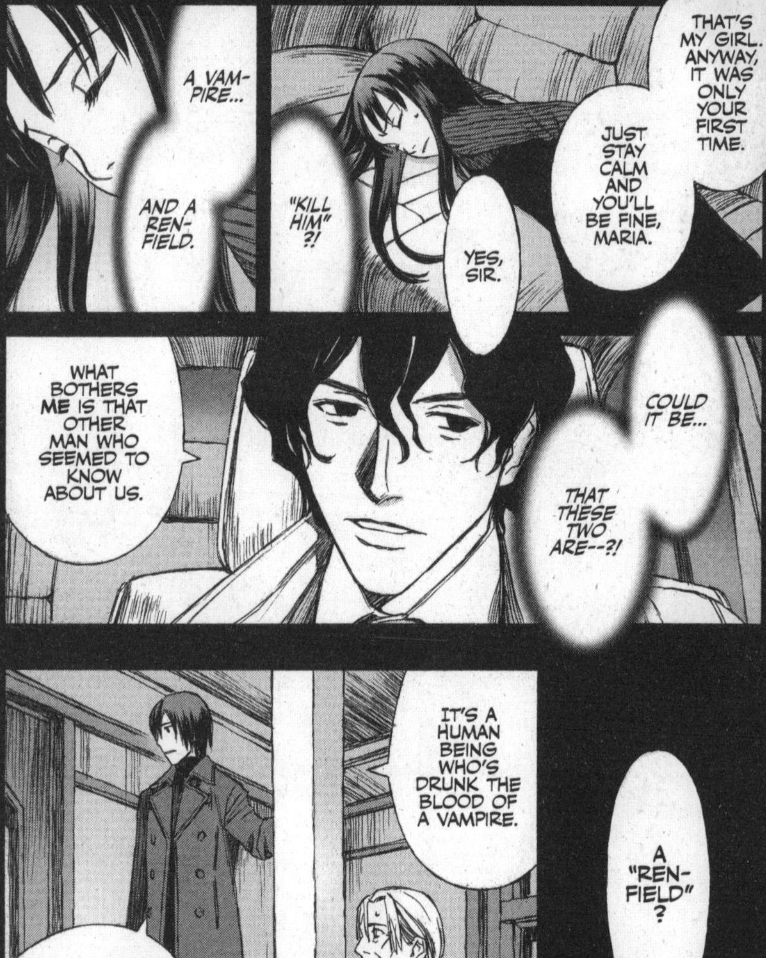
THAT'S MY GIRL. ANYWAY, IT WAS ONLY YOUR FIRST TIME.
JUST STAY CALM AND YOU'LL BE FINE, MARIA.
YES, SIR.
"KILL HIM"?!
A VAMPIRE...
AND A RENFIELD.
COULD IT BE...
THAT THESE TWO ARE--?!
WHAT BOTHERS ME IS THAT OTHER MAN WHO SEEMED TO KNOW ABOUT US.
A "RENFIELD"?
IT'S A HUMAN BEING WHO'S DRUNK THE BLOOD OF A VAMPIRE.
IN EXCHANGE FOR LIMITED IMMORTALITY AND CERTAIN VAMPIRIC ABILITIES, THEY BIND THEIR SOULS TO A VAMPIRE.

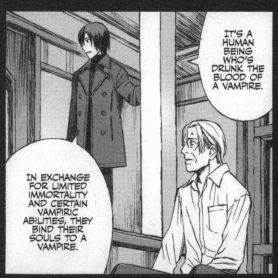

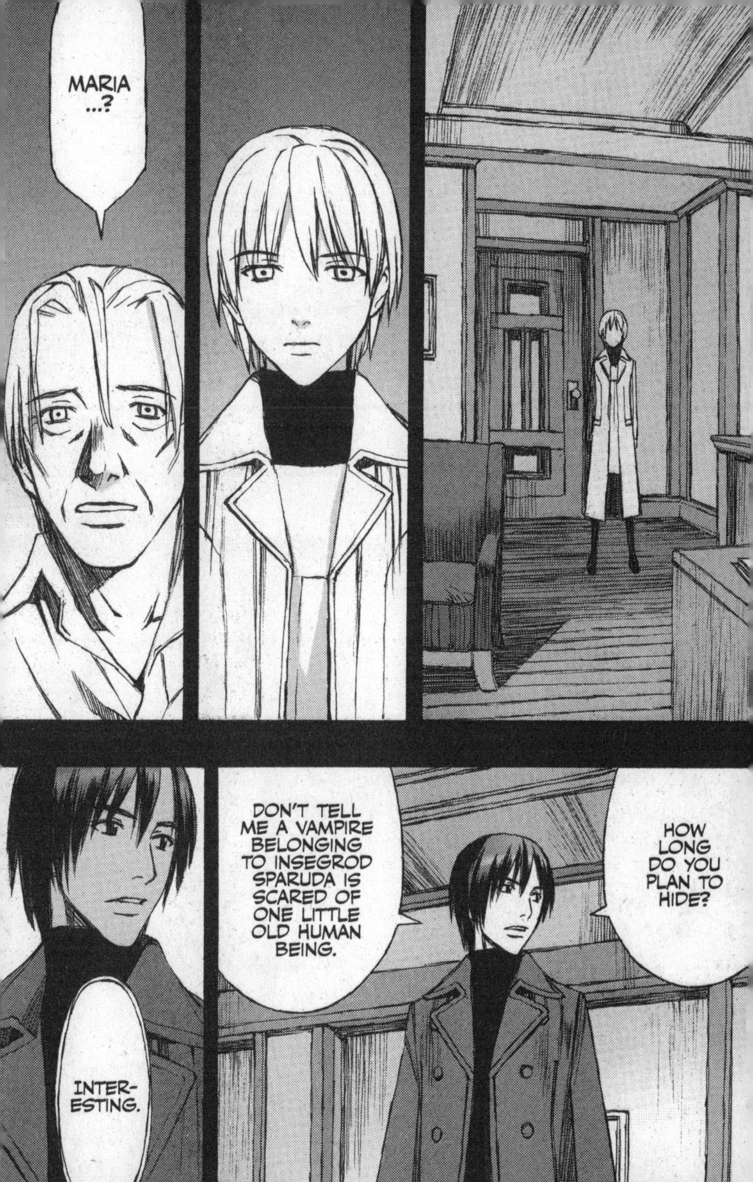
MARIA ...?
HOW LONG DO YOU PLAN TO HIDE?
DON'T TELL ME A VAMPIRE BELONGING TO INSEGROD SPARUDA IS SCARED OF ONE LITTLE OLD HUMAN BEING.
INTER-ESTING.

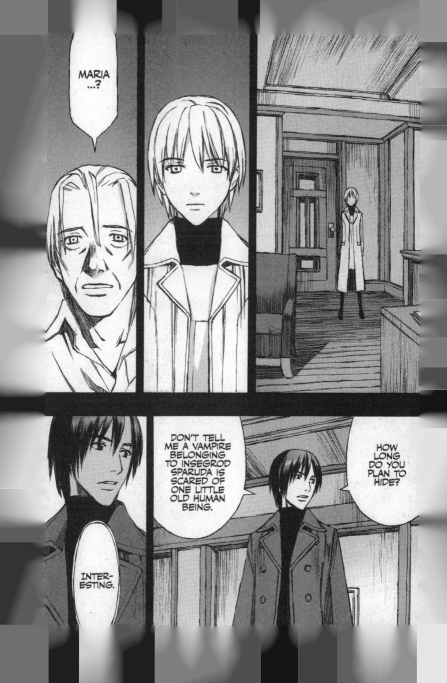

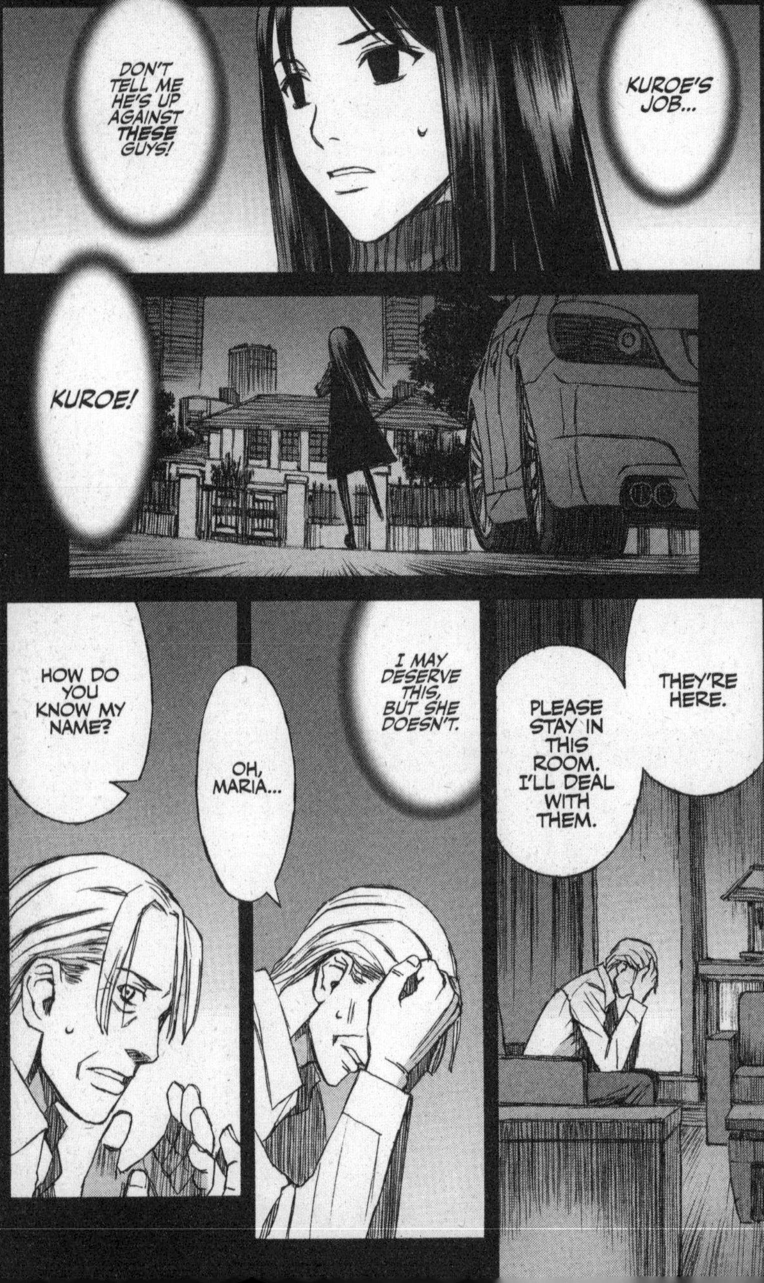
KUROE'S JOB...
DON'T TELL ME HE'S UP AGAINST THESE GUYS!
KUROE!
THEY'RE HERE.
PLEASE STAY IN THIS ROOM. I'LL DEAL WITH THEM.
I MAY DESERVE THIS, BUT SHE DOESN'T.
OH, MARIA...
HOW DO YOU KNOW MY NAME?

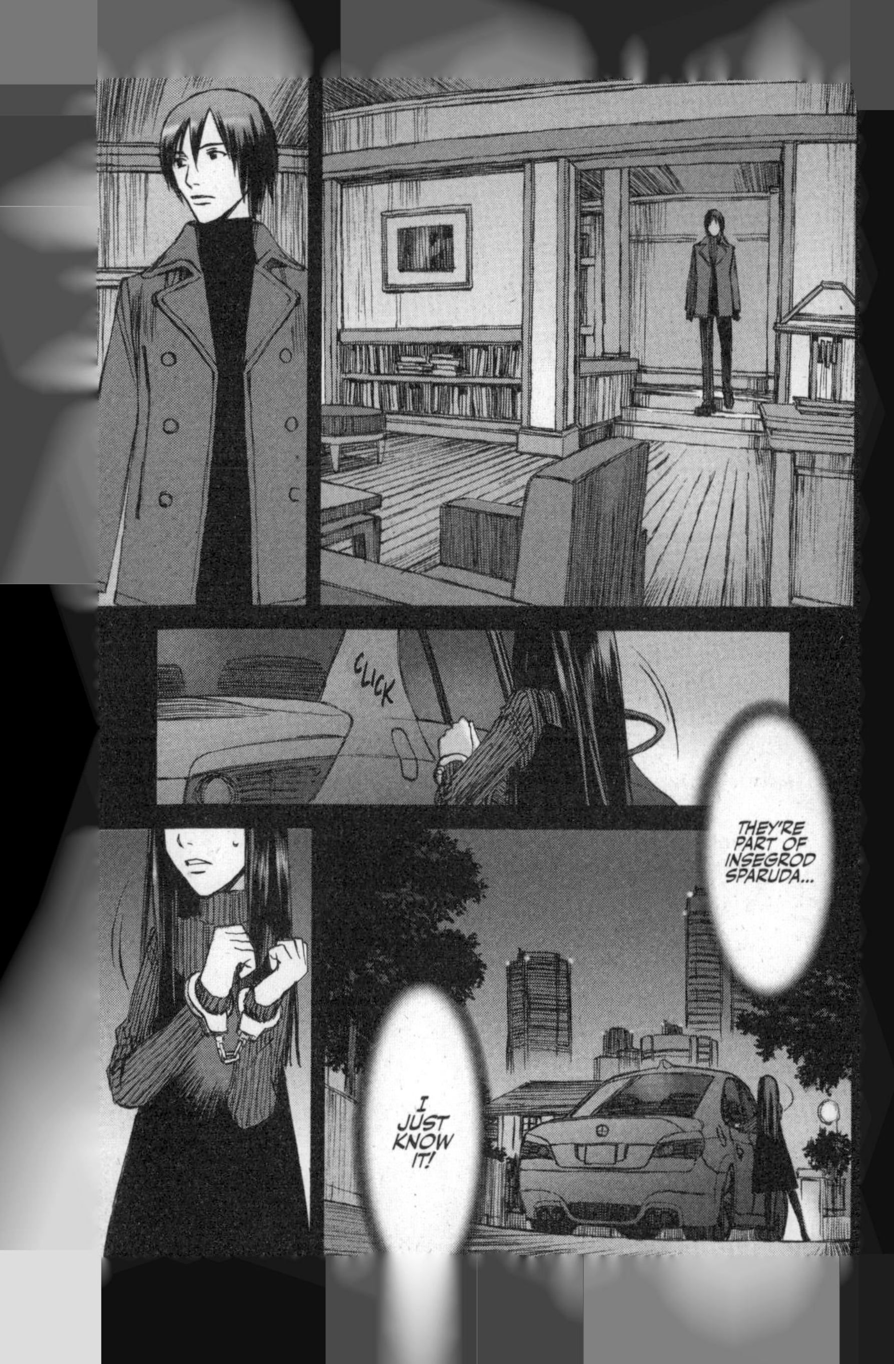
CLICK
THEY'RE PART OF INSEGROD SPARUDA...
I JUST KNOW IT!

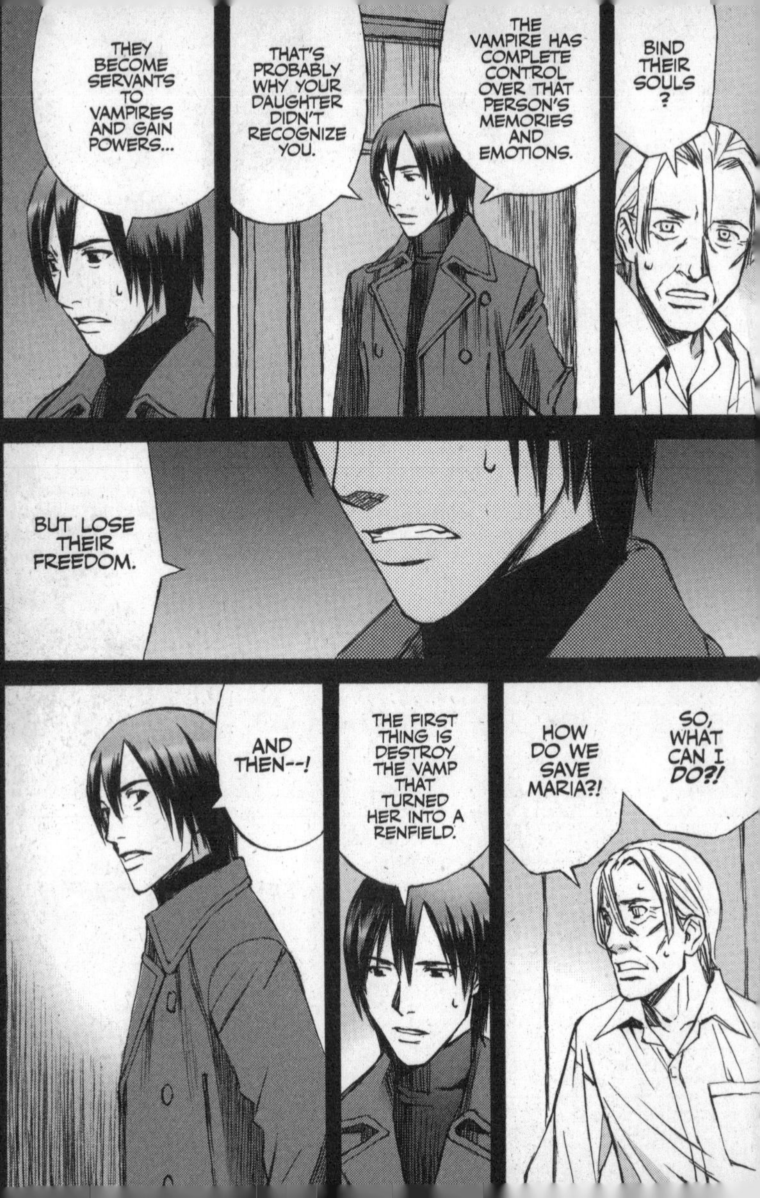
BIND THEIR SOULS?
THE VAMPIRE HAS COMPLETE CONTROL OVER THAT PERSON'S MEMORIES AND EMOTIONS.
THAT'S PROBABLY WHY YOUR DAUGHTER DIDN'T RECOGNIZE YOU.
THEY BECOME SERVANTS TO VAMPIRES AND GAIN POWERS...
BUT LOSE THEIR FREEDOM.
SO, WHAT CAN I *DO?!*
HOW DO WE SAVE MARIA?!
THE FIRST THING IS DESTROY THE VAMP THAT TURNED HER INTO A RENFIELD.
AND THEN--!

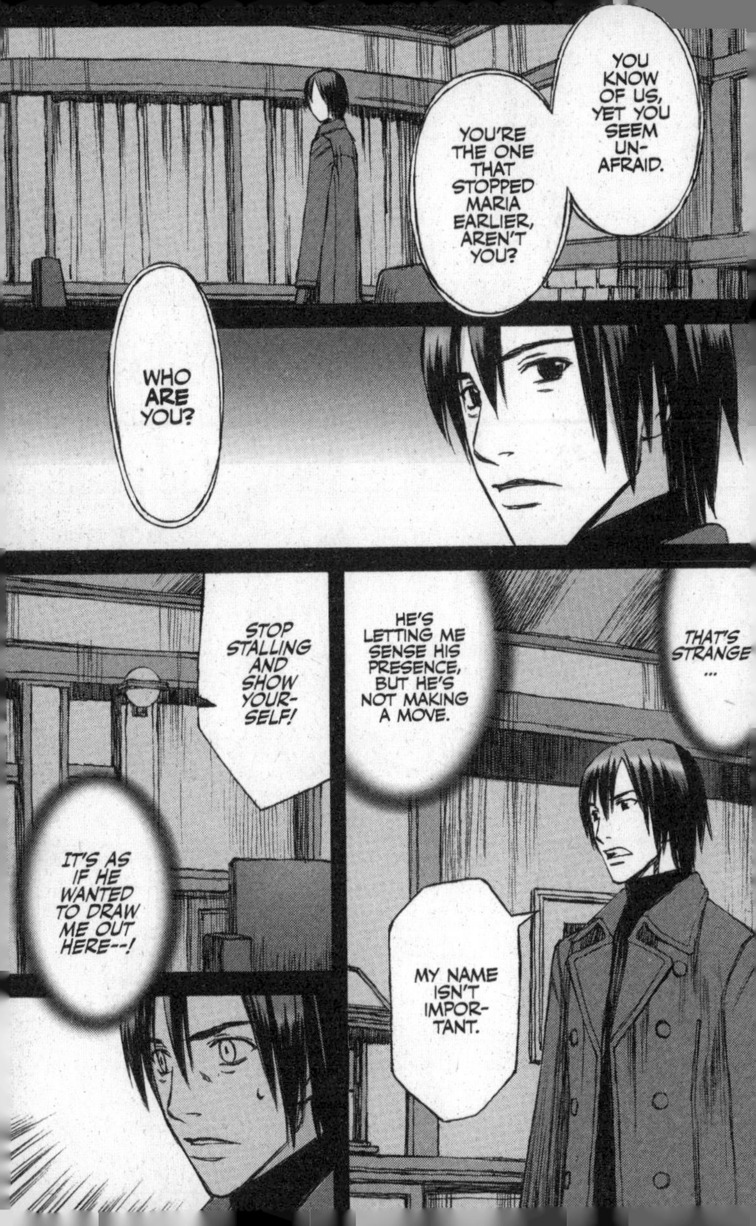
YOU KNOW OF US, YET YOU SEEM UN-AFRAID.
YOU'RE THE ONE THAT STOPPED MARIA EARLIER, AREN'T YOU?
WHO ARE YOU?
THAT'S STRANGE...
HE'S LETTING ME SENSE HIS PRESENCE, BUT HE'S NOT MAKING A MOVE.
MY NAME ISN'T IMPORTANT.
STOP STALLING AND SHOW YOUR-SELF!
IT'S AS IF HE WANTED TO DRAW ME OUT HERE--!

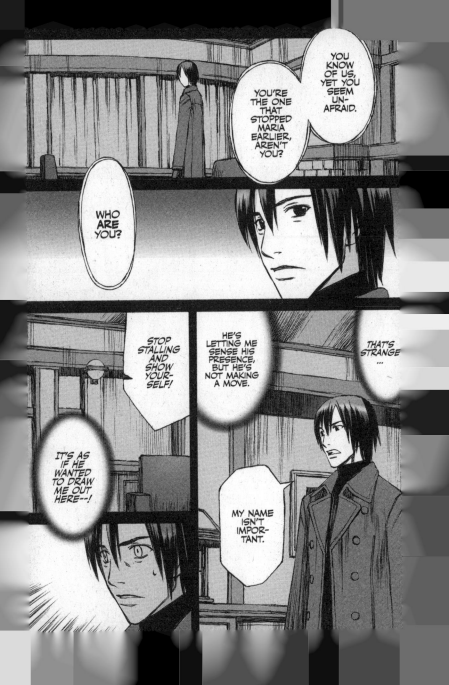

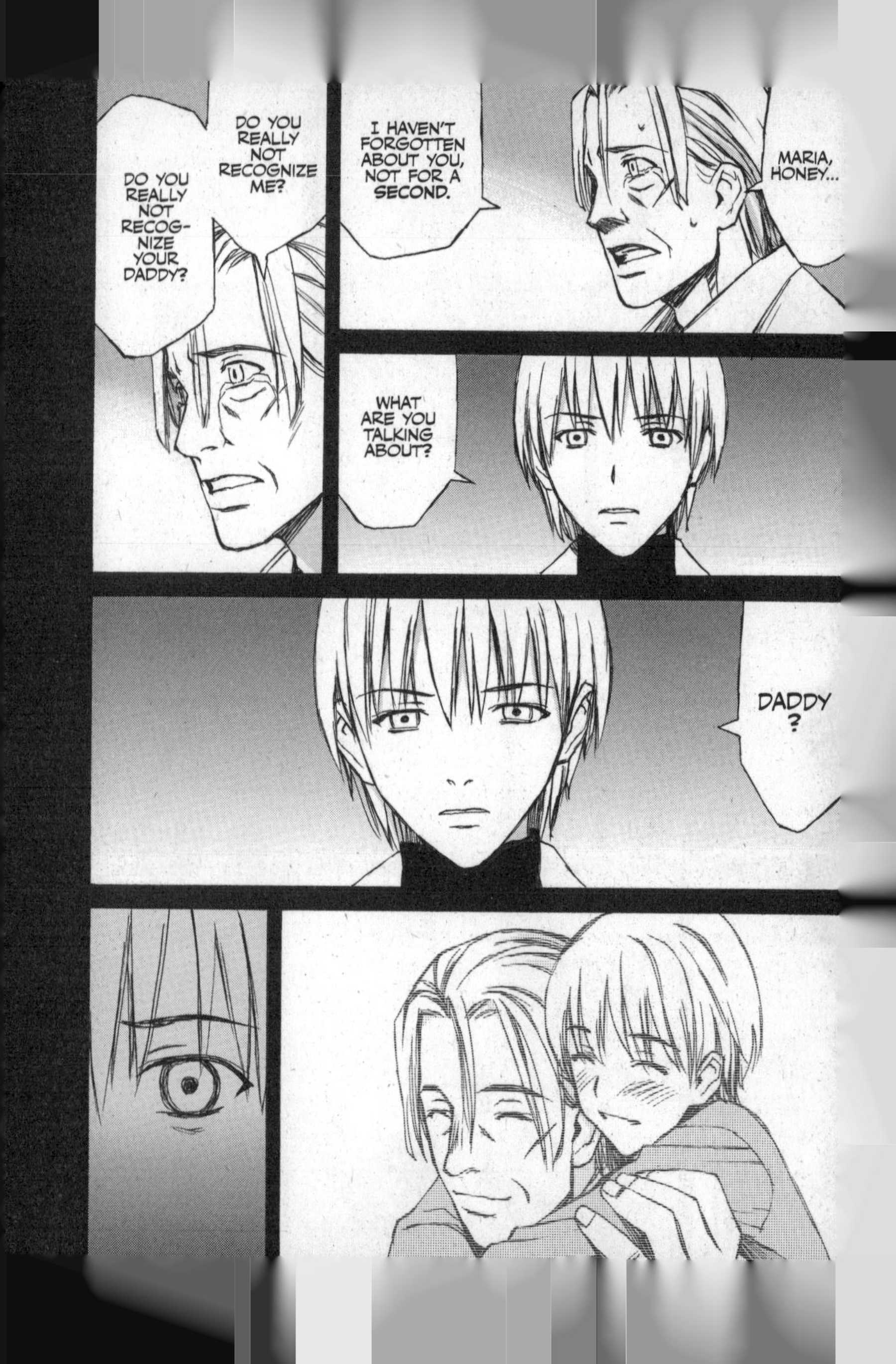
MARIA, HONEY...
I HAVEN'T FORGOTTEN ABOUT YOU, NOT FOR A SECOND.
WHAT ARE YOU TALKING ABOUT?
DO YOU REALLY NOT RECOGNIZE ME?
DO YOU REALLY NOT RECOG-NIZE YOUR DADDY?
DADDY?

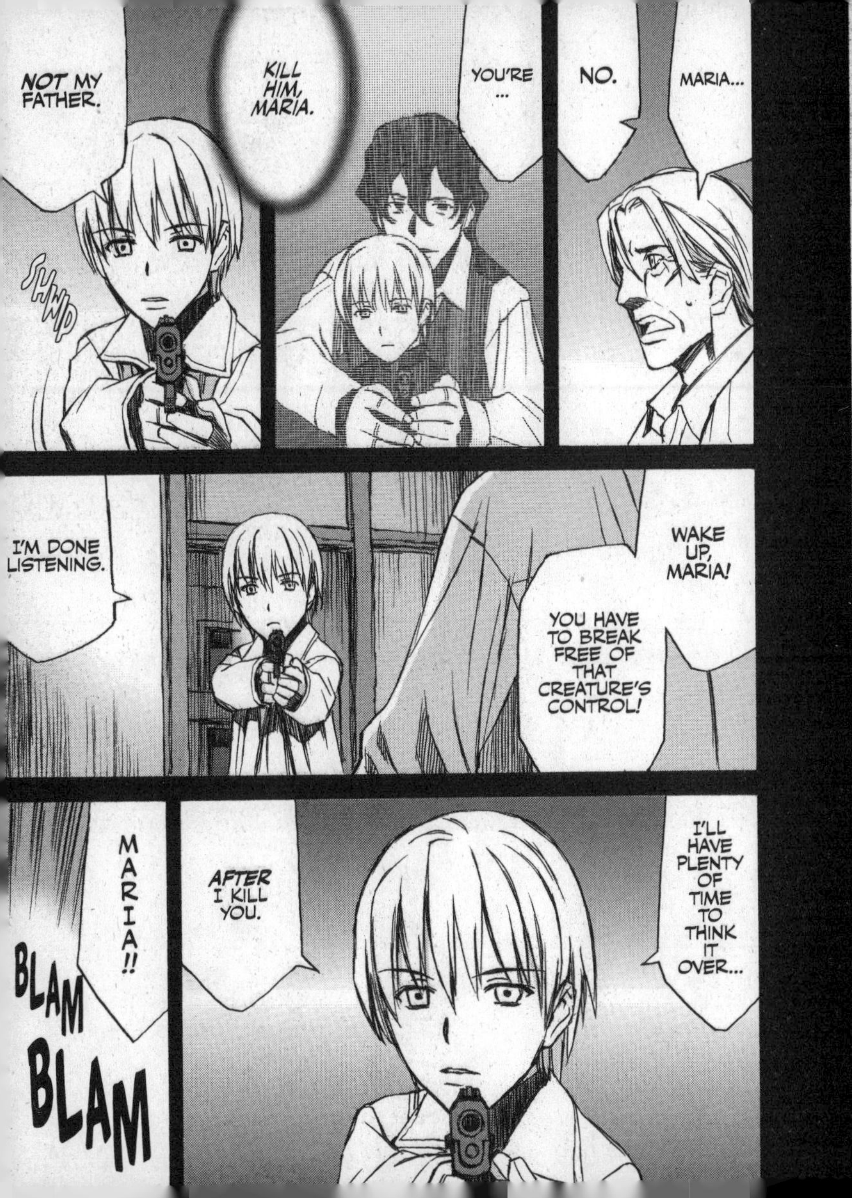
MARIA...
NO.
YOU'RE ...
KILL HIM, MARIA.
NOT MY FATHER.
SHWIP
WAKE UP, MARIA!
YOU HAVE TO BREAK FREE OF THAT CREATURE'S CONTROL!
I'M DONE LISTENING.
I'LL HAVE PLENTY OF TIME TO THINK IT OVER...
AFTER I KILL YOU.
MARIA!!
BLAM BLAM

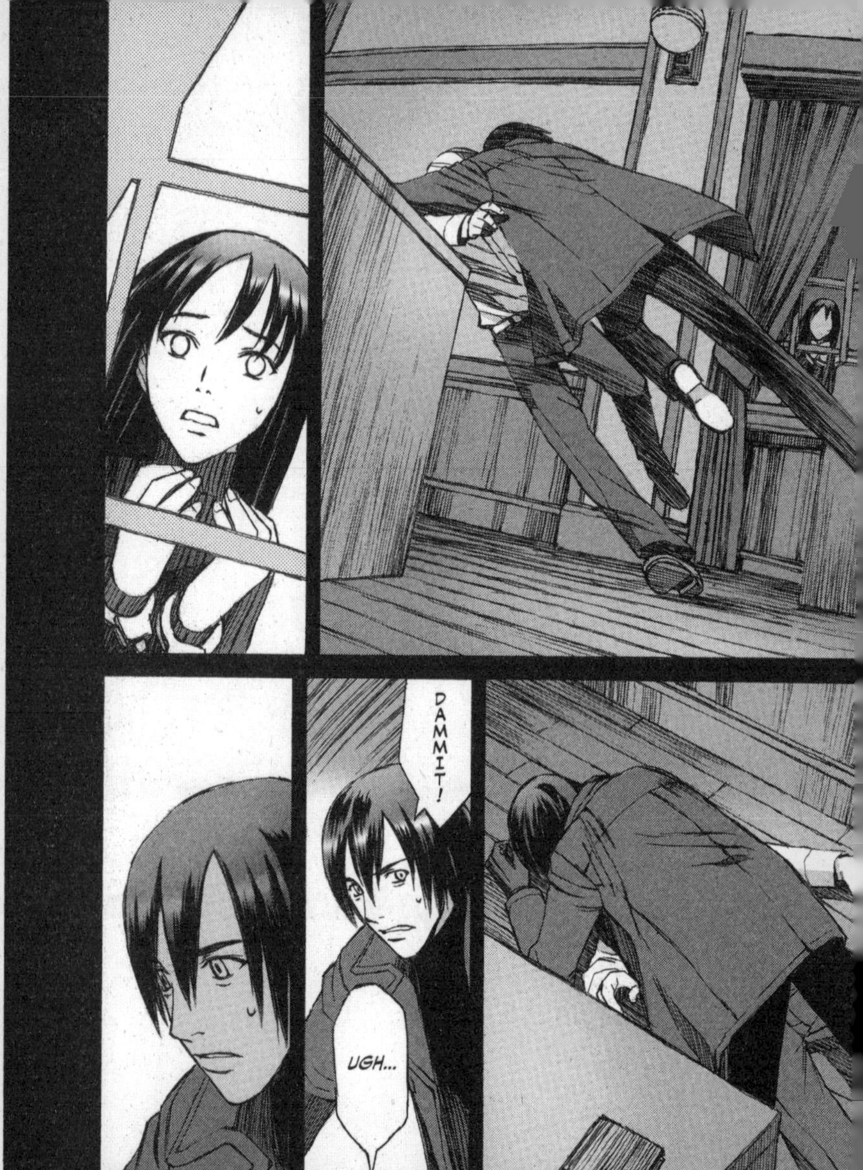
DAMMIT!
UGH...

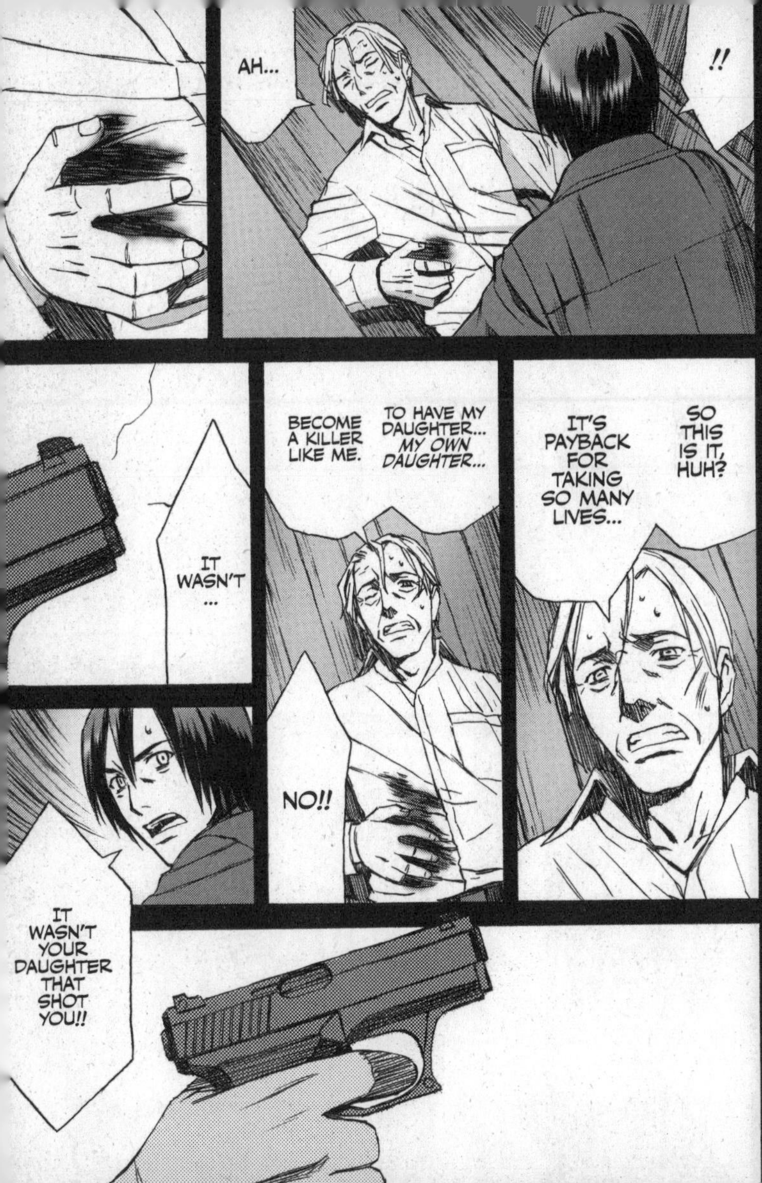
!!
AH...
SO THIS IS IT, HUH?
IT'S PAYBACK FOR TAKING SO MANY LIVES...
TO HAVE MY DAUGHTER... *MY OWN DAUGHTER...*
BECOME A KILLER LIKE ME.
NO!!
IT WASN'T ...
IT WASN'T YOUR DAUGHTER THAT SHOT YOU!!

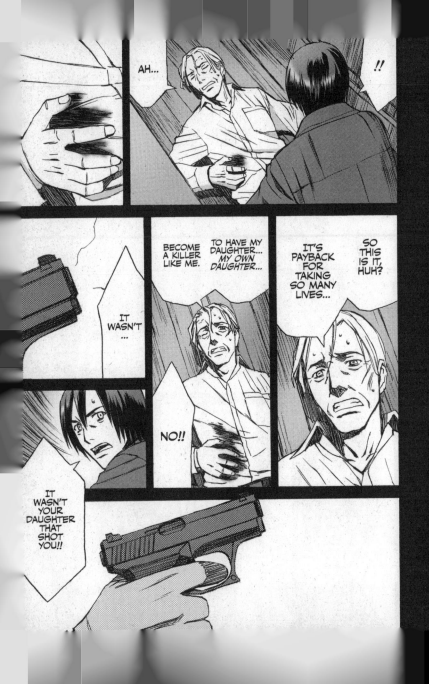

FINISH HIM OFF, MARIA.

AND IF THAT OTHER HUMAN GETS IN THE WAY, KILL HIM AS WELL.

I'LL BE OUTSIDE.

TAp

!!

BLAM

BLAM

YOU BAS-TARD!!

YES, FATHER.

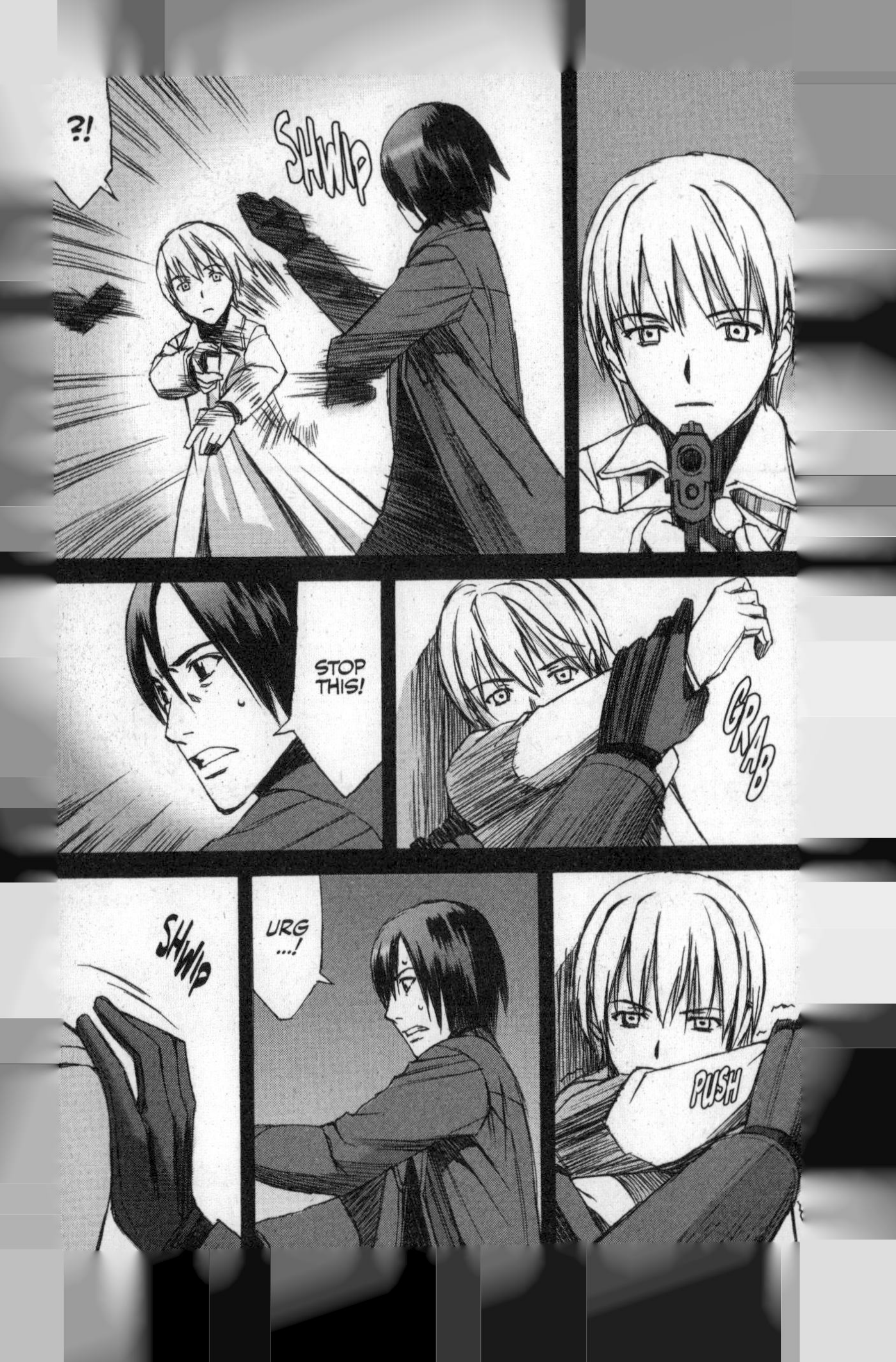
SHWIP
?!
GRAB
STOP THIS!
PUSH
URG ...!
SHWIP

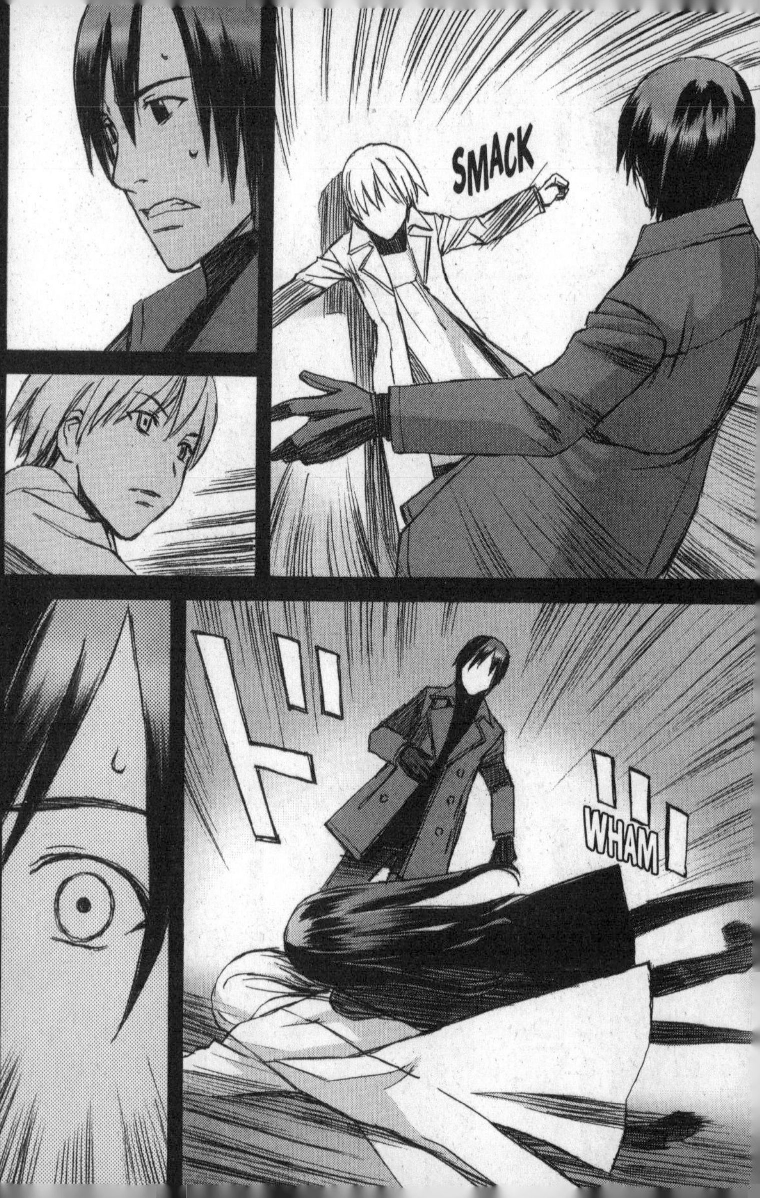
SMACK
ド
WHAM

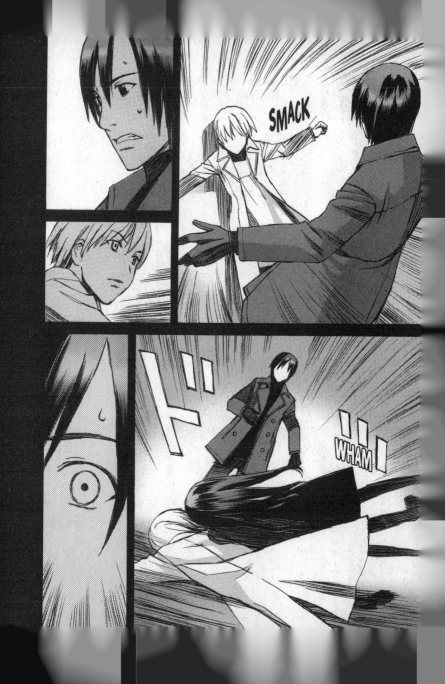

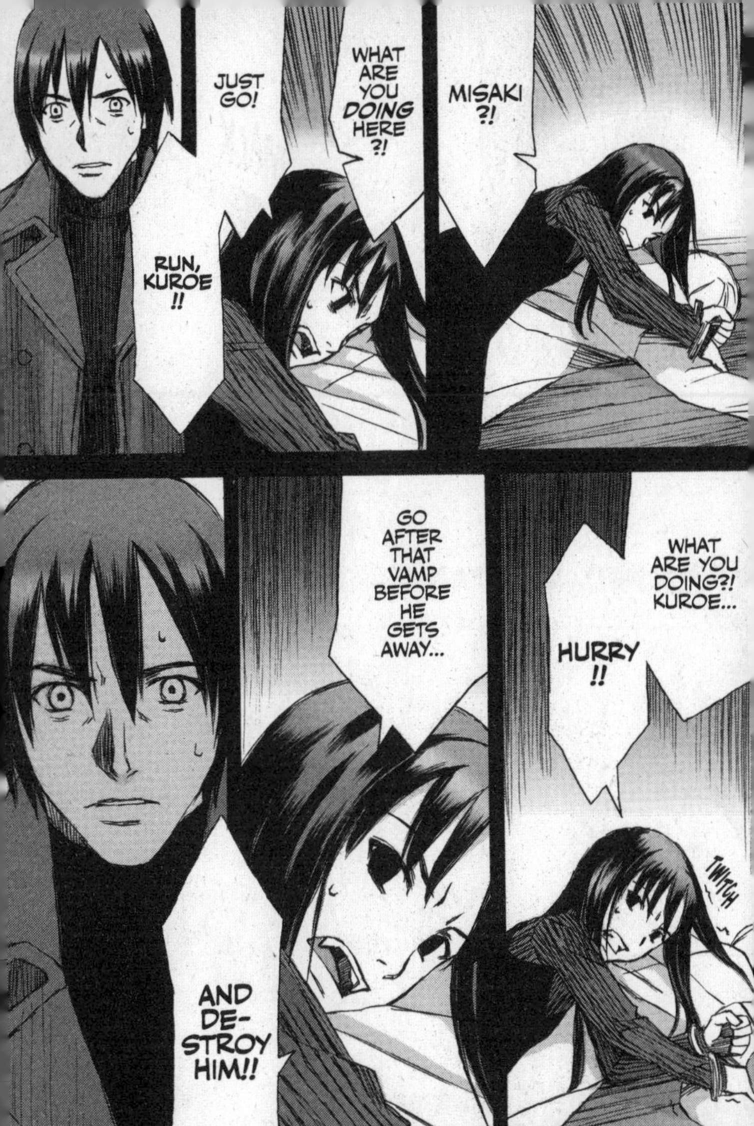
MISAKI?!
WHAT ARE YOU DOING HERE?!
JUST GO!
RUN, KUROE!!
WHAT ARE YOU DOING?! KUROE...
HURRY!!
TWITCH
GO AFTER THAT VAMP BEFORE HE GETS AWAY...
AND DE-STROY HIM!!

Episode 14
WHY CRY? part 3

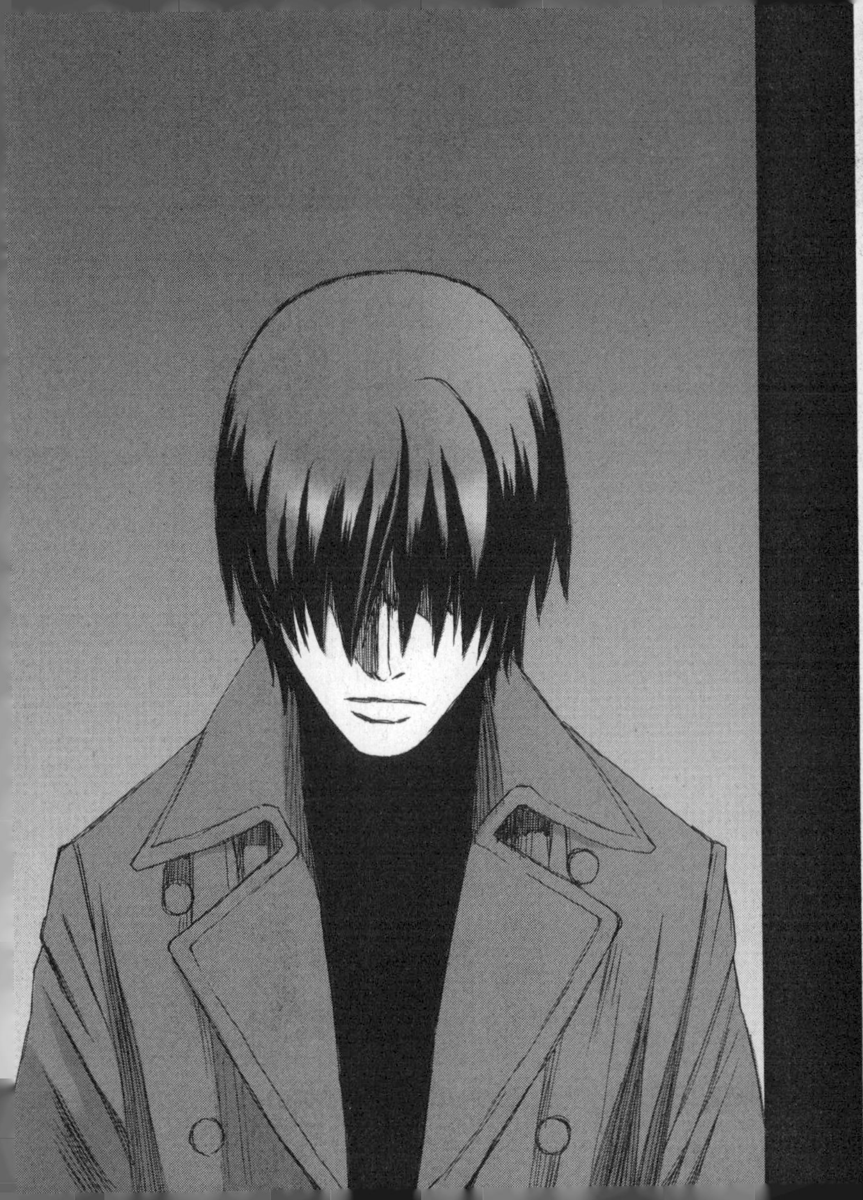

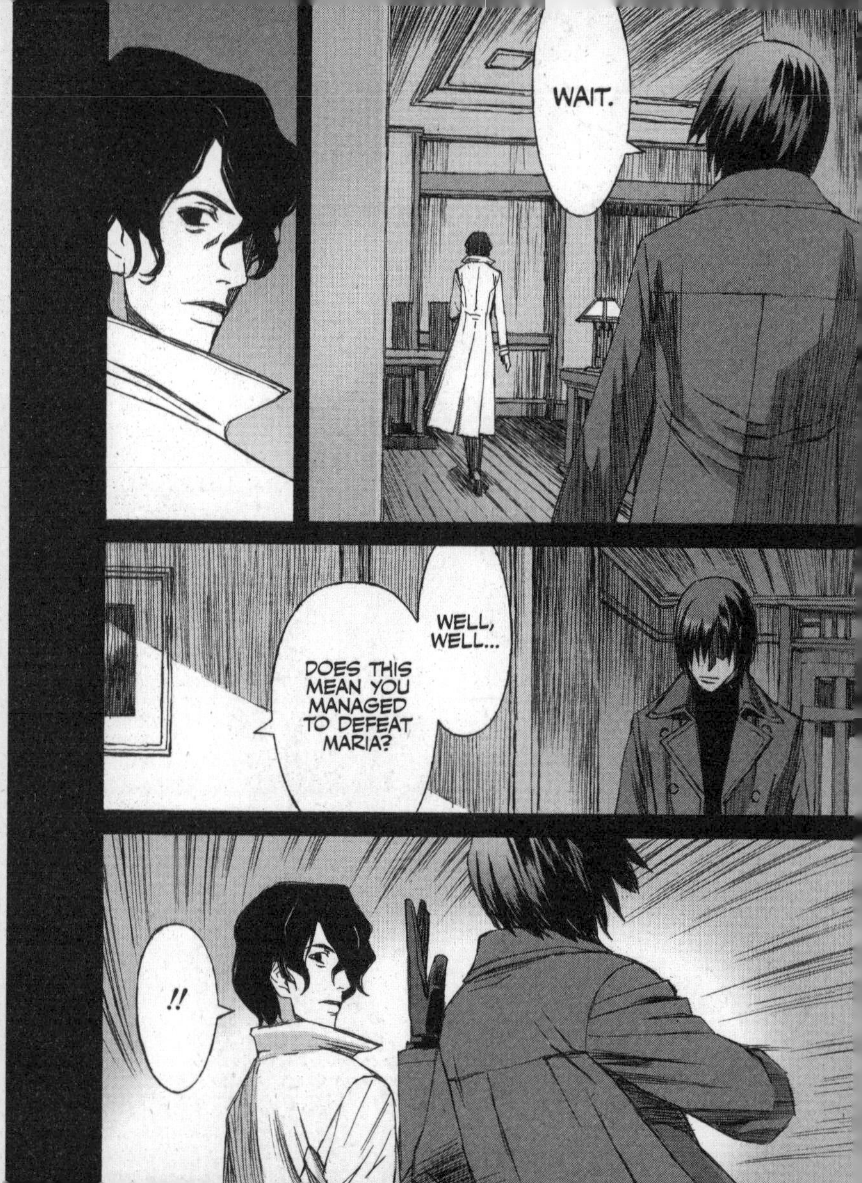
WAIT.
WELL, WELL...
DOES THIS MEAN YOU MANAGED TO DEFEAT MARIA?
!!

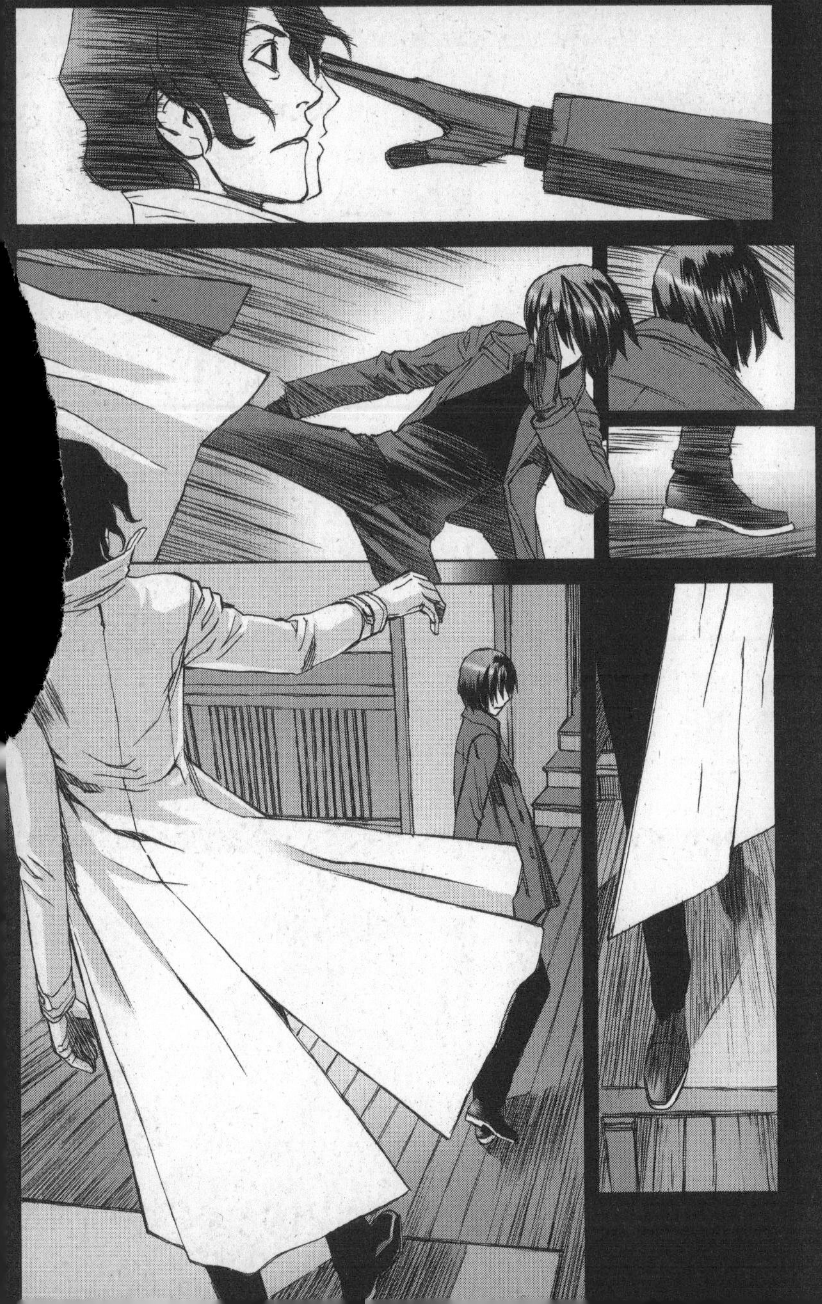

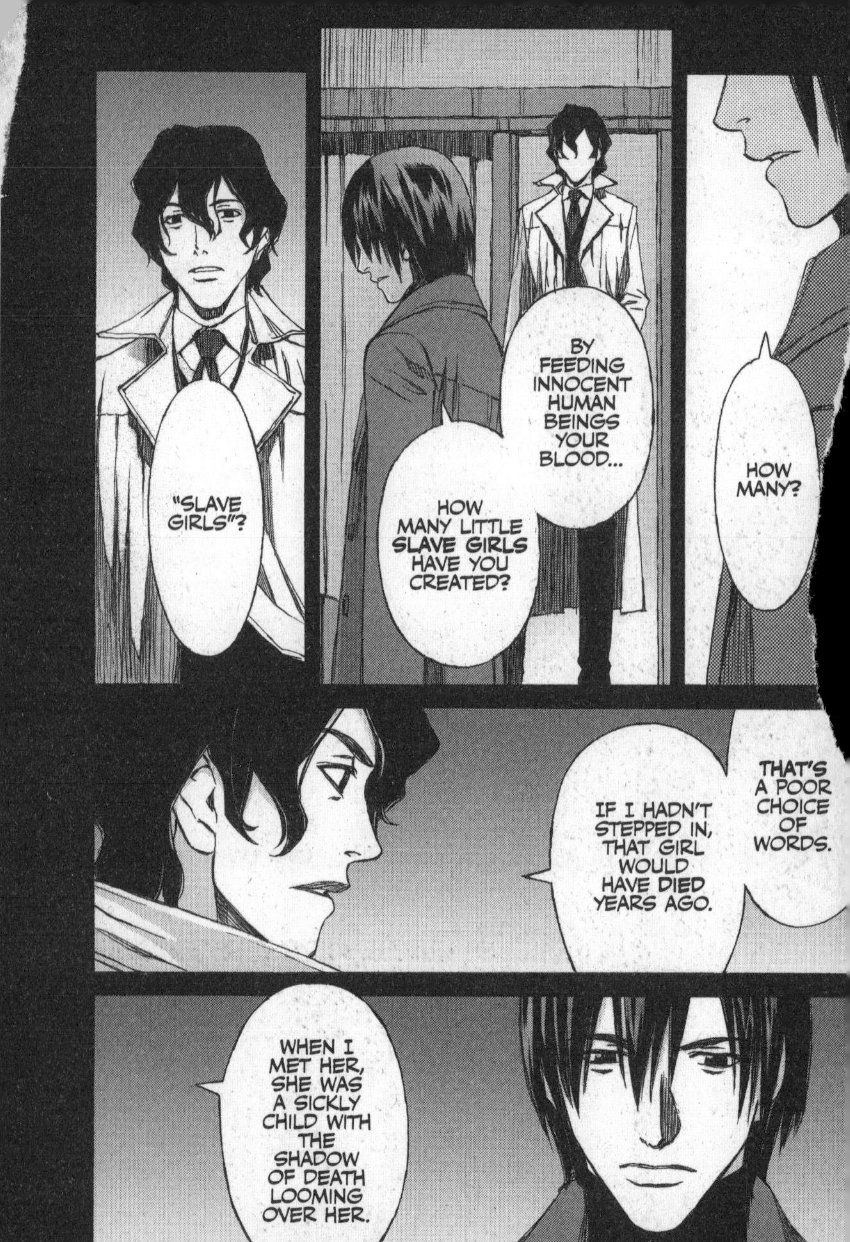
HOW MANY?
BY FEEDING INNOCENT HUMAN BEINGS YOUR BLOOD...
HOW MANY LITTLE SLAVE GIRLS HAVE YOU CREATED?
"SLAVE GIRLS"?
THAT'S A POOR CHOICE OF WORDS.
IF I HADN'T STEPPED IN, THAT GIRL WOULD HAVE DIED YEARS AGO.
WHEN I MET HER, SHE WAS A SICKLY CHILD WITH THE SHADOW OF DEATH LOOMING OVER HER.

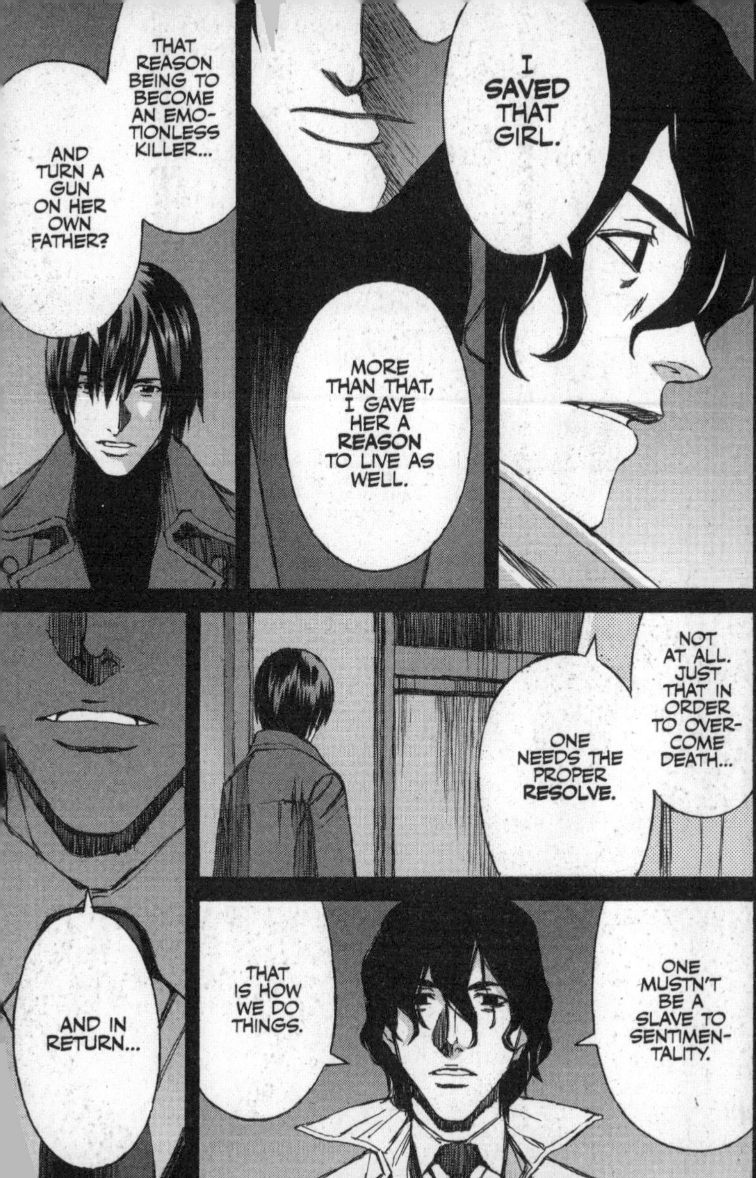
I SAVED THAT GIRL.
MORE THAN THAT, I GAVE HER A REASON TO LIVE AS WELL.
THAT REASON BEING TO BECOME AN EMO-TIONLESS KILLER...
AND TURN A GUN ON HER OWN FATHER?
NOT AT ALL. JUST THAT IN ORDER TO OVER-COME DEATH...
ONE NEEDS THE PROPER RESOLVE.
ONE MUSTN'T BE A SLAVE TO SENTIMENT-TALITY.
THAT IS HOW WE DO THINGS.
AND IN RETURN...

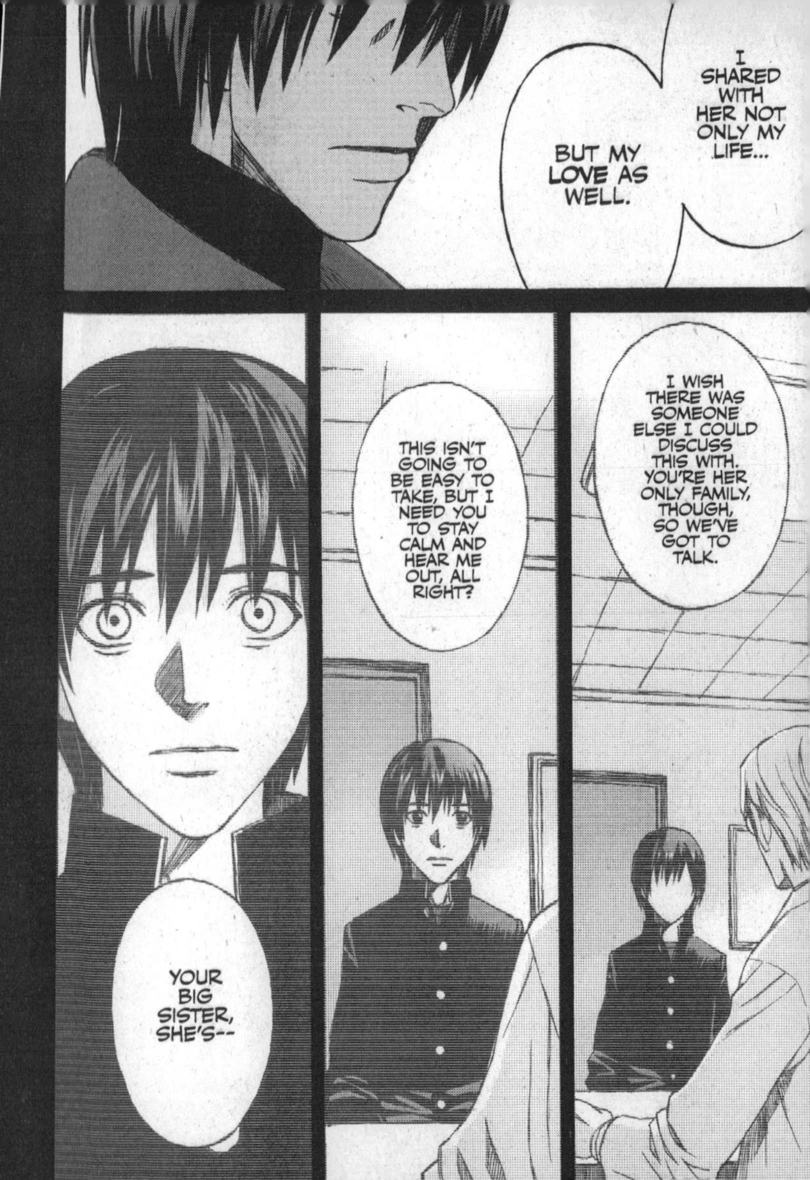
I SHARED WITH HER NOT ONLY MY LIFE...
BUT MY LOVE AS WELL.
I WISH THERE WAS SOMEONE ELSE I COULD DISCUSS THIS WITH. YOU'RE HER ONLY FAMILY, THOUGH, SO WE'VE GOT TO TALK.
THIS ISN'T GOING TO BE EASY TO TAKE, BUT I NEED YOU TO STAY CALM AND HEAR ME OUT, ALL RIGHT?
YOUR BIG SISTER, SHE'S--

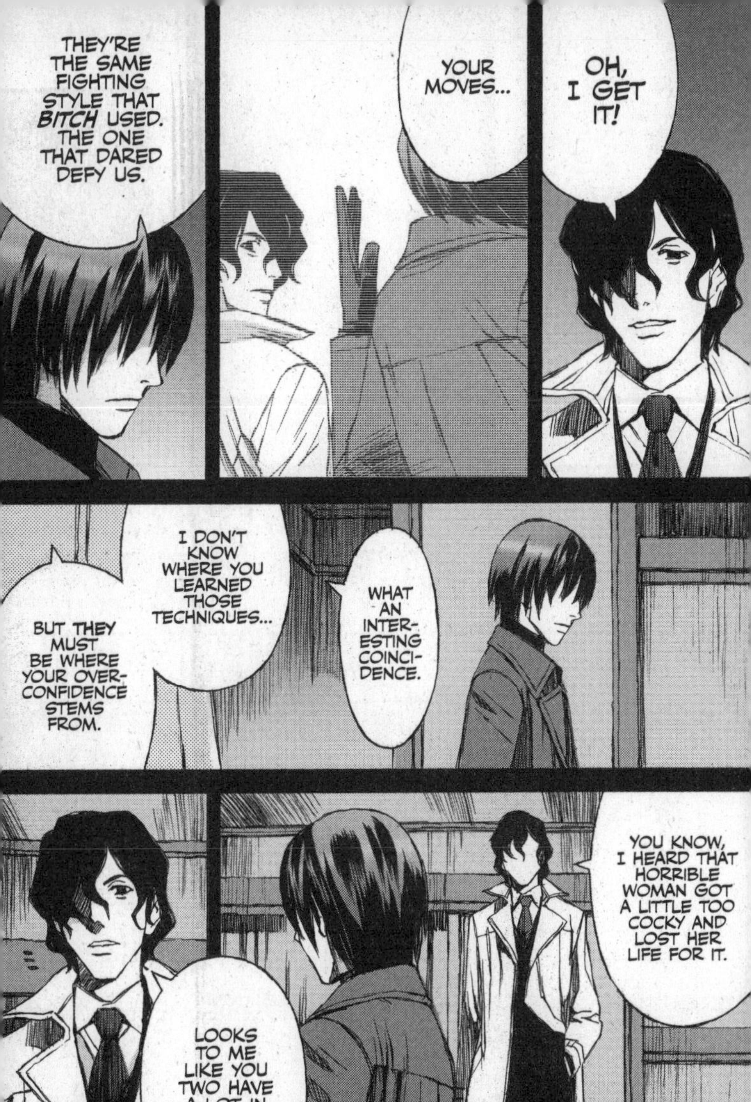
OH, I GET IT!
YOUR MOVES...
THEY'RE THE SAME FIGHTING STYLE THAT *BITCH* USED. THE ONE THAT DARED DEFY US.
WHAT AN INTER-ESTING COINCI-DENCE.
I DON'T KNOW WHERE YOU LEARNED THOSE TECHNIQUES...
BUT THEY MUST BE WHERE YOUR OVER-CONFIDENCE STEMS FROM.
YOU KNOW, I HEARD THAT HORRIBLE WOMAN GOT A LITTLE TOO COCKY AND LOST HER LIFE FOR IT.
LOOKS TO ME LIKE YOU TWO HAVE A LOT IN COMMON.

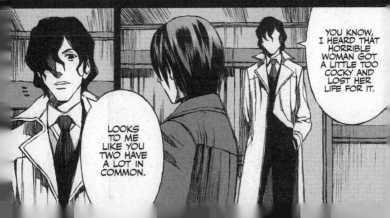

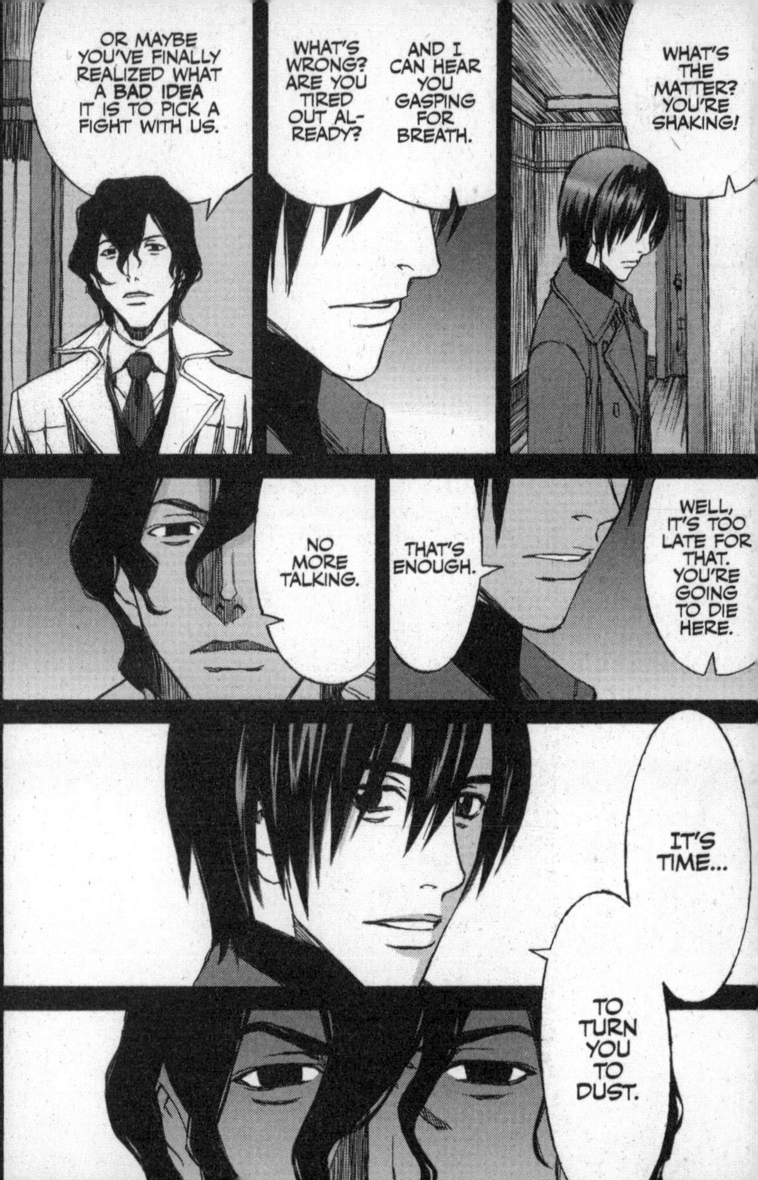
WHAT'S THE MATTER? YOU'RE SHAKING!
AND I CAN HEAR YOU GASPING FOR BREATH.
WHAT'S WRONG? ARE YOU TIRED OUT AL-READY?
OR MAYBE YOU'VE FINALLY REALIZED WHAT A **BAD IDEA** IT IS TO PICK A FIGHT WITH US.
WELL, IT'S TOO LATE FOR THAT. YOU'RE GOING TO DIE HERE.
THAT'S ENOUGH.
NO MORE TALKING.
IT'S TIME...
TO TURN YOU TO DUST.

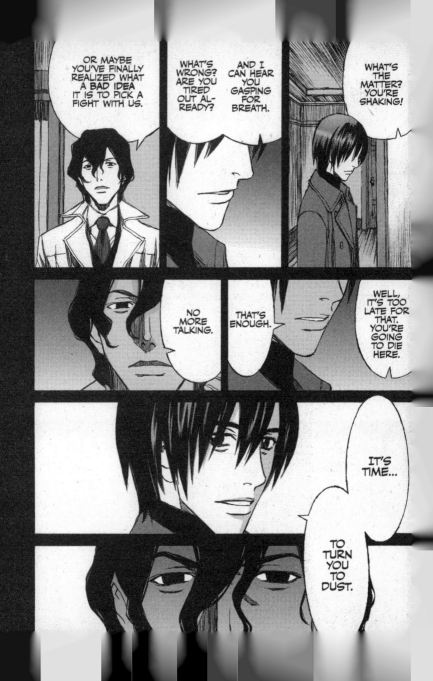

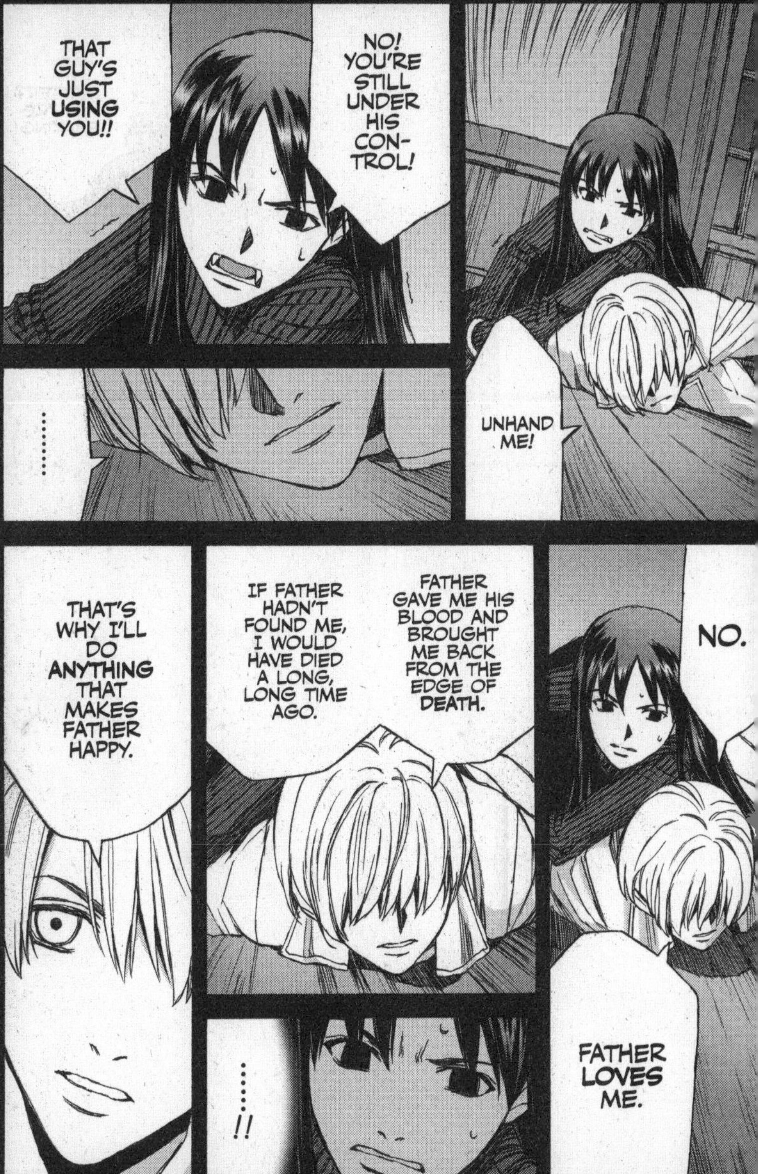

UNHAND ME!
NO! YOU'RE STILL UNDER HIS CON-TROL!
THAT GUY'S JUST **USING** YOU!!
......
NO.
FATHER LOVES ME.
FATHER GAVE ME HIS BLOOD AND BROUGHT ME BACK FROM THE EDGE OF **DEATH.**
IF FATHER HADN'T FOUND ME, I WOULD HAVE DIED A LONG, LONG TIME AGO.
......!!
THAT'S WHY I'LL DO **ANYTHING** THAT MAKES FATHER HAPPY.

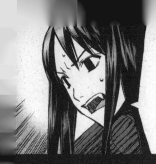

WOW, YOU'VE REALLY DRUNK THE KOOL-AID!
THEY TURN PEOPLE INTO SLAVES!!
TO VAMPIRES OF INSEGROD SPARUDA...
REN-FIELDS ARE JUST TOOLS THEY CAN USE AND TOSS ASIDE!
THAT'S NOT TRUE!!
FATHER LOVES ME! HE SAID SO HIMSELF!!
HE LOVES ME!!
IF HE REALLY LOVED YOU...
REACH

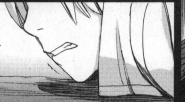

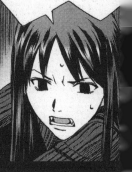

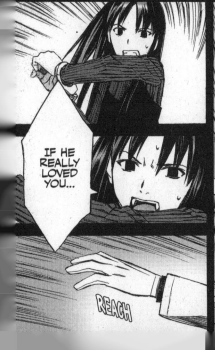

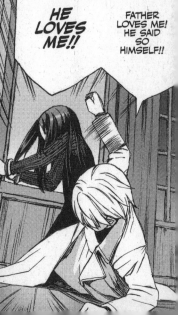

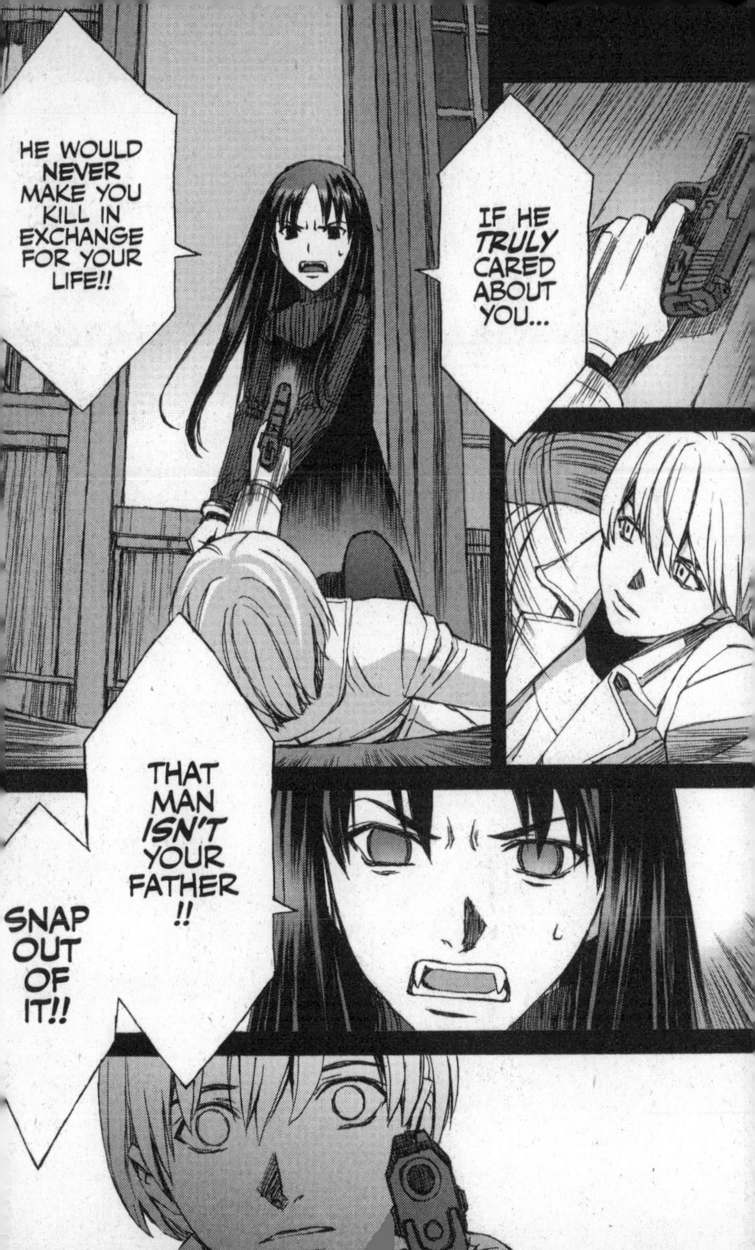
IF HE TRULY CARED ABOUT YOU...
HE WOULD NEVER MAKE YOU KILL IN EXCHANGE FOR YOUR LIFE!!
THAT MAN ISN'T YOUR FATHER!!
SNAP OUT OF IT!!

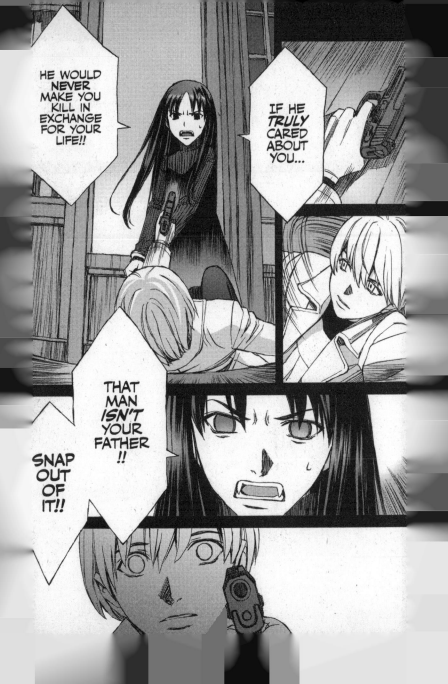

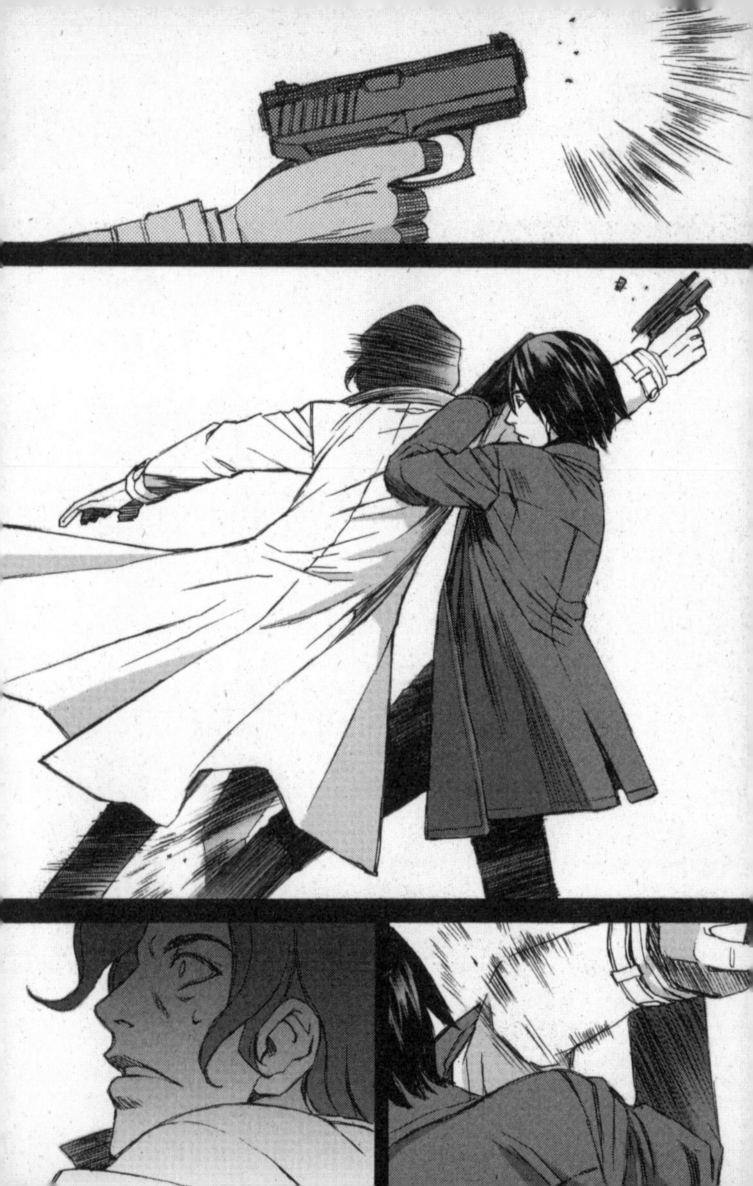

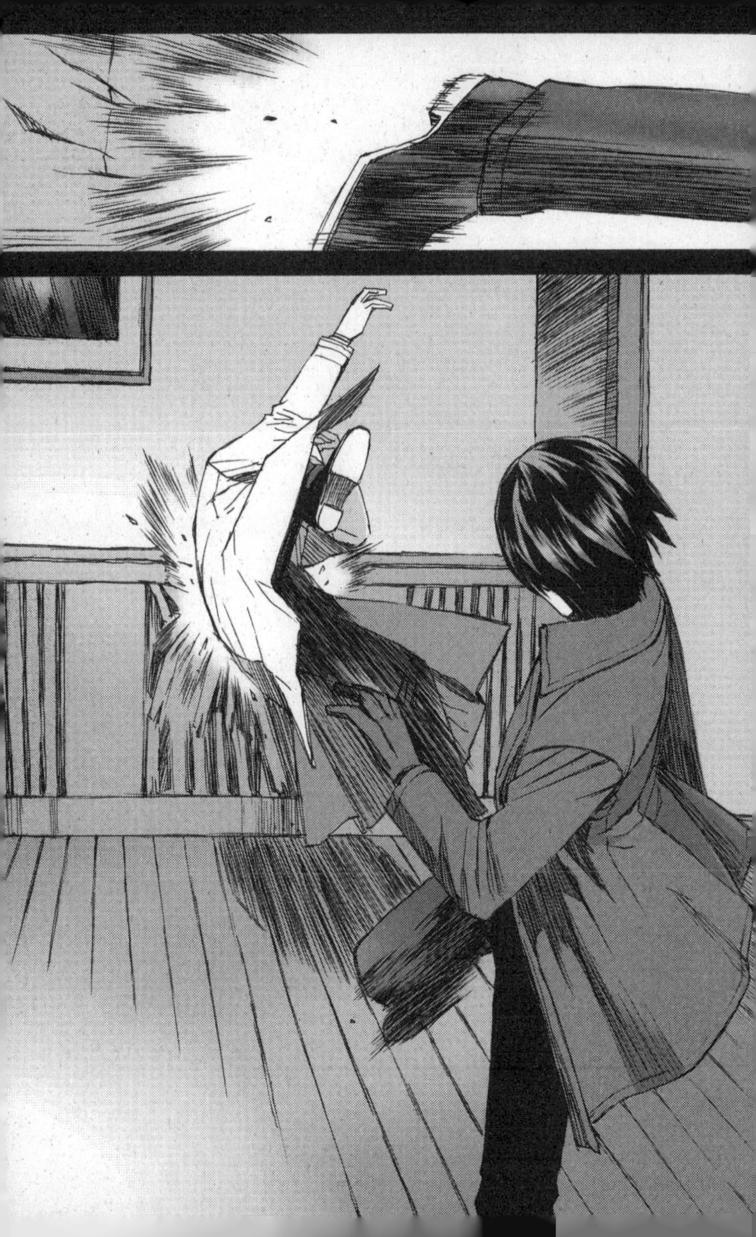

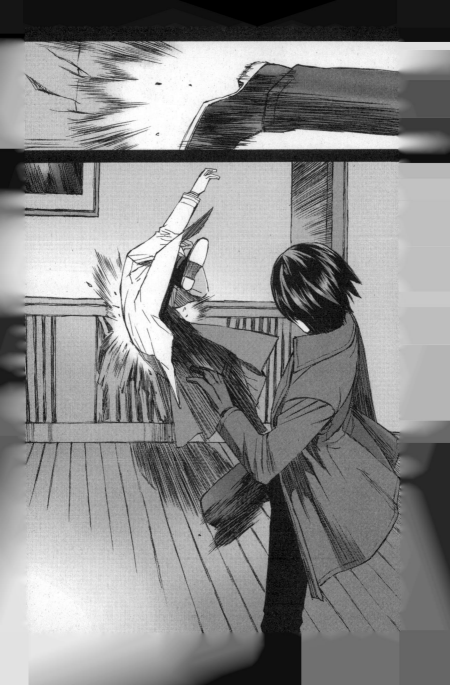

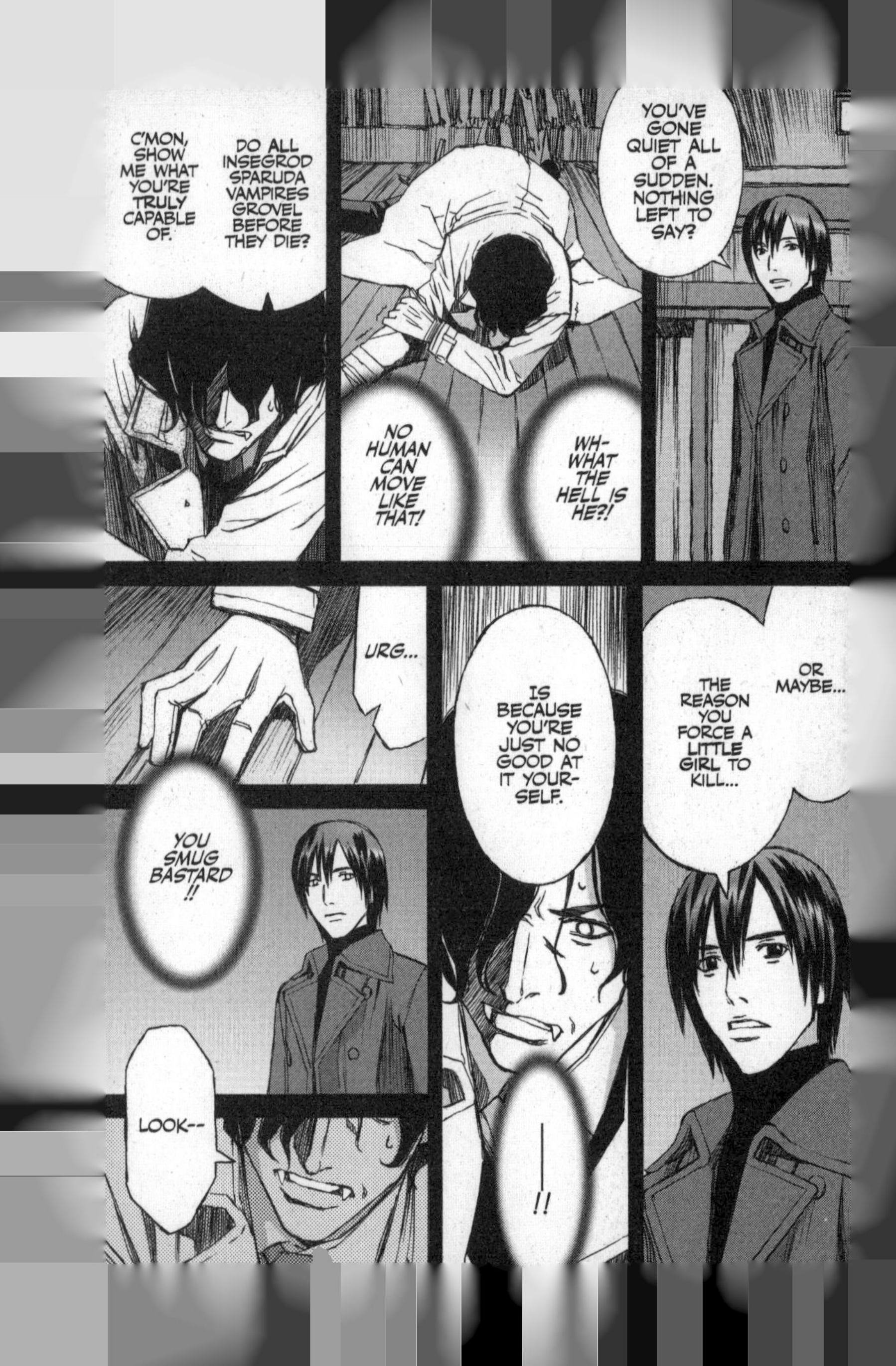
YOU'VE GONE QUIET ALL OF A SUDDEN. NOTHING LEFT TO SAY?
WH-WHAT THE HELL IS HE?!
NO HUMAN CAN MOVE LIKE THAT!
DO ALL INSEGROD SPARUDA VAMPIRES GROVEL BEFORE THEY DIE?
C'MON, SHOW ME WHAT YOU'RE TRULY CAPABLE OF.
OR MAYBE...
THE REASON YOU FORCE A LITTLE GIRL TO KILL...
IS BECAUSE YOU'RE JUST NO GOOD AT IT YOURSELF.
——!!
URG...
YOU SMUG BASTARD!!
LOOK--

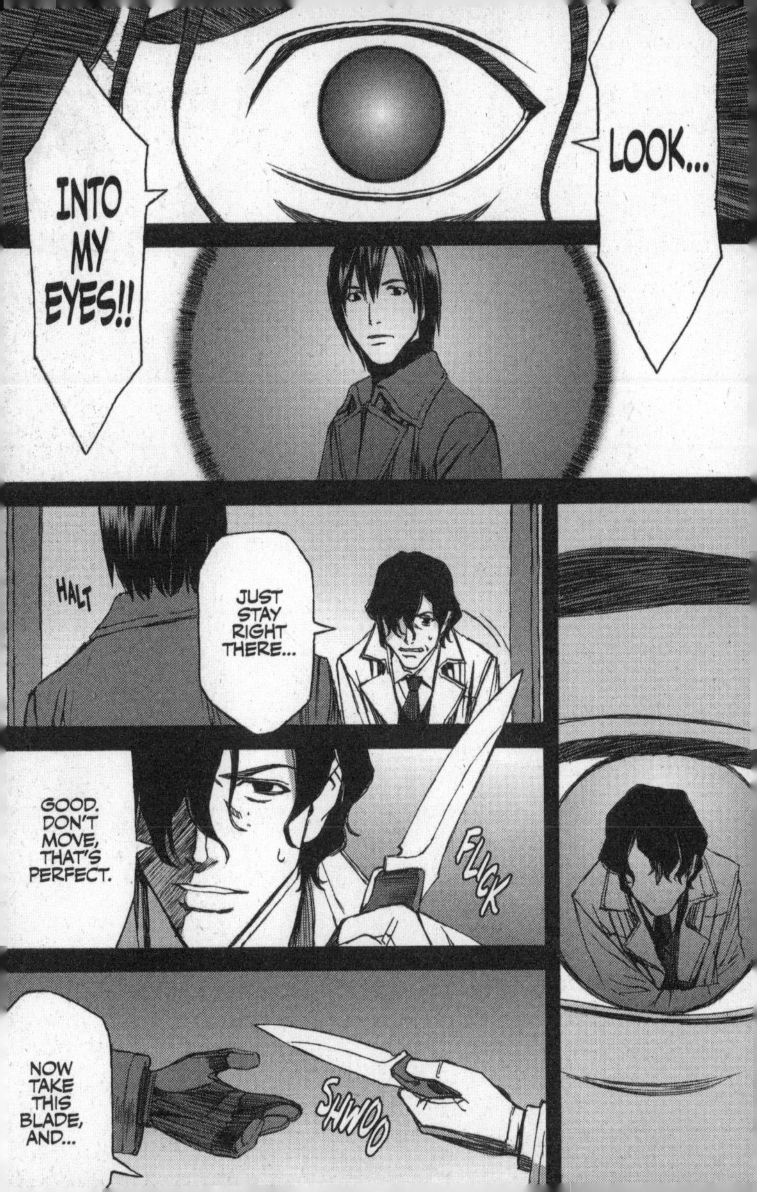
LOOK...
INTO MY EYES!!
HALT
JUST STAY RIGHT THERE...
GOOD. DON'T MOVE, THAT'S PERFECT.
FLICK
NOW TAKE THIS BLADE, AND...
SHWOO

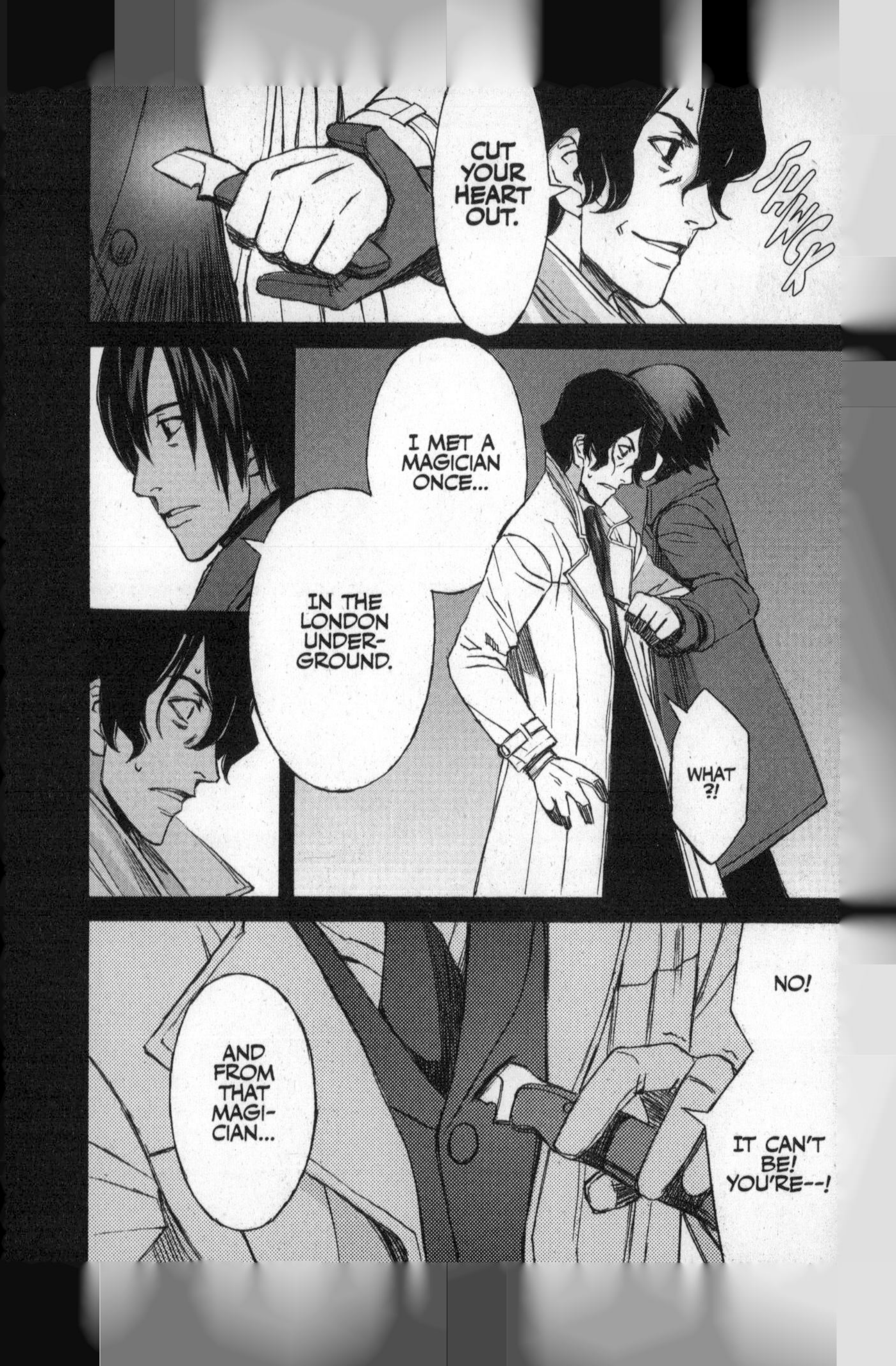
SHWNGK
CUT YOUR HEART OUT.
I MET A MAGICIAN ONCE...
IN THE LONDON UNDERGROUND.
WHAT?!
NO!
AND FROM THAT MAGI-CIAN...
IT CAN'T BE! YOU'RE--!

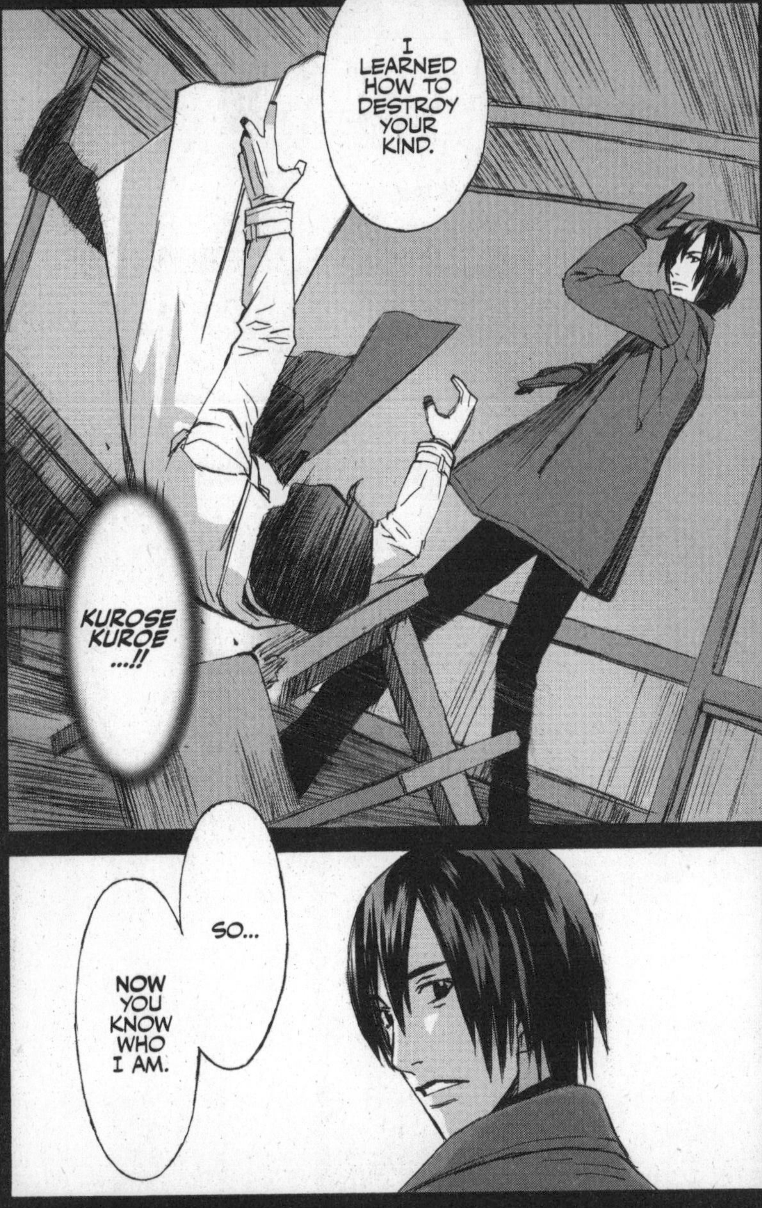
I LEARNED HOW TO DESTROY YOUR KIND.
KUROSE KUROE ...!!
SO...
NOW YOU KNOW WHO I AM.

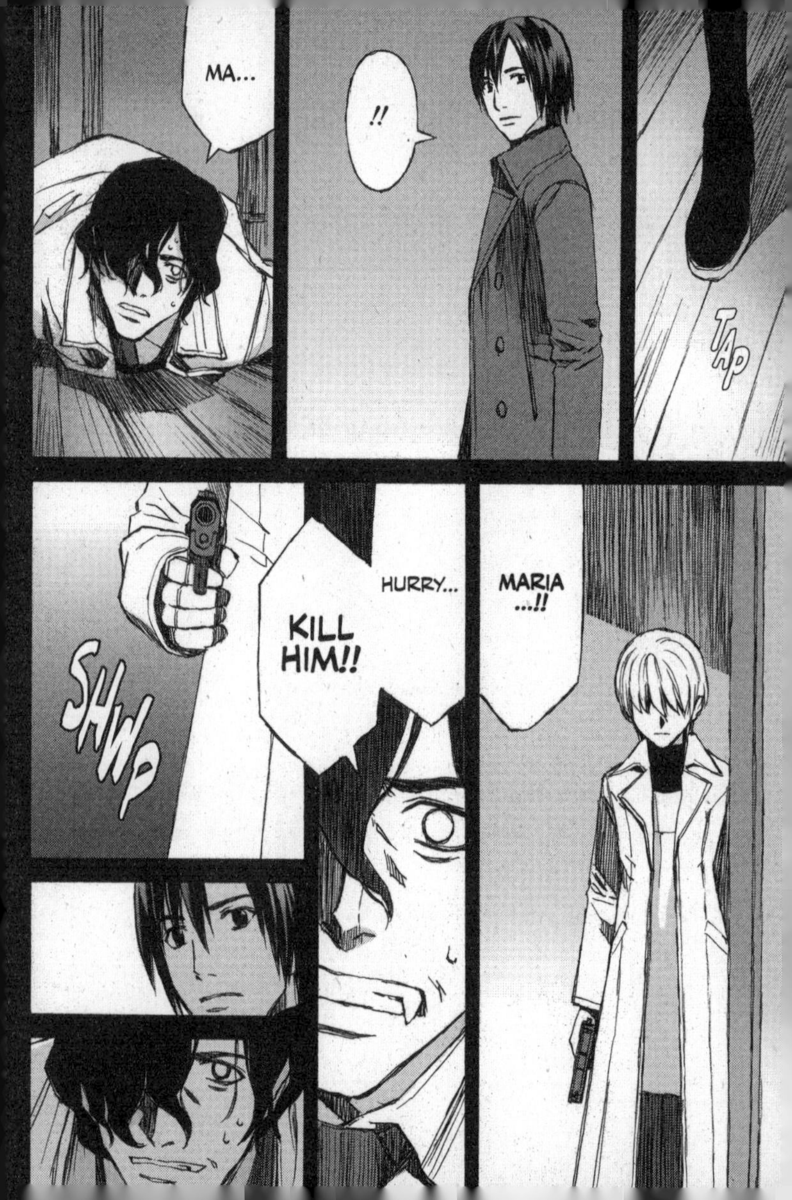
TAP
!!
MA...
MARIA ...!!
HURRY...
KILL HIM!!
SHWP

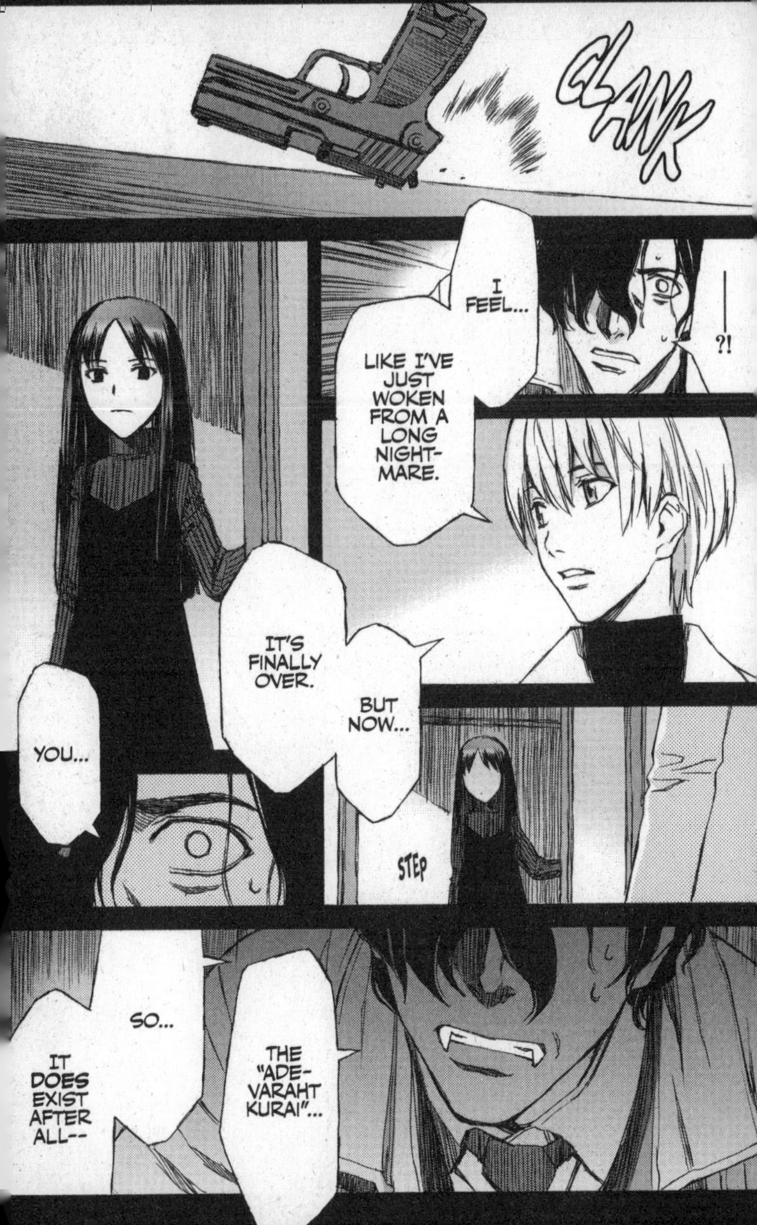
CLANK
—?!
I FEEL...
LIKE I'VE JUST WOKEN FROM A LONG NIGHT-MARE.
IT'S FINALLY OVER.
BUT NOW...
STEP
YOU...
SO...
THE "ADE-VARAHT KURAI"...
IT DOES EXIST AFTER ALL--

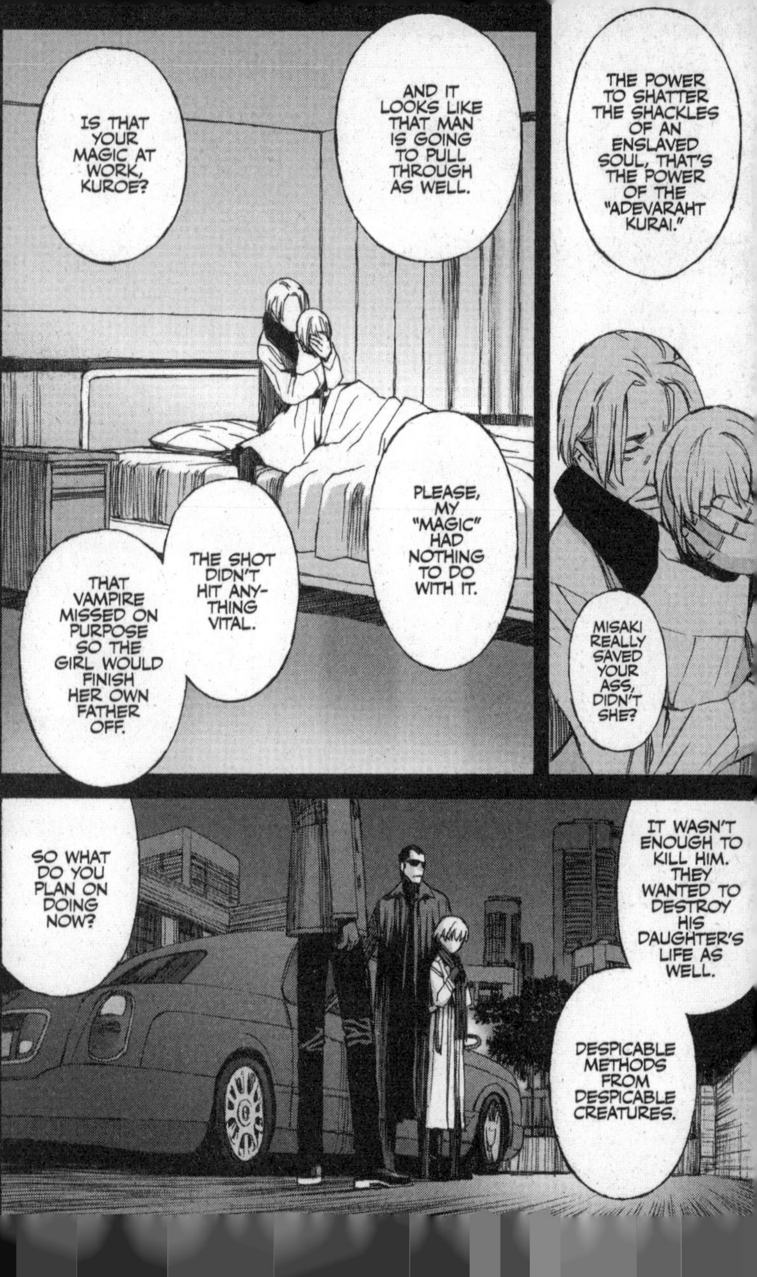
THE POWER TO SHATTER THE SHACKLES OF AN ENSLAVED SOUL, THAT'S THE POWER OF THE "ADEVARAHT KURAI."
MISAKI REALLY SAVED YOUR ASS, DIDN'T SHE?
AND IT LOOKS LIKE THAT MAN IS GOING TO PULL THROUGH AS WELL.
IS THAT YOUR MAGIC AT WORK, KUROE?
PLEASE, MY "MAGIC" HAD NOTHING TO DO WITH IT.
THE SHOT DIDN'T HIT ANY-THING VITAL.
THAT VAMPIRE MISSED ON PURPOSE SO THE GIRL WOULD FINISH HER OWN FATHER OFF.
IT WASN'T ENOUGH TO KILL HIM. THEY WANTED TO DESTROY HIS DAUGHTER'S LIFE AS WELL.
DESPICABLE METHODS FROM DESPICABLE CREATURES.
SO WHAT DO YOU PLAN ON DOING NOW?

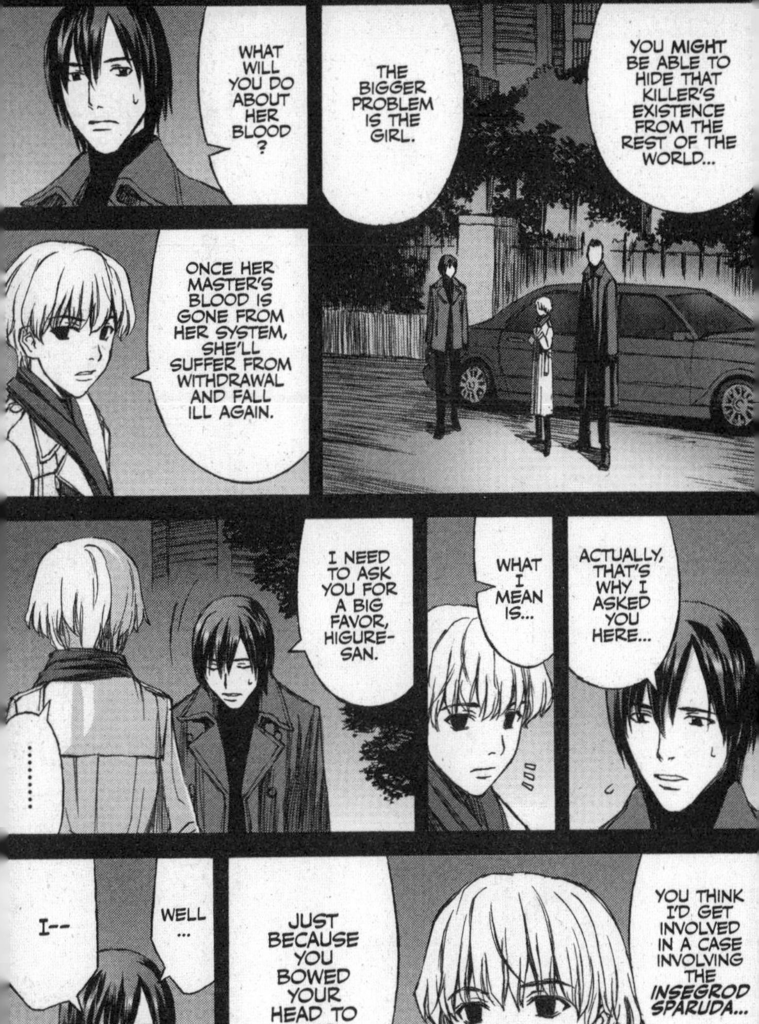
YOU MIGHT BE ABLE TO HIDE THAT KILLER'S EXISTENCE FROM THE REST OF THE WORLD...
THE BIGGER PROBLEM IS THE GIRL.
WHAT WILL YOU DO ABOUT HER BLOOD?
ONCE HER MASTER'S BLOOD IS GONE FROM HER SYSTEM, SHE'LL SUFFER FROM WITHDRAWAL AND FALL ILL AGAIN.
ACTUALLY, THAT'S WHY I ASKED YOU HERE...
WHAT I MEAN IS...
I NEED TO ASK YOU FOR A BIG FAVOR, HIGURE-SAN.
......
YOU THINK I'D GET INVOLVED IN A CASE INVOLVING THE *INSEGROD SPARUDA*...
JUST BECAUSE YOU BOWED YOUR HEAD TO ME?
WELL...
I--

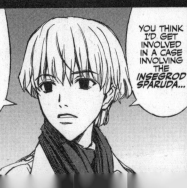

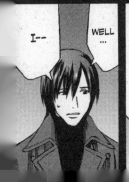

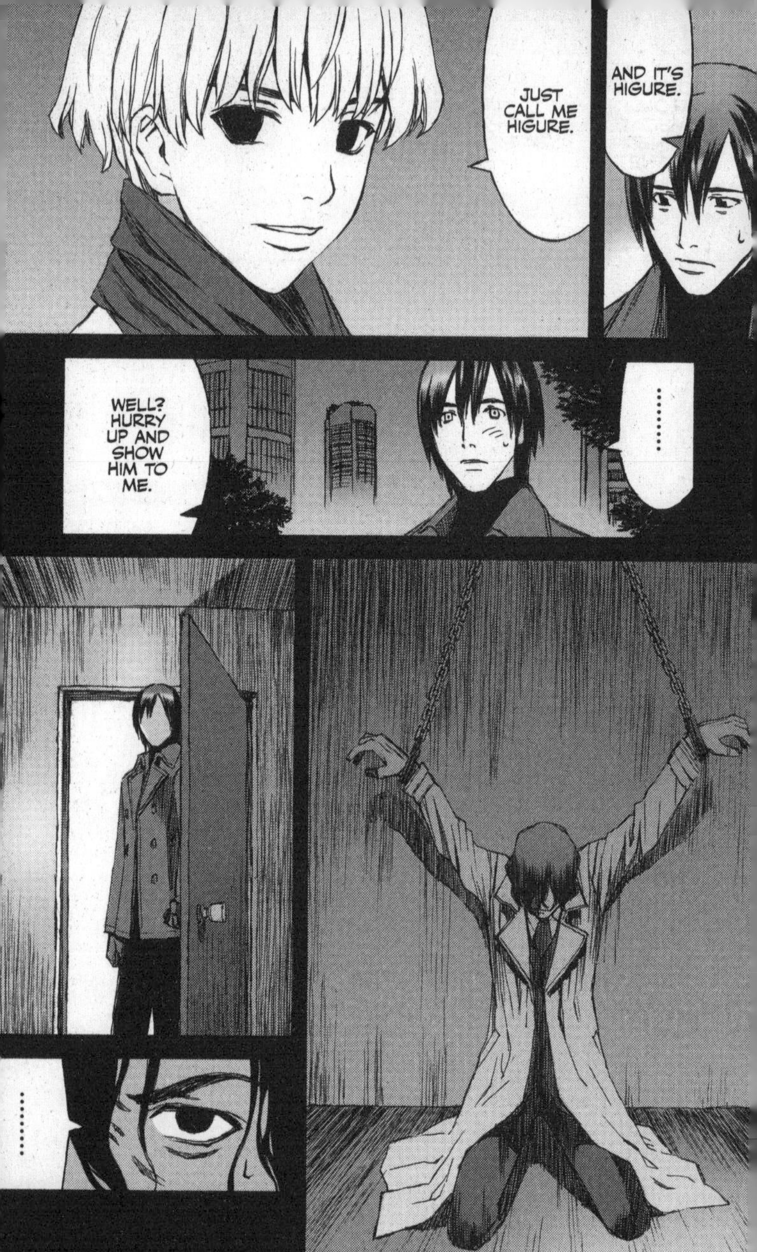
AND IT'S HIGURE.
JUST CALL ME HIGURE.
……
WELL? HURRY UP AND SHOW HIM TO ME.
……

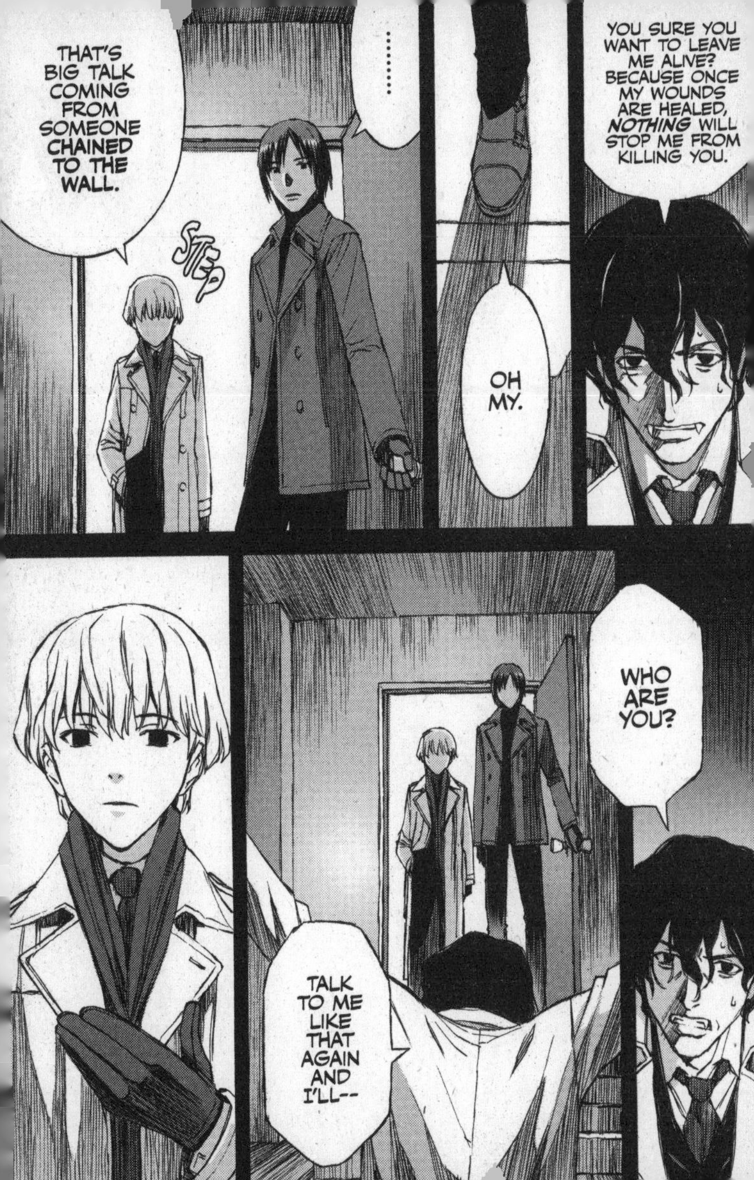
YOU SURE YOU WANT TO LEAVE ME ALIVE? BECAUSE ONCE MY WOUNDS ARE HEALED, *NOTHING* WILL STOP ME FROM KILLING YOU.
OH MY.
......
THAT'S BIG TALK COMING FROM SOMEONE CHAINED TO THE WALL.
STEP
WHO ARE YOU?
TALK TO ME LIKE THAT AGAIN AND I'LL--

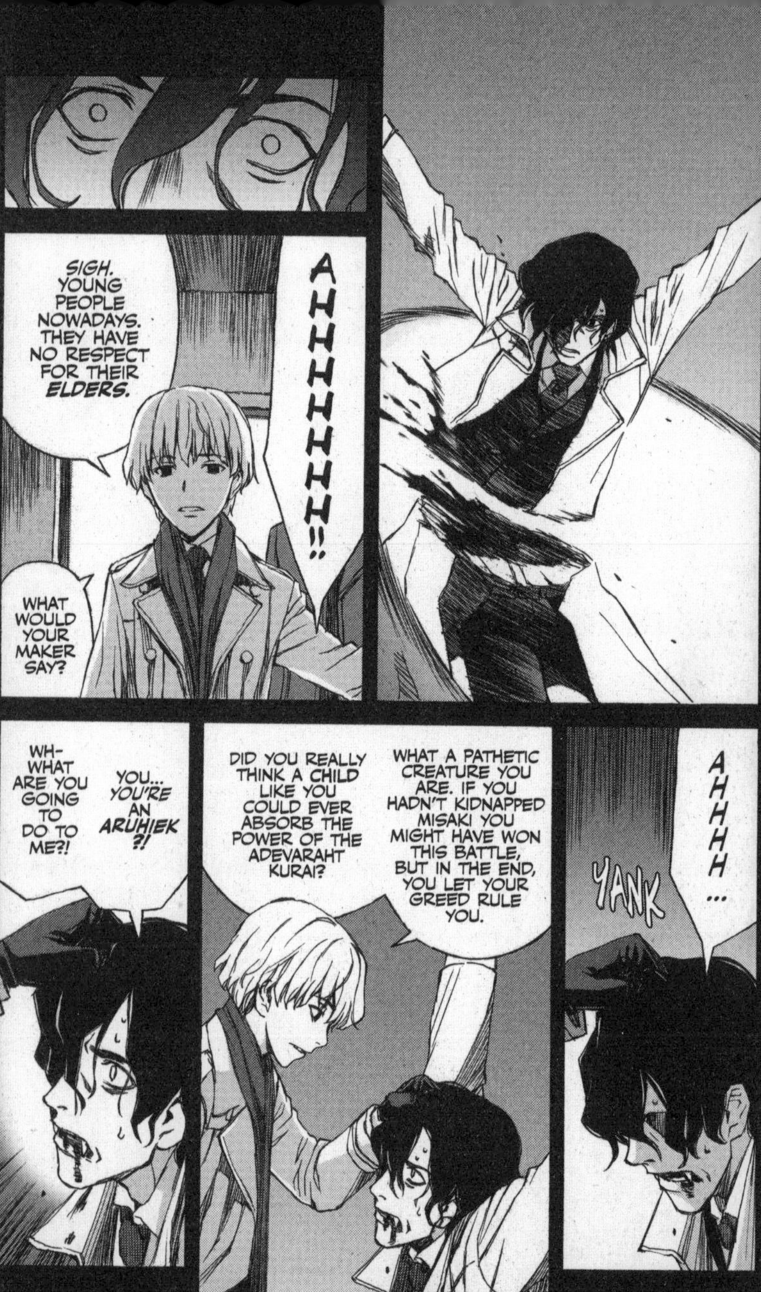
AHHHHHHHH!!
SIGH. YOUNG PEOPLE NOWADAYS. THEY HAVE NO RESPECT FOR THEIR *ELDERS.*
WHAT WOULD YOUR MAKER SAY?
AHHHH...
YANK
WHAT A PATHETIC CREATURE YOU ARE. IF YOU HADN'T KIDNAPPED MISAKI YOU MIGHT HAVE WON THIS BATTLE, BUT IN THE END, YOU LET YOUR GREED RULE YOU.
DID YOU REALLY THINK A CHILD LIKE YOU COULD EVER ABSORB THE POWER OF THE ADEVARAHT KURAI?
YOU... *YOU'RE* AN *ARUHIEK ?!*
WH- WHAT ARE YOU GOING TO DO TO ME?!

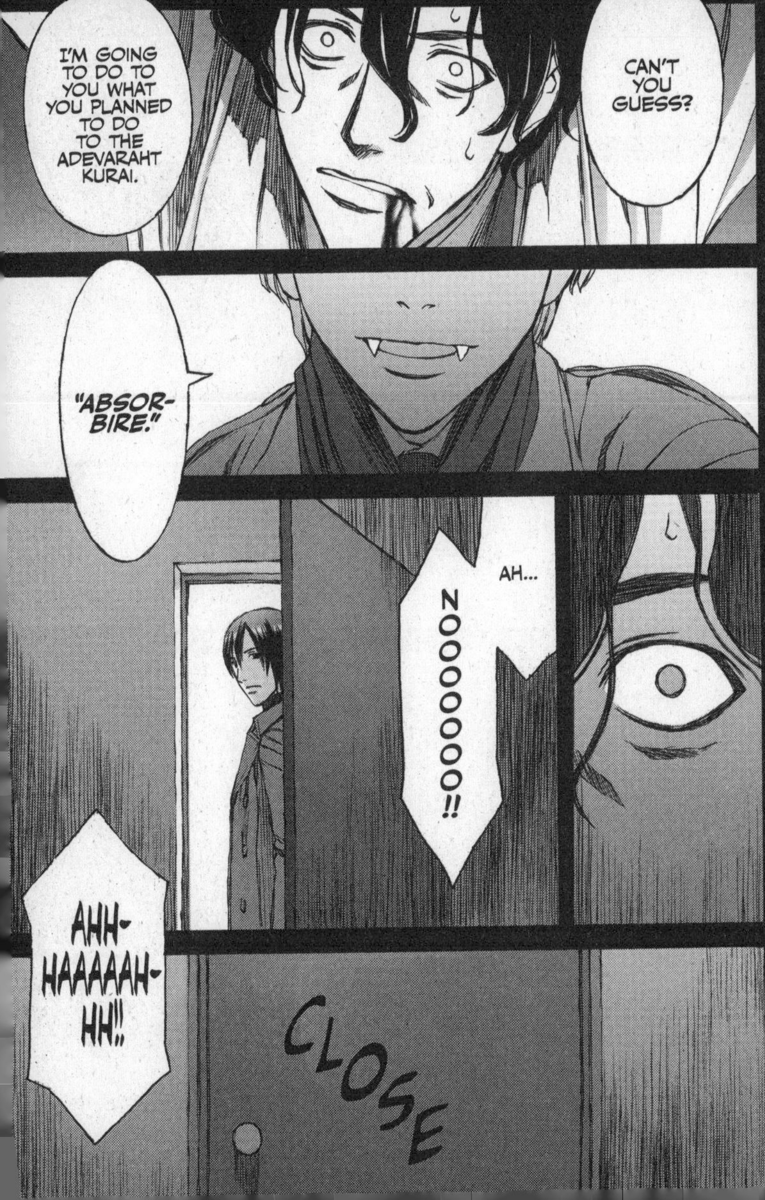
CAN'T YOU GUESS?
I'M GOING TO DO TO YOU WHAT YOU PLANNED TO DO TO THE ADEVARAHT KURAI.
"ABSORBIRE."
AH...
NOOOOOOOOO!!
AHH-HAAAAAH-HH!!
CLOSE

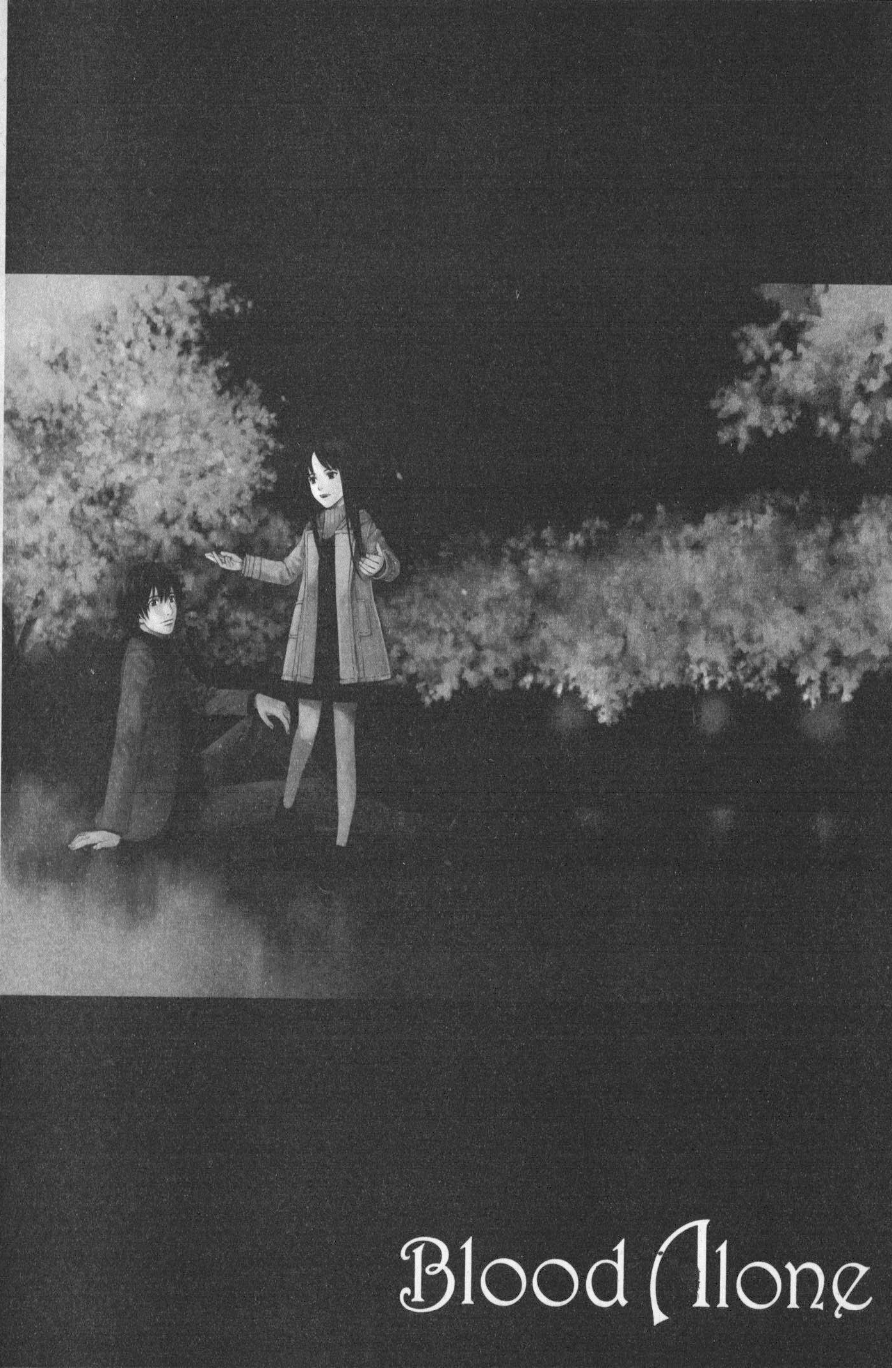
Blood Alone

Episode 15

CHERRY BLOSSOM

Sakura

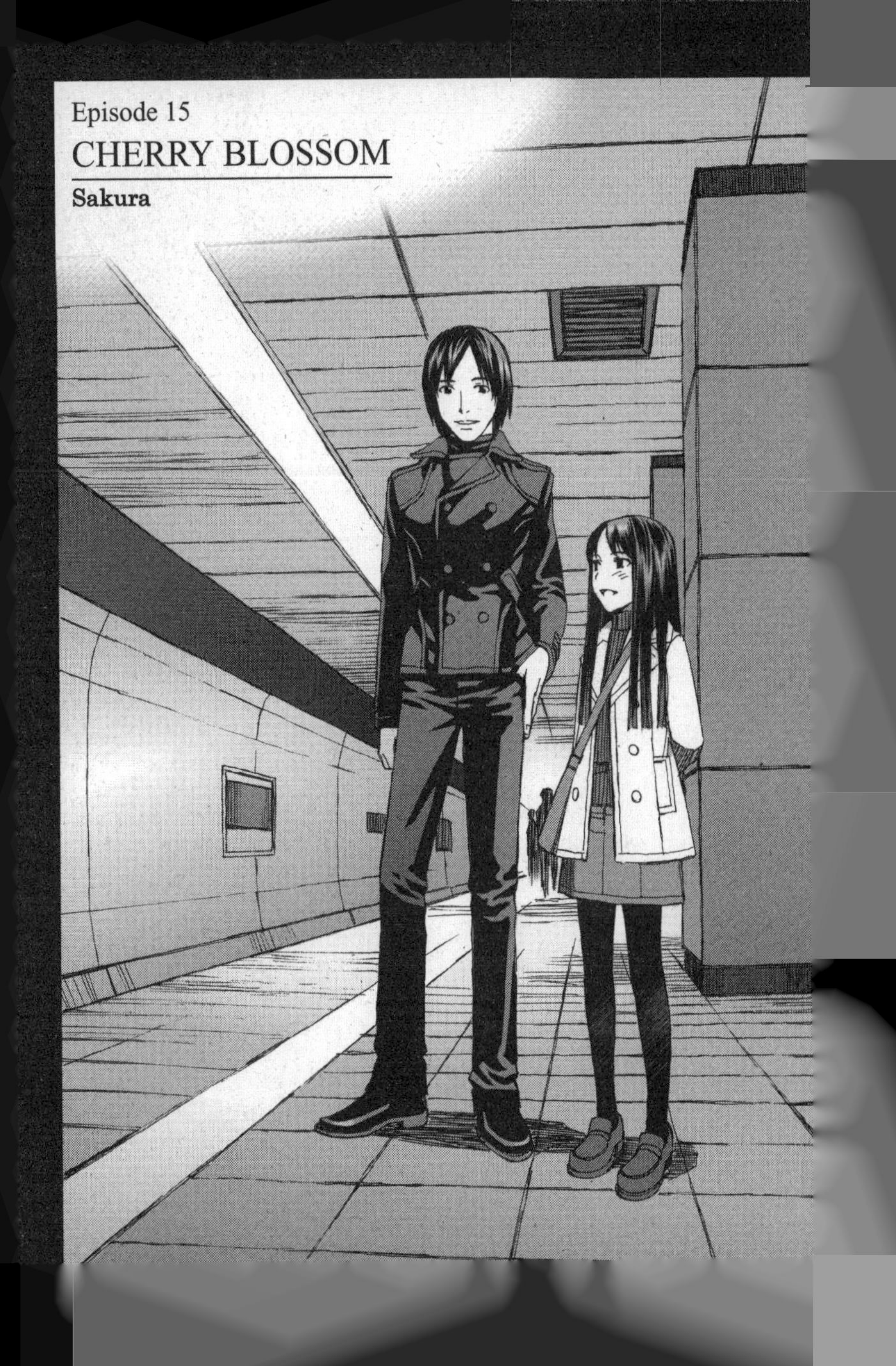

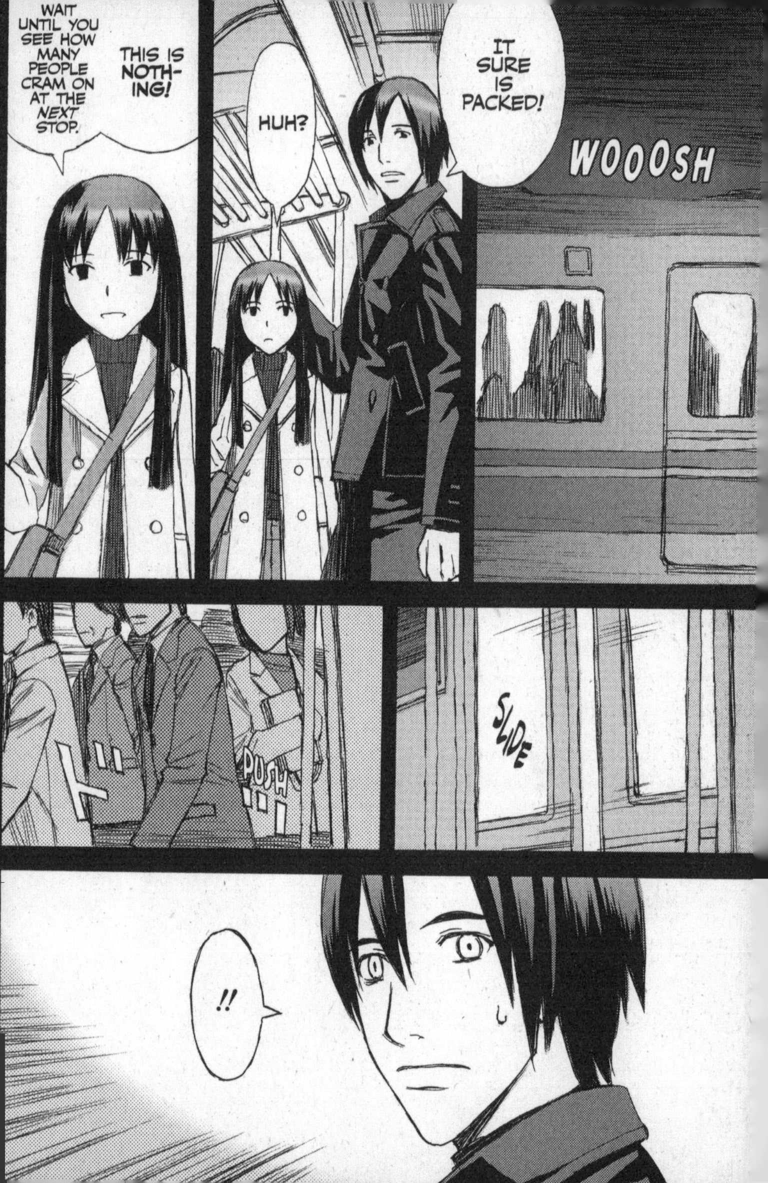
WOOOSH
IT SURE IS PACKED!
HUH?
THIS IS NOTHING!
WAIT UNTIL YOU SEE HOW MANY PEOPLE CRAM ON AT THE *NEXT* STOP.
SLIDE
PUSH
!!

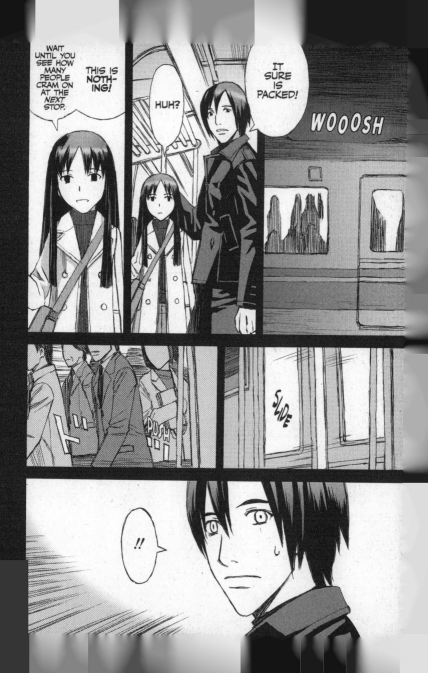

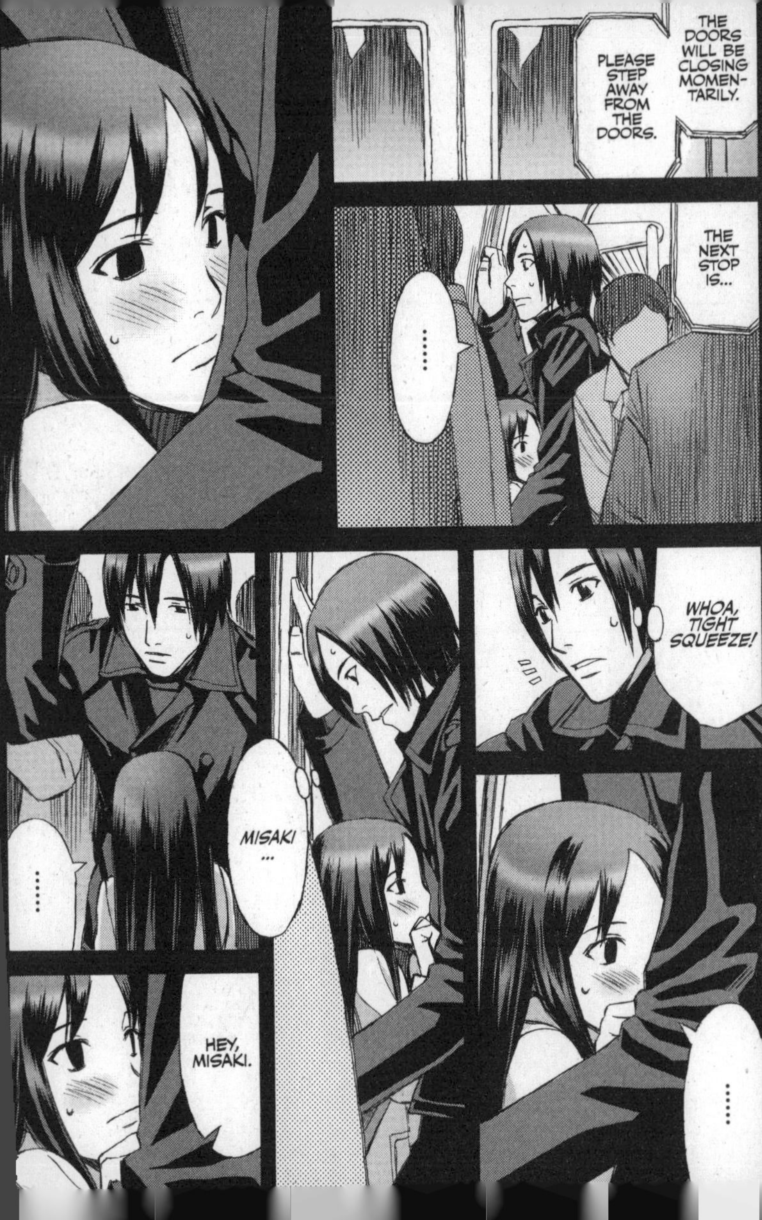
THE DOORS WILL BE CLOSING MOMENTARILY.
PLEASE STEP AWAY FROM THE DOORS.
THE NEXT STOP IS...
……
WHOA, TIGHT SQUEEZE!
……
MISAKI ...
……
HEY, MISAKI.

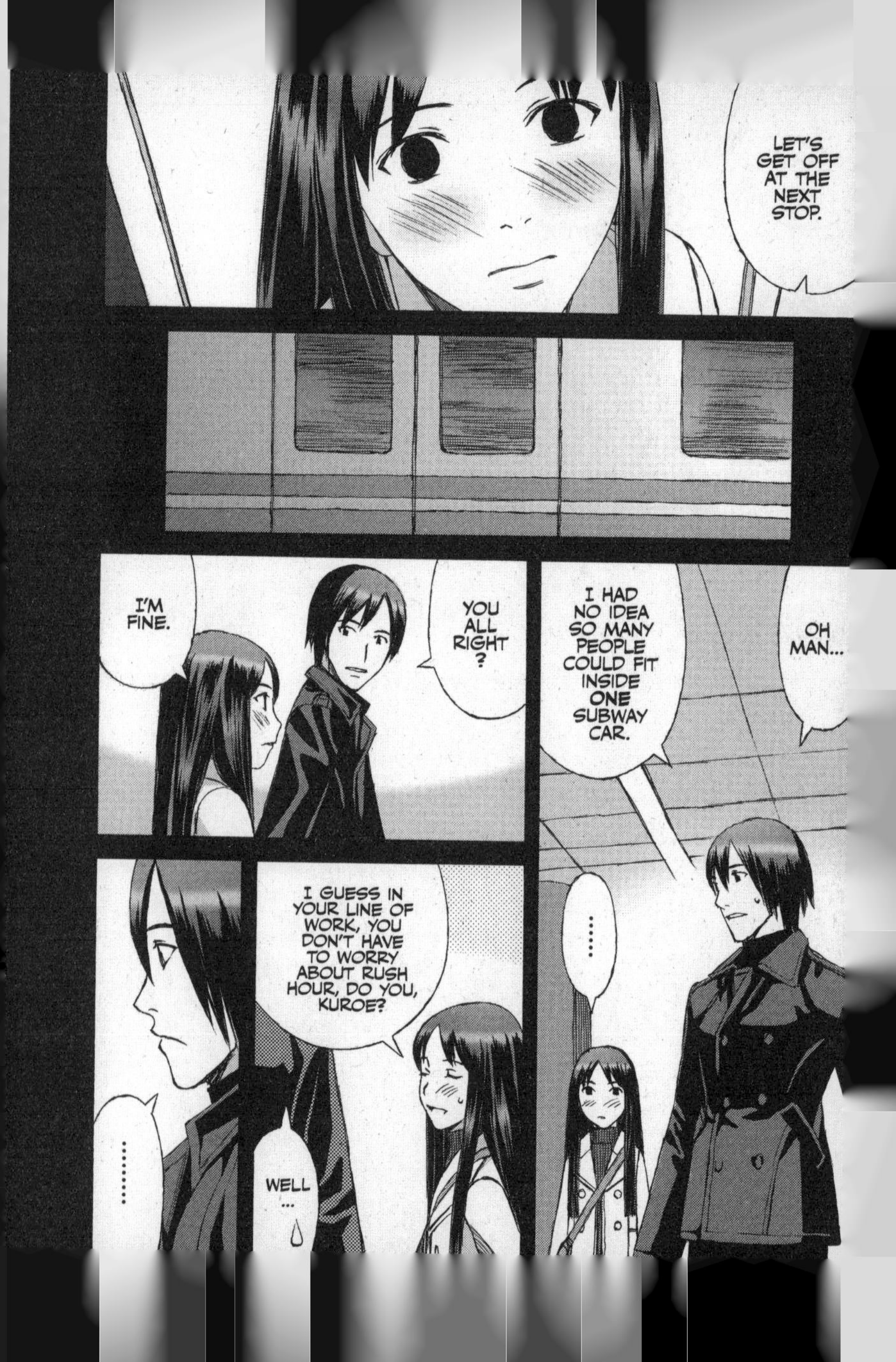
LET'S GET OFF AT THE NEXT STOP.
OH MAN...
I HAD NO IDEA SO MANY PEOPLE COULD FIT INSIDE ONE SUBWAY CAR.
......
YOU ALL RIGHT?
I'M FINE.
I GUESS IN YOUR LINE OF WORK, YOU DON'T HAVE TO WORRY ABOUT RUSH HOUR, DO YOU, KUROE?
WELL...
......

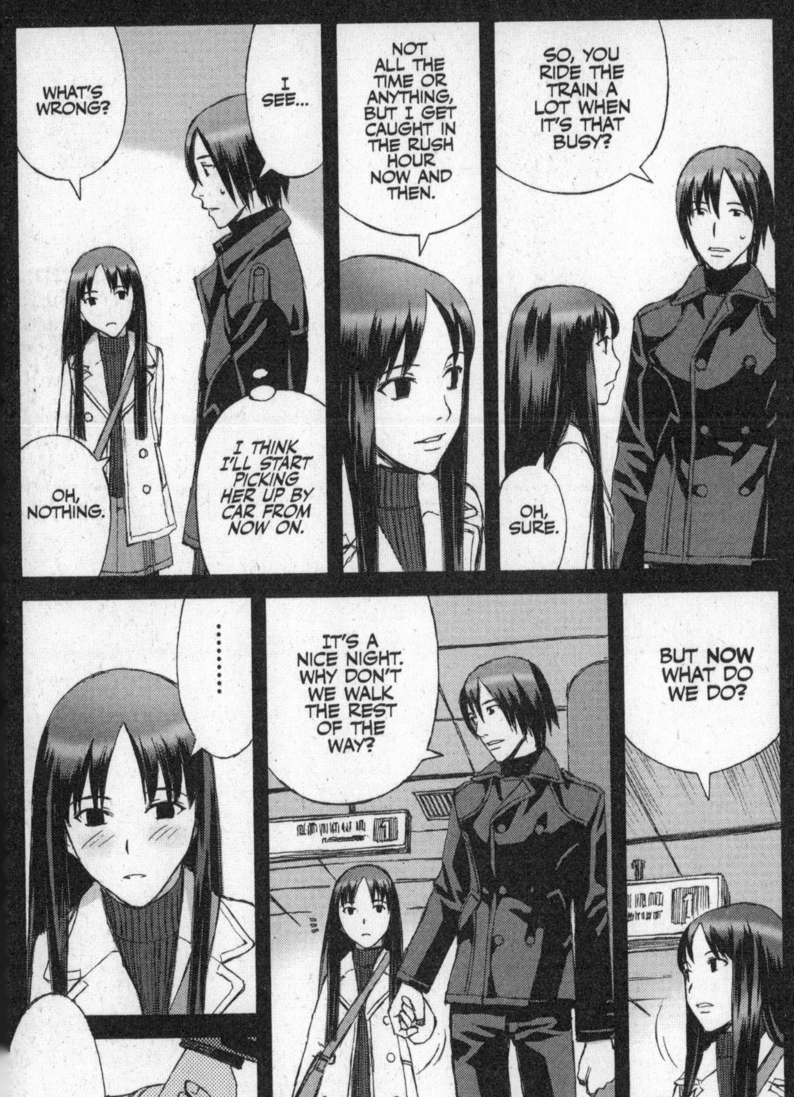
SO, YOU RIDE THE TRAIN A LOT WHEN IT'S THAT BUSY?
OH, SURE.
NOT ALL THE TIME OR ANYTHING, BUT I GET CAUGHT IN THE RUSH HOUR NOW AND THEN.
I SEE...
I THINK I'LL START PICKING HER UP BY CAR FROM NOW ON.
WHAT'S WRONG?
OH, NOTHING.
BUT NOW WHAT DO WE DO?
WE'RE STILL TWO STATIONS AWAY FROM OUR STOP.
IT'S A NICE NIGHT. WHY DON'T WE WALK THE REST OF THE WAY?
......
SURE.

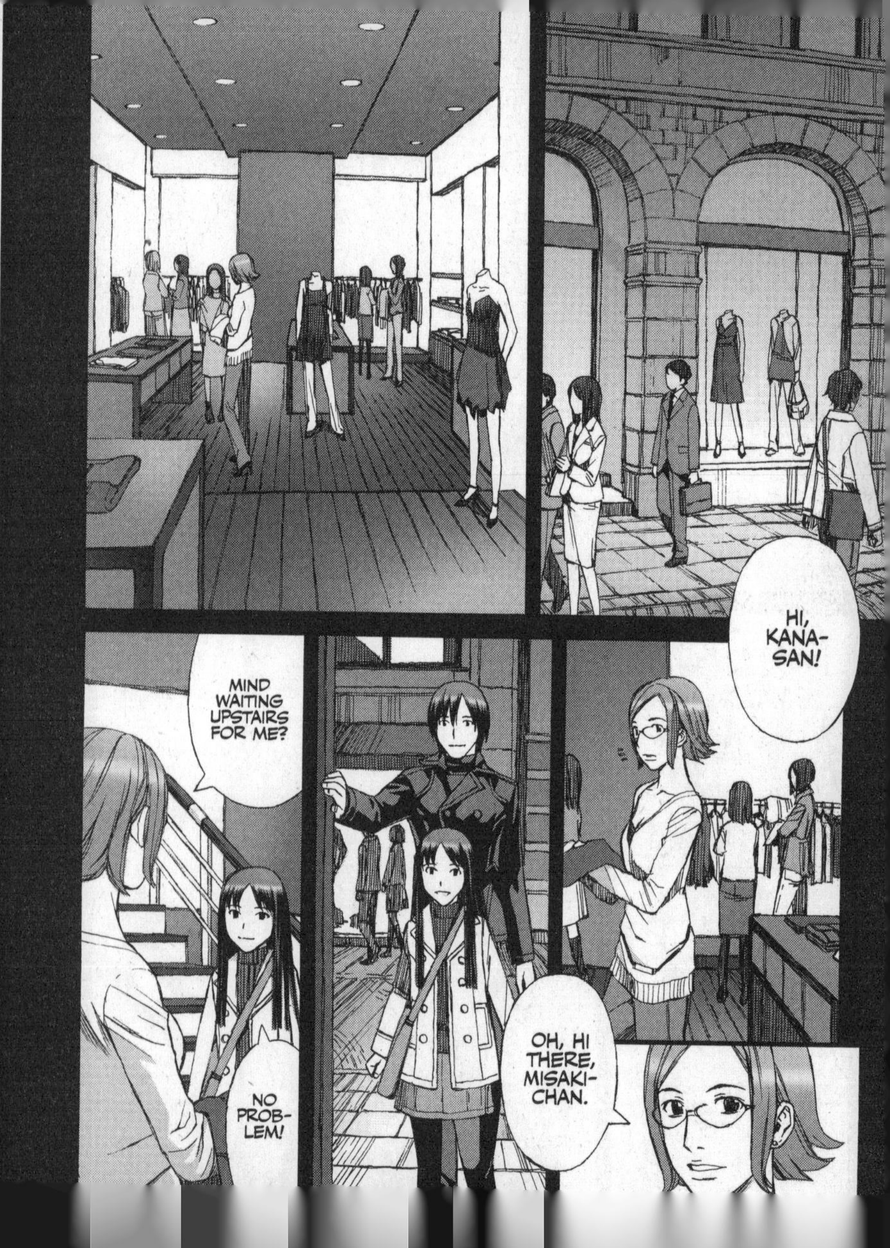
HI, KANA-SAN!
OH, HI THERE, MISAKI-CHAN.
MIND WAITING UPSTAIRS FOR ME?
NO PROB-LEM!

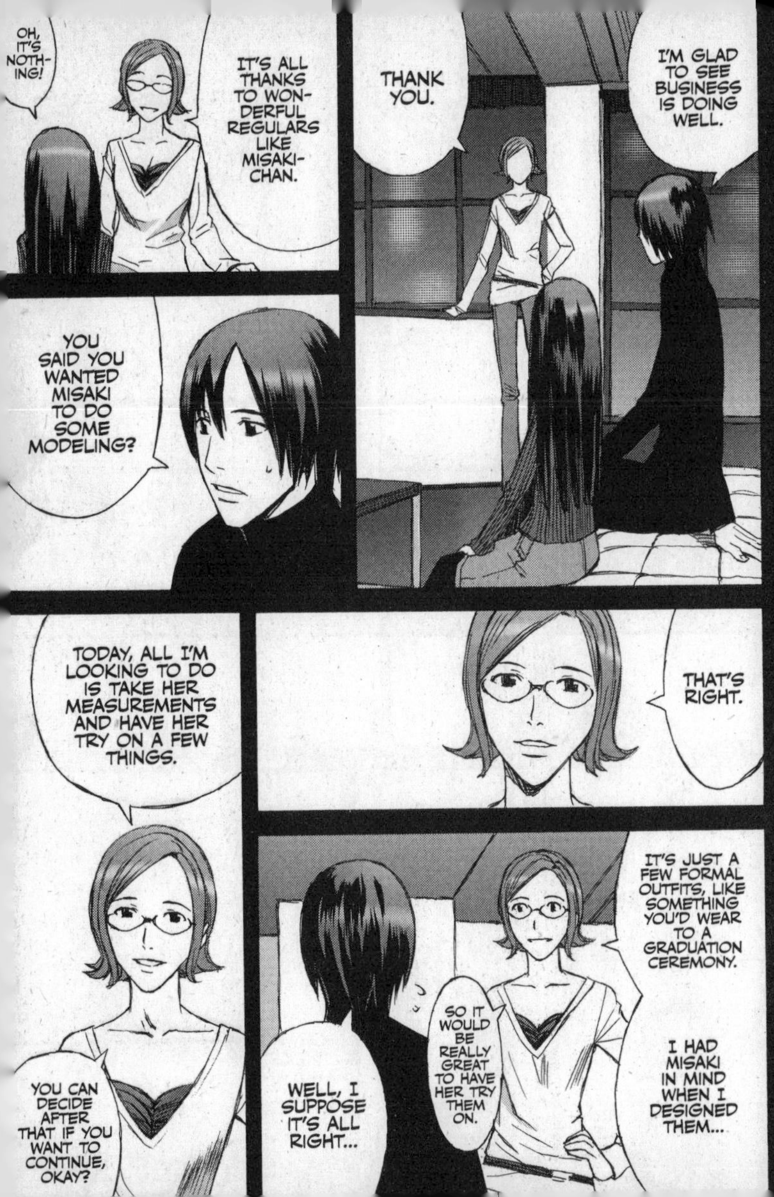
I'M GLAD TO SEE BUSINESS IS DOING WELL.
THANK YOU.
IT'S ALL THANKS TO WONDERFUL REGULARS LIKE MISAKI-CHAN.
OH, IT'S NOTHING!
YOU SAID YOU WANTED MISAKI TO DO SOME MODELING?
THAT'S RIGHT.
IT'S JUST A FEW FORMAL OUTFITS, LIKE SOMETHING YOU'D WEAR TO A GRADUATION CEREMONY.
I HAD MISAKI IN MIND WHEN I DESIGNED THEM...
SO IT WOULD BE REALLY GREAT TO HAVE HER TRY THEM ON.
WELL, I SUPPOSE IT'S ALL RIGHT...
TODAY, ALL I'M LOOKING TO DO IS TAKE HER MEASUREMENTS AND HAVE HER TRY ON A FEW THINGS.
YOU CAN DECIDE AFTER THAT IF YOU WANT TO CONTINUE, OKAY?

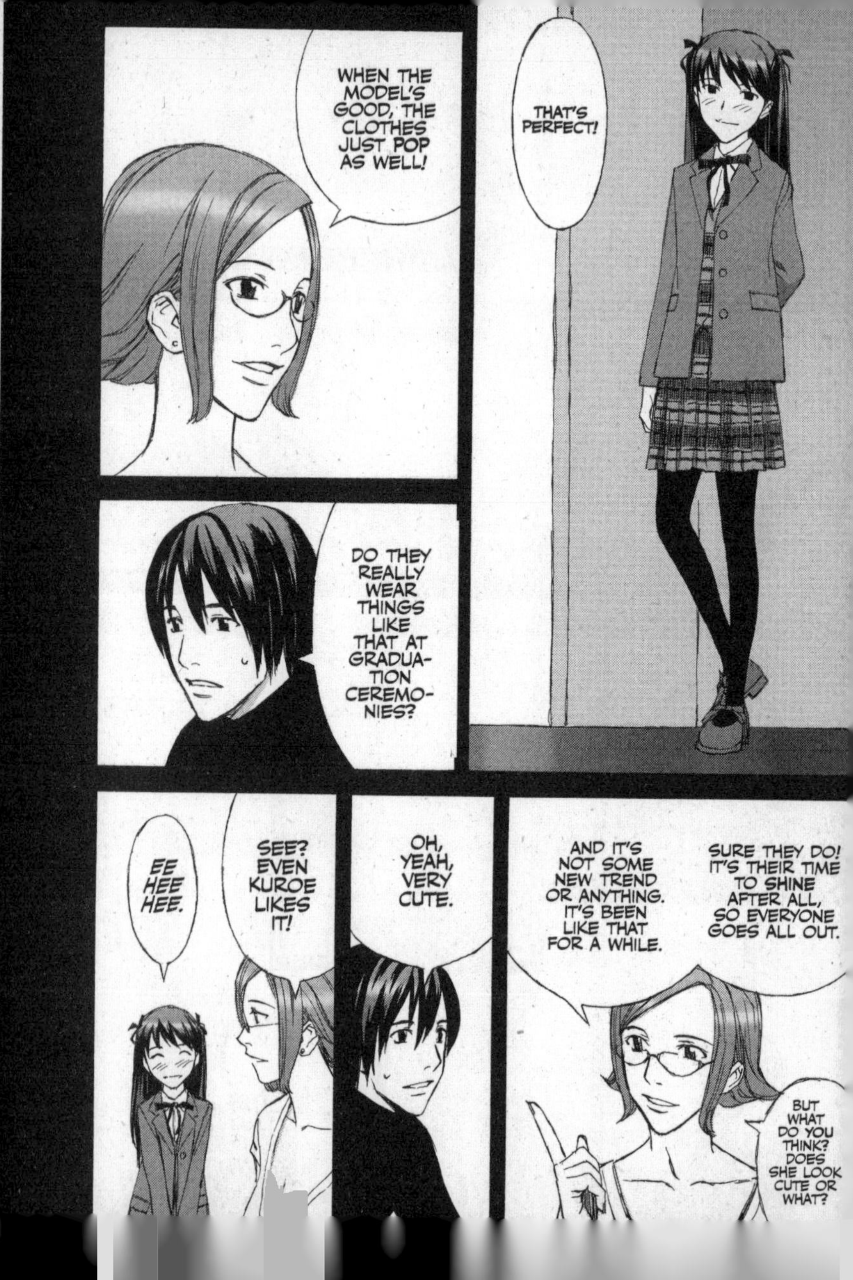
THAT'S PERFECT!
WHEN THE MODEL'S GOOD, THE CLOTHES JUST POP AS WELL!
DO THEY REALLY WEAR THINGS LIKE THAT AT GRADUATION CEREMONIES?
SURE THEY DO! IT'S THEIR TIME TO SHINE AFTER ALL, SO EVERYONE GOES ALL OUT.
AND IT'S NOT SOME NEW TREND OR ANYTHING. IT'S BEEN LIKE THAT FOR A WHILE.
BUT WHAT DO YOU THINK? DOES SHE LOOK CUTE OR WHAT?
OH, YEAH, VERY CUTE.
SEE? EVEN KUROE LIKES IT!
EE HEE HEE.

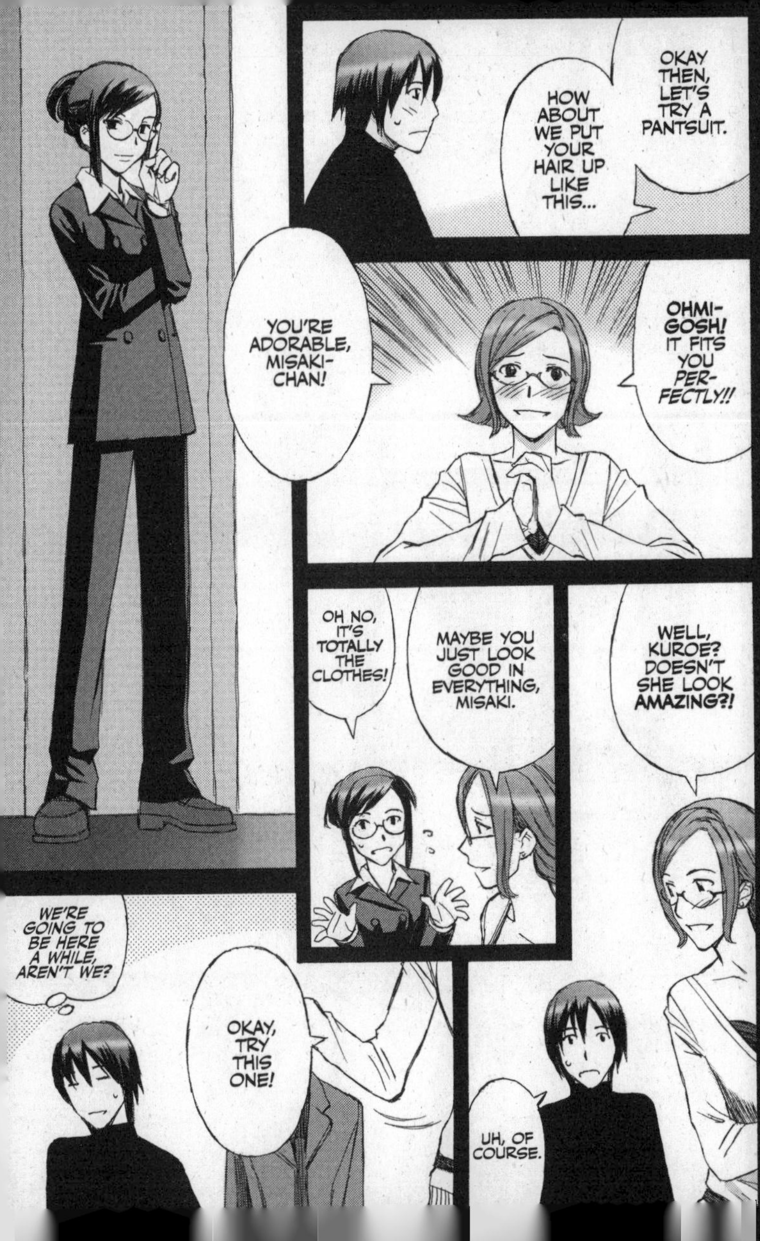
OKAY THEN, LET'S TRY A PANTSUIT.
HOW ABOUT WE PUT YOUR HAIR UP LIKE THIS...
OHMI-GOSH! IT FITS YOU PER-FECTLY!!
YOU'RE ADORABLE, MISAKI-CHAN!
WELL, KUROE? DOESN'T SHE LOOK AMAZING?!
MAYBE YOU JUST LOOK GOOD IN EVERYTHING, MISAKI.
OH NO, IT'S TOTALLY THE CLOTHES!
UH, OF COURSE.
OKAY, TRY THIS ONE!
WE'RE GOING TO BE HERE A WHILE, AREN'T WE?

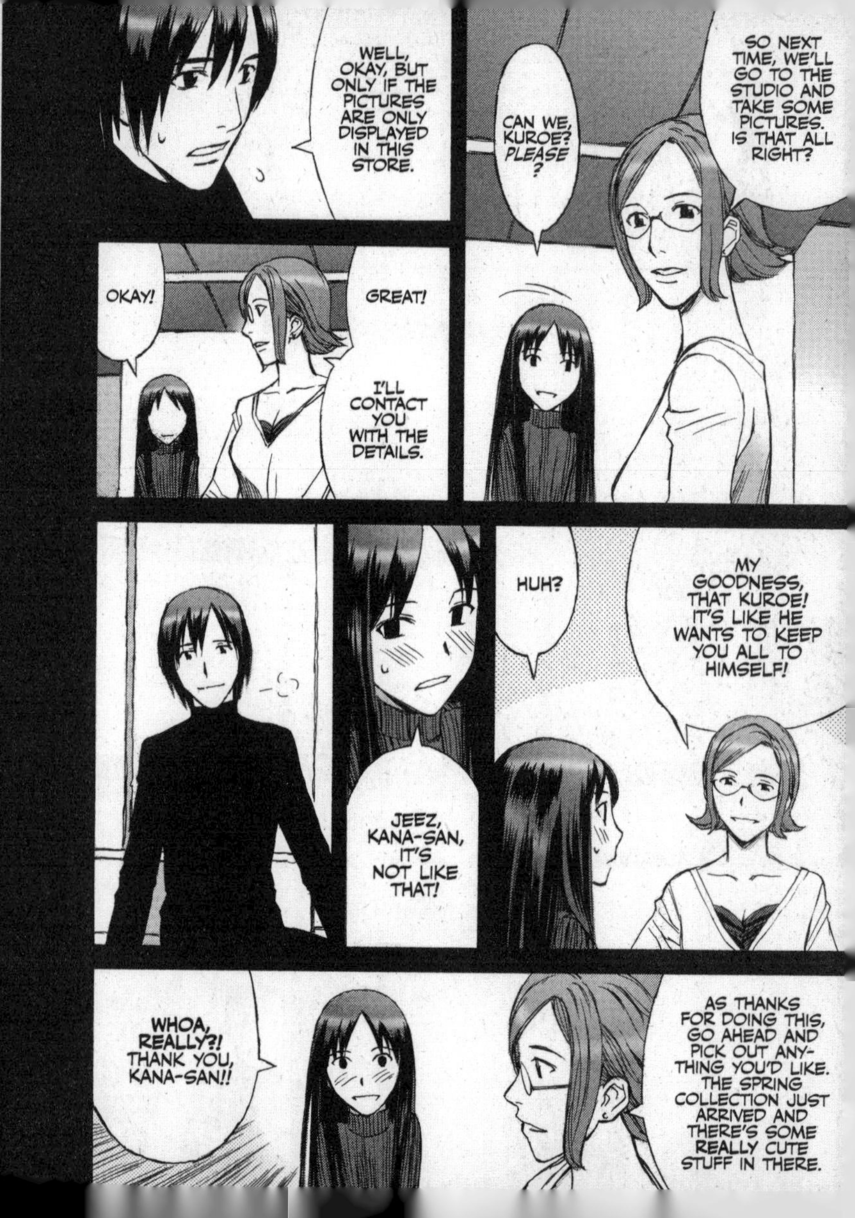

SO NEXT TIME, WE'LL GO TO THE STUDIO AND TAKE SOME PICTURES. IS THAT ALL RIGHT?
CAN WE, KUROE? *PLEASE*?
WELL, OKAY, BUT ONLY IF THE PICTURES ARE ONLY DISPLAYED IN THIS STORE.
GREAT!
I'LL CONTACT YOU WITH THE DETAILS.
OKAY!
MY GOODNESS, THAT KUROE! IT'S LIKE HE WANTS TO KEEP YOU ALL TO HIMSELF!
HUH?
JEEZ, KANA-SAN, IT'S NOT LIKE THAT!
AS THANKS FOR DOING THIS, GO AHEAD AND PICK OUT ANY-THING YOU'D LIKE. THE SPRING COLLECTION JUST ARRIVED AND THERE'S SOME REALLY CUTE STUFF IN THERE.
WHOA, REALLY?! THANK YOU, KANA-SAN!!

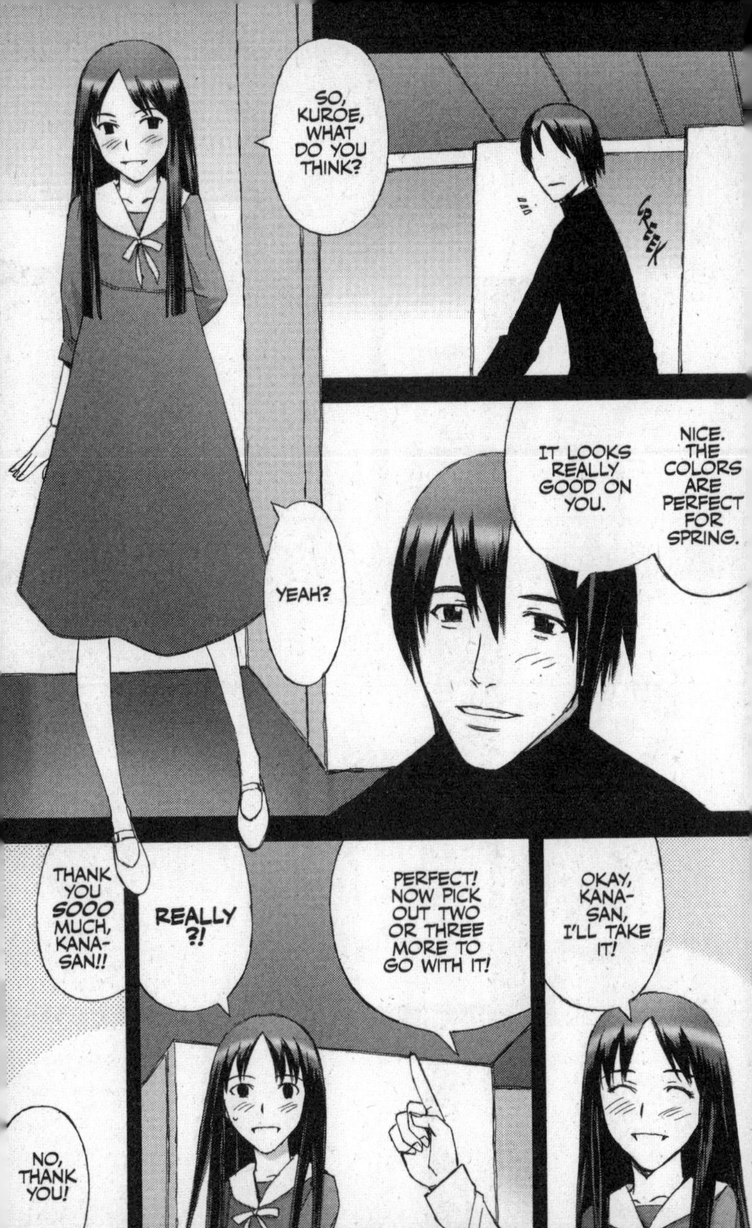
CREEEK
...
NICE. THE COLORS ARE PERFECT FOR SPRING.
IT LOOKS REALLY GOOD ON YOU.
SO, KUROE, WHAT DO YOU THINK?
YEAH?
OKAY, KANA-SAN, I'LL TAKE IT!
PERFECT! NOW PICK OUT TWO OR THREE MORE TO GO WITH IT!
REALLY ?!
THANK YOU SOOO MUCH, KANA-SAN!!
NO, THANK YOU!

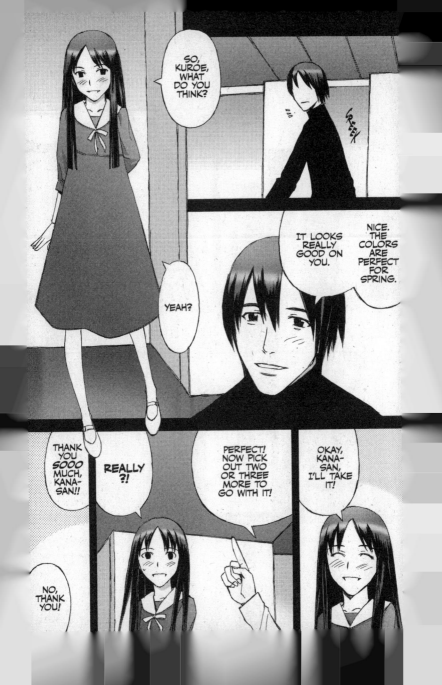

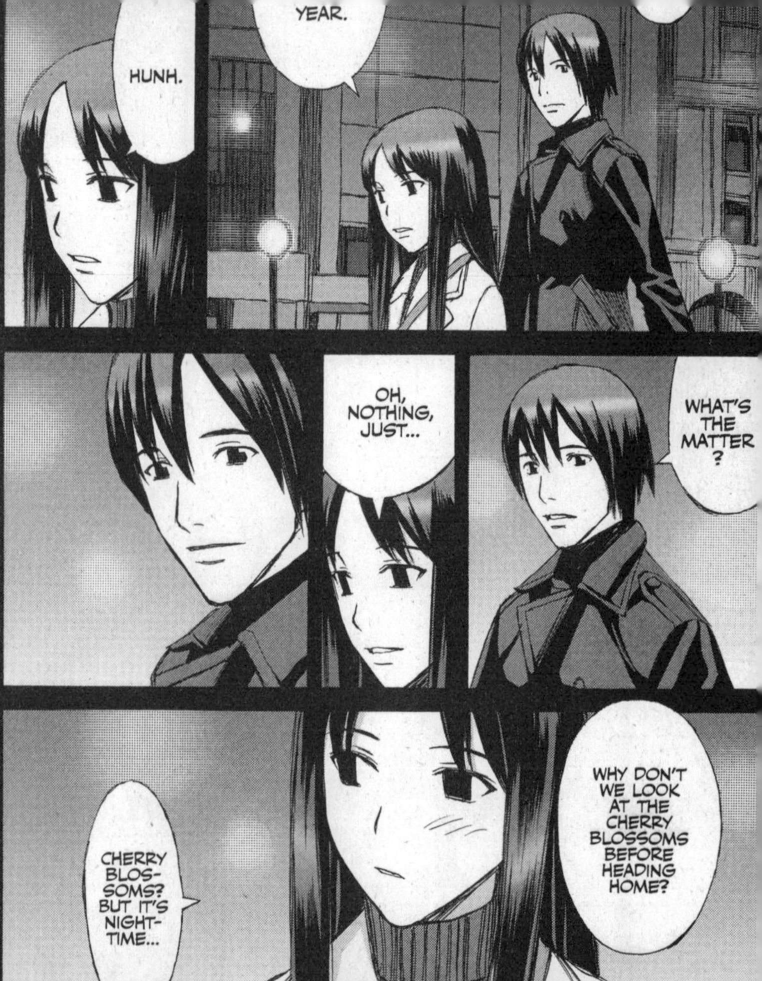
YEAR.
HUNH.
WHAT'S THE MATTER?
OH, NOTHING, JUST...
WHY DON'T WE LOOK AT THE CHERRY BLOSSOMS BEFORE HEADING HOME?
CHERRY BLOSSOMS? BUT IT'S NIGHTTIME...

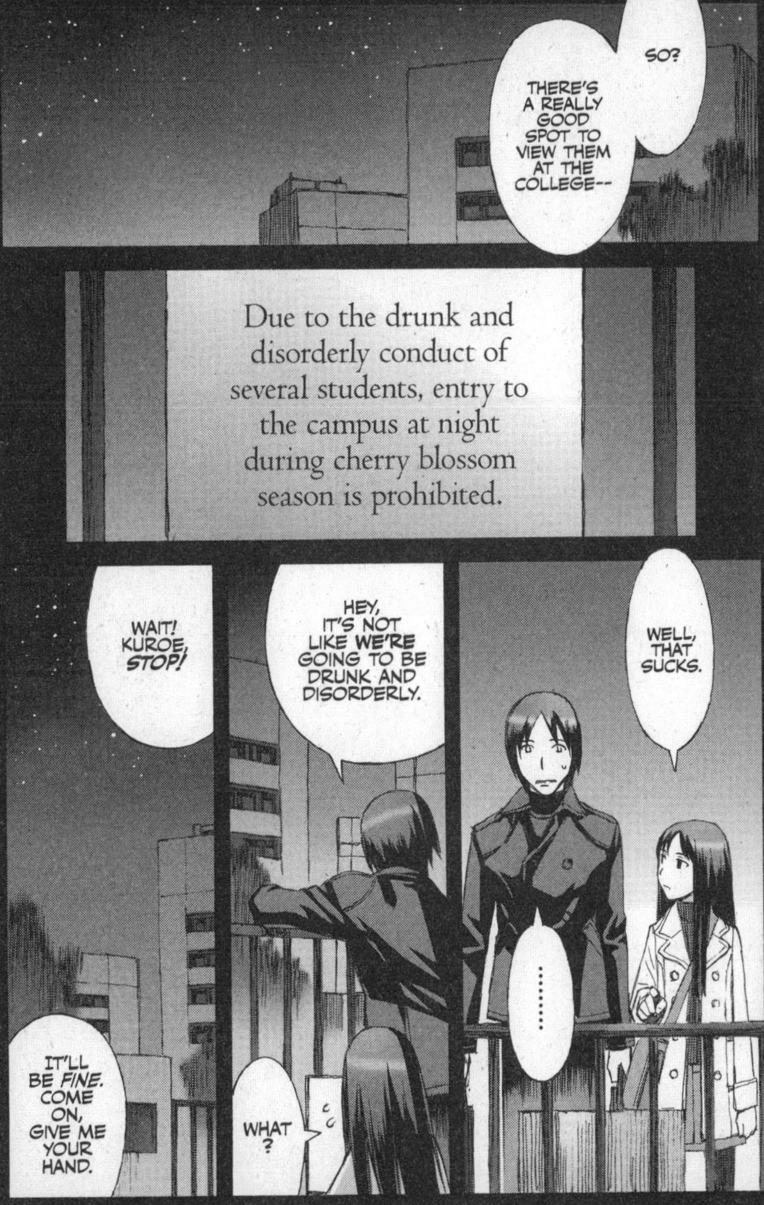
SO?
THERE'S A REALLY GOOD SPOT TO VIEW THEM AT THE COLLEGE--
Due to the drunk and disorderly conduct of several students, entry to the campus at night during cherry blossom season is prohibited.
WELL, THAT SUCKS.
......
HEY, IT'S NOT LIKE WE'RE GOING TO BE DRUNK AND DISORDERLY.
WHAT?
WAIT! KUROE, STOP!
IT'LL BE FINE. COME ON, GIVE ME YOUR HAND.

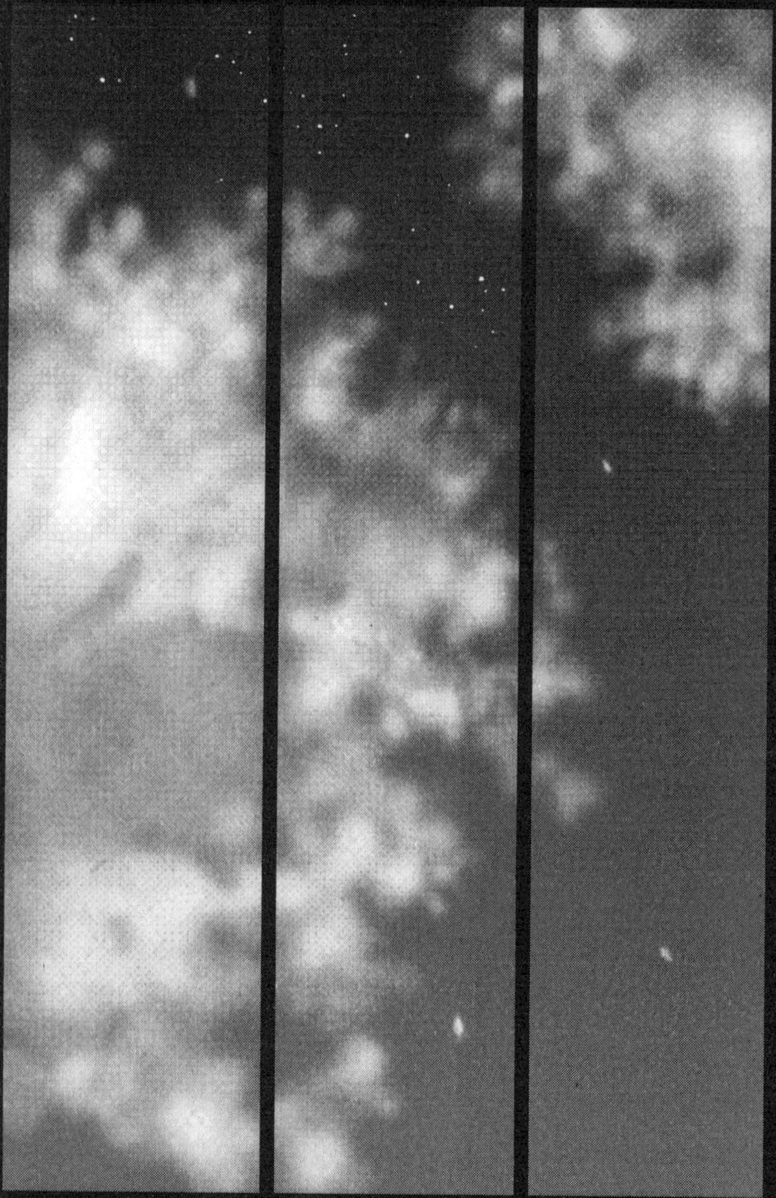

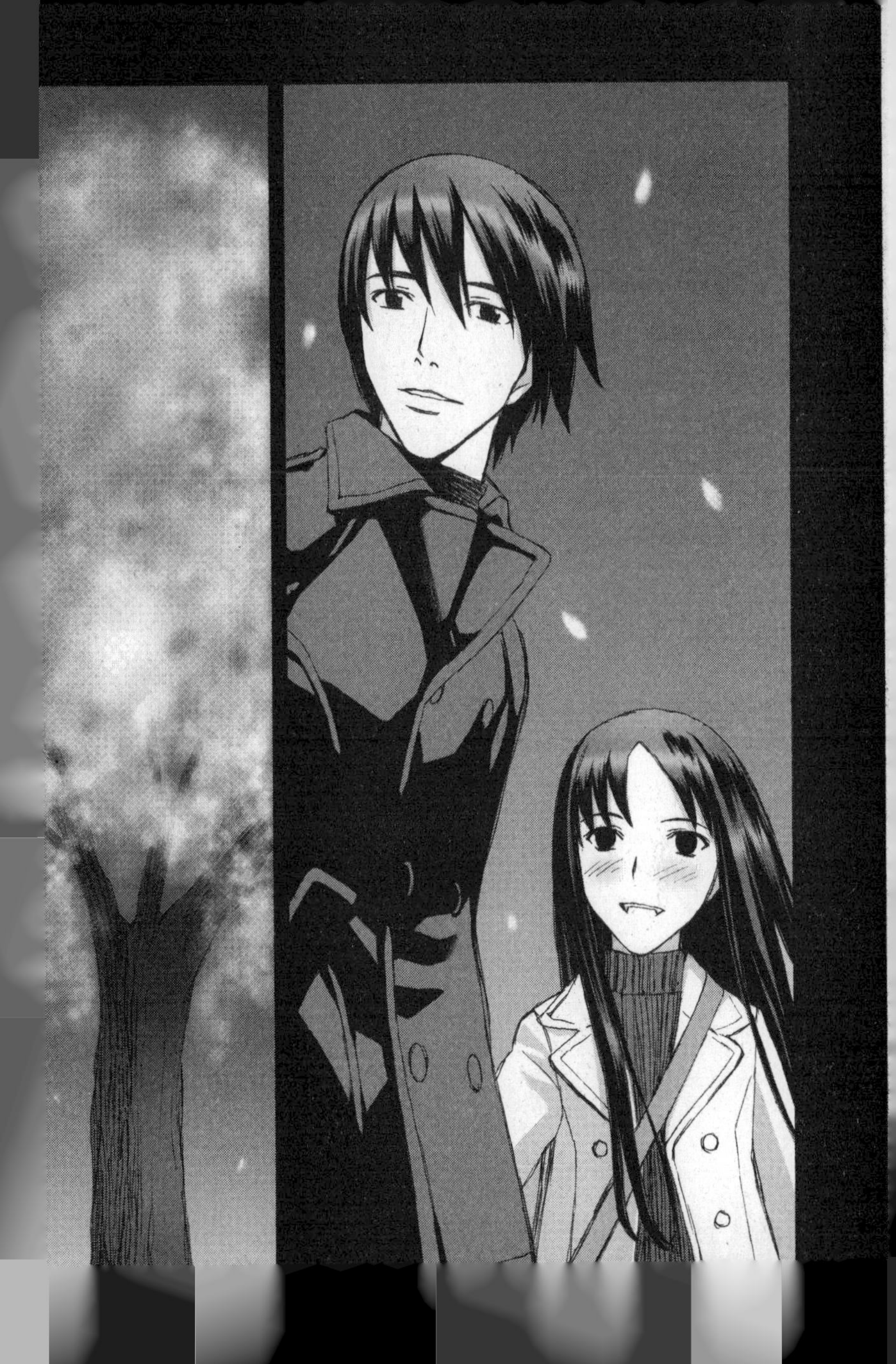

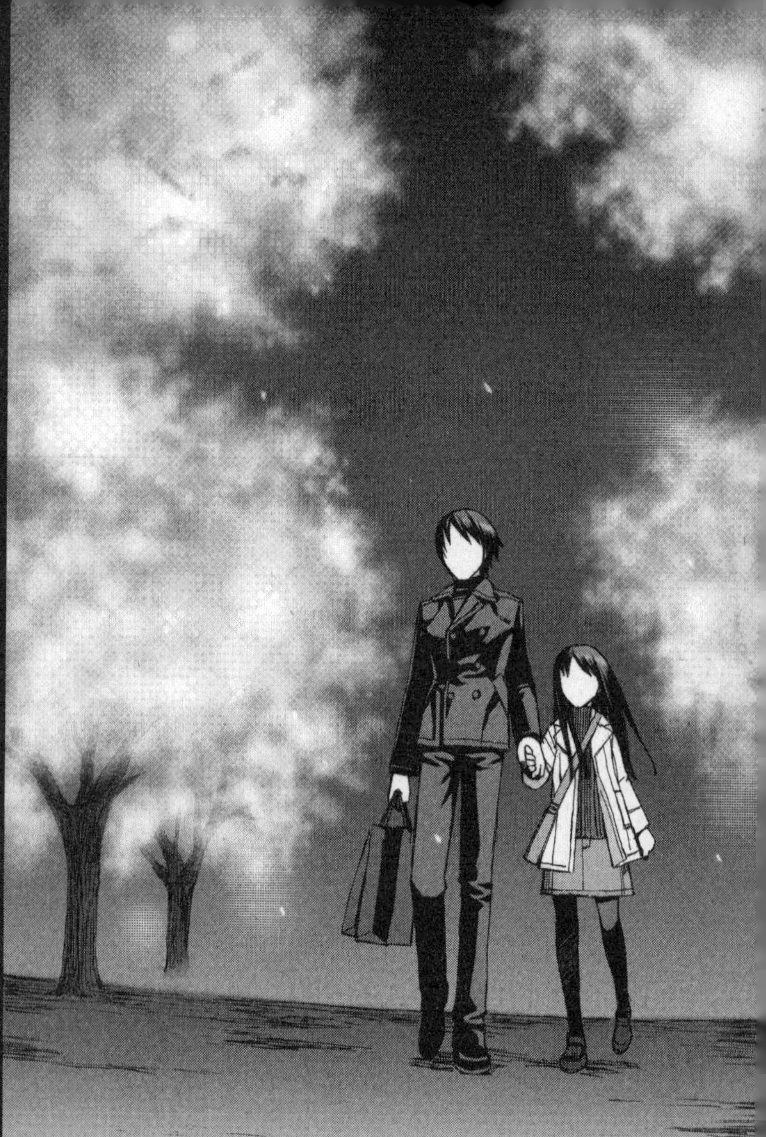

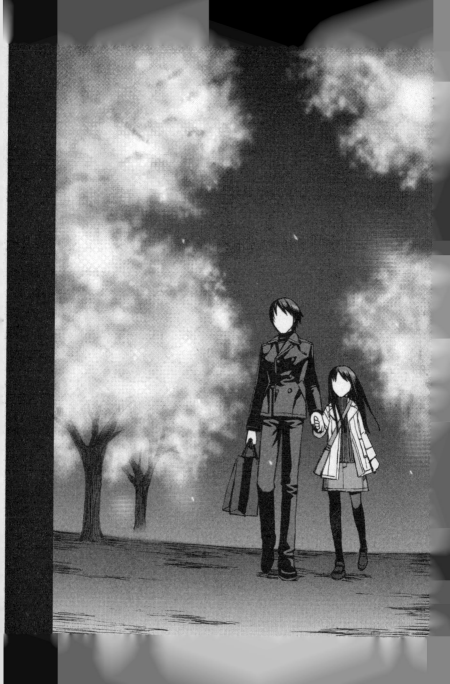

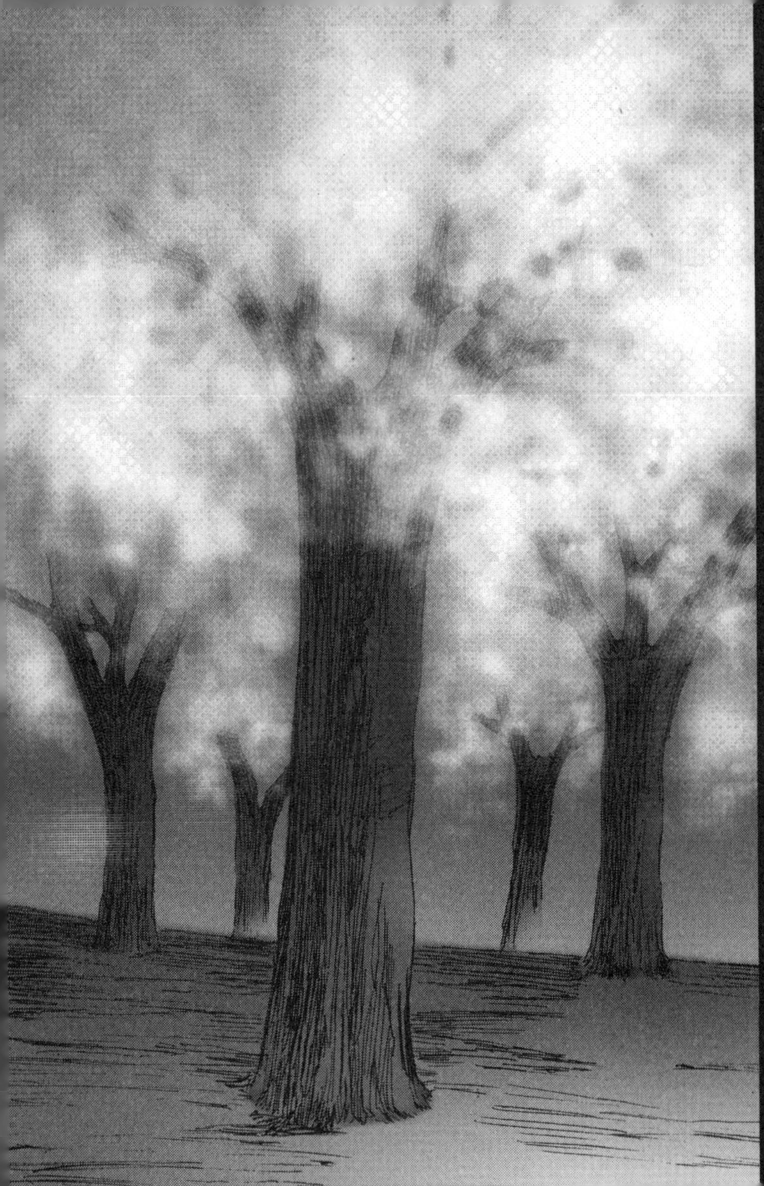

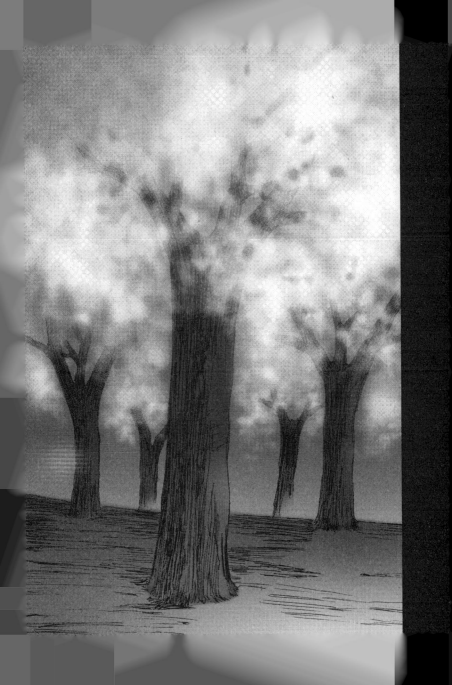

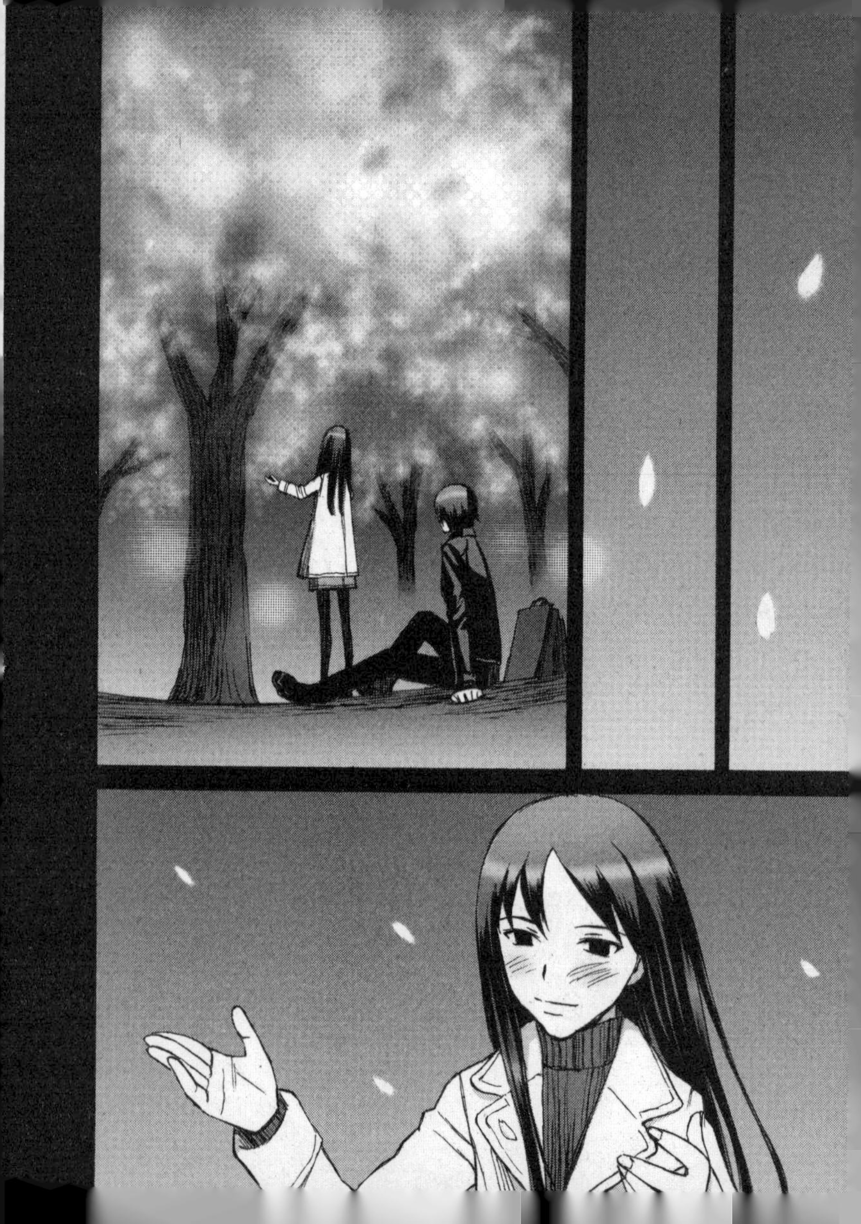

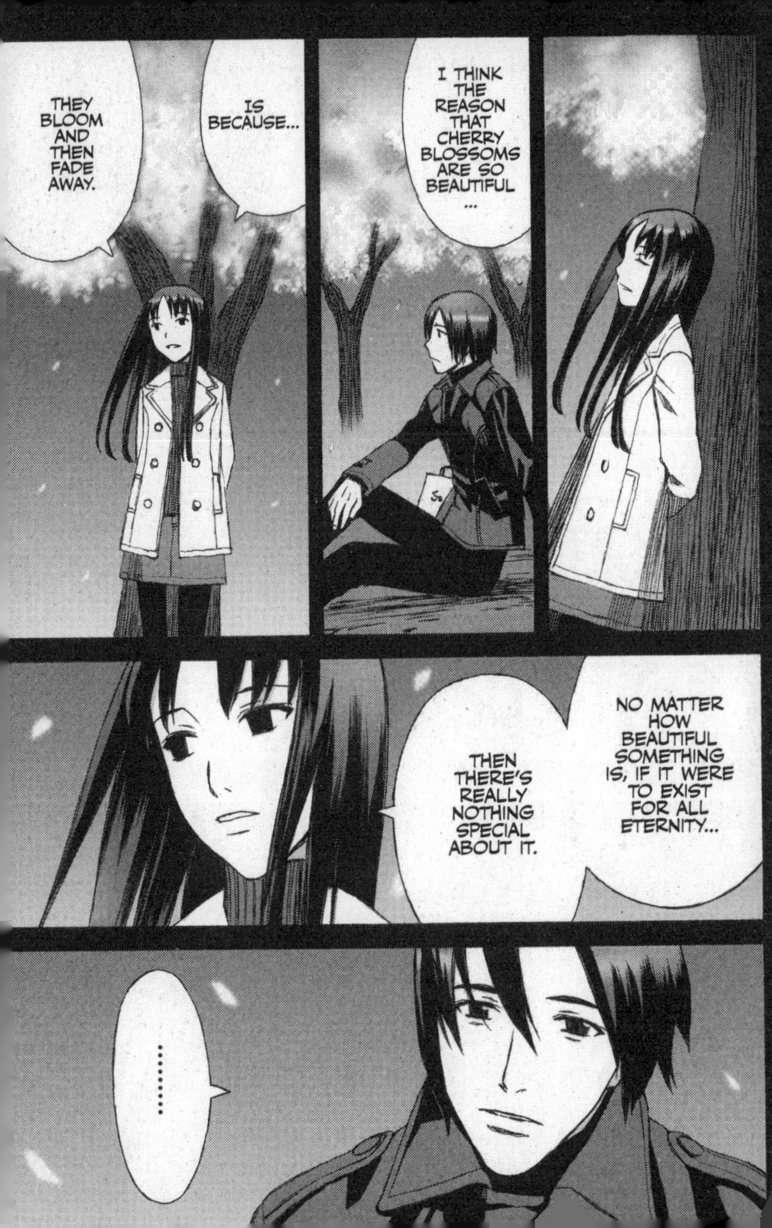
I THINK THE REASON THAT CHERRY BLOSSOMS ARE SO BEAUTIFUL ...
IS BECAUSE...
THEY BLOOM AND THEN FADE AWAY.
NO MATTER HOW BEAUTIFUL SOMETHING IS, IF IT WERE TO EXIST FOR ALL ETERNITY...
THEN THERE'S REALLY NOTHING SPECIAL ABOUT IT.
....

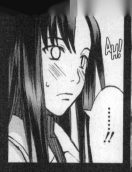

WELL, IF THAT'S THE CASE, YOU'LL BE FINE, MISAKI.
YOU HAVEN'T EVEN BLOOMED, AFTER ALL.
AH!
......!!
HEY, WHAT'S THAT SUPPOSED TO MEAN?
BUT...
IF YOU HAD, I'M SURE...

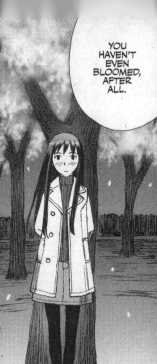

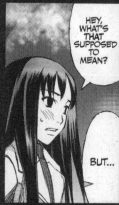

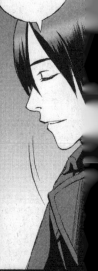

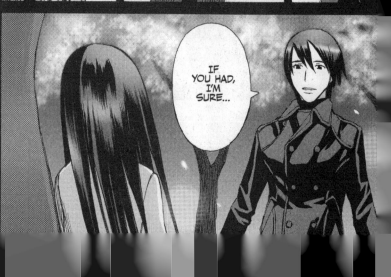

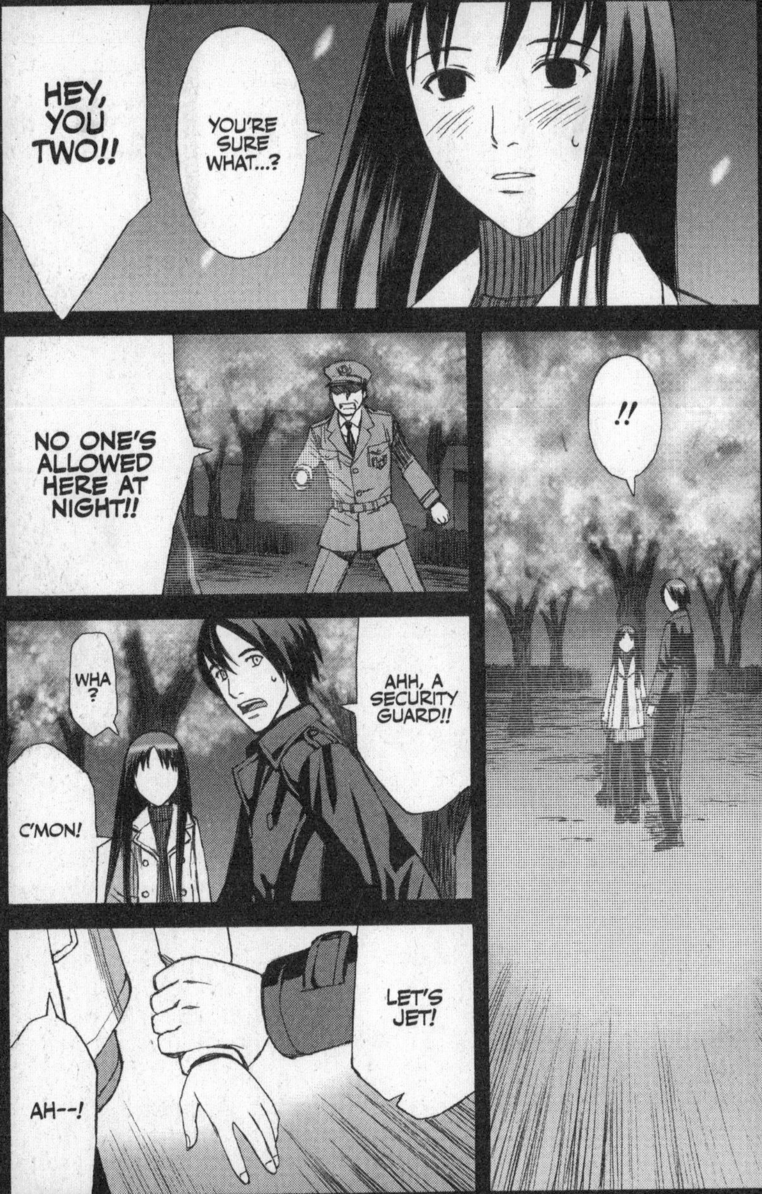
YOU'RE SURE WHAT...?
HEY, YOU TWO!!
!!
NO ONE'S ALLOWED HERE AT NIGHT!!
AHH, A SECURITY GUARD!!
WHA?
C'MON!
LET'S JET!
AH--!

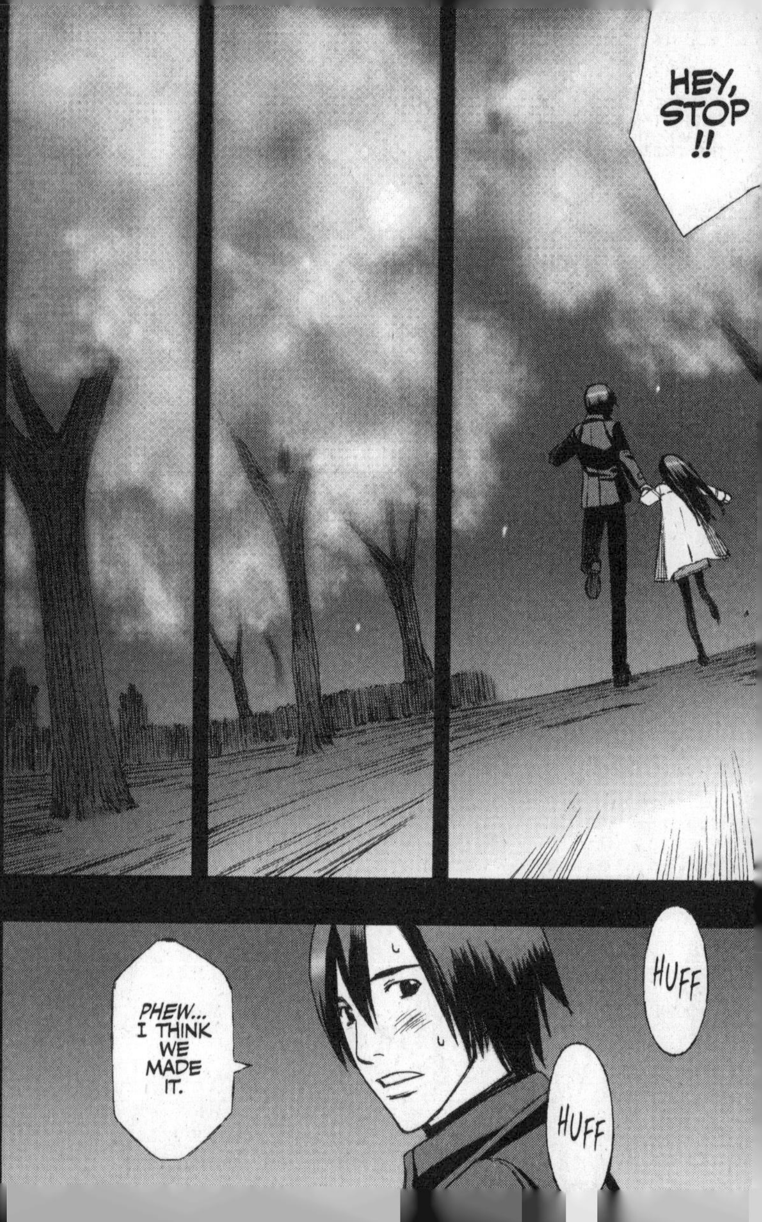
HEY, STOP !!
HUFF
HUFF
PHEW... I THINK WE MADE IT.

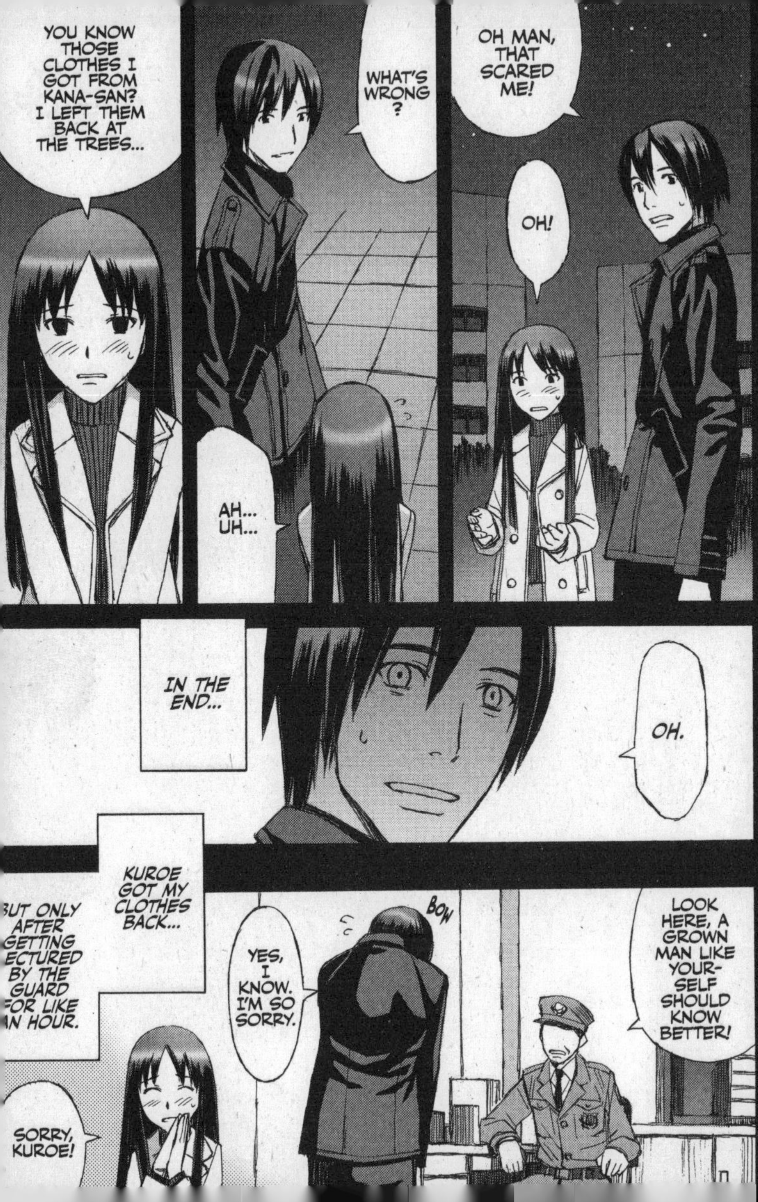

OH MAN, THAT SCARED ME!
OH!
WHAT'S WRONG?
AH... UH...
YOU KNOW THOSE CLOTHES I GOT FROM KANA-SAN? I LEFT THEM BACK AT THE TREES...
OH.
IN THE END...
LOOK HERE, A GROWN MAN LIKE YOUR-SELF SHOULD KNOW BETTER!
BOW
YES, I KNOW. I'M SO SORRY.
KUROE GOT MY CLOTHES BACK...
BUT ONLY AFTER GETTING LECTURED BY THE GUARD FOR LIKE AN HOUR.
SORRY, KUROE!

Episode 16
MY FIRST MEMORY
Our Shared Memory

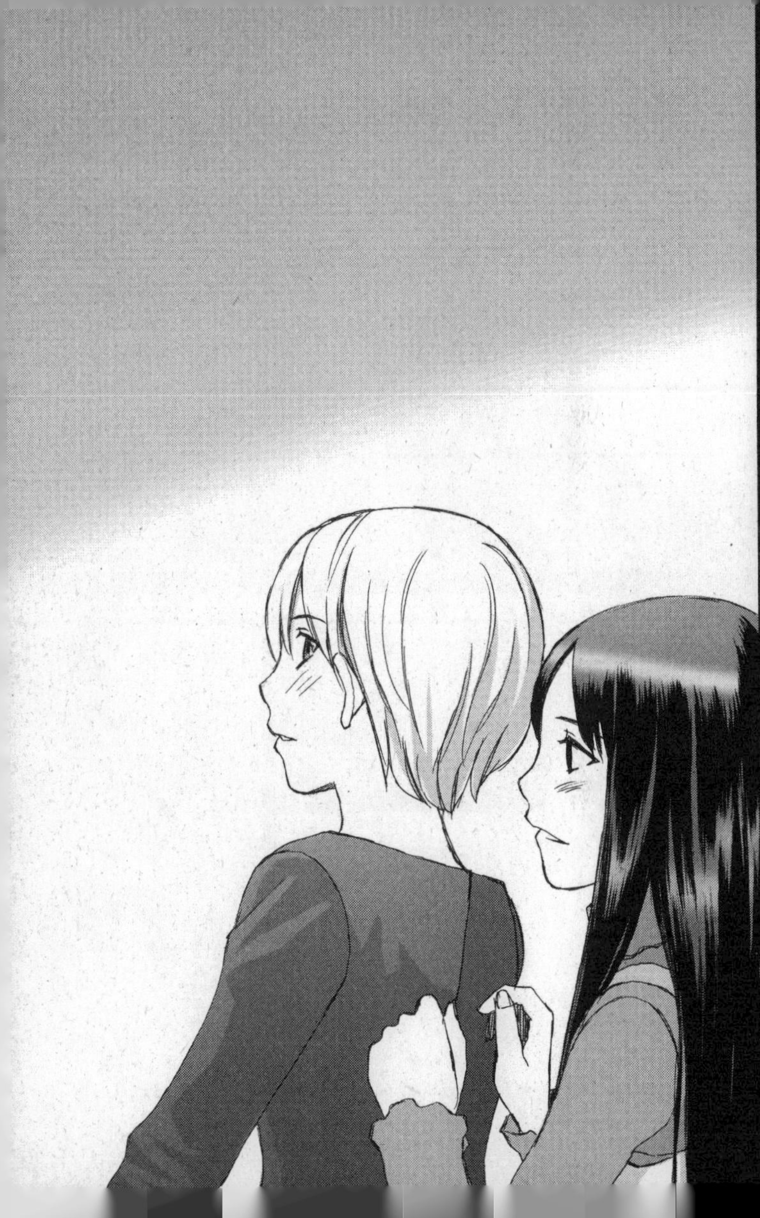

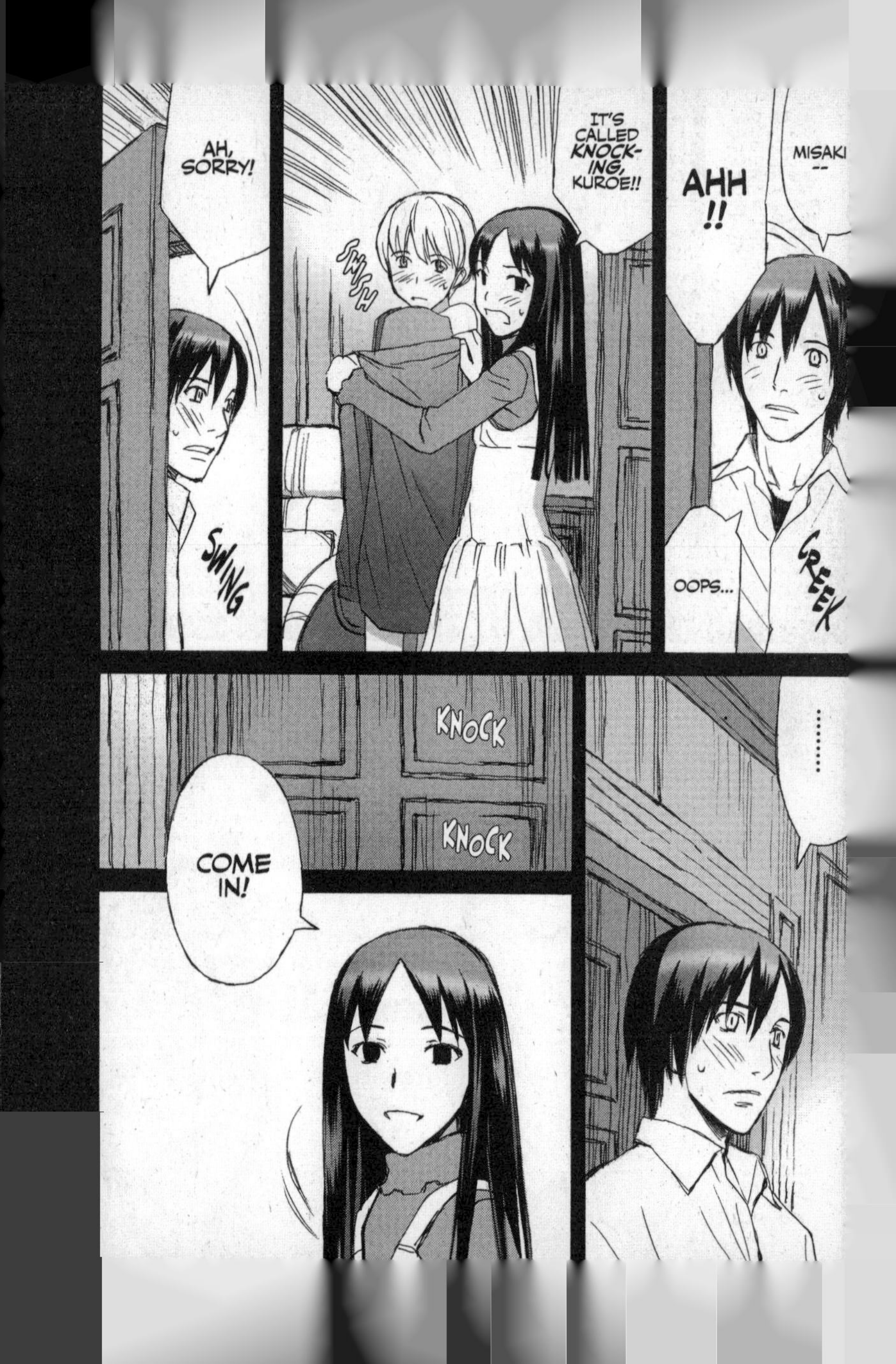
MISAKI --
AHH !!
CREEK
OOPS...
IT'S CALLED KNOCKING, KUROE!!
SWISH
AH, SORRY!
SWING
......
KNOCK
KNOCK
COME IN!

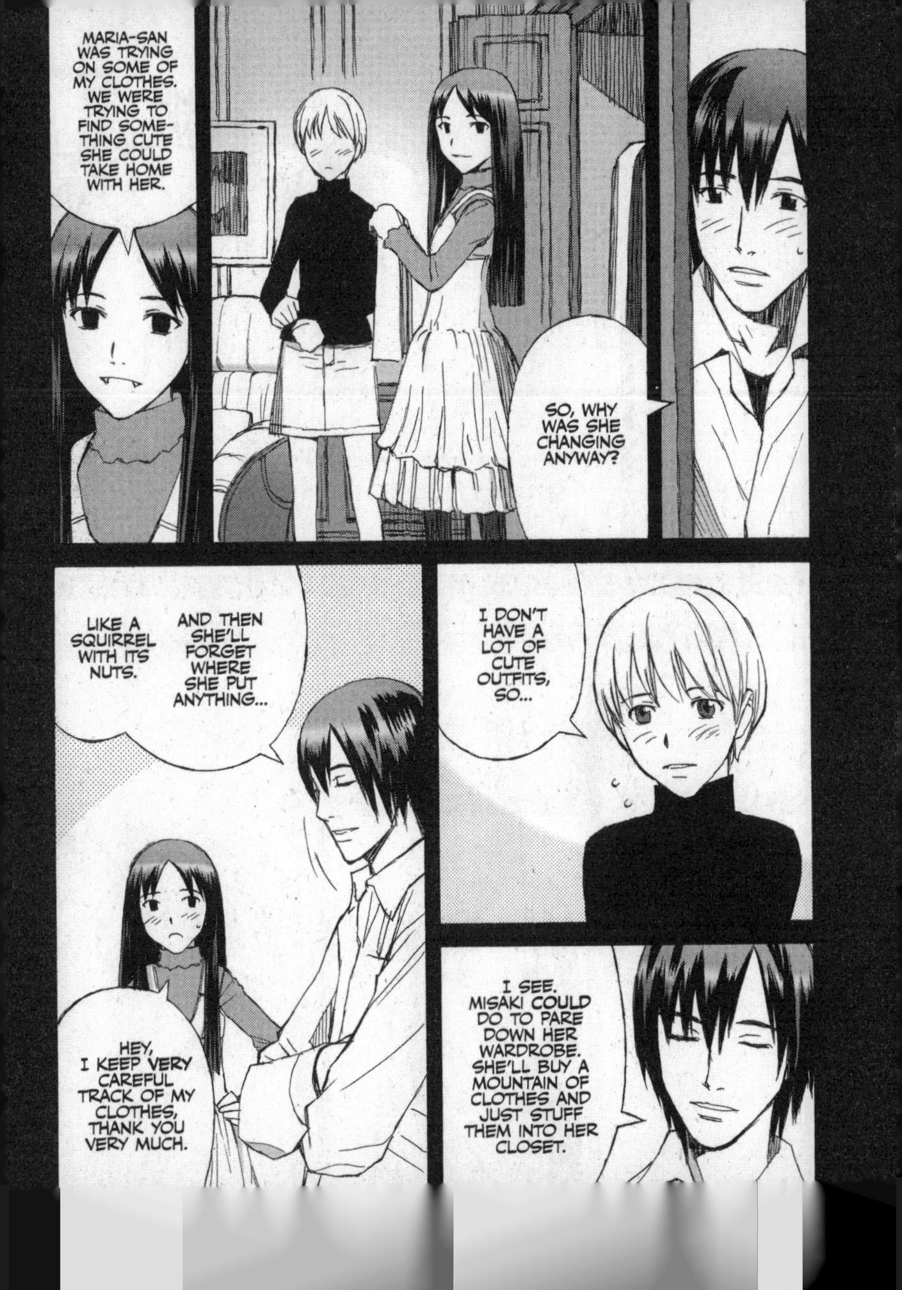
SO, WHY WAS SHE CHANGING ANYWAY?
MARIA-SAN WAS TRYING ON SOME OF MY CLOTHES. WE WERE TRYING TO FIND SOME-THING CUTE SHE COULD TAKE HOME WITH HER.
I DON'T HAVE A LOT OF CUTE OUTFITS, SO...
I SEE. MISAKI COULD DO TO PARE DOWN HER WARDROBE. SHE'LL BUY A MOUNTAIN OF CLOTHES AND JUST STUFF THEM INTO HER CLOSET.
AND THEN SHE'LL FORGET WHERE SHE PUT ANYTHING...
LIKE A SQUIRREL WITH ITS NUTS.
HEY, I KEEP VERY CAREFUL TRACK OF MY CLOTHES, THANK YOU VERY MUCH.

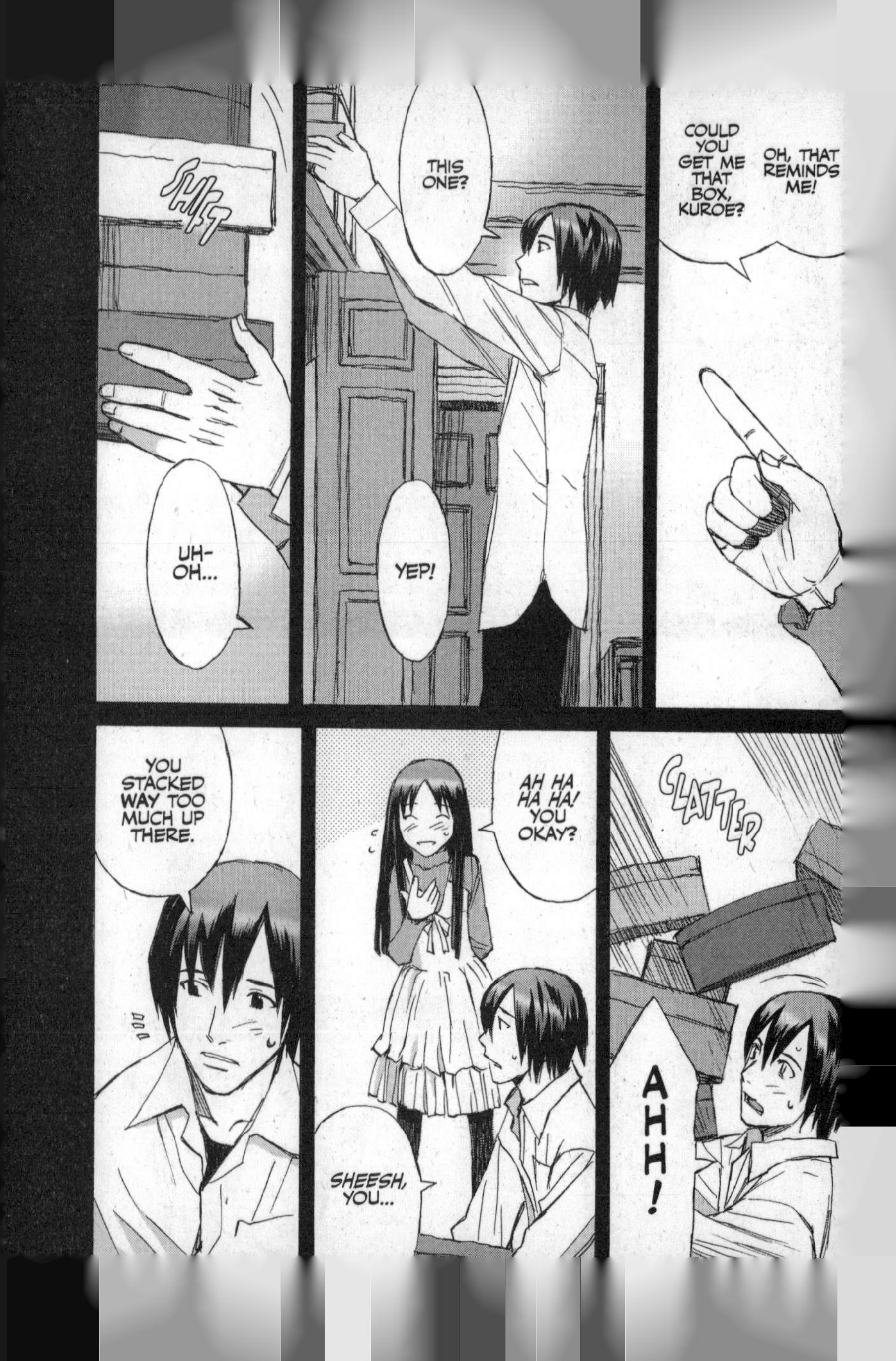
OH, THAT REMINDS ME!
COULD YOU GET ME THAT BOX, KUROE?
THIS ONE?
YEP!
SHFT
UH-OH...
CLATTER
AHH!
AH HA HA HA! YOU OKAY?
SHEESH, YOU...
YOU STACKED WAY TOO MUCH UP THERE.

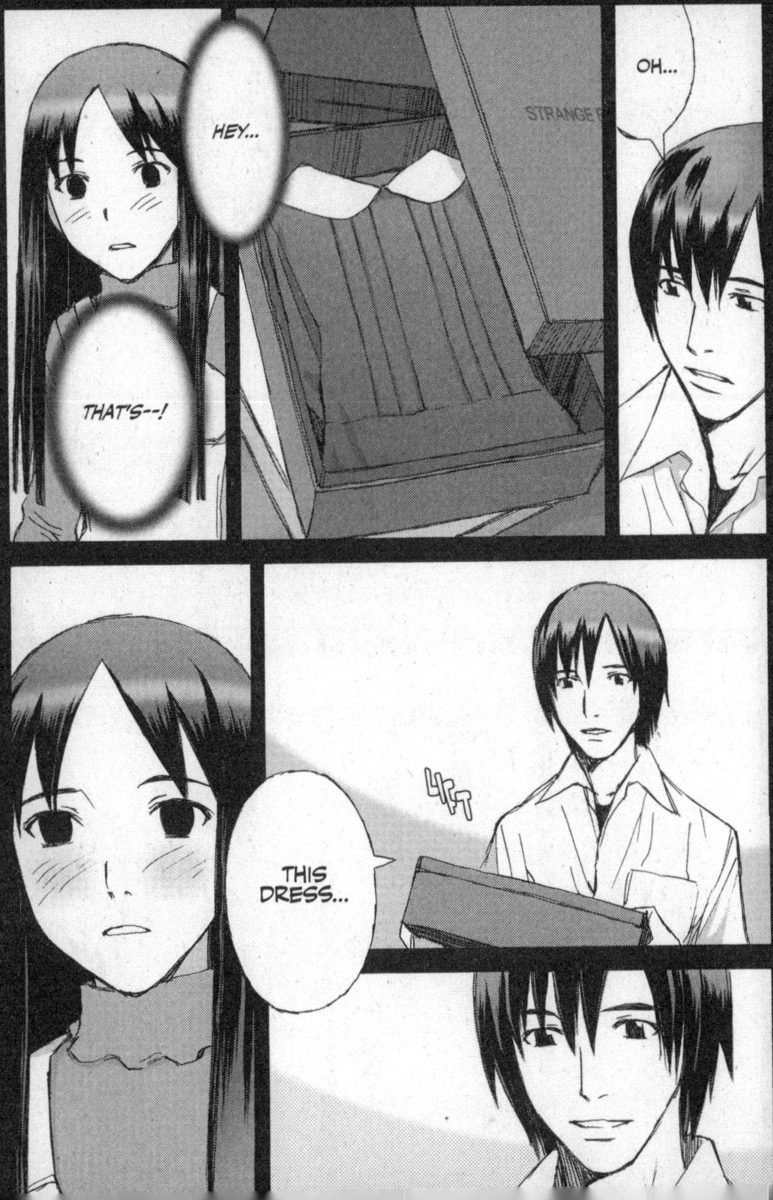
OH...
STRANGE
HEY...
THAT'S--!
LIFT
THIS DRESS...

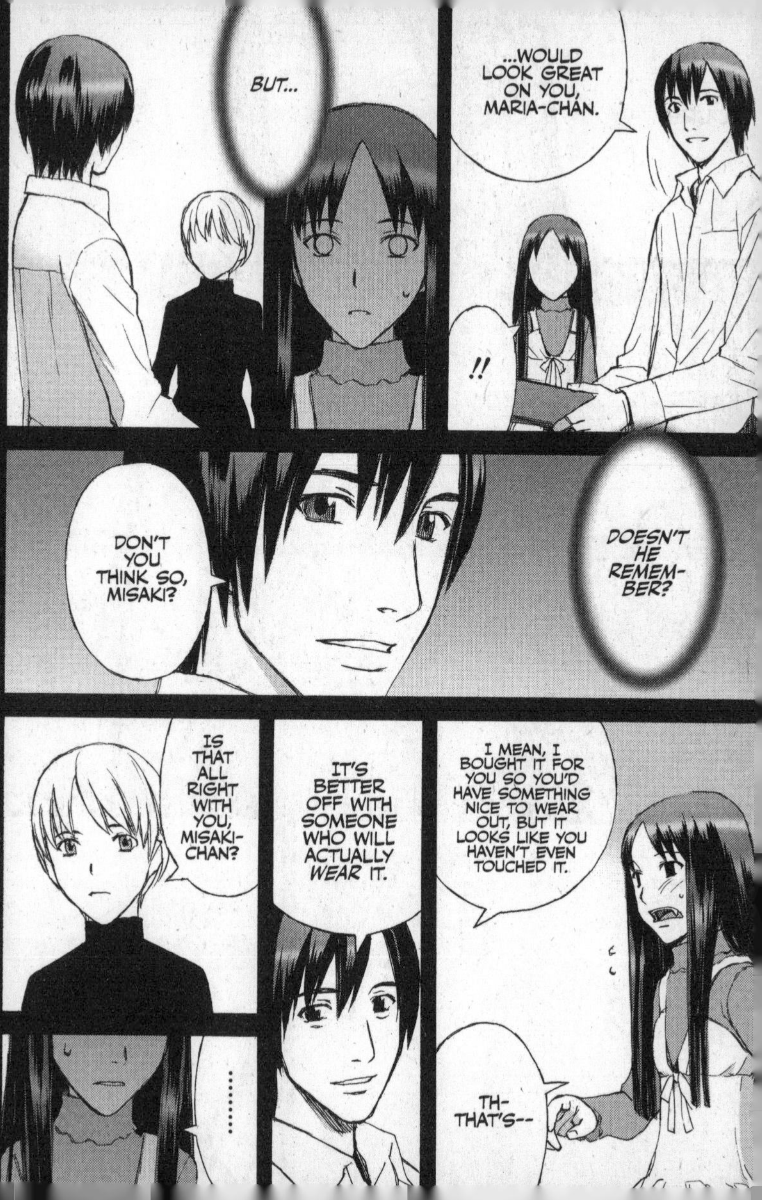
...WOULD LOOK GREAT ON YOU, MARIA-CHAN.
!!
BUT...
DOESN'T HE REMEMBER?
DON'T YOU THINK SO, MISAKI?
I MEAN, I BOUGHT IT FOR YOU SO YOU'D HAVE SOMETHING NICE TO WEAR OUT, BUT IT LOOKS LIKE YOU HAVEN'T EVEN TOUCHED IT.
TH- THAT'S--
IT'S BETTER OFF WITH SOMEONE WHO WILL ACTUALLY *WEAR* IT.
IS THAT ALL RIGHT WITH YOU, MISAKI-CHAN?
......

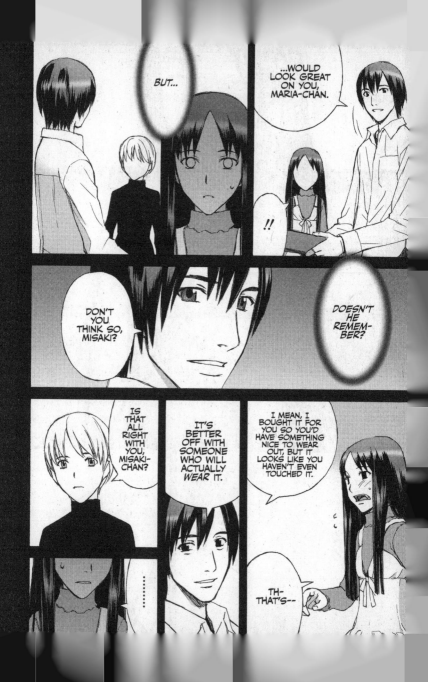

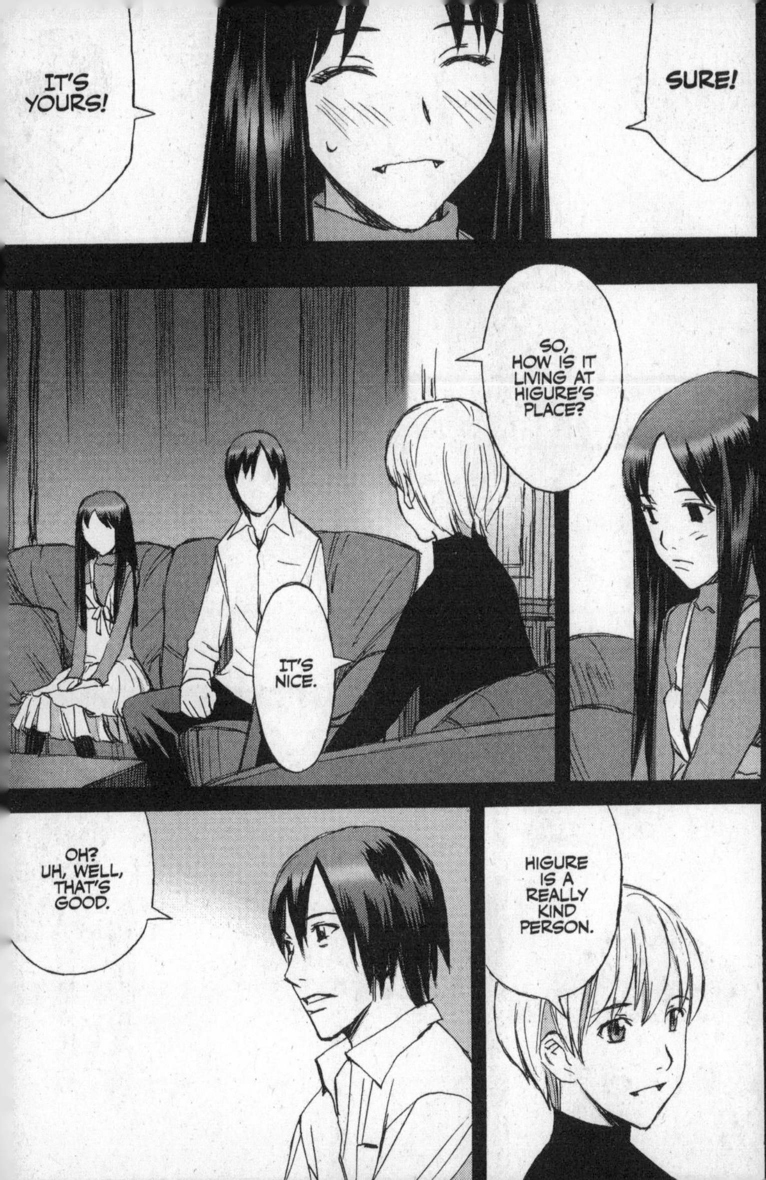
SURE!
IT'S YOURS!
SO, HOW IS IT LIVING AT HIGURE'S PLACE?
IT'S NICE.
HIGURE IS A REALLY KIND PERSON.
OH? UH, WELL, THAT'S GOOD.

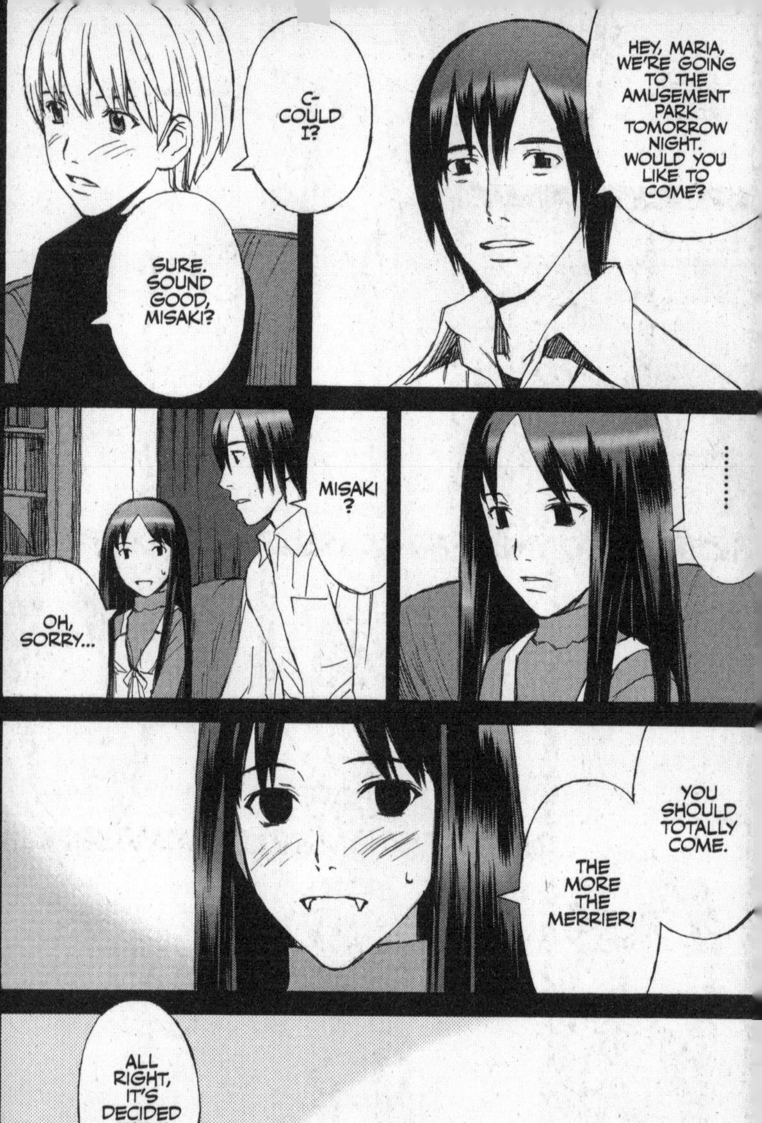
HEY, MARIA, WE'RE GOING TO THE AMUSEMENT PARK TOMORROW NIGHT. WOULD YOU LIKE TO COME?
C-COULD I?
SURE. SOUND GOOD, MISAKI?
......
MISAKI?
OH, SORRY...
YOU SHOULD TOTALLY COME.
THE MORE THE MERRIER!
ALL RIGHT, IT'S DECIDED THEN!

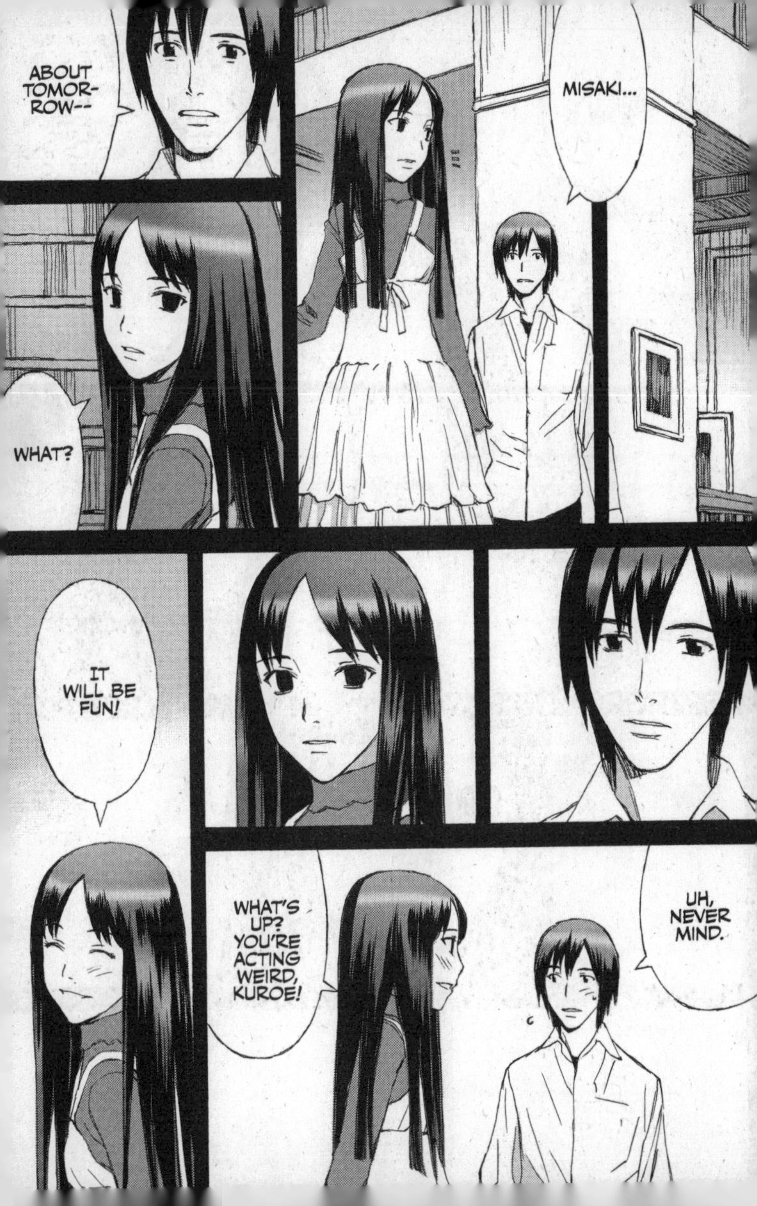
MISAKI...
ABOUT TOMOR-ROW--
WHAT?
UH, NEVER MIND.
WHAT'S UP? YOU'RE ACTING WEIRD, KUROE!
IT WILL BE FUN!

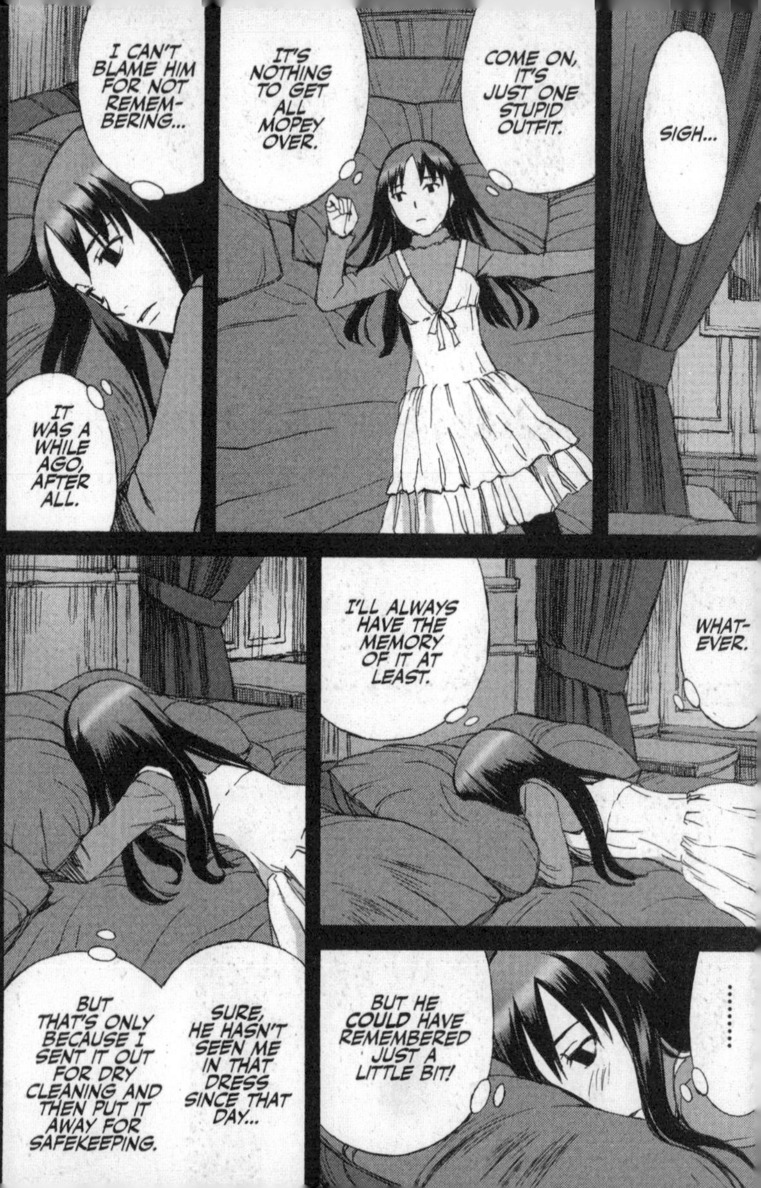
SIGH...
COME ON, IT'S JUST ONE STUPID OUTFIT.
IT'S NOTHING TO GET ALL MOPEY OVER.
I CAN'T BLAME HIM FOR NOT REMEMBERING...
IT WAS A WHILE AGO, AFTER ALL.
WHATEVER.
I'LL ALWAYS HAVE THE MEMORY OF IT AT LEAST.
....
BUT HE COULD HAVE REMEMBERED JUST A LITTLE BIT!
SURE, HE HASN'T SEEN ME IN THAT DRESS SINCE THAT DAY...
BUT THAT'S ONLY BECAUSE I SENT IT OUT FOR DRY CLEANING AND THEN PUT IT AWAY FOR SAFEKEEPING.

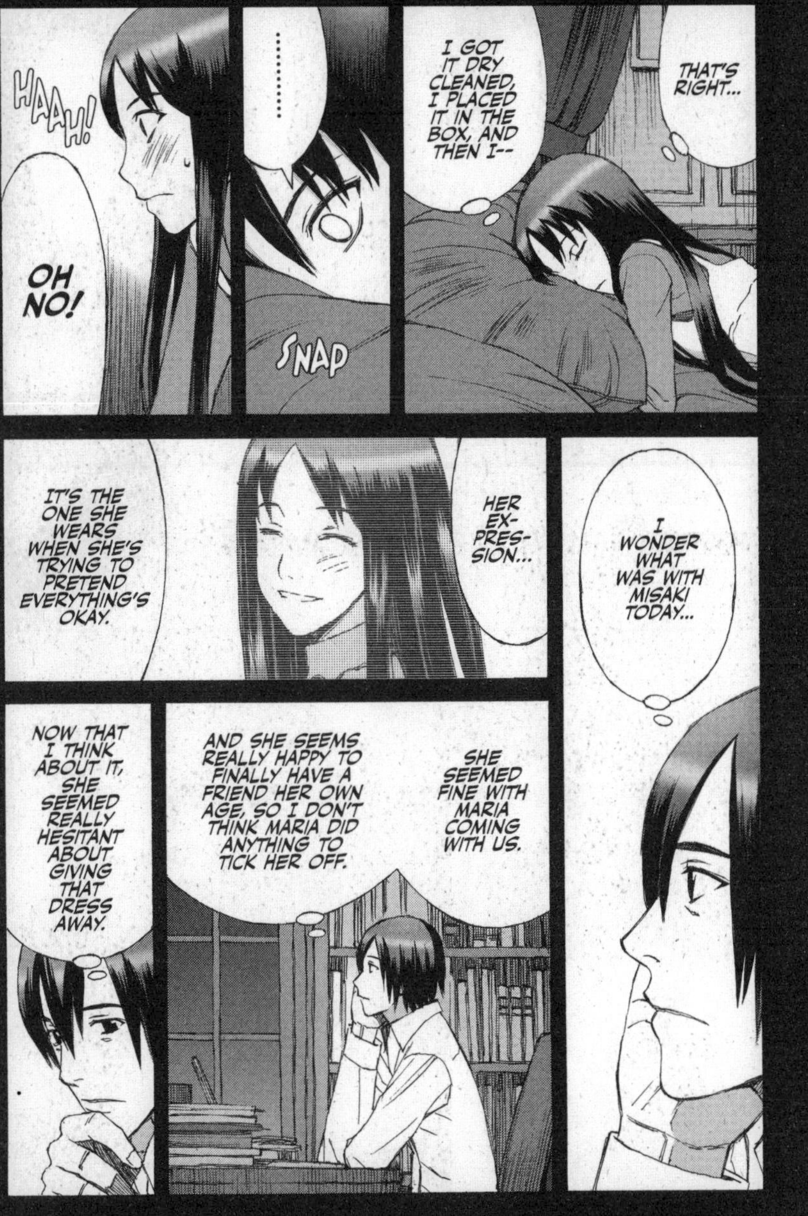
THAT'S RIGHT...
I GOT IT DRY CLEANED, I PLACED IT IN THE BOX, AND THEN I--
......
SNAP
HAAAH!
OH NO!
I WONDER WHAT WAS WITH MISAKI TODAY...
HER EX-PRES-SION...
IT'S THE ONE SHE WEARS WHEN SHE'S TRYING TO PRETEND EVERYTHING'S OKAY.
SHE SEEMED FINE WITH MARIA COMING WITH US.
AND SHE SEEMS REALLY HAPPY TO FINALLY HAVE A FRIEND HER OWN AGE, SO I DON'T THINK MARIA DID ANYTHING TO TICK HER OFF.
NOW THAT I THINK ABOUT IT, SHE SEEMED REALLY HESITANT ABOUT GIVING THAT DRESS AWAY.

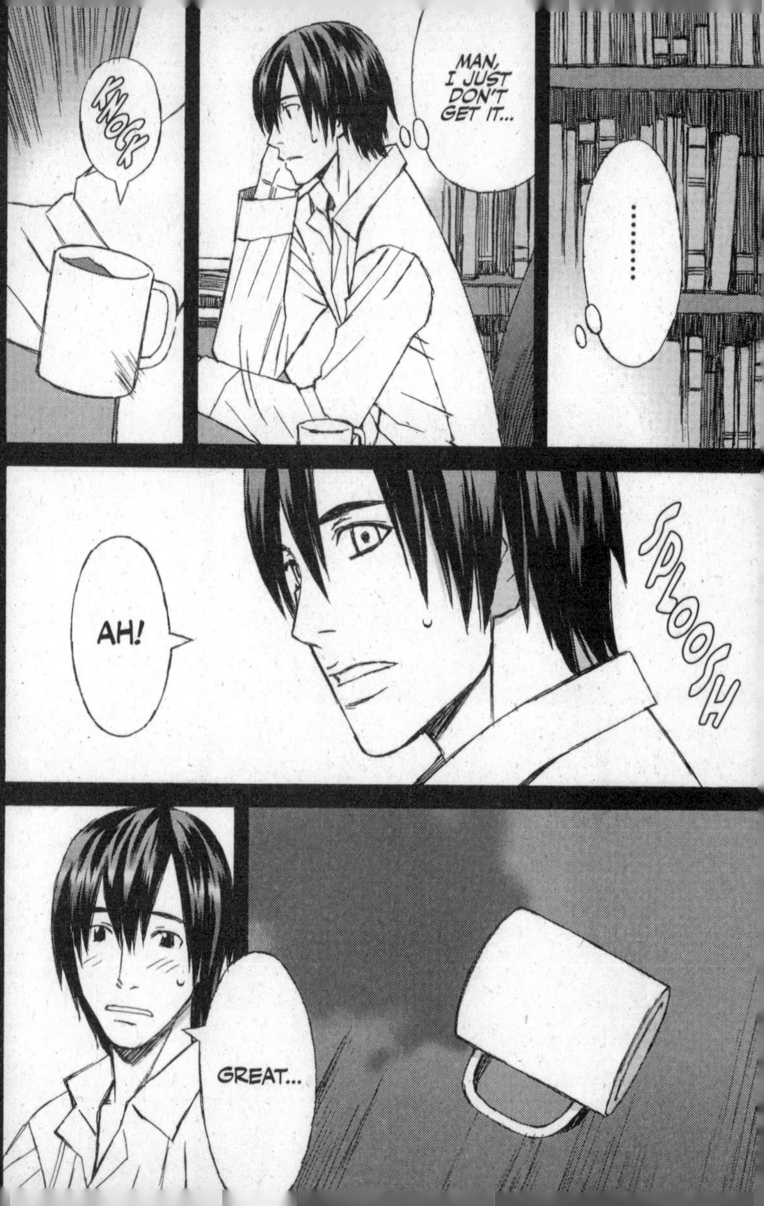
......
MAN, I JUST DON'T GET IT...
KNOCK
SPLOOSH
AH!
GREAT...

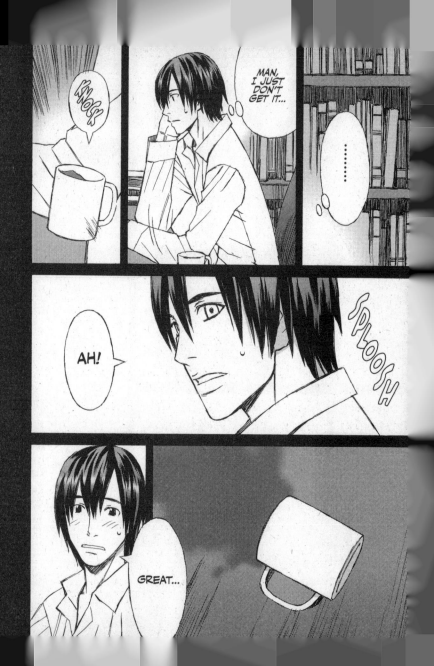

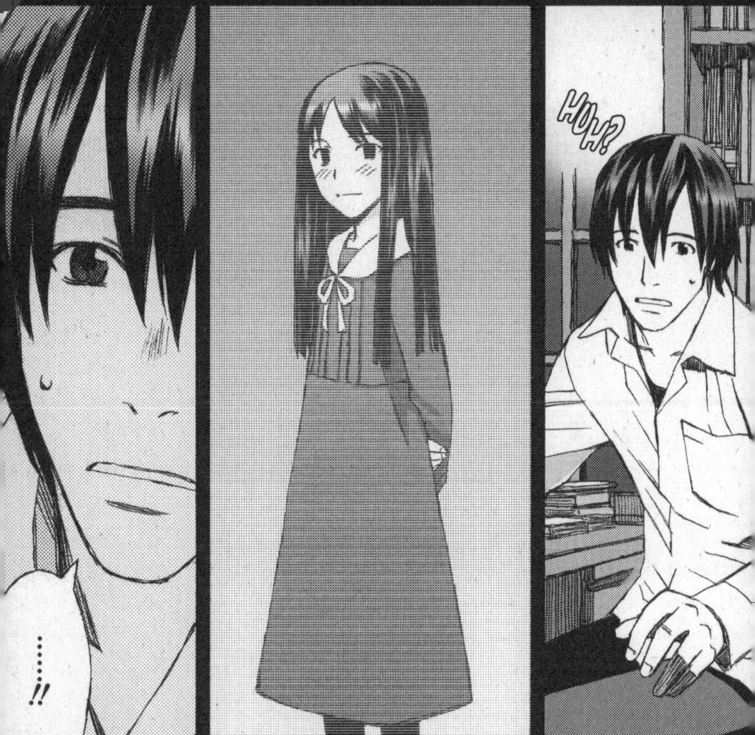
HUH?
......!!
WAIT...
WAS THAT THE DRESS SHE--?!

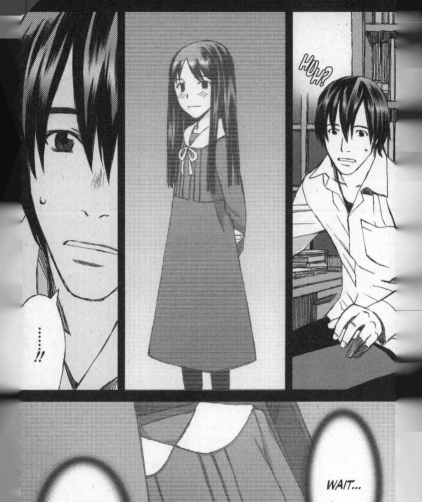

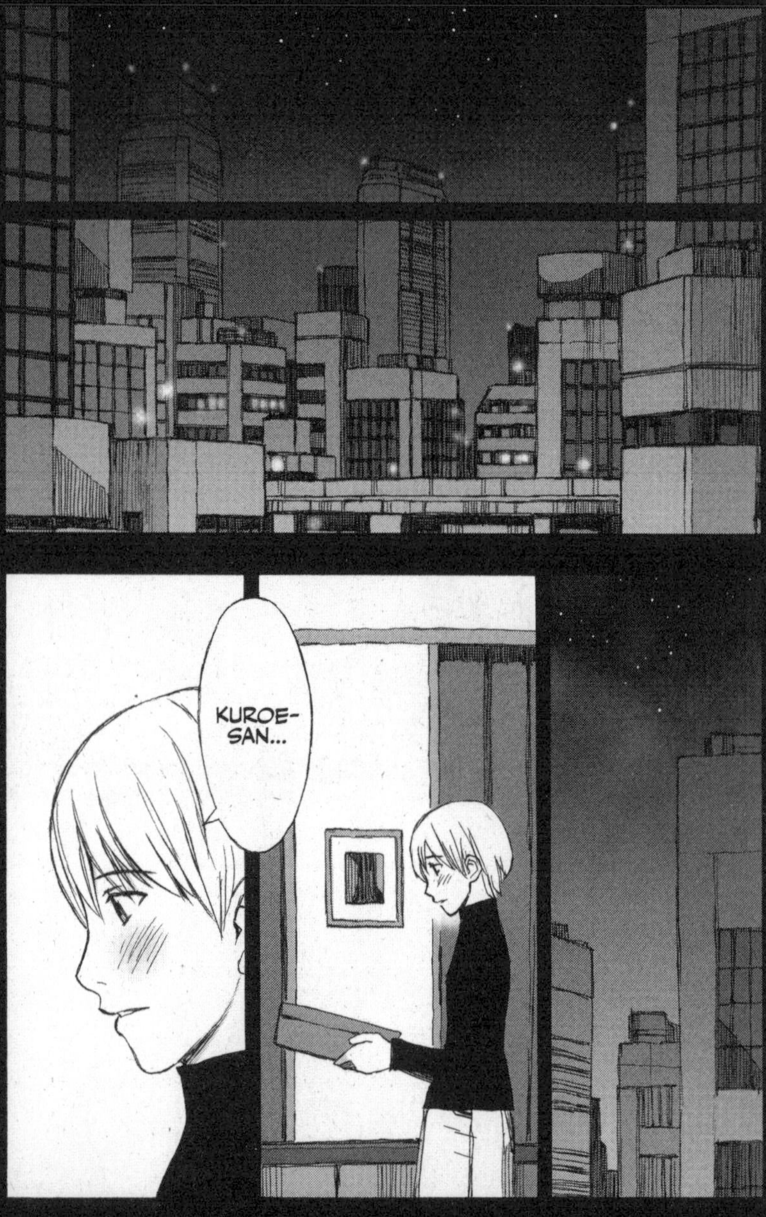
KUROE-SAN...

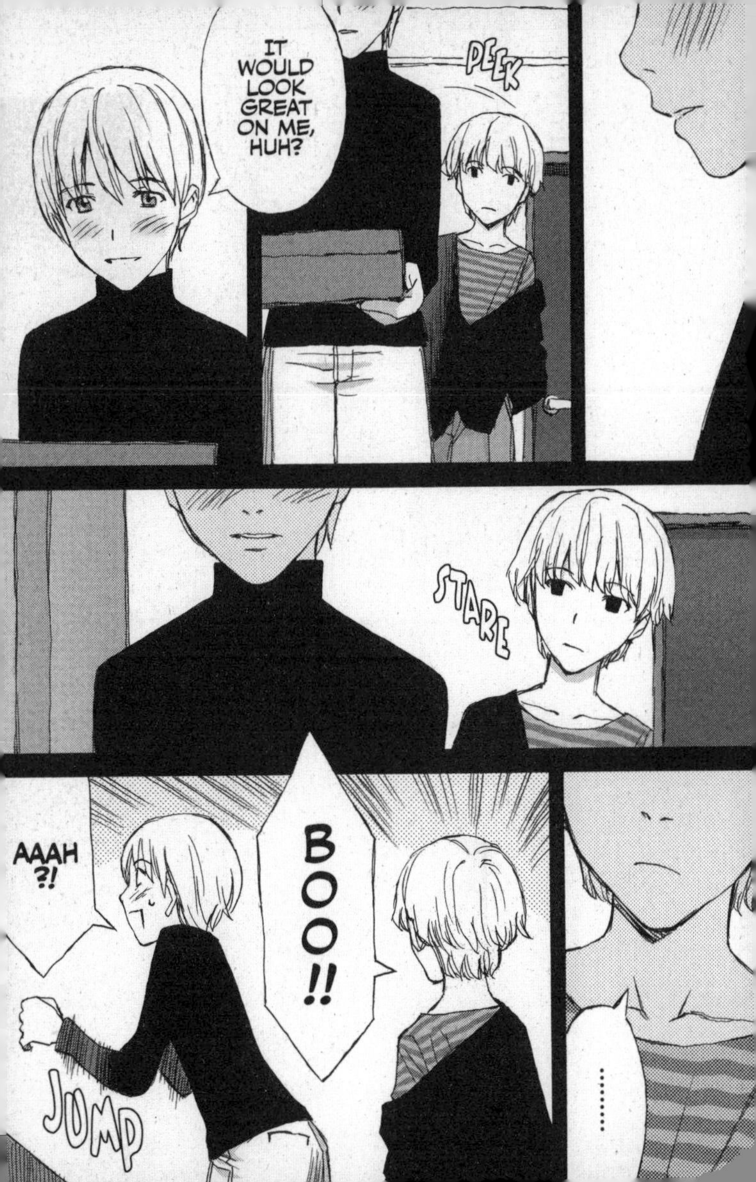
PEEK
IT WOULD LOOK GREAT ON ME, HUH?
STARE
……
BOO!!
AAAH ?!
JUMP

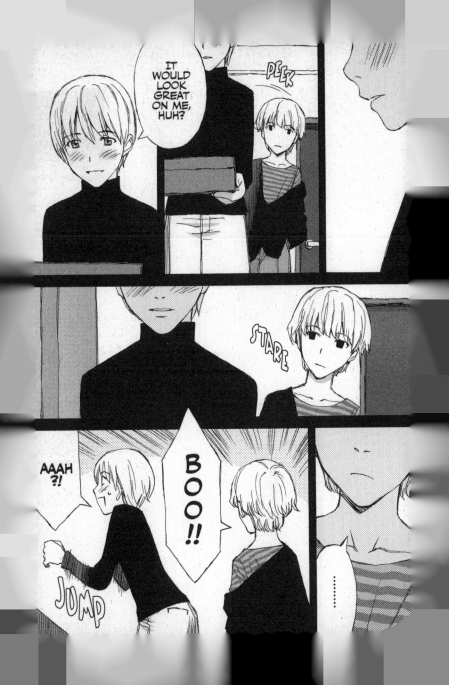

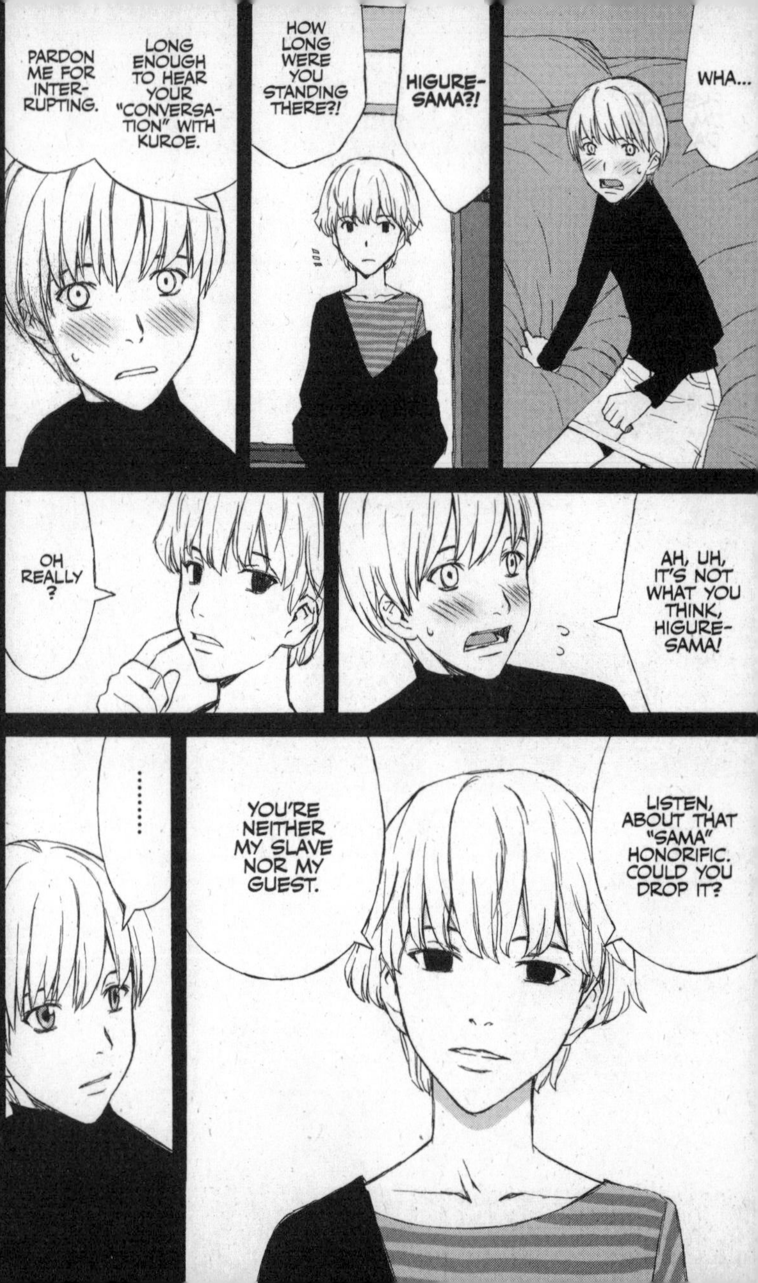
WHA...
HIGURE-SAMA?!
HOW LONG WERE YOU STANDING THERE?!
LONG ENOUGH TO HEAR YOUR "CONVERSATION" WITH KUROE.
PARDON ME FOR INTER-RUPTING.
AH, UH, IT'S NOT WHAT YOU THINK, HIGURE-SAMA!
OH REALLY?
LISTEN, ABOUT THAT "SAMA" HONORIFIC. COULD YOU DROP IT?
YOU'RE NEITHER MY SLAVE NOR MY GUEST.
......

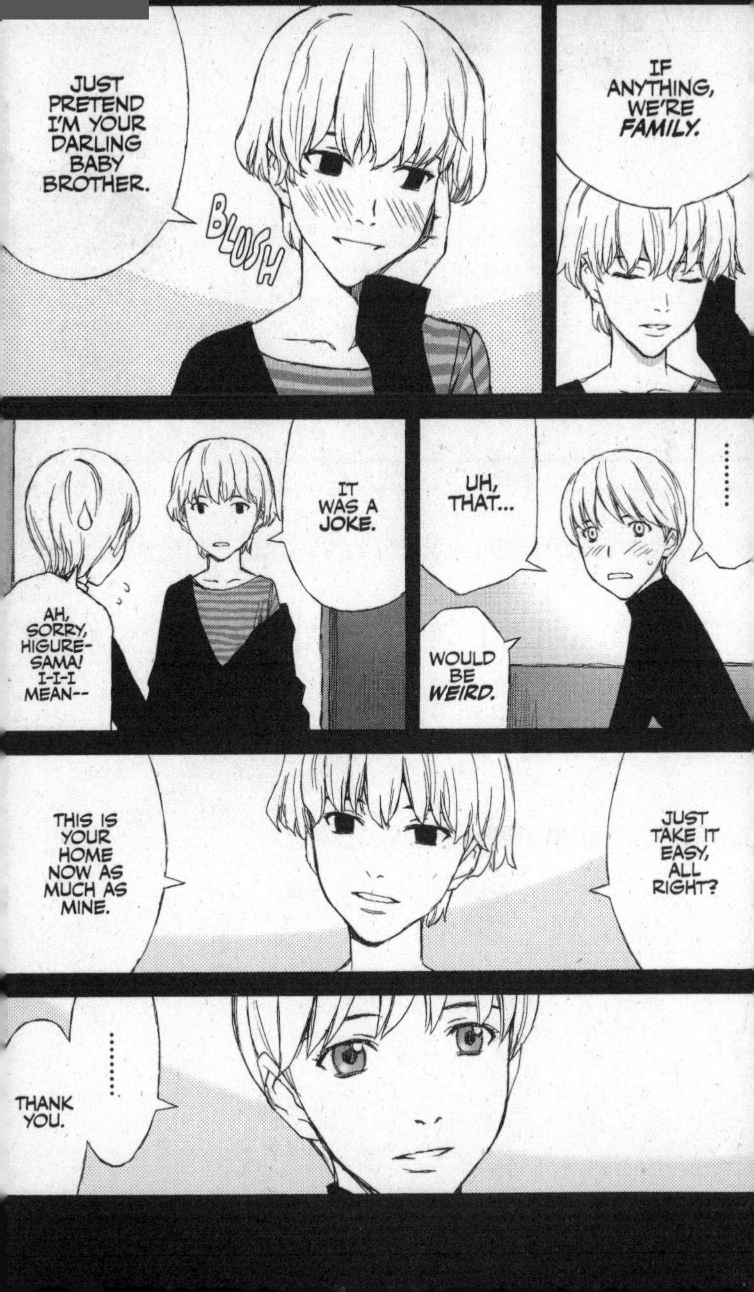
IF ANYTHING, WE'RE *FAMILY.*
JUST PRETEND I'M YOUR DARLING BABY BROTHER.
BLUSH
......
UH, THAT...
WOULD BE *WEIRD.*
IT WAS A JOKE.
AH, SORRY, HIGURE-SAMA! I-I-I MEAN--
JUST TAKE IT EASY, ALL RIGHT?
THIS IS YOUR HOME NOW AS MUCH AS MINE.
......
THANK YOU.

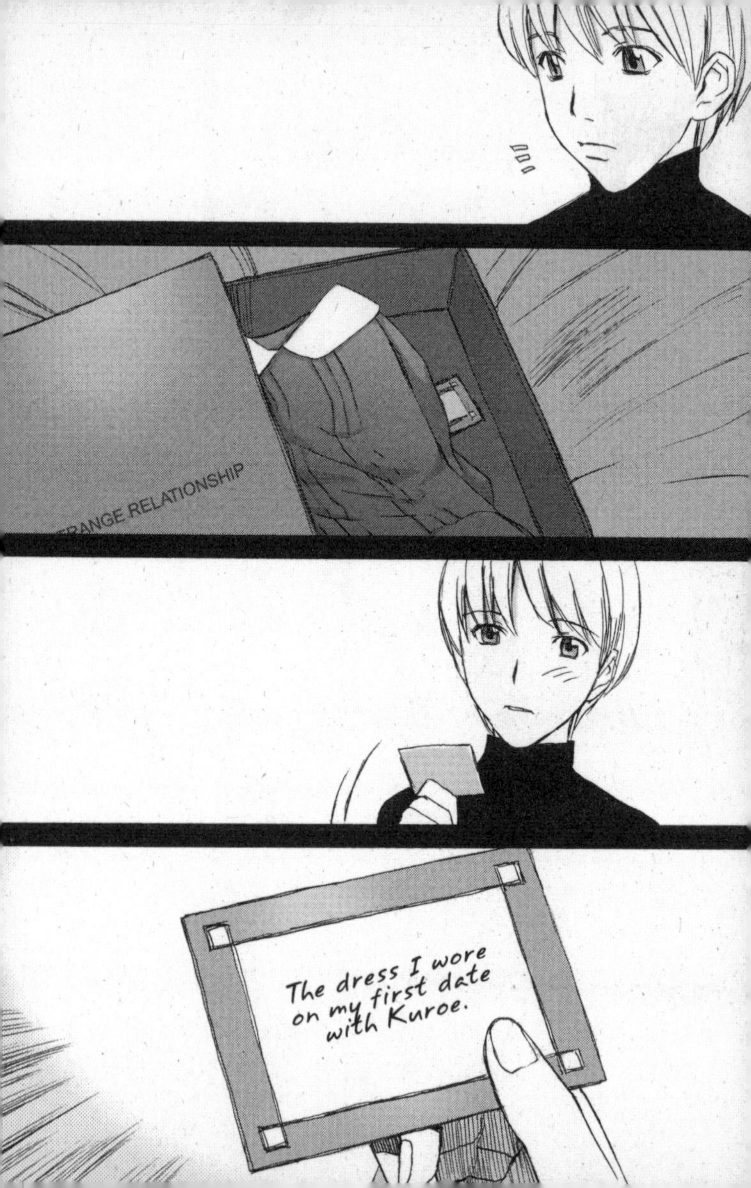
RANGE RELATIONSHIP
The dress I wore on my first date with Kuroe.

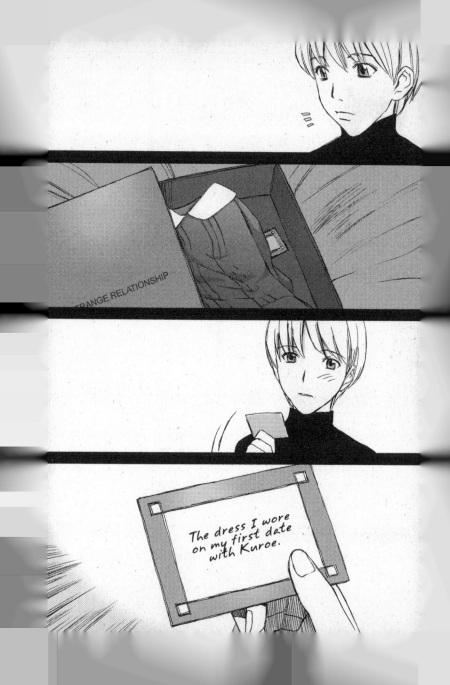

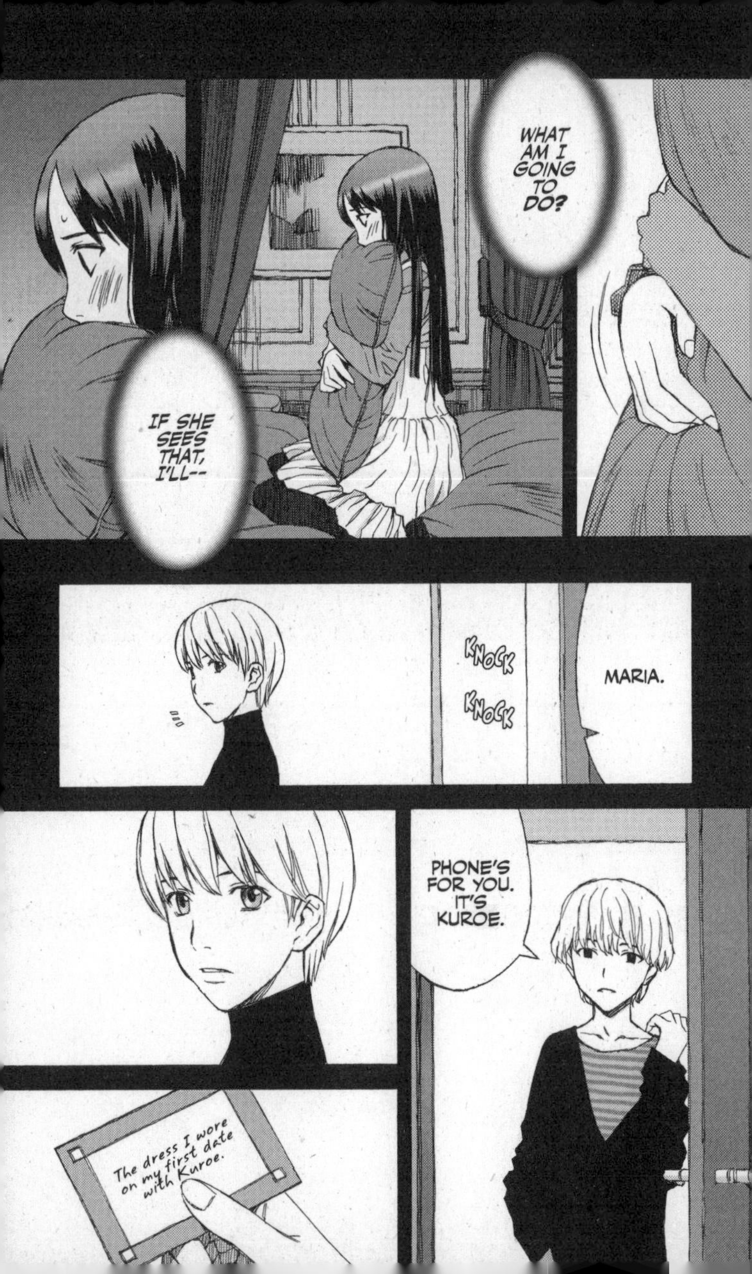
WHAT AM I GOING TO DO?
IF SHE SEES THAT, I'LL--
MARIA.
KNOCK
KNOCK
PHONE'S FOR YOU. IT'S KUROE.
The dress I wore on my first date with Kuroe.

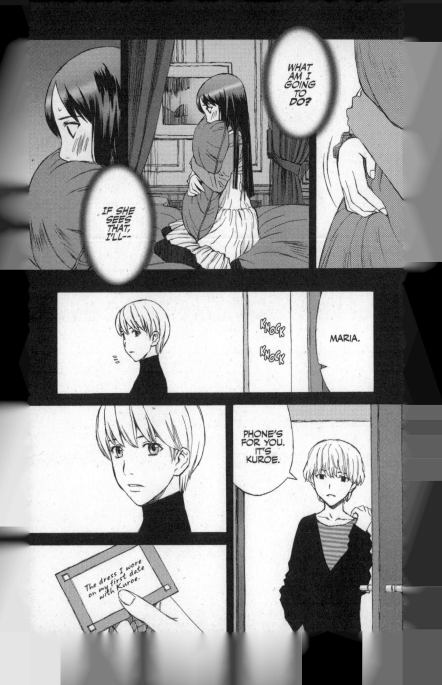

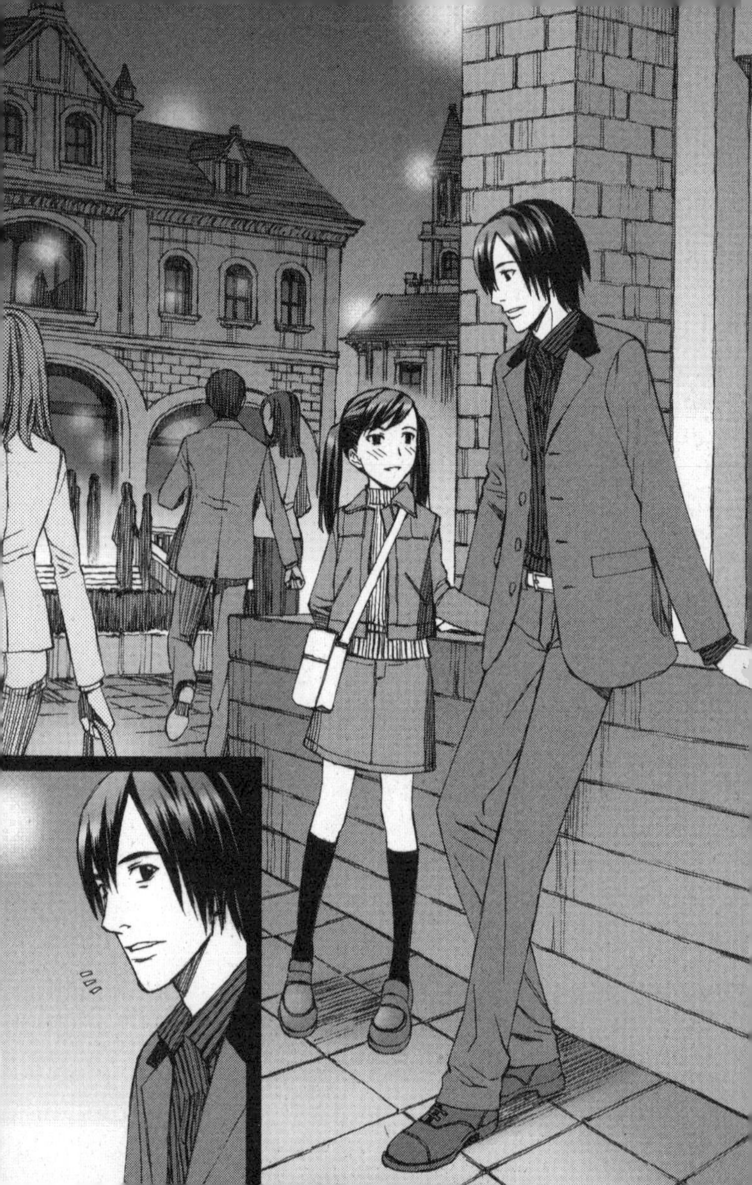

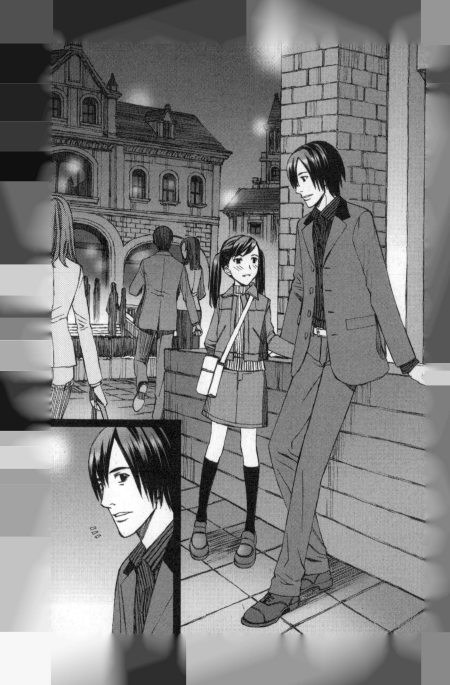

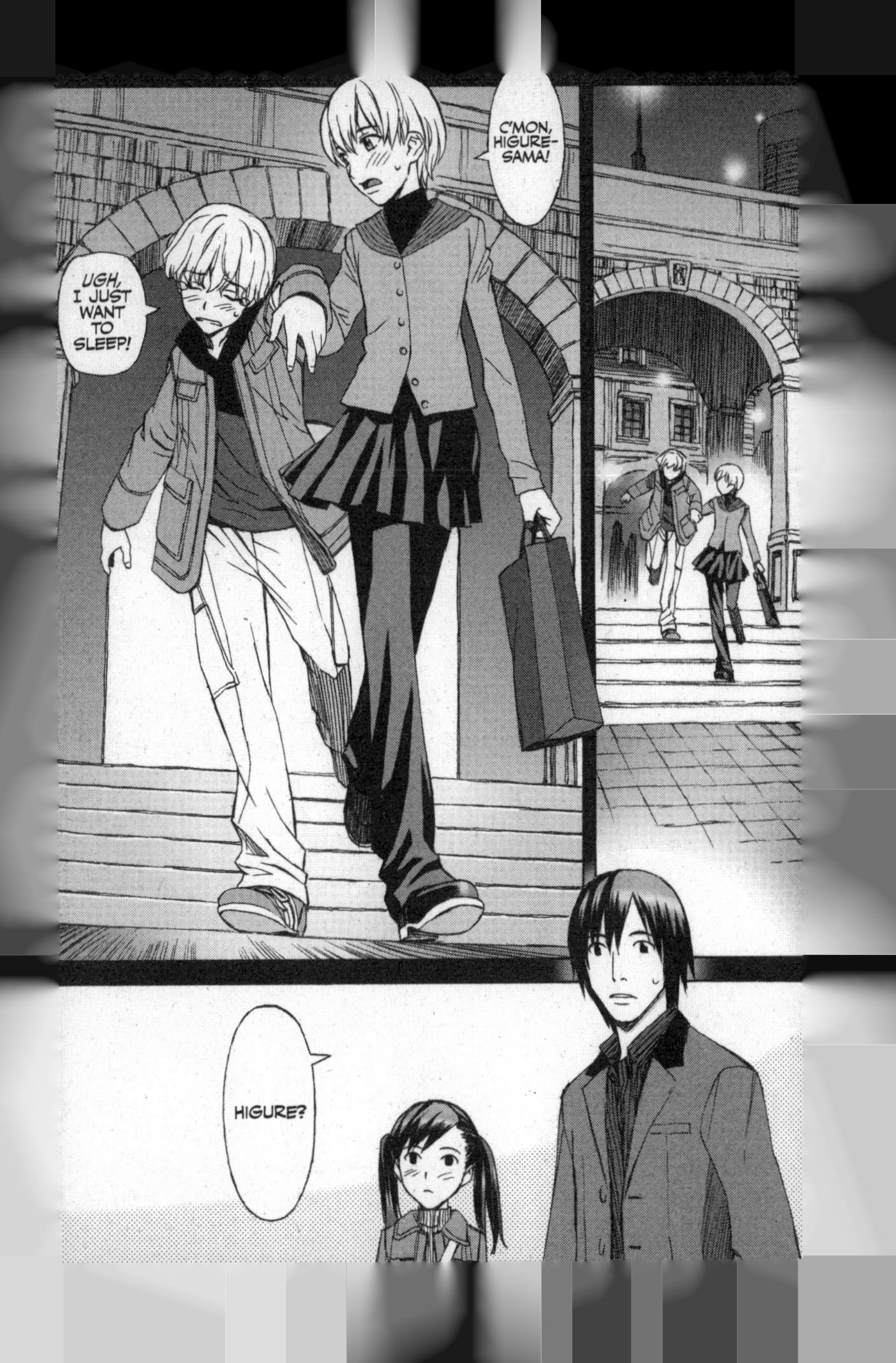
C'MON, HIGURE-SAMA!
UGH, I JUST WANT TO SLEEP!
HIGURE?

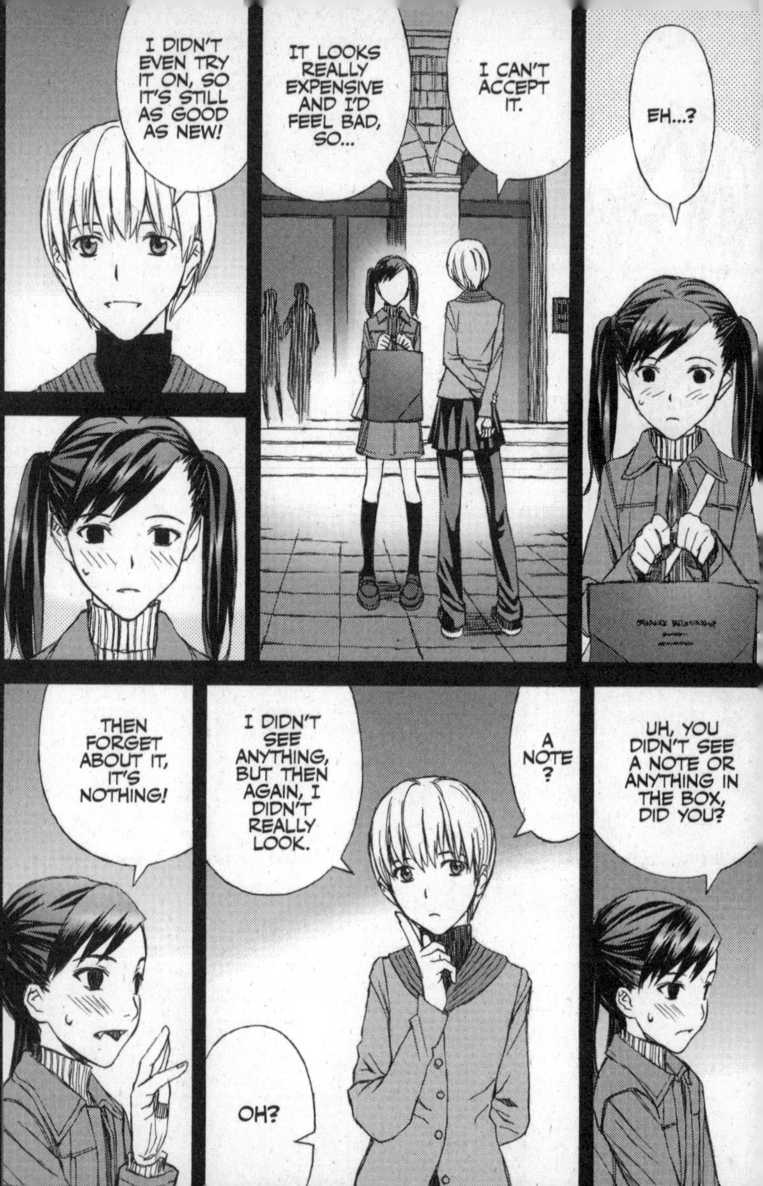
EH...?
I CAN'T ACCEPT IT.
IT LOOKS REALLY EXPENSIVE AND I'D FEEL BAD, SO...
I DIDN'T EVEN TRY IT ON, SO IT'S STILL AS GOOD AS NEW!
UH, YOU DIDN'T SEE A NOTE OR ANYTHING IN THE BOX, DID YOU?
A NOTE?
I DIDN'T SEE ANYTHING, BUT THEN AGAIN, I DIDN'T REALLY LOOK.
OH?
THEN FORGET ABOUT IT, IT'S NOTHING!

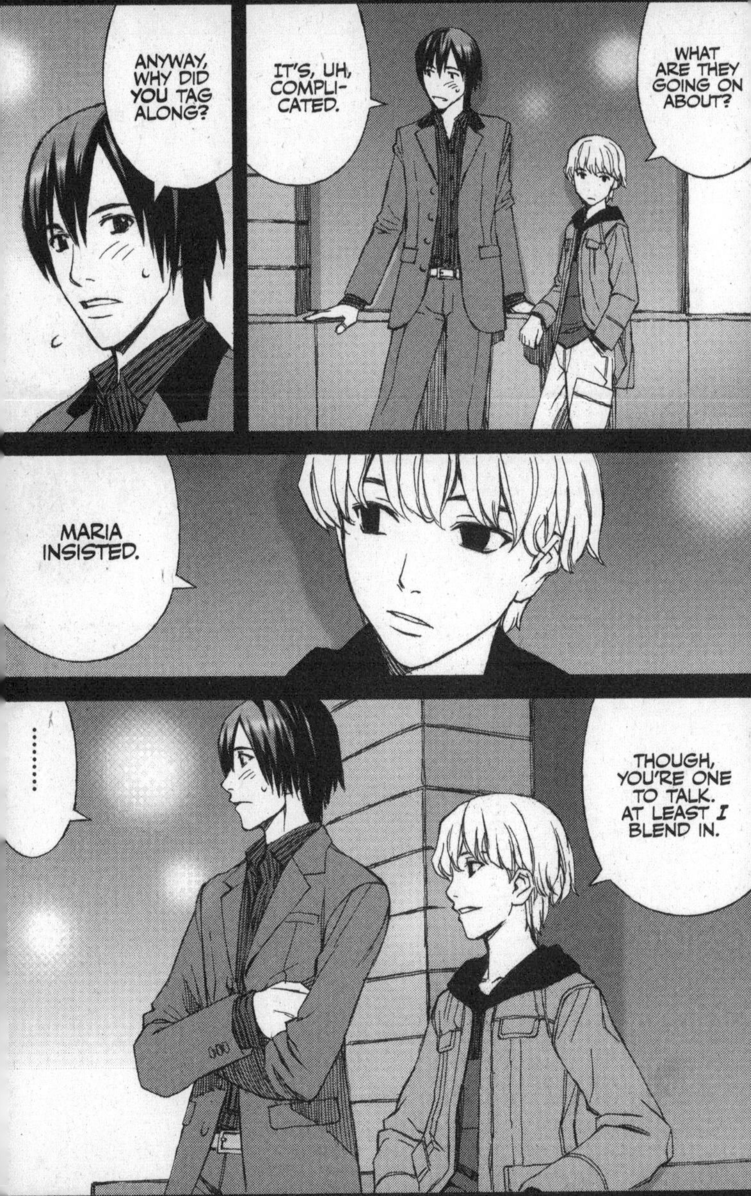
WHAT ARE THEY GOING ON ABOUT?
IT'S, UH, COMPLI-CATED.
ANYWAY, WHY DID YOU TAG ALONG?
MARIA INSISTED.
THOUGH, YOU'RE ONE TO TALK. AT LEAST *I* BLEND IN.
....

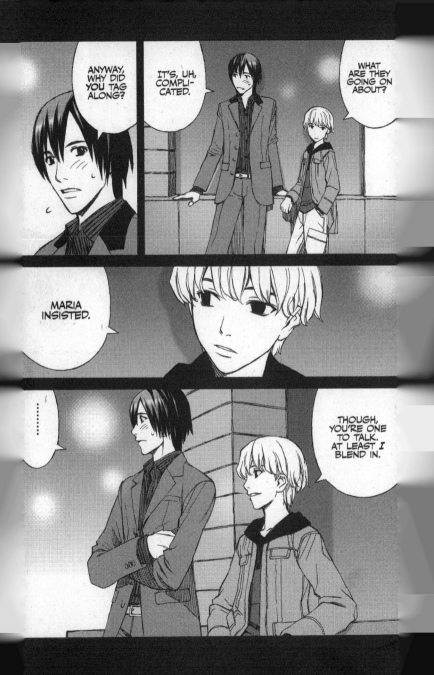

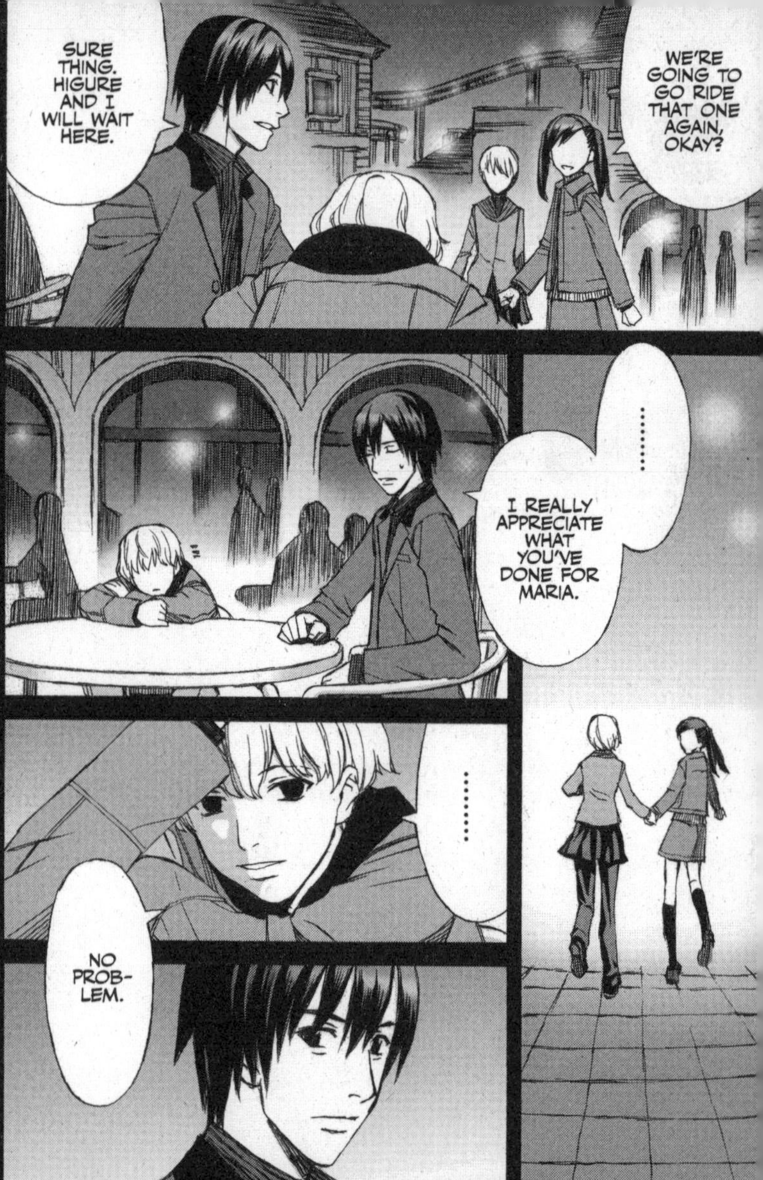
WE'RE GOING TO GO RIDE THAT ONE AGAIN, OKAY?
SURE THING. HIGURE AND I WILL WAIT HERE.
......
I REALLY APPRECIATE WHAT YOU'VE DONE FOR MARIA.
......
NO PROB-LEM.

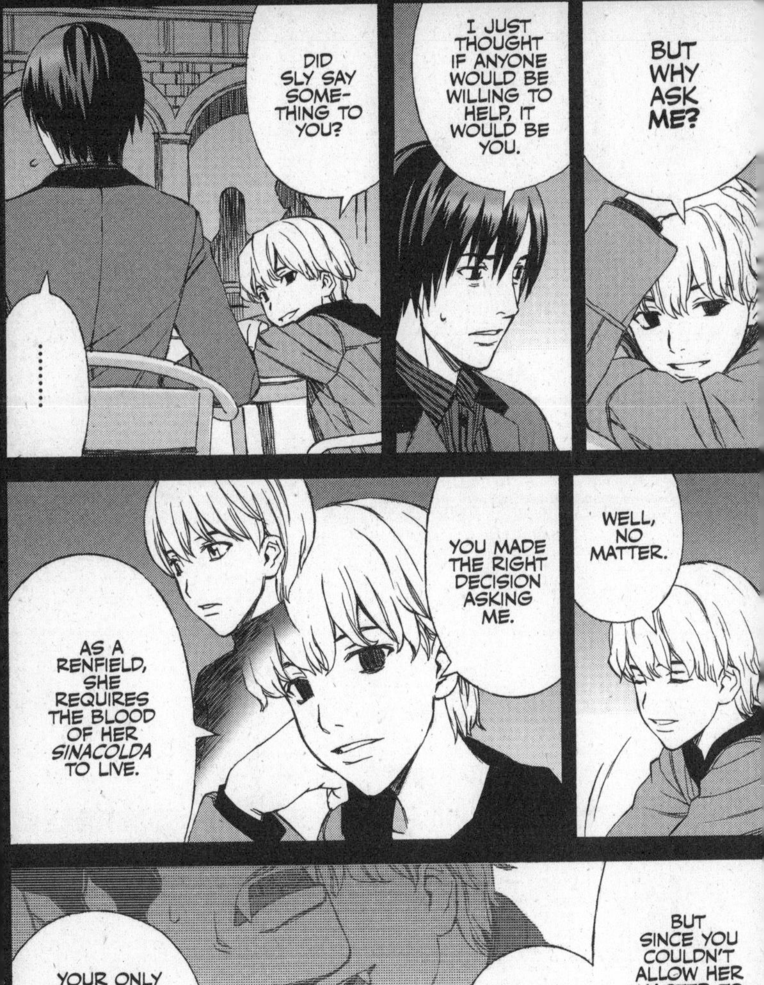
BUT WHY ASK ME?
I JUST THOUGHT IF ANYONE WOULD BE WILLING TO HELP, IT WOULD BE YOU.
DID SLY SAY SOMETHING TO YOU?
....
WELL, NO MATTER.
YOU MADE THE RIGHT DECISION ASKING ME.
AS A RENFIELD, SHE REQUIRES THE BLOOD OF HER *SINACOLDA* TO LIVE.
BUT SINCE YOU COULDN'T ALLOW HER MASTER TO SURVIVE...
YOU HAD TO FIND ANOTHER VAMPIRE CARRYING THE *SAME BLOODLINE*.
YOUR ONLY OPTION WAS TO HAVE ANOTHER VAMPIRE COMMIT ABSORBIRE AND TAKE IN HIS BLOOD AS THEIR OWN.

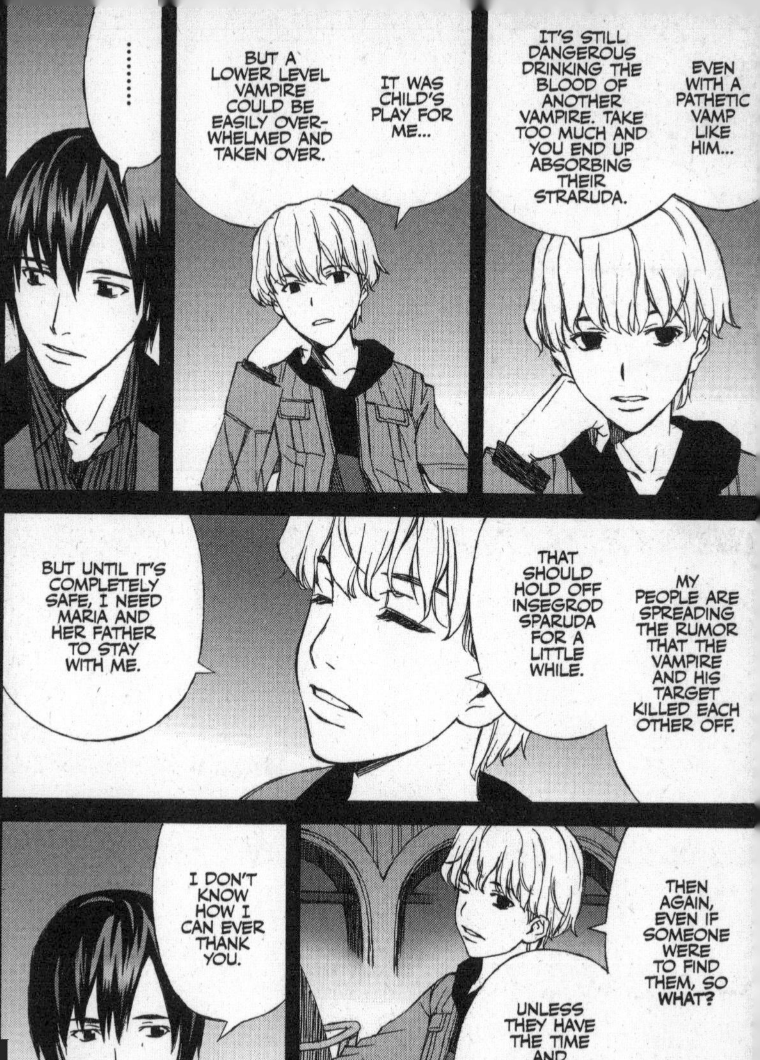
EVEN WITH A PATHETIC VAMP LIKE HIM...
IT'S STILL DANGEROUS DRINKING THE BLOOD OF ANOTHER VAMPIRE. TAKE TOO MUCH AND YOU END UP ABSORBING THEIR STRARUDA.
IT WAS CHILD'S PLAY FOR ME...
BUT A LOWER LEVEL VAMPIRE COULD BE EASILY OVER-WHELMED AND TAKEN OVER.
......
MY PEOPLE ARE SPREADING THE RUMOR THAT THE VAMPIRE AND HIS TARGET KILLED EACH OTHER OFF.
THAT SHOULD HOLD OFF INSEGROD SPARUDA FOR A LITTLE WHILE.
BUT UNTIL IT'S COMPLETELY SAFE, I NEED MARIA AND HER FATHER TO STAY WITH ME.
THEN AGAIN, EVEN IF SOMEONE WERE TO FIND THEM, SO WHAT?
UNLESS THEY HAVE THE TIME AND RESOURCES TO GO AFTER MY ENTIRE CLAN, THEY'LL LET IT GO.
I DON'T KNOW HOW I CAN EVER THANK YOU.

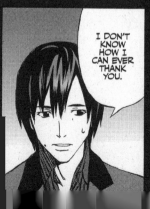

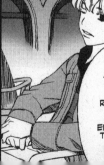

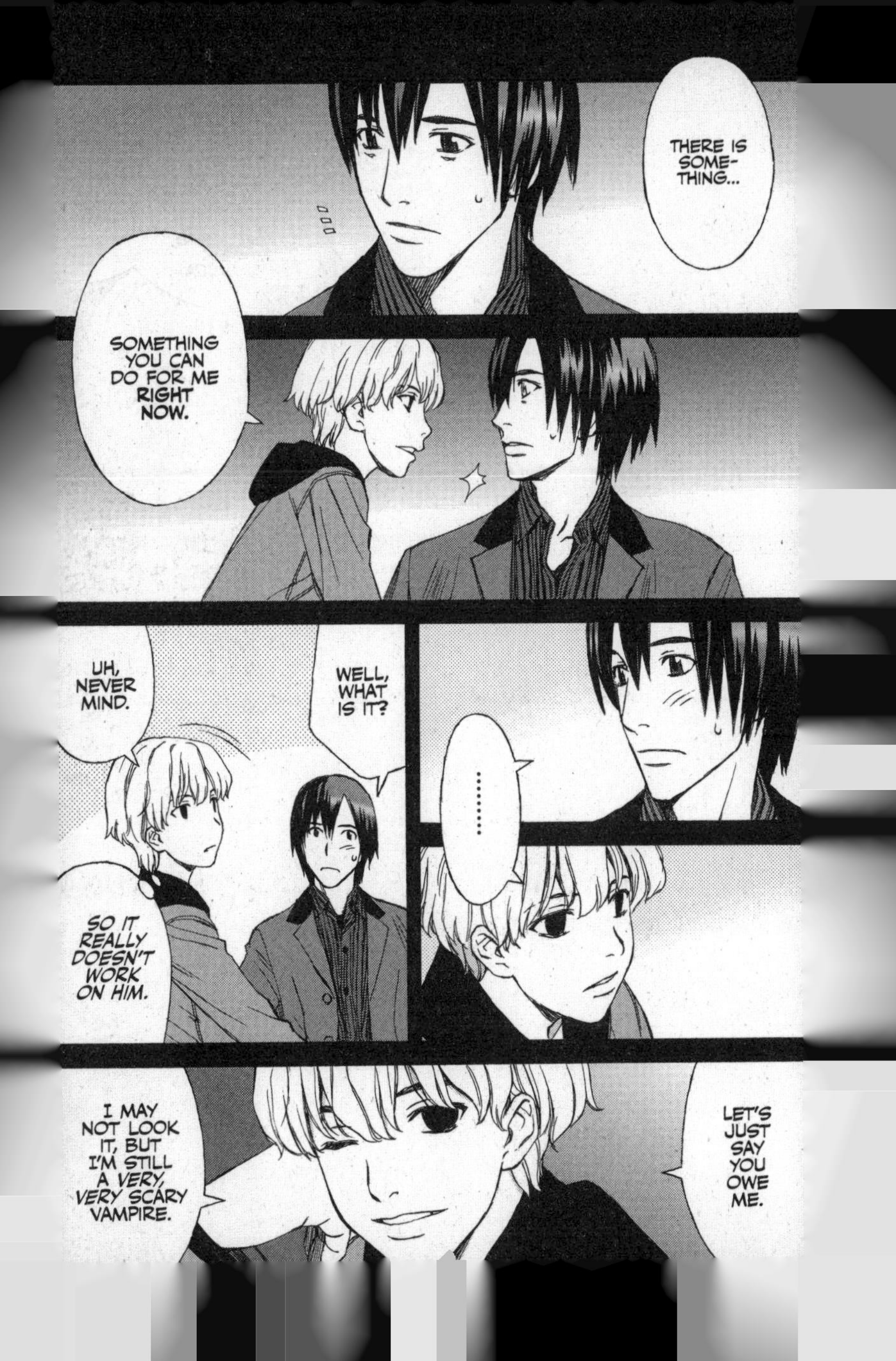
THERE IS SOME-THING...
SOMETHING YOU CAN DO FOR ME RIGHT NOW.
......
WELL, WHAT IS IT?
UH, NEVER MIND.
SO IT REALLY DOESN'T WORK ON HIM.
LET'S JUST SAY YOU OWE ME.
I MAY NOT LOOK IT, BUT I'M STILL A *VERY*, *VERY* SCARY VAMPIRE.

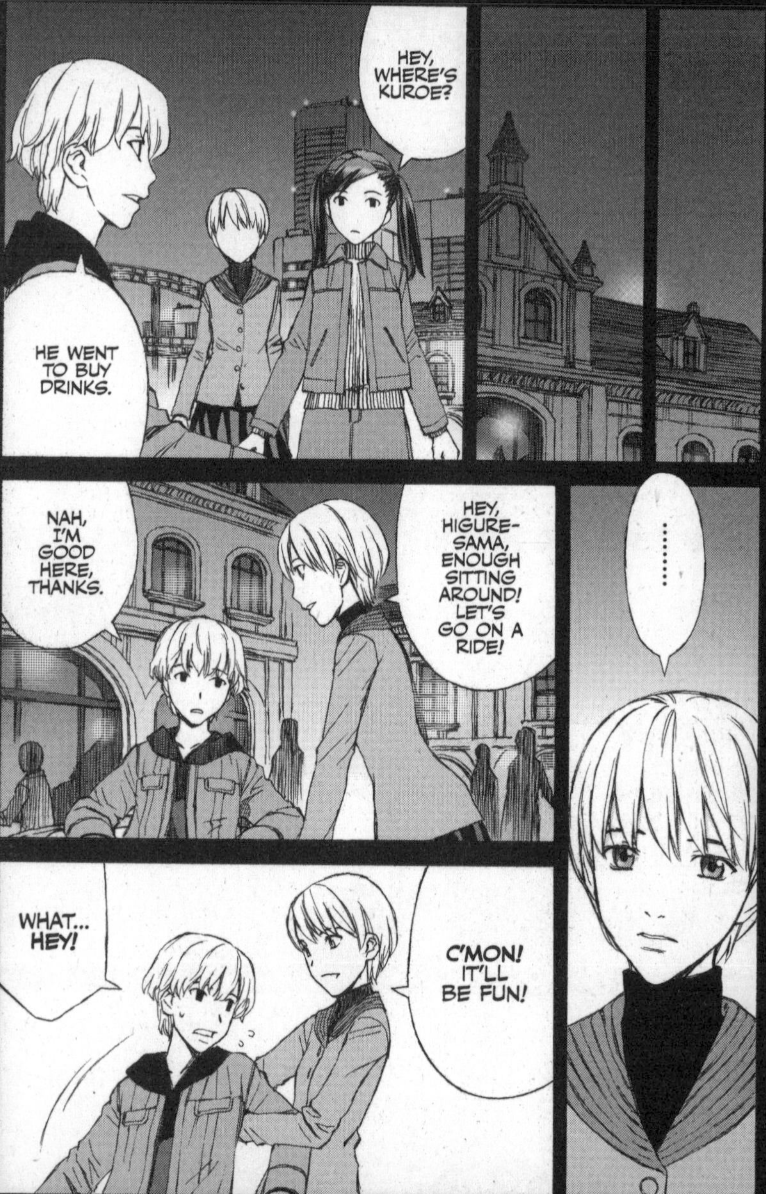
HEY, WHERE'S KUROE?
HE WENT TO BUY DRINKS.
......
HEY, HIGURE-SAMA, ENOUGH SITTING AROUND! LET'S GO ON A RIDE!
NAH, I'M GOOD HERE, THANKS.
C'MON! IT'LL BE FUN!
WHAT... HEY!

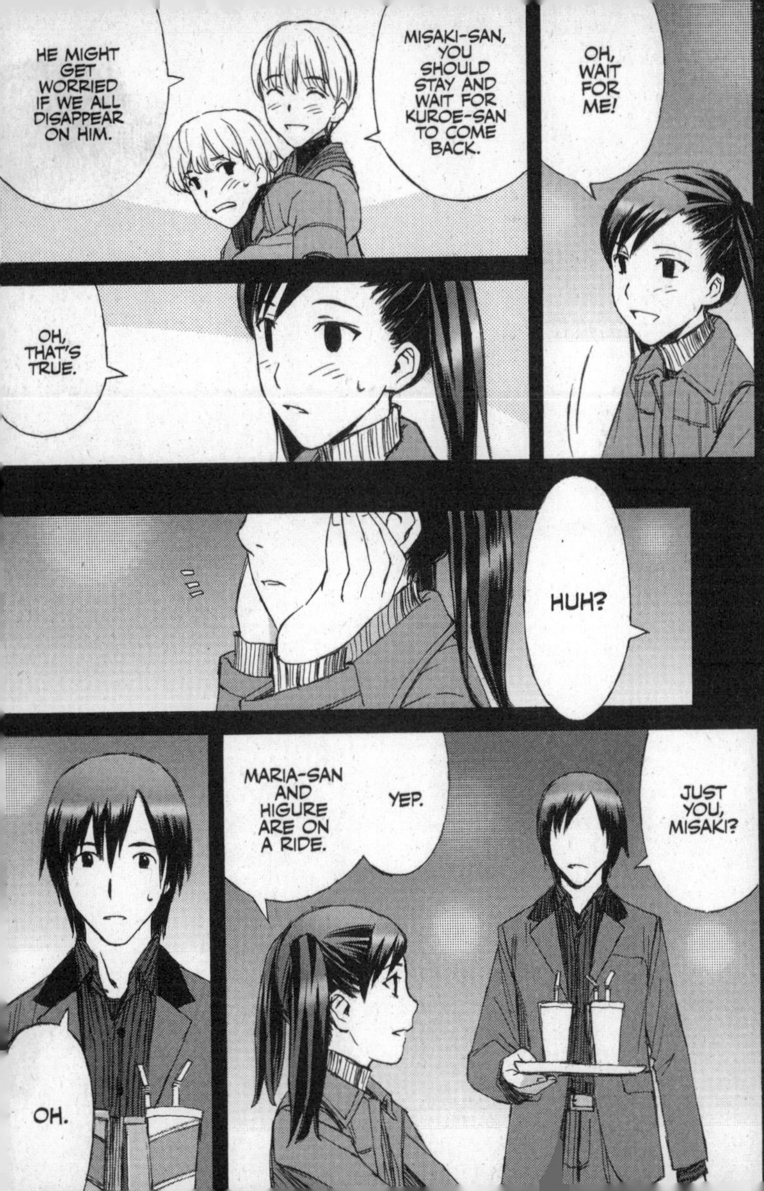
OH, WAIT FOR ME!
MISAKI-SAN, YOU SHOULD STAY AND WAIT FOR KUROE-SAN TO COME BACK.
HE MIGHT GET WORRIED IF WE ALL DISAPPEAR ON HIM.
OH, THAT'S TRUE.
HUH?
JUST YOU, MISAKI?
YEP.
MARIA-SAN AND HIGURE ARE ON A RIDE.
OH.

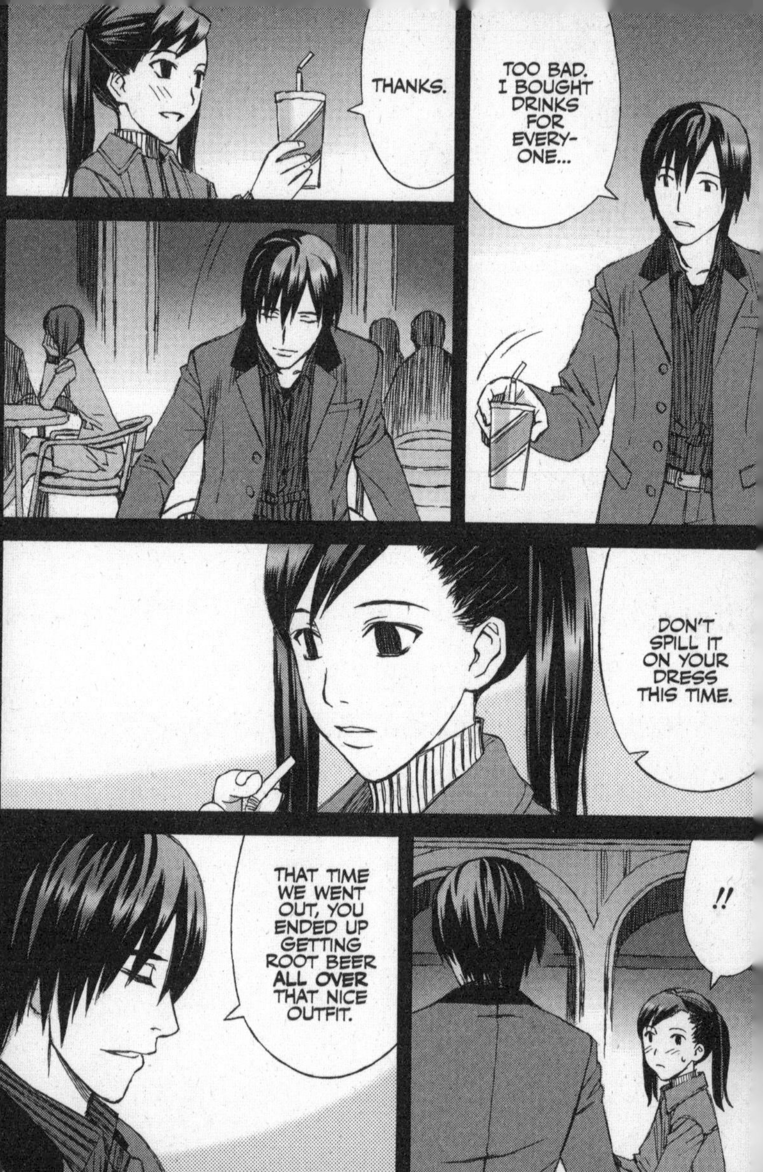
TOO BAD. I BOUGHT DRINKS FOR EVERY-ONE...
THANKS.
DON'T SPILL IT ON YOUR DRESS THIS TIME.
!!
THAT TIME WE WENT OUT, YOU ENDED UP GETTING ROOT BEER ALL OVER THAT NICE OUTFIT.

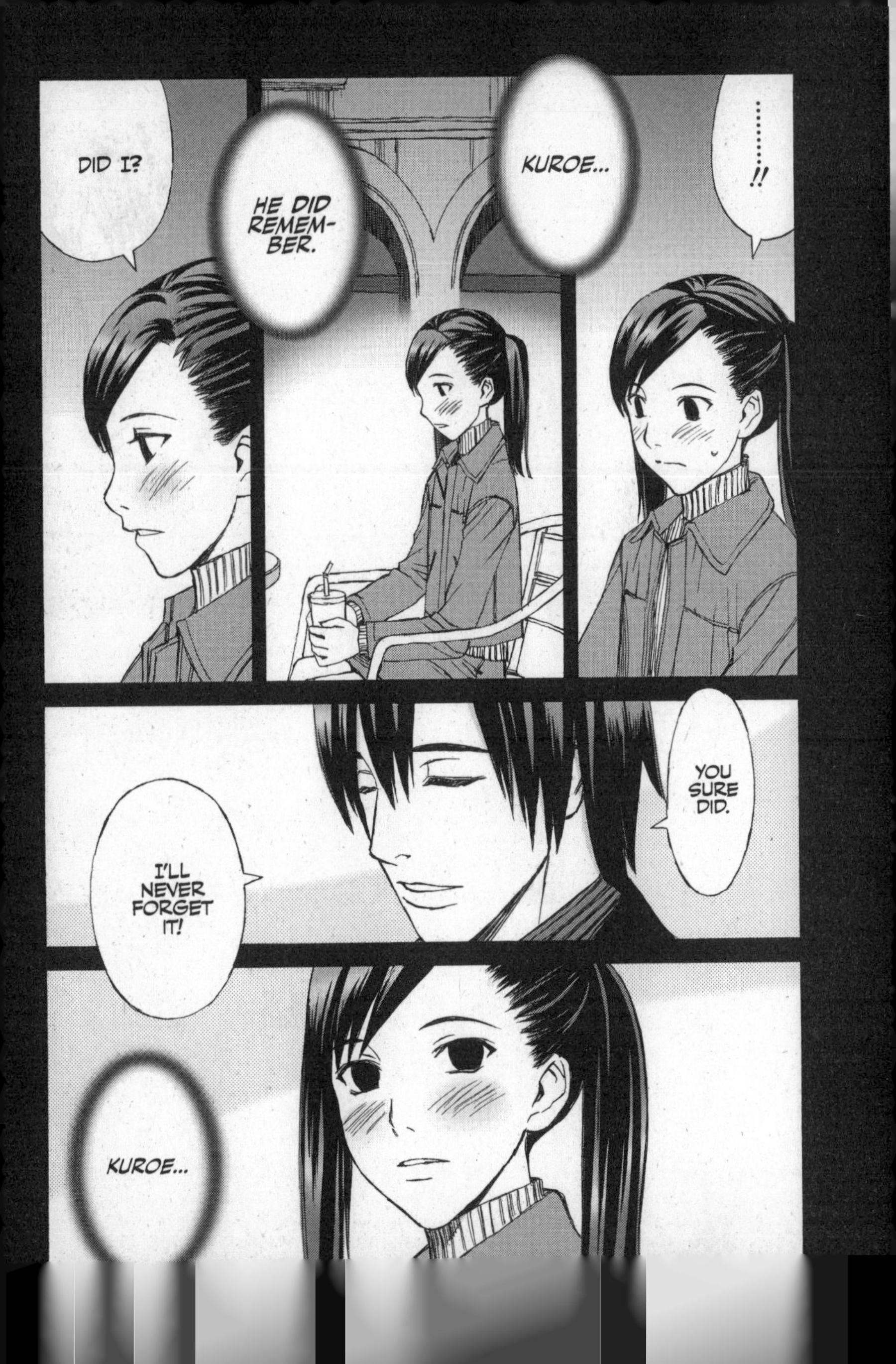
......!!
KUROE...
HE DID REMEMBER.
DID I?
YOU SURE DID.
I'LL NEVER FORGET IT!
KUROE...

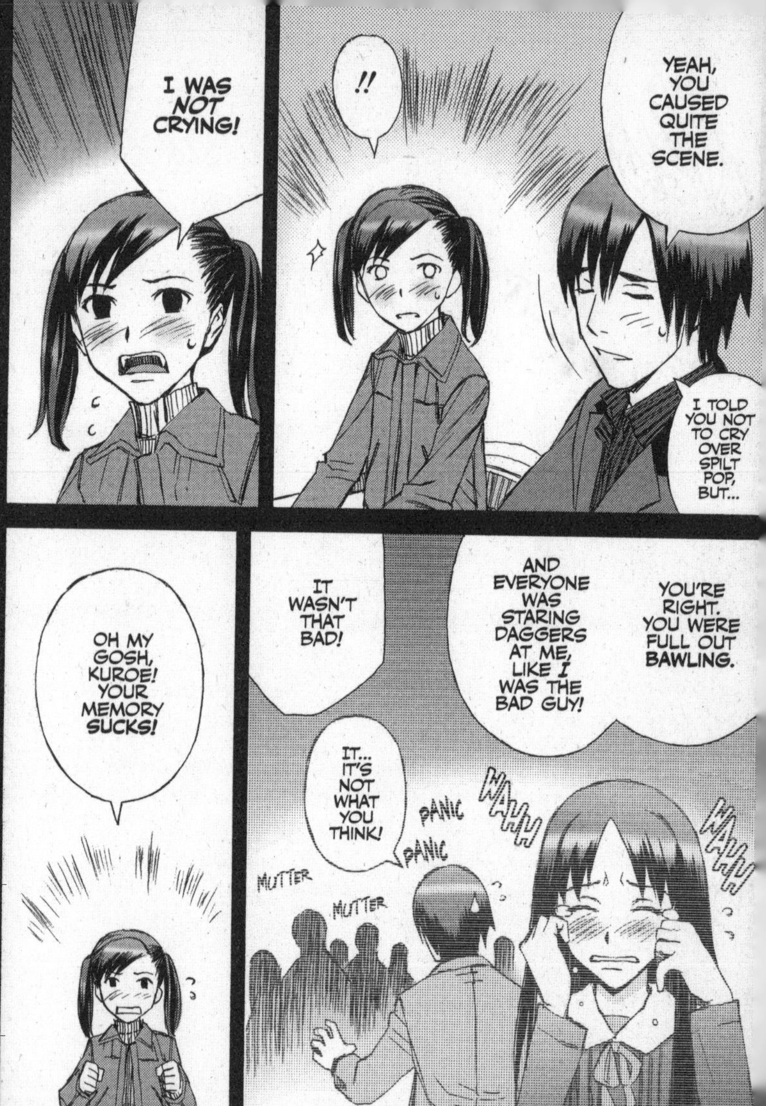
YEAH, YOU CAUSED QUITE THE SCENE.
!!
I TOLD YOU NOT TO CRY OVER SPILT POP, BUT...
I WAS NOT CRYING!
YOU'RE RIGHT. YOU WERE FULL OUT BAWLING.
AND EVERYONE WAS STARING DAGGERS AT ME, LIKE I WAS THE BAD GUY!
IT WASN'T THAT BAD!
WAAH
WAAH
IT... IT'S NOT WHAT YOU THINK!
PANIC
PANIC
MUTTER
MUTTER
OH MY GOSH, KUROE! YOUR MEMORY SUCKS!

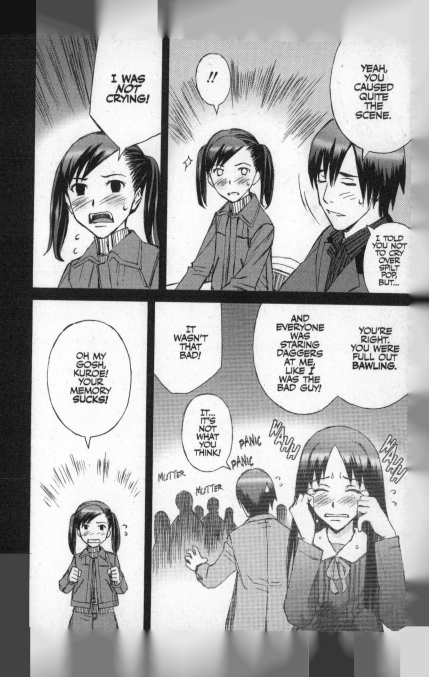

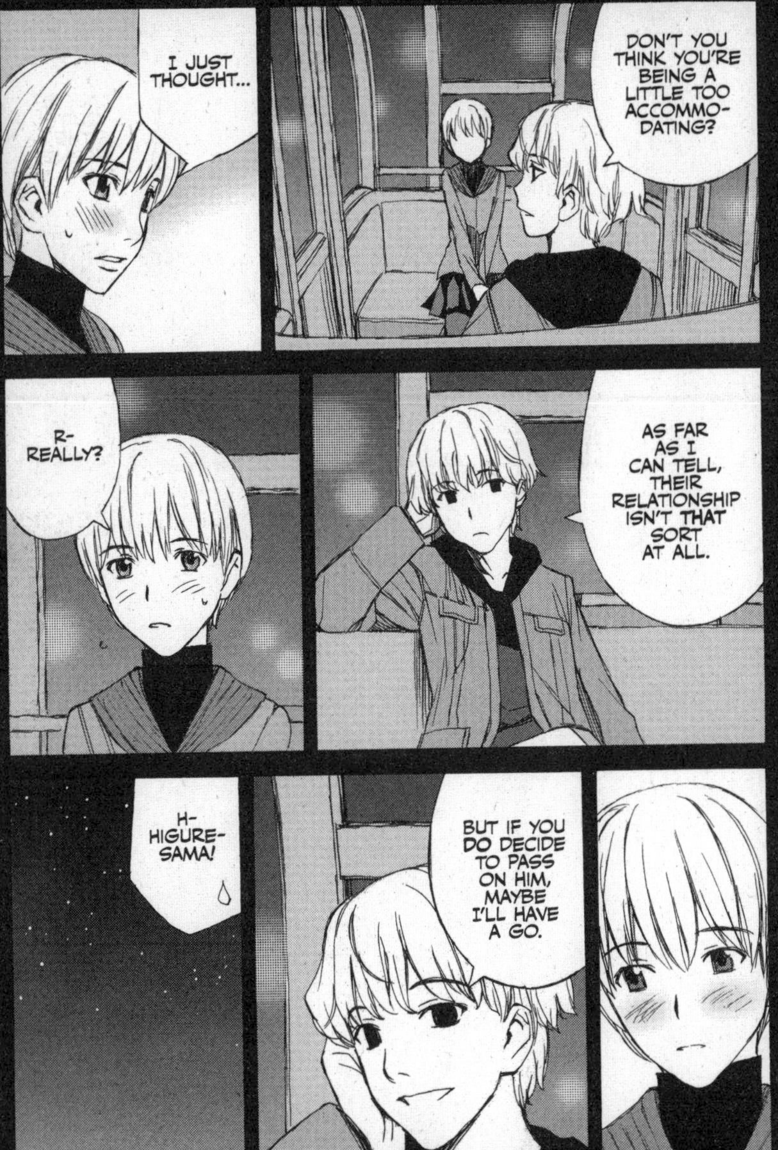
DON'T YOU THINK YOU'RE BEING A LITTLE TOO ACCOMMO-DATING?
I JUST THOUGHT...
AS FAR AS I CAN TELL, THEIR RELATIONSHIP ISN'T THAT SORT AT ALL.
R-REALLY?
BUT IF YOU DO DECIDE TO PASS ON HIM, MAYBE I'LL HAVE A GO.
H-HIGURE-SAMA!

I SHOULD HAVE REMEMBERED SOONER.

I'M SORRY.

IT'S ALL RIGHT.

IT'S JUST A SILLY OLD DRESS.

THAT'S RIGHT.

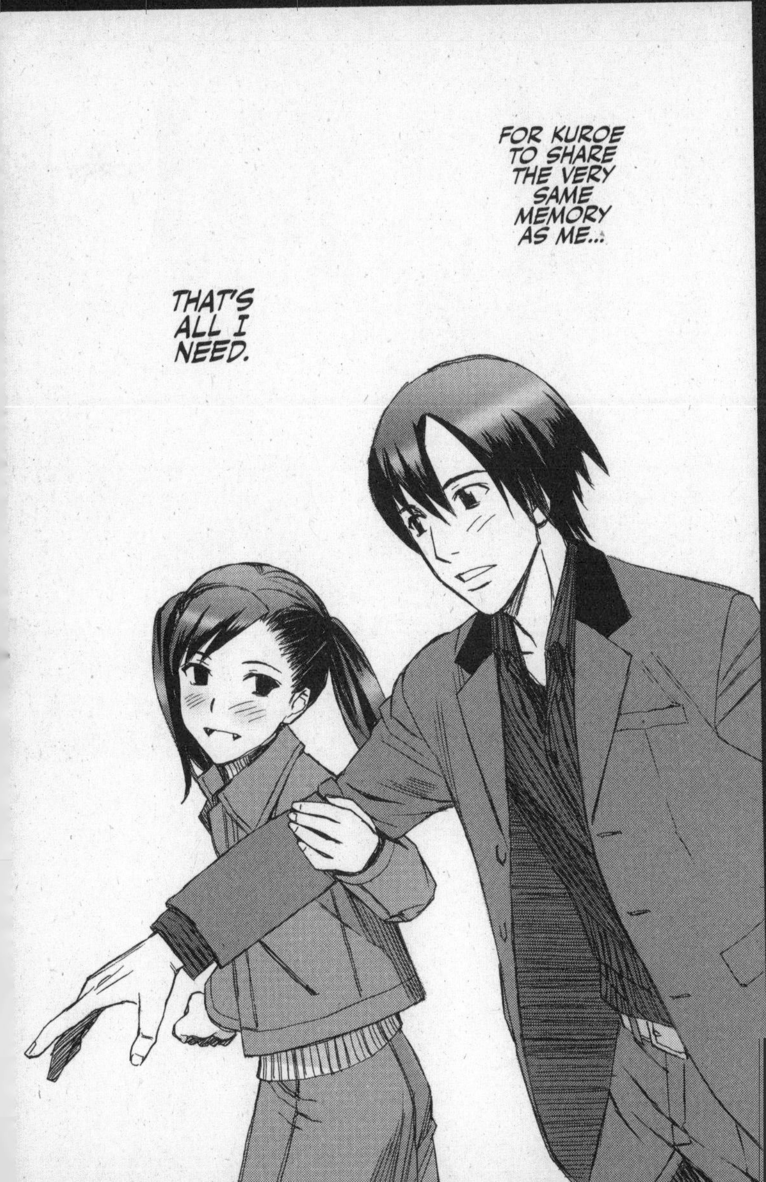
FOR KUROE TO SHARE THE VERY SAME MEMORY AS ME...
THAT'S ALL I NEED.

Episode 17
MIDNIGHT SWIM
A Starry Night Swim

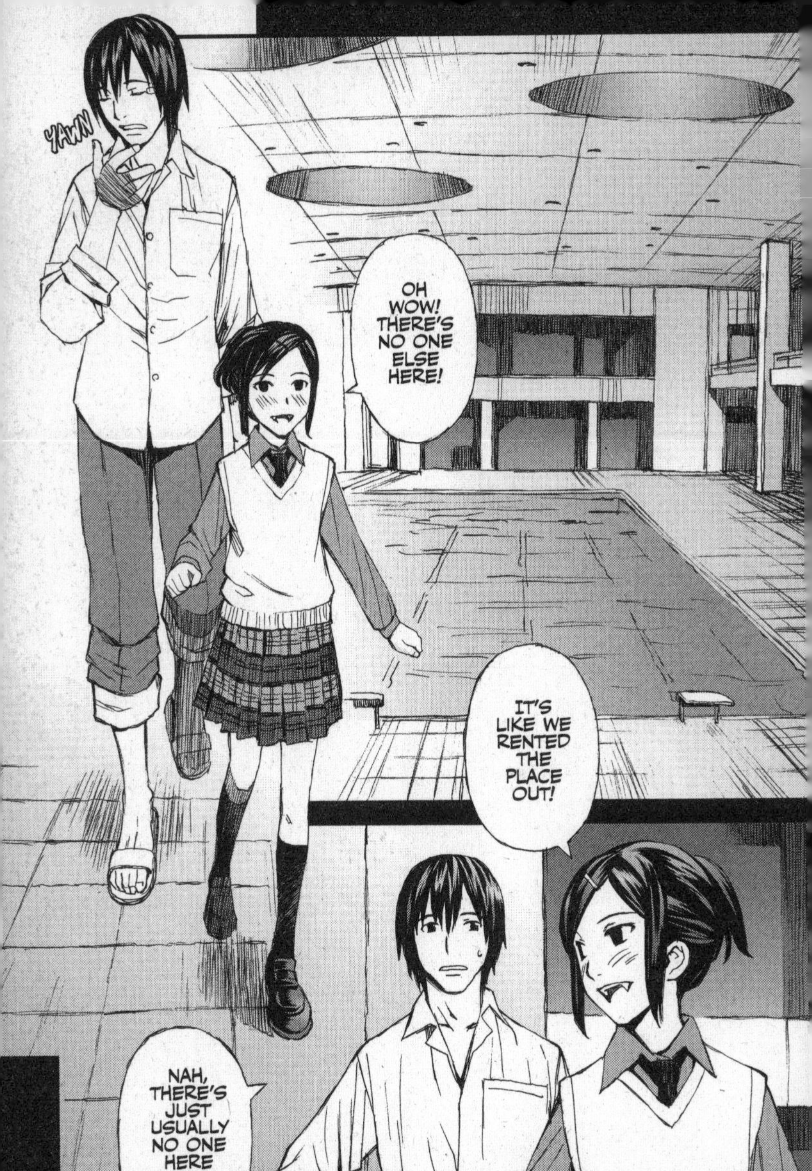
YAWN
OH WOW! THERE'S NO ONE ELSE HERE!
IT'S LIKE WE RENTED THE PLACE OUT!
NAH, THERE'S JUST USUALLY NO ONE HERE THIS LATE.

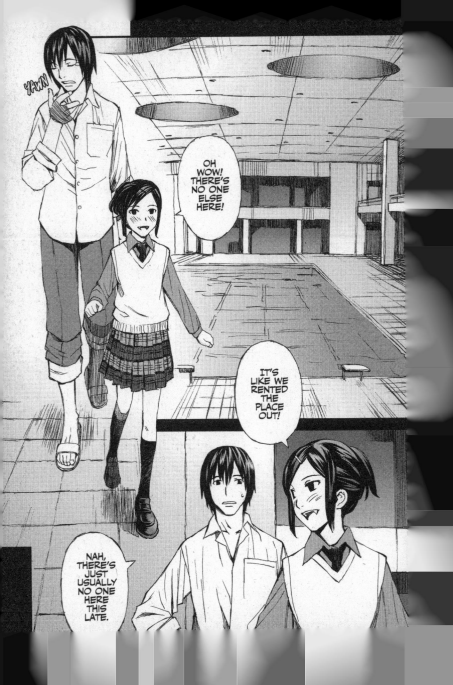

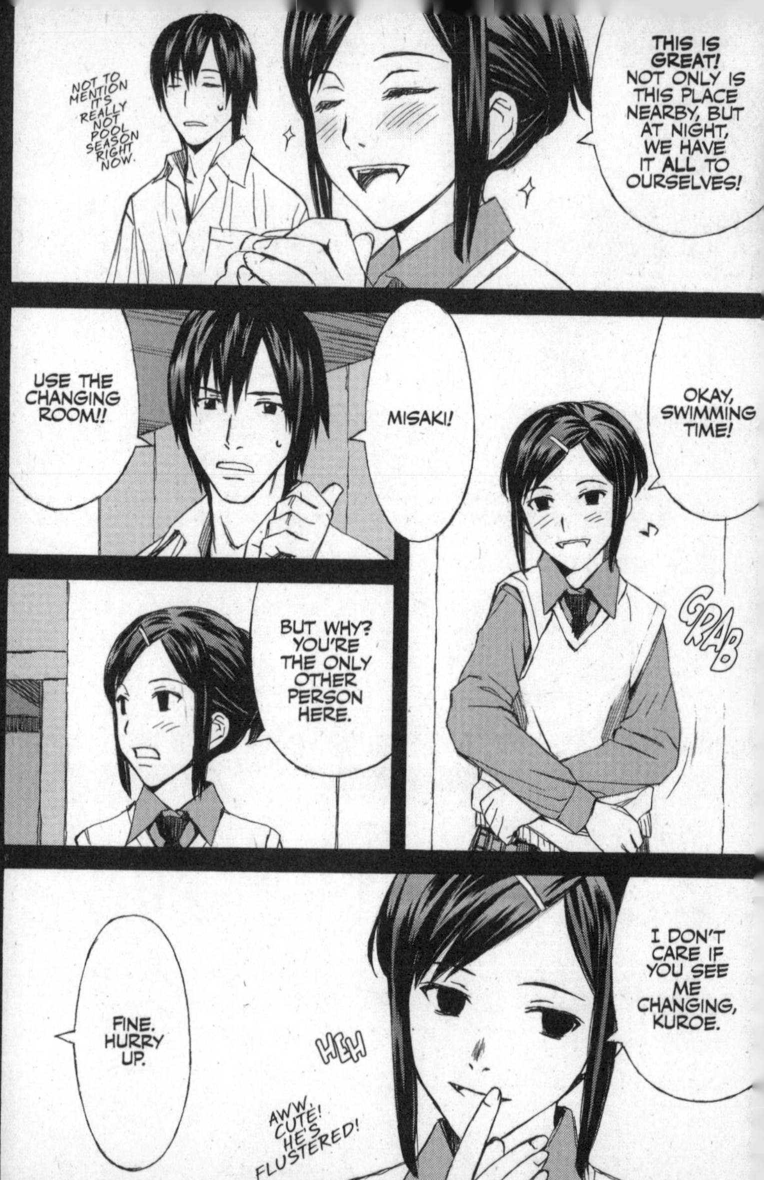
THIS IS GREAT! NOT ONLY IS THIS PLACE NEARBY, BUT AT NIGHT, WE HAVE IT ALL TO OURSELVES!
NOT TO MENTION IT'S REALLY NOT POOL SEASON RIGHT NOW.
OKAY, SWIMMING TIME!
GRAB
MISAKI!
USE THE CHANGING ROOM!!
BUT WHY? YOU'RE THE ONLY OTHER PERSON HERE.
I DON'T CARE IF YOU SEE ME CHANGING, KUROE.
HEH
AWW, CUTE! HE'S FLUSTERED!
FINE. HURRY UP.

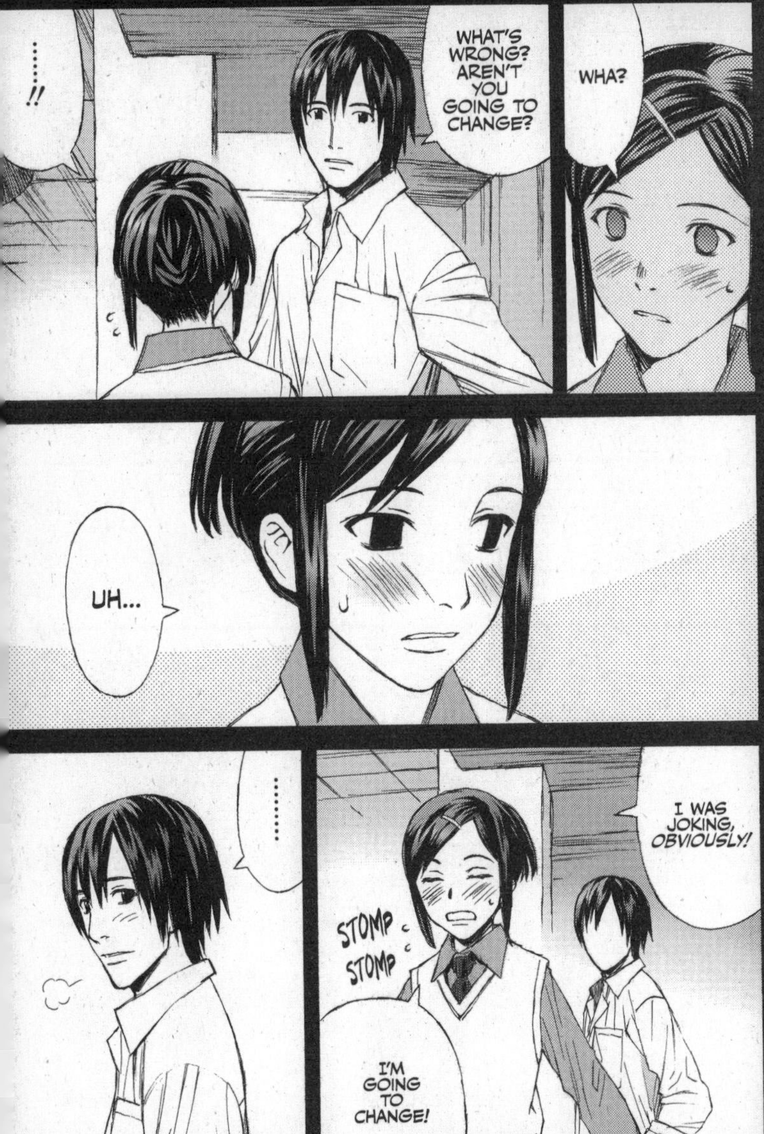
WHA?
WHAT'S WRONG? AREN'T YOU GOING TO CHANGE?
......!!
UH...
I WAS JOKING, OBVIOUSLY!
STOMP STOMP
I'M GOING TO CHANGE!
....

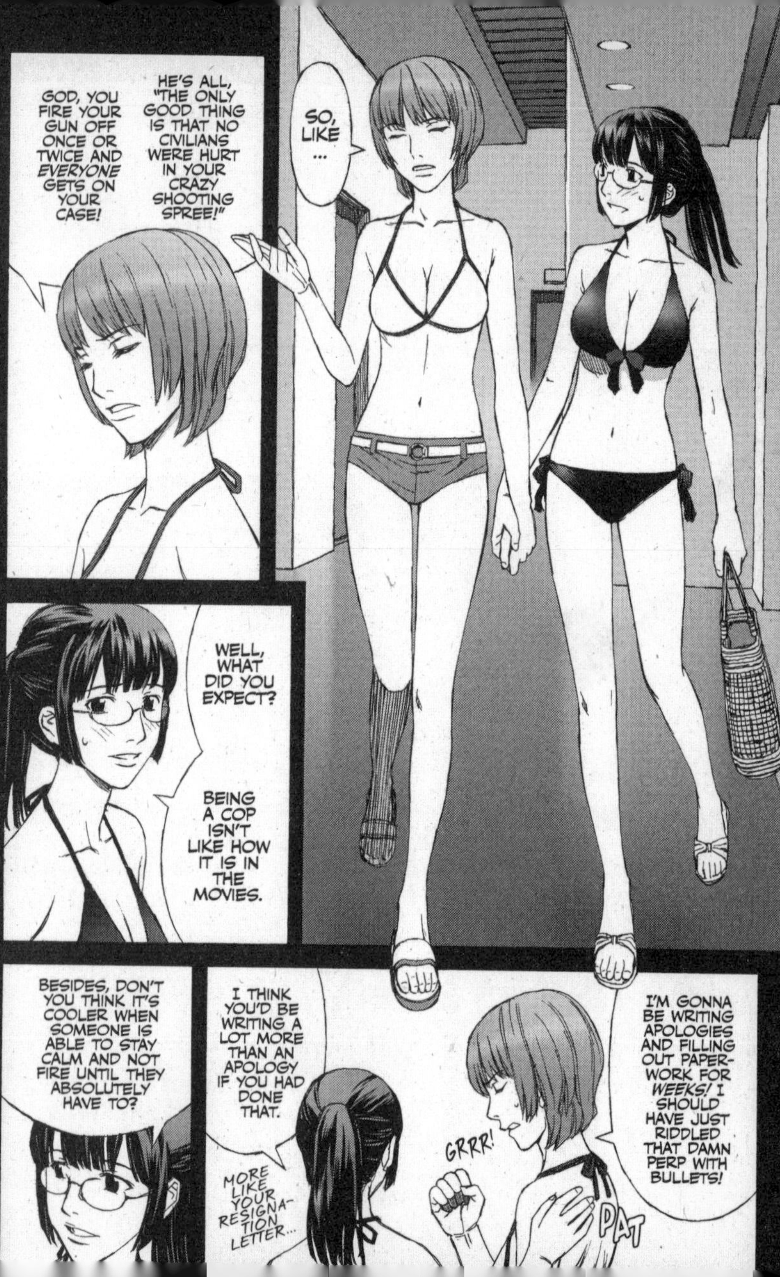
SO, LIKE ...
HE'S ALL, "THE ONLY GOOD THING IS THAT NO CIVILIANS WERE HURT IN YOUR CRAZY SHOOTING SPREE!"
GOD, YOU FIRE YOUR GUN OFF ONCE OR TWICE AND *EVERYONE* GETS ON YOUR CASE!
WELL, WHAT DID YOU EXPECT?
BEING A COP ISN'T LIKE HOW IT IS IN THE MOVIES.
I'M GONNA BE WRITING APOLOGIES AND FILLING OUT PAPERWORK FOR *WEEKS!* I SHOULD HAVE JUST RIDDLED THAT DAMN PERP WITH BULLETS!
I THINK YOU'D BE WRITING A LOT MORE THAN AN APOLOGY IF YOU HAD DONE THAT.
GRRR!
MORE LIKE YOUR RESIGNATION LETTER...
PAT
BESIDES, DON'T YOU THINK IT'S COOLER WHEN SOMEONE IS ABLE TO STAY CALM AND NOT FIRE UNTIL THEY ABSOLUTELY HAVE TO?

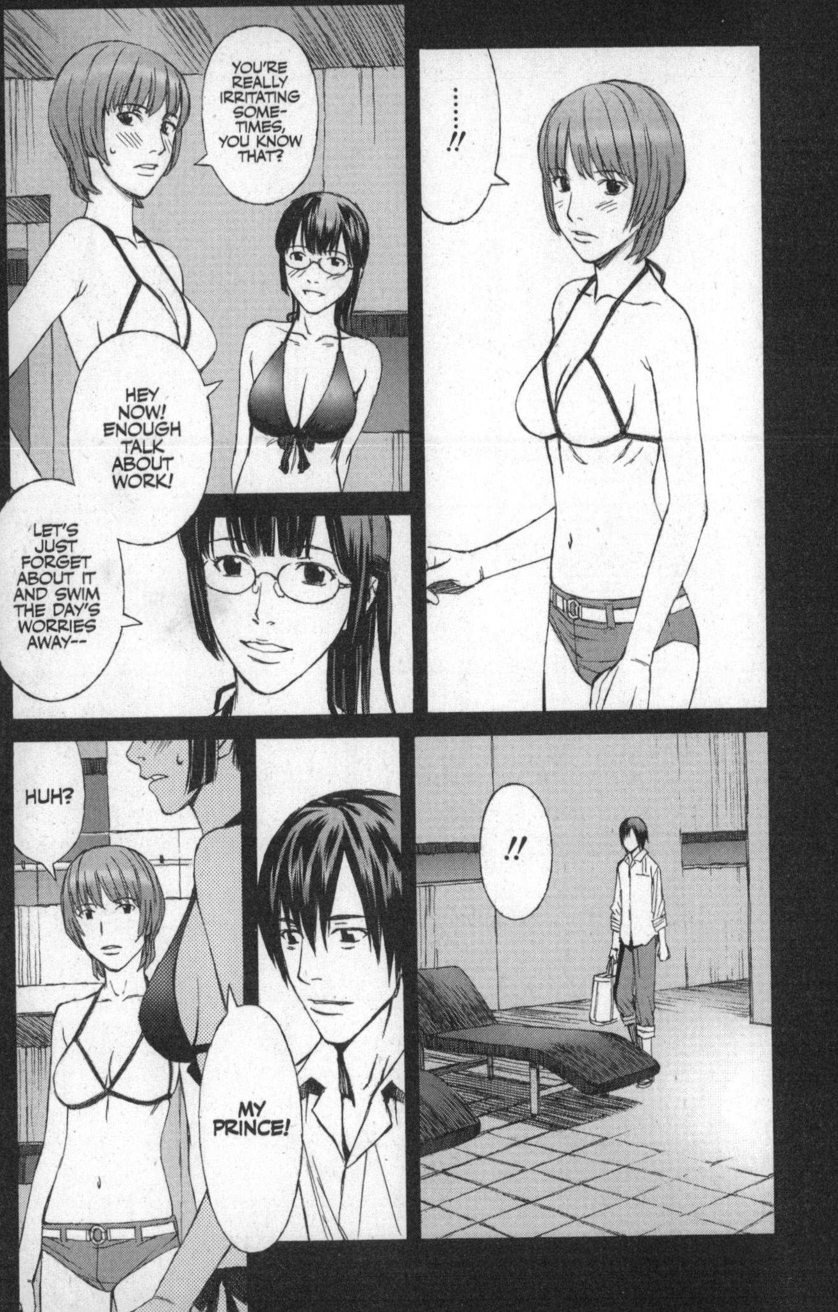
......!!
YOU'RE REALLY IRRITATING SOME-TIMES, YOU KNOW THAT?
HEY NOW! ENOUGH TALK ABOUT WORK!
LET'S JUST FORGET ABOUT IT AND SWIM THE DAY'S WORRIES AWAY--
!!
MY PRINCE!
HUH?

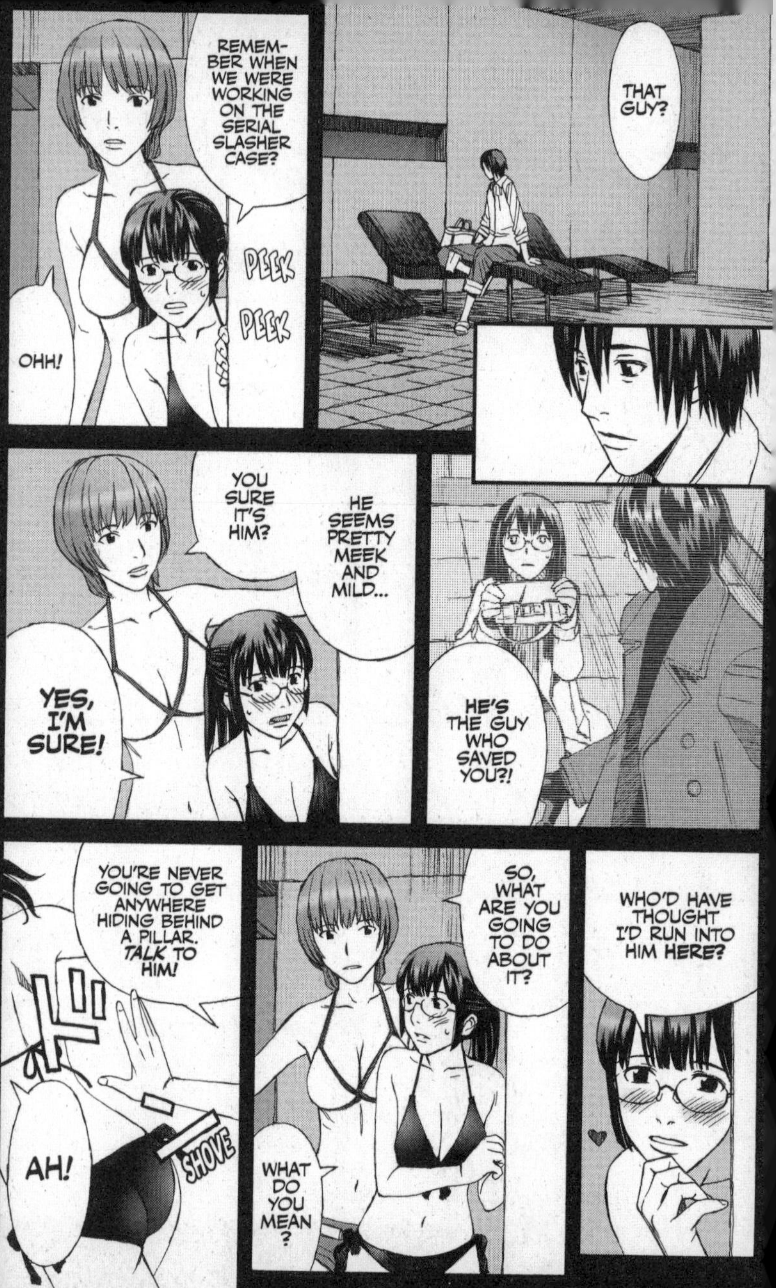
THAT GUY?
REMEMBER WHEN WE WERE WORKING ON THE SERIAL SLASHER CASE?
PEEK
PEEK
OHH!
HE'S THE GUY WHO SAVED YOU?!
YOU SURE IT'S HIM?
HE SEEMS PRETTY MEEK AND MILD...
YES, I'M SURE!
WHO'D HAVE THOUGHT I'D RUN INTO HIM HERE?
SO, WHAT ARE YOU GOING TO DO ABOUT IT?
WHAT DO YOU MEAN?
YOU'RE NEVER GOING TO GET ANYWHERE HIDING BEHIND A PILLAR. *TALK* TO HIM!
SHOVE
AH!

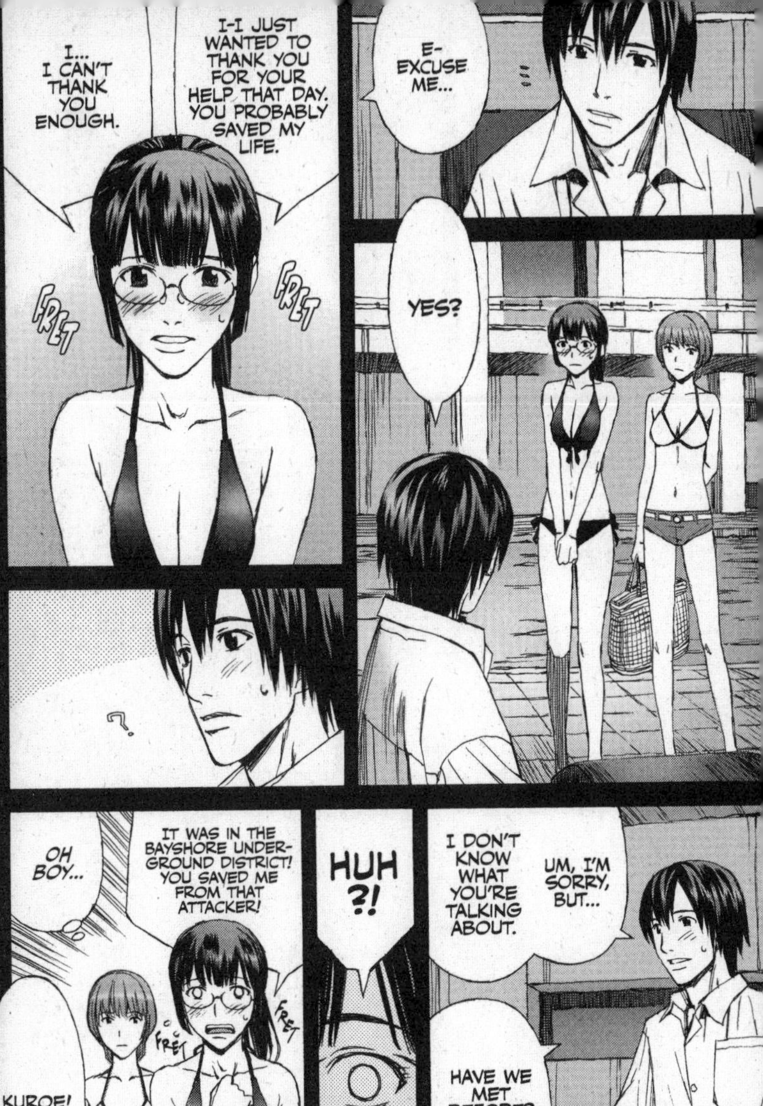
E-EXCUSE ME...
YES?
I-I JUST WANTED TO THANK YOU FOR YOUR HELP THAT DAY. YOU PROBABLY SAVED MY LIFE.
I... I CAN'T THANK YOU ENOUGH.
FRET
FRET
?
UM, I'M SORRY, BUT...
I DON'T KNOW WHAT YOU'RE TALKING ABOUT.
HAVE WE MET BEFORE?
HUH ?!
IT WAS IN THE BAYSHORE UNDER-GROUND DISTRICT! YOU SAVED ME FROM THAT ATTACKER!
OH BOY...
FRET
FRET
KUROE!

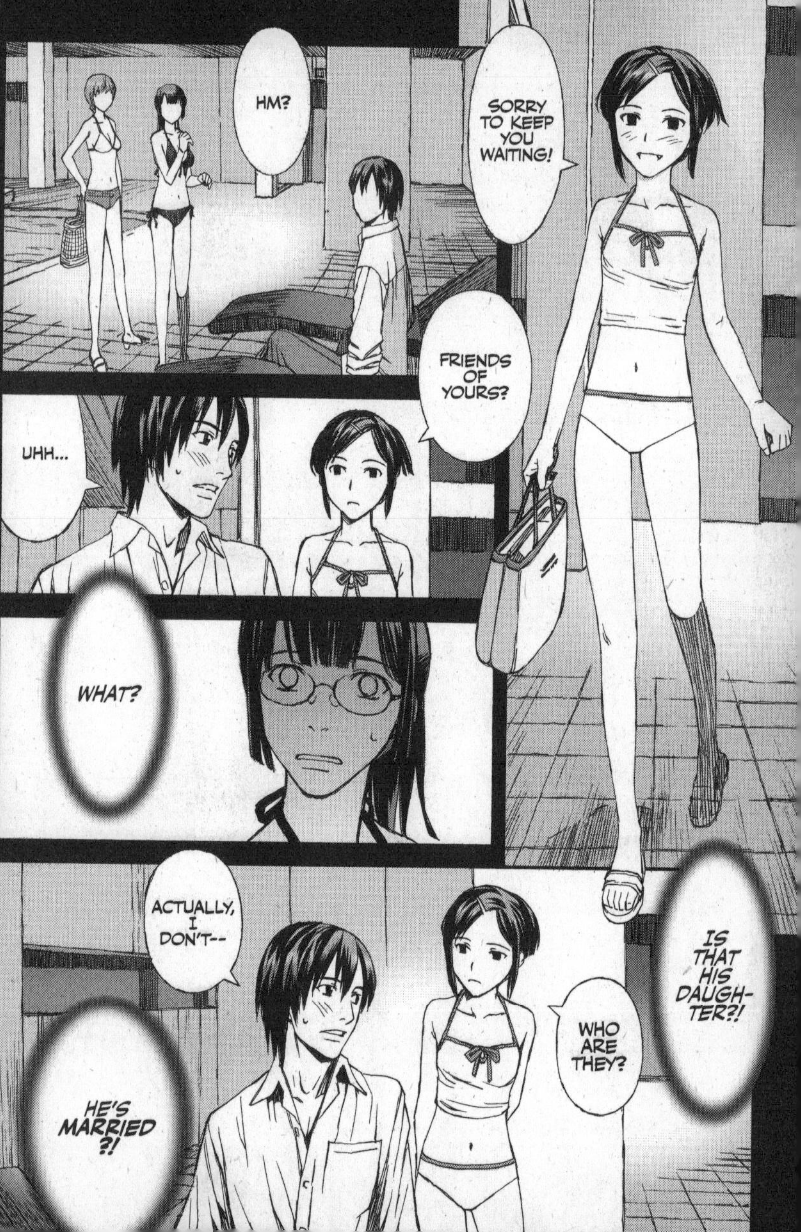
SORRY TO KEEP YOU WAITING!
FRIENDS OF YOURS?
HM?
UHH...
WHAT?
IS THAT HIS DAUGHTER?!
WHO ARE THEY?
ACTUALLY, I DON'T--
HE'S MARRIED ?!

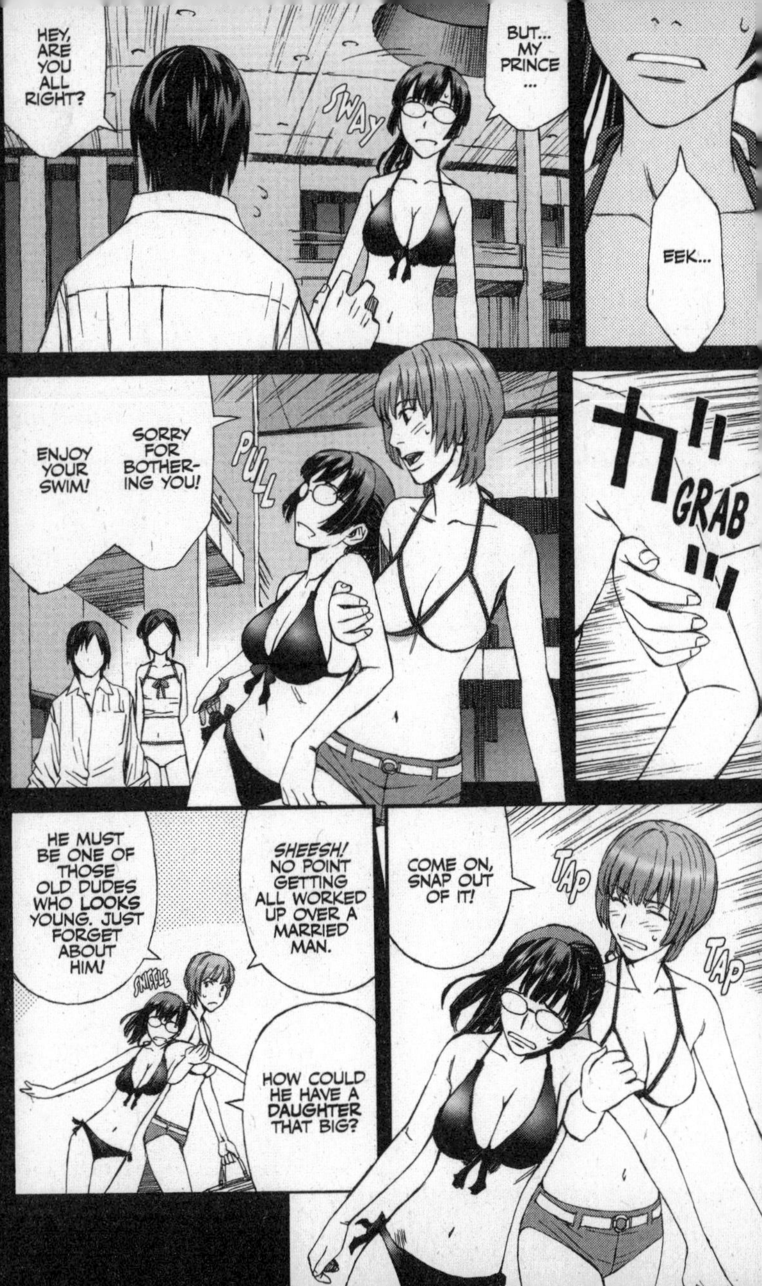
EEK...
BUT... MY PRINCE ...
SWAY
HEY, ARE YOU ALL RIGHT?
カッ
GRAB
PULL
SORRY FOR BOTHERING YOU!
ENJOY YOUR SWIM!
TAP
TAP
COME ON, SNAP OUT OF IT!
SHEESH! NO POINT GETTING ALL WORKED UP OVER A MARRIED MAN.
HE MUST BE ONE OF THOSE OLD DUDES WHO LOOKS YOUNG. JUST FORGET ABOUT HIM!
SNIFFLE
HOW COULD HE HAVE A DAUGHTER THAT BIG?

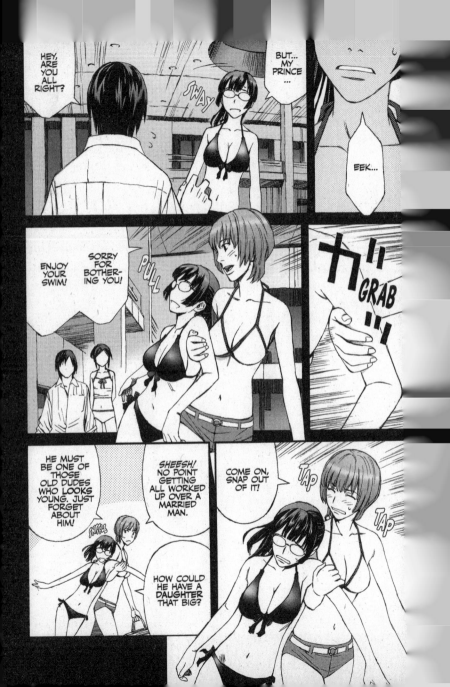

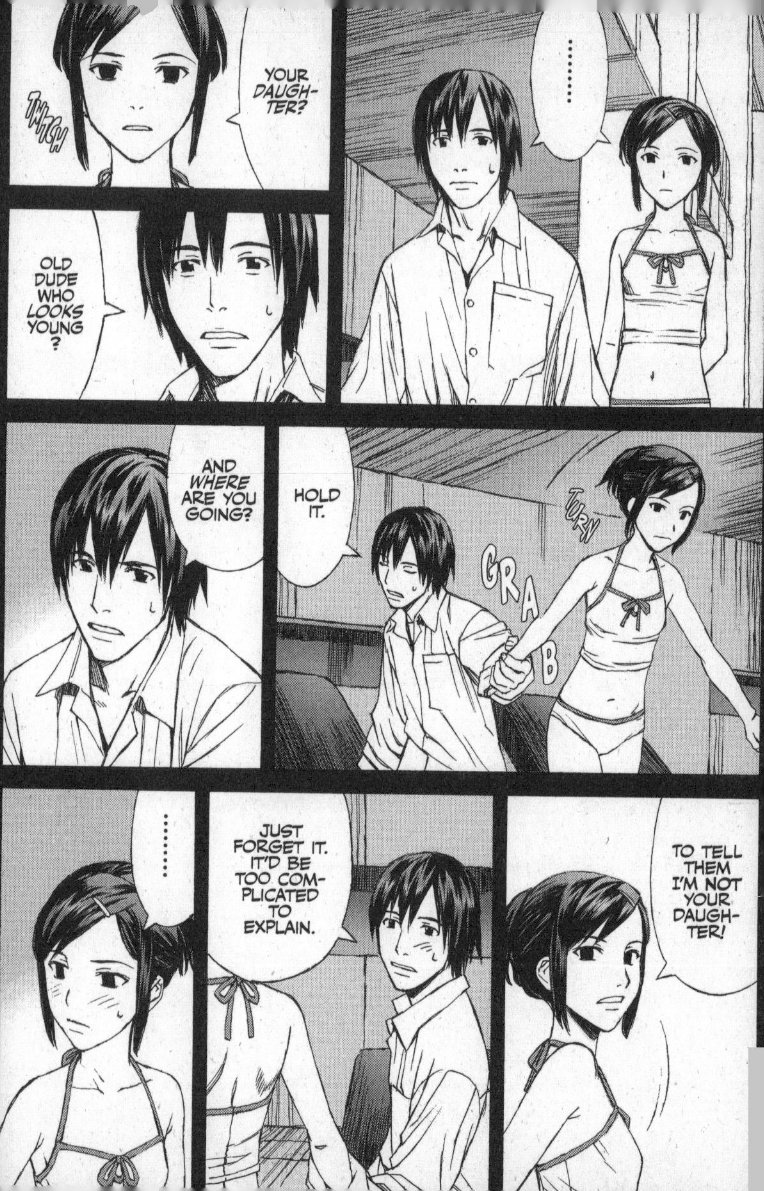
……
YOUR DAUGHTER?
TWITCH
OLD DUDE WHO LOOKS YOUNG?
HOLD IT.
TURN
GRAB
AND WHERE ARE YOU GOING?
TO TELL THEM I'M NOT YOUR DAUGHTER!
JUST FORGET IT. IT'D BE TOO COMPLICATED TO EXPLAIN.
……

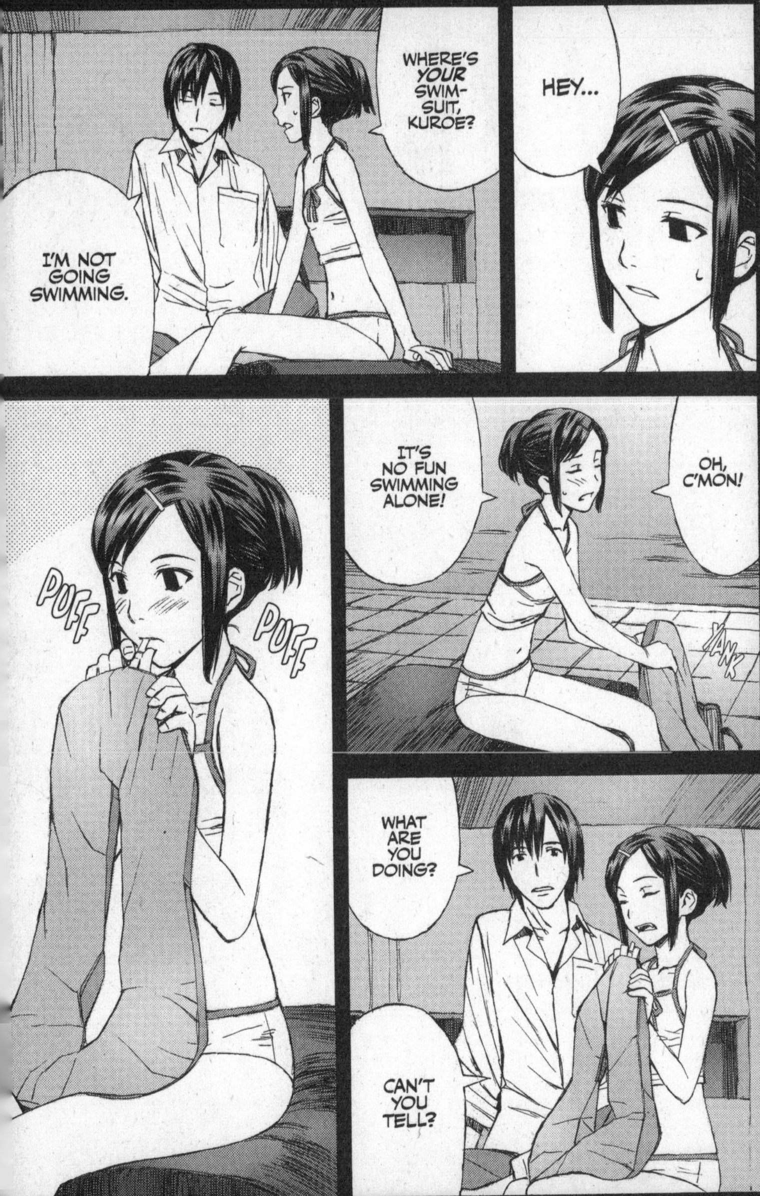
HEY...
WHERE'S *YOUR* SWIM-SUIT, KUROE?
I'M NOT GOING SWIMMING.
OH, C'MON!
IT'S NO FUN SWIMMING ALONE!
YANK
WHAT ARE YOU DOING?
CAN'T YOU TELL?
PUFF
PUFF

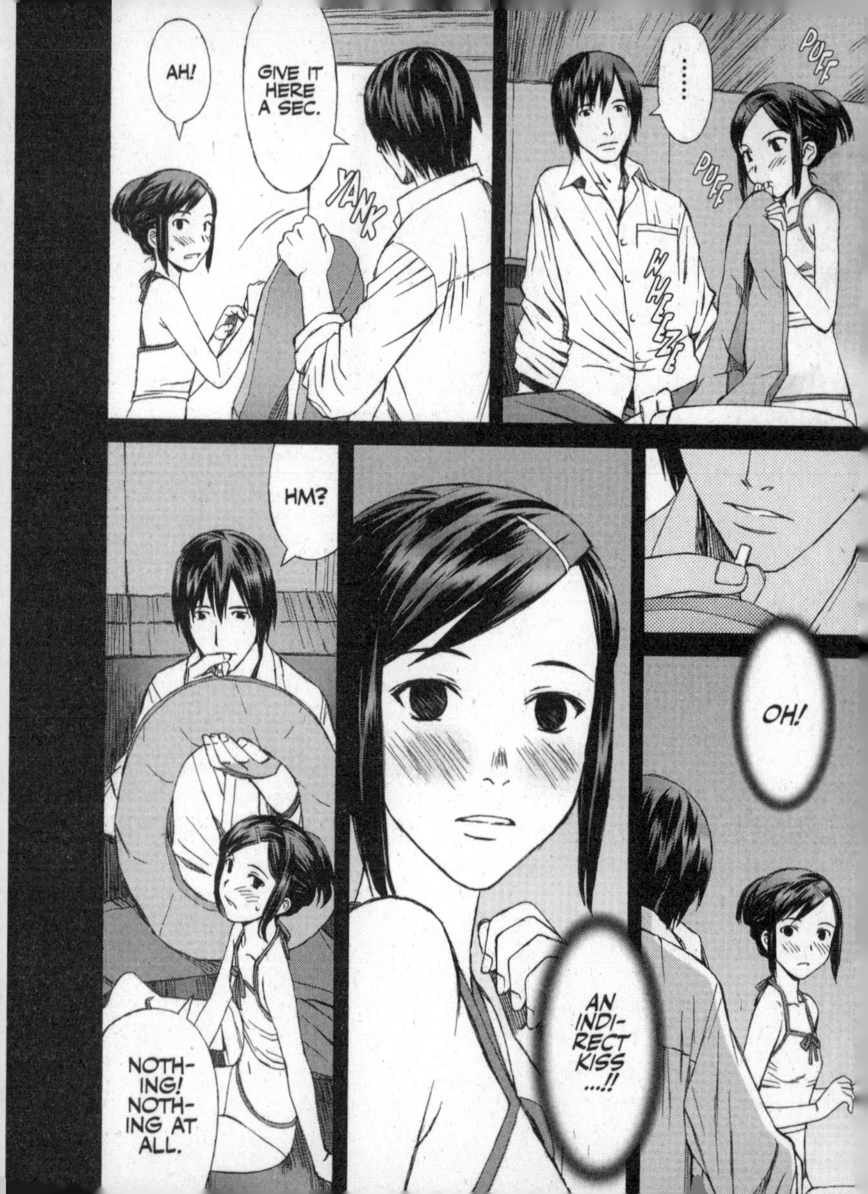
......
PUFF
PUFF
WHEEZE
GIVE IT HERE A SEC.
AH!
YANK
OH!
AN INDI-RECT KISS ...!!
HM?
NOTH-ING! NOTH-ING AT ALL.

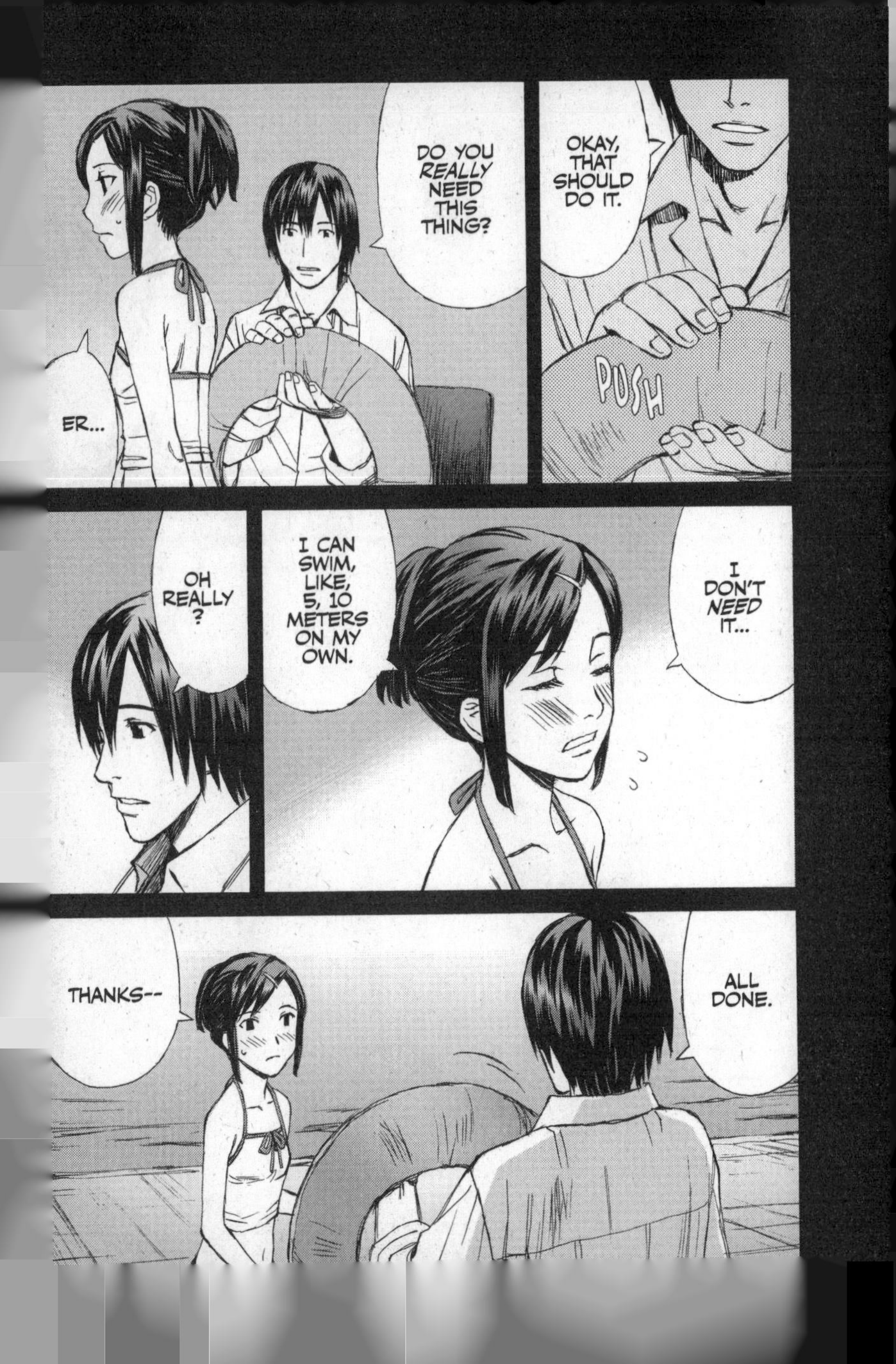
OKAY, THAT SHOULD DO IT.
PUSH
DO YOU REALLY NEED THIS THING?
ER...
I DON'T NEED IT...
I CAN SWIM, LIKE, 5, 10 METERS ON MY OWN.
OH REALLY?
ALL DONE.
THANKS--

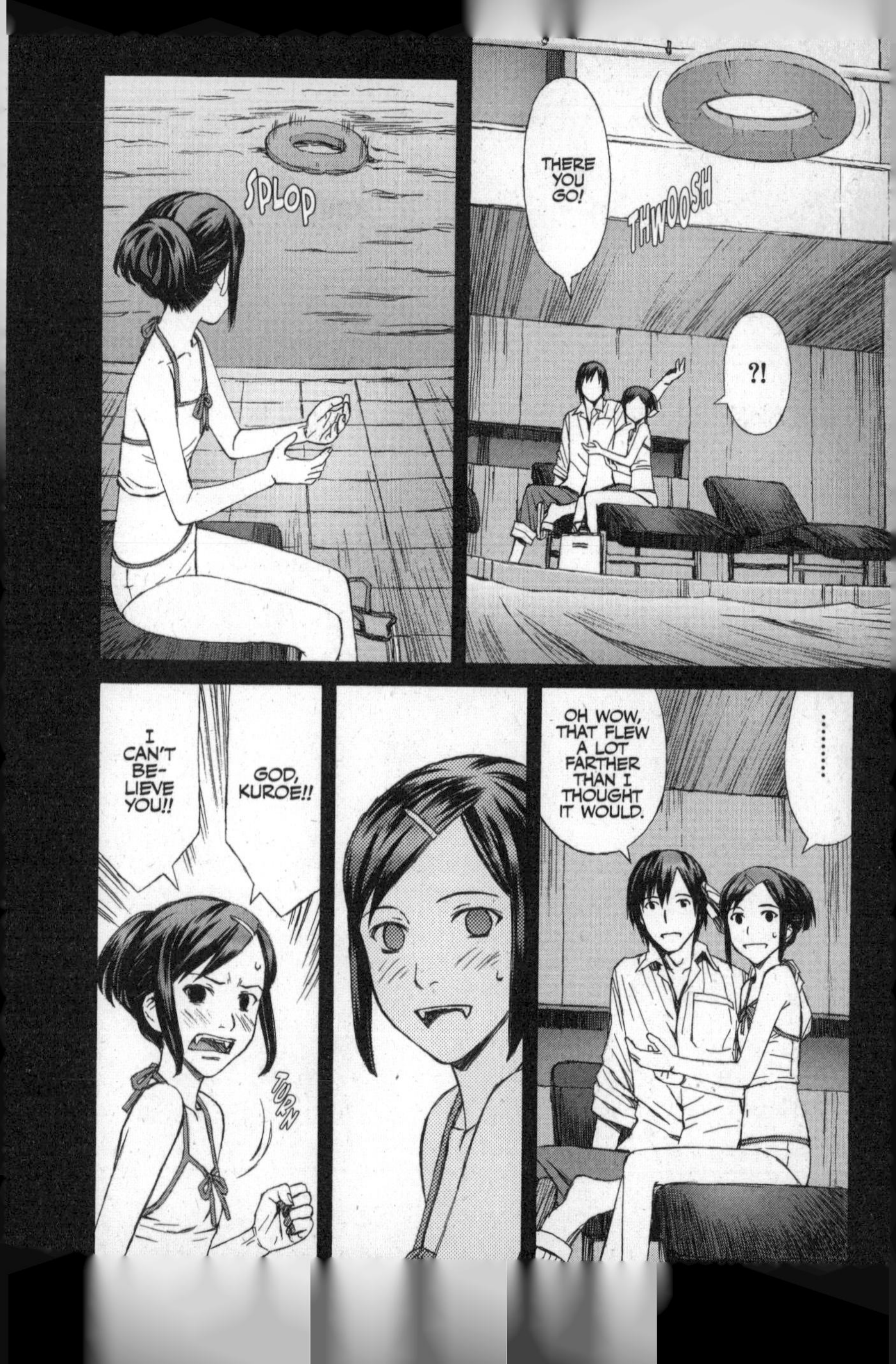
THERE YOU GO!
THWOOSH
?!
SPLOP
......
OH WOW, THAT FLEW A LOT FARTHER THAN I THOUGHT IT WOULD.
GOD, KUROE!!
I CAN'T BE-LIEVE YOU!!
TURN

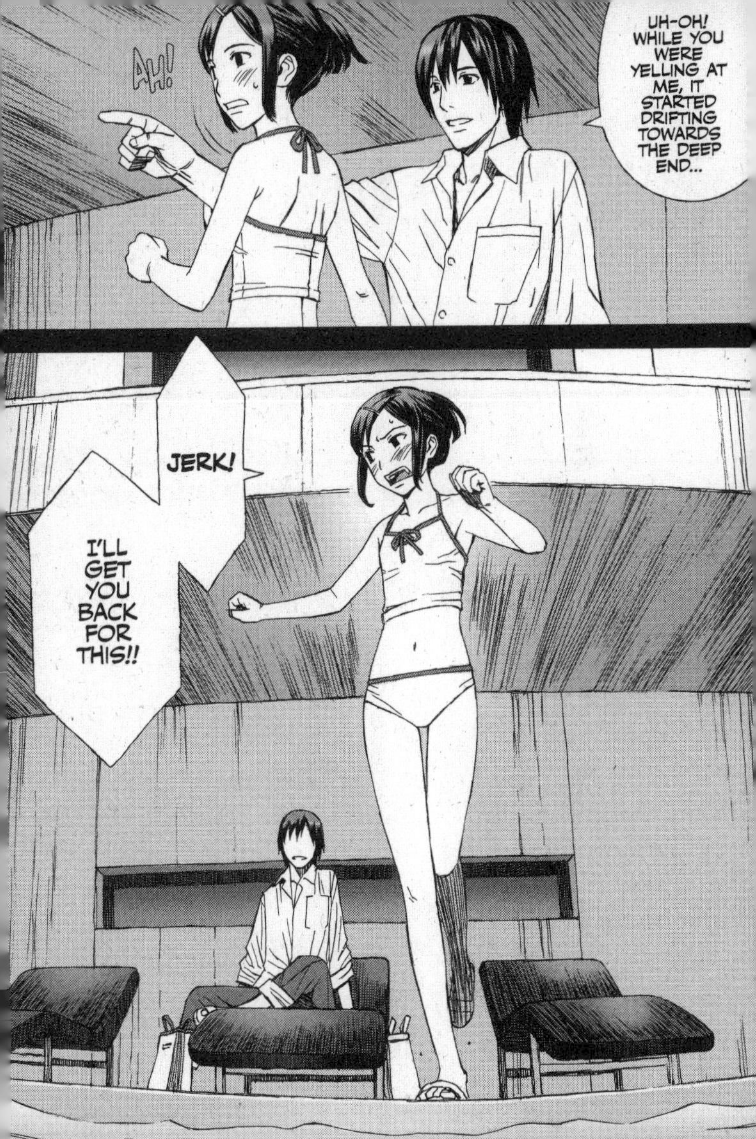
UH-OH! WHILE YOU WERE YELLING AT ME, IT STARTED DRIFTING TOWARDS THE DEEP END...
AH!
JERK!
I'LL GET YOU BACK FOR THIS!!

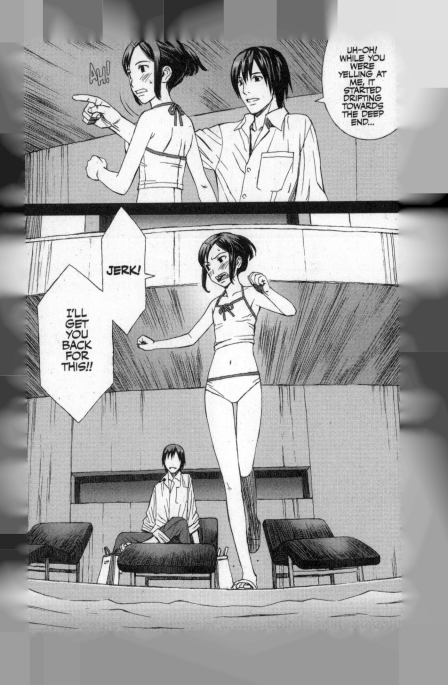

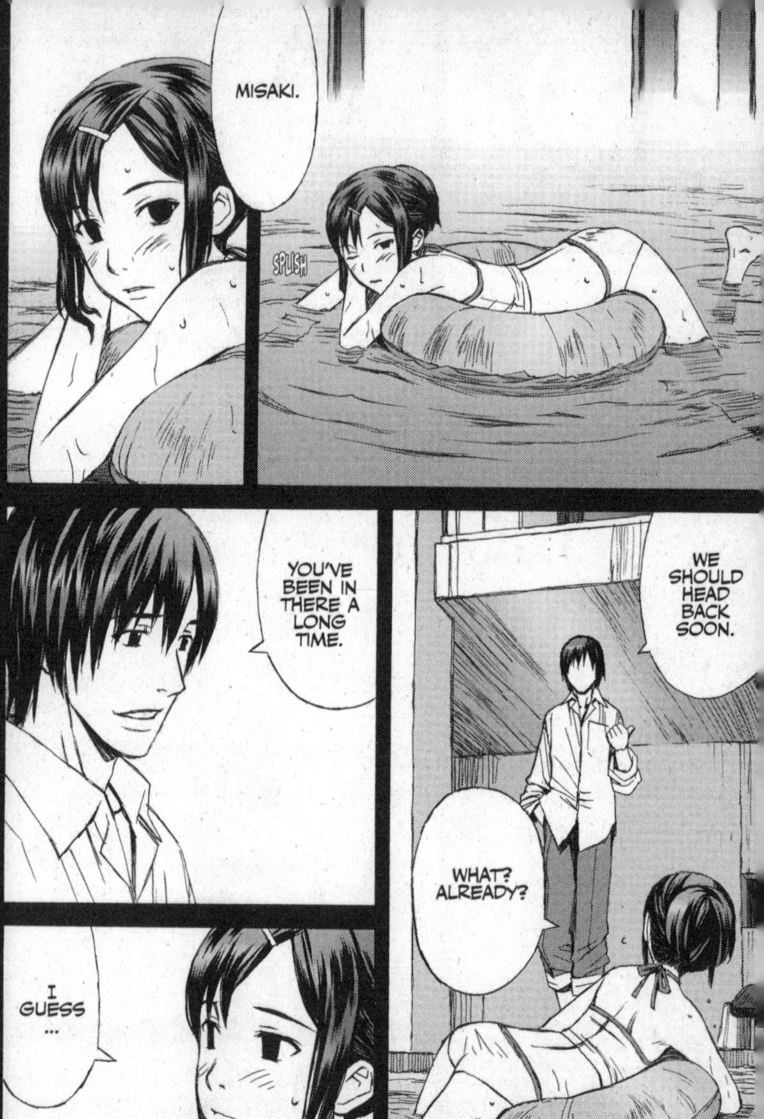
MISAKI.
SPLISH
WE SHOULD HEAD BACK SOON.
WHAT? ALREADY?
YOU'VE BEEN IN THERE A LONG TIME.
I GUESS ...

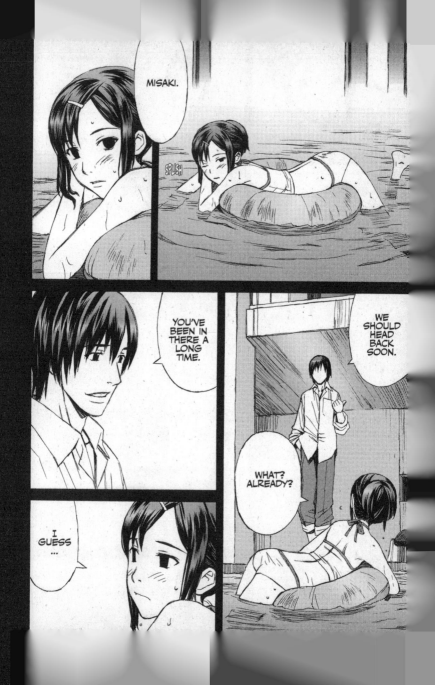

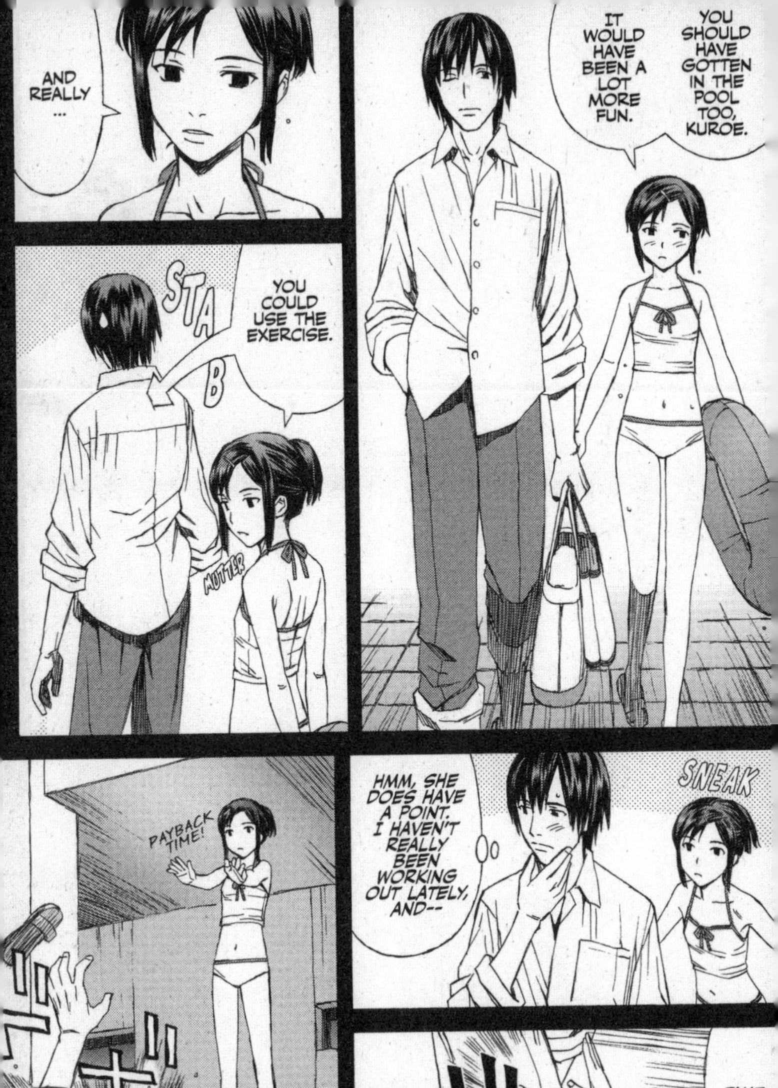

YOU SHOULD HAVE GOTTEN IN THE POOL TOO, KUROE.
IT WOULD HAVE BEEN A LOT MORE FUN.
AND REALLY ...
STAB
YOU COULD USE THE EXERCISE.
MUTTER
SNEAK
HMM, SHE DOES HAVE A POINT. I HAVEN'T REALLY BEEN WORKING OUT LATELY, AND--
TAKE THAT!!
SHOVE
AHH!
PAYBACK TIME!
SPLOOSH!

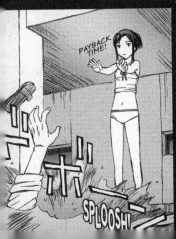

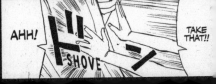

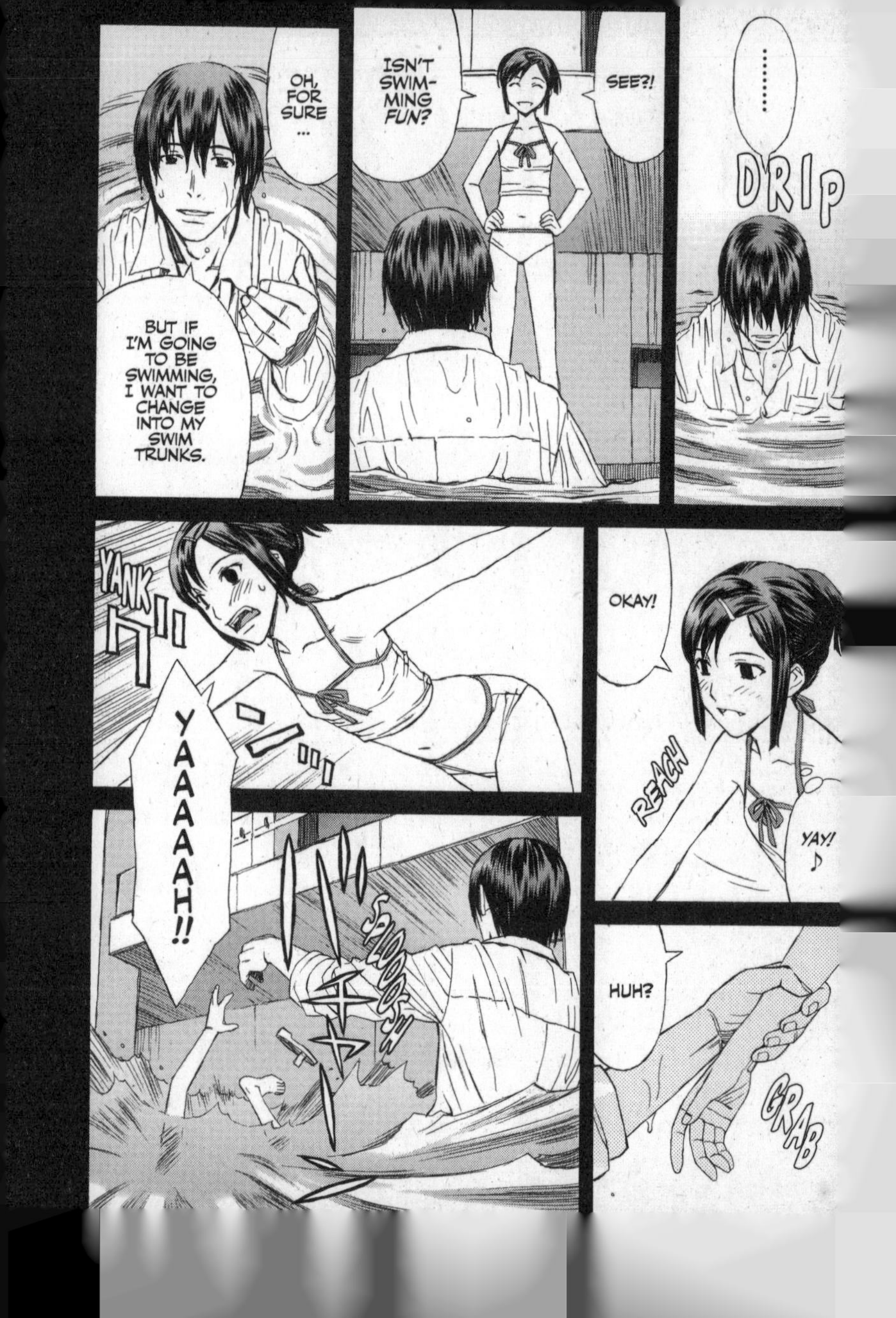
......
DRIP
SEE?!
ISN'T SWIM-MING FUN?
OH, FOR SURE ...
BUT IF I'M GOING TO BE SWIMMING, I WANT TO CHANGE INTO MY SWIM TRUNKS.
OKAY!
REACH
YAY! ♪
HUH?
GRAB
YANK
YAAAAAAH!!
SPLOOOSH

KUROE!

SPLASH

COUGH! COUGH!

SPLASH

WAAAH!

SPLASH

SPLASH

GRRRR

AH HA HA! HAVING FUN NOW?

YOU DORK!!

SMACK

SMACK

WHAT...?

PANT

PANT

LIFT

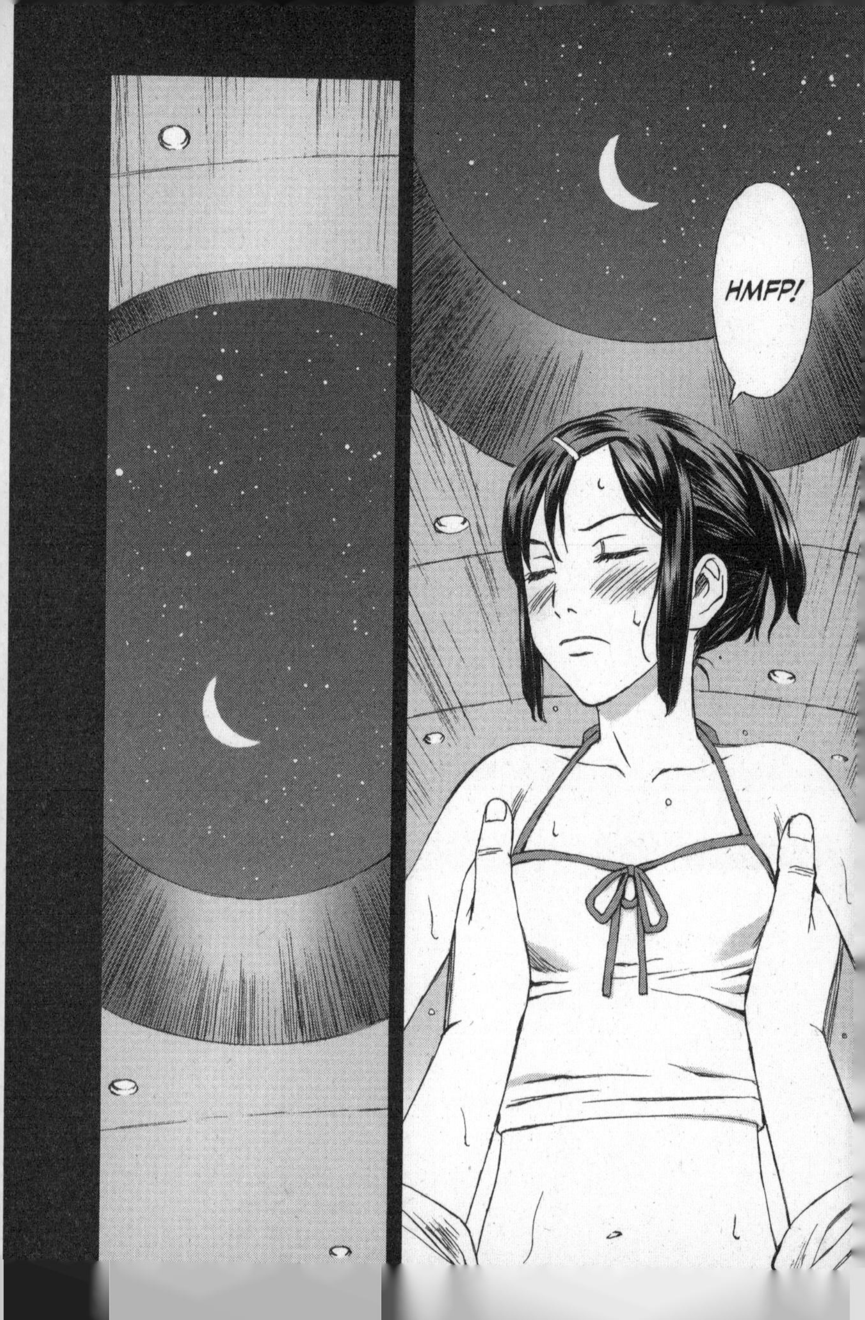
HMFP!

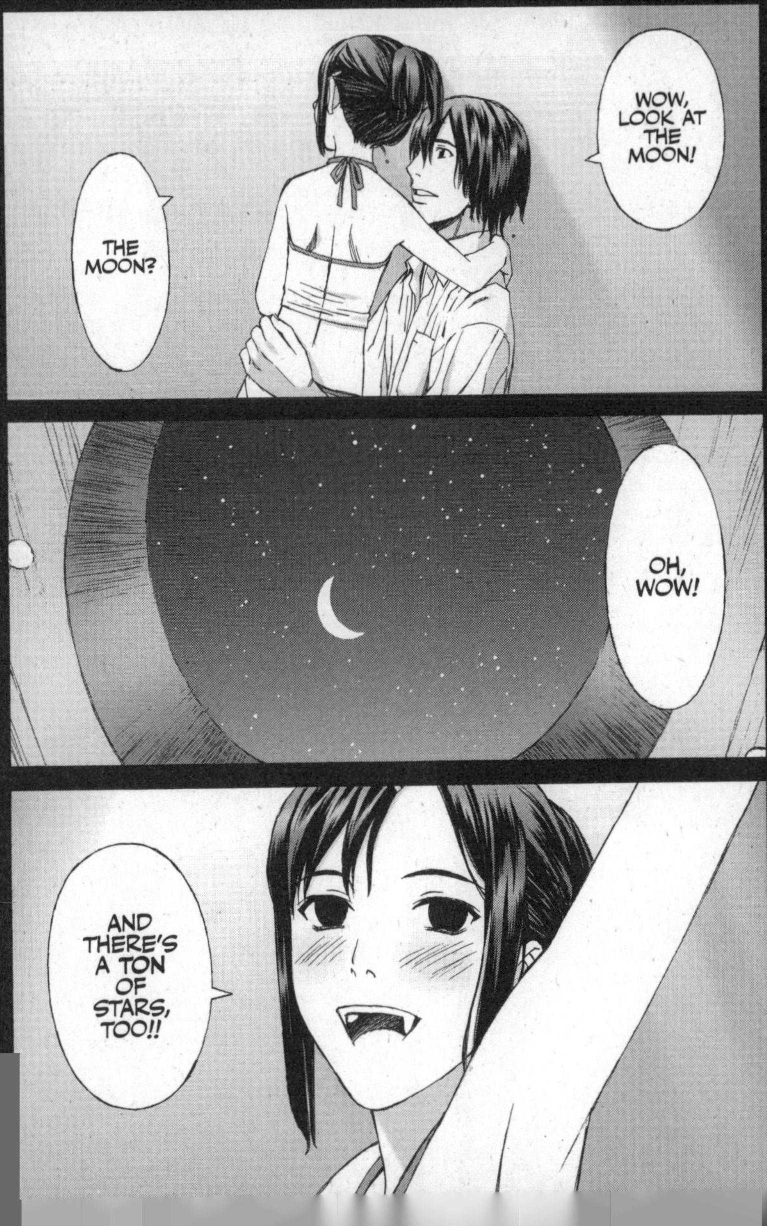
WOW, LOOK AT THE MOON!
THE MOON?
OH, WOW!
AND THERE'S A TON OF STARS, TOO!!

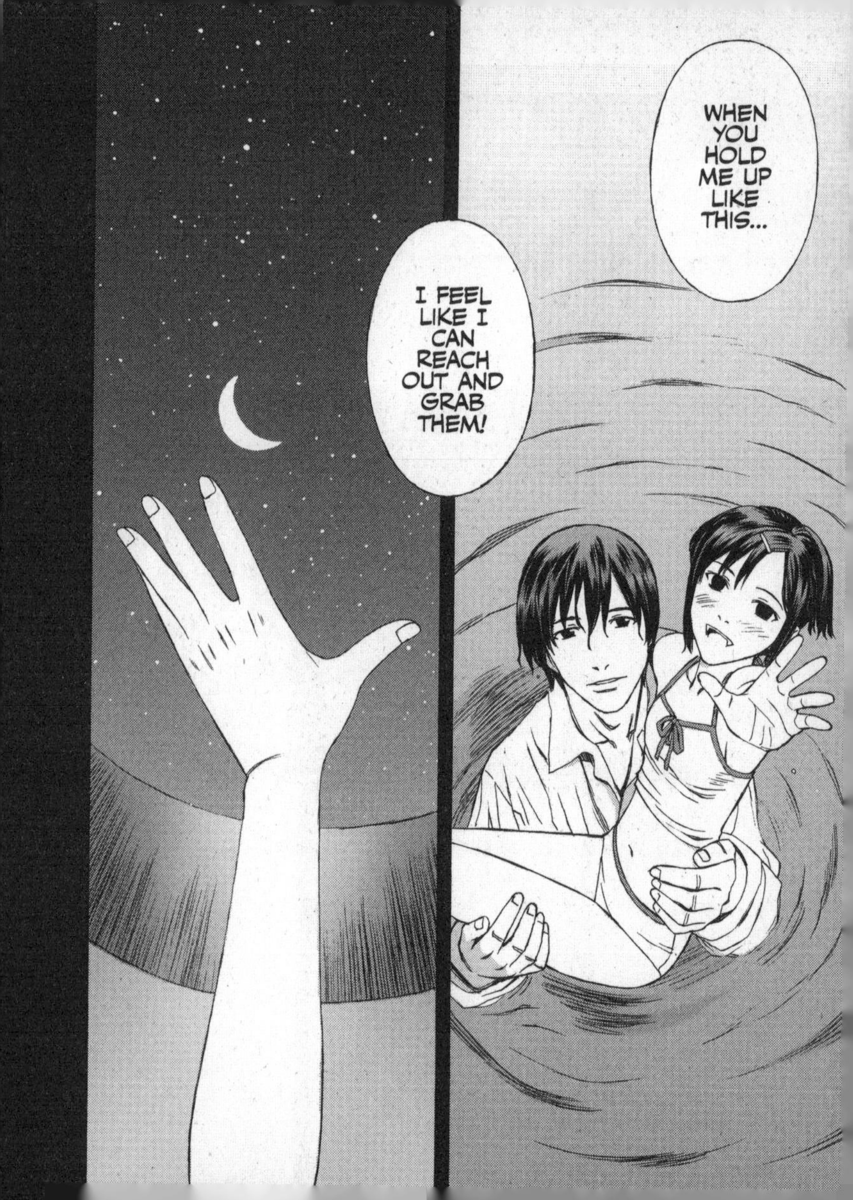
WHEN YOU HOLD ME UP LIKE THIS...
I FEEL LIKE I CAN REACH OUT AND GRAB THEM!

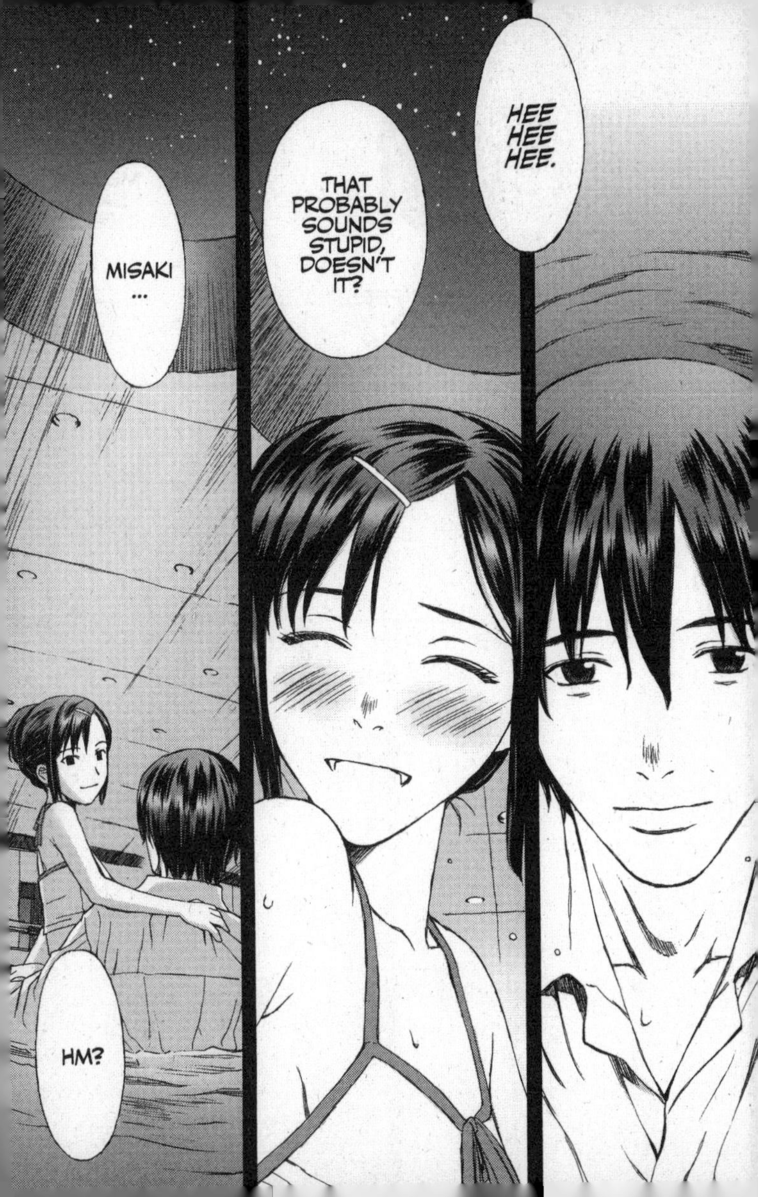
HEE HEE HEE.
THAT PROBABLY SOUNDS STUPID, DOESN'T IT?
MISAKI ...
HM?

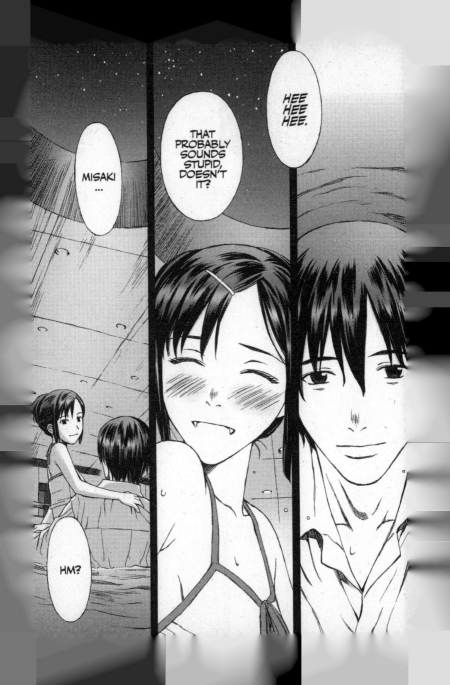

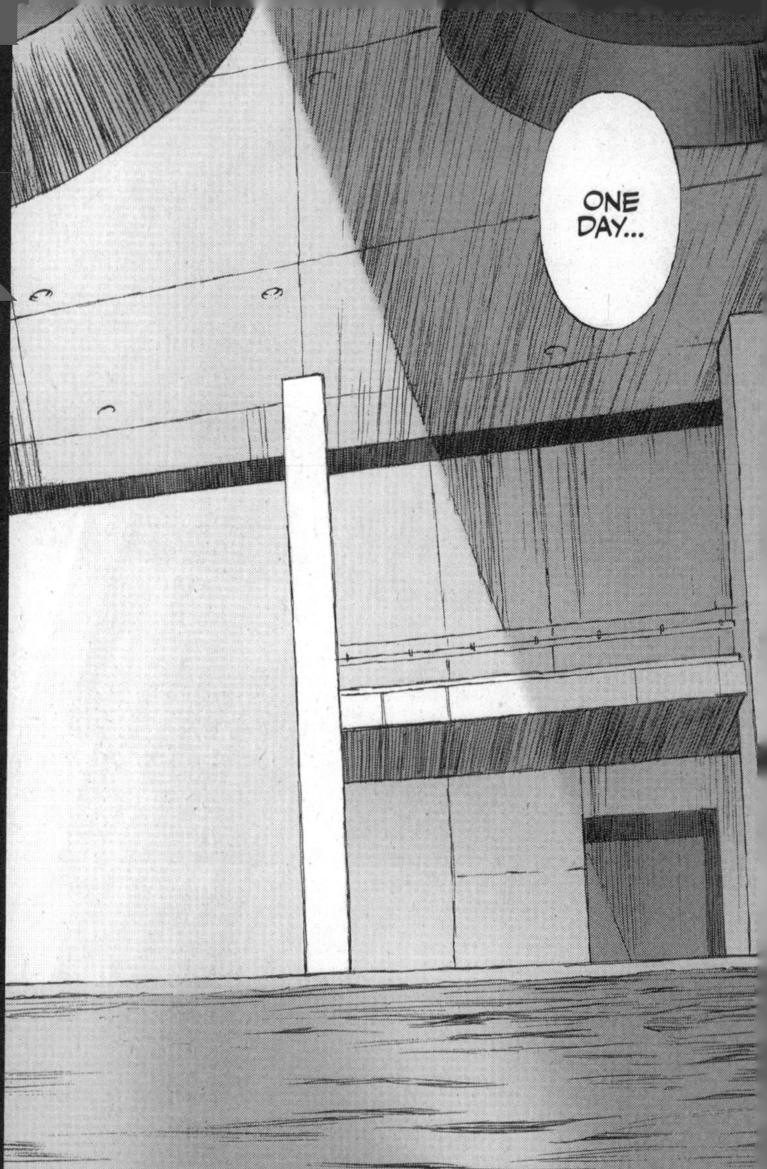
ONE DAY...

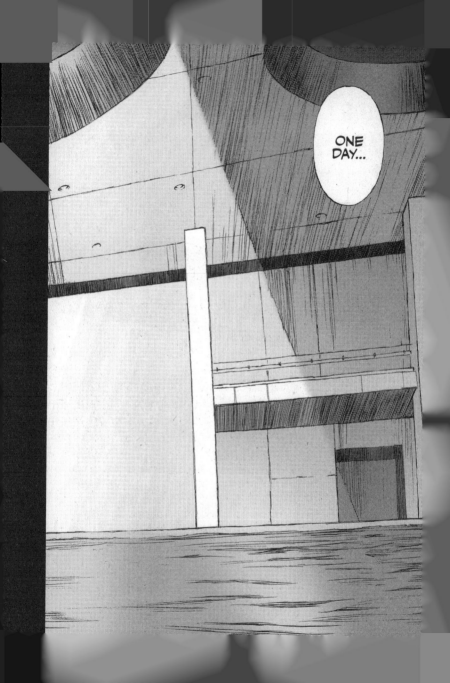

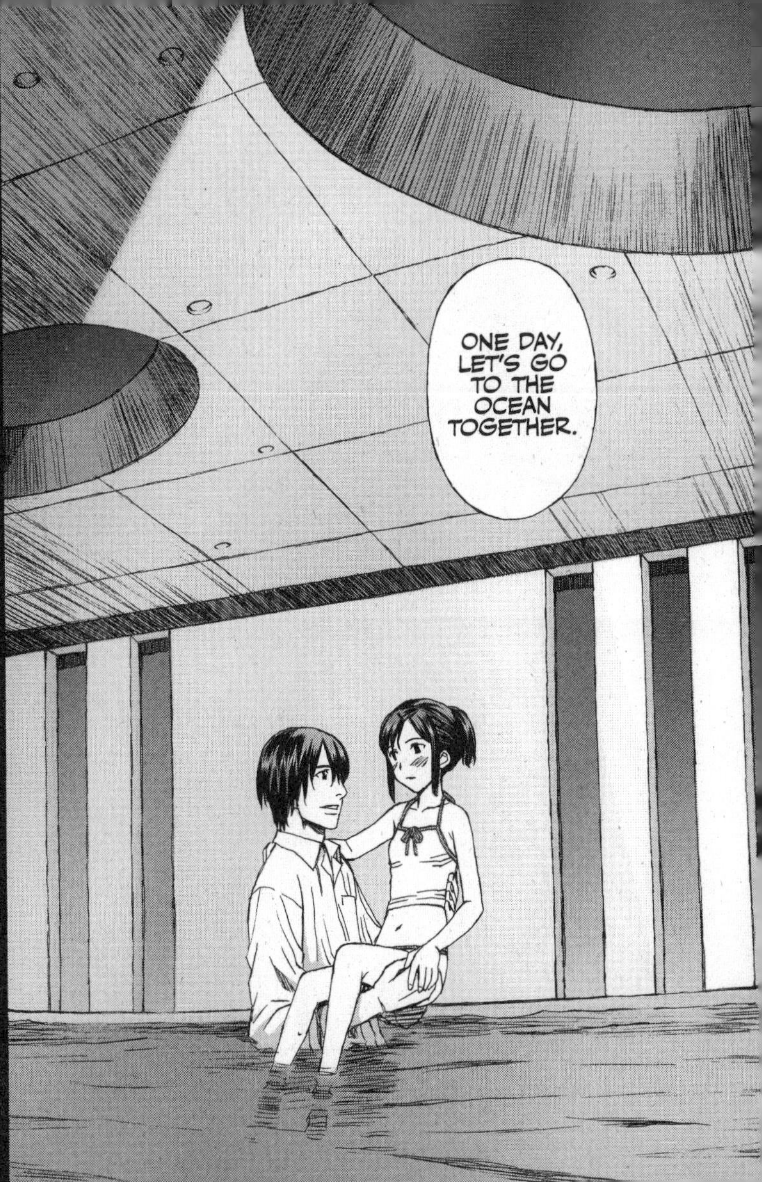
ONE DAY, LET'S GO TO THE OCEAN TOGETHER.

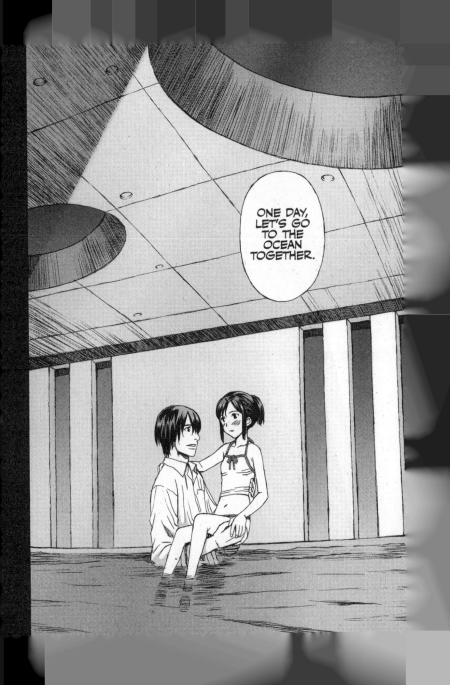

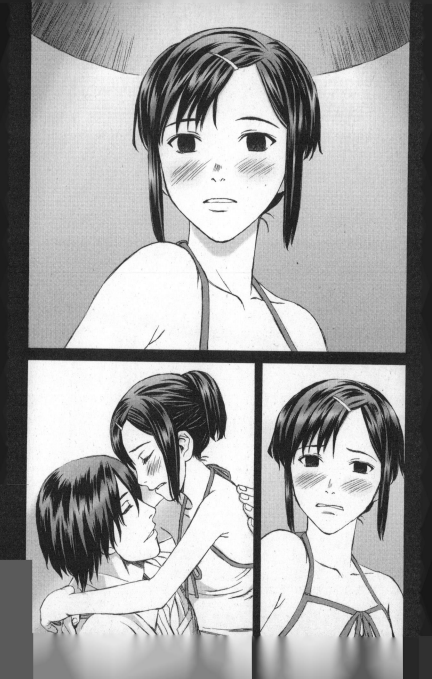

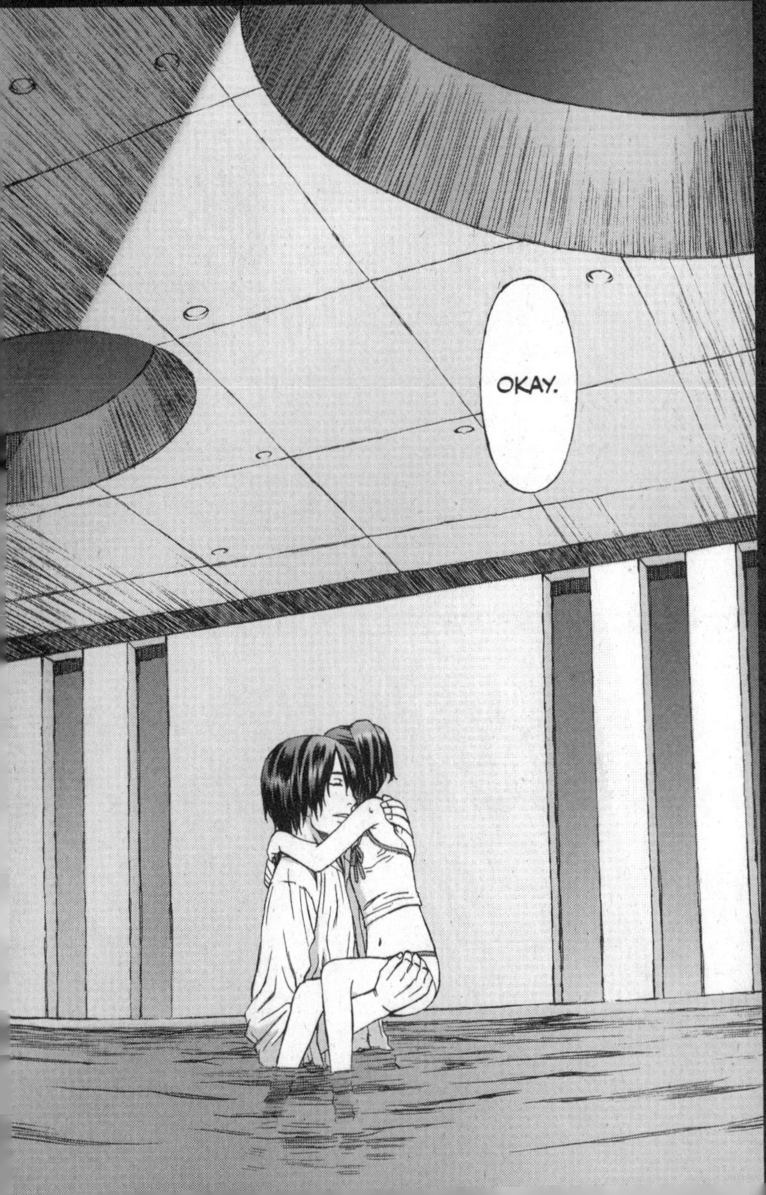
OKAY.

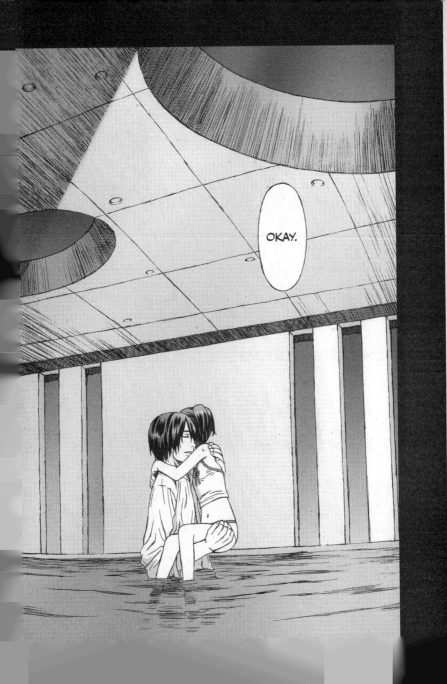

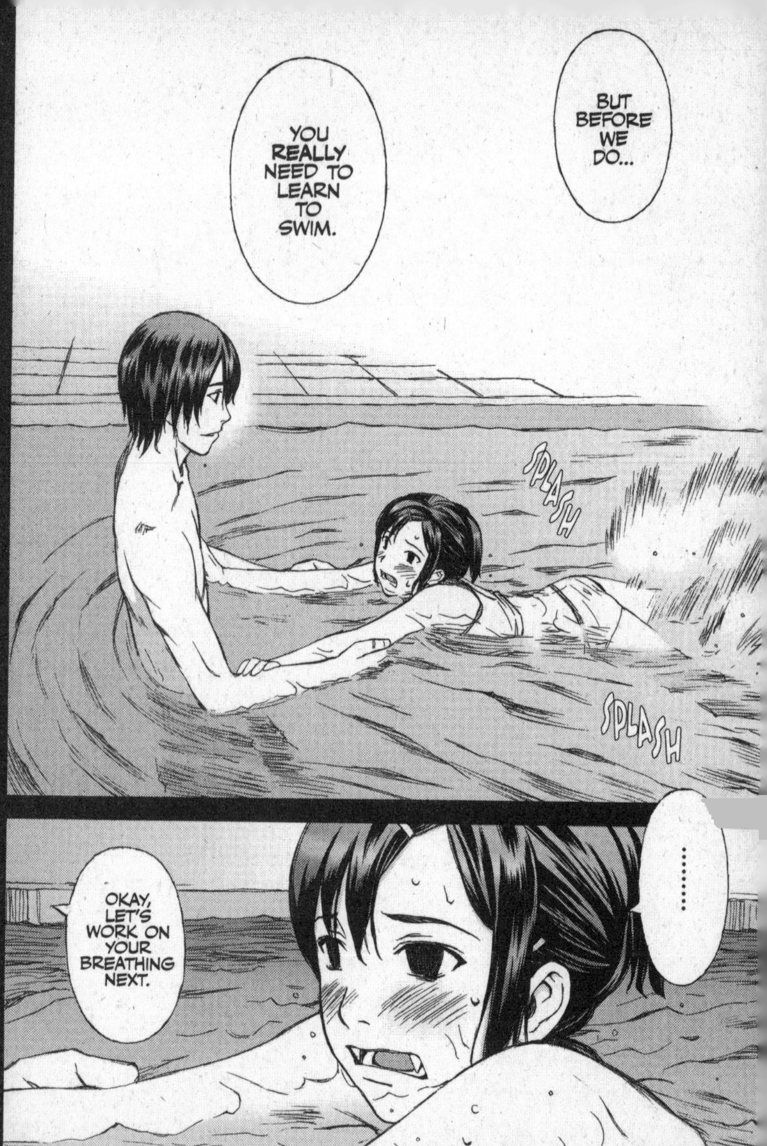
BUT BEFORE WE DO...
YOU REALLY NEED TO LEARN TO SWIM.
SPLASH
SPLASH
......
OKAY, LET'S WORK ON YOUR BREATHING NEXT.

Episode 18
MIDNIGHT CRUISE
Her True Face

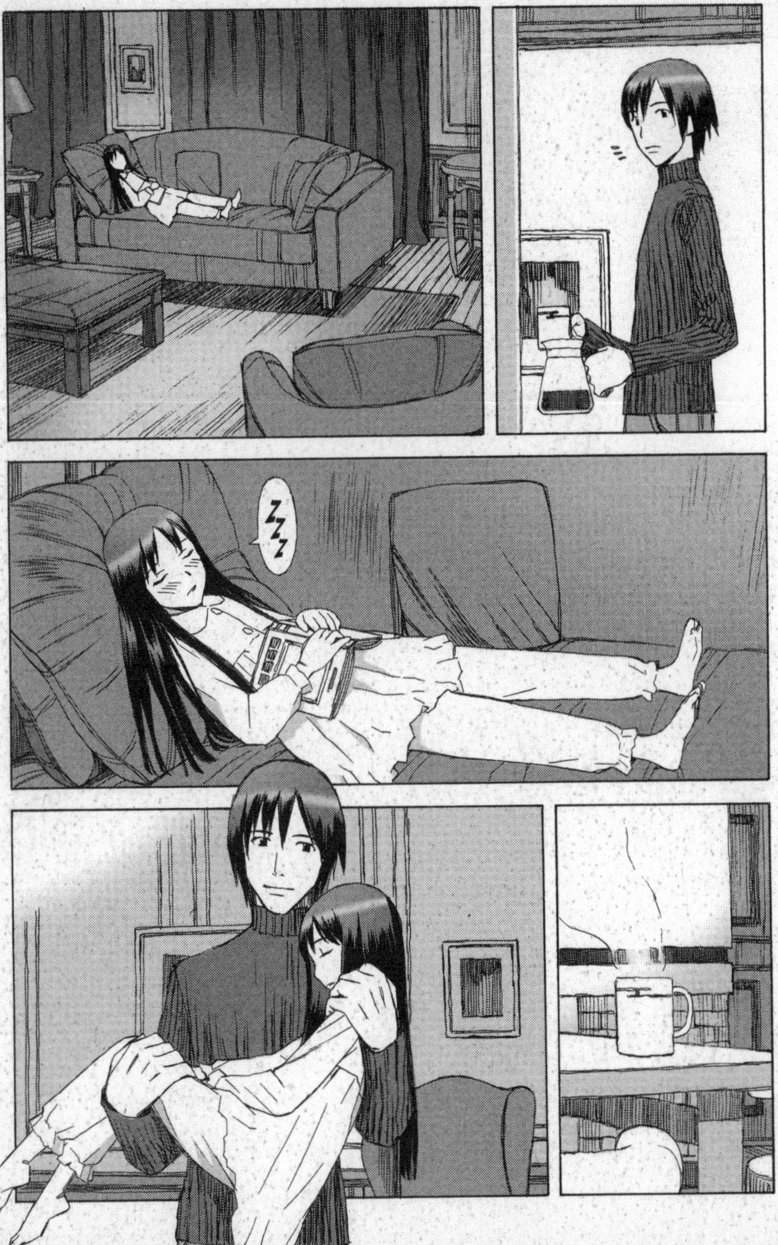
ZZZ

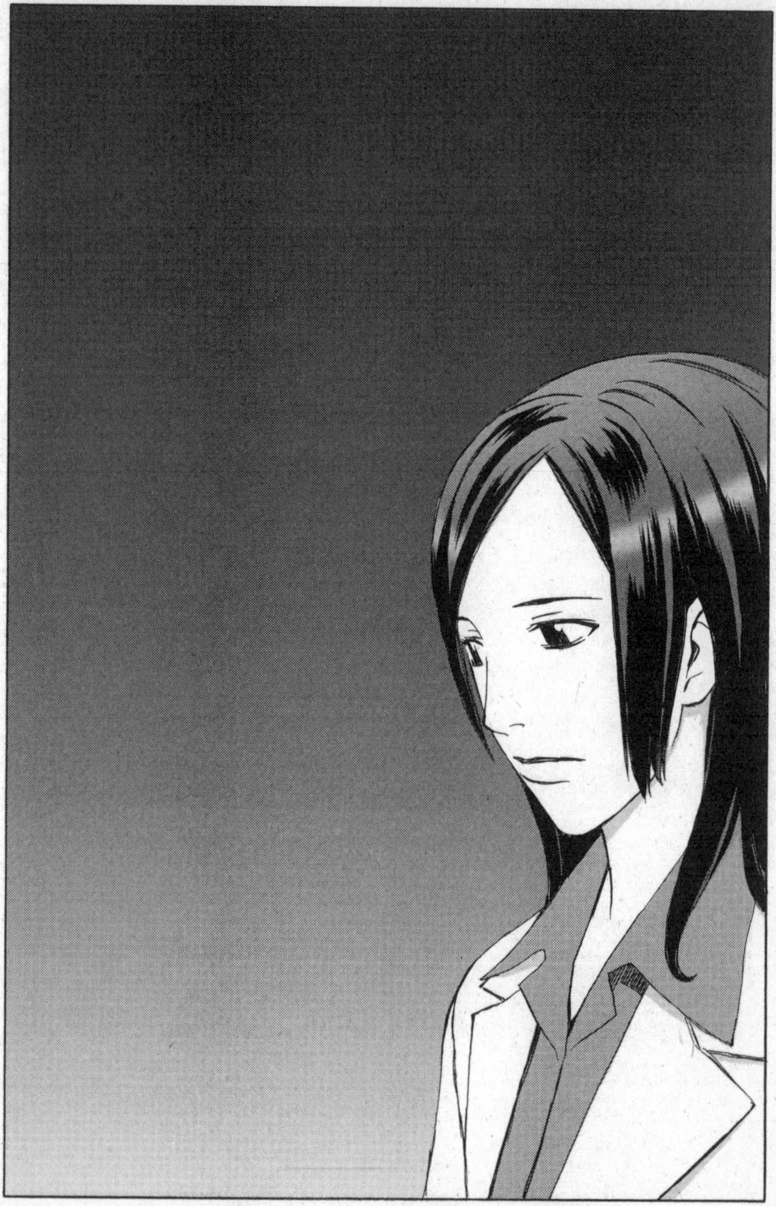

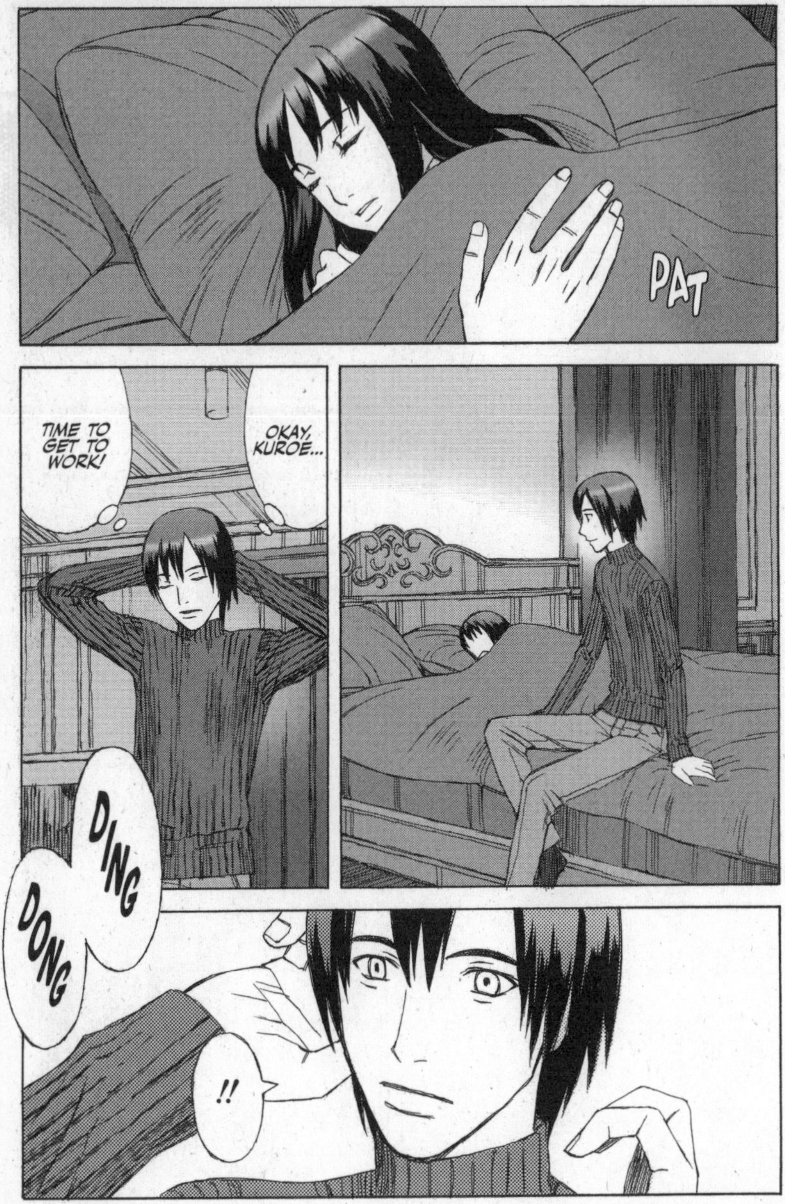
PAT
OKAY, KUROE...
TIME TO GET TO WORK!
DING DONG
!!

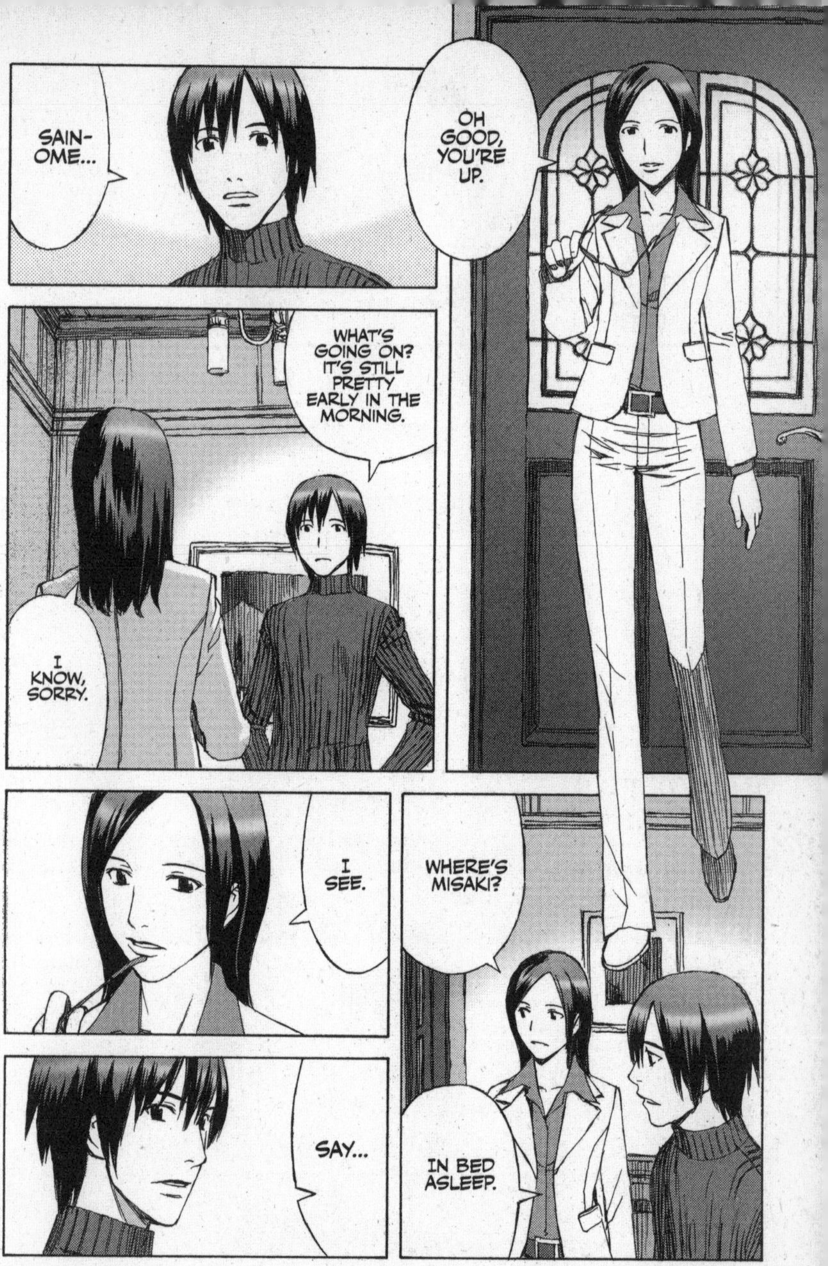
OH GOOD, YOU'RE UP.
SAIN-OME...
WHAT'S GOING ON? IT'S STILL PRETTY EARLY IN THE MORNING.
I KNOW, SORRY.
WHERE'S MISAKI?
IN BED ASLEEP.
I SEE.
SAY...

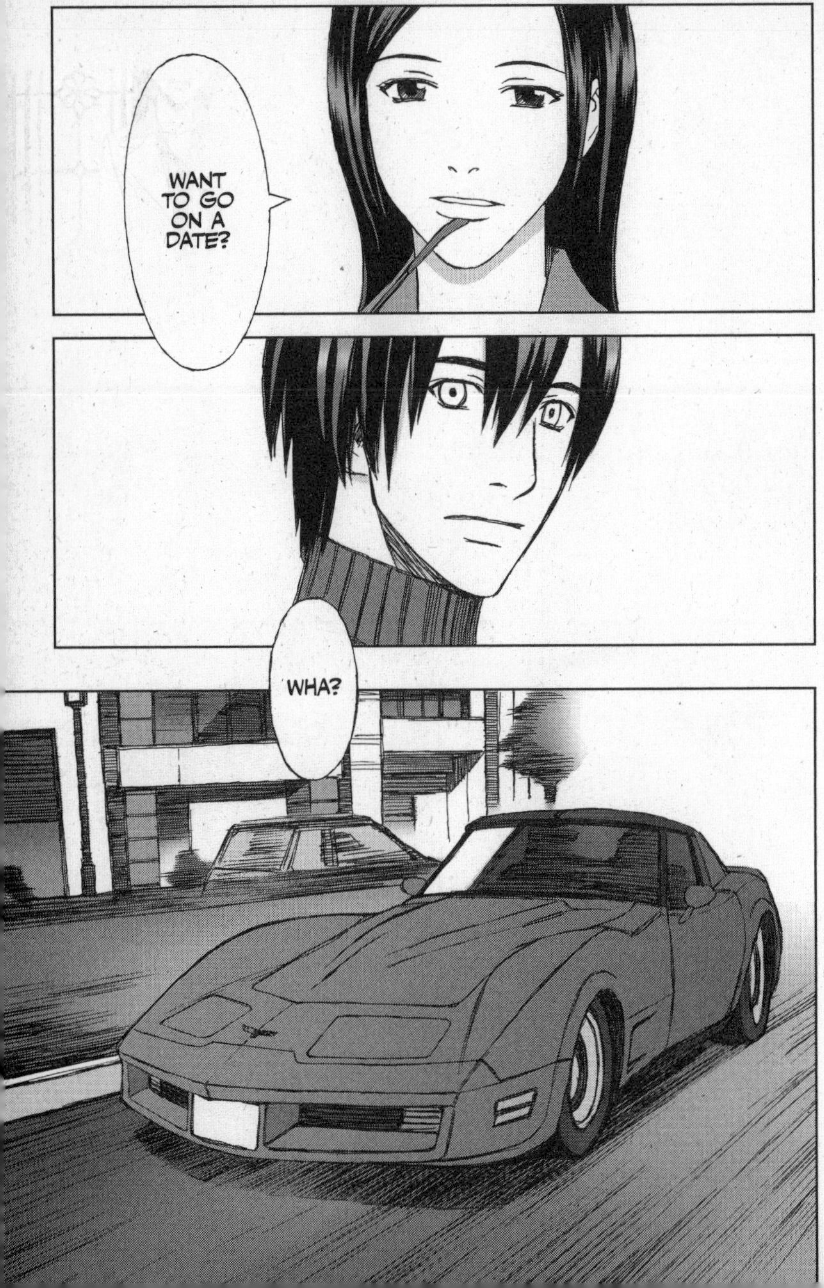
WANT TO GO ON A DATE?
WHA?

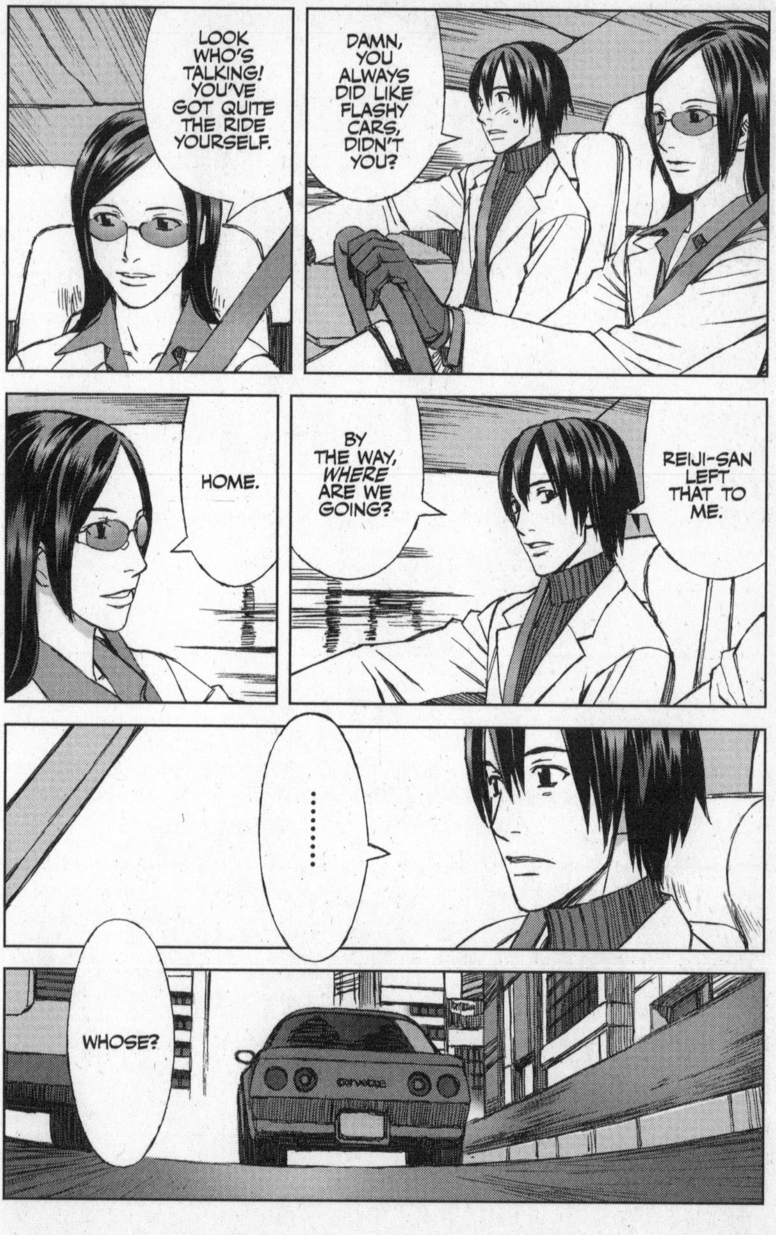
DAMN, YOU ALWAYS DID LIKE FLASHY CARS, DIDN'T YOU?
LOOK WHO'S TALKING! YOU'VE GOT QUITE THE RIDE YOURSELF.
REIJI-SAN LEFT THAT TO ME.
BY THE WAY, *WHERE* ARE WE GOING?
HOME.
....
WHOSE?

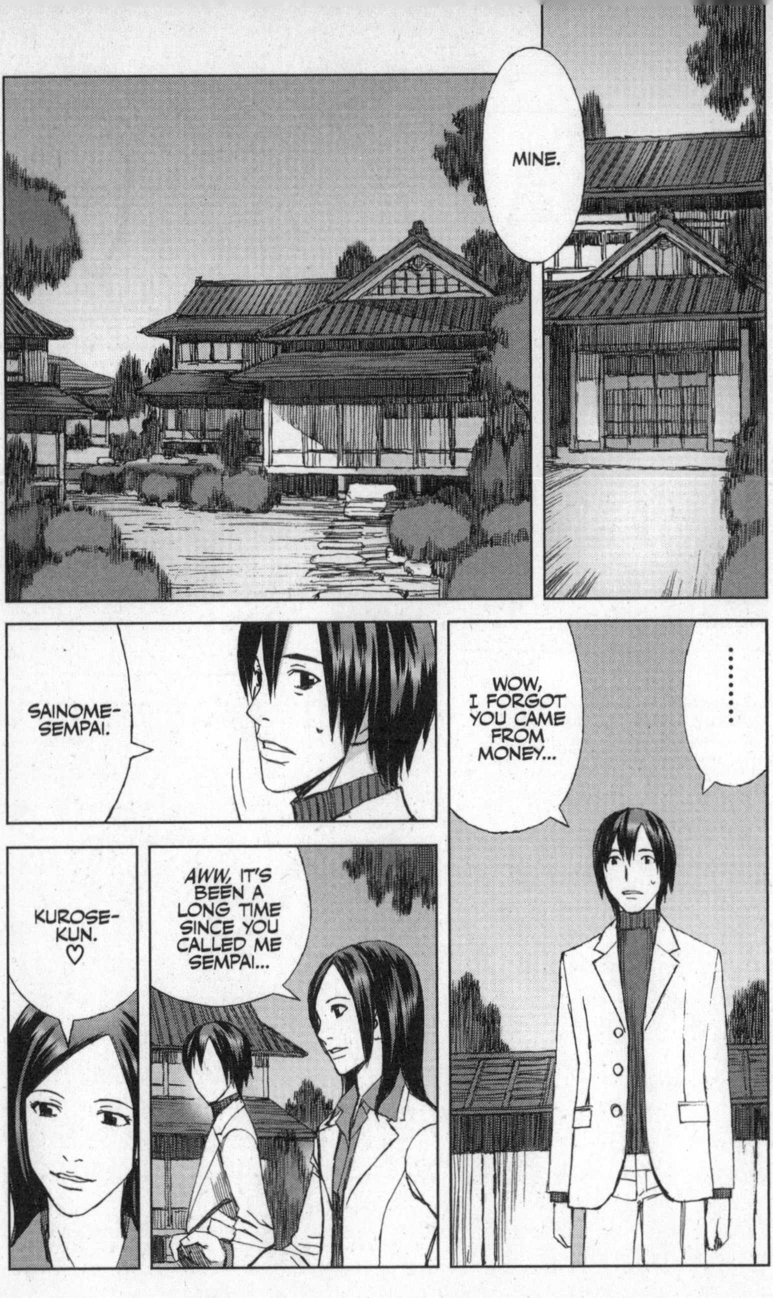
MINE.
......
WOW, I FORGOT YOU CAME FROM MONEY...
SAINOME-SEMPAI.
AWW, IT'S BEEN A LONG TIME SINCE YOU CALLED ME SEMPAI...
KUROSE-KUN. ♡

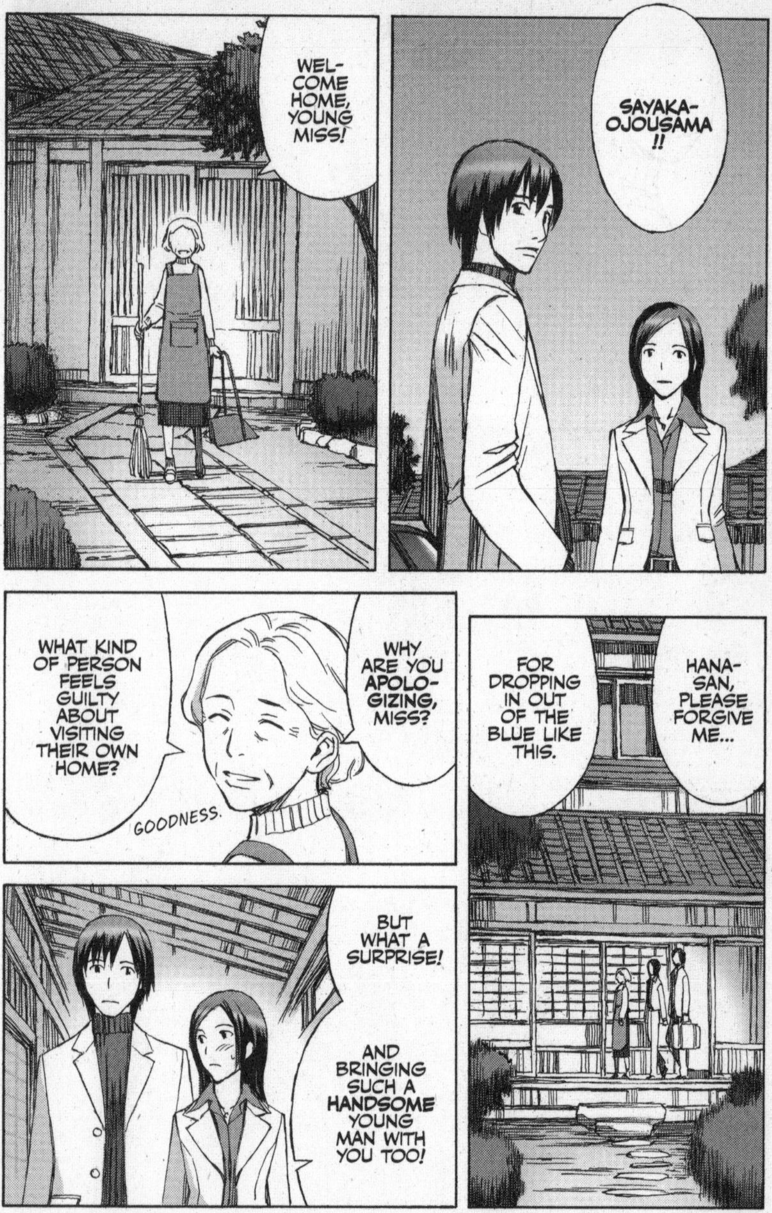
SAYAKA-OJOUSAMA !!
WEL-COME HOME, YOUNG MISS!
HANA-SAN, PLEASE FORGIVE ME...
FOR DROPPING IN OUT OF THE BLUE LIKE THIS.
WHY ARE YOU APOLOGIZING, MISS?
WHAT KIND OF PERSON FEELS GUILTY ABOUT VISITING THEIR OWN HOME?
GOODNESS.
BUT WHAT A SURPRISE!
AND BRINGING SUCH A HANDSOME YOUNG MAN WITH YOU TOO!

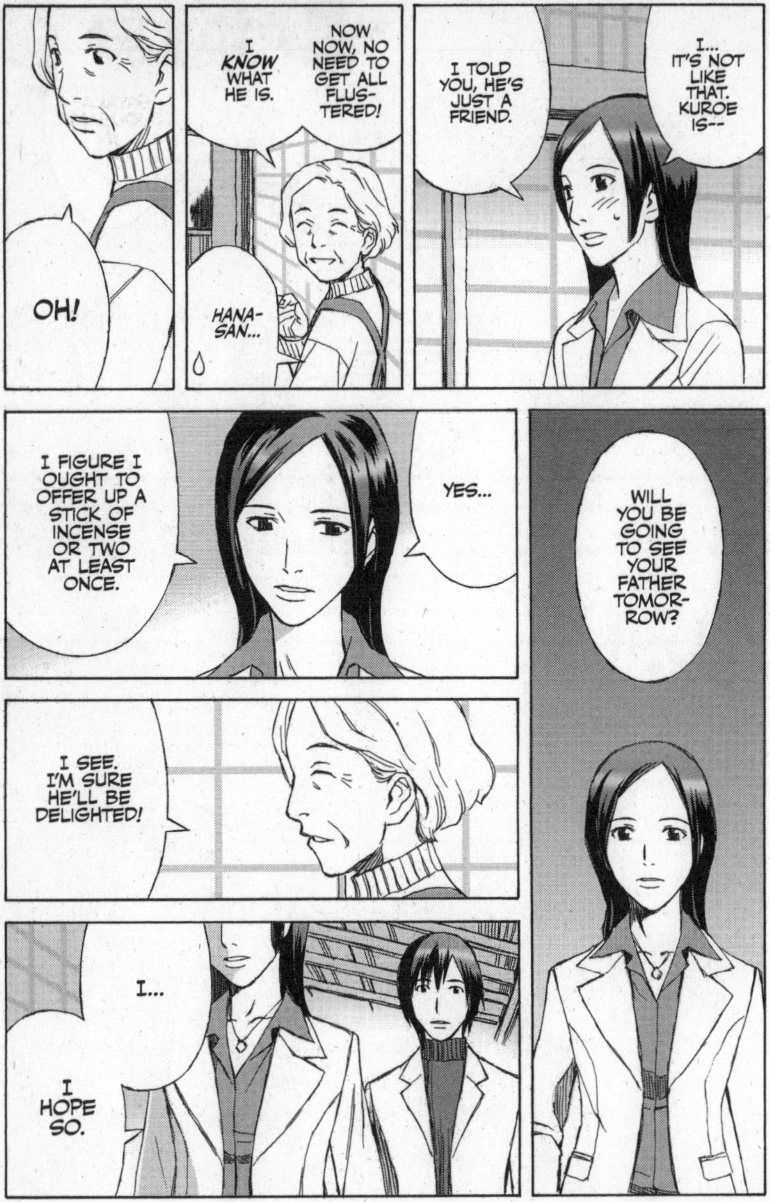
I... IT'S NOT LIKE THAT. KUROE IS--
I TOLD YOU, HE'S JUST A FRIEND.
NOW NOW, NO NEED TO GET ALL FLUS-TERED!
I *KNOW* WHAT HE IS.
HANA-SAN...
OH!
WILL YOU BE GOING TO SEE YOUR FATHER TOMOR-ROW?
YES...
I FIGURE I OUGHT TO OFFER UP A STICK OF INCENSE OR TWO AT LEAST ONCE.
I SEE. I'M SURE HE'LL BE DELIGHTED!
I...
I HOPE SO.

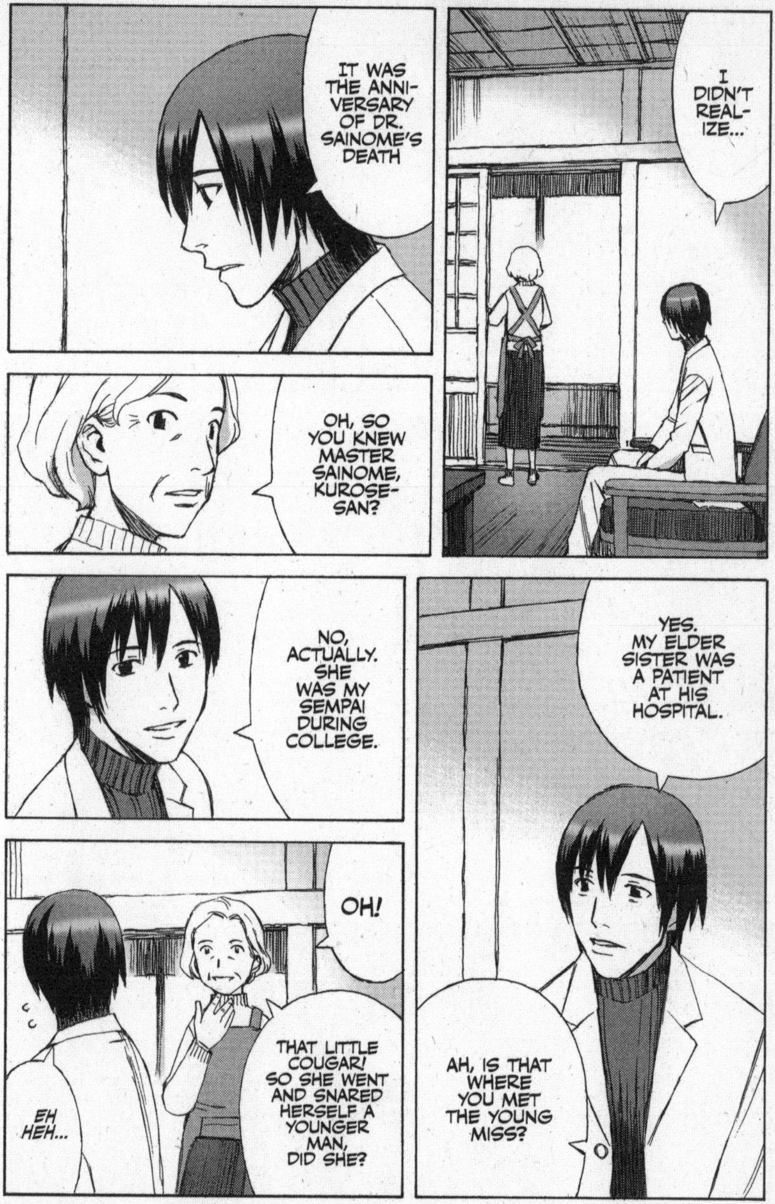
I DIDN'T REALIZE...
IT WAS THE ANNIVERSARY OF DR. SAINOME'S DEATH
OH, SO YOU KNEW MASTER SAINOME, KUROSE-SAN?
YES. MY ELDER SISTER WAS A PATIENT AT HIS HOSPITAL.
AH, IS THAT WHERE YOU MET THE YOUNG MISS?
NO, ACTUALLY. SHE WAS MY SEMPAI DURING COLLEGE.
OH!
THAT LITTLE COUGAR! SO SHE WENT AND SNARED HERSELF A YOUNGER MAN, DID SHE?
EH HEH...

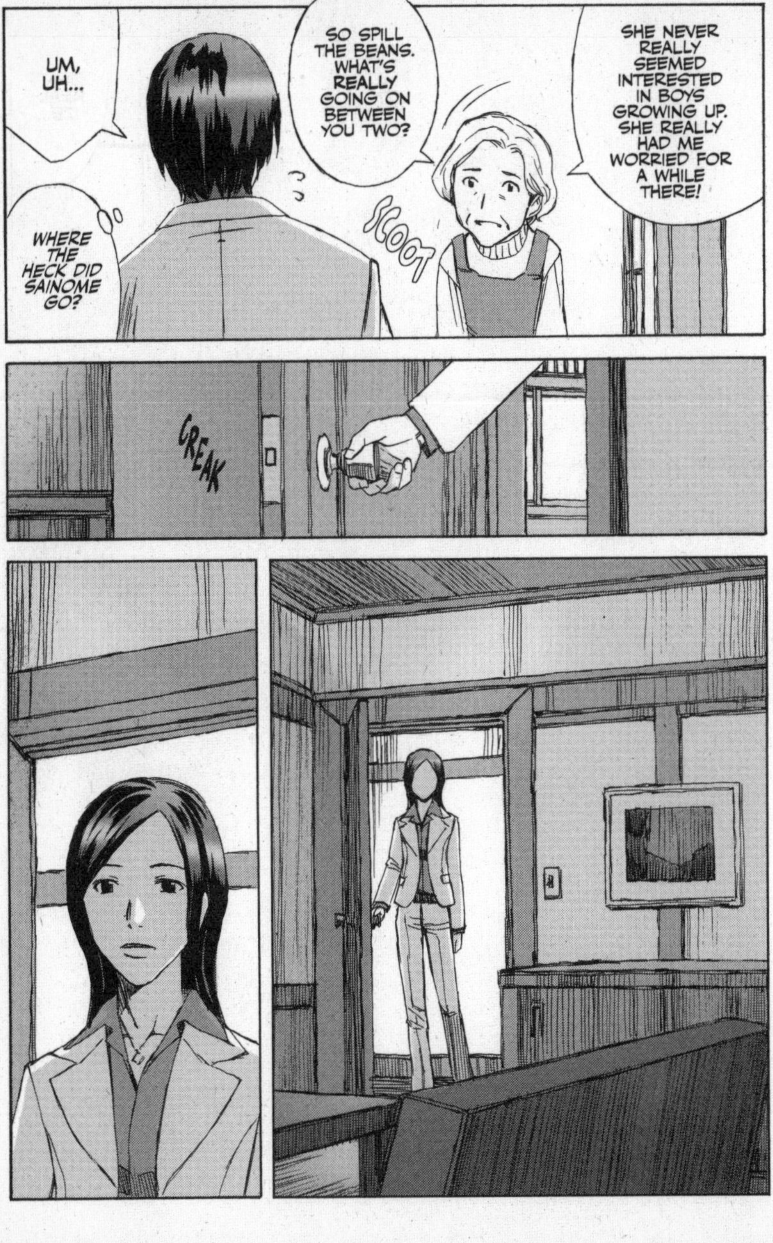
SHE NEVER REALLY SEEMED INTERESTED IN BOYS GROWING UP. SHE REALLY HAD ME WORRIED FOR A WHILE THERE!
SO SPILL THE BEANS. WHAT'S **REALLY** GOING ON BETWEEN YOU TWO?
SCOOT
UM, UH...
WHERE THE HECK DID SAINOME GO?
CREAK

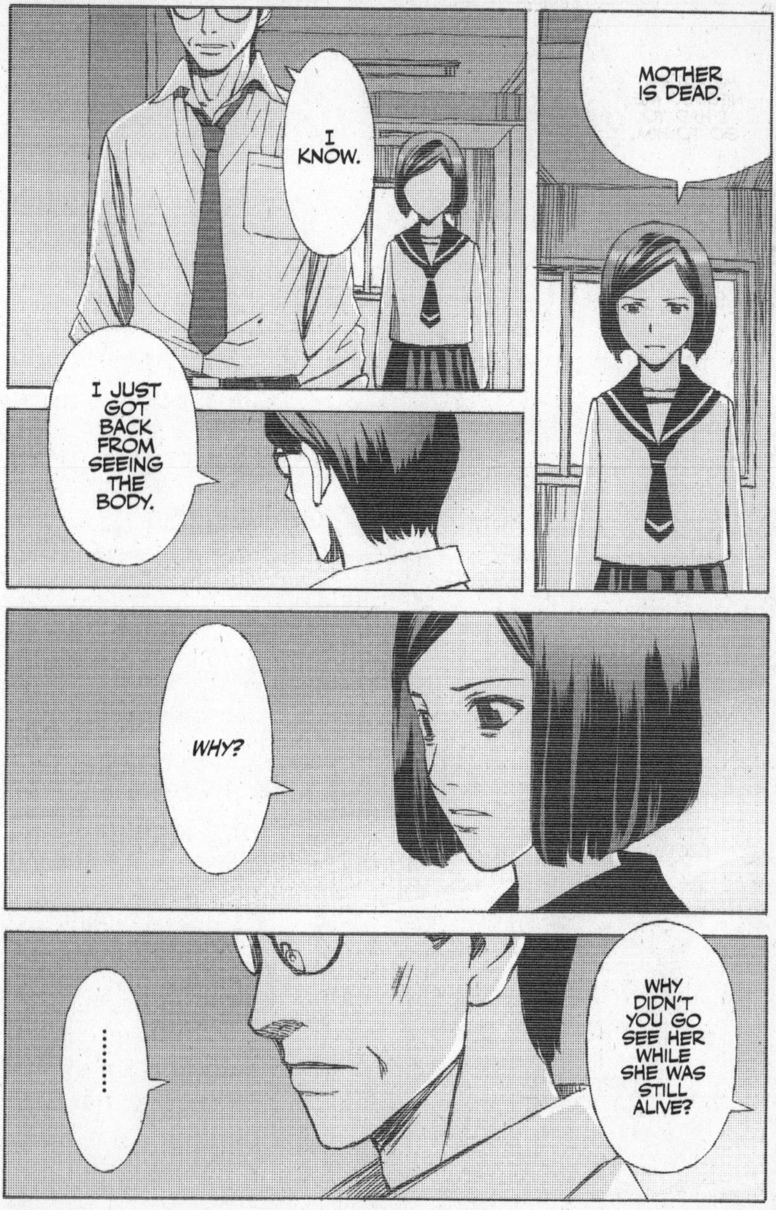
MOTHER IS DEAD.
I KNOW.
I JUST GOT BACK FROM SEEING THE BODY.
WHY?
WHY DIDN'T YOU GO SEE HER WHILE SHE WAS STILL ALIVE?
……

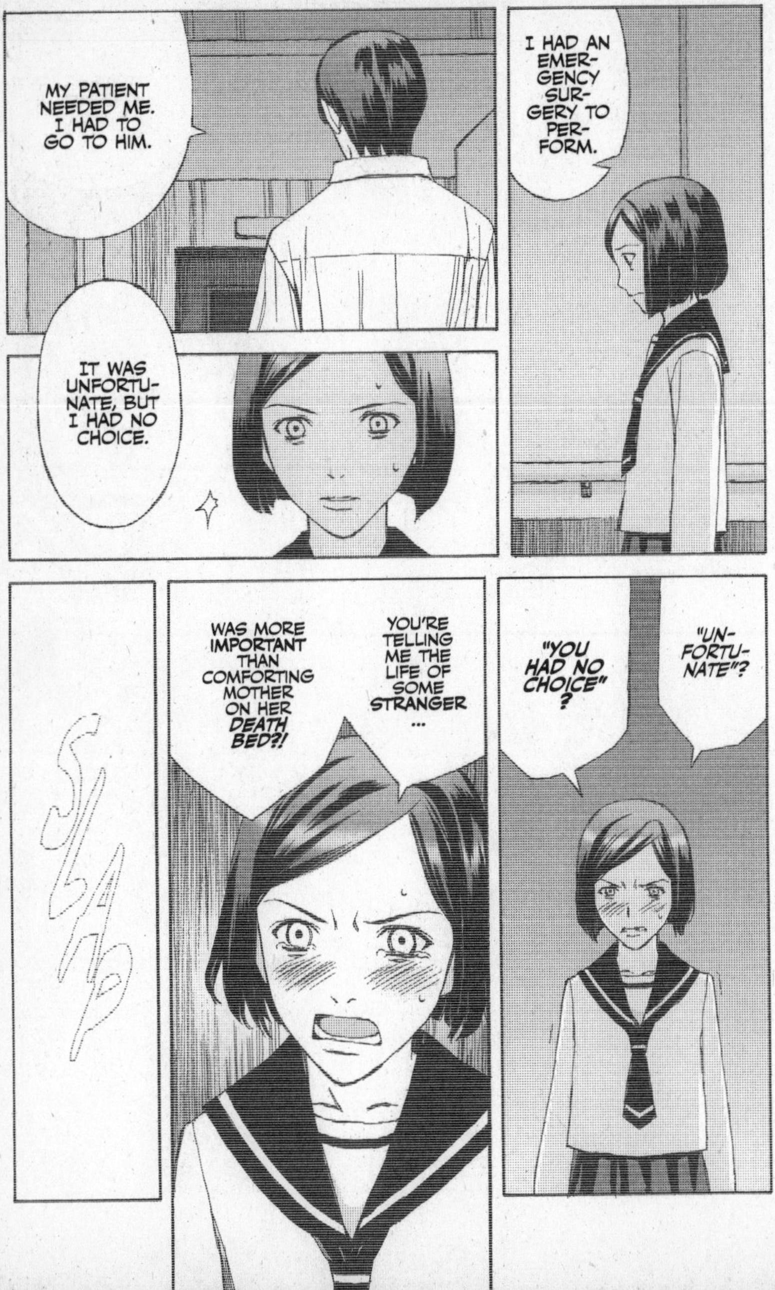
I HAD AN EMERGENCY SURGERY TO PERFORM.
MY PATIENT NEEDED ME. I HAD TO GO TO HIM.
IT WAS UNFORTUNATE, BUT I HAD NO CHOICE.
"UNFORTUNATE"?
"YOU HAD NO CHOICE"?
YOU'RE TELLING ME THE LIFE OF SOME STRANGER...
WAS MORE IMPORTANT THAN COMFORTING MOTHER ON HER *DEATH BED?!*
SLAP

I KNOW THIS IS UPSETTING, BUT PLEASE DON'T EVER TALK LIKE THAT AGAIN.

SAYAKA ...!!

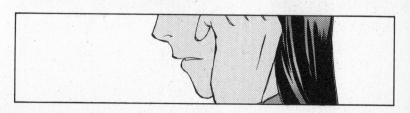

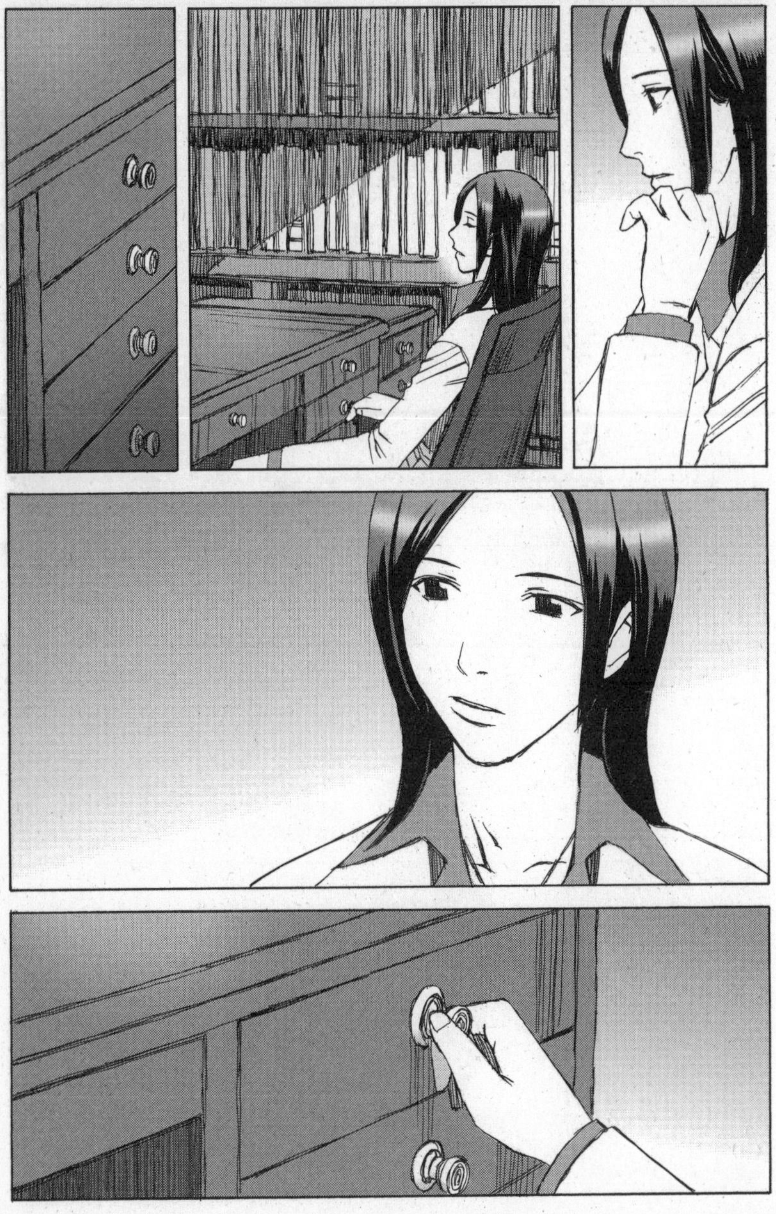

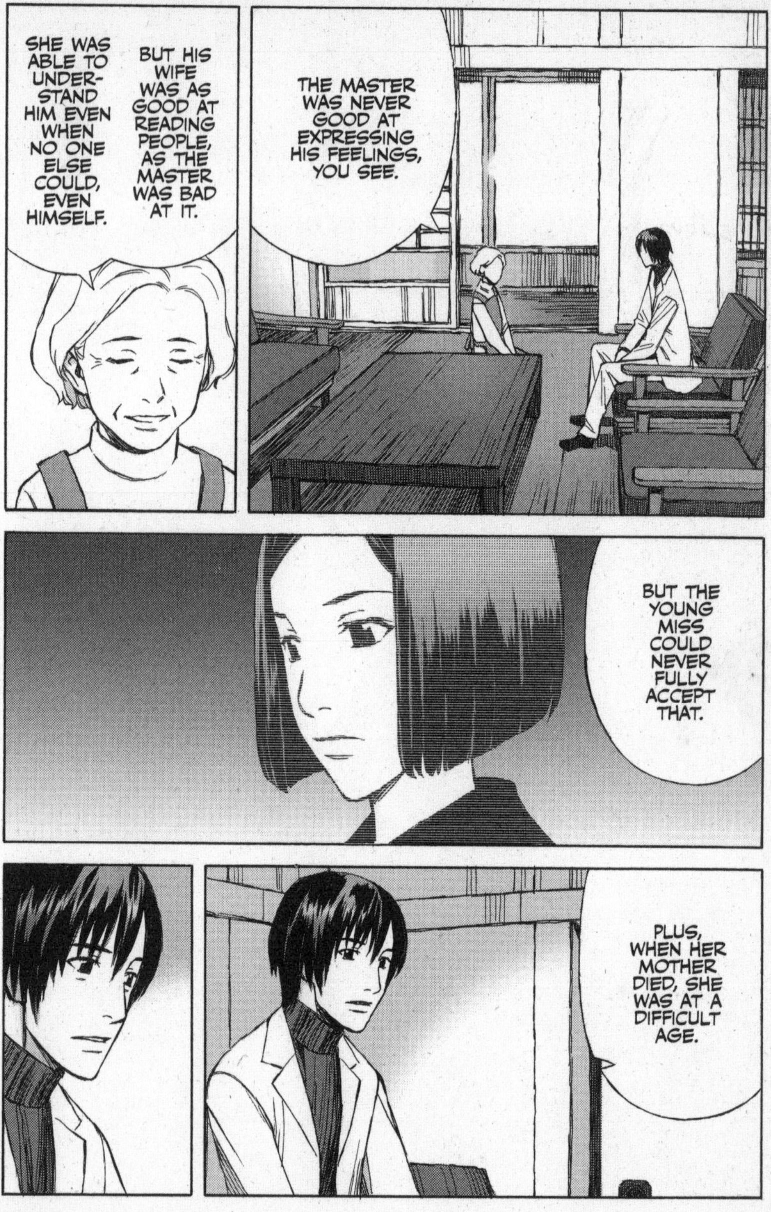
THE MASTER WAS NEVER GOOD AT EXPRESSING HIS FEELINGS, YOU SEE.
BUT HIS WIFE WAS AS GOOD AT READING PEOPLE, AS THE MASTER WAS BAD AT IT.
SHE WAS ABLE TO UNDER-STAND HIM EVEN WHEN NO ONE ELSE COULD, EVEN HIMSELF.
BUT THE YOUNG MISS COULD NEVER FULLY ACCEPT THAT.
PLUS, WHEN HER MOTHER DIED, SHE WAS AT A DIFFICULT AGE.

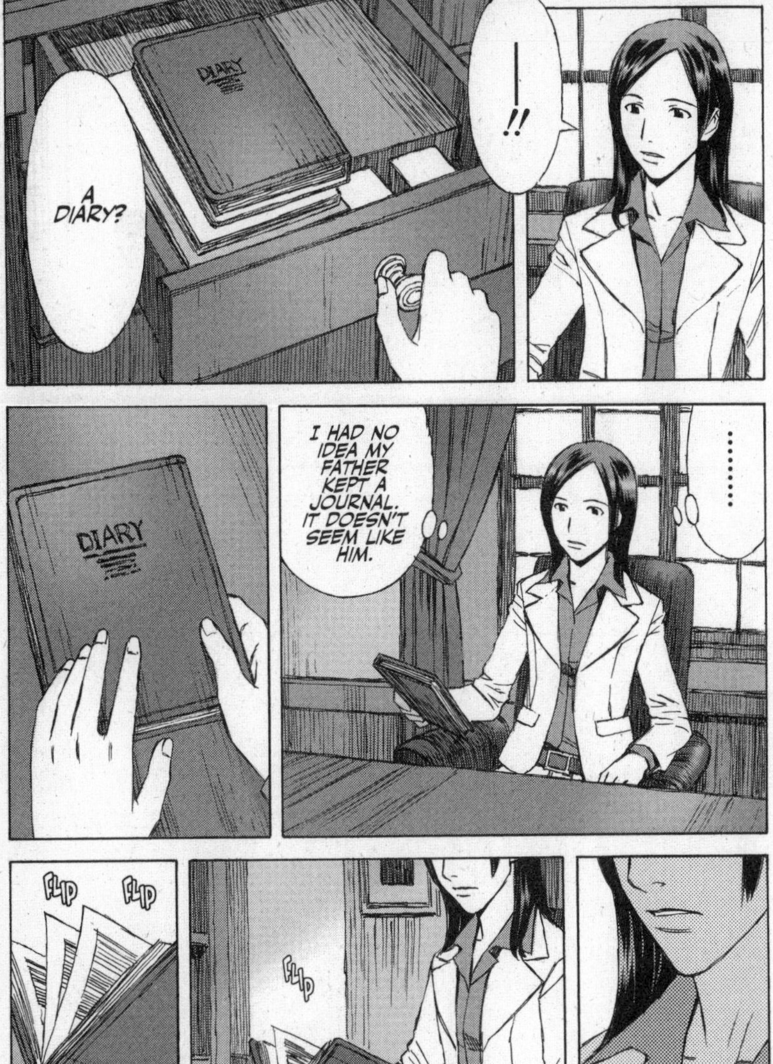

!!
A DIARY?
......
I HAD NO IDEA MY FATHER KEPT A JOURNAL. IT DOESN'T SEEM LIKE HIM.
FLIP
FLIP FLIP

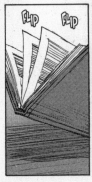

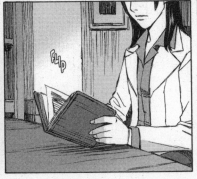

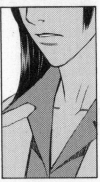

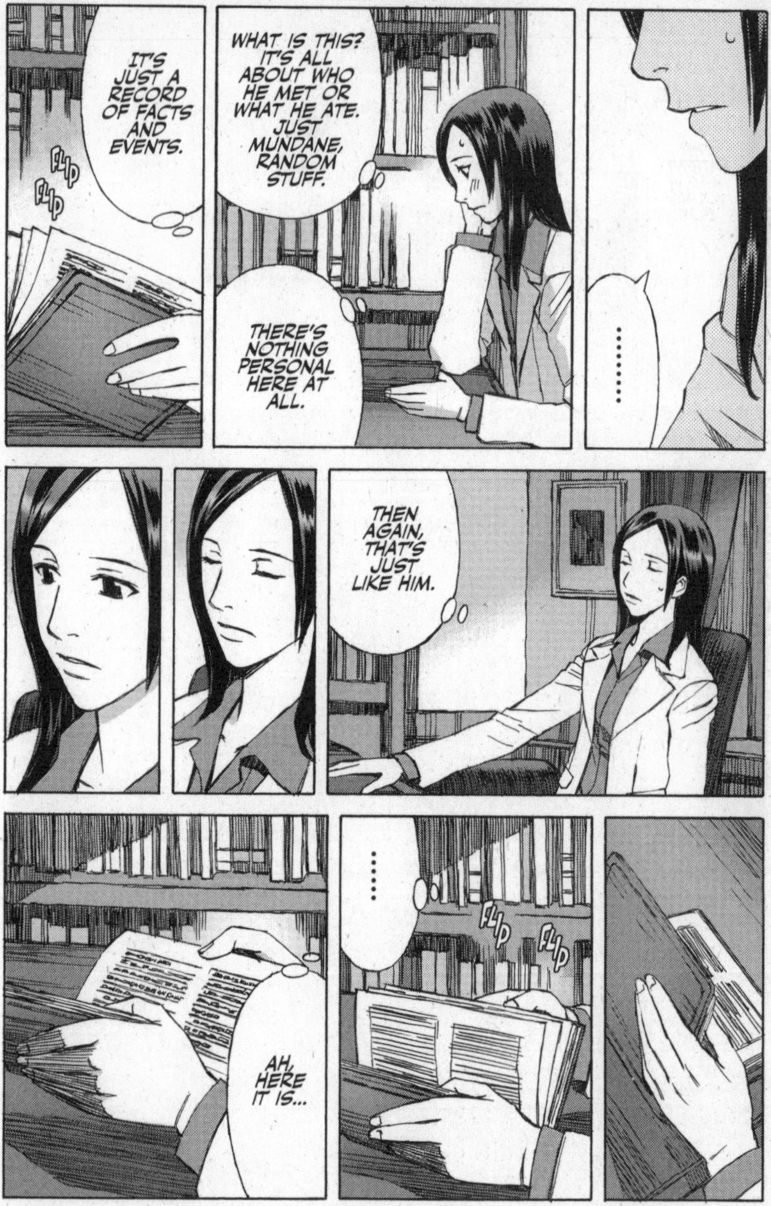
......
WHAT IS THIS? IT'S ALL ABOUT WHO HE MET OR WHAT HE ATE. JUST MUNDANE, RANDOM STUFF.
THERE'S NOTHING PERSONAL HERE AT ALL.
IT'S JUST A RECORD OF FACTS AND EVENTS.
FLIP
FLIP
THEN AGAIN, THAT'S JUST LIKE HIM.
......
FLIP
FLIP
AH, HERE IT IS...

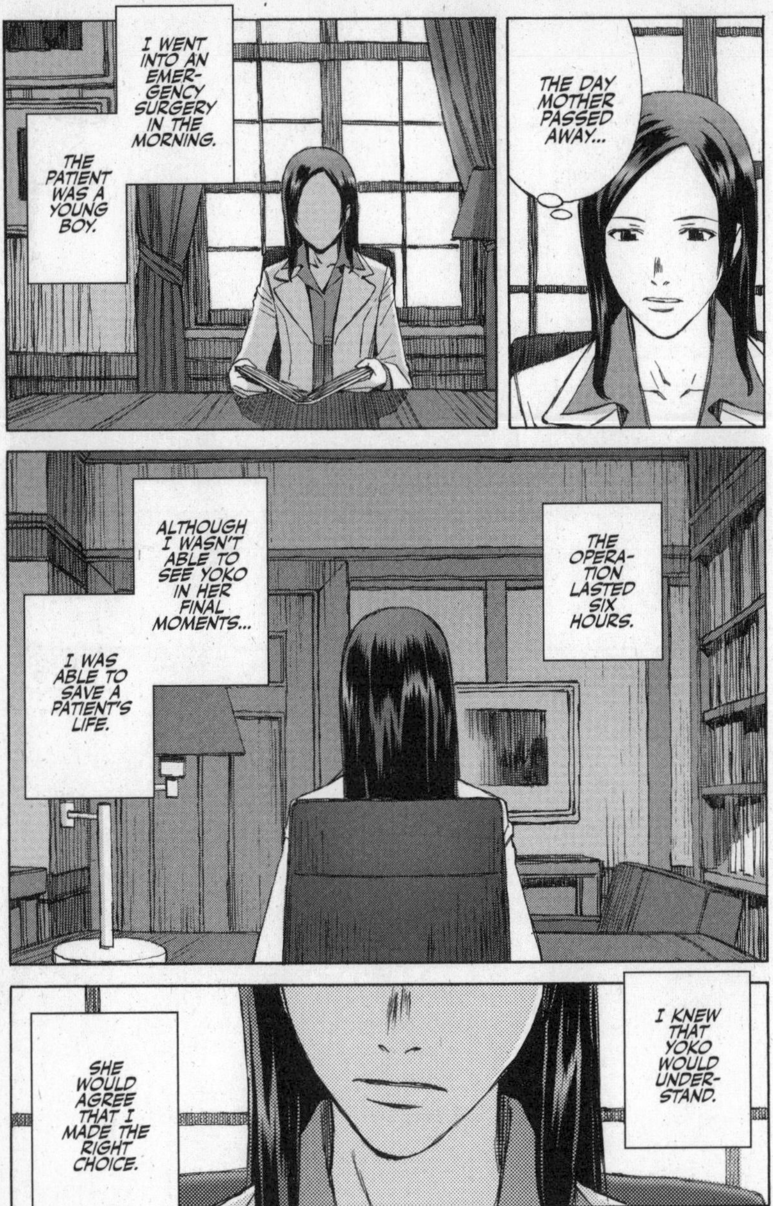
THE DAY MOTHER PASSED AWAY...
I WENT INTO AN EMER-GENCY SURGERY IN THE MORNING.
THE PATIENT WAS A YOUNG BOY.
THE OPERA-TION LASTED SIX HOURS.
ALTHOUGH I WASN'T ABLE TO SEE YOKO IN HER FINAL MOMENTS...
I WAS ABLE TO SAVE A PATIENT'S LIFE.
I KNEW THAT YOKO WOULD UNDER-STAND.
SHE WOULD AGREE THAT I MADE THE RIGHT CHOICE.

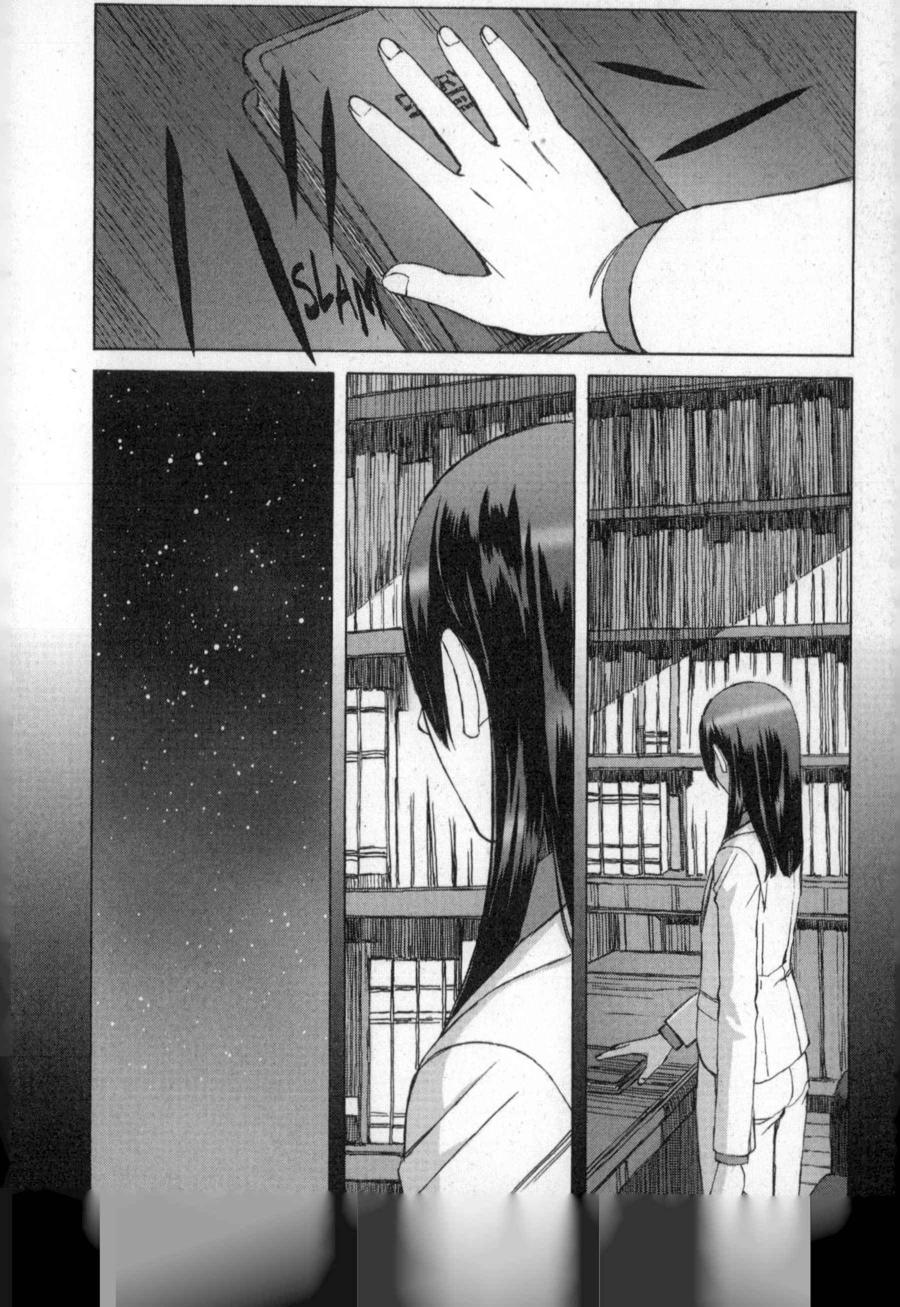
SLAM

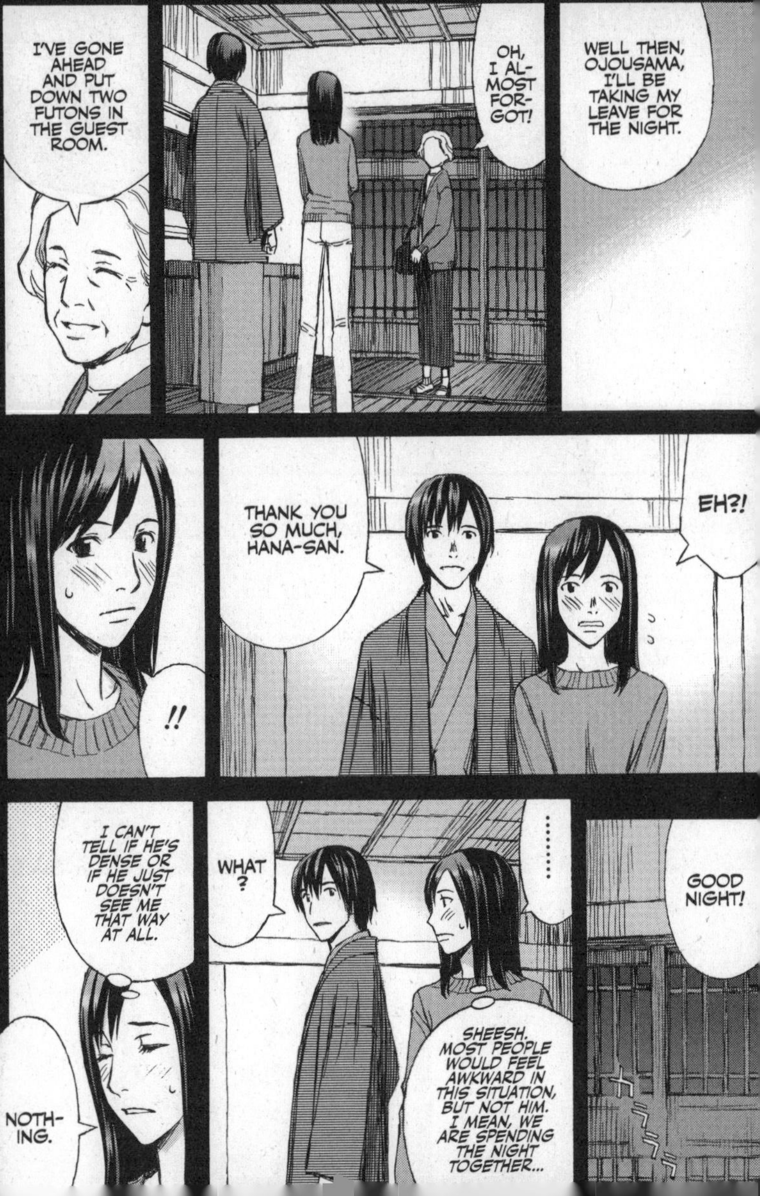
WELL THEN, OJOUSAMA, I'LL BE TAKING MY LEAVE FOR THE NIGHT.
OH, I AL-MOST FOR-GOT!
I'VE GONE AHEAD AND PUT DOWN TWO FUTONS IN THE GUEST ROOM.
EH?!
THANK YOU SO MUCH, HANA-SAN.
!!
GOOD NIGHT!
カラララ
......
WHAT?
SHEESH. MOST PEOPLE WOULD FEEL AWKWARD IN THIS SITUATION, BUT NOT HIM. I MEAN, WE ARE SPENDING THE NIGHT TOGETHER...
I CAN'T TELL IF HE'S DENSE OR IF HE JUST DOESN'T SEE ME THAT WAY AT ALL.
NOTH-ING.

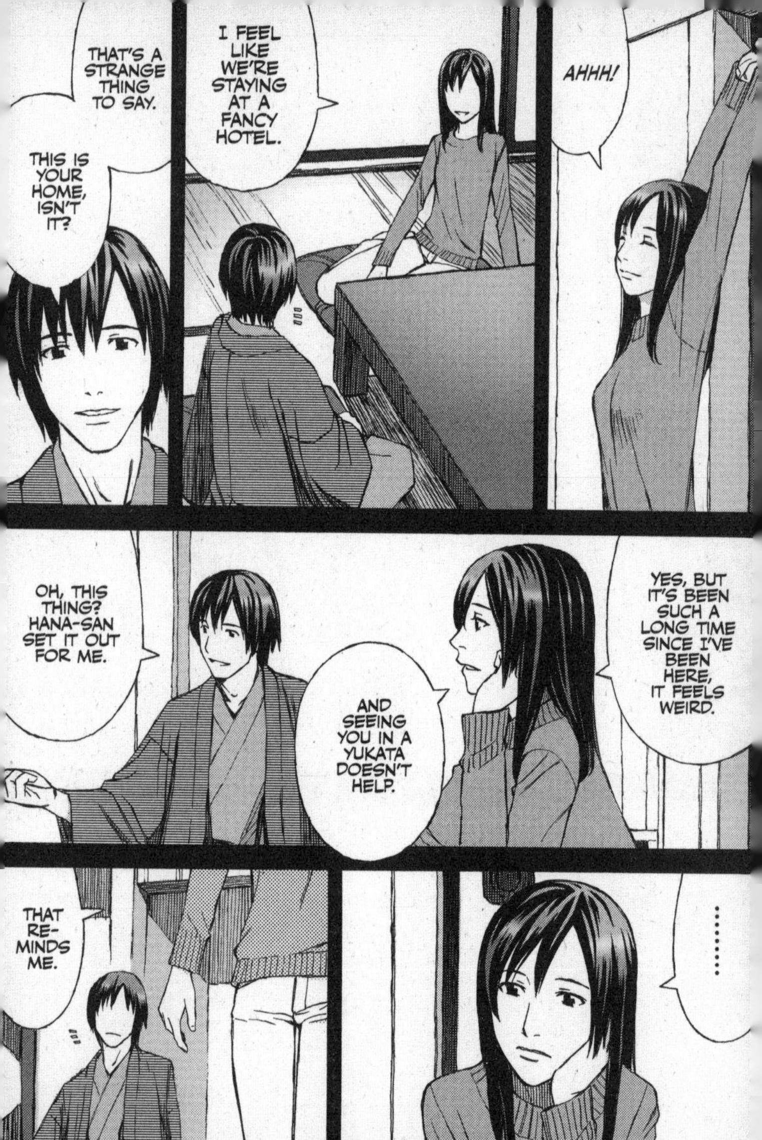
AHHH!
I FEEL LIKE WE'RE STAYING AT A FANCY HOTEL.
THAT'S A STRANGE THING TO SAY.
THIS IS YOUR HOME, ISN'T IT?
YES, BUT IT'S BEEN SUCH A LONG TIME SINCE I'VE BEEN HERE, IT FEELS WEIRD.
AND SEEING YOU IN A YUKATA DOESN'T HELP.
OH, THIS THING? HANA-SAN SET IT OUT FOR ME.
....
THAT RE-MINDS ME.

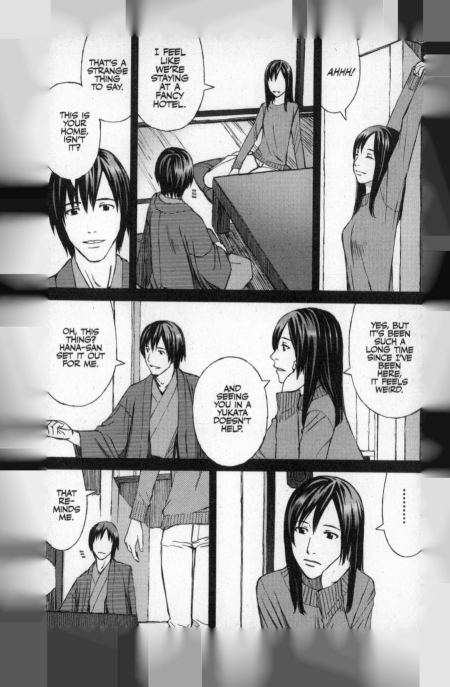

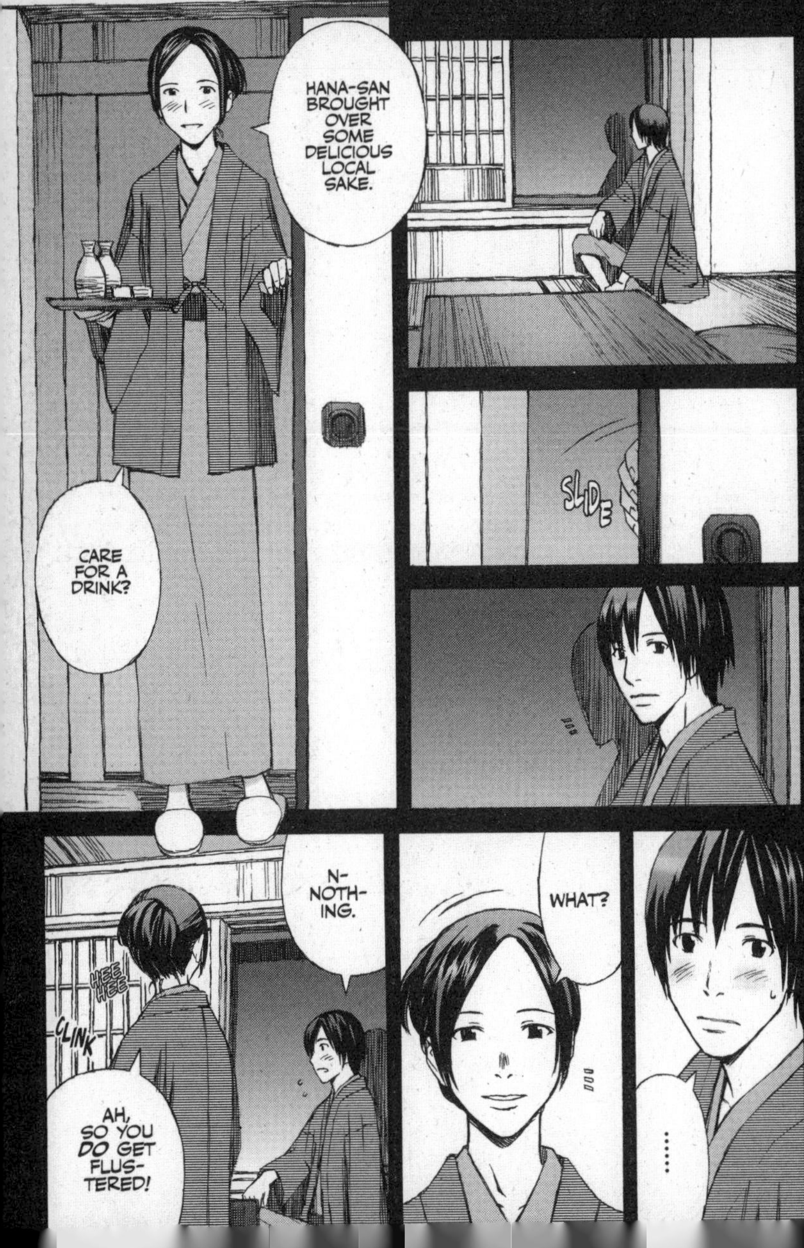
SLIDE
HANA-SAN BROUGHT OVER SOME DELICIOUS LOCAL SAKE.
CARE FOR A DRINK?
......
WHAT?
N-NOTHING.
HEE HEE
CLINK
AH, SO YOU DO GET FLUSTERED!

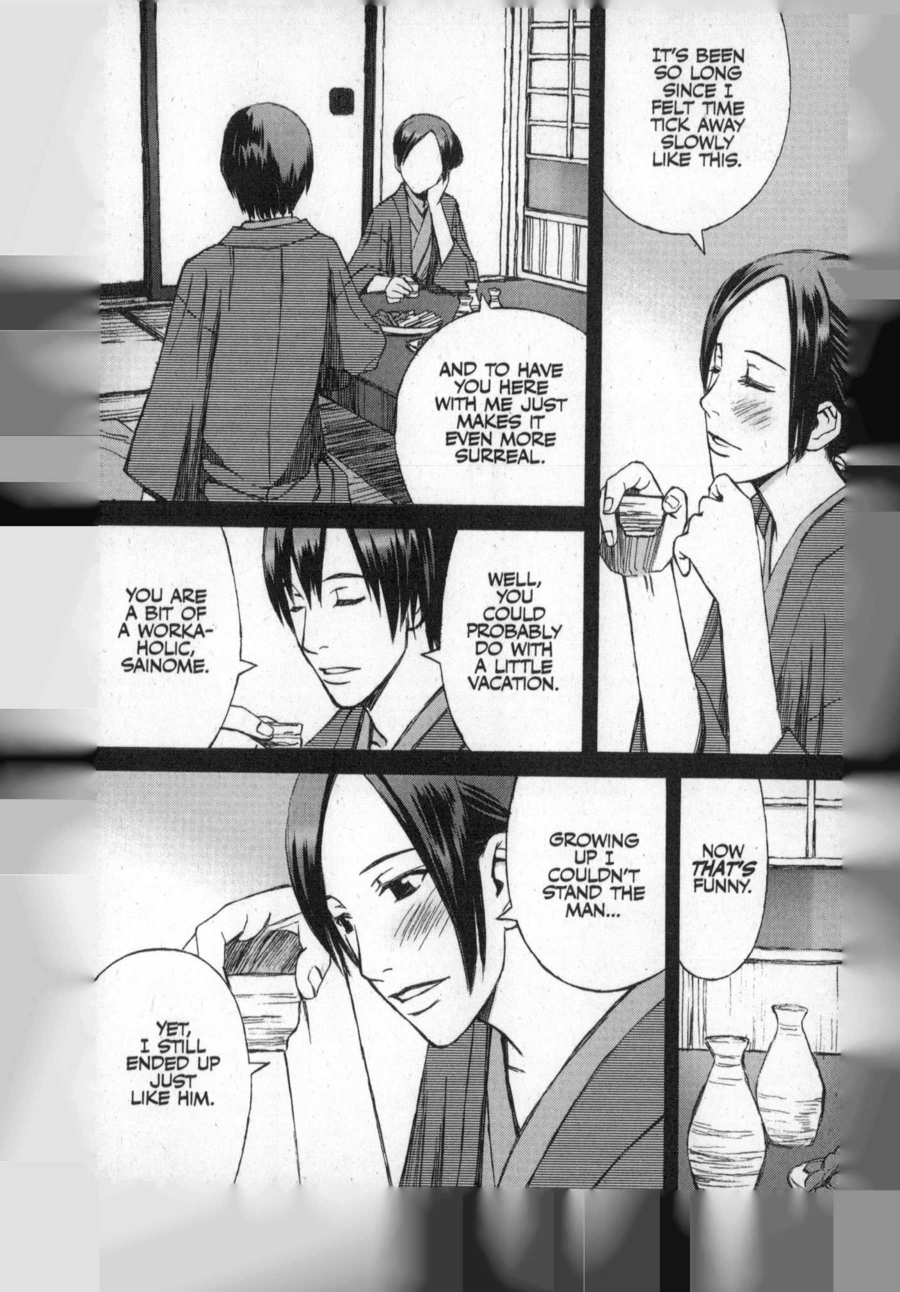
IT'S BEEN SO LONG SINCE I FELT TIME TICK AWAY SLOWLY LIKE THIS.
AND TO HAVE YOU HERE WITH ME JUST MAKES IT EVEN MORE SURREAL.
WELL, YOU COULD PROBABLY DO WITH A LITTLE VACATION.
YOU ARE A BIT OF A WORKA-HOLIC, SAINOME.
NOW *THAT'S* FUNNY.
GROWING UP I COULDN'T STAND THE MAN...
YET, I STILL ENDED UP JUST LIKE HIM.

YOU MEAN DR. SAIN-OME?
YEAH.
HE NEVER CARED ABOUT HIS FAMILY, ONLY WORK.
HE NEVER ONCE PRAISED ME...
OR SCOLDED ME FOR THAT MATTER.
WELL, EXCEPT FOR THAT ONE TIME.
HE WAS A MUCH BETTER DOCTOR THAN A FATHER.

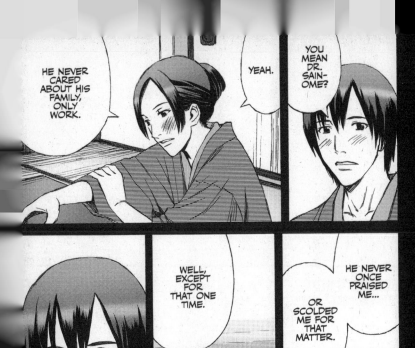

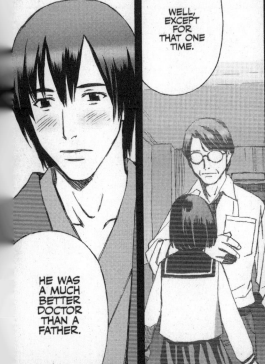

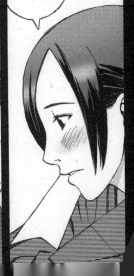

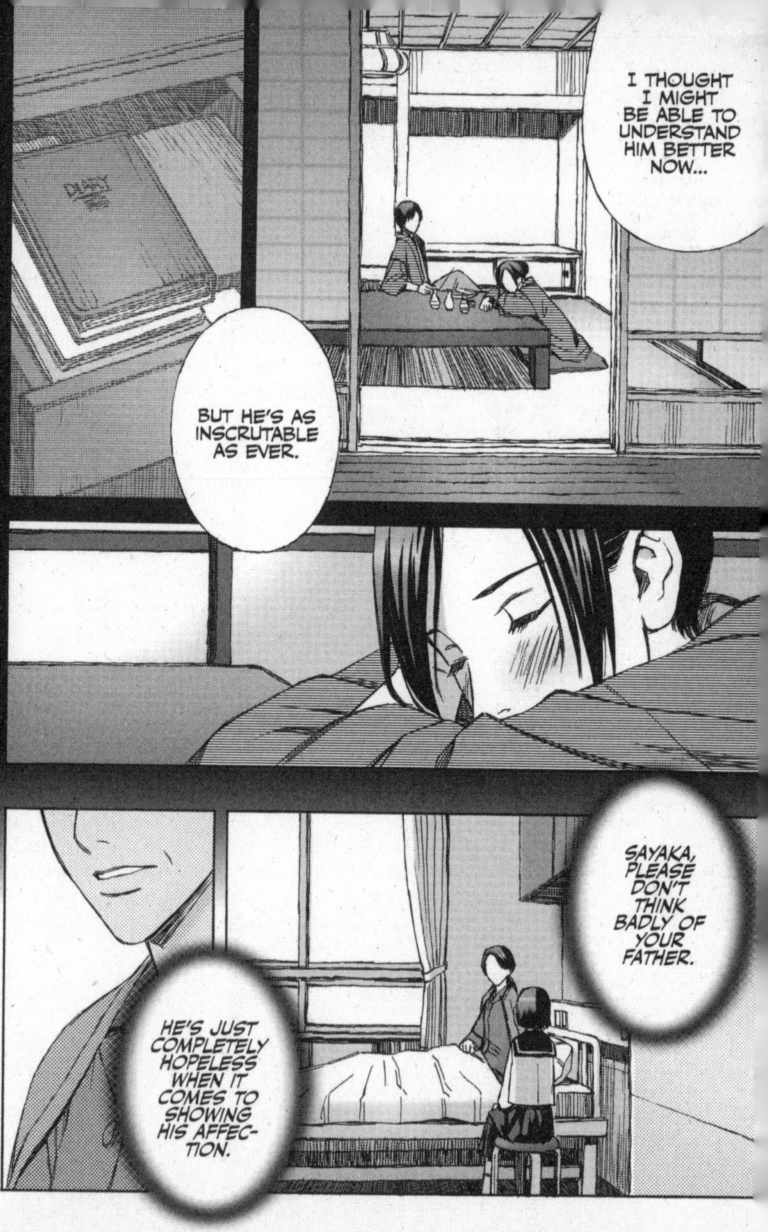
I THOUGHT I MIGHT BE ABLE TO UNDERSTAND HIM BETTER NOW...
BUT HE'S AS INSCRUTABLE AS EVER.
SAYAKA, PLEASE DON'T THINK BADLY OF YOUR FATHER.
HE'S JUST COMPLETELY HOPELESS WHEN IT COMES TO SHOWING HIS AFFEC-TION.

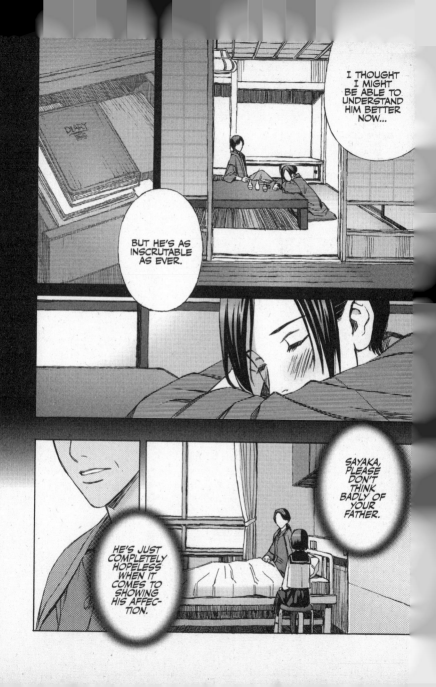

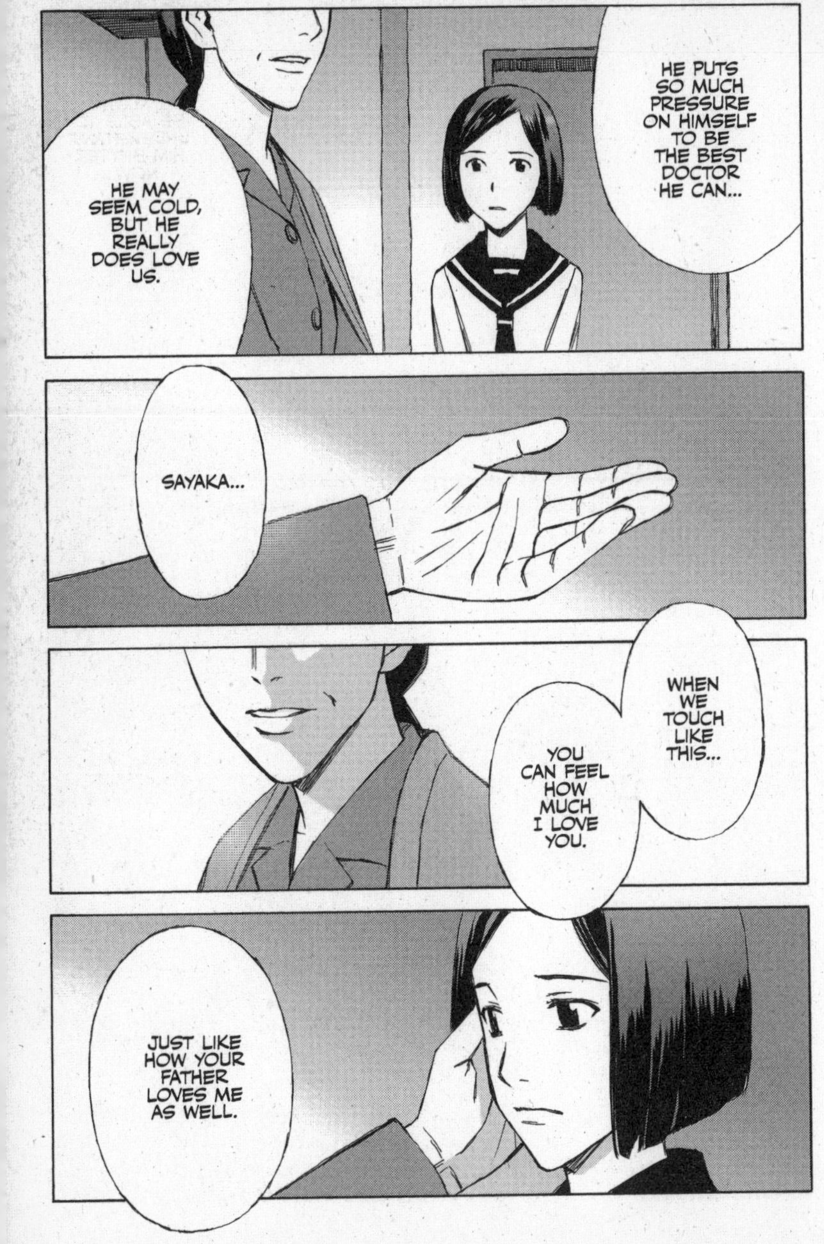
HE PUTS SO MUCH PRESSURE ON HIMSELF TO BE THE BEST DOCTOR HE CAN...
HE MAY SEEM COLD, BUT HE REALLY DOES LOVE US.
SAYAKA...
WHEN WE TOUCH LIKE THIS...
YOU CAN FEEL HOW MUCH I LOVE YOU.
JUST LIKE HOW YOUR FATHER LOVES ME AS WELL.

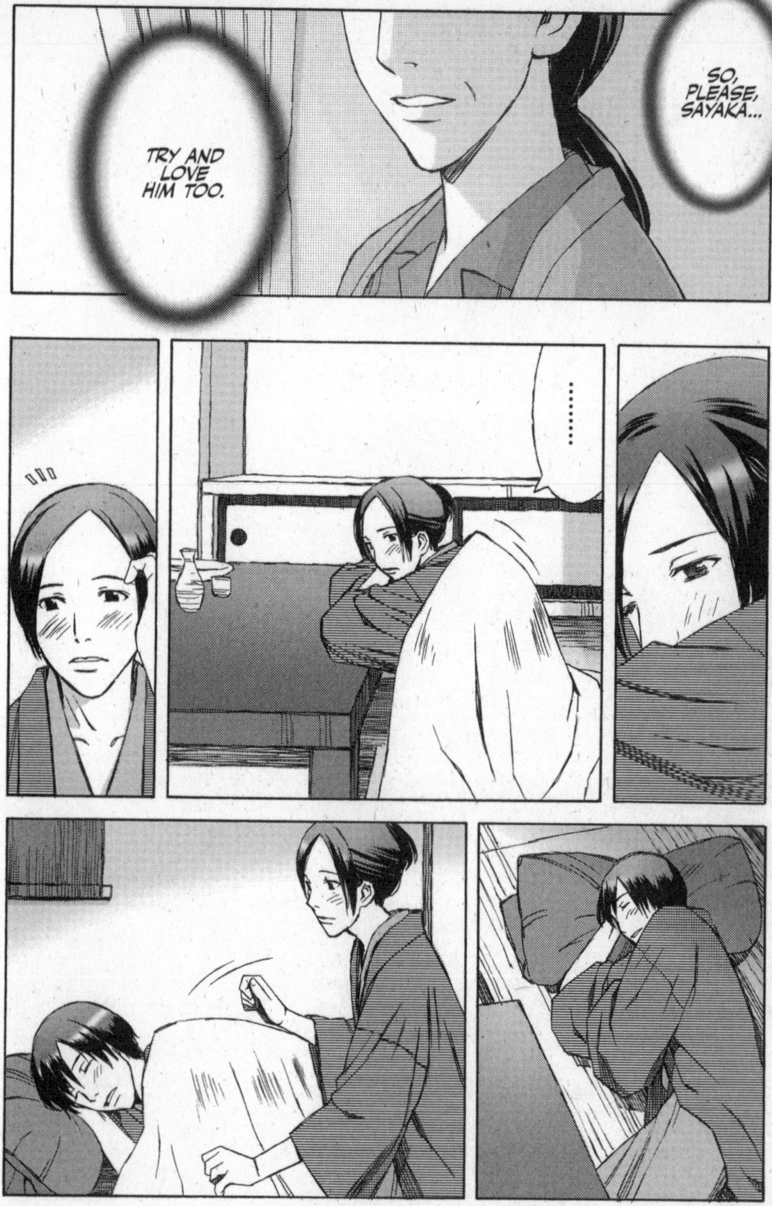
SO, PLEASE, SAYAKA...
TRY AND LOVE HIM TOO.
......

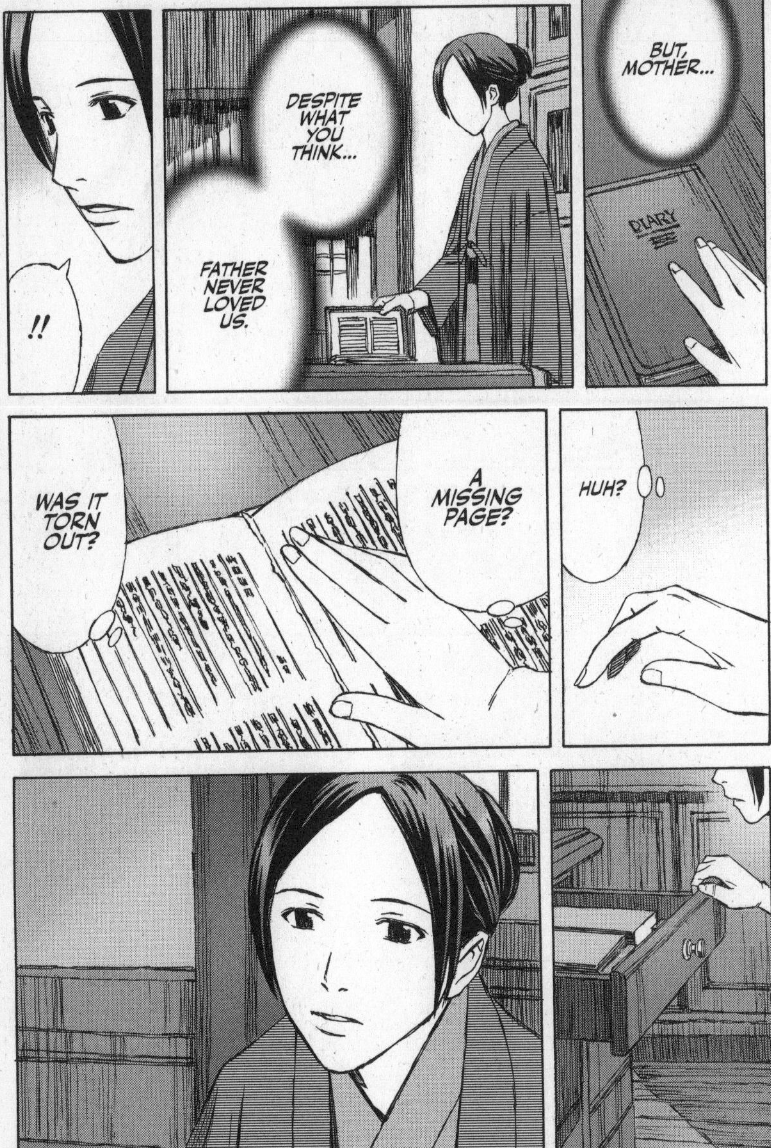
BUT, MOTHER...
DESPITE WHAT YOU THINK...
FATHER NEVER LOVED US.
!!
HUH?
A MISSING PAGE?
WAS IT TORN OUT?

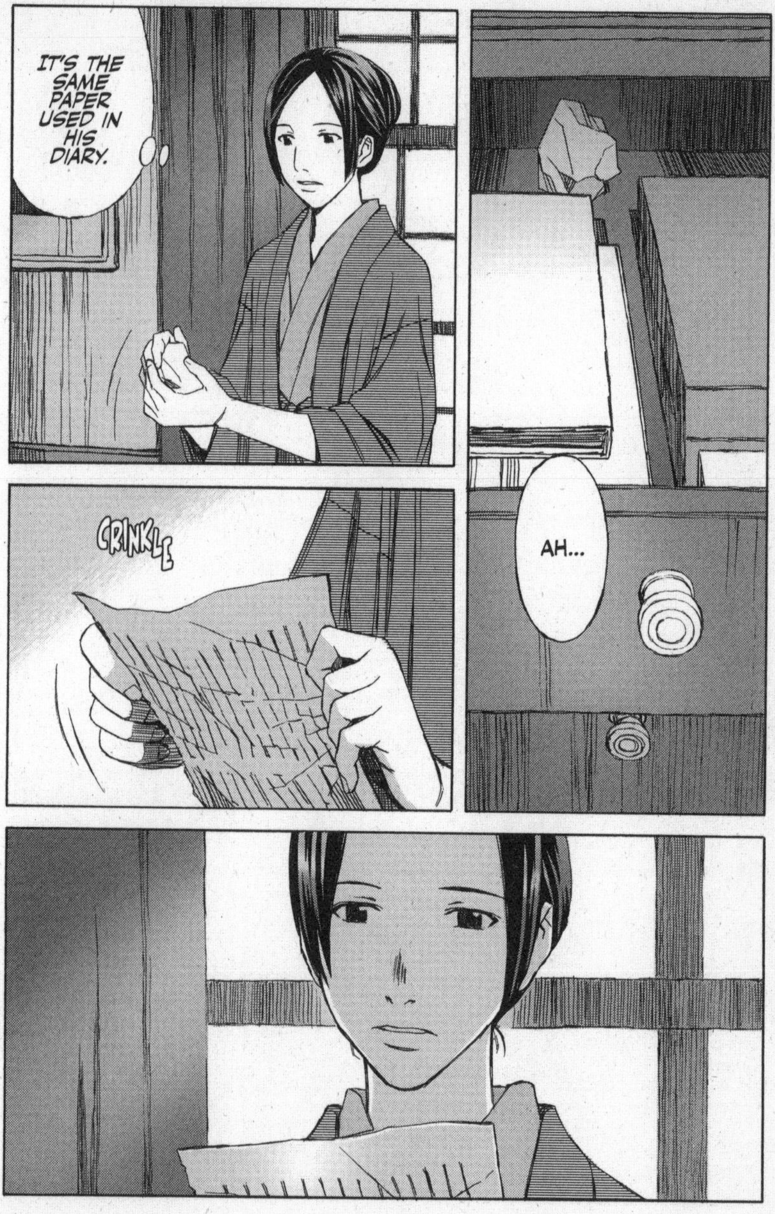
IT'S THE SAME PAPER USED IN HIS DIARY.
AH...
CRINKLE

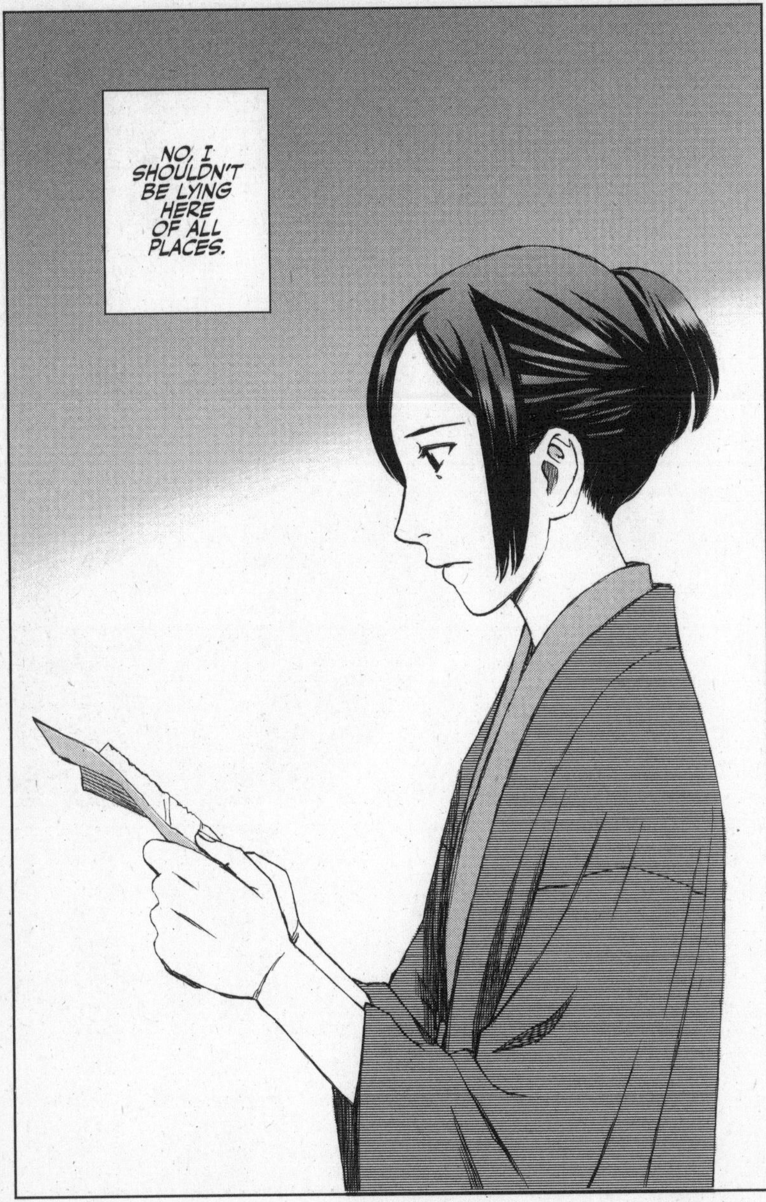
NO, I SHOULDN'T BE LYING HERE OF ALL PLACES.

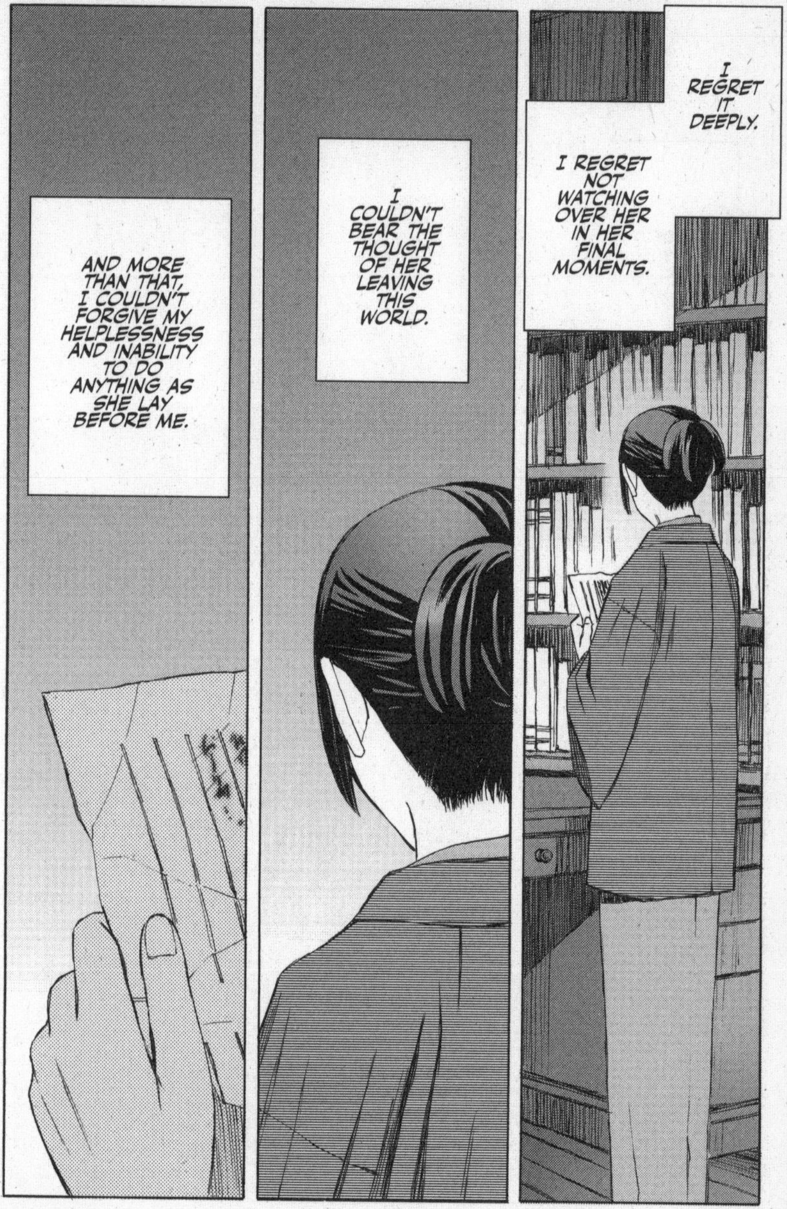
I REGRET IT DEEPLY.
I REGRET NOT WATCHING OVER HER IN HER FINAL MOMENTS.
I COULDN'T BEAR THE THOUGHT OF HER LEAVING THIS WORLD.
AND MORE THAN THAT, I COULDN'T FORGIVE MY HELPLESSNESS AND INABILITY TO DO ANYTHING AS SHE LAY BEFORE ME.

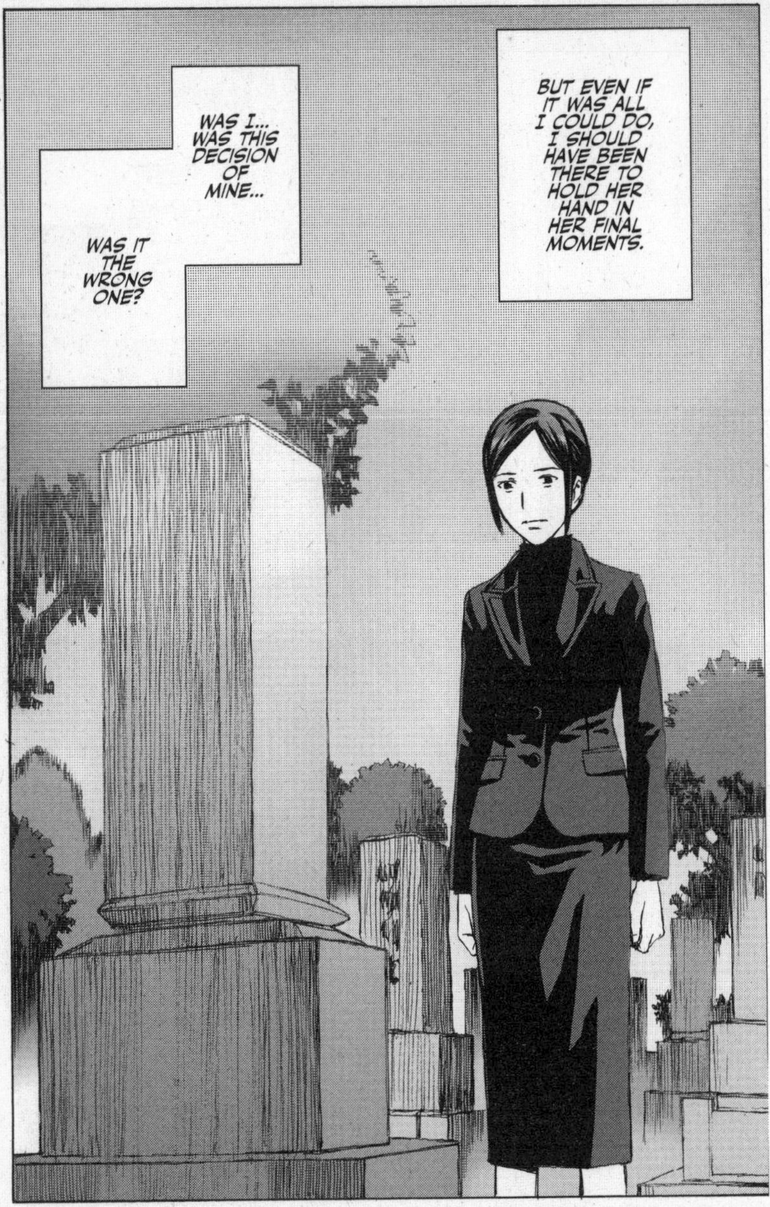
BUT EVEN IF IT WAS ALL I COULD DO, I SHOULD HAVE BEEN THERE TO HOLD HER HAND IN HER FINAL MOMENTS.
WAS I... WAS THIS DECISION OF MINE...
WAS IT THE WRONG ONE?

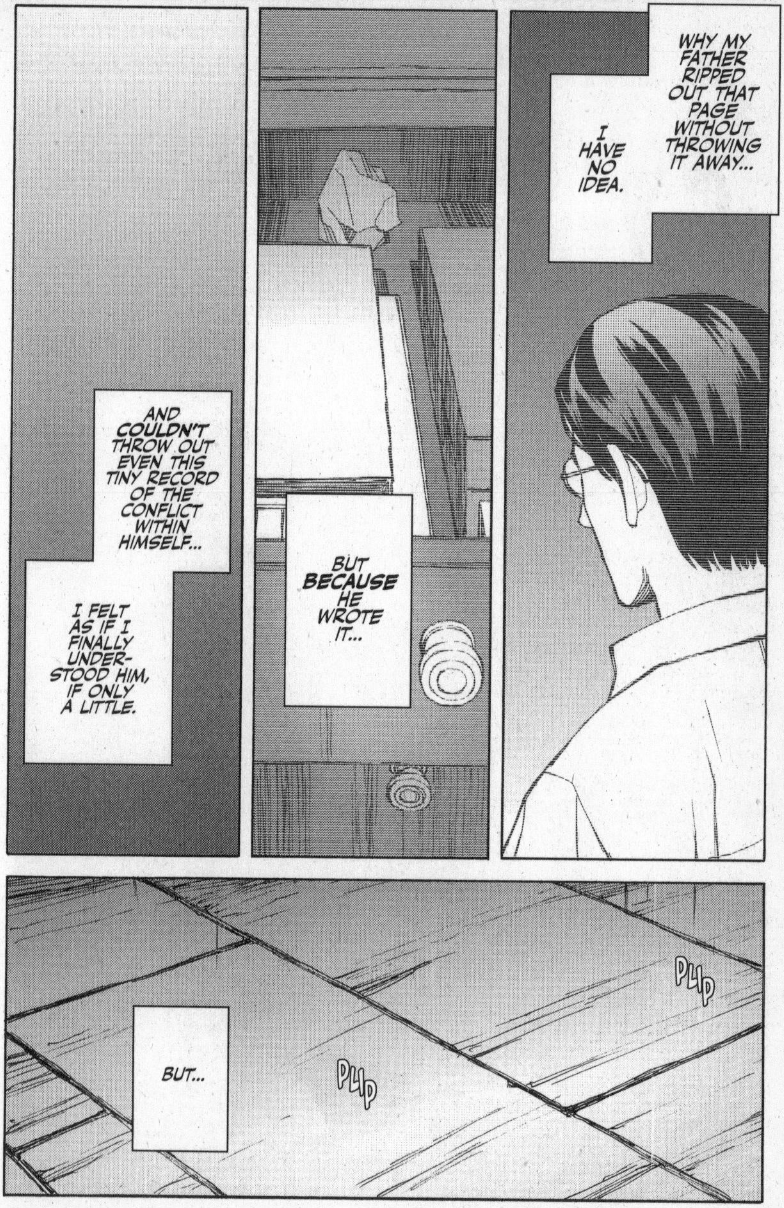
WHY MY FATHER RIPPED OUT THAT PAGE WITHOUT THROWING IT AWAY...
I HAVE NO IDEA.
BUT BECAUSE HE WROTE IT...
AND COULDN'T THROW OUT EVEN THIS TINY RECORD OF THE CONFLICT WITHIN HIMSELF...
I FELT AS IF I FINALLY UNDER-STOOD HIM, IF ONLY A LITTLE.
PLIP
BUT...
PLIP

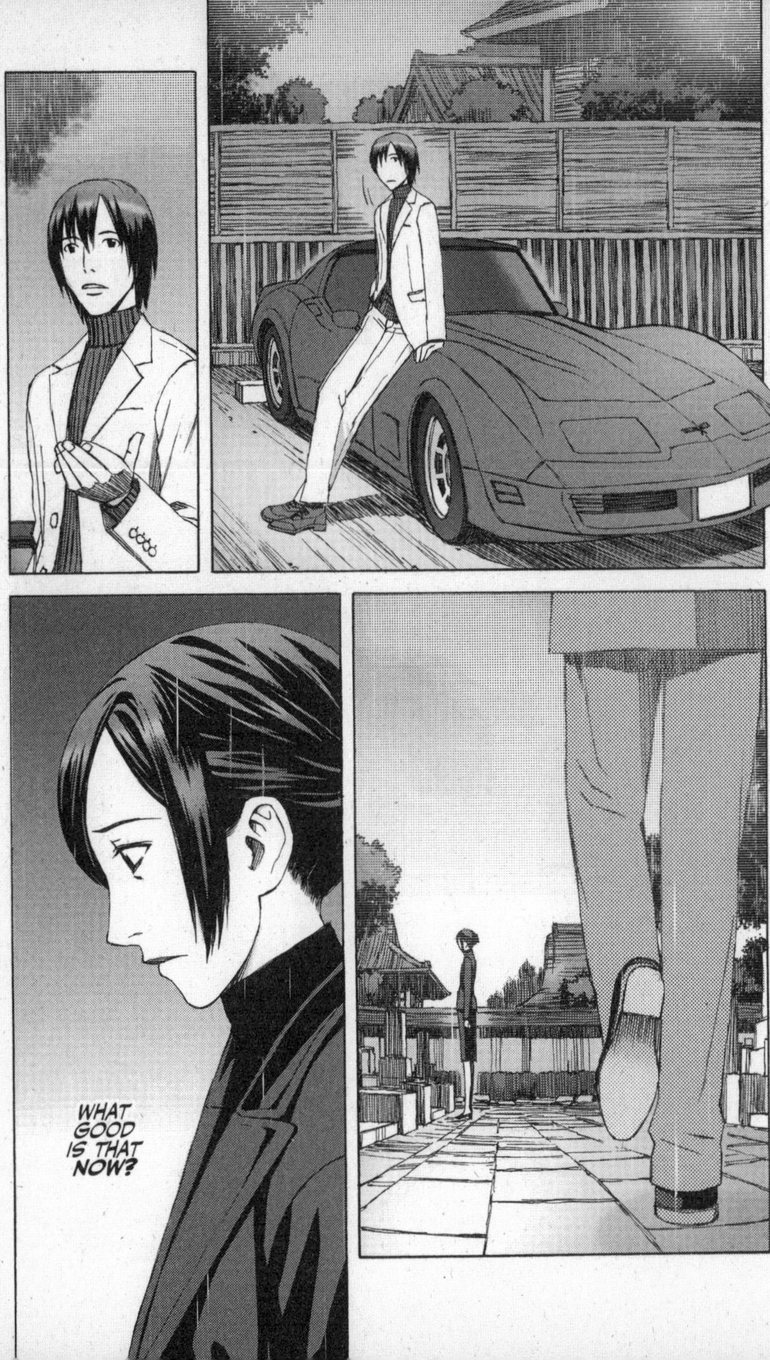
WHAT GOOD IS THAT NOW?

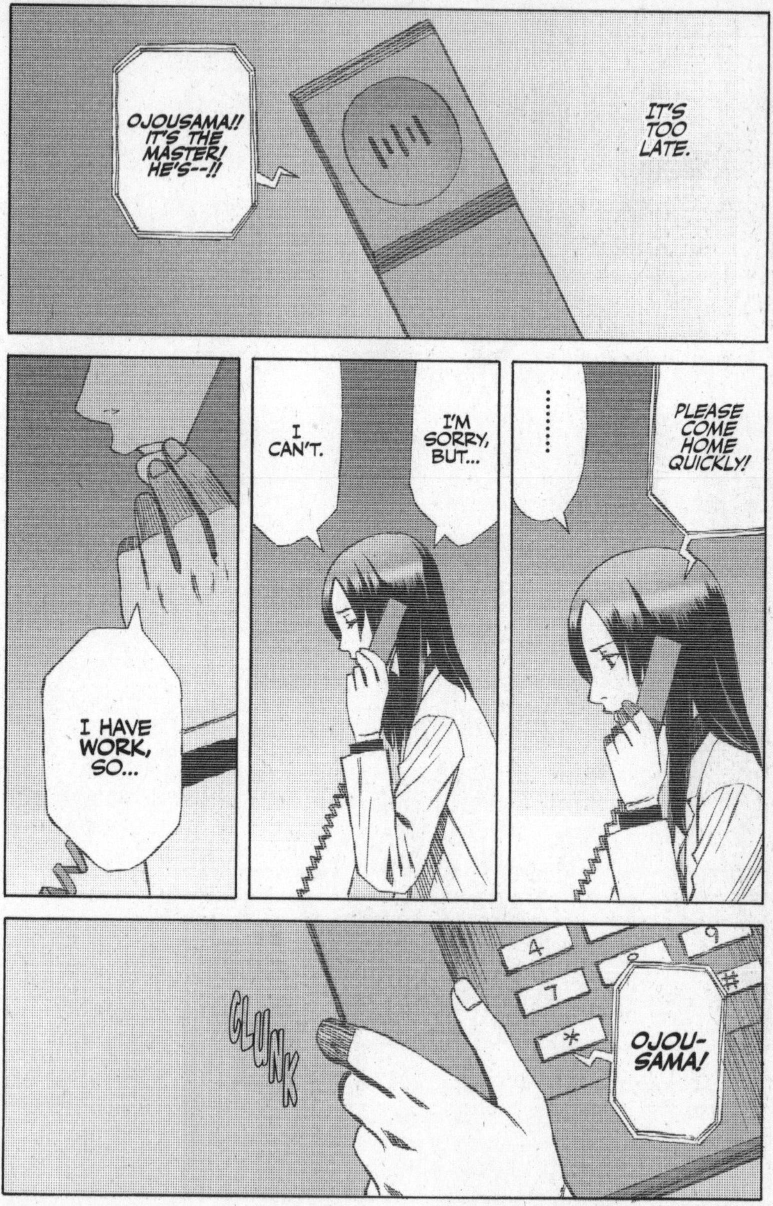
IT'S TOO LATE.
OJOUSAMA!! IT'S THE MASTER! HE'S--!!
PLEASE COME HOME QUICKLY!
……
I'M SORRY, BUT...
I CAN'T.
I HAVE WORK, SO...
OJOU-SAMA!
CLUNK

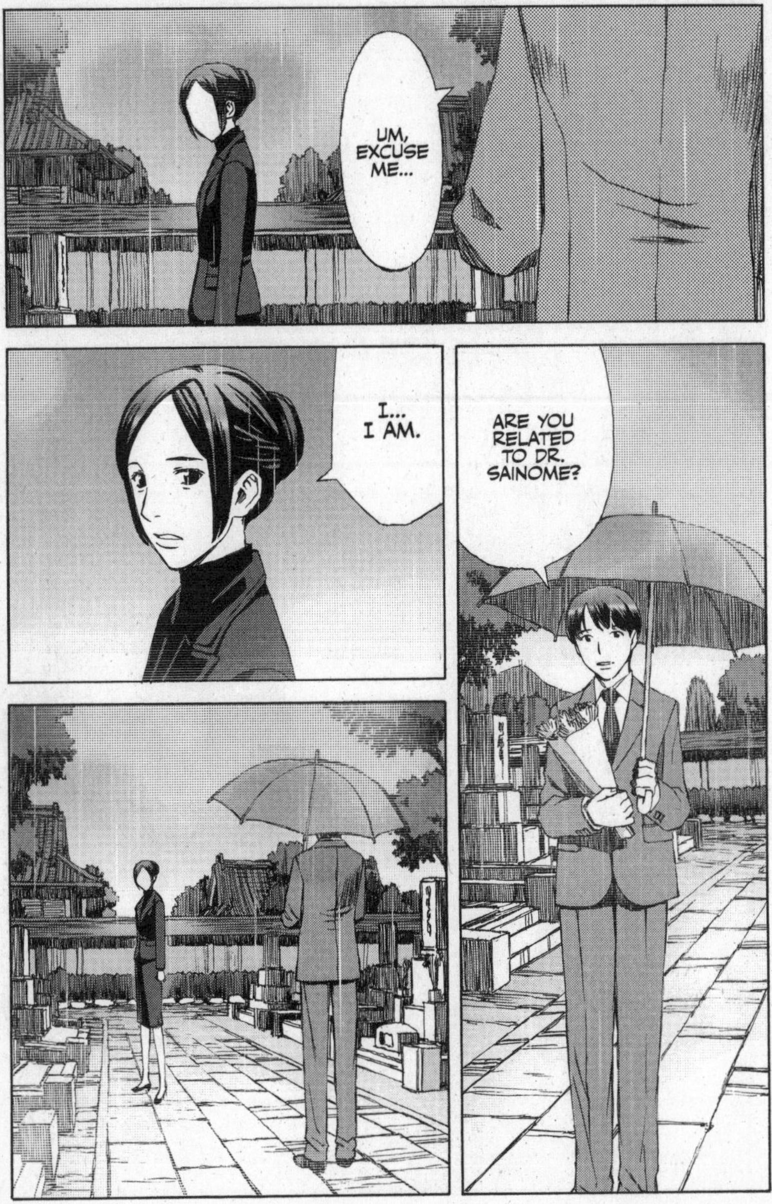
UM, EXCUSE ME...
ARE YOU RELATED TO DR. SAINOME?
I... I AM.

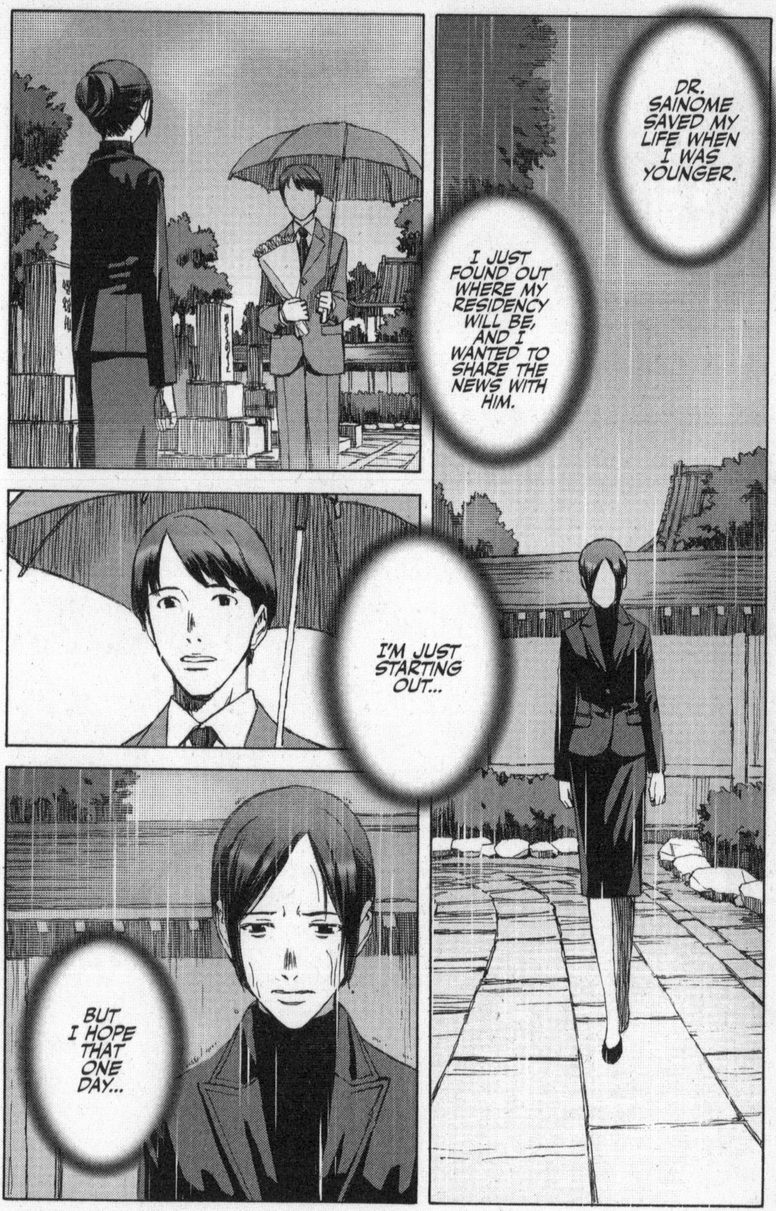
DR. SAINOME SAVED MY LIFE WHEN I WAS YOUNGER.
I JUST FOUND OUT WHERE MY RESIDENCY WILL BE, AND I WANTED TO SHARE THE NEWS WITH HIM.
I'M JUST STARTING OUT...
BUT I HOPE THAT ONE DAY...

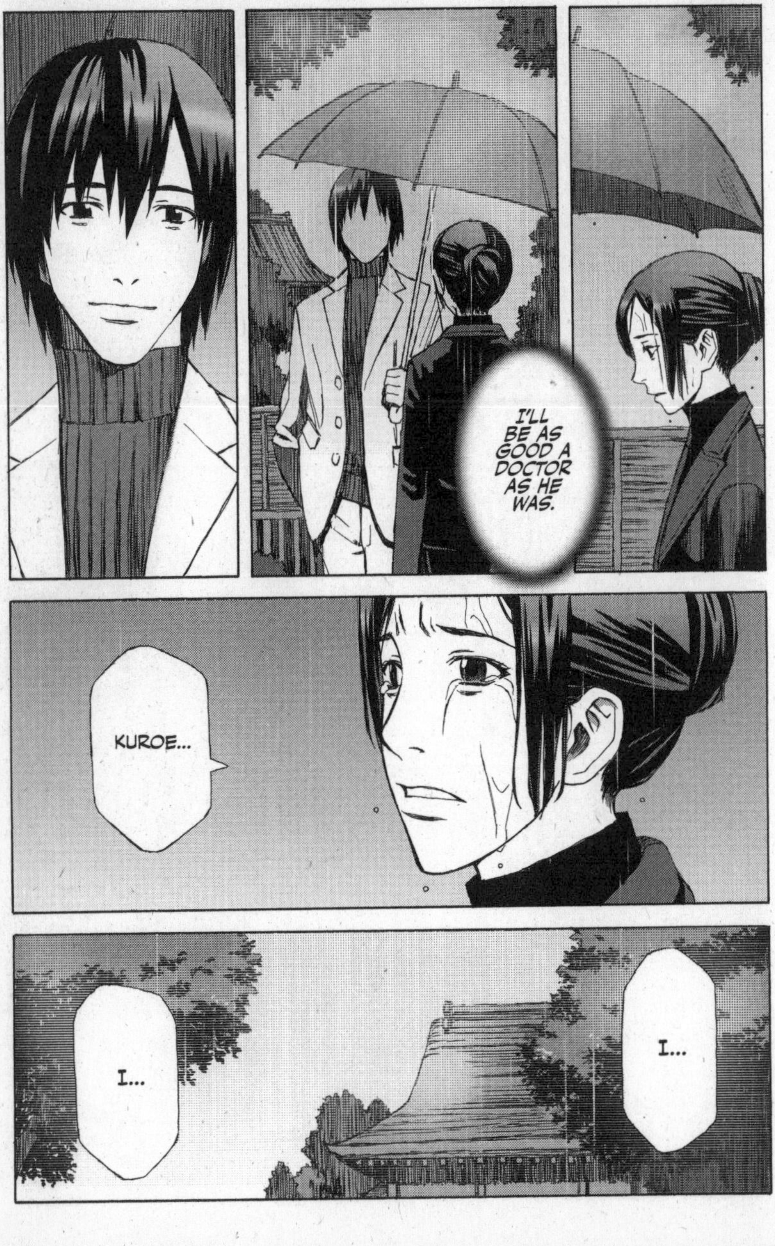
I'LL BE AS GOOD A DOCTOR AS HE WAS.
KUROE...
I...
I...

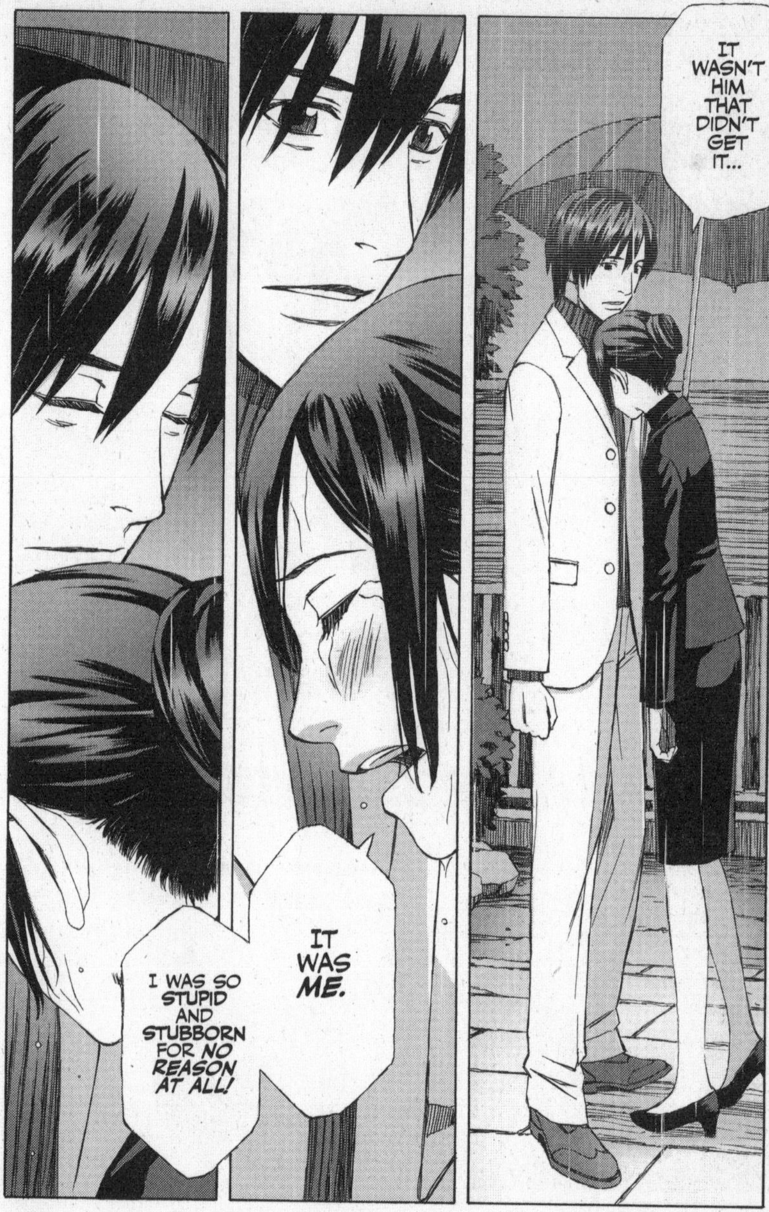
IT WASN'T HIM THAT DIDN'T GET IT...
IT WAS *ME.*
I WAS SO **STUPID** AND **STUBBORN** FOR ***NO REASON AT ALL!***

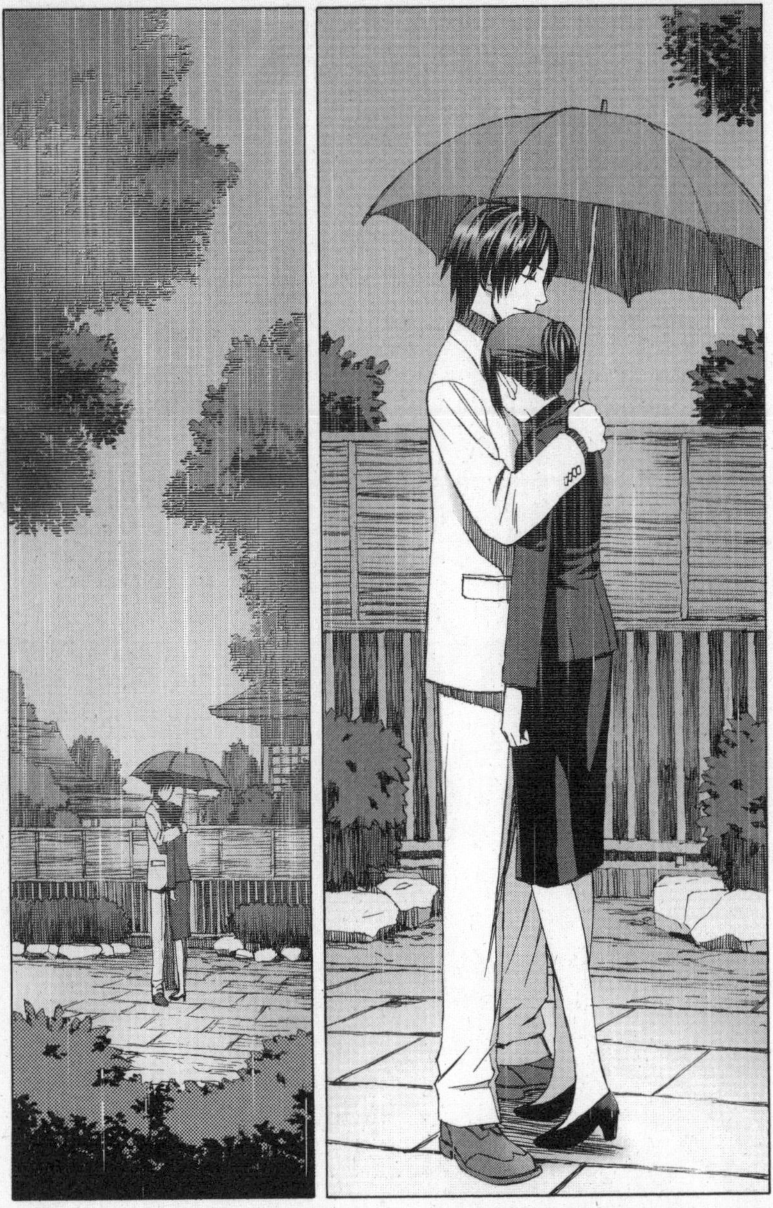

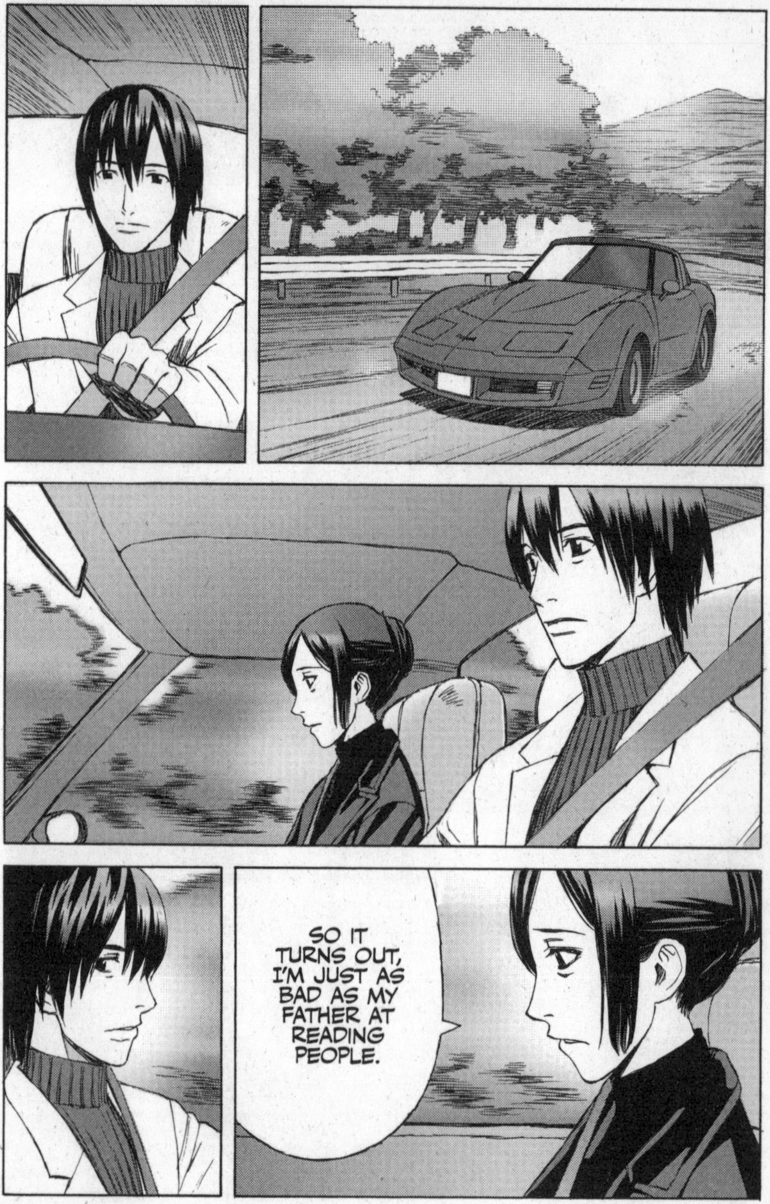
SO IT TURNS OUT, I'M JUST AS BAD AS MY FATHER AT READING PEOPLE.

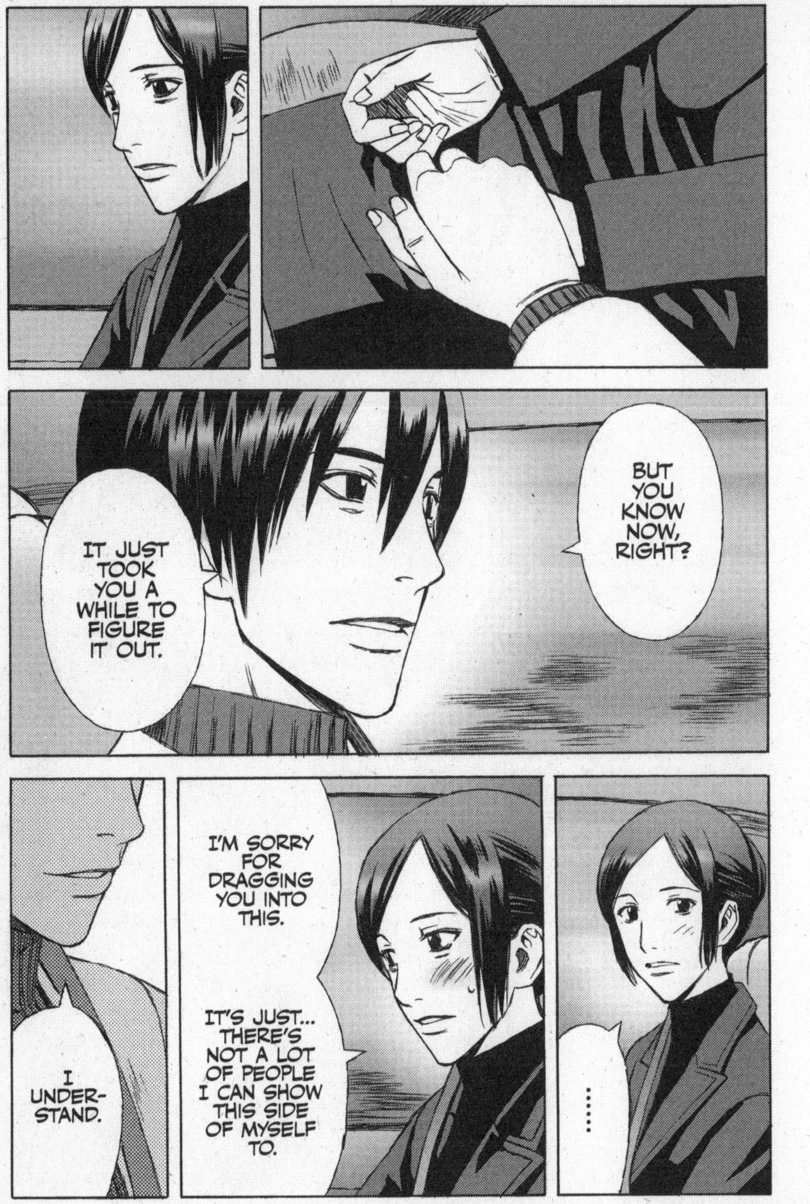
BUT YOU KNOW NOW, RIGHT?
IT JUST TOOK YOU A WHILE TO FIGURE IT OUT.
......
I'M SORRY FOR DRAGGING YOU INTO THIS.
IT'S JUST... THERE'S NOT A LOT OF PEOPLE I CAN SHOW THIS SIDE OF MYSELF TO.
I UNDER-STAND.

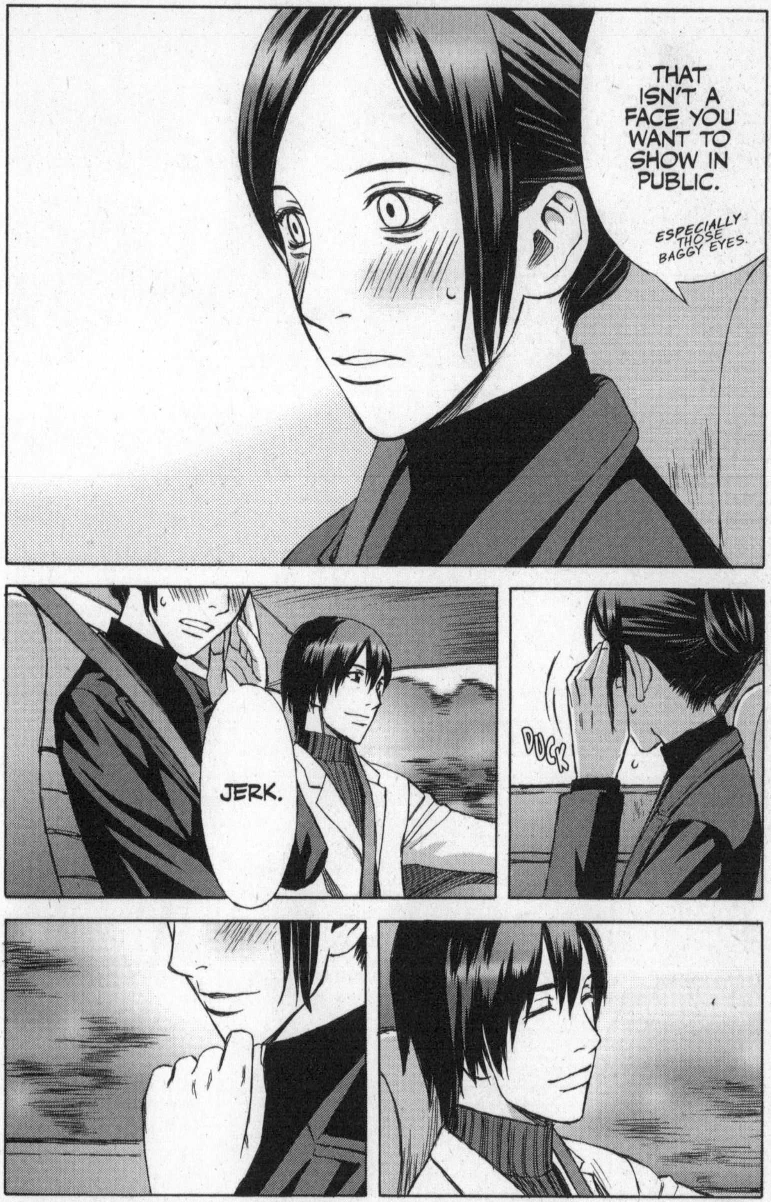
THAT ISN'T A FACE YOU WANT TO SHOW IN PUBLIC.
ESPECIALLY THOSE BAGGY EYES.
DUCK
JERK.

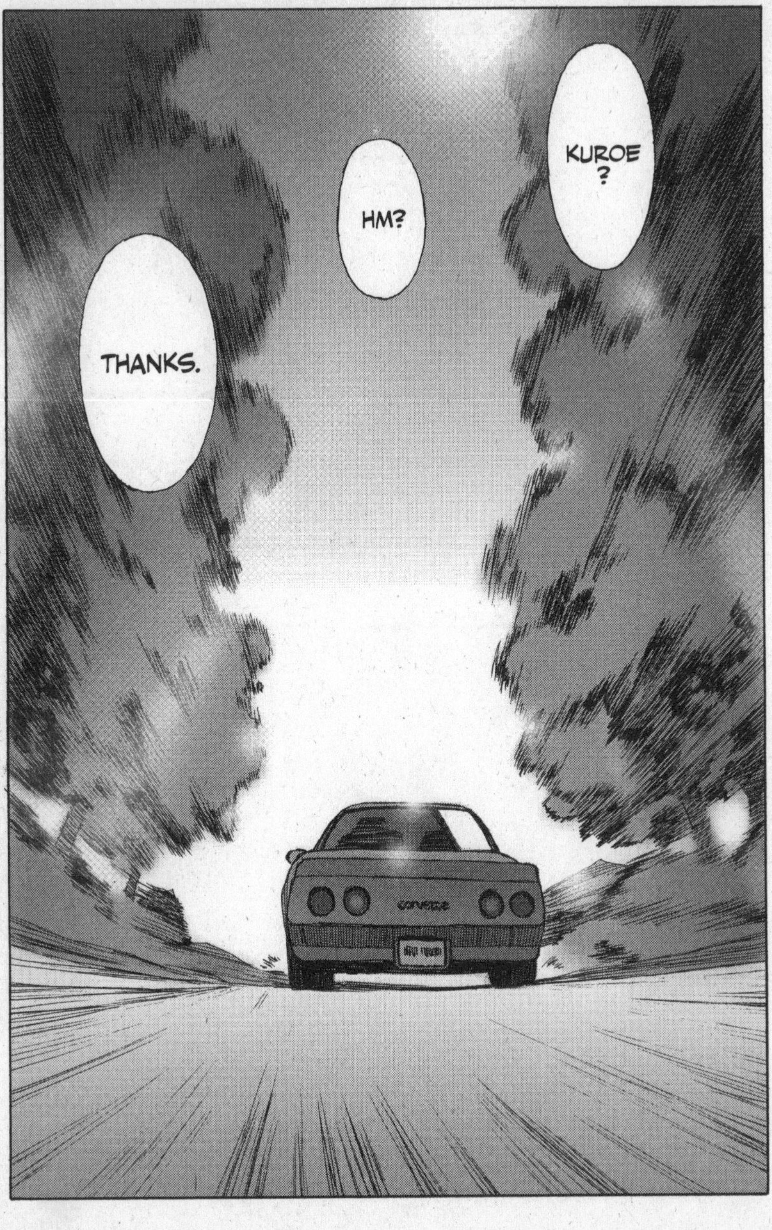
KUROE?
HM?
THANKS.

Episode 19

HOME ALONE

A Room Without You

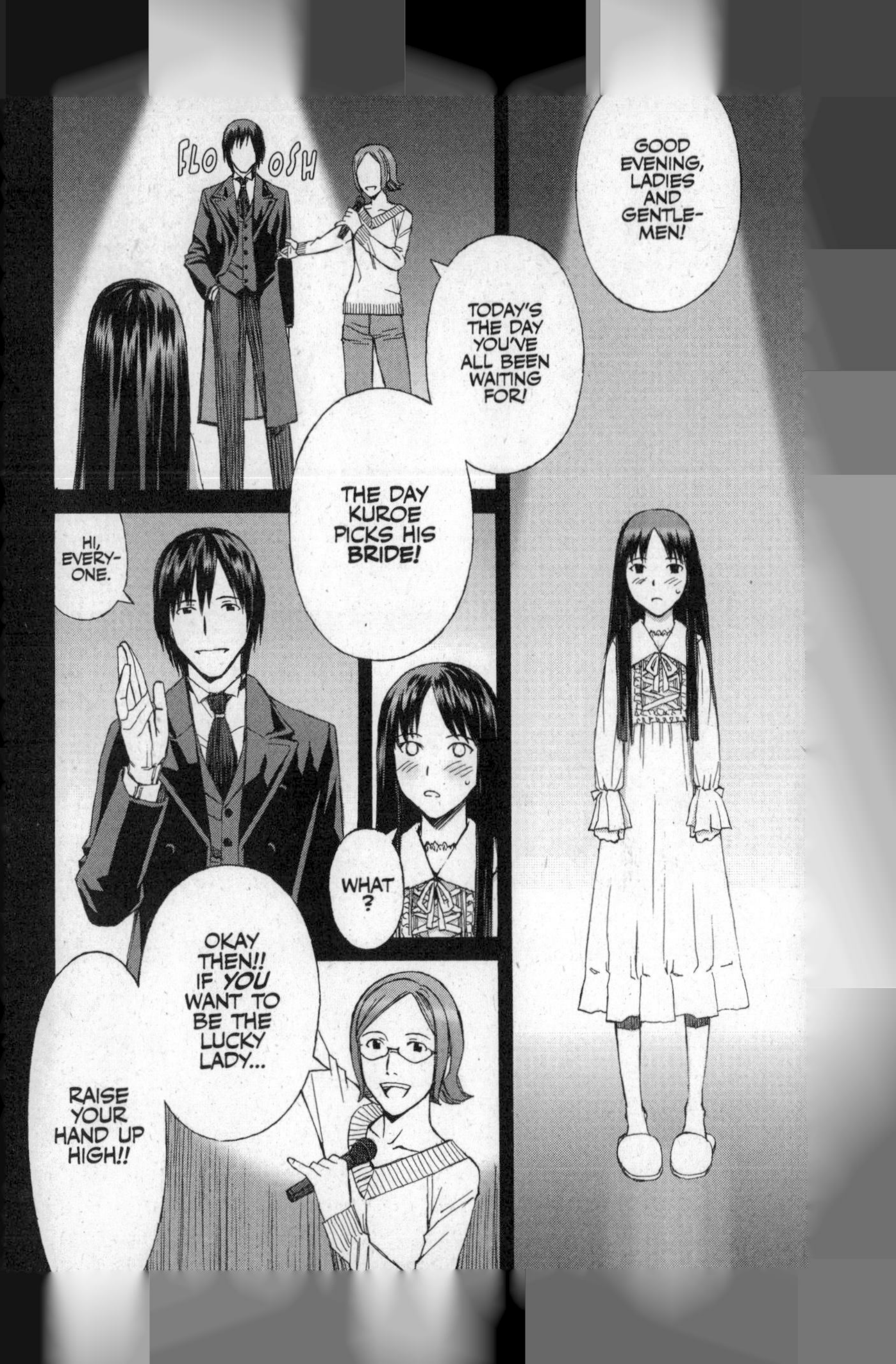
GOOD EVENING, LADIES AND GENTLE-MEN!
FLOOSH
TODAY'S THE DAY YOU'VE ALL BEEN WAITING FOR!
THE DAY KUROE PICKS HIS BRIDE!
WHAT?
OKAY THEN!! IF *YOU* WANT TO BE THE LUCKY LADY...
RAISE YOUR HAND UP HIGH!!
HI, EVERY-ONE.

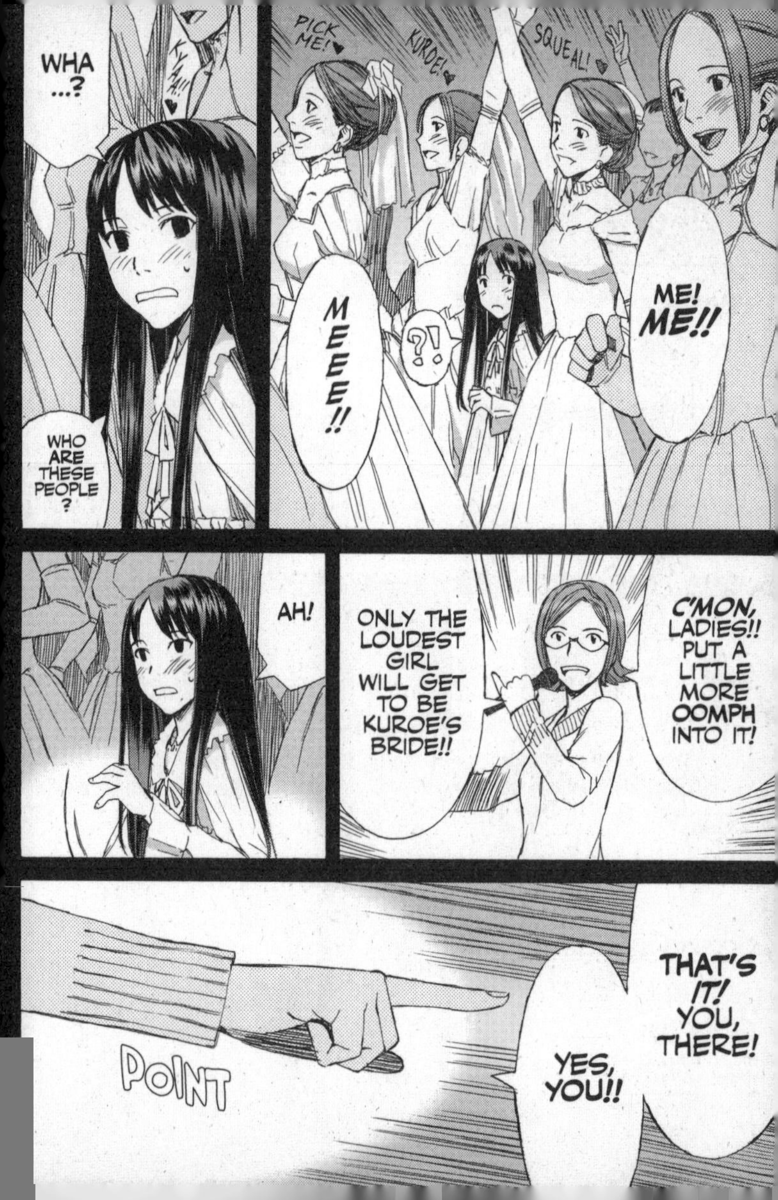
SQUEAL!
KUROE!
PICK ME!
ME! ME!!
?!
MEEE!!
KYAAA!!
WHA ...?
WHO ARE THESE PEOPLE?
C'MON, LADIES!! PUT A LITTLE MORE OOMPH INTO IT!
ONLY THE LOUDEST GIRL WILL GET TO BE KUROE'S BRIDE!!
AH!
THAT'S IT! YOU, THERE!
YES, YOU!!
POINT

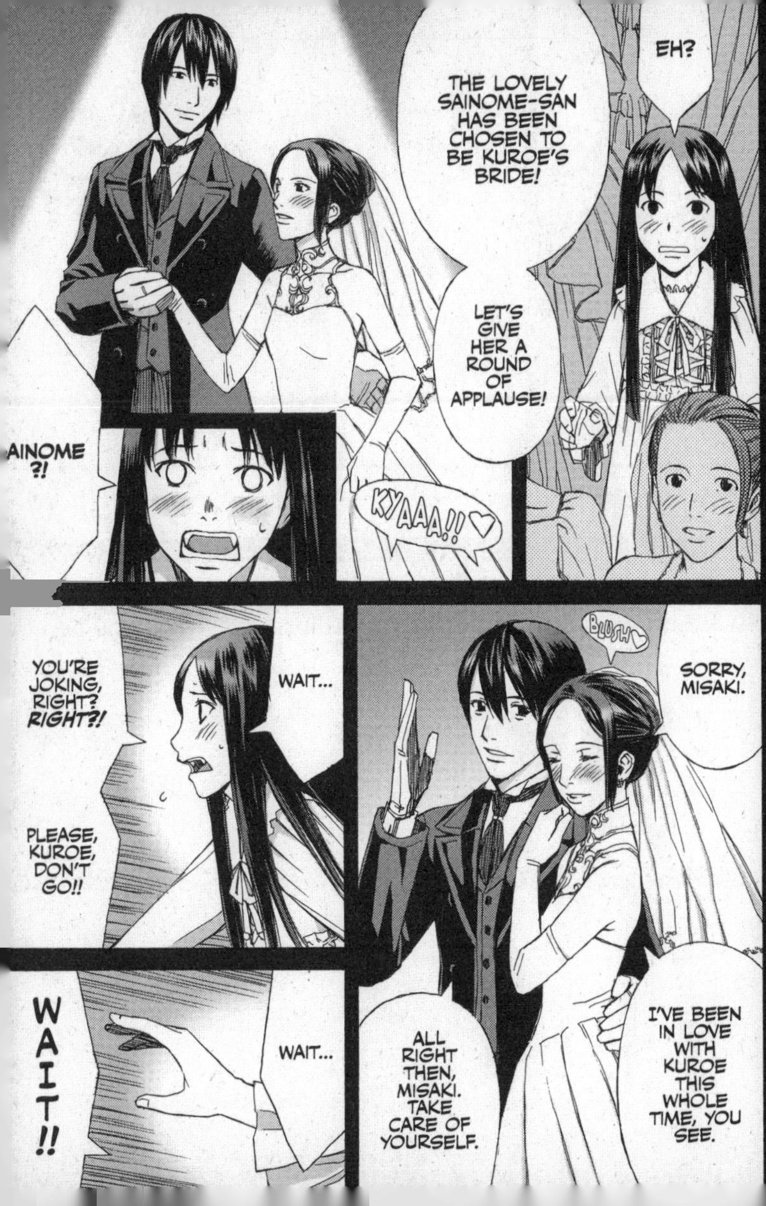
THE LOVELY SAINOME-SAN HAS BEEN CHOSEN TO BE KUROE'S BRIDE!
EH?
LET'S GIVE HER A ROUND OF APPLAUSE!
KYAAA!! ♥
AINOME ?!
BLUSH ♥
SORRY, MISAKI.
I'VE BEEN IN LOVE WITH KUROE THIS WHOLE TIME, YOU SEE.
ALL RIGHT THEN, MISAKI. TAKE CARE OF YOURSELF.
WAIT...
YOU'RE JOKING, RIGHT? *RIGHT?!*
PLEASE, KUROE, DON'T GO!!
WAIT...
WAIT!!

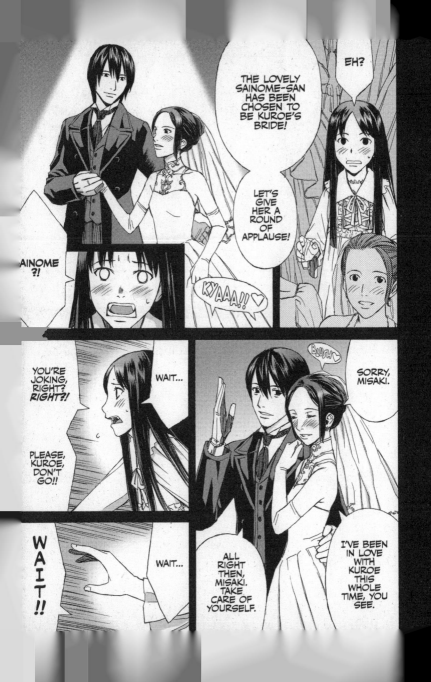

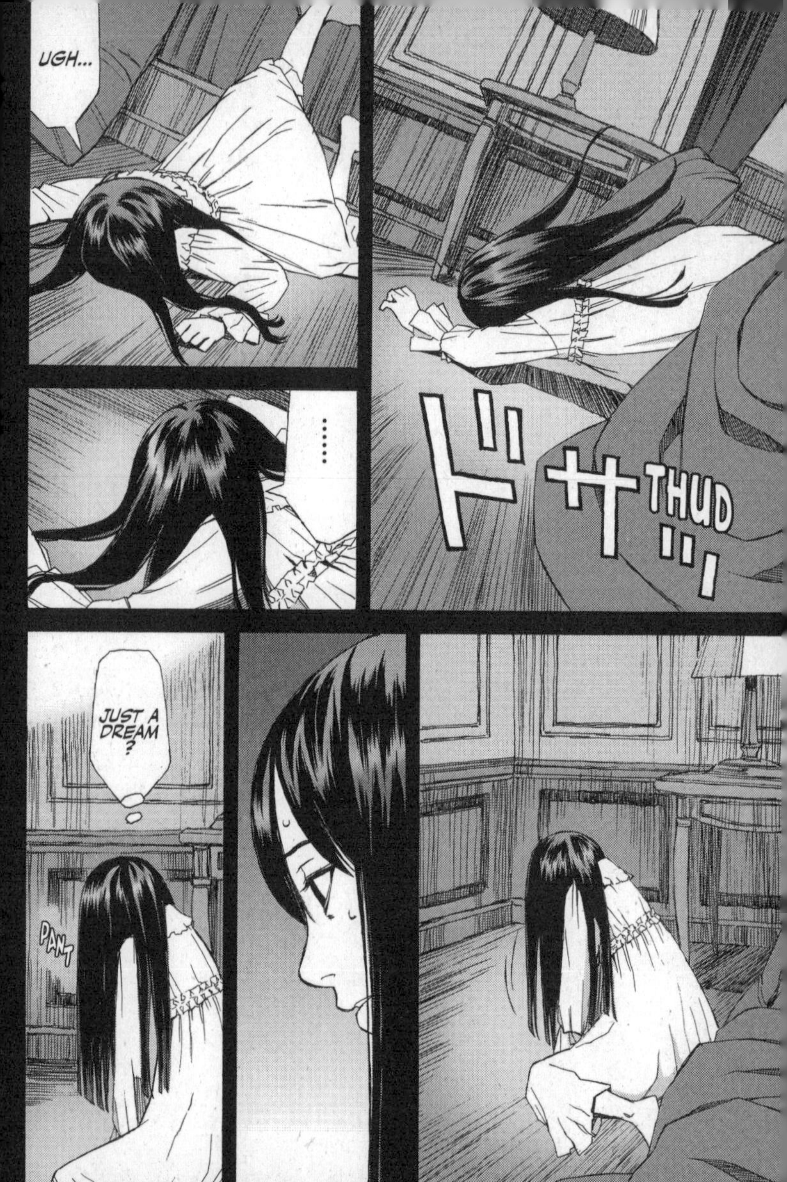
ドサ
THUD
UGH...
......
JUST A DREAM?
PANT

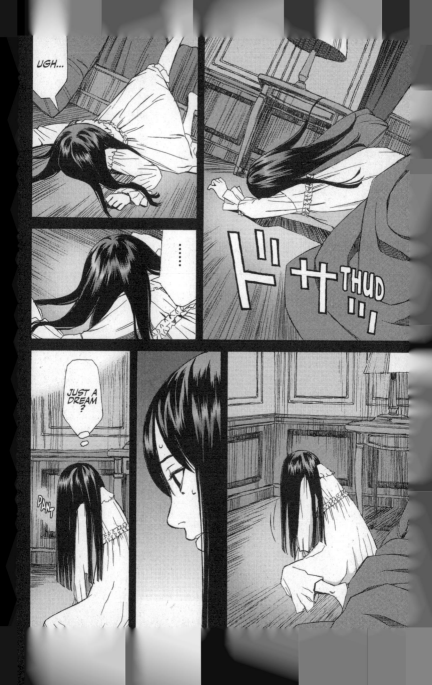

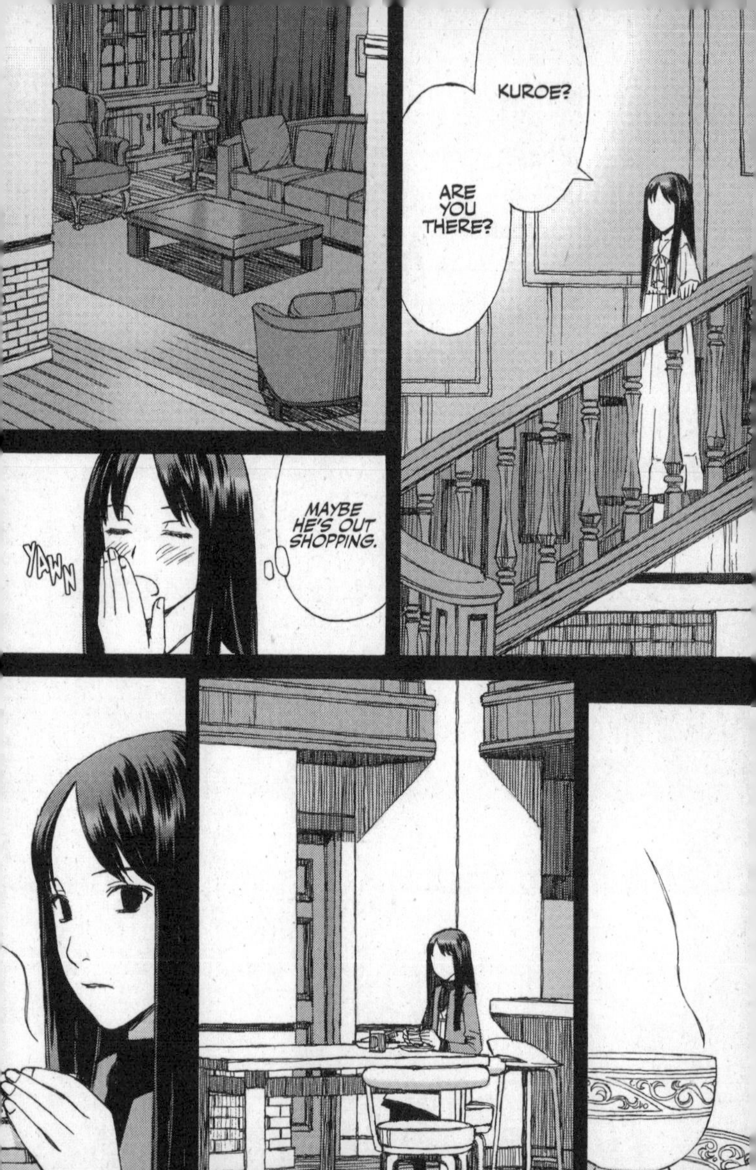
KUROE?
ARE YOU THERE?
MAYBE HE'S OUT SHOPPING.
YAWN

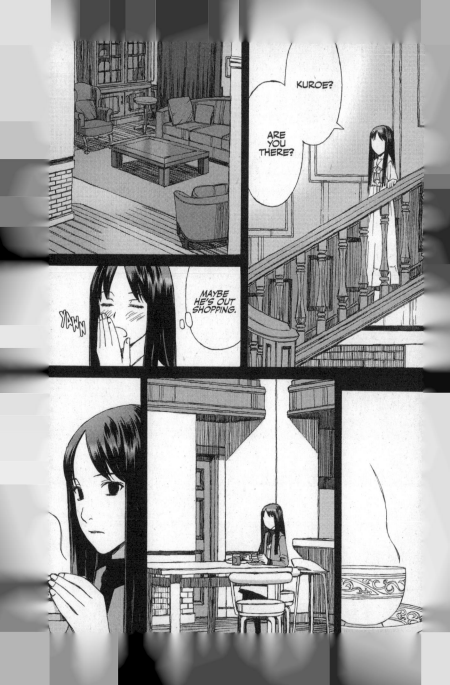

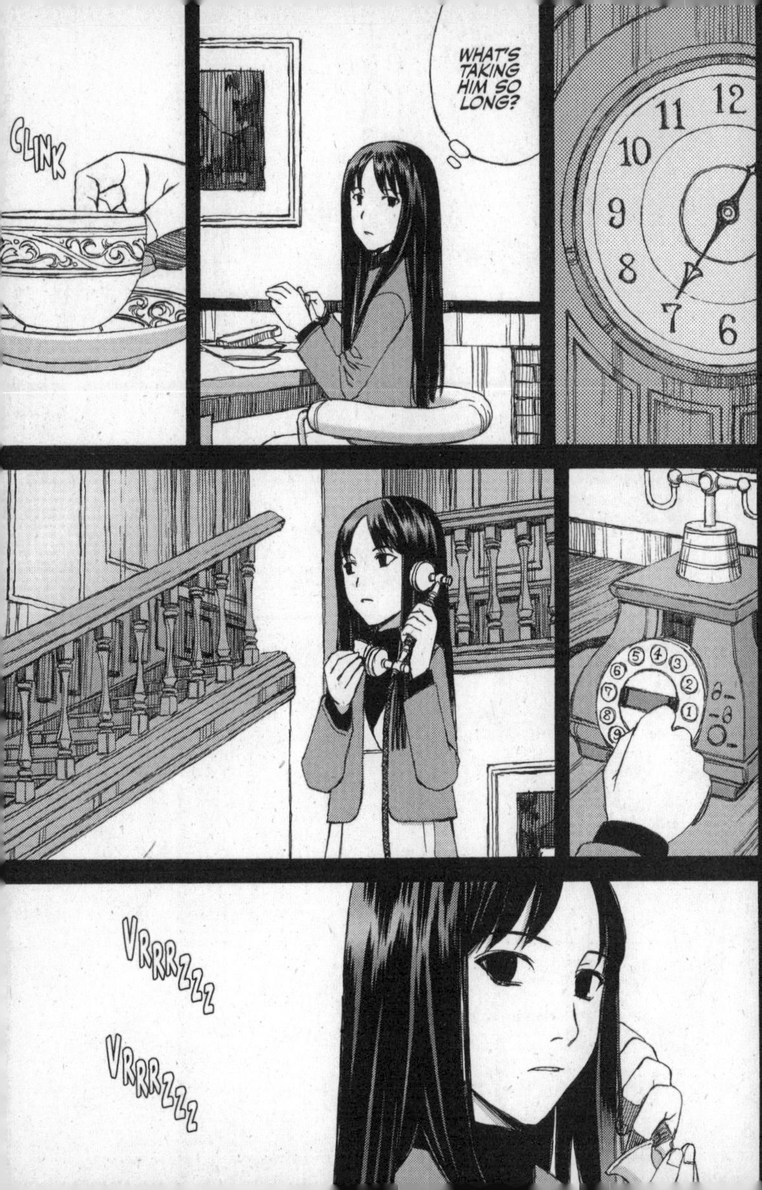
WHAT'S TAKING HIM SO LONG?
CLINK
VRRRZZZ
VRRRZZZ

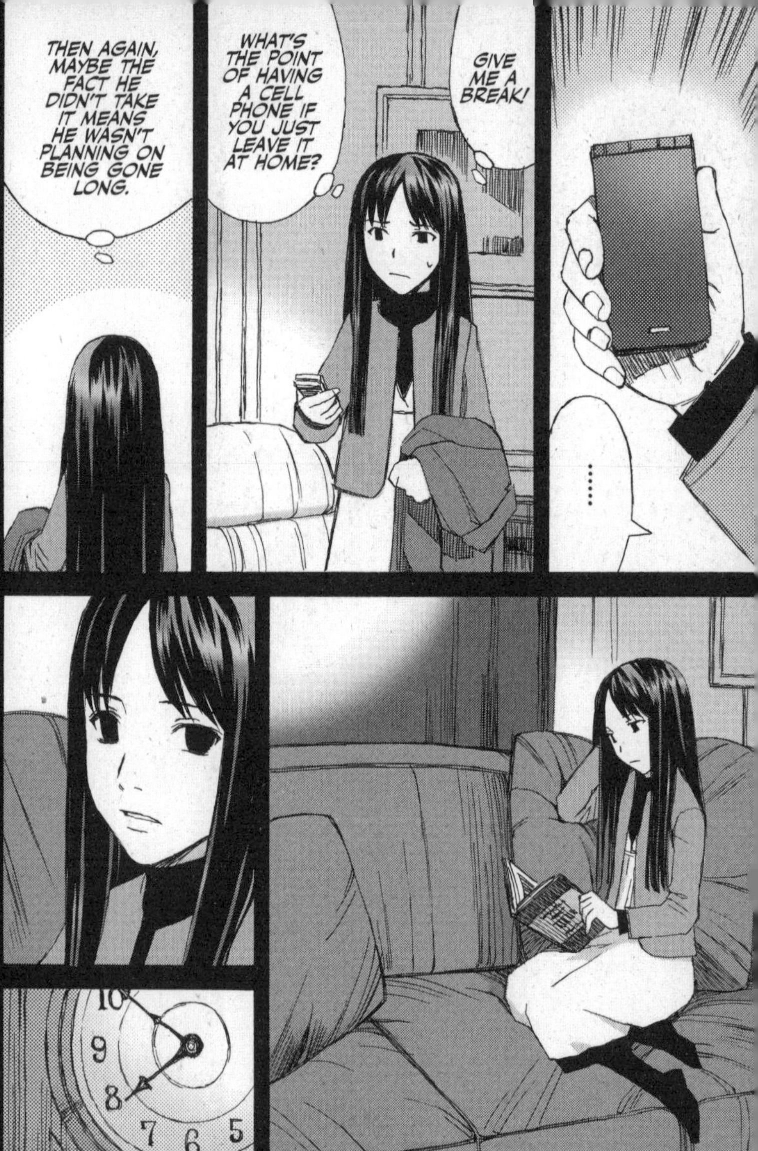
GIVE ME A BREAK!
......
WHAT'S THE POINT OF HAVING A CELL PHONE IF YOU JUST LEAVE IT AT HOME?
THEN AGAIN, MAYBE THE FACT HE DIDN'T TAKE IT MEANS HE WASN'T PLANNING ON BEING GONE LONG.

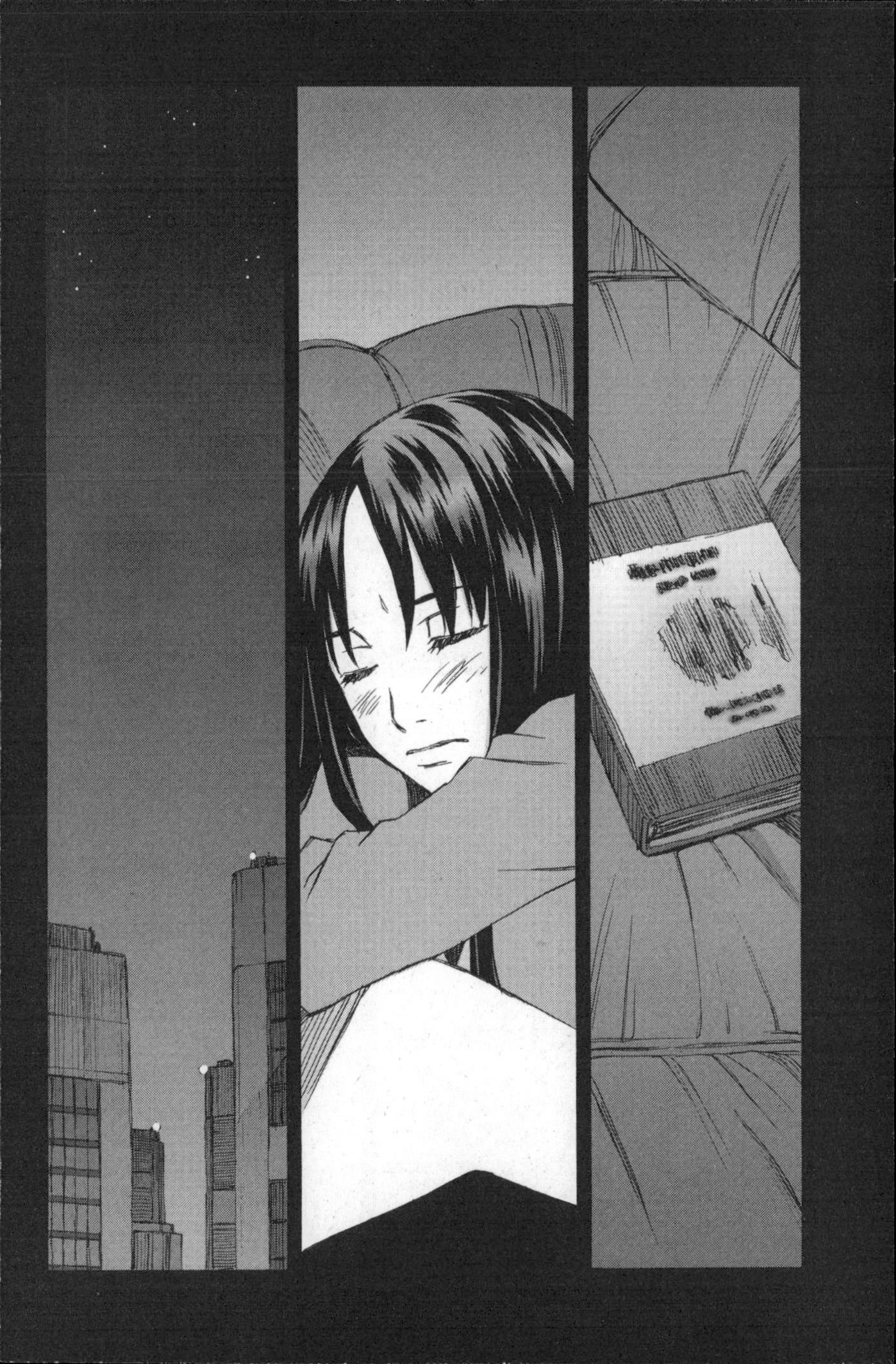

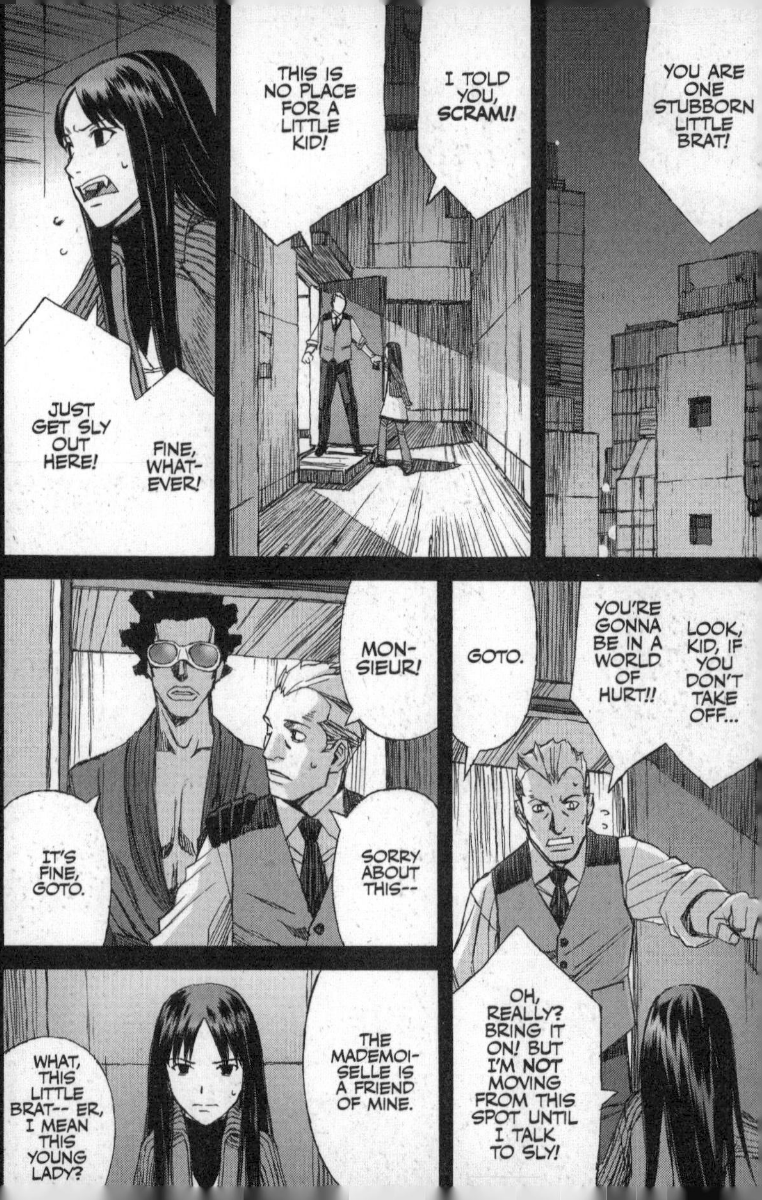
YOU ARE ONE STUBBORN LITTLE BRAT!
I TOLD YOU, SCRAM!!
THIS IS NO PLACE FOR A LITTLE KID!
FINE, WHAT-EVER!
JUST GET SLY OUT HERE!
LOOK, KID, IF YOU DON'T TAKE OFF...
YOU'RE GONNA BE IN A WORLD OF HURT!!
GOTO.
OH, REALLY? BRING IT ON! BUT I'M NOT MOVING FROM THIS SPOT UNTIL I TALK TO SLY!
MON-SIEUR!
SORRY ABOUT THIS--
IT'S FINE, GOTO.
THE MADEMOI-SELLE IS A FRIEND OF MINE.
WHAT, THIS LITTLE BRAT-- ER, I MEAN THIS YOUNG LADY?

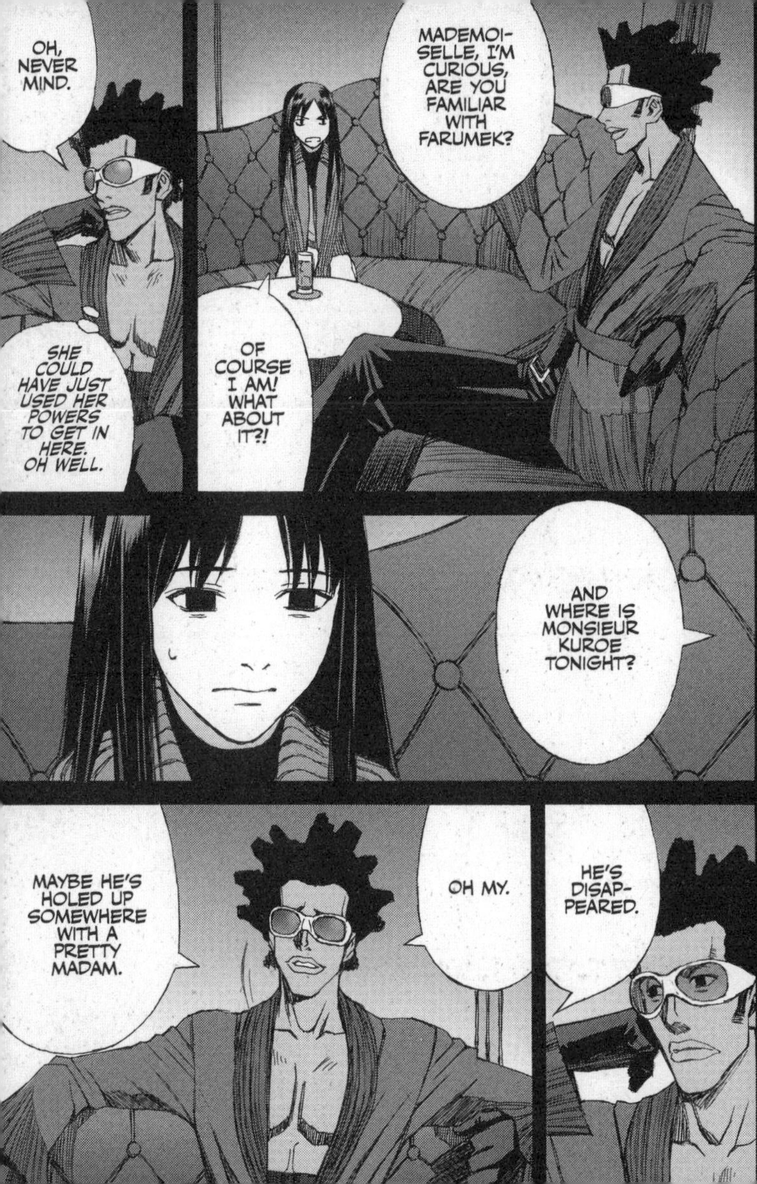
MADEMOI-SELLE, I'M CURIOUS, ARE YOU FAMILIAR WITH FARUMEK?
OF COURSE I AM! WHAT ABOUT IT?!
OH, NEVER MIND.
SHE COULD HAVE JUST USED HER POWERS TO GET IN HERE. OH WELL.
AND WHERE IS MONSIEUR KUROE TONIGHT?
HE'S DISAP-PEARED.
OH MY.
MAYBE HE'S HOLED UP SOMEWHERE WITH A PRETTY MADAM.

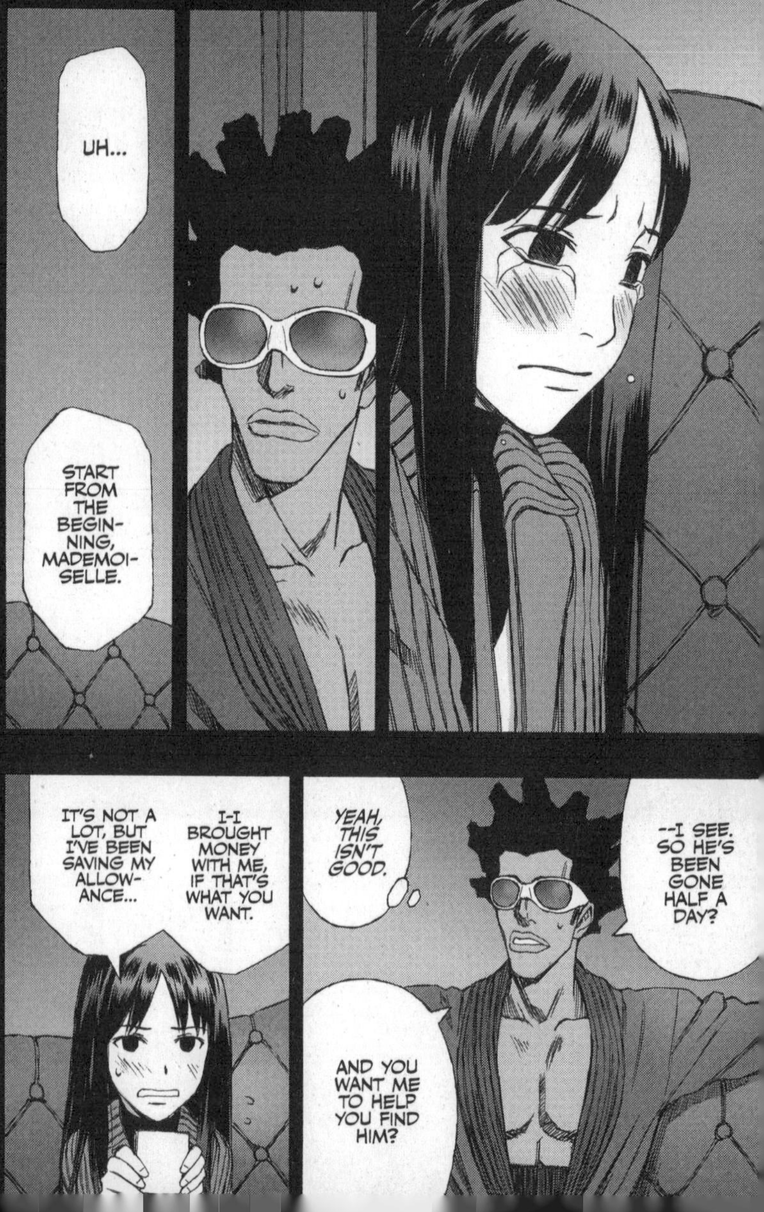
UH...
START FROM THE BEGINNING, MADEMOISELLE.
--I SEE. SO HE'S BEEN GONE HALF A DAY?
YEAH, THIS ISN'T GOOD.
AND YOU WANT ME TO HELP YOU FIND HIM?
I-I BROUGHT MONEY WITH ME, IF THAT'S WHAT YOU WANT.
IT'S NOT A LOT, BUT I'VE BEEN SAVING MY ALLOWANCE...

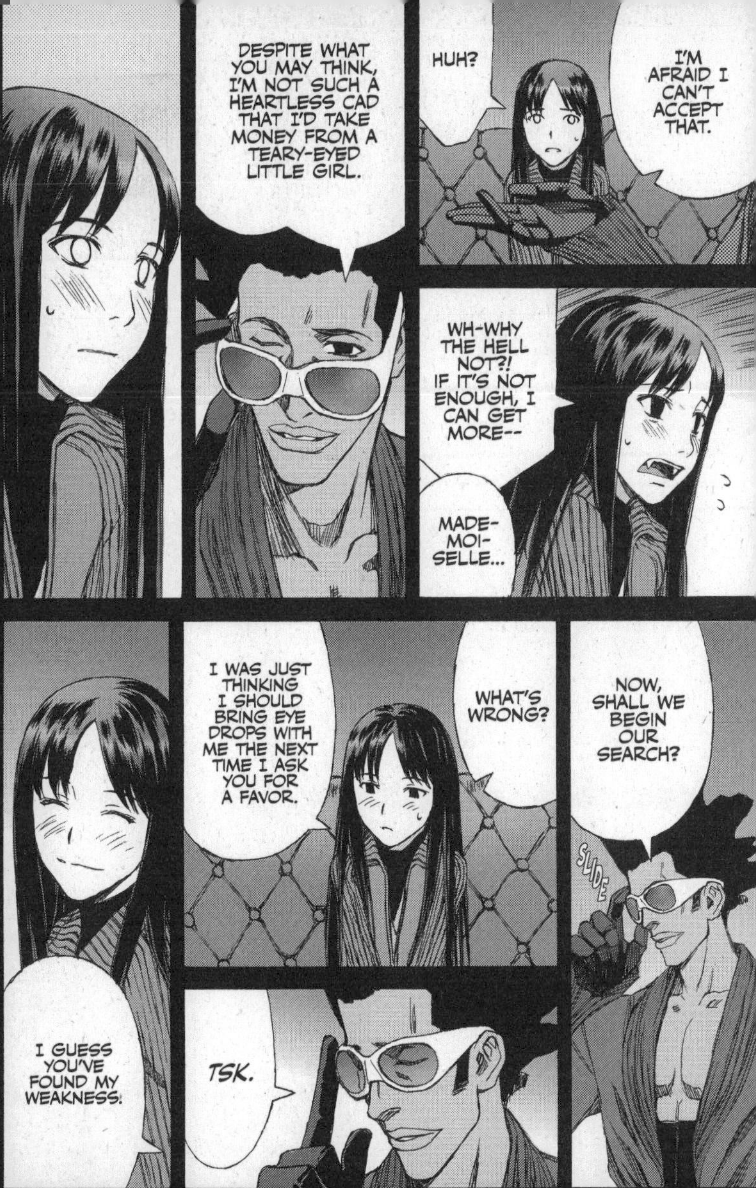
I'M AFRAID I CAN'T ACCEPT THAT.
HUH?
WH-WHY THE HELL NOT?! IF IT'S NOT ENOUGH, I CAN GET MORE--
MADE-MOI-SELLE...
DESPITE WHAT YOU MAY THINK, I'M NOT SUCH A HEARTLESS CAD THAT I'D TAKE MONEY FROM A TEARY-EYED LITTLE GIRL.
NOW, SHALL WE BEGIN OUR SEARCH?
SLIDE
WHAT'S WRONG?
I WAS JUST THINKING I SHOULD BRING EYE DROPS WITH ME THE NEXT TIME I ASK YOU FOR A FAVOR.
TSK.
I GUESS YOU'VE FOUND MY WEAKNESS.

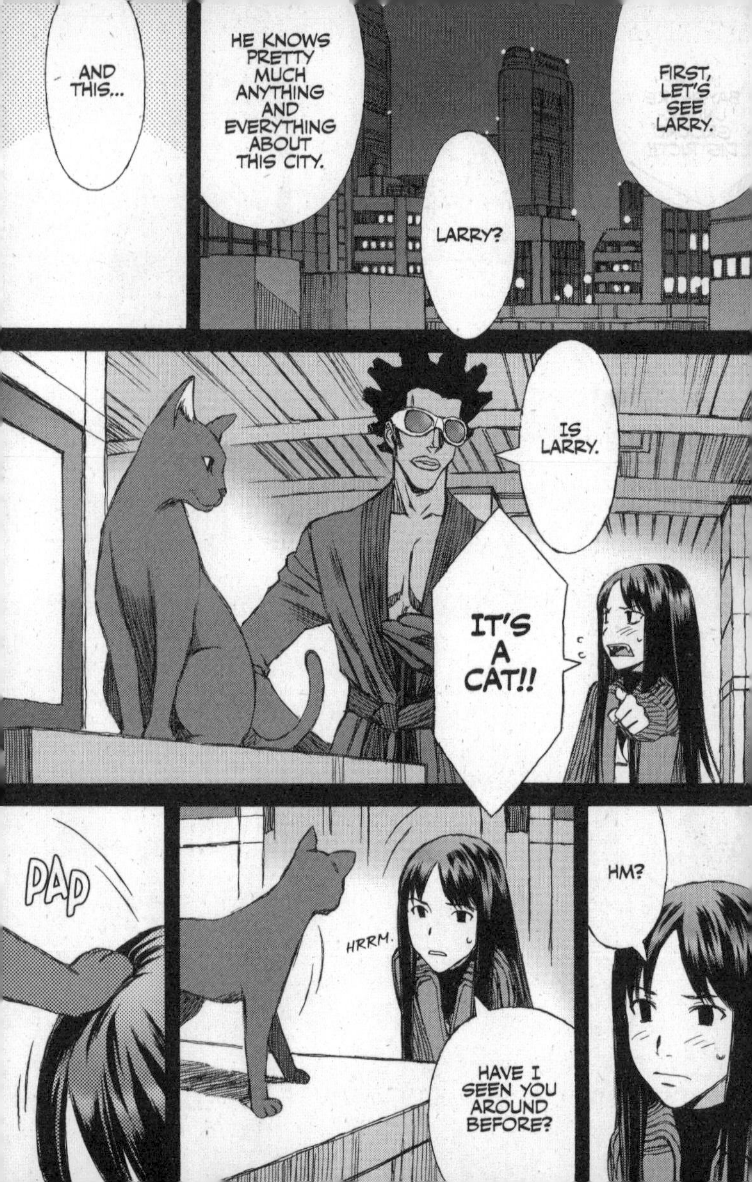
FIRST, LET'S SEE LARRY.
LARRY?
HE KNOWS PRETTY MUCH ANYTHING AND EVERYTHING ABOUT THIS CITY.
AND THIS...
IS LARRY.
IT'S A CAT!!
HM?
HAVE I SEEN YOU AROUND BEFORE?
HRRM.
PAP

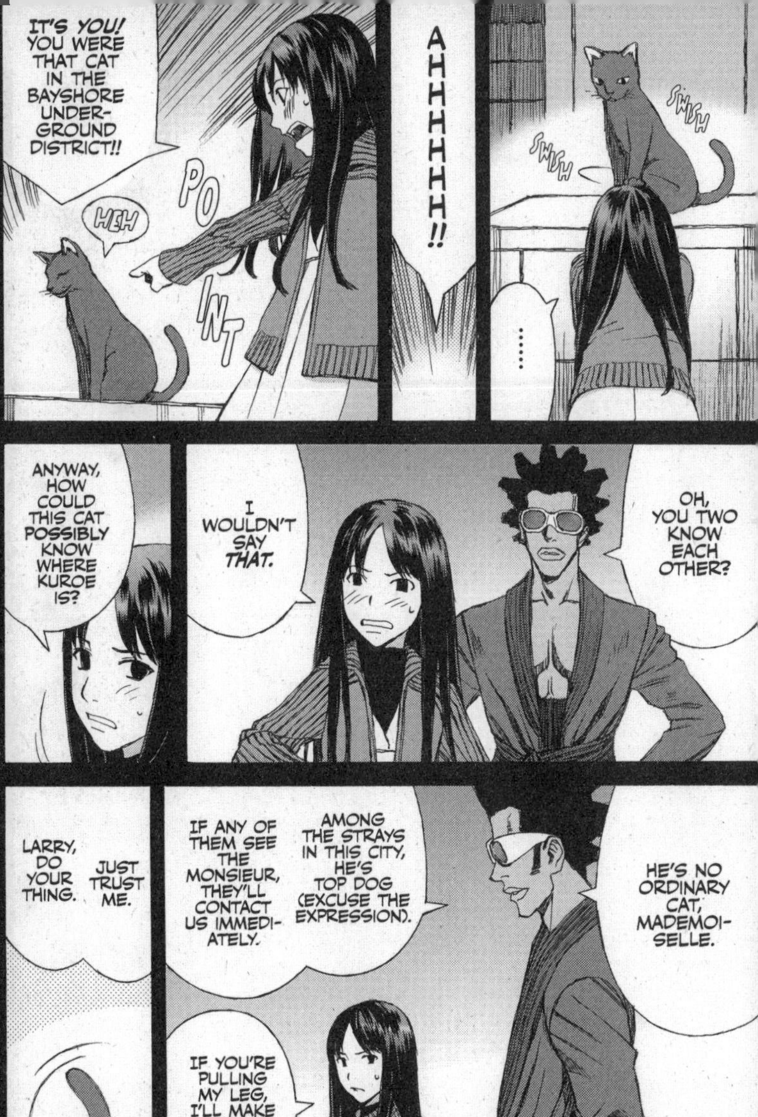
SWISH
SWISH
......
AHHHHHH!!
IT'S YOU! YOU WERE THAT CAT IN THE BAYSHORE UNDER-GROUND DISTRICT!!
HEH
POINT
OH, YOU TWO KNOW EACH OTHER?
I WOULDN'T SAY THAT.
ANYWAY, HOW COULD THIS CAT POSSIBLY KNOW WHERE KUROE IS?
HE'S NO ORDINARY CAT, MADEMOI-SELLE.
AMONG THE STRAYS IN THIS CITY, HE'S TOP DOG (EXCUSE THE EXPRESSION).
IF ANY OF THEM SEE THE MONSIEUR, THEY'LL CONTACT US IMMEDI-ATELY.
IF YOU'RE PULLING MY LEG, I'LL MAKE YOU REGRET IT.
LARRY, DO YOUR THING.
JUST TRUST ME.

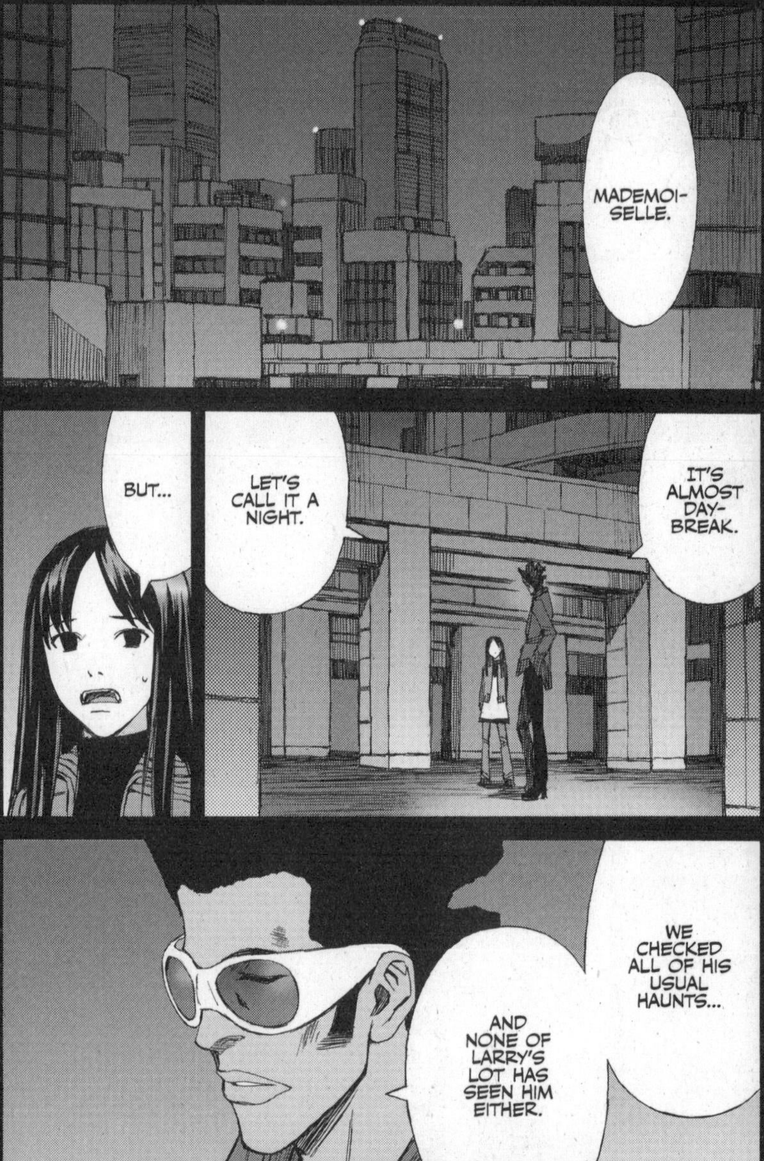
MADEMOI-
SELLE.
IT'S ALMOST DAY-BREAK.
LET'S CALL IT A NIGHT.
BUT...
WE CHECKED ALL OF HIS USUAL HAUNTS...
AND NONE OF LARRY'S LOT HAS SEEN HIM EITHER.

THERE'S NOTHING MORE WE CAN DO TONIGHT.
JUST LEAVE THE REST UP TO ME. YOU GO HOME AND RELAX.
I'LL CONTACT YOU AS SOON AS I HEAR SOMETHING.
OKAY.
THANK YOU.
LISTEN, DON'T WORRY YOUR PRETTY LITTLE HEAD.
MONSIEUR KUROE WOULD **NEVER** JUST TAKE OFF AND LEAVE YOU BEHIND, RIGHT?
RIGHT...
HE PROBABLY JUST...

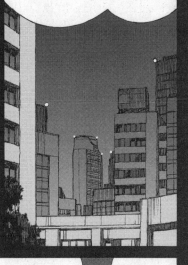

TIME TO HIM- SELF?

YEAH.

MONSIEUR KUROE PROBABLY JUST NEEDED A LITTLE TIME TO HIMSELF.

NOW, ALLOW ME TO WALK YOU HOME.

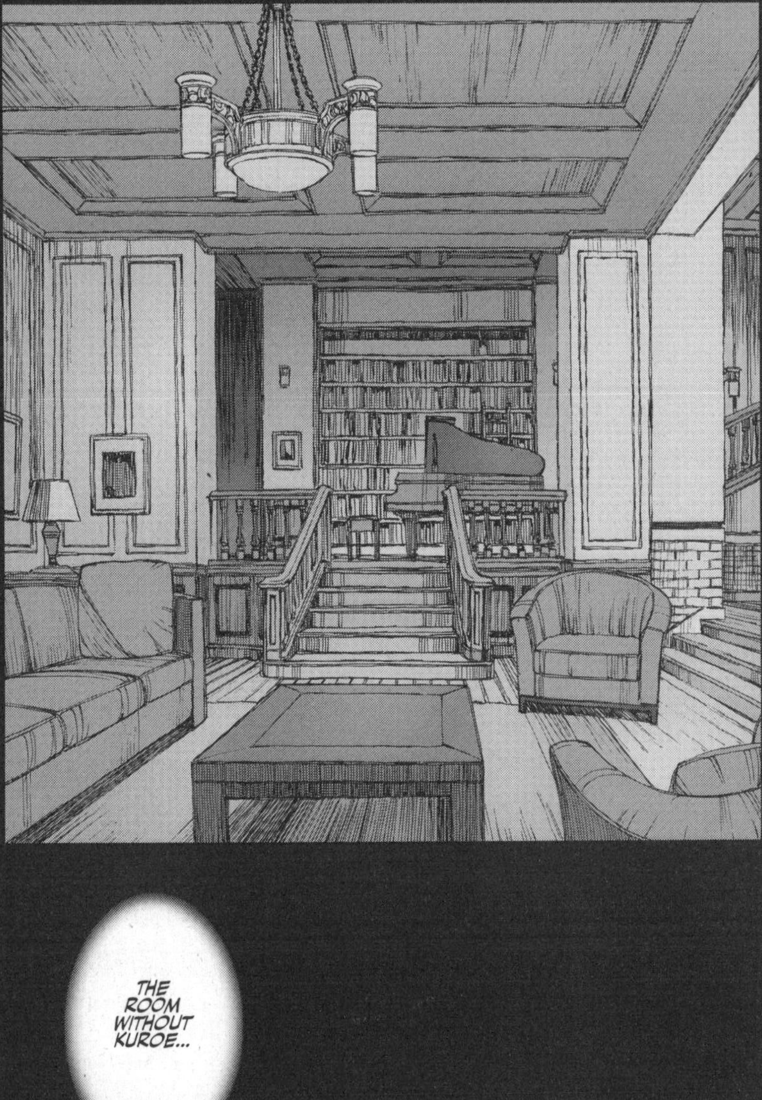
THE ROOM WITHOUT KUROE...

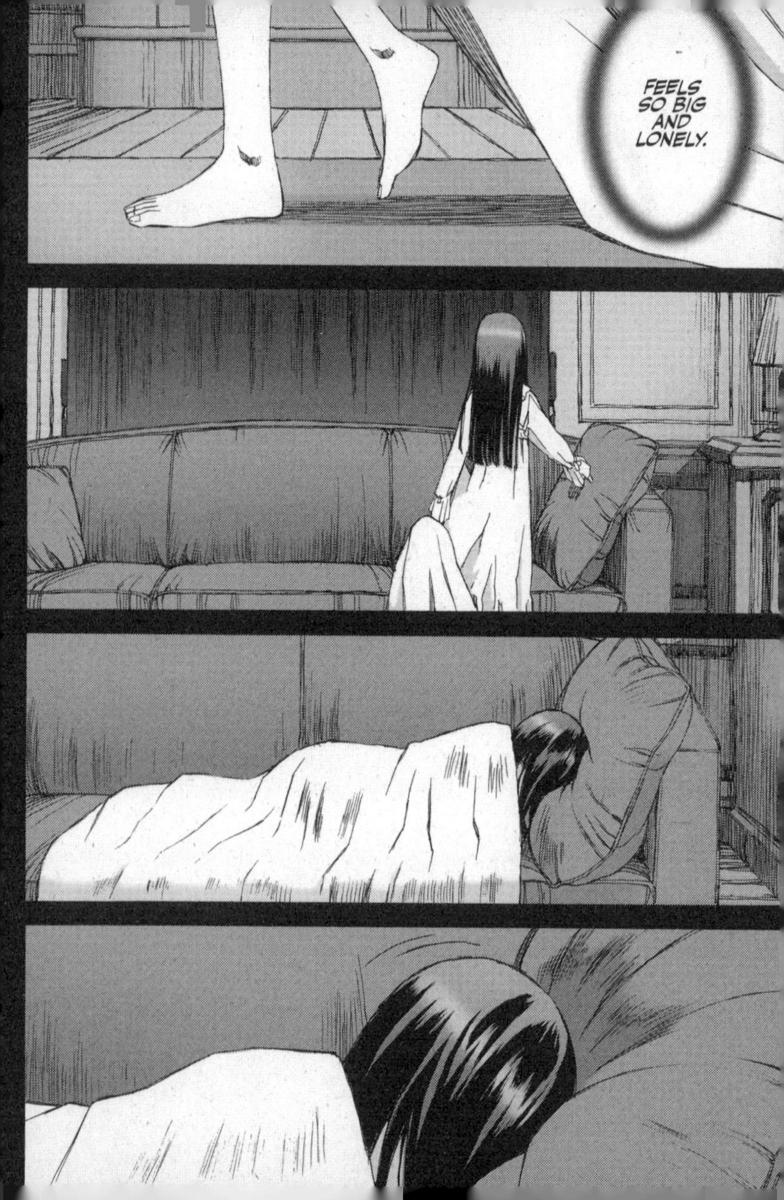
FEELS SO BIG AND LONELY.

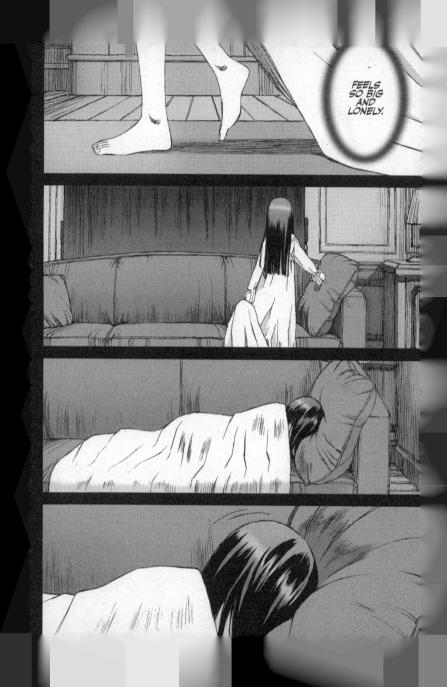

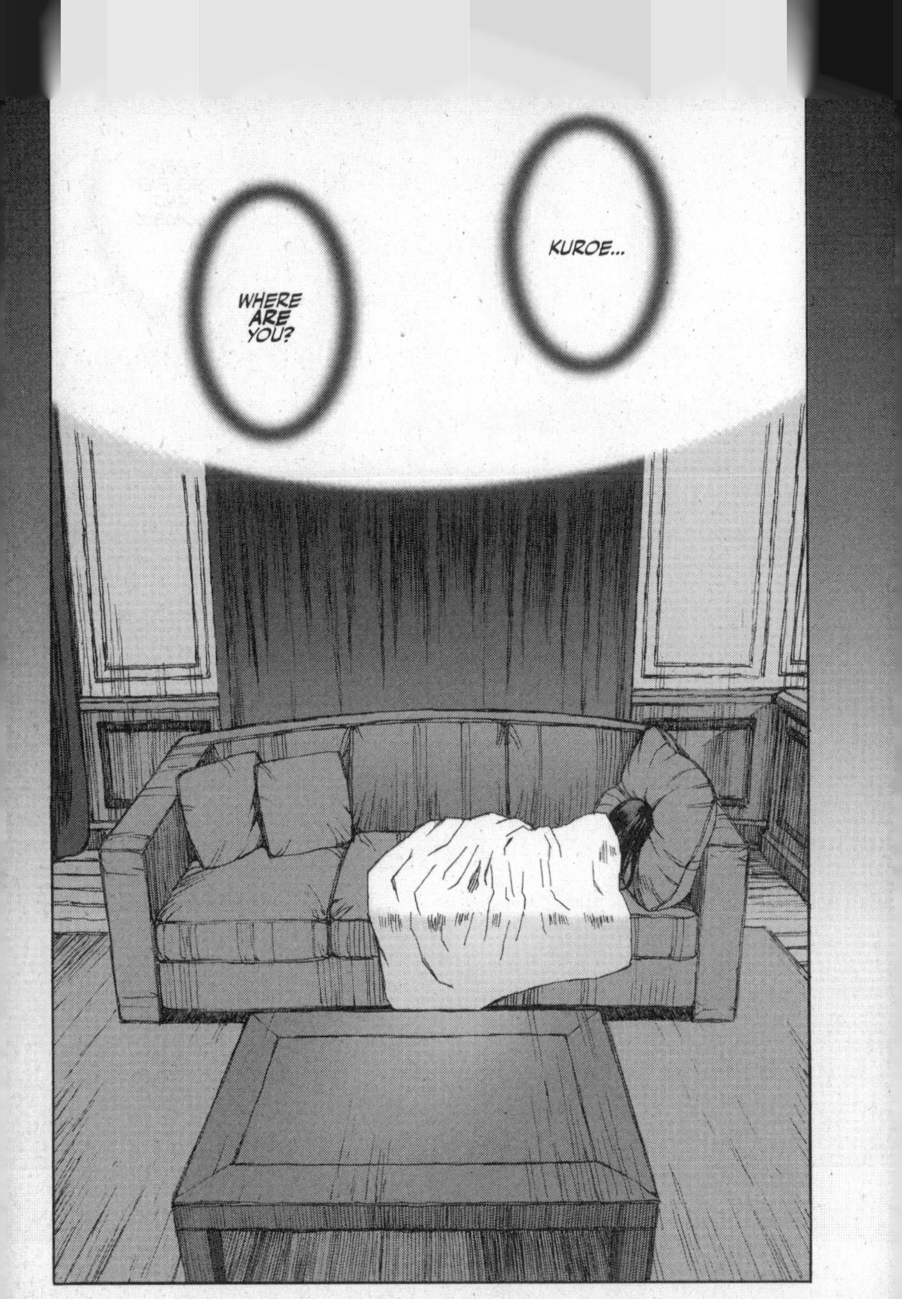
KUROE...
WHERE ARE YOU?

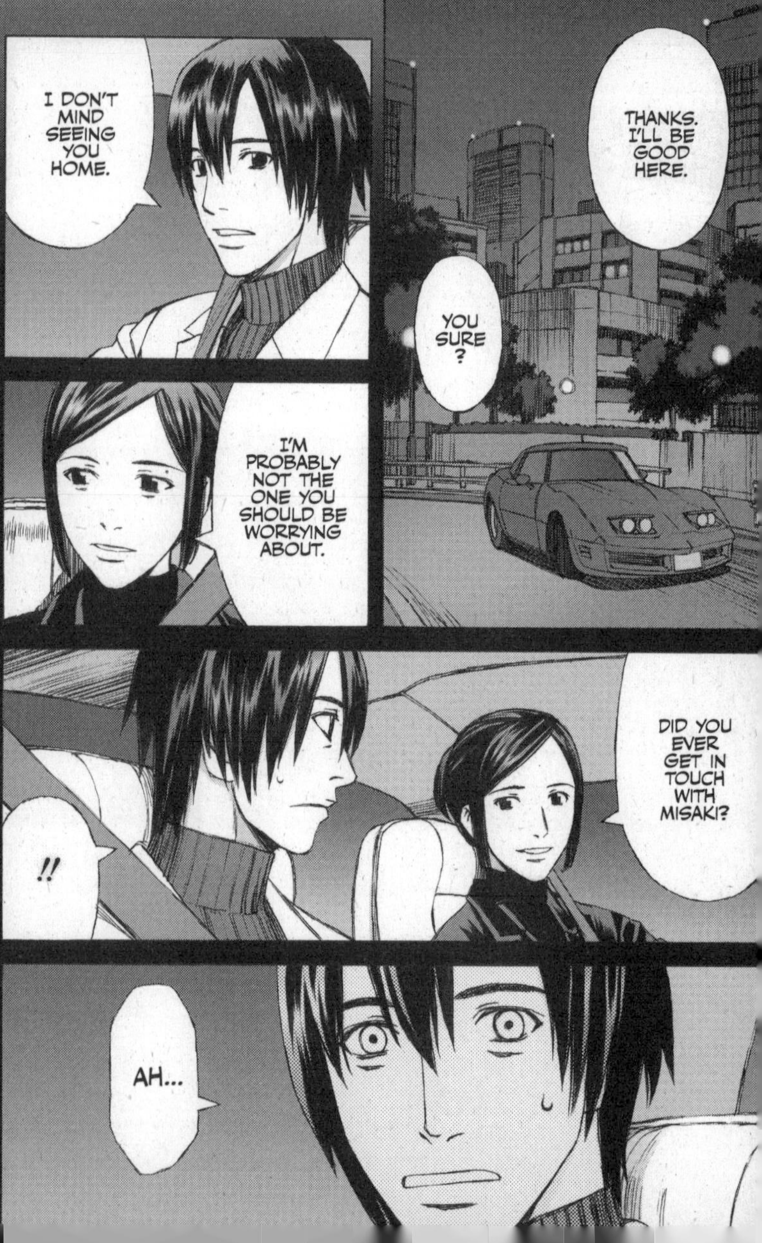
THANKS. I'LL BE GOOD HERE.
YOU SURE?
I DON'T MIND SEEING YOU HOME.
I'M PROBABLY NOT THE ONE YOU SHOULD BE WORRYING ABOUT.
DID YOU EVER GET IN TOUCH WITH MISAKI?
!!
AH...

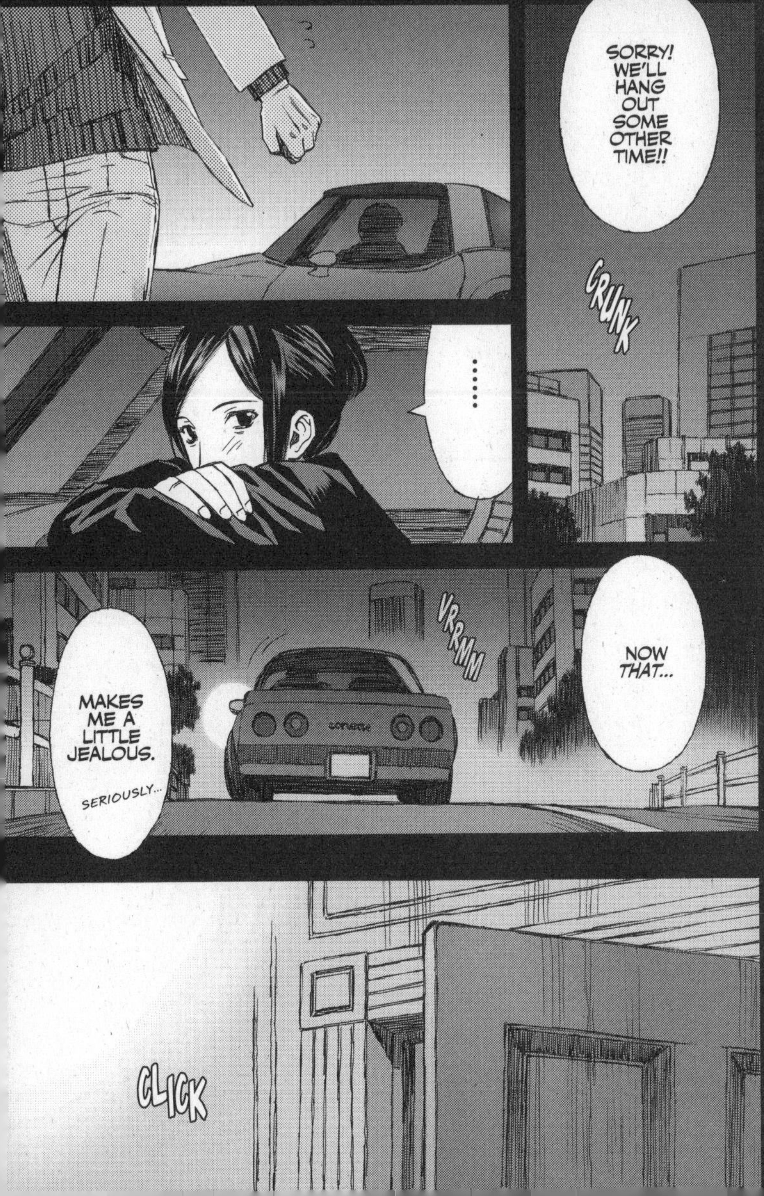
SORRY! WE'LL HANG OUT SOME OTHER TIME!!
CRUNK
......
NOW THAT...
VRRMM
MAKES ME A LITTLE JEALOUS.
SERIOUSLY...
CLICK

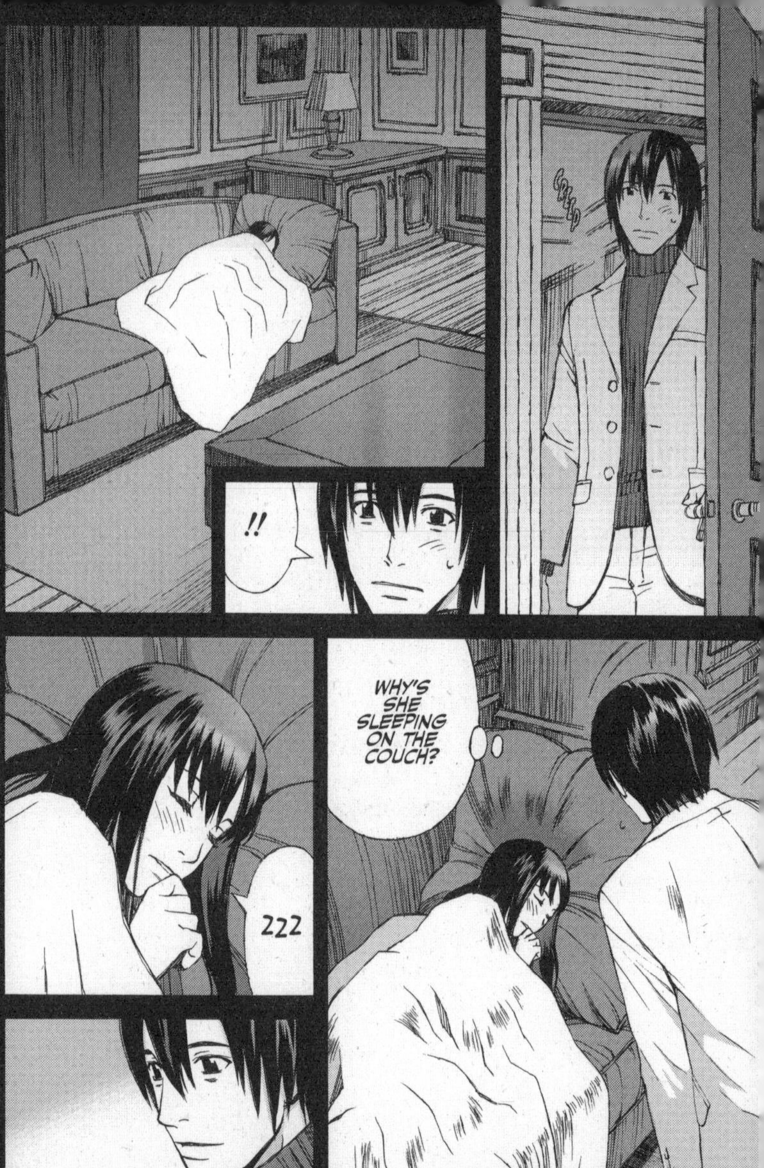
!!
WHY'S SHE SLEEPING ON THE COUCH?
ZZZ

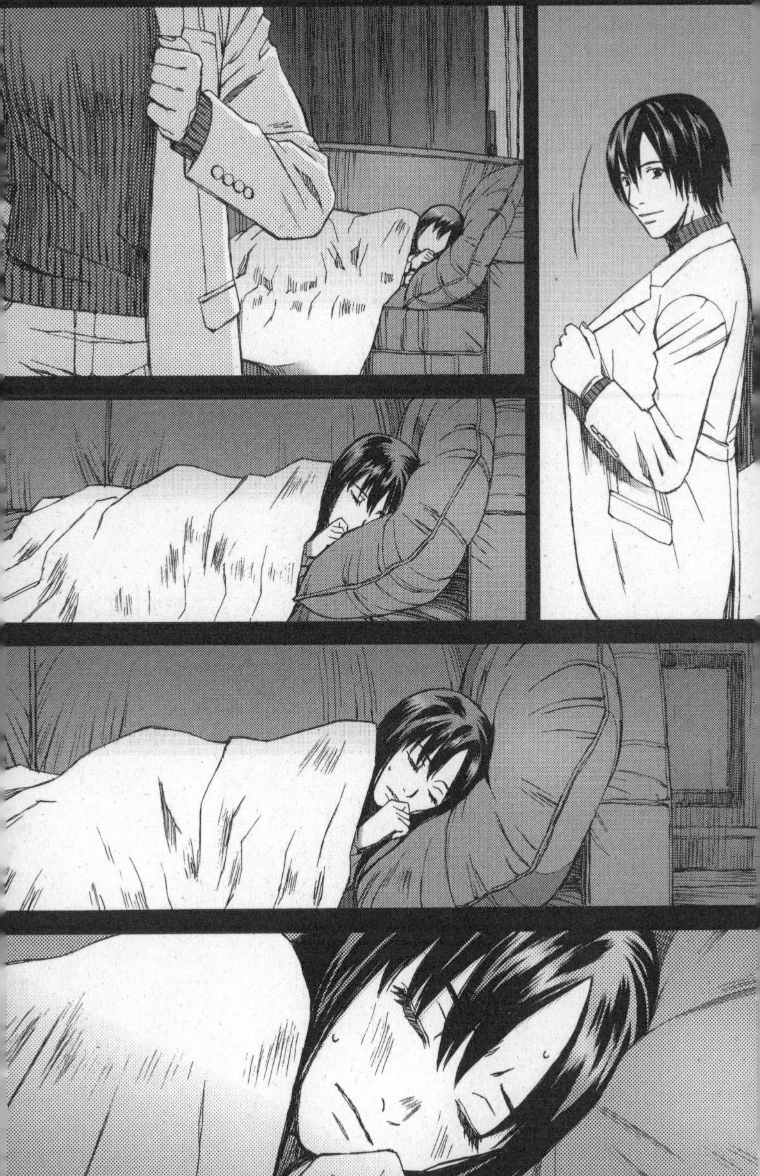

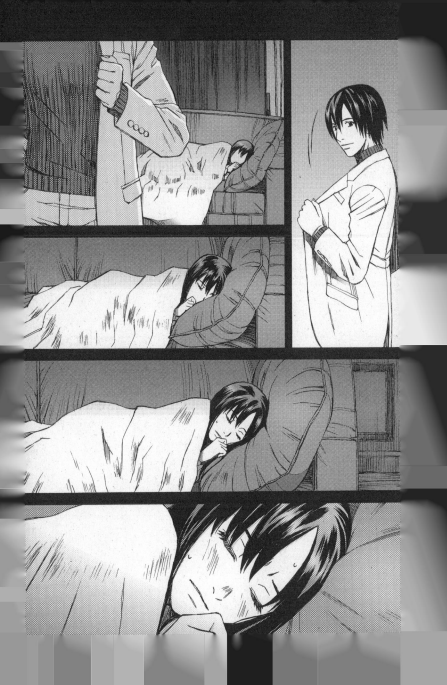

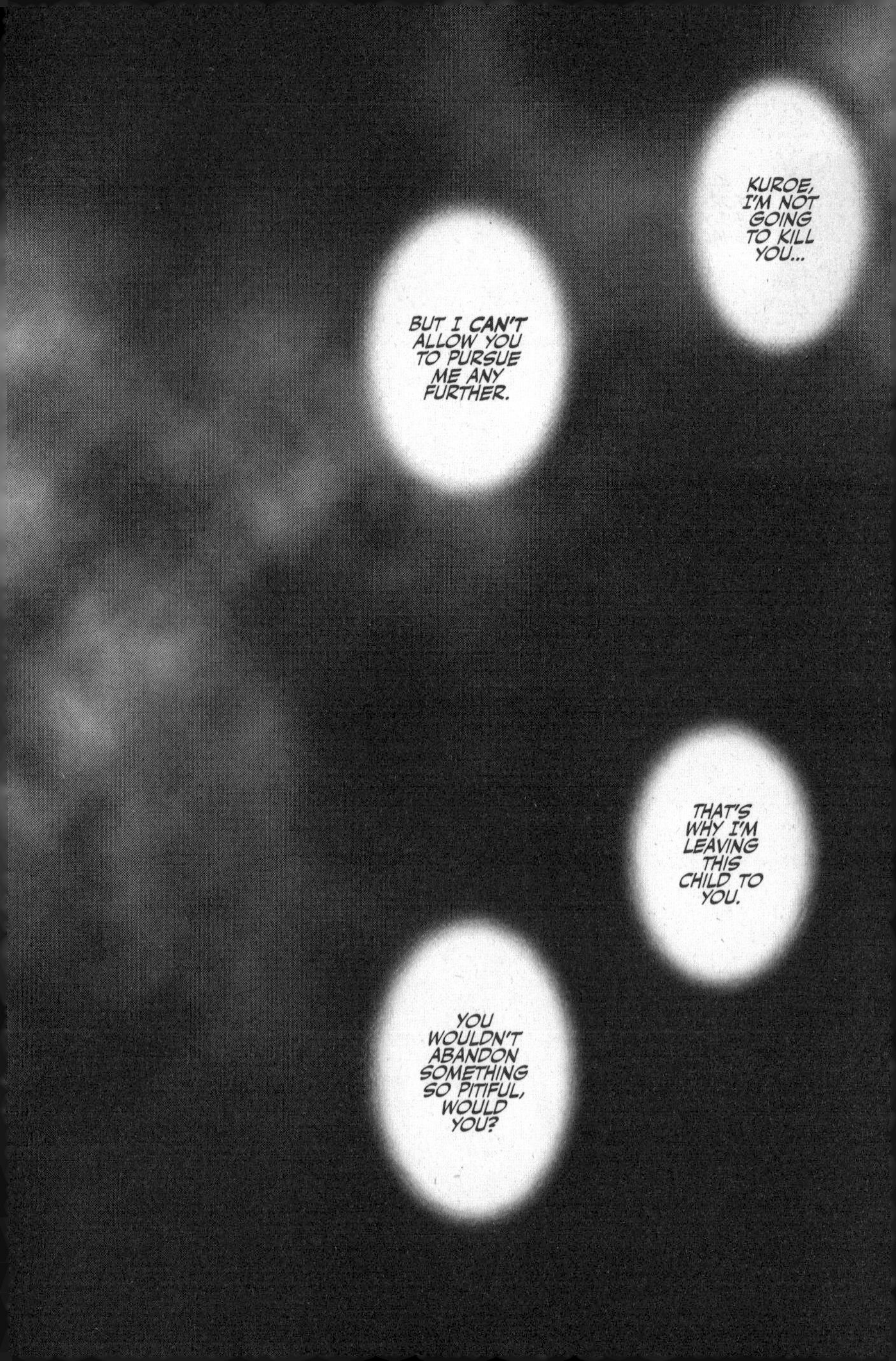
KUROE, I'M NOT GOING TO KILL YOU...
BUT I CAN'T ALLOW YOU TO PURSUE ME ANY FURTHER.
THAT'S WHY I'M LEAVING THIS CHILD TO YOU.
YOU WOULDN'T ABANDON SOMETHING SO PITIFUL, WOULD YOU?

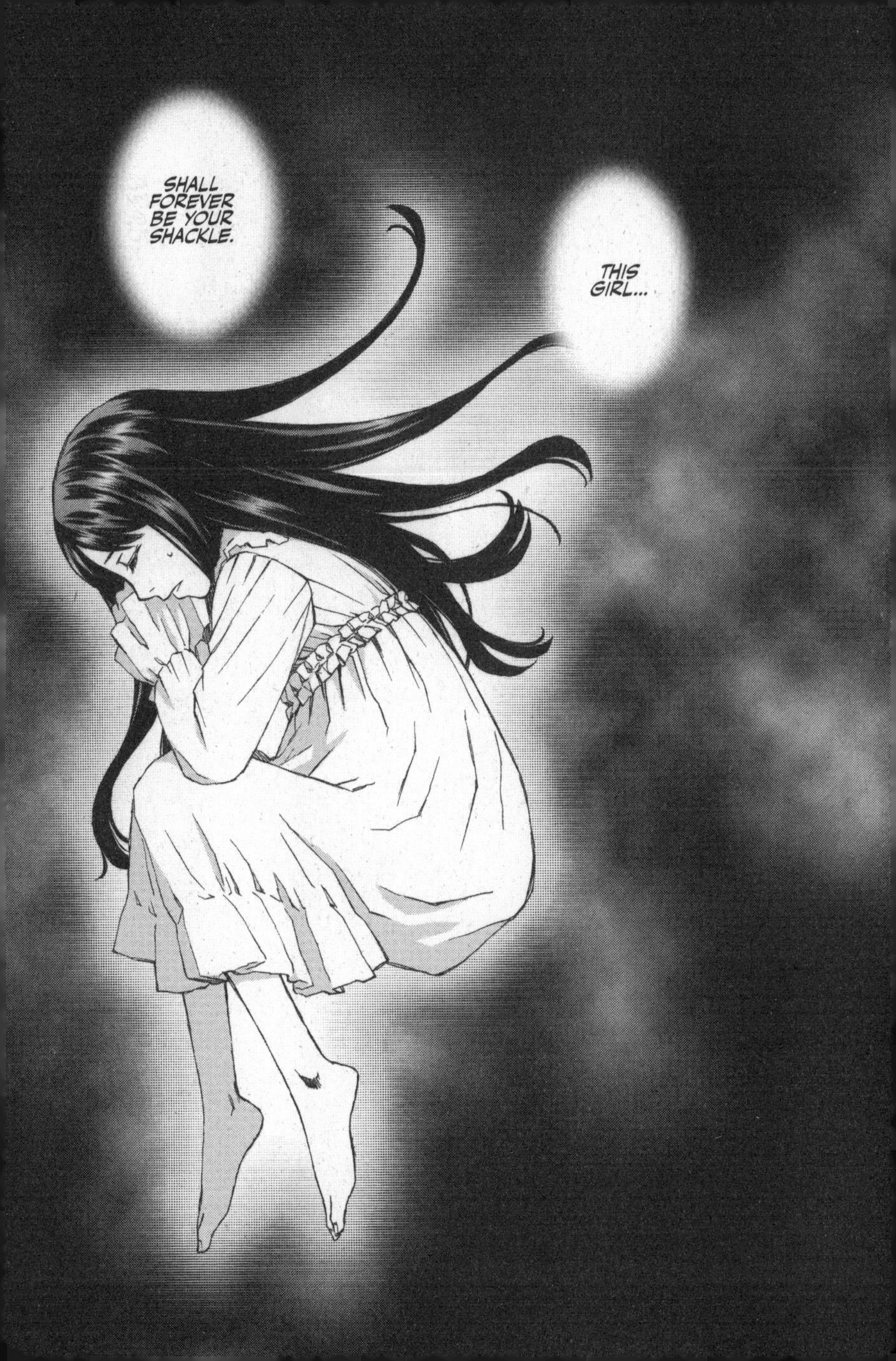
THIS GIRL...
SHALL FOREVER BE YOUR SHACKLE.

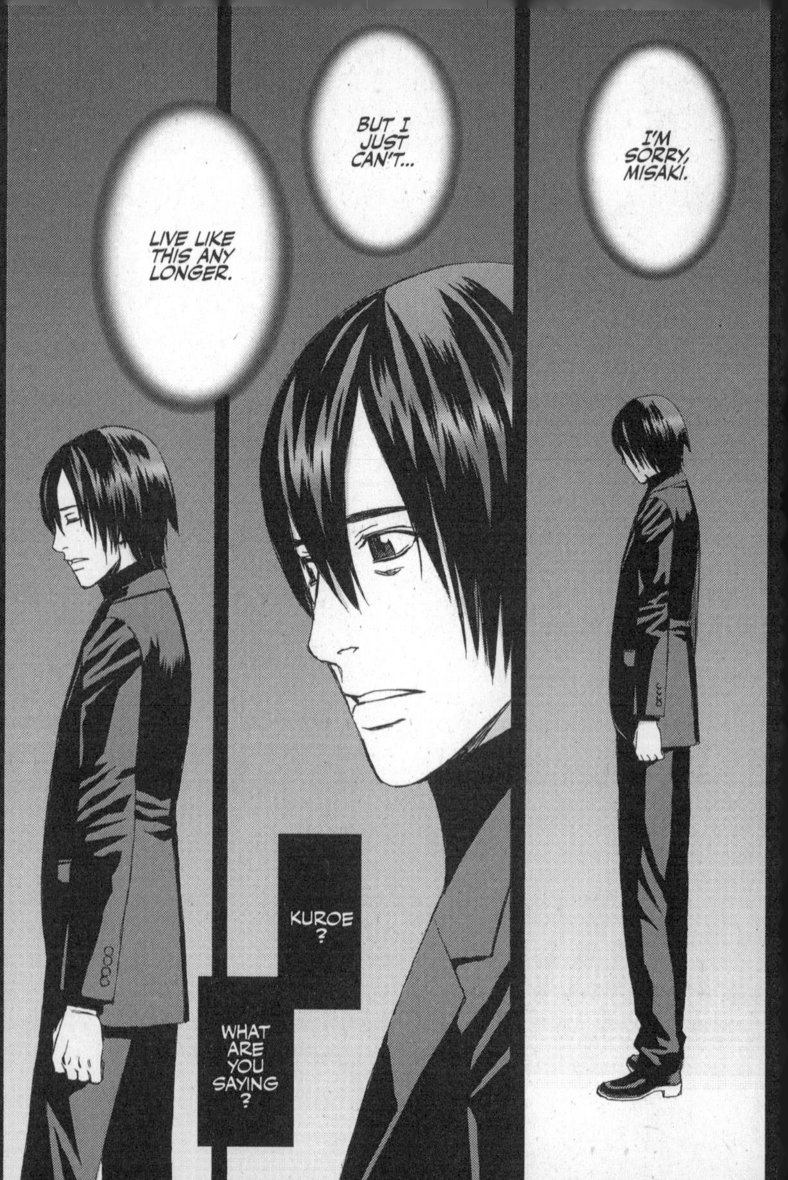
I'M SORRY, MISAKI.
BUT I JUST CAN'T...
KUROE?
WHAT ARE YOU SAYING?
LIVE LIKE THIS ANY LONGER.

I HAVE SOMEONE INCREDIBLY IMPORTANT TO ME THAT I'VE NEVER FORGOTTEN.
AND IT'S TIME I WENT AND FOUND HER.
SO...
TAKE CARE, MISAKI.
—!!
KUROE!!

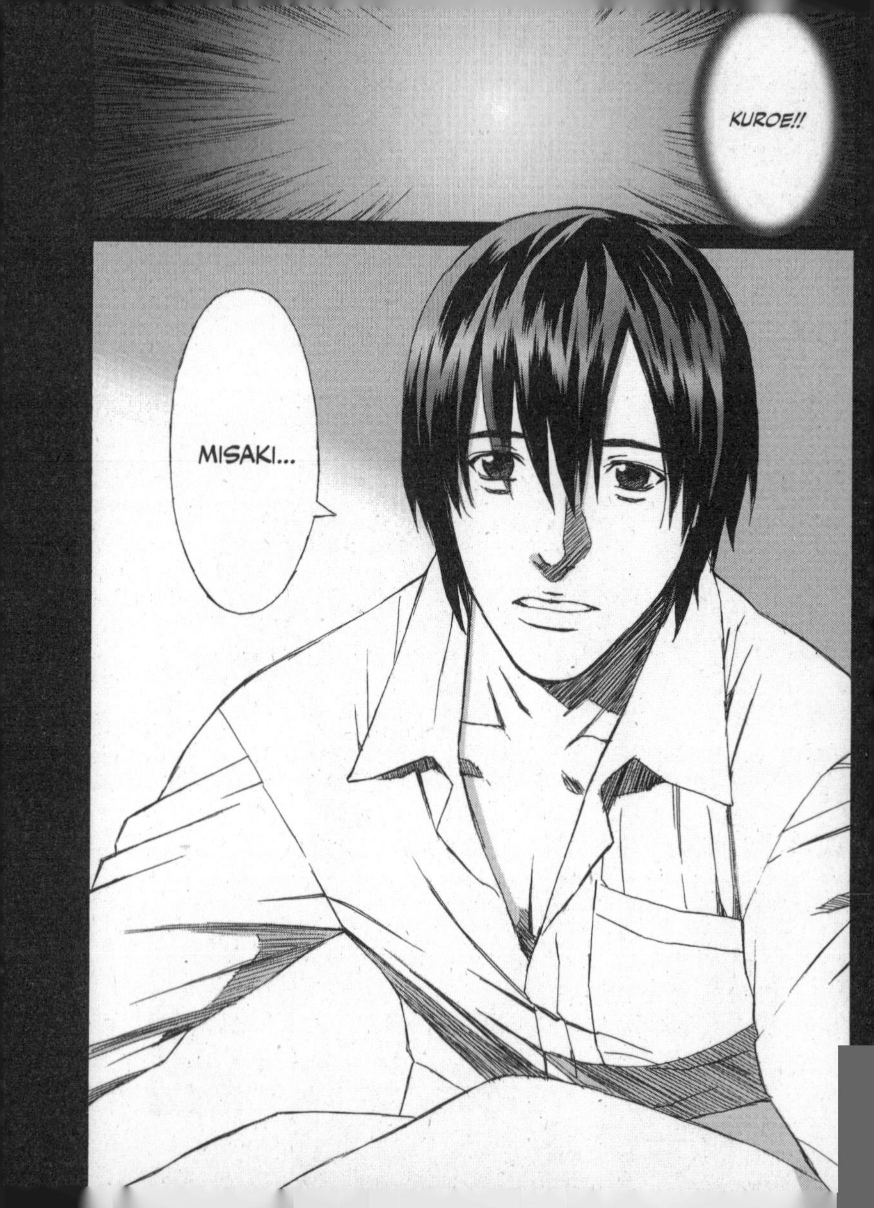
KUROE!!
MISAKI...

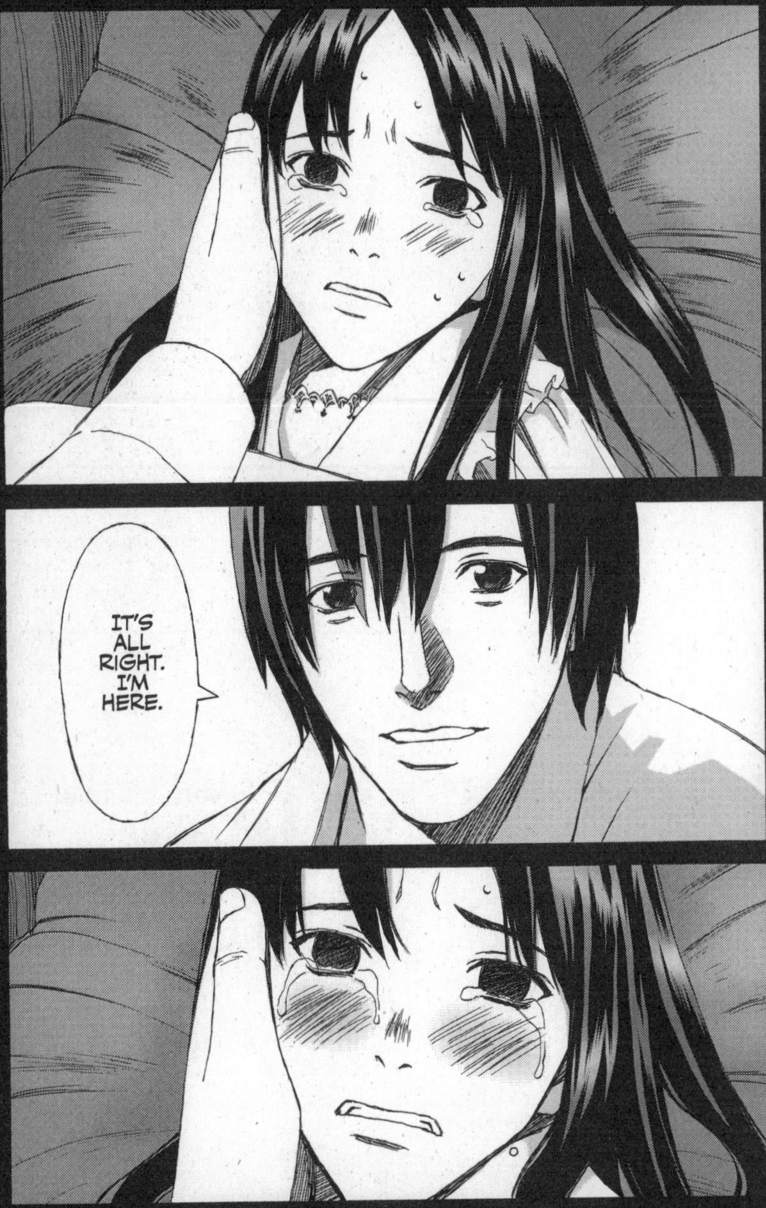
IT'S ALL RIGHT. I'M HERE.

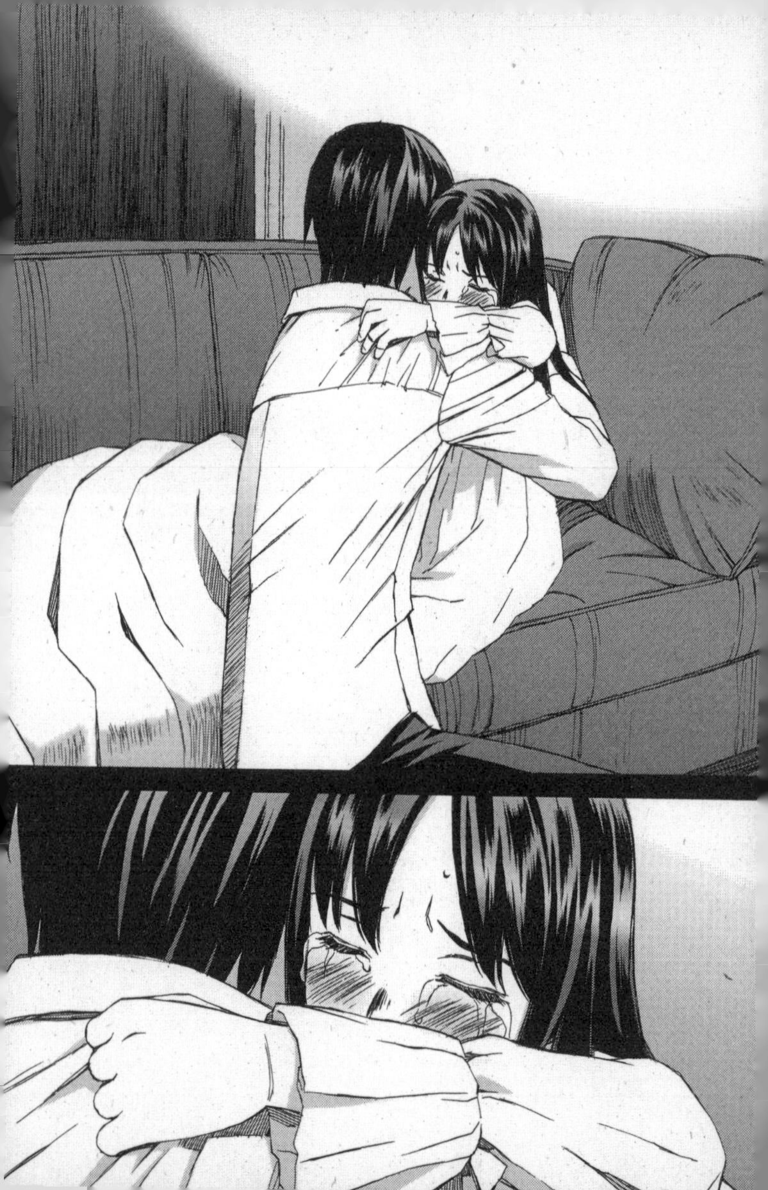

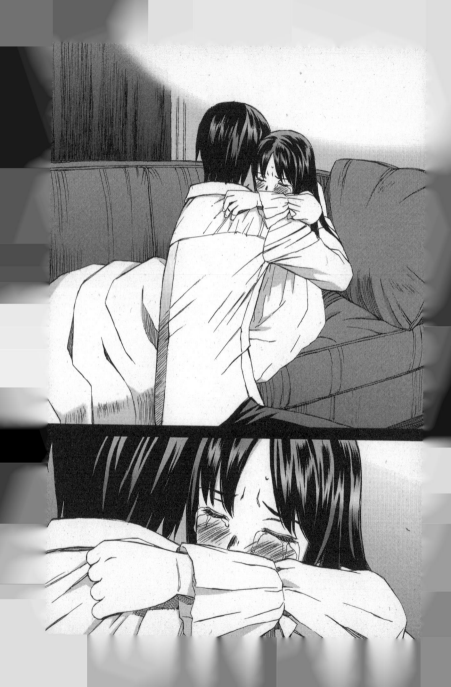

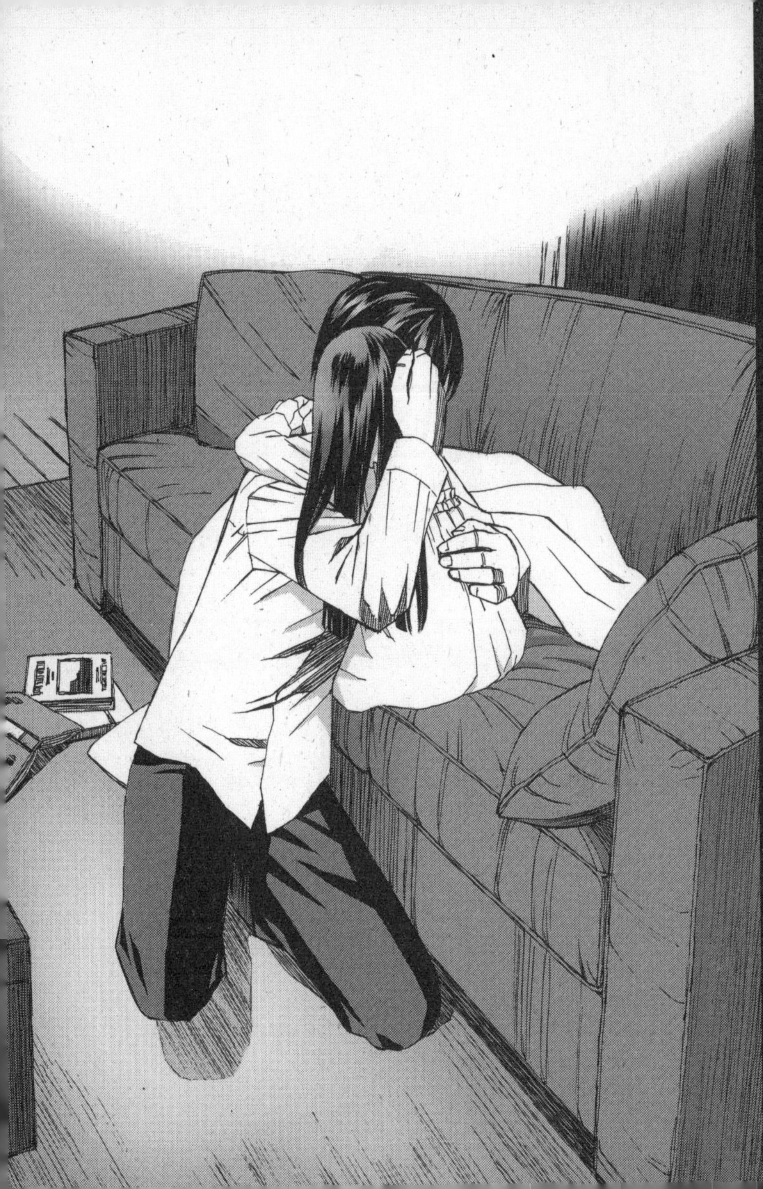

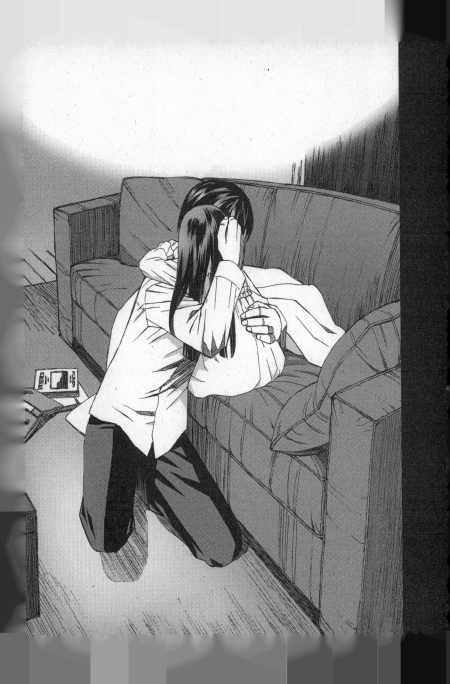

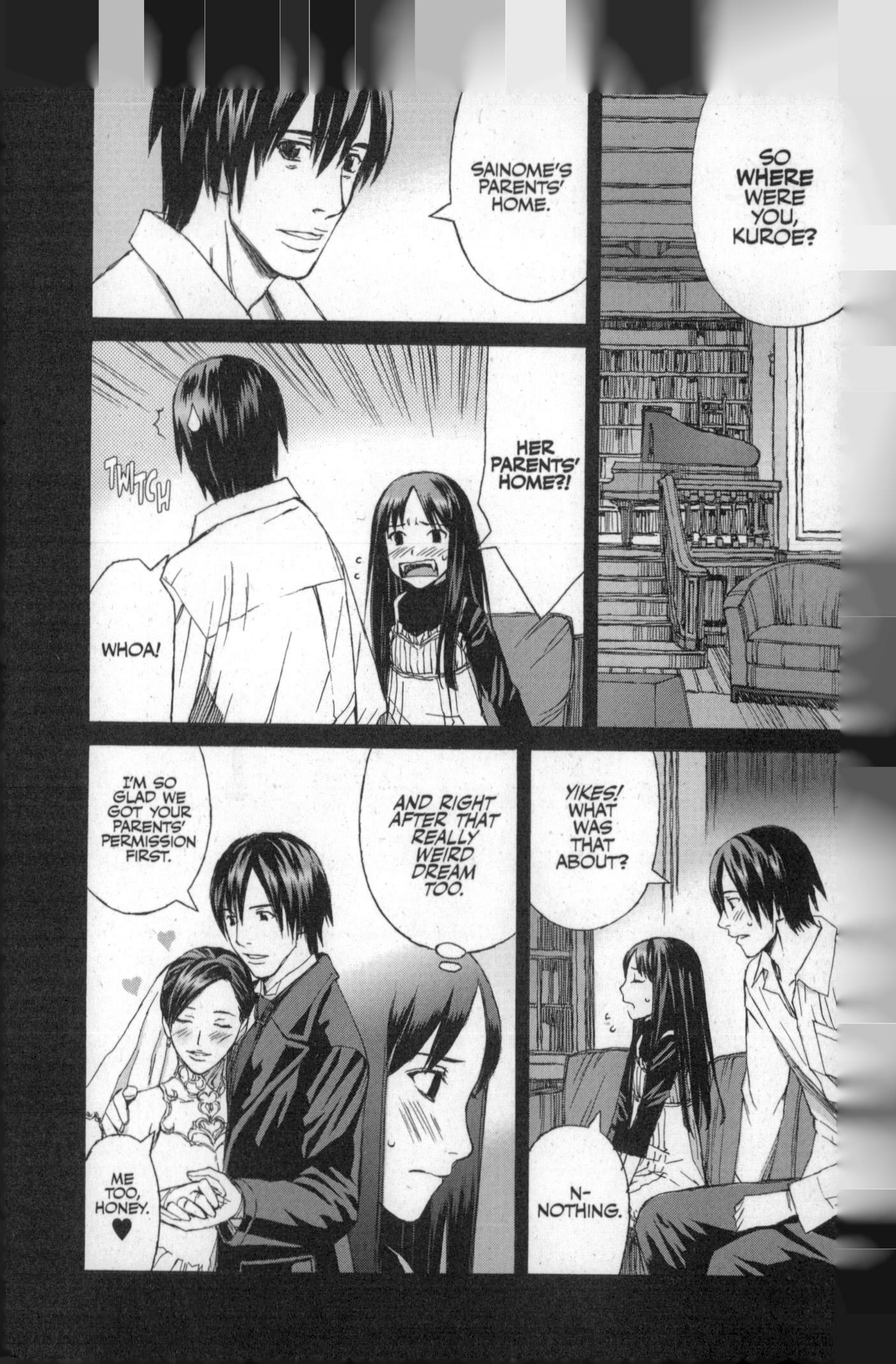
SO WHERE WERE YOU, KUROE?
SAINOME'S PARENTS' HOME.
HER PARENTS' HOME?!
TWITCH
WHOA!
YIKES! WHAT WAS THAT ABOUT?
N-NOTHING.
AND RIGHT AFTER THAT REALLY WEIRD DREAM TOO.
I'M SO GLAD WE GOT YOUR PARENTS' PERMISSION FIRST.
ME TOO, HONEY. ♥

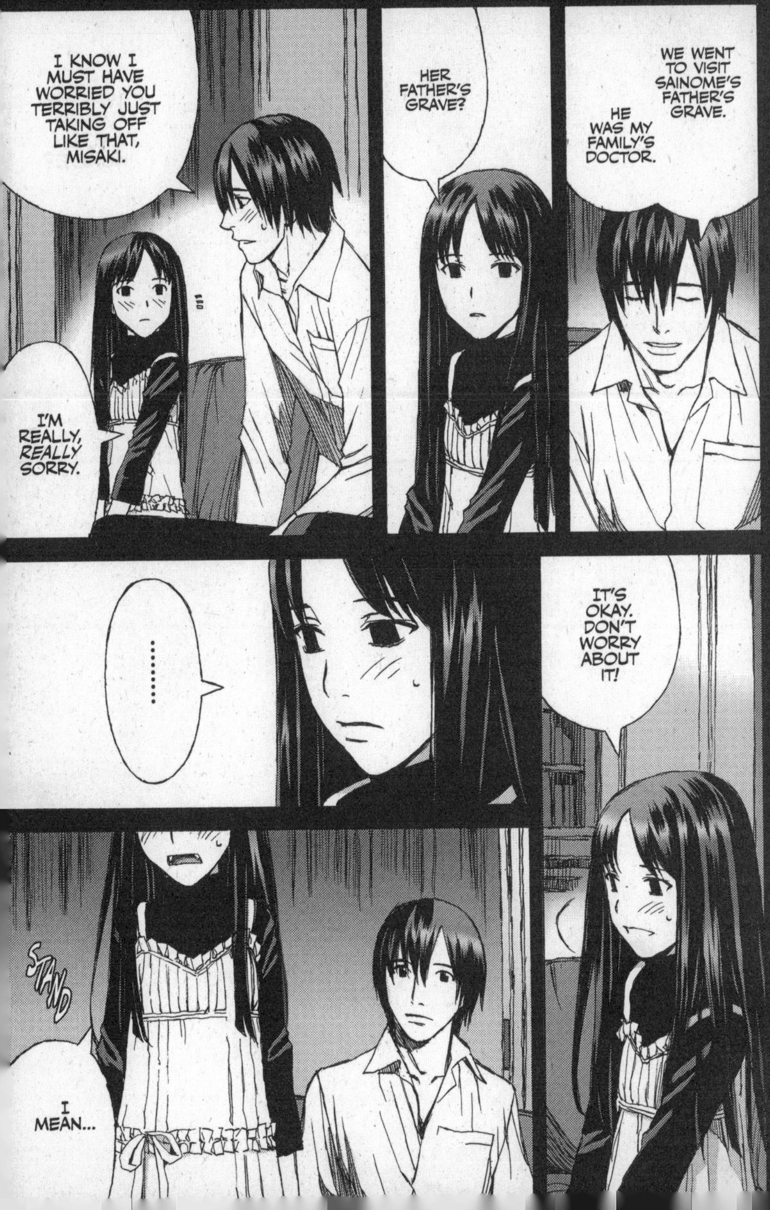
WE WENT TO VISIT SAINOME'S FATHER'S GRAVE.
HE WAS MY FAMILY'S DOCTOR.
HER FATHER'S GRAVE?
I KNOW I MUST HAVE WORRIED YOU TERRIBLY JUST TAKING OFF LIKE THAT, MISAKI.
I'M REALLY, *REALLY* SORRY.
IT'S OKAY. DON'T WORRY ABOUT IT!
......
STAND
I MEAN...

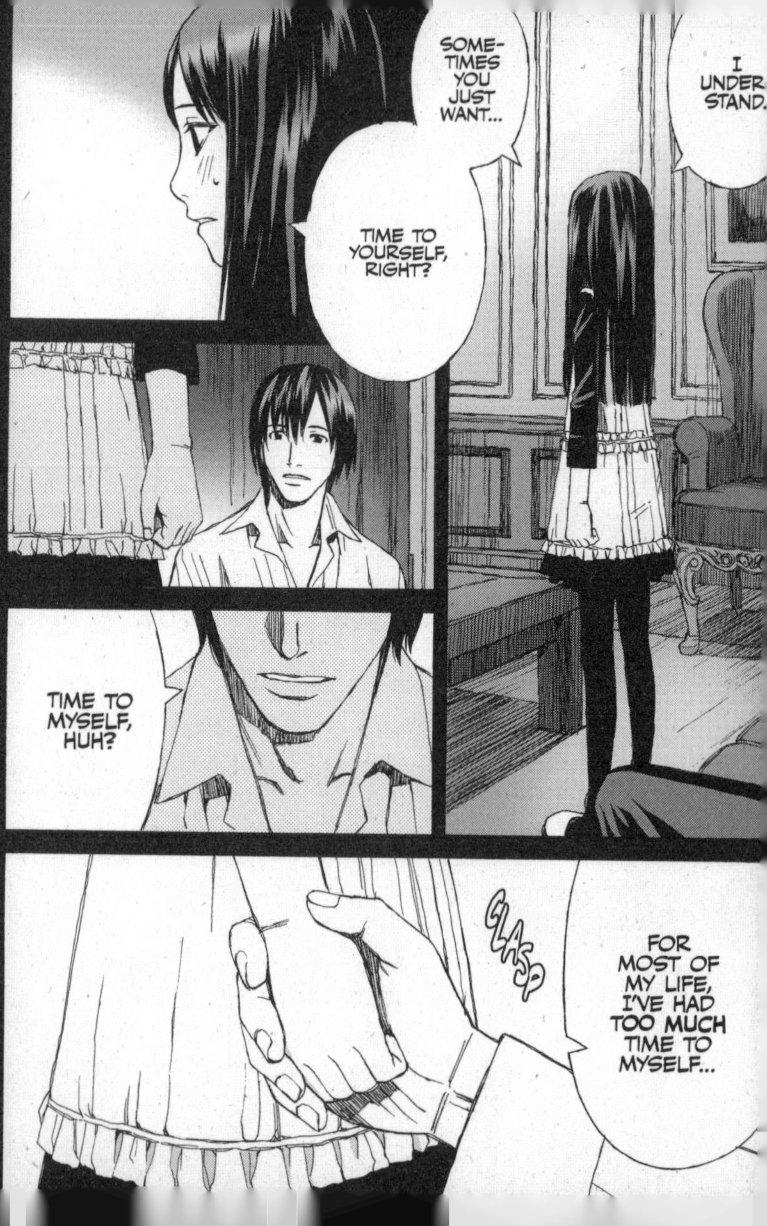
I UNDERSTAND.
SOMETIMES YOU JUST WANT...
TIME TO YOURSELF, RIGHT?
TIME TO MYSELF, HUH?
FOR MOST OF MY LIFE, I'VE HAD TOO MUCH TIME TO MYSELF...
CLASP

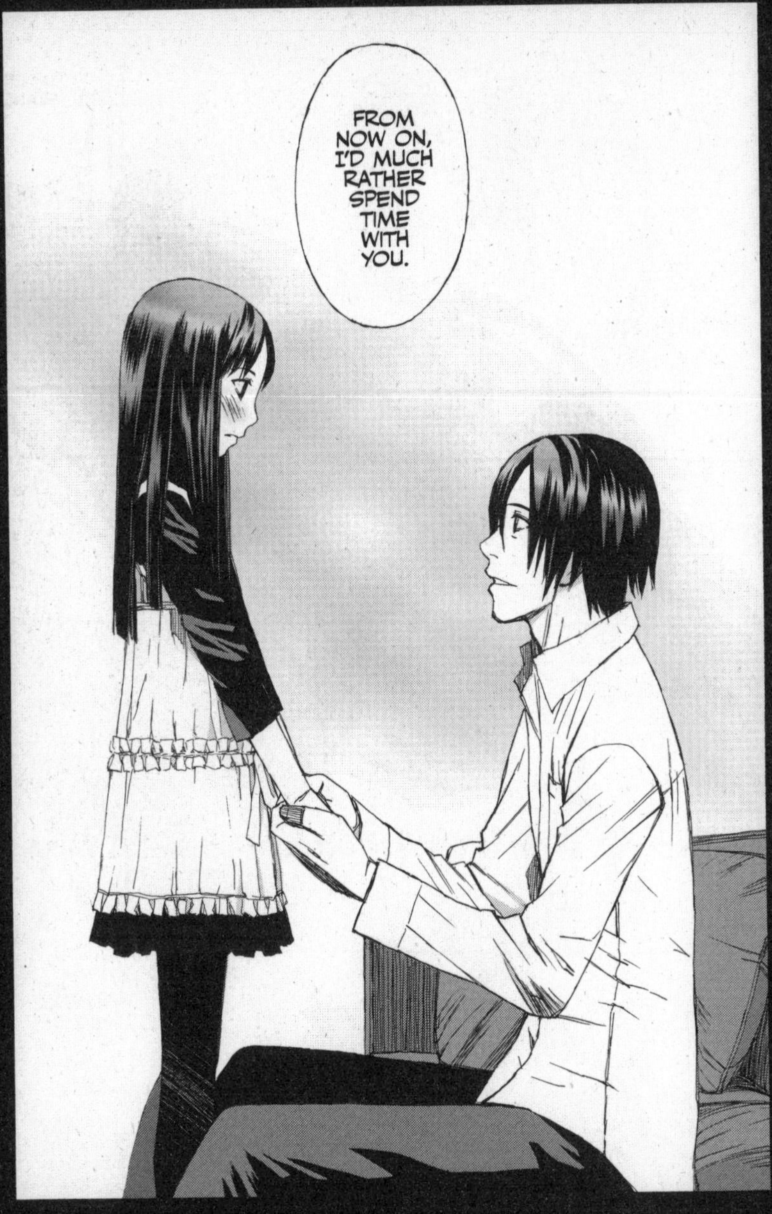
FROM NOW ON, I'D MUCH RATHER SPEND TIME WITH YOU.

Appendix

AFTER THE DANCE

Sainome Afterwards

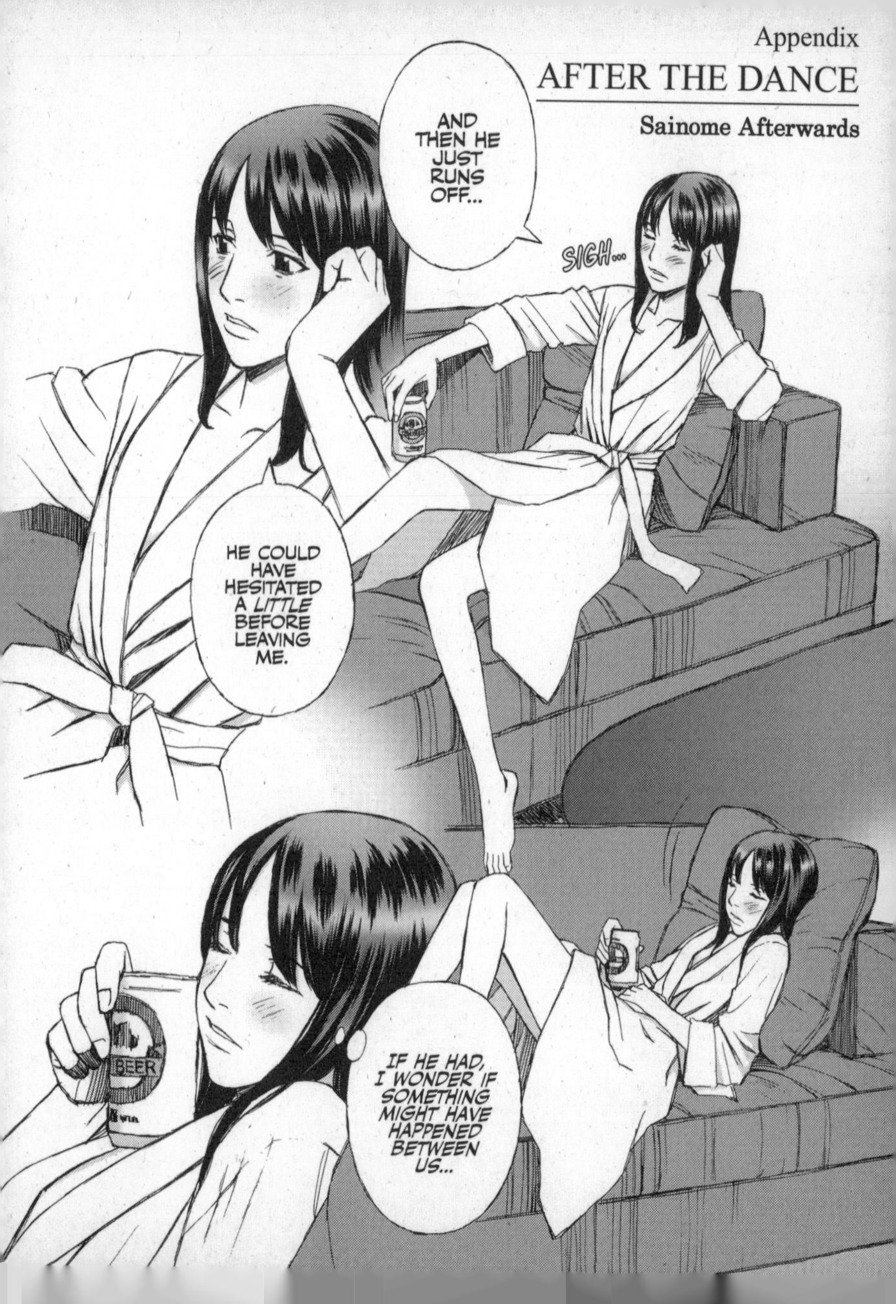
AND THEN HE JUST RUNS OFF...
SIGH...
HE COULD HAVE HESITATED A *LITTLE* BEFORE LEAVING ME.
BEER
IF HE HAD, I WONDER IF SOMETHING MIGHT HAVE HAPPENED BETWEEN US...

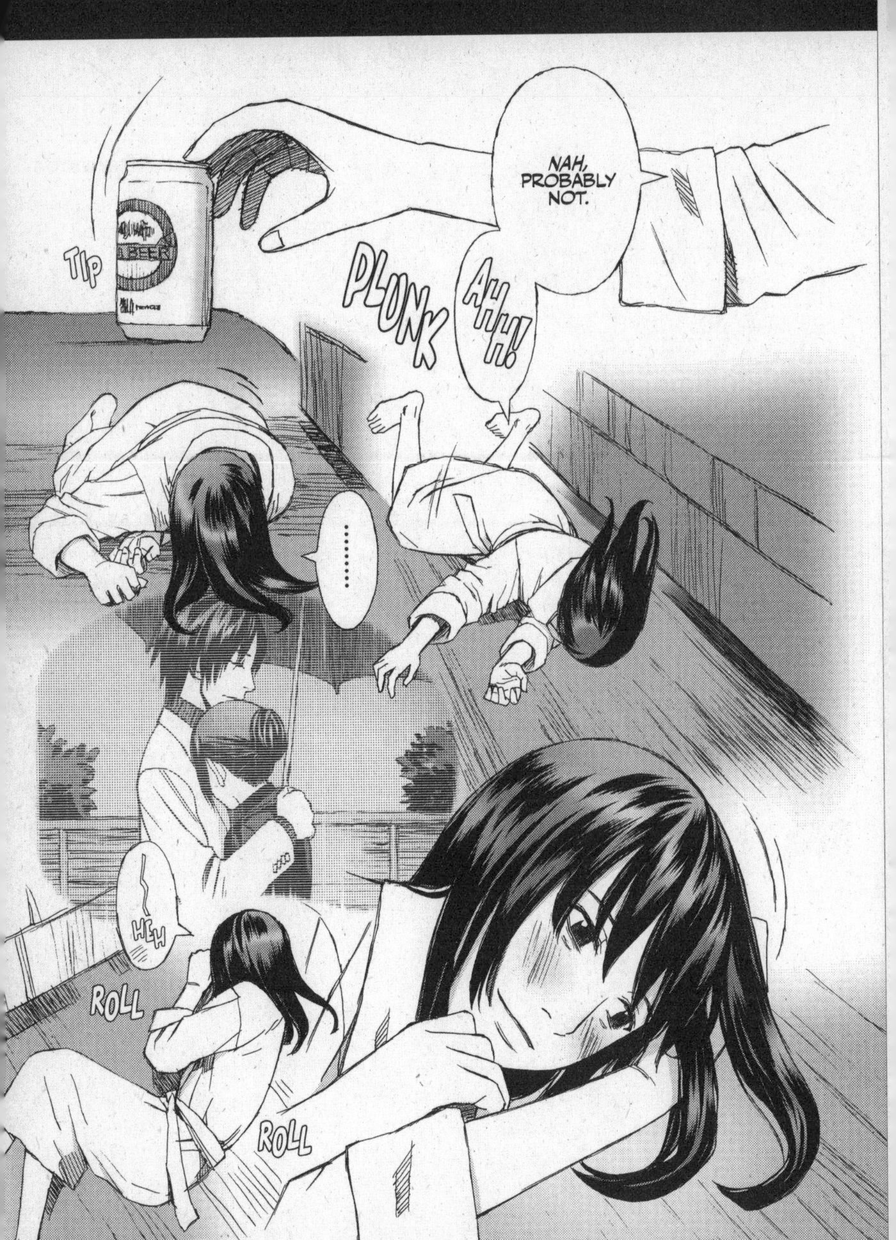
NAH, PROBABLY NOT.
AHH!
PLUNK
TIP
......
HEH
ROLL
ROLL
to be continued

TRANSLATION NOTES

Episode 1
Renfield – In *Blood Alone*, the term Renfield refers to humans who are bound to vampires by a taste of their blood. The name Renfield comes from a character in Bram Stoker's Dracula. In the book, Renfield is an insane man controlled by the title's famous vampire. Another common term often used in vampire fiction is a "thrall."

Episode 5
Shunin – An honorific similar to "boss."

Episode 18
Ojousama – The honorific Hana uses to address Sainome is one typically used for the daughter of a well-to-do family.

Ryokan – When Sainome says that her home feels like a fancy hotel, what she's actually referring to is a *ryokan*, a traditional Japanese inn.

Yukata – The *yukata* Kuroe is wearing is similar to ones guests at a *ryokan* would wear. It's a light kimono worn in the summer.

Blood Alone

Blood Alone

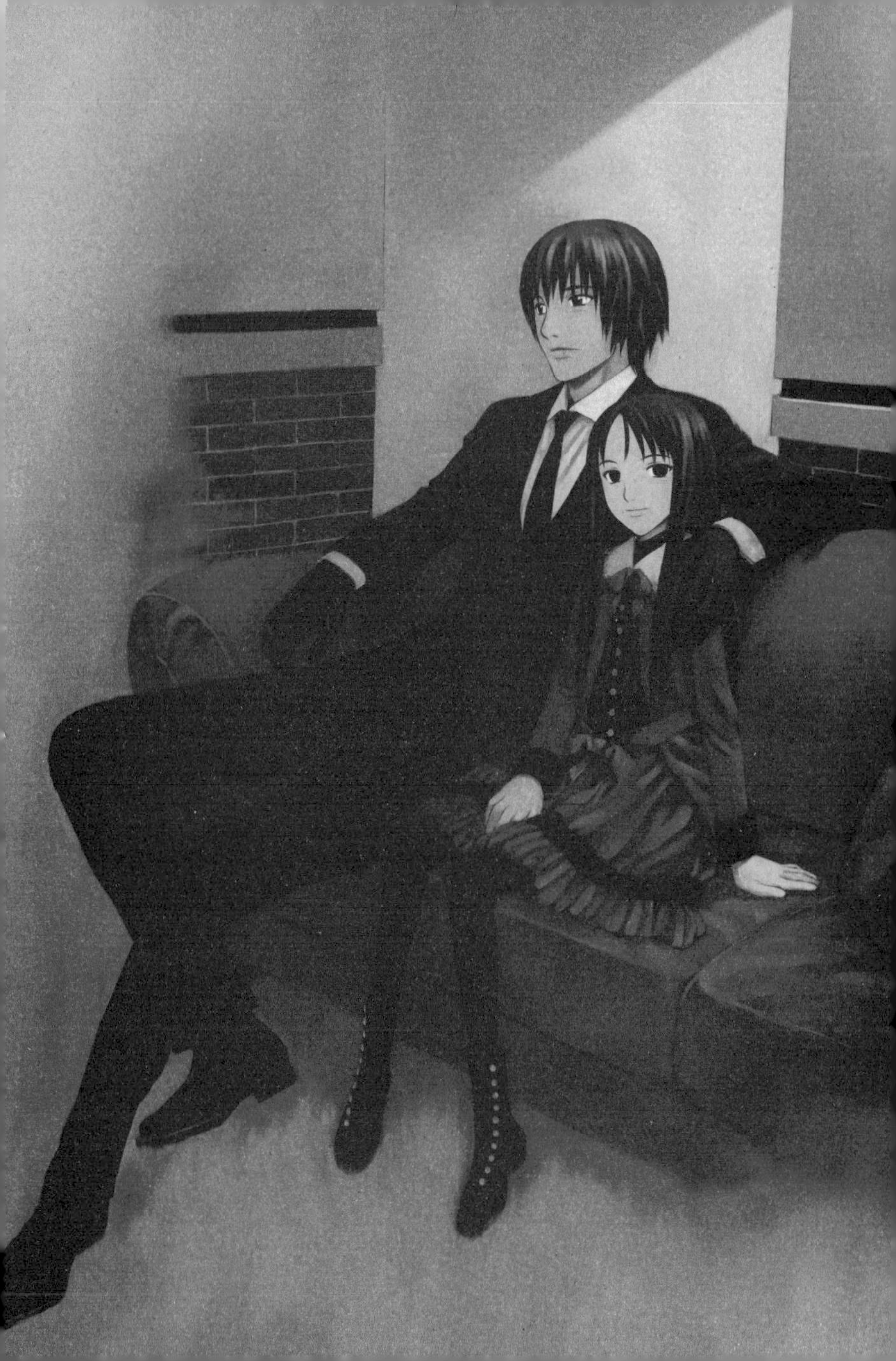

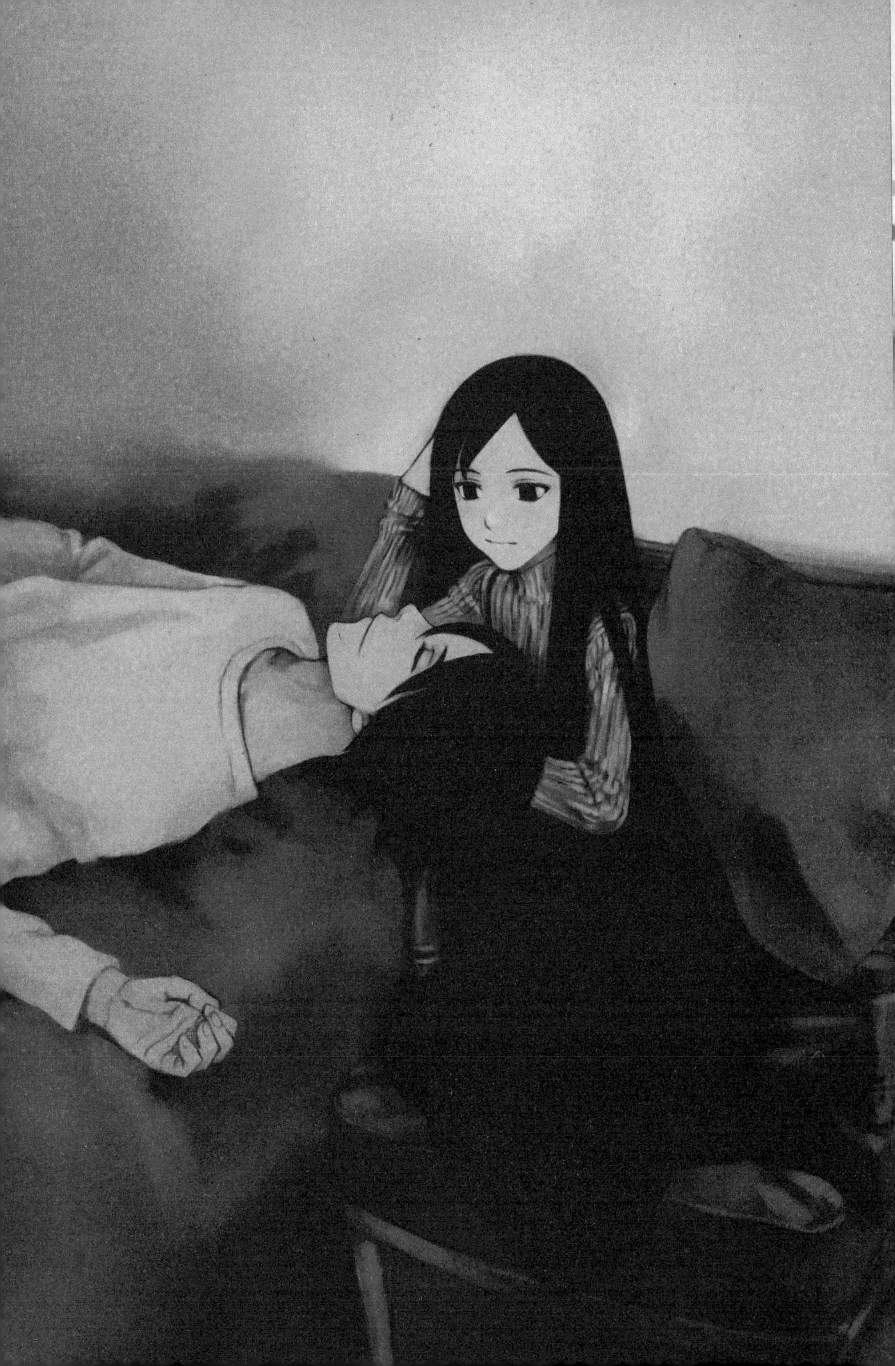

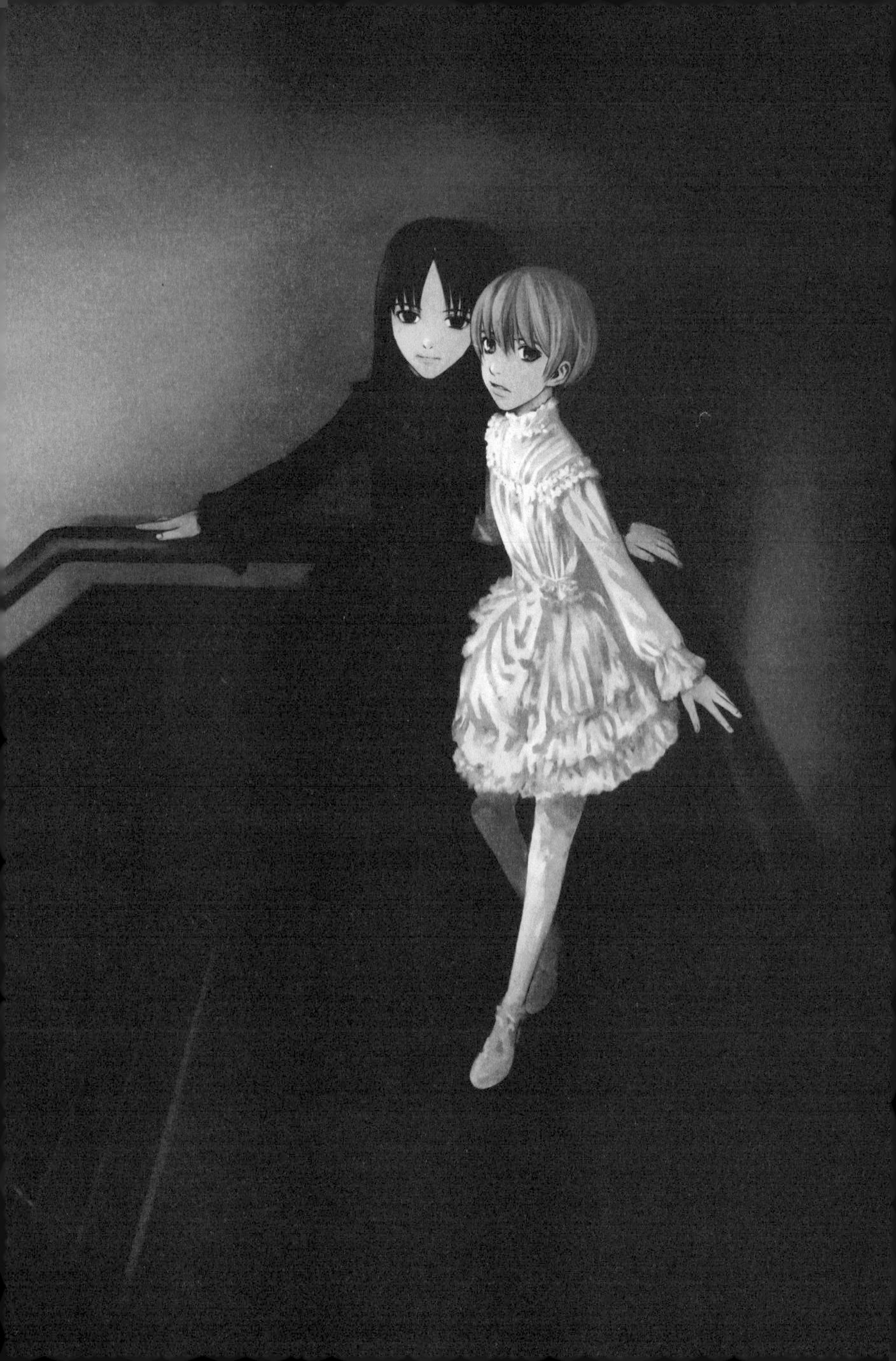

FROM THE TEAM THAT BROUGHT YOU AOI HOUSE COMES...
VAMPIRE
CHEERLEADERS
SPECIAL PREVIEW
Featuring art by Shiei, the artist of AMAZING AGENT LUNA!

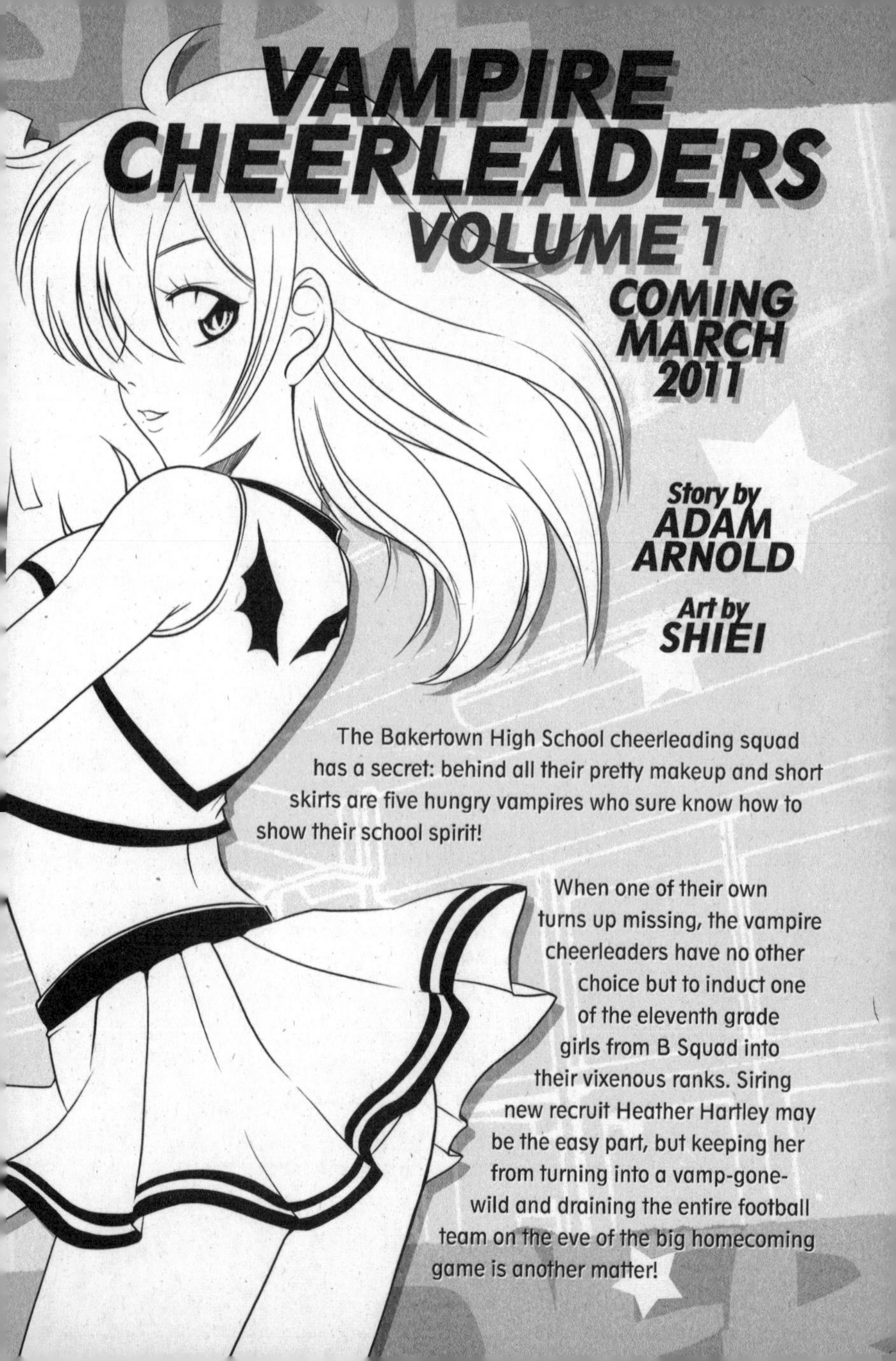
VAMPIRE CHEERLEADERS
VOLUME 1
COMING MARCH 2011
Story by ADAM ARNOLD
Art by SHIEI
The Bakertown High School cheerleading squad has a secret: behind all their pretty makeup and short skirts are five hungry vampires who sure know how to show their school spirit!
When one of their own turns up missing, the vampire cheerleaders have no other choice but to induct one of the eleventh grade girls from B Squad into their vixenous ranks. Siring new recruit Heather Hartley may be the easy part, but keeping her from turning into a vamp-gone-wild and draining the entire football team on the eve of the big homecoming game is another matter!

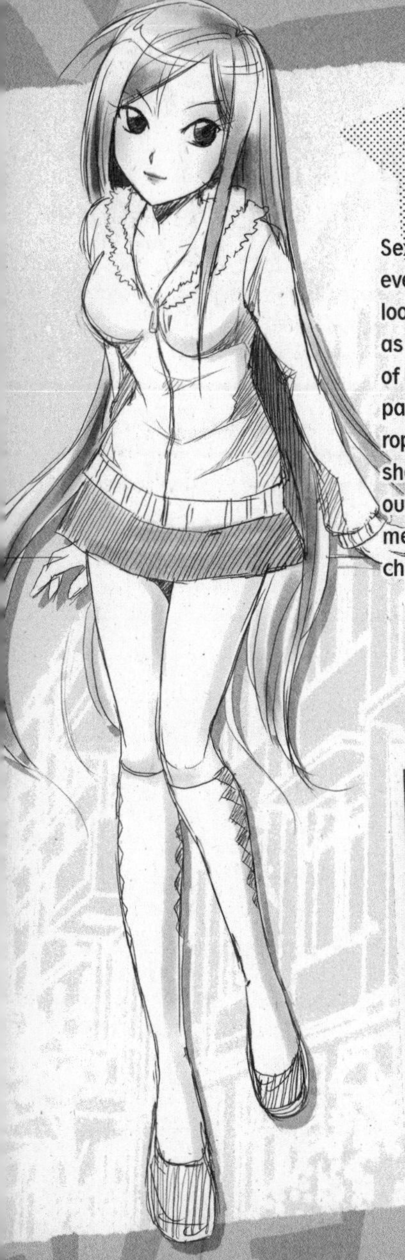

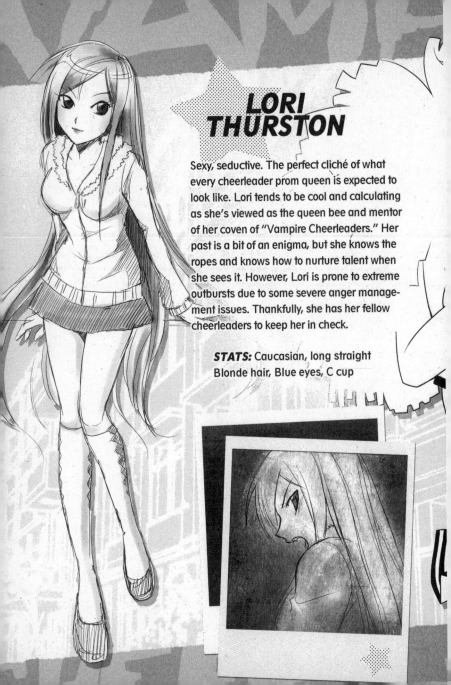

LORI THURSTON

Sexy, seductive. The perfect cliché of what every cheerleader prom queen is expected to look like. Lori tends to be cool and calculating as she's viewed as the queen bee and mentor of her coven of "Vampire Cheerleaders." Her past is a bit of an enigma, but she knows the ropes and knows how to nurture talent when she sees it. However, Lori is prone to extreme outbursts due to some severe anger management issues. Thankfully, she has her fellow cheerleaders to keep her in check.

STATS: Caucasian, long straight Blonde hair, Blue eyes, C cup

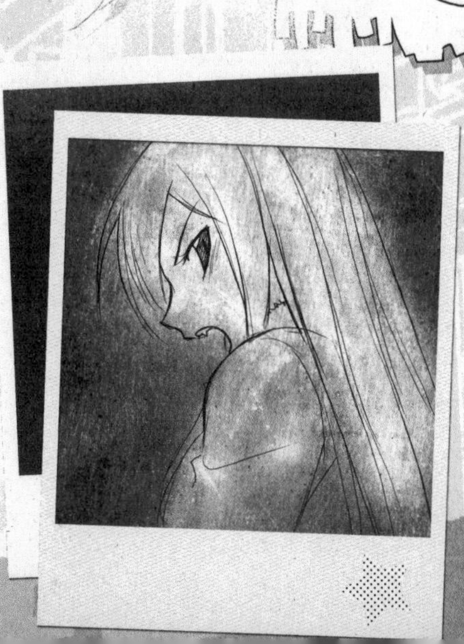

HEATHER HARTLEY

An eleventh grader on the B Squad who is seen as a goodie-two-shoes. Indeed, Heather's parents are overbearing and avid churchgoers, so Heather has lived a sheltered life. Once Heather gets turned into a vampire, however, a whole new world opens up for her.

STATS: Caucasian, Short (Petite), Brown hair done in a single pony tail in the back, Green eyes, B cup

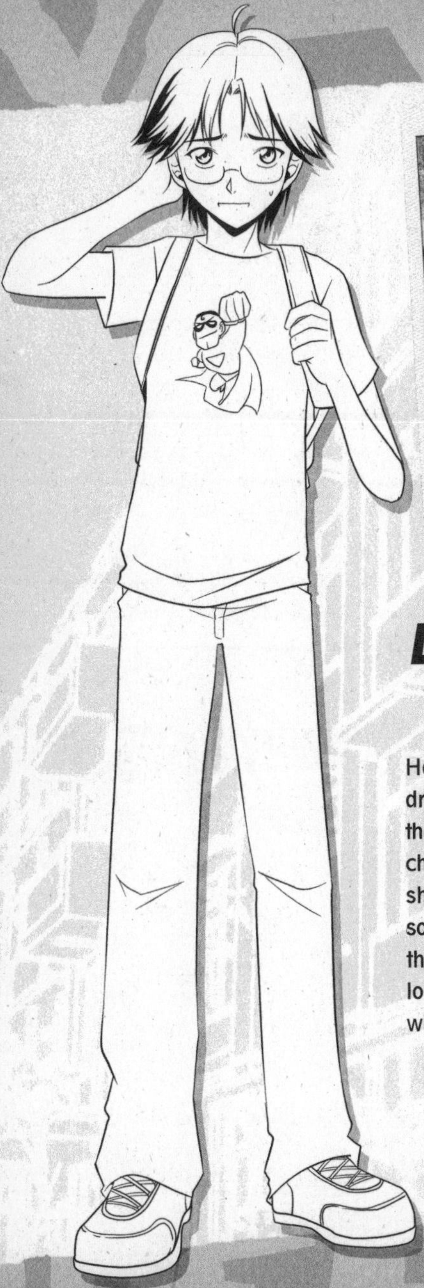

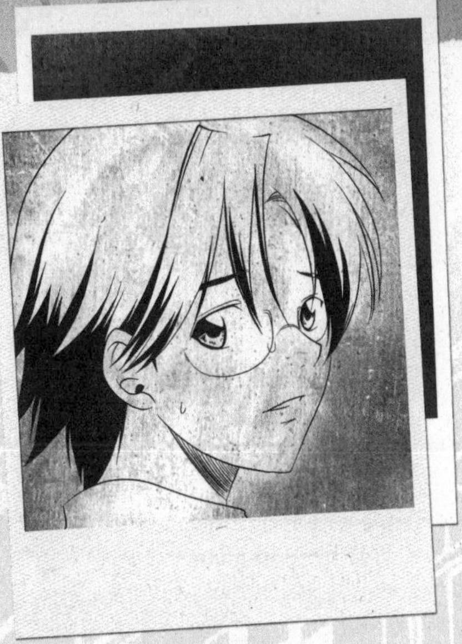

LEONARD DUVALL

Heather's best friend. A geek that dresses in fandom t-shirts and swears that he's discovered that the Bakertown cheerleaders are all vampires. Kinda shy/nervous. Has a crush on Heather, so it breaks his heart to see her go from the sweet girl he's crushed on for so long into a wild creature of the night with loose morals.

STATS: Caucasian, Brown hair, Blue eyes.

ZOE WELLER
CO-CAPTAIN

Zoe has a good head on her shoulders and is Lori's right-hand woman. Unfortunately, Zoe seems to get rubbed the wrong way by Suki at every turn. The two always seem to be at each other's throats over the most trivial things. Playful rivalry? Or something else...?

STATS: African American, Brown/Black hair, Brown eyes, C cup

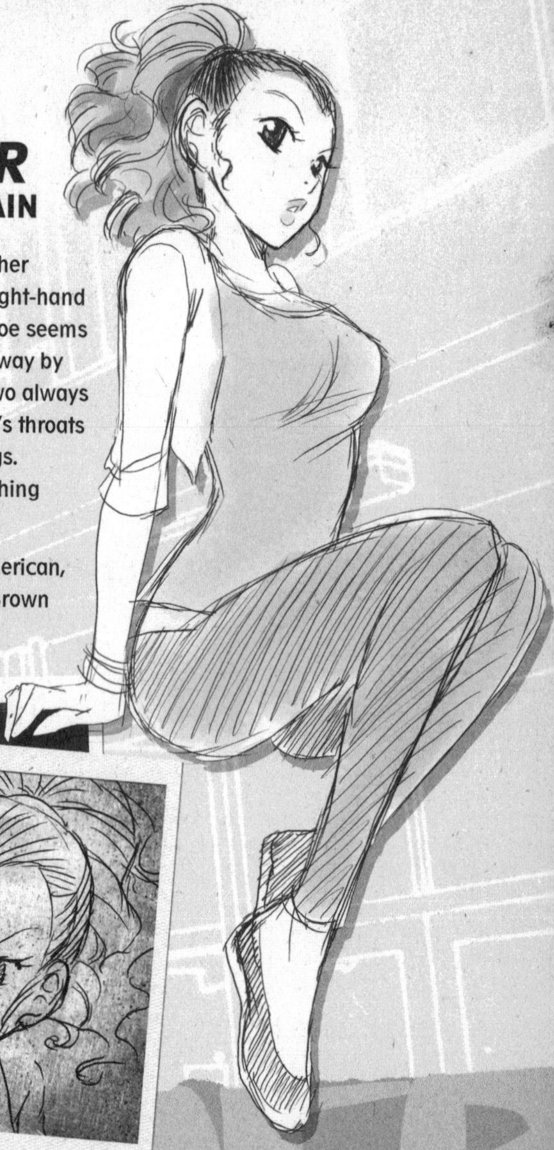

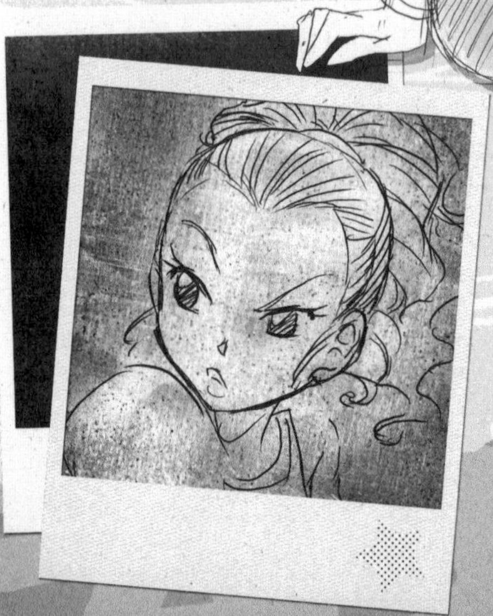

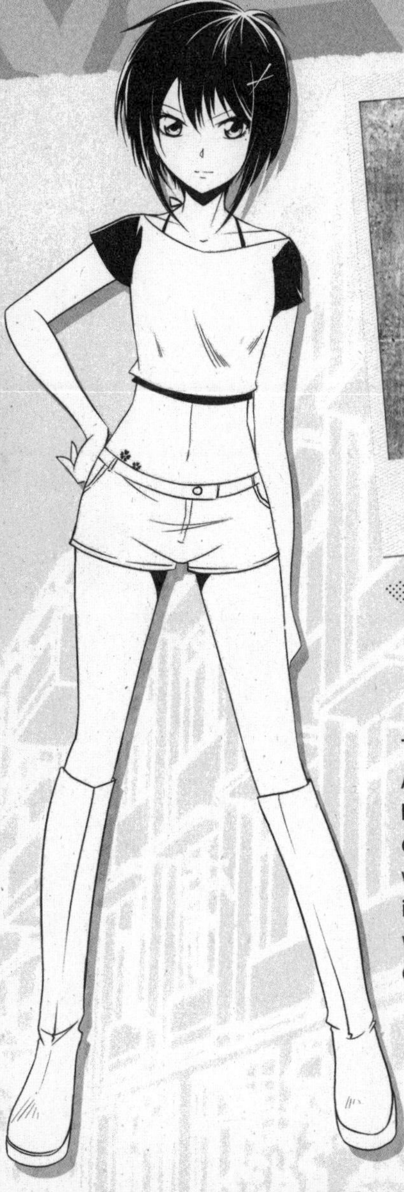

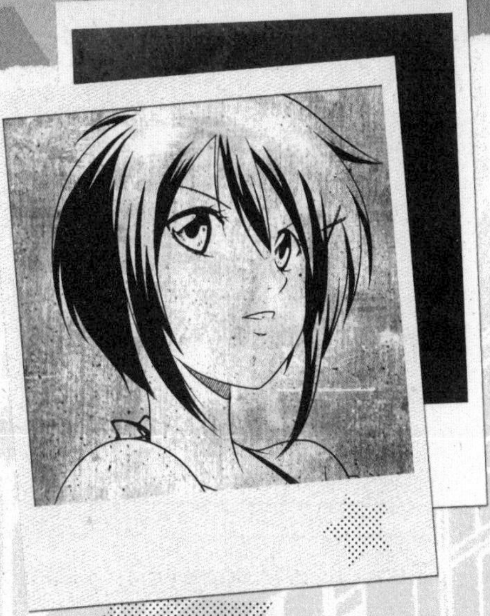

SUKI TAFT

CO-CAPTAIN

The bad seed. She knows guys dig Asian chicks and she knows just how to use her talents to bleed 'em dry (pun intended). Always saying whatever's on her mind...even when it's totally inappropriate and the wrong thing at the wrong time. Has a friendly(?) rivalry with Zoe.

STATS: Asian American, Black hair with highlights, Brown eyes but sometimes wears colored contacts, A cup

LESLEY CHANDRA
TEAM TREASURER

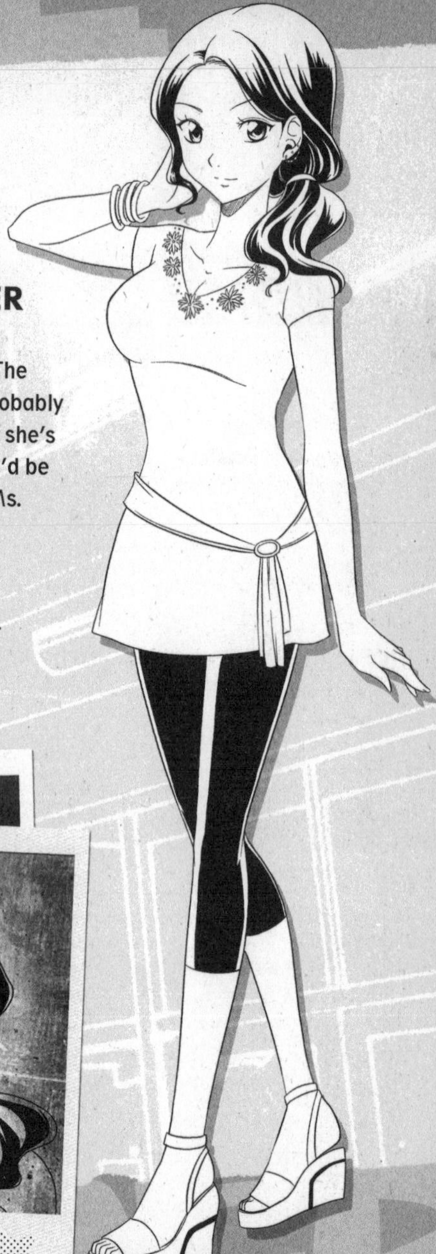

Pleasant personality, friendly. The voice of reason in the group. Probably the smartest of all the girls. But she's also got a wild side. In fact, you'd be surprised to know that she's "Ms. Kama Sutra" in a cheerleading costume.

STATS: East Indian American, Black/Brown hair, Brown eyes, D cup

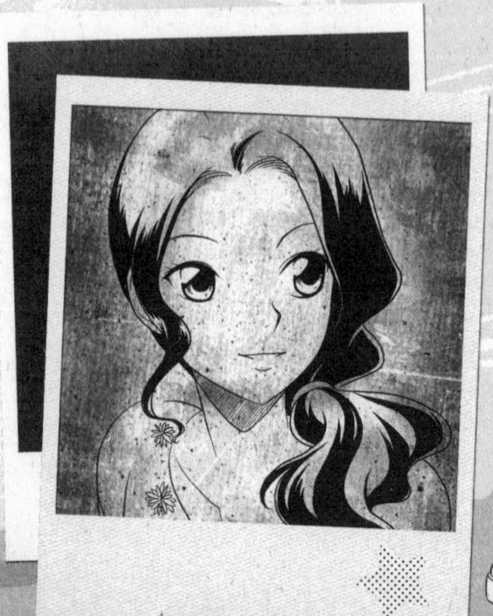

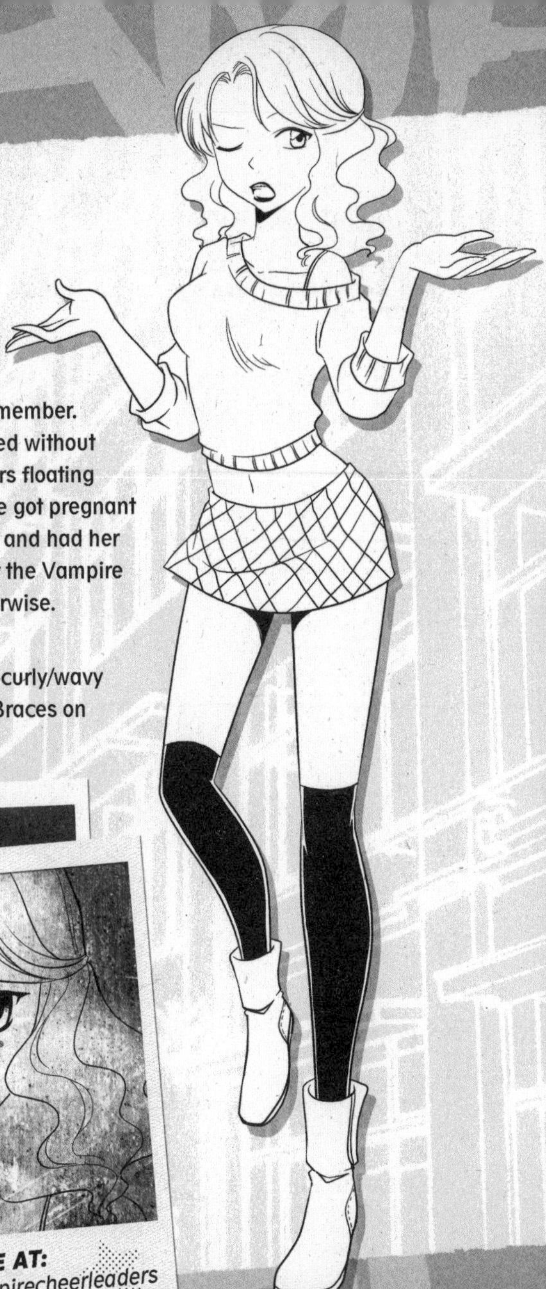

CANDICE

The team's former fifth member. She's up and disappeared without a trace. One of the rumors floating around school is that she got pregnant and her parents freaked and had her sent to a monastery. But the Vampire Cheerleaders know otherwise.

STATS: Caucasian, semi-curly/wavy hair, Brown eyes, C cup, Braces on her teeth.

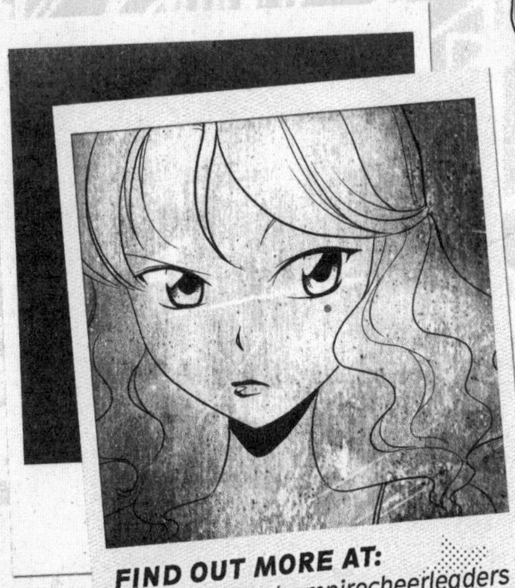

FIND OUT MORE AT:
facebook.com/vampirecheerleaders

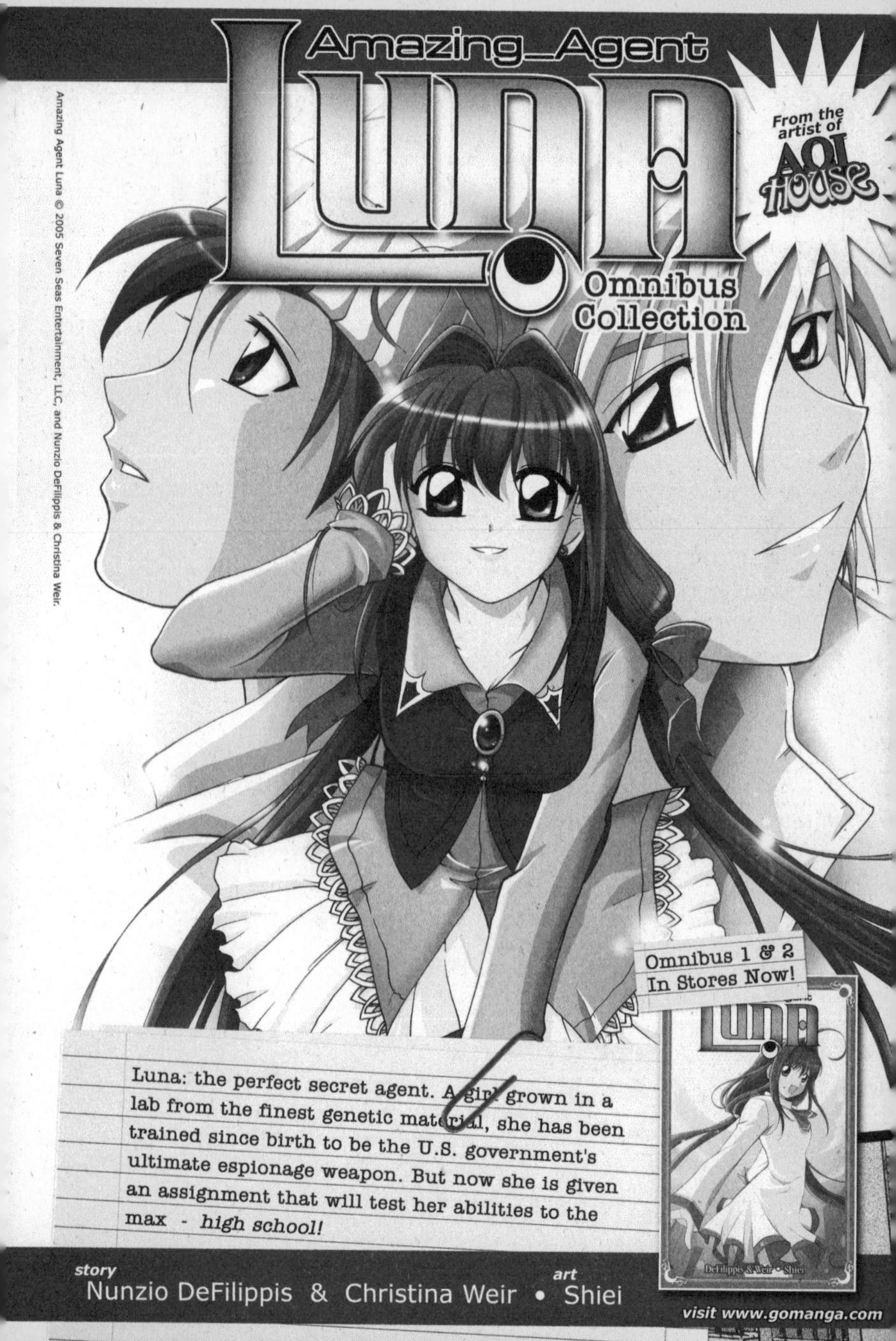

Amazing Agent
Luna
Omnibus Collection
From the artist of AOI House
Omnibus 1 & 2 In Stores Now!
Luna: the perfect secret agent. A girl grown in a lab from the finest genetic material, she has been trained since birth to be the U.S. government's ultimate espionage weapon. But now she is given an assignment that will test her abilities to the max - *high school!*
story Nunzio DeFilippis & Christina Weir • art Shiei
DeFilippis & Weir • Shiei
visit www.gomanga.com
Amazing Agent Luna © 2005 Seven Seas Entertainment, LLC, and Nunzio DeFilippis & Christina Weir.

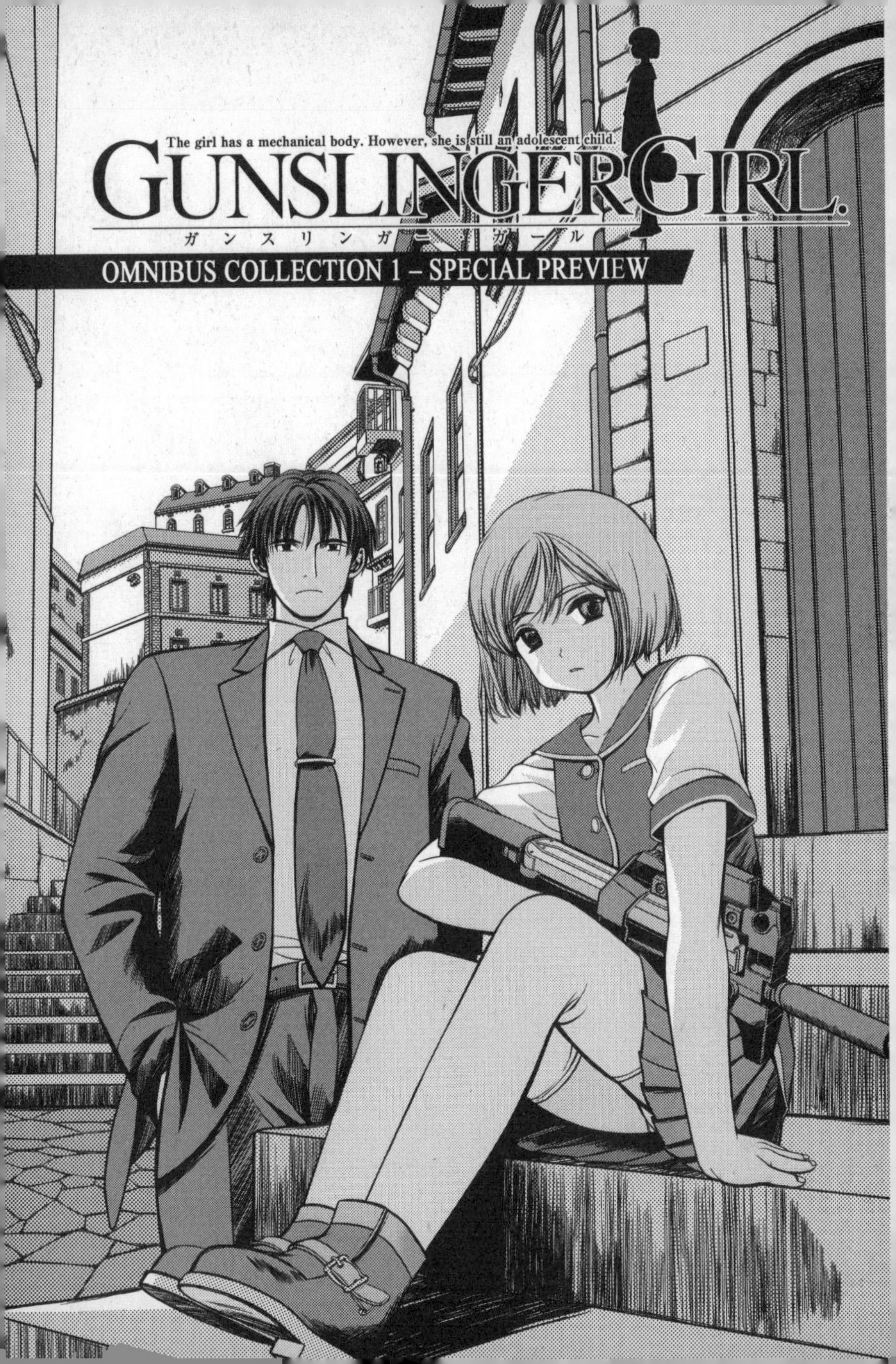
The girl has a mechanical body. However, she is still an adolescent child.
GUNSLINGER GIRL.
ガンスリンガー ガール
OMNIBUS COLLECTION 1 – SPECIAL PREVIEW

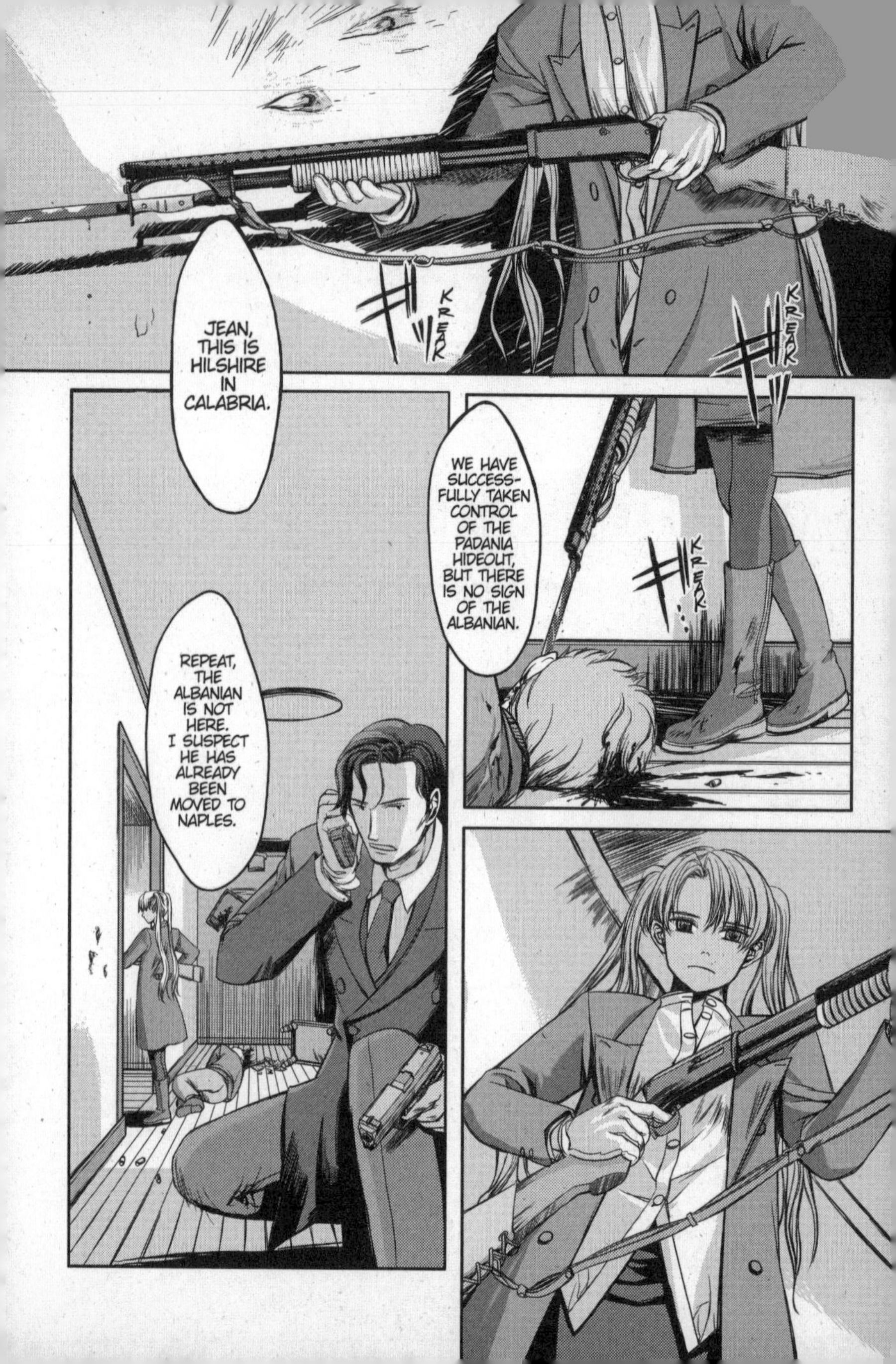
KREAK
KREAK
JEAN, THIS IS HILSHIRE IN CALABRIA.
WE HAVE SUCCESSFULLY TAKEN CONTROL OF THE PADANIA HIDEOUT, BUT THERE IS NO SIGN OF THE ALBANIAN.
KREAK...
REPEAT, THE ALBANIAN IS NOT HERE. I SUSPECT HE HAS ALREADY BEEN MOVED TO NAPLES.

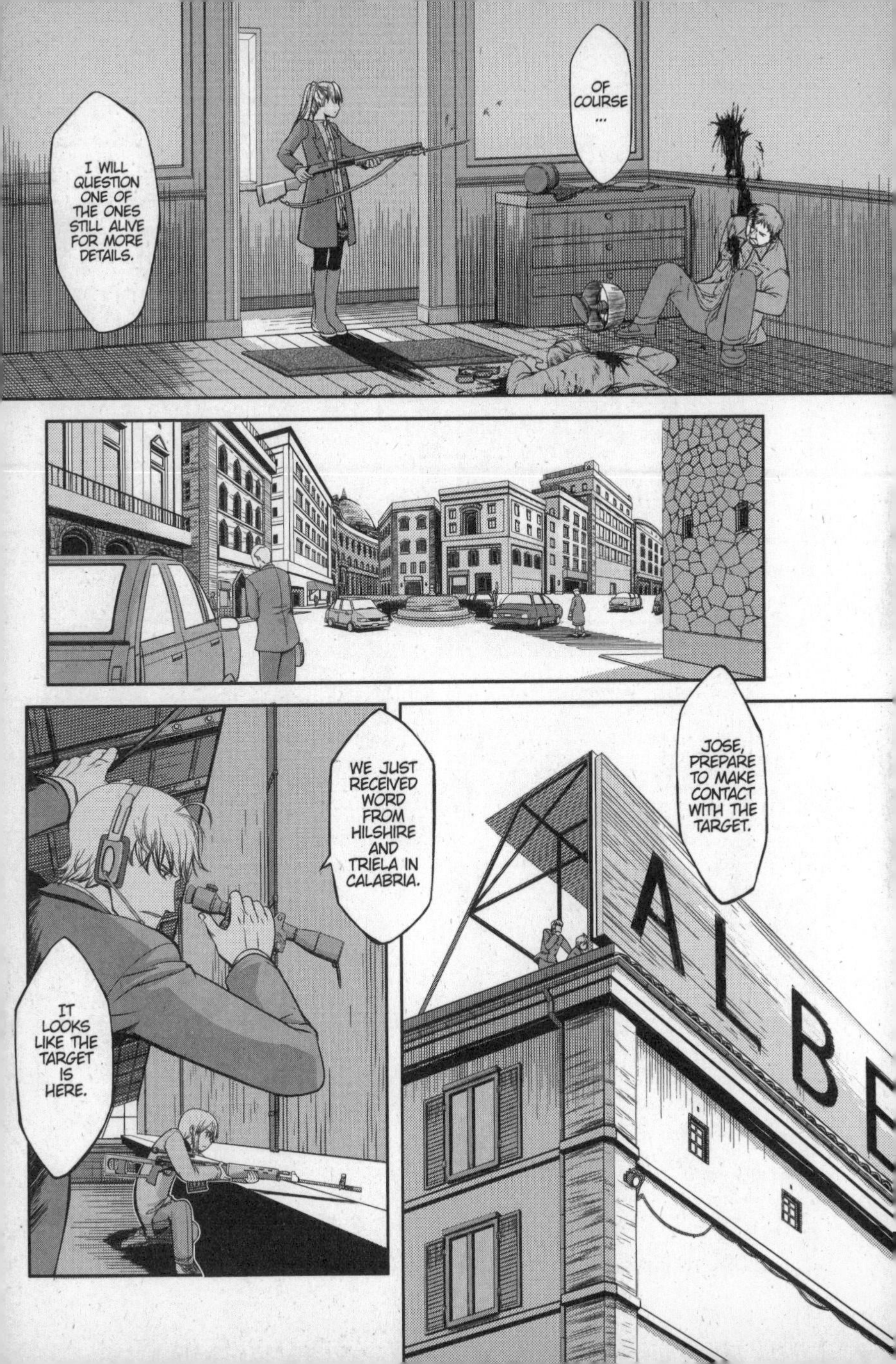
OF COURSE ...
I WILL QUESTION ONE OF THE ONES STILL ALIVE FOR MORE DETAILS.
JOSE, PREPARE TO MAKE CONTACT WITH THE TARGET.
ALBE
WE JUST RECEIVED WORD FROM HILSHIRE AND TRIELA IN CALABRIA.
IT LOOKS LIKE THE TARGET IS HERE.

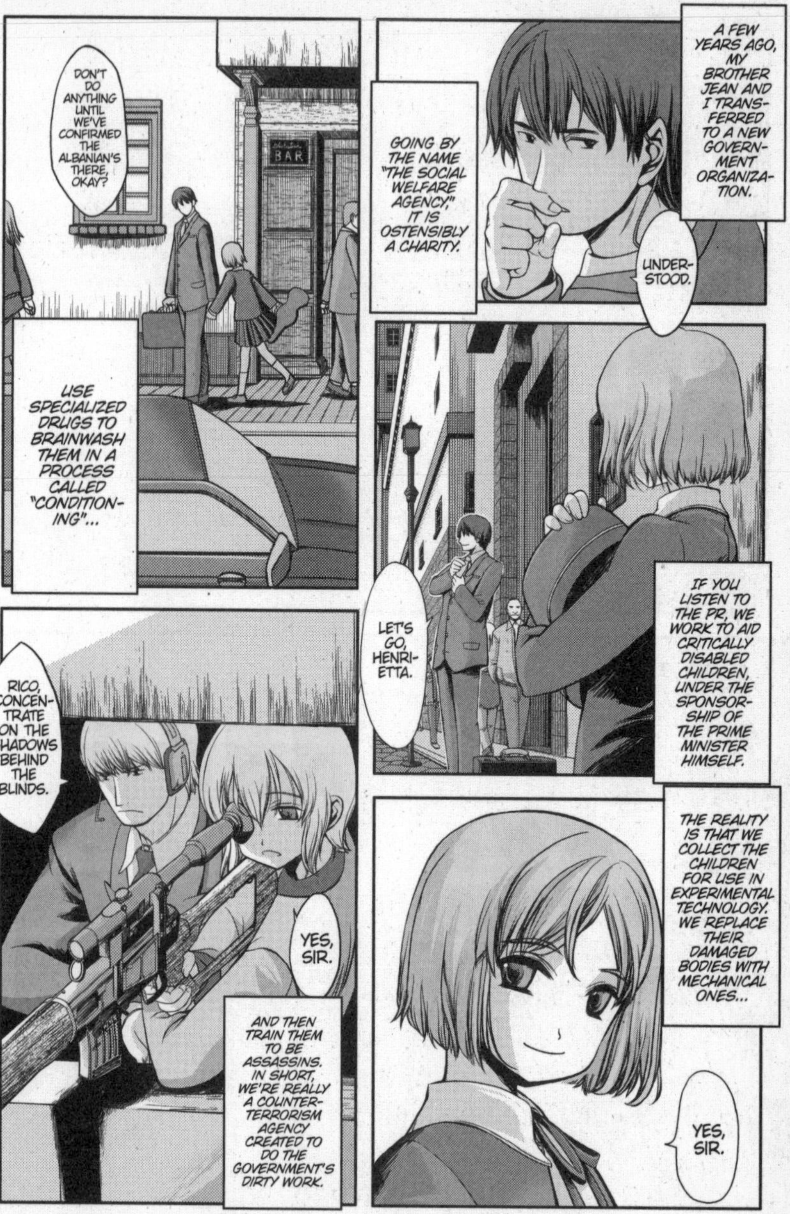
A FEW YEARS AGO, MY BROTHER JEAN AND I TRANSFERRED TO A NEW GOVERNMENT ORGANIZATION.
GOING BY THE NAME "THE SOCIAL WELFARE AGENCY," IT IS OSTENSIBLY A CHARITY.
UNDERSTOOD.
IF YOU LISTEN TO THE PR, WE WORK TO AID CRITICALLY DISABLED CHILDREN, UNDER THE SPONSORSHIP OF THE PRIME MINISTER HIMSELF.
LET'S GO, HENRIETTA.
THE REALITY IS THAT WE COLLECT THE CHILDREN FOR USE IN EXPERIMENTAL TECHNOLOGY. WE REPLACE THEIR DAMAGED BODIES WITH MECHANICAL ONES...
YES, SIR.
DON'T DO ANYTHING UNTIL WE'VE CONFIRMED THE ALBANIAN'S THERE, OKAY?
BAR
USE SPECIALIZED DRUGS TO BRAINWASH THEM IN A PROCESS CALLED "CONDITIONING"...
RICO, CONCENTRATE ON THE SHADOWS BEHIND THE BLINDS.
YES, SIR.
AND THEN TRAIN THEM TO BE ASSASSINS. IN SHORT, WE'RE REALLY A COUNTERTERRORISM AGENCY CREATED TO DO THE GOVERNMENT'S DIRTY WORK.

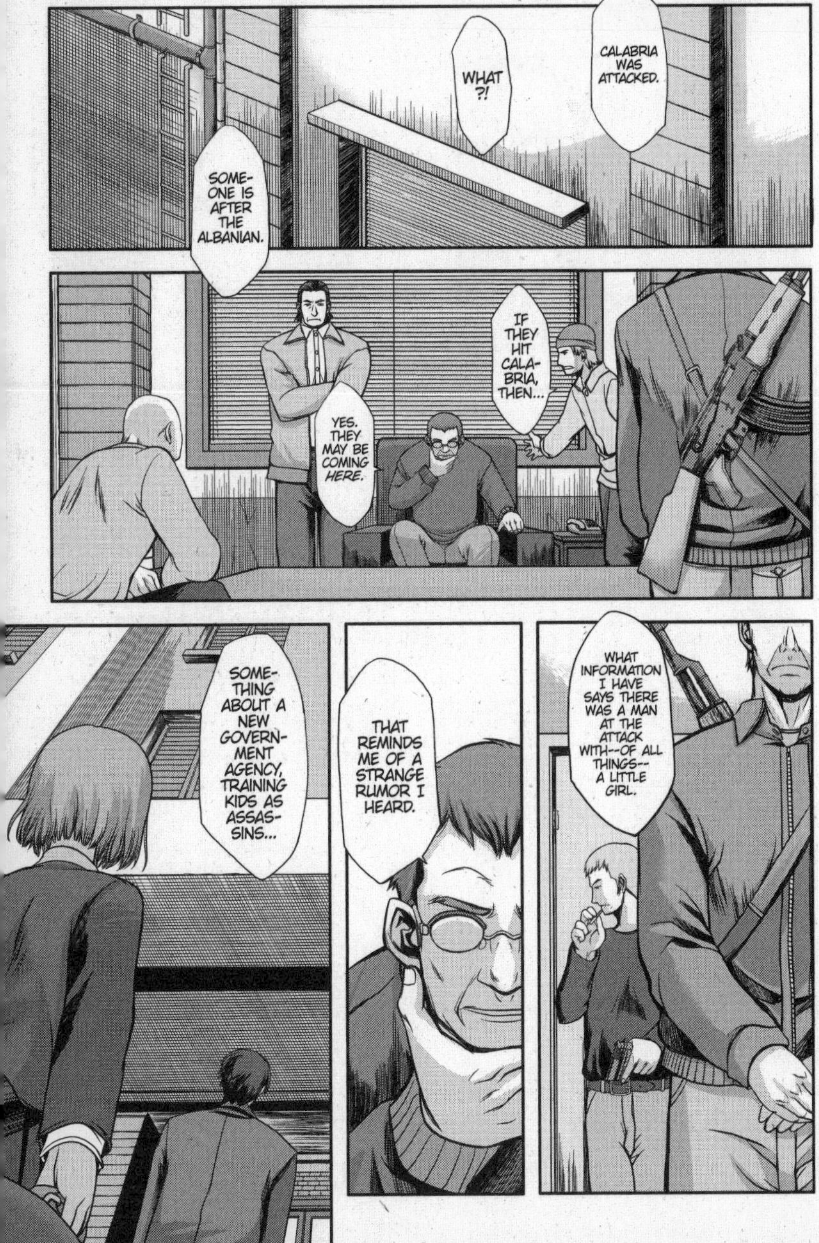
CALABRIA WAS ATTACKED.
WHAT?!
SOMEONE IS AFTER THE ALBANIAN.
IF THEY HIT CALABRIA, THEN...
YES. THEY MAY BE COMING HERE.
WHAT INFORMATION I HAVE SAYS THERE WAS A MAN AT THE ATTACK WITH--OF ALL THINGS--A LITTLE GIRL.
THAT REMINDS ME OF A STRANGE RUMOR I HEARD.
SOMETHING ABOUT A NEW GOVERNMENT AGENCY, TRAINING KIDS AS ASSASSINS...

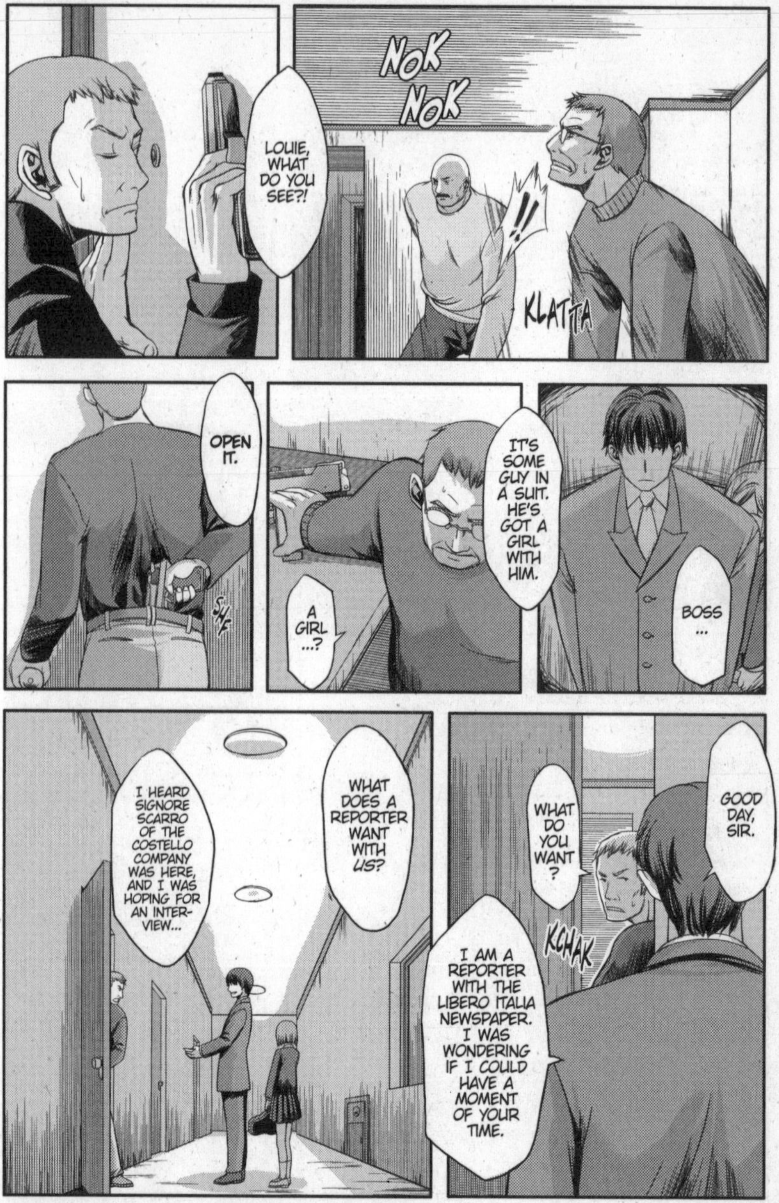
NOK NOK
!!
KLATTA
LOUIE, WHAT DO YOU SEE?!
BOSS...
IT'S SOME GUY IN A SUIT. HE'S GOT A GIRL WITH HIM.
A GIRL...?
OPEN IT.
SHF
GOOD DAY, SIR.
WHAT DO YOU WANT?
KCHAK
I AM A REPORTER WITH THE LIBERO ITALIA NEWSPAPER. I WAS WONDERING IF I COULD HAVE A MOMENT OF YOUR TIME.
WHAT DOES A REPORTER WANT WITH US?
I HEARD SIGNORE SCARRO OF THE COSTELLO COMPANY WAS HERE, AND I WAS HOPING FOR AN INTERVIEW...

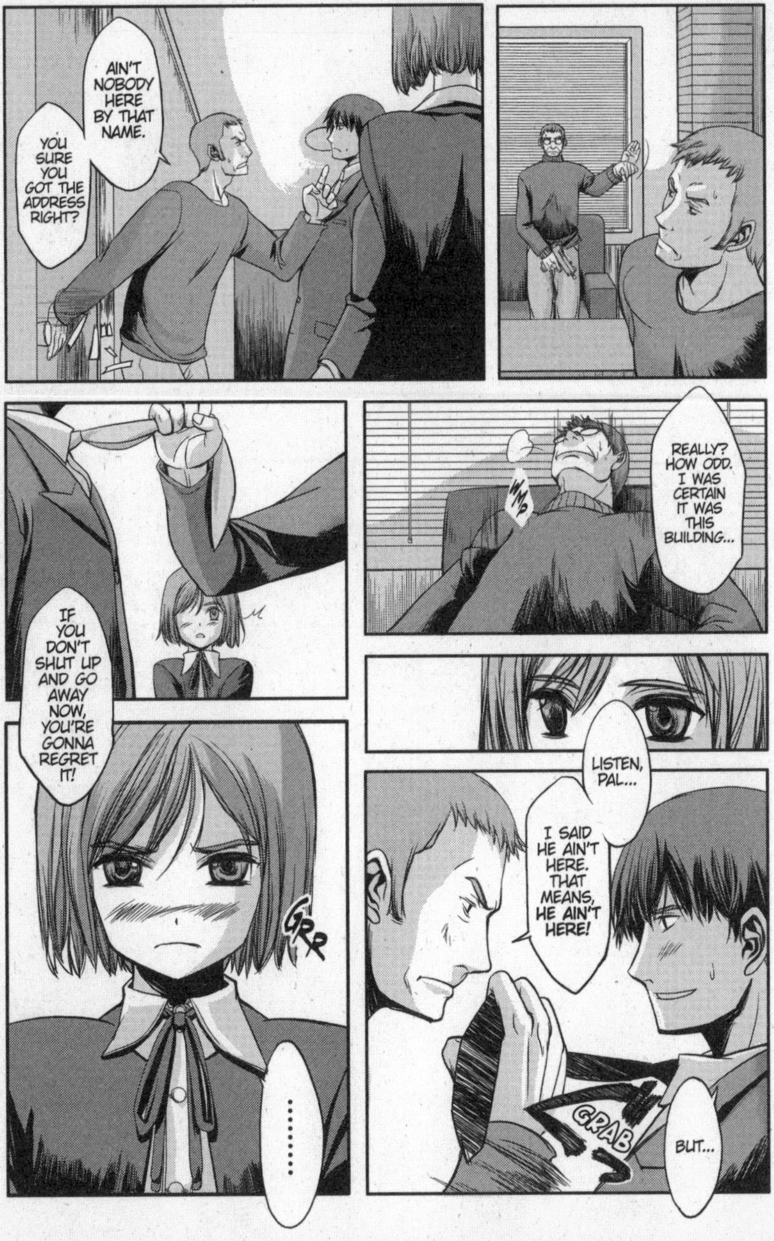
AIN'T NOBODY HERE BY THAT NAME.
YOU SURE YOU GOT THE ADDRESS RIGHT?
REALLY? HOW ODD. I WAS CERTAIN IT WAS THIS BUILDING...
WHP
LISTEN, PAL...
I SAID HE AIN'T HERE. THAT MEANS, HE AIN'T HERE!
GRAB
BUT...
IF YOU DON'T SHUT UP AND GO AWAY NOW, YOU'RE GONNA REGRET IT!
GRR
....

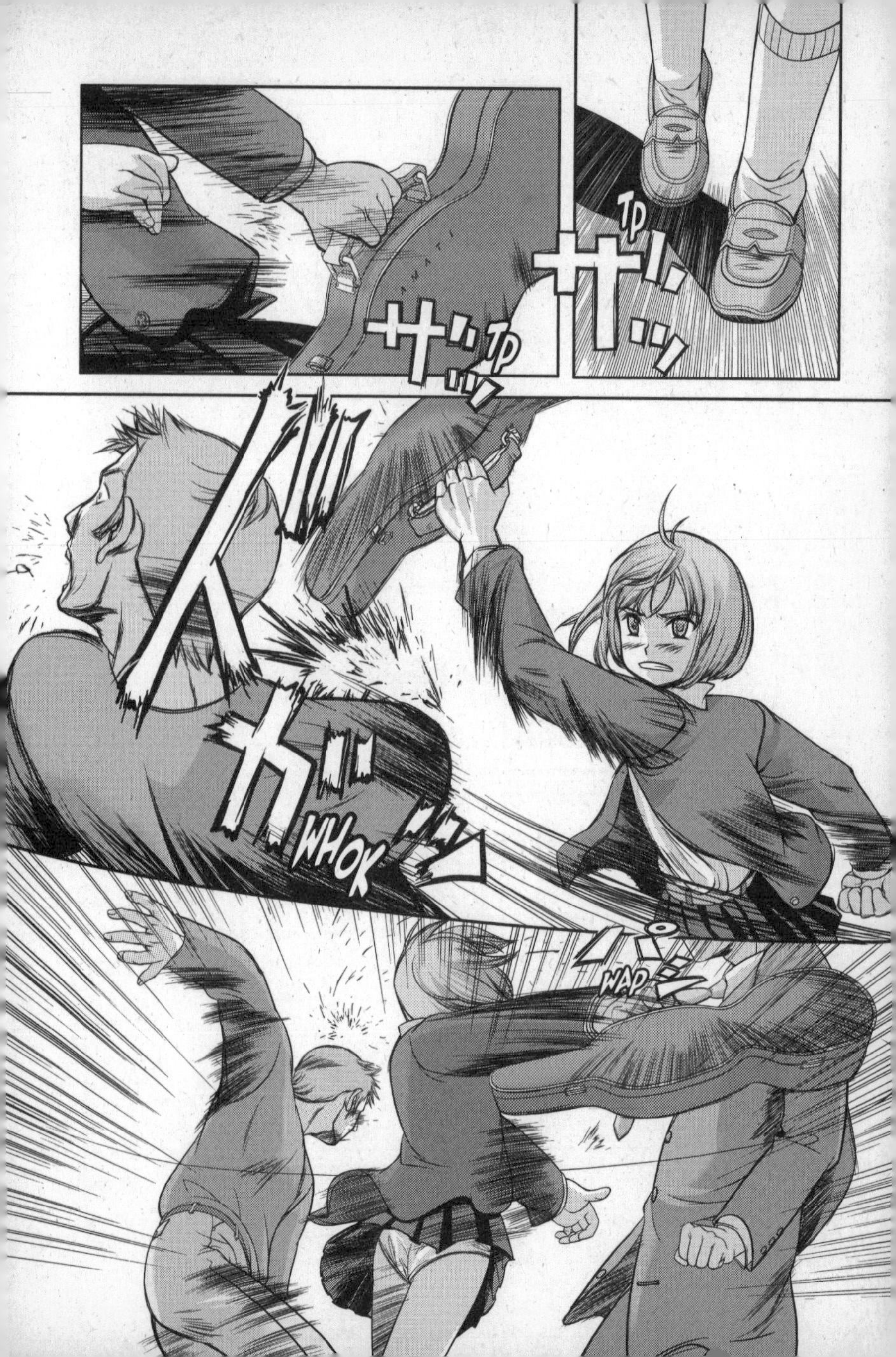
TP
TP
WHOK
WAP

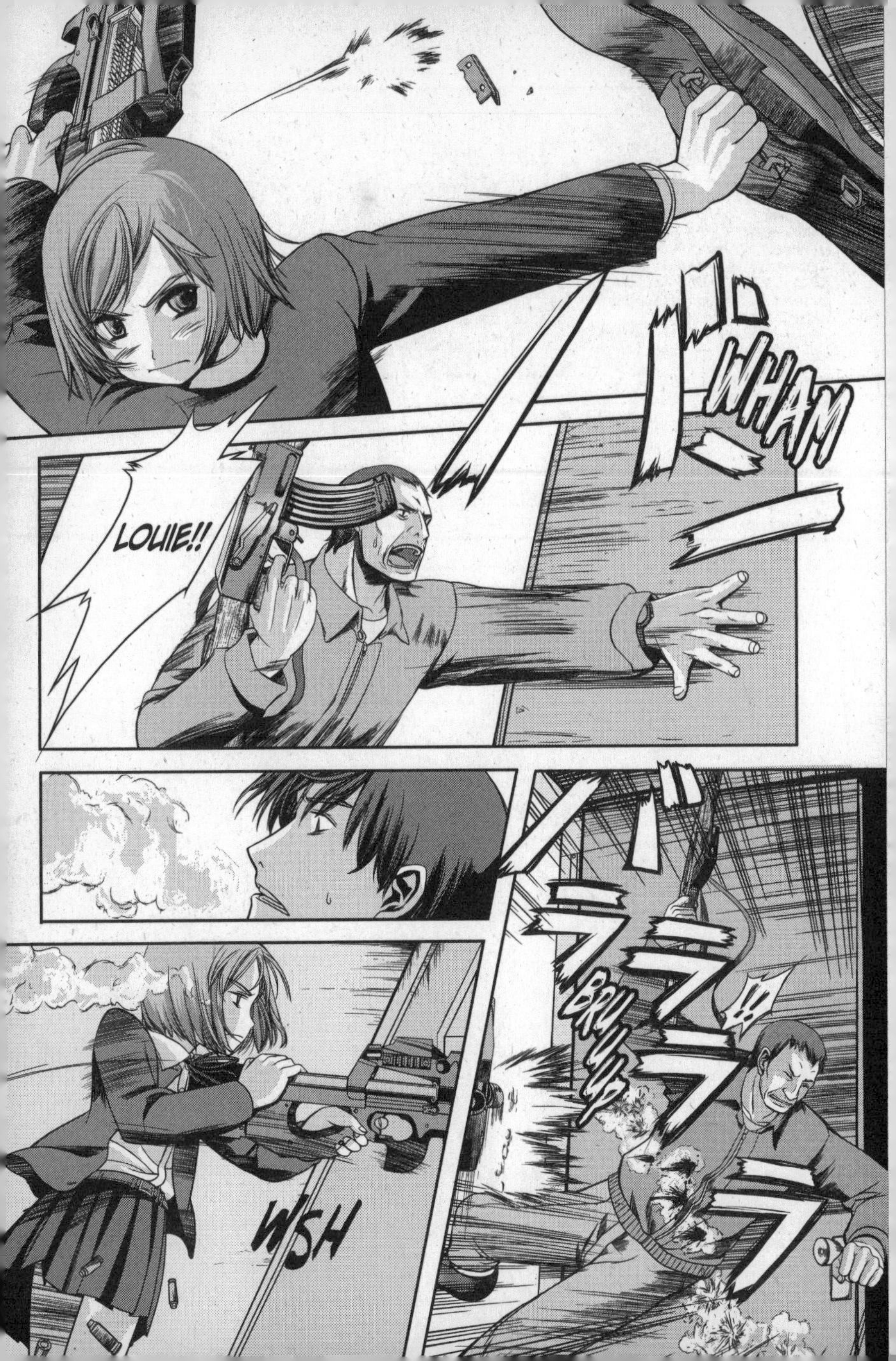

WHAM
LOUIE!!
!!
BRUUUP
WSH

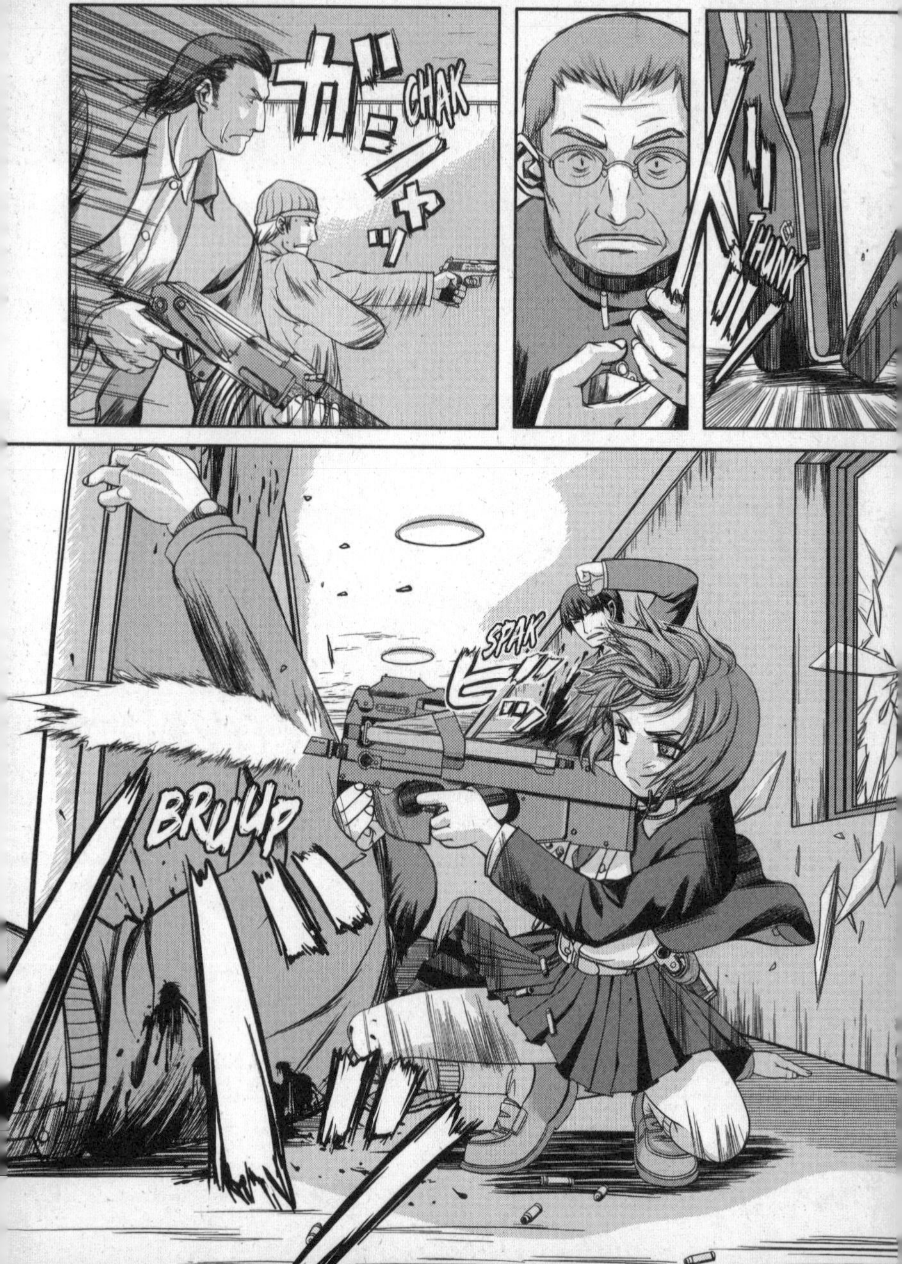
THUNK
CHAK
SPAK
BRUUP

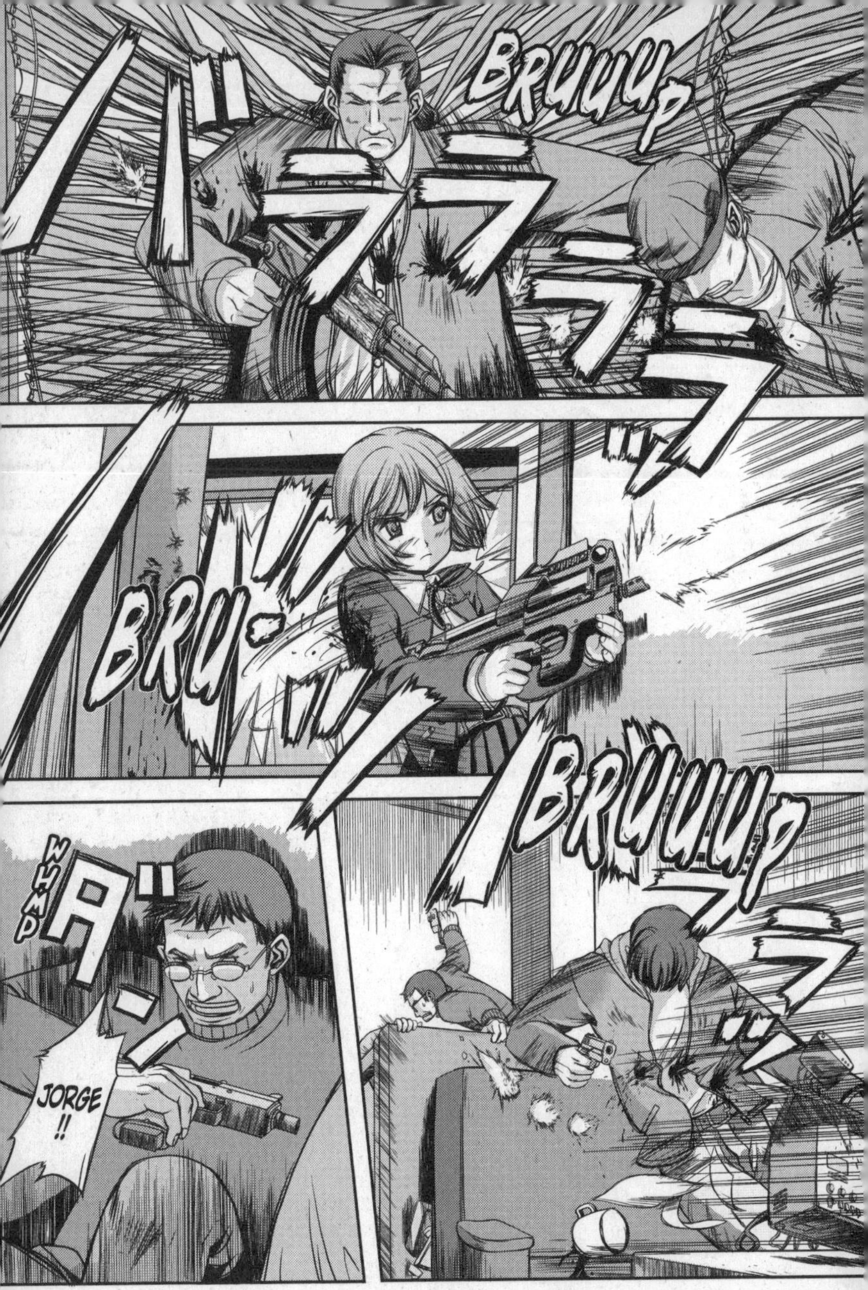
BRUUUP
BRU-
BRUUUP
WHMP
JORGE !!

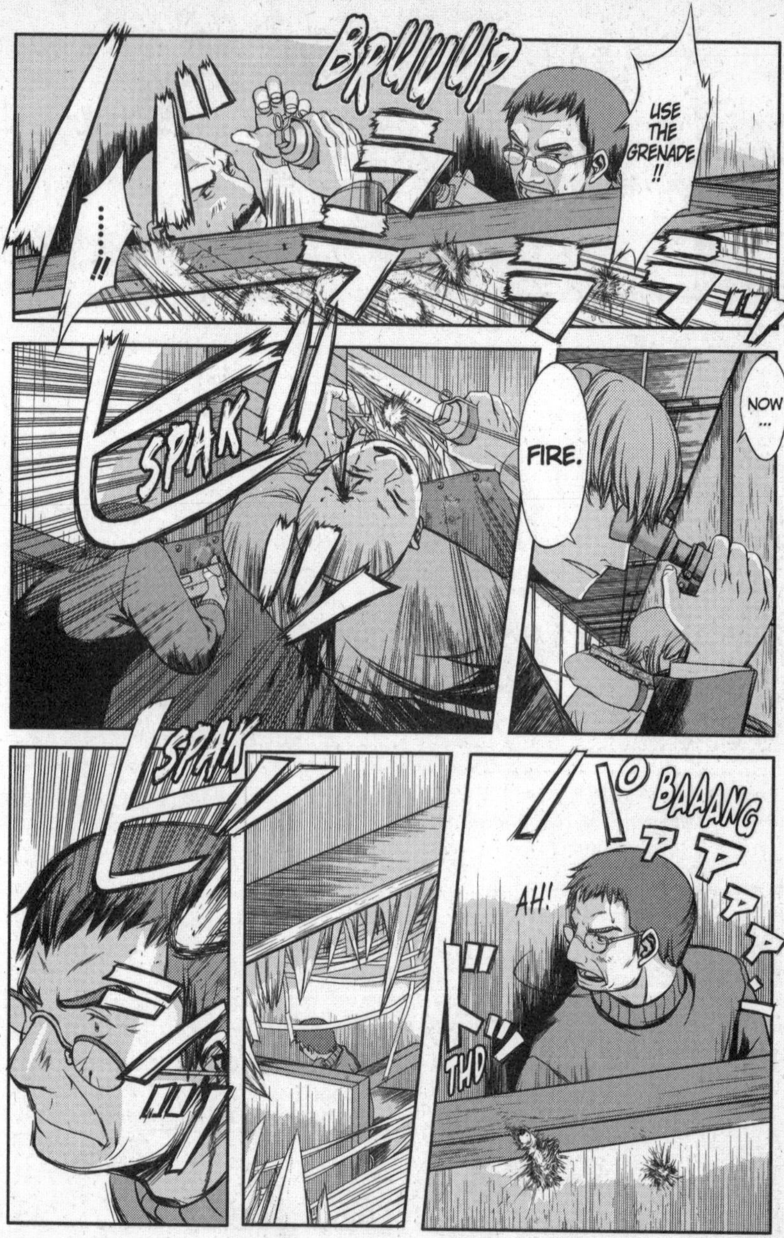
USE THE GRENADE !!
BRUUUP
NOW ...
FIRE.
SPAK
BAAANG
AH!
THD
SPAK

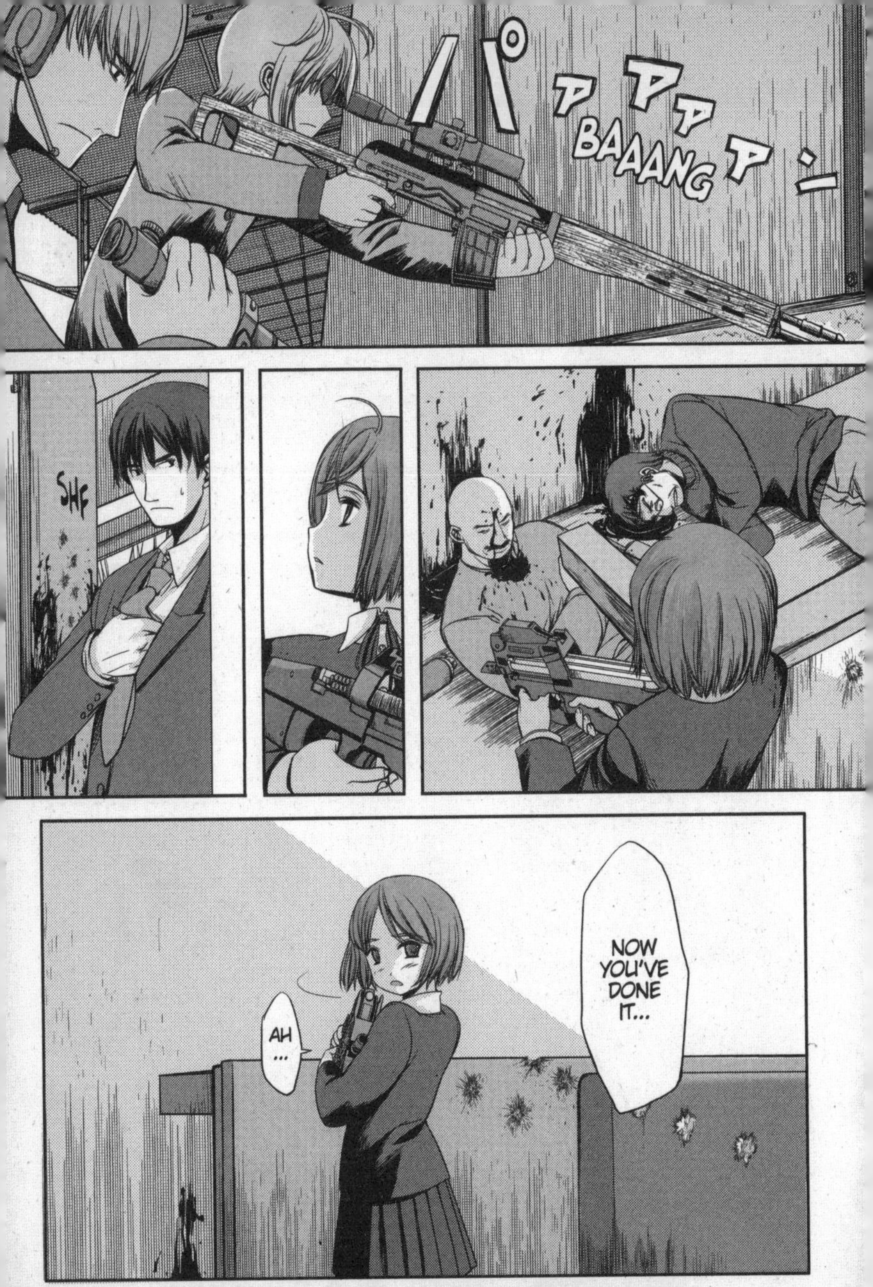
パァァァァン
BAAANG
SHF
NOW YOU'VE DONE IT...
AH ...

Continued in Gunslinger Girl Omnibus Collection 1!

THE END

YOU'RE READING THE WRONG WAY

This is the last page of
Blood Alone
Omnibus Collection 1

This book reads from right to left, Japanese style. To read from the beginning, flip the book over to the other side, start with the top right panel, and take it from there.

If this is your first time reading manga, just follow the diagram. It may seem backwards at first, but you'll get used to it! Have fun!